Your guide to

AF754618

MEDICAL LANGUAGE LAB FOR

MEDICAL TERMINOLOGY

Mastering Word Building

Medical Language Lab

Your journey to medical terminology SUCCESS BEGINS HERE!

Medical Language Lab for Medical Terminology guides you step by step from basic through advanced levels of writing and speaking proficiency.

Don't miss everything that's waiting for you online to make learning less stressful and save you time. Follow the instructions on the inside front cover to use the access code to unlock your resources today.

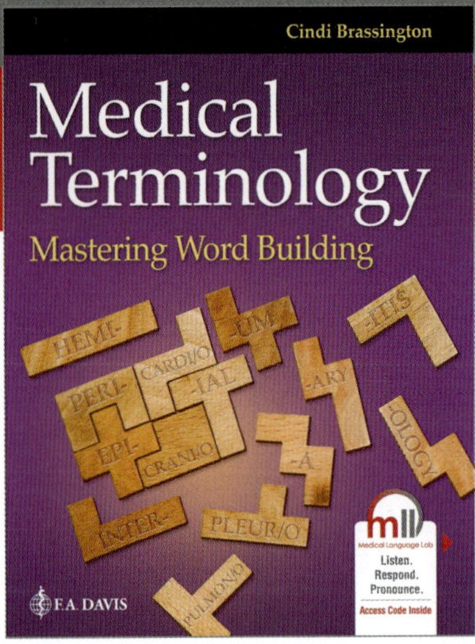

STEP #1

LEARN

Build a solid foundation with your text.

Prepare for your role as a professional.
An evolving **case study** threaded throughout each body system chapter demonstrates medical terminology at work in professional practice.

CASE STUDY

Jessica is a 24-year-old woman who had a gastric bypass surgery last year. At 5 ft 4 in. tall, Jessica previously weighed 320 lb, with a BMI (body mass index) of 54.9. A BMI of 30 or higher is categorized as obese and increases risk of diabetes, heart disease, hyper-tension, elevated cholesterol, gastroesophageal reflux disease (GERD), obstructive sleep apnea, depression, and back and knee

ELEMENT REVIEW
esophag/o = esophagus
-stenosis = condition of narrowing

Esophagus

The food moves down from the pharynx into the **esophagus**, a muscular tube that moves food to the stomach. The esophagus is approximately 10 in. long and passes through an opening in the diaphragm into the abdominal cavity. The passage of food from the esophagus to the stomach is controlled by a muscular ring called the **lower esophageal sphincter** (LES). Food is moved down the esophagus by the coordinated contractions of muscles called **peristalsis**. As the food reaches the LES, the sphincter opens to allow the food bolus to enter the stomach. It then closes to prevent food from refluxing back into the esophagus.

Build your vocabulary.
Element Reviews in the margins break medical terms from their adjoining paragraphs into their color-coded parts to show how the word parts build the terms. Prefixes are coded **green**; suffixes are coded **blue**; and combining forms (word root + a vowel) are coded **orange**.

Make the connections.
Detailed **photographs** and **illustrations** with concise explanations make often complex concepts easy to understand and easy to remember.

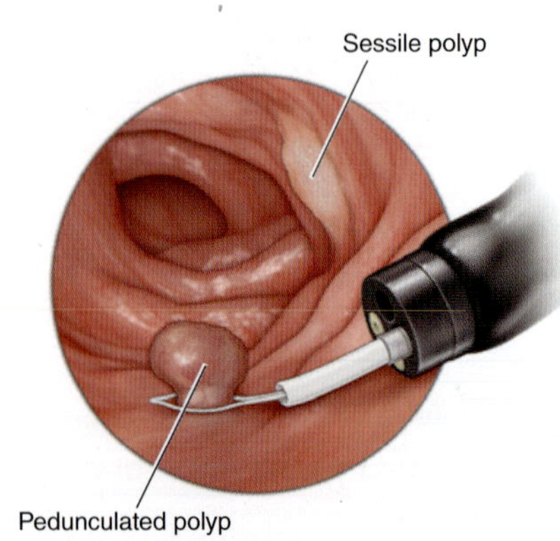

Figure 5-8 Two forms of polyps: a sessile polyp is attached by a base to the mucosa, and a pedunculated polyp is attached by a stalk.

Uncorrected page proofs may vary upon publication.

MEDICAL DOCUMENTATION

Knowledge of terms related to normal anatomy and pathological conditions enables you to understand medical documentation such as history and physical examinations, operative reports, discharge summaries, laboratory reports, and x-ray reports. Apply your knowledge by answering the questions that follow the report.

Operative Report

Patient name: Jessica W
Date of Birth: 04/14/1997
Patient ID: 9835784
Admitting Physician: Irene Carlisle, MD
Date of admission: September 16, 2023
Preoperative diagnosis: acute cholecystitis
Postoperative diagnosis: acute cholecystitis
Surgeon: William Morgan, MD
Operation: Laparoscopic cholecystectomy
Anesthesia: General endotracheal
Anesthetist: Bethany Chambers, CRNA

Procedure: After informed consent was obtained, the patient was brought to the operating room and placed in the supine position. General endotracheal anesthesia was induced, and the CRNA was present for the entire procedure. The patient was prepped and draped in the usual sterile fashion. A no. 11-blade scalpel was used to make a small infraumbilical skin incision along the midline. The fascia was elevated between Ochsner clamps and incised. A figure-of-eight stitch of 2-0 Vicryl was placed through the edge of the fascia. The 11-mm port was placed into the abdomen, and pneumoperitoneum was established. Upon adequate pneumoperitoneum, the laparoscope was introduced. Three additional ports were placed under direct visualization. An 11-mm port was placed in the epigastric area, two 5-mm ports were placed in the right upper quadrant. The patient was moved to a reverse Trendelenburg position and rotated to the left. The fundus of the gallbladder was retracted superiorly and laterally. The infundibulum was retracted inferiorly and laterally. Electrocautery was used to dissect the peritoneum down around the base of the gallbladder. The triangle of Calot was carefully opened. The cystic duct was identified heading to the base of the gallbladder. The cystic artery was also identified within the triangle of Calot. After the triangle of Calot had been dissected, a clip was placed high up on the cystic duct near the junction with the gallbladder. The cystic artery was clipped twice proximally and once distally. Scissors were the introduced and used to make a small opening in the cystic duct, and the cystic artery was divided.

An intraoperative cholangiogram was obtained and revealed good flow through the cystic du into the common bile duct and into the duodenum without filling defects. The cholangiocatheter was removed and two clips were placed distal to the ductotomy on the cystic duct. The cystic duct was then divided using scissors. The gallbladder was moved up and away using electrocautery and was removed through the epigastric port. The gallbladder and contents were sent to pathology for analysis. The liver bed was then irrigated and suctioned. All disse tion areas were inspected and found to be hemostatic. No bile leakage was observed, and a clips were in place. The right gutter over the edge of the liver was irrigated and suctioned un

See terminology in context.
Medical documentation introduces you to the use of terminology as it's used in the real-world, preparing you to read and interpret the patient charts, reports, research materials, and technical articles that you'll encounter throughout your career.

MEDICAL DOCUMENTATION—cont'd

Questions

Apply your knowledge by answering the following questions.

1. The cholecystectomy was not an "open" procedure and was done via a ______________
2. Jessica was moved to a reverse Trendelenburg position, which means ______________
3. An incision was made in the infraumbilical area. In your own words, where is this? ______________
4. Dissect and define the term *endotracheal* ______________
5. In the term *pneumoperitoneum*, what does *pneumo* refer to? ______________
6. Dissect and define the term *cholecystectomy*. ______________
7. Dissect and define *electrocautery*. ______________
8. The gallbladder was grasped and moved in what direction for removal? ______________
9. The gallbladder was removed through which port? ______________
10. Dissect and define the term *hemostatic*. ______________
11. What instrument/procedure is used to see the internal structures of Jessica's anatomy? ______________

Develop your skills.
Critical-thinking questions after each medical document test your understanding of and illustrate how medical communication is central to a variety of health-care scenarios.

Pathology Report

, gallstones
acute cholecystitis
s: acute cholecystitis with perforation and gangrene
container labeled gallbladder with stones.
D 9835784

n: The specimen consists of a large collapsed gallbladder measuring tween 4.0 and 7.2 cm in fundal diameter. The gallbladder is partially a patent cystic duct. The gallbladder shows an area of perforation own-tan dull serous, including the areas of thinning. Four black ent within the lumen and measure from 1.7 to 0.6 cm in diameter. The gic, edematous, and varies up to 0.9 cm in thickness. The mucosa nce, alternating between red-brown and greenish appearance with

CAREER EXPLORATION: DIETICIAN

After Jessica's gastric bypass surgery and subsequent weight loss, she is inspired to go back to school to become a dietician. She learned so much about eating well for good health that she felt inspired to share her knowledge with others. She enrolled in her local university and learned that there are two distinct educational degrees in the field of nutrition to help different patient populations. RDNs, registered dietician nutritionists, work most often in a hospital setting providing acute care such as parenteral nutrition (tube feeding). Certified nutrition specialists (CNSs) are trained to work in chronic care and private clinical practices such as physician offices and wellness centers. RDNs are trained in conventional medicine, meaning they are trained to follow the US Department of Agriculture guidelines and their training incorporates general recommendations for the population at large. CNSs are trained to work with patients on personalized nutritional plans. While both careers are important, Jessica feels that her personal experiences are best used in a one-on-one consultation with clients. She opts for the CNS certification and earns her master's degree, completes 1,000 hours of supervised clinical training, and completes the Certified Nutrition Specialists test from the Board for Certification of Nutrition Specialists (BCNS). She joins a private practice that specializes in eating disorders in children. Jessica loves her job and helping her clients gain understanding of how food fuels the body. She remains friends with Janelle, the clinical dietician who advised her during her hospital stay and inspired her new career. The two collaborate and have a booth at the annual health fair sponsored by the hospital to share good nutritional practices for people in their community.

Explore the opportunities.
Career Exploration presents a variety of health-care professions to illustrate how they interact with patients and the health-care team.

STEP #3

ASSESS

Build mastery. Attain fluency.

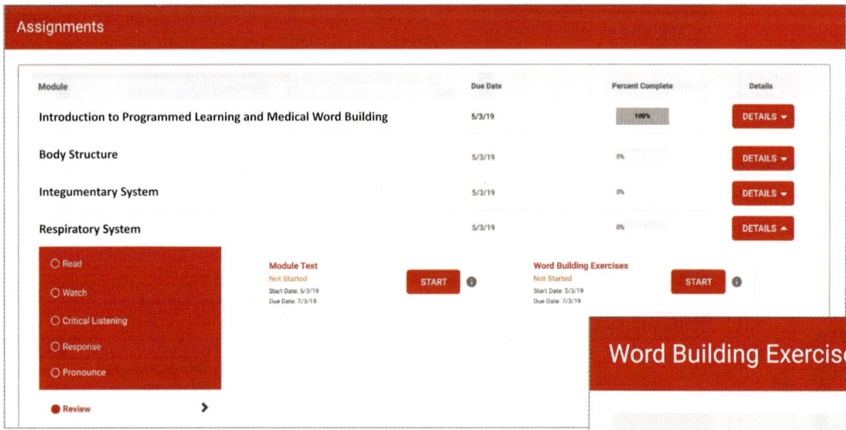

Identify your strengths and weaknesses. After you complete the learning activities for each module, a **Module Test** assesses your understanding of the content. You'll immediately know what areas require additional review.

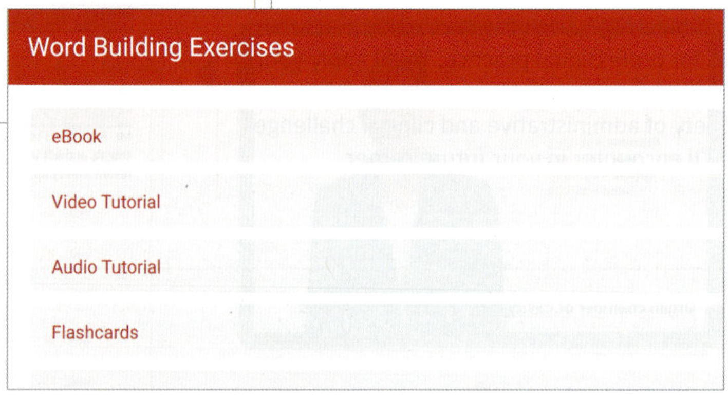

Turn weaknesses into strengths. The results of your Module Tests create a **review program** that focuses on the topic areas you need to spend more time on. Choose the media formats that best suit your learning style.

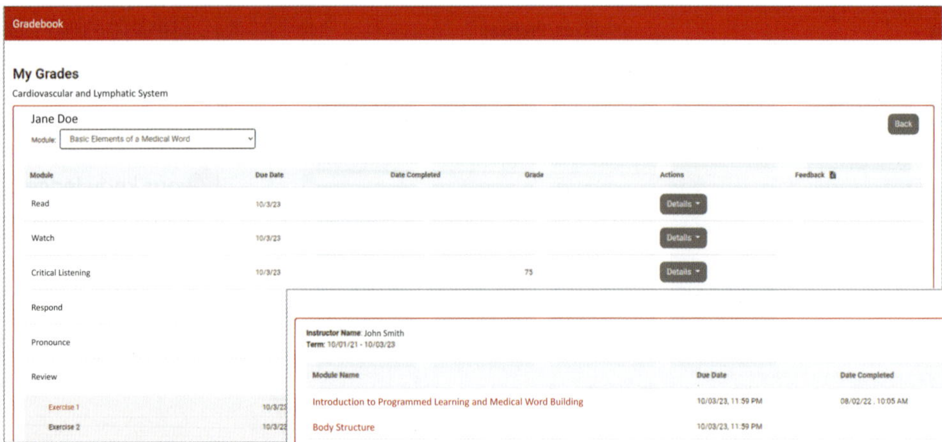

Measure your progress. The **Student Lesson Gradebook** tells you what lessons you've completed (or haven't completed) and the grades you've earned.

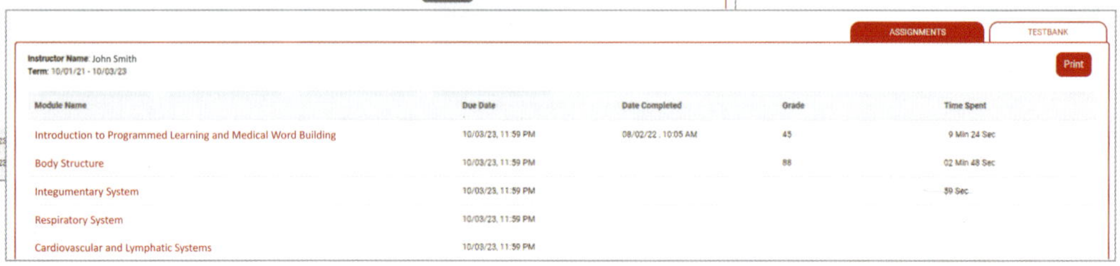

Review your performance. The **Student Activity Gradebook** drills down to show you how you've performed on specific assignments and tracks how long it takes you to complete each one.

Online content subject to change upon publication.

Medical Terminology

Mastering Word Building

Medical Terminology

Mastering Word Building

Cindi Brassington, MS, CMA (AAMA)

F.A. DAVIS
Philadelphia

Reviewers

The author and F. A. Davis thank the reviewers who read the manuscript and provided their comments and suggestions for improving this textbook.

Christine L. Albright, PhD
Associate Professor, Instructor for Medical Terminology
Classics
University of Georgia
Athens, Georgia

Tammy Albright, CMA (AAMA)
Associate Professor
Medical Assisting
Wake Technical Community College
Raleigh, North Carolina

Beatrice Avila, MEd, RHIA, CCSP, CCMA
Program Director
Health Information Technology
St Philips College
San Antonio, Texas

Dora P. Bailey, B.S., A.A.S.
Adjunct Instructor
Health and Wellness
Durham Technical Community College
Durham, North Carolina

Beth Bentz, MS, CTRS, ADC,
Adjunct Professor/Instructor
Recreation and Leisure
Mohawk Valley Community College
Utica, New York

Holly M Berebitsky, CMA
Director of Medical Assisting, Phlebotomy, Medical Billing and Coding, HIT
Medical Assisting
Mohave Community College
Kingman Arizona

Jennifer Campbell, OT/L, PhD
Endowed Chair of Online Learning, Professor Health Sciences
Online Learning/Health Science
Tulsa Community College
Tulsa, Oklahoma

Kelly Cary, MHA, CMA
Program Coordinator
Healthcare Administration
SUNY Brockport
Brockport, New York

Terrie Ciez, Ed, D., RDMS, RDCS, RT
Professor
Health Sciences
College of DuPage
Glen Ellyn

Mary Jo Daniels, MSN, RN
Professional Nursing Instructor
1st Semester Nursing
Casper College
Casper, WY

Lisa DesNoyers, MPH, RHIA, SME
Program Director for Health Information Management
BioHealth Informatics
Indiana University, Purdue University Indianapolis (IU)
Indianapolis, Indiana

Leon Deutsch, RMA, BS. M.Ed.
Medical Assisting Program Director
Medical Assisting
Collin College
Allen, Texas

Pronunciation Guide

The pronunciations in this textbook are from *Taber's Cyclopedic Medical Dictionary*, 24th edition, published by F. A. Davis Company. Diacritical marks are used to provide the pronunciations.

The diacritical macron mark ¯ over a vowel means the vowel is pronounced using its long sound. The breve mark ˘ over a vowel means the vowel is pronounced using its short sound.

ā = say	ă = sofa	a = at, bat	
ē = meet	ĕ = met	e = bed, dread, cred	
ī = eye	ĭ = in	i = it, did	
ō = oh	ŏ = dog	o = got, lot, pawn	oo = food
ū = you	ŭ = up	u = put, foot	

These same examples of vowels using diacritical marks appear at the bottom of each Combining Form table to help you remember them.

For each term, the accented (emphasized) syllable is capitalized. For example, the pronunciation "AK-sent" indicates that the first syllable is emphasized when pronouncing the word *accent*.

The Latin and Greek used in medical terminology also have special guidelines that can help you when you see an unfamiliar term.

- If *e* or *es* comes at the end of a Latin or Greek word, they are often pronounced as separate syllables; *syncope* or *nares* (NĀR-ēz, the plural of naris, or nostril).
- When a word ends in *i* to form a plural, the *i* is pronounced *eye,* such as in fungi (FŪN-jī).
- When *c* and *g* come before *e, i,* and *y* in Greek or Latin words, they are pronounced as a soft *s* or *j*: celebrate, circle, ginger, gym, fungi.
- For the vowel combination *ae,* the first vowel is often silent, and the *e* is long. Ulnae (ŬL-nē) is the plural of ulna, the large medial bone of the forearm.
- The *p* in *pneumo-* is silent and the *n* is pronounced, as in pneumonia (noo-MŌN-yă).
- If the *pn* combination is in the middle of a word, the *p* and *n* are pronounced separately; for example, hypnotic, or apnea (ap-NĒ-ă), which is the temporary stopping of breathing.
- The *p* in *ps* at the beginning of a word is silent, and the *s* is pronounced, as in psychotic.

CHAPTER
1

Elements of Medical Words

LEARNING OBJECTIVES

Upon completion of the chapter, you will be able to:

1. List the three basic component parts of words.
2. Define word roots and combining forms.
3. Correctly apply the combining form rules for word roots.
4. Correctly choose noun versus adjective forms of words.
5. Correctly choose singular versus plural forms of words.
6. Define eponyms and provide examples.

Medical terminology can be thought of as the "language of medicine" and can be studied like a foreign language. As for spoken languages, you must use memorization of word elements to create a body of knowledge. You can then use the memorized elements to create many medical terms. There are grammatical rules to follow to create words, and these rules may also be applied in order to analyze words for their meanings. With this process, you can build a working knowledge of medical terms that describe our anatomy, physiology, diseases, and treatments. Anatomy is the study of how our bodies are constructed and organized. Physiology is the study of how our bodies function. Diseases are dysfunctions of the body, and treatments are medications, surgical procedures, and physical therapy that can reduce symptoms or cure disease. When you understand medical terminology, you will be able to communicate effectively with patients and colleagues.

KEY TERMS

Adjective	Eponym	Prefix	Suffix
Combining vowel	Noun	Root	

Word Roots, Prefixes, and Suffixes

The three types of word elements, parts that compose medical terms, are named by their placement within the word. As the names imply, **prefixes** are at the beginning of words, **suffixes** appear at the end of the word, and **roots** are the main component of the word. While all words do not necessarily have a prefix, all words must have a suffix. Prefixes and suffixes are explored in further detail in Chapters 2 and 3.

Word Roots

The word root is the foundation of a medical word and expresses the basic meaning of the term. Most word roots are derived from Greek and Latin terms. Word roots can be modified (changed) to create different words, but they retain the central meaning of the word element. For example, the root **cardi/o-** means heart. Anytime **cardi/o-** appears in a medical word, the heart is central to its meaning. Adding a suffix, such as **-ology**, which means "the study of," creates the word *cardiology*, the study of the heart. Adding another suffix, **-ium**, changes the word element to a **noun**. Nouns are words that name a person, place, or thing. Nouns usually function as the subject of a sentence or the object of a verb (action word) in a sentence. The *cardium* refers to the heart. Additionally, adding a prefix, such as **peri-**, which means "around," produces a related word. The pericardium is the outermost layer of the heart. A different suffix, **-al**, changes the noun to an **adjective**, a word that describes a noun. The pericardial sac is the space around the heart that contains fluid and keeps it supple. (Notice that *pericardial* cannot stand alone; it needs a noun such as *sac*).

As shown in Table 1-1, medical roots have a combining vowel, most commonly the letter *o*, which acts as the "glue" to connect a suffix to the word root. If a suffix begins with a consonant, for example the suffix **-megaly**, which means enlargement, the root *cardi-* needs a vowel to bridge the two-word elements to create the word *cardiomegaly*. This facilitates ease of pronunciation. Notice that when **-itis** is added to the word root **gastr/o-**, the combining vowel *o* is dropped. Because **-itis** starts with the vowel *i*, the root *gastr-* doesn't need its combining *o*.

The rules of suffixes will be further discussed in Chapter 3. For now, memorize the meanings of the terms in Table 1-1 so that you can begin to practice creating and deciphering terms.

Word Roots Practice

Using only the word elements in the lists, create medical terms for the corresponding meanings. Remember to apply the vowel rules to add the word endings.

Roots	Suffixes
cardi/o	-oma
dermat/o	-algia
gastr/o	-ology
hepat/o	-itis
my/o	-megaly
nephr/o	-ologist

1. Specialist who treats diseases and disorders of the heart ____________________
2. Muscle pain ____________________
3. Inflammation of the liver ____________________
4. Enlargement of a kidney ____________________
5. The study of the skin ____________________
6. Tumor of a kidney ____________________
7. Enlargement of the stomach ____________________
8. Specialist who diagnoses and treat disorders of the kidneys ____________________
9. Inflammation of the skin ____________________
10. The study of the liver ____________________

TABLE 1-1 Common Medical Roots With Their Combining Vowels

Medical Root	Meaning	Example (Pronunciation)	Example Definition
arth/o	joint	arthritis (ar-THRĪT-ĭs)	inflammation of a joint
arteri/o	artery	arterial (ar-TĒR-ē-ăl)	pertaining to arteries
bronch/o	bronchus	bronchitis (brong-kīt′ĭs)	inflammation of the bronchi
cardi/o	heart	cardiomegaly (kăr-dē-ō-MĔG-ă-lē)	enlargement of the heart
chondr/o	cartilage	chondral (KŎN′drăl)	pertaining to cartilage
dermat/o	skin	dermatologist (dĕr-mă-TŎL-ō-jĭst)	specialist who studies the skin
encephala/o	brain	encephalopathy (en-sef-ă-LOP-ă-thē)	disease of the brain
enter/o	intestines	enteric (en-TER-ik)	pertaining to the intestines
hemat/o	blood	hematologist (hē-mă-, hĕm-ă-TŌ-mă)	specialist who studies the blood
gastr/o	stomach	gastritis (gas-TRĪT-ĭs)	inflammation of the stomach
hepat/o	liver	hepatology (hĕp-ă-TŎL-ō-jē)	study of the liver
mast/o	breast	mastectomy (mas-TEK-tŏ-mē)	surgical removal of a breast
my/o	muscle	myalgia (mī-ĂL-jē-ă)	muscle pain
neur/o	nerves	neurologist (nū-RŎL-ō-jĭst)	specialist who studies nerves
nephr/o	kidney	nephroma (nĕ-FRŌ-mă)	tumor of the kidney
oste/o	bone	osteoid (OS-tē-oyd)	resembling bone
pancreat/o	pancreas	pancreatitis (pang-krē-ă-TĪT-ĭs, pan-krē-ă-TĪT-ĭs)	inflammation of pancreas
phleb/o	vein	phlebotomy (flĕ-BOT-ĕŏ-mē)	incision into a vein
pulmon/o	lung	pulmonary (PŬL-mō-nĕ-rē)	pertaining to the lung
ur/o	urine	urology (ū-RŎL-ō-jē)	the study of urine, urinary system

ā = say, ă = sofa, ē = meet, ĕ = met, ī = eye, ĭ = in, ō = oh, ŏ = dog, ū = you, ŭ = up, oo = food

Words With Multiple Roots

Some medical words refer to more than one subject and thus have multiple roots (Table 1-2). Words such as *cardiovascular* refer to both the heart and vessels. *Gastroesophageal* refers to both the stomach and esophagus. The "drop the vowel" rule does not extend to root-to-root combinations. The pronunciation of words with multiple roots allows for double vowels, for instance, gastroesophageal (ga·strow·uh·saa·fuh·**jee**·uhl).

A variety of suffixes mean "pertaining to" and make the word an adjective, a word that describes a noun. Remember that each of these words cannot stand alone and needs a noun to modify (describe).

> ***Study Tip***
> Create notecards to memorize combining forms and their meanings. On one side write the combining form, and on the other side write the meaning. Refer to the cards and quiz yourself often.

Words With Multiple Roots Practice

1. Define the Word Elements

After making notecards and memorizing the word elements from Table 1-1, test your knowledge by giving the root and combining form for the definitions below.

1. Urine ______________________
2. Kidneys ______________________
3. Lungs ______________________
4. Breast ______________________

TABLE 1-2 Sample of Medical Terms With Multiple Roots

Root Combinations	Meaning	With Suffix Meaning "Pertaining to"*	Example Phrase
atrioventricular	pertaining to the atria and ventricles	-ar	atrioventricular function
cardiopulmonary	pertaining to the heart and lungs	-ary	cardiopulmonary resuscitation
cardiothoracic	pertaining to the heart and chest	-ic	cardiothoracic surgery
gastroesophageal	pertaining to stomach and esophagus	-eal	gastroesophageal reflux dx
hepatorenal	pertaining to the liver and kidneys	-al	hepatorenal syndrome

*Suffixes that mean "pertaining to" include -al, -ar, -ary, -eal, and -ic. You will learn more suffixes in Chapter 3.

5. Vein ____________________
6. Muscle ____________________
7. Bones ____________________
8. Cartilage ____________________
9. Nerves ____________________
10. Heart ____________________
11. Brain ____________________
12. Skin ____________________
13. Intestine ____________________
14. Blood ____________________
15. Joint ____________________

Study Tip

Memorizing word elements instead of full medical words will save you an enormous amount of time. Think about how many medical terms exist; *Taber's Cyclopedic Medical Dictionary*, 24th Edition, contains over 2500 pages of medical terms! By memorizing word elements, you will be able to build your medical vocabulary efficiently. Medical professionals use this method every day.

2. Create Words With Suffixes

Use the following suffixes to create words for the meanings listed.

-oma	-ologist	-ic
-algia	-itis	-megaly
-ology		

1. Pain in the cartilage ____________________
2. The study of the nerves and nervous system ____________________
3. Enlargement of the liver and spleen ____________________
4. Tumor in a muscle ____________________
5. Inflammation of a breast ____________________
6. Specialist who studies the kidneys ____________________
7. Bone pain ____________________
8. Inflammation of the pancreas ____________________
9. Pertaining to the heart and chest ____________________
10. Specialist who studies the skin ____________________

HISTORY OF MEDICAL TERMS LOST AND LATER FOUND

The ancient Greek term *diabetes mellitus* is composed of two distinct terms. *Diabetes* means "flowing through," *mellitus* means "pleasant tasting, or sweet as honey." In ancient China and Japan, doctors observed that dogs were drawn to some people's urine. Examination of the urine showed a sweet odor and taste. This term was adopted by the Romans as they carefully preserved translations of Greek into Latin, and it continues to be used today. The huge medical encyclopedia, *De Medicinia*, is Latin for "about medicine." It was written by Roman nobleman Cornelius Celsus in the 9th or 10th century and recorded all that was then known about both Greek and Roman medicine. It was lost until the 15th century and was then printed in 1478.

Multiple Word Elements for the Same Meanings

As you expand your medical vocabulary, you will see that the same meaning can sometimes be derived from more than one word element. Table 1-3 shows you a few of these terms.

Singular Versus Plural Words

As in any spoken language, there are rules for a singular object versus many of the same objects. You can hand your friend a bag or several bags. However, the plural forms of words are not always as simple as adding an *S* to the end. If you hand your friend a box, you might then hand him several boxes. Medical terminology is no different: you will need to understand and apply some rules when making a term singular or plural. Table 1-4 gives the rules for singular and plural forms.

TABLE 1-3 Examples of Roots With Common Meanings

Root Forms	Meaning	Example	Example Definition
dermat/o	skin	dermatology	the study of skin
derm/o	skin	dermabrasion	scraping of skin
cutane/o	skin	subcutaneous	pertaining to under the skin
hemat/o	blood	hematology	the study of the blood
hem/o	blood	hemolysis	destruction of blood
mast/o	breast	mastectomy	surgical removal of the breast
mamm/o	breast	mammography	recording of the breast
nephr/o	kidney	nephrologist	specialist who studies the kidney
ren/o	kidney	renal	pertaining to the kidneys

TABLE 1-4 Rules for Singular and Plural Forms

Singular	Plural	Rule	Singular Example	Plural Example
a	ae	retain a and add e	vertebra	verterbrae
ax	aces	drop x, add ces	thorax	thoraces
en	ina	drop en, add ina	lumen	lumina
is	es	drop is, add es	metastasis	metastases
ix or ex	ices	drop ix, add ices	appendix	appendices
on	a	drop on, add a	ganglion	ganglia
um	a	drop um, add a	diverticulum	diverticula
us	i	drop us, add i	alveolus	alveoli
y	ies	drop y, add ies	pathology	pathologies
ma	mata	drop ma, add mata	granuloma	granulomata

Singular Versus Plural Words Practice

Using the rules for singular and plural forms, fill in the chart and include the rule. The first one has been done for you as an example.

Singular	Plural	Rule
bacterium	*bacteria*	*drop um, add a*
1. bronchus	______	______
2. ______	gliomata	______
3. fornix	______	______
4. ______	deformities	______
5. carcinoma	______	______
6. apex	______	______
7. ______	nares	______
8. coccus	______	______
9. axilla	______	______
10. ______	diagnoses	______
11. therapy	______	______

Eponyms

While many medical terms are defined by their roots, prefixes, and suffixes, other medical terms cannot be defined through this process. An eponym is a name for a disease, procedure, or body function that is named after a person, often the physician or researcher

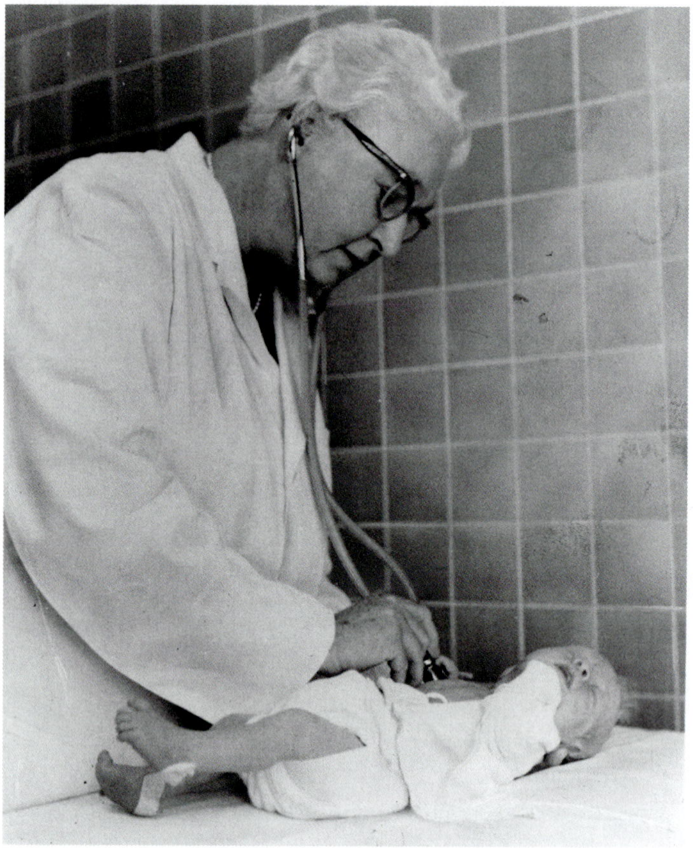

Figure 1-1 Dr. Virginia Apgar.

who discovered the disease, such as Parkinson's disease, a neurological disorder. James Parkinson was a British physician who discovered the chronic degenerative disease. Other examples of eponyms include the following.

Apgar score: Virginia Apgar, MD, American obstetric anesthesiologist who developed the system for evaluating an infant's physical condition at birth (Fig. 1-1).
Cushing's syndrome: Harvey Williams Cushing, MD, American neurosurgeon first to describe the pituitary disease that presents as Cushing's syndrome.
Hodgkin's disease: Thomas Hodgkin, British physician and pathologist who described the blood and lymphatic disease now known as Hodgkin's disease.
Lou Gehrig's disease: Lou Gehrig was an American professional baseball player who became afflicted with amyotrophic lateral sclerosis; thus, its common name is Lou Gehrig's disease.

ELEMENT REVIEW

Look for Element Reviews throughout this book's later chapters to remind you of what word elements mean.

amyotrophic lateral sclerosis
a- = without
my/o = muscle
-trophic = pertaining to growth
later/o = side
-al = pertaining to
scler/o = hardening
-osis = condition

Bell's palsy: Unilateral facial paralysis named after Scottish surgeon Sir Charles Bell who discovered the function of facial nerves and the paralytic disorder.
Crohn's disease: A form of irritable bowel syndrome named for Dr. Burrill B. Crohn, who described the disease in 1932.
Graves' disease: The most common form of hyperthyroidism, which is named for Dr. Robert Graves.

ELEMENT REVIEW
hyper- = excessive
thyroid/o = thyroid
-ism = condition

Guidelines for Pronunciation

In addition to the components of words to create medical terms, rules for pronunciation will guide you in proper pronunciation of terms. It is important to note that regional accents affect medical terms as well as general language. Keeping this in mind, you will find some guidelines with examples in Table 1-5 to help you correctly pronounce medical terms.

Be sure to use the Medical Language Lab at medicallanguagelab.com. The lab provides audio files of medical terms to help you practice your pronunciations.

TABLE 1-5 Guidelines for Pronunciation

Rule	Pronunciation	Examples
Word begins with C		
If the C is followed by e, i, y	pronounced as a soft "c" like an "ss" sound	**ce**rvix, **ce**cum, **ci**rrhosis, **ci**rcumcision, **cy**anosis, **cy**st
If the C is followed by a, o, u	pronounced as a hard "c" like a "k" sound	**ca**theter, **ca**vity, **co**ugh, **co**unt, **cu**be, **cu**mulative
If the C is followed by a consonant	pronounced as a hard "c" like a "k" sound	**ch**ronic, **cl**amp, **cr**anium
If the word begins with S or PS	pronounced with an "ss" sound	**s**aliva, **ps**ychology,
If the word begins with SK, SC, SCH	pronounced with an "sk" sound	**sk**eletal, **sc**lera, **sc**iatica, **sch**ool
If the word begins with K, Ch	pronounced with a hard "k" sound	**k**yphosis, **k**inesiology, **ch**ancre, **ch**romatosis
If the word begins with J or Ge, Gi	pronounced with a "j" sound	**j**aundice, **j**oint, **ge**riatric, **gi**ngiva
If the word begins with N or PN, KN	pronounced with an "n" sound	**n**euroma, **pn**eumonia, **kn**ee
If the word root ends with ge, gi	pronounced as a "j" sound	laryn**gi**tis, pharyn**ge**al
If the word root ends in ga, go	pronounced as a hard "g," a "guh" sound	esopha**go**cele, pha**go**cytosis, laryn**ga**lgia
If the word root begins with Z or X	pronounced with a "z" sound	**z**ygote, **x**eroderma

Pronunciation Practice

Mark the pronunciation rule for each of the following words; the first one is done for you:

Word	Pronunciation Rule
Chromosome	*Word begins with Ch, hard K*
1. Meningocele	______________________
2. Jejunum	______________________
3. Pneumothorax	______________________
4. Cyanotic	______________________
5. Collagen	______________________
6. Cutaneous	______________________
7. Schizophrenia	______________________
8. Cornea	______________________

CHAPTER REVIEW

Fill in the Blanks

Complete the sentences using the following terms:
adjectives, combining vowel, eponym, nouns, prefix, root, suffix

1. The "glue" that binds a word root to a suffix is the ______________.
2. All words must end with a ______________.
3. A word named for a person is an ______________.
4. The word element at the beginning of a word is a ______________.
5. If a suffix begins with a vowel, the ______________ is dropped.
6. The basic foundation of a word is the ______________.
7. Words that end in -al, -ar, -ous are ______________.
8. Words that can be the subject of a sentence are ______________.
9. Not all words have a ______________.
10. Crohn's disease is an example of an ______________.

Circle the Correct Choice

1. bacteria	singular	plural
2. bacterium	noun	adjective

3. bronchial	noun	adjective
4. hepatorenal	noun	adjective
5. virus	singular	plural
6. alveolus	singular	plural
7. atria	noun	adjective
8. atria	singular	plural
9. cocci	singular	plural
10. venous	noun	adjective

Build the Terms

Using the word endings in the list, create medical words for the following meanings.

-al	-ology	-itis
-oma	-ologist	-megaly
-algia		

1. Enlargement of the liver ______________________
2. Pain in the eye ______________________
3. Pertaining to the heart muscle ______________________
4. Inflammation of the breast ______________________
5. Study of the kidneys ______________________
6. Study of blood ______________________
7. Tumor of bone ______________________
8. Inflammation of cartilage ______________________
9. Muscle pain ______________________
10. Study of the stomach and intestines ______________________
11. Specialist who diagnoses and treats the heart ______________________
12. Inflammation of the brain ______________________
13. Nerve pain ______________________
14. Pertaining to the liver and kidneys ______________________
15. Pertaining to the lungs ______________________

Identify the Terms

Complete the sentence with the appropriate medical word.

1. The ______________________ examined Mr. Williams' heart.
2. Mrs. Jones complains of pain in her muscles, also known as ______________________.
3. Curtis suffers from an inflammation of the liver, also called ______________________.
4. Curtis sees what specialist for his problem in no. 3? ______________________.
5. Gary is in medical school studying the skin, a profession known as ______________________.
6. Upon graduating, Gary will become a ______________________.
7. Julie has a tumor in the cartilage of her chest, known as a ______________________.
8. Hannah complains of inflammation of the skin, also known as ______________________.
9. Joseph suffers from an inflammation of his liver, called ______________________.
10. Wendy has ______________________ function tests to evaluate how her lungs are working.
11. If Lydia has difficulty urinating, to what department should she go? ______________________.
12. The medical term that refers to the liver and kidneys is ______________________.
13. The medical term that refers to the heart and lungs is ______________________.
14. If Susie is having digestive trouble, she should see what specialist? ______________________.
15. Susie is diagnosed with inflammation of the intestines, also known as ______________________.

CHAPTER

2

Prefixes and Suffixes

LEARNING OBJECTIVES

Upon completion of the chapter, you will be able to:

1. Define a prefix and state the rule for using prefixes in words.
2. Identify at least 20 prefixes for numbers, colors, measurements, and negatives.
3. Identify at least eight prefixes that describe position or direction.
4. Define a suffix and state the rule for using suffixes in words.
5. Identify at least 15 suffixes that make the word a noun.
6. Identify at least 15 suffixes that make the word an adjective.
7. Identify at least 10 suffixes that pertain to body system specialties and specialists.
8. Identify at least 10 suffixes that describe diagnostic, therapeutic, and surgical procedures or instruments.
9. Identify at least four suffixes that describe categories of medications.
10. Demonstrate the ability to create at least 20 words using prefixes and suffixes

After reading this chapter, you will expand your knowledge of prefixes and suffixes in medical terms. You will be able to decipher components that compose a medical term, identifying the root (or subject) of the term, the prefix, and the suffix. Based upon the suffix attached to the root, you will be able to identify the term as a singular noun, a plural noun, or an adjective.

KEY TERMS

Adjective suffix
Anatomical position
Combined suffixes
Noun suffixes
Prefix

The Relationship of Prefixes to Word Roots

As you learned in Chapter 1, a word root is the foundation of a medical word and expresses the basic meaning of the term. A word can be modified by the addition of a **prefix**, a word element attached to the beginning of the word. Prefixes have defined meanings, and when used with a variety of word roots, the meaning of the prefix does not change.

For example, the prefix **dys-** means poor, bad, difficulty, or labored. When added to a variety of word roots, it describes difficulty of that term (Table 2-1).

The prefix **a-** means *without*, so if we add *a* as the prefix to the word roots in Table 2-1, the meanings of the words change to the inability to perform the function that is described by the word root (Table 2-2).

Prefixes are attached to roots to describe numbers, measurements, positions, direction, color, and negatives. Prefixes that indicate a number are not only found in medical terms but also in terms you are already familiar with (Table 2-3). For example, a bicycle is

TABLE 2-1 The Prefix Dys-

Word	Prefix	Root	Definition	Ending	Definition
dyspnea	dys	pne/o	to breathe	-a	difficulty breathing
dysphagia	dys	phagi/o	to swallow	-ia	difficulty swallowing
dyspepsia	dys	pepsi/o	to digest	-ia	difficulty digesting
dyskinesia	dys	kinesi/o	to move	-ia	difficulty moving

TABLE 2-2 The Prefix A-

Word	Prefix	Root	Definition	Ending	Definition
apnea	a-	pne/o	to breathe	-a	cessation of breathing
aphagia	a-	phagi/o	to swallow	-ia	absence of swallowing
apepsia	a-	pepsi/o	to digest	-ia	inability to digest
akinesia	a-	kinesi/o	to move	-ia	lack of movement

TABLE 2-3 Prefixes Used to Denote Numbers and Measurements

Prefix	Meaning	Example (Pronunciation)	Example Meaning
bi-	two	bilingual (BĪ-LĪNG-gwăl)	being able to speak two languages
hemi-	one-half	hemiplegia (hĕm-ē-PLĒ-jē-ă)	paralysis of one-half of the body
hyper-	excessive	hyperpyrexia (hī-pĕr-pī-REK-sē-ă)	excessive high fever
hypo-	under, below normal amount	hypoesthesia (hī-pō-es-THĒ-zh[ē-]ă)	less than normal sensation
mono-	one	monocular (mŏn-ŏk-ū-lar)	concerning or affecting one eye
multi-	many	multicellular (mŭl-tĭ-SĔL-ū-lăr)	an organism of many cells
nulli-	none	nullipara (nŭl-ĬP-ă-ră)	a woman who has never given birth
poly-	many, much	polymyositis (pol-ē-mī-ŏ-SĪ-tĭs)	inflammation of many muscles
primi-	first	primigravida (prī-mĭ-GRAV-ĭd-ă)	a woman who is pregnant for the first time
quadri-	four	quadriplegia (kwŏd-rĭ-PLĒ-jē-ă)	paralysis of all four limbs

TABLE 2-3 Prefixes Used to Denote Numbers and Measurements—cont'd

Prefix	Meaning	Example (Pronunciation)	Example Meaning
semi-	One-half	semipermeable (sĕm-ē-PER-mē-ă-bl)	pertaining to cell membranes that permit passage of some materials but not others
tetra-	four	tetraparesis (te-tră-pă-RĒ-sĭs)	weakness in all four limbs
tri-	three	trichotomy (trī-KŎT-ō-mē)	division into three parts
uni-	one	uniarticular (ū-nē-ăr-TĬK-ū-lăr)	pertaining to one joint

ā = say, ă = sofa, ē = meet, ĕ = met, ī = eye, ĭ = in, ō = oh, ŏ = dog, ū = you, ŭ = up, oo = food

different from a unicycle or a tricycle. We know the number of wheels of each cycle based on the number prefix.

Prefixes are used to describe a position or a direction in the body (Table 2-4). It is important to remember that we visualize a person in the anatomical position (discussed further in Chapter 3).

TABLE 2-4 Prefixes to Describe Position or Direction

Prefix	Meaning	Example (Pronunciation)	Example Meaning
ab-	away from	abduction (ab-DŬK-shŏn)	movement away from midline
ad-	toward, increase	adduction (ă-DŬK-shŏn)	movement toward midline
ambi-	both, both sides	ambidextrous (am-bi-DEK-strŭs)	able to write or work well with either hand
ante-	before, in front	antecubital (ant-ē-KŪ-bĭt-ăl)	area at the front of the elbow
circum-	around	circumduction (sĭr-kum-DŪK-shŏn)	movement around an axis
dia-	through	diarrhea (dī-ă-RĒ-ă)	passage of watery stool through the gastrointestinal tract
ecto-	outside	ectopic (ek-TOP-ik)	outside the normal location
endo-	within	endoscopy (en-DOS-kŏ-pē)	process of inspecting inside
epi-	upon, over	epigastric (ep-ĭ-GAS-trik)	upon the stomach
ex-	out, away from, outside	exudate (EK-syu-dāt)	any fluid released from body

Continued

TABLE 2-4 Prefixes to Describe Position or Direction—cont'd

Prefix	Meaning	Example (Pronunciation)	Example Meaning
exo-	outside, away from	exoserosis (ĕks-ō-sĕr-Ō-sĭs)	oozing of serum
extra-	outside, beyond	extracorporeal (eks-tră-kor-POR-ē-ăl)	outside the body
hypo-	under, below, beneath	hypoesthesia (hī-pō-es-THĒ-zh[ē-]ă)	less than normal sensation
in-	inside, within	intubate (IN-too-bāt)	insert a tube in the body
infra-	beneath, below	infrapatellar (in-fră-pă-TEL-ăr)	pertaining to under the knee
inter-	between	intercostal (int-ĕr-KOS-tăl)	between the ribs
intra-	within	intravenous (in-tră-VĒ-nŭs)	within a vein
juxta-	near, beside	juxtaglomerular (jŭks-tă-glŏ-MER-yŭ-lăr)	near or adjacent to glomerulus
meso-	middle	mesoderm (MES-ŏ-dĕrm, MEZ-ŏ-dĕrm)	middle layer of skin
para-	near, beside, next to	paracervical (păr-ă-SĔR-vĭ-kăl)	located near the cervix
peri-	around	periodontal (per-ē-ō-DONT-ăl)	located around a tooth
pre-	before, in front of	prenatal (prē-NĀT-ăl)	before birth
pro-	before, in front of	prognosis (prog-NŌ-sĭs)	knowledge before
re-	back, again	reinfection (rē-ĭn-FĔK-shŭn)	second infection, same organ
retro-	backward, behind	retroperitoneal (re-trō-per-ĭt-ŏn-Ē-ăl)	behind the peritoneum
sub-	under, below	sublingual (sŭb-LING-gwăl)	under the tongue
super-	above, beyond	superovulation (soo-pĕr-ŏv-ū-LĀ-shŭn)	increased frequency of ovulation
supra-	above, over	suprahepatic (soo-pră-hē-PĂT-ĭk)	located above the liver
trans-	through, across	transdermal (trănz-DĔRM-ăl)	through the skin

ā = say, ă = sofa, ē = meet, ĕ = met, ī = eye, ĭ = in, ō = oh, ŏ = dog, ū = you, ŭ = up, oo = food
GI, gastrointestinal.

Prefixes can be used to express a lack of, not, or against (Table 2-5).

Prefixes can describe the color of a reaction, the color of a body part, a growth, a rash, or body fluids (Table 2-6). Some color-related word roots are used as prefixes, and some are used as word roots; thus, these combining forms are shown.

Some prefixes modify word elements and are not categorized above. Table 2-7 shows prefixes that describe medical terms, and they will be used in the body system chapters of this text.

TABLE 2-5 Prefixes Used to Denote Negatives

Prefixes	Meaning	Example (Pronunciation)	Example Meaning
a-	without	apnea (ăp-NĒ-ă)	without breathing
an-	without, no, not	analgesia (an-ăl-JĒ-zh[ē]-ă)	without pain
ana-	not, without	anaplasia (an-ă-PLĀ-zh(ē)-ă)	without formation, development
anti-	against	antibiotic (ant-i-bī-OT-ik)	med to destroy microorganisms
contra-	against	contraindicated (kon-tră-in-dĭ-KĀT-ĕd)	against indications, such as a medication during pregnancy or in a patient with liver disease
dis-	free of, to undo	disability (dis-ă-BIL-ĭt-ē)	physical, mental, or functional impairment
im-	not	imbalance (im-BAL-ăns)	lack of balance
in-	inside, within, not	incontinence (in-KONT-ĭn-ĕns)	loss of voluntary control of urine excretion
non-	not	nontoxic (nŏn-TŎK-sĭk)	not poisonous

ā = say, ă = sofa, ē = meet, ĕ = met, ī = eye, ĭ = in, ō = oh, ŏ = dog, ū = you, ŭ = up, oo = food

TABLE 2-6 Prefixes and Combining Forms Used to Denote Colors

Prefix/Combining Form	Meaning	Example (Pronunciation)	Example Meaning
alb-	white	albino (al-BĪ-nō)	a person with a marked lack of pigment in skin, eyes
albin/o-	white	albinism (AL-bĭ-nizm)	condition of abnormally white skin, absence of pigment
chlor/o	green	chloronychia (klō-rō-NĬK-ē-ă)	green nail syndrome
cirrh/o	yellow, tawny	cirrhosis (sĭ-rō-sĭs)	chronic degenerative disease of the liver, resulting in yellowing of the skin and liver

Continued

TABLE 2-6 Prefixes and Combining Forms Used to Denote Colors—cont'd

Prefix/Combining Form	Meaning	Example (Pronunciation)	Example Meaning
cyan/o	blue	cyanuria (sī-ă-nū-rē-ă)	voiding of blue urine
eosin/o	red, rosy	eosinophil (ē-ŏ-SIN-ŏ-fil)	a leukocyte that stains red with an acid dye
erythr/o	red	erythrocyte (ĕ-RITH-rŏ-sīt)	a red blood cell
glauc/o	gray, silver	glaucoma (glaw-KŌ-mă)	disorder of the eye, increased intra-ocular pressure causing dull, gray gleam of the affected eye
jaund/o	yellow	jaundice (JON-dĭs)	yellow discoloration of the skin
leuk/o	white	leukocyte (LOO-kŏ-sīt)	any of several types of white blood cells
melan/o	black	melanoma (mel-ă-NŌ-mă)	malignant tumor of darkly pig-mented skin cells
poli/o	gray	poliomyelitis (pō-lē-ō-mī-ĕl-ĪT-ĭs)	inflammation of the gray matter of the spinal cord
purpur/o	purple	purpura (PŬR-pyŭ-ră)	collection of blood beneath the skin surface, pinpoint hemorrhages with a purple/red color
xanth/o	yellow	xanthoderma (zan-thŏ-DĚR-mă)	yellow discoloration of skin

ā = say, ă = sofa, ē = meet, ĕ = met, ī = eye, ĭ = in, ō = oh, ŏ = dog, ū = you, ŭ = up, oo = food

TABLE 2-7 Common Prefixes

Prefix	Meaning	Example (Pronunciation)	Example Meaning
bio-	life	biology (bī-OL-ŏ-jē)	the study of life
brady-	slow	bradypnea (brăd-ĭp-NĒ-ă)	slowed breathing
con-	together, with	congenital (kŏn-JEN-ĭ-tăl)	born with, appearing at birth
dys-	bad, poor, labored	dyspnea (dis[p]-NĒ-ă)	difficulty breathing
eu-	normal, good	euphoria (ū-FOR-ē-ă)	good feelings
hetero-	different	heterocellular (hĕt-ĕr-ō-SĔL-ū-lăr)	composed of different types of cells

TABLE 2-7 Common Prefixes—cont'd

Prefix	Meaning	Example (Pronunciation)	Example Meaning
homeo-	likeness, sameness	homeostasis (hō-mē-ō-STĀ-sĭs)	constancy of the internal environment of the body
homo-	same	homolateral (hō-mō-LĂT-ĕ-răl)	on the same side
hydro-	water	hydronephrosis (hī-drō-nĕf-RŌ-sĭs)	water retention within the kidney
idio-	individual, distinct	idioventricular (ĭd-ē-ō-vĕn-TRĬK-ū-lăr)	pertaining to the cardiac ventricle only
meta-	beyond, change	metamorphosis (mĕt-ă-MOR-fĭs)	process of changing shape
pseudo-	false	pseudoneoplasm (soo-dō-NĒ-ō-plăsm)	false or phantom tumor
sym-	joined, together	symbiosis (sim-bē-Ō-sĭs)	two organisms living together in close association
syn-	joined, together	synthesis (sĭnthĕ-sĭs)	a combining of separate elements or substances to form a coherent whole
ultra-	beyond, excess	ultrasound (ŬL-tră-sownd)	sound waves above 20,000 cycles/sec

ā = say, ă = sofa, ē = meet, ĕ = met, ī = eye, ĭ = in, ō = oh, ŏ = dog, ū = you, ŭ = up, oo = food

Word-Building Practice

Read each definition and complete the term using the prefixes and combining forms provided. Refer to word roots presented in Chapter 1 to complete the word.

ante-	hemi-	peri-
anti-	hyper-	poly-
bi-	hypo-	post-
brady-	infra-	pre-
contra-	inter-	primi-
dys-	intra-	retro-
ecto-	leuk/o-	semi-
endo-	melan/o-	tachy-
erythr/o-	multi-	tri-
eu-	pan-	uni-
exo-	para-	xanth/o-

1. between the ribs ______________________
2. a red blood cell ______________________

3. the period of time after a surgical procedure ______________________
4. difficulty breathing ______________________
5. a woman who is pregnant for the first time ______________________
6. partial paralysis of half of the body ______________________
7. pertaining to within a vein ______________________
8. a fast heart rate ______________________
9. a slow heart rate ______________________
10. care given before a woman gives birth ______________________
11. an instrument to look inside of the body ______________________
12. a medication that cannot be used for a specific patient or condition ______________________
13. a darkly pigmented skin cancer ______________________
14. a white blood cell ______________________
15. pertaining to under the liver ______________________
16. pertaining to under the kneecap ______________________
17. pertaining to both sides ______________________
18. the valve of the heart that contains three cusps ______________________
19. pertaining to beneath the eyeball ______________________
20. to bear many children ______________________

The Relationship of Suffixes to Word Roots

The word root is the foundation of a medical word and expresses the basic meaning of the term. Many words don't have a prefix, but every term *must* have a suffix. All word roots depend upon a suffix. The suffix tells the reader the word is a noun (plural or singular) or an adjective and thus guides its usage in sentences and the expression of thoughts.

Recall that linking suffixes to combining forms follows one of two rules:

Rule 1: When a suffix begins with a consonant, a combining vowel is used with the word root to link the root and the suffix.
Example: cardiomegaly: **cardi/o** = heart, **-megaly** = enlargement

Rule 2: When the suffix begins with a vowel, the word root can be attached directly to the suffix and does not need the combining vowel.
Example: carditis: **cardi/o** = heart, **-itis** = inflammation

It is important to note that word elements, roots, prefixes, and suffixes retain the same meaning from word to word. Thus, **-megaly** will always mean "enlargement." You can use the suffix to describe the enlargement of a variety of body parts:

Gastromegaly means "enlargement of the stomach" (**gastr/o** = stomach).
Hepatomegaly means "enlargement of the liver" (**hepat/o** = liver).
Acromegaly means "enlargement of extremities" (**acr/o** = extremities).

Note that **-megaly** starts with the letter *M* (a consonant); thus, each of the word roots in the examples brings its combining vowel to make the word.

We can also use the same root and a variety of suffixes to build medical terms. Table 2-8 shows how the root **hepat/o**, meaning "liver," can be used to create many terms related to the liver.

Elements Retain Their Meaning

It is important to note that word elements may be used as a prefix, a root, or a suffix, but they retain their meaning no matter where they are placed in a word.

For example: **path/o** means disease.

It can be used as the root of a word.
Pathology means "the study of disease:" **path/o** = disease, **-logy** = the study of
It also retains its meaning if it is used as a suffix.
Encephalopathy means "disease of the brain:" **-en** = within, **cephal/o** = head, **-pathy** = noun ending meaning "disease."
Encephalopathic: **-pathic** = adjective ending meaning "pertaining to disease."

By memorizing word roots and suffixes, you will be able to both build and decipher many medical terms and thus build your medical vocabulary.

Noun Suffixes

Many of the suffixes attached to a medical term make the term a noun. **Noun suffixes** attached to a combining form can be the subject of a sentence. As stated in Chapter 1, a noun is a person, place, thing, or quality. Table 2-9 lists suffixes that form nouns.

Many noun suffixes denote a condition and are listed in Table 2-10.

Specialties and Specialists

Suffixes may describe the various body systems and the specialists who treat diseases and disorders of those systems (Table 2-11). Suffixes used to describe a practitioner or a field of study are noun suffixes; therefore, the word can be the subject of a sentence.

TABLE 2-8 Suffixes and the Root Hepat/o

Word	Suffix	Suffix Meaning	Example Meaning
hepatitis	-itis	inflammation	inflammation of the liver
hepatomegaly	-megaly	enlargement	enlargement of the liver
hepatic	-ic	pertaining to the	pertaining to the liver
hepatology	-ology	the study of	the study of the liver

TABLE 2-9 Suffixes that Form Nouns

Suffix	Meaning	Example (Pronunciation)	Example Meaning
-a	noun ending	erythema (er-ĭ-THĒ-mă)	reddening of the skin
-e	noun ending	dermatome (DĔR-mă-tōm)	instrument to cut the skin
-er	person who . . .	ultrasonographer (ŭl-tră-sŏ-NOG-ră-fĕr)	person who administers ultrasound
-iatry	medical treatment / profession	psychiatry (Sī-KĪ-a-trē)	treatment of diseases and disorders of the mind
-ion	action, process	contraction (kŏn-TRAK-shŏn)	action that shortens muscle
-ist	practitioner	podiatrist (pŏ-DĪ-ă-trist)	specialist in the treatment of feet
-ole	small	arteriole (ar-TĒR-ē-ōl)	small artery
-tion	process of	parturition (păr-tū-RĬSH'ŭn)	the act of giving birth
-ula	small	uvula (Ū-vyŭ-lă)	small projection at the back of the throat
-ule	small	venule (VEN ūl)	smallest vein that connects to a capillary
-um	singular noun	peritoneum (per-it-ŏ-NĒ-ŭm)	serous membrane of the abdomen
-us	singular noun	coccus (KOK-ŭs)	singular form for a bacterium type

ā = say, ă = sofa, ē = meet, ĕ = met, ī = eye, ĭ = in, ō = oh, ŏ = dog, ū = you, ŭ = up, oo = food

TABLE 2-10 Noun Suffixes Denoting a Condition

Suffix	Meaning	Example (Pronunciation)	Example Meaning
-esis	condition	diuresis (dī-yŭ-RĒ-sĭs)	secretion of a large amount of urine
-ia	condition	quadriplegia (kwŏd-rĭ-PLĒ-jē-ă)	paralysis of all four limbs
-ism	condition	alcoholism (AL-kŏ-hol-izm)	disease of dependence upon alcohol
-osis	condition	scoliosis (skō-lē-Ō-sĭs)	condition of a lateral bend of the spine
-y	condition	retinopathy (ret-ĭn-OP-ă-thē)	disease state of the retina

ā = say, ă = sofa, ē = meet, ĕ = met, ī = eye, ĭ = in, ō = oh, ŏ = dog, ū = you, ŭ = up, oo = food

TABLE 2-11 Suffixes to Describe a Practitioner or a Field of Study

Suffix	Meaning	Example (Pronunciation)	Example Meaning
-ician	specialist in a field of study	obstetrician (ob-stĕ-TRISH-ăn)	specialist in pregnancy and childbirth
-iatrics	relating to medicine, providers or providing	pediatrics (pē-dē-ĂT-rĭks)	field of medicine pertinent to children or medical treatment
-iatry	medical treatment, profession	podiatry (pō-DĪ-ă-tr)	field of medicine pertinent to feet
-iatrist	one who treats, provider	psychiatrist (sī-KĪ-ă-trĭst)	specialist in mental health
-ist	one who treats, provider	optometrist (ŏp-TŎM-ĕ-trĭst)	specialist who measures and treats disorders of eyes
-logist	specialist in the study of	gynecologist (gīn-ĕ-KOL-ō-jĭst)	specialist in the study of women's health
-logy	study of	cardiology (kăr-dē-ŎL-ō-jē)	the study of the heart
-practor	specialist	chiropractor (kī-rō-PRAK-tŏr)	specialist who uses hands to treat the body

ā = say, ă = sofa, ē = meet, ĕ = met, ī = eye, ĭ = in, ō = oh, ŏ = dog, ū = you, ŭ = up, oo = food

Instruments and Procedures

Suffixes can be used to describe medical instruments or surgical and diagnostic procedures (Table 2-12). Procedures vary and may be performed in a medical office (outpatient setting) or in a hospital surgery setting (inpatient). Most instrument suffixes are primarily used for tools that measure or diagnose. Instruments and procedures are nouns and therefore can be the subject of a sentence.

TABLE 2-12 Suffixes to Describe Medical Instruments or Surgical and Diagnostic Procedures

Suffix	Meaning	Example (Pronunciation)	Example Meaning
-centesis	surgical puncture	amniocentesis (am-nē-ō-sen-TĒ'sĭs)	surgical puncture and removal of amniotic fluid for lab analysis
-clasis	breaking	osteoclasis (os'tē-ŏ-kla-sĭs)	surgical fracture to correct bone deformity
-desis	binding or surgical fusion	arthrodesis (ar-THROD'ĕ-sĭs)	fusion of a joint
-ectasis	stretching/ dilation	bronchiectasis (brong-kē-EK-tă-sĭs)	chronic dilation of a bronchus or bronchi damaged from infection
-ectomy	surgical removal	tonsillectomy (tŏn-sĭl-ĔK-tō-mē)	surgical removal of tonsils

Continued

TABLE 2-12 Suffixes to Describe Medical Instruments or Surgical and Diagnostic Procedures—cont'd

Suffix	Meaning	Example (Pronunciation)	Example Meaning
-gram	record or picture	electrocardiogram (ē-lĕk-trō-KĂR-dē-ō-grăm)	record of electrical activity of the heart
-graph	instrument to record	electrocardiograph (ē-lĕk-trō-KĂR-dē-ō-grăf)	instrument used to record electrical activity of the heart
-graphy	process of recording	electrocardiography (ē-lĕk-trō-kăr-dē-ŎG-ră-fē)	process of recording the electrical activity of the heart
-meter	instrument to measure	thermometer (thĕr-MOM-ĕt-ĕr)	instrument to measure temperature
-metry	process of measuring	pelvimetry (pĕl-VĬM-ĕ-trē)	process of measuring the dimensions of the pelvis
-opsy	process of viewing	biopsy (BĪ-op-sē)	removal of small sample of living tissue for analysis
-pexy	surgical fixation	cystopexy (SĬS-tō-pĕk-sē)	surgical fixation of the bladder to the wall of the abdomen
-plasty	surgical repair	rhinoplasty (RĪ-nō-plăs-tē)	surgical repair of the nose
-rrhaphy	suturing	cardiorrhaphy (kăr-dē-OR-ă-fē)	suturing of the heart
-scope	instrument to view	otoscope (Ō-tō-skōp)	instrument to view the interior ear
-scopy	process of viewing	otoscopy (ō-TŌS-kō-pē)	process of viewing the ear
-stat	instrument to stop/control	hemostat (HĒ-mŏ-stat)	instrument to control bleeding
-stomy	creation of a new opening	colostomy (kŏ-LOS-tŏ-mē)	surgical creation of a new opening between the colon and surface of the body
-tomy	incision into	phlebotomy (flĕ-bot-ŏ-mē)	incision into a vein
-tripsy	crushing	lithotripsy (LITH-ŏ-trip-sē)	crushing of a stone

ā = say, ă = sofa, ē = meet, ĕ = met, ī = eye, ĭ = in, ō = oh, ŏ = dog, ū = you, ŭ = up, oo = food

Adjective Suffixes

Adjectives are words that describe or modify nouns. The **adjective suffix** describes the word root to which it is attached. The definition of the adjective suffix form is the same as its corresponding noun form, but the adjective suffix acts as a descriptor. These adjective suffix forms cannot be the subject of a sentence. Before we can compare noun suffix and

TABLE 2-13 Adjective Suffixes Meaning "Pertaining to"

Suffix	Meaning	Example (Pronunciation)	Example Meaning
-ac	pertaining to	cardiac (KĂR-dē-ăk)	pertaining to the heart
-al	pertaining to	duodenal (doo-ŏ-DĒN-ăl)	pertaining to the duodenum
-ar	pertaining to	vascular (VAS-kyŭ-lăr)	pertaining to blood vessels
-ary	pertaining to	coronary (KOR-ō-ner-ē)	pertaining to the blood vessels of the heart
-eal	pertaining to	esophageal (ē-sof-ă-JĒ-ăl)	pertaining to the esophagus
-ic	pertaining to	pediatric (pē-dē-ĂT-rĭk)	pertaining to the children
-ical	pertaining to	neurological (noo-rŏ-LOJ-ĭ-kăl)	pertaining to the study of nerves
-ile	pertaining to	febrile (FĒ-brĭl)	pertaining to fever
-ory	pertaining to	auditory (OD-ĭ-tōr-ē)	pertaining to hearing
-ous	pertaining to	venous (VĒ-nŭs)	pertaining to veins
-tic	pertaining to	cyanotic (sī-ăn-ŎT-ĭk)	pertaining to condition of blueness

ā = say, ă = sofa, ē = meet, ĕ = met, ī = eye, ĭ = in, ō = oh, ŏ = dog, ū = you, ŭ = up, oo = food

corresponding adjective suffix forms, we must understand the largest group of adjective suffixes: those that mean "pertaining to" (Table 2-13). There are no rules that govern which "pertaining to" suffix is used; thus, you must memorize common root + suffix combinations.

When using adjectives, there must be a noun that is modified. The words from Table 2-6 are used in sentences to give some examples of this rule.

1. *The pediatric office is located near the hospital.* The word *pediatric* describes the type of office.
2. *The patient was found to have a duodenal ulcer.* The word *duodenal* describes the location of the ulcer.
3. *The vascular surgeon was consulted.* The word *vascular* describes the type of surgeon.
4. *The coronary arteries were occluded (blocked).* The word *coronary* describes the location of the arteries.
5. *The patient was found to have esophageal cancer.* The word *esophageal* describes the type of cancer.
6. *The patient was transferred to the cardiac care unit.* The word *cardiac* describes the type of care unit.
7. *The patient was given a neurological examination.* The word *neurological* describes the type of examination.
8. *Covid is often a febrile infection.* The word *febrile* describes the quality of the infection.

9. *The auditory tube is in the middle ear.* The word *auditory* describes the function of the tube.
10. *The phlebotomist draws venous blood from the patient.* The word *venous* describes the type of blood.
11. *The unconscious patient appears cyanotic.* The word *cyanotic* describes the appearance of the patient.

Corresponding Noun and Adjective Suffixes

Suffixes can describe a condition, a feeling, or a quality. Most of the suffixes listed in Table 2-14 are noun suffixes, but a few are also shown in their adjective suffix forms. As noted previously, the definition of the adjective form is the same as the corresponding noun form, but it acts as a descriptor. Some of the suffixes listed are **combination suffixes,** suffixes that comprise two elements. Often, combination suffixes are made up of a specific condition followed by **-osis**; thus, the combination suffixes specify the condition. Examples include **-lithiasis** (condition with a stone) or **-stenosis** (condition of narrowing). When memorizing the adjective form, add "pertaining to" to the definition of the noun form. It is important to understand both the meaning of the suffix and its noun or adjective form.

TABLE 2-14 Suffixes to Describe a Condition, Feeling, or Quality

Noun/Adjective	Suffix	Meaning	Example (Pronunciation)	Definition
Noun	-algesia	pain	analgesia (an-ăl-JĒ-zh[ē]-ă)	without pain
Adjective	-algesic	pertaining to pain	analgesic medication (an-ăl-JĒ-zik med-ĭ-KĀ-shŏn)	pertaining to without pain
Noun	-algia	pain	myalgia (mī-AL-j[ē-]ă)	muscle pain
Noun	-blast	immature	osteoblast (OS-tē-ō-blast)	immature bone cell
Noun	-cele	hernia	rectocele (REK-tŏ-sēl)	herniation of the rectum (anus)
Adjective	-cidal	pert to causing death	suicidal (SOO-ĭ-sīd-ăl)	an impulse to kill one's self
Noun	-cide	causing death	suicide (SOO-ĭ-sīd)	the act of killing one's self
Noun	-cyte	cell	osteocyte (OS-tē-ŏ-sīt)	a bone cell
Noun	-dynia	pain	arthrodynia (ar'thrō-dĭn ē-ă)	joint pain
Noun	-gen	producing, forming	carcinogen (KARS-ĭn-ŏ-jen)	a substance that causes cancer
Noun	-genesis	producing, forming	osteogenesis (os-tē-ō-JEN-ĕ-sĭs)	process of forming of bone

TABLE 2-14 Suffixes to Describe a Condition, Feeling, or Quality—cont'd

Noun/Adjective	Suffix	Meaning	Example (Pronunciation)	Definition
Adj	-genic	pert to producing, forming pollution	carcinogenic (kar-sĭ-nō-JEN-ik)	pert to a substance that causes cancer
Noun	-gravida	pregnant	primigravida (prī-mĭ-GRAV-ĭd-ă)	first pregnancy
Noun	-iasis	condition	sialolithiasis (sī-ă-lō-lĭ-THĪ-ă-sĭs)	condition of a stone in the salivary gland
Noun	-ism	condition, theory	hirsutism (HĬR-sŭ-tizm)	condition of excessive body hair in a male distribution pattern
Noun	-itis	inflammation	bronchitis (brong-KĪT-ĭs)	inflammation of the bronchi
Noun	-lepsy	seizure	narcolepsy (NĂR-kō-lĕp-sē)	condition of daytime sleepiness
Noun	-lith	stone	cholelith (KŌ-lĭ-lĭth)	gallstone
Noun	-lithiasis	condition of a stone	cholelithiasis (kō-li-lith-Ī-ă-sĭs)	condition of a gallstone
Noun	-lysis	destruction	rhabdomyolysis (rab-dō-mī-OL-ĭ-sĭs	destruction of skeletal muscle
Adj	-lytic	pert to destruction	hemolytic (hē-mŏ-LIT-ik)	disease of the newborn, blood disorder caused by incompatibility of maternal and fetal blood
Noun	-mania	frenzy, madness	egomania (ē-gō-MĀ-nē-ă)	abnormal self-esteem
Noun	-megaly	enlargement	hepatomegaly (hep-ăt-ō-MEG-ă-lē)	enlargement of the liver
Noun	-oid	resembling	lipoid (LĬP-oyd)	resembling fat
Noun	-oma	tumor	lipoma (li-PŌ-mă)	fatty tumor
Noun	-opia	vision	hyperopia (hī-pĕr-Ō-pē-ă)	farsightedness
Noun	-osis	condition	cyanosis (sī-ă-NŌ-sĭs)	condition of blueness (of the skin)
Noun	-pathy	disease	cardiopathy (kăr-dē-ŎP-ă-thē)	disease of the heart
Adj	-pathic	pert to disease	encephalopathic (ĕn-sĕf-ă-lō-PATH-ik)	pertaining to disease of the brain

Continued

TABLE 2-14 Suffixes to Describe a Condition, Feeling, or Quality—cont'd

Noun/Adjective	Suffix	Meaning	Example (Pronunciation)	Definition
Noun	-penia	decreased amount	erythropenia (ĕ-rĭth-rō-PĒ-nē-ă)	decreased amount of red blood cells)
Noun	-philia	attraction to	hemophilia (hē-mŏ-FIL-ē-ă)	bleeding disorder (attraction/ affinity to bleed)
Noun	-phobia	fear	arachnophobia (ă-rak-nō-FŌ-bē-ă)	a fear of spiders
Noun	-plasia	formation	dysplasia (dis-PLĀ-zh[ē-]ă)	abnormal development, formation
Noun	-plegia	paralysis, stroke	hemiplegia (hĕm-ē-PLĒ-jē-ă)	paralysis on one side of the body
Adj	-plegic	pert to paralysis	hemiplegic patient (hĕm-ē-PLĒ-jĭk PĀ-shĕnt)	pert to paralysis on one side of the body
Noun	-pnea	to breath	tachypnea (tak-ē-NĒ-ă)	abnormally rapid breathing
Noun	-ptosis	drooping	blepharoptosis (blĕf-ă-rō-tō-sĭs)	drooping of upper eyelid
Noun	-rrhage	rupture	hemorrhage (HEM-[ŏ]răj)	blood loss
Noun	-rrhea	discharge, flow	rhinorrhea (rī-nŏ-RĒ-ă)	a runny nose
Noun	-rrhexis	rupture of a body part	cardiorrhexis (kăr-dē-ō-RĔK-sĭs)	rupture of the heart
Noun	-sclerosis	condition of hardening	arteriosclerosis (ar-tēr-ē-ō-sklĕ-RŌ-sĭs)	hardening of the arteries
Noun	-stasis	stop, control	hemostasis (hē-mŏ-STĀ-sĭs)	to stop, control bleeding
Noun	-stenosis	narrowing	tracheostenosis (trā-kē-ō-stĕn-Ō-sĭs)	narrowing of the trachea
Noun	-uria	urine	hematuria (hē-mă-TOOR-ē-ă)	blood in the urine

ā = say, ă = sofa, ē = meet, ĕ = met, ī = eye, ĭ = in, ō = oh, ŏ = dog, ū = you, ŭ = up, oo = food

Drug Suffixes

The suffixes in the generic names of medications often identify the medication's classification (Table 2-15). The therapeutic classification categorizes drugs by the type of disease or conditions they can treat. The pharmacological classification is based on the drug's mechanism of action. As you get into the practice of breaking words into elements, you will be able to categorize some of the generic medications by their suffix.

TABLE 2-15 Examples of Medication Suffixes

Suffix	Drug Class	Example	Body System
-pril	antihypertensive	benazepril	cardiovascular
-zosin	antihypertensive	terazosin	cardiovascular
-olol	antihypertensive	metoprolol	cardiovascular
-statin	cholesterol lowering	lovastatin	cardiovascular
-azole	anti-fungal	fluconazole	dermatologic
-cillin	antibiotic	penicillin	immune system
-cycline	antibiotic	tetracycline	immune system
-prazole	proton pump inhibitors	pantoprazole	gastrointestinal
-ipramine	antidepressant	desipramine	neurologic
-zepam	benzodiazepines	clonazepam	neurologic
-terol	bronchodilator	albuterol	respiratory

SUMMARY

- Prefixes are located at the beginning of a medical term and change the meaning of the word.
- Not all medical terms have a prefix.
- All medical terms must include a suffix.
- The suffix of a word determines if it is a noun (singular or plural) or an adjective.
- Word elements retain their meaning no matter their position within a medical term.
- Roots must retain their combining vowel if the suffix begins with a consonant.
- Roots must drop their combining vowel if the suffix begins with a vowel.
- Generic medications can often be classified by their suffix.

Medical Language Lab

Visit the Medical Language Lab at medicallanguagelab.com. Use it to improve your recognition and understanding of terms in medical documentation.

CHAPTER REVIEW

Identify the Prefixes

Mark the correct definition for the prefix listed.

1. ante-
   a. against
   b. before
   c. below
   d. less than

2. hemi-
   a. below
   b. too much
   c. half
   d. painful, difficult

3. dys-
   a. below
   b. too much
   c. half
   d. painful, difficult

4. contra-
   a. against
   b. below
   c. above
   d. too much

5. sym-
   a. joined, together
   b. without
   c. behind
   d. above

6. pseudo-
   a. against
   b. false
   c. without
   d. under, below

7. tachy-
   a. hardening
   b. slow
   c. rapid, fast
   d. together, with

8. ad-
   a. together, with
   b. against
   c. hardening
   d. softening

9. supra-
   a. below
   b. above
   c. beyond
   d. against

10. quadri-
    a. many
    b. limbs
    c. four
    d. without

11. anti-
    a. before
    b. after
    c. without
    d. against

12. post-
    a. after
    b. before
    c. without
    d. against

13. epi-
    a. together, with
    b. many
    c. upon
    d. same

14. non-
    a. not
    b. against
    c. below
    d. above

Complete the Terms

Read each definition and complete the term using the prefixes and combining forms provided:

an-	epi-	intra-	pre-
ante-	erythr/o	leuk/o	primi-
anti-	eu-	melan/o	retro-
bi-	ex-	multi-	semi-
brady-	hemi-	pan-	tachy-
contra-	hyper-	para-	tri-
dys-	hypo-	peri-	uni-
ecto-	infra-	poly-	xer/o
endo-	inter-	post-	xanth/o

1. A medication to reduce pain is a(n) ____________ *algesic.*
2. An injection within the muscle is called ____________ *muscular.*
3. High blood pressure is commonly called ____________ *tension.*
4. A medication to kill a pathogen is called ____________ *biotic.*
5. The lining of the uterus is called the ____________ *metrium.*
6. Good or normal breathing is called ____________ *pnea.*
7. A condition of low calcium in the bloodstream is called ____________ *calcemia.*
8. A woman who has given birth to one infant is ____________ *parous.*
9. Pertaining to below the skin ____________ *cutaneous.*
10. Turning backward ____________ *version.*
11. A toxin that destroys white blood cells is ____________ *cytotoxin.*
12. The term that means pertaining to upon the retina of the eye ____________ *retinal.*
13. The term meaning pertaining to many joints ____________ *articular.*
14. Abnormal outward protrusion of the eyeball ____________ *opthalamos.*
15. Condition of abnormally slow eating or swallowing ____________ *phagia.*
16. Condition of a decrease in all types of blood cells ____________ *cytopenia.*
17. Period of pregnancy between conception and onset of labor ____________ *partum.*
18. Pertaining to several glands ____________ *glandular.*
19. Pertaining to the opposite side ____________ *lateral.*
20. Paralysis of the lower portion of the body ____________ *plegia.*

Circle the Correct Nouns or Adjectives

Using your knowledge of noun and adjective suffixes, circle the word that fits the sentence provided.

1. The patient had inflammation in the ______ sac. pericardium pericardial
2. The heart surgery was performed by the ______. cardiologist cardiology
3. The ______ lines the abdomen. peritoneum peritoneal
4. The bluish color of the patient's skin is called ______. cyanotic cyanosis

5. The patient is dependent upon alcohol, a disease known as ______.	alcoholic	alcoholism
6. Jane suffers from ______ heart disease.	hypertensive	hypertension
7. The baby was transferred to the ______ care unit.	neonatal	neonate
8. After eating a large meal, Tyrone complained of ______ pain.	epigastric	epigastrium
9. Lasix is a drug that causes the body to increase the amount of urine secreted. This increase is known as ______.	diuresis	diuretic
10. A medication to relieve pain, such as Tylenol or aspirin, belongs to a category of medications known as ______.	analgesics	analgesia

Complete the Sentences

Complete each sentence by placing the provided medical terms in their correct place.

1. electrocardiogram, electrocardiography, electrocardiograph

   The medical assistant performs the ____________________ procedure by using the ____________________ machine to create the ____________________ image that can be placed in the patient's chart.

2. pathology, pathologist, adenopathic, adenopathy

   The provider palpated the patient's neck to assess signs of ____________________. The culture was sent to the ____________________ laboratory, and the findings were reported by the ____________________. The patient suffers from an ____________________ disorder.

3. hemostasis, hemolytic, hemopathology, hemostat, hemolysis

   An incompatible blood transfusion will result in ____________________. ____________________ is the analysis of the cellular elements of blood, bone marrow to diagnose and treat disease. ____________________ disease of the newborn is a congenital disorder. Bleeding is controlled during surgery by a process known as ____________________, using an instrument known as a ____________________.

CHAPTER

3

Structures of the Human Body

LEARNING OBJECTIVES

Upon completion of the chapter, you will be able to:

1. Identify and define the combining forms, roots, prefixes, and suffixes introduced in the chapter.
2. Spell medical terms related to the structure of the human body.
3. Describe the levels of organization of the body, anatomical position, and body planes.
4. Define and use directional terms.
5. Describe the dorsal, ventral, cranial, spinal, thoracic, and abdominopelvic body cavities.
6. Discuss the differences between the dorsal and ventral body cavities.
7. Discuss the differences between the abdominal, pelvic, and abdominopelvic body cavities.
8. Describe the quadrants and regions of the abdominopelvic cavity.
9. Identify and discuss major pathological terms of the human body.
10. Identify and discuss major diagnostic and therapeutic treatments of the human body.
11. Define abbreviations pertaining to the structure of the human body.

After reading this chapter, you will expand your knowledge of medical terms related to the structure of the human body. You will understand how the body is organized from the smallest level, the cell, to the entire body. You will know the divisions of the body, the organs found within, and how to use anatomical terms to discuss their relationship. You will be able to use word elements presented to understand unfamiliar terms and to build your medical vocabulary.

KEY TERMS

Abdominopelvic cavity
Anatomical plane
Anatomical position
Anterior
Appendicular
Asymptomatic
Atoms
Axial
Cell
Cell membrane
Connective (tissue)
Coronal
Cranial cavity
Cytoplasm
Deep
Deoxyribonucleic acid
Distal
Dorsal cavity
Epithelial (tissue)
Etiology
Frontal
Gene
Homeostasis
Inferior
Lateral
Medial
Metabolism
Midline
Midsagittal
Molecule
Muscular (tissue)
Nervous (tissue)
Nucleus
Organ
Organelle
Organism
Pelvic cavity
Posterior
Proximal
Quadrant
Sagittal
Sign
Spinal cavity
Superficial
Superior
Symptom
System
Thoracic cavity
Tissue
Transverse
Ventral cavity

Levels of Organization of the Body

Before learning about all the organ systems of the body, it is helpful to understand how the body is organized; that is, how the cells that compose the body are grouped together to create larger structures and how these structures are, in turn, grouped to form increasingly complex structures. The levels of organization of the human body, from simple to complex, are chemical, cell, tissue, organ, system, and organism (Fig. 3-1).

Chemical

The smallest level of organization is the chemical level. All matter is built with **atoms**. Atoms are composed of positively charged protons, negatively charged electrons, and electrically neutral neutrons. Protons and neutrons are found in the nucleus of an atom and the electrons orbit around them in the electron cloud. Examples of atoms include oxygen, hydrogen, and iron. When two or more atoms bond together, they form molecules. **Molecules** are the building blocks of the human body. Examples of molecules are water, glucose, and proteins.

Cells

ELEMENT REVIEW
multi- = many
cellul/o = consisting of cells
-ar = pertaining to

Humans are multicellular organisms composed of trillions of cells. **Cells** are the smallest unit of life and the building blocks of the body. There are several kinds of cells, each with its own structure and function (Fig. 3-2). Despite differences in structure and function, all cells have at least three components in common: the cell membrane, cytoplasm, and

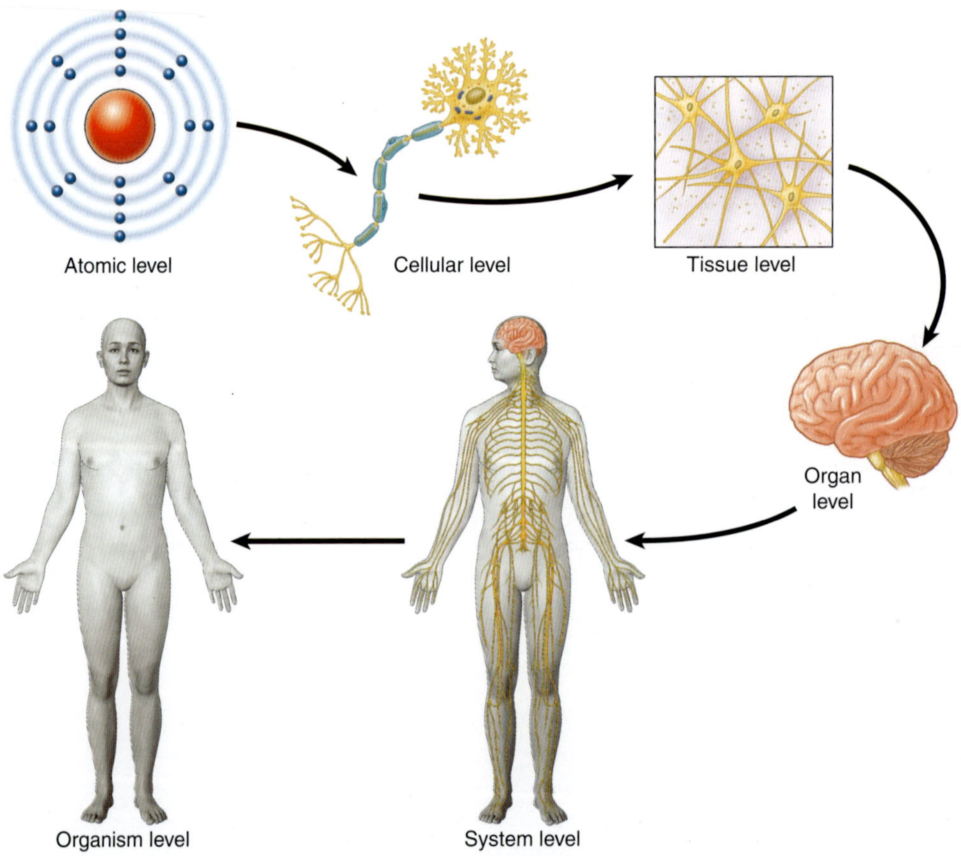

Figure 3-1 The organization of the human body.

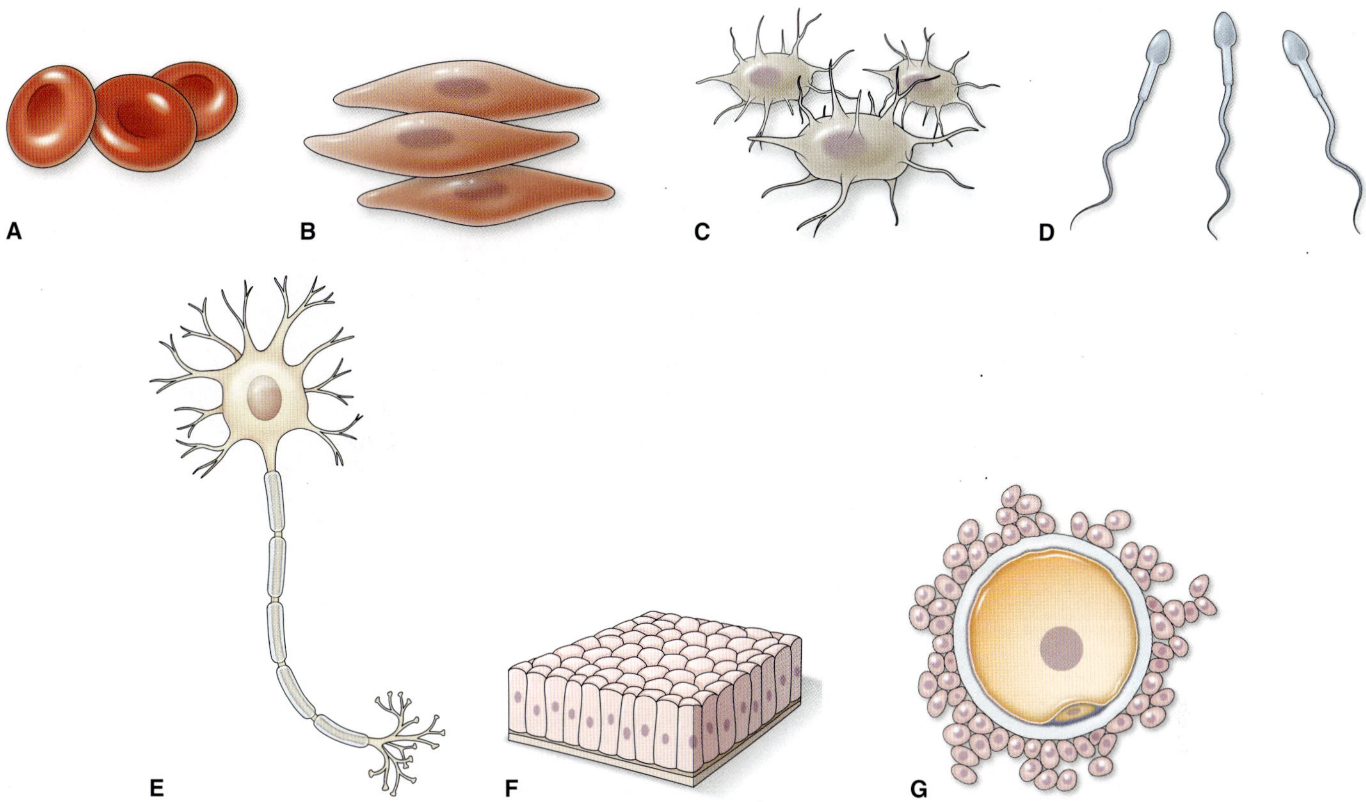

Figure 3-2 Examples of cells in the human body. (A) Red blood cells, (B) smooth muscle cell, (C) bone cell, (D) sperm cell, (E) nerve cell, (F) columnar epithelial cell, and (G) ovum cell.

nucleus (Fig. 3-3). The **cell membrane** defines the extent of the cell, separating the inside of the cell from its surrounding environment. The **cytoplasm** is considered the "body" of the cell and is a semifluid, sticky substance. Finally, the **nucleus** is the "brain" of the cell, containing the genetic material that controls and directs the cell. Genetic material may be found in two forms, chromosomes and chromatin. Chromosomes are a condensed form of deoxyribonucleic acid (DNA) that are formed immediately prior to mitosis, or cell reproduction, so that the DNA is accurately copied and distributed to the two daughter cells, ensuring the genetic information is transmitted correctly. The unit of hereditary is known as a gene, which is a segment of DNA that contains the instructions for a function. When the cells are not replicating, DNA is found in the form of chromatin, threadlike strands that actively control the functioning of the cell.

Cells also contain various **organelles**, tiny structures inside the cell that perform other functions necessary to life. The organelles present in each cell vary depending on its function. The various organelles are listed in Table 3-1.

Tissues

In order for the cells to work together, they must be organized into larger structures. The second level of organization, **tissues**, are groups of similar cells that work together to perform a function. The study of tissues is *histology*. There are four main tissue types: epithelial, connective, muscular, and nervous tissue (Fig. 3-4). Each tissue type has subtypes that vary in shape, structure, arrangement, and function.

ELEMENT REVIEW
hist/o = tissue
-ology = the study of

Epithelial Tissue

Epithelial tissues compose the outermost layer of skin; line the inside of the body cavities and hollow organs; cover the surface of internal organs; and form membranes, ducts, and

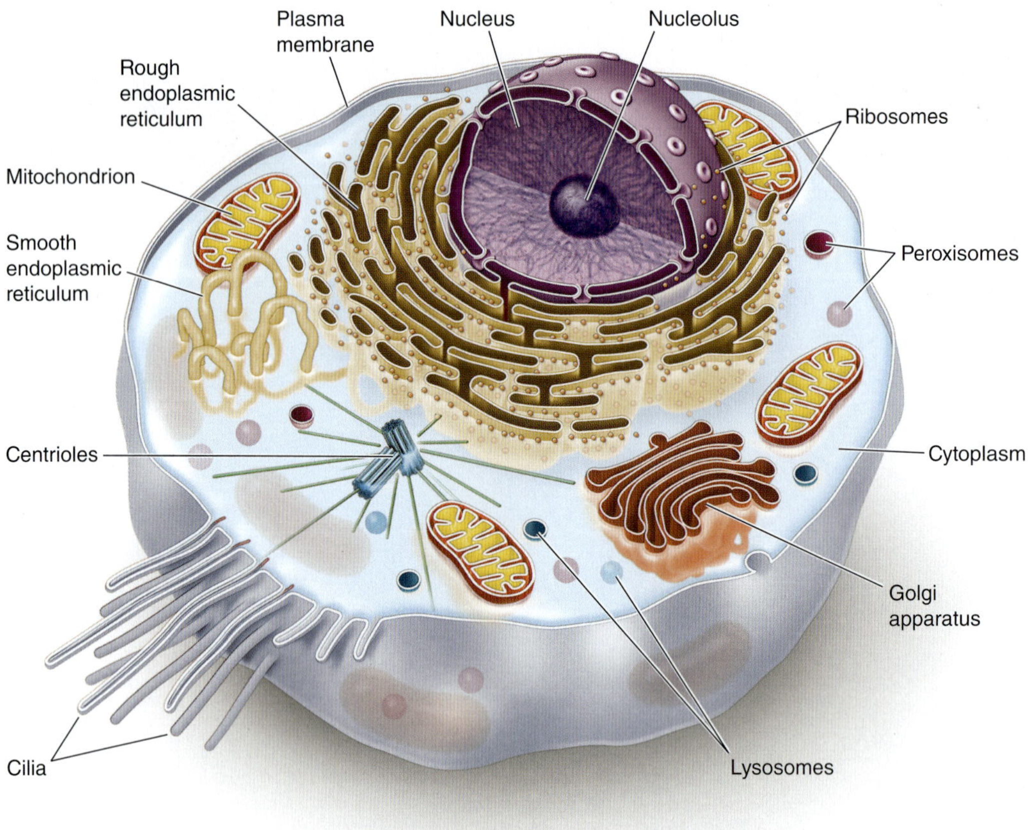

Figure 3-3 The structures of the cell.

TABLE 3-1 Organelles of the Cell

Organelle	Function
Centrioles	Organize and produce the cytoskeleton
Cytoskeleton	Provide structural support, play a role in cell motility, cell reproduction, and transport of substances in the cell
Golgi apparatus	Sort, modify, and package proteins for export from the cell
Lysosomes	Detoxify organic substances
Mitochondria	Produce energy in the form of ATP
Peroxisomes	Detoxify nonorganic substances
Ribosome	Synthesize proteins
Rough endoplasmic reticulum	Modify proteins for use outside the cell
Smooth endoplasmic reticulum	Produce lipids, store calcium

ATP, adenosine triphosphate.

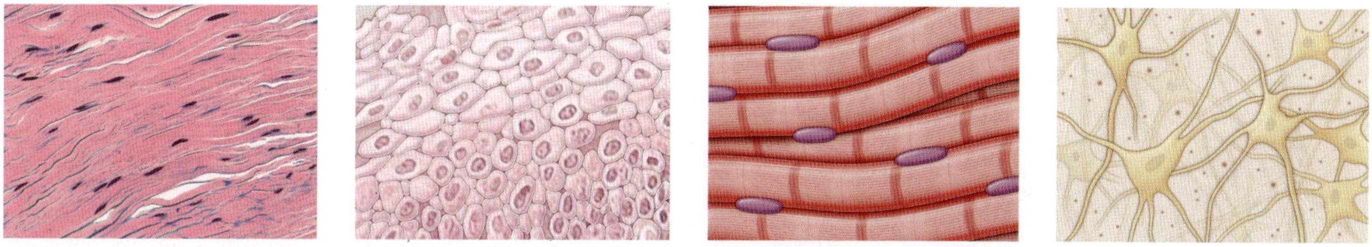

Figure 3-4 Tissue types of the body.

glands. The cells are tightly packed and most commonly found arranged as large, sheetlike tissues that vary in thickness. The epithelial tissues have six main functions:

- Protection: The sheetlike arrangement protects underlying structures from physical, mechanical, or chemical damage, prevents the entry of pathogens (disease-causing microbes), restricts water loss, and forms barriers between organs or systems.
- Sensation: Specialized cells within the epithelium detect stimuli and changes in the environment. These sensory cells are found throughout the skin as well as contained in the eyes, ears, and tongue.
- Secretion: Glands are specialized organs that create and release substances such as hormones, enzymes, sweat, and oil. The glands are composed of epithelial tissue.
- Absorption: The small intestine is lined with epithelial cells; these cells are responsible for absorbing nutrients from the digestive tract into the body.
- Excretion: The removal of waste products from the body is facilitated by the kidneys, which filter waste products from the blood and into the urine. In addition, some waste products are excreted via sweat.
- Diffusion: The movement of substances from an area of high concentration to an area of low concentration often occurs across a membrane in the body. However, this membrane must be very thin to allow effective movement of the substances. Thin layers of epithelial cells found in the blood capillaries and lungs allow gases, liquids, nutrients, and waste products to diffuse from one part of the body to another.

Connective Tissue

Connective tissue is the most abundant tissue in the body as well as the most varied in structure. **Connective tissue** protects, supports, and connects the other tissues of the body, binding structures together, holding organs in place, separating organs from each other, and providing storage areas. It is found surrounding muscle cells and connecting the muscles to bones or other muscles. Bone is a solid form of connective tissue that protects underlying organs. Blood is a liquid connective tissue that protects the body from diseases. To be classified as connective tissue, the tissue must contain specialized cells surrounded by a nonliving matrix.

Muscle Tissue

Muscle tissue has a primary function—to produce movement—in addition to several secondary functions. The secondary functions of muscle are to provide joint stability, maintain posture, and generate heat. There are three type of muscle tissue:

- Skeletal muscle tissue is also known as striated or voluntary muscle. Skeletal muscle displays striations, or stripes, when viewed microscopically. Skeletal muscle is found attached to bones and is responsible for moving the body.
- Cardiac muscle is also known as myocardium and is found in the walls of the heart. It is a striated and involuntary muscle responsible for contraction of the heart to pump blood throughout the body.

ELEMENT REVIFW
my/o = muscle
cardi/o = heart
-ium = noun ending

- Smooth muscle is also known as visceral muscle. Smooth muscle lacks striations and is involuntary. It is found in the walls of hollow organs, such as the stomach, esophagus, large intestine, small intestine, blood vessels, bladder, and uterus. It functions to move substances through the body.

Nervous Tissue

Unlike the other tissue types, nervous tissue does not have multiple tissues in its classification. **Nervous tissue** is composed of neurons and neuroglia. Neurons are cells that are specialized to be excitable and conductive, allowing them to send electrochemical signals throughout the body. Neuroglia are the support cells. These cells work together to form nervous tissue, which controls and coordinates the activities of the body.

Organs

When two or more tissue types are combined to perform a function, they create organs. **Organs** are anatomically distinct structures; each performs specific functions necessary to maintain life. Examples of organs are the heart, lungs, liver, and stomach.

Systems

Organs do not function alone. Instead, they function in groups, known as **systems**, to perform major physiological functions of the body. For example, the urinary system separates toxins and excess fluid from the blood and excretes liquid waste from the body. Individual organs of the urinary system have different functions that combine to allow liquid to be excreted from the body. The kidneys separate wastes to form urine, ureters carry the urine to the bladder, which temporarily stores it, and the urethra carries the urine out of the body. Each organ has a specific function that combines with the functions of additional organs to perform a major physiological task of the body.

The human body has 11 distinct systems (Fig. 3-5). While each body system has a set of organs that contribute to its function, the organs are not restricted to one system only. In fact, most organs perform functions associated with multiple systems. For example, while the kidneys are part of the renal system, they play a key role in the maintenance of blood pressure, which is regulated by both the cardiovascular and endocrine systems. The 11 systems are listed in Table 3-2, along with selected organs and functions.

Organism

The highest level of organization is the organism. An **organism** is a living being that can perform all functions of life. All the cells, tissues, organs, and systems work together to maintain homeostasis, the steady state of the body.

Homeostasis can also be called *dynamic equilibrium*. Dynamic equilibrium means that although our bodies are constantly changing (dynamic), the state of the body exists within a healthy, stable range of parameters. As you explore the various systems of the human body, you will see how homeostatic mechanisms control body temperature, blood pressure, pH, levels of hydration, and much more.

Levels of Organization of the Body Review

Match the word to the description.

cell	endocrine	reproductive (female)
connective	epithelial	urinary
cytoplasm	nucleus	

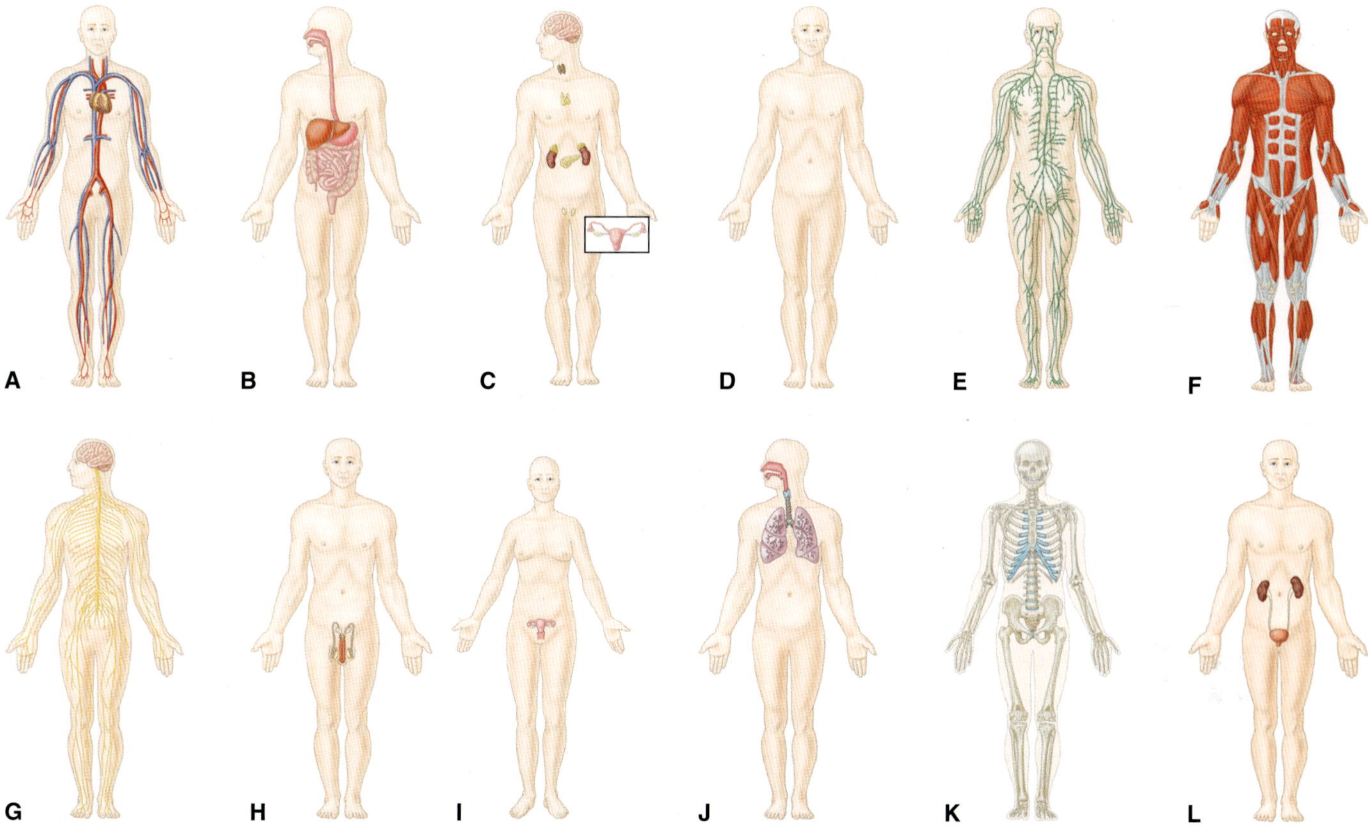

Figure 3-5 Organ systems of the body. (A) Cardiovascular, (B) digestive, (C) endocrine, (D) integumentary, (E) lymphatic, (F) muscular, (G) nervous, (H) reproductive (male), (I) reproductive (female), (J) respiratory, (K) skeletal, (L) urinary.

1. Body system that contains the pancreas, thyroid, ovaries, and testes ______________
2. Body system that contains the ovaries, uterus, and mammary glands ______________
3. Organelle that contains the genetic material ______________
4. Simplest living structure ______________
5. System in which the ureters, kidneys, bladder, and urethra are found ______________
6. Tissue type defined by the presence of a matrix ______________
7. Tissue type that forms sheets to enclose and protect ______________
8. Semifluid considered the body of the cell ______________

Anatomical Position and Divisions

Medical professionals have developed a standard language to accurately describe and discuss complaints regarding the human body. However, these terms are accurate only when all medical professionals are viewing the body in the same orientation. This orientation is known as the **anatomical position**. In the anatomical position, the body is erect, with the head facing forward and arms by the sides with the palms forward. Feet are slightly

ELEMENT REVIEW
Anatomy = the structure of an organism
-ical = pertaining to

TABLE 3-2 Organ Systems of the Human Body

Organ System	Organs	Functions
Cardiovascular	heart, blood vessels, blood	transports nutrients and wastes
Digestive	esophagus, stomach, large intestine, small intestine, liver	processes food for absorption removes solid wastes
Endocrine	ovaries, testes, thyroid, thymus, pancreas, pineal, pituitary	releases hormones regulates body functions
Integumentary	skin, hair, and nails	protects and encloses the body sensory reception
Lymphatic	lymph vessels, lymph nodes, spleen, thymus	protects from disease returns excess fluid to the blood
Muscular	muscles and tendons	enables movement maintains body temperature
Nervous	brain, spinal cord, nerves	detects and interprets sensory information creates body responses
Reproductive	male: penis, testes, prostate, seminal vesicles, epididymis	produces sex hormones (estrogen and testosterone)
	female: vagina, uterus, fallopian tubes, mammary glands, ovaries	produces gametes (ova and sperm)
Respiratory	lungs, trachea, larynx	brings in oxygen releases carbon dioxide
Skeletal	bones, joints, tendons, and ligaments	supports and protects the body stores minerals and fat
Urinary	bladder, ureters, kidneys, urethra	maintains water balance removes liquid wastes

apart with the heels lifted. Anatomical left and right are used, indicating left and right as perceived by the patient. The body may also be divided into the axial and appendicular regions. The **axial** part of the body is composed of the head, neck, and trunk. The **appendicular** portion of the body includes the limbs and their attachments, either the shoulders or the hips (Fig. 3-6). Once in anatomical position, the body planes, directional terms, and body cavities may be used to accurately describe the body.

Body Planes

Anatomical planes are imaginary lines on which the body or organ is divided. Each time the body or organ is divided on a plane, two sections are created. The body can be divided along three main planes: sagittal, transverse, and coronal. A **sagittal** plane vertically divides the body into right and left pieces. If the plane divides the body into two identical mirror image pieces, it is known as the **midsagittal** plane. The line upon which a midsagittal plane is cut is known as the **midline**. A **transverse** plane may also be known as a horizontal plane and divides the body into superior (top) and inferior (bottom) sections. A **frontal** or **coronal** plane divides the body into anterior (front) and posterior (back) sections (Fig. 3-7).

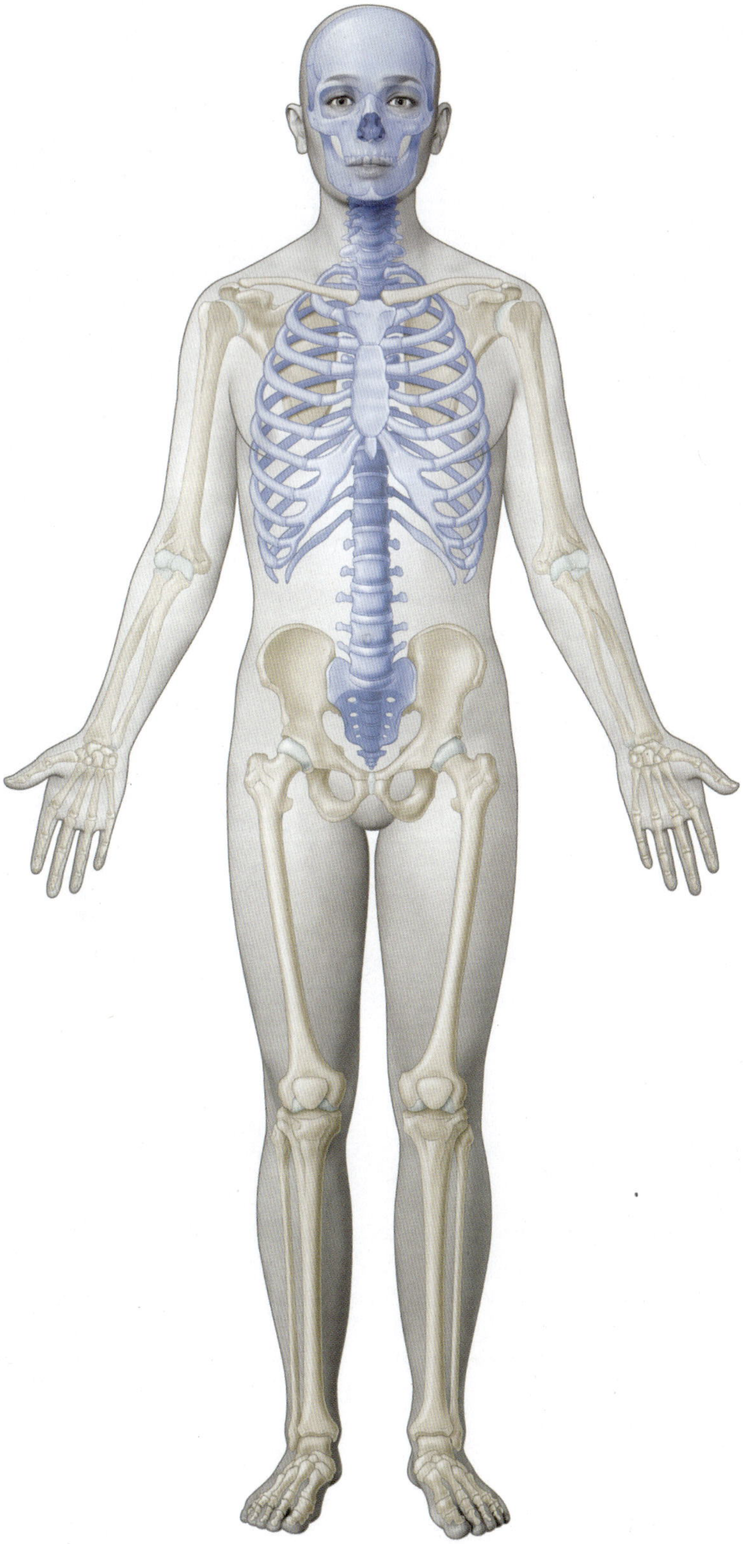

Figure 3-6 The anatomical position.

Directional Terms

Directional terms are used to describe the position of organs or body parts in relationship to each other (Fig. 3-8). They are also used to describe the location of any signs or symptoms a patient is experiencing. Table 3-3 lists the directional terms, their definitions, and examples of their use.

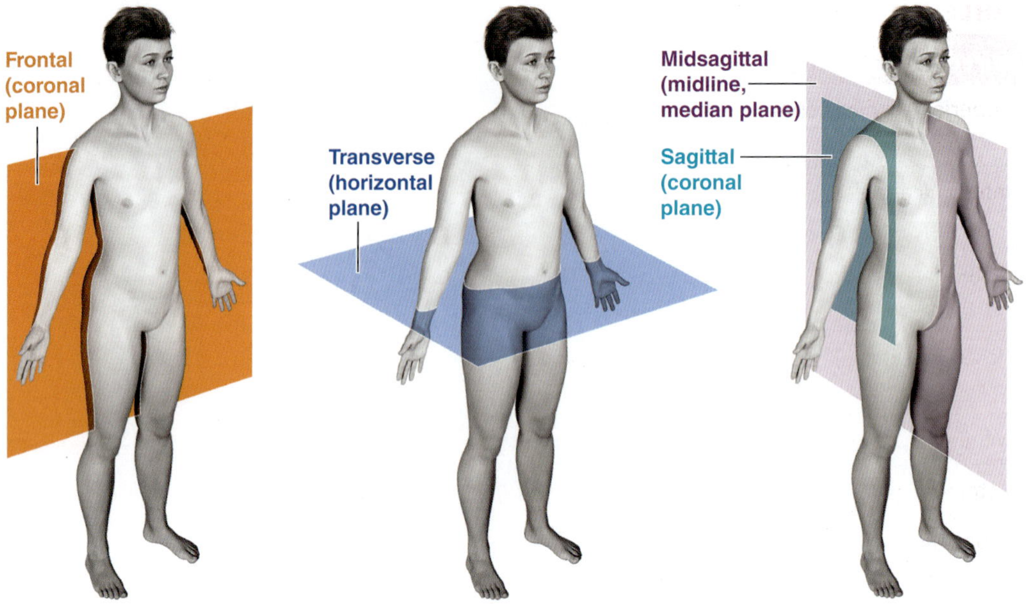

Figure 3-7 Planes of the body.

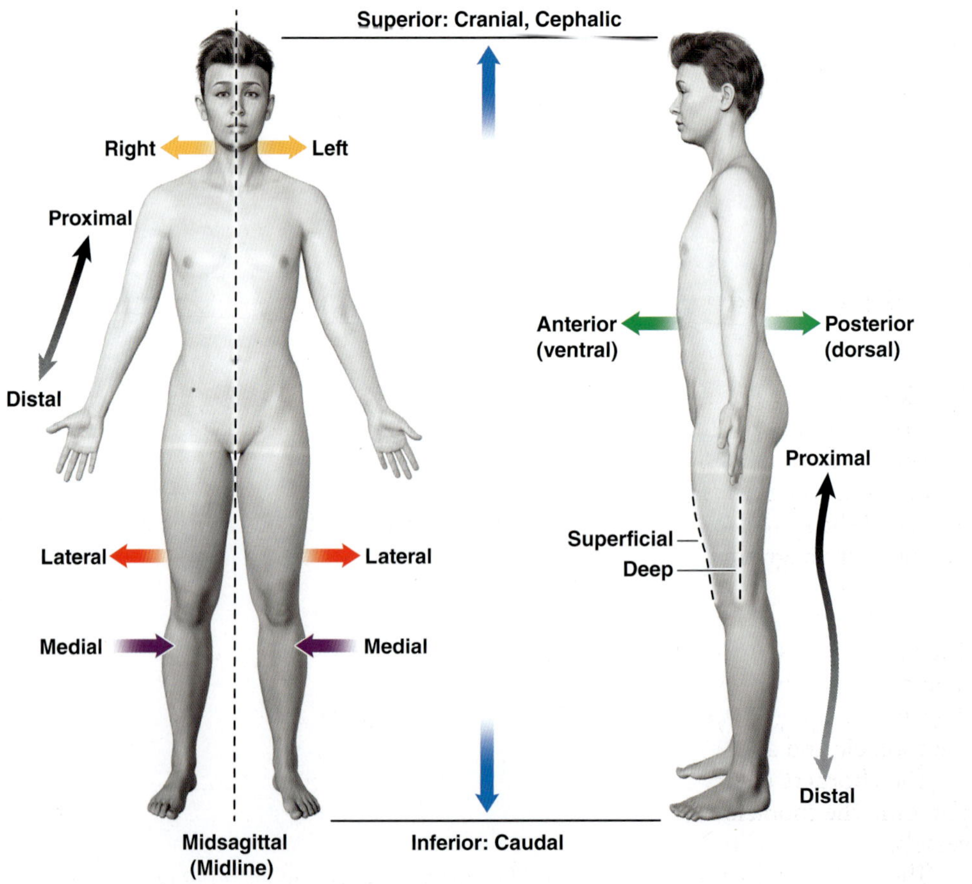

Figure 3-8 Directional terms.

TABLE 3-3 Directional Terms, Their Definition, and Example of Use

Directional term	Definition	Example
Superior (cranial, cephalic)	toward the head, above	The head is superior to the neck. The diaphragm is cranial to the bladder.
Inferior (caudal)	toward the tail, below	The mouth is inferior to the eyes. The lungs are caudal to the trachea.
Anterior (ventral)	toward the front, belly side	The esophagus is anterior to the spine. The liver is ventral to the gallbladder.
Posterior (dorsal)	toward the back	The kidneys are posterior to the large intestine. The spine is dorsal to the trachea.
Medial	closer to the midline	The heart is medial to the lungs.
Lateral	further from the midline	The eyes are lateral to the nose.
Proximal	closer to the point of attachment (often the shoulder or hip)	The elbow is proximal to the wrist. The knee is proximal to the toes.
Distal	further from the point of attachment (often the shoulder or hip)	The ankle is distal to the thigh. The fingers are distal to the palm.
Superficial	closer to the surface	The skin is superficial to the muscles.
Deep	further from the surface	The bone is deep to the muscles.
Ipsilateral	on the same side	The left leg is ipsilateral to the left arm.
Contralateral	on the opposite side	The right arm is contralateral to the left leg.

Body Cavities

A body cavity is a space that contains and protects internal organs. These cavities allow the body to maintain its internal organization during changes in the size and position of the internal organs. There are two main body cavities, named for their location: the dorsal (posterior) cavity and the ventral (anterior) cavity (Fig. 3-9).

Dorsal Cavity

The **dorsal cavity** is found in the back of the body and contains organs of the nervous system. It is subdivided into the cranial and spinal cavities. The **cranial cavity** is defined by the skull and contains the brain. The **spinal cavity** is defined by the vertebrae of the spinal column and contains the spinal cord. Although these two subdivisions are continuous (the brain and the spinal cord are connected), there is a defined line between the two cavities—the foramen magnum of the skull.

Ventral Cavity

The **ventral cavity** is found in the front of the body; it is the space in the torso and abdomen that contains a significant number of the internal organs, including the organs of digestion, respiration, elimination, and reproduction. The ventral cavity is subdivided into the thoracic and abdominopelvic cavities.

The **thoracic cavity** is the chest cavity, which is defined by the rib cage and the diaphragm. The thoracic cavity contains the heart, lungs, trachea, esophagus, and great blood vessels.

The **abdominopelvic cavity** is the largest cavity of the body; it is divided from the thoracic cavity by the diaphragm. Due to its size, the abdominopelvic cavity can be further

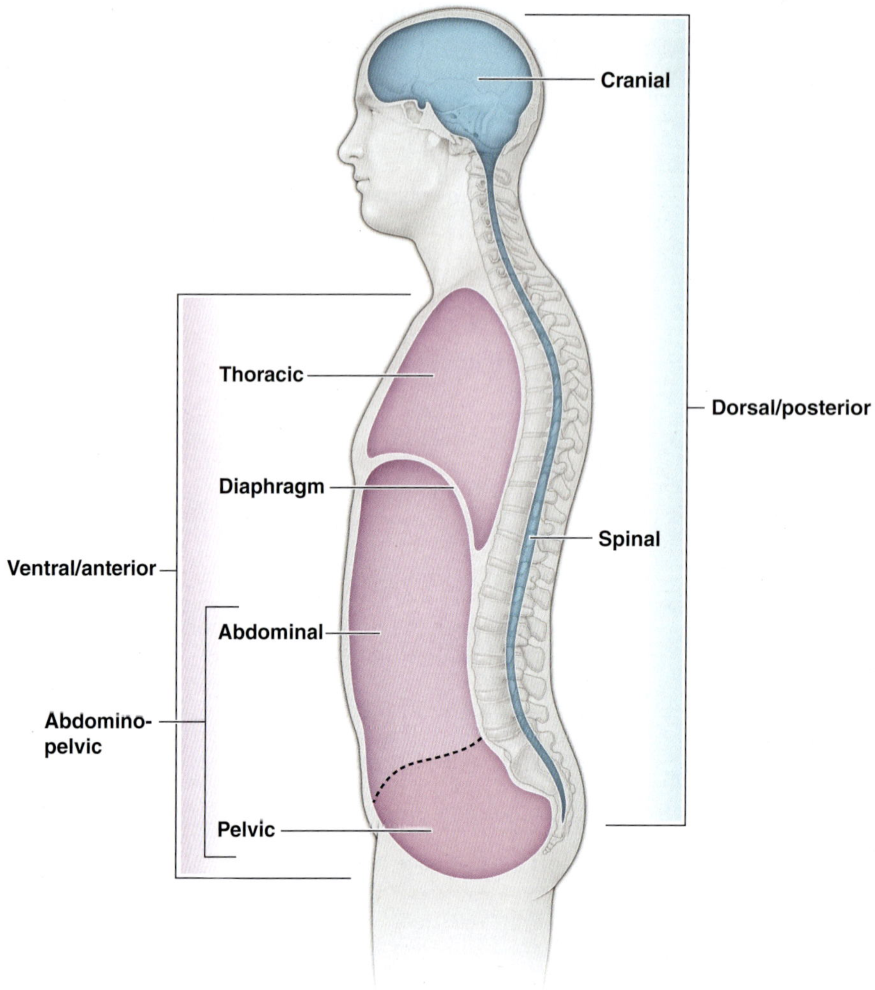

Figure 3-9 Cavities of the body.

divided into the **abdominal cavity** and the **pelvic cavity.** There is no distinct line separating these cavities; instead, they are defined by the organs they contain. The abdominal cavity primarily contains organs of digestion, such as the stomach, large intestine, and small intestine. In contrast, the pelvic cavity contains the organs of reproduction and elimination, such as the urinary bladder, ovaries, uterus, prostate, and seminal vesicles.

For descriptive and diagnostic purposes, the abdominopelvic cavity is described using either four quadrants or nine regions. These divisions allow medical professions to describe the exact location of an area of concern in the abdominopelvic cavity, such as for a patient complaint, suspicious mass that should undergo additional investigation, or incision location.

Quadrants of the Abdominopelvic Cavity

The four **quadrants** of the abdominopelvic cavity are defined by one horizontal and one vertical line that intersect at the navel (bellybutton) (Fig. 3-10). The four quadrants of the abdominopelvic cavity are:

- Left upper quadrant (LUQ): This quadrant contains the stomach, spleen, a kidney, and part of the liver, pancreas, small intestine, and large intestine.
- Right upper quadrant (RUQ): This quadrant contains the gallbladder and part of the liver, pancreas, small intestine, and large intestine.

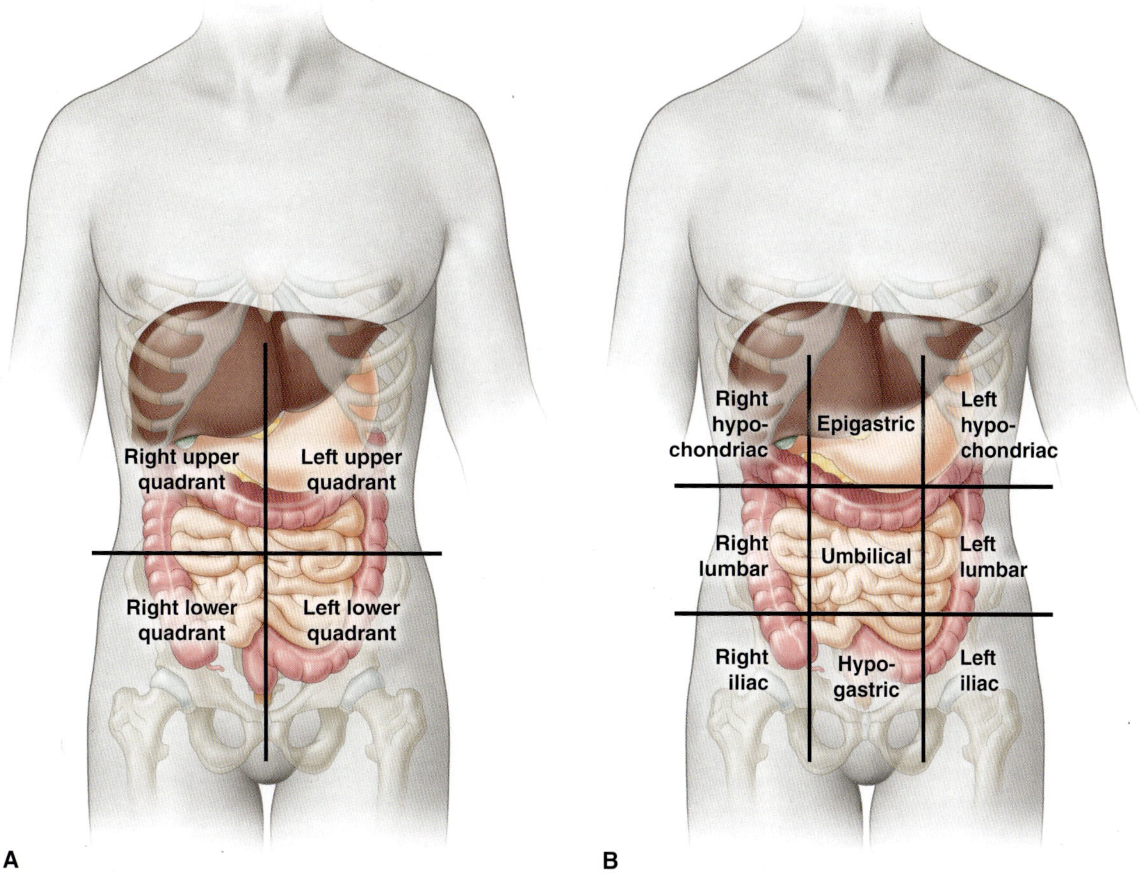

Figure 3-10 (A) Abdominopelvic quadrants. (B) Abdominopelvic regions.

- Left lower quadrant (LLQ): This quadrant contains the left ovary and fallopian tube, left ureter, and part of the bladder, uterus, small intestine, and large intestine.
- Right lower quadrant (RLQ): This quadrant contains the right ovary and fallopian tube, right ureter, and part of the bladder, uterus, small intestine, and large intestine.

Nine Regions of the Abdominopelvic Cavity

The more detailed division of the abdominopelvic cavity is nine regions rather than four quadrants. To create these divisions, two vertical lines are drawn from the midpoint of the collarbones. The horizontal lines are drawn at the height of the ninth rib and the top of the pelvis. Remember that the upper boundary of these regions is the diaphragm; none of the thoracic organs are included in these regions. The nine regions of the abdominopelvic cavity are as follows:

- Right hypochondriac: Upper right region directly below the cartilages connecting the ribs to the sternum. Contains the gallbladder and part of the liver.
- Left hypochondriac: Upper left region directly below the cartilages connecting the ribs to the sternum. Contains part of the liver, stomach, spleen, and pancreas.
- Epigastric: Region over the stomach. Contains part of the liver, stomach, and pancreas.
- Right lumbar: Right, middle, lateral region. Contains part of the small intestine, large intestine, and right kidney.
- Left lumbar: Left, middle, lateral region. Contains part of the small intestine, large intestine, and left kidney.
- Umbilical: In the center of the abdomen, overlying the navel.
- Right iliac: Also known as the right inguinal region. Right, inferior, lateral region. Contains part of the small intestine and large intestine.

ELEMENT REVIEW
epi- = upon
hypo- = under, below
chondr/o = cartilage
lumb/o = loins, lower back
gastr/o = stomach
-ar = pertaining to
-ic = pertaining to

- Left iliac: Also known as the left inguinal region. Left, inferior, lateral region. Contains part of the small intestine and large intestine.
- Hypogastric: Middle inferior region, directly below the navel. Contains the bladder and part of the small intestine and large intestine.

Anatomical Positions and Divisions Review

1. Anatomical Planes

Match the word to the description:

abdominal	dorsal	spine
contralateral	medial	thoracic
coronal	pelvic	transverse
cranial	right upper quadrant	umbilical
diaphragm	sagittal	

1. Divides the body into right and left pieces ______________________
2. Divides the body into superior and inferior pieces ______________________
3. Divides the body into anterior and posterior pieces ______________________
4. Closer to the midline ______________________
5. Farther from the point of attachment ______________________
6. Term for two structures on opposite sides of the body ______________________
7. the cranial and spinal cavities combine to form this cavity ______________________
8. The quadrant of the abdominopelvic cavity that contains the spleen ______________________
9. The region of the abdominopelvic cavity overlying the navel ______________________
10. The region of the spinal column that articulates with ribs ______________________
11. The stomach is found in this cavity. ______________________
12. The urinary bladder is found in this cavity. ______________________
13. The dividing line between the thoracic and abdominopelvic cavities ______________________
14. The cavity containing the brain ______________________
15. The connection between the brain and the rest of the body ______________________

Identify each plane of the body shown in Figure 3-11.

1. coronal ____________
2. midsagittal ____________
3. sagittal ____________
4. transverse ____________

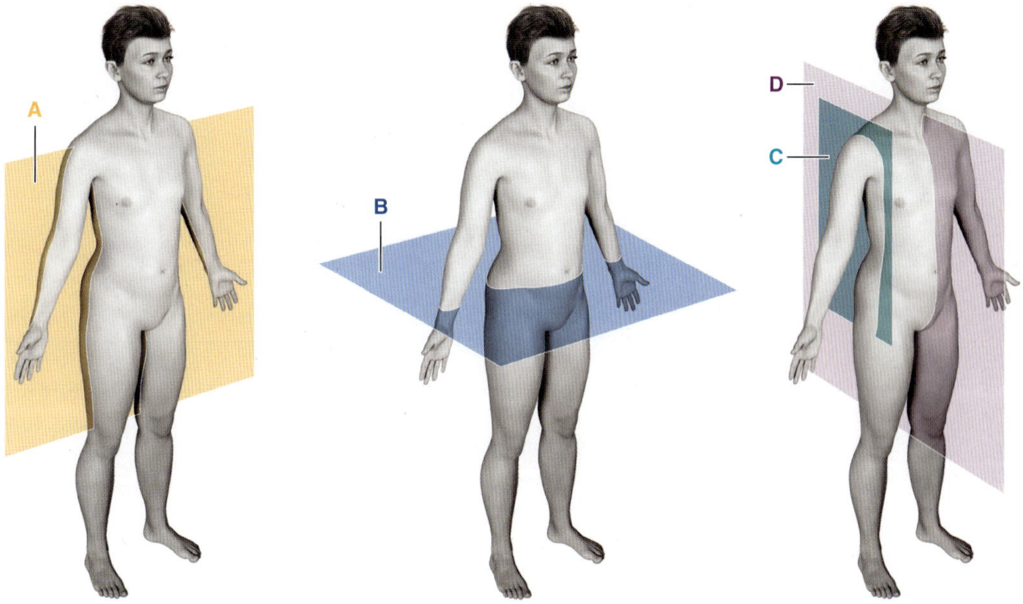

Figure 3-11 Identify the planes of the body.

2. Identify the Directional Terms

Match the directional term(s) to the letters shown on Figure 3-12. Some answers are used more than once.

1. anterior ____________
2. caudal ____________
3. cephalic ____________
4. cranial ____________
5. deep ____________
6. distal ____________
7. dorsal ____________
8. inferior ____________
9. lateral ____________
10. medial ____________
11. posterior ____________
12. proximal ____________
13. superficial ____________
14. superior ____________
15. ventral ____________
16. midsagittal ____________

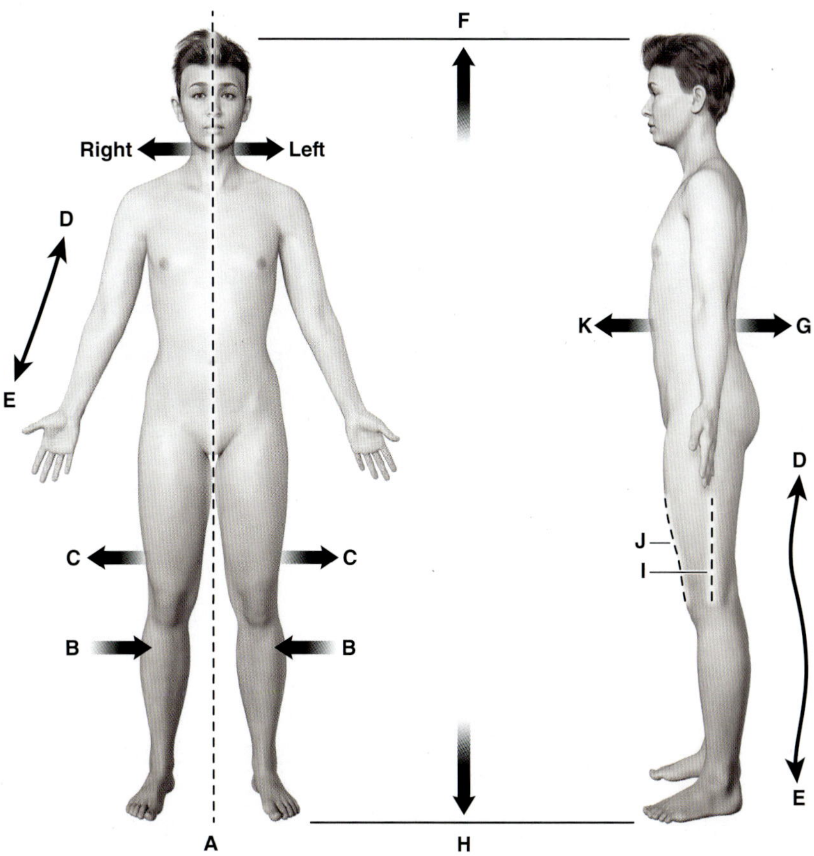

Figure 3-12 Identify the directional terms.

3. Match the Directional Term

Match the word to the description. Some descriptions fit multiple words.

anterior	distal	posterior
caudal	dorsal	proximal
cephalic	inferior	superficial
contralateral	ipsilateral	superior
cranial	lateral	ventral
deep	medial	

1. above, toward the head ______________, ______________, ______________
2. away from the midline ______________
3. below, toward the tail ______________, ______________
4. closer to the midline ______________
5. closer to the point of attachment ______________
6. closer to the surface ______________
7. further from the point of attachment ______________
8. further from the surface ______________
9. on opposite sides ______________
10. on the same side ______________
11. toward the back ______________, ______________
12. toward the front ______________, ______________

4. Identify the Opposite Term

For each of the following terms, write the directional term that could be used to indicate the opposite direction.

1. anterior ______________
2. caudal ______________
3. cephalic ______________
4. contralateral ______________
5. cranial ______________
6. deep ______________

7. distal ______________________________

8. dorsal ______________________________

9. inferior ______________________________

10. ipsilateral ______________________________

11. lateral ______________________________

12. medial ______________________________

13. posterior ______________________________

14. proximal ______________________________

15. superficial ______________________________

16. superior ______________________________

17. ventral ______________________________

5. Complete the Sentence

Complete each sentence with the appropriate term. There may be more than one term that correctly completes the sentence.

1. The heart is ______________________________ to the lungs.

2. The diaphragm is ______________________________ to the large intestine.

3. The liver is ______________________________ to the spleen.

4. The gallbladder is ______________________________ to the liver.

5. The left kidney is ______________________________ to the stomach.

6. The hand is ______________________________ to the elbow.

7. The small intestine is ______________________________ to the skin.

8. The shoulder is ______________________________ to the wrist.

9. The knee is ______________________________ to the foot.

10. The ear is ______________________________ to the eye.

11. The shoulder is ______________________________ to the ribcage.

12. The sternum is ______________________________ to the arm.

13. The mouth is ______________________________ to the nose.

14. The thumb is ________________________________ to the fingers.

15. The chin is ________________________________ to the nose.

16. The forehead is ________________________________ to the mouth.

17. The skin is ________________________________ to the muscles.

18. The spine is ________________________________ to the trachea.

6. Identify the Body Cavities

Match each cavity of the body to the letters shown in Figure 3-13:

1. abdominal cavity

   ____

2. abdominopelvic cavity

   ____

3. cranial cavity

   ____

4. diaphragm

   ____

5. dorsal/posterior cavity

   ____

6. pelvic cavity

   ____

7. spinal cavity

   ____

8. thoracic cavity

   ____

9. ventral/anterior cavity

   ____

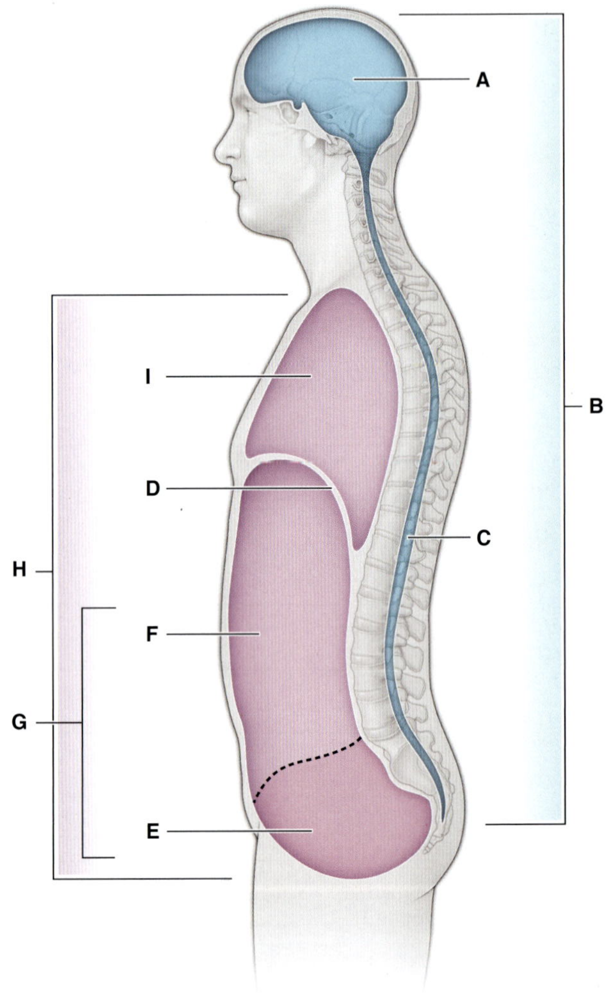

Figure 3-13 Identify the body cavities.

7. Name the Cavity

Name the cavity in which the following organs are found. Some organs are found in multiple cavities; name each one.

1. bladder __________, __________, __________
2. brain __________, __________
3. heart __________, __________
4. kidney __________, __________, __________
5. large intestine __________, __________, __________
6. liver __________, __________, __________
7. lungs __________, __________
8. ovaries __________, __________, __________
9. pancreas __________, __________, __________
10. small intestine __________, __________, __________
11. spinal cord __________, __________
12. stomach __________, __________, __________
13. uterus __________, __________, __________
14. ureter __________, __________, __________

8. Write the Quadrants and Regions

Write out the full term for each of the following abbreviations:

1. LLQ ____________________
2. LUQ ____________________
3. RLQ ____________________
4. RUQ ____________________

9. Identify the Quadrants and Regions

Match each quadrant and region of the abdominopelvic cavity to the letters shown on Figure 3-14.

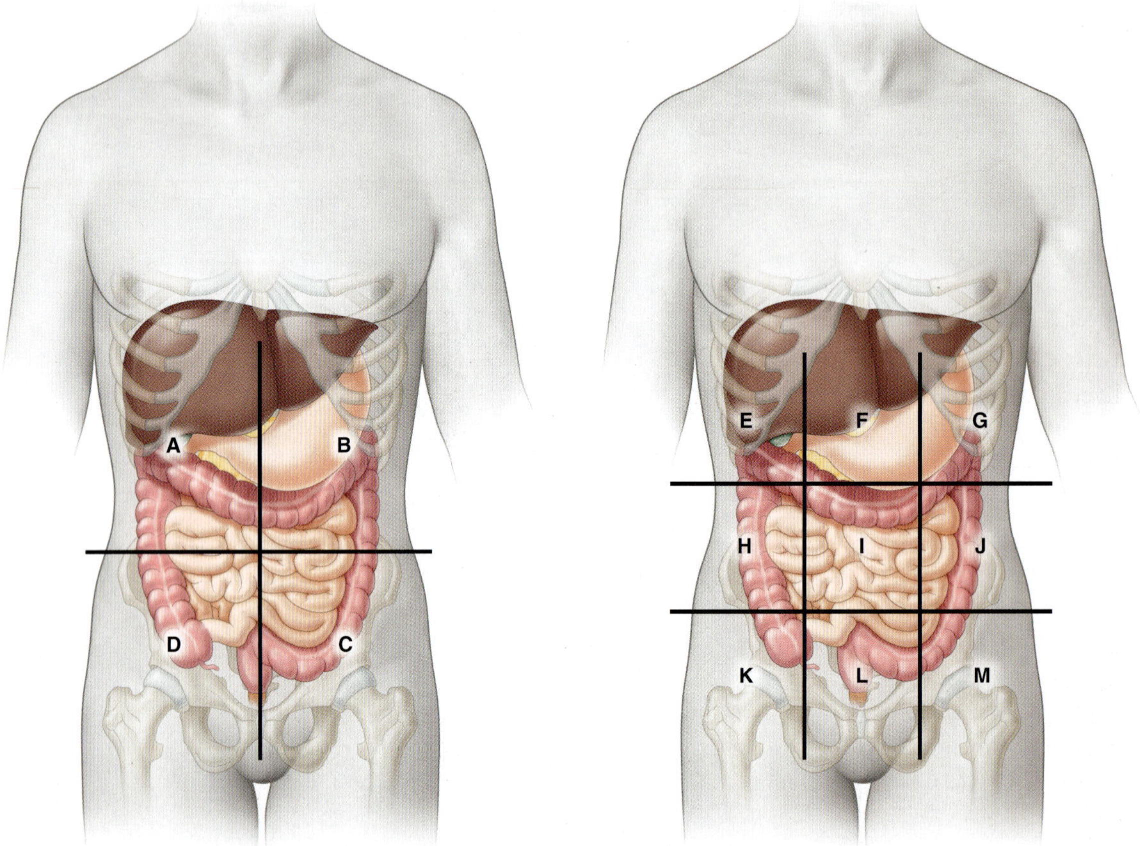

Figure 3-14 Identify the quadrants and regions.

1. epigastric ______
2. hypogastric ______
3. left hypochondriac ______
4. left iliac ______
5. left lower quadrant ______
6. left lumbar ______
7. left upper quadrant ______
8. right hypochondriac ______
9. right iliac ______
10. right lower quadrant ______
11. right lumbar ______
12. right upper quadrant ______
13. umbilical ______

10. Match the Organ to the Quadrant

Match each organ to the quadrant in which you would find the majority of the organ.

All quadrants	LUQ	RLQ
LLQ	On the midline	RUQ

1. bladder ______________
2. gallbladder ______________
3. large intestine ______________
4. left kidney ______________
5. left ovary ______________
6. liver ______________
7. pancreas______________
8. right fallopian tube ______________
9. right kidney ______________
10. right ureter ______________
11. small intestine ______________
12. spleen ______________
13. stomach ______________
14. uterus______________

Word Building With Combining, Prefix, and Suffix Forms

The following word roots, prefixes, and suffixes are commonly used in medical terms for the anatomy and pathologies of the body systems. Combining vowels for word roots are included. Once you learn these word elements, you will have the knowledge you need to understand the meaning of new terms you will encounter as a health-care professional.

The list contains examples of terms that use the word elements and provide pronunciation guides. Be sure to use the pronunciation guide so that you will learn to say the terms correctly.

The Medical Language Lab at the website medicallanguagelab.com provides audio files to help you practice your pronunciations.

Combining Form	Meaning	Example (Pronunciation)	Example Definition
abdomen/o	abdomen	abdominocentesis (ab-dom-i-nō-sen-TĒ-sis)	surgical puncture of the abdomen to remove fluid
anter/o	in front	anterior (an-TĒR-ē-ŏr)	pertaining to in front of
arthr/o	joint	arthroscopy (ăr-THRŎS-kō-pē)	viewing of the joint
cardi/o	heart	cardiology (kăr-dē-ŎL-ō-jē)	study of the heart
caud/o	toward the tail	caudal (KOD-ăl)	pertaining to toward the tail
cephal/o	toward the head	cephalic (sĕ-FAL-ĭk)	pertaining to toward the head

Continued

Combining Form	Meaning	Example (Pronunciation)	Example Definition
cervic/o	neck	cervical (SĔR-vĭ-kăl)	pertaining to the neck
chondr/o	cartilage	chondritis (kŏn-drĭtĭs)	inflammation of the cartilage
crani/o	skull	craniocele (KRĀ-nē-ō-sēl)	protrusion of the brain from the skull
cyan/o	blue, bluish	cyanosis (sī-ă-NŌ-sĭs)	blue discoloration of the skin due to lack of oxygen
cyt/o	cell	cytobiology (sī-tō-bī-ŎL-ō-jē)	biology of cells
dist/o	away from the point of attachment	distal (DIS-tăl)	pertaining to away from the point of attachment
dors/o	back	dorsiflexion (dor-sĭ-FLEK-shŏn)	bending a body part toward the posterior aspect of the body
encephal/o	brain	encephalogram (ĕn-SĔF-ă-lō-grăm)	x-ray of the brain
gastr/o	stomach	gastroparesis (gas-trō-pă-RĒ-sĭs)	delayed emptying of food from the stomach into the small bowel
hepat/o	liver	hepatoma (hĕp-ă-TŌ-mă)	a liver tumor
infer/o	inferior, below	inferiorly (in-FĒR-ē-ŏr-lē)	pertaining to below
lapar/o	abdomen	laparoscopy (lap-ă-ROS-kŏ-pē)	abdominal exploration with an endoscope
later/o	lateral, away from the midline	laterality (lat-ĕ-RAL-ĭt-ē)	the preference of most people for using one side of the body over the other
lymph/o	lymph	lymphadenectomy (lim-fad-ĕn-EK-tŏ-mē)	surgical removal of a lymph node
medi/o	toward the midline, middle	mediolateral (mēd-ē-ō-LAT-ĕ-răl)	pertaining to the middle and side of a structure
muscul/o	muscle	musculoskeletal (mŭs-kyŭ-lō-SKEL-ĕt-ăl)	pertaining to the muscles and skeleton
neur/o	nerves	neuropathy (noo-ROP-ă-thē)	any disease of the nerves
ocul/o	eye	oculomotor (ŎK-ū-lō-mō-tor)	relating to eye movements
organ/o	organ	organogenesis (or-gă-nō-JEN-ĕ-sĭs)	the formation and development of body organs
poster/o	behind, toward the back	posterior (pŏs-TĒ-rē-or)	pertaining to or located at or toward the rear of the body

Combining Form	Meaning	Example (Pronunciation)	Example Definition
proxim/o	toward the point of attachment	proximal (PROK-sĭ-măl)	pertaining to nearest the point of attachment
pulmon/o	lungs	pulmonary (PŬL-mō-nĕ-rē)	pertaining to the lungs
sacr/o	sacrum	sacrococcygeal (sā-krō-kok-SIJ (-ē-) -ăl)	pertaining to the sacrum and coccyx
spin/o	spine	spinocerebellar (SPĪ-nō-sĕr-ĕ-BĔL-ăr)	pertaining to the spinal cord and cerebellum
thorac/o	chest	thoracotomy (THŌ-răk-ŎT-ō-mē)	surgical incision of the chest wall
thyr/o	thyroid	thyrotoxic (thī-rō-TŎKS-ĭk)	excess circulating thyroid hormone
umbilic/o	navel	infraumbilical (in-fră-ŭm-BIL-ĭ-kăl)	pertaining to below the navel
ventr/o	toward the front, belly	ventral (VEN-trăl)	pertaining to toward the belly of the organism
viscer/o	internal organs	visceromegaly (VIS-ĕ-rō-MEG-ă-lē)	generalized enlargement of the abdominal internal organs

ā = say, ă = sofa, ē = meet, ĕ = met, ī = eye, ĭ = in, ō = oh, ŏ = dog, ū = you, ŭ = up, oo = food

Prefix Form	Meaning	Example (Pronunciation)	Example Definition
ante-	before, forward	antecubital (ant-ē-KŪ-bĭt-ăl)	pertaining to in front of the elbow
bi-	two	biarticular (bī-ar-TIK-yā-lār)	pertaining to two joints
dys-	bad, difficult, painful, abnormal	dysfunction (dis-FŬNGK-shŏn)	abnormal, inadequate, or impaired action of an organ or part
endo-	within	endobronchial (en-dŏ-BRONG-kē-ăl)	within a bronchus
epi-	above	epicranium (ep-i-KRĀ-nē-ŭm)	the soft tissue covering the cranium (skull)
extra-	outside, beyond	extracellular (eks-tră-SEL-yŭ-lăr)	located or occurring outside a cell
hemi-	half	hemiplegia (hĕm-ē-PLĒ-jē-ă)	paralysis of one side of the body
homeo-	same, similar	homeotherm (HŌ-mē-ŏ-thĕrm)	an organism that maintains a constant body temperature
hyper-	above, excessive	hypersecretion (hī-pĕr-si-KRĒ-shŏn)	excessive release of a substance by a cell, gland, tissue, or organism

Continued

Prefix Form	Meaning	Example (Pronunciation)	Example Definition
hypo-	below, deficient	hypocalcemia (hī-pō-kal-SĒ-mē-ă)	an abnormally low amount of calcium in the blood
infra-	below, inferior	infraclavicular (in-fră-klă-VIK-yŭ-lăr)	below the clavicle
inter-	between	interatrial (int-ĕr-RĀ-trē-ăl)	between the atria of the heart
intra-	within	intra-abdominal (in-tră-ab-DOM-ĭn-ăl)	within the abdomen
supra-	above, beyond, superior	suprarenal (soo-pră-RĒ-năl)	located above the kidney

ā = say, ă = sofa, ē = meet, ĕ = met, ī = eye, ĭ = in, ō = oh, ŏ = dog, ū = you, ŭ = up, oo = food

Suffix Form	Meaning	Example (Pronunciation)	Example Definition
-al	pertaining to	sural (SŪ-răl)	Pertaining to the calf of the leg
-ar	pertaining to	muscular (MŬS-kyŭ-lăr)	Pertaining to the muscles
-cyte	cell	hepatocyte (HEP-ăt-ŏ-sīt)	Liver cell
-genesis	formation, produce	carcinogenesis (kar-sĭ-nō-JEN-ĕ-sĭs)	The formation or production of cancerous cells
-glia	glue	neuroglia (noo-ROG-lē-ă)	Supporting cells of the nervous system
-ia	pertaining to	acystia (ā-SIS-tē-ă)	Congenital absence of the bladder
-ic	pertaining to	nephric (NEF-rik)	Pertaining to the kidneys
-megaly	enlargement	acromegaly (ak-rō-MEG-ă-lē)	Excess growth hormone in adults resulting in boney enlargements
-ous	pertaining to	anomalous (ă-NOM-ă-lŭs)	Deviating from normal; irregular
-phagia	to eat, swallow	aphagia (ă-FĀ-j(ē-)ă)	Inability to swallow
-plasm	formed, plasma	neoplasm (NĒ-ŏ-plazm)	Formation of a new growth
-plasty	surgical repair	angioplasty (AN-jē-ŏ-plas-tē)	Surgical repair of blood vessels
-rrhea	flow, discharge	rhinorrhea (rī-nŏ-RĒ-ă)	A thin watery discharge from the nose

Suffix Form	Meaning	Example (Pronunciation)	Example Definition
-scopy	to view, examine	cystoscopy (sis-TOS-kŏ-pē)	Examination of the bladder with a camera
-stasis	stop, control	hemostasis (hē-MŌ-stā-sĭs)	Stopping of bleeding
-tomy	incision into	valvulotomy (val-vyŭ-LOT-ŏ-mē)	The process of cutting through a valve

ā = say, ă = sofa, ē = meet, ĕ = met, ī = eye, ĭ = in, ō = oh, ŏ = dog, ū = you, ŭ = up, oo = food

Combining Forms Practice

1. Build the Terms

Using only the word elements listed, create terms to match the definition.

Prefixes	Combining Forms		Suffixes	
endo-	anter/o	organ/o	-al	-ior
homeo-	cardi/o	poster/o	-ary	-megaly
inter-	crani/o	pulmon/o	-cyte	-plasm
intra-	cyt/o	sacr/o	-genesis	-scopy
	lapar/o	thorac/o	-ic	-stasis
		viscer/o		

1. enlargement of an organ ______________________
2. formation of cells ______________________
3. maintenance of stable state ______________________
4. pertaining to an internal organ ______________________
5. pertaining to the front and back ______________________
6. pertaining to the heart and lungs ______________________
7. pertaining to inside the lungs ______________________
8. pertaining to within the brain ______________________
9. plasma in a cell ______________________
10. examination of the abdomen ______________________

2. Decipher the Terms

Separate each term into its prefix (if any), combining form, and suffix. Next, translate the word parts and then give the common definition of the term.

1. epigastric

   Prefix: ______________________ *Suffix:* ______________________

   Combining Form: ______________________

   Meaning: ______________________

2. endocardium

   Prefix: ______________________ *Suffix:* ______________________

   Combining Form: ______________________

   Meaning: ______________________

3. neuroglia

   Prefix: ______________________ *Suffix:* ______________________

   Combining Form: ______________________

   Meaning: ______________________

4. cardiothoracic

   Prefix: ______________________ *Suffix:* ______________________

   Combining Form: ______________________

   Meaning: ______________________

5. homeostasis

   Prefix: ______________________ *Suffix:* ______________________

   Combining Form: ______________________

   Meaning: ______________________

6. hypochondriac

   Prefix: ______________________ *Suffix:* ______________________

   Combining Form: ______________________

   Meaning: ______________________

7. contralateral

Prefix: ____________________ *Suffix:* ____________________

Combining Form: ____________________

Meaning: ____________________

8. cytoplasm

Prefix: ____________________ *Suffix:* ____________________

Combining Form: ____________________

Meaning: ____________________

9. multicellular

Prefix: ____________________ *Suffix:* ____________________

Combining Form: ____________________

Meaning: ____________________

10. umbilical

Prefix: ____________________ *Suffix:* ____________________

Combining Form: ____________________

Meaning: ____________________

Diseases and Conditions

Diseases and disorders of the body may be caused by many different mechanisms. The **etiology** is the cause of a disease or disorder. The first step in evaluation by a provider is to assess the signs and symptoms the patient exhibits. A **sign** is an objective health issue that can be seen or measured by the provider (Table 3-4). A **symptom** is a subjective experience that only the patient can detect. Some diseases and disorders are **asymptomatic**, the patient has no indications of the disease or disorder. However, these diseases and disorders may be detected via signs. An example of an asymptomatic disease is hypertension, or high blood pressure. This disease presents as asymptomatic but may be detected during routine screening of the blood pressure.

Diseases and disorders can be categorized by their causation. The etiologies of disease are described below.

Autoimmune disorders occur when the body mistakenly produces antibodies that attack the body's cells, rather than foreign cells. Examples of autoimmune diseases include Crohn's disease, rheumatoid arthritis, Hashimoto's thyroiditis, and celiac disease.

ELEMENT REVIEW
auto- = self

Cancer is always caused by mutations (changes) to a cell's DNA. The mutations leading to cancer will have one of three effects on the cell: rapid growth, uncontrolled growth, or further mutations. These mutations may be inherited, such as the *BRCA1* and *BRCA2* genes, which carry a 75% risk of developing breast or ovarian cancer. Many mutations are caused by environmental, lifestyle, or behavioral choices. Carcinogenic environmental

TABLE 3-4 Examples of Signs and Symptoms

Sign	Symptom
Bleeding	abdominal cramps
Blood pressure	anorexia (lack of appetite)
Breathing rate	anxiety
Cough	body aches
Cyanosis	breathlessness
Edema (swelling)	dizziness
Fever	fatigue
Heart rate	itching
Hives	loss of taste or smell
Nasal discharge	pain
Rash	thirst
Respiratory sounds	urinary urgency
Swollen lymph nodes	weakness

exposures include asbestos, radiation, and smog. Lifestyle and behavioral choices include exposure to alcohol and tobacco, diets high in processed foods, obesity, early sexual activity, and exposure to sexually transmitted infections (STIs). In addition to STIs, other infections, such as *Helicobacter pylori*, the bacterial cause of stomach ulcers, and tuberculosis may lead to cancer.

The term **congenital** describes a disease or disorder that is present at birth, rather than acquired. Congenital diseases have many different causes, including environmental exposures while in utero, genetic causes, and malformation. Examples include club foot, spina bifida, cerebral palsy, and Down's syndrome (trisomy 21).

Deficiency diseases occur when the body lacks one or more essential nutrients or dietary elements, typically a vitamin or mineral. The lack of the nutrient or element may be due to the body's inability to absorb it from the intestinal tract (malabsorption), poor nutritional intake, medications, altered metabolism, or other health conditions. The most common deficiency disease is iron-deficiency anemia. Other deficiency diseases include goiters (iodine deficiency), night blindness (vitamin A deficiency), rickets (vitamin D deficiency), and osteomalacia (calcium deficiency).

Hereditary diseases are diseases or disorders that are passed from parent to child and are classified as genetic or nongenetic.

- In genetic hereditary diseases, gene(s) inherited from a parent have a mutation that alters the controlled function. Some genetic diseases require that the mutation be passed on from both parents whereas other diseases are expressed if only one copy is passed down. Examples of genetic diseases include sickle cell anemia, hemophilia, cystic fibrosis, and Huntington's disease.
- In nongenetic hereditary diseases, external forces such as diet and stress during gestation impact gene expression by the child after birth. Nongenetic hereditary diseases include heart disease, stroke, diabetes, autism, ADHD, and dementia.

Idiopathic diseases are diseases or disorders with no known cause. Some diseases are always idiopathic, such as chronic pelvic pain, while others may have idiopathic forms, such as peripheral neuropathy. Peripheral neuropathy may be caused by diabetes mellitus, a vitamin B deficiency, or HIV; however, in up to 40% of cases, the root cause cannot be isolated.

Infectious diseases are diseases caused by a microbe invading the body. These microbes may be viruses, bacteria, fungi, or parasites. Examples of infectious diseases include influenza (viral), strep throat (bacterial), athlete's foot (fungal), yeast infections (fungal), and malaria (parasitic).

- Noncommunicable infectious diseases cannot be transmitted directly from person to person. Instead, they must pass through another organism to infect a human. Examples of noncommunicable infectious diseases include malaria, Lyme disease, and trichinosis. Malaria (a parasite) is transmitted via a mosquito bite, whereas Lyme (a bacterium) is transmitted via tick bite. Trichinosis is infection by a parasitic worm (*Trichinella*) and is transmitted through consumption of undercooked pork.
- Communicable infectious diseases are diseases transmitted directly from person to person. Communicable diseases may be viral, bacterial, fungal, or parasitic. Viral examples of communicable diseases include COVID-19, influenza, HIV, and hepatitis. Bacterial examples of communicable diseases include tuberculosis, pertussis (whooping cough), and chlamydia. Fungal examples of communicable diseases include ringworm, athlete's foot, vaginal yeast infections, and thrush (oral yeast infections). Parasitic examples of communicable diseases include giardiasis and trichomoniasis.
- Contagious diseases are a subset of communicable diseases that are easily transmitted from person to person. Consider the ease of transmitting influenza or tuberculosis from one person to another; simply being in the presence of an infected individual is enough to transmit the disease. Other communicable diseases are harder to transmit, such as HIV, which requires the exchange of bodily fluids. HIV is considered communicable but not contagious.

Metabolic disorders occur when the body's metabolism does not work correctly. **Metabolism** comprises all the chemical processes that occur in the cells and body to sustain life. Diabetes mellitus is an example of a metabolic disorder. In insulin-dependent diabetes mellitus, the pancreas does not produce enough insulin, preventing the body from using glucose. In non-insulin-dependent diabetes mellitus, the pancreas produces insulin, but cells of the body do not respond to the hormone and take up the glucose. In phenylketonuria, the body either does not produce any, or enough, phenylalanine hydroxylase, an enzyme that breaks down amino acids. Excess amino acids build up in the body and cause brain damage.

ELEMENT REVIEW
meta- = change

Degenerative diseases and disorders are caused by a reduction in function or change in structure that worsens over time and are strongly linked to aging. Some degenerative diseases may worsen or develop depending on lifestyle choices, such as exercise and diet choices, whereas the same choices may improve the prognosis of other degenerative diseases. Examples of degenerative diseases include Alzheimer's disease, dementia, osteoporosis, osteoarthritis, and Parkinson's disease.

Psychological disorders, sometimes referred to as mental health conditions, are disorders characterized by an abnormal condition of the brain that impacts the way a person thinks, feels, behaves, relates to others, and relates to the surroundings. These disorders are usually associated with distress or an inability to function. Examples of psychological disorders include anxiety disorders, depression, post-traumatic stress disorder, schizophrenia, and eating disorders.

Trauma is a physical injury that has a sudden onset and that may result in wounds, broken bones, or organ damage. Traumatic injuries are divided into blunt force trauma and penetrating trauma. In blunt force trauma, an object or force hits the body, resulting in damage such as concussions, broken bones, bleeding, and cuts. Blunt force trauma may be the result of a motor vehicle accident, playing sports, falling, and assault. Penetrating trauma occurs when an object pierces the skin and body, creating an open wound, and may be the result of shootings, stabbings, explosions, or impalement (falling onto an object).

While understanding the etiology of disease enables medical providers to fully treat and assist patients, it is important to note that some diseases and disorders have multiple etiologies. Three examples of these variations are diarrhea, migraines, and cardiovascular disease.

Diarrhea is the frequent passage of loose and watery stool. Most individuals will experience diarrhea at some point in their life. Diarrhea may be caused by gastroenteritis, an infection of the intestinal tract. This infection may be caused by bacteria (*Escherichia coli* or cholera), viruses (Norovirus), or parasites (*Giardia*). Diarrhea may also have a noninfectious etiology, such as an allergy or food sensitivity, especially to dairy and wheat. Inflammatory bowel diseases, such as Crohn's disease, lead to the inability of the intestinal tract to absorb the water, resulting in diarrhea.

Migraines are headaches that cause severe throbbing pain or a pulsing sensation along with nausea, vomiting, and sensitivity to light, sound, or smell. Some individuals also experience visual disturbances, known as auras, either prior to or with the onset of the migraine. Not only does the cause of the migraine vary between individuals, but also the trigger for the onset of the migraine varies. In rare cases, tumors may be the cause of a migraine. More commonly, nutritional deficiencies, especially magnesium, or a serotonin imbalance are the causes of a migraine. Other hormonal changes associated with menstrual periods, pregnancy, and menopause may be a trigger for a migraine. Alcohol, chocolate, lack of sleep, high stress levels, and food additives are also known to trigger migraines.

Cardiovascular diseases are a group of diseases or disorders of the heart and blood vessels. This group includes coronary artery disease, cerebrovascular disease (stroke), rheumatic heart disease, congenital heart disease, peripheral artery disease, deep vein thrombosis, and pulmonary embolism. Given the range of diseases considered part of this group, it should not be surprising that there is an equally varied number of etiologies and presentations.

Some causes of cardiovascular disease are bacterial infections that damage the heart structures, malformations of the heart structure during fetal development, narrowing or blockage of blood flow through the arteries, and damage to veins from surgery or inflammation. Cardiovascular disease is often asymptomatic, but it may also present a wide variety of symptoms, depending on the etiology. Common symptoms include chest pain, pressure, heaviness, or discomfort; shortness of breath; fatigue; fainting or dizziness; irregular heartbeats; nausea; stomach cramps; and weakness. Narrowing or blockage of blood flow may lead to swelling, pain, or cramps in one or both legs; cool or red skin on the legs; numbness or tingling in the face or limb, often only on one side of the body; and difficulty walking, talking, or seeing.

Diagnostic and Surgical Procedures

Auscultation: A noninvasive procedure using a stethoscope to listen to sounds of internal organs. May be used to identify diseases/disorders of the heart, lungs, and alimentary canal.

Biopsy: An invasive procedure in which a sample of tissue is removed for testing. Cancers, ulcers, kidney and liver diseases, and endometriosis may be identified through the use of a biopsy.

Comprehensive metabolic panel: A blood test used to monitor the body's function and done as part of a regular checkup. This tests for the levels of 14 substances in the blood: glucose, calcium, sodium, potassium, carbon dioxide, chloride, albumin, total protein, alkaline phosphatase, alanine transaminase, aspartate aminotransferase, bilirubin, blood urea nitrogen, and creatinine.

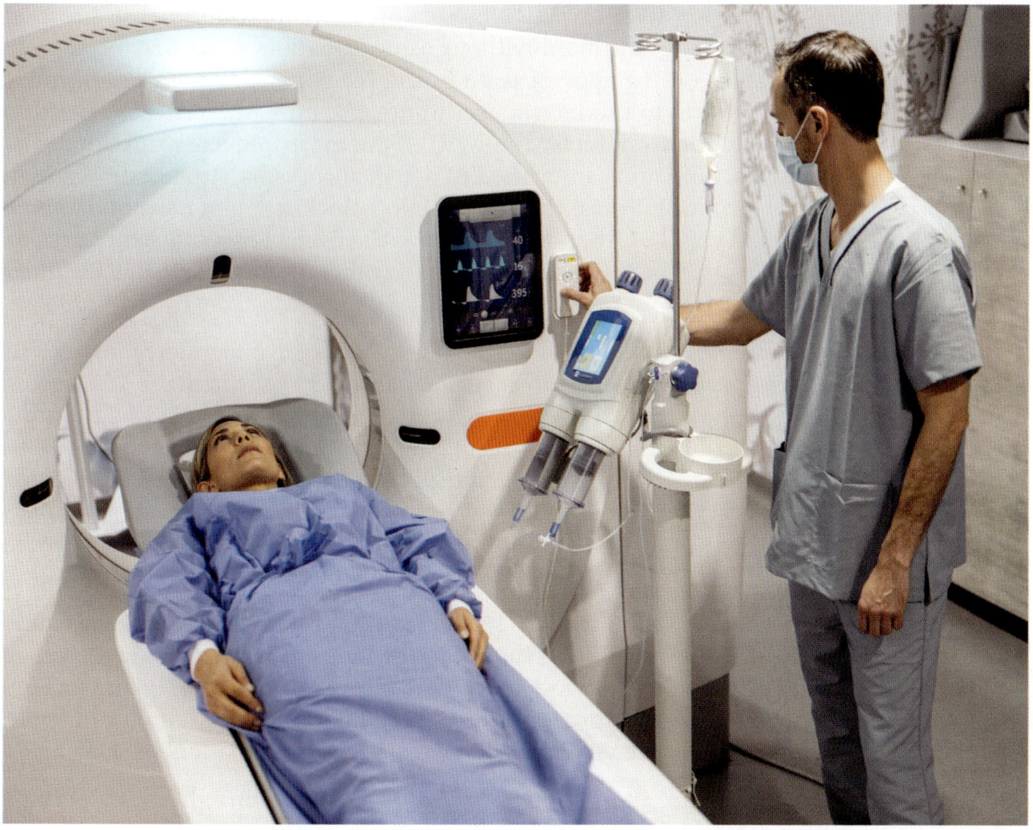

Figure 3-15 CT scans create cross-sectional images of a patient's body.

Computed tomography (CT): CT scans are a radiographic technique that selects levels in the body and blurs structures above and below it to create "slices" of images (Fig. 3-15). These images are combined via computer processing to create cross-section images of organs. CT scans can visualize the majority of the body and may be used to identify diseases, disorders, or injuries. They may also be used to plan or follow up on surgical or radiation treatment.

Debridement: Debridement is the removal of dead or infected tissue in a wound, and helps to promote healing by removing a source of nutrients for bacteria as well as the bacteria. Debridement also allows topical treatments to make direct contact with the wound to enhance their efficacy.

Electroencephalogram (EEG): A noninvasive procedure that records the electrical activity of the brain using electrodes attached to the scalp. EEGs are used to detect unusual electrical activity in the brain and diagnose brain disorders/dysfunction, such as seizures.

Electrocardiogram (EKG): A noninvasive test that records the electrical activity of the heart. A 12-lead EKG is done by attaching 10 electrodes to the body: one on each limb and the remaining six on the chest. EKGs provide information on the health of the heart and may be used to identify arrhythmias, blocked arteries, heart damage or failure, or heart attacks.

Endoscopy: An endoscopy is done by inserting into the body a long, flexible tube with a camera to examine a hollow organ or cavity. In addition to a camera, cutting tools, balloons, and cauterization tools may be inserted to allow for sampling of tissues, widening of lumina, or cauterization of blood vessels. Endoscopies may be used to identify diseases/disorders of the alimentary canal (either via the mouth or rectum), respiratory tract, urinary tract, and female reproductive system. In addition, endoscopes may be used to view normally closed cavities through a small incision, such as joints (arthroscopy), the abdominal cavity (laparoscopy), or the chest cavity (thoracoscopy).

Magnetic resonance imaging (MRI): MRI is a noninvasive procedure that provides visualization of soft tissue, bone, and fluid without using radiation. MRI may be with or without contrast depending on the type of testing. The machine uses a strong magnetic field and radio frequency waves to produce images of organs and tissues. It can be used to diagnose disorders of many body systems. The MRI is the most frequently used imaging test of the brain and spinal cord and can be used to detect aneurysms, strokes, tumors, and trauma. MRIs may also be done to assess the size, function, thickness, and movement of the heart and associated blood vessels. Other organs, such as the liver, kidneys, spleen, pancreas, uterus, prostate, and bones, may be assessed for tumors or other disorders and abnormalities using an MRI.

Positron electron tomography (PET): A PET scan is a radiologic imaging technique that uses a radioactive tracing agent attached to sugar to show metabolic activity. The tracing drug is injected into a vein, typically in the arm, and circulates through the body in the blood. The more metabolically active a cell or tissue, the more the tracing agent is absorbed into the cell or tissue (Fig. 3-16). PET scans are most commonly used to detect or diagnose cancer, heart disease, or brain disorders. In both cancers and brain disorders, an accumulation of the tracing agent may indicate an area of concern, and in heart disease, a decrease in accumulation of the tracing agent may indicate an area of concern.

Pulmonary function test (PFT): Pulmonary function tests are a noninvasive way to measure the capacity, rate of air flow, and gas exchange in the lungs. The most common type of PFT is spirometry, which measures the air flow into and out of the lungs. PFTs may be used to diagnose a variety of respiratory disorders or diseases, including asthma, chronic obstructive pulmonary disorder, or a restricted airway due to tumors, inflammation, or scarring.

Urinalysis: Urinalysis is a quick and noninvasive test that provides insight into a person's overall health. It may detect and manage a wide variety of diseases, such as urinary tract infections, kidney disease, diabetes, liver disease, and preeclampsia. A complete urinalysis

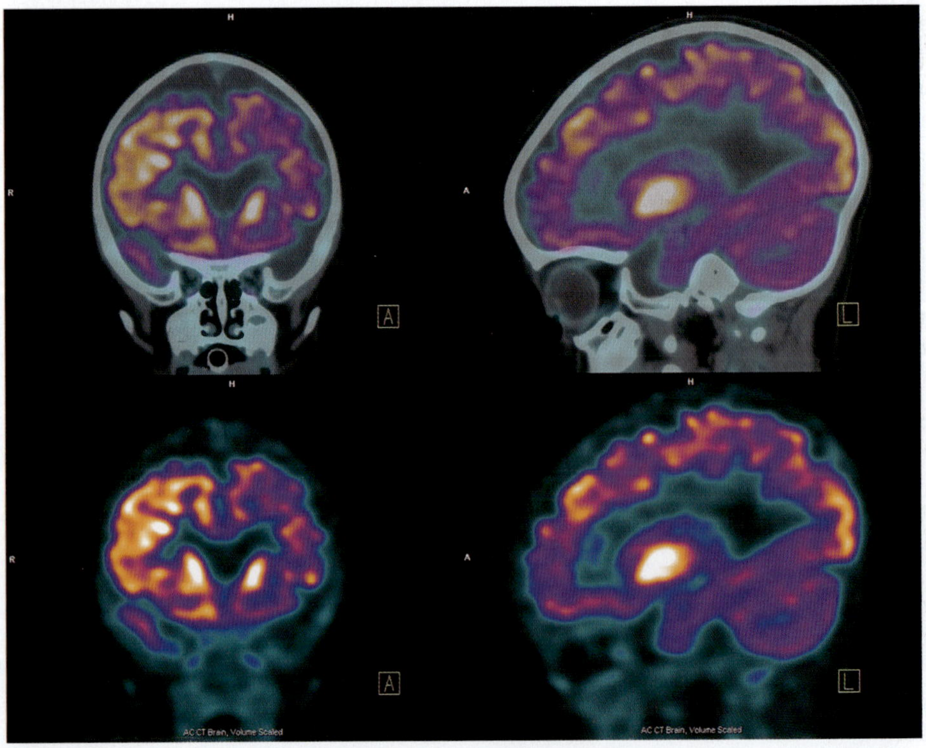

Figure 3-16 PET scan of the brain. The more metabolically active areas of the brain will retain more of the radioactive tracer that can be detected by the scanner. In this image, the more active areas are orange.

examines the physical, chemical, and microscopic components of the urine. Physical components analyzed include the volume, color, clarity, odor, and concentration of the urine whereas chemical components look at protein, glucose, urobilinogen, bilirubin, ketones, and nitrite levels; the presence of red or white blood cells; and pH. The microscopic component involves examining the urine for casts, cells, crystals, and microbes.

Ultrasound (UT): Also known as a sonogram, ultrasound is a noninvasive procedure using high-frequency sound waves to show a picture of internal organs. One of the most frequent uses of ultrasound is to view the uterus, ovaries, and fetus during pregnancy. Ultrasounds may also be used to examine the gallbladder and its duct system, blood flow, breast lumps, and the thyroid, as well as guiding needles for biopsies or other treatment.

X-ray: An x-ray is a noninvasive procedure that uses radiation to create images of internal structures, including bones and soft tissues. They may be done with or without a contrast agent. Most often, x-rays are used to diagnose damage to bones, including fractures, infections, arthritis, and bone cancer. X-rays are also used to look for lung infections or other lung conditions, breast cancer, an enlarged heart, digestive tract dysfunction, or swallowed objects.

Diagnostics and Procedures Review

1. Fill in the Blanks

Fill in the blanks to answer the questions.

1. a blood test considered part of a normal checkup ____________________
2. a noninvasive method to listen to internal organs ____________________
3. a nonradioactive method to scan the body ____________________
4. a radiographic technique that allows visualization of cross-sections of organs ____________________
5. a test of lung function ____________________
6. imaging study used to monitor fetal development ____________________
7. imaging study that requires the use of a contrast agent ____________________
8. most common method to detect broken bones ____________________
9. noninvasive test that may detect or manage multiple diseases/disorders ____________________
10. provides information about metabolic activity of cells and tissues ____________________
11. recording of the electrical activity of the brain ____________________

12. removal of a sample of tissue for testing ______________________

13. test used to identify heart damage ______________________

14. the removal of dead or infected tissue ______________________

15. use of a camera on a long, flexible tube to view hollow organs and cavities ______________________

2. Sign or Symptom

Determine if each of the following complaints would be considered a sign or a symptom and circle your answer.

1. Abdominal pain	Sign	Symptom
2. Blood in the stool	Sign	Symptom
3. Edema of the legs	Sign	Symptom
4. Heart palpitations	Sign	Symptom
5. High blood pressure	Sign	Symptom
6. Joint stiffness	Sign	Symptom
7. Nausea	Sign	Symptom
8. Severe itching	Sign	Symptom
9. Tachycardia	Sign	Symptom
10. Wheezing	Sign	Symptom

Structure of the Human Body Abbreviations

The list below provides some common abbreviations pertaining to the structure of the human body and their meanings.

A&P anatomy and physiology

Abd abdomen

AP anteroposterior

BP blood pressure

CNS central nervous system

CO_2 carbon dioxide

DNA deoxyribonucleic acid

Dx diagnosis

GI gastrointestinal

HIV human immunodeficiency virus

HR heartrate

Ht height

Hx history

IDDN insulin dependent diabetes mellitus

LAT lateral

LLQ left lower quadrant

LUQ left upper quadrant

NIDDM Noninsulin dependent diabetes mellitus

O_2 oxygen

P pulse

PERRLA pupils are equal, round, and reactive to light and accommodation

PNS peripheral nervous system

RLQ	right lower quadrant
RR	respiratory rate
RUQ	right upper quadrant
SOB	shortness of breath
T	temperature
Wt	weight

Abbreviations Review

Choose the correct definition for the abbreviation.

1. A&P
   a. abdomen & pelvis
   b. anatomical & physiological
   c. anatomy & physiology
   d. anterior & posterior

2. Abd
   a. abdomen
   b. airway or breathing diagnosis
   c. already been done
   d. arterial blood diagnostics needed

3. AP
   a. anatomical position
   b. anatomy and physiology
   c. anteroposterior
   d. appropriate

4. BP
   a. belly pressure
   b. benign procedure
   c. blood present
   d. blood pressure

5. DNA
   a. deoxyribonucleic acid
   b. diabetes not applicable
   c. diagnosis not attempted
   d. do not attempt

6. Dx
   a. deep
   b. diagnosis
   c. digestion
   d. digital

7. GI
   a. gastrointestinal
   b. glioma
   c. goiter indicated
   d. gums infected

8. HR
   a. heartrate
   b. hepatitis r virus
   c. hernia
   d. hormone replacement

9. Hx
   a. hemoglobin
   b. history
   c. hypoxemia
   d. hypoxia

10. LAT
    a. lactose tolerated
    b. lateral
    c. left
    d. liver alanine transferase

11. LLQ
    a. left lower quadrant
    b. likely lower quadriplegia
    c. low levels quantified
    d. lower left quadrant

12. RLQ
    a. resistant levels quantified
    b. right left quadrant
    c. right lower quadrant
    d. right lung quit

13. LUQ
    a. lateral upper quadrant
    b. left lateral quadrant
    c. left upper quadrant
    d. left, lateral, upper quadrant

14. RUQ
    a. respiratory–upper question
    b. right umbilical quadrant
    c. right upper quadrant
    d. round upper quadrant

15. T
    a. temper
    b. temperature
    c. therapy
    d. thoracic

MEDICAL DOCUMENTATION

Knowledge of terms related to normal anatomy and pathological conditions enables you to understand medical documentation such as history and physical exams, operative reports, discharge summaries, laboratory reports, and x-ray reports. Read the following routine history and physical exam and answer the questions that follow.

Routine History and Physical Exam

Date: 3/9/2023

History and Physical Examination

Demographics

Patient Name: Lena W
DOB: January 24, 1985
Gender: Female
Race: White, non-Hispanic

Marital status: Married
Medical Insurance: Blue Cross Blue Shield
Chief complaint: "I'm here for my annual physical"

History of Present Illness

The patient is a 38-year-old female returning for her annual physical. She states she feels well aside from lingering soreness from a previously twisted ankle and occasional numbness in toes (bilaterally).

Past Medical History

- Dyspareunia (noted 11/20/2015)
- Dysmenorrhea (noted 11/20/2015)
- Migraines
- Obesity
- External hemorrhoids without bleeding (noted 12/28/2022)

Surgical History

- Cesarean section (3/9/2021; 5/25/2019)
- Tonsillectomy (6/3/2008)
- Wisdom tooth extraction (8/22/1999)
- Supraumbilical hernioplasty (7/10/1985)

Psychiatric History

- None

Allergy

- Codeine (other: hyperactivity)
- Penicillin (anaphylaxis)

Alcohol Use

- Rarely (0–1 drink per month)

Tobacco Use

- Never

Smokeless Tobacco Use

- Never

Other Drug Use

- Marijuana (2007)

Current Medication

- Ferrous sulfate (iron) 325-mg tablet
- Ascorbic acid (vitamin C) 500-mg chewable tablet

MEDICAL DOCUMENTATION—cont'd

- Magnesium 250-mg tablet
- Cyanocobalamin (vitamin B-12) 2500-mg chewable tablet
- Multivitamin tablet
- Fluticasone 50-mcg/spray nasal spray
- Levonorgestrel (Liletta) 19.5 mcg/day IUD

Family History

- Mother: Endometriosis, hyperlipidemia
- Father: Hypertension, hyperlipidemia, NIDDM
- Sibling (Sister): Depression

Review of Systems

- Vital signs
  - BP: 104/80
  - P: 77 bpm
  - T: 99.1°F
  - RR: 20
  - O_2 saturation: 99%
  - Wt: 222 lb (Note: 15 lb loss from previous physical)
  - Height: 5'7"
- Constitutional – Denies weight, weakness, fever, or chills.
- Eyes – Denies changes in vision, blurry vision, excessive eye discharge, dry eyes, floaters, or eye pain.
- Ears/Nose/Mouth/Throat
  - Ears: Denies tinnitus, earache, and decrease in hearing.
  - Nose: Denies runny nose, epistaxis, or decreased in smelling. Throat/Mouth: Denies sore throat, oral lesions or sores, voice hoarseness, difficulty/painful swallowing, facial pain, postnasal drip, or jaw pain.
- Cardiovascular – Denies chest discomfort, palpitations, chest pain, or leg edema.
- Respiratory – Denies shortness of breath, hemoptysis, wheezing, pleuritic pain, or coughing.
- GI – Her normal bowel pattern is every day. Denies any nausea, hematemesis, melena, diarrhea, vomiting, constipation, or any bloody stool.
- GU – Denies painful urination, frequent urination, nocturia, and hematuria.
- Musculoskeletal – Denies joint pain, muscle pain, back pain, swollen joints, stiff joints, or walking difficulties.
- Integumentary – Denies rashes, itching, dryness, or any genital lesions.
- Endocrine – Denies increased thirst, hunger, cold or hot intolerance, and excessive sweating.
- Neurological – Denies numbness, dizziness, headache, or paresthesia.
- Psychiatric/Mental Health – Denies thoughts of suicide, sadness, and anxiety.
- Hematologic/Lymphatic – Denies any swollen and painful lymph nodes.
- Allergies – No new allergies.
- General: Well-developed, well-nourished, alert, cooperative female in no apparent distress. Excellent cognitive function. Denies unintentional weight loss, weakness, fever, or chills.
- HEENT (head, eye, ears, nose, and throat)
  - Normocephalic
  - Denies changes in vision, blurry vision, excessive discharge, floaters, dry eyes, and eye pain. Pupils are equal, round, and reactive to light and accommodation. Extraocular movements intact.
  - Denies tinnitus, earache, and decreased hearing. Tympanic membranes benign.

Continued

MEDICAL DOCUMENTATION—cont'd

- Denies epistaxis or decreased smelling. States occasional runny nose due to environmental allergies.
- Denies sore throat, oral sores, dysphagia, facial pain, postnasal drip, and jaw pain. Oropharynx is nonerythematous.

- Neck
  - Denies stiffness or pain.
  - Supple, no lymphadenopathy or thyromegaly.
- Lungs
  - Denies shortness of breath, hemoptysis, wheezing, pain, or coughing.
  - Clear to percussion and auscultation bilaterally.
- Cardiovascular
  - Denies chest discomfort, palpitations, or chest pain.
  - Regular rate and rhythm. No murmurs, rubs, or gallops. No carotid bruits appreciated upon auscultation.
- Abdominal
  - Normal bowel movements daily.
  - Denies any nausea, vomiting, hematemesis, melena, diarrhea, constipation, or bloody stool.
  - Obese, soft, nontender, nondistended with no hepatosplenomegaly. Normoactive bowel sounds upon auscultation.
- Extremities
  - Nonedematous.
- Skin
  - Denies rashes, itching, dryness, or lesions.
  - Warm and dry. No cyanosis or pallor present.
- Genitourinary
  - Denies painful urination, frequent urination, nocturia, and hematuria.
  - Genitalia normal.
  - Mild external hemorrhoids.
  - The stool is hemoccult negative.
- Musculoskeletal
  - Denies joint pain, muscle pain, swollen or stiff joints, walking difficulties.
- Neurological
  - Denies dizziness or paresthesia.
  - Complaint of headache.
  - Complaint of numbness in toes.
    - Pinprick test normal.
  - Cranial nerves II through XII are grossly intact.
  - Deep tendon reflexes +2/4 bilaterally in both upper and lower extremities.
  - Good grip strength noted bilaterally with no involuntary movements.
  - Sensation is intact to pain and light touch.

Questions

1. Many of the tests were done "bilaterally" (percussion and auscultation of the lungs, deep tendon reflex, grip strength). What does this mean? ______________________

2. Seven vital signs were noted using abbreviations. Define five of the seven abbreviations. ______________________

MEDICAL DOCUMENTATION—cont'd

3. What abbreviation could be used to shorten the phrase "Pupils are equal, round, and reactive to light and accommodation"? ______________________
4. What does extraocular mean? ______________________
5. Three different organs were examined and found not enlarged. Which organs? ______________________
6. The patient had a supraumbilical hernioplasty. In your own words, where in the body did this occur? ______________________
7. Break up "normocephalic" into its word parts and define it. ______________________
8. Which body system is affected by dyspareunia and dysmenorrhea? ______________________
9. What does nonerythematous mean? Which region of the body (in your own words) did it describe? ______________________
10. What is hyperlipidemia? ______________________
11. What is hypertension? ______________________
12. What is indicated by the abbreviation NIDDM? ______________________
13. Does the patient have pain or difficulty swallowing? ______________________
14. Which body part(s) has the patient had surgically removed? ______________________

CHAPTER

4

The Integumentary System

LEARNING OBJECTIVES

Upon completion of the chapter, you will be able to:

1. Identify and define the combining forms, roots, prefixes, and suffixes introduced in the chapter.
2. Spell medical terms related to the integumentary system.
3. Describe the major organs of the integumentary system.
4. Describe the five functions of skin.
5. Discuss how people can recognize signs of skin cancer and the importance of seeking medical care.
6. Discuss how skin changes can be indicative of disorders such as diabetes or cardiovascular disease.
7. Identify and discuss major pathological terms of the integumentary system.
8. Identify and discuss major diagnostic and therapeutic treatments of the integumentary system.
9. Identify the major categories of medications used to treat skin pathologies.
10. Define abbreviations of the integumentary system

After reading this chapter, you will expand your knowledge of medical terms related to the integumentary system. You will understand how the skin protects us from pathogens, regulates body temperature, keeps organs warm and moist, and acts as an organ for the elimination of toxins. You will be able to use the word elements presented to understand unfamiliar terms and to build your medical vocabulary.

We begin this chapter with a case study of Travis, who has a skin disorder. The case study introduces some of the medical terms relevant to the integumentary system. Throughout the chapter, we will revisit the story of Travis to understand his skin disorder and how medical interventions can improve a patient's quality of life.

CASE STUDY

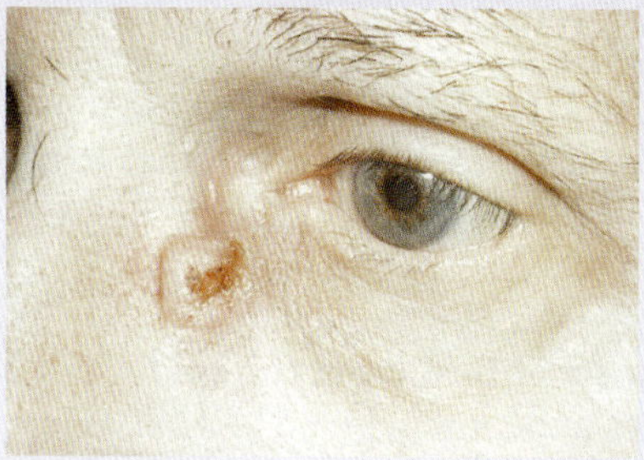

Travis is a 68-year-old man who has noticed an area of red, raised irritated skin on the side of his nose. The lesion sometimes bleeds when the nosepiece of his glasses rubs the spot. He has ignored it for a few years, but recently the area of irritation has become darker and larger and is often sore, bleeding more often. He also felt small bumps on the lesion. His wife, Claire, told him to see a dermatologist, but he argued that he had enough of doctors with his primary care physician and his cardiologist. Claire makes the appointment and convinces Travis to see Dr. Xavier Torres, the dermatologist affiliated with their primary care provider. Travis and Claire meet with Dr. Torres who examines the lesion on Travis's nose. He explains that

Continued

CASE STUDY, continued

the growth is a basal cell carcinoma, the most common form of skin cancer (accounting for 80% of skin cancers). Dr. Torres assures them that with excision (removal) Travis will recover fully. Basal cell carcinoma (BCC) commonly occurs on parts of the skin that are exposed to sunlight (like the nose), so Travis is advised to wear sunscreen on his face and other parts of the body that are exposed. Claire suggests that he wear a hat while working in the garden. While some BCC lesions can be removed in the office, the lesion on Travis is too large for a simple excision. Dr. Torres explains that he will do the procedure at the hospital so that Travis can have general anesthesia. Travis has a preoperative EKG because he has hypertension and a pacemaker. The EKG findings are normal, and the BCC excision is scheduled.

KEY TERMS

Apocrine glands
Arrector pili
Carotene
Collagen
Corium
Cuticle
Dermis
Eccrine glands
Epidermis
Hair bulb
Hair follicle
Hair root
Hair shaft
Hypodermis
Keratin
Lunula
Melanin
Melanocyte
Nail plate
Nail root
Papillary region
Pore
Reticular region
Sebaceous glands
Strata
Subcutaneous layer
Sudoriferous glands

Structures and Physiology

The skin is the organ of protection that covers our bodies. The skin is part of the integumentary system and is comprised of skin, hair, nails, and sweat and oil glands. The integumentary system performs five functions essential for good health:

- Protection from microorganisms and harmful effects of ultraviolet light,
- Regulation of body temperature,
- Sensory organ for sensations of touch, pain, heat, cold,
- Elimination of toxic wastes, water, salts, and some fats through perspiration,
- Synthesis of vitamin D, essential for bone growth, development, and maintenance.

The skin is arranged in layers: five layers of the epidermis and two layers of the dermis (Fig. 4-1). While the subcutaneous layer is not part of the skin, it is an important connection of the skin to the internal structures of the body.

Epidermis

The outermost layer, the **epidermis**, is a dynamic, water-resistant covering of the body that does not contain blood or a nerve supply (Fig. 4-2). The uppermost cells are constantly being shed, requiring replacement by deeper cells. The cells of the epidermis are arranged in the following five layers called **strata** and flatten as they migrate toward the surface of the body.

Stratum corneum is the outermost layer of cells consisting of 20 to 50 rows of flattened, dead cells. These cells are lost daily and replaced by deeper cells in a process called desquamation.

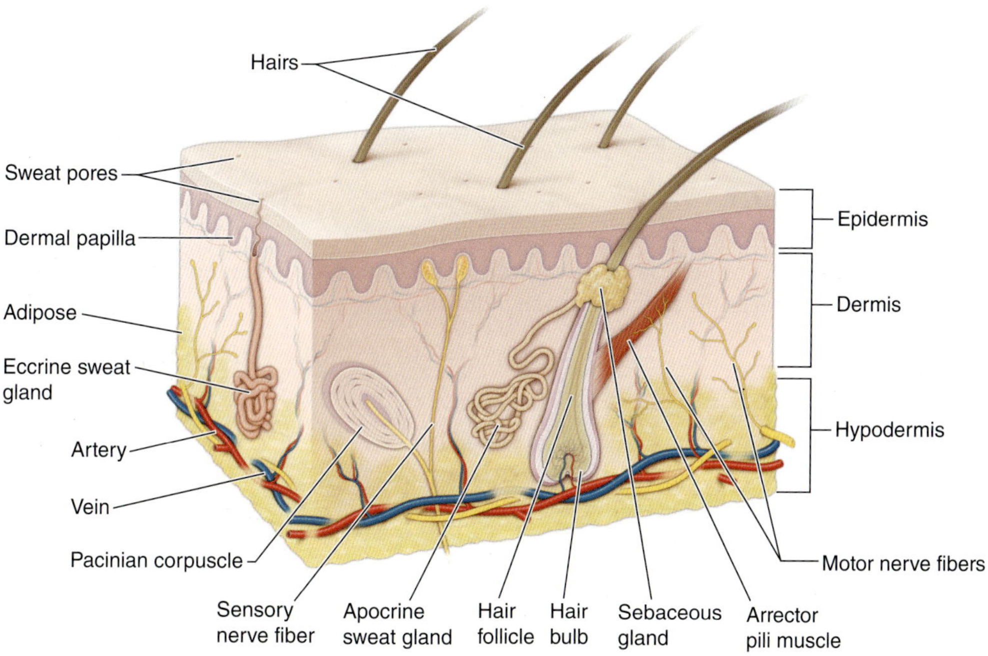

Figure 4-1 Structures of the skin.

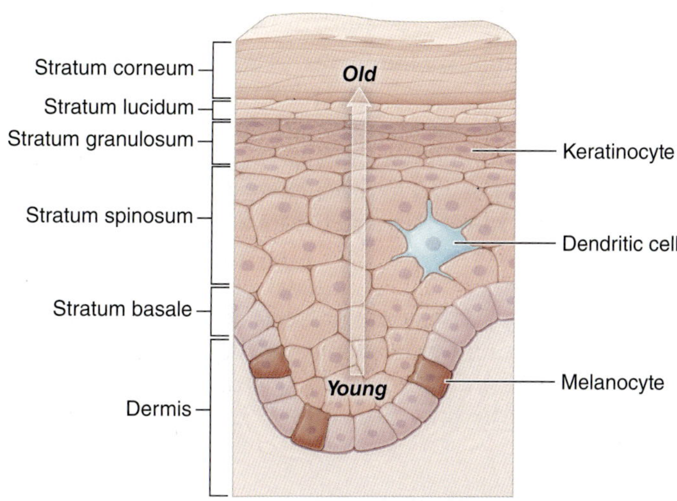

Figure 4-2 The layers of the epidermis.

Stratum lucidum is present only in the thick skin of the palms and soles of the feet. It consists of three to four rows of flattened dead cells that are mostly transparent. **Stratum granulosum** is comprised of three to five rows of partially flattened **keratinocytes**, cells containing small granules in their cytoplasm. These granular cells are comprised of proteins that transform into **keratin**. Keratin is the waterproofing component of skin that also prevents fluids from evaporating through the skin. The **Stratum spinosum** is a multilayered arrangement of cuboid cells. Most of the cells are keratinocytes. The keratinocytes contain desmosomes that have a spiny appearance, giving the layer its name. The remaining cells are dendritic cells, which defend against microorganisms and tumor cells by phagocytosis, the process of engulfing potential pathogens.

ELEMENT REVIEW
kerat/o = keratin
-cyte = cell
corne/o = hard
lucidi/o = clear
spin/o = spiny, prickly
-um = pertaining to
granul/o = granular
-ar = pertaining to

ELEMENT REVIEW
bas/o = base, bottom
-ale = pertaining to

Stratum basale, the deepest layer of the epidermis, is also called the *stratum germinativum*. It comprises a single layer of columnar or cuboidal cells. They are the only cells of the epidermis that undergo cell division via mitosis. The newly produced cells are constantly pushed toward the surface of the skin as new cells are created.

PHYSIOLOGY FACT

Fingerprints and footprints are formed at the 10th week of gestation in the mother's womb. The stratum basale creates new cells that fold and bend, creating the patterns that will be the fingerprints unique to each individual.

Study Tip

You can remember the five layers of the epidermis with the mnemonic Come Let's Get Sun Blocked: **C**orneum. **L**ucidium, **G**ranulosum, **S**pinosum and **B**asal

Skin Color

ELEMENT REVIEW
melan/o = black
-cyte = cell

The color of skin is determined by **melanocytes**, cells that secrete **melanin**, or dark protein. The greater the amount of melanin, the darker the skin color. Production of melanin by melanocytes is regulated by the genes in the DNA of the melanocytes, thus skin color is an inherited trait. The production of melanin can be increased by exposure to ultraviolet light. Sunlight stimulates melanocytes to produce more melanin. The effect is tanning of the skin. Tanning is the skin's effort to protect from additional damage. Although it may be visually appealing, there is no "healthy tan." The function of melanocytes is to protect the skin from the harmful effects of UV (ultraviolet) light that can break apart DNA within the nuclei of skin cells and cause mutations. Excessive exposure to sunlight can overwhelm the melanocytes, resulting in sunburn or skin cancer.

Additionally, **carotene** is a skin pigment of the stratum corneum and the dermis that gives an orange-yellow hue to the skin.

PHYSIOLOGY FACT

The color of skin is also affected by increased blood flow to the skin, causing a pink or red appearance. It can be due to vigorous exercise, which increases blood flow. Increased blood flow to the surface can also be triggered by the sympathetic nervous system during embarrassment or emotional distress. It appears most prominently in very lightly pigmented people.

Dermis

The dermis, or **corium**, is a region of connective tissue that lies directly beneath the basal layer of the epidermis. The dermis contains glands and sensory nerves that create an important connection of the skin's surface to the underlying structures of the body. The cells are not arranged in a tight waterproof form as is the epidermis, and they are scattered far apart. In a healthy person, the extracellular material of the dermis contains large amounts of **collagen**, a protein-containing substance that gives firmness to the layer. This dense, spongy firmness of the dermis affords the body protection from mechanical injury and compression. The dermis extends to the stratum basale of the epidermis, supplying it with nourishment and helping to remove waste. The dermis may be divided into two layers, the papillary region, adjacent to the epidermis, and the reticular region, which is deeper.

The **papillary region** contains fingerlike projections (papillae) that extend toward the epidermis and provides the bumpy surface to the skin. In the palms, fingers, soles of the feet and the toes, the papillae projecting into the epidermis form contours to the skin surface. The result is ridges in the skin such as those seen in fingerprints and footprints.

The **reticular region** lies deep to the papillary region and is usually much thicker. It has a high concentration of collagen, elastic, and reticular fibers that run through it, hence its name. The elastic nature of the reticular region gives it both strength and flexibility. As we age, the proteins of these elastic fibers decline in production and the appearance of wrinkles occurs. Within the reticular region, accessory organs of the skin include sebaceous glands, sweat glands, receptors, nails, and the roots of hair.

The Subcutaneous Layer

The **subcutaneous** layer, also called the **hypodermis**, is not part of the skin but rather connects the skin to the internal structures of the body. Strands of collagen extend from the dermis through the hypodermis to the muscle layer below. Lying below the dermis, the subcutaneous layer consists of connective tissue and adipose (fat) tissue. The hypodermis provides insulation from extreme heat and a shock-absorbing cushion against injury. The adipose tissue is a reserve for energy storage. The thickness of the subcutaneous layer varies over different parts of the body. It is most abundant in the abdomen and thighs and less so in the chest and arms. Diet, metabolism, and activity/exercise level account for variations in total body fat storage.

PHYSIOLOGY FACT

In general, people with more stored fat in the abdomen and thighs will feel warmer than lean people as they have more insulation.

The Accessory Organs

In addition to the layers of skin, the integumentary system includes hair, a variety of glands, and nails (Fig. 4-3). These structures have different functions as discussed next.

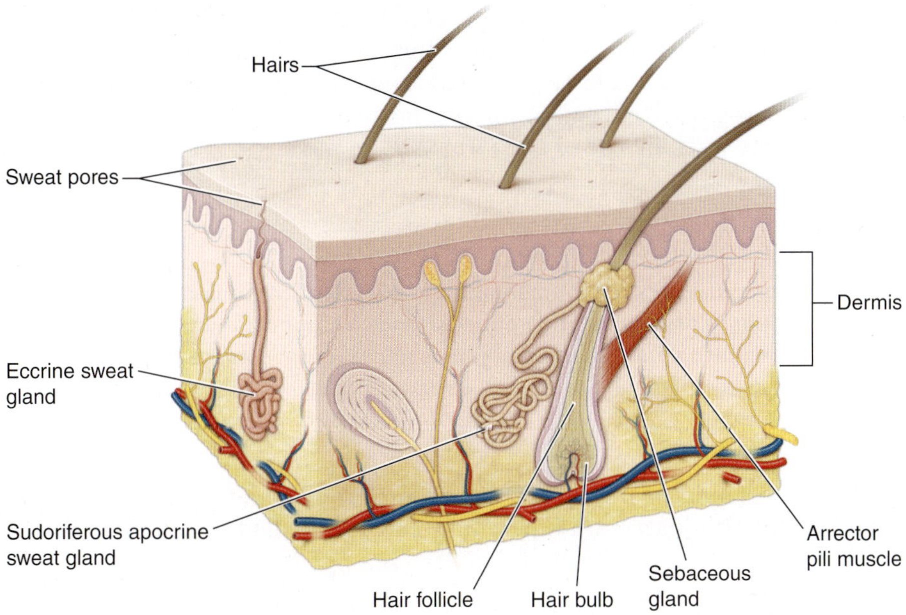

Figure 4-3 Accessory organs.

Hair

Hair is a long, slender filament made of collagen and protects the skin from damage from sunlight, debris, and injury. The base of a hair cell is the **hair root**, which is embedded in the **hair follicle**. The distal base of the hair root and hair follicle is slightly larger than the hair shaft and acts as an anchor with a bulb-like appearance, thus it is called the **hair bulb**. Arising from the follicle is the **hair shaft**, the portion we can see above the skin. Hair covers most of the human body, except for the palms of the hands and the soles of the feet, the lips, and nipples. Oxygen and nutrients from blood vessels around the hair bulb form the hair. Pigment-producing melanocytes in the hair bulb account for the color of hair, which is genetically determined. Surrounding each hair follicle is a small muscle called **arrector pili**, meaning "to stand up." Contraction of this muscle causes the hair to protrude straight up from the skin, giving the appearance of bumps. Commonly called "goose bumps," this is seen on the skin when we are cold or frightened.

PHYSIOLOGY FACT

The differences in hair color—blonde, brown, black, and red—result from varying concentrations of melanin and are mainly determined by genetic inheritance. Additionally, a unique type of melanin containing iron results in red hair. As we age, the quantity of melanin decreases causing hair to turn gray or white.

Skin Glands

ELEMENT REVIEW
ex/o = outside
-crine = to secrete
hyp/o = under, below
dermis = skin

Adjacent to the arrector pili is the **sebaceous gland**. Sebaceous glands are exocrine glands that produce an oily substance called sebum. They are nearly always associated with hair follicles, and they act to lubricate both the hair and the skin. Sebum prevents dryness of skin and inhibits the growth of bacteria on the surface of the skin. Sebaceous gland activity rises during puberty with the rise of sex hormones.

PHYSIOLOGY FACT

Although normal quantities of sebum inhibit the growth of bacteria on the surface of the skin, its increased presence during puberty tends to support and attract colonies of bacteria. Bacteria then enters sebaceous glands and ducts and cause localized inflammation, known as pimples.

Another gland found in the skin is the **sudoriferous gland**, commonly known as a sweat gland. Sweat glands secrete a watery substance, also called perspiration, that is made of water, salts, and a small amount of metabolic wastes. Secretion of sweat helps to regulate body temperature as sweat evaporates from skin. Each sweat gland originates as a coiled tube in the dermis and ends with an opening to the surface of the skin, called a **pore**. There are two forms of sweat glands: eccrine and apocrine glands.

Eccrine glands are found throughout the body and secrete sweat to regulate body temperature. To a lesser degree, eccrine glands also aid the kidneys in ridding the body of metabolic wastes.

Apocrine glands begin to function during puberty in response to sex hormones. The sweat they produce also contains proteins that promote the growth of bacteria on the skin. The microorganisms on the surface of the skin break down the proteins for food and release sulfur-containing waste materials, giving the sweat a foul odor. Apocrine glands are found in the armpits and groin and are active primarily during emotional stress.

Nails

The distal ends of our fingers and toes are protected by the nails. Nails are formed from the compressed outer layer of the stratum corneum and contain a large amount of keratin, giving nails a hard consistency. The visible portion of the nail, the **nail plate**, overlies the nail bed. The distal edge of the nail is called the free edge, and the **cuticle** is a small flap of stratum corneum that overlies the proximal edge of the nail. Deep to the cuticle, the **nail root** contains active stratum basale known as the *nail matrix*, which produces new nail cells by mitosis. The newly formed cells are pushed outward and thus the nails grow. A small part of the nail matrix can be seen through the nail body as a light-colored crescent called the **lunula**.

PHYSIOLOGY FACT

The appearance of a person's nails is influenced by changing metabolic conditions of the body; thus their appearance can help to diagnose many health conditions and dietary deficiencies (Fig. 4-4). Yellow nails may indicate thyroid disease, liver disorder, or AIDS. Brittle cracked nails may indicate a calcium deficiency. Pitted or concave nails may indicate poor circulation of blood.

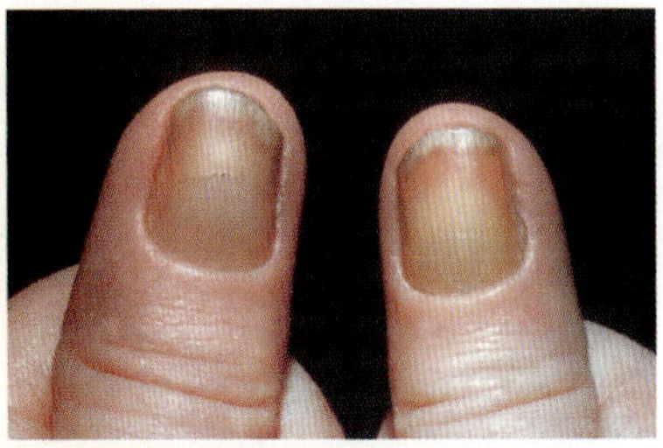

Figure 4-4 Yellow nail syndrome.

Receptors

An important feature of our skin is perception. When touch is integrated with sight and sound, we perceive the world around us. Skin contains the distal ends of neurons, cells that transmit sensory information to the brain. The various types of receptors transmit different sensations to the brain (Fig. 4-5):

Meissner (tactile) corpuscles are located in the papillary region (superficial) of the dermis and detect fine or light touch.

Free nerve endings are located in the dermis and respond to a variety of changes in temperature, pressure, and pain.

Pacinian (lamellar) corpuscles are located in the subcutaneous tissues as well as other parts of the body, such as the pancreas, penis, clitoris, and nipples. They detect deep or heavy pressure.

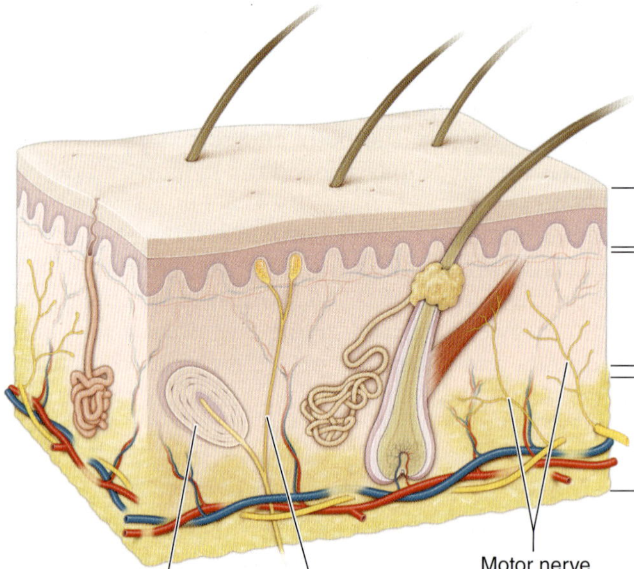

Figure 4-5 Types of skin receptors.

STRUCTURES AND PHYSIOLOGY REVIEW

1. Match the Words

Match the words to their descriptions.

adipose	epidermis	stratum basale
apocrine	keratin	stratum corneum
arrector pili	lunula	stratum lucidium
carotene	melanin	sudoriferous
dermis	melanocyte	
eccrine	pore	

1. Another term for fat ________________
2. Pigment that gives skin a yellow hue ________________
3. Cells that secrete pigment-producing substance ________________
4. Opening in the skin for either sweat or oil to escape ________________
5. The "clear" layer of the epidermis ________________
6. The most prominent type of sweat glands ________________
7. The deepest layer of the epidermis ________________
8. A muscle that causes hair to stand up ________________
9. The name for sweat glands ________________

10. The pigment that darkens hair and skin ______________________

11. The thick layer that lies beneath the epidermis ______________________

12. The outermost layer of the epidermis ______________________

13. The light-colored crescent on nails ______________________

14. Sweat glands that secrete protein-containing sweat ______________________

15. Gives skin waterproofing ______________________

Structures and Physiology Word-Building Practice

1. Nouns and Adjectives

Complete the chart of nouns and their adjective forms.

Noun form	Adjective form
sebum	______________________
epidermis	______________________
hypodermis	______________________
papilla	______________________
follicle	______________________

2. Prefixes

Choose from the list of prefixes to build a word for the definitions below:

a-, an-	without	melan-	large
epi-	upon	sub-	under, below
hyper-	excessive	xantho-	yellow
hypo-	decreased amount	xero-	dry
macro-	large		

1. Dry skin ______________________

2. The top layer of skin ______________________

3. Yellow skin ______________________

4. Condition of excessive hair growth ______________________

5. Condition of decreased amount of melanin in the skin ______________________

6. Absence of color ______________________

7. Pertaining to under the skin ______________________

3. Singular and Plural Forms

Complete the chart of singular and plural forms.

papilla	________
hair	________
________	bacteria
fungus	________
________	nevi
virus	________

Word-Building With Combining, Prefix, and Suffix Forms

The following word roots, prefixes, and suffixes are commonly used in medical terms for the anatomy and pathology of the integumentary system. Combining vowels for word roots are included. Memorizing these elements will help you understand new terms that you may encounter as a medical assistant, dermatologist, nurse, or physical therapist, or as another health-care professional.

The lists contain examples of terms that utilize the word elements as well as a pronunciation guide. Be sure to use the pronunciation guide so that you can learn to say the terms correctly.

Medical Language Lab

The Medical Language Lab at medicallanguagelab.com provides audio files to help you practice your pronunciations.

Combining Form	Meaning	Example (Pronunciation)	Definition
adip/o	fat	adipoid (Ă-dĭ-poyd)	resembling fat
albin/o	white	albicans (AL-bĭ-kanz)	to make white
bas/o	base	basal (BĀ-săl)	pertaining to the base
cutane/o	skin	cutaneous (kū-TĀ-nē-ŭs)	pertaining to skin
chromat/o	color	chromatic (krō-MĂT-ĭk)	pertaining to color
cirrh/o	yellow	cirrhosis (sĭ-RŌ-sĭs)	abnormal condition of yellow
cyan/o	blue	cyanosis (sī-ă-NŌ-sĭs)	abnormal condition of blue
derm/o	skin	dermatome (DĔR-mă-tōm)	instrument to incise skin

Combining Form	Meaning	Example (Pronunciation)	Definition
dermat/o	skin	dermatitis (dĕr-mă-TĪT-ĭs)	inflammation of skin
erythem/o	red	erythema (ĕr-i-THĒ-mă)	reddening of the skin
erythr/o	red	erythrocyte (ĕ-RĬTH-rŏ-sīt)	red blood cell
hidr/o	sweat	hidrosis (hī-DRŌ-sĭs)	abnormal condition of sweat
kerat/o	horny, hard tissue, cornea	keratinase (KĔR-ă-tĭ-nās)	enzyme that hydrolyzes keratin
melan/o	black	melanin (MĔL-ă-nĭn)	pigment that gives dark color to skin and hair
myc/o	fungus	mycology (mī-KŎL-ō-jē)	the study of fungi
necr/o	dead	necrotic (nĕk-KRŎT-ĭk)	pertaining to dead tissue
onych/o	nail	onychomalacia (ŏn-ĭ-kō-mă-LĂ-shē-ă)	softening of nails
pil/o	hair	piloerection (pī-lō-e-REK-shŏn)	elevation of hair above the skin
rhytid/o	wrinkles	rhytidoplasty (RĬT-ĭ-dō-plas-tē)	surgical correction of wrinkles
trich/o	hair	trichopathy (trĭk-ŎP-ă-thē)	disease of the hair
scler/o	hardening	scleroderma (sklĕ-RŌ-dĕr-mă)	hardening of the skin
seb/o	sebum	seborrhea (sĕ-bō-RĒ-ă)	flow or discharge of sebum
xanth/o	yellow	xanthoderma (zan-thō-DĔR-mă)	yellow skin
xer/o	dry	Xerosis (zēr-ō-sĭs)	condition of dryness

ā = say, ă = sofa, ē = meet, ĕ = met, ī = eye, ĭ = in, ō = oh, ŏ = dog, ū = you, ŭ = up, oo = food

Prefix	Meaning	Example (Pronunciation)	Definition
a-	without	achromat (ā-KRŌ-mă)	absence of color of the skin
hyper-	excessive	hypertrophy (hī-PĔR-trŏ-fē)	excessive growth
hypo-	under, below	hypodermis (hī-pŏ-DĔR-mĭs)	under the skin

Continued

Prefix	Meaning	Example (Pronunciation)	Definition
intra-	within	intradermal (in-tră- DĔR-măl)	within the skin
sub-	under, below	subcutaneous (sŭb-kū-TĀ-nē-ŭs)	under the skin

ā = say, ă = sofa, ē = meet, ĕ = met, ī = eye, ĭ = in, ō = oh, ŏ = dog, ū = you, ŭ = up, oo = food

Suffix	Meaning	Example (Pronunciation)	Definition
-ectomy	surgical removal	rhytidectomy (rĭd-ĭ-DEK-tō-mē)	surgical removal of wrinkles
-iasis	condition	trichiasis (trĭk-Ī-ă-sĭs)	condition of hair
-ic	pertaining to	hypodermic (hī-pō-DĔR-mĭk)	pertaining to under the skin
-itis	inflammation	dermatitis (dĕr-mă-TĪT-ĭs)	inflammation of the skin
-ology	study of	histology (hĭs-TŎL-ŏ-jē)	the study of the tissue
-oma	tumor	squamous cell carcinoma (SKWĀ-mŭs sel kar-sĭn-Ō-mă)	tumor of squamous epithelium
-osis	condition	onychomycosis (on-i-kō-mī-KŌ-sĭs	fungal infection (condition) of nails
-plasty	surgical repair	dermatoplasty (dĕr-mă-TŌ-plas-tē)	surgical repair of skin

ā = say, ă = sofa, ē = meet, ĕ = met, ī = eye, ĭ = in, ō = oh, ŏ = dog, ū = you, ŭ = up, oo = food

Combining Forms Practice

1. Build the Terms

*Using **only** the word parts in the lists, create medical terms for the indicated meanings.*

Prefixes	Combining Forms		Suffixes	
a-	adip/o	melan/o	-a	-lysis
epi-	albin/o	myc/o	-al	-ology
hyper-	cutane/o	necr/o	-ectomy	-oma
hypo-	cirrh/o	onych/o	-ia	-osis
intra-	cyan/o	phag/o	-iasis	-ous
par-	derm/o	pil/o	-ic	-plasty
sub-	dermat/o	rhytid/o	-itis	-rhea
	erythr/o	trich/o		
	hidr/o	scler/o		

Prefixes	Combining Forms		Suffixes
	kerat/o	seb/o	
	leuk/o	xanth/o	
		xer/o	

1. Surgical repair of wrinkles ____________________
2. Condition of excessive sweating ____________________
3. Blue condition ____________________
4. Dry skin ____________________
5. Condition of compulsive eating of hair ____________________
6. Tumor of keratin ____________________
7. Condition of hardening and inflammation ____________________
8. Surgical removal of fat ____________________
9. Disease of hair caused by fungus ____________________
10. The study of mortality statistics ____________________
11. Pertaining to within the epidermis ____________________
12. Destruction of skin ____________________
13. Abnormal redness of the skin ____________________
14. White spots or streaks on the nails ____________________
15. Nail biting (eating) ____________________
16. Increased amount of discharge of sebum ____________________
17. Yellow skin ____________________
18. Pertaining to under the skin ____________________
19. Pertaining to the hair and sebaceous glands ____________________
20. The study of skin ____________________

2. Decipher the Terms

Separate each term into its prefix (if any), combining form, and suffix. Next, translate the word parts and then give the common definition of the term.

1. Lipocyte

   Prefix: __________ *Combining Form:* __________ *Suffix:* __________

   Meaning: ______________________________

2. Transcutaneous

Prefix: ______________ *Combining Form:* ______________ *Suffix:* ______________

Meaning: ____

3. Albino

Prefix: ______________ *Combining Form:* ______________ *Suffix:* ______________

Meaning: ____

4. Hypermelanosis

Prefix: ______________ *Combining Form:* ______________ *Suffix:* ______________

Meaning: ____

5. Erythema

Prefix: ______________ *Combining Form:* ______________ *Suffix:* ______________

Meaning: ____

6. Melanoma

Prefix: ______________ *Combining Form:* ______________ *Suffix:* ______________

Meaning: ____

7. Cyanoderma

Prefix: ______________ *Combining Form:* ______________ *Suffix:* ______________

Meaning: ____

8. Onychopathy

Prefix: ______________ *Combining Form:* ______________ *Suffix:* ______________

Meaning: ____

9. Rhytidectomy

Prefix: ______________ *Combining Form:* ______________ *Suffix:* ______________

Meaning: ____

10. Dermabrasion

Prefix: ______________ *Combining Form:* ______________ *Suffix:* ______________

Meaning: ____

Visit the Medical Language Lab at medicallanguagelab.com. Use it to enhance your word-building skills for the word parts covered in this chapter.

CASE STUDY, continued

Travis and Claire arrive at the hospital early in the morning for his BBC removal. He does not eat breakfast, as he has been instructed. Bethany, the certified nurse anesthetist, interviews Travis prior to the procedure. She asks him if he has had anesthesia in the past and if he had any problems with it. He stated that he had a pacemaker inserted 2 years ago with no problems. He also had a hip replacement without complications. Travis is brought to the operating room and placed under laryngeal mask airway anesthesia in the supine position. Travis tolerated the BBC excision well and was brought to the postoperative recovery room. Claire was able to talk with Dr. Torres, who explained that the procedure went well and that the BCC was removed with clear margins, meaning all of the tumor was removed. The tissue was sent to pathology. Dr. Torres tells Claire that when Travis is awake, he will explain the findings in the pathology report and give discharge instructions to Travis.

Integumentary System Diseases and Disorders

Diseases of the integumentary system are often visible, so the process of diagnosing these diseases often starts with visual inspection of the skin. Diseases and disorders of the skin include cysts, calluses, infections, scrapes, acne, burns, lacerations (cuts), and both cancerous and noncancerous tumors.

Common Signs and Symptoms

The skin and accessory organs work to provide protection, regulate temperature, and act as organs of detoxification. As such, there are signs and symptoms common to disorders of the integumentary system (Table 4-1). The presence of these signs and/or symptoms will prompt the provider to investigate to attain a specific diagnosis.

TABLE 4-1 Common Signs and Symptoms

Common Signs	Common Symptoms
Paleness	Itching
Erythema (redness)	Feeling of tightness of skin
Dryness	Feeling hot or cold
Rashes	Pain
Alopecia (hair loss)	Paresthesia (numbness)
Scaly skin	Burning sensation
Jaundice (yellowing)	
Cysts, boils, furuncles	
Exudates	

Pathological Conditions of the Integumentary System

Abrasion: Scrape of the skin, rubbing the mucous membrane away because of friction.

Abscess: A localized collection of pus in an area of inflammation.

Acne vulgaris: Commonly occurs during adolescence due to the increase in sex hormones. Common sites of the lesions are face, chest, back, and neck. The lesions can be whiteheads (closed comedos) or blackheads (open comedos). The condition is caused by increased secretion of sebum, and the skin takes on an oily appearance. Treatment may consist of application of antibiotic creams, frequent cleansing of the skin, and avoiding makeup that may clog pores. Patients may be tempted to "pop" both whiteheads and blackheads, leading to scarring of the skin. After puberty, patients may elect to have dermabrasion to reduce the appearance of acne scars.

ELEMENT REVIEW
actin/o = ray
-ic = pertaining to

Actinic keratosis: Appearance of rough sandpaper-like skin in areas that are exposed to sunlight such as the face or ears. Prevention strategy is to cover the skin and/or apply sunscreen. Liquid nitrogen can be applied to lesions to prevent progression to cancers.

Alopecia: Complete or partial hair loss (Fig. 4-6). It may be a result of normal aging or a reaction to medications such as chemotherapy, endocrine disorders, or skin disease.

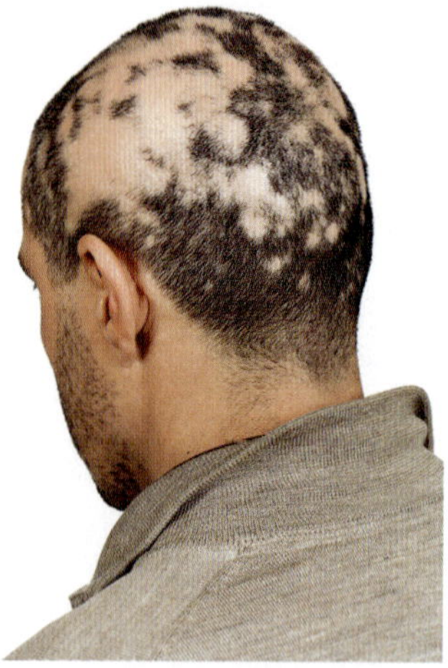

Figure 4-6 Alopecia.

Basal cell carcinoma (BCC): Malignant epithelial cell tumor originating in the stratum basale (Fig. 4-7). It is the most common malignant skin cancer, accounting for 80% of skin cancers. BCC is seen primarily in areas exposed to sunlight such as the face, especially the nose. If left untreated, it can progress to destruction of a body part (such as the nose). Treatments depend on the severity of the lesion and include excision, curettage and electrodesiccation, cryosurgery, or radiation. While the lesions rarely metastasize to other regions of the body, they do recur, especially with lesions greater than 2 cm in diameter.

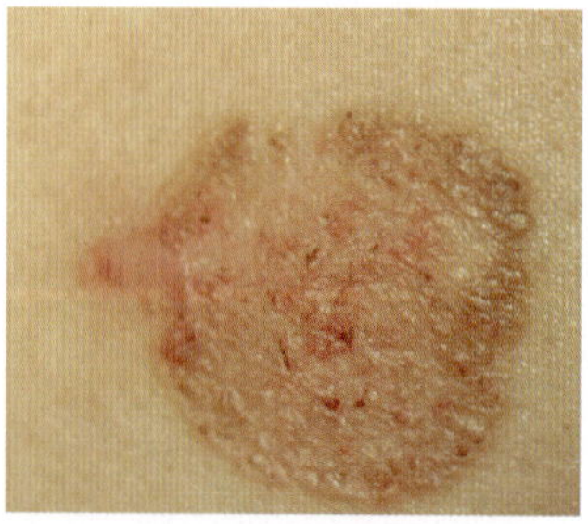

Figure 4-7 Basal cell carcinoma.

Bulla: Term for a large blister or skin vesicle that is filled with clear fluid.

Burn: Injured or destroyed skin caused by flame, heat, caustic chemicals, radiation, or electricity (Fig. 4-8). Burns are categorized based on the depth of the injury:

First-degree burns, such as sunburns, involve the epidermis only. The affected skin appears red, with some localized swelling. These burns will heal with the peeling off of the burned layer within a few days. Treatment consists of application of aloe and topical corticosteroids, and staying away from sun exposure. Fair skinned people, prone to sunburn, are advised to use high SPF (sun protection factor) sunscreen and to avoid direct sunlight in midday.

Second-degree burns are the most painful burns and involve both the epidermis and the dermis but do not damage lower-lying hair follicles or sweat and sebaceous glands. The skin will heal within 2 to 3 weeks if kept clean and no infection occurs. The affected skin appears red, with painful blisters that can be large and contain clear fluid. The blisters can burst and risk infection. Infection can delay wound healing and cause permanent scarring.

ELEMENT REVIEW
all/o = another
aut/o = self
xen/o = strange, foreign

ELEMENT REVIEW
necr/o = dead
-osis = condition

Third-degree burns cause necrosis of the epidermis, dermis, and possibly some of the subcutaneous tissues. The skin appears black, tan, white, or bright red and can be wet or dry. Loss of tissue shows a sunken appearance with eschar (dry crust) and coagulated capillaries. The burns are often not painful because nerve endings are also burned, but the edges of the site will be painful. Pain will ensue as tissue heals. Treatment is prolonged and painful and includes debridement, which involves taking away dead tissue to allow for new skin to grow. The patient may also require skin grafts (dermatoplasty) that are used to cover large areas of burns. The grafts can be taken from other areas of the patient's body (autograft), from human donors (allograft), from animals such as pigs (xenograft), or a synthetic skin made in a laboratory. Complications of fluid loss, dehydration, and infection are common, and patients are often treated in the hospital

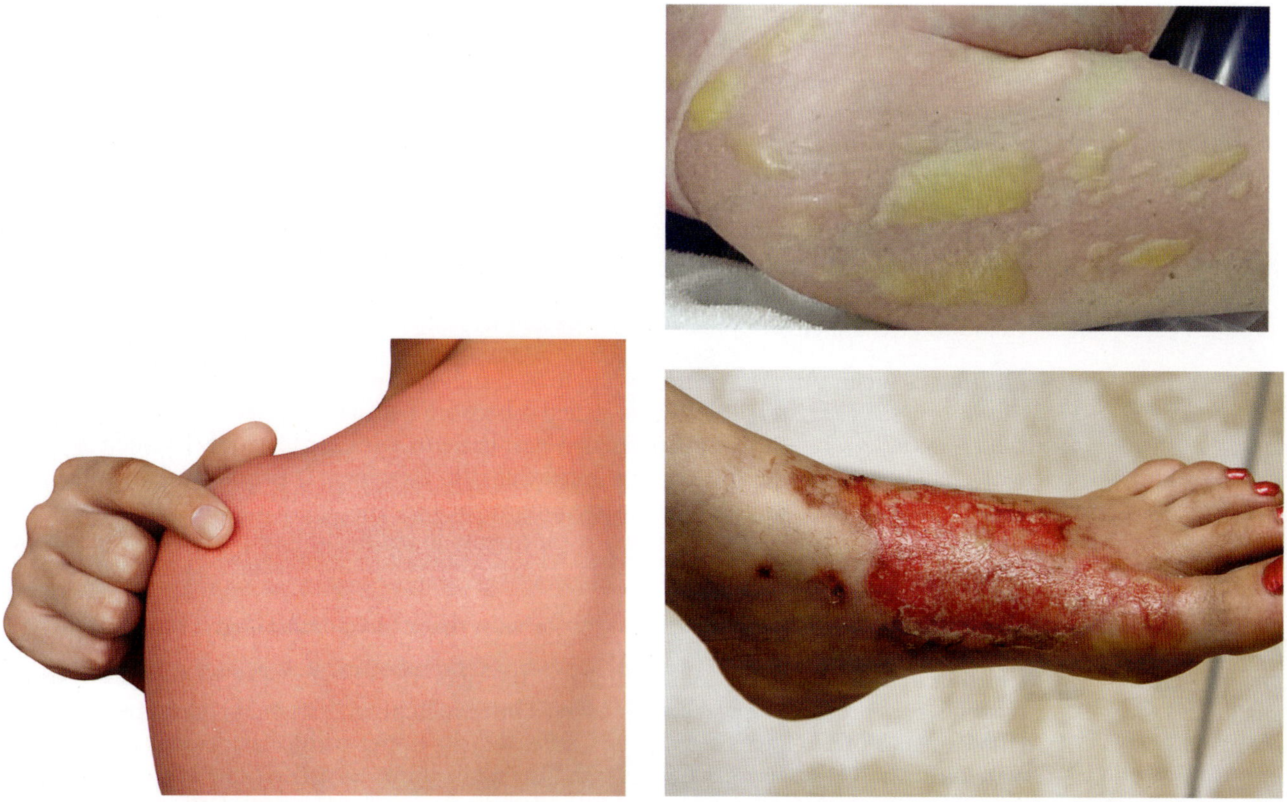

Figure 4-8 Burn categories.

so that a sterile environment can minimize infection. Survival of third-degree burns depends on the percentage of the body burned, the location of the burns, the age of the patient, and any comorbidities.

Callus: Localized area of hyperplasia caused by friction, pressure, or weight-bearing. Commonly seen on the soles of the feet and the palms of the hands of people who perform manual labor. Prevention includes wearing work gloves and applying protection creams. Properly fitted shoes, with adequate cushioning or shoe inserts will decrease pressure.

ELEMENT REVIEW
hyper- = excessive
-plasia = formation

Carbuncle: Deep skin lesion that starts as a painful, inflamed node (Fig. 4-9). Skin appears reddened and "tight." As the skin layer thins, a pus-filled lesion is seen, which later perforates, and pus exudes. Treatment consists of antibiotics and warm compresses.

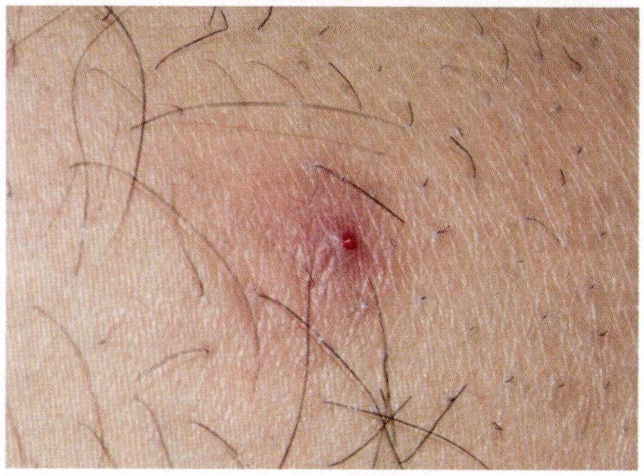

Figure 4-9 Carbuncle.

Cellulitis: A spreading bacterial infection of the skin and subcutaneous tissues, usually caused by streptococcal or staphylococcal infections. It may occur after an insect bite or other wound. It is often seen in the lower legs, where the skin "weeps" and a clear fluid exudate appears. Risk factors include diabetes, lymphedema, venous stasis, or venous insufficiency. Treatment consists of antibiotics (oral or IV depending on severity), sterile wound care, and elevating the legs.

Comedo: Lesions associated with acne vulgaris. Two forms are open comedo, called a blackhead, and a closed comedo, called a whitehead.

Corn: A horny thickening of the skin usually caused by pressure or friction. Often seen in the feet if shoes are too tight. Treatment consists of well-fitted shoes; podiatrists may remove corns with a scalpel or application of a keratolytic agent to dissolve the corn. Patients with diabetes or peripheral vascular disease are advised to inspect their feet because they may not feel development of a corn or other foot lesion and risk progression of lesions or infections.

Cyst: A broad term used to denote a closed sac or pouch that contains fluid, semifluid, or solid material. Cysts vary greatly; those arising from sebaceous glands are filled with sebum, keratin, and epithelial debris. Other forms of cysts arise from bones, teeth (odontogenic cysts), nerve roots (ganglion cysts), Bartholin's glands, ovaries (see Chapter 12, The Female Reproductive System), and the scrotal sac, known as a hydrocele (see Chapter 13, The Male Reproductive System).

ELEMENT REVIEW
odont/o = teeth
-genic = producing, forming

Decubitus ulcer: An area of necrosis due to unrelieved pressure preventing circulation to the skin tissue (Fig. 4-10). It is also called a bedsore because it is seen in neglect of bedridden patients who cannot move themselves. Patients with sensory deficits, such as those with spinal cord injuries, strokes, or coma are at risk. Treatment is primarily directed at prevention by frequent turning or repositioning in the bed and application of skin protection to bony parts. If lesions occur, antibiotic ointments to aid healing of partial thickness sores are implemented.

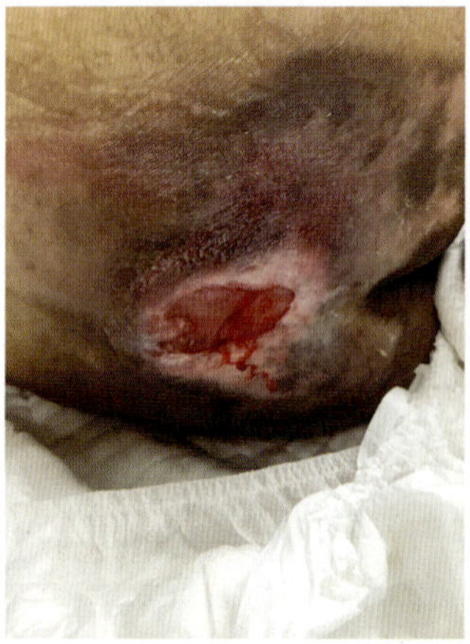

Figure 4-10 Decubitus ulcer.

Ecchymosis: Superficial bleeding under the skin that causes darkening; a bruise.

Eczema: Acute or chronic skin condition with erythema (redness of skin), papules, vesicles, pustules, scales, crusts, or scabs, which cause intense itching (Fig. 4-11). Common sites are elbows, backs of the knees, ears, hands, feet, and the upper trunk. The lesions can weep or ooze serum and later become thick and hardened in a process called lichenification, causing permanent scarring. Causes of eczema include environmental or food allergies, irritating chemicals, genetic predisposition, medications, scratching the skin, or sun exposure. Treatment is directed at the cause: avoiding the allergen, sun exposure, perfume, etc. Antihistamines may reduce itching, especially at night. Staying hydrated and using a humidifier in winter are recommended. Children and infants are most affected, and symptoms reduce as the child grows.

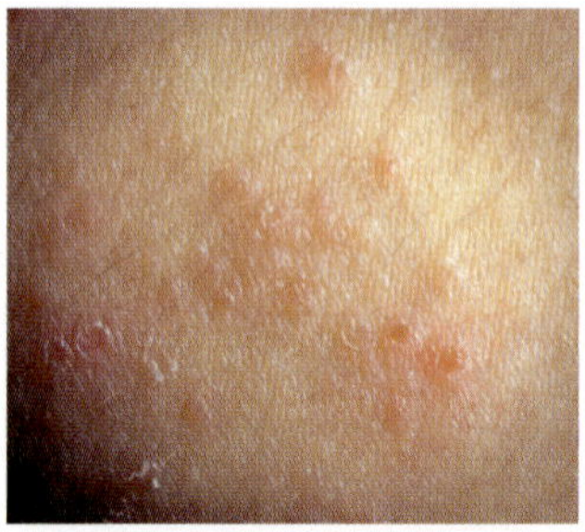

Figure 4-11 Eczema.

Fissure: A small cleft or crack in the skin, commonly seen on the margin of the anus, fingertips, or in athletes foot infections.

Folliculitis: Inflammation of hair follicles including a bumpy red rash. Lesions may be tender and pus-filled. They are commonly seen on the neck, armpit, and groin areas. Causes include exposure to contaminated bath, swimming pool, or spa water. The infection is self-limiting and will resolve without treatment within 2 weeks.

Frostbite: Severe tissue and cell injury from exposure to cold temperature causing freezing. The intracellular water turns to ice, damaging blood supply to the cells. Most commonly seen on the nose, ears, fingers, and toes. Preventive measures include limiting time in extreme cold and wearing warm, dry clothing. Treatment consists of gently rewarming the skin with warm water and drinking warm fluids. Because rewarming frostbitten skin can be painful, analgesics and NSAIDs can be given. If severe, frostbite can lead to necrosis of tissue and loss of a body part such as fingers or toes.

Furuncle: Infection of a hair follicle and its adjacent sebaceous gland, creating a dome-shaped lesion. It is also called a boil and usually is seen on the neck, face, axilla (armpit), or buttocks. As they progress and become larger, they fill with pus and cellular debris. Treatment consists of warm, moist compresses to encourage drainage and relieve pressure. Oral antibiotics and incision and drainage (I&D) is necessary for larger furuncles.

Gangrene: Necrosis of tissue due to a lack of blood supply. Can be caused by frostbite, crush injuries, or uncontrolled diabetes mellitus. Treatments include vasodilating and thrombolytic agents to stop the progression of tissue death. It may require surgical removal of the dead tissue.

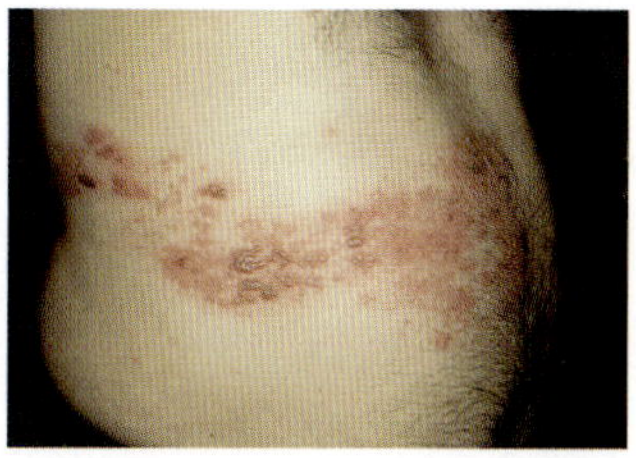

Figure 4-12 Shingles.

Herpes zoster: An acute viral infection, also called shingles, characterized by painful eruptions on the skin following a nerve pathway of spinal or cranial nerves (Fig. 4-12). According to the Centers for Disease Control and Prevention (CDC), "Approximately 1 out of 3 people in the United States will develop herpes zoster during their lifetime."

The rash is always unilateral and is most common in adults over the age of 50. Acute eruption of the infection is caused by reactivation of the latent varicella virus that causes chicken pox. Symptoms include a painful unilateral rash, fever, severe itching, GI discomfort, headache, and fatigue. The lesions appear as closed but they erupt and ooze within 3 to 5 days and are highly contagious. Patients are advised not to share towels or linens when the vesicles are oozing to prevent spread to family members. The lesions crust and dry within 2 to 3 weeks, but recurrence of herpes zoster is possible. According to the CDC the precise rate of recurrence is not known. Treatment may consist of analgesics, antivirals, and corticosteroids if inflammation becomes severe. The most common complication of shingles, postherpetic neuralgia, is characterized by pain that lasts 3 months or longer after the rash has resolved. Patients complain of sensitivity to light touch, itching, burning, and numbness. The vaccine for herpes zoster may prevent its occurrence.

ELEMENT REVIEW
post- = after
herpet/o = herpes
-ic = pertaining to

Impetigo: Scabby bacterial skin infection characterized by yellow to red weeping, crusted, or pus-filled lesions appearing on the nose and mouth (Fig. 4-13). Highly contagious and commonly seen in children. Prevention includes proper skin hygiene. Treatment includes topical antibiotics, cleansing, and drying the skin. Family members are encouraged not to share towels and face cloths to prevent the spread of infection.

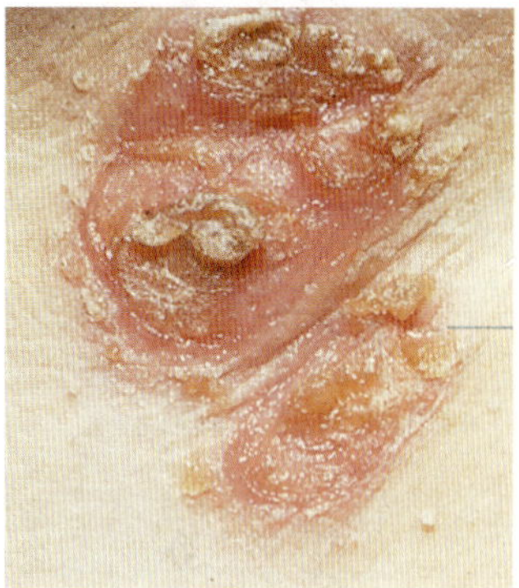

Figure 4-13 Impetigo.

Laceration: A tear in the flesh, often caused by accidental injury with a sharp instrument such as a kitchen knife or household tool. Treatment depends on the severity of the injury. Washing the wound, stopping bleeding with compression, and applying a clean bandage is often satisfactory. Deeper, larger lacerations may require suturing. Paying attention to where the hand and the blade are in the kitchen or workshop can prevent injury.

Macule: A flat, discolored spot on the skin, which may be darker or lighter than surrounding skin. Examples include freckles, petechiae, and vitiligo.

Malignant melanoma: An aggressive form of cancer originating from melanocytes in nevi (moles) (Fig. 4-14). The circular moles change in shape, becoming irregular as they increase in size. Diameter of lesions increases to 6 mm or more, and the colors can vary. People at risk of malignant melanoma include those with a light complexion and/or family history. Risk increases with excessive sun exposure. Most melanomas are invasive, spreading throughout the lymphatic system and metastasizing to other organs, often with fatal results. Diagnosis of malignant melanoma begins with visual inspection and follows the ABCD acronym:

A. Asymmetry—pigmented flat and elevated lesions that are not rounded like a mole.
B. Borders—brown pigmented lesions that spread in irregular shapes.
C. Color—variations red, black, brown, or pale that change over time.
D. Diameter—lesions with suspicious characteristics that measure 6 mm or greater.

Prevention of lesions includes wearing sunscreen, limiting direct sun exposure and inspecting skin to obtain early diagnosis. Treatment for lesions is to remove them with a scalpel.

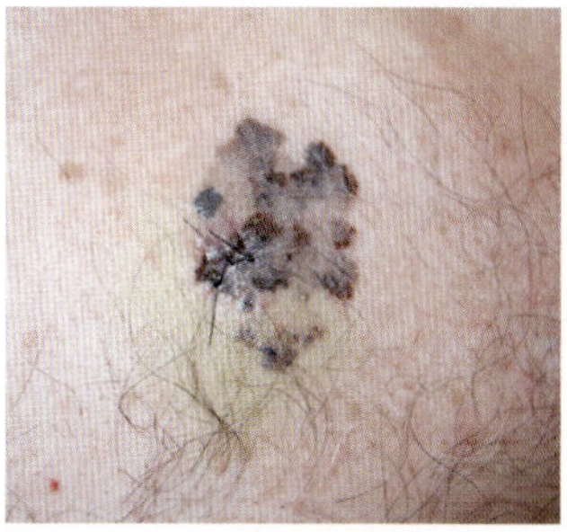

Figure 4-14 Malignant melanoma.

Melasma: Tan to brown and sharply defined patches of skin that develop symmetrically on the forehead, temples, cheeks, or upper lip. It often occurs during pregnancy, in women using oral birth control, or in patients with underlying liver disease. Exposure to sunlight increases hyperpigmentation.

ELEMENT REVIEW
onych/o = nail
crypt/o = hidden
-osis = condition

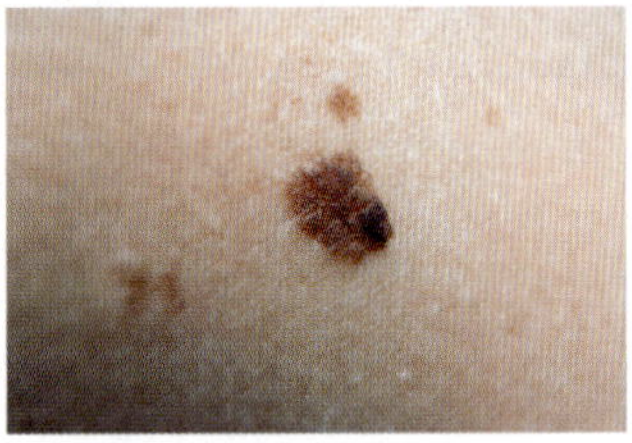

Figure 4-15 Papule.

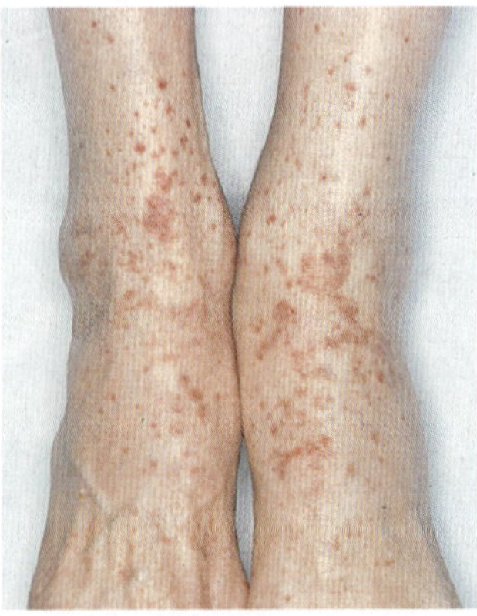

Figure 4-16 Petechiae.

ELEMENT REVIEW
psor/i = itching
-iasis = condition

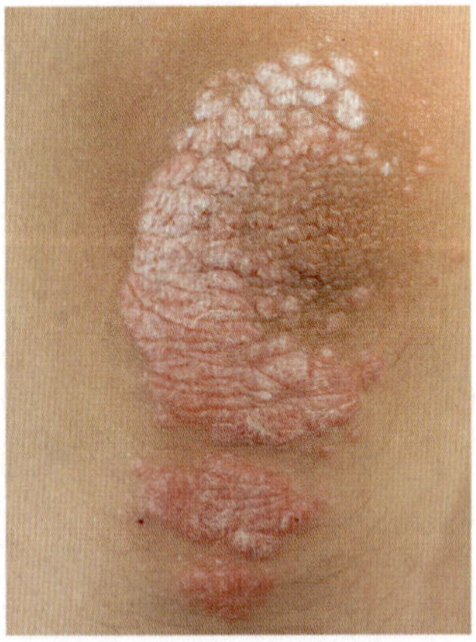

Figure 4-17 Psoriasis.

Nevus: A dark brown flat or raised round spot created by an accumulation of melanocytes, also called a mole. Changes in the size or shape of nevi should be monitored by the patient as these changes may lead to melanoma.

Onychocryptosis: An ingrown toenail, most commonly seen in the great toe.

Papule: A small, raised bump on the skin, such as a nevus (mole) (Fig. 4-15).

Paronychia: Acute or chronic infection at the margins of the fingernails or toenails. The nails become painful, red, thickened, warm, and may exude pus. Treatment consists of application of moist heat, antibiotics, or surgical drainage.

Pediculosis: Infestation of the head, body, or pubic region with lice. The eggs attach to the hair shaft then hatch and feed off blood of the skin causing itching. The condition is highly transmittable as lice can jump from person to person. The condition is often seen in school children and often diagnosed by a school nurse. Treatment with application of a pediculicide such as Nix resolves the infection, but washing of linens, combs, and hairbrushes is also recommended to prevent return of infection.

Petechiae: Pinpoint red spots from bleeding under the skin often caused by platelet deficiencies and febrile illnesses (Fig. 4-16). It is also seen in exertion such as lifting heavy weights or pushing during childbirth.

Psoriasis: Chronic skin condition affecting 1% to 2% of the population, characterized by red papules and scaly silvery plaques with defined borders (Fig. 4-17). Common sites are the elbows, knees, skin, ears, buttocks, and hairline. The lesions are itchy, dry, cracked, and painful. Infection from scratching may occur, forming pustules. The disease presents most often from age 10 to 40 years old and has a genetic predisposition. There is no cure for chronic psoriasis, but palliative treatments consist of topical corticosteroids, vitamin D, UV light therapies, keratolytics, and methotrexate.

Puncture: Any wound made by a sharp, pointed instrument; may vary in depth.

Pustule: A small blister filled with pus that may rupture spontaneously or be "popped" to express pus.

Rosacea: Chronic redness to the cheeks, forehead, and around the eyes commonly occurring in people of northern European ancestry age 30 to 50 years. It is more common in women than in men. To prevent rosacea, recommendations are to limit sun exposure, wear a hat, and use sunscreen. Patients may also see an increase in red appearance with specific food triggers; avoiding these foods is recommended. Treatments may consist of oral antibiotics.

Scabies: Highly contagious infestation of skin with *Sarcoptes scabiei,* itch mites. The skin is reddened, and itchy, with the presence of insect burrows and secondary bacterial infections. Common sites are the folds of wrists, elbows, waistline, and the web of the fingers. Treatment consists of application of topical scabicide creams and washing of linens, towels, and clothing with hot water to prevent reinfection.

Scales: Small, dry flakes of skin that increase in diseases such as psoriasis and tinea pedis and after scratching the skin (Fig. 4-18).

Scleroderma: A gradual thickening of the dermis in which the skin becomes anchored to the underlying tissue. The severity of the disorder can be mild to life-threatening. No cause has been identified, and treatment is directed at decreasing symptoms with antineoplastics and physical therapy to prevent loss of range of motion of joints.

Sebaceous cyst: A small sac under the skin, filled with keratin, sebum, and cellular debris arising from a sebaceous gland. Common sites are the back, neck, or axilla. The cysts can be drained and removed surgically with a local anesthetic.

Seborrheic keratosis: Benign, flat, irregularly shaped skin tumors of various colors (yellow, gray or brown), with a waxy appearance. It is commonly seen in older adults and is of unknown etiology. Treatment by excision resolves the lesions, and new skin growth appears within 1 week.

Squamous cell carcinoma: Malignancy of squamous cells, often on sun-exposed areas of the body (Fig. 4-19). The lesions have a scaly, crusty appearance and grow much faster than basal cell carcinoma. Common sites are the top of the nose, forehead, ears, backs of the hands, and lower lip. Lesions may bleed and become painful and infected. Treatment by surgical removal with clear margins or cryosurgery will resolve the lesions.

Sudoresis: Also known as hyperhidrosis, is profuse or excessive sweating. It is often caused by an underlying health condition such as heart disease or menopause. Treatment is directed at the cause of the condition.

Tinea: Infection with ringworm characterized by red, round patches with elevated borders (Fig. 4-20). Treatment with topical antifungals resolves the infection. Common sites include:

Tinea capitis: Scalp (more common in children)
Tinea corporis: Body, most common in hot, humid climates
Tinea cruris: Groin, also known as "jock itch"
Tinea pedis: Feet, also known as "athlete's foot"

Ulcer: lesion of the skin or mucous membrane with inflammation, redness, necrosis, and loss of tissue.

Urticaria: Acute vasodilation of the skin caused by acute allergic reaction. It is characterized by multiple discreet swellings (wheals) and intense itching. Common sites are the truck, back, face, and scalp. Treatment with antihistamines reduces swelling and itching.

Vesicle: Small, clear fluid-filled lesion.

Vitiligo: Chronic, progressive skin disease characterized by loss of local melanocytes leading to loss of pigmentation (Fig. 4-21). Common sites are hands, face, and genitals. The cause is unknown, but it may be an autoimmune disorder in which antibodies attack melanocytes. Affected areas should be protected from sunlight with SPF sunscreen. Cosmetic coverage with makeup is common.

Wart: Small, benign tumor caused by various strains of HPV (human papilloma virus). Hypertrophy of the epidermis causes the lesions to be raised and hard. Often seen in children ages 9 to 12; common sites are the backs of hands and fingers. Treatment with keratolytics resolves the warts.

Wheal: Itchy, round, raised skin lesion with a white center and a pink-red periphery. Often seen in insect bites, urticaria, anaphylaxis.

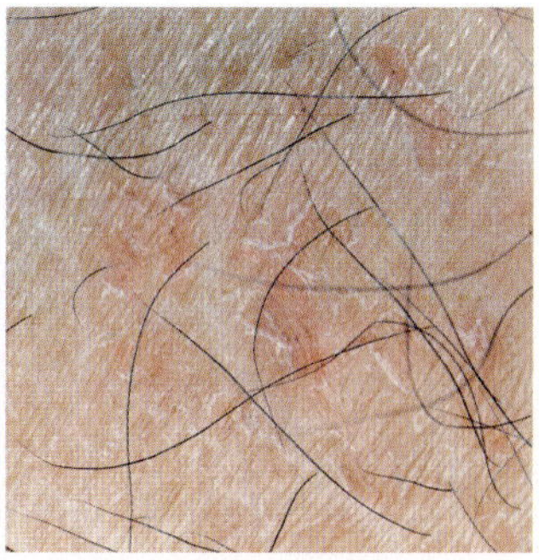
Figure 4-18 Scales.

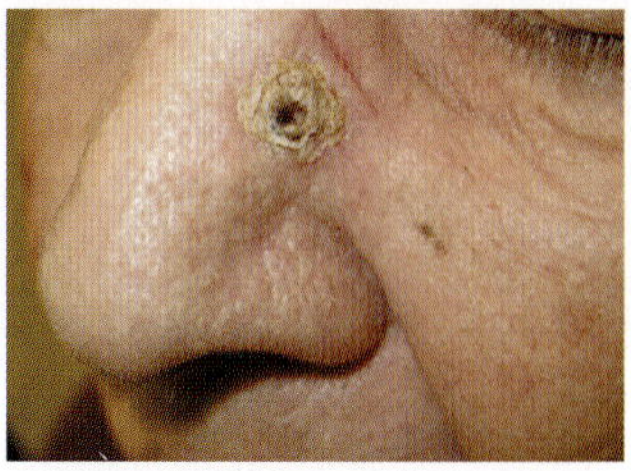
Figure 4-19 Squamous cell carcinoma.

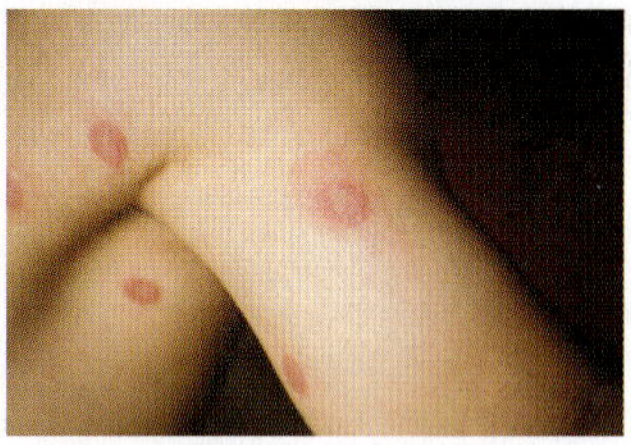
Figure 4-20 Tinea.

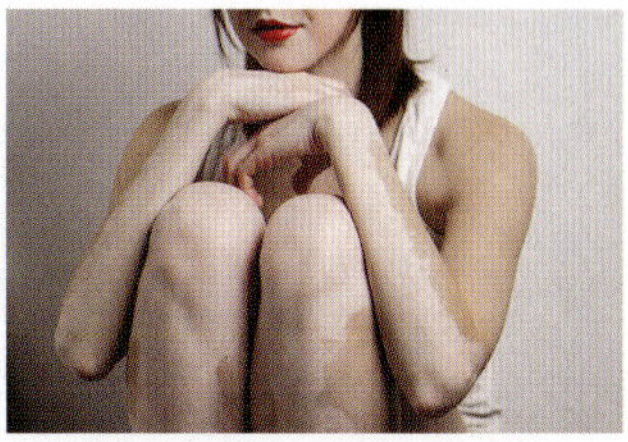
Figure 4-21 Vitiligo.

Pathology Word-Building Practice

1. Build the Terms

*Using **only** the word parts in the lists, create medical terms for the indicated meanings.*

Prefixes	Combining Forms		Suffixes	
a-	adip/o	melan/o	-a	-oma
hyper-	albin/o	myc/o	-ectomy	-osis
hypo-	cutane/o	necr/o	-ia	-ous
intra-	cirrh/o	onych/o	-iasis	-plasty

Prefixes	Combining Forms		Suffixes	
par-	cyan/o	pil/o	-ic	-phagia
sub-	derm/o	rhytid/o	-itis	-rrhea
	dermat/o	trich/o	-lysis	-trophy
	erythema/o	scler/o	-ology	
	erythr/o	seb/o		
	hidr/o	xanth/o		
	kerat/o	xer/o		
	lip/o			

1. condition of dry skin ______________________
2. the study of the skin ______________________
3. excessive growth ______________________
4. a yellow tumor ______________________
5. destruction of fat ______________________
6. inflammation of the nails ______________________
7. surgical repair of wrinkles ______________________
8. condition of decreased amount of sweating ______________________
9. black tumor ______________________
10. discharge of sebum ______________________
11. infection of the margins of the nails ______________________
12. pertaining to the oil glands ______________________
13. condition of "hard" skin ______________________
14. inflammation of the skin ______________________
15. reddening of the skin ______________________

2. Prefixes

Choose from the list of prefixes to build a word for the definitions below.

Prefixes

a-	hypo-	macro-
epi-	inter-	par-
hyper-	intra-	sub-

1. Pertaining to below the skin __________
2. A needle used to deliver medication under the skin __________
3. Infection of the margins of the nails __________
4. Layer under the dermis __________
5. Pertaining to within the skin __________
6. Pertaining to within the cell __________
7. Lack of growth or development __________
8. Condition of excessive keratin __________
9. Large cell __________
10. Outermost layer of skin __________

3. Suffixes

Choose from the list of suffixes to build a word for the definitions below.

-iasis	-ology	-phagia
-ic	-oma	-rrhea
-itis	-osis	
-lysis	-plasty	

1. excessive discharge of oil __________
2. tumor of squamous cell __________
3. condition of keratin __________
4. destruction of skin __________
5. nail biting __________
6. chronic skin disorder with silver plaques __________
7. pertaining to the discharge of sebum __________
8. infestation with lice __________
9. inflammation of hair follicles __________
10. medical term for a bruise __________

CAREER EXPLORATION: AESTHETIC NURSE

While in nursing school, Emily had horrible acne. She tried various topical creams and facewashes and was careful to eat a healthy diet, low in oil and fat. As a struggling nursing student, Emily could not afford to get dermatological treatment for her acne because it was not covered by her parents' health insurance plan. She wore makeup to hide the acne and acne scars, but she was embarrassed about her appearance. Upon graduating from nursing school, she got a job on a medical surgical floor at the local hospital. One of the nurses Emily works with, Regina, has beautiful skin. Emily asked Regina what soap she uses, and Regina told her she had horrible acne as a teen. She later had a procedure called dermabrasion to correct acne scars. Emily went to a dermatologist's office for a consult. She was surprised to learn that the procedure is not performed by the dermatologist, but by an aesthetic nurse specialist. The nurse specialist who performed Emily's procedure was a friend from nursing school, Carla, who was two semesters ahead of Emily. Carla explained that she worked in the hospital for 6 months and realized that she wanted to work in an outpatient setting. She always loved art and aesthetics, so she investigated aesthetic nursing. She went on to tell Emily there are many in-person and virtual programs, such as the American Association of Aesthetic Medicine and Surgery. Emily had four treatments with Carla and loved the outcome. She was able to wear no makeup as the acne scars were almost invisible. Emily's mom was so impressed with the results that she made an appointment with Carla for a Botox treatment to reduce the forehead lines that she had begun noticing. Carla explained that the Botox certification can be obtained by registered nurses and other health-care providers who learn how to evaluate, mark, and inject patients with botulinum toxins and dermal fillers. Emily decided to become an aesthetic nurse and join the dermatology practice with Carla. She enrolled in a self-paced online program and enjoyed learning about the various procedures. The fast-growing dermatology practice hired her, and her new career began. She loves seeing young patients, both men and women, and the transformation in their self-esteem when she removes the acne scars. She often tells her story to her patients and feels a connection to them. Later, she expanded her knowledge of aesthetic nursing by becoming certified in Botox injections, chemical peels, and nonsurgical face lifts.

Integumentary System Diagnostic Procedures

Diagnostic procedures of the skin, along with visual inspection and patient interview, can be used to identify the cause of illness and therefore direct the provider to the appropriate care.

Allergy Testing

ImmunoCAP: A blood test that measures IgE antibodies in the blood and allows the provider to see if antibodies are created in response to a specific food or an environmental allergy.

Scratch testing procedure: A small amount of a suspected allergen is scratched into the skin of the back. Several allergens are usually tested at once, and the clinician must keep a record of the placement of each allergen. Reactions to the various allergens are recorded, such as redness and inflammation. The test is no longer common because more accurate blood testing has been established.

Skin biopsy: The removal of a small piece of tissue for histological analysis. Gross and microscopic analysis is used to establish a diagnosis. Several types of biopsies of skin can be obtained:

Excisional biopsy: An entire tumor or lesion is removed.
Incisional biopsy: A portion of a lesion is removed with a scalpel.
Punch biopsy: A piece of a lesion is removed with a cookie-cutter-type instrument.
Shave biopsy: A scalpel or a razor blade is used to shave lesions above the surface of the skin.

Woods lamp: Used in the examination of the skin using ultraviolet light.

Integumentary System Therapeutic Procedures

Therapeutic procedures for the skin may be medically necessary to cure disease or to prevent disease progression. Some procedures are, however, cosmetic and may not be funded by medical insurance plans. The health-care professional should be aware of the noncovered procedures and treatment prices to inform patients prior to procedures and to avoid billing confusion or disputes.

Botox: Injection of botulinum toxin into the muscles of the face to reduce the appearance of wrinkles and frown lines.

Cautery: Application of heat or caustic chemical to burn and scar the skin, causing coagulation of tissue.

Chemical peel: Application of a chemical solution to reduce the appearance of wrinkles, uneven pigmentation, scars, tattoos, and removal of blemishes.

Cryosurgery: Application of subfreezing temperature to freeze and destroy tissue. Local anesthetic is used on the surface of the lesion and liquid nitrogen is applied to the surface. The procedure is used for primary basal cell carcinomas that are small and present low risk, for squamous cell carcinomas, and for warts. While the procedure causes little pain and can be performed in the out-patient dermatology office, there is a longer healing time as compared to an excision. The wound may be painful, swollen, and sometimes may blister.

Curettage and electrodessication: A combination procedure involving scraping away abnormal tissue and the application of electrodessication to destroy the base of a tumor with low-voltage electricity. The treatment is used for basal cell carcinomas that are less than 2 cm in diameter and superficial (not involving deeper tissues). It can also be used to excise small squamous cell carcinomas (of 1 cm or less) with distinct borders. As with cryosurgery, wound healing is prolonged and may be painful.

Debridement: Removal of cellular debris, foreign objects, dirt, and necrotic tissue to allow wound healing and prevent infection. The procedure may be performed surgically or medically in the outpatient setting. Debridement of burns is often performed directly after hydrotherapy.

Dermabrasion: A wire brush or diamond burr is used to resurface and smooth the skin removing small scars, moles (nevi), fine wrinkles, and tattoos.

Dermaplaning: A dermatome, an instrument like an electric razor, is used to resurface the skin, decreasing the appearance of small scars, moles (nevi), wrinkles, and tattoos.

Dermatoplasty: Surgical transplantation of living skin to correct defect from trauma or disease; it is also called a skin graft. Often used to correct loss of skin in third-degree burns. Postoperatively, both sites (donor and graft) must be monitored for signs of infection or graft rejection, such as redness or fever. Fluid balance and proper nutrition are emphasized to promote healing.

Electrodessication: Destruction of tissue by use of electrical spark to remove surface lesions.

Escharotomy: Incision into necrotic tissue resulting from a severe burn. After a burn, the tissue scabs form a dry crust called eschar. Removal of this tissue prevents wound infection and relieves tightness of the affected skin. Sterile surgical incision into the area promotes blood flow and prevents further necrosis and gangrene.

Laser resurfacing: Uses short pulses of light to remove fine lines and reduce the appearance of wrinkles and uneven pigmentation.

Liposuction: Aspiration of fat through a cannula placed under the dermis to alter the contours of the body. After the procedure, pressure dressings are applied to reduce sagging of the skin.

Mohs surgery: Surgical treatment for skin cancers that have a high rate of recurrence, such as large tumors, and tumors where the edges are not well-defined or in certain locations, such as the nose, ears, forehead and scalp. It can be used to treat basal cell carcinoma, squamous cell carcinoma, and malignant melanoma. The patient is given a local anesthetic and remains awake for the procedure. The surgeon removes a thin layer of the tumor and the surrounding skin. The removed tissue is observed under a microscope while the patient waits. The surgeon then removes more tissue and repeats the process until no cancer cells are observed under the microscope. The wound is then sutured or allowed to heal without sutures, depending on the size and location of the wound. The procedure is time-consuming but offers a high cure rate.

Procedures and Diagnostics Review

Fill in the blanks to provide the term defined.

1. An acute or chronic infection with erythema, papules, scales, crusts, and scabs that presents in childhood ________________
2. The most common form of skin cancer ________________
3. Death of tissue ________________
4. An incision into necrotic tissue that is a result of a severe burn ________________
5. Acute viral infection that is unilateral and follows a nerve pathway of the cranium or spine ________________
6. Chronic redness of the face, common in women aged 30 to 50, aggravated by sun exposure ________________
7. Using short pulses of light to remove wrinkles or fine lines ________________
8. Destruction of tissue by an electrical spark ________________
9. The most painful degree of a burn ________________
10. Complete or partial hair loss ________________

11. Examination of the skin with an ultraviolet light ______________________

12. A tear of flesh that can be of varying thickness ______________________

13. Noninfectious chronic skin condition with silvery plaques with defined borders ______________________

14. Ringworm infection of the scalp ______________________

15. Benign skin lesion caused by HPV ______________________

16. Another term for a skin graft ______________________

17. Blood test for allergies ______________________

18. Removal of a small piece of tissue with a "cookie cutter" ______________________

19. The medical term for an ingrown toenail ______________________

20. Skin lesion that is commonly called a mole ______________________

CASE STUDY, completed

After waking from surgery, Travis is thirsty and eager for discharge. Dr. Torres explains that the pathologist confirmed the diagnosis of BCC. The pathologist saw infundibulocystic hyperplasia in the epidermis. Claire and Travis look confused, so Dr. Torres explains that infundibulocystic means nodular tumors (which is why the side of his nose felt "bumpy") and hyperplasia means excessive growth (the tumor was getting larger). He further explains to Travis and Claire that he excised the carcinoma and sutured the nose. He then applied a sterile dressing. Travis cannot get the dressing wet, but Dr. Torres discussed with Claire how to change the dressing each evening. Dr. Torres tells them to contact the office if there is any localized bleeding or if Travis has a fever. Dr. Torres discharges Travis home with instructions to come to his office in 1 week for inspection of the nose and suture removal. He also gives them written discharge instructions and general skin care advice on preventing further BBC lesions. Dr. Torres explains that he was able to do an excision of the BCC since it was small, but if larger areas of BCC appear, he may have to perform Mohs surgery, where the lesion is removed layer by layer and analyzed under a microscope. He emphasizes sun protection as a preventive measure.

CRITICAL THINKING QUESTIONS

1. The excised tissue was sent to the pathology laboratory. Dissect the word *pathology* into its elements. ______________________

2. The excised tissue showed infundibulocystic hyperplasia. Dissect and define the terms. ______________________

3. Dissect and define the term *anesthesia*. ______________________

4. Travis suffers from hypertension, which is also called ______________________

5. Why are discharge instructions given both verbally and written? ______________________

Continued

CASE STUDY, completed

6. A surgical procedure to remove tissue is called a/an ______________________

7. Why can't Travis get the dressing wet? ______________________

8. Dr. Torres performs surgical procedures of the skin. What type of physician performs such surgeries? ______________________

9. Why is Travis told to return if he has a fever or bleeding? ______________________

10. Travis's tumor is a basal cell carcinoma. Which layer of the skin is involved? ______________________

Medications for the Integumentary System

Table 4-2 includes medications to alleviate symptoms of burns, abrasions, blisters, inflammation, calluses, and infections from bacteria, fungi, or parasites. Medications can also treat hair loss, oily skin lesions, scaling of skin, and cancer. Medications are administered topically or orally depending on their mechanism of action.

TABLE 4-2 Medications for the Integumentary System

Classification	Examples	Common Use/Action
Antifungal (topical)	Clotrimazole, Mycelex, Lotrimin, Gyne-Lotrimin, nystatin, Mycostatin	Fungal infections such as ringworm, athlete's foot, jock itch, vaginal yeast infection, and diaper rash
Antipsoriatic agents	cyclosporin, Gengraf, Neoral, Enbrel, methotrexate, Trexall	Psoriasis, psoriatic arthritis, dandruff, rheumatoid arthritis, skin cancer
Benzoyl peroxide	Benzoyl peroxide (generic), Clearskin, PanOxyl	Treatment of acne (most common in teen years)
Corticosteroids (topical)	hydrocortisone, Cortaid, dexamethasone, Decadron	Inflammation and rashes caused by allergic reactions, psoriasis or eczema
Fluorouracil (topical)	Fluorouracil, Efudex, Carac	Scaly skin, superficial basal cell carcinoma
Immunomodulators (topical)	Pimecrolimus, Elidel, tacrolimus, Protopic	Severe atopic dermatitis, superficial basal cell carcinoma
Keratolytics	salicylic acid, Compound W, Clearasil, Stridex, ammonium lactate, Lac-Hydrin lotion	Treatment of acne, dandruff, seborrhea, or psoriasis. Removal of warts, corns, calluses
Retinoids	Tretinoin, Retin-A, Renova, Tazorac	Treatment of severe acne, reduce appearance of wrinkles
Scabicides and pediculicides	Lindane, permethrin, Nix	Treatment of lice or scabies

Medications Review

Using the table of medications, complete the chart below. The first medication has been done for you.

Medication	Classification (mechanism)	Therapeutic Use (What is it used for?)
Carac	*Fluoracil*	*Scaly skin, superficial basal cell carcinoma*
Lotrimin	______________	______________
Nix, Lindane	______________	______________
Retin-A	______________	______________
Protopic	______________	______________
Hydrocortisone	______________	______________
Clearskin	______________	______________
Compound W	______________	______________
Gyne-Lotrimin	______________	______________

Integumentary Abbreviations

The list below provides some common abbreviations pertaining to the integumentary system and their meanings.

BCC	basal cell carcinoma
Bx, bx	biopsy
C&S	culture and sensitivity
decub.	decubitus ulcer, pressure sore
derm	dermatology
DLE	discoid lupus erythematosus
EAHF	eczema, asthma and hay fever
FANA	fluorescent antinuclear antibody
FH	family history
FS	frozen section
Hx	history
ID	intradermal
IP	ice pack
I&D	incision and drainage
IV	intravenous
MHP	moist heat pack
MM	malignant melanoma
OTC	over the counter
PPD	purified protein derivative
PSS	progressive systemic scleroderma
SCC	squamous cell carcinoma
SLE	systemic lupus erythematosus
Subq, subcu	subcutaneous
TENS	transcutaneous electrical nerve stimulation
ung	ointment
UV	ultraviolet
XP, XDP	xeroderma pigmentosum

Abbreviations Review

Choose the correct definition for the abbreviation:

1. UV
   a. Unvascular
   b. Ultraviolet
   c. Ultimately viral
   d. Ultravector

2. SCC
   a. Squamous carcinogenic cell
   b. Squamous carrier cell
   c. Squamous calcium cell
   d. Squamous cell carcinoma

3. MHP
   a. Multiple heat packs
   b. Moist heat pack
   c. Moist heart pack
   d. Malignant heart palpitations

4. ung
   a. under the skin
   b. under nails
   c. under granulosum
   d. ointment

5. I&D
   a. Incision and drainage
   b. Incised drainage
   c. Incision and debridement
   d. Incised debridement

6. decub
   a. debrided ulcer
   b. decubitus ulcer
   c. dead tissue ulcer
   d. decubodial ulcer

7. BCC
   a. Basement cell cancer
   b. Basal cell cancer
   c. Basal cell creation
   d. Basal cell carcinoma

8. XDP
   a. Xeroderma pigmentosum
   b. Xeroderma and damaged pigment
   c. Xerosis and damaged pigment
   d. Xerosis pigmentosum

9. TENS
   a. Transelectrical nerve stimulation
   b. Transcaudal nerve stimulation
   c. Transcutaneous electrical nerve stimulation
   d. Transdermal electrical nerve stimulation

10. Subq
    a. Subquality
    b. Subcutaneous
    c. Subsequent
    d. Substandard

11. SLE
    a. Systemic lupus erythematosus
    b. Systemic lupus erythema
    c. Systemic lymphoid erythematosus
    d. Systemic leuko erythematosus

12. FANA
    a. Fluorescent antigen antibody
    b. Fluorescent antinuclear antineoplasm
    c. Fluid antinuclear antibody
    d. Fluorescent antinuclear antibody

13. PSS
    a. Progressive skin scleroderma
    b. Progressive scleral scleroderma
    c. Progressive systemic scleroderma
    d. Progressive stomach scleroderma

14. ESHF
    a. Eczema, asthma, and hay fever
    b. Eosinophilic asthma and hay fever
    c. Eczema, asthenia, and hay fever
    d. Eczema, asthma, and high fluids

15. FS
    a. Frozen section
    b. Frozen skin
    c. Frozen squamous cells
    d. Frozen slides

MEDICAL DOCUMENTATION

Knowledge of terms related to normal anatomy and pathological conditions enables you to understand medical documentation such as History & Physical Exams, operative reports, discharge summaries, laboratory reports, and x-ray reports. Read the following Procedure Report and Surgical Pathology report and answer the questions that follow each document.

Procedure Report

Excision of Basal Cell Carcinoma of the Nose

Date: 11/16/2024
Patient: Travis J
DOB: 04/14/1954
ID#: 78630000

Surgeon: Xavier Torres, MD
Anesthetist: Bethany Chambers, CRNA

Procedures performed:

1. Excision of lesion, right side of bony nasal pyramid
2. Frozen section sent to pathology consultation showing basal cell carcinoma with clear margins
3. V-Y closure

Procedure in Detail: The patient was placed in the supine position, and after adequate induction of general laryngeal mask airway anesthesia, the patient was prepped with Betadine scrub and draped with towels in a sterile field. The line of proposed circular excision of the right dorsum of the bony nasal pyramid was outlined with a marking pen. The area was infiltrated with local anesthetic solution, and the lesion was excised as outlined. The 12-o'clock border was marked with a marking pen and was submitted for frozen-section pathology consultation, showing basal cell carcinoma with clear margins. VY flaps were outlined approximately 1.3 cm × 2.4 cm long, one on the left and one on the right side of the nose. These areas were infiltrated with local anesthetic solution. The flaps were elevated as outlined. Several small bleeders were identified and controlled by electrocautery. The flaps were rotated into the defect, and the wound edges were approximated with interrupted 5-0 black nylon sutures. A dressing of Steri-Strips was applied. Total blood loss was approximately 5 mL. Instrument count was performed and was correct. He tolerated the procedure well and was taken to the recovery room.

Electronically signed
Xavier Torres, MD
Dermatology

Questions

1. How was bleeding controlled during the procedure? ______________________

____

2. How was the anesthesia given to Travis? ______________________

____

3. Into what surgical position was Travis was placed? ______________________

____

4. Look up the phrase *interrupted sutures*. In your own words, what does that mean? ________

____

Continued

MEDICAL DOCUMENTATION—cont'd

5. The lesion was excised, which means ______________________________

____

Surgical Pathology Report

Date: 11/16/2024 DOB: 04/14/1954
Patient: Travis J ID#: 78630000

Diagnosis: Basal cell carcinoma, right side of nasal bony pyramid
Gross description:
Skin ellipse, right side of nasal bony pyramid 1.2 × 2.4 cm
Excision depth 0.2 cm
Skin surface: central pigmented lesion 0.9 × 2.1 cm
Notes: Serially sectioned and entirely submitted in one cassette for microscopic examination.
Microscopic examination: Sections show infundibulocystic basal cell carcinoma with basaloid keratinocytes distributed in the epidermis. No lymphohistiocytic infiltrate is noted.

Electronically signed
Grace Medford, MD
Pathologist

Questions

1. Break up the word *basaloid* into its elements. ______________________________
2. Break up the word *lymphohistiocytic* into its elements ______________________________
3. Is there any lymphatic infiltrate of the tumor? ______________________________
4. What characteristics of the lesion are described in the gross description? ______________________________
5. What does the term "microscopic description" mean? ______________________________

Visit the Medical Language Lab at medicallanguagelab.com. Use it to improve your recognition and understanding of terms in medical documentation.

CHAPTER REVIEW

Complete the Sentences

Using medical terms from this chapter, complete the sentences.

1. The outermost layer of the epidermis is called the ______________________________.
2. Hair does not grow on the following parts of the body: ______________________________.
3. The substance that is responsible for the color of skin is ______________________________.
4. The specialist who diagnoses and treats diseases of the skin is called ______________________________.
5. The two types of sweat glands are ______________________________.
6. The oil secreted on the surface of the skin is called ______________________________.

7. The light-colored crescent on fingernails is called the ______________________.

8. The small muscle next to hair shafts that cause hairs to "stand up" is called ______________________.

9. Lice infestation is called ______________________.

10. A fungal infection of the nails is called ______________________.

11. Overgrowth of the horny layer of the epidermis is a condition called ______________________.

12. Skin tumors that are assessed by the ABCD acronym are ______________________.

13. Ringworm infection in the groin region is called ______________________.

14. Term that means hardening of the skin is ______________________.

15. A thickening of tissue of the hand or foot due to friction is ______________________.

16. Combination procedure of scraping away abnormal tissue and then using low-voltage electricity to remove remaining tissue is called ______________________

17. Freezing tissue to destroy it is called ______________________

18. Diagnostic procedure that involves irritating the skin with allergens is ______________________.

19. Injection of toxin to paralyze facial muscles and reduce appearance of wrinkles is ______________________.

20. Procedure to reduce the appearance of tattoos, scars, uneven pigmentation by short pulses of light is called ______________________.

Spelling

Circle the word that is spelled correctly.

1. keratinocyte karatinoctye
2. lunala lunula
3. arrector pili arrector pilli
4. eczema egzema
5. appocrine apocrine
6. psoriasis soriasis
7. melanin melenin
8. exudate exadate
9. sebecous sebaceous
10. carcinoma carcinioma

Abbreviations

Define the following abbreviations.

1. IP ______________________________
2. MM ______________________________
3. OTC ______________________________
4. DLE ______________________________
5. PPD ______________________________
6. FH ______________________________
7. derm ______________________________
8. C&S ______________________________
9. ID ______________________________
10. IV ______________________________

Identify the Anatomical Structures

Match the following structures of the skin to the letters shown in Figure 4-22.

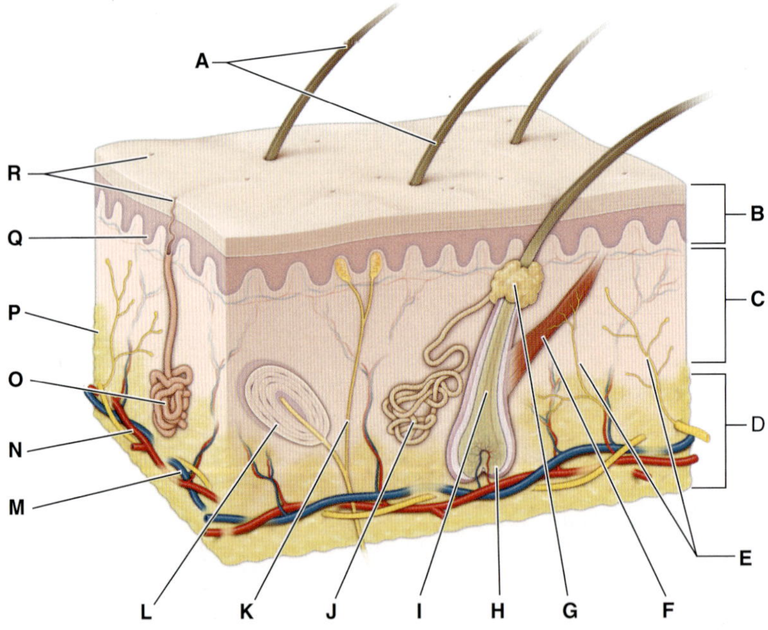

Figure 4-22 Identify the structures of the skin.

1. _____ adipose cells	7. _____ epidermis
2. _____ apocrine gland	8. _____ hair shaft
3. _____ blood vessel	9. _____ nerve fiber
4. _____ capillary	10. _____ pores
5. _____ dermis	11. _____ sebaceous gland
6. _____ eccrine gland	12. _____ subcutaneous layer

Match the following structures of the epidermis to the letters shown in Figure 4-23.

1. ______ dendritic cell
2. ______ keratinocyte
3. ______ melanocyte
4. ______ stratum basale
5. ______ stratum corneum
6. ______ stratum granulosum
7. ______ stratum lucidum
8. ______ stratum spinosum

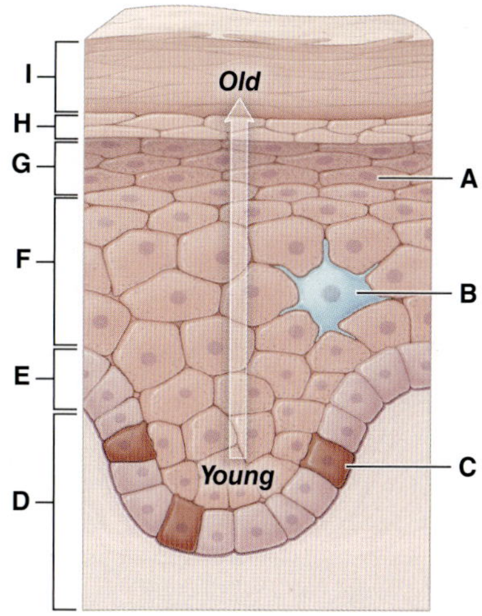

Figure 4-23 Identify the structures of epidermis.

CHAPTER

5

The Digestive System

LEARNING OBJECTIVES

Upon completion of the chapter, you will be able to:

1. Identify and define the combining forms, roots, prefixes, and suffixes introduced in the chapter.
2. Spell medical terms related to the digestive system.
3. Describe the major organs of the digestive system.
4. Discuss the difference between the alimentary canal and the accessory organs of digestion.
5. Describe the processes of the digestive system: mastication, digestion (chemical and mechanical), absorption, and elimination of wastes.
6. Describe the macronutrients and micronutrients and how they function to fuel the body.
7. Identify and discuss major pathological terms of the digestive system.
8. Identify and discuss major diagnostic and therapeutic treatments of the digestive system.
9. Identify the major categories of medications used to treat digestive pathologies.
10. Define abbreviations of the digestive system.

After reading this chapter, you will have expanded your knowledge of medical terms related to the digestive system. You will understand how the body breaks down food as fuel for maintenance, growth, and development and how waste is eliminated. You will be able to use the word elements presented to understand unfamiliar terms and to build your medical vocabulary. We begin this chapter with the story of Jessica, a young woman who had struggled with her weight, poor nutrition, and subsequent gastrointestinal symptoms and interventions. Throughout the chapter, we will revisit the story of Jessica to understand what happens with a nutritional disorder and how medical interventions can improve patient quality of life.

CASE STUDY

Jessica is a 24-year-old woman who had a gastric bypass surgery last year. At 5 ft 4 in. tall, Jessica previously weighed 320 lb, with a BMI (body mass index) of 54.9. A BMI of 30 or higher is categorized as obese and increases risk of diabetes, heart disease, hypertension, elevated cholesterol, gastroesophageal reflux disease (GERD), obstructive sleep apnea, depression, and back and knee

Continued

CASE STUDY, continued

pain/injury. She was unable to control her hunger, eating more and more. Her parents are both obese and suffer from type 2 diabetes and heart disease. They encouraged Jessica to have the surgical procedure to avoid future health problems associated with severe obesity. After the procedure, Jessica has worked hard to control her food portions and increase exercise, and she has lost 153 lb. At 167 lb, she has more energy, goes for long walks with her friends, and feels happier than she has in years.

Lately, Jessica has been suffering from abdominal pain, cramping, nausea, and diarrhea. She makes an appointment to see Dr. Morgan, her gastroenterologist, who orders a cholecystogram, a diagnostic procedure to view her gallbladder. The test showed multiple stones in the gallbladder and common bile duct. Jessica was admitted for a cholecystectomy, surgical removal of her gallbladder.

KEY TERMS

Ascending colon	Descending colon	Ileocecal sphincter	Pylorus
Accessory organs	Duodenum	Incisors	Rugae
Acini cells	Esophagus	Liver	Saliva
Alimentary canal	Enzymes	Lower esophageal sphincter	Salivary glands
Anus	Feces	Macronutrients	Sigmoid colon
Ascending colon	Fundus	Mastication	Soft palate
Bile	Gallbladder	Micronutrients	Splenic flexure
Body (of the stomach)	Gingivae	Molars	Teeth
Bolus	Glucose	Nutrients	Tongue
Cecum	Glycogenesis	Oral cavity	Transverse colon
Chyme	Hard palate	Peristalsis	Uvula
Defecation	Hepatic flexure	Pharynx	Vermiform appendix

Structures and Physiology

The gastrointestinal system organs consist of the **alimentary canal**, the organs that food passes through, and the **accessory organs** that add to chemical digestion (Fig. 5-1). The alimentary canal comprises the mouth, teeth, esophagus, stomach, small intestines, and large intestines. The three accessory organs are the liver, gallbladder, and the pancreas, which add digestive enzymes and chemicals.

The organs of the digestive system have many functions:

- to ingest food,
- to detoxify foods, killing any pathogens,
- to break down food through physical and chemical processes,
- to distribute nutrients through the intestinal wall to the bloodstream, and
- to eliminate waste.

Oral Cavity

Food starts its path in the mouth, which is also called the **oral cavity** (Fig. 5-2). The oral cavity consists of the lips, which surround the mouth, and the cheeks, which form the sides

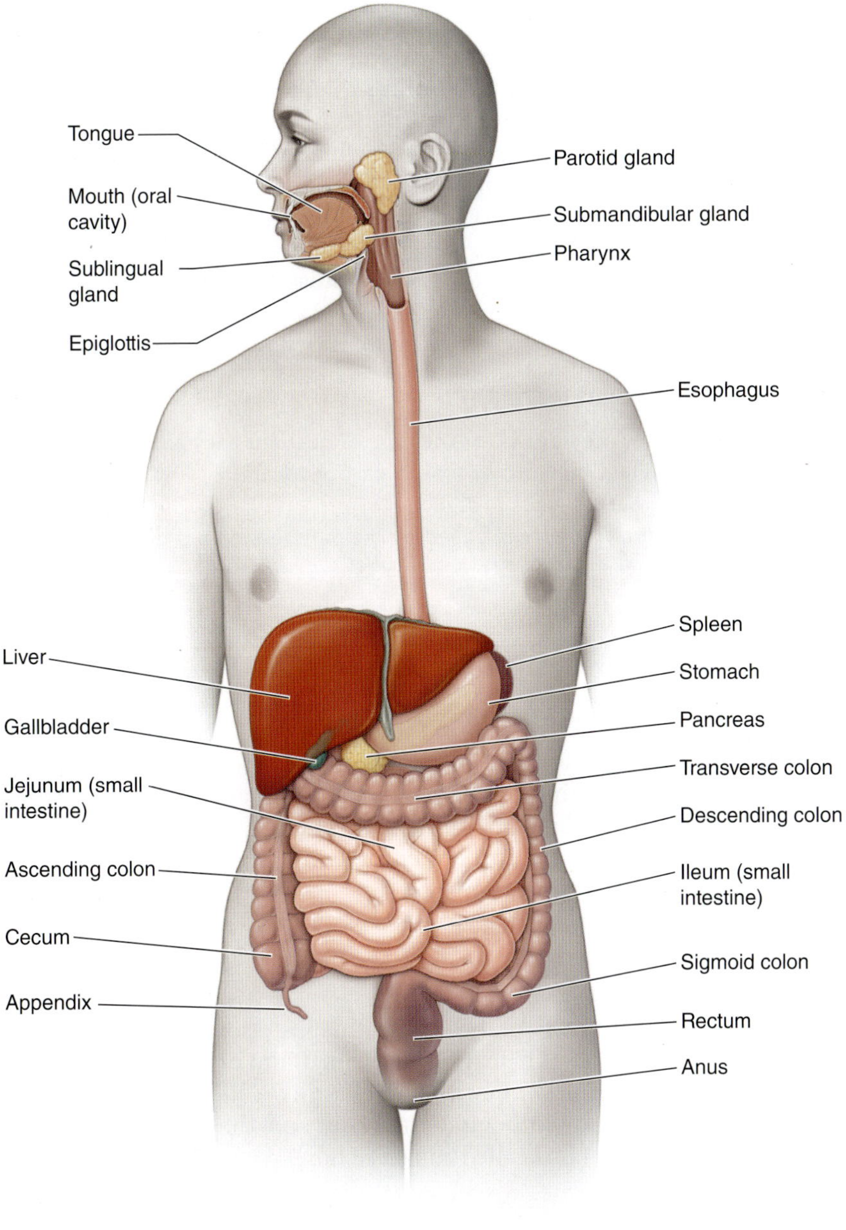

Figure 5-1 The gastrointestinal system.

of the oral cavity. The lips and cheeks hold food in the mouth and create a space for **mastication**, the process of chewing food. The **hard palate** is the bony, hard surface that forms the anterior, upper roof of the mouth. The **soft palate** is the posterior and upper portion of the mouth; it is made of skeletal muscle and soft connective tissue and lies closer to the throat. At the end of the soft palate, there is a cone-shaped projection called the **uvula**. The uvula aids in digestion and swallowing but also helps us produce speech. The **tongue** is a solid muscular structure located at the floor of the mouth. The tongue is the main organ of taste and assists in mastication and swallowing. The upper surface of the tongue is moist, pink, and covered in small rough projections called papillae, which contain taste buds. During the process of chewing, the tongue moves the food around the taste buds, and we perceive tastes of sweet, salty, sour, bitter, and umami (savory). The tongue helps to mix the food with saliva.

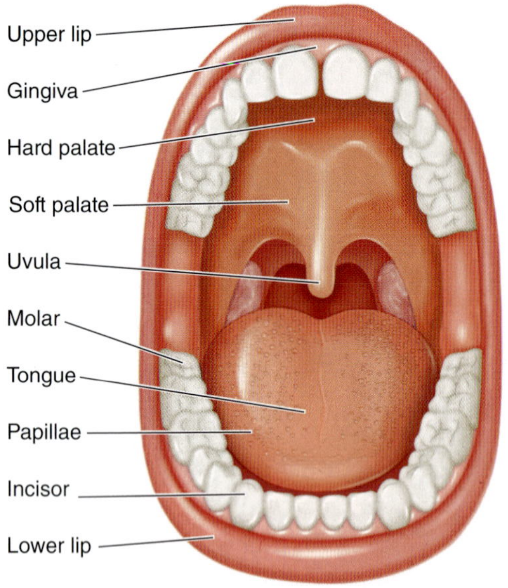

Figure 5-2 The oral cavity.

Salivary Glands

The **salivary glands** secrete **saliva**, a watery fluid that contains mucus and enzymes. **Enzymes** are chemicals that help to break down food into **nutrients**, smaller molecules that can be used by the body for energy. Enzymes found in saliva include amylase, which digests carbohydrates, and lipase, which begins digestion of fats. Saliva works to add fluid and chemically digest food. The salivary glands are in three groups, the parotids, submandibular, and sublingual. The mucus aids in lubrication so that the chewed and lubricated ball of food, the **bolus**, can be swallowed and enter the pharynx.

TERMINOLOGY FACT

Enzymes are named for the type of nutrient they aid in digesting.

- Amylase digests amylose (a carbohydrate).
- Protease digests proteins.

More enzymes are released by the pancreas to aid digestion in the small intestines.

Teeth

ELEMENT REVIEW
gingivi/o = gums
-itis = inflammation

Teeth function to chew (masticate) food in the mouth. The food is softened by saliva and torn by **incisors**, the teeth in the front of the mouth, and ground up by **molars**, the teeth in the back of the mouth. The **gingiva** surrounds the teeth, anchoring them in place. Gingivae (plural) are commonly called the gums and must remain healthy to promote chewing and therefore digestion. Gingivitis, acute or chronic inflammation of the gums, can cause pain and tooth loss and compromise digestion.

Pharynx

ELEMENT REVIEW
pharyng/o = pharynx
-eal = pertaining to

The throat or **pharynx** adjoins the oral cavity at the posterior end and is common to the digestive and respiratory tracts. The pharynx is divided into oropharynx, laryngopharynx, and nasopharynx. As their names imply, the oropharynx is located at the back of the oral cavity, the nasopharynx is located behind the nose, and the laryngopharynx is located further down near the larynx (also called the voice box).

Esophagus

ELEMENT REVIEW
esophag/o = esophagus
-stenosis = condition of narrowing

The food moves down from the pharynx into the **esophagus**, a muscular tube that moves food to the stomach. The esophagus is approximately 10 in. long and passes through an opening in the diaphragm into the abdominal cavity. The passage of food from the esophagus to the stomach is controlled by a muscular ring called the **lower esophageal sphincter** (LES). Food is moved down the esophagus by the coordinated contractions of muscles called **peristalsis**. As the food reaches the LES, the sphincter opens to allow the food bolus to enter the stomach. It then closes to prevent food from refluxing back into the esophagus.

TERMINOLOGY FACT

Although it is not part of the cardiovascular system, the LES is sometimes called the cardiac sphincter because of its location directly anterior to the heart.

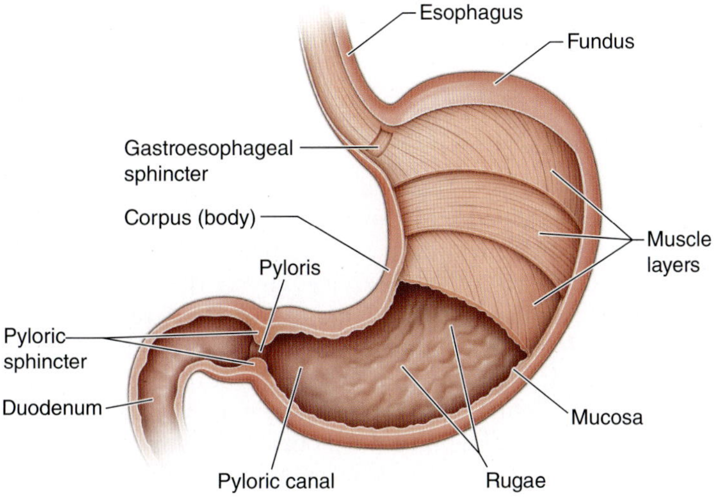

Figure 5-3 The stomach.

Stomach

The stomach is located in the upper left quadrant of the abdomen and is comprised of layered muscle, glands, and an endothelial lining (Fig. 5-3). It is divided into three areas. The upper rounded portion of the stomach, called the **fundus**, rises to the left and slightly above the LES. Next, the **body** of the stomach lies below the fundus and curves to the right. The **pylorus** is the lower tubular portion of the stomach and ends with the pyloric sphincter that leads to the small intestine. When the stomach is empty, the stomach muscles contract, and we feel the need to eat. The mucus membrane of the lining of the stomach contains **rugae**, a series of folds or depressions that allow the stomach to expand when full. Upon filling the stomach, the musculature of the stomach allows it to move and mix the digesting food. The various glands of the stomach secrete gastric juices that contain digestive enzymes and hydrochloric acid (HCL). HCL kills potential pathogens by keeping the pH of the stomach environment very acidic. The pH of the human stomach is approximately 2.0. Other digestive enzymes break down the food bolus, which is now called **chyme**. The stomach secretes 1.2 to 1.5 L of gastric juice each day. Table 5-1 shows the source and function of gastric juice.

TABLE 5-1 Gastric Secretions and Their Function

Secretion	Source	Function
Gastrin	Gastrin (G) cells in the lining of the stomach	Stimulates release of HCL and pepsinogen
Pepsinogen	Zymogenic cells	Inactive form of pepsin
Pepsin	Converted from pepsinogen in the presence of HCL	Chemical digestion of proteins
HCL	Parietal cells	Creates acidic environment to kill pathogens and activate pepsinogen
Mucus	Mucous cells	Creates protective layer of mucus to prevent ulceration
Intrinsic factor	Parietal cells	Promotes absorption of vitamin B_{12} across the wall of the small intestine

After the chyme is mixed with the gastric secretions, it is released in small amounts through the pyloric sphincter and into the **duodenum**, the first portion of the small intestine.

Small Intestine

The small intestine is a coiled structure that is approximately 20 ft long, filling most of the abdominal cavity. It is divided into three sections: the duodenum, jejunum, and the ileum. The first section, the duodenum, is approximately 12 in. long and extends in a C shape from the pylorus of the stomach. It receives chyme from the stomach and digestive juices from the accessory organs that contribute to the digestive process via the common bile duct. The second portion, the jejunum, is approximately 8 ft long. The last section, the ileum, is approximately 12 ft long and ends at the ileocecal junction. The small intestine, also called the small bowel, is the chief organ of nutrient absorption. It performs the final stages of chemical digestion that begin in the mouth and stomach and move chyme along the intestines by peristaltic waves. The mucous membrane of the small intestines is lined with millions of tiny fingerlike projections called villi (Fig. 5-4). The long length of the

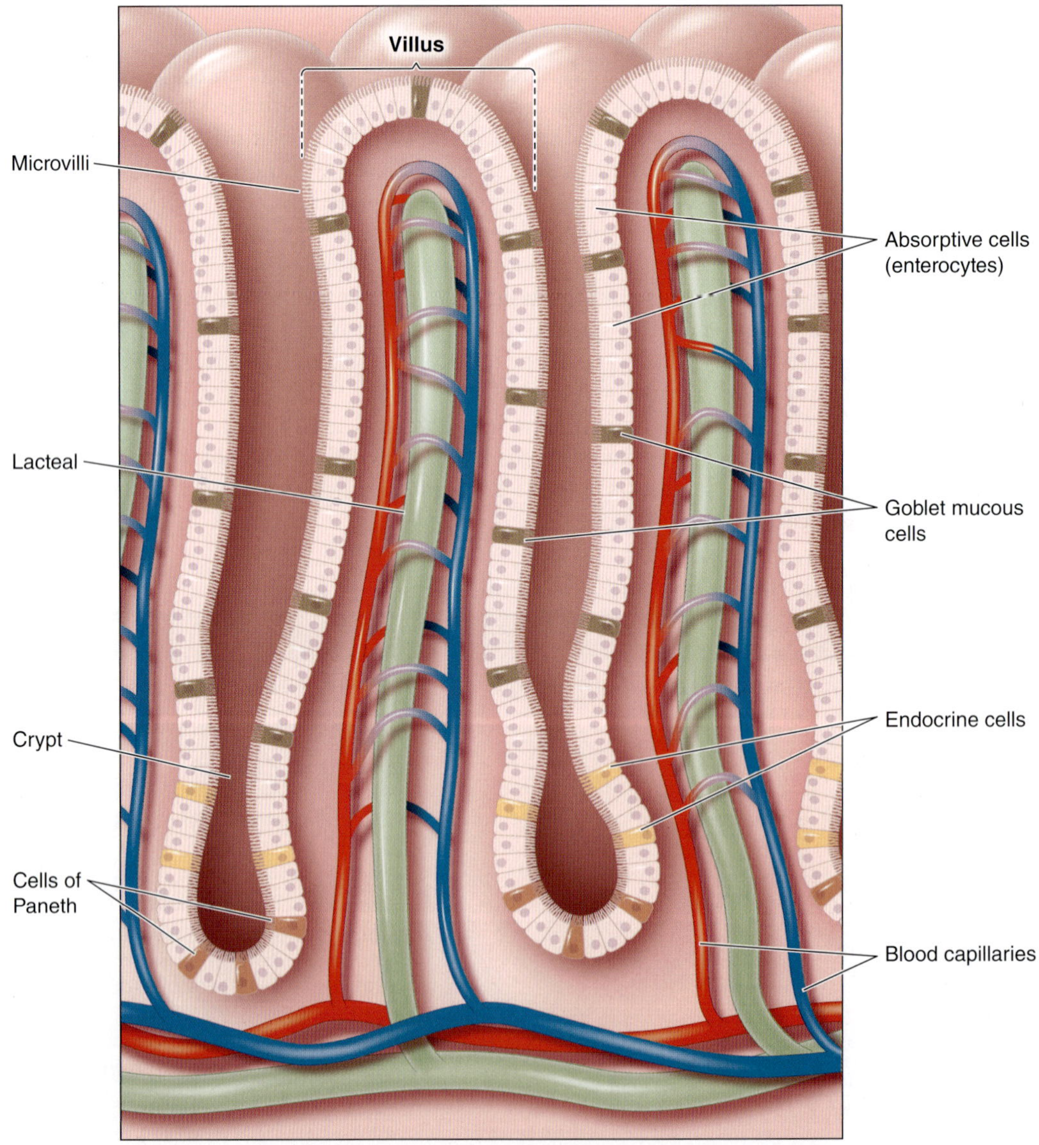

Figure 5-4 Villi of the wall of the small intestine.

small intestines and the villi create a large surface area for absorption of nutrients. The villi are surrounded by blood capillaries, where nutrients are transported to the bloodstream.

ELEMENT REVIEW
ile/o = ileum
cec/o = cecum
-al = pertaining to
peri- = around
-stalsis = contraction

Large Intestine

The large intestine begins at the ileocecal junction and ends at the anus. The ileocecal junction contains a muscular ring called the **ileocecal sphincter**. It opens to allow chyme to flow from the ileum to the **cecum**, the first section of the large intestine. The sphincter closes to prevent the flow of waste back into the ileum.

The large intestine is divided into the cecum, colon, and rectum. The cecum is a blind pouch on the right side of the abdomen, extending 2 to 3 in. beyond the ileocecal sphincter, which receives chyme from the ileum of the small intestine. At the base of the cecum, there is a small thin structure called the **vermiform appendix**. The appendix is 3 to 8 in. long and 0.5 in. in diameter and hangs down from the colon; the distal end is closed. The function of the appendix is unknown although it is theorized that it may contain beneficial bacteria that can protect from pathogenic bacteria. The largest portion of the large intestine is the colon. The colon is divided into four sections named for the direction in which the material inside is flowing. The **ascending colon** begins at the ileocecal junction, curving upward on the right side of the abdomen toward the liver. When the ascending colon reaches the bottom of the liver, it turns horizontally to the left at the **hepatic flexure**, where it is now called the **transverse colon**. The transverse colon continues leftward toward the bottom of the spleen. It turns downward at the **splenic flexure** and is now called the **descending colon**. It follows a downward path along the left side of the abdomen to then make an s-shaped curve to the **sigmoid colon**. The sigmoid colon connects to the rectum. The rectum is the last 7 to 8 in. of the colon and connects to the **anus**, the opening through which feces exit the body. **Feces**, the solid waste products of digestion, are eliminated by the process of **defecation**. The anal sphincter lies in the folds between the buttocks and controls the process of elimination. The function of the large intestine is to resorb fluid from the digested chyme flowing toward the anus. Water is continuously drawn away from the chyme until the feces is a solid material. If chyme flows too quickly through the large intestine, water remains in the feces, and the watery material is termed *diarrhea*.

ELEMENT REVIEW
hepat/o = liver
-cyte = cell

Accessory Organs of Digestion

The accessory organs of digestion are the salivary glands (previously discussed), liver, pancreas, and gallbladder (Fig. 5-5). The **liver** is located under the diaphragm and lies to the right side. It is the largest gland of the body, weighing approximately 3 to 4 lb in an adult. The liver is enclosed by a fibrous connective tissue that extends to its interior and divides it into the right and left lobes. The liver is held in place by the falciform ligament suspended from the diaphragm and the anterior abdominal wall.

The liver functions as both a digestive and endocrine organ. Its digestive function is to produce **bile**, a chemical that emulsifies fats, making them smaller and soluble in the watery fluid of the intestines. Bile is a yellowish-green secretion that contains bile salts, bile pigments, and cholesterol. The bile is stored in a pear-shaped sac called the **gallbladder**, which is located next to the duodenum. The gallbladder holds the bile until it is needed to digest fat, at which time the bile flows through the cystic duct to the common bile duct into the duodenum, where it can mix with the digesting chyme.

In addition to the production of bile, the liver has many other functions.

ELEMENT REVIEW
chol/e = bile
cyst/o = sac
cholecyst/o = gallbladder

- The liver recycles iron from old red blood cells (RBCs) which are destroyed in the spleen, and converts the remaining portion into bile pigments or waste material excreted in the feces.
- It synthesizes vitamin K-dependent plasma proteins: albumin, globulins, and clotting factors.

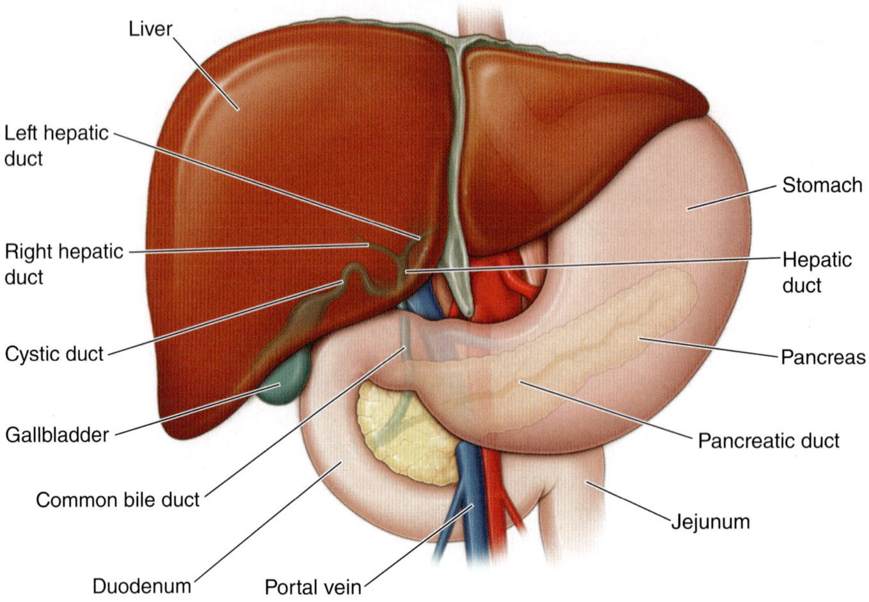

Figure 5-5 The liver, gallbladder, and pancreas.

- The liver metabolizes amino acids.
- It metabolizes fat. The liver synthesizes cholesterol and other lipoproteins that transport fat to tissues. It converts fatty acids to ketones to be used for energy.
- The liver is an organ of detoxification of harmful substances such as medications, alcohol, heavy metals, and ammonia.
- The liver stores the fat-soluble vitamins A, D, E, K, and vitamin B_{12}, as well as iron and copper.

ELEMENT REVIEW
glyc/o = sugar
neo- = new
-genesis =formation
glycogen/o = glycogen
-lysis = destruction

The liver converts excess blood glucose into glycogen for storage in the liver cells in a process called **glycogenesis**. When blood glucose declines, the glycogen can be cleaved into glucose molecules and released into the bloodstream. This process is called glycogenolysis, breaking down glycogen. It can also be called gluconeogenesis because new glucose is being formed. **Glucose** is the source of fuel for all metabolic processes of the body.

The **pancreas** is a soft, elongated organ of approximately 6 to 9 in. that lies in the upper left quadrant of the abdomen. It extends across the abdomen from its head near the duodenum to its tail, which touches the spleen. The middle section is called the body. The pancreas functions as both an exocrine and an endocrine organ. The digestive work of the pancreas is done by the **acini cells**, the secretory cells that compose 90% of the organ. The other 10% are the islets of Langerhans, which are part of the endocrine system. Acini cells encircle the ends of pancreatic ducts that secrete a mixture of alkaline digestive enzymes collectively called pancreatic juice (Table 5-2). The average adult produces

TABLE 5-2 Pancreatic Secretions and Their Function

Composition of Pancreatic Juice	Function
Bicarbonate ions (pH 8.4 to 8.9)	Neutralize acid in chyme
Trypsinogen	Converts to trypsin for protein digestion
Chymotripsinogen	Converts to chymotrypsin for protein digestion
Amylase	Coverts starch to maltose
Lipase	Digests emulsified fats

500 to 1,200 mL of pancreatic juice each day. The alkaline nature of the juice is important in raising the pH of the chyme as it leaves the acidic media of the stomach.

ELEMENT REVIEW
pancreat/o = pancreas
-ic = pertaining to

Nutrition

The digestive system functions to take fuel into the body. The food substances that prompt chemical reactions or provide energy necessary for the metabolic work of the body are called **nutrients**. These nutrients can be divided into macronutrients, which provide calories, and noncaloric components called **micronutrients**. The macronutrients are carbohydrates, fats, and proteins that can be converted to energy in the body. The term **calorie** refers to the quantity of energy needed to raise 1 g of water 1°C. The **micronutrients** do not contain calories but provide essential components for chemical reactions in the body, such as the enzymes used for digestion. Complete nutrition relies on adequate quantities of food containing these nutrients. The caloric value and micronutrients of food are written on food package labels and can be used as a guide for complete nutrition (Fig. 5-6). When food is abundant but highly processed, poor food quality and overeating can lead to both obesity and malnutrition.

Nutrition Facts	
6 servings per container	
Serving size	**1 bar (80g)**
Amount per serving	
Calories	**360**
	% Daily Value*
Total Fat 12g	**16%**
Saturated Fat 10g	**50%**
Trans Fat 0g	
Cholesterol 30mg	**10%**
Sodium 160mg	**7%**
Total Carbohydrate 41g	**15%**
Dietary Fiber 2g	**5%**
Total Sugars 29g	
Includes 28g Added Sugars	**55%**
Sugar Alcohol 3g	
Protein 20g	**38%**
Vitamin D 0mcg	0%
Calcium 230mg	15%
Iron 1.9mg	10%
Potassium 240mg	4%

* The % Daily Value (DV) tells you how much a nutrient in a serving of food contributes to a daily diet. 2,000 calories a day is used for general nutrition advice.

Figure 5-6 The nutrition label from an energy bar.

Structures and Physiology Review

Match the word to the description:

cecum	large intestines	rugae
chyme	liver	small intestines
duodenum	mastication	stomach
esophagus	molars	tongue
gallbladder	pancreas	uvula
hepatic flexure	peristalsis	villi
incisors	pylorus	

1. The process of chewing food ________________
2. The point where the ascending colon turns to the left ________________
3. Teeth that grind food ________________
4. Fingerlike projections of the small intestines that absorb nutrients ________________
5. Storage pouch for bile ________________
6. Accessory organ that produces bile ________________
7. Resorbs water from chyme ________________
8. Tube that receives food from the pharynx ________________
9. Partially digested food mixed with digestive juices ________________

10. Lower tubular portion of the stomach ______________________
11. Aids in digestion and production of sound and speech ______________________
12. The first section of the small intestine ______________________
13. Solid mass of muscle in the mouth that provides sense of taste ______________________
14. Muscular action that moves food through the digestive system ______________________
15. The 2- to 3-in. blind pouch extending beyond the ileocecal junction ______________________
16. Folds in the stomach it is when empty ______________________
17. Anterior teeth used to cut food ______________________
18. Provides an acidic media for digestion and detoxification of food ______________________
19. Twenty feet long, major organ of digestion ______________________
20. Secreted bicarbonate ions to increase pH of chyme ______________________

Structures and Physiology Word-Building Practice

1. Nouns and Adjectives

Complete the chart of nouns and adjective forms of words.

Noun	Adjective
anus	____________
____________	cecal
dentition	____________
digestion	____________
duodenum	____________
nutrition	____________
peristalsis	____________
pancreas	____________
pylorus	____________
____________	villous

2. Prefixes

Use the listed prefix to build a word for each definition.

a-	dia-	supra-
peri-	sub-	endo-
an-	dys-	eu-
meta-		

1. Normal speaking ________________
2. Pertaining to above the liver ________________
3. Inability to swallow ________________
4. Discharge of watery stool ________________
5. Difficulty digesting ________________
6. A scope used to look within the body ________________
7. Pertaining to under the stomach ________________
8. Pertaining to around a tooth ________________
9. Without appetite ________________
10. The sum of all chemical changes of the body ________________

3. Singular and Plural Forms

Complete the chart of singular and plural forms.

Singular	Plural
diverticulum	________________
________________	gingivae
________________	papillae
________________	rugae
tooth	________________

Word Building With Combining, Prefix, and Suffix Forms

The following word roots, prefixes, and suffixes are commonly used in medical terms for the anatomy and pathology of the digestive system. Combining vowels for word roots are included. Memorizing these word elements will help you understand new terms that you may encounter in the field of gastroenterology as a medical assistant, clinical dietician, nurse, or other professional working in gastroenterology or internal medicine.

The list contains examples of terms that use the combining forms and a pronunciation guide. Be sure to use the pronunciation guide so that you learn to say the terms correctly.

Medical Language Lab

The Medical Language Lab at medicallanguagelab.com provides audio files to help you practice your pronunciations.

Combining Form	Meaning	Example (Pronunciation)	Example Definition
abdomin/o	abdomen	abdominal (ab-DŎ-mĭ-năl)	pertaining to the abdomen
amyl/o	starch	amylase (AM-ĭ-lās)	enzyme to digest starch
appendic/o	appendix	appendicitis (ă-pĕn-dĭ-SĪ-tĭs)	inflammation of the appendix
bil/i	bile	biliary (BĬL-ē-ār-ē)	pertaining to bile
bucc/o	cheek	buccal (BŬK-kăl	pertaining to the cheek
cec/o	cecum	ileocecal (ĬL-ē-SE-kăl	pertaining to the ileum and cecum
celi/o	abdomen	celiocentesis (SĒ-lē-ō-sĕn-tē-sĭs)	puncture of the abdomen
cheil/o	lips	cheiloplasty (KĪ-lō-plas-tē)	surgical repair of lips
chol/e	bile	cholelith (KŎL-ĭ-lĭth)	bile stone
cholecyst/o	gallbladder	cholecystitis (KŎ-lĕ-sis-tĭt-ĭs)	inflammation of the gallbladder
choledoch/o	common bile duct	choledocholithiasis (KŎ-lĕd-ō-kō-lĭ-THĪ-ă-sĭs)	condition of a stone in the common bile duct
cirrh/o	yellow	cirrhosis (sĭ-RŌ-sĭs)	yellow, hardening of the liver
col/o	colon	coloenteritis (ko-lŏ-ĕn-tĕ-Ī-tĭs)	inflammation of the small intestine and colon
colon/o	colon	colonoscope (ko-LŎN-skōp)	instrument to view the colon
dent/o	tooth	dentistry (DĔNT-ĭ-strē)	branch of medicine that deals with teeth
duoden/o	duodenum	duodenal (dū-ŏ-DĔN-ăl)	pertaining to the duodenum
enter/o	intestine	enterocele (ĔNT-ĕ-rō-sēl)	hernia of the intestine
esophag/o	esophagus	esophageal (ē-sŏf-ă-GĒ-ăl)	pertaining to the esophagus
gastr/o	stomach	gastroenterology (găs-trō-ĕn-tĕr-ŎL-ă-jē)	branch of medicine for stomach and intestines
gingiv/o	gums	gingivitis (jĭn-jĭ-VĪ-tĭs)	inflammation of the gums
gloss/o	tongue	glossolingual (glŏs-ō-LĬNG-gwăl)	pertaining to the gums and lips
gluc/o	sugar	gluconeogenesis (gloo-kō-nē-ō-JĔN-ĕ-sĭs)	production of sugar

Combining Form	Meaning	Example (Pronunciation)	Example Definition
glyc/o	sugar	glycolysis (glī-KOL-ĭ-sĭs)	breakdown of sugar
hepat/o	liver	hepatitis (hĕp-ă-TĪ-tĭs)	inflammation of the liver
ile/o	ileum	ileostomy (ĬL-ē-os-tŭ-mē)	creation of a surgical passage in the ileum
jejun/o	jejunum	jejunorrhaphy (jē-jū-nŏ-RĂ-fē)	suturing of the jejunum
lapar/o	abdominal wall	laparoscopy (lăp-ă-ROS-kŏ-pē)	process of viewing through the abdominal wall
lingu/o	tongue	lingual (LĬNG-gwăl)	pertaining to the tongue
lip/o	fat	lipoprotein (lip-ō-PRŌ-tēn)	made of fat and protein
lith/o	stone	lithiasis (lith-Ī-ă-sĭs)	condition of stones
odont/o	teeth	orthodontist (or-thō-DŎN-tĭst)	specialist to straighten teeth
or/o	mouth	oral hygiene (ŌR-ăl HĪ-jēn)	pertaining to sanitary practice of the mouth
palat/o	palate	palatoglossal (PAL-ăt-ăl-GLŎS-ăl)	pertaining to the palate and tongue
pancreat/o	pancreas	pancreatitis (păn-krē-ă-TĪ-tĭs)	inflammation of the pancreas
pharyng/o	pharynx	pharyngeal (făr-ĬN-jē-ăl)	pertaining to the pharynx
peritone/o	peritoneum	peritoneal (per-ĭt- ŏ-NĒ- ăl)	pertaining to the peritoneum
proct/o	anus, rectum	proctologist (prŏk-TOL-ŏ-jĭst)	specialist of the rectum/anus
rect/o	rectum	anorectal (ā-nō-RĔK-tăl)	pertaining to the anus and rectum
sial/o	salivary gland	sialolith (sī-AL-ō-lĭth)	stone of the salivary gland
sigmoid/o	sigmoid colon	sigmoidoscopy (sĭg-MOY-dō-kŏ-pē)	procedure to view the sigmoid colon
splen/o	spleen	splenectomy (splē-NEK-tŏ-mē)	surgical removal of the spleen
steat/o	fat	steatorrhea (stē-ă-tō-Rē-ă)	passage of fatty stool
stomat/o	mouth	stomatitis (stō-mă-TĪ-tĭs)	inflammation of the mouth

ā = say, ă = sofa, ē = meet, ĕ = met, ī = eye, ĭ = in, ō = oh, ŏ = dog, ū = you, ŭ = up, oo = food

Prefix Form	Meaning	Example (Pronunciation)	Example Definition
a-, an-	without	achlorhydria (ā-klor-HĪ-drē-ă)	lack of stomach acid
dys-	bad, labored	dysphagia (dis-FA-j(ē-)ă)	difficulty swallowing, eating
hyper-	excessive	hyperemesis (hī-PĔR-EM-ĕ-sĭs)	excessive vomiting
hypo-	decreased	hypoglossal (hī-pŏ-GLŎS-ăl)	located under the tongue

ā = say, ă = sofa, ē = meet, ĕ = met, ī = eye, ĭ = in, ō = oh, ŏ = dog, ū = you, ŭ = up, oo = food

Suffix Form	Meaning	Example (Pronunciation)	Example Definition
-ase	enzyme	protease (PROT-ē-ās)	enzyme to digest proteins
-centesis	puncture	abdominocentesis (ab-dom-i-nŏ-sen-TĒ-sĭs)	surgical puncture of the abdomen
-ectasis	stretching/ dilation	gastrectasis (găs-trek-TĀ-sĭs)	stretching of the stomach
-ectomy	surgical removal	cholecystectomy (kō-lē-sĭs-TĔK-tŏ-mē)	surgical removal of the gallbladder
-lysis	destruction	glycogenolysis (glī-kō-jĕ-NOL-ĭ-sĭs)	destruction of glycogen
-ostomy	creation of new	colostomy (kŏ-LOS-tō-mē)	creation of new opening of the colon to the abdominal wall
-pepsia	digestion	eupepsia (yū-PEP-sē-ă)	healthy digestion
-phagia	to eat	polyphagia (pŏl-ē-FA-j(ē-)ă)	excessive hunger
-plasty	surgical repair	cheiloplasty (KĪ-lō-plas-tē)	surgical repair of the lips
-ptosis	downward displacement	gastroptosis (găs-TRŌP-tō-sĭs)	downward displacement of the stomach
-tripsy	crushing	lithotripsy (LITH-ŏ-trip-sē)	crushing of a stone

ā = say, ă = sofa, ē = meet, ĕ = met, ī = eye, ĭ = in, ō = oh, ŏ = dog, ū = you, ŭ = up, oo = food

Combining Forms Practice

1. Build the Terms

Using only the word elements listed, create terms to match the definition.

Prefixes	Combining Forms		Suffixes	
a-, an-	abdomin/o	hepat/o	-al	-lysis
sub-	amyl/o	hyper-	-ase	–megaly
	dent/o	hypo-	-cele	-ostomy
	duoden/o	lingu/o	-centesis	-pepsia
	enter/o	lip/o	-ectasis	–phagia
	esophag/o	lith/o	-ectomy	-plasty
	gastr/o	pancreat/o	-ic	-tripsy
	gingiv/o	rect/o		
	gloss/o	splen/o		
	gluc/o	stomat/o		

1. Pertaining to the stomach ________________
2. Enlargement of the spleen ________________
3. Pertaining to the pancreas ________________
4. Difficulty digesting ________________
5. Pertaining to under the tongue ________________
6. Surgical joining of proximal colon and sigmoid colon ________________
7. Presence of a stone in the common bile duct ________________
8. Excision of all or part of the liver ________________
9. Hernia of the esophagus ________________
10. Condition of stones in the pancreas ________________
11. Surgical puncture of the abdomen ________________
12. Surgical repair of the tongue ________________
13. Crushing of a salivary stone ________________
14. Pertaining to teeth ________________
15. Pertaining to the rectum and sigmoid colon ________________

2. Decipher the Terms

Separate each term into its prefix (if any), combining form, and suffix. Next, translate the word parts and then give the common definition of the term.

1. hypoglossal

   Prefix: __________ *Combining Form:* __________ *Suffix:* __________

   Meaning: ______________________________

2. sublingual

Prefix: ______________ *Combining Form:* ______________ *Suffix:* ______________

Meaning: ____

3. gingivectomy

Prefix: ______________ *Combining Form:* ______________ *Suffix:* ______________

Meaning: ____

4. hematemesis

Prefix: ______________ *Combining Form:* ______________ *Suffix:* ______________

Meaning: ____

5. cheiloplasty

Prefix: ______________ *Combining Form:* ______________ *Suffix:* ______________

Meaning: ____

6. abdominocentesis

Prefix: ______________ *Combining Form:* ______________ *Suffix:* ______________

Meaning: ____

7. protease

Prefix: ______________ *Combining Form:* ______________ *Suffix:* ______________

Meaning: ____

8. gastroenterologist

Prefix: ______________ *Combining Form:* ______________ *Suffix:* ______________

Meaning: ____

9. lipolysis

Prefix: ______________ *Combining Form:* ______________ *Suffix:* ______________

Meaning: ____

10. dentilingual

Prefix: ______________ *Combining Form:* ______________ *Suffix:* ______________

Meaning: ____

Digestive System Diseases and Disorders

Pathological conditions of the gastrointestinal system can have a variety of causes, including infections, cancers, congenital abnormalities, trauma, or structural defects. Because the purpose of the gastrointestinal system is to fuel the body, pathologies of the gastrointestinal system can affect other organ systems.

Common Signs and Symptoms

The digestive system breaks down food into usable nutrients and provides the body with energy. The signs and symptoms of disorders of the gastrointestinal system are common across a variety of diseases and disorders (Table 5-3).

Pathological Conditions of the Gastrointestinal System

Achalasia: Decreased motility of the lower esophagus and constriction of the LES causes food accumulation in the lower esophagus. Nerve impulses cause the LES to relax and open, allowing food to enter the stomach. Barium swallow and upper endoscopy are used to diagnose the disorder.

ELEMENT REVIEW
end/o = within
-scopy = procedure to look

Anal fistula: An abnormal passage in the skin near the anus usually connecting to the rectum.

TABLE 5-3 Common Signs and Symptoms

Common Signs	Common Symptoms
Achlorhydria (absence of HCL in gastric secretions)	Anorexia (loss of appetite)
Aphagia (inability to swallow)	Bloating (feeling of abdominal distention)
Ascites (abnormal accumulation of fluid in the peritoneal cavity)	Fatigue (lack of energy)
Borborygmus (audible abdominal sounds of hyperactive intestinal peristalsis)	Heartburn (chest pain and sour/burning taste in the mouth)
Cachexia (general ill health, malnutrition, weight loss, muscle loss)	Nausea (uncomfortable feeling that may lead to vomiting)
Constipation (passage of hard stool, can be painful)	Pruritis ani (itching of the skin in the perianal area)
Diarrhea (frequent passage of watery, loose stool)	
Emaciation (excessive weight loss, leading to low BMI)	
Eructation (act of bringing up air from the stomach to the mouth, belching)	
Flatulence (passing of air through the rectum)	
Icterus, jaundice (yellowing of the skin, sclera of the eyes, due to increased bilirubin in the blood)	
Melena (abnormal black tarry stool)	
Steatorrhea (excessive fat in the feces)	
Vomiting, emesis (expelling of stomach contents through the esophagus and out the mouth)	

Aphthous stomatitis: Infectious, inflammatory, ulcerated lesions in the mouth, lips, tongue, and sides of the cheeks. The lesions are also called canker sores. While the cause is unknown, possible causes are food or drug allergies, emotional stress, viral infection, and hormonal imbalances. Topic analgesics can reduce symptoms, which usually resolve in 1 to 2 weeks.

Appendicitis: Acute inflammation and infection of the vermiform appendix that may lead to rupture. Signs and symptoms include fever, nausea, anorexia, and abdominal pain. The cause of the inflammation is a fecal obstruction at the opening to the appendix. As the fecal matter collects, bacteria can multiply and cause infection, formation of pus, and inflammation. If the appendix ruptures, the bacteria and feces will spill out into the peritoneum, causing peritonitis.

Barrett's esophagus: Characterized by replacement of squamous epithelium of the distal esophagus with metastatic columnar epithelium. The cellular changes are a result of chronic exposure of the esophagus to stomach acid. Stomach acid splashes up (refluxes) into the esophagus, thus causing damage. Diagnosis is confirmed with endoscopy. If left untreated, the disease can progress to adenocarcinoma of the distal esophagus.

Figure 5-7 Gallstones can be surgically removed from the gallbladder or common bile duct.

ELEMENT REVIEW
chol/e = bile
doch/o = duct
-lithiasis = condition with a stone

Celiac disease: Caused by a sensitivity to gluten found in wheat, barley, rye, and oats. Signs and symptoms include steatorrhea (passage of large, foul-smelling, fatty stools), gas, bloating, abdominal distention, and malnutrition. Symptoms can occur in infants when they start eating cereals or may not develop until adulthood. Effective treatment consists of elimination of gluten in the diet.

Cholelithiasis (gallstones): Gallstones are hard stones made of cholesterol that can lodge in the common bile duct, cystic duct, or the gallbladder (Fig. 5-7). Symptoms include right-sided epigastric pain that often radiates to the upper back, along with nausea and vomiting. Symptoms increase when the patient eats fatty foods. Diagnosis is confirmed by history of symptoms and ultrasound to view the stones. Medication (Chenodiol) to dissolve the stones and reduce the liver's production of cholesterol can be administered. Surgical removal of the gallbladder, a cholecystectomy, via laparoscopy can decrease pain and maldigestion. After cholecystectomy, patient education in dietary choices can also help to reduce symptoms.

CASE STUDY, continued

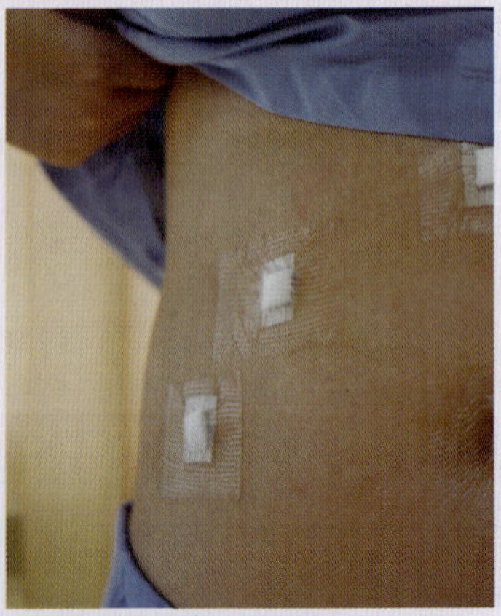

Let's return to Jessica's story. Jessica is admitted to the hospital on Tuesday morning after fasting since midnight. Dr. Morgan performs the laparoscopic cholecystectomy, and Jessica is sent to the recovery room. Upon waking from anesthesia, she is encouraged to rest and drink fluids. While many patients can go home the same day, Dr. Morgan keeps her in the hospital overnight for observation because of her complex medical history. Dr. Morgan explains to Jessica that her gallbladder was inflamed, perforated, and contained several large stones. The gallbladder and its contents are sent to the pathology laboratory for analysis. He further explains that the pain and nausea she had previously experienced should subside, but she still needs to eat a healthy diet and limit her portion sizes as she has been doing for the past year. He explains that good nutrition is very important to prevent weight gain and asks Janelle, the hospital's registered dietician, to visit Jessica before she is discharged tomorrow.

Cirrhosis is a degenerative disease of the hepatocytes where fat infiltrates the lobules of the liver. The liver cells are unable to function normally, becoming fibrous and eventually hardening (cirrhosis). It is most commonly caused by chronic alcoholism or viral infection. It can also be an autoimmune disorder called primary biliary cirrhosis or caused by right-sided heart failure. Eventually, the hardening progresses to an increased resistance to blood flow within the liver called portal hypertension. Obstruction of blood flow within the liver causes multisystem problems such as encephalopathy and esophageal varices. If left untreated, liver failure will occur.

ELEMENT REVIEW
cirrh/o = yellow
-osis = condition

Colitis, ulcerative (UC): Chronic inflammation of the mucous membrane of the lining of the colon that leads to ulceration. It commonly affects the anus, rectum, and distal colon, but it sometimes includes the entire large intestine. Symptoms include abdominal pain, spasms, and chills. Signs include fever, weight loss, and watery diarrhea with passage of mucus, pus, and blood. In severe cases, multiple bloody bowel movements daily will cause severe anemia. Diagnosis is confirmed by colonoscopy, sigmoidoscopy, barium enema, or computed tomography (CT) scan. Treatment includes corticosteroids to reduce inflammation and sulfasalazine (5-ASA) for its antibiotic and anti-inflammatory properties. Surgical removal of part of the colon is warranted in severe cases. Patients with a history of UC are at an increased risk of colon cancer.

ELEMENT REVIEW
col/o = colon
-itis = inflammation

Colorectal cancer: The second leading cause of cancer deaths in the United States and affects approximately 6% of U.S. citizens. Most cancers of the large intestines are adenocarcinomas and occur in the rectal area. Signs and symptoms include rectal bleeding and pain. The etiology of colorectal cancer is unknown, but risk factors include high-fat, low-residue diets, processed foods, and lack of physical exercise. Patients with Crohn's disease or ulcerative colitis are at increased risk. Family history of rectal polyps also increases risk. Diagnosis is confirmed by rectal examination, barium enema, sigmoidoscopy, and/or colonoscopy. Treatment options include chemotherapy, brachytherapy, radiation, monoclonal antibodies, or surgical removal of diseased section of the colon.

Colorectal polyps: Small outgrowths of tissue projecting from the mucous membrane of the colon or rectum (Fig. 5-8). They vary in size and shape and may be benign or precancerous. Polyps are usually asymptomatic. Presence of polyps is very common, found in 1 in 4 patients upon their first colonoscopy at age 50. Routine colonoscopy is recommended at age 50 and repeated every 10 years, unless more frequent testing is recommended as in the case of pathologies of the large intestines. Polyps are removed during the colonoscopy procedure, and biopsy will be obtained to determine if they are cancerous. Treatment for recurrent polyps is dietary avoidance of fried fatty foods, eggs, and processed meats such as bacon, hot dogs, and cold cuts.

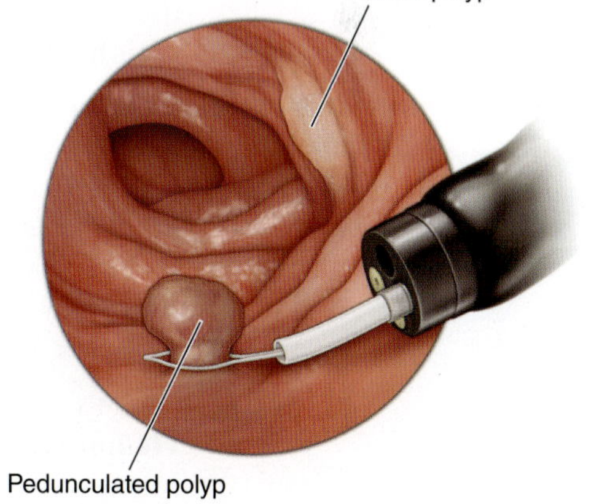

Figure 5-8 Two forms of polyps: a sessile polyp is attached by a base to the mucosa, and a pedunculated polyp is attached by a stalk.

Crohn's disease: An acute and chronic inflammation of the bowel that can lead to swelling and obstruction. Symptoms include nausea and abdominal tenderness. Signs include blood in both diarrhea and vomit. As the disease progresses, the patient may show signs of malnutrition. Although the exact etiology is unknown, food allergies and immunological dysregulation are thought to be contributing factors. Diagnosis is confirmed by colonoscopy. Treatment is dietary restriction and corticosteroids when inflammation increases.

Dental caries: Dental cavities are caused by acid-forming microorganisms that decalcify the enamel, the hard outer surface of teeth and dentin, the middle layer of teeth. These microorganisms collect in the mouth by fermentation of sugars. Proper oral hygiene, brushing after meals, and daily flossing removes plague. Plaque is the sticky residue of bacteria that forms between and on the surface of teeth. Additionally, topical application of fluoride increases the enamel's resistance to acids.

ELEMENT REVIEW
dent/o = teeth
-al = pertaining to

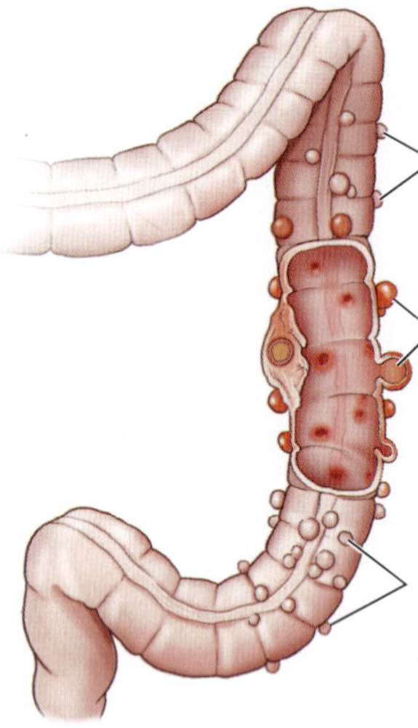

Figure 5-9 Diverticulosis and diverticulitis.

Diverticulosis and diverticulitis: Outpouches or herniations of the muscular layer of the large intestine, most commonly the sigmoid colon, are called diverticula (Fig. 5-9). These areas of stressed tissue are not normal to the colon. *Diverticular disease* is the term used to describe both diverticulosis, the presence of diverticula and diverticulitis, the presence of inflamed diverticula. Thus, diverticulitis is more advanced and symptomatic than diverticulosis. Diverticulosis does not progress to diverticulitis in most patients, but preventive patient education is necessary to reduce symptoms and disease progression. Commonly occurring in patients over age 45, diverticular disease is caused by diets low in fiber and lack of physical exercise. Symptoms include pain and cramping. Signs include fever, increased flatulence, and elevated white blood cell counts. Diagnosis is confirmed by barium enema or proctoscopy. Treatment includes replacement of lost fluids and electrolytes, antibiotics, analgesics, and stool softeners if indicated.

Dysentery: Painful intestinal inflammation and infection due to eating food or drinking water contaminated with pathogenic bacteria, protozoa, parasites, lead, mercury, or pesticides. Signs include watery diarrhea that may contain blood and mucus, passing of gas, and an elevated white blood cell count. Symptoms include pain, cramping, and urge to defecate. Treatment with antibiotics and rehydration will resolve dysentery, but prevention of future infections is key. Patient teaching includes frequent handwashing, storing foods in a refrigerator below 40° F, and separating raw and cooked foods to prevent cross contamination.

Esophageal varices: Swollen, twisted veins at the distal end of the esophagus caused by portal hypertension. The increased intrahepatic pressure causes the vessels of the esophageal veins to increase, making them susceptible to hemorrhage. The varices are commonly seen in patients with cirrhosis of the liver. Treatment is directed at the underlying liver disease by using antihypertensives, by detoxifying the liver, or by liver transplant if advanced disease is present.

Gastroesophageal reflux disease (GERD): Backflow of the contents of the stomach into the esophagus because of incompetent LES. Treatment consists of antacids and sitting upright after eating.

ELEMENT REVIEW
gastr/o = stomach
-paresis = partial paralysis

Gastroparesis: Delayed emptying of food from the stomach into the small intestines. Symptoms include heartburn, nausea, vomiting, and an immediate feeling of fullness upon eating. The condition may occur in patients receiving parenteral nutrition. It is also a complication seen in patients with chronic renal failure, spinal cord injury, multiple sclerosis, Parkinson's disease, severe emotional stress, uncontrolled diabetes mellitus, and amyloidosis. It may occur during pregnancy because of elevated progesterone levels. It is diagnosed by upper endoscopy. Treatments include medications to increase motility and dietary changes.

Hemorrhoids: Distended and swollen veins around the rectum and anus. They can be internal (inside of the sphincter) or external (on the outside of the sphincter). Internal hemorrhoids can become constricted and painful and can bleed as they get larger and extrude to the outside of the anus. External hemorrhoids don't usually bleed, and they cause minimal pain. Treatment with topical anti-inflammatory creams can decrease swelling of external hemorrhoids. Internal hemorrhoids may need surgical removal. Increasing dietary fluid and use of stool softeners can decrease symptoms.

ELEMENT REVIEW
hepat/o = liver
-itis = inflammation

Hepatitis: Acute or chronic inflammation of the liver, hepatitis, can be caused by viruses, bacteria, infection, drugs, alcohol, toxins, or parasites. Symptoms include abdominal and gastric pain, tenderness at the liver, joint pain, anorexia, and lethargy. Signs include jaundice and elevated liver enzymes. The most common cause of hepatitis is viral infection of three types: hepatitis A, hepatitis B, and hepatitis C.

Hepatitis A: Frequently transmitted by the fecal-oral route due to poor hygiene, contaminated water, or shellfish. With antiviral medication, most patients completely recover.
Hepatitis B: Transmitted by blood or body fluids contaminated with the virus. The disease can progress to cause loss of liver function, cirrhosis, liver failure, or even death. Treatment with Vemlidy, an antiviral medication, can cause remission of symptoms.
Hepatitis C: Transmitted by intravenous administration of contaminated blood products or when drug users share contaminated needles. It can progress to the chronic stage and cause permanent liver damage.

> ***Study Tip***
> The causes of viral hepatitis: A = anus, B = blood, C = community.

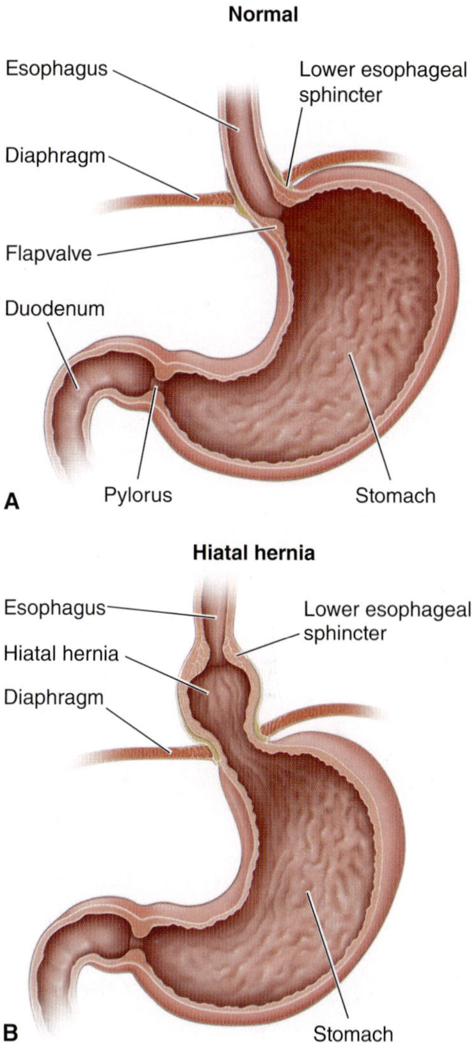

Figure 5-10 Hiatal hernia. (A) Normal esophagus through the diaphragm. (B) Hiatal hernia above the diaphragm.

Hiatal hernia: Upward protrusion of the stomach above the wall of the diaphragm (Fig. 5-10) caused by weakness of the muscle of the diaphragm. The disorder may be asymptomatic or may cause acid reflux as acid from the stomach flows back up into the esophagus. Diagnosis is confirmed by an x-ray or a barium swallow. Treatment consists of antacids, histamine receptor antagonists, dietary changes, and sitting upright while eating to ease food down into the stomach. If symptoms persist, surgical correction is performed by strengthening the esophageal hiatus, the notch where the esophagus and stomach are separated by the diaphragm.

Herpetic stomatitis: Inflammatory infection of the oral cavity with lesions caused by a recurrent viral infection that is thought to lie dormant until reactivated by fever, upper respiratory infection, or exposure to sunlight. The lesions have a clear fluid exudate, can be painful, and are highly contagious. Resolving in 5 to 7 days, they can appear on the lips, palate, tongue, and gums and are commonly called cold sores. Treatments include topical analgesics and anesthetics to reduce pain. Immunocompromised patients may be treated with intravenous acyclovir.

Hirchsprung's disease: An absence of the autonomic ganglia of smooth muscle of the intestines responsible for peristalsis, also known as congenital megacolon. Intestinal peristalsis, which moves food through the alimentary canal, is weak or absent. Feces don't move and collect in the bowel, causing distention called *megacolon*. The disease is commonly diagnosed during early infancy when the infant fails to pass the first stool. Diagnosis is confirmed by barium enema, and the quantity of affected tissue is determined by biopsy. Surgical removal of the aganglionic section of the colon is performed. Medications may be needed to promote proper motility as the child grows.

ELEMENT REVIEW
mega- = large

Ileus: Partial obstruction of the intestine caused by twisting of the bowel, lack of peristalsis, adhesions, or tumors. Diagnosis is confirmed by x-ray or CT scan. Treatment is directed at the cause of obstruction.

Intestinal obstruction: Complete intestinal obstruction is a medical emergency requiring quick diagnosis and treatment within 24 hours to prevent death. Signs include altered bowel sounds, distention, and vomiting. Symptoms include nausea, abdominal pain, and weakness. Causes of obstruction may include the following:
- chronic inflammation causing decreased diameter in the lumen of the intestine
- postsurgical adhesions
- tumors that block the intestine
- hernias that can become incarcerated, causing blockage

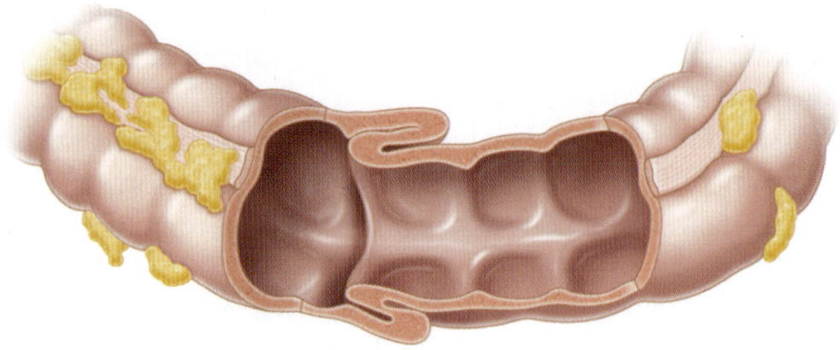

Figure 5-11 Intussusception.

- volvulus, where the bowel twists on itself
- intussusception, "telescoping" of the bowel

Diagnosis is confirmed by x-ray, barium enema, complete blood count, and blood chemistry studies. Placement of an intestinal tube is the first treatment. If the tube placement does not alleviate the obstruction, surgical correction is indicated.

Intussusception: Telescoping of intestines from the proximal to the distal intestine at the ileocecal region, causing partial obstruction (Fig. 5-11). It is usually seen in infants and young children. Signs and symptoms include vomiting, blood in stool, and severe abdominal pain. Diagnosis is confirmed by barium enema. The pressure of the barium enema can also resolve the intussusception. If the procedure does not resolve the telescoping, immediate surgical correction is required.

Irritable bowel syndrome (IBS): An increase of motility of the small and large intestines that increases upon emotional stress. Symptoms include abdominal pain, nausea, passing of foul-smelling gas. Signs include diarrhea more often than constipation, but both may intermittently occur. No diagnostic testing can confirm IBS, but tests such as a barium enema are used to rule out other diagnoses. Treatment is directed at reduction of emotional stresses and good food and sleep habits.

Obesity: Condition of having too much body fat due to eating too much and exercising too little. Contributing factors include psychological factors (depression/boredom leading to overeating), hypothyroidism, some medications, polycystic ovarian syndrome, insulin resistance, and Cushing's syndrome. Obesity is categorized according to BMI with increasing risk of health conditions including diabetes, heart disease, respiratory distress, musculoskeletal injuries to the knees and/or lower back. Treatments may include modification of diet, psychological counseling, increasing exercise, or weight-loss surgery if for class II or III obesity as it could be life-threatening if left untreated.

- Overweight, BMI 25 to 29.9
- Class I obesity, BMI 30 to 34.9
- Class II obesity, BMI 35 to 39.9
- Class III obesity, more than 40

ELEMENT REVIEW
leuk/o = white
plakia- = plaque

Oral leukoplakia: Precancerous lesions of gray, white, yellowish raised patches caused by chronic irritation by use of tobacco or alcohol.

Oral thrush: Fungal infection caused by *Candida albicans* infection of the mouth causing sore, creamy white patches on the tongue or inside of the cheeks. It occasionally affects newborns. The disorder is common to immunocompromised patients or people receiving chemotherapy, long-term antibiotics, or corticosteroids. Diagnosis is confirmed by scraping and testing a sample of the white matter. Treatment with daily antifungal rinse of fluconazole for 14 consecutive days will resolve the condition.

Pancreatitis: Inflammation of the pancreas that can be acute or chronic.

Acute pancreatitis presents quickly as mild pancreatic edema or severe inflammation causing necrotizing hemorrhagic pancreatitis. Signs include rigid abdominal distention;

decreased bowel sounds; hypotension; fever; and cold, clammy skin. Symptoms include severe continuous epigastric and abdominal pain that radiates to the back. Pain is most pronounced after eating a fatty meal or drinking alcohol. In addition to alcoholism, causes of acute pancreatitis include trauma, postsurgical infection, metabolic disorders, or ruptured peptic ulcers. Complications include abscess, diabetes mellitus, renal failure, ascites, heart failure, hypovolemic shock, respiratory distress, multiple organ failure, and death. Treatment is inpatient monitoring directed at pain relief and decreasing GI irritation (nasogastric [NG] tube and npo status).

Chronic pancreatitis A progressive destruction of pancreatic cells causing fibrosis, atrophy, calcification, and fatty degeneration. It is caused by chronic alcoholism, malnutrition, surgery, or cancer. Signs and symptoms are similar to acute pancreatitis but also include large fatty stools, and weight loss. Treatment includes pancreatic enzymes, antiemetics, antacids, and insulin if needed.

Peptic ulcers: Sores arising from the mucous membrane lining the gastrointestinal tract as a result of the bacterium *Helicobacter pylori* or from abnormalities of pH in the stomach. Ulcers can be acute or chronic, shallow or deep. Acute ulcers are most commonly shallow and do not extend completely through the wall of the stomach, resolving with minimal symptoms. Chronic ulcers go deep into the wall of the stomach and can create a hole in the wall called a perforation. A perforated ulcer will require surgical correction. Symptoms of ulcers include bloating after meals, indigestion, heartburn, nausea. Treatment includes antacids, decreasing alcohol and tobacco use, and antibiotics if *H. pylori* is the cause of the ulcer.

Periodontal disease: An inflammation of the gums around the teeth, which can lead to infection and tooth loss. As plaque accumulates around the base of the teeth from fermentation of carbohydrates, bacteria can colonize, causing infection. Gingivitis, inflammation of the gums, progresses. Discoloration of teeth, bleeding gums, and pain upon chewing are also common. As the disease progresses, pyorrhea, drainage of pus, from the gum line occurs. Treatment with surgical replacement of diseased tissue is needed in severe cases.

ELEMENT REVIEW
peri- = around
odont/o = teeth
-al = pertaining to

Volvulus: Rotation of the loops of the bowel causing intestinal obstruction.

Pathology Word-Building Practice

1. Build the Terms

*Using **only** the word parts in the lists provided, create medical terms for the indicated meanings.*

Prefixes	Combining Forms		Suffixes
an-, a-	an/o	gastr/o	-al
dys-	appendic/o	odont/o	-dynia
hyper-	cirrh/o	or/o	-emesis
mega-	cholecyst/o	pancreat/o	-ia
peri-	choledoch/o	py/o	-iasis
	colon/o	pylor/o	-itis
	dent/o	rect/o	-lith
	diverticul/o	rexi/o	-osis
	esophag/o	steat/o	-phagia
	hepat/o	sial/o	-plakia
	leuk/o		-rrhea
			-stenosis

1. Excessive vomiting __________
2. Having an extremely large colon __________
3. Inflammation of the liver __________
4. A condition of having no appetite __________
5. Difficulty swallowing __________
6. Discharge, flow of pus __________
7. Condition of hardening, scarring (related to the liver) __________
8. White patches that appear on the tongue __________
9. Passage of fatty stools __________
10. Inflammation of the gallbladder __________
11. Stone in a salivary gland __________
12. Condition of having diverticula __________
13. Condition of a stone in the common bile duct __________
14. Pertaining to the teeth __________
15. Stomach pain __________
16. Pertaining to around the teeth __________
17. Narrowing or stricture of the pylorus __________
18. Pertaining to the rectum __________
19. Narrowing of the esophagus __________
20. Inflammation of the pancreas __________

2. Prefixes

Choose from the list of prefixes to build a word for the definitions below.

dia-	macro-	supra-
dys-	micro-	trans-
hemi-	peri-	
infra-	poly-	

1. Abnormally fast discharge of chyme through the GI system __________
2. Excessive eating __________

3. Pertaining to under the liver ______________________
4. Pertaining to around the anus ______________________
5. Pertaining to above the spleen ______________________
6. Through or across the abdominal wall ______________________
7. Having unusually small teeth ______________________
8. Having an abnormally large tongue ______________________
9. Difficulty swallowing, eating ______________________
10. Surgical removal of half of the stomach ______________________

3. Suffixes

Choose from the list of suffixes to build a word for the definitions below.

-eal	-ostomy	-rrhea
-ectomy	-pathy	-scopy
-ic	-plasty	-stenosis
-itis	-ptosis	-toxic
-oma		

1. Swollen twisted veins of the lower esophagus ______________________
2. Procedure to look at the sigmoid colon ______________________
3. Discharge of pus from infected gums ______________________
4. Surgical correction of the lips ______________________
5. Surgical removal of the vermiform appendix ______________________
6. Poisonous to the liver ______________________
7. Narrowing of the esophagus ______________________
8. Tumor of fat ______________________
9. Pertaining to the duodenum and the liver ______________________
10. Downward displacement of the colon ______________________

Digestive System Diagnostic Procedures

Abdominal CT: A radiographic technique that selects levels in the body and blurs structures above and below it to create "slices" of images (Fig. 5-12). When performed on the abdomen, these pictures can identify disease/disorders of the liver, gallbladder, bile ducts, intestines, pancreas, kidneys, and bladder.

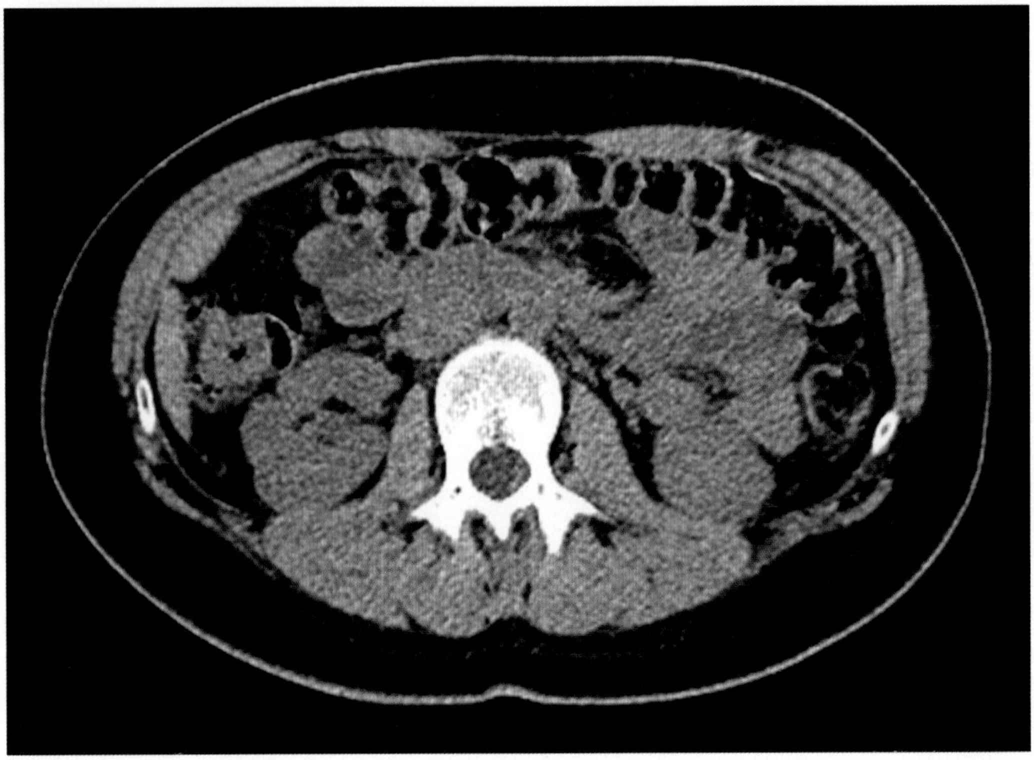

Figure 5-12 Abdominal CT scan. The vertebra appears white because bones are denser than the soft tissues of the intestines to the sides and top of the spine. The spinal column is seen as the dark center where it passes through the vertebra. The ribs are seen curving around the top edges of the anterior body.

Abdominal ultrasound: A noninvasive procedure using high-frequency sound waves to show a picture of internal organs. Disease/disorders of the liver, gallbladder, bile ducts, intestines, pancreas, kidneys, and bladder can be identified.

Alanine aminotransferase (ALT): ALT blood levels obtained from a serum sample. Normal values are 5 to 35 IU/L. Elevated ALT, a hepatocellular enzyme, is seen in liver disease such as cirrhosis, hepatotoxicity due to medications or street drugs, hepatic necrosis or tumors, obstructive jaundice, or pancreatitis. (ALT is formerly known as serum glutamic pyruvic transaminase: SGOT).

Alkaline phosphatase (ALP): An intestinal enzyme found in highest concentrations in the liver, the biliary tract, and bone. Normal values are 20 to 140 IU/mL. Increased ALP is seen in cirrhosis, biliary obstruction, liver cancer, intestinal ischemia, necrosis, and jaundice. It may be elevated during pregnancy and childhood. Decreased ALP is seen in zinc, magnesium or protein deficiencies, celiac disease, or excessive B vitamin ingestion.

Amylase: A digestive enzyme normally secreted from the pancreas into the duodenum via the pancreatic duct. Normal serum amylase is 56 to 190 IU/L. If the pancreatic duct is blocked, the enzyme leaks into the free peritoneum and is absorbed into the bloodstream via the intrapancreatic lymph, causing a rise in serum level. Elevated levels are seen in pancreatitis, perforated peptic ulcers, perforated or necrotic bowel, duodenal obstruction, or acute cholecystitis.

Barium enema: Procedure using radiopaque barium to observe the lower intestinal tract. After colonic cleansing with laxative and enema, barium sulfate is administered into the rectum and retained in the lower intestinal tract while x-rays are taken. The radiopaque barium will show stenosis, tumors, diverticula, and polyps. Since patient preparation requires npo from midnight the night before the procedure, barium enemas are most often scheduled in the morning.

Barium swallow: The swallowing of barium sulfate while the patient is being x-rayed. The barium enters the esophagus and into the stomach. As the material moves down the alimentary canal, esophageal pathologies such as varices, strictures, tumors, and obstruction can be observed. As the material enters the stomach and duodenum, pathologies such as tumors, hiatal hernias, and obstructions can be observed. Because the procedure is done while the patient is swallowing, the motility of the upper GI is also observed. Achalasia, a slowed motility, can be diagnosed.

Capsule endoscopy (wireless endoscopy): The visualization of the gastrointestinal tract using a camera pill. The camera, about the same size as a vitamin, is swallowed to relay pictures of the entire length of the small intestine. The digital pictures can show areas that other diagnostic procedures may not be able to show. The patient swallows the camera pill with a glass of water and wears a recording device on a belt. The patient is instructed to eat normally for approximately 8 hours, then the data on the recording device is transferred to a computer for viewing. As the camera moves through the alimentary canal, it does not disrupt the normal activity of the gastrointestinal tract and passes naturally via a bowel movement. While the procedure can be useful in diagnosing ulcers, tumors, intestinal bleeding, and inflammatory bowel disease, it is not appropriate for patients with dysphagia (difficulty swallowing), a history of intestinal obstruction or narrowing, or the presence of a pacemaker.

Cholecystography: The visualization of the gallbladder using radiopaque pills with an iodine-based dye. The test can show gallstones, gallbladder polyps, cancers, or duct obstruction. It is not as accurate as a gallbladder ultrasound. The image it produces is called the cholecystogram.

ELEMENT REVIEW
chol/e = bile
cyst/o = sac
-graphy = process of recording

Colonoscopy: An invasive procedure that provides direct visualization of the lining of the large intestine by a fiberoptic colonoscope. The patient preparation requires colonic cleansing with laxatives and enema. The procedure can help to diagnose colonic polyps, tumors (both benign and malignant), and the cause of persistent rectal bleeding, chronic diarrhea or constipation, or loss of appetite (anorexia). The procedure can be used both diagnostically to identify areas of pathology and therapeutically, as polyps can be removed by a snare instrument during the procedure.

CT colonoscopy (virtual colonoscopy): A noninvasive procedure that obtains views of the colon without the use of a scope. It provides two- and three-dimensional images of the colon and can identify polyps or other lesions. Unlike fiberoptic colonoscopy, it cannot be used therapeutically because polyps cannot be removed. Patient preparation of colonic cleansing with laxatives and enema is the same as that for the invasive colonoscopy. A small tube is inserted only 2 in. into the patient's rectum to allow air to be administered into the colon. The air expands the walls of the colon to help see any polyps. It may be used for patients at a low risk of polyps or for those who may be concerned with invasive procedures; however, it is not considered a substitute for conventional colonoscopy.

Endoscopic retrograde cholangiopancreatography (ERCP): A flexible fiberoptic scope with a light is passed through the esophagus, stomach, and into the duodenum. Passage of the tube is viewed on a screen during its placement. The physician locates the ampulla of Vater, the passageway that connects the common bile duct and the pancreatic duct to the duodenum. Patient preparation is npo the night before the procedure, and the patient is placed under light sedation. Once the tube is placed, a sampling of digestive fluid is obtained before a contrast medium is injected for x-ray analysis. The size and filling of the pancreatic and biliary ducts can be observed. Abnormal findings may include strictures of the biliary tree, tumors, gallstones, and cysts.

ELEMENT REVIEW
chole/o = bile
angi/o = vessel
pancreat/o = panceas
-graphy = process of recording

Esophagogastroduodenoscopy (EGD): Direct visualization of the esophagus, stomach, and duodenum by a fiberoptic endoscope. EGD may be used therapeutically to aspirate fluid or coagulate areas of bleeding (by using a laser). Diagnostically, it can show tumors, esophagitis, gastroesophageal varices, and bleeding ulcers.

Gastric analysis: A nasogastric tube is placed to obtain sample of gastric fluid. The fluid is analyzed to determine its pH and to detect the presence of blood, bacteria, bile, or abnormal cells. An alternative procedure has the patient ingest Diagnex, a resin dye that turns blue in the presence of acid. The HCL in the stomach should react with the dye, which is absorbed by the bowel and excreted in the urine in approximately 2 hours. If the urine does not turn blue, it indicates absence of HCL in the stomach, a condition called hypochlorhydria.

Gastric emptying tests: Tests utilized to assess the rate of food moving from the stomach into the small intestine. These tests are commonly used to diagnose gastroparesis.

Gastric emptying breath test (GEBT): The patient consumes a solid or liquid that contains carbon-13. As the material is absorbed in the intestines, it should be metabolized and be present in the breath in increasing quantities. Samples of breath are measured over a few hours to evaluate absorption.

Scintigraphy: The patient eats a light meal of eggs and toast that contains a small amount of a radioactive marker. A scanner is used to view the rate of movement of the radioactive bolus from the stomach to the small intestines.

Liver biopsy: A test used to diagnose liver conditions. If liver disease is suspected, a needle is placed into the liver through the abdominal wall. The tissue is then examined and can show hepatitis, abscess, tumor, or infiltrative disease.

Liver scan: A procedure to examine the liver. After IV injection of a radioactive compound that is taken up by the Kupffer cells of the liver, distribution is detected by a radiation detector. It may be used to detect cysts, abscesses, tumors, granulomas, or infiltrative disease of the liver.

Magnetic resonance imaging (MRI): A noninvasive procedure that provides visualization of soft tissue, bone, and fluid without using radiation. MRI may be done with or without contrast, depending on the type of testing. The machine uses a strong magnetic field and radiofrequency waves to produce images of organs and tissues and can be used to diagnose disorders of many body systems. GI disorders that can be identified by MRI include esophageal stricture, bile stones in the gallbladder or ducts, liver disease, and bowel inflammation or obstruction. People with implanted metal devices such as rods, wires, or pacemakers cannot undergo MRI procedures because the strong magnetic field will cause the metal to move and harm the patient. Additionally, the patient must lie in the MRI tube, thus a claustrophobic patient may not be able to tolerate the test. Premedication or testing in an "open" MRI scanner may allow these patients to have an MRI.

ELEMENT REVIEW
trans- = through, across
hepat/o = liver
-ic = pertaining to

Percutaneous transhepatic cholangiography (PTC): Examination of the bile duct structure by injecting contrast medium into the intrahepatic bile duct and viewing the flow of the contrast material. As the contrast flows, obstructions, strictures, sclerosis, anatomical variations, tumors, or cysts may be identified. If the cause of disease is extrahepatic, a catheter may be placed for external drainage of the bile duct. Rare postprocedure complications include bleeding, peritonitis, or septicemia.

48-hour pH study: An analysis that can detect how long gastric secretions reflux into the esophagus and determine the severity of GERD. A radio-transmitting capsule is placed into the esophagus by a nasal catheter. A small amount of suction adheres the capsule to the wall of the esophagus. During the 48-hour study, the patient eats, drinks, and maintains normal activity. No antacid medications are taken during the testing period. The capsule collects pH readings and transmits the data via radiofrequency telemetry to a recorder. The patient is asked to record meals, activities, and symptoms of heartburn, chest pain, and belching. At the end of the 48-hour study, the data recorder is returned to the endoscopy laboratory for data analysis. The capsule will detach from the esophageal wall within 5 to 7 days and will pass in the stool.

Serum bilirubin: Bilirubin is an orange-yellow pigment that is a product of RBC breakdown that can be measured in serum. Normal total serum bilirubin is 0.1 to 1.0 mg/dL.

Because clearance of bilirubin is a liver function, an increase can be a sign of liver dysfunction. Bilirubin will be elevated by hepatic damage, cirrhosis, hepatitis, metastatic liver disease, or extrahepatic duct obstruction.

Serum glutamic-oxaloacetic transaminase (SGOT): Also called aspartate aminotransferase (AST). SGOT is an enzyme that has very high concentration in liver cells. Normal adult level of SGOT/AST is 8 to 20 U/L. Increased levels are seen in cirrhosis, hepatotoxicity due to drug abuse, metastatic liver disease, acute pancreatitis, and hepatic necrosis.

Small bowel follow through: A test performed by oral administration of barium sulfate with x-rays of the GI tract at timed intervals as the barium progresses to the small intestines. Delayed transit time for the barium to get to the small intestines is observed in obstructions (malignant and benign). Decreased intestinal motility will also increase transit time. Decreased transit time is seen in malabsorption disease, as the barium flows too quickly through the body. Inflammatory disease, malabsorption syndrome, congenital defects, malrotations, or perforations may be diagnosed with this study.

Stool analysis for occult blood (also called a stool guaiac): Using guaiac as a reagent, analysis of a stool sample to look for the presence of blood. A positive test prompts the need for further study as the presence of blood in stool does not determine the location of the bleeding. Bleeding may indicate tumors, polyps, varices, IBS, ulcers, ischemic bowel disease, hemorrhoids, gastritis, esophagitis, diverticulosis, or diverticulitis.

Stool culture: Stool specimen placed on various culture mediums (plates) and microorganism colonies grown to identify specific pathogen(s). Patients are instructed to avoid mixing the stool sample with urine as it could inhibit the growth of bacteria. Abnormal pathogens found in stool include parasitic, protozoan, or bacterial forms that cause enterocolitis.

Urinary bilirubin: Urine test to check for the presence of bilirubin (which should be negative). Positive findings are an indication of gallstones, liver metastasis, or extrahepatic duct obstructions.

Digestive System Therapeutic Procedures

Abdominocentesis: Insertion of a needle into the abdominal cavity to remove excess fluid. The patient is placed in a seated position in order to remove large amounts of fluid, called ascites. The procedure reduces abdominal pressure and improves breathing. The fluid is sent to the pathology laboratory for analysis to look for infection or increased levels of amylase, indicative of pancreatitis.

Appendectomy: The surgical removal of an inflamed and/or ruptured appendix. It is performed either in an open procedure or laparoscopically (if no rupture is evident). Antibiotics are administered postoperatively to prevent subsequent infection.

ELEMENT REVIEW
append/o = appendix
-ectomy = surgical removal
cheil/o = lips
-plasty = surgical correction

Cheiloplasty: Surgical correction of a defect of the lip either of a congenital anomaly or due to trauma.

Cholecystectomy: Surgical removal of the gallbladder performed via a laparoscopy or an open procedure, depending on the extent of inflammation and quantity and location of gallstones. If stones are lodged in the ducts, an open procedure with common bile duct exploration will be necessary during surgery. Placement of a T-tube in the duct to drain bile and reduce edema may also be required (Fig. 5-13). The T-tube may remain for several weeks. Before it is removed, an x-ray will be performed to make sure no stones are left in the duct while it heals.

Colostomy: The surgical creation of a new opening on the abdominal wall for feces to exit the body. The incised colon and new opening may be permanent or temporary, allowing

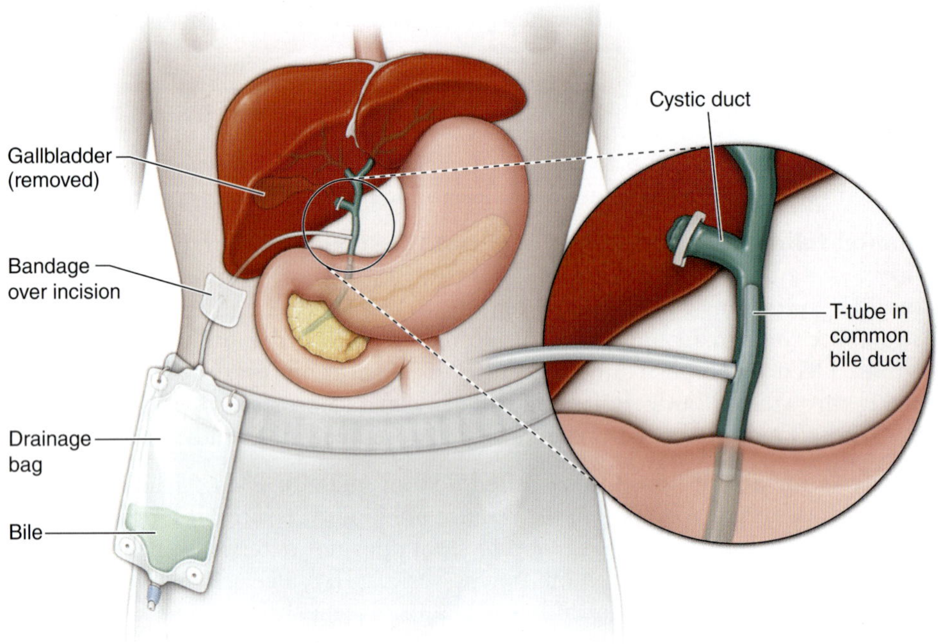

Figure 5-13 Cholecystectomy.

the bowel to heal from trauma, surgery, or chronic inflammation. Patient education must emphasize keeping the stoma (new opening) clean to avoid infection and embarrassing odor.

ELEMENT REVIEW
stoma = new opening
extra- = outside
corpor/o = body
-eal = pertaining to
lith/o = stone
-tripsy = crushing

Extracorporeal shock wave lithotripsy (ESWL): An alternative to an open procedure to remove gallstones. ESWL uses shock waves to crush gallstones, enabling the gallbladder to contract and pass the stones. The contractions of the gallbladder can be painful, so the patient is offered analgesics and advised to rest after the procedure. Hematuria (blood in the urine) and nausea are also normal postprocedure complaints.

Gastric banding: Laparoscopic placement of an adjustable silicone band around the upper portion of the stomach, creating a small pouch that limits the volume of food the patient can consume (Fig. 5-14). A port is placed under the skin so that saline can be added or removed to adjust the band. Patients are instructed to eat more slowly and to limit fluid with meals to avoid dumping syndrome.

Gastric bypass: Also known as Roux-en-Y bypass. A gastric bypass is a weight-loss surgery that reduces the size of the stomach so that the patient eats less. A small pouch is created and connects directly to the small intestine, "bypassing" most of the stomach and the first section of the small intestines (Fig. 5-15). It is performed on patients with a BMI of 34 or more and for whom nonsurgical weight-loss strategies have failed.

ELEMENT REVIEW
gastr/o = stomach
-ic = pertaining to

Gastric lavage: Irrigation and washing out of the stomach contents with sterile water or saline. The procedure is performed before and after surgery to remove irritants and toxins from the stomach. It may also be performed prior to endoscopy to clear passageway of the scope.

ELEMENT REVIEW
herni/o = hole
-rrhaphy = sewing, suturing

Herniorrhaphy: Surgical repair of a hernia to close the defect. It can be performed with sutures, mesh, or wires, depending on the size and location of the defect.

Nasogastric intubation: Instillation of a tube through the nose and into the stomach for feeding, instillation of medications, and fluids. The NG tube may be used to relieve gastric distention by removing secretions, gas, or food.

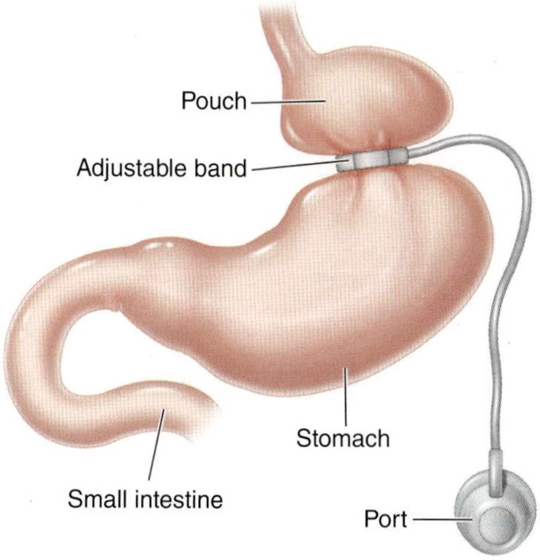

Figure 5-14 Gastric banding.

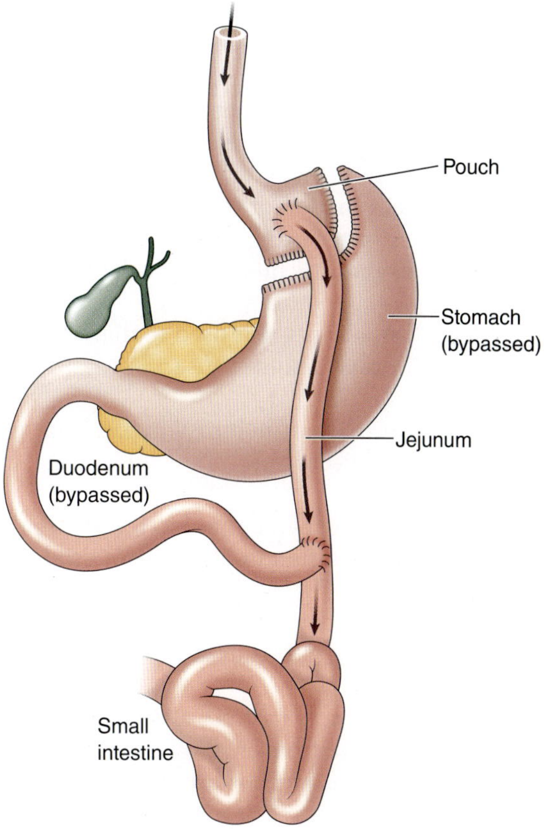

Figure 5-15 Gastric bypass.

Procedures and Diagnostics Review

Fill in the blanks to complete the sentences or answer the questions.

1. A patient born with a congenital deformity of the lips can have a surgical correction called a ____________________.
2. Insertion of a needle into the abdominal cavity to remove fluid is called ____________________.
3. A tube placed through the nose into the stomach is called a ____________________.
4. Surgical repair of a hernia is called ____________________.
5. Surgical removal of the gallbladder is called ____________________.
6. Weight-loss surgeries to reduce the capacity of the stomach ____________________.
7. Gastric breath test analysis is used to diagnose what disorder? ____________________.

8. The procedure that uses sterile water or saline instilled into the stomach is called ______________________.

9. The procedure that uses shock waves to crush gallstones is called ______________________.

10. Examination of the bile duct and adjacent structures using a contrast medium in the intrahepatic bile duct is called ______________________.

11. A stool culture is used to diagnose which disorders and its cause? ______________________.

12. Elevated serum bilirubin can be a sign of what disorders? ______________________.

13. Which enzyme that has a very high concentration in liver cells is used to diagnose hepatitis? ______________________.

14. Diagnex blue is used in what type of test? ______________________.

15. The devices that use a strong magnetic field and radiofrequency waves to produce images of organs and tissues are ______________________.

CASE STUDY, completed

Jessica meets with Janelle, the registered dietician, who explains that without a gallbladder, Jessica must be careful to avoid foods that are high-fat, fried, or greasy. The liver still produces bile, the substance needed to digest fat, but it continuously drains directly from the liver to the small intestines. It may be harder and take longer for the fat to be digested. Janelle goes on to explain that the best way to avoid painful symptoms of gas, bloating, and diarrhea is to limit meals to 3 grams or less of fat. Additionally, caffeine and high-sugar foods can cause diarrhea and need to be avoided. Jessica explains that she has lost a lot of weight since her gastric bypass procedure and has been eating small portions and increasing her exercise. Janelle advises her to continue her healthful habits and to report any symptoms of persistent diarrhea, nausea, vomiting, or jaundice.

CRITICAL THINKING QUESTIONS

1. What type of surgeon performed Jessica's gastric bypass? ______________________.
2. Jessica suffered from gallstones, a disorder called: ______________________.
3. Surgical removal of the gallbladder is called: ______________________.
4. The gallbladder removal was conducted through the wall of the abdomen, a surgical approach called: ______________________.
5. Obese patients risk sleep apnea; define the term. ______________________.

CASE STUDY, completed

6. Jessica was admitted npo from midnight on, which means: ______________________.

7. Using an online source, calculate Jessica's BMI after her weight loss: 5 ft 4 in. and 167 lb. ______________________.

8. Poor nutrition can lead to hypercholesterolemia. Break down the term into the elements. ______________________.

9. What digestive enzyme is normally stored in the gallbladder? ______________________.

10. What term means "pertaining to the stomach"? ______________________.

CAREER EXPLORATION: DIETICIAN

After Jessica's gastric bypass surgery and subsequent weight loss, she is inspired to go back to school to become a dietician. She learned so much about eating well for good health that she felt inspired to share her knowledge with others. She enrolled in her local university and learned that there are two distinct educational degrees in the field of nutrition to help different patient populations. RDNs, registered dietician nutritionists, work most often in a hospital setting providing acute care such as parenteral nutrition (tube feeding). Certified nutrition specialists (CNSs) are trained to work in chronic care and private clinical practices such as physician offices and wellness centers. RDNs are trained in conventional medicine, meaning they are trained to follow the US Department of Agriculture guidelines and their training incorporates general recommendations for the population at large. CNSs are trained to work with patients on personalized nutritional plans. While both careers are important, Jessica feels that her personal experiences are best used in a one-on-one consultation with clients. She opts for the CNS certification and earns her master's degree, completes 1,000 hours of supervised clinical training, and completes the Certified Nutrition Specialists test from the Board for Certification of Nutrition Specialists (BCNS). She joins a private practice that specializes in eating disorders in children. Jessica loves her job and helping her clients gain understanding of how food fuels the body. She remains friends with Janelle, the clinical dietician who advised her during her hospital stay and inspired her new career. The two collaborate and have a booth at the annual health fair sponsored by the hospital to share good nutritional practices for people in their community.

Medications for the Digestive System

The medications for the digestive system shown in Table 5-4 include those to alleviate symptoms of abdominal pain, gas, bloating, heartburn, weight gain or loss, nausea, vomiting, diarrhea, or constipation. Various medications work to increase or decrease function by changing muscle tone, changing the rate of food passage through the alimentary canal, or replacing enzymes.

TABLE 5-4 Medications

Therapeutic Classification	Examples	Common Use/Action
Antacids	Magnesium hydroxide, milk of magnesia, calcium carbonate, TUMS, Maalox, Mylanta	Peptic ulcers, GERD, indigestion
Appetite suppressants	Phentermine, Adipex-P, Zantryl	Obesity
Antidiarrheals	Bismuth sulfate, Pepto-Bismol, diphenoxylate with atropine, Lomotil, Kaopectate	Diarrhea
Antiemetics	Chlorpromazine, Thorazine, Compazine, Dramamine, diphenhydramine, Benadryl	Nausea, vomiting, motion sickness prophylaxis
Antiflatulents	Simethicone, Alka-Seltzer, Gas-X, Mylanta Gas	Intestinal gas
Antifungals	Nystatin, Mycostatin	Thrush
anthelmintics	Ivermectin, Vermox	Parasitic infection of the gastrointestinal tract
Antispasmodics	Dicyclomine, Bentyl	IBS, diverticulitis, peptic ulcers
Bowel evacuants	Golightly, GlycoLax	PREP for colonoscopy, surgical procedures
Dopamine antagonists	Domperidone, Motilium, Zofran	To increase gastric motility
Enzyme digestive agents	Lactase, Lactaid, papain, bromelain, lipase	Indigestion due to low or absent digestive enzymes
Gallstone-solubilizing agents	Ursodiol	Gallstones
GI stimulants	Reglan, Propulsid	GERD
H. pylori agents (antibiotic)	Amoxicillin, clarithromycin, Flagyl, tetracycline	Peptic ulcer due to *H. pylori* infection
H2-receptor antagonists	Tagamet, Pepcid, Zantac	Gastric ulcer, duodenal ulcer, GERD
Laxatives/stool softeners	Psyllium, Metamucil, Colace, Dulcolax, MiraLAX	Constipation
Lipase inhibitors	Orlistat, alli, Xenical	Obesity
Prostaglandins	Misoprostol, Cytotec	Gastric or duodenal ulcers
Proton pump inhibitors	Esomeprazole, Nexium, Prevacid, Protonix	Duodenal ulcers, GERD, benign gastric ulcers
Mucosal protectants	Carafate	Ulcers

Medications Review

Using the table of medications, complete the chart below. The first one has been done for you.

Medication Name	Classification (mechanism)	Therapeutic Use (What is it used for?)
Esomeprazole, Nexium	*Proton pump inhibitor*	*Ulcers, GERD*
Bentyl	______________	______________
Orlistat	______________	______________

Medication Name	Classification (mechanism)	Therapeutic Use (What is it used for?)
Thorazine		
Maalox		
Phentermine		
TUMS		
Carafate		
GoLYTELY		
Cytotec		

Digestive System Abbreviations

The list below provides some common abbreviations pertaining to the digestive system and their meanings.

ac	before meals (ante cibum)
ALT	alanine aminotransferase
AST	aspartate aminotransferase (formerly called SGOT, serum glutamic-oxaloacetic transaminase)
Ba	barium
BE	barium enema
bid	twice a day
CT	computed tomography
EGD	esophagogastroduodenoscopy
ERCP	endoscopic retrograde cholangiopancreatography
FBS	fasting blood sugar
GB	gallbladder
GBS	gallbladder series
GEBT	gastric emptying breath test
GERD	gastroesophageal reflux disease
GI	gastrointestinal
GI	gastrointestinal series
GTT	glucose tolerance test
HAV	hepatitis A virus
HBV	hepatitis B virus
HCL	hydrochloric acid
IBS	irritable bowel syndrome
IVC	intravenous cholangiography
LES	lower esophageal sphincter
LFT	liver function test
MRI	magnetic resonance imaging
NVD	nausea, vomiting, diarrhea
NG	nasogastric
npo	nothing by mouth
pc	after meals (post cibum)
pp	postprandial
PPG	postprandial glucose
PTC, PTHC	percutaneous transhepatic cholangiogram
SBO	small bowel obstruction
SBS	small bowel series
SGOT	serum glutamic-oxaloacetic transaminase (now called AST)
SGPT	serum glutamic pyruvic transaminase
TPN	total parenteral nutrition
UGI series	upper gastrointestinal series

Abbreviations Review

Choose the correct definition for the abbreviation:

1. PTCH
   a. percutaneous transhepatic cholangiogram
   b. percutaneous transhepatic colonogram
   c. pericutaneous transhepatic cholangiogram
   d. pericutaneous transhepatic colonogram

2. GTT
   a. glycogen tolerance test
   b. glucose tolerance test
   c. glycogen taste test
   d. glucose taste test

3. SGPT
   a. serum glutamic pyruvic transaminase
   b. serum glucose pyruvic transaminase
   c. serum glycogen pyruvic transaminase
   d. serum galactose pyruvic transaminase

4. BE
   a. bariatric elimination
   b. barium elimination
   c. barium enema
   d. barium expulsion

5. NVD
   a. nausea vomiting defecation
   b. nausea vomiting diarrhea
   c. natural vomiting and diarrhea
   d. no vomiting or diarrhea

6. LES
   a. luminal esophageal stretching
   b. lower esophageal stretching
   c. luminal esophageal sphincter
   d. lower esophageal sphincter

7. TPN
   a. temporary parenteral nutrients
   b. total parenteral nutrients
   c. total parenteral nutrition
   d. temporary parenteral nutrition

8. HCL
   a. hydrochloric acid
   b. hydrogen chlorine liquid
   c. hydrogen containing liquid
   d. hydrochloric liquid

9. GERD
   a. gastroenteric reflux disease
   b. gastroenterocolic reflux disease
   c. gastrointestinal reflux disease
   d. gastroesophageal reflux disease

10. pc
    a. after meals
    b. before meals
    c. with meals
    d. once per day

11. CT
    a. computerized tomography
    b. computed tomography
    c. computational tomography
    d. compared tomography

12. FBS
    a. fecal blood smear
    b. fetal blood scan
    c. fasting blood scan
    d. fasting blood sugar

13. ERCP
    a. endoscopic retrograde cholangiopancreatography
    b. enteroscopic retrograde cholangiopancreatography
    c. enterocolic retrograde cholangiopancreatography
    d. endoscopic retrograde cholangiopancreatography

14. npo
    a. no postoperative care
    b. nothing by mouth
    c. nothing per operation
    d. no preoperative care

15. ALT
    a. alanine aminotransferase
    b. amino alaninotransferase
    c. alanine lipotransferase
    d. amino lipotransferance

MEDICAL DOCUMENTATION

Knowledge of terms related to normal anatomy and pathological conditions enables you to understand medical documentation such as history and physical examinations, operative reports, discharge summaries, laboratory reports, and x-ray reports. Apply your knowledge by answering the questions that follow the report.

Operative Report

Patient name: Jessica W
Date of Birth: 04/14/1997
Patient ID: 9835784
Admitting Physician: Irene Carlisle, MD
Date of admission: September 16, 2023
Preoperative diagnosis: acute cholecystitis
Postoperative diagnosis: acute cholecystitis
Surgeon: William Morgan, MD
Operation: Laparoscopic cholecystectomy
Anesthesia: General endotracheal
Anesthetist: Bethany Chambers, CRNA

Procedure: After informed consent was obtained, the patient was brought to the operating room and placed in the supine position. General endotracheal anesthesia was induced, and the CRNA was present for the entire procedure. The patient was prepped and draped in the usual sterile fashion. A no. 11-blade scalpel was used to make a small infraumbilical skin incision along the midline. The fascia was elevated between Ochsner clamps and incised. A figure-of-eight stitch of 2-0 Vicryl was placed through the edge of the fascia. The 11-mm port was placed into the abdomen, and pneumoperitoneum was established. Upon adequate pneumoperitoneum, the laparoscope was introduced. Three additional ports were placed under direct visualization. An 11-mm port was placed in the epigastric area, two 5-mm ports were placed in the right upper quadrant. The patient was moved to a reverse Trendelenburg position and rotated to the left. The fundus of the gallbladder was retracted superiorly and laterally. The infundibulum was retracted inferiorly and laterally. Electrocautery was used to dissect the peritoneum down around the base of the gallbladder. The triangle of Calot was carefully opened. The cystic duct was identified heading to the base of the gallbladder. The cystic artery was also identified within the triangle of Calot. After the triangle of Calot had been dissected, a clip was placed high up on the cystic duct near the junction with the gallbladder. The cystic artery was clipped twice proximally and once distally. Scissors were then introduced and used to make a small opening in the cystic duct, and the cystic artery was divided.

An intraoperative cholangiogram was obtained and revealed good flow through the cystic duct into the common bile duct and into the duodenum without filling defects. The cholangiocatheter was removed and two clips were placed distal to the ductotomy on the cystic duct. The cystic duct was then divided using scissors. The gallbladder was moved up and away using electrocautery and was removed through the epigastric port. The gallbladder and contents were sent to pathology for analysis. The liver bed was then irrigated and suctioned. All dissection areas were inspected and found to be hemostatic. No bile leakage was observed, and all clips were in place. The right gutter over the edge of the liver was irrigated and suctioned until dry. All ports were removed under direct vision. The abdominal cavity was allowed to deflate. The fascia at the epigastric port site was closed with two 2-0 Vicryl stitches. The fascia at the umbilical port was closed by tying the previously placed stitch. All skin incisions were closed with subcuticular sutures of 4-0 Monocryl. Marcaine (0.25%) with epinephrine was infiltrated to all port sites. Sponge and instrument counts were correct. The patient tolerated the procedure well and transferred to postoperative recovery.

Electronically signed
William Morgan, MD

Continued

MEDICAL DOCUMENTATION—cont'd

Questions

Apply your knowledge by answering the following questions.

1. The cholecystectomy was not an "open" procedure and was done via a ____________________
2. Jessica was moved to a reverse Trendelenburg position, which means ____________________
3. An incision was made in the infraumbilical area. In your own words, where is this? ____________________
4. Dissect and define the term *endotracheal* ____________________
5. In the term *pneumoperitoneum*, what does *pneumo* refer to? ____________________
6. Dissect and define the term *cholecystectomy.* ____________________
7. Dissect and define *electrocautery.* ____________________
8. The gallbladder was grasped and moved in what direction for removal? ____________________
9. The gallbladder was removed through which port? ____________________
10. Dissect and define the term *hemostatic.* ____________________
11. What instrument/procedure is used to see the internal structures of Jessica's anatomy? ____________________

Pathology Report

Specimen(s): gallbladder, gallstones
Preoperative diagnosis: acute cholecystitis
Postoperative diagnosis: acute cholecystitis with perforation and gangrene
Received in formalin in a container labeled gallbladder with stones.
09/16/2023–Jessica W. ID 9835784

Macroscopic description: The specimen consists of a large collapsed gallbladder measuring 14.2 cm in length and between 4.0 and 7.2 cm in fundal diameter. The gallbladder is partially opened and attached to a patent cystic duct. The gallbladder shows an area of perforation through a mottled red-brown-tan dull serous, including the areas of thinning. Four black spherical calculi are present within the lumen and measure from 1.7 to 0.6 cm in diameter. The wall is irregular, hemorrhagic, edematous, and varies up to 0.9 cm in thickness. The mucosa shows a patchy appearance, alternating between red-brown and greenish appearance with obvious areas of purulence. No plaques, polyps, or areas of induration are observed. Representative sections are submitted.

Microscopic description: Sections of the gallbladder show multiple areas of mucosal ulceration and transmural necrosis with marked acute and chronic ulceration. There is also extensive edema in the wall of the gallbladder with fresh hemorrhage. Areas containing intact mucosa show mucous cell metaplasia in the epithelium with patchy inflammatory cell infiltrate. No Rokitansky-Aschoff sinuses are present.

MEDICAL DOCUMENTATION—cont'd

Diagnosis

1. Gallbladder cholecystectomy with acute gangrenous cholecystitis
2. Lithiasis, four stones
3. Mild, chronic cholecystitis

Electronically signed,
Gary Davidson, MD

Questions

Apply your knowledge by answering the following questions:

1. Size and color of the gallbladder are described in what section of a pathology report? ________________
2. What eponym appears in the pathology report? ________________
3. What word is used to describe cellular changes? ________________
4. Is the gallbladder intact? What word describes the condition of the gallbladder? ________________.
5. The gallbladder has areas of dead tissue. This is described in the report as ________________

CHAPTER REVIEW

Complete the Sentence

1. The point where the ascending colon turns left toward the liver is the ________________.
2. The muscular action that moves food down the alimentary canal is called ________________.
3. The second section of the small intestine is called the ________________.
4. Distended, swollen veins in the distal rectum or anus are called ________________.
5. Fungal infection of the mouth and tongue is called ________________.
6. Inflammation of the gums is called ________________.
7. The collection of a stool sample with growth of colonies of microorganisms to identify specific pathogens is a ________________.

8. The most dangerous category of obesity with a BMI of more than 40 is ______________________________.

9. Bowel evacuants, such as GoLYTELY, are used for ______________________________.

10. The process of chewing food is called ______________________________.

11. Swollen, twisted veins of the esophagus are called ______________________________.

12. Telescoping of a portion of the intestines is called ______________________________.

13. Insertion of a needle to remove excess fluid in the abdomen is called ______________________________.

14. Creation of a new opening on the abdominal wall for feces to exit the body is called a ______________________________.

15. Yellow discoloration of the body caused by high levels of bilirubin is called ______________________________.

16. The pancreatic enzyme that is abnormally increased in acute pancreatitis is ______________________________.

17. Surgical correction of a deformity of the lips due to congenital anomaly or injury is called ______________________________.

18. The most severe form of liver disease, causing portal hypertension, is ______________________________.

19. Liver process of converting sugar into a complex form for storage is called ______________________________.

20. An abnormal collection of fluid in the abdominal cavity is called ______________________________.

Spelling

Circle the word that is spelled correctly.

1. ascities	ascites
2. biliruben	bilirubin

3. borborygmus	borborygmys
4. choledocolithiasis	choledocholithiasis
5. cholecystitis	cholocystitis
6. gastroesophageal	gastresophageal
7. gingivitus	gingivitis
8. glucaneogenesis	gluconeogenesis
9. jaundise	jaundice
10. masticration	mastication
11. melena	melana
12. oropharynx	oralpharynx
13. pancreatectosmy	pancreatectomy
14. peritanitis	peritonitis
15. rugae	rugea

Abbreviations

Define the following abbreviations:

1. ac ______________________________
2. Ba ______________________________
3. GI ______________________________
4. HBV ______________________________
5. LFT ______________________________
6. IVC ______________________________
7. MRI ______________________________
8. PPG ______________________________
9. SBS ______________________________
10. UGI ______________________________

Identify the Anatomical Structures

Match the following structures of the gastrointestinal system to the letters shown in Figure 5-16.

1. ______ ascending colon
2. ______ anus
3. ______ appendix
4. ______ cecum
5. ______ descending colon
6. ______ duodenum
7. ______ esophagus
8. ______ gallbladder
9. ______ ileum
10. ______ jejunum
11. ______ liver
12. ______ mouth
13. ______ pancreas
14. ______ parotid gland
15. ______ pharynx
16. ______ rectum
17. ______ sigmoid colon
18. ______ stomach
19. ______ tongue
20. ______ transverse colon

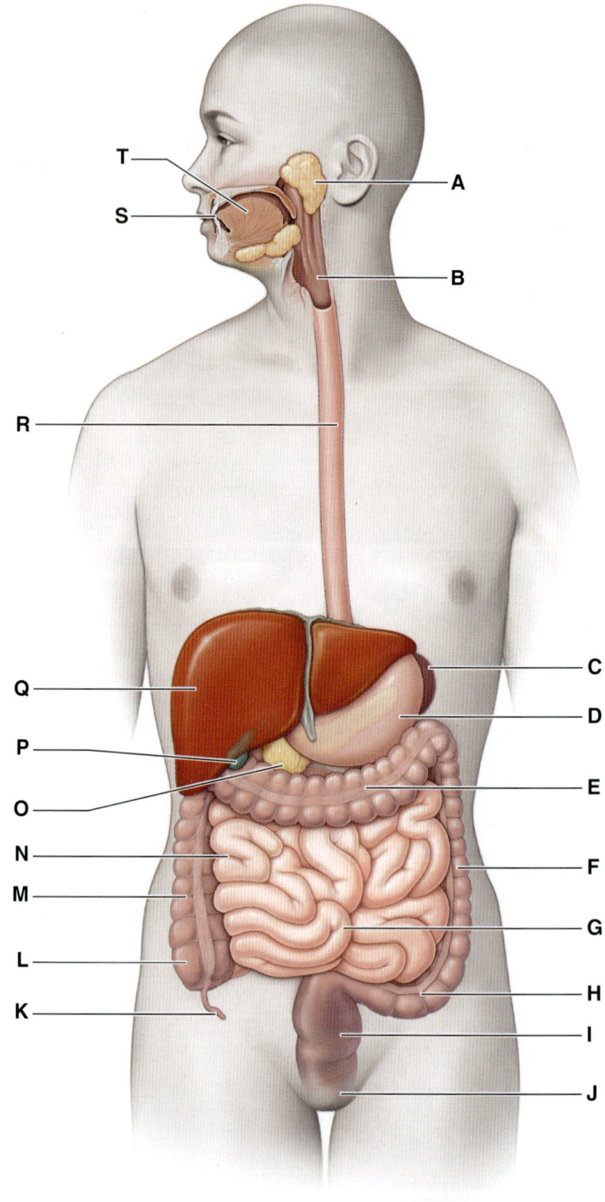

Figure 5-16 Identify the structures of the gastrointestinal system.

Match the following structures of the oral cavity to the letters shown in Figure 5-17.

1. ______ gingiva
2. ______ hard palate
3. ______ incisor
4. ______ lower lip
5. ______ molar
6. ______ papillae
7. ______ soft palate
8. ______ tongue
9. ______ upper lip
10. ______ uvula

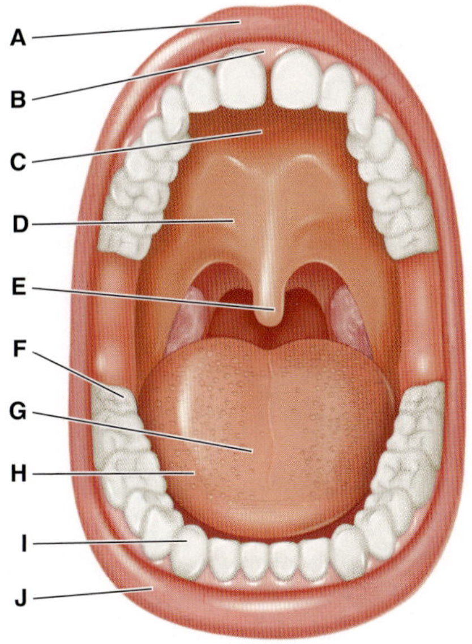

Figure 5-17 Identify the structures of the oral cavity.

Match the following structures of the stomach to the letters shown in Figure 5-18.

1. ______ corpus (body)
2. ______ duodenum
3. ______ esophagus
4. ______ fundus
5. ______ lower esophageal sphincter (LES)
6. ______ muscle layers
7. ______ pyloric canal
8. ______ pyloric sphincter
9. ______ pylorus
10. ______ rugae

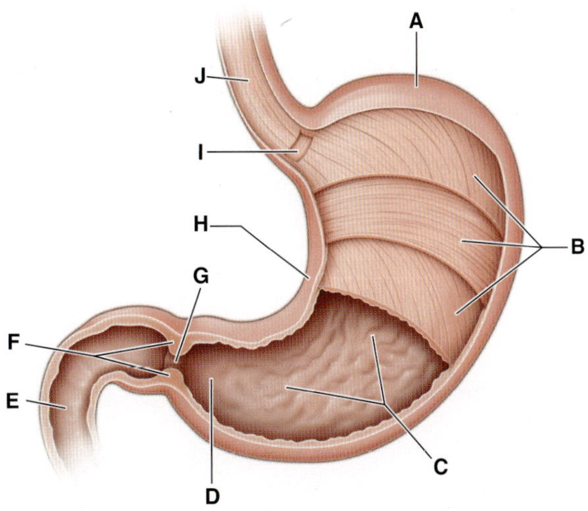

Figure 5-18 Identify the structures of the stomach.

Define the Terms

Identify the words from the following definitions.

1. Inflammation of the gallbladder ______________________.
2. Specialist who diagnoses and treats disorders of the digestive system ______________________.
3. A liver cell ______________________.
4. Condition of dryness of the mouth ______________________.

5. Creation of "new" sugar ______________________.
6. Pertaining to the cheek ______________________.
7. Crushing of a stone ______________________.
8. Bad or difficult digestion ______________________.
9. Surgical removal of one-half of the stomach ______________________.
10. Surgical repair of a hernia ______________________.
11. Passage of watery stool ______________________.
12. Junction of the small and large intestine ______________________.
13. Mixture of food and digestive juices ______________________.
14. Emulsifying agent produced in the liver ______________________.
15. The wormlike structure at the end of the cecum ______________________.

Visit the Medical Language Lab at medicallanguagelab.com. Use it to enhance your word-building skills for the word parts covered in this chapter.

CHAPTER

6

The Respiratory System

LEARNING OBJECTIVES

Upon completion of the chapter, you will be able to:

1. Identify and define the combining forms, roots, prefixes, and suffixes introduced in the chapter.
2. Spell medical terms related to the respiratory system.
3. Describe the major organs of the respiratory system.
4. Describe the difference between internal and external respiration.
5. Describe the pathway of air as it travels from the nasal passages to the capillaries of the lungs.
6. Describe six breath sounds.
7. Identify and discuss major pathological terms of the respiratory system.
8. Identify and discuss major diagnostic and therapeutic treatments of the respiratory system.
9. Identify the major categories of medications used to treat respiratory pathologies.
10. Define abbreviations of the respiratory system.

After reading this chapter, you will have expanded your knowledge of medical terms related to the respiratory system. You will understand how air enters the nose and how oxygen and carbon dioxide are exchanged in the lungs to supply all the cells of the body. You will be able to use the word elements presented to understand unfamiliar terms and to build your medical vocabulary. We begin this chapter with the story of Jennifer, a young woman with a history of asthma who seeks treatment for an acute respiratory infection. Throughout the chapter, we will revisit the story of Jennifer to understand what happens with respiratory infections and how proper diagnosis and medications can improve patient quality of life.

CASE STUDY

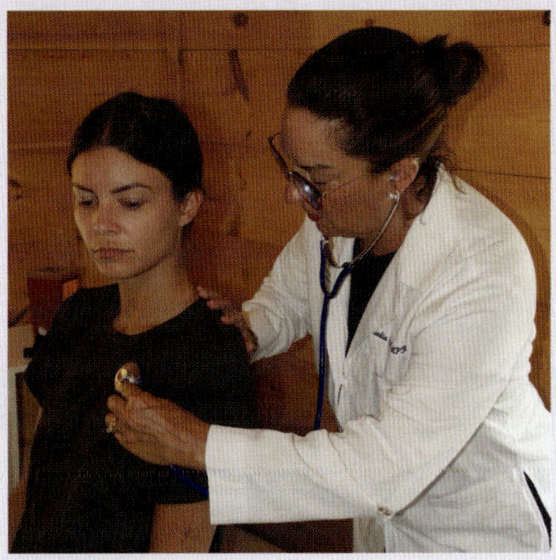

Jennifer has suffered from asthma since she was 9 years old and began playing soccer and softball. At that time, her pediatrician gave her a metered dose inhaler, and the medical assistant taught how to use it when breathing became difficult, especially during sports. Jennifer always kept her albuterol inhaler with her. Albuterol, a medication known as a bronchodilator, helps her exchange oxygen and carbon dioxide in the lungs.

During her childhood, Jennifer's parents made sure she ate a healthy diet and got plenty of rest. Now a college student, she tries to maintain the healthy habits she was taught, but right before final exams, she develops what felt like bronchitis,

Continued

CASE STUDY, continued

a tightness in her chest and some fatigue. She has been studying, working part-time, and not eating well or getting enough sleep, but she thought she could get through final exams. Jennifer tries to manage her symptoms with her albuterol inhaler, some decongestants, and extra sleep. She gets progressively worse, and her roommate, Laura, is concerned that Jennifer's breathing is labored, she isn't hungry, and she looks very pale. Laura takes Jennifer's temperature, and it is 101.3°F. Laura is a nursing student and knew that she needed to get Jennifer to the campus infirmary.

At the infirmary, the nurse practitioner, Kristen, listens to Jennifer's lungs and hears wheezing, a whistling sound of air getting in and out of inflamed airways. Jennifer complains of fatigue and headache, and she is coughing up thick, yellow mucus. She says that sometimes the coughing is so violent that it causes sharp chest pain and that last night she experienced chills. She states, "I just couldn't get warm, I was shaking." Kristen explains that she can hear how difficult it is for Jennifer to get air in and out of the alveoli, the tiny air sacs in the lungs where gases are exchanged. Kristen orders a chest x-ray, which shows some fluid and inflammation in her lungs, consistent with the wheezing she heard with the stethoscope. Kristen then orders a sputum culture. The sputum culture shows Streptococcus pneumoniae, the most common form of bacteria that causes pneumonia. Kristen explains to Jennifer that bacterial pneumonia often occurs after a viral infection, such as the flu, or for people with chronic respiratory disease, such as asthma. Jennifer mentions that a week ago Laura was sick with a sinus infection, and that's when Jennifer also started to feel tired and headachy. Kristen goes on to explain that the S. pneumoniae germ normally lives in our upper respiratory tract, but it can reach the lower respiratory tract. If it does, it can cause pneumonia in times of stress, such as during final exams. In fact, it infects up to 900,000 Americans each year.

Because Jennifer's pneumonia is caused by a bacterial infection, Kristen prescribes ciprofloxacin, an antibiotic, at 500 mg twice per day. She also prescribes prednisone, an oral corticosteroid to help reduce lung inflammation and aid Jennifer's breathing. She advises Jennifer to rest, drink plenty of fluids, and come back to the infirmary the next week to see how she is doing. Kristen asks Laura to call the infirmary or dial 911 if Jennifer does not respond to the antibiotics and steroids. Jennifer may need hospitalization, where intravenous antibiotics and supplemental oxygen may be required. This scares both Jennifer and Laura, but they agree and thank Kristen.

A week later, Jennifer returns to the clinic where she tells Kristen, "Thank you so much! I feel so much better. The fever and chills are gone, I am breathing easier and got a good night's sleep for the past few days. Laura took great care of me, and she is taking her finals today. I was able to ask my professors for an extension, so I am taking finals next Monday." Kristen listens to Jennifer's breathing, and the wheezing has subsided. She also notices Jennifer is no longer pale. Kristen tells Jennifer, "Your lungs sound good, but please do not ignore symptoms in the future. If you had come in sooner, I would have been treating your bronchitis, not pneumonia." Jennifer replies "Yes, I learned my lesson, I can't put off getting care if my symptoms progress." Kristen says, "Good luck on your final exams and stay healthy."

KEY TERMS

Adenoids	Bronchi	Cellular respiration	Epiglottis
Alveoli	Bronchial tree	Cilia	External respiration
Aspiration	Bronchioles	Diaphragm	Exhalation

KEY TERMS—cont'd

Expiration	Larynx	Respiratory center	Trachea
Glottis	Lung	Respiratory rate	Ventilation
Goblet cells	Nostrils	Septum	Vital signs
Inhalation	Pharynx	Spirometer	Vocal cords
Internal respiration	Pleura	Tonsils	
Inspiration	Respiration	Total lung capacity	

Structures and Physiology

The respiratory system consists of a series of tubes or airways that move gases in and out of the capillaries of the lungs (Fig. 6-1). The respiratory system is divided into the upper and lower airways. The upper airway consists of the mouth, nose, sinuses, and pharynx. The lower airway consists of the trachea, lungs, bronchus, and alveoli. Additionally, the diaphragm provides the spontaneous muscular action that supports the continuous work of the respiratory system.

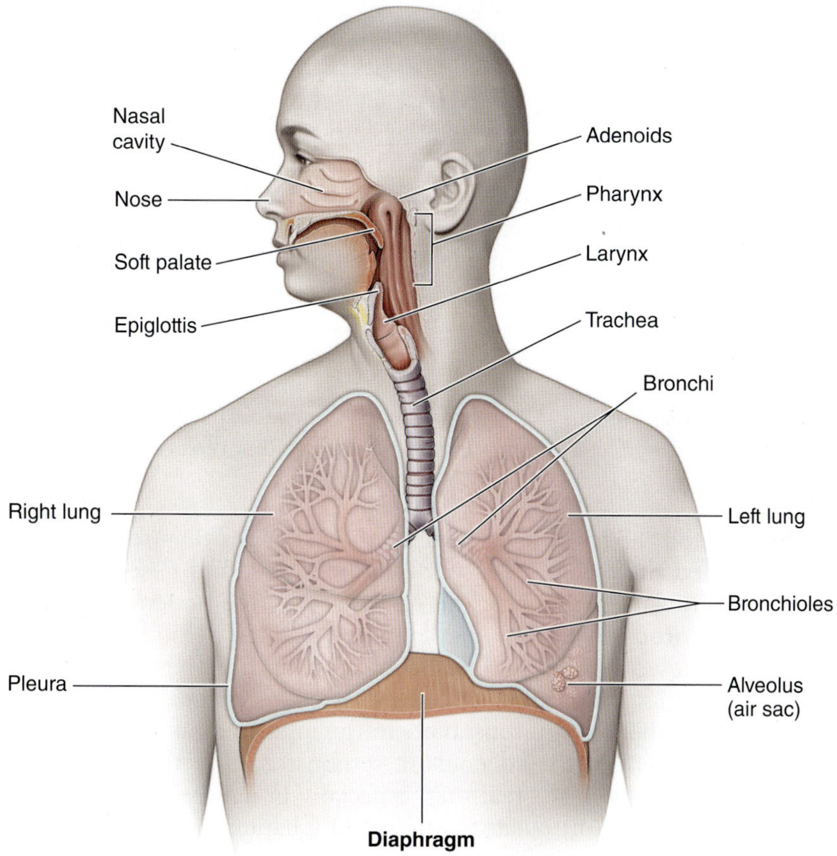

Figure 6-1 The respiratory system.

The respiratory system organs are responsible for important functions:

- Distribution of oxygen to all the cells of the body
- Removal of carbon dioxide from the cells
- Regulation of acid-base (pH) levels in the bloodstream by continually adjusting the CO_2 level
- Protection of the body by filtering out airborne pathogens and pollutants
- Contribution to the production of sound via the vocal cords

Respiration

The spontaneous exchange of gases between the air and the body is a process known as **respiration.** In concert with the cardiovascular system, oxygen-rich blood is delivered to the tissues where it can be used by cells for metabolic processes that are necessary to sustain life. Additionally, carbon dioxide is removed from the cells and released into the lungs to be exhaled.

Oxygen inhaled circulates to the bloodstream via capillaries in the lungs. Oxygen is distributed to cells of the body; carbon dioxide is removed from the cells and moved into the bloodstream. This exchange of gases within the body is known as **internal respiration**, also known as **cellular respiration.** Once carbon dioxide has been removed from the cells and enters the bloodstream, it is transported back to the lungs, then leaves the body in our exhale. When we inhale, we take in oxygen from the environment. This exchange of gases from the environment into the body is called **external respiration**, also known as **ventilation.**

Air enters the body via the nose and mouth. The nose is comprised of bone and cartilage covered with skin. The **nostrils** (also called nares) are the opening of the nose, and they are lined with hair to trap debris before it can enter the deeper structures of the respiratory tract. As air enters the nose, it passes into the nasal cavity, which is divided into a right and left side by a **septum**, a wall of bony tissue that gives structure to the nose. Once air enters the nasal cavity, it passes through the paranasal sinuses, which are cavities within the skull that respond to pressure differences between the skull and the environment. The interior of the nose and the sinuses are lined with hairlike projections, called **cilia**, that trap foreign material such as dirt and dust toward the throat for elimination in a cough. The sinuses are hollow, which lightens the head and enhances the sound of the voice. Sinuses expand when the atmospheric pressure is low, such as when it is raining or very muggy. We may feel this expansion and pressure as a sinus headache.

PHYSIOLOGY FACT

If we have a stuffy nose, we can still breathe through our mouths. This redundancy ensures that respiration, a vital process for life, continues uninterrupted.

ELEMENT REVIEW
nas/o = nose
-pharynx = pharynx
laryng/o = larynx
or/o = mouth

Air that has entered the nasal cavity and paranasal sinuses then reaches the **pharynx**, the airway (also called the throat) that connects the mouth and nose to the larynx. The pharynx is divided into three sections: the nasopharynx, the uppermost section located behind the nose; the oropharynx, the middle section located behind the mouth; and the laryngopharynx, the lower section located behind the larynx. The nasopharynx contains two masses of lymphatic tissue called the **adenoids** or pharyngeal tonsils. The adenoids filter out bacteria and other foreign substances in the inhaled air as they pass through the nasopharynx. Enlargement of the adenoids in response to infection or a large quantity of dust or debris can compromise breathing, especially in children. The palatine **tonsils**, located on either side of the soft palate, as shown in Chapter 5, are also lymphatic tissue that filters pathogens. The pharynx serves not only as the passageway for air to the lungs but also for food and liquids to enter the digestive system. A small tongue-shaped flap of cartilage called the **epiglottis** is located at the distal end of the pharynx and covers the **glottis**, the opening of the larynx. During swallowing, the epiglottis moves downward as the larynx moves upward to seal off the larynx. This directs food and liquid into the esophagus, which lies posterior to the trachea, thus preventing **aspiration**, food or liquids entering the lower respiratory tract.

PHYSIOLOGY FACT

The epiglottis acts as the traffic cop directing air to the respiratory system and food to the digestive system.

Air now enters the **larynx**, also called the voice box (see Fig. 6-1). Two long, parallel folds of tissue called the **vocal cords** stretch across the upper larynx. When air rushes between the vocal cords during exhalation, the vocal cords vibrate. The vibration generates sound waves that can be converted to speech when the muscles of the pharynx, jaw, and tongue work together to produce specific sounds. When we sleep, this vibration may cause snoring. The pitch of the voice is determined by the size and structure of the vocal cords. The larynx averages 4 to 5 cm long in adults; males have a slightly larger voice box compared to females, accounting for a deeper voice.

The larynx connects the pharynx to the **trachea**, also called the windpipe. The trachea is approximately 12 cm long and 2.5 cm wide and consists of a muscular tube embedded with 16 to 20 rings of cartilage. The cartilage rings are rigid and keep the trachea open to allow a continuous, uninterrupted flow of air. The inner wall of the trachea is composed of a mucous membrane lining embedded with tiny, hairlike projections called **cilia**. The trachea contains many **goblet cells**, which secrete mucus. The cilia trap debris in the mucus and moves it back up toward the pharynx for removal. Once the mucus reaches the pharynx, it is either swallowed or expelled as sputum.

PHYSIOLOGY FACT

Vocal cords are not covered in cilia, and they can accumulate mucus. To remove mucus, we may cough to clear the throat.

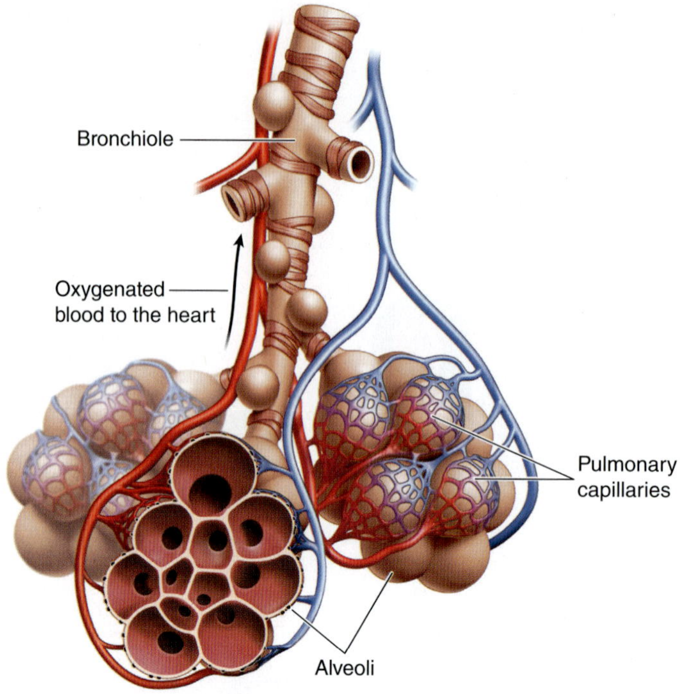

Figure 6-2 The alveoli and capillaries.

The trachea divides into two branches called the right and left primary **bronchi**. Each primary bronchus (singular) leads to the lung on the right or the left. The bronchi are also constructed of consecutive cartilage rings that hold each bronchus open for the passage of air. The primary bronchi extend a short distance before they branch into secondary and tertiary bronchi. This branching is called the **bronchial tree**. It further divides and subdivides into smaller tubes called **bronchioles**. The bronchioles end at grapelike clusters called **alveoli** (Fig. 6-2). The alveoli are sacs of air that have extremely thin walls, allowing gases to filter to the blood capillaries that surround each alveolus (singular). Each lung contains approximately 300 million microscopic alveoli covered by an expansive capillary bed with a rich blood supply. As air enters the alveoli, they expand and fill with air. They then contract and partially deflate as air is absorbed into each adjacent capillary. The blood becomes oxygenated and is ready to be pumped to the heart for systemic distribution. The alveoli take up carbon dioxide from the capillaries, and it is pushed to the bronchioles to the bronchus to the trachea to the larynx to the pharynx to the mouth and nose, and out of the body.

ELEMENT REVIEW
alveol/o = alveoli
-ar = pertaining to

PHYSIOLOGY FACT

The larynx contains many different areas of cartilage. The largest is called the thyroid cartilage. As the larynx grows during puberty, the thyroid cartilage needs room to expand and grow so it pushes anteriorly (forward). In males we see the prominent bump called the Adam's Apple. The voice is also changing during this time causing a squeaky sound. It is temporary, but often embarrassing for young men.

The **lungs** are two spongy organs that lie lateral to the mediastinum and contain the alveoli and capillaries where the work of internal respiration is done. The uppermost portion of the lung is called the apex, and the lowest part is called the base, which rests on the diaphragm. The portion of the lung near the midline where blood vessels, nerves, and the bronchial tubes enter and exit is called the hilum. The left lung has an indentation anterior to the hilum called the cardiac depression where the heart resides, making the left lung smaller than the right.

The lungs are divided into lobes, three on the right lung and two on the left lung. In adults, the right lung weighs approximately 630 grams and the left weighs 570 grams. The lungs are covered in a bilayer membrane called the **pleura**. The visceral pleura lies directly on the outside membrane of each lung, and the parietal pleura lines the inner wall of the thoracic space. The term *interpleural* refers to the space between the two layers and contains a small amount of fluid called pleural fluid. This fluid space allows for the lungs to smoothly expand and contract in response to the air being pushed in or out of the lungs. The lungs are not a muscle and therefore do not expand and contract on their own. The lungs are inflated and compressed by the chief muscle of respiration, the **diaphragm**. The diaphragm is a thin dome-shaped muscle that lies below the two lungs and separates the lungs from the abdominal cavity. When we inhale, the diaphragm moves down to increase the size of the thoracic cavity and allow the lungs to fill with air. The quantity of air a person can inhale is called **total lung capacity**. On average, adults can hold 6000 mL of air. When we exhale, the diaphragm moves up, decreasing the size of the thoracic cavity, thus pushing air out of the lungs. The air then moves to the trachea, along the respiratory tract, and eventually out the nose.

ELEMENT REVIEW
inter- = between
pleur/o = pleura
cost/o = ribs
-al = pertaining to

The diaphragm also functions to increase pressure in the abdominal cavity, which aids in urination, defecation, and vomiting.

The Cycle of Respiration

The diaphragm is directed by the **respiratory center**, a group of neurons located in the brainstem. It is governed by the autonomic nervous system; thus, we breathe continuously and spontaneously. The respiratory cycle starts when the phrenic nerve stimulates the diaphragm to contract, moving downward and expanding the thoracic cavity. This creates a negative pressure in the thorax and causes air to move into the lungs; this is called **inhalation** or **inspiration**.

The neurons of the respiratory center produce rhythmic impulses and send them to the diaphragm and external costal muscles to stimulate the muscles to contract. After 1 to 3 seconds of activity, the neurons stop abruptly. When the diaphragm relaxes, it rises up into the thoracic cavity, increasing pressure within the thorax and causing the air to be forced out of the lungs. This process is called **exhalation** or **expiration**. There is no input from the respiratory center signaling the diaphragm and external costal muscles to relax, thus exhaling is a passive activity. The intercostal muscles that lie between the ribs assist the diaphragm in changing the volume of the thoracic cavity by elevating and lowering the rib cage.

Many pathologies of the respiratory system will cause effective exhaling to become effortful.

Respiratory Volume

Many factors influence the quantity of air moving in and out of our lungs. Activities that require more oxygen to tissues such as exercise increase the volume of air in and out of the lungs. Conversely, sleep or just sitting and reading requires less oxygen. The respiratory system adapts to the changing need for oxygen by changing both the volume of air and the **respiratory rate**, how many breaths per minute we exchange. Respiratory volume can be measured by a spirometer. During the test, a patient breathes through a mouthpiece into the instrument that records the volume of air inhaled and exhaled. It is a useful test to evaluate baseline normal respiratory quantities and to quantify loss of respiratory function in a variety of respiratory diseases. Table 6-1 shows average respiratory volumes.

TABLE 6-1 Average Respiratory Volumes

Type	Abbreviation	Definition	Average Normal Volume
Tidal volume	TV	Amount of air moving in and out of the lungs during restful breathing	500 mL
Inspiratory reserve volume	IRV	Maximum quantity of air that can be inhaled forcibly over the tidal volume	3,100 mL
Expiratory reserve volume	ERV	Maximum quantity of air that can be exhaled forcibly over the tidal volume	1,200 mL
Residual volume	RV	Amount of air remaining in the lungs after forced expiration	1,200 mL
Vital capacity	VC	Total quantity of exchangeable air, determined by the formula VC = TV + IRV + ERV	4,800 mL
Total lung capacity	TLC	Total quantity of air contained in the fully inflated respiratory system, determined by the formula TLC = VC + RV	6,000 mL

PHYSIOLOGY FACT

The process of respiration is governed by the autonomic nervous system and happens without thinking about it. However, unlike many autonomic body functions such as digestion or release of hormones, we sometimes exert conscious control over our breathing. We can take intentionally large breaths, or we can hold our breath for short periods of time (think about when you dive into water). After holding your breath for an extended time, the overwhelming urge to breathe causes you to resume breathing. This urge is caused by a buildup of carbon dioxide (CO_2) in the bloodstream making the blood more acidic. The pH of blood must remain slightly alkaline between 7.35 to 7.45 on the pH scale. When blood becomes more acidic (less than 7.35 on the pH scale), the urge to breathe is triggered. Inhaling oxygen-rich air brings oxygen into the bloodstream and exhaling allows CO_2 to be eliminated in the exhaled air. Thus, the drive to breathe is triggered by CO_2 build up and a low pH. If you hold your breath for long enough, you will pass out and then begin to breathe again spontaneously. You may also develop a headache from hypercapnia and hypoxemia.

ELEMENT REVIEW
hyper- = excessive, above
-capnia = condition of carbon dioxide
hypo- = under, below
-oxia = condition of oxygenation

The Respiratory Rate

The rate of respiration is one of the **vital signs** (temperature, pulse, respirations), and is measured by a medical assistant or nurse during a routine physical. Establishing a baseline of vital signs (temp/pulse/resp when the patient is feeling well), allows the practitioner to use that information when a patient is sick. For example, some people have a higher or lower body temperature when he/she is feeling well. The degree of deviation away from the baseline values can be used to quantify how sick the patient is.

Because basal respiration rates can increase when there is an increased need for oxygen, or to counter buildup of carbon dioxide, the respiratory rate is an important vital sign to monitor. Alteration to lung functions such as pneumonia, upper respiratory tract infections, bronchitis, asthma, or chronic obstructive pulmonary disease (COPD) all cause impaired gas exchange in the lungs. This impairment of lungs will cause acidosis (low blood pH) and hypercapnia (increased blood CO_2), which increases the respiratory rate controlled

TABLE 6-2 Normal Respiratory Values

Age of Patient (Year)	Respiratory Range (Breaths Per Minute)
Premature infant	40–90
Newborn	30–60
Year 1	20–40
Year 2	20–30
Year 5	20–25
Year 15	15–20
Adult	8–20

by the respiratory control center in the brain. Additionally, sympathetic stress leads to an increased respiratory rate. When we are frightened or anxious, we may hyperventilate (an increasing rate and depth of breathing). Measuring the respiratory rate is just the first step in diagnosing an illness. Normal respiratory rates are shown in Table 6-2. Infants and children have faster normal respiratory rates because their lung volumes are lower compared to body mass than adults. Additionally, infants and children metabolize nutrients at a higher rate than adults due to growth and development. They need more oxygen, and thus need to eliminate more carbon dioxide than adults to support their growing bodies.

Structures and Physiology Review

Match the words to their descriptions.

adenoids	epiglottis	paranasal sinuses
alveoli	external respiration	pharynx
bronchi	glottis	pleura
bronchial tree	goblet cells	respiration
bronchioles	internal respiration	septum
bronchus	larynx	sputum
cilia	nostrils	total lung capacity
diaphragm	palatine tonsils	trachea

1. Also called the voice box ______________________
2. Bony partition that divides the nose right and left ______________________
3. Also called the windpipe ______________________
4. Exchange of gases within the body ______________________
5. Mucus producing cells that line the trachea ______________________
6. Quantity of air that can be forced into the lungs by inhalation ______________________

7. Cavities in the skull that respond to changes in pressure ____________________

8. Hairlike projections on mucus membranes that sweep away dirt ____________________

9. Small tongue-like flap that acts as a "traffic cop" for air and food ____________________

10. Also called the throat ____________________

11. Expelled mucus ____________________

12. Microscopic air sacs within the lungs ____________________

13. Structures that branch from the trachea and enter the lungs at the hilum ____________________

14. The chief muscle of respiration ____________________

15. Lymphatic tissue located in the nasopharynx ____________________

16. Entrance of the nose ____________________

17. Exchange of gases between the lungs and the environment ____________________

18. The opening of the larynx ____________________

19. The branching divisions of the bronchi ____________________

20. Lymphatic tissue located on either side of the soft palate ____________________

Structures and Physiology Word-Building Practice

1. Nouns and Adjectives

Complete the chart of nouns and their adjective forms.

Noun Form	Adjective Form
alveoli	________________
apnea	________________
________________	bronchial
epiglottis	________________
________________	hypoxic
________________	laryngeal
pleura	________________
trachea	________________
diaphragm	________________
________________	nasal

2. Singular and Plural Forms

Complete the chart of singular and plural forms.

________________	alveoli
________________	bronchi
bronchiole	________________
lobe	________________
________________	capillaries

Word Building With Combining, Prefix, and Suffix Forms

The following word roots, prefixes, and suffixes are commonly used in medical terms for the anatomy and pathology of the respiratory system. Combining vowels for word roots are included. Memorizing these elements will help you understand new terms that you may encounter as a respiratory therapist or as another health-care professional.

The list contains examples of terms that utilize the combining forms and a pronunciation guide. Be sure to use the pronunciation guide so that you can learn to say the terms correctly.

The Medical Language Lab at medicallanguagelab.com provides audio files to help you practice your pronunciations.

Root Form	Meaning	Example (Pronunciation)	Definition
adenoid/o	adenoids	adenoidectomy (ăd-ĕ-noyd-ĔK-tō-mē)	surgical removal of the adenoids
alveol/o	alveolus	alveolar (ăl-VĒ-ō-lăr)	pertaining to the alveoli
anthrac/o	black, coal	anthracosis (ăn-thră-KŌ-sĭs)	black lung disease
atel/o	incomplete	atelectasis (ăt-ĕ-LĔK-tă-sĭs)	incomplete expansion of lungs
bronch/i, bronch/o	bronchus	bronchial (BRŎNG-kē-ăl)	pertaining to the bronchus
coni/o	dust	pneumoconiosis (nū-mō-kō-nē-Ō-sĭs)	disease of lungs caused by dust
laryng/o	larynx (voice box)	laryngitis (lăr-ĭn-JĪ-tĭs)	inflammation of the larynx
lob/o	lobe	lobectomy (lō-BĔK-tō-mē)	surgical excision of a lobe of the lung
nas/o	nose	nasal (NA-zăl)	pertaining to the nose
ortho/o	straight	orthopnea (or-THŎP-nē-ă)	"straight" breathing, sitting up

Continued

Root Form	Meaning	Example (Pronunciation)	Definition
ox/o	oxygen	hypoxic (hī-PŎK-sik)	pertaining to low oxygenation
pector/o	chest	pectoral (PĔK-tō-răl)	pertaining to the chest
pharyng/o	pharynx, throat	pharynoscope (făr-ĬN-gō-skōp)	instrument to view the throat
phren/o	diaphragm, mind	phrenic (FREN-ik)	pertaining to the diaphragm
pleur/o	pleura	pleurodesis (ploo-rŏ-DĒ-sĭs)	adhesions in the pleura
pneum/o, pneumon/o	air, lung	pneumonectomy (noo-MŌ-NEK-tŏ-mē)	surgical excision of a lung
pulmon/o	lung	pulmonary (PŬL-mō-nĕ-rē)	pertaining to the lungs
rhin/o	nose	rhinoplasty (RĪ-nō-plăs-tē)	surgical correction of the nose
spir/o	to breathe	spirometry (spī-RŎM-ĕ-trē)	process of measuring breathing
steth/o	chest	stethoscope (STĔTH-ō-skōp)	instrument to listen to the chest sounds
thorac/o	chest	thoracocentesis (thō-ră-cō-sĕn-TĒ-sĭs)	puncture and aspirate the chest
trache/o	trachea	tracheotomy (TRĀ-kē-ō-tō-mē)	incision into the trachea
tonsill/o	tonsils	tonsillitis (TON-sĭl-ī-tĭs)	inflammation of the tonsils

ā = say, ă = sofa, ē = meet, ĕ = met, ī = eye, ĭ = in, ō = oh, ŏ = dog, ū = you, ŭ = up, oo = food

Suffix	Meaning	Example (Pronunciation)	Definition
-capnia	carbon dioxide	hypercapnia (hī-pĕr-KĂP-nē-ă)	excessive carbon dioxide (in the blood)
-ectasis	expansion	bronchiectasis (brŏng-kē-ĔK-tă-sĭs)	expansion, dilation of the bronchioles
-osmia	smell	anosmia (a-NOZ-mē-ă)	lack of sense of smell
-ostomy	new opening	tracheostomy (trā-kē-ŎStō-mē)	creation of a new opening in the trachea
-phonia	voice	dysphonia (dis-FŌ-nē-ă)	difficulty speaking or producing sound
-pnea	to breathe	apnea (ăp-NĒ-ă)	inability to breathe, cessation of breathing

Suffix	Meaning	Example (Pronunciation)	Definition
-ptysis	spitting	hemoptysis (hē-MŎP-tĭ-sĭs)	spitting up blood
-rrhea	copious discharge	rhinorrhea (rī-nŏ-RĒ-ă)	a runny nose
-thorax	chest	pneumothorax (nū-mō-THŌ-răks)	air in the chest cavity (outside of the lung)

ā = say, ă = sofa, ē = meet, ĕ = met, ī = eye, ĭ = in, ō = oh, ŏ = dog, ū = you, ŭ = up, oo = food

Prefix	Meaning	Example (Pronunciation)	Definition
a-, an-	without	apnea (ăp-NĒ-ă)	cessation of breathing
brady-	slow	bradypnea (brăd-ĭp-NĒ-ă)	abnormally slowed breathing
eu-	normal, good	eupnea (ūp-NĒ-ă)	normal breathing
inter-	between	intercostal (int-ĕr-KOS-tăl)	between the rib
tachy-	fast, rapid	tachypnea (tak-ē-NĒ-ă)	abnormally fast breathing

ā = say, ă = sofa, ē = meet, ĕ = met, ī = eye, ĭ = in, ō = oh, ŏ = dog, ū = you, ŭ = up, oo = food

Combining Forms Practice

1. Build the Terms

*Using **only** the word elements in the lists, build words for the definitions.*

Prefixes	Combining Forms		Suffixes	
a-, an-	adenoid/o	pharyng/o	-al	-meter
brady-	alveol/o	phren/o	-ar	-metry
eu-	atel/o	pneum/o	-ary	-osis
hyper-	bronch/i	pneumon/o	-capnia	-osmia
hypo-	bronch/o	pulmon/o	-centesis	-pnea
inter-	coni/o	rhin/o	-eal	-ptysis
tachy-	laryng/o	spir/o	-ectasis	-phonia
	nas/o	thorac/o	-ectomy	-rrhea
	ortho/o	tonsill/o	-ia	-thorax
	ox/o	trache/o	-itis	-tomy

1. Instrument to measure oxygen ____________________
2. Deficiency of oxygen (in the blood) ____________________

3. Pertaining to the lungs ______
4. Excessive breathing ______
5. Inflammation of the tonsils ______
6. Process of measuring breathing ______
7. Normal amount of carbon dioxide (in the blood) ______
8. Inflammation of nasal passages ______
9. Pertaining to the larynx ______
10. Any condition caused by inhalation of dust ______
11. Incision into the trachea ______
12. Pertaining to the throat ______
13. Pertaining to between the alveoli ______
14. "Straight" breathing ______
15. Slowed breathing ______

2. Define the Terms

1. interlobitis ______
2. bronchopulmonary ______
3. phrenectomy ______
4. pharyngitis ______
5. pectoral ______
6. tachypnea ______
7. alveolar ______
8. thoracocentesis ______
9. tracheobronchial ______
10. aphonia ______

CASE STUDY, continued

Let's check in on Jennifer 10 years later and see how she is doing. After graduating from college, Jennifer started her career, got married, and had two children. Her asthma symptoms are manageable. She sometimes uses her albuterol inhaler at the gym, but she hasn't had pneumonia since that horrible episode in college. When the COVID-19 pandemic caused Jennifer's employer to close, she lost her job, and her children could no longer attend daycare. Fortunately, her husband is now able to work from home. The family has settled into their new routine, and Jennifer and her husband, Jim, make sure to get the kids outside for fresh air and exercise.

Now that Jennifer and Jim are double vaccinated and received their booster shots, they start socializing with friends again. The day after they go to a Memorial Day picnic, Jennifer wakes up with a horrible headache, muscle aches, and fatigue. She suspects that she may have been infected with COVID-19. She read on the CDC.gov website that while vaccines are effective in preventing infection, serious illness, and death, they are not 100% effective. Vaccinated people can still get COVID-19. She makes an appointment and goes to a pharmacy that offers a drive-up COVID test. Jennifer gets her results within 24 hours; she tests positive for COVID-19. Jennifer calls her primary care provider and schedules a telemedicine visit. Telemedicine visits have become a way for patients to be seen by a provider but not spread communicable infections such as COVID-19. Because the patient stays home and attends the visit on a secure platform, the provider and the patient can see and hear each other without physical contact.

The medical assistant speaks with Jennifer, schedules the visit, and explains to Jennifer that she will receive an email link to the visit. She will log on and wait for the provider to start the visit. Jennifer follows the instructions and meets with Dr. Wilson. Jennifer explains to Dr. Wilson that she has a history of asthma controlled with albuterol sulfate inhaler and had pneumonia 10 years ago as a college student. Dr. Wilson asks Jennifer about her symptoms. Jennifer explains that she woke up yesterday with a horrible headache, muscle aches, some mild trouble breathing, and her sense of smell is diminished. She is concerned that she will transmit COVID-19 to her children as they are too young to be vaccinated. Dr. Wilson explains that while she can transmit the virus to her children, transmission is less likely because she is fully vaccinated. Also, her symptoms will probably not be severe. The doctor states, "When a fully vaccinated person gets the virus, we call it a breakthrough infection. But even when fully vaccinated people develop symptoms, they tend to be less severe than for unvaccinated people, and they are much less likely to die from COVID-19."

Dr. Wilson prescribes Paxlovid, a combination of two antiviral drugs (nirmatrelvir and ritonavir) approved to treat COVID-19. Additionally, Dr. Wilson advises Jennifer to quarantine from her husband and children for the next 10 days. He advises her to rest and use her albuterol inhaler if needed for breathing. She should respond to the antiviral prescription, and her symptoms should decrease soon. He asks Jennifer to schedule a follow-up telemedicine visit in 2 weeks or sooner if her symptoms do not resolve.

Respiratory System Diseases and Disorders

Normal respiration produces **vesicular breath sounds**. The sounds heard are low pitched as the air flows easily through the open airways. The provider will use an instrument called a **stethoscope** to listen to the sounds of respiration.

Common Signs and Symptoms

Abnormalities in the sounds, along with other signs and symptoms, are indicative of respiratory or cardiac illness and are described in Table 6-3 and Table 6-4.

TABLE 6-3 Abnormal Breath Sounds

Sound	Description
Cheyne-Stokes respirations	Fluctuations in the depth of respirations. The patient breathes deeply for a short period of time, then slightly, then not at all. The breathing pattern is indicative of heart failure or brain damage.
Crackle/rale	Intermittent sounds caused by spasms, hyperplasia, exudates, or when air enters moisture-filled alveoli.
Diminished breath sounds	Lack of sounds while listening with a stethoscope due to decreased air movement.
Rhonchi	Continuous sounds of air moving during both inspiration and expiration in the larger airways. The sound resembles snoring.
Stridor	High-pitched, harsh sound caused by swelling or obstruction in the upper airway. Stridor may be life-threatening and requires immediate intervention.
Rub (pleural friction rub)	A loud, grating sound heard over the lungs due to inflammation of the pleura.
Wheeze	Whistling sound caused by narrowing of the lumen of the respiratory passages. Heard in asthma, croup, hay fever, emphysema, and COPD.

TABLE 6-4 Common Signs and Symptoms

Common Signs	Common Symptoms
Abnormal breath sounds; also called adventitious sounds.	Chest pain (thoracodynia) (patient reports tightness and pain in the chest)
Bradypnea (abnormally slowed respirations of less than 12 rpm)	Exercise intolerance (patient reports inability to breathe with exertion)
Cough (may be dry or productive)	Shortness of breath (patient reports effortful ventilation)
Types of sputum in productive coughs	Orthopnea (patient reports inability to breathe lying supine)
-mucoid (resembling mucus)	
-mucopurulent (containing mucus and pus)	
-purulent (containing pus)	
-serous (resembling serum, a clear watery fluid that is less viscous than other types of sputum)	
Cyanosis (blue appearance to the skin, nailbeds, lips)	
Erythema (redness of the skin, can be related to respiratory distress)	
Fever (elevated body temperature)	
Tachypnea (abnormally fast breathing of more than 39 rpm)	

PHYSIOLOGY FACT

Patients with COPD may present as blue (cyanosis) or pink (erythema) based on the underlying cause of the COPD. If COPD is due to chronic bronchitis, this leads to an increase in lung volume from overexertion in breathing. Typically, the patients have a chronic cough and may be overweight or obese. The patient cannot effectively exchange O_2 and CO_2, giving the skin a blueish tint. If COPD is due to emphysema, the most common cause is smoking. Patients are often malnourished, appear lean, and may lose weight. They have a pinkish complexion as they huff and puff, trying to catch their breath. This gives them a pink coloring in the cheeks and the face.

Pathological Conditions of the Respiratory System

Diseases and disorders of the respiratory system can be caused by infections, genetic abnormalities, environmental factors such as pollutants or cigarette smoke, or trauma. Diagnosing the cause of the respiratory disorder will direct the provider to the appropriate therapies.

Upper Respiratory Conditions

Coryza: Also called a common cold or rhinitis. It is characterized by inflammation of the respiratory mucous membranes of the upper respiratory tract. Symptoms include a cough, nasal discharge, sore throat, sneezing, headache, lethargy, muscle aches, and chills. The patient may also have a fever.

Croup: A childhood disease marked by a distinctive barking, hoarse cough, inspiratory stridor, tachypnea, and laryngeal spasm. The symptoms can cause extreme anxiety to the parents and the child as the sound of stridor is pronounced. Treatment with a humidifier and cool mist vaporizers will reduce symptoms. Croup may be caused by acute obstruction of the larynx due to allergens, infection, or a foreign object.

Deviated nasal septum: Deviation of the nasal septum away from the midline caused by trauma such as a broken nose or a congenital abnormality. It causes an inability to draw air in and out of both nostrils. It may result in headache, sinus congestion, nasal pain, and dyspnea. Surgical correction to realign the septum along the midline can decrease symptoms of pain and dyspnea.

Diphtheria: Caused by *Corynebacterium diphtheriae* bacterium and presents as a sore throat, dysphonia (difficulty speaking), and fever. A white plaque coating may be observed over the airway. As the disease progresses, the bacterium release toxins into the bloodstream that quickly damage the heart and nerves. This can lead to heart failure, paralysis, and death. Diphtheria is uncommon in the United States because the childhood vaccine recommendations include a DPT immunization, which protects the child from diphtheria, pertussis, and tetanus.

Epiglottitis: A swelling of the epiglottis that results from infection with *Haemophilus influenzae* type B (Hib), streptococci, or staphylococci. The infections usually occur in children ages 2 to 5 years. Signs and symptoms include a sore throat, high fever, dysphagia (difficulty swallowing), and stridor. The swelling can obstruct airflow and lead to death. In the United States, children are immunized against Hib, formerly the primary causative agent of epiglottitis; thus, the incidence has drastically declined.

Epistaxis: A nosebleed. It can be caused by vigorously blowing the nose, fragile blood vessels within the nose, picking at crusted mucus in the nose, or by an injury, such as a punch to the nose.

Laryngitis: Inflammation of the larynx usually leading to dysphonia (an inability to speak), hoarseness, cough, and dysphagia (difficulty swallowing). Laryngitis is common with overuse in professions such as singers, lecturers, and preachers. Treatment for laryngitis depends on the severity of symptoms. Resting the voice, lozenges, avoiding irritants such as smoke or harsh chemicals are advised for mild cases. More severe laryngitis can be a complication of chronic bronchitis and may require antibiotics.

Obstructive sleep apnea: Absence of breathing during sleep caused by temporary blockage of the upper airway. The disorder affects 10% of middle-aged men and 5% of middle-aged women. It is more common in obese adults. When airflow is obstructed during sleep, patients make loud snorting and snoring sounds as they gasp for breath. Symptoms include intermittent snoring and disordered breathing and is often first observed by the patient's sleeping partner. Daytime sleepiness and falling asleep at work or while driving make it a serious condition. Treatment is with a continuous positive airway pressure (CPAP) machine that delivers continuous airflow through an air mask. The pressurized airflow keeps the airway open during sleep. Corrective surgery of structural defects in the upper airway helps a small number of patients.

Pertussis: An acute upper respiratory infection caused by the *Bordetella pertussis* bacterium, commonly known as "whooping cough." The disease commonly affects young children and infants and is characterized by fever, sneezing, dry cough, irritability, and anorexia (loss of appetite). It is therefore commonly misdiagnosed as coryza (a common cold). As the disease progresses, the coughing becomes more violent, and the child is unable to rest. Coughing may become severe enough to cause vomiting. Treatment with antibiotics is effective if caught early, and antitussive medications will help the child rest. Pertussis can be prevented by immunization with a DPT vaccine, a standard childhood vaccine recommended by the Centers for Disease Control and Prevention (CDC).

Pharyngitis: Inflammation of the pharynx, also called a sore throat. The most common cause of pharyngitis is a viral infection, but bacterial infection may also occur. Signs and symptoms include red, raw pharyngeal membranes, swollen palatine tonsils (may include white pus spots or exudate). The cervical lymph nodes are enlarged and painful to palpation. Fever, malaise, difficulty swallowing, and soreness of the throat are common. A provider will order a rapid throat culture, and if the causative organism is streptococcus, it is called "strep throat." Treatment with oral antibiotics and rest will resolve pharyngitis.

Sinusitis: Inflammation of the nasal sinuses, especially the paranasal sinuses. Symptoms include pain and pressure in the face and malaise. Signs include purulent nasal discharge and, sometimes, a fever. Causes include allergens or a complication of an upper respiratory infection. If the cause is bacterial infection, sinusitis is treated with antibiotics. Decongestants and icepacks applied to the face and analgesics can relieve pain and pressure.

ELEMENT REVIEW
epiglott/o = epiglottis
pharyng/o = pharynx
sinus/o = sinuses
tonsill/o = tonsils
-itis = inflammation
a- = without
-pnea= to breath

Tonsillitis: Inflammation and infection of the palatine tonsils. Symptoms include sore throat, snoring, and difficulty swallowing. Signs include fever and enlarged, red tonsils that may exude yellow or white pus. Acute tonsillitis may cause chills. Treatment with bedrest, liquid diet, antipyretics, analgesics, and saline gargles often resolve tonsillitis. If the cause is a bacterial infection, antibiotics are recommended. Chronic tonsillitis may require a tonsillectomy to remove the site of chronic infection.

Lower Respiratory Conditions

Anthracosis: An accumulation of carbon deposits in the lungs due to inhalation of smoke or coal dust. The disease is also called black lung disease or coal workers' pneumoconiosis. The bronchioles and alveoli become clogged with coal dust and are no longer able to exchange oxygen and carbon dioxide. Black dots on the lungs, called *coal macules*, result in weakening and dilation of the bronchioles, causing overinflation.

Asbestosis: A lung infection caused by inhalation of asbestos particles. The inhaled particles penetrate the bronchioles and alveolar walls causing diffuse interstitial fibrosis. Symptoms include a dry cough, chest pain, dyspnea upon exertion, or in advanced disease, dyspnea at rest. Advanced disease can also lead to cor pulmonale or pulmonary hypertension. Diagnosis is confirmed by changes observed on chest x-ray, lung CT scan, and pulmonary function

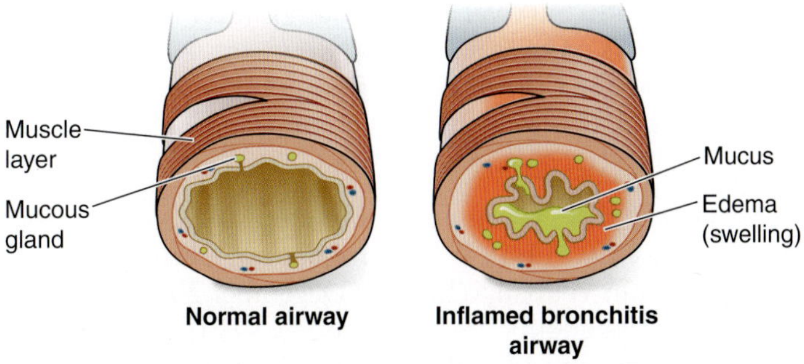

Figure 6-3 Normal and asthmatic bronchiole.

tests. Treatment consists of administration of supplemental oxygen if arterial blood gases indicate hypoxemia with ordinary air. Exposure to asbestos has been linked to lung cancers such as mesothelioma and bronchogenic carcinoma, and its latency period may be 20 years or more.

ELEMENT REVIEW
anthrac/o = coal
-osis = condition
mesotheli/o = lining of the pleura or peritoneum
carcin/o = cancer
-oma = tumor
bronch/o = bronchus
-genic = pertaining to production, cause
pulmon/o = lung
-ary = pertaining to

Asthma: Occurs most commonly in childhood and early adulthood and is characterized by paroxysmal (sudden and recurrent) dyspnea, accompanied by wheezing. It is caused by spasms of the bronchial tubes and swelling of the mucous membranes (Fig. 6-3). Asthma attacks begin with a sudden bout of coughing and a sensation of tightness in the chest. Slow, labored breathing with wheezing then follows. The patient exerts a lot of force to expel air, and sitting hunched forward aids the labored breathing. Attacks can last from 30 minutes to a few hours and are frightening for the patient as they gasp for air. Exercise, exposure to pollutants, and mental distress can initiate asthma attacks. Treatment with inhaled bronchodilators and corticosteroids are often prescribed. If the patient produces a lot of thick mucus, mucolytics (drugs that thin the consistency of mucus) can help the patient expel it through productive coughing. Most patients diagnosed with asthma will carry an inhaler with them for use as needed. Acute attacks of asthma may lead to status asthmaticus, a medical emergency that does not respond to medication and lasts longer than 24 hours.

Atelectasis: Partial collapse of alveoli causing inability to exchange oxygen and carbon dioxide. The condition may be caused by obstruction with a mucous plug, hypoventilation secondary to pain, or by compression of the lung or bronchi by tumors or enlarged lymph nodes.

Bronchiectasis: Chronic dilation of the bronchi causing loss of structure and production of thick purulent sputum, wheezing, and hemoptysis (coughing up blood). Clubbing of the fingers is often seen because peripheral circulation is compromised. Patients are prone to repeated pulmonary infections. The condition may be acquired or congenital, occurring in one or both lungs (usually affecting the lower lung). Acquired bronchiectasis may be caused by obstruction or infection with tuberculosis, pertussis, or bronchial pneumonia. Congenital cause is most commonly cystic fibrosis. Diagnosis is confirmed with a chest x-ray, lung CT scan, or cultures taken during bronchoscopy. Treatment consists of oral or IV antibiotics for 7 to 10 days and postural drainage and percussive therapy to expel sputum. Aerosols may be useful to alleviate bronchospasm.

ELEMENT REVIEW
bronchi/o = bronchus
-ectasis = stretching, expansion
-dilator = dilation, medication to open airways

Bronchitis: Inflammation of the mucous membrane of the bronchus commonly caused by infection. Symptoms include wheezing, dyspnea, and chest pain. Acute bronchitis is caused by viral or, rarely, a bacterial infection. Other causes include exposure to cigarette smoke or pollutants. It is usually self-limiting, resolving with rest, analgesics, antipyretics, and fluids. If the cause is a bacterial infection, oral antibiotics may speed the recovery rate.

Bronchogenic carcinoma: Also known as lung cancer, a malignant tumor that originates in the bronchi. The disease is caused by cigarette smoking or exposure to secondhand smoke. Signs and symptoms include persistent cough, hemoptysis, chest pain, a raspy voice, fatigue, and shortness of breath. Survival rates for lung cancer are low because most are not diagnosed until the cancer has metastasized to other organs. More than 50% of tumors are too advanced for excision by the time of diagnosis. Treatment may consist of chemotherapeutics or palliative care to make the patient as comfortable as possible for the remainder of their life.

ELEMENT REVIEW
pan- = all
-demic = pertaining to people, crowd
an- = without
-osmia = the sense of smell
a- = without
-geusia = the sense of taste

COVID-19: The contagious disease caused by the severe acute respiratory syndrome coronavirus 2 (SARS-COV2). COVID-19 is an acronym for COronaVIrus Disease of 2019. The first case was identified in Wuhan, China, in December 2019. The virus spread quickly across the globe, causing a pandemic. Symptoms of COVID-19 vary, but often include fever, cough, fatigue, dyspnea, and loss of smell (anosmia) and taste (ageusia). Preventive measures include decreasing person-to-person transmission by physical or social distancing, quarantining, ventilation of indoor spaces, covering coughs and sneezes, hand washing, and keeping unwashed hands away from the face. The use of face masks or coverings has often been recommended in public settings to minimize the risk of transmissions. Cases confirmed by nasal swab testing are treated with remdesivir or Paxlovid as recommended by the CDC. Treatment has progressed to focusing on prevention with vaccines.

Chronic obstructive pulmonary disease (COPD): A group of diseases where the alveoli are destroyed, making exchange of oxygen and carbon dioxide difficult. COPD is progressive and can be fatal as the number of alveoli involved increases. The most common cause of COPD is smoking, but some people develop COPD from repeated exposure to secondhand smoke. The disease affects millions of Americans and accounts for 500,000 hospital admissions each year. Signs and symptoms include dyspnea upon exertion, and as chronic wet cough with thick mucopurulent sputum. Symptom management is with inhaled bronchodilators, low-flow oxygen, and antibiotics if bacterial infection is also present. Smoking cessation and regular exercise are advised but patient compliance is often problematic.

Cystic fibrosis (CF): Fatal genetic disorder of the lungs and digestive systems that causes normally thin secretions in the digestive and respiratory tracts to be thick. It is caused by a genetic defect in the gene responsible for moving salt in and out of cells. The thickened mucus in the respiratory tract causes blockages in the bronchi and alveoli. Respiratory signs and symptoms include a salty sweat, persistent cough with thick mucus, recurrent sinusitis, stuffy nose, and lung infections. Gastrointestinal signs and symptoms include foul-smelling greasy stool, weight loss or poor weight gain in infants and small children, and intestinal blockage. Treatment with acetylcysteine to thin mucus and allow the patient to expel mucus and bronchodilators to open respiratory passages are used in concert with respiratory therapy. Respiratory therapy with percussion to the back and chest helps to loosen mucus. Although treatments for CF have improved over time, the life expectancy of a CF patient is 50 years.

Emphysema: A chronic respiratory disease characterized by hyperinflated alveoli or destruction of the alveolar walls (Figure 6-4). The disease is progressive, affecting more and more alveoli and the most common cause is cigarette smoke. Often the damage to the lungs is permanent before diagnosis is made. Because the alveoli are distended, the expiration of air is most difficult. Patients report a feeling of not being able to get air out of the lungs and must "force" the air out. They may appear "barrel chested" due to this difficulty exhaling. Treatment with smoking cessation, bronchodilators, mucolytics, and supplemental oxygen offers some relief. Patient compliance with smoking cessation is essential, especially if supplemental oxygen is prescribed.

ELEMENT REVIEW
muc/o = mucus
-lytic = pertaining to destruction
py/o = pus
-thorax = thoracic cavity

Empyema: A collection of pus in the pleural cavity, also known as pyothorax. Signs and symptoms include fever, night sweats, chest pain, anorexia, dyspnea, and weight loss. Treatments include antibiotics and aspiration of pleural fluid.

Hyaline membrane disease: Also known as respiratory distress syndrome of the newborn. It is most common in premature infants that weigh less than 5 lb and are 37 weeks gestation or less. It is caused by the premature lungs not having sufficient surfactant, the liquid

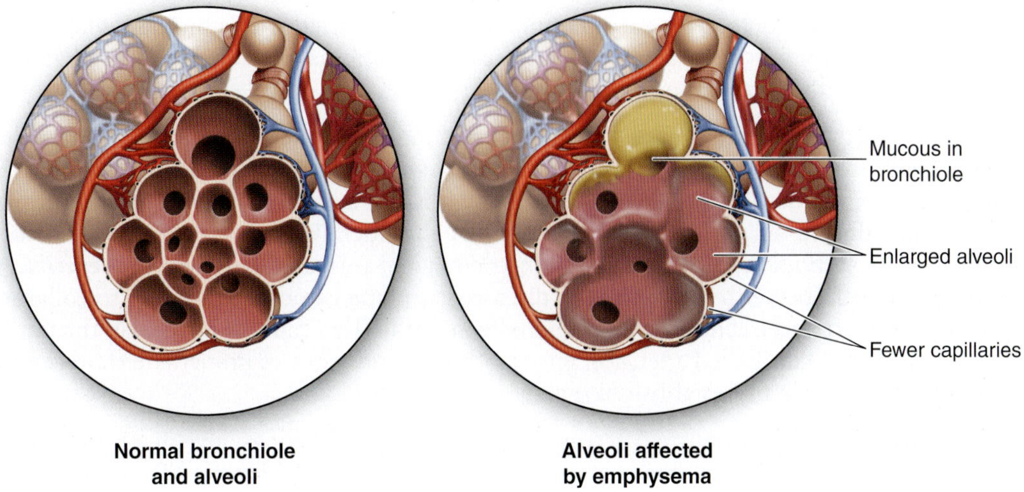

Figure 6-4 Cross-sections of healthy alveoli clusters and the hyperinflated alveoli demonstrated with emphysema.

that coats the inside of the lungs and allows for smooth respiration. Signs and symptoms include tachypnea, tachycardia, retraction of the rib cage during inspiration, cyanosis, flaring nostrils, and a grunting sound during expiration. Treatment may consist of an endotracheal tube, mechanical breathing, supplemental oxygen, and administration of an artificial surfactant. The infant is often sedated to ease the baby's pain during treatment.

Influenza: Highly contagious viral infection transmitted by airborne droplets, it is commonly called "the flu." Common symptoms are sore throat, fever, body aches, chills, headache, cough, and fatigue. Influenza is often self-limiting within 3 to 10 days. Treatment consisting of bed rest, fluids, and analgesics will decrease time of recovery. Annual flu shots are available to people 6 months and older and may increase resistance to annual flu that can be common each fall/winter.

Lung abscess: A localized collection of pus and necrotic debris in the lung caused by an infection. Signs and symptoms include productive cough with purulent and bloody sputum (hemoptysis). It is commonly caused by aspiration of nasopharyngeal mucus into the lungs of patients with impaired consciousness. It is diagnosed by chest x-ray or sputum cultures. Treatment with IV antibiotics and percutaneous, endobronchial, or surgical drainage of the abscess may be necessary if antibiotics do not resolve the abscess.

Pleural effusion: Excess collection of fluid and air in the pleural space resulting in a compression of the underlying lung. It is usually secondary to COPD and signs and symptoms follow the primary disease. Diagnosis of pleural effusion is confirmed by chest x-ray and listening to breath sounds that will indicate the presence of fluid. Treatment with thoracentesis resolves the collection of fluid.

Pleurisy (pleuritis): Inflammation of the visceral and parietal pleura causing them to rub against each other. Normally there is a space between the bilayer of tissue and some interstitial fluid that decreases friction upon movement. Pleurisy can be secondary to other respiratory illnesses and treatment is directed at the cause. Symptoms include a sharp pain during respiration, more pronounced during inspiration. The pleural rub can be heard with a stethoscope confirming diagnosis.

Pneumonia: Inflammation of the lungs caused by a viral, bacterial, or fungal infection. Signs and symptoms include dyspnea, productive cough, sinus congestion, and chest pain. A sputum culture is used to diagnose the causative agent and direct appropriate care with antibiotic, antiviral, or antifungal medication. Some mild cases of pneumonia are self-limiting, but symptoms can progress quickly, so patients are advised to seek care. Prednisone, a corticosteroid, to decrease inflammation is often paired with a bronchodilator and the appropriate anti-infective agent. Severe cases of pneumonia may require hospitalization and treatment with intravenous antibiotics.

Pneumothorax: A collection of air outside of the lung in the pleural cavity. Air enters the pleura cavity from a perforation through the chest wall causing the lung to collapse. The pneumothorax can occur spontaneously from lung disease and presents as a sharp, stabbing pain in the affected side with referral pain to the shoulder. Most cases are mild and will resolve with rest. Pneumothorax is caused by trauma and is treated based on the severity. A severe pneumothorax, either due to lung disease or trauma can cause the lung to collapse, shifting the heart and trachea toward the unaffected side. This causes pressure on the unaffected side to build up, called a tension pneumothorax, and requires immediate thoracentesis to inflate the lung and establish oxygen.

Pulmonary edema: An abnormal accumulation of fluid in the lungs, alveoli, or interstitial spaces. It is most commonly caused by congestive heart failure where the amount of blood received in the lungs from the right side of the heart is too much for the left ventricle of the heart to remove in the cycle of circulation. This overload of blood causes a backup of fluid that leaks through the capillary walls of the alveoli and into the airways. Signs and symptoms include a sense of suffocation, dyspnea, cyanosis, and pallor. This emergency condition requires immediate medical attention with supplemental oxygen, vasodilators, diuretics, and morphine to control severe pain and panic.

Pulmonary embolism: A sudden obstruction of a pulmonary blood vessel caused by debris or a blood clot. Signs and symptoms include cough, chest pain, and breathlessness. The embolus can be solid or liquid and can lead to necrosis of tissue called an infarct. Pulmonary embolism is a serious concern; in fact, in 25% of cases, patients exhibit no signs before their sudden death.

Silicosis: Inflammation of the lungs from inhaling silica (quartz) dust. The lungs form nodules that increase in number and size, later forming dense masses of fibrous tissue (fibroids). As the lungs lose the ability to expand fully, secondary emphysema develops. The condition is caused by occupational exposure to silica dust over a period of 10 to 25 years before symptoms of dyspnea, weakness, weight loss, and cough occur. It may be diagnosed by a lung biopsy or bronchial lavage. Treatment is palliative as no cure is available. Bronchodilators, supplemental oxygen, and smoking cessation will slow progression of the disease.

Sudden infant death syndrome (SIDS): Also known as crib death, SIDS is the unexplained death of a seemingly healthy infant who stops breathing during sleep. Infants are found in the crib, often in the same position as they were placed hours before, with no signs of struggling to resume breathing. It occurs between the second week and first year of life and affects 7,000 infants each year in the United States. Premature babies, males, and those infants living in poverty are most affected. Infants at risk for SIDS are monitored during sleep and are sometimes placed on an apnea alarm to alert caregivers if the infant stops breathing.

Tuberculosis (TB): An infectious disease caused by the *Mycobacterium tuberculosis* tubercule bacillus. It is a contagious disease transmitted by droplets sneezed or coughed into the air by an infected person. The mycobacterium can settle in the lungs, lying dormant until the immune system is compromised and the bacterium begins to multiply. Signs and symptoms include coughing up green sputum, chest pain, dyspnea, fever, night sweats, anorexia, and fatigue. It is diagnosed by tuberculin skin testing using a purified protein derivative (PPD) and confirmed by presence of nodules on a chest x-ray (most commonly seen in the apex of the lung). A sputum culture will confirm the presence of acid-fast bacillus. Treatment with a 9- to 12-month course of antibiotics and vitamins is advised. Because TB is highly contagious for a long period of time, each state department of public health requires reporting of active TB cases. Reporting procedures vary state to state but will include name, address, age, sex, HIV status, and occupation of the patient. Reports must be submitted within 24 hours of confirmation of disease.

Pathology Word-Building Practice

1. Prefixes

Choose from the list of prefixes to build a word for the definitions below.

a-, an-	slow	hypo-	insufficient
eu-	normal	tachy-	rapid
hyper-	excessive		

1. fast breathing ____________________
2. excessive carbon dioxide ____________________
3. a lack of breathing ____________________
4. insufficient oxygen ____________________
5. normal breathing ____________________

2. Suffixes

Use the list of suffixes to build a word for the definitions below.

-ar	pertaining to	-itis	inflammation
-ary	pertaining to	-osis	condition
-dynia	pain	-rrhea	discharge
-ectasis	stretching or dilation	-stenosis	condition narrowing
-edema	swelling		

1. Pain in the chest ____________________
2. Inflammation of the tonsils ____________________
3. Narrowing of the trachea ____________________
4. Swelling of the lungs ____________________
5. Lung disease caused by inhaling silica dust ____________________
6. Pertaining to the lungs ____________________
7. Inflammation of the larynx ____________________
8. Stretched or dilated bronchi ____________________
9. Discharge from the nose ____________________
10. Pertaining to the alveoli ____________________

Respiratory System Diagnostic Procedures

CAREER EXPLORATION: RESPIRATORY THERAPIST

When I was growing up, my brother, Leon, who has cystic fibrosis, had a respiratory therapist (RT) come to our house to do his treatments. John performed percussive therapy on Leon's back and chest to help him cough up mucus. I didn't think it was gross since I loved my brother and was curious about his treatments. John would explain to me what he was doing and how he was positioning Leon to help him get rid of sputum in a process called postural drainage. From then on, I knew I wanted to become an RT. My brother was 15 years older than me, so when he died at 35, I was still in college. I enrolled in an RT program and learned that RTs treat a variety of patients, from young children to the elderly. I graduated, earning a bachelor's degree in RT, then I took my state licensing exam. In addition to treating patients with cystic fibrosis, I now treat patients with asthma, COPD, and even patients who are on ventilators. My job is primarily in a hospital, but sometimes I treat patients in the outpatient respiratory clinic too. I love that I often work with the same patients over a period of time and get to know them and their families. I have worked with tiny 4-pound babies with premature lungs to a 95-year-old gentleman with COPD. My job includes patient education, where I teach patients how to use respiratory medications with a nebulized mist inhaler, nebulizer, or inhaler. I also go to patients' homes, set up life support systems, and teach caregivers to monitor equipment. As technology has progressed, patients with cystic fibrosis are living longer. I have a patient, Lenore, who has CF and is 43 years old. She is able to work as a medical coder at the hospital, which was unheard of for people with CF a few years ago. I admire her hard work, both with her disease and her profession. She and I have become good friends, and she reminds me of my brother Leon. Recently, I ran into John at a respiratory therapist continuing education program. He was excited to see that I became an RT. I hope that I can inspire someone to become an RT too. Read that again . . . get it? *Inspire* someone to become an RT!

Physical Examination

Assessment of respiratory illnesses always starts with examination by looking at and listening to the patient. Information gathered during the physical examination will be used to determine further diagnostic testing and guide treatment.

Inspection: Visual inspection of the external body, including color of the skin, bruises, movements, and posture. Noting how the patient sits, upright or hunched forward, and noting the patient's speech and breath patterns will inform the practitioner of respiratory distress or comfort.

Palpation: Use of the hands to feel the external surface of the body. Noting skin turgor, tone, dryness, and muscle tone. Patient response to touch, such as tenderness, is also noted.

Auscultation: Use of a stethoscope to listen to sounds within the body. The chest and back is auscultated during normal respiration and when the patient is asked to take a deep breath. Heart sounds and breath sounds are noted. The abdomen is auscultated to listen to bowel sounds.

Percussion: Tapping on the body lightly with the fingertips to elicit sound and determine position, size, and consistency of underlying structures. Gases, fluid, and solids under the skin will produce different sounds upon percussion.

Clinical and Imaging Tests

Bronchoscopy: Examination of the interior of the bronchi with a fiberoptic scope. The bronchoscope is inserted into the nose and passes through the pharynx, larynx, and trachea into the bronchus. The procedure is done with the patient in the supine or seated position and under light sedation (awake). A local anesthetic is sprayed into the throat to prevent gagging during the procedure. The procedure is used diagnostically to obtain fluid or biopsied masses for laboratory analysis. Therapeutically the procedure can be used to remove obstructions such as thick mucus plugs, or foreign objects that may have been aspirated into the bronchus.

Chest x-ray: Chest x-ray allows the provider to see the internal structures of the chest for diagnosis (Fig. 6-5). X-rays are now digital and can be uploaded into a patient's electronic medical record. Fluid, pus, and masses in the lungs can be viewed.

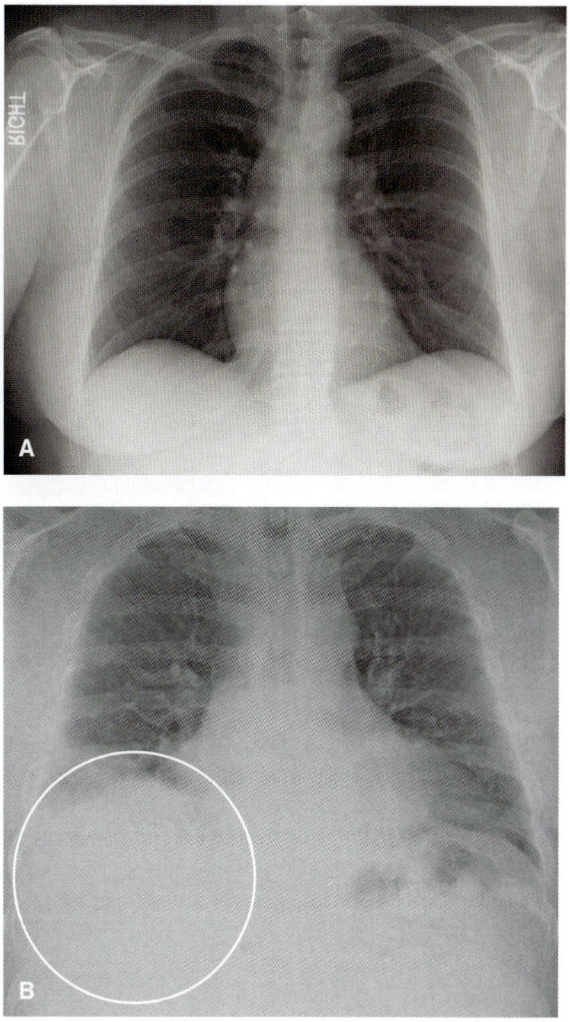

Figure 6-5 Two chest x-rays: (A) normal chest, (B) x-ray of lobar pneumonia.

Computed tomography pulmonary angiography: A contrast dye is injected intravenously and observed in a CT scan. Abnormalities of pulmonary circulation such as blood clots, areas of stenosis, aneurysms, congenital defects of vessels, and vessel occlusions can be identified.

Laryngoscopy: Examination of the interior of the larynx using a flexible, lighted scope. The device is called a laryngoscope or an endoscope. The procedure is performed in the medical office, and a local anesthetic is sprayed into the throat to prevent gagging. It can be used to diagnose masses, damage to vocal cords, or remove foreign objects stuck in the upper airway.

Nuclear perfusion lung scan: Radioactive marker is inhaled or given in an intravenous injection to observe the pattern of radioactive activity in the lungs. Areas that do not show radioactivity are indicative of blockage of blood flow.

Mediastinoscopy: Use of a thin, flexible, lighted scope with a camera to view the mediastinum, the space behind the sternum. The procedure can be used to remove lymph nodes in patients with lung cancer. It can be used to assess inflammation, infection, or thymoma, and cancer of the thymus gland.

Polysomnography: Also called a sleep study, polysomnography is performed at a hospital or clinic where the patient is monitored during sleep (Fig. 6-6). Electrodes are placed on the head so that brainwaves can be monitored while the patient sleeps to assess stages of sleep. Heart rate, breathing and oxygenation of the blood are also monitored. The test can be used to diagnose sleep apnea, narcolepsy, chronic insomnia, periodic limb movement disorders, REM (rapid eye movement), and sleep behavior disorders such as sleepwalking.

Pulmonary function tests: A group of tests used to measure a patient's breathing capacity. An instrument called a **spirometer** measures the volume of air that the patient can move in and out of the lungs.

Pulse oximetry: Indirect measurement of saturation of peripheral oxygen (SpO_2), commonly known as "O_2 sat." The device is placed on the patient's finger while vital signs are being assessed. An O_2 sat for a patient with healthy lungs is 96% to 99%. O_2 sat levels below 96% are indicative of an inability to get oxygen delivered to the peripheral body cells.

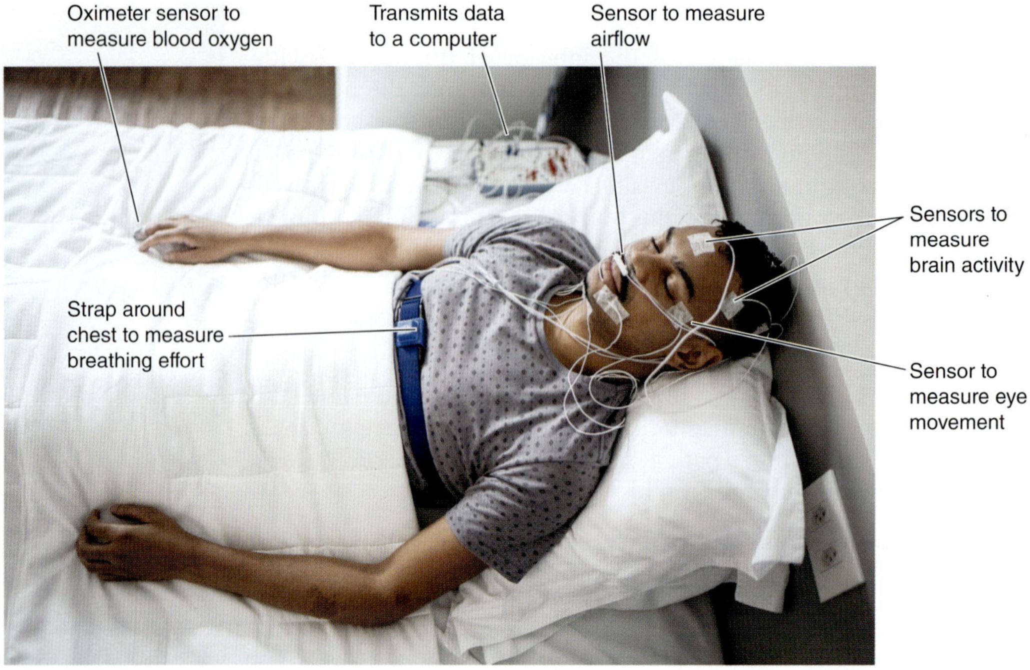

Figure 6-6 Polysomnography.

Laboratory Tests

Arterial blood gases: Blood is taken from an artery, usually from the wrist, groin, or above the elbow to measure oxygen and carbon dioxide levels and pH balance in arterial blood. The test can be used to evaluate respiratory and kidney function and evaluate the effectiveness of supplemental oxygen therapy.

Mantoux test: PPD is injected intradermally to identify if the patient has been exposed to tuberculosis (Fig. 6-7). Formation of a wheal indicates a positive finding.

Sputum culture: Analysis of mucus or fluid coughed up from the lungs. The sputum is cultured, allowing microorganisms to multiply to be identified as the cause of an infection.

Sweat test: The skin of the forearm is washed and patted dry, and a pad soaked in pilocarpine, a chemical that stimulates the sweat glands, is placed on the skin. The amount of chloride in the sweat sample is then measured. The sweat test is considered the most

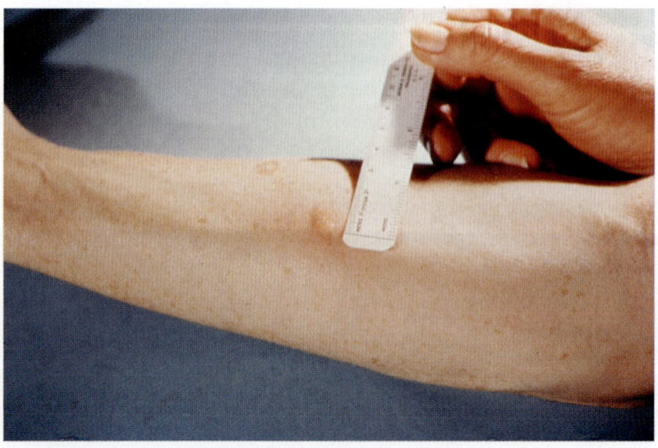

Figure 6-7 Positive PPD test.

reliable test to diagnose cystic fibrosis because patients with CF have high quantities of salt in their sweat.

Throat culture: Analysis of mucus taken from the back of the throat on a cotton swab. The mucus is cultured, allowing microorganisms to multiply to be identified as the cause of an infection. A rapid strep culture can be done and read in the doctor's office, and a patient can be given a prescription the same day.

Respiratory System Therapeutic Procedures

Upper Airway Therapeutic Procedures

Aerosol therapy: Bronchodilator and antispasmodic medications are converted from a liquid to an aerosol spray and administered by a nebulizer into the lungs (Fig. 6-8). It is also called inhalation therapy.

Antral lavage: Irrigation (washing) of sinuses for patients who do not respond to decongestant medications.

Endotracheal intubation: Also called intubation. A flexible plastic tube is placed from the mouth into the trachea to maintain an open airway (Fig. 6-9). It is often done as an emergency procedure in unconscious patients who are not spontaneously breathing.

Intermittent positive pressure breathing (IPPB): Technique used to provide short-term or intermittent mechanical ventilation via mouthpiece or mask for the purpose of promoting lung expansion, mobilizing bronchial secretions, and delivering aerosol medication.

Septoplasty: Surgical correction of a deviated septum to increase ease of air intake into the nasal cavity (Fig. 6-10).

Tracheostomy: Placement of a surgically created hole in the trachea to provide an alternative airway for breathing. Once the surgical hole is created, a tracheostomy tube is inserted into the neck and secured with a strap placed around the neck. The tube may be temporary or permanent based on the patient's illness. Conditions that may require a tracheostomy include burns or corrosion of the throat, severe neck and mouth trauma, chronic lung disease, coma, anaphylaxis, injury to the larynx, or cancer of the head and neck.

Figure 6-8 Aerosol therapy with a bronchodilator.

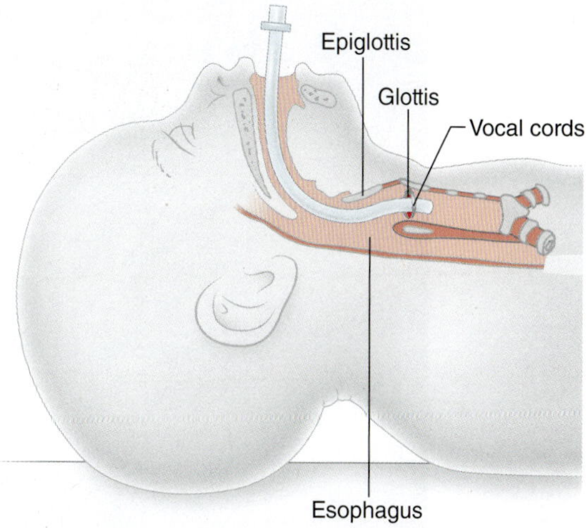

Figure 6-9 Endotracheal intubation.

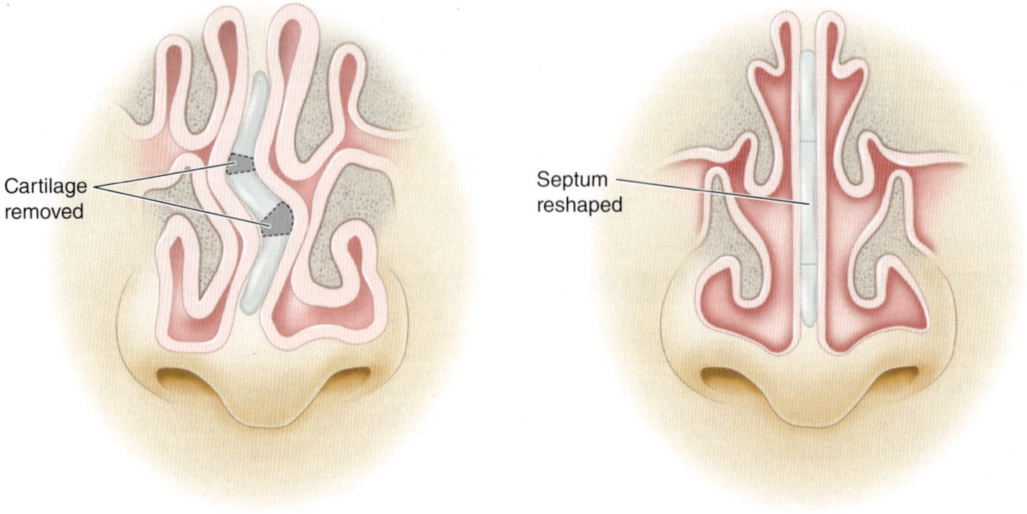

Figure 6-10 Septoplasty.

Lower Airway Therapeutic Procedures

Continuous positive airway pressure (CPAP) machine: The most commonly prescribed machine for sleep apnea. An air mask and hose are attached to the machine. The mask is worn at night to force air from the machine into the lungs (Fig. 6-11). The continuous flow of air decreases interruptions of sleep by gently keeping the tongue, uvula, and soft palate from shifting down the airway and obstructing the flow of air.

Lung transplant: Implantation of a donor lung in cases of severe lung disease.

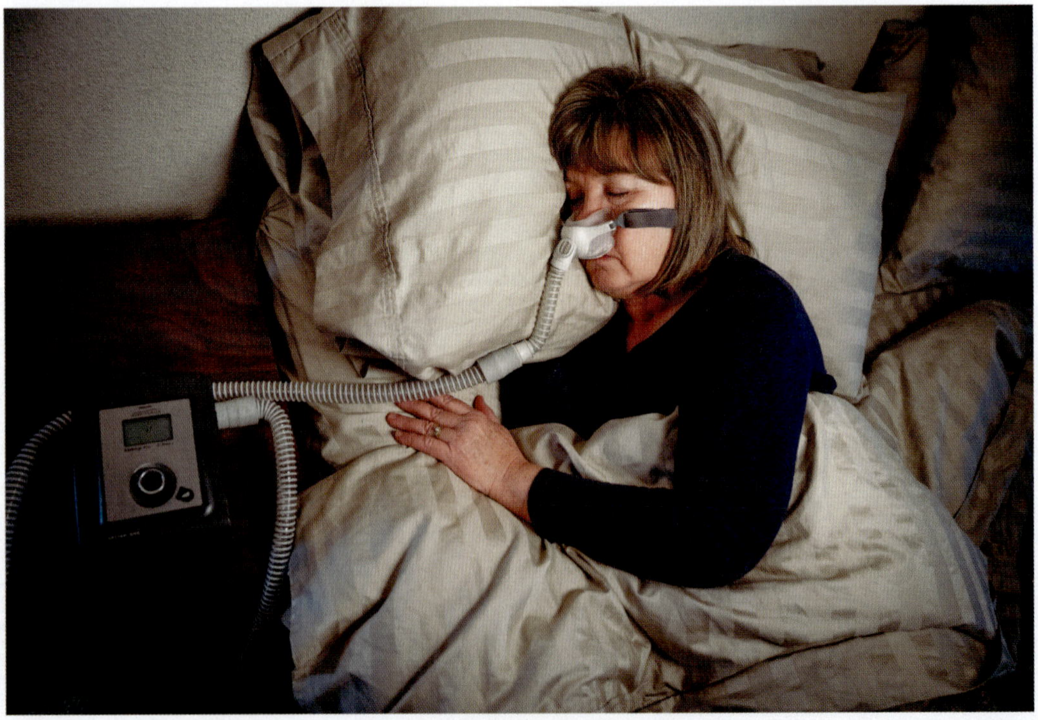

Figure 6-11 Patient using a CPAP machine.

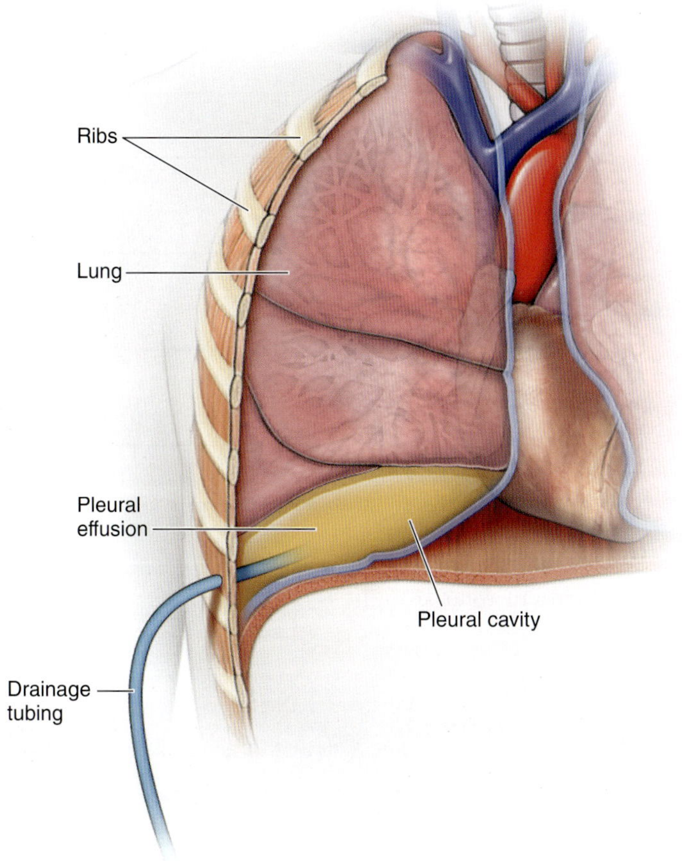

Figure 6-12 Thoracentesis.

Pleurectomy: The excision of all or part of the pleura to remove a tumor of a pleural mesothelioma. It preserves the lung in cases of operable mesothelioma. Also called decortication.

Postural drainage: The patient is placed in various positions to help bring up secretions from the bronchi and lungs. The procedure is often performed by a respiratory therapist.

Pneumonectomy: Surgical removal of a diseased lung or a lung severely damaged by trauma. It can also be performed for cases of extensive unilateral tuberculosis, bronchiectasis, or multiple abscesses of the lung.

Thoracentesis (thoracentesis): Surgical puncture and drainage of the pleural cavity (Fig. 6-12). It can be used to drain excess fluid or to take a sample for laboratory analysis.

Procedures and Diagnostics Review

Answer the following questions.

1. Which blood test can give the provider information about both respiratory and renal function? ______________________

2. If a patient had severe unilateral tuberculosis in the right lung, what surgical procedure may be recommended? ______________________

3. The process in which a patient is asked to take a deep breath and the practitioner listens. ______________________

4. What medical device is used in question 3? ______________________

5. This device tells you the patient's "O_2 sat". ______________________

6. What type of test is performed while the patient is sleeping? ______________________

7. What is monitored during the test in question 4? ______________________

8. What test uses an intravenous contrast dye observed in a CT scan? ______________________

9. Using the fingertips to tap on the body and listen for sounds is called ______________________

10. What machine can a patient wear at night to help his breathing? ______________________

CASE STUDY, completed

Jennifer takes the Paxlovid as prescribed by Dr. Wilson. She asks her sister, Lisa, to move into her spare bedroom and care for her children while she quarantines from her family. Lisa takes the young children out to the playground, makes their meals, and gives them baths. Jim sleeps on a blowup mattress in his office to give Jennifer the master bedroom and bathroom. Jennifer meets with Dr. Wilson again on a telemedicine visit 2 weeks after her diagnosis. She states she is feeling better. She slept a lot during the past 2 weeks, but her energy is resuming. Dr. Wilson is pleased and states that a return of her energy and the headaches resolving are great signs. He advises her that she can resume contact with her husband and children. Jennifer is so happy because COVID-19 has taken such an emotional toll on her and her family. She tells Dr. Wilson that her sense of smell is still diminished. He advises her that it may take weeks or even months, and some patients do not recover their sense of smell. He does think that hers will return since her COVID symptoms were not severe. Jennifer thanks Dr. Wilson. She tells Lisa and Jim that quarantine is lifted!

CRITICAL THINKING QUESTIONS

1. What comorbidities may have made Jennifer more susceptible to a COVID-19 infection? ______________________

2. Pulmonary edema is the common term for fluid in lungs, but edema means "swelling." Using the word parts you have learned so far, create a single-word medical term that means "fluid in the lungs." ______________________

3. Jennifer was prescribed Ciprofloxacin to treat her pneumonia. What category of drug is Ciprofloxacin, and which part of the drug name tells you this category? ______________________

4. Jennifer complained of difficulty breathing. The medical term is ______________________

5. Jennifer experienced a loss of appetite when she had pneumonia. The medical term is ______________________

CASE STUDY, completed

6. What is the medical term for the inflammation of the tiny air sacs in Jennifer's lungs? ______________________
7. What test did Kristen use to prescribe medication for Jennifer's pneumonia? ______________________
8. One symptom of Jennifer's COVID-19 infection is the inability to smell, which is called ______________________
9. Jennifer experienced muscle pain and headaches. The medical terms are ______________________
10. Why did Dr. Wilson see Jennifer on a telemedicine visit and not a traditional office visit? ______________________

Medications for the Respiratory System

Medications for the respiration system include those to alleviate symptoms of dyspnea, cough, inflammation, excess mucus production, infection, nasal congestion, and cancer (Table 6-5). Medications are administered by inhalation or orally, depending on their mechanism of action.

TABLE 6-5 Medications for the Respiratory System

Classification	Examples	Common Use/Action
Anticholinergics	Atrovent, Spiriva	Dilation of bronchi
Anti-influenza	Relenza, Tamiflu	Reduces severity and duration of symptoms of influenza
Antitussives	dextromethorphan, Robitussin, codeine	Coughing cessation
Antivirals (COVID-19)	Paxlovid, remdesivir	COVID-19 infection
Beta-adrenergic agonists	Albuterol, Proventil, Ventolin	Dilation of bronchi
Decongestants	phenylephrine, Dimetapp, Sudafed, Triaminic, pseudoephedrine, Chlor-Trimeton, Contac Cold	Decrease fluid in respiratory passages
Expectorants	guaifenesin, Mucinex	Promote more productive cough to clear mucus in the respiratory tract
Glucocorticoids	beclomethasone, Beclovent, budesonide, Pulmicort	Decrease inflammation in the respiratory tract
Mast cell stabilizers	cromolyn sodium, Intal, nedocromil, Tilade aerosol	Prevention of asthma attacks
Mucolytics	acetylcysteine, Mucomyst	Thin mucus in respiratory tract
Oxygen	oxygen	Treatment of apnea
Respiratory stimulants	theophylline, caffeine citrate, Cafcit	Treatment of apnea
Smoking cessation aids	Wellbutrin, Zyban, Nicorette, Chantix	Decrease symptoms of nicotine cravings
Xanthines	aminophylline, theophylline, Theo-Dur Sprinkles	Relief of asthma symptoms

Medications Review

Using the table of respiratory medications, complete the chart below. The first one has been done for you as an example.

Medication Name	Classification (mechanism)	Therapeutic Use (What is it used for?)
Cafcit	*Respiratory stimulant*	*Treatment of apnea*
Chantix	______________	______________
Robitussin	______________	______________
Spiriva	______________	______________
remdesivir	______________	______________
Mucomyst	______________	______________
Pulmicort	______________	______________
Albuterol	______________	______________
Mucinex	______________	______________
Tamiflu	______________	______________
Intal	______________	______________
theophylline	______________	______________

Respiratory Abbreviations

ABGs	arterial blood gases
AFB	acid-fast bacilli
AIDS	acquired immunodeficiency syndrome
AP	anteroposterior
ARD	acute respiratory disease
ARDS	adult respiratory distress syndrome
ARF	acute respiratory failure
CDC	Centers for Disease Control and Prevention
CF	cystic fibrosis
CO_2	carbon dioxide
COPD	chronic obstructive pulmonary disease
CPAP	continuous positive airway pressure
CPR	cardiopulmonary resuscitation
CTPA	computed tomography pulmonary angiography
CXR	chest x-ray
DPT	diphtheria, pertussis, tetanus
HMD	hyaline membrane disease
IPPB	intermittent positive pressure breathing
LLL	left lower lobe (lung)
LUL	left upper lobe
MDI	metered dose inhaler
NMI	nebulized mist inhaler
O_2	oxygen

OSA obstructive sleep apnea	RLL right lower lobe
PA posteroanterior	RUL right upper lobe
Pco_2 partial pressure of carbon dioxide	SIDS sudden infant death syndrome
PCP pneumocystis pneumonia, primary care physician	SOB shortness of breath
PFT pulmonary function test	SpO_2 saturation of peripheral oxygen
pH degree of acid or base	T and A tonsillectomy and adenoidectomy
Po_2 partial pressure of oxygen	TB tuberculosis
PPD purified protein derivative	TPR temperature, pulse, respiration
R respiration	URI upper respiratory infection

Abbreviations Review

Chose the correct definition for the abbreviation:

1. URI
   a. Ultra respiration intake
   b. Upper respiratory infection
   c. Upper respiration intake
   d. Upper respiration initiation

2. RLL
   a. Respiration lower level
   b. Respiration lowered level
   c. Right lower lobe
   d. Right level of lung

3. SOB
   a. Shortness of breath
   b. Status of breathing
   c. Status of bronchi
   d. Status of bronchioles

4. TPR
   a. Total pressure of respiration
   b. Total pulmonary respiration
   c. Total pulse and respiration
   d. Temperature, pulse, respiration

5. ABG
   a. Autonomic blood gases
   b. Arterial blood gases
   c. Arterial blood globulins
   d. Autonomic blood globulins

6. AP
   a. Autonomic perfusion
   b. Anteroposterior
   c. Autonomic pulmonary
   d. Anterior pulmonary

7. PPD
   a. Purified protein derivative
   b. Posterior protein derivative
   c. Positive pressure derivation
   d. Positive protein derivative

8. OSA
   a. Obstructive sinus asthma
   b. Obstructive septal adenoma
   c. Obstructive sleep apnea
   d. Obstructive sleep asthma

9. MDI
   a. Metered dose inhaler
   b. Metered dose inhalation
   c. Metered dose intake
   d. Metric dose inhaled

10. IPPB
   a. Interlobular positive pressure breathing
   b. Intermittent positive pressure breathing
   c. Interstitial positive pressure breathing
   d. Intercostal positive pressure breathing

MEDICAL DOCUMENTATION

Knowledge of terms related to normal anatomy and pathological conditions enables you to understand medical documentation such as history and physical examinations, operative reports, telemedicine visit summaries, discharge summaries, laboratory reports, and x-ray reports. Apply your knowledge by answering the questions that follow the report.

Operative Report

Patient Name: Augustus S.
Medical Record No.: 584300
Date of Operation: March 1, 2023
Preoperative Diagnosis: Right upper lobe mass on CT scan.
Postoperative Diagnosis: Right upper lobe mass on CT scan.
Operation: Bronchoscopy

Surgeon: Saul Hochman, MD
Assistant: Jennifer Austin, PA-C
Anesthesia: IV sedation and topical.
Drains: None
Specimens: Multiple washings and biopsies.
Complications: None
Estimated Blood Loss: Minimal

Indications for Procedure: The patient is a 58-year-old white male, who was admitted to our hospital with chest pain upon exertion and at rest. A subsequent CT scan of chest revealed a mass located in the right upper lobe of the lung. Bronchoscopy is indicated to evaluate the mass and obtain washings and biopsy for pathology.

Procedure: After explaining the risks and benefits of the procedure, the patient agreed to undergo the procedure, and informed consent was e-signed and placed in the electronic chart. The patient was taken to the operating room and placed on the operating table in the supine position. Patient was prepped and draped in the usual sterile manner. Two liters of oxygen was applied nasally along with IV sedation. After topical anesthetic of 2% Xylocaine with lidocaine jelly and Cetacaine spray, the Olympus fiberoptic bronchoscope was introduced into the patient's right cavity, and passed along the nasal cavity floor, through the nasal pharynx, epiglottis, posterior pharynx, and into the bronchial tree.

The findings showed that the posterior pharynx, epiglottis, and true vocal cords were all of normal anatomy. The trachea and main carina were also normal. The entire bronchial tree along the major airway was examined and found to be normal.

No abnormalities were noted on the left side. There was, however, compression on the anterior segment of the right upper lobe. There also appeared to be an approximately 1.5 × 3.0-cm submucosal mass located in the bronchus intermedius between the right upper lobe and right middle lobe. Multiple washings, brushings, and biopsies were taken from the right upper lobe and bronchus intermedius. The specimens were sent for cytology and routine pathology. The patient tolerated the procedure well, and there were no complications. The patient was taken to the recovery room in stable condition.

____

Saul Hochman, MD

Questions

1. Mr. S complained of chest pain, for which the medical term is ________________.
2. What objective findings were obtained prior to the procedure? ________________

   ____
3. What test was used to diagnose Mr. S's condition? ________________
4. The specimens were sent for cytology analysis. "Cytology" means ________________.

MEDICAL DOCUMENTATION—cont'd

5. The specimens were sent to the pathology laboratory. What does that department look for? ____________________
6. Describe the direction the patient is facing when placed in the supine position.____________________
7. What medication is used to prevent the patient from gagging?____________________
8. How was the anesthetic administered to the patient?____________________
9. What does submucosal mean?____________________
10. A sample of tissue was removed. Tissue removed and analyzed is called a __________.

TELEMEDICINE VISIT

June 3, 2022
Patient: Jennifer G

DOB 07-23-1994
Medical Record Number- 9470104

Assessment: COVID-19 infection

Discussion/Summary: Telehealth visit conducted, and the limitations of the visit were discussed with the patient.

Clinical Intake: Benefits and limitations of telemedicine visit were discussed with the patient as follows: "Telephone and video visits have many benefits. You can visit a provider without traveling and avoid contact in the waiting room with other patients who may be sick. Certain portions of an examination cannot be done using video and lab tests cannot be drawn. If you have concerns or questions, please discuss this with your provider." The patient agreed to the visit and the aforementioned limitation of telemedicine.

Plan

1. Start Paxlovid 3 tablets per dose twice a day for 5 days
2. Quarantine from family for 10 days
3. Continue albuterol sulfate inhaler, 2 puffs every 4 hours, as needed

History of Present Illness The patient reports that she has received two Pfizer COVID-19 vaccines and subsequently one booster. She reports mild redness at the vaccine site, but no other side effects. She attended a party 2 days ago and believes that is the cause of her infection. She went to a drugstore drive thru for a rapid COVID-19 test; the test is positive.

Review of Systems: Constitutional, eye, otolaryngeal, cardiovascular, pulmonary, gastrointestinal, genitourinary, neurological, psychiatric, endocrine, and hematological are normal except as noted:
Constitutional fever: 99.4°F, anorexia
ENT: Mild sore throat, no dysphagia
Cardiovascular: No edema
Respiratory: Coughing and wheezing, mild dyspnea controlled with albuterol sulfate, anosmia
Gastrointestinal: Loss of appetite, no abdominal pain
Neurological: No dizziness

Physical Examination: Patient is W/D adult female in no acute distress.
Eyes: the sclera and conjunctiva are normal, extraocular movements are intact.

Continued

TELEMEDICINE VISIT—cont'd

Neck: appearance of the neck is normal.
Pulmonary: normal respiratory rate and rhythm, no tremor is seen.
Psychiatric: oriented to person, place and time, insight and judgment were intact, the affect and speech patterns are normal. The patient reports anxiety about positive COVID-19 test.

Active Problems Headache, dyspnea, anosmia, fatigue, anxiety.

Current medications Albuterol sulfate HFA, inhale 2 puffs every 4 hours, as needed.

Allergies No known drug allergies

Signature
Electronically signed
Justin Wilson, MD 06/03/2021 4:17pm EST

Questions

1. What do W/D and W/N stand for? ______________________
2. Jennifer reports mild redness at the vaccine site; what is the medical term for this redness? ______________________
3. Jennifer states she has no appetite; the medical term is: ______________________
4. Jennifer complains of anosmia, which means: ______________________
5. She does not complain of abdominal pain. To which part of which body system does this refer? ______________________
6. Her sclera and conjunctiva are normal. To what body system do these terms refer? ______________________
7. What does extraocular mean? ______________________
8. Jennifer does not suffer from dysphagia, which means: ______________________
9. To what structures of the body does *otolaryngeal* refer? ______________________
10. Telemedicine visits are limited in examination procedures to which assessment process? ______________________
11. Jennifer takes her albuterol sulfate "as needed." What is the medical abbreviation for "as needed"? ______________________
12. How many tablets of Paxlovid will Jennifer take each day? ______________________
13. How many tablets in total are prescribed? ______________________

CHAPTER REVIEW

Identify the Anatomical Structures

Match the structures of the respiratory system from the following list to the letters shown in Figure 6-13.

1. ______ adenoids
2. ______ alveolus (air sac)
3. ______ bronchi
4. ______ diaphragm
5. ______ epiglottis
6. ______ larynx
7. ______ left lung
8. ______ nasal cavity
9. ______ nose
10. ______ pharynx
11. ______ pleura
12. ______ right lung
13. ______ sinuses
14. ______ soft palate
15. ______ trachea

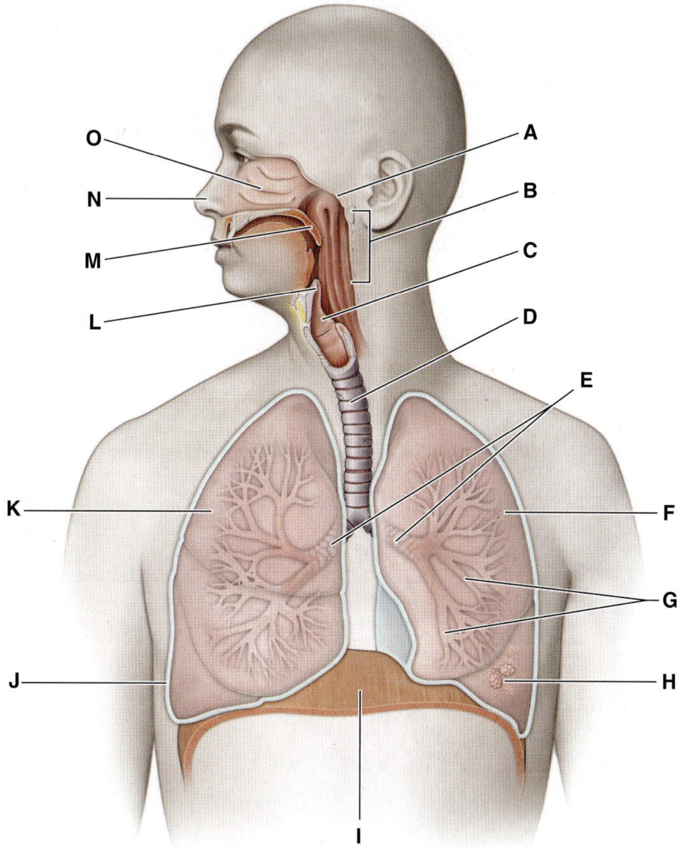

Figure 6-13 Identify the structures of the respiratory system.

Complete the Sentence

Using medical terms from this chapter, complete the sentence.

1. The medical term for a nosebleed is ______________________________.
2. The classification of medications used to liquefy respiratory secretions is __________ ______________________________.
3. Abnormally fast breathing is called ______________________________.
4. The medical term for the voice box is ______________________________.
5. The classification of medications that relieves or suppresses the urge to cough is _____ ______________________________.
6. The chief muscle of respiration is the ______________________________.

7. The area of the lung near the midline where blood vessels, nerves, and the bronchial tubes enter and exit is called the ______________________________.

8. The high-pitched harsh upper airway sound, which may be life-threatening, is called ______________________________.

9. The term for the exchange of O_2 and CO_2 between body cells and the blood capillaries is ______________________________

10. A skill taught to medical or laypersons to restore a victim's breathing and circulation is ______________________________.

11. Mucus or fluid coughed up from the lungs is known as ______________________________.

12. The intradermal injection of tuberculin purified protein under the skin is the ______________________________ test.

13. The measurement of the volume of air that can be exhaled after maximum inspiration is called the ______________________________.

14. The term for creating a mouth-like opening into the trachea is ______________________________.

15. The respiratory disease caused by inhaled coal dust is known as ______________________________.

Spelling

Circle the correctly spelled terms in the pairs of terms.

1. ventilation ventiliation
2. diptheria diphtheria
3. asthma azthma
4. bronchoscopy broncoscopy
5. corzya coryza
6. emphysema emphyzema
7. bronchoectasis bronchiectasis
8. hemotysis hemoptysis
9. cor pulmonale cor pulmonade
10. pleurisy pleuirsy
11. pneumothorac pneumothorax

12. perfusion parfusion
13. sputim sputum
14. tuberculosis tubreculosis
15. thoracentesis thoraccocentesis

Abbreviations

Define the following abbreviations:

1. SIDS ______
2. CPR ______
3. AIDS ______
4. RLL ______
5. TB ______
6. Po_2 ______
7. IPPB ______
8. AFB ______
9. CF ______
10. CDC ______

Decipher the Terms

Separate each term into its prefix (if any), combining form, and suffix. Next, translate the word parts and then give the common definition of the term. Pulmonary has been done for you as an example.

pulmonary

Prefix: *None* *Combining Form:* *Pulmon/o = lungs* *Suffix:* *-ary = pertaining to*

Meaning: *referring to the lungs*

1. bradypnea

Prefix: ______ *Combining Form:* ______ *Suffix:* ______

Meaning: ______

2. laryngitis

Prefix: ______ *Combining Form:* ______ *Suffix:* ______

Meaning: ______

3. pleurodynia

Prefix: ________ *Combining Form:* ________ *Suffix:* ________

Meaning: ________

4. pneumothorax

Prefix: ________ *Combining Form:* ________ *Suffix:* ________

Meaning: ________

5. hypoxia

Prefix: ________ *Combining Form:* ________ *Suffix:* ________

Meaning: ________

6. bronchoscopy

Prefix: ________ *Combining Form:* ________ *Suffix:* ________

Meaning: ________

7. orthopnea

Prefix: ________ *Combining Form:* ________ *Suffix:* ________

Meaning: ________

8. bronchiectasis

Prefix: ________ *Combining Form:* ________ *Suffix:* ________

Meaning: ________

9. dysphonia

Prefix: ________ *Combining Form:* ________ *Suffix:* ________

Meaning: ________

10. nasopharynx

Prefix: ________ *Combining Form:* ________ *Suffix:* ________

Meaning: ________

11. hypercapnia

Prefix: ________ *Combining Form:* ________ *Suffix:* ________

Meaning: ________

12. pleural

Prefix: ______________ *Combining Form:* ______________ *Suffix:* ______________

Meaning: ____

13. thoracotomy

Prefix: ______________ *Combining Form:* ______________ *Suffix:* ______________

Meaning: ____

14. epiglottitis

Prefix: ______________ *Combining Form:* ______________ *Suffix:* ______________

Meaning: ____

15. dyspnea

Prefix: ______________ *Combining Form:* ______________ *Suffix:* ______________

Meaning: ____

CHAPTER

7

The Cardiovascular System

LEARNING OBJECTIVES

Upon completion of the chapter, you will be able to:

1. Identify and define the combining forms, roots, prefixes, and suffixes introduced in the chapter.
2. Spell medical terms related to the cardiovascular system.
3. Describe the major organs of the cardiovascular system: the heart, arteries, veins and capillaries, and their functions.
4. Describe the flow of blood through the heart, lungs, and body.
5. Describe the conduction system of the heart and how it regulates the heartbeat.
6. Define and discuss blood pressure and pulse and identify the major pulse points.
7. Identify and discuss major pathological terms of the cardiovascular system.
8. Identify and discuss major diagnostic and therapeutic treatments of the cardiovascular system.
9. Identify the major categories of medications used to treat cardiac pathologies.
10. Define abbreviations of the cardiovascular system.

We start this chapter with the story of Nico, who has a history of high blood pressure and high cholesterol. The case study introduces some of the medical terms relevant to the cardiovascular system. Throughout the chapter, we will revisit the story of Nico to understand his diagnosis and how management of his condition improves his quality of life. Additionally, this chapter will discuss the normal anatomy and physiology of the cardiovascular system, additional pathologies of the cardiovascular system, and treatments for these conditions. You will be able to use word elements presented to understand unfamiliar terms and to build your medical vocabulary.

CASE STUDY

Nico is a 66-year-old retired long-haul truck driver who has HTN (high blood pressure) and hyperlipidemia (high cholesterol). He tries to exercise and lose some weight, but he has some bad dietary habits from his years being on the road. His wife and daughter encourage him to eat vegetables, but he is a "meat and potato" guy. He takes a pill for high blood pressure and a statin to lower his cholesterol. Nico wakes up early on Sunday morning with angina (chest pain) and nausea. He thinks about the food he ate at his daughter's nursing school graduation party yesterday and thinks "this must be heartburn." But the pain gets worse; it has never been this severe. Reluctantly, he wakes his wife and says, "I think I need to go to the emergency department."

Continued

CASE STUDY, continued

Marla looks at her husband and is frightened at how his skin looks gray, and he is sweating profusely. She says "Yes, let's go right away. I'll get Lindsay to drive so I can sit in the backseat with you." Lindsay gives him an aspirin and says, "Dad, chew on this aspirin and sip some water."

KEY TERMS

Aorta
Aortic valve
Apex
Apical pulse
Artery
Atrioventricular (AV) node
Bicuspid valve (Mitral valve)
Blood pressure
Bundle of His
Capillaries
Cardiac cycle
Depolarization
Diastole
Diastolic pressure
Foramen ovale
Inferior vena cava
Left atrium
Left ventricle
Mediastinum
Mitral valve (bicuspid valve)
Pulmonary circulation
Pulmonary valve
Pulse points
Purkinje fibers
Right atrium
Right ventricle
Septum
Sinoatrial (SA) node
Superior vena cava
Systemic circulation
Systole
Systolic pressure
Tricuspid valve
Vein
Venule

Structures and Physiology of the Cardiovascular System

The cardiovascular system, also called the circulatory system, comprises the heart and blood vessels. Blood vessels include the arteries, arterioles, veins, venules, and capillaries. The functions of the cardiovascular system are to:

- pump blood to the tissues and cells of the body,
- distribute oxygen (O_2) and nutrients to the tissues and cells, and
- remove carbon dioxide (CO_2) and other waste products from the tissues and cells.

The Heart

ELEMENT REVIEW
cardi/o = heart
my/o = muscle
end/o = inside
epi- = outside
peri- = around

The heart is a hollow muscular organ made of cardiac muscle fibers. It is about the size of a closed fist, and its purpose is to pump blood to all parts of the body through a closed vascular network. It beats 60 to 100 times per minute for an entire lifetime. Located in the center of the chest, it is protected by the sternum, or breastbone. It is slightly to the left of the midline in an area between the lungs called the **mediastinum**. The wall of the heart has three layers: the outermost layer is the epicardium, the middle muscular layer is the myocardium, and the inner lining is the endocardium. The heart is enclosed in a sturdy fibrous membrane called the pericardium, or pericardial sac, which also contains a small amount of fluid called pericardial fluid.

The heart has four chambers (Fig. 7-1): the two upper "holding" chambers, the right and left atrium, and two larger lower "pumping" chambers, the right and left ventricles. The left ventricle is larger and more muscular than the right because of its greater workload, pumping blood to the entire body (systemic circulation) (Fig. 7-2). The right ventricle also pumps blood but back to the lungs for reoxygenation (pulmonary circulation). The walls of the ventricles are thicker and more muscular than the atria because they take blood away from the heart to the lungs (right) and body (left).

The right and left sides of the heart are divided by a thick layer of muscle tissue called the **septum**.

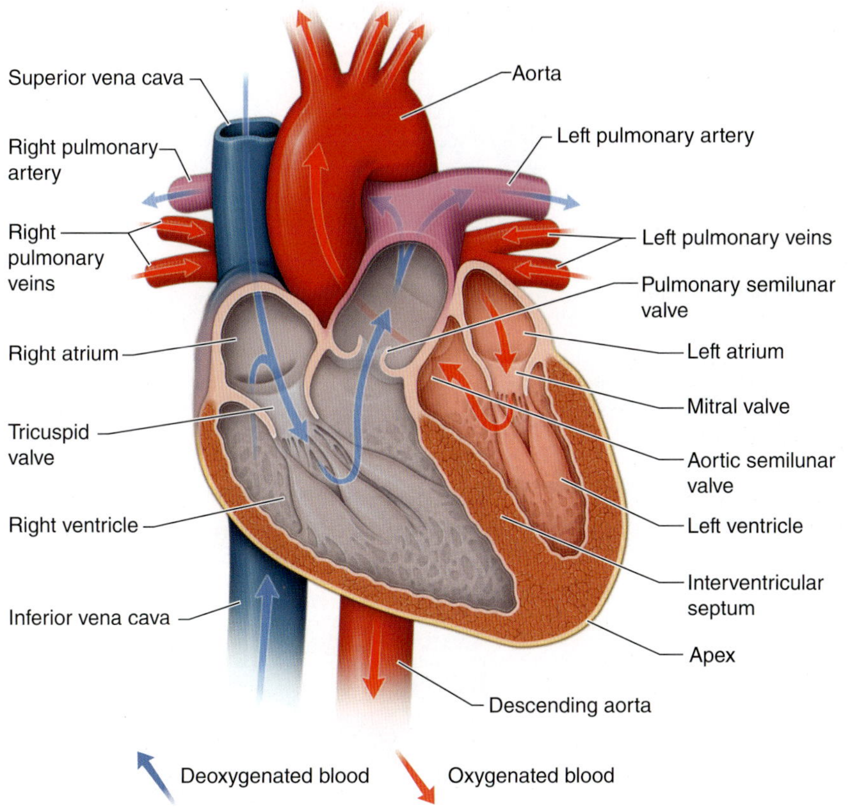

Figure 7-1 The heart.

The heart has four valves. The **tricuspid valve** exits the right atrium into the right ventricle, and the mitral, or **bicuspid valve**, exits the left atrium into the left ventricle. The **pulmonary semilunar valve** exits the right ventricle into the pulmonary artery, and the **aortic valve** exits the left ventricle into the aorta.

The largest part of the heart, the tip of the left ventricle, is known as the **apex**. This site is best for listening to sounds from the mitral valve and is where the **apical pulse** is best heard. Listening to (auscultating) the apical pulse for 1 full minute is considered the most accurate method of measuring heart rate.

ELEMENT REVIEW
pulmon/o = lungs
-ary = pertaining to

The Path of Blood

Circulation is the one-way flow of blood to and from the heart. Blood flows through both sides of the heart simultaneously, and each side pumps blood to different parts of the body. The left side of the heart delivers oxygenated blood to the body while the right side of the heart delivers deoxygenated blood to the lungs. The body is composed of trillions of cells that all need a continuous supply of O_2 and nutrients. As the cells of the body metabolize food for energy, they also produce waste products that must be eliminated. The cardiovascular system continuously provides O_2 and nutrients while simultaneously getting rid of CO_2 and waste.

Deoxygenated waste-filled blood is carried by the **superior vena cava** (SVC) and the **inferior vena cava** (IVC) to the right side of the heart. The superior vena cava brings deoxygenated blood from the head and neck to the right atrium. The IVC (the largest vein in your body) brings deoxygenated blood from the rest of the body to the right atrium.

The right atrium pumps blood downward through the tricuspid valve into the **right ventricle**. The tricuspid valve closes to prevent backflow of blood. As the right ventricle

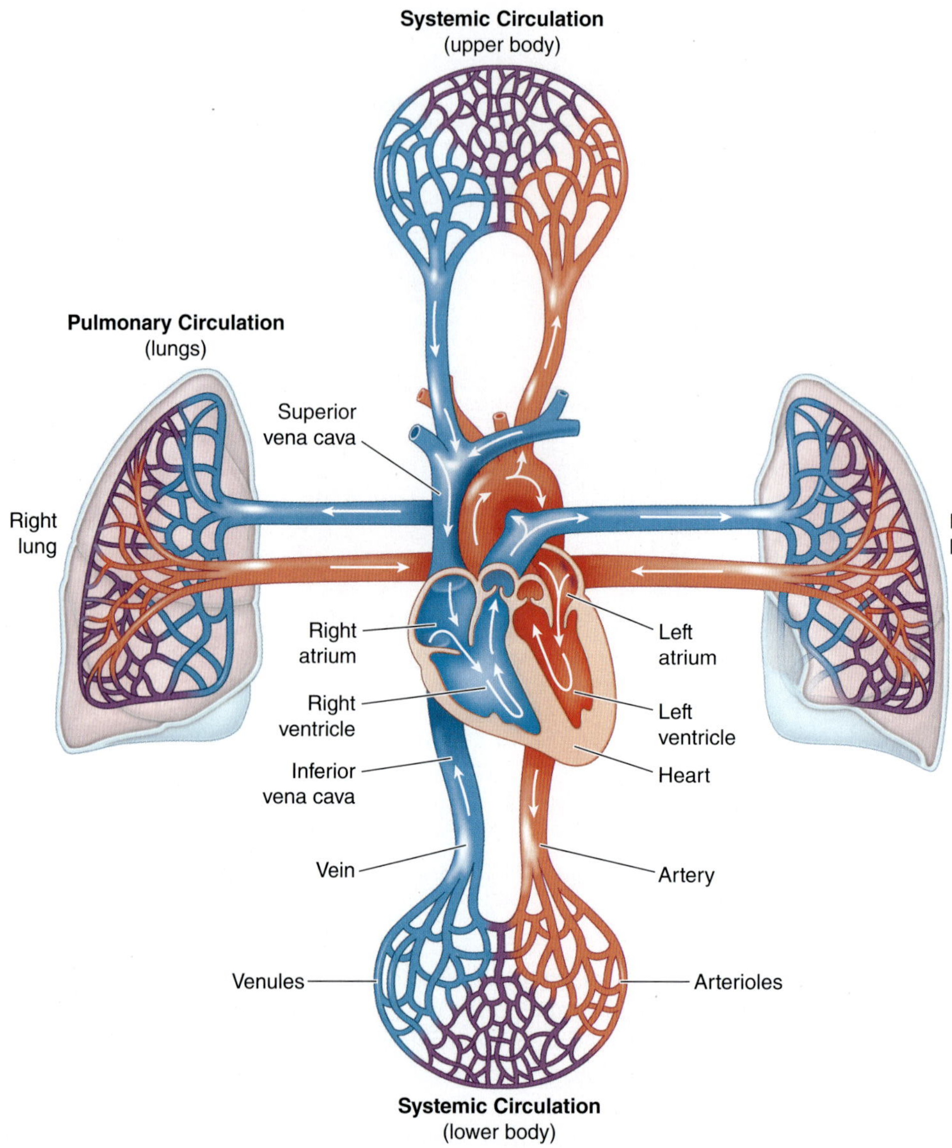

Figure 7-2 Pulmonary and systemic circulation, a one-way flow.

contracts, blood is forced up and out through the pulmonary valve into the pulmonary arteries. The pulmonary valves close to prevent backflow of blood back into the right ventricle. The pulmonary arteries then carry deoxygenated blood to the lungs. The pulmonary artery is the only artery in your body that carries deoxygenated blood.

After gaseous exchange occurs in the lungs, the oxygenated blood returns to the **left atrium** via the pulmonary veins. The pulmonary veins are the only veins in your body that transport *oxygen-rich* blood. As the left atrium contracts, blood is pushed downward through the **mitral valve** (bicuspid) into the **left ventricle**. The mitral valve closes to prevent backflow of blood into the left atrium. Blood is then pumped or pushed upward and out through the **aortic valve** into the **aorta**. The aortic valve closes to prevent backflow of blood to the left ventricle. The aorta transports blood to the rest of the body from arteries to arterioles to capillaries. The blood then starts back to the heart via venules, veins, and finally to the superior vena cava and IVC back to the right atrium. Arteries and veins get larger as they get closer to the heart; the aorta is the largest artery, and the IVC is the largest vein.

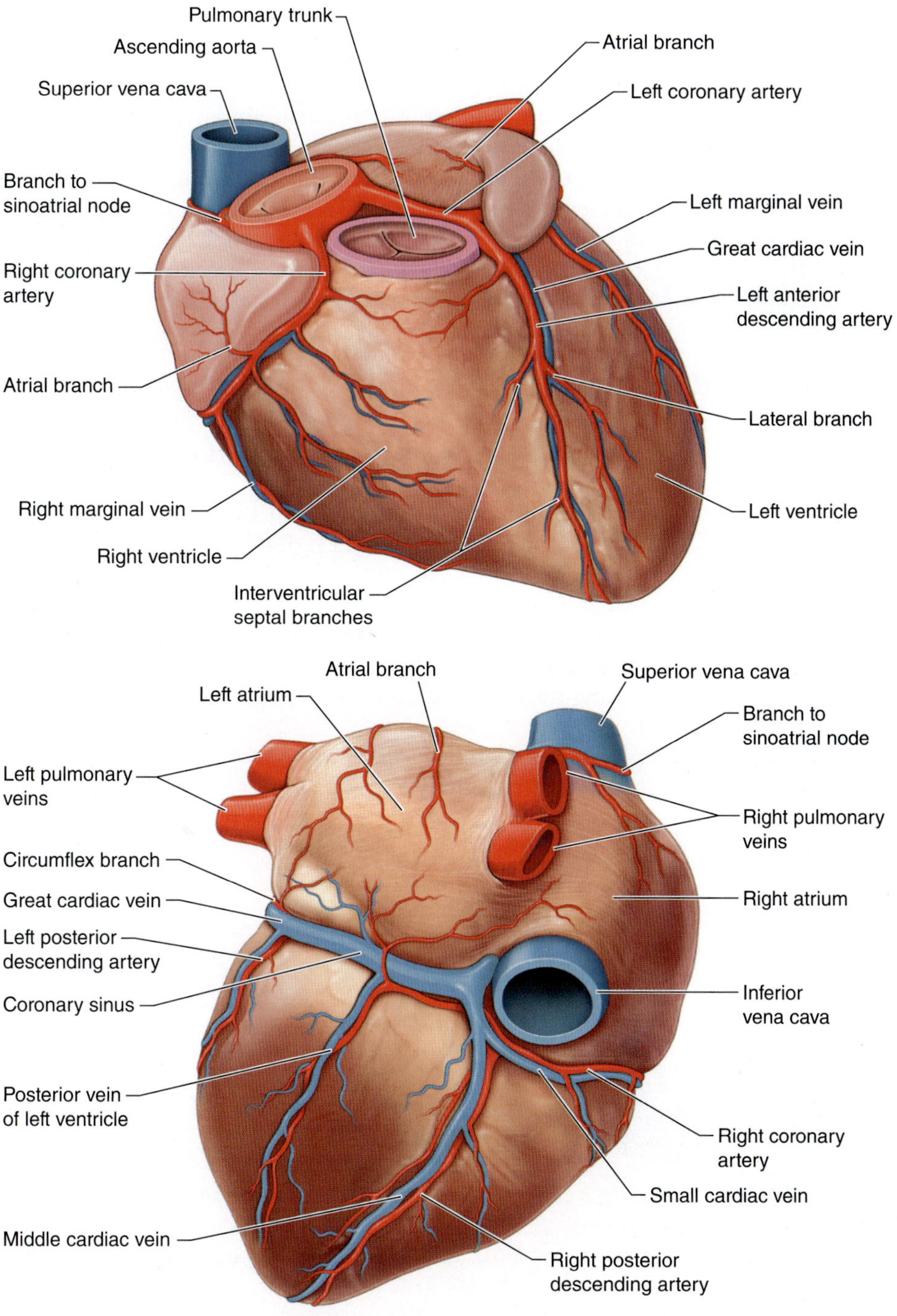

Figure 7-3 The coronary arteries.

The Coronary Arteries

In addition to supplying blood to all the tissues of the body, the heart itself needs a tremendous amount of blood. The coronary arteries, shown in Figure 7-3, originate at the top of the left ventricle near the aorta. The right and left coronary arteries branch out to supply both ventricles. The heart uses approximately three times more oxygen than other organs or tissues of the body. Proper myocardial function relies on the blood supply of the coronary arteries.

The Conduction System

ELEMENT REVIEW
cardi/o = heart
my/o = muscle
-cyte = cell

The heart rate is regulated by the autonomic nervous system, meaning that you don't have voluntary control over the beating of the heart. The heartbeat relies on a cluster of specialized cells (modified cardiomyocytes) in the right atrium called the **sinoatrial (SA) node**. It is commonly called the pacemaker of the heart, and it initiates an electrical impulse about 60 to 100 times per minute. Each of these impulses is transmitted throughout all muscle cells of the heart, resulting in electrical **depolarization**. Depolarization is the electrical change in cardiac muscle cells in which the inside of the cells become positive in relation to the outside. This depolarization causes individual cardiac muscle cells in the atria to contract in unison. The normal rhythm of the heart is called *normal sinus rhythm*, named for the SA node.

While the cardiac rate is governed by the autonomic nervous system, it is also influenced by outside factors. For example, it accelerates during exercise and slows down at rest or during sleep.

ELEMENT REVIEW
atri/o = atrium
ventricul/o = ventricle
-ar = pertaining to

Within the floor of the right atrium is a backup pacemaker, the **atrioventricular (AV) node**. It receives the impulse from the SA node and transmits it onward to both ventricles via the atrioventricular bundle, also called the **bundle of His**, and the **Purkinje fibers**, located in the right and left ventricles. The electrical signal is distributed throughout the septum and ventricles to create coordinated muscular contraction. As the electrical impulse is transmitted throughout the ventricles, all ventricular muscle fibers must contract in unison. This contraction occurs just slightly after the contraction of the atria, and the combination of the two results in one complete heartbeat. This entire process is repeated with each heartbeat forming the cardiac cycle. The sequencing of the conduction pathway is shown in Figure 7-4.

Impulse transmission through the conduction system can be recorded on graph paper or a computer screen by an instrument called an *electrocardiograph*, also known as an EKG. The machine records the electrical activity of the heart and is represented by a wave

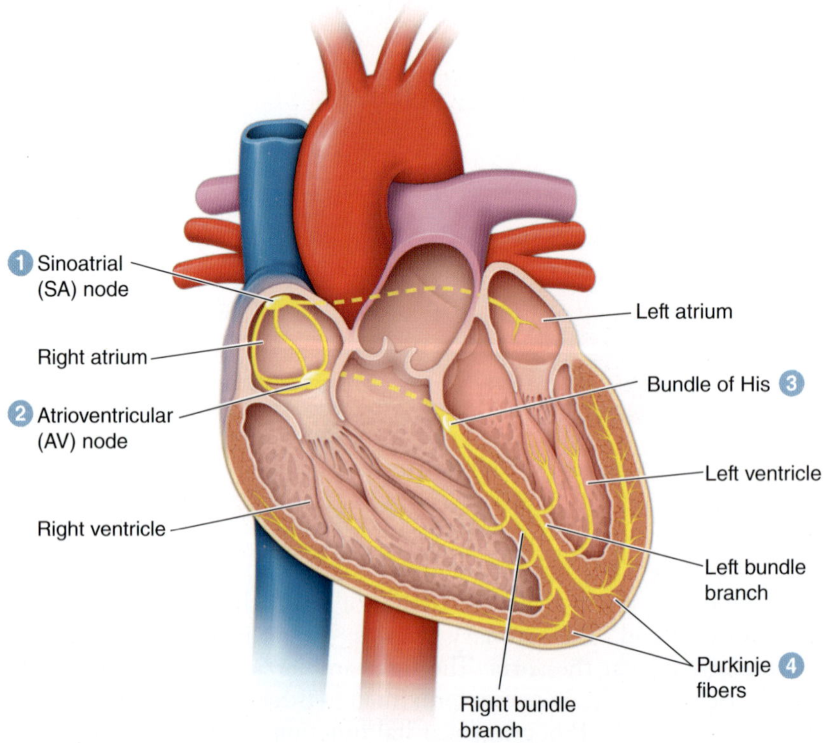

Figure 7-4 The conduction pathway sequence.

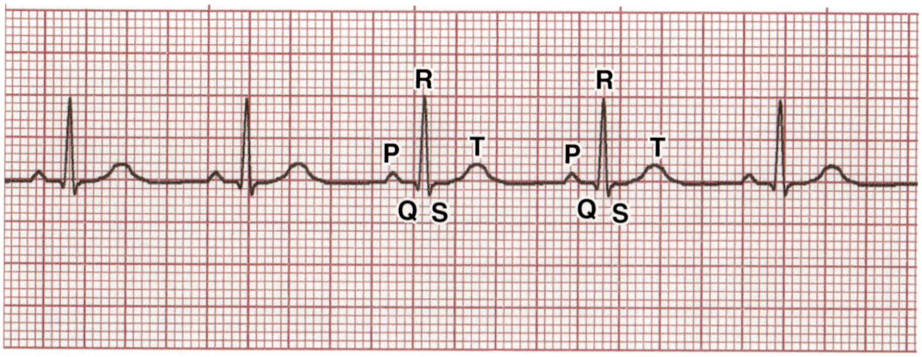

Figure 7-5 An ECG of a normal sinus rhythm.

complex (Fig. 7-5). The letters P, Q, R, S, and T are associated with specific electrical events within the heart:

The P wave is the depolarization (contraction) of the atria,
the QRS complex is the depolarization (contraction) of the ventricles, and
the T wave follows as the ventricles repolarize.

The Cardiac Cycle

The coordinated contraction and relaxation of the four heart chambers creates each heartbeat and is known as the **cardiac cycle**. Each cardiac cycle takes approximately 0.8 seconds. The pressure created by pumping blood, known as **blood pressure**, is written as two numbers, with one written over the other: for example, 120/80. The upper number, called the **systolic pressure**, is a measurement of the highest pressure exerted against artery walls during ventricular contraction or **systole**. The lower number, called the **diastolic pressure**, measures the lowest pressure exerted against artery walls during ventricular relaxation, or **diastole**. Several factors influence blood pressure:

- Resistance of blood flow in the blood vessels
- The muscular pumping action of the heart
- Viscosity (thickness) of the blood flowing in the arteries
- The elasticity of the arteries
- The total volume of blood in the vascular system

Large arteries in the body that have a strong pulse and are easily palpated are known as **pulse points** (Fig. 7-6). These points, sometimes called pressure points, may be compressed to slow bleeding in the case of hemorrhage.

The Blood Vessels

There are three types of blood vessels: arteries, capillaries, and veins. The aorta, the largest artery of the body, delivers oxygen-rich blood from the heart to various parts of the body via

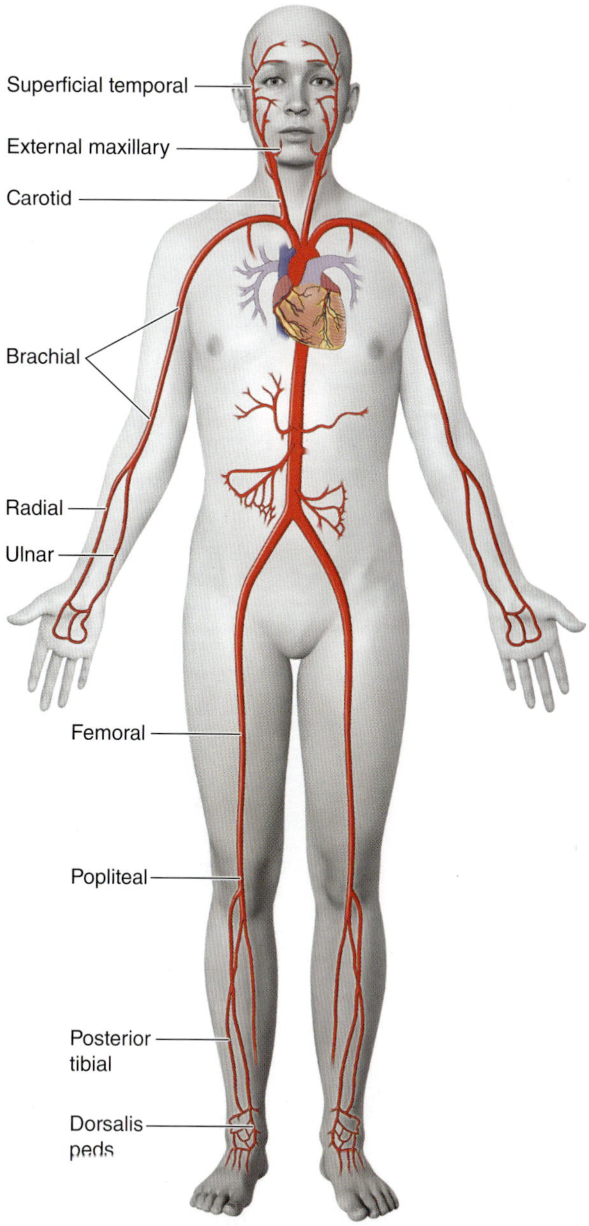

Figure 7-6 Pulse points. Find your radial and carotid pulse points. Can you measure your beats per minute?

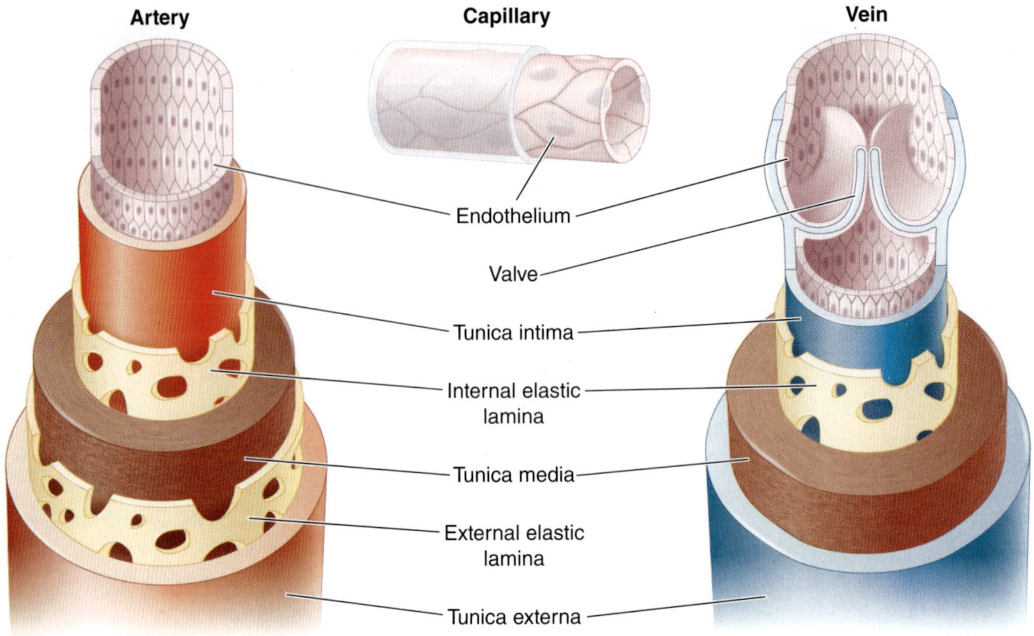

Figure 7-7 The layers of the arterial, venal, and capillary walls.

systemic circulation. As blood leaves the aorta, it moves through smaller and smaller arteries.

Blood is propelled through the arteries by the pumping action of the heart. The **artery** walls must be thick and muscular because they carry blood under high pressure. The layers of the arterial walls are shown in Figure 7-7. The middle layer, the tunica media, is made up of smooth muscle and elastic fibers that allow the artery wall to expand slightly under pressure. The tunica externa, the outer layer, is made of connective tissue, which gives it both strength and flexibility. The inner lining, the tunica intima, affords the lumen a smooth inner surface to promote ease of blood flow.

The smallest arteries, called arterioles, have thinner walls than do the arteries, and are made of mostly smooth muscle which has much fewer elastic properties. Arterioles terminate in capillary beds. **Capillaries** are the tiniest blood vessels in the body and are where the exchange of gases and nutrients occurs. Capillary walls are only one cell thick, making them semipermeable, meaning oxygen and nutrients can exit the capillary. The capillaries can also pick up carbon dioxide and waste from the tissue cells. This exchange is systemic, happening all over the body to ensure exchange of O_2, nutrients, and CO_2. Blood low in O_2 and high in CO_2 leaves the capillaries and enters tiny veins called **venules**. The numerous venules become larger **veins** as they get closer to the heart. Veins must push blood up against gravity. Venous blood travels under much less pressure than does arterial blood, so contraction of skeletal muscles facilitates the venous blood flow against gravity. Large veins, especially in the abdomen, have smooth muscle within the vein that uses peristalsis to push blood back toward the heart.

Additionally, veins have one-way valves to prevent backflow (see Fig. 7-7). If a vein starts bleeding, these valves also slow the blood loss. Arteries don't have these valves so blood from a damaged artery flows more quickly. Venous blood continues flowing through larger and larger veins until it returns to the heart via the SVC and IVC. Blood is then sent to the lungs in a process called **pulmonary circulation**, in which carbon dioxide is released and oxygen is picked up by the blood.

PHYSIOLOGY FACT

Veins bleed more slowly than arteries because the valves act like locks (gates) on a canal; more blood loss occurs only after the valves open and blood refills the damaged portion of the vein.

Fetal Circulation

The circulatory system of a fetus differs from that of a newborn infant. The fetus depends on maternal blood vessels to provide exchange of O_2, CO_2, nutrients, and waste. Respiration does not involve the lungs of the fetus. Instead, the placenta and maternal blood vessels provide O_2 and nutrients to the umbilical arteries. CO_2 and waste products are carried away from the fetus by way of the umbilical vein (Fig. 7-8).

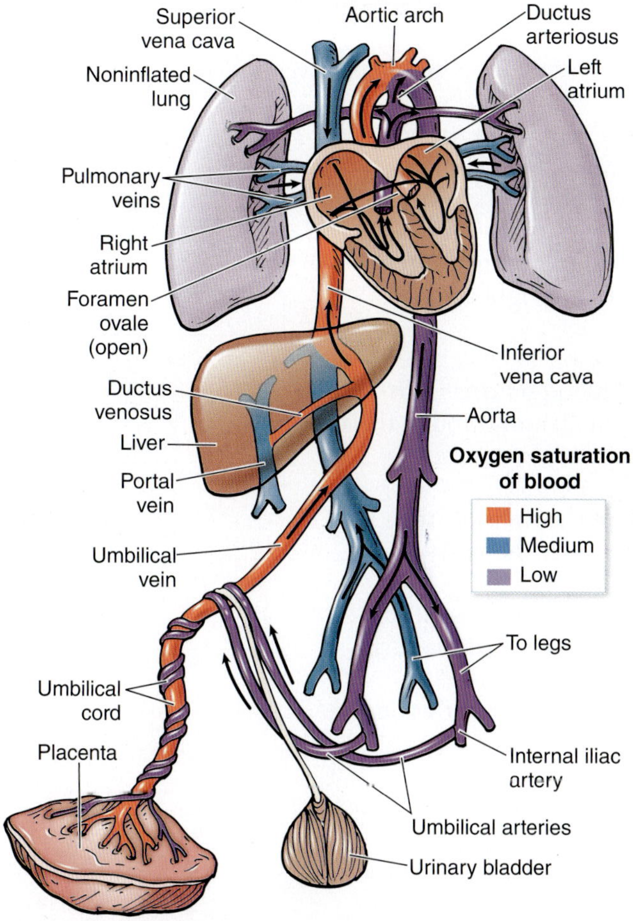

Figure 7-8 The circulatory system of a fetus.

The umbilical cord contains two arteries that carry deoxygenated blood away from the fetus to the placenta. Oxygenation of the blood occurs in the placenta, and O_2-rich blood returns to the fetus via the umbilical vein. Most of the blood in the umbilical vein enters the IVC through the ductus venosus and is then delivered to the right atrium of the fetus. Some of this blood passes to the right ventricle, but most passes through the **foramen ovale**, a small opening in the atrial septum that will close shortly after birth. The ductus arteriosus shunts most of the blood out of the pulmonary arteries into the aorta, bypassing the nonfunctioning lungs of the fetus.

STRUCTURES AND PHYSIOLOGY REVIEW

1. Match the Words

Match the words to their descriptions.

aortic semilunar valve	epicardium	pulse points
apex	mediastinum	septum
arterioles	mitral valve	sinoatrial node
auscultating	myocardium	vena cavae
capillaries	pericardial fluid	ventricles
cardiac cycle	pericardium	venules
coronary arteries	pulmonary veins	

1. Vessels that originate from the aorta, resembling a crown, encircling the heart and supply blood to the heart ________________
2. The thick muscular layer of tissue dividing the left and right sides of the heart ________________
3. Deoxygenated blood returns from the body to the right atrium through these inferior and superior structures. ________________
4. The sturdy fibrous membrane that encloses and protects the heart ________________
5. The valve that exits the left ventricle and allows blood to flow to the aorta ________________
6. The smallest veins that directly connect to capillaries ________________
7. The process of "listening to" heart sounds ________________
8. The valve that is located between the left atrium and ventricle ________________

9. Locations on the body with a strong pulse that are easily palpated ______________________

10. The structure called the "natural pacemaker" of the heart ______________________

11. The repeated and continuous contraction and relaxation of the four heart chambers ______________________

12. The large muscular layer of the heart ______________________

13. The area between the lungs slightly left of the center of the chest ______________________

14. The two lower (pumping) chambers of the heart ______________________

15. The lubricating fluid that reduces friction as the heart contracts and relaxes ______________________

16. Very small arteries ______________________

17. The outermost layer of the heart ______________________

18. Vessels that transport oxygen-rich blood to various parts of the body ______________________

19. The largest part of the heart; the lower left area ______________________

20. The smallest vessels of the circulatory system that are just one cell thick and allow O_2 and CO_2 to diffuse across their membrane ______________________

Structures and Physiology Word-Building Practice

1. Nouns and Adjectives

Complete the chart of nouns and their adjective forms.

Noun Form	Adjective Form
1. myocardium	______________________
2. apex	______________________
3. ______________________	ventricular
4. atria, atrium	______________________
5. vein	______________________
6. thrombolysis	______________________

7. pericardium ______________________

8. ______________________ hypertensive

9. ______________________ diaphoretic

10. artery ______________________

2. Prefixes

Choose from the list of prefixes to build a word for the definitions below:

bi-	two	myo-	muscle
con-	together, with	pre-	before
echo-	sound	pro-	before, forward
endo-	in, within, inner	re-, retro-	behind, back
macro-	large	tri-	three
micro-	small		

1. Pertaining to the inner lining of the heart ______________________
2. The valve that has three "cusps" ______________________
3. The valve that has two "cusps" ______________________
4. The inner lining of the heart ______________________
5. Process of recording the heartbeat with sound ______________________
6. Unusual smallness of the heart ______________________
7. The period in the heart's cycle before the systole ______________________
8. Pertaining to the heart muscle ______________________

3. Singular and Plural Forms

Complete the chart of singular and plural forms. Refer to singular and plural forms table in Chapter 2.

Singular	Plural
1. atrium	______________________
2. ______________________	ventricles
3. apex	______________________
4. artery	______________________
5. vein	______________________
6. ______________________	capillaries
7. ______________________	Vena cavae

Word Building With Combining, Prefix, and Suffix Forms

The following word roots, prefixes, and suffixes are commonly used in medical terms for the anatomy and pathology of the cardiovascular system. Combining vowels for word roots are included. Memorizing these word elements will enable you to understand new terms you may encounter in the field of cardiology, or as a physical therapist, medical assistant, nurse, EKG technician, and many other health professions.

The list contains examples of terms that utilize the combining forms as well as a pronunciation guide. Be sure to use the pronunciation guide so that you can learn to pronounce the terms correctly.

The Medical Language Lab at medicallanguagelab.com provides audio files to help you practice your pronunciations.

Combining Form	Meaning	Example (Pronunciation)	Definition
angi/o	vessel	angioma (an-JĒ-ō-mă)	tumor of a vessel
aort/o	aorta	aortic (ā-ORT-ĭk)	pertaining to the aorta
arteri/o	artery	arteriosclerosis (ăr-tē-rē-ō-sklĕ-RŌ-sĭs)	abnormal condition of hardening of an artery
ather/o	thick, fatty	atherosclerotic (ath-ĕ-rŏ-sklĕ-RŌ-tĭk)	pertaining to thick fatty deposits in arteries
atri/o	atria	atrioventricular (ā-trē-ō-vĕn-TRĬK-ū-lăr)	pertaining to the atria and the ventricles
cardi/o	heart	bradycardia (brād-ē-KĂR-dē-ă)	condition of a slow heart rate
coron/o	heart	coronary (KOR-ō-nă-rē)	pertaining to the heart
electr/o	electricity	electrocardiography (ē-lĕk-trō-KĂR-dē-ō-grăfe)	process of recording electrical activity of the heart
phleb/o	vein	phlebotomy (flĕb-ō-tōmē)	incision into a vein
scler/o	hardening	sclerotic (sklĕ-RŌ-ĭk)	pertaining to abnormal condition of
thromb/o	thrombus (clot)	thromboangiitis (thrŏm-bō-an-jē-ĪT-ĭs)	inflammation of a blood vessel with clot formation
valv/o	valve	valvotomy (văl-VŎT-ō-mē)	cutting into or incision of a valve
valvul/o	valve	valvulotome (VĂL-vū-lō-mē)	an instrument for incising (cutting) into a valve
vascul/o	blood vessel	vasculopathy (văs-kū-LŎP-ă-thē)	any disease or disorder affecting blood vessels
vas/o	vessel	vasoconstriction (văs-OR-kŏn-strĭk-shŭn)	decrease in the diameter of blood vessels, decreasing blood flow and increasing pressure

Continued

Combining Form	Meaning	Example (Pronunciation)	Definition
ven/o	vein	venectasia (vē-nek-TĀ-zē-ă)	dilation of a vein
ventricul/o	ventricle	ventriculotomy (věn-trĭk-ū-LŎ-tō-mē)	surgical incision into a ventricle

ā = say, ă = sofa, ē = meet, ĕ = met, ī = eye, ĭ = in, ō = oh, ŏ = dog, ū = you, ŭ = up, oo = food

Prefix	Meaning	Example (Pronunciation)	Definition
brady-	slow	bradycardia (brād-ē-KĂR-dē-ă)	abnormally slow heart rate
hyper-	excessive, fast	hypertension (hī-pĕr-TEN-shŏn)	high blood pressure
hypo-	diminished, slow	hypotension (hī-pō-TEN-shŭn)	low blood pressure
peri-	around	pericardial (per-ĭ-KAR-dē-ăl	pertaining to around the heart
tachy-	fast	tachycardia (tak-ē-KARD-ĕ-ă)	abnormally fast heart rate

ā = say, ă = sofa, ē = meet, ĕ = met, ī = eye, ĭ = in, ō = oh, ŏ = dog, ū = you, ŭ = up, oo = food

Suffix	Meaning	Example (Pronunciation)	Definition
-ar	pertaining to	ventricular (vĕn-TRĬK-ū-lăr)	pertaining to the ventricles
-gram	record	electrocardiogram (ē-lĕk-trō-KĂR-dē-ō-grăm)	electrical recording of the heart
-graphy	process of recording	echocardiography (ĕk-ō-KĂR-dē-ō-grăm)	process of recording the heart with sound
-ial	pertaining to	myocardial (mī-ō-KĂR-dē-ăl)	pertaining to heart muscle
-itis	inflammation	phlebitis (flē-BĪ-tĭs)	inflammation of a vein
-megaly	enlargement	cardiomegaly (KĂR-dē-ō-MĔG-ă-lē)	enlargement of the heart
-osis	condition	arteriosclerosis (ăr-tē-rē-ō-sklĕ-RŌ-sĭs)	condition of hardening of arteries
-pathy	disease	cardiomyopathy (KĂR-dē-ō-mī-OP-ă-thē)	disease of heart muscle
-stasis	stop, control	hemostasis (hē-mŏ-STĀ- sĭs)	stopping or controlling blood flow

ā = say, ă = sofa, ē = meet, ĕ = met, ī = eye, ĭ = in, ō = oh, ŏ = dog, ū = you, ŭ = up, oo = food

Combining Forms Practice

1. Build the Terms

*Using **only** the word parts in the lists provided, create medical terms for the indicated meanings.*

Prefixes	Combining Forms		Suffixes	
a-	angi/o	phleb/o	-ar	-oma
an-	aort/o	scler/o	-ary	-plasty
brady-	arteri/o	thromb/o	-al	-rrhaphy
tachy-	ather/o	valv/o	-edema	-rrhexis
	atri/o	valvul/o	-gram	-sis
	cardi/o	vas/o	-ia	-stasis
	coron/o	vascul/o	-itis	-stenosis
	electr/o	ven/o	-lytic	-sclerosis
		ventricul/o	-ic	

1. pertaining to the aorta ____________________
2. condition of a slow heart ____________________
3. pertaining to the heart and blood vessels ____________________
4. abnormal condition of narrowing of a vein ____________________
5. suturing of the heart ____________________
6. an image of the aorta ____________________
7. removal of thick fatty plaque ____________________
8. surgical repair of a vein ____________________
9. stopping the flow of blood ____________________
10. pertaining to the aorta ____________________
11. hardening of fatty plaque ____________________
12. pertaining to the ventricles ____________________
13. inflammation of a vein with the presence of a clot ____________________
14. pertaining to the heart muscle ____________________
15. Condition of a fast heart (rate) ____________________

2. Decipher the Terms

Separate each term into its prefix (if any), combining form, and suffix. Next, translate the word parts, and then give the common definition of the term.

1. arteriovenous

   Prefix: ______________ *Combining Form:* ______________ *Suffix:* ______________

   Meaning: ____

2. angiorrhexis

   Prefix: ______________ *Combining Form:* ______________ *Suffix:* ______________

   Meaning: ____

3. cardiomyocyte

   Prefix: ______________ *Combining Form:* ______________ *Suffix:* ______________

   Meaning: ____

4. cardiogenesis

   Prefix: ______________ *Combining Form:* ______________ *Suffix:* ______________

   Meaning: ____

5. valvoplasty

   Prefix: ______________ *Combining Form:* ______________ *Suffix:* ______________

   Meaning: ____

6. myocardium

   Prefix: ______________ *Combining Form:* ______________ *Suffix:* ______________

   Meaning: ____

7. echocardiogram

   Prefix: ______________ *Combining Form:* ______________ *Suffix:* ______________

   Meaning: ____

8. electrocardiography

   Prefix: ______________ *Combining Form:* ______________ *Suffix:* ______________

   Meaning: ____

9. thrombolytic

Prefix: ______________ *Combining Form:* ______________ *Suffix:* ______________

Meaning: ____

10. atheroma

Prefix: ______________ *Combining Form:* ______________ *Suffix:* ______________

Meaning: ____

CASE STUDY, continued

Nico, his wife, and daughter get to the emergency department of the local hospital. Lindsay explains to the intake nurse that her dad is complaining of chest pain (angina). The nurse observes that Nico is sweating (diaphoresis) and is pale. She takes his BP, which reads 150/98 mm Hg. His temperature is normal at 98.4, respirations are 18/min and labored. He appears to be in acute distress. The ED provider prescribes a nitroglycerin patch to dilate coronary blood vessels, Vicodin to decrease Nico's chest pain, and metoprolol to decrease his elevated blood pressure. The pain subsides as Nico rests. An EKG and blood tests are performed. Marla and Lindsay wait with Nico to see why he developed his symptoms so quickly, and more importantly, what can be done for him.

Cardiovascular System Diseases and Disorders

Good nutrition and exercise will help the cardiovascular system contribute to overall good health. Unfortunately, not everyone enjoys good health, and there are many diseases and disorders of the cardiovascular system. Treatments for cardiovascular diseases and disorders can be surgical correction, pharmacological therapy, and/or lifestyle changes, which are discussed in further detail in this chapter.

Common Signs and Symptoms

Patients with cardiovascular diseases and disorders may describe a list of common complaints, objective signs, and subjective symptoms to their health-care providers and support staff (Table 7-1). The observant medical assistant will look for these signs and symptoms when caring for patients who may suffer from cardiovascular diseases and disorders.

Pathological Conditions of the Heart

Angina pectoris: The sensation of pain and pressure and a symptom of heart disease, most commonly of coronary artery disease. Pain and pressure can be felt in the chest, shoulders, arms, jaw, or neck, which is caused by insufficient blood and oxygen (ischemia) to the heart.

Cardiac tamponade: Compression of the heart due to excess fluid within the pericardial sac that prevents the ventricles from adequately filling and pumping blood. If left untreated, it is a life-threatening emergency. Treatment is most often pericardiocentesis to remove the excess fluid and relieve pressure on the heart.

ELEMENT REVIEW
peri- = around
cardi/o = heart
-centesis = surgical puncture and aspiration of fluid

TABLE 7-1 Common Signs and Symptoms

Common Signs	Common Symptom
Bradycardia (HR under 60 bpm)	Anorexia (lack or loss of appetite)
Cyanosis (slightly blueish or gray discoloration of the skin due to reduced hemoglobin in the blood)	Anxiety (uneasy feeling of worry or dread)
	Chest pain (tightness, aching, crushing feeling in the chest)
Dyspnea (difficulty breathing, shortness of breath) *Both a sign and symptom	Fatigue (feeling tired and weak, state of exhaustion)
Edema (excess fluid accumulation; swelling, often in the legs)	Headache (cephalgia; acute or chronic diffuse pain in the head, with location on the head that may vary)
Fever (elevated normal body temperature often accompanies infection)	
Pallor (paleness, lack of color in the skin)	Nausea (unpleasant sensation that can precede vomiting; can be brought on by chest pain)
Sweat (excessive perspiration; also called hyperhidrosis)	
Tachycardia (a resting HR of over 100)	Palpitation (rapid, violent, throbbing pulsations felt by the patient)
Vomiting (forcible ejection of the stomach contents out of the mouth)	Weakness (lack of normal [baseline] physical strength)

Congestive heart failure: The inability of the heart to pump enough blood to meet the body's metabolic needs. Left-sided cardiac failure (the left ventricle is unable to pump sufficient quantities of blood that enters from the lungs) causes pulmonary edema, dyspnea (difficulty breathing), fatigue, and anxiety. Right-sided cardiac failure, or **cor pulmonale** (the right ventricle cannot pump sufficient quantities of blood to the lungs from the venous system), causes edema in the lower extremities, weight gain, hepatomegaly (enlargement of the liver), ascites (fluid buildup in the abdominal cavity), anorexia (loss of appetite), nocturia (frequent nighttime urination), and weakness.

Coronary artery disease: Narrowing of the coronary arteries to the extent that the myocardium does not receive adequate blood supply (Fig. 7-9). The condition is caused by arteriosclerosis and atherosclerosis and can cause clots to form and lead to thrombotic occlusion (blockage).

Endocarditis: An infection or inflammation of the membrane lining of the heart. It may affect the inside of one or more heart chambers and any of the heart valves. Endocarditis is commonly caused by streptococcal bacteria (or other pathogenic organisms) originating in other parts of the body such as the skin, intestinal tract, and respiratory tract and traveling to the heart via the bloodstream. The condition can lead to deformity of the valves and result in a heart murmur.

Mitral valve prolapse: The abnormal displacement of the valve into the atrium during ventricular systole (when the heart is pumping). Commonly caused by a thickening of the valve. Ten percent of the population has the condition, although many individuals with MVP are asymptomatic.

Mitral valve stenosis: The mitral valve, located between the left atrium and ventricle, fails to open completely due to thickening of the valve (Fig. 7-10). It is often caused by previous bouts of rheumatic carditis.

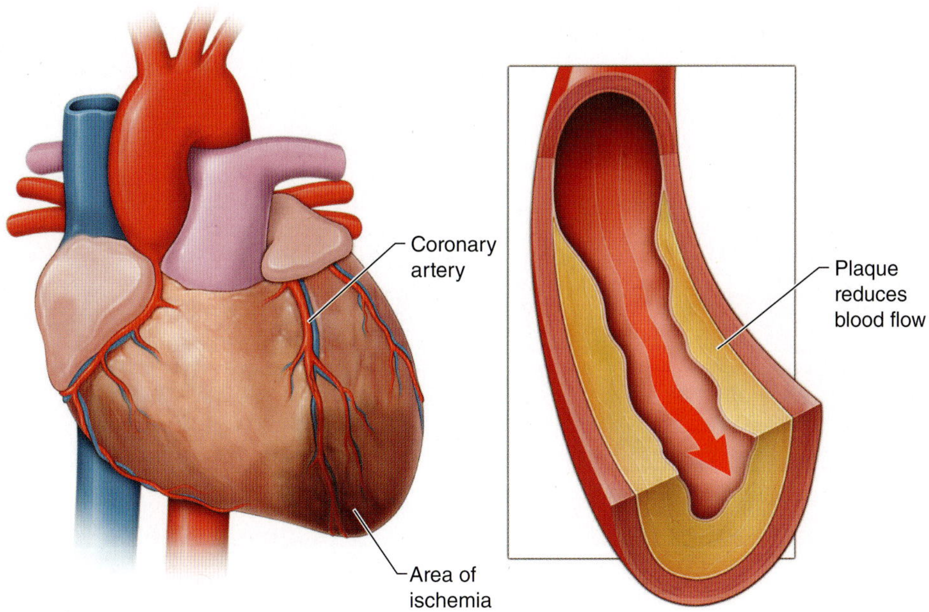

Figure 7-9 Coronary artery disease.

PHYSIOLOGY FACT

Patients with mitral stenosis may have a heart murmur or other abnormal heart sound.

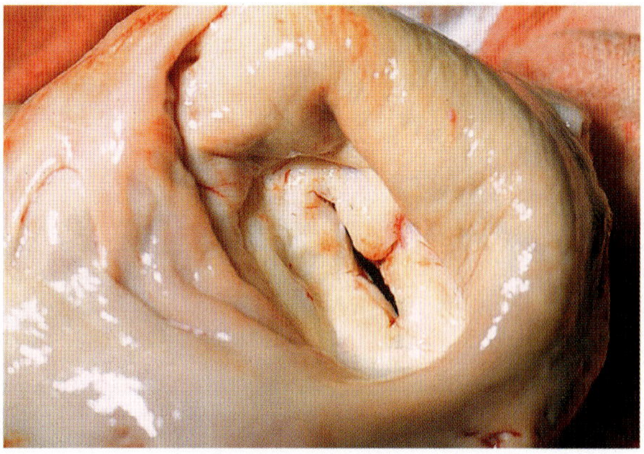

Figure 7-10 Mitral valve stenosis.

Mitral valve regurgitation: An incomplete closure of the mitral valve (located between the left atrium and left ventricle) that allows blood to flow back into the left atrium, often causing an extra heart sound (murmur) (Fig. 7-11). It is also called mitral insufficiency or mitral incompetence.

Murmur: A blowing or swishing sound in addition to the normal heart sounds, arising from blood flowing through the heart. It is commonly caused by backflow of blood in the valves, but it may or may not indicate an abnormality or cause symptoms.

Myocardial infarction (MI): Commonly called a heart attack. Defined as death of heart muscle caused by occlusion (blockage) of blood and oxygen in a coronary artery (Fig. 7-12). Signs and symptoms include heavy pressure or squeezing chest pain, tingling in the left arm to the fourth and fifth fingers of the left hand, and abdominal pain. Patients may mistake the pain for indigestion. Initial treatment is directed at minimizing damage to the heart by pain relief, rest, and stabilization of heart rhythm, and reducing the workload of the heart. Hospital medications include aspirin, nitroglycerin, thrombolytics, beta blockers, and morphine. The first 24 to 48 hours after a heart attack are most critical, with 35% of patients dying within the first 12 hours after MI.

Surgical treatment with stent placement and/or coronary artery bypass graft may be used to open clogged coronary arteries. Medication regimes after a heart attack include

- anticoagulant therapy to prevent subsequent blockages,
- antihypertensives to reduce high blood pressure,
- antilipidemics to lower cholesterol, and
- post-MI education on good dietary and exercise habits to decrease chance of subsequent heart attack.

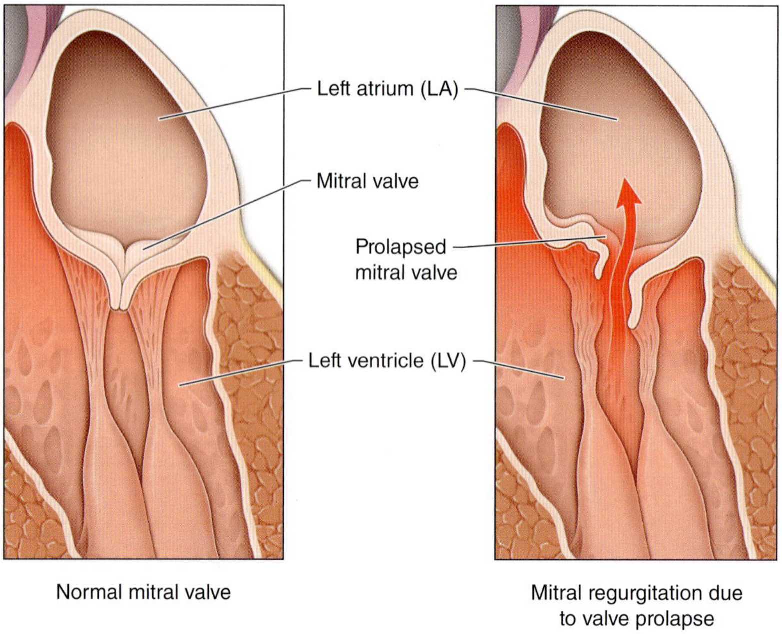

Figure 7-11 Mitral regurgitation.

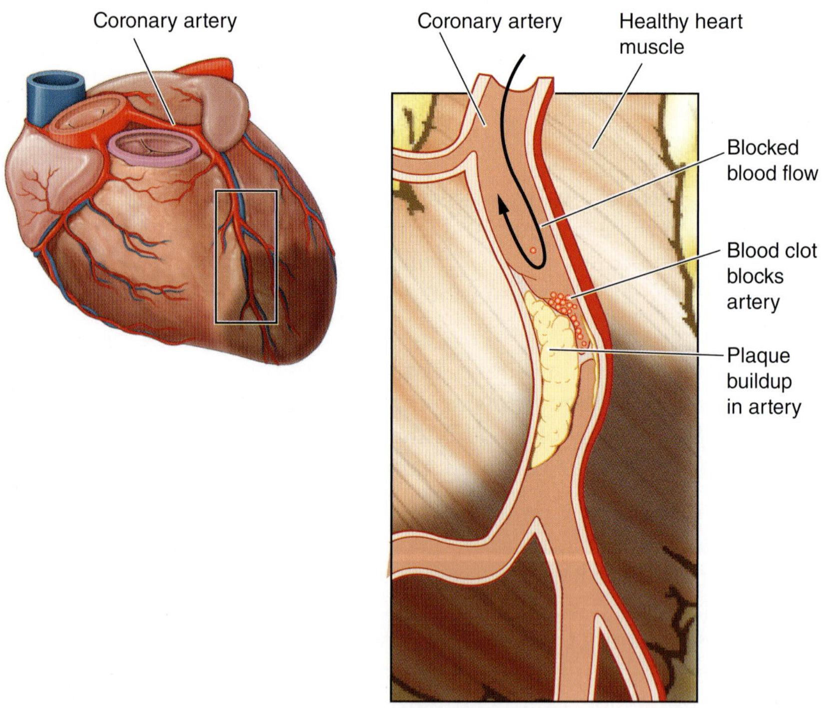

Figure 7-12 Myocardial infarction.

PHYSIOLOGY FACT

Think about the story of Nico. Lindsay tells Nico to chew the aspirin and not swallow it. Chewing the aspirin and then drinking water gets the medication into the bloodstream quickly where it can help dissolve a clot that is forming in one of Nico's coronary arteries. The aspirin should be 325-mg regular strength and without enteric coating.

Myocarditis: Condition in which the muscular middle layer of the heart wall becomes inflamed. Common causes include bacterial, viral, fungal, or parasitic infections. Some individuals with myocarditis are asymptomatic, while others may complain of chest pain, fatigue, heart palpitations, syncope, dizziness, mild dyspnea, and joint pain. Other signs include abnormal heart rhythm or fever.

Pericarditis: A condition in which the pericardium, the saclike fibrous membrane that surrounds the heart, becomes inflamed. It may be acute or chronic and may have a variety of causes such as a bacterial infection, neoplasms (tumors), viral infection, myocardial infarction (heart attack), trauma, or tuberculosis. Symptoms include dyspnea that is relieved by sitting up (orthopnea), tachycardia, fever, and fatigue. Common sign of pericarditis is a pericardial friction rub heard on auscultation (a grating sound).

ELEMENT REVIEW
orth/o = straight
-pnea = to breathe

Rheumatic heart disease: A complication of rheumatic fever in which inflammation and damage occurs to parts of the heart. Most commonly affected are the heart valves.

PHYSIOLOGY FACT

Chronic rheumatic disease is the most common reason for heart valve replacement in the United States.

Arrhythmias

Atrial flutter: A condition in which the contractions of the atria become very rapid (between 250 to 350 bpm). It is treated with medication to slow and strengthen the heartbeat. If management of the condition by medication fails, cardioversion (electrical shock) can slow the heart rate and restore a normal rhythm.

Atrial fibrillation: The most common arrythmia (Fig. 7-13). Rapid, yet incomplete contraction of the atria results in uncontrolled quivering. The rate of the contraction can be as high as 350 to 600 beats per minute. At these rates, the ventricles cannot contract efficiently or recover adequately between contractions. The condition leads to hypotension (low blood pressure), angina (pain), and congestive heart failure.

Ventricular tachycardia: A condition wherein the ventricles of the heart beat at 100+ beats per minute and don't have time to fill with blood to pump out of the heart (Fig. 7-14). It may occur in either the right or left ventricle, leaving the blood flow out of the heart lacking. Signs and symptoms include palpitations, angina, fatigue, dizziness, and dyspnea.

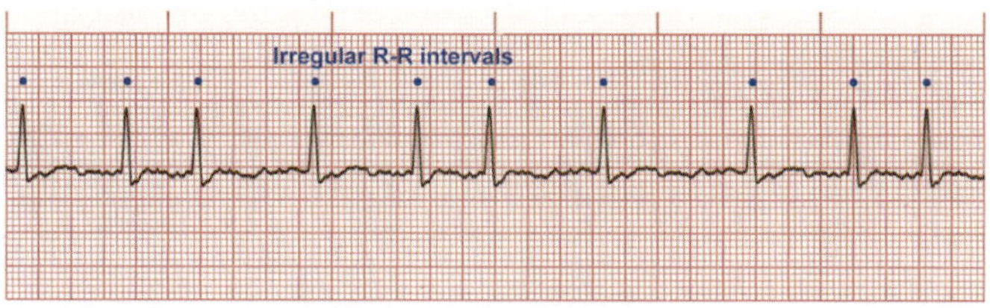

Figure 7-13 ECG strip showing atrial fibrillation.

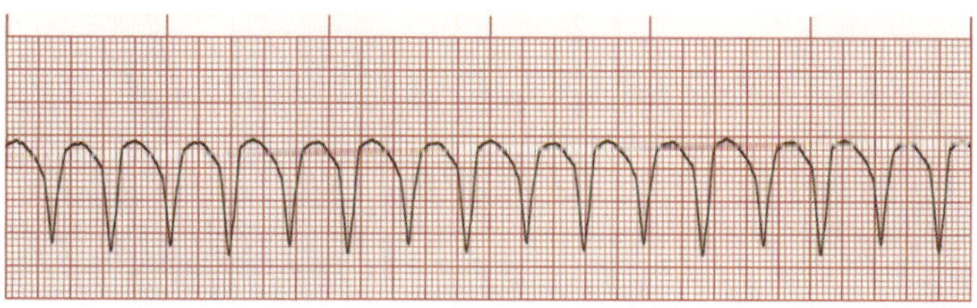

Figure 7-14 ECG strip showing ventricular tachycardia.

Treatment may include implantation of a cardioverter to reestablish normal rate and rhythm. It may become a life-threatening arrhythmia requiring CPR, electrical defibrillation, and cardioversion.

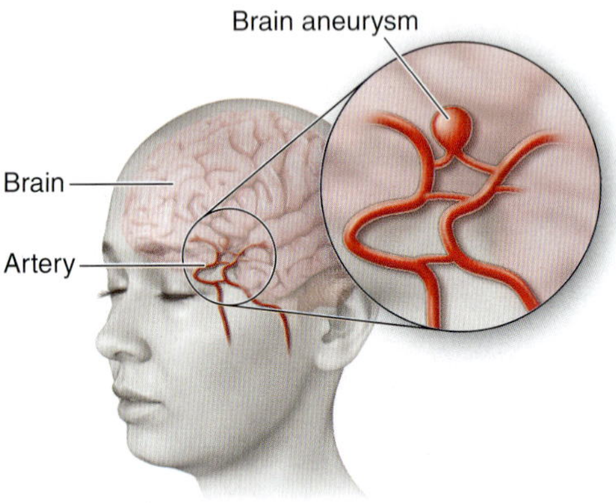

Figure 7-15 Brain aneurysm.

Pathological Conditions of the Blood Vessels

Aneurysm: A localized abnormal dilation in the wall of a blood vessel (usually an artery) due to weakness in the vessel wall (Fig. 7-15). Commonly caused by hypertension (increased pressure on the artery walls) and atherosclerosis (hardened fatty plaque in the arteries). Aneurysm of the arteries of the brain and abdominal aorta are most common.

Angiospasm: Involuntary spasmodic muscle contraction of smooth muscle that may cause cramping or angina.

Angiostenosis: Narrowing of the vessel, especially a blood vessel.

Arteriosclerosis: Hardening of the arteries. The thickening, loss in elasticity, and loss in contractility of arterial walls.

Arteriorrhexis: A ruptured artery. May occur if an aneurysm ruptures the arterial wall.

Atheroma: Deposits of fatty plaque in the walls of an artery that bulge into the lumen causing a narrowing.

ELEMENT REVIEW
arteri/o = artery
scler/o = hard
ather/o = fatty plaque
-osis = condition

Atherosclerosis: A common form of arteriosclerosis marked by cholesterol-lipid-calcium deposits in the walls of arteries that may restrict blood flow (Fig. 7-16).

Deep vein thrombosis (DVT) (thrombophlebitis): An inflammation of a vein associated with the formation of a thrombus (clot) (Fig. 7-17). It most frequently occurs in the lower legs, thighs, and pelvic area. It is caused by poor venous circulation, which may be due to obesity, sitting for long periods of time, or damage to leg veins.

Embolus: Sudden obstruction of a blood vessel by debris such as cholesterol-containing plaque, bacteria, or cancer cells that have broken away from a thrombus (clot) elsewhere in the body. If the point of obstruction is the coronary artery, then it can result in a myocardial infarction (heart attack).

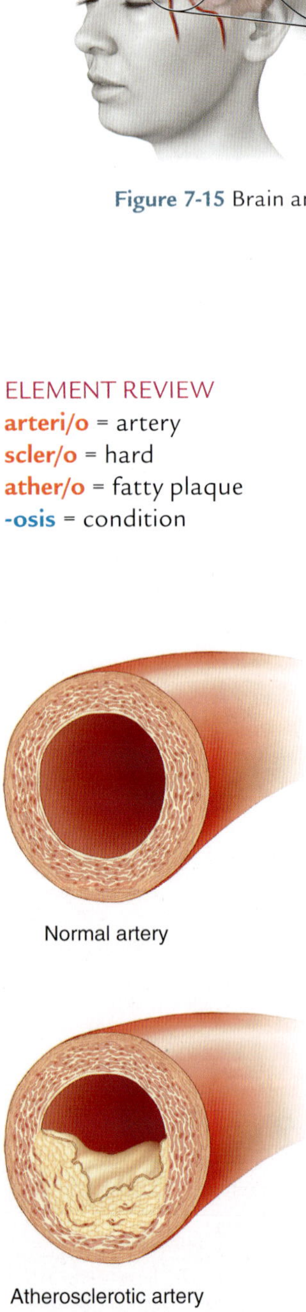

Figure 7-16 Atherosclerosis.

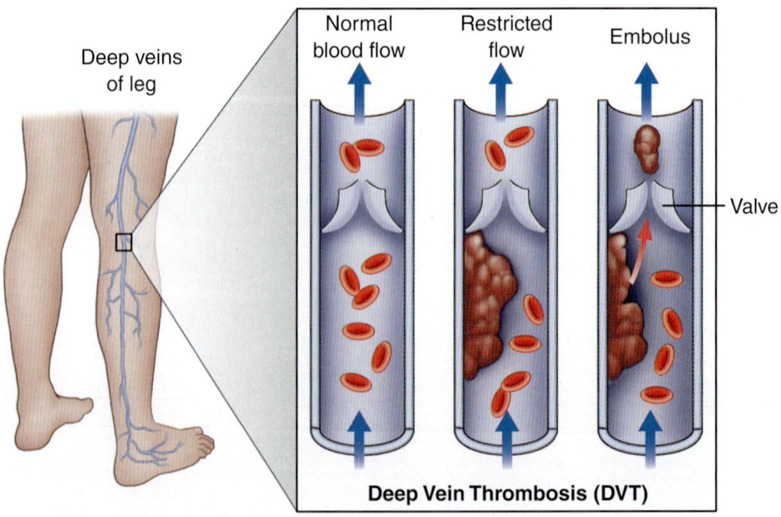

Figure 7-17 Deep vein thrombosis.

Hypertension (HTN): Commonly known as high blood pressure. The heart must work harder to pump blood against the increased resistance of excessive pressure in the arteries. HTN, if left untreated, can lead to coronary artery disease, heart failure, stroke, peripheral vascular disease, kidney failure, and retinopathy. Diagnosis is obtained by three separate blood pressure readings over several weeks' time measuring the systolic pressure above 140, the diastolic pressure above 90, or both.

Stage 1: systolic of 140 to 159 or diastolic of 90 to 99.

Stage 2: systolic 160 or above or diastolic 100 or above.

Prehypertension: systolic readings between 120 and 140 and/or diastolic readings between 80 and 90.

Risk factors for hypertension include pregnancy, obesity, tobacco use, family history of hypertension, and diabetes.

Hypotension: Decrease in systolic and diastolic blood pressure; can occur from shock, hemorrhage, dehydration, infection, cancer, or anemia.

Peripheral artery disease (PAD): A condition of partial or complete obstruction of the arteries of the extremities (more common in the legs, but can occur in the arms). PAD is caused by arteriosclerosis and atherosclerosis. It most commonly develops in the femoral, popliteal, tibial, and peroneal arteries of the legs.

Raynaud's phenomenon: Intermittent attacks of vasoconstriction of the arterioles that cause a decrease of blood flow to fingers and toes (Fig. 7-18). As the attack progresses, pallor (whitish color) occurs, then cyanosis (blue), then redness, before returning to normal color. Numbness, tingling, and a burning sensation accompany the color changes and resolve with application of heat or return to normal color. The disorder can be brought on by cold or emotional stress. The disorder is often idiopathic (of unknown origin). Treatment consists of antianxiety medication and avoidance of extreme cold.

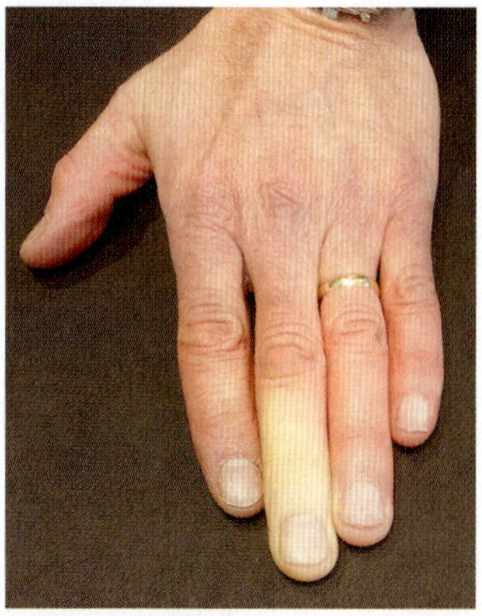
Figure 7-18 Raynaud phenomenon.

Thromboangiitis obliterans (TAO) (Buerger's disease): Characterized by chronic, recurring inflammation and clot formation in small vessels without atherosclerosis. It is most often seen in men aged 20 to 40 who smoke cigarettes or chew tobacco. Treatment requires cessation of smoking and use of chewing tobacco. If the patient continues to use tobacco, gangrene can occur, and amputation of affected extremities may be necessary.

EPONYM FACT

The eponym *Buerger's disease* comes from Leo Buerger, MD (1879–1943), an Austrian-born U.S. surgeon, pathologist, and urologist who characterized the vascular disorder related to tobacco use.

Varicose veins: Enlarged, dilated, superficial veins that are twisted and dilated from incompetent valves that are designed to keep blood flowing back to the heart (Fig. 7-19). Varicosities develop in veins of the lower legs because blood must flow up against gravity back to the heart. The condition can develop during pregnancy or is brought on by obesity or genetics. The condition can be asymptomatic or cause aching, muscle cramping, and a feeling of fatigue in the legs. Treatments can include wearing compression stockings, elevating the legs, or surgical treatments such as sclerotherapy or vein stripping.

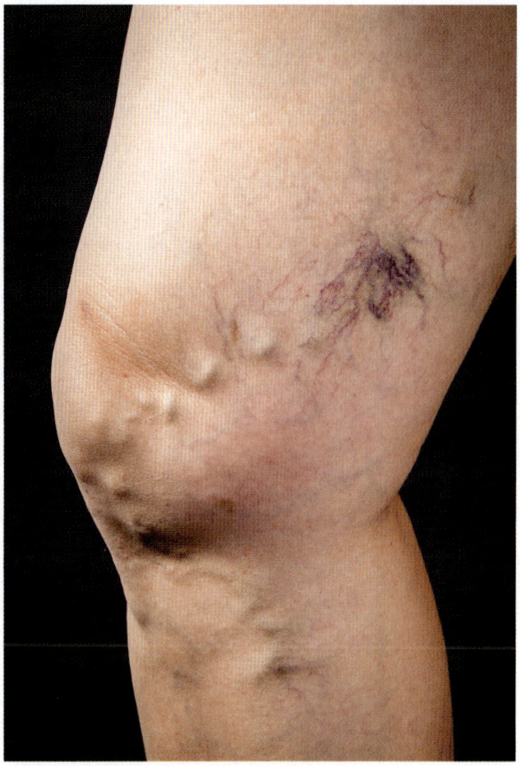
Figure 7-19 Varicose veins.

PHYSIOLOGY FACT

Severe varicose veins increase the risk of DVT.

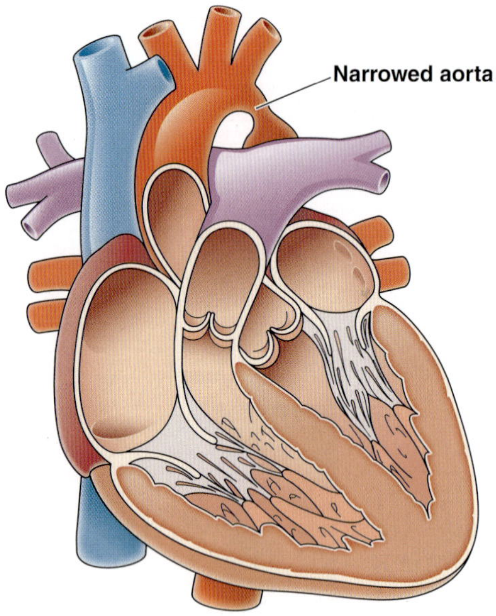

Figure 7-20 Coarctation.

Congenital Heart Diseases

Coarctation of the aorta: A congenital heart defect characterized by a narrowed aorta, causing increased blood pressure in the upper extremities and decreased pressure in the lower extremities (Fig. 7-20). Diagnosis is based on findings of a contrast in pulsations and blood pressure in the upper versus lower extremities. The femoral, popliteal, and pedal pulses are weak or delayed. The carotid and brachial pulses are strong and bounding. Surgical correction of the stricture can cure the condition if found early.

Patent ductus arteriosus (PDA): An opening between the pulmonary artery and the aorta, called the ductus arteriosus, provides fetal circulation. Shortly after birth, the connections should close. Failure of the duct to close is a congenital heart anomaly that usually requires surgical correction.

Tetralogy of Fallot: A group of four congenital defects: pulmonary stenosis, interventricular septal defect, dextroposition (a shift to the right) of the aorta, and hypertrophy of the right ventricle (Fig. 7-21). Most infants appear cyanotic, especially when crying, feeding, or straining during a bowel movement as there is an increased need for oxygen during these activities. Surgical correction of the multiple defects is required.

Transposition of great vessels: A condition in which the aorta arises from the right ventricle (instead of the left) and delivers deoxygenated blood to systemic circulation. This blood is then returned from the body tissues back to the right ventricle. Blood does not become oxygenated because it does not pass through the lungs. The infant presents with severe cyanosis at birth and needs surgical correction to establish oxygenation of blood for life.

ELEMENT REVIEW
tetra- = four
-ology = study of
sten/o = narrowing
-osis = condition
inter- = between/among
ventricul/o = ventricle
-ar = pertaining to
hyper- = excessive
-trophy = growth
sept/o = septum
-al = pertaining to

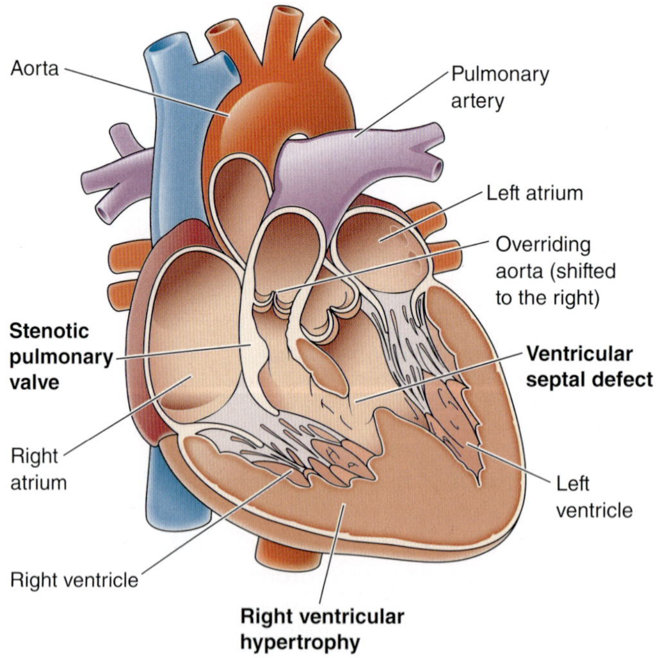

Figure 7-21 Tetrology of Fallot.

Pathology Word-Building Practice

1. Prefixes

Choose from the list of prefixes to build a word for the definitions below.

brady-	ischi/o	re-, retro-
hyper-	micro-	tachy-
hypo-	pre-	

1. The term that means low blood pressure ________________
2. The term that means high blood pressure ________________
3. Slow heart rate ________________
4. Fast heart rate ________________
5. Blockage/deficiency of blood supply ________________

2. Suffixes

Use the list of suffixes to build a word for the definitions below.

-ary	-megaly	-sclerosis
-dynia	-oid	-stasis
-edema	-pathy	-stenosis
-lysis	-rrhexis	-tension

1. Increased blood pressure *hyper*________________
2. Stopping or slowing of blood flow in veins *veno*________________
3. Condition of hardening of arteries *arterio*________________
4. Narrowing of a vein *phlebo*________________
5. Disease of the heart muscle *cardiomyo*________________
6. Swelling of a vessel *angio*________________
7. A ruptured artery *arterio*________________
8. Narrowing of the aorta *aorto*________________
9. Pertaining to the heart *coron*________________
10. Enlargement of the heart *cardio*________________

Cardiovascular System Diagnostic Procedures

CAREER EXPLORATION: CARDIAC VASCULAR NURSE

After graduating from nursing school, I began my career on a medical surgical floor, commonly called "med surg." On an evening shift, I was caring for a patient who went into cardiac arrest. I called a cardiac "code blue," and the rapid response team arrived within minutes to the bedside. The rapid response team worked quickly to assess and stabilize my patient's heart rate and blood pressure. This experience got me interested in caring for cardiac patients. I took online courses, studied, and passed the certification exam. I now use the credential: cardiac vascular nurse, board certified (CV-BC). I work in the Cardiac Intensive Care Unit and work closely with a team of professionals to care for our patients:

Cardiologists who assess and prescribe medications, perform surgery
Physical therapists who help patients gain cardiac function through monitored exercise
Clinical dieticians who advise patients on heart healthy diets
Social workers who help rehab and discharge planning
Phlebotomists who come up to the floor to draw labs

The following list gives some examples of common cardiac procedures and tests.

Cardiac scan: A specialized form of x-ray that can detect calcium-containing plaque in the coronary arteries. Also called a coronary calcium scan.

Doppler ultrasonography: Uses high-frequency sound waves to create an image of the heart. The speed and the direction of the blood flow is shown by the Doppler technology, thus identifying blood clots and DVTs.

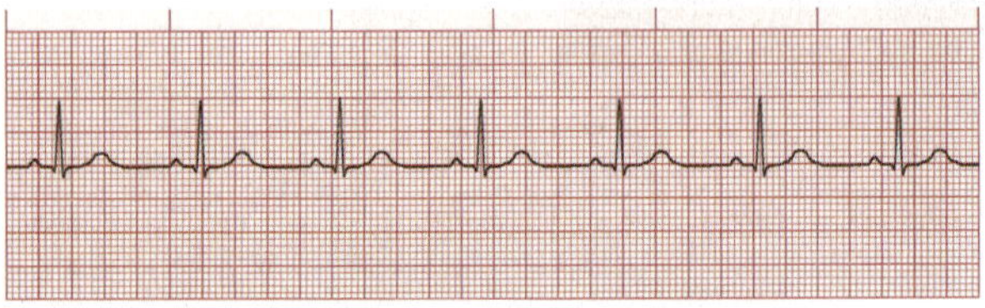

Figure 7-22 Normal ECG strip.

Echocardiography (ECHO): Uses sound wave echoes to visualize the heart and cardiac valves.

Electrocardiography (ECG, EKG): The process of recording electrical activity of the heart by placing electrodes on the chest and extremities (Fig. 7-22).

Event recorder (loop recorder): Portable monitoring device that records arrhythmias and transmits heart rhythms by telephone to a central laboratory. Unlike the Holter monitor, it is activated by arrhythmia and is not recording continuously.

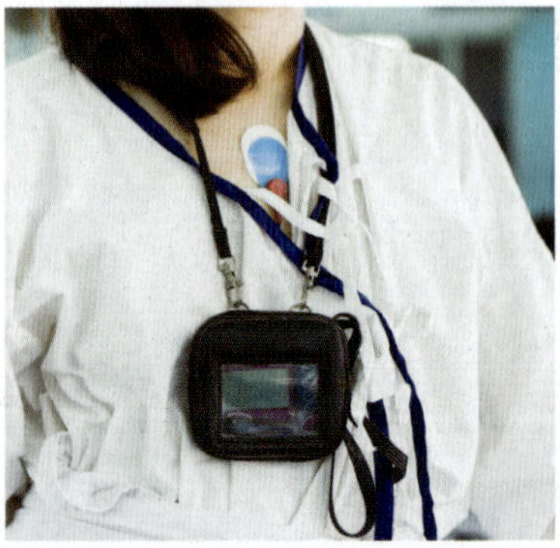

Figure 7-23 Holter monitor.

Holter monitor: Portable ECG device small enough to be worn by a patient during normal activity that records heart rhythm for 24 to 48 hours (Fig. 7-23).

International normalized ratio (INR): Standardized measurement of oral anticoagulant therapy used to adjust warfarin dosage based on prothrombin time (PT). It is used to maintain a balance between clot prevention and excessive bleeding.

Partial thromboplastin time (PTT): Measurement of blood-clotting time for patients taking heparin to balance prevention of blood clots and excessive bleeding.

Prothrombin time (PT): Measurement of blood-clotting time for patients taking warfarin to balance prevention of blood clots and excessive bleeding. Test is used in conjunction with INR.

Pulse oximetry: Measurement of pulse rate and saturation of peripheral oxygen (SpO_2) in the blood. The pulse oximeter is placed on the patient's finger and detects the oxygenated blood versus deoxygenated blood by use of an infrared light (Fig. 7-24). Normal SpO_2 is 95% to 100%. An SpO_2 of lower than 92% may indicate respiratory distress.

Figure 7-24 Pulse oximeter.

Stress test: Monitoring of a patient's heart while patient is exercising on a treadmill or bicycle. Blood supply to coronary arteries is assessed.

Transesophageal echocardiography (TEE): Study of the heart via a probe placed in the esophagus.

Troponin: A blood test that shows the cardiac isoforms troponin T or troponin I released from heart muscle upon damage to the heart. While it is considered the most accurate blood test to confirm a diagnosis of a heart attack (MI), other causes of an increase in troponins can include acute renal failure, strenuous exercise, systemic inflammation, acute pulmonary embolism, and sepsis.

Cardiovascular System Therapeutic Procedures

Interventions to correct electrical and structural abnormalities of the heart and vascular system can include surgical revision, defibrillation by external or implanted devices, or implantation of a pacemaker.

Aneurysmectomy: surgical removal of the sac of an aneurysm.

Angiography: Diagnostic or therapeutic radiography (radiological imaging) of the heart and blood vessels using a radiopaque contrast medium to visualize and repair pathological obstructions of coronary arteries.

Automated external defibrillator (AED): A computer-driven defibrillator that can be used by the general public and is available in office buildings, airplanes, etc. (Fig. 7-25). The device analyzes the patient's rhythm, selects the appropriate energy level, charges the machine, and delivers a shock to the patient to reestablish normal rhythm.

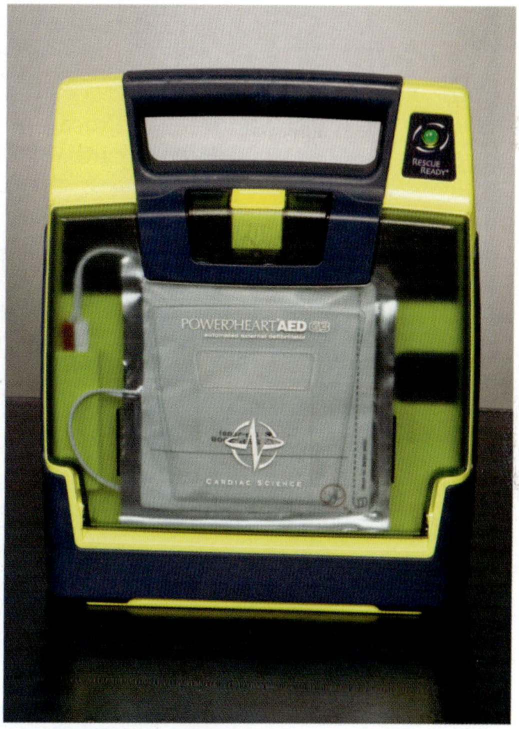

Figure 7-25 Automated external defibrillator.

Automatic implanted cardioverter defibrillator (AICD): A small surgically implanted defibrillator capable of detecting and treating life-threatening arrhythmias in high-risk patients.

Cardiac catheterization: Injection of a radiopaque dye that shows up under radiology and used to evaluate heart vessels and valves (Fig. 7-26).

Cardiopulmonary resuscitation (CPR): The application of manual external compression and artificial respiration when a patient is not breathing and/or heartbeat is not spontaneous. The procedure is taught to both medical and nonmedical personnel and is performed in order of CAB: compressions, airway, and breathing.

Cardioversion: Restoration of a normal sinus rhythm (NSR) by chemical or electrical means.

Coronary artery bypass graft (CABG): Surgical establishment of a shunt that creates an alternate route for blood flow around an area of coronary arterial obstruction. (Fig. 7-27).

Defibrillation: Delivery of an electric shock that completely depolarizes the myocardium and produces a brief period of asystole (no rhythm), allowing the sinoatrial node (SA) to recover and restore a NSR.

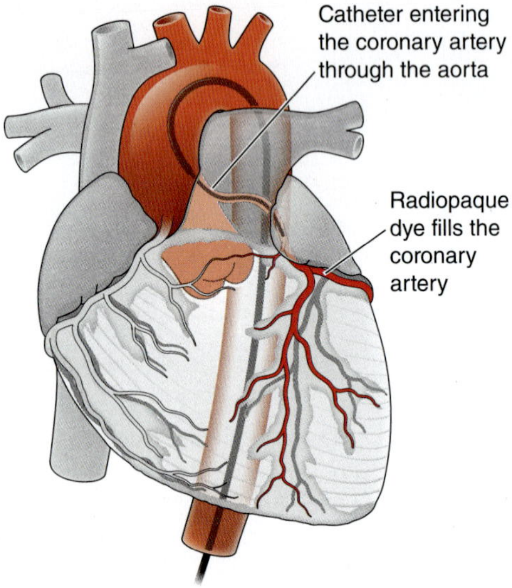

Figure 7-26 Cardiac catheterization.

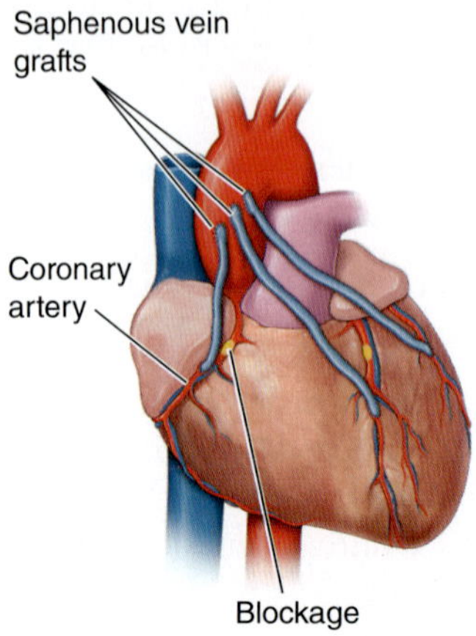

Figure 7-27 Coronary artery bypass graft.

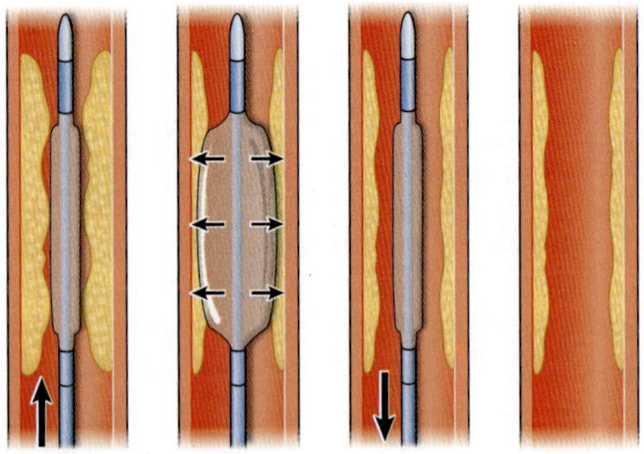

Figure 7-28 Percutaneous transluminal coronary angioplasty.

Pacemaker: Surgically implanted device that triggers the mechanical contractions of the heart (replacing the function of the SA node) by emitting periodic electrical discharges. A transcutaneous pacemaker delivers electricity through the chest wall; an internal or implantable pacemaker delivers electricity inside the body.

Percutaneous transluminal coronary angioplasty (PTCA): Treatment of a narrowed coronary artery via inflation and deflation of a balloon on a double-lumen catheter inserted through the right femoral artery (Fig. 7-28).

Procedures and Diagnostics Review

1. Process of using sound to visualize internal cardiac structures ________________
2. Blood test used to assess risk of blood clots and excessive bleeding ________________
3. Delivery of electric shock to depolarize the myocardium ________________
4. Treatment of a narrowed coronary artery with a balloon catheter ________________
5. Device used to measure oxygen in blood and the pulse rate ________________
6. Surgically implanted device that replaces the function of the SA node ________________
7. The use of drugs or electricity to terminate arrythmia ________________
8. Condition in which body tissues contain excess fluid ________________

9. Use of contrast media to look at anatomy of the heart ____________________

10. Emergency procedure that follows CAB: compression, airway, breathing. ____________________

11. A recording device worn by a cardiac patient for 2 to 4 days ____________________

12. Rapid, violent, or throbbing pulsations or a rapid heartbeat ____________________

13. Radiographic procedure to assess calcium deposits in arteries of the heart ____________________

14. Surgical device implanted to detect and prevent arrhythmias ____________________

15. Monitoring of a patient's heart while exercising on a treadmill or bicycle ____________________

16. Surgical procedure to create an alternate route of obstructed blood flow ____________________

17. A blood test that shows the cardiac enzymes released from heart muscle upon damage to the heart ____________________

18. Feeling of worry, uneasiness, or dread of future events ____________________

19. A group of four congenital heart defects ____________________

20. Chest pain due to heart disease ____________________

CASE STUDY, completed

While Nico rests, the ED team led by Dr. Giordano, the on-call cardiologist, gets Nico's blood test result, which reveals his troponin level is 0.27 ng/mL. Dr. Giordano explains that troponin I is a cardiac and skeletal muscle protein that binds to actin in thin myofilaments. Troponin I prevents myosin from binding to actin in relaxed muscle. Normally, the amount of troponin in the bloodstream is undetectable. A troponin level of 0.04 to 0.39 ng/mL means there is a problem with the heart and is indicative of a heart attack.

Dr. Giordano now recommends that Nico have a procedure called a coronary angioplasty, also called percutaneous coronary intervention. He explains that it is a procedure used to open clogged heart arteries. Angioplasty uses a tiny balloon catheter that is inserted in a blocked blood vessel to help widen it and improve blood flow to Nico's heart. Dr. Giordano also explains to Nico, Marla, and Lindsay that he will place a small wire mesh tube called a stent. The stent will hold the artery wall open and decrease the chance of it narrowing again. The stent will also be coated with a medication that will help keep Nico's artery open. After signing the informed consent, Nico is taken for the angioplasty procedure. During the procedure, Dr. Giordano makes an incision in Nico's groin and inserts a catheter into the artery. Dr. Giordano then threads the catheter upward to the affected blood vessel around the heart. A contrast dye is used to visually guide and assess the arterial blockage. The catheter contains the inflatable balloon that displaces the plaque, opening up the artery. Once the procedure is completed, Dr. Giordano tells Marla and Lindsay that Nico did well and is in the recovery room.

Continued

CASE STUDY, completed

CRITICAL THINKING QUESTIONS

1. What are Nico's symptoms (subjective findings) that cause him to go to the emergency department? ____________________
2. What are some signs (measurable objective findings) of Nico's heart disease? ____________________
3. Nico appears diaphoretic, which means ____________________
4. Dr. Giordano is a heart specialist, also known as a ____________________
5. Nico has hypertension, which means ____________________
6. Dissect the term angioplasty into its elements. ____________________
7. Nico had a heart attack, also called a ____________________
8. Nico has a blockage of blood in the arteries of the heart. What is the medical term for blockage of blood? ____________________
9. What does the insertion of the balloon catheter do? ____________________
10. Nico is taking a statin drug because he has what condition? ____________________
11. What is the name of the small wire tube inserted, and what is it used for? ____________________
12. When are cells of the heart starved of blood and oxygen, and what happens to them? What is the medical term? ____________________
13. As deposits of fat collect in arteries, what does this cause? What is the medical term for the condition? ____________________

Medications for the Cardiovascular System

A variety of medications can be prescribed to improve the function of the heart by promoting healthy heart rate and rhythm, preventing clotting, decreasing blood pressure, and reducing lipid levels in the blood. Table 7-2 shows the classification of the medications, their uses, and some examples. It is important to understand why a patient is taking a particular medication and that a patient may be prescribed more than one cardiac medication to affect multiple conditions. A variety of medications can be prescribed to improve the function of the heart by promoting healthy heart rate and rhythm, preventing clotting, decreasing blood pressure, and reducing lipid levels in the blood.

TABLE 7-2 Medications for the Cardiovascular System

Classification	Examples	Common Use/Action
ACE inhibitors	benazepril, Lotensin, Cozaar	Block stress hormones and relieve stress on the heart's pumping action
Antianginals	nitroglycerin (oral, sublin-gual, or skin patches) Dilatrate-SR, Nitro-Dur	Prevent, reduce, relieve angina pain
Antiarrhythmics	amiodarone, Procan, procainamide	Control irregular heartbeat, maintain normal heart rate and rhythm
Antihypertensives	Catapres, Cardura, Aldomet	Reduce blood pressure by relaxing and widening blood vessels
Anticoagulants and platelet inhibitors	Lovenox, warfarin, Plavix	Slow blood clotting and reduce the risk of strokes and heart attacks caused by blood clotting in small blood vessels
Beta blockers	atenolol (Tenormin), Coreg	Treat HTN and angina, block stress hormones, relax blood vessels
Calcium channel blockers	Norvasc, Vascor, Cardizem	Restrict calcium into the cells of the heart and blood vessels to prevent narrowing and spasming and to reduce the heart's workload and need for O_2
Digitalis glycosides	digoxin (Lanoxin)	Strengthen the heart muscle, treat irregular heart rhythms, improve exercise tolerance
Diuretics (water pills)	Lasix, Diuril	Reduce blood pressure by reducing blood volume (increase urinary output)
Lipid medications (blood cholesterol lowering); statins	Lipitor, lovastatin (Altoprev)	Lower serum cholesterol
Lipid medications (blood cholesterol lowering); fibrates	Tricor, gemfibrozil	Lower serum cholesterol
Lipid medications (blood cholesterol lowering); bile acid sequestrants	Welchol, Questran	Lower serum cholesterol
Lipid medications (blood cholesterol lowering); other	Niacin	Lower serum cholesterol

**Medications Review

Using the table of cardiac medications, complete the chart below. The first one has been done for you as an example.

Medication Name	Classification (mechanism)	Therapeutic Use (What is it used for?)
Diuril	*Diuretic*	*To reduce blood pressure*
1. Nitroglycerin	__________	__________
2. lovastatin	__________	__________
3. Vascor	__________	__________
4. Plavix	__________	__________
5. Questran	__________	__________
6. Tenormin	__________	__________
7. Lotensin	__________	__________
8. Lovenox	__________	__________
9. Cozaar	__________	__________
10. procainamide	__________	__________

Cardiology Abbreviations

The list below provides some common cardiovascular abbreviations and their meanings.

AED automated external defibrillator

AF atrial fibrillation

AMI acute myocardial infarction

AS arteriosclerosis

ASA acetylsalicylic acid, commonly called aspirin

ASD atrial septal defect

ASHD arteriosclerotic heart disease

AV, A-V atrioventricular

BBB bundle branch block

BP blood pressure

bpm beats per minute

CABG coronary artery bypass graft

CAD coronary artery disease

cath catheterization

CC cardiac catheterization, chief complaint

CCU cardiac care unit

CHF congestive heart failure

CK creatine kinase

CoA coarctation of the aorta

CP chest pain

CPR cardiopulmonary resuscitation

CSD congenital septal defect

CV cardiovascular

DVT deep vein thrombosis

ECG, EKG electrocardiogram

ECHO echocardiography

fib fibrillation
HTN hypertension
ICD implantable cardioverter defibrillator
IV intravenous
LVH left ventricular hypertrophy
MI myocardial infarction, mitral insufficiency
mm Hg millimeters of mercury
MR mitral regurgitation
MS mitral stenosis
MVP mitral valve prolapse
P pulse
PAC premature atrial contraction
PDA patent ductus arteriosus
PTCA percutaneous transluminal coronary angioplasty
PVC premature ventricular contraction
PVD peripheral vascular disease
S1 first heart sound
S2 second heart sound
SA, S-A sinoatrial
SK streptokinase
V fib ventricular fibrillation
VSD ventricular septal defect
VT ventricular tachycardia

Abbreviations Review

Chose the correct definition for the abbreviation:

1. VT
   a. Vascular tension
   b. Ventricular tachycardia
   c. Vascular tachycardia
   d. Ventricular tension

2. PVD
   a. Peripheral vascular disease
   b. Paroxysmal vascular disease
   c. Patent vascular disorder
   d. Peripheral ventricular disease

3. ASHD
   a. Atherosclerotic heart disease
   b. Arteriosclerotic heart disease
   c. Atrial septal heart disease
   d. Arterioseptal heart disease

4. MI
   a. Mitral insufficiency
   b. Myocardial infarction
   c. Mitral inclusion
   d. A & B only

5. CABG
   a. Cardiac atrial bypass graft
   b. Coronary atrial bypass graft
   c. Cardiac artery bypass graft
   d. Coronary artery bypass graft

6. SA, S-A
   a. Sinoatrial
   b. Septoatrial
   c. Syncope attack
   d. Sinoarterial

7. CHF
   a. Congestive heart failure
   b. Coronary heart fatigue
   c. Coronary heart failure
   d. Congestive heart fatigue

8. BBB
   a. Bundle branch bifurcation
   b. Bundle branch blockage
   c. Bundle of His blocked
   d. Bundle of His bifurcated

9. DVT
   a. Deep vein thrombosis
   b. Distal vein thrombosis
   c. Deep ventricular thrombosis
   d. Distal ventricular thrombosis

10. VSD
   a. Vascular sinus defect
   b. Vascular septal defect
   c. Ventricular septal defect
   d. Ventricular sinus defect

MEDICAL DOCUMENTATION

Knowledge of terms related to normal anatomical and pathological conditions enables you to understand medical documentation such as history and physical exams, operative reports, discharge summaries, laboratory reports, and x-ray reports. Apply your knowledge by answering the questions that follow this procedure report.

Percutaneous Transluminal Coronary Angioplasty

Patient: Nico G.
Date of Birth: 08/18/1957
Medical Record Number: 123987
Date: 07/12/20XX

Referring Physician: Hector R., MD
Cardiologist: Kenneth G., MD
Indications for Examination: angina pectoris, coronary atherosclerosis.

Procedure Performed: Percutaneous Transluminal Coronary Angioplasty

Procedure Technique: Under local anesthesia, a 6F introducer was placed in the right femoral artery. Following placement of the arterial sheath, 10,000 units of heparin were administered as a bolus followed by continuous infusion at a rate of 2000 units per hour. Left heart catheterization was performed. Coronary arteriography and left ventriculography were then performed. Following the procedure, the sheath was left in place. The patient tolerated the procedure well. Angioplasty and stenting was performed on the left LAD and left circumflex lesions. He was taken to recovery in stable condition.

Findings: Diagnostic catheterization, left heart catheterization to LAD.

Impression: Severe left anterior descending and left circumflex artery disease.

Recommendations:

1. ASA 81 mg PO after dinner for 1 year
2. Clopidogrel (Plavix) 75 mg PO after lunch for 1 year
3. Medical treatment of hyperlipidemia and hypertension upon assessments postprocedure
4. Referral to cardiac dietician for weight management

Electronically signed
Kenneth G., MD

Questions

1. Nico complained of angina pectoris, which is the medical term for ____________
2. Dr. Giordano inserted the catheter in Nico's right ____________ artery.
3. Visualization/recording of the ventricles of the heart is done by a procedure called a ____________.
4. The term that means surgical repair of a vessel is ____________.
5. Nico will be evaluated for hyperlipidemia, which is ____________.
6. Nico is advised to take ASA 80 mg every night after dinner. What medication is that? ____________
7. What is ASA taken for (therapeutic use)? ____________
8. Nico is prescribed Plavix, which is the trade name for clopidogrel. What is the classification and therapeutic use of Plavix? ____________

MEDICAL DOCUMENTATION—cont'd

9. In the document, LAD refers to the ____________.

10. Nico's postprocedure medications are to be taken PO, which means ____________.

Discharge Summary

Read the discharge summary and define the bolded abbreviations and terms.

Discharge Summary

Patient: Helen J Date: September 24, 20XX
ID # 38760244

HISTORY: This 65-year-old black female was brought to the emergency department unresponsive. **CPR** was begun by EMTs on the scene. During transport, the portable **EKG** demonstrated **ventricular fibrillation**. Advanced cardiac life support procedure was followed.

HOSPITAL COURSE: The patient was brought to the **CCU**. Her daughter confirmed previous cardiac history, including a myocardial infarction and subsequent **CABG**. She also had a history of **hypertension**, **hyperlipidemia**, and diabetes. The patient's condition deteriorated, and she was in coma during the entire hospitalization. In consultation with the cardiologist, her daughter was told of the severity of her condition and that extensive myocardial tissue death had occurred due to **ischemia**.

LABORATORY DATA: Chest x-ray showed **cardiomegaly** and right upper lobe infiltrate. **Arterial** blood gases indicated that mechanical ventilation was offering minimal support.

DISPOSITION: The patient expired on hospital day 2 with her family present.

1. CPR ____________________
2. EKG ____________________
3. ventricular fibrillation ____________________
4. CCU ____________________
5. CABG ____________________
6. hypertension ____________________
7. hyperlipidemia ____________________
8. ischemia ____________________
9. cardiomegaly ____________________
10. arterial ____________________

Continued

MEDICAL DOCUMENTATION—cont'd

SOAP Note

Define the bolded words in the document.

Patient name: June G. Date: May 15, 20XX

ID # 7892596

SUBJECTIVE: June is a 32-year-old female who presents with **edema**, redness, and tenderness of the right posterior lower extremity, specifically most painful at the popliteal space. Pain and swelling have been present for the last 48 hours and gets worse at the end of a work day. She reports no trauma or injury but works long hours on her feet as a waitress. She takes oral birth control pills but no other medications. She takes a multivitamin each day, nonsmoker, social drinker.

OBJECTIVE: Upon visual inspection, localized **erythema**, induration (areas of hardened tissue), tenderness, and edema is noted in the right lower extremity. **Varicose veins** are noted distally and proximally.

ASSESMENT: Chronic venous insufficiency with **superficial thrombophlebitis**. No deep vein **thrombosis** is noted.

PLAN:

1. Ibuprofen 60 mg **BID** (with food).
2. Wear compression stockings while working.
3. Apply warm compresses to the affected area for 30–60 minutes **TID**.
4. Elevate legs as needed.
5. Return to the clinic in 2 weeks or sooner if symptoms worsen.

Define the Terms

1. Edema ______________________________
2. erythema ______________________________
3. varicose veins ______________________________
4. superficial ______________________________
5. thrombophlebitis ______________________________
6. thrombosis ______________________________
7. BID ______________________________
8. TID ______________________________

Visit the Medical Language Lab at the website medicallanguagelab.com. Use it to improve your recognition and understanding of terms in medical documentation.

CHAPTER REVIEW

Identify the Anatomical Structures

Match the structures of the heart from the following list to the letters shown in Figure 7-29.

1. ______ aorta
2. ______ bicuspid valve
3. ______ inferior vena cava
4. ______ left atrium
5. ______ left ventricle
6. ______ pulmonary artery
7. ______ pulmonary vein
8. ______ right atrium
9. ______ right ventricle
10. ______ septum
11. ______ superior vena cava
12. ______ tricuspid valve

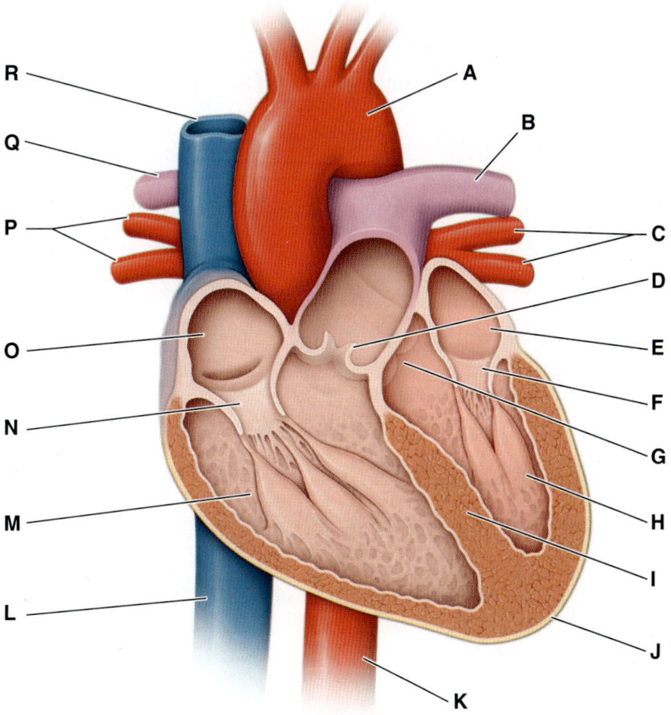

Figure 7-29 Label the structures of the heart.

Complete the Sentence

Using medical terms from this chapter, complete the sentence.

1. Mrs. G had surgery to unblock a narrowed coronary artery via inflation and deflation of a balloon. The procedure is called a ______________________.
2. The term *hypertension* means elevated ______________________.
3. Atorvastatin is a medication used to reduce ______________________.
4. Patent ductus arteriosus is a condition a person is born with, meaning it is a ______________________ condition.
5. Enlarged, superficial, dilated veins are called ______________________.
6. The contraction phase of the heart beat that forces blood into the aorta and the pulmonary arteries is called the ______________________.
7. Inflammation of a vein is called ______________________.
8. Compression of the heart due to excess fluid in the pericardium is a serious condition called ______________________.

9. Mr. M. takes a medication that prevents or reduces chest pain. The type of medication is a ______________________________.

10. Joe responded to an emergency in which he saw a man had collapsed and had no pulse or spontaneous respirations. Joe performed ______________________ until EMS arrived.

11. An elevated ______________________ level can be an indication of a heart attack, but it also can be the result of sepsis or strenuous exercise.

12. The medical term for a heart attack is a ______________________________.

13. The structure that divides the heart into the right and left sides is called the ______________________________.

14. The thick-walled vessels that carry oxygenated blood away from the heart are called ______________________________.

15. The relaxation phase of the cardiac cycle is called the ______________________.

16. The pressure exerted on the walls of the arteries is called ______________________.

17. ______________________ is an emergency medication used to relieve pain in the chest (angina pectoris).

Spelling

Circle the correctly spelled terms in the pairs of terms.

1.	varicose	vericose
2.	arteriosclerosis	arterosclerosis
3.	rhumatic	rheumatic
4.	aneurism	aneurysm
5.	cyanosis	syanosis
6.	thrombophlebitis	thrombaphlebiltis
7.	edema	adema
8.	mitral valve	mitrol valve
9.	myocardial infarction	myocardial infraction
10.	eckocardiography	echocardiography
11.	nitroglycerine	nitroglycerin

Abbreviations

Define the following abbreviations:

1. MI ______________________________
2. CABG ______________________________
3. BBB ______________________________
4. DVT ______________________________
5. ASHD ______________________________
6. CHF ______________________________
7. SA ______________________________
8. EKG ______________________________
9. CCU ______________________________
10. MVP ______________________________

Decipher the Terms

Separate each term into its prefix (if any), combining form, and suffix. Next, translate the word parts and then give the common definition of the term. Cardiovascular *has been done for you as an example.*

Cardiovascular

Prefix: None *Combining Form:* cardi/o = heart, vascul/o = blood vessels

Suffix: -ar = pertaining to

Meaning: referring to the lungs

1. Cardiomyopathy

   Prefix: __________ *Combining Form:* __________ *Suffix:* __________

   Meaning: ______________________________

2. ischemia

   Prefix: __________ *Combining Form:* __________ *Suffix:* __________

   Meaning: ______________________________

3. bradycardia

   Prefix: __________ *Combining Form:* __________ *Suffix:* __________

   Meaning: ______________________________

4. atrioventricular

Prefix: ______________ *Combining Form:* ______________ *Suffix:* ______________

Meaning: ____

5. electrocardiography

Prefix: ______________ *Combining Form:* ______________ *Suffix:* ______________

Meaning: ____

6. echocardiography

Prefix: ______________ *Combining Form:* ______________ *Suffix:* ______________

Meaning: ____

7. thrombophlebitis

Prefix: ______________ *Combining Form:* ______________ *Suffix:* ______________

Meaning: ____

8. arteriosclerosis

Prefix: ______________ *Combining Form:* ______________ *Suffix:* ______________

Meaning: ____

9. atherosclerosis

Prefix: ______________ *Combining Form:* ______________ *Suffix:* ______________

Meaning: ____

10. atheroma

Prefix: ______________ *Combining Form:* ______________ *Suffix:* ______________

Meaning: ____

11. pericardium

Prefix: ______________ *Combining Form:* ______________ *Suffix:* ______________

Meaning: ____

12. cardiologist

Prefix: ______________ *Combining Form:* ______________ *Suffix:* ______________

Meaning: ____

13. arrythmia

Prefix: ______________ *Combining Form:* ______________ *Suffix:* ______________

Meaning: ____

14. angioplasty

Prefix: ______________ *Combining Form:* ______________ *Suffix:* ______________

Meaning: ____

15. endocardial

Prefix: ______________ *Combining Form:* ______________ *Suffix:* ______________

Meaning: ____

mll Medical Language Lab

Visit the Medical Language Lab at the website medicallanguagelab.com. Use it to enhance your study and reinforcement of the medical terms and word parts covered in this chapter.

CHAPTER

8

The Blood, Lymphatic, and Immune Systems

LEARNING OBJECTIVES

Upon completion of the chapter, you will be able to:

1. Identify and define the combining forms, roots, prefixes, and suffixes introduced in the chapter.
2. Spell medical terms related to the blood, lymphatic, and immune systems.
3. Describe the major organs of the blood, lymphatic, and immune systems.
4. Describe the functions of the various blood cells.
5. Describe the four blood types A, B, AB, and O.
6. Compare and contrast the two types of immunity: humoral and cell-mediated immunity.
7. Describe the flow of lymph and how it regulates fluid volume in and out of the circulatory system.
8. Identify and discuss major pathological terms of the blood, lymphatic, and immune systems.
9. Identify and discuss major diagnostic and therapeutic treatments of the blood, lymphatic, and immune systems.
10. Identify the major categories of medications used to treat blood, lymphatic, and immune pathologies.
11. Define abbreviations of the blood, lymphatic, and immune systems.

We begin this chapter with the story of Lucy, a woman with sickle cell anemia, an inherited blood disorder that compromises oxygen delivery to cells of the body. Lucy's weakened condition causes her to fall at home. She is subsequently hospitalized and treated for her sickle cell disease and her injuries. After reading this chapter, you will expand your knowledge of medical terms related to the blood, lymphatic, and immune systems. You will understand how the body maintains oxygenation and defends against pathogens. You will be able to use word elements presented to understand unfamiliar terms and to build your medical vocabulary. Throughout the chapter, we will revisit the story of Lucy to understand what happens with a blood disorder and how medical interventions can improve a patient's quality of life.

CASE STUDY

Lucy is a 49-year-old woman who has been living with sickle cell anemia. Eight months ago, her spouse of 18 years died of Covid-19. Zuki had been a critical care nurse, who during the pandemic, often slept at the hospital to protect her immunocompromised partner. Lucy suffered from horrible loneliness and depression. As a practicing attorney, her firm allowed her to work from home during the pandemic, but Lucy's depression got so bad that she couldn't concentrate. She moved in with her niece for both financial and emotional support. She has been going to grief counseling, but lately has had insomnia, lack of appetite, leg pain, and severe depression.

Continued

CASE STUDY, continued

She complained of difficulty getting her breath. Lucy felt her heart racing and noticed yellowing in the whites of her eyes.

This afternoon, her niece found her in the kitchen unconscious and bleeding from her head and called an ambulance. Lucy is transported to the emergency department where Dr. Collins, the on-call hematologist examines her and orders blood work. She regains consciousness but remains confused. She does not remember falling or hitting her head on the side of the counter. The ED physician assistant stitched her head wound as Dr. Collins talks with Melanie, Lucy's niece and next of kin.

After reviewing Lucy's blood work, Dr. Collins asks Melanie about Lucy's sickle cell disease. Melanie says that Lucy complained of horrible back and leg pain yesterday but is diligent about taking her medications. Melanie explains that Lucy takes Endari to prevent crisis and hydroxyurea to prevent abnormal cell formation. Additionally, Lucy doesn't drink alcohol and is always careful to stay hydrated and warm.

KEY TERMS

Acquired immunity	Eosinophil	Lymph	Phagocytosis
Agglutination	Erythrocyte	Lymph node	Phlebotomy
Agranulocyte	Fibrinogen	Lymphocyte	Plasma
Albumin	Globulin	Macrophage	Serum
Anaphylaxis	Granulocyte	Monocyte	Spleen
Antibodies	Hematopoiesis	Natural immunity	Thrombocyte
Antigen	Hemoglobin	Neutrophil	Thymus
Basophil	Immune reaction	Pancytopenia	Tonsils
Blood	Immunity	Pathogen	Vaccination
Coagulation	Leukocyte		

Structures and Physiology of the Blood, Lymphatic, and Immune System

All the cells of the human body require a steady supply of oxygen and nutrients to carry out the many complex metabolic functions needed for life. Additionally, all cells require disposal of metabolic waste and maintenance of their environment. The body must be protected from pathogens and provide a balanced environment for cellular function. Specifically, the blood functions to:

- Deliver oxygen and nutrients to all tissues of the body
- Remove carbon dioxide and waste from the body
- Play an important role in the immune system through a variety of WBCs (white blood cells)

The lymphatic system helps to maintain fluid balance in the body. The lymphatic fluid, lymph vessels, nodes, and organs provide immunity through antibody production.

Blood

Blood is the liquid pumped by the heart to the arteries, veins, and capillaries of the body. The total blood volume for an average adult female is 4 to 5 liters and 5 to 6 liters for an adult male. Blood accounts for approximately 8% of our total body weight. Blood pH is slightly alkaline at 7.35 to 7.45 and must be tightly controlled for good health. The blood comprises both liquid and cells with distinct functions (Fig. 8-1).

Serum is the liquid portion of blood and contains no cells or clotting factors. Plasma is the blood fluid plus the blood clotting agents. See Table 8-1 for differences in serum versus plasma. **Plasma** is a yellow or straw-colored fluid that is approximately 90% water. The remaining 10% are solutes, substances dissolved in the solution, consisting of electrolytes, proteins, fats, glucose, bilirubin, and dissolved gases. The largest group of plasma solutes are the plasma proteins, which are created in the liver and have regulatory functions. The three categories of plasma proteins are albumins, globulins, and fibrinogen.

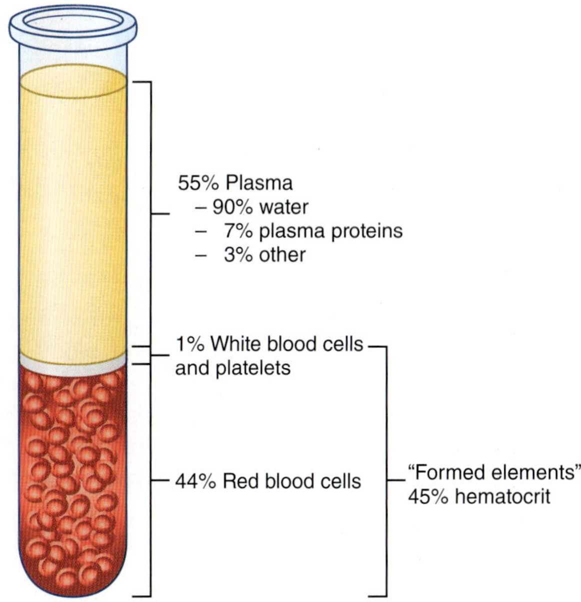

Figure 8-1 The components of whole blood.

1. **Albumins** are the most abundant at 60% of the plasma proteins. They function to maintain normal blood pressure and volume by attracting water into the capillaries through a process called osmosis. Fluid from the lesser concentration of solute flows to the greater concentration to equilibrate (even) the fluids. The balance of interstitial fluid (outside of the bloodstream) and fluid inside of the bloodstream is maintained by albumins.
2. **Globulins** make up approximately 36% of the plasma proteins. There are three types of globulins: alpha, beta, and gamma. Alpha and beta globulins transport lipids (fats) and fat-soluble vitamins (ADEK) in the bloodstream. Gamma globulins are antibodies, which are part of the immune system.

TABLE 8-1 Difference Between Serum and Plasma

Characteristics	Serum	Plasma
Definition	Noncellular liquid part of the blood remaining after the coagulation.	Plasma is the clear and yellowish fluid part of the blood.
Composition	Serum is the fluid from blood without the clotting factors. It contains albumin and globulins.	Plasma is the blood fluid that also contains fibrinogen (clotting factors).
Volume	Volume of serum is compared to plasma.	Plasma volume is greater than serum, which is 55% of total volume of blood.
Isolation	Serum is allowed to clot for 15–30 min, centrifuged for 5–10 min at 2500 rpm.	Plasma is acquired by spinning for 5–10 minutes at 2500 rpm.
Use of anticoagulants	Serum is obtained without use of anticoagulants.	Anticoagulants—heparin, oxalate or EDTA—are necessary to separate plasma.
Composition (antibodies)	Serum contains antibodies and cross reacts with recipient antigen. It can be used to create antiserum for bites and stings of venomous animals.	Blood plasma contains antibodies, a type of protein that can fight a substance considered foreign to the host body.
Density	Serum has a density of approximately 1.024 g/mL It is 90% water.	Plasma has a density of approximately 1.025 g/mL. It is 92%–95% water.
Uses	Serum is used diagnostically to determine blood group-ABO and in a variety of blood tests: DNA testing, hCG levels (pregnancy test), cholesterol, and glucose.	Plasma is used therapeutically to increase blood volume in cases of burns, trauma, shock, hemophilia.

3. **Fibrinogen** constitutes only 4% of the total plasma proteins, but they are the largest molecules. Fibrinogen is essential for the process of blood clotting, also called coagulation.

> ***Study Tip***
> Use the pneumonic SS: serum is smaller than plasma.

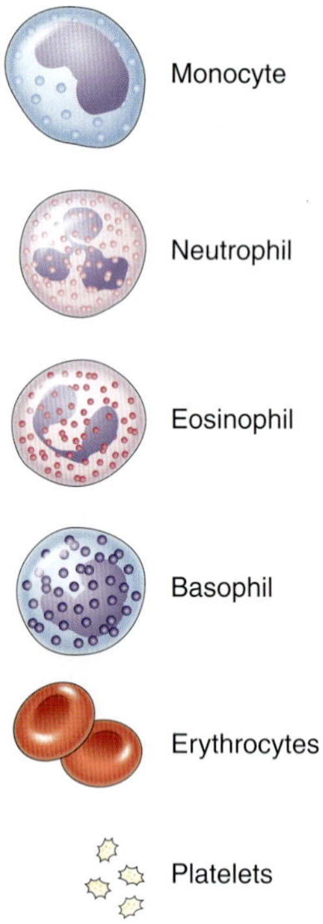

Figure 8-2 Blood cells include erythrocytes (RBCs), neutrophils, eosinophils, basophils, monocytes, lymphocytes, and platelets.

Blood Cells

The cells of blood are formed in a process called **hematopoiesis**, occurring in the red bone marrow. Production of blood cells occurs in specific regions of the body: the skull, sternum, ribs, vertebrae, and pelvis. All blood cells develop as undifferentiated stem cells called hemocytoblasts. As the blood cells mature, they undergo differentiation to become specific types of blood cells (Fig. 8-2). The seven types of blood cells are erythrocytes, leukocytes (divided into five distinct forms: neutrophils, eosinophils, basophils, monocytes, lymphocytes), and platelets.

ELEMENT REVIEW
hem/o = blood
cyt/o = cell
-blast = immature or undifferentiated cell
hemat/o = blood
-poiesis = production, development

Red Blood Cells

Erythrocytes, red blood cells (RBCs), function to carry oxygen to tissues and pick up carbon dioxide for release via the lungs in our exhaled air. The cells are biconcave-shaped disks that afford a large surface area for the bonding of oxygen (Fig. 8-3). Each RBC contains **hemoglobin**, which consists of heme (iron) and globin (protein). Oxygen is attracted to the hemoglobin molecule within each RBC. Upon bonding with oxygen, oxyhemoglobin is responsible for the bright red color of blood. Uptake of oxygen in the lungs to the RBCs allows the transport of oxygen to all cells of the body. The biconcave shape also enables it to absorb carbon dioxide from tissues in systemic circulation. The RBC is now deoxygenated, containing deoxyhemoglobin giving the blood a duller red color. This continuous process is dependent upon the heart (pumping the blood to all parts of the body) and the lungs reoxygenating the blood.

Erythrocytes are formed in the red bone marrow in a process called erythropoiesis. As they develop, they decrease in size and extrude (get rid of) their nuclei. They also construct hemoglobin, the iron protein molecule that functions to attract oxygen. After a lifespan of approximately 120 days, RBCs rupture and release hemoglobin and cell fragments. Hemoglobin breaks down into hemosiderin, an iron compound, and several bile pigments. Most hemosiderin returns to the bone marrow and is reused to form new RBCs. The bile pigments are excreted by the liver into the feces. Erythrocytes are the most numerous of the formed elements in blood.

ELEMENT REVIEW
hem/o = blood
-globin = protein

> **PHYSIOLOGY FACT**
> Healthy Adult RBC Counts
> Males have 4.5 to 6 million RBCs per cubic millimeter of blood.
> Females have approximately 4.2 to 4.8 million RBCs per cubic millimeter of blood.

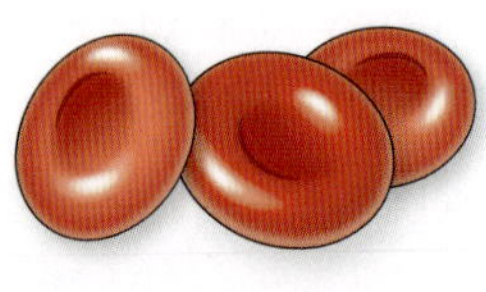

Figure 8-3 The shape of the RBC allows hemoglobin to pick up oxygen and deliver it to tissues.

White Blood Cells

WBCs, or **leukocytes**, are larger than erythrocytes but much fewer in number. Their function is to protect the body from **pathogens** or foreign substances; they remove debris from injured tissues and aid in the healing process. A mature leukocyte retains its nucleus after development but does not contain hemoglobin. It therefore is not involved in oxygen transport. Leukocytes are divided into two categories: granulocytes and agranulocytes.

TABLE 8-2 Types of Granulocytes

Granulocyte Type	WBCs, %	Staining	Function
Neutrophils	60%–70%	Minimal staining	Remain fairly neutral; phagocytic, engulfing and destroying bacteria
Eosinophils	2%–4%	Red-rosy color in acid stain; nucleus with two lobes	Increase in number in response to allergic reactions
Basophils	Less than 1%	Stain dark blue with base dye	Secrete histamine and heparin during allergic reactions

Granulocytes

Three of the five types of leukocytes are granular: **neutrophils**, **eosinophils**, and **basophils**. As the category implies, they all contain granules in their cytoplasm. In the laboratory, these cells can be stained with various dyes as the granules will absorb the dyes (Table 8-2). The various colors, as well as the shapes of the nuclei, allow the laboratory technician to identify the different WBCs under the microscope.

Agranulocytes

The two forms of agranulocytes are monocytes and lymphocytes. As their name implies, they have no granules within the cytoplasm and do not stain a dark color when observed under a microscope. **Monocytes** are the largest of the WBCs and have a kidney-bean shaped nucleus. They comprise 3% to 8% of total WBCs and protect the body by engulfing pathogens in a process called **phagocytosis**. **Lymphocytes** comprise 20% to 25% of all WBCs. They have a large, spherical-shaped nucleus and play an important role in the immune system. Some lymphocytes are phagocytes (engulfing bacteria), whereas others produce antibodies that destroy bacteria. Lymphocytes are divided into two main categories: T cells and B cells.

ELEMENT REVIEW
phag/o = to eat
cyt/o = cell
-osis = condition

T cells are derived from the thymus gland and make up 75% of the lymphocytes. They function to destroy tumor cells and cells infected by bacteria.

B cells make up 25% of the lymphocytes. Upon activation by a pathogen, they produce antibodies to specific infections.

ELEMENT REVIEW
thromb/o = clot

Thrombocytes

A **thrombocyte**, also known as a platelet, is not actually a cell but rather a cell fragment of a very large bone marrow cell called a *megakaryocyte*. The function of platelets is to start the chemical reactions for blood clotting, also called **coagulation**. When a capillary ruptures, platelets adhere to each other and to the cut edges of the vessel forming a platelet plug. Some of the platelets then disintegrate as they flow over the damaged blood vessel, releasing thromboplastin. Thromboplastin converts prothrombin into thrombin, which is the active form of the enzyme. Calcium ions and other clotting factors aid the reaction. Thrombin then converts fibrinogen into fibrin. The fibrin threads then form a clot, adhering to the damaged tissue. This series of chemical reactions is called the clotting cascade (Fig. 8-4). The average platelet count ranges from 250,000 to 500,000 platelets per cubic millimeter of blood.

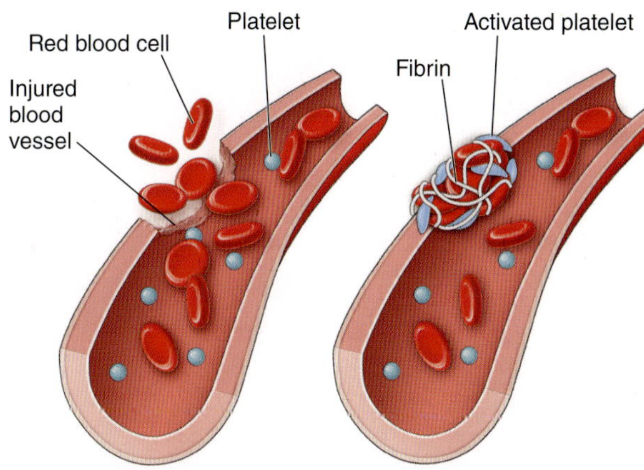

Figure 8-4 The chemical reactions necessary for clot formation start with the platelets.

Blood Types

While RBCs all function to deliver oxygen and carbon dioxide, they do differ among individuals. The surface of the RBCs contains chemicals called antigens. An **antigen**, also called an agglutinogen, can stimulate the body to produce antibodies. **Antibodies** are chemical substances programmed to attack foreign invaders. Based on the antigens of the RBCs, the corresponding produced antibodies will not attack. The body "recognizes" their own antigens, and no attack is prompted. If the antigen is not recognized by the antibody, an incompatibility will arise. This becomes important when we consider transfusing blood of one person to another. We call the patient the "recipient" and the person giving the blood a "donor." If the antigens on the surface of the RBCs of the donor are not compatible with the antibodies circulating in the plasma of the recipient, **agglutination** (clumping of cells) occurs.

Antigens on the surface of RBCs can be categorized into four groups: A, B, AB, and O. This is referred to as the "blood type." Antigen A has anti-B antibody, antigen B has anti-A antibody. Antigen–antibody combinations are shown in Table 8-3.

Illness, surgery, or injury may require a patient to receive blood (Table 8-4). The American Red Cross holds blood drives where healthy adults may donate their blood for use in hospitals and emergency departments. Upon donation, the blood is screened for disease, and the blood type is confirmed. Units of blood are stored and distributed to hospitals all over the country.

In addition to the ABO system, another form of antigen on the RBCs is known as the Rh factor. This antigen is named for the rhesus monkey where it was first studied. Humans can be Rh positive (Rh+) or Rh negative (Rh–). Agglutination will occur if a person with Rh negative blood is transfused with Rh positive blood. Conversely, a patient with Rh positive blood can receive Rh-negative blood without agglutination. It can be said that Rh-negative blood is "allergic" to Rh positive blood (although the reaction is not a true "allergy" but rather an incompatibility).

There is another concern, specifically with women who are Rh negative. If she becomes pregnant with an Rh-positive baby (inheriting the Rh type from the father), the maternal blood may mix with the fetal blood, causing production of anti-Rh antibodies. The first pregnancy may progress normally, but subsequent pregnancies are at risk. The exposure of the maternal blood to the Rh-positive antigen causes her blood to recognize Rh-positive

TABLE 8-3 ABO Blood Types

Blood Type	Antigen Present on the RBC	Antibody Present in Plasma
A	A	Anti-B antibody
B	B	Anti-A antibody
AB	AB	No antibodies
O	O	Both anti-A and anti-B antibodies

TABLE 8-4 Who Can You Donate to? Who Can You Receive From?

Blood Type	Donate to	Receive From
A	A, AB	A, O
B	B, AB	B, O
AB	AB only	All (universal receiver)
O	All (universal donor)	O only

antigen as foreign to her body. Anti-Rh antibodies will cross the placenta and react with the Rh antigens on the RBCs of the fetus. Destruction of the fetal blood cells will cause loss of the pregnancy.

To prevent this devastating possibility, Rh-negative mothers are given an injection of Rh immune globulin (RhoGAM) during week 28 of pregnancy. Administration of the injection prevents the development of anti-Rh antibodies in the mother's bloodstream.

The Lymphatic System

The lymph system is made up of fluid, vessels, nodes, organs, and cells that play an important role in the immune system and fluid regulation. As such, the lymphatic system is considered part of the circulatory system because it consists of moving fluid (lymph), which is derived from blood and returns to blood via lymphatic vessels. To protect the body from infection each of the lymphatic organs—including the thymus, spleen, and tonsils—use different mechanisms.

Lymph and Lymph Vessels

Lymph is clear, colorless fluid derived from blood and fluids that collect in the body. It contains proteins, electrolytes, fats, glucose, and lymphocytes.

The smallest lymph vessels, lymphatic capillaries, collect fluid that filters out of blood capillaries. Water and solutes continually filter out of blood capillaries and into the interstitial space (space outside of organs and tissues). This fluid needs to be removed to prevent an accumulation of fluid called edema (swelling). This fluid flowing from the blood capillaries to the lymphatic vessels is now called lymph. Lymph vessels contain valves to prevent backflow of fluid just like the valves in the veins. Unlike the cardiovascular system, the lymphatic system delivers fluid in one direction, from the tissues of the body back toward the thoracic cavity to the right lymphatic duct and the thoracic duct (Fig. 8-5). These two ducts are the only points of entry of lymph fluid into the bloodstream. Lymphatic drainage from the right side of the head and neck flows into the right lymphatic duct. Lymph from all other parts of the body flow directly into the thoracic duct. The right lymphatic duct empties into the right subclavian vein whereas the thoracic duct empties into the left subclavian vein. Thus, the lymphatic fluid is returned to the bloodstream.

Lymph nodes (also called glands) are a specialized group of tissues located at intervals along the path of the lymph vessels. They function to destroy pathogens, filter and remove impurities, and move the lymph fluid toward venous circulation. The major concentration of lymph nodes is found in the cervical, submandibular, axillary, and inguinal areas. Within the lymph vessels, macrophages will engulf and destroy the bacteria through phagocytosis. **Macrophages** are specialized immune cells located in lymph nodes, but they also are found in the liver, spleen, lungs, brain, and spinal cord. As lymph flows through the stationary lymph nodes, old cells, dead cells, and bacteria (killed by the macrophages) are filtered out so that they will not enter the bloodstream (Fig. 8-6).

ELEMENT REVIEW
macr/o = large
-phage = to eat
lymph/o = lymph
-edema = swelling

Thymus

The **thymus** gland is located in the middle of the chest near the mediastinum just under the sternum. It is an endocrine gland that secretes the hormone thymosin. Thymosin acts to stimulate red bone marrow to produce T lymphocytes (T cells). T lymphocytes migrate from the red bone marrow and mature in the thymus gland. Upon maturation, these cells enter the bloodstream and circulate throughout the body. They attack foreign and abnormal cells. Development of the thymus gland begins at 5 weeks gestation and continues to function through childhood and into puberty. It decreases in size and function and is dormant by age 40.

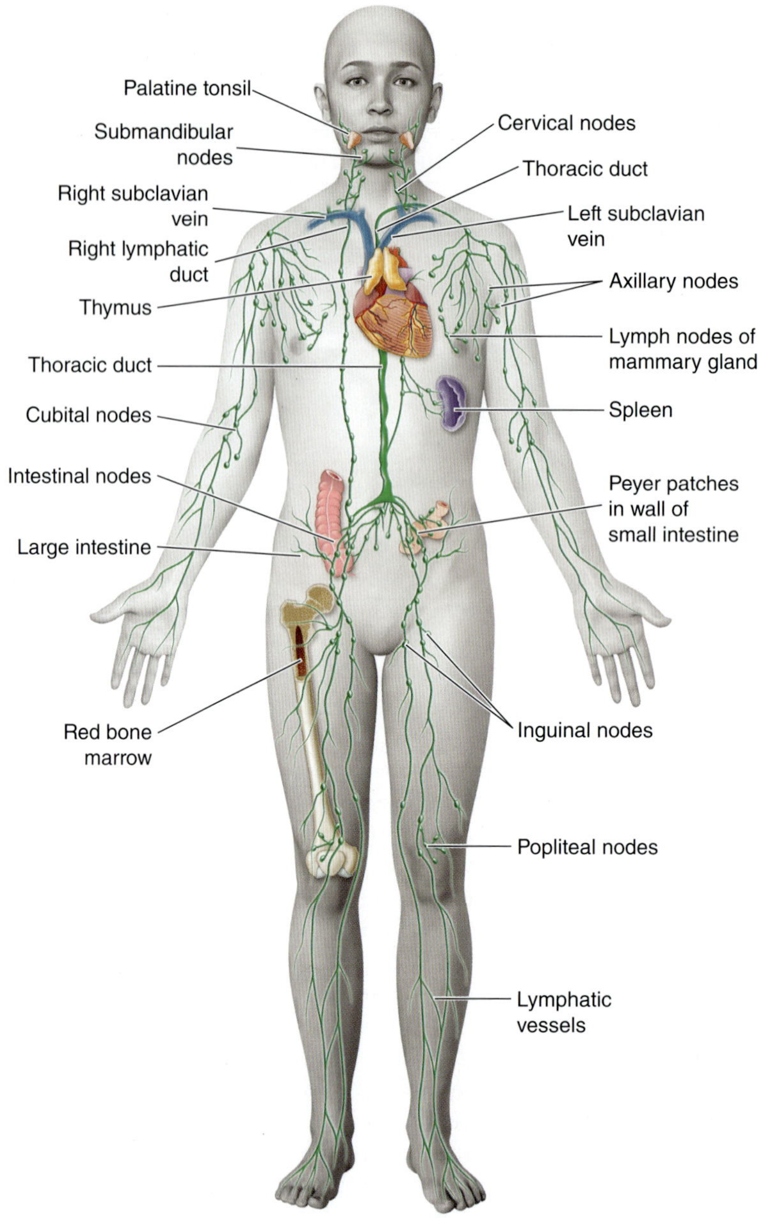

Figure 8-5 Lymph flows through the lymph nodes, vessels, and organs to the right lymphatic duct and the thoracic duct.

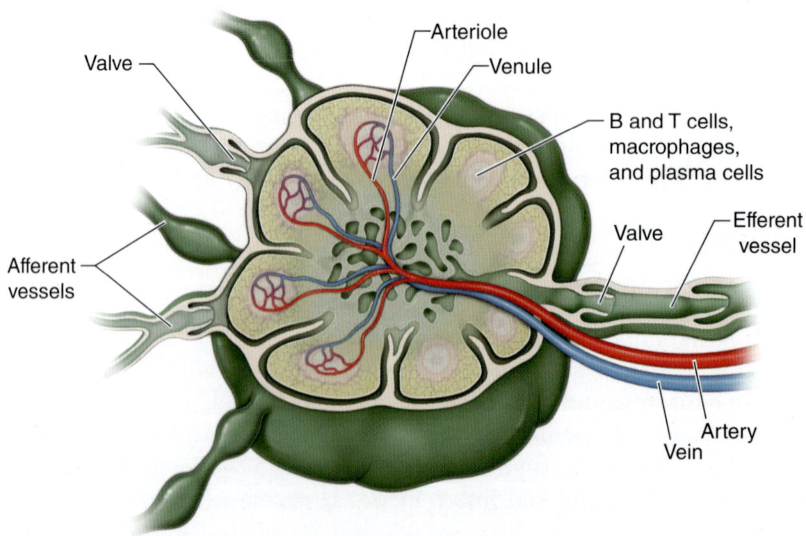

Figure 8-6 Lymphatic nodes and ducts

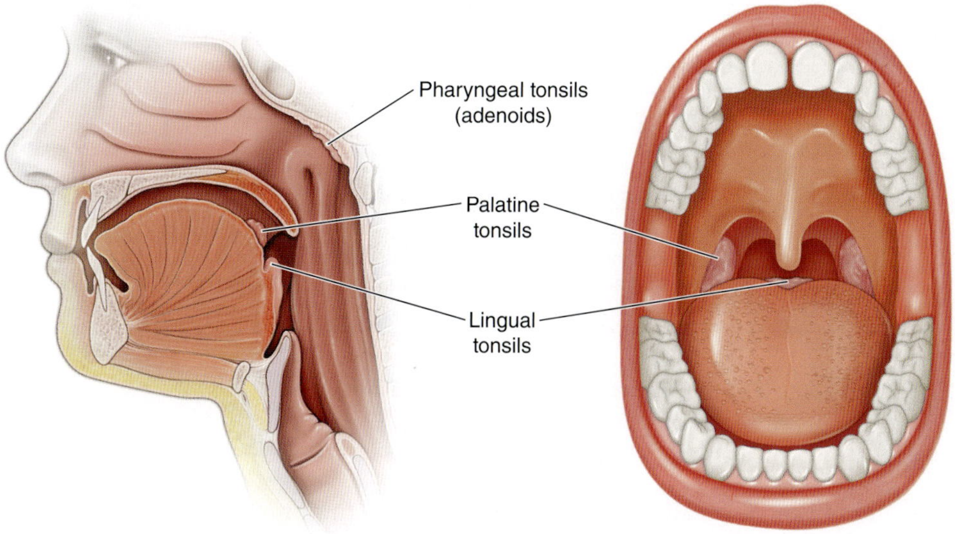

Figure 8-7 Pharyngeal, palatine, and lingual tonsils

Spleen

The **spleen** is the largest lymph organ and is in the left upper quadrant of the abdomen below the diaphragm and behind the stomach. Macrophages in the spleen remove pathogens and filter blood the same way lymph nodes filter lymph fluid. Additionally, macrophages in the spleen remove old RBCs from circulation, breaking them down and forming bile. Bile is then sent to the liver for excretion. Its function to destroy and remove old RBCs gives the spleen the nickname the "graveyard of RBCs." The spleen serves as a storage reservoir for blood. The venous sinuses of the spleen can hold up to a cup of blood, which can be released into circulation in an emergency such as a hemorrhage. Although the spleen plays a vital role in the immune system and is a backup reservoir for blood, if injured it may be removed in a procedure called a splenectomy. The need for a splenectomy is usually due to the spleen rupturing in a trauma (auto accident, fall).

ELEMENT REVIEW
splen/o = spleen
-ectomy = surgical removal

Tonsils

The **tonsils** are three masses of lymphatic tissue, located at the back of the throat (Fig. 8-7):

- Pharyngeal tonsils (also known as adenoids) lie near the opening of the nasal cavity and into the pharynx.
- Palatine tonsils are located on each side of the throat at the back of the oral cavity.
- Lingual tonsils are located at the base of the tongue.

ELEMENT REVIEW
tonsill/o = large
-itis = inflammation

Tonsils are the first line of defense against bacteria and other pathogens that can enter the body through the nose and mouth. This repeated contact with potential pathogens makes the tonsils susceptible to chronic infection and inflammation.

The Immune System

The lymphatic system is an important part of the immune system, protecting the body from disease-producing organisms (pathogens) and other foreign microorganisms. **Immunity**, the state of being protected or resistant to disease, can be natural or acquired.

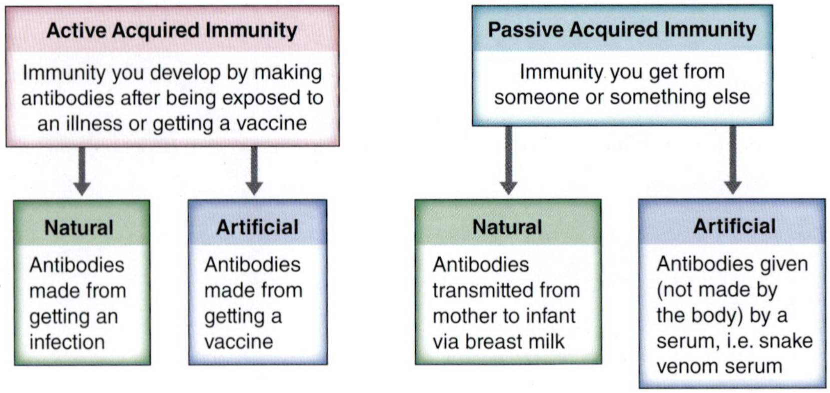

Figure 8-8 Types of acquired immunity.

Natural Immunity

Natural immunity, also called "genetic immunity," is the protection we are born with. Some pathogens that are harmful to animals cannot affect humans because of the natural immunity we enjoy from birth. For example, humans do not suffer from feline infectious peritonitis (FIP). FIP is an alpha-coronavirus, and the corona viruses that can make humans sick are beta viruses. This natural immunity is a permanent state of immunity to a specific disease.

Acquired Immunity

Acquired immunity is immunity the body develops after birth to a specific agent. This protection can be attained by having received immunizations against the disease or having and recovering from the disease itself. Thus, acquired immunity can be divided into two categories: passive acquired immunity and active acquired immunity (Fig. 8-8).

> ***Study Tip***
> Active = I make the antibodies. Passive = the antibodies are given to me.

Passive acquired immunity is acquired artificially by injecting antibodies from the blood of humans or animals to protect the patient from a specific disease. This immunity is immediate but short-lived, lasting only a few weeks. An example of passive immunity is the administration of gamma globulin (blood protein containing antibodies) to patients who have been exposed to specific viruses such as hepatitis B or toxins such as snake venom. Another example of passive immunity is maternal antibodies that cross the placenta and confer immunity to the fetal blood. This provides the newborn passive immunity for the first year of life, prior to development of his or her own antibodies. This differs from baby to baby as exposure of mothers to viruses differ, in contrast to genetic immunity to certain animal infections enjoyed by all humans.

Active acquired immunity can be attained naturally by contracting a specific disease and recovering or artificially by being inoculated by a vaccine, antigen, or toxoid. Natural acquired immunity is the result of the disease itself, such as measles or chicken pox. The patient experiences symptoms of the disease, and in the process of fighting the infection, develops enough antibodies to prevent recurrence of the disease. Artificial acquired immunity is the result of **vaccination** with an antigen or toxoid to stimulate the body to form antibodies. For example, the measles-mumps-rubella vaccine (MMR) exposes the child to a mild strength of the disease, enough to stimulate the formation of antibodies but not enough to cause the disease itself. Often, the vaccines are attenuated, meaning the virus is weakened but still viable enough to stimulate the body to produce antibodies. Common attenuated vaccines include MMR, yellow fever, and some flu vaccines. Other vaccines are inactivated (or killed) and consist of only a fragment of the pathogen. Because inactivated vaccines produce less of an immune response, these vaccines often require subsequent vaccination (boosters) to confer long-term immunity. Examples of inactivated vaccines include polio, pertussis, rabies, and some flu vaccines.

Children receive routine vaccinations throughout their early years of life to confer protection against childhood diseases (Table 8-5). Other vaccines, such as malaria and typhoid, are offered for specific diseases for overseas travel.

Corona Virus Vaccine

The COVID-19 pandemic led to the rapid development of the COVID vaccine. Currently, three vaccines are available. All three vaccines are inactivated vaccines and do not contain the live virus.

Two mRNA vaccines are currently available from Pfizer and Moderna that contain harmless genetic material from the COVID-19 virus. This material instructs our cells to create a protein unique to the virus. The body then builds T lymphocytes and B lymphocytes specific to the COVID-19 virus if future infection occurs.

Vector vaccines available from Johnson & Johnson and Janssen contain a virus that is genetically similar to COVID-19. The virus is similar enough to act as a stand-in and prompt immune response to a COVID-19 infection. Like the mRNA vaccines, administration of the vaccine prompts T lymphocytes and B lymphocytes to remember how to fight future infections with COVID-19.

Immune Reaction

The **immune reaction**, also called the *immune response*, is a defense function of the body by which invading antigens (pathogens) are destroyed. Antigens trigger the immune response during an interaction with a myriad of cells of the body. The two types of immune responses are humoral and cell mediated.

Humoral immune response occurs when B lymphocytes encounter specific invading antigens. This interaction produces immunoglobulins, protein antibodies directed to destroy the antigen. These antibodies are all gamma globulins and can be divided into five categories:

1. **Immunoglobulin (IgM).** The first antibody that bacteria encounter, causes agglutination of bacteria, 5%-10% of antibodies in circulating blood.
2. **Immunoglobulin G (IgG).** Enhances phagocytosis and neutralizes bacteria and viral toxins. Most common and abundant antibody at 75% to 90% of antibodies in circulating blood. IgG migrates to the site of infection and reacts with the antigen to destroy it.
3. **Immunoglobulin E (IgE).** Most effective antibody against parasitic infections, it is a potent antibody but comprises only 0.01% of antibodies in circulating blood.
4. **Immunoglobulin A (IgA).** Protects the body from bacterial growth and colonization and comprises 10% to 15% of antibodies in circulating blood.
5. **Immunoglobulin D (IgD).** Specific function is unknown, with less than 0.5% of antibodies in circulating blood.

Study Tip

Use these mnemonics to remember the Ig categories:

IgM—Master, first responder
IgG—Greatest number
IgE—Environmental allergens
IgA—Against bacteria, antibacterial
IgD—Don't know

TABLE 8-5 Childhood Vaccine Schedule: Birth to 15 Months

Vaccine	Birth	1 Month	2 Months	4 Months	6 Months	9 Months	12 Months	15 Months
Hepatitis B (HepB)	1st dose	←2nd dose→				←3rd dose→		
Rotavirus (RV) RV1 (2-dose series); RV5 (three-dose series)			1st dose	2nd dose	See Notes			
Diphtheria, tetanus, and acellular pertussis (DTaP: <7 yr)			1st dose	2nd dose	3rd dose			←4th dose→
Haemophilus influenzae type b			1st dose	2nd dose	See Notes			3rd or 4th dose See Notes
Pneumococcal conjugate (PCV13, PCV15)			1st dose	2nd dose	3rd dose			←4th dose→
Inactivated poliovirus (IPV) (<18 yr)			1st dose	2nd dose		←3rd dose→		
COVID-19 (1vCOV-mRNA, 2vCOV-mRNA, 1vCOV-aPS)					2- or 3-dose primary series and booster (See notes.)			
Influenza (IIV4) OR influenza (LAIV4)					Annual vaccination 1 or 2 doses			
Measles-mumps-rubella (MMR)					Recommended ages for certain high-risk groups. See notes		←1st dose→	
Vericella (VAR)					Recommended ages for certain high-risk groups. See notes.		←1st dose→	
Meningococcal (MenACWY-D: ≥9 mo, MenACWY-CRM: ≥2 mo, MenACWY-TT: ≥2 y)			Recommended ages for certain high-risk groups. See notes.					

NOTES

- Consult relevant Advisory Committee on Immunization Practices (ACIP) statements for detailed recommendations.
- For calculating intervals between doses, 4 weeks = 28 days. Intervals of ≥4 months are determined by calendar months.
- Within a number range (e.g., 12–18), a dash (–) should be read as "through."
- Vaccine doses administered ≤4 days before the minimum age or interval are considered valid. Doses of any vaccine administered ≥5 days earlier than the minimum age or minimum interval should not be counted as valid and should be repeated as age appropriate. **The repeat dose should be spaced after the invalid dose by the recommended minimum interval.** For further details, see Table 3-2, Recommended and Minimum Ages and Intervals Between Vaccine Doses, in *General Best Practice Guidelines for Immunization*.
- Information on travel vaccination requirements and recommendations is available at https://www.cdc.gov/travel/.
- For vaccination of persons with immunodeficiencies, see Table 8-1, Vaccination of persons with primary and secondary immunodeficiencies, in *General Best Practice Guidelines for Immunization*, Immunization in Special Clinical Circumstances (In: Kimberlin DW, Barnett ED, Lynfield Ruth, Sawyer MH, eds. *Red Book: 2021–2024 Report of the Committee on Infectious Diseases.* 32nd ed. Itasca, IL: American Academy of Pediatrics; 2021:72–86).

(Adapted from Child and Adolescent Immunization Schedule by Age, Birth to 15 Months. Centers for Disease Control and Prevention. https://www.cdc.gov/vaccines/schedules/hcp/imz/child-adolescent.html#birth-15. Accessed June 14, 2023.)

Cell-mediated immune response involves T lymphocytes. Immature T lymphocytes originate in bone marrow stem cells and migrate to the thymus gland where they mature. Mature T lymphocytes enter the bloodstream, circulating and providing defense against disease by attacking foreign and/or abnormal cells. They migrate to the lymph node and lymph organs. When they encounter a specific invading antigen, they multiply rapidly and engulf and ingest the antigen. This rapid multiplication of cells creates memory cells. As the name implies, these cells remember the antigen and are ready to attack if they see the antigen again.

Although both the humoral and cell-mediated immune reactions attack specific antigens, there are differences in the two reactions. During the humoral reaction, B cells form Ig immunoglobulins (antibodies) as listed earlier to destroy extracellular pathogens such as microbes and their toxins. During the cell-mediated reaction, T cells destroy infected cells directly; no antibodies are formed. They kill intracellular microbes, viruses, bacteria, parasites, and tumor cells.

Study Tip

Use these mnemonics to remember the function of T and B cells:

T cells—Take down immediately.
B cells—Be right back with an immunoglobulin.

Structures and Physiology Review

Match the Terms

Match the terms to their description.

agglutination	fibrinogen	phagocytosis
antigen	hematopoiesis	spleen
basophils	leukocytes	thymus
coagulation	lymph	tonsils
erythrocyte	megakaryocyte	vaccination

1. Artificial stimulation of the body to produce antibodies to a specific pathogen ____________________
2. Process in the bone marrow to produce blood cells ____________________
3. Large bone marrow cell ____________________
4. Clear fluid that collects from blood and fluids in the body ____________________
5. Process of "cell eating" ____________________
6. The largest lymph organ, located in the upper left quadrant of the abdomen ____________________
7. The plasma protein necessary for clotting ____________________
8. The lymphatic tissue located in the throat ____________________

9. The endocrine gland that secretes thymosin ________________
10. Stimulates the body to produce antigens ________________
11. The medical term for a red blood cell ________________
12. Clumping of cells ________________
13. The process of blood clotting ________________
14. General term meaning white blood cells ________________
15. Cells that secrete histamine and heparin during allergic reactions ________________

Structures and Physiology Word-Building Practice

1. Nouns and Adjectives

Complete the chart of nouns and adjectives.

	Noun Form	Adjective Form
1.	__________	anemic
2.	__________	serous
3.	pathogen	__________
4.	__________	coagulopathic
5.	__________	splenic
6.	phagocyte	__________
7.	__________	eosinophilic
8.	chromatin	__________

2. Prefixes

Choose from the list of prefixes to build a word for the definitions below:

a-, an-	hypo-	micro-
ante-	inter-	pan-
anti-	intra-	poly-
hemi-	macro-	poikilio-
hyper-	mega-	pro-sub-

1. Large bone marrow cell ________________
2. Irregularly shaped cell ________________

3. Deficiency of all cells (blood) ____________________
4. Initiating protein that is converted to thrombin ____________________
5. Form of anemia pertaining to abnormally small cells ____________________
6. Reduction in quantity of circulating blood cells (RBCs) ____________________
7. Form of anemia characterized by excessive color of RBCs ____________________
8. Form of anemia characterized by decreased color of RBCs ____________________
9. Form of anemia characterized by abnormally large cells ____________________
10. Type of medication to reduce clotting ____________________

Word Building With Combining, Prefix, and Suffix Forms

The following word roots, prefixes, and suffixes are commonly used in medical terms for the anatomy and pathology of the blood, lymphatic, and immune systems. Combining vowels for word roots are included. Memorizing these word elements will help you understand new terms that you may encounter in the field of hematology as a medical assistant, medical laboratory technologist, nurse, phlebotomist, or other professional working in hematology or immunology.

The list contains examples of terms that utilize the combining forms and a pronunciation guide. Be sure to use the pronunciation guide so that you can learn to say the terms correctly.

The Medical Language Lab at medicallanguagelab.com provides audio files to help you practice your pronunciations.

Combining Form	Meaning	Example (Pronunciation)	Example Definition
aggluntin/o	to clump	agglutination (ă-gloot-ĭn-Ā-shŏn)	process of clumping
coagul/o	clotting	coagulopathy (kō-ag-yŭ-LOP-ă-thē)	disease/disorder of clotting
eosin/o	red, rosy	eosinophil (Ē-ŏ-SIN-ŏ-FIL)	granulocyte that stains red
erythr/o	red	erythrocyte (ĕ-RITH-rō-sīt)	red blood cell
hem/o	blood	hemolytic (hē-mŏ-LIT-ik)	pertaining to destruction of blood

Continued

Combining Form	Meaning	Example (Pronunciation)	Example Definition
hemat/o	blood	hematologist (HĒ-mō-tŏl-ō-jĭst)	specialist who treats diseases and disorders of blood
kary/o	nucleus	megakaryocyte (mĕg-ă-KĂR-ē-ō-sīt)	large bone marrow cell
leuk/o	white	leukocytopenia (loo-kō-sī-tō-PĒ-nē-ă)	deficiency in no. of WBCs
lymph/o	lymph	lymphatic (lim-FAT-ik)	pertaining to the lymphatic system
lymphaden/o	lymph gland	lymphadenopathy (lĭm-FĂD-ĕ-NOP-ă-thē)	disease of lymph glands
lymphangi/o	lymph vessel	lymphangiosarcoma (lĭm-făn-jē-ō-săr-KŌ-mă)	malignant neoplasm of lymph vessels
nucle/o	nucleus	anuclear (ā-NŪ-klē-ăr)	pertaining to a cell without nucleus
phag/o	to eat, swallow	phagocytosis (FĂG-ō-sī-TŌ-sĭs)	process of cell digesting pathogens
poikil/o	irregular	poikilocytosis (poy-kĭ-lŏ-sī-TŌ-sĭs)	condition of irregular cells
pyret/o	fever	pyretic (pi-RĔT-ĭk)	pertaining to fever
splen/o	spleen	splenectomy (splē-NEK-tŏ-mē)	surgical removal of the spleen
thromb/o	a clot	thrombosis (thrŏm-BŌ-sĭs)	condition of a clot
thym/o	thymus	thymoma (thī-MŌ-mă)	tumor of the thymus gland
tonsill/o	tonsil	tonsillitis (tŏn-sĭl-Ī-tĭs)	inflammation of the tonsils

ā = say, ă = sofa, ē = meet, ĕ = met, ī = eye, ĭ = in, ō = oh, ŏ = dog, ū = you, ŭ = up, oo = food

Prefix Form	Meaning	Example (Pronunciation)	Example Definition
a-, an-	without	agranulocyte (ā-GRAN-yū-lō-sīt)	WBC that doesn't contain granules
macro-	large	macrophage (MAK-rŏ-fāj)	large circulating monocytes
micro-	small	microthrombus (mī-krō-THRŎM-bŭs)	microscopic clump of fibrin, platelets, & RBCs
morpho-	shape	morphology (mor-FŎl-ō-jē)	the study of the shape (of cells)

ā = say, ă = sofa, ē = meet, ĕ = met, ī = eye, ĭ = in, ō = oh, ŏ = dog, ū = you, ŭ = up, oo = food

Suffix Form	Meaning	Example (Pronunciation)	Example Definition
-blast	immature	erythroblast (ĕr-RĬTH-rō-blăst)	immature RBC
-cyte	cell	phagocyte (FĂG-ō-sīt)	WBC that digests microorganisms
-cytosis	condition of cells	leukocytosis (loo-kō-sī-TŌ-sĭs)	condition of WBCs
-emia	blood condition	polycythemia (pol-ē-sī-THĒ-mē-ă)	condition of all blood cells
-globin	protein	hemoglobin (HĒ-mŏ-glō-bĭn)	blood protein
-lysis	destruction	hemolysis (hē-MŌL-ĭ-sĭs)	destruction of blood cells
-phil	love of	eosinophil (Ē-ŏ-SIN-ŏ-fil)	WBC that stains red, rosy
-poiesis	formation	hematopoiesis (he-mă-tŏ-poy-Ē-sĭs)	formation of blood cells

ā = say, ă = sofa, ē = meet, ĕ = met, ī = eye, ĭ = in, ō = oh, ŏ = dog, ū = you, ŭ = up, oo = food

Combining Forms Practice

1. Build the Terms

Using only the word elements listed, build terms for the definitions listed.

Prefixes	Combining Forms		Suffixes
an-, a-	agglutin/o	macro-	-ectomy
-blast	coagul/o	morpho-	-ic
-cytosis	eosin/o	phag/o	-lysis
	erthry/o	poikil/o	-ology
	hem/o	splen/o	-osis
	hemat/o	thromb/o	-oma
	kary/o		-pathy
	leuk/o		-penia
	lymph/o		-phil
			-poiesis

1. condition of RBCs ____________________
2. disease of the spleen ____________________
3. the study of the blood ____________________
4. formation of blood cells ____________________
5. irregularly shaped cells ____________________
6. condition of WBCs ____________________

7. WBC that stains rosy red ______________________
8. process of cell engulfing bacteria ______________________
9. immature red blood cell ______________________
10. the study of the shape and structure of cells ______________________

2. Decipher the Terms

Give the definition for the terms listed.

1. lymphoma ______________________
2. thrombosis ______________________
3. leukocytopenia ______________________
4. anemia ______________________
5. macrophage ______________________
6. lymphoblast ______________________
7. coagulopathy ______________________
8. erythropoiesis ______________________
9. splenic ______________________
10. thrombolytic ______________________

Visit the Medical Language Lab at medicallanguagelab.com. Use it to enhance your study and reinforcement of the medical terms and word parts covered in this chapter.

Blood, Lymphatic, and Immune System Diseases and Disorders

The blood, lymphatic, and immune system provide oxygenation to cells as well as protection from pathogens. As such, the signs and symptoms of disorders of these systems are common across a variety of diseases and disorders (Table 8-6). The presence of these signs and/or symptoms will prompt the provider to investigate to attain a specific diagnosis.

Pathological Conditions of the Blood, Lymphatic, and Immune System

Diseases of the blood include a variety of anemias and other disorders of RBCs, white blood cells, and disorders related to platelets. These conditions can be inherited or caused by disease, toxins, poor diet, or trauma.

TABLE 8-6 Common Signs and Symptoms

Common Signs	Common Symptoms
Paleness	Fatigue
Low blood counts such as anemias	Lethargy
Opportunistic infections	Loss of appetite (anorexia)
Low blood pressure	Cravings for nonfoods (pica)
Low body temperature	Feeling cold
Excessive bleeding	Depression
	Lack of concentration
	Mental confusion

Anemias

Anemia is a decrease in hemoglobin, the oxygen transporting protein complex, within RBCs. While there are several classifications of anemias, signs and symptoms of anemia are common to all forms. These signs and symptoms include fatigue, paleness of the skin, headaches, syncope (fainting), numbness and tingling, loss of appetite, swelling in the lower extremities, and dyspnea (difficulty breathing).

Aplastic anemia: Also called bone marrow depression anemia, characterized by **pancytopenia**, a decrease in all the formed elements, RBCs, WBCs, and platelets. It can occur due to infection or damage to stem cells of the bone marrow, but the cause is unknown in approximately 70% of cases. It can also be caused by chemotherapeutics, certain antibiotics (chloramphenicol), or exposure to radiation. Aplastic anemia is treated with blood transfusions until the patient's bone marrow can form blood cells (upon conclusion of chemotherapeutics or radiation). A bone marrow transplant from a close tissue match can also provide treatment.

ELEMENT REVIEW
pan- = all
cyt/o = cell
-penia = decreased number

Hemolytic anemia: The destruction of RBCs (hemolysis) from an intrinsic or extrinsic cause. Intrinsic causes include structural defects in hemoglobin formation or cell membrane weakness. Extrinsic causes include infections, toxins, chemicals, trauma, or artificial heart valves.

Iron-deficiency anemia: The most common form of anemia. The hemoglobin of the RBCs lacks iron, preventing oxygen delivery to cells of the body. It can arise from lack of iron in the diet or an inability to absorb iron. It also can be caused by chronic blood loss from heavy menstrual periods or gastrointestinal bleeding. In addition to the general symptoms of anemia, patients with iron-deficiency anemia may suffer from brittle nails, cracks at the corners of the mouth (cheilosis), soreness of the tongue, and pica. Pica is cravings to eat unusual items such as clay or starch. The condition is treated with iron supplementation.

Pernicious anemia: Caused by a deficiency of mature RBCs to form. These immature cells are large, nucleated cells that are inefficient in delivering oxygen to tissues. They vary in size, a condition called **anisocytosis**, and they are irregularly shaped (**poikilocytosis**). Pernicious anemia is caused by a lack of vitamin B_{12}, an important factor in RBC maturation. Normally, B_{12} binds with intrinsic factor (a protein secreted in the stomach), which protects the vitamin until it reaches the ileum for absorption into the bloodstream. The condition can be caused by gastric surgery that decreases the surface area of the stomach and therefore limits intrinsic factor secretion. It can be of autoimmune cause and is more prevalent in patients 60 years or older. Destruction of erythroblasts may result in elevated bilirubin levels causing yellowish (jaundiced) skin. The condition is treated with vitamin B_{12} injections.

ELEMENT REVIEW
an- = without, not
is/o = same, equal
cyt/o = cell
-osis = condition
poikil/o = varied, irregular
cyt/o = cell
-osis = condition

Sickle cell: A chronic hereditary anemia in which RBCs are shaped like a crescent or sickle. These crescent-shaped RBCs clump and form clots or thromboses. The clots can then occlude small blood vessels and cause tissue hypoxia (low oxygen). These areas of infarction (lack of O_2) are very painful. Areas of occlusion include hands, feet, and the abdominal cavity. As the oxygen concentration increases, the cells begin to resume the normal RBC shape. But frequent changes in the shape of the RBC, normal to sickle and back again, weakens the blood cell, leading to hemolysis. The disorder is caused by one gene (sickle cell trait) or two genes (sickle cell disease). It is most common in people of African and Mediterranean descent. Complications of sickle cell anemia can include heart murmurs, congestive heart failure, enlargement of the liver, jaundice, gallstones, hematuria, decreased urine concentration (leading to dehydration), osteomyelitis, ulcers on the lower extremities, and vision complications. Patients with sickle cell disease are advised not to have children; patients with sickle cell trait are advised to have their partner tested for the trait prior to pregnancy to avoid passing two genes to their offspring.

CASE STUDY, continued

Dr. Collins explains that RBCs, erythrocytes, are normally flexible, allowing them to bend to get into small blood vessels and deliver oxygen. The doctor goes on to explain that sickle cells are shaped like a crescent, and they are harder and less flexible than normal RBCs. This causes them to get stuck in small blood vessels. Lucy's acute pain was caused by a sickle cell crisis, acute pain caused by sickled cells blocking small blood vessels that carry blood to the bones. The pain is most common in the back, knees, legs, arms, chest, or stomach. The pain can be throbbing, sharp, or dull, but in Lucy's case it was so intense that she lost consciousness. Melanie told Dr. Collins that Lucy had complained of a headache and extreme fatigue for the past 2 days. Melanie asks Dr. Collins what else can she do to help? What other complications does Lucy risk? Should Lucy take an iron supplement?

PHYSIOLOGY FACT

Taking iron supplements is contraindicated for sickle cell patients. The mishappen cells are not caused by a lack of iron. Supplements may cause harm because the extra iron can build up in the body and cause organ damage.

Granulocytosis: The abnormal elevation in granulocytes circulating in the bloodstream. In response to allergic conditions (asthma, parasitic infections), eosinophils (one of the three granulocytes) will become elevated. This condition is called **eosinophilia.** In some forms of leukemia, basophils (another of the granulocytes) are elevated (**basophilia**).

Hemochromatosis: A rare genetic iron metabolism disorder that causes iron deposits throughout the body. It is usually a complication of one of the hemolytic anemias. The disorder is more common in men, and symptoms present at age 40. Patients have a bronze skin color, can suffer from congestive heart failure, fatigue, liver failure, arthralgia (joint pain), and diabetes as secondary complications. Treatment consists of **phlebotomy**, withdrawing venous blood from a patient at regular intervals to decrease iron stores.

Hemophilia: The two common forms of **hemophilia** are caused by inherited inadequacies of coagulation (clotting). **Hemophilia A**, also called classic hemophilia, is the most common (approximately 80%) and is a result of absence of factor VIII. The blood clotting cascade requires specific chemicals or "factors" to complete the process of clot formation.

Nearly all cases are reported in males. Signs and symptoms include bleeding gums and mouth and hematuria (blood in the urine). Treatment for episodes of bleeding includes transfusion with factor VIII or fresh plasma.

Hemophilia B: Also called Christmas disease, accounts for 10% to 15% of hemophilias and is caused by a lack of factor IX. The clotting process stops because the chemical reaction caused by factor IX does not occur. Differentiation of hemophilia type A vs B is done in a laboratory to discern the missing factor. Other forms of hemophilia are Von Willebrand's disease and Rosenthal's disease and account for only 5% to 10% of cases.

Leukemia: An excessive increase in immature WBCs leading to infection, anemia, and thrombocytopenia (a decrease in platelets). There are subcategories of leukemias based on the abnormal WBCs and whether the condition is acute or chronic. Acute forms of leukemia develop rapidly and quickly present with thrombocytopenia, progressive anemia, infected lesions in the throat and mouth, hyperpyrexia (high fever), and severe infection. Acute leukemia is more common in children. Chronic leukemias are more commonly seen in adults with gradual progression of the disease.

Acute myelogenous leukemia (AML) is predominated by immature granulocytes (neutrophils, eosinophils, and basophils). Acute lymphocytic leukemia (ALL) is predominated by immature lymphocytes and is more common to children and adolescents. Chronic myelogenous leukemia (**CML**) is predominantly both immature and mature granulocytes in the blood and bone marrow.

Chronic lymphocytic leukemia (CLL) is predominated by large amounts of lymphocytes in the spleen, bone marrow, and lymph nodes.

Because bone marrow produces large numbers of abnormal leukocytes, symptoms of all types of leukemias include infection, fever, sores of the throat and mouth, pneumonia, cystitis, and septicemia. Symptoms related to the decreased platelets include petechiae (pinpoint hemorrhages on the skin), epistaxis (nosebleeds), hematuria (blood in the urine), bruising, hematomas, scleral or retinal hemorrhage. Treatments include radiation, chemotherapy, and bone marrow transplantation.

ELEMENT REVIEW
idi/o = individual, distinct, self-produced, unknown
-pathic = pertaining to disease
hem/o = blood
-rrhage = burst forth, rupture

Idiopathic thrombocytopenia purpura: The body produces an antiplatelet factor, destroying its own platelets. This decrease in platelets causes hemorrhages under the skin, giving patients red-purple skin discolorations. Treatments include splenectomy to stop platelet destruction and corticosteroids. As the name suggests, the cause is unknown.

Multiple myeloma: An infiltration of malignant plasma cells into bone marrow. These cells produce excessive numbers of antibodies that can destroy the skeletal system, causing multiple fractures. Additionally, there is a reduction of normal antibodies to fight infection, thus the patient is at an increased risk of infection, hypercalcemia (increased blood calcium), anemia, and renal damage. Treatment consists of chemotherapy, but survival statistics are poor.

Polycythemia vera: An abnormal increase in the number of RBCs, granulocytes, and thrombocytes causing an increase in blood viscosity (thickness). Congestion in the liver and spleen with too many RBCs and thromboses (clots) in other areas is common. Symptoms include headaches, vertigo (dizziness), and cyanosis of the face. Polycythemia vera eventually can lead to congestive heart failure. Treatment includes periodic removal of blood via phlebotomy and myelotoxic medications to suppress the bone marrow's production of cells.

ELEMENT REVIEW
myel/o = bone marrow
-toxic = poison

Thalassemia: An inherited form of hemolytic anemia in which alpha or beta hemoglobin chains are defective, causing an inability to transport oxygen. Deficiency of normal hemoglobin causes RBCs to be hypochromic and microcytic. The disorder is most common in people of Mediterranean descent and is treated with frequent transfusions to sustain life. The frequent transfusions, however, can cause accumulation of iron in the liver, heart, and pancreas. Organ failure may then occur.

Diseases and Disorders of the Immune System

Acquired immunodeficiency syndrome (AIDS): HIV (human immunodeficiency virus) is diagnosed by the presence of antibodies to the infection. HIV is a slow-growing virus that typically begins with an acute infection. As the disease progresses, T cells are compromised, with their count going from 1600 (normal) to 800, reduced by approximately one-half. Symptoms of HIV include headache, stiffness in the neck, malaise, fever, night sweats, abdominal cramps, diarrhea, and skin rashes. Patients can stay in this stage of infection for years before T cells decrease to 200 or less, which is defined as AIDS. This leaves the patient vulnerable to opportunistic infections and cancers such as Kaposi's sarcoma. The HIV infection is transmitted via blood transfusion, drug use/abuse with contaminated needles, or sexual intercourse with an infected partner. An HIV-positive mother can transmit the virus to her unborn baby during pregnancy. Treatments include a cocktail of several anti-viral drugs and management of symptoms as they arise.

Cytomegalovirus: A herpes-type virus that causes serious illness in immunocompromised patients, including AIDS patients and organ-transplanted patients who are being treated with immunosuppressive medications to avoid transplant rejection. Common sites of the infection are the gastrointestinal system or the retina.

Graft vs host disease (GVH): An immunological injury suffered by a recipient of a bone marrow graft. The donated lymphoid cells attack the recipient (host). Common sites of damage include the skin, liver, and gastrointestinal tract. GVH occurs in 50% of all allogenic (from another person) bone marrow transplants.

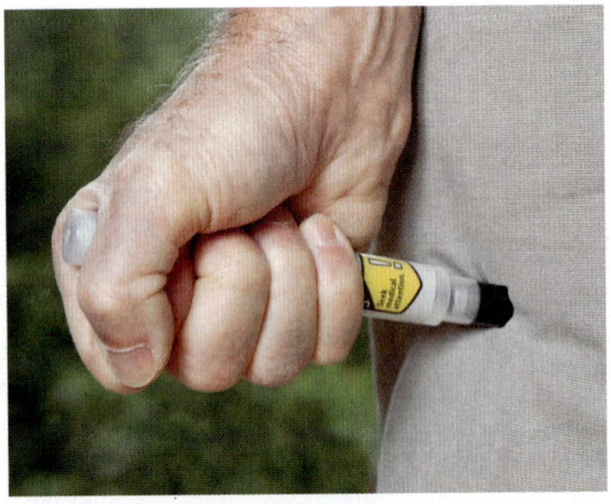

Figure 8-9 EPIPEN.

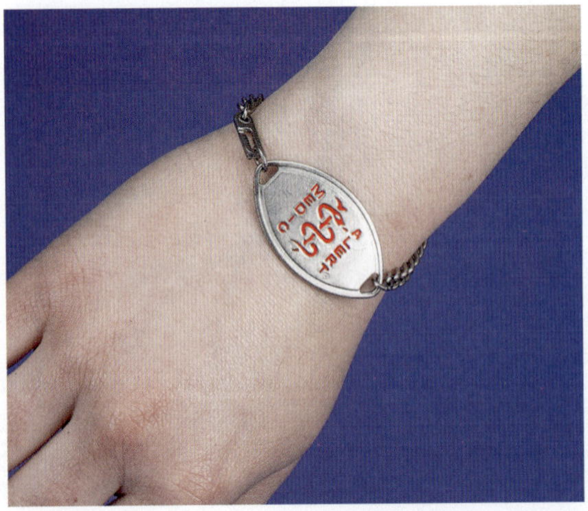

Figure 8-10 Medic alert bracelet.

Hypersensitivity (Allergy): The abnormal excessive response of the immune system to a particular stimulus. In an effort to protect the body from foreign materials, antibodies mistakenly attack healthy cells. The formation of the antibodies creates a hypersensitivity or allergic reaction. This allergic reaction is caused by an allergen, a substance that is not itself harmful but that causes the body to overreact. When a person reacts to a specific item, he or she is said to be allergic to that substance. Examples of allergens are foods such as peanuts, strawberries, eggs, or shellfish. Other allergens are found in the environment such as grass, pollens, ragweed, bee and wasp stings. Still other allergens are medications such as penicillin or other antibiotics. The hypersensitivity reaction can vary from mild to life-threatening. Some mild reactions include a skin rash, runny nose, hives, or itchy eyes. A severe and sometimes fatal hypersensitive reaction that can occur to previously encountered antigens is called **anaphylaxis** or anaphylactic shock. The first exposure to the antigen does not cause a reaction but sensitizes the patient to the substance for subsequent hypersensitive reactions. The second severe reaction is caused by the antigen–antibody complex, creating a massive secretion of histamine. This flood of histamine causes swelling and can occlude the throat causing an inability to breathe. Treatment for severe allergic reaction is administration of epinephrine, usually with an EPIPEN (Fig. 8-9). Once a patient knows that they have such a severe and potentially life-threatening reaction to a substance, they will be prescribed an EPIPEN to carry with them at all times and, of course, told to avoid the offending allergen(s). Patients with severe medication allergies can also wear medic alert bracelets (Fig. 8-10).

Hypersplenism: The painful enlargement of the spleen. It can be due to hemolytic anemias, portal hypertension, lymphomas, tuberculosis, malaria, or inflammatory/connective tissue disease. Symptoms include pain in the upper left side of the abdomen, with the spleen easily palpated upon examination. Treatment for the underlying condition will decrease symptoms. A splenectomy is performed if the enlargement is severe (at risk for a rupture).

Kaposi's sarcoma: A malignant neoplasm associated with AIDS. The sarcoma typically presents as lesions on the skin (tiny red to purple macules) that grow into larger nodules or plaques. It can also cause lesions in the mucous membranes, lungs, and visceral organs. Visceral lesions can cause gastrointestinal bleeding and anemia. Lymphatic lesions will cause swollen lymph nodes and localized edema. Pulmonary lesions will cause shortness of breath and dyspnea (difficulty breathing). Treatments include radiation, chemotherapy, and laser cryotherapy to skin lesions.

Lymphoma: A neoplasm of lymphoid tissue that can be divided into Hodgkin's disease and non-Hodgkin's lymphoma. Hodgkin's disease, named for Thomas Hodgkin (1798–1866), a British physician, is characterized by the Reed-Sternberg (RS) cell. RS cells are malignant cells of the lymph nodes. These malignancies are first observed in the cervical nodes and progress to the other nodes and the spleen. Males are affected twice as often as females. Signs and symptoms include enlarged, painful lymph nodes, splenomegaly, night sweats, low-grade fever, anorexia, leukocytosis, and anemia. Localized radiation therapy is used if contained to the cervical lymph nodes. Further spread of the disease warrants chemotherapy. Non-Hodgkin's lymphoma is classified as any other lymphoma that does not contain the RS cells. Signs and symptoms are similar to Hodgkin's and radiation and chemotherapy are used to stop growth of lymphomas and cure the disease.

Mononucleosis: Usually caused by the **Epstein-Barr virus** (EBV), mononucleosis is a benign acute infection of the B lymphocytes and primarily affects young adults (14 to 20 years old). It is named the "kissing disease" because it is transmitted via saliva. The infection of the B lymphocytes causes the body to produce antibodies by B and T lymphocytes to fight the infection. As such, the lymphoid tissue becomes swollen, causing enlarged, sore lymph nodes in the cervical and sometimes the axillary nodes. Additionally, the spleen may become tender. The infection can last 1 to 3 weeks with signs and symptoms including fatigue, fever, chills, diaphoresis (sweating), sore throat, headache, skin rash, and anorexia. Diagnosis is confirmed by elevated lymphocyte count and physical examination. Treatment consists of bedrest, analgesics, and corticosteroids (if necessary for swelling). Fatigue may last up to 3 months postinfection.

Myasthenia gravis: An autoimmune disorder in which acetylcholine receptor sites are attacked by antibodies. This causes a disconnect in the neuromuscular junctions, impairing muscle function. The disorder is more common in women, usually occurring at age 20 to 40 years. Symptoms may present gradually or suddenly, most noticeably in the muscles of the face causing drooping eyelids and difficulty swallowing or speaking. Muscle fatigue is more pronounced later in the day or after exercise. Weakness can progress to paralysis. Treatment is restricted activity, a soft or liquid diet, and anticholinesterase drugs (Mestinon). Patients may also benefit from periodic corticosteroids to reduce inflammation.

***Pneumocystis* pneumonia (PCP):** A subacute opportunistic infection caused by the fungus *Pneumocystis jirovecii* (previously classified as *Pneumocystis carinii)*, which can be found worldwide. It is the most common opportunistic infection of AIDS patients, affecting 75% to 80%. Signs and symptoms include fever, dry cough, tachypnea (rapid breathing), dyspnea (difficulty breathing), and hypoxemia. As symptoms progress and exchange of air is impaired, swelling of alveoli (air sacs in the lungs) occurs, as does accumulation of protein-rich foamy fluid.

Sarcoidosis: Caused by granulomas forming primarily in the lungs (90%) but also in the lymph nodes, eyes, liver, or other organs. The granulomas start as small, round lesions that may spontaneously resolve or grow larger, leading to fibrosis. It is most commonly seen in African American women from 20 to 40 years of age. Mortality is less than 3%, but some patients suffer permanent disability of the lungs or eyes. Treatment consists of corticosteroids to suppress granuloma formation and growth.

Systemic lupus erythematosus (SLE): An inflammatory connective tissue disease that is caused by autoantibodies being created and attacking lymph, blood, and connective tissue vessels. The SLE autoantibodies and their corresponding antigens travel throughout the body and frequently cause damage in the kidneys. They may also travel to the brain, lungs, skin, muscles, spleen, heart, GI tract, or peritoneum, which is why it is named *systemic*.

Pathology Word-Building Practice

1. Build the Terms

*Using **only** the word parts in the lists provided, create medical terms for the indicated meanings.*

Prefixes	Combining Forms		Suffixes	
a-	aden/o	lymph/o	-al	-itis
an-	bas/o	neutr/o	-ar	-lysis
macro-	cyt/o	poikli/o	-ary	-oma
micro-	eosin/o	septic/o	-cocci	-osis
mega-	erythr/o	ser/o	-cyte	-pathy
pan-	hem/o	splen/o	-edema	-penia
	hemato/o	strept/o	-emia	-phil
	kary/o	thromb/o	-genesis	-poiesis
	leuk/o	tonsill/o	-ic	-stasis

1. varied or irregular cells ________________________
2. pertaining to abnormally small cells ________________________
3. disease of glands ________________________
4. blood protein ________________________
5. presence of pathogens in the blood ________________________
6. decreased amount of all blood cells ________________________
7. inflammation of the tonsils ________________________
8. pertaining to the spleen ________________________
9. condition of RBCs ________________________
10. large, nucleated cell ________________________
11. tumor of lymph cells ________________________

12. inflammation of lymph glands ________________
13. swelling of lymph ________________
14. abnormal condition where cells are round ________________
15. destruction of blood cells ________________
16. condition of a clot ________________
17. abnormal condition of a lack of blood ________________
18. gram-positive twisted chains of bacteria ________________
19. decreased number of neutrophils ________________
20. disease of blood ________________

2. Prefixes

Choose from the list of prefixes to build a word for the definitions below.

an-	micro-	pan-
hyper-	mono-	poly-
macro-		

1. type of anemia characterized by abnormally small cells ________________
2. large WBC that engulfs pathogens ________________
3. category of conditions that mean of a lack of blood cells ________________
4. abnormal increase in the number of RBCs ________________
5. a marked reduction in the number of all blood cells ________________
6. benign, self-limiting acute infection of B lymphocytes ________________
7. syndrome of deficiency of blood cells and enlargement of the spleen ________________
8. condition of unequal size of cells ________________
9. mononuclear phagocyte ________________
10. an abnormally large thrombocyte ________________

3. Suffixes

Choose from the list of suffixes to build a word for the definitions below.

-blast	-itis	-oma
-cytosis	-lytic	-pathy
-emia	-penia	-phage

1. immature RBC ____________________
2. neoplasm of lymphoid tissue ____________________
3. decreased number of neutrophils ____________________
4. large cell that eats pathogens ____________________
5. condition of WBCs ____________________
6. inflammation of the tonsils ____________________
7. pertaining to destruction of blood ____________________
8. disease of the spleen ____________________
9. decrease in the number of RBCs ____________________
10. blood condition of WBCs ____________________

Order	Tube Color	Additive
1	Yellow	SPS Sterile media bottles
2	Light blue	Sodium citrate
3	Red plastic	Clot activator
	Red glass	No additive
	Red and gray SST	Gel separator tube with clot activator
	Gold SST	Gel separator tube with clot activator
	Orange RST	Gel separator tube with thrombin
	Royal blue	Clot activator
4	Light green PST	Gel separator tube with heparin
	Green	Heparin
	Royal blue	Heparin
5	Lavender	EDTA
	Pink	EDTA
	Tan	EDTA
	Royal blue	EDTA
	White PPT	Gel separator with EDTA
6	Gray	Potassium oxalate Sodium fluoride
7	Yellow	ACD

Figure 8-11 Order of draw and additives for blood tests.

Blood, Lymphatic, and Immune System Diagnostic Procedures

Diagnostic procedures of the blood, lymphatic, and immune system not only rely on many blood tests but also some biopsies and imaging to diagnose some cancers.

Blood Tests

Blood testing requires phlebotomy, withdrawing venous blood from a patient, into various blood tubes that contain preservatives or anticoagulants, depending on the type of test. The tables below show the blood tests, normal ranges, and some causes of abnormalities. The blood to be tested must be collected in the proper tube.

Different blood collection tubes have reagents that preserve the blood for various tests. The reagents are indicated by the color of the tube stopper. The working phlebotomist will memorize the reagents in each of the colored tube stoppers and the order of drawing for tests (Fig. 8-11).

- Complete blood count (CBC): A series of tests performed on venous blood and is often a part of a routine checkup. It can help to diagnose a variety of disorders such as anemias, infections, disease of the immune system, and blood cancers.

Name of Test	Definition	Normal Range Females	Normal Range Males	Notes
Red blood cell count	No. of circulating RBCs	4.2–5.4	4.7–6.1	Low in iron-deficiency anemias or blood loss
Hemoglobin (Hgb) g/dL	No. grams of Hgb per milliliter of blood	12–16 g/dL	14–18 g/dL	Decreased in iron-deficiency anemias or blood loss. Increased in polycythemia vera, congestive heart failure, COPD, dehydration, severe burns
Hct	RBC/total blood volume, %	37% to 47%	42% to 52%	Increased in dehydration, polycythemia vera, shock. Decreased in anemia, leukemia, bone marrow failure, poor nutrition, multiple myeloma
Mean corpuscular volume (femto liter, fL)	Average size of RBCs	78–100	78–100	Elevated in macrocytic anemias, decreased in microcytic anemias
Mean corpuscular hemoglobin	Average amount of Hgb in RBCs	27.0–32.0	27.0–32.0	Elevated in macrocytic anemia, decreased in microcytic anemias
Mean corpuscular hemoglobin concentration	Amount of hemoglobin in packed cells (hemoglobin divided by hematocrit)	310–370	310–370	Increased in smokers or during pregnancy; decreased in anemias: iron deficiency, pernicious, and hemolytic
Red cell distribution width	Difference in size and volume of RBCs	11.5–15.0	11.5–15.0	Elevated in nutritional deficiencies of vitamin B_{12}, iron, folate
Platelets ×10 9/L	No. of platelets in milliliter of blood	150–400	150–400	Elevated essential thrombocythemia or reactive thrombocytosis
WBC × 10 9/L	No. of WBCs in milliliter of blood	4.0–11.0	4.0–11.0	Increased in a variety of infections, inflammation decreased in lupus, rheumatoid arthritis, HIV, AIDS, cancer, effect of chemotherapy

- Differential WBCs. The differential WBCs are often run together with the CBC.

Name of Test	Normal Range	Notes
Lymphocytes	1.0–4.5	Elevated in viral infections, leukemia; decreased in HIV and AIDS
Neutrophils	2.0–7.5	Elevated in bacterial and viral infections
Eosinophils	0.04–0.40	Elevated in allergic reactions, asthma, parasitic infections
Basophils	Less than 0.1	Elevated in lymphoma or leukemia

- Other blood tests

Type of Test	Definition	Normal Values	Notes
Bleeding time	Determines how fast small blood vessels in the skin stop bleeding	2–7 minutes	Increased in platelet dysfunction, von Willibrand's disease, hemophilia
C-reactive protein (CRP)	Measures CRP, a protein made in the liver and is a nonspecific marker of inflammation	0 to 0.65, optimal 0.66 to 2.00, healthy 2.01 to 3.00, moderate risk 3 or higher, high risk	Increased in cardiovascular disease, pneumonia, COPD, irritable bowel syndrome, lupus, rheumatoid arthritis

Continued

Type of Test	Definition	Normal Values	Notes
Enzyme-linked immunosorbent assay (ELISA)	Tests for antibodies to AIDS virus, or other viruses, such as Lyme disease	Neg = no disease Pos = presence of disease	Positive test indicates disease but should be confirmed with a Western blot test (detects antibodies to confirm ELISA results)
Erythrocyte sedimentation rate (ESR) Measured in mm/hr	Rate at which RBCs settle out of a tube of unclotted blood	0–10 mm/hr	Increased in pneumonia, acute MI, severe anemia, kidney failure, obesity, cancer Decreased in congestive heart failure, sickle cell anemia, polycythemia vera, angina pectoris
Glucose (fasting)	Measurement of blood glucose	80–99 mg/dL	Increased in diabetes mellitus or prediabetes Decreased in hypoglycemia, high-intensity exercise, fasting, very low carbohydrate diet
Hemoglobin A1c Measured as percentage of glycated RBCs	Measures average blood glucose over past 3 months (lifetime of RBC)	Less than 6.5%	Increased in poorly controlled blood glucose Deceased (less than 5%) in people with very strict diets
Lipid profile	Measurement of variety of lipids in the bloodstream	Total = 400–800 mg/dL Triglycerides = 40–150 mg/dL Cholesterol = less than 200 mg/dL Phospholipids = 150–380 mg/dL Fatty acids = 9–15 mmol/L	Increased levels cause increased risk of atherosclerosis and heart disease. Very low levels can be indicative of higher risk of cancer or hemorrhagic stroke
Partial thromboplastin time (PTT)	Assessment of various blood clotting factors Used to monitor heparin administration	60–70 sec	Increased in vitamin K deficiency, leukemia, heparin administration, cirrhosis of the liver, clotting factor deficiencies (hemophilia), decreased in disseminated intravascular coagulation, early stages of cancer
Prothrombin time (PT)	Used to assess clotting factors I and II (fibrinogen and prothrombin) Used to monitor effectiveness of warfarin therapy	10–13.4 sec	Prolonged in patients with insufficient clotting factors I and/or II PT > 30 = high risk for hemorrhage
Prostate-specific antigen (PSA)	Men only; measures amount of PSA in blood	0–0.4 ng/mL	Increased in prostatitis or prostate cancer
Reticulocyte count	Measurement (%) of immature erythrocytes	0.5%–1.5%	Increased in hemolytic anemia, sickle cell anemia, leukemia, pregnancy, and post hemorrhage. Decreased in pernicious and aplastic anemias, cirrhosis of the liver, folic acid deficiency, bone marrow failure, chronic infection, postradiation therapy
Rouleax	Aggregation of RBCs that look like a stack of coins (seen under a microscope)	Does not occur in normal circulation	Seen in patients with multiple myeloma, inflammatory disease or cancer

Other Diagnostic Tests

While many diagnostic tests rely on a blood sample, other tests require sampling of tissue, imaging, and contrast medium.

Bone marrow biopsy: Bone marrow samples taken by needle aspiration or surgical resection. The marrow is analyzed to diagnose abnormalities such as leukemia, anemias, and conditions of increased or decreased platelet formation.

CT scan (CAT): X-ray images taken after injection of a contrast medium. Used to diagnose abnormalities of lymphoid organs such as spleen, thymus, or lymph nodes.

Lymphangiogram: X-ray images taken after injection of a contrast medium into the lymph vessels of the hand or foot. As the lymph flows to the thoracic cavity, the contrast medium can outline abnormalities and help to diagnose and stage lymphomas.

Schilling test: A diagnostic test for pernicious anemia. The patient is given oral radioactive cobalt that is tagged with vitamin B_{12}. Absorption in the gastrointestinal tract is evaluated by the level of radioactive B_{12} excreted in the urine. Normal value should be 8% to 40% of the B_{12} excreted collected over 24 hours. A decreased amount of excreted B_{12} indicates an inability to absorb B_{12} due to pernicious anemia.

CAREER EXPLORATION: PHLEBOTOMIST

Our high school held a blood drive where I volunteered to check patients in and provide snacks after people donated their blood. I observed phlebotomists drawing blood and talked with the nurse supervisor about becoming a phlebotomist. I enrolled in a phlebotomy program at the community college and became a certified phlebotomist in 6 months. Now I work for the American Red Cross and travel to local community centers, churches, and businesses to work at blood drives. We even went back to my high school, and I drew blood from the principal and my former math teacher. I love seeing a variety of people in our community and being a part of collecting much-needed blood for our national supply. I am currently back in school pursuing a degree as a medical laboratory technician. I hope to work in a hospital laboratory, specifically in the hematology department. I guess you could say it's "in my blood."

Blood, Lymphatic, and Immune System Therapeutic Procedures

Therapeutic procedures of the blood and immune system include surgical procedures, medications, and dietary changes to eliminate disease or manage symptoms of blood, lymphatic, and immune disorders.

Allergy shots: Regular injections administered over a period of time (usually 3 to 5 years) to stop or reduce allergy attacks. The allergy shots contain a tiny amount of the allergen (offending agent) to stimulate the immune system to react, but not enough to cause a full-blown allergic reaction. Over time, the dose of allergens is increased in the shots to cause a desensitization to the allergens. This prevents natural exposure to the allergens to cause symptoms.

Blood transfusion: Patients may be transfused blood after surgery, trauma, or disease. The donor blood must be compatible with the recipient's blood type.

Bone marrow transplant: Patients with leukemia, myeloma, lymphoma, or aplastic anemias have a dysfunction of immune cells, leaving the patient unable to fight infection. Bone marrow transplant with healthy cells will offer the patient immunity to infection. Prior to the transfusion, chemotherapy or total body radiation is performed to destroy all malignant cells of the bone marrow. The recipient and donor must be tissue and blood matched to prevent rejection of the cells. Healthy bone marrow cells are infused intravenously to the recipient. After transplantation, the patient must take immunosuppressant medications to prevent transplant rejection. Complications of bone marrow transplantation include serious infections, rejection of transplanted cells (GVH), and relapse of the original disease.

Diet management for food allergy: Food allergies can be managed with either avoidance of the offending food or desensitization with allergy shots or tiny amounts of the offending food being ingested. Because some severe food allergies can be life-threatening, desensitization must always be done under the care of a provider.

Tonsillectomy: Surgical removal of pharyngeal (adenoid), palatine, and lingual tonsils. Also called a tonsillectomy and adenoidectomy. The removal is recommended in cases of recurrent infection.

Splenectomy: Surgical removal of the spleen. It may be performed as an emergency surgery in response to rupture of the spleen due to injury or in response to severe enlargement presenting risk of rupture.

Medications for the Blood, Lymphatic, and Immune System

Table 8-7 lists common medications for the blood, lymphatic, and immune system used to fight infection, normalize values of vital blood components, and prevent harmful autoimmune responses.

Medications Review

Using the table of medications, complete the chart below. The first one has been done for you.

Medication Name	Classification (mechanism)	Therapeutic Use (What is it used for?)
Tetracycline	*antibiotic*	*infections gram pos or neg*
1. Plavix	____________	____________
2. Prograf	____________	____________
3. Zyrtec	____________	____________
4. Iodine-125	____________	____________
5. Biktarvy, Dovato	____________	____________
6. Remdesivir	____________	____________
7. Bexxar	____________	____________
8. Amoxicillin	____________	____________
9. interferon alfa-2a (Roferon)	____________	____________

TABLE 8-7 Medications the Blood, Lymphatic, and Immune Systems

Classification	Examples	Common Use/Action
Antihistamines	diphenhydramine (Bendryl) loratadine (Claritin) cetirizine (Zyrtec)	Allergies, can be used prophylactically prior to medications that may cause allergic reaction
Immunosuppressants	Corticosteroids Prograf	Autoimmune diseases: lupus, rheumatoid arthritis, organ transplant
Amino acid	Endari (glutamine)	Increases glutamine in Sickle cell anemia
Antibiotic—penicillins	amoxicillin, penicillin Amoxil Ticar	Common infections with gram positive or gram-negative bacteria
Antibiotics—cephalosporins *often used for patients with allergy to pencillins	cephalexin, Keflex, Ceclor	Nosocomial (hospital acquired) surgical infections, pneumonia
Antibiotics—tetracylines	doxycycline, tetracycline	Common infections with gram positive or gram-negative bacteria
Antibiotics—macrolides	erythromycin Zithromax, Z-pak	Used to combat infections that are resistant to penicillin
Anticoagulants	warfarin (Coumadin) heparin	Used to prevent heart attack and stroke
Antifungals	Topical: clotrimazole (Lotrimin) Systemic (oral): fluconazole (Diflucan), miconazole Monistat	Fungal infections
Antimetabolites	leucovorin (Wellcovorin)	Cancers: lung, metastatic breast, pancreatic, ovarian and GI tumors
	hydroxyurea (Droxia)	Sickle cell anemia, chronic myelogenous leukemia
Antiplatelet agents	aspirin, Plavix	Prevent heart attack, stroke in patients with history of MI
Antivirals	acyclovir Tamiflu Remdesivir (approved for Covid-19 infection)	Viral infections
Antiretrovirals	Biktarvy, Dovato, AZT	HIV infection
Biological response modifiers	interferon alfa-2a (Roferon) interferon alfa-2b (Intron A)	Anemia, malignant melanoma, aids related Kaposi's sarcoma, Hepatitis B & C
hematopoetics	ferrous sulfate, vitamin B12	Various anemias
Immunomodulators	lenalidomide (Revlimid)	Multiple myeloma
Monoclonal antibodies	alemtuzumab (Campath) tositumomab (Bexxar)	Colon, lung, head, neck, breast cancers, leukemia, non-Hodgkin lymphoma
	crizanlizumab (Adakveo)	Anticoagulant specific to sickle cells
Radioactive isotopes	Brachytherapy seeds: iodine-125, iridium-194, palladium-103, thulium-170	Prostate, lung, cervical, endometrial and bile duct cancers

CASE STUDY, completed

Lucy is admitted for rest and observation after her head injury. Because she is aware of her sickle cell disease, Dr. Collins advises her to continue her medications but also discusses the risk for splenic sequestration, a condition in which a large number of sickle cells get trapped in the spleen, causing enlargement. Symptoms can appear suddenly and include weakness, pale lips, fast breathing, left-sided abdominal pain, and fast heart rate. This is a life-threatening condition, so Lucy and Melanie are advised to come back to the hospital immediately if she has these symptoms. Treatment for splenic sequestration includes blood transfusion or, in severe cases, a splenectomy. Dr. Collins also advises that Lucy continue with grief counseling and consider antidepressant medication if her symptoms persist. Regular eye examinations and frequent handwashing are advised to prevent retinal damage and infection.

CRITICAL THINKING QUESTIONS

1. What term means pertaining to the spleen? ______________________
2. Sickle cell anemia can sometimes cause a fast heart rate. What is its medical term? ______________________
3. Which type of blood cells are malformed in sickle cell disease? ______________________
4. What are common symptoms of sickle cell anemia (remember symptoms are subjective)? ______________________
5. What are common signs of sickle cell anemia (remember signs are objective and measurable)? ______________________
6. Why did Lucy's partner, a critical care nurse, start sleeping at the hospital during the pandemic? ______________________
7. What type of physician treats blood disorders? ______________________
8. Lucy suffers from an inability to sleep. The medical term is ______________________.
9. The white of Lucy's eyes appear yellow. This is called ______________________.
10. Sickle cell anemia can cause ischemia, which means ______________________.

Blood, Lymphatic, and Immune Abbreviations

Ab	antibody
Ag	antigen
ABO	blood groups: A, B, AB, O
ALL	acute lymphatic leukemia
AML	acute myelogenous leukemia
AIDS	acquired immune deficiency syndrome
ARC	AIDS-related complex
BMT	bone marrow transplant
CBC	complete blood count
CMV	cytomegalovirus
Diff	differential (WBC counts)
ELISA	enzyme-linked immunosorbent assay

EBV Epstein-Barr virus	KS Kaposi's sarcoma
ESR erythrocyte sedimentation rate	LDL low-density lipoprotein
GVH graft vs host disease	Lymph lymphocyte
Hct hematocrit	PT prothrombin time
Hgb or Hb hemoglobin	PTT partial thromboplastin time
HDL high-density lipoprotein	RA rheumatoid arthritis
HIV human immunodeficiency virus	RBC red blood cells
Histo histology	SLE systemic lupus erythematosus
ITP idiopathic thrombocytopenia purpura	VLDL very low-density lipoprotein
	WBC white blood cells

Abbreviations Review

Choose the correct definition for each of the abbreviations listed.

1. SLE
   a. Systemic leukocytic extrusion
   b. Systemic lupus erythematosus
   c. Systemic lupus extrusion
   d. Systemic leukocytic erythrematosus

2. RA
   a. Rheumatic arthritis
   b. Rheumatic arthrosis
   c. Rheumatoid arthritis
   d. Rheumatoid arthrosis

3. PTT
   a. Partial thromboplastin time
   b. Partial thrombic time
   c. Partial T-cell time
   d. Partial thrombolytic time

4. HIV
   a. Human immunodeficiency virus
   b. Human idiopathic virus
   c. Humoral immunodeficiency virus
   d. Humoral idiopathic virus

5. ESR
   a. Erythrocyte settle rate
   b. Erythrocyte separation rate
   c. Erythrocyte sedimentation rate
   d. Erythrocyte separation ratio

6. AML
   a. Acquired myelogenous leukemia
   b. Acquired myelogenic leukemia
   c. Acute myelogenous leukemia
   d. Acute myelogenic leukemia

7. HDL
   a. High-density lipoprotein
   b. High-density leukocyte
   c. High-differential leukocyte
   d. High-differential lipoprotein

8. KS
   a. Karocyte sarcoma
   b. Karocytic sarcoma
   c. Kaposi's sarcoma
   d. Kaposi's sclerosis

9. ELISA
   a. Enzyme-linked immunosorbent assay
   b. Enzyme-link immunodeficiency assay
   c. Enzyme-linked immunosorbent assessment
   d. Enzyme-linked immunodeficiency assessment

10. Ag
   a. Blood type A
   b. Agglutination
   c. Antigen
   d. Immunoglobulin type Ag

11. PT
   a. Prothrombin time
   b. Physical therapist
   c. Partial thromboplastin
   d. Partial therapeutic time

12. VLDL
    a. Very low-density leukocyte
    b. Very low differentiated leukocyte
    c. Very low-density lipoprotein
    d. Very low differentiated lipoprotein

13. Ab
    a. Blood type with antigens A and B
    b. Abdominal cavity
    c. Antibeta complex
    d. Antibodies

14. Hct
    a. Hemochromatic
    b. Hemoclasis
    c. Hemolytic cyclic treatment
    d. Hematocrit

15. Hgb
    a. Hemoglobin
    b. Hemolysis type B
    c. Hemolytic globulins
    d. Hemogranular complex

MEDICAL DOCUMENTATION

Knowledge of terms related to normal anatomical and pathological conditions enables you to understand medical documentation such as history and physical examinations, operative reports, discharge summaries, laboratory reports, and x-ray reports. Read the inpatient history and physical examination and answer the questions that follow.

Inpatient History and Physical Examination

Name: Joseph L.
DOB: 07-11-1955

Reason for Admission: The patient is a 76-year-old gentleman with a diagnosis of large B-cell lymphoma who is transferred from the MICU for chemotherapy.

HPI: Joe noticed his medical problems this last fall with difficulty urinating, frequent night-time urination, and a distended bladder. He states, "I never feel like I'm empty." He was treated last year by a urologist, who diagnosed him with a UTI. CT scan showed prostatic hypertrophy and abdominal lymphadenopathy.

He had noticed a significant and increasing weight loss. He was seen by infectious disease specialist, hematology, oncology, and a parasitologist as Joe had recently traveled to Singapore. Parasite testing was negative.

He was found unresponsive by his daughter this morning and was brought to the hospital for evaluation. His daughter states that he has been confused for the last few days but had refused transport to the hospital. A serial abdominal scan with guided biopsy was performed. Pathology confirmed diffuse large B-cell lymphoma. He was transferred from the MICU to oncology.

Physical Examination: The patient is extremely debilitated and is barely able to lift his arms or sit up without assistance. He is alert and oriented ×3, but his affect is flat. He states he is "tired all the time and never hungry." He later fell asleep during this examination. He understands that he has been diagnosed with cancer and is here for possible chemotherapy.

He has a Foley catheter. His lungs show rhonchi, and breath sounds are dull, especially on the left. Abdomen is soft, with normal bowel sounds. Extremities show pitting edema.

Laboratory Data: Elevated bilirubin, hypoalbuminemia at 1.5, increased alkaline phosphatase. Hct 30.7, platelet count is 62,000. UTI showed *Pseudomonas*, which was sensitive to amikacin.
Impression: The patient is suffering from diffuse large B-cell lymphoma. It is likely that his continued weight loss, anorexia, and debilitation are all related to the disease process of lymphoma. After extensive discussion with his daughter, we explained that without treatment he would likely die of lymphoma. However, given his debilitated condition, he is likely to die from chemotherapy also. His daughter wishes to go ahead with chemotherapy, so he was transferred to the oncology service.

MEDICAL DOCUMENTATION—cont'd

Upon discussion with Dr. Espinosa, it was suggested that the patient receive Cytoxan and prednisone. We will hold the doxorubicin and vincristine pending further laboratory tests. If he has a good response to Cytoxan, his medication therapy will be reviewed and modified.

At this point, a family meeting with his daughter and son-in-law is scheduled for tomorrow to discuss chemotherapy planning. We want to make sure the family understands the risks of him worsening with further therapy; however, no other options are available currently. His code status is full code, and this will also be discussed at the family meeting tomorrow.

Questions

1. Joe is said to have anorexia, which means ______________________________
____
2. What symptoms does Joe complain of? ______________________________
____
3. What signs of disease are present? ______________________________
____
4. What type of physician diagnosed Joe's urinary tract infection? ______________
____
5. Joe's Hct is 30.7. Look at the chart of blood values. Is that normal? ____________
6. Joe's blood shows hypoalbuminemia; dissect the word into its elements and define it.
____
7. Joe has prostatic hypertrophy. The term *hypertrophy* means ______________
____
8. Dissect and define the word *oncology*. ______________________________
9. Joe is diagnosed with lymphadenopathy; break the word into the elements and define it.
____
10. A CT scan was performed; is this test diagnostic or therapeutic? ______________
11. Cytoxan is a medication belonging to what classification?______________
____
12. How was Joe's cancer diagnosed?______________________________

DISCHARGE SUMMARY

Patient: Lucy W.
DOB: 11/17/1965

CHIEF COMPLAINT: Head wound secondary to sickle cell crisis

HISTORY OF PRESENT ILLNESS: The patient is a 57-year-old black female with a past medical history of sickle cell disease. She was transported to the ED by ambulance after suffering a head injury at home. CT scan of the head was negative for skull fracture or brain bleeding. She received 11 stitches in the ED and was transferred to the medicine floor for observation and review of her sickle cell disease.

PAST MEDICAL HISTORY: Her history is significant for sickle cell disease. No diabetes, no hypertension, no asthma, no heart disease. She has had previous hospitalizations for sickle cell crisis, most recently 3 years ago.

PAST SURGICAL HISTORY: Tonsillectomy at age 7, uterine ablation 12 years ago.

ALLERGIES: Tetracycline

CURRENT MEDICATIONS:

Endari, 2 10-gram packets per day, mixed with food or liquid

Hydroxyurea, 500-mg capsule, 1 per day
Ibuprofen, prn for pain

SOCIAL HISTORY: Patient is recently retired, widowed, and living with her niece. She denies cigarette smoking and alcohol.

FAMILY HISTORY: Mother has sickle cell trait, father had sickle cell trait, and he is deceased. She has no siblings. She has an uncle with diabetes.

REVIEW OF SYSTEMS: Febrile at 99.2, no chills. The patient reports trouble sleeping and loss of appetite. She weighs 147 lb and reports a 5-lb weight loss in the past 2 weeks. No sore throat, no chest pain, mild diarrhea and gas. She complains of nausea. No dysuria, no hematuria, no burning on micturition. Musculoskeletal: moderate back pain and mild pain in legs. She reports mental depression.

PHYSICAL EXAMINATION: Vital signs: temperature 99.2, pulse 76 bpm, respirations 20 breaths per minute, blood pressure 110/72, oxygen saturation 98% on room air.

General: The patient is alert and awake, oriented x3.

HEENT: Head laceration (sutured) on the right forehead with mild bruising. Pupils equal, round, reactive to light and accommodation, bilaterally. Yellowish sclera is observed. Ears: no discharge, TMs normal. Throat: moist mucous membranes. Nose: mild congestion, Neck: soft and supple, no lymphadenopathy. Chest: symmetrical heart: heart sounds S1 and S2 are normal, no murmur. Lungs: clear to auscultation bilaterally. Abdomen: soft bowel sounds are present. Nontender, nondistended. Slight tenderness on epigastric region. Extremities: slight cyanosis observed in her hands; hands are cold to the touch. No clubbing or edema. Neurological: neurologically intact; deep tendon reflexes present and symmetrical.

HOSPITAL COURSE: The patient was admitted to the medicine floor with a diagnosis of sickle cell crisis and was started on folic acid, 1 mg po, once daily and infusion with Adakveo. Chest x-ray was negative for fluid or pathology. She was seen for a mental health consult and set up an appointment with psychiatry.

She was discharged on day 3, advised to resume her sickle cell medication, and advised to follow up with her primary physician.

DISCHARGE SUMMARY—cont'd

Questions

1. No lymphadenopathy is noted. Dissect and define the term. ____________________
2. Lucy presents with slight cyanosis, which means ____________________.
3. Which term means blood in the urine? ____________________
4. There is slight tenderness in the epigastric region. Where is that? ____________________
5. Lucy takes ibuprofen prn, which means ____________________.
6. What does HEENT stand for? ____________________
7. Lucy is febrile, which means ____________________.
8. The term *musculoskeletal* refers to which body systems? ____________________
9. Dissect the term *pathology* into its elements and define it. ____________________
10. Lucy does not have edema, which means ____________________.

CHAPTER REVIEW

Complete the Sentence

1. A white blood cell is called a ____________________.
2. Injection of a contrast medium into lymph vessels is a ____________________.
3. The process of white blood cells engulfing pathogens is ____________________.
4. Irregularly shaped RBCs are called ____________________.
5. Measurement of the percentage of each type of circulating WBC is ____________________.
6. Destruction of blood is ____________________.
7. Microscopic examination of bone marrow is ____________________.
8. Hereditary bleeding disorder is called ____________________.
9. Systemic inflammatory connective tissue disease is called ____________________.
10. The blood test used to screen for antibodies to AIDS virus and other diseases such as Lyme's disease is ____________________.
11. The name of the blood profile that measures triglycerides, HDL, LDL, and VLDL levels is ____________________.
12. The condition of enlargement of the spleen is ____________________.

13. The measurement of the percent of volume RBCs in whole blood is ______________.

14. An abnormal increase in circulating granulocytes in response to infection is called ______________________________.

15. The state of being resistant to disease is ______________________.

Spelling

Circle the correct spelling in the word pairs.

1. anemia	anemea
2. cytomorfology	cytomorphology
3. hemaglobin	hemoglobin
4. hematocrit	hematocript
5. hemostasis	hemastasis
6. imunologist	immunologist
7. luekocytopenia	leukocytopenia
8. lymphadenopathy	lymphadanopathy
9. mononucleosis	mononuecleosis
10. polycytemia vera	polycythemia vera
11. meylogenous	myelogenous
12. reticulocyte	reticulacyte
13. septecemia	septicemia
14. spleenomegaly	splenomegaly
15. thrombosus	thrombosis

Abbreviations

Define the following abbreviations from the chapter.

1. ALL ______________________________
2. CBC ______________________________
3. PT ______________________________
4. CMV ______________________________
5. ARC ______________________________

6. ITP ______________________________

7. SLE ______________________________

8. GVH ______________________________

9. RBC ______________________________

10. Hgb ______________________________

Identify the Anatomical Structures

Match the types of blood cells to the letters shown in Figure 8-12.

1. ______ basophil
2. ______ eosinophil
3. ______ erythrocytes
4. ______ monocyte
5. ______ neutrophil
6. ______ platelets

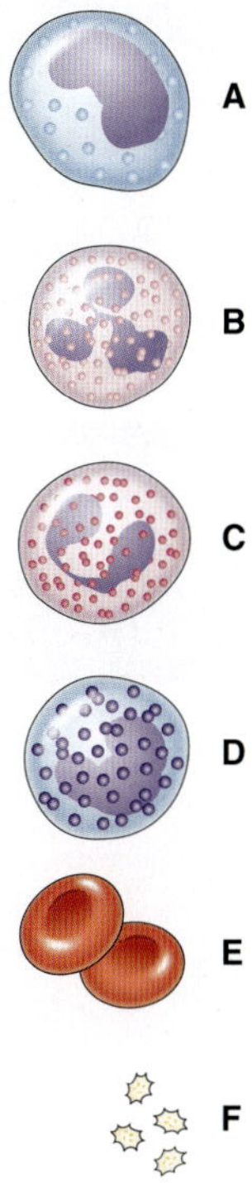

Figure 8-12
Identify the structures of the blood cell.

Match the following structures of the lymphatic system to the letters shown in Figure 8-13.

1. ______ axillary nodes
2. ______ cervical nodes
3. ______ inguinal nodes
4. ______ left subclavian vein
5. ______ lymphatic vessels
6. ______ lymph nodes of mammary gland
7. ______ palatine tonsil
8. ______ Peyer's patches
9. ______ red bone marrow
10. ______ right lymphatic duct
11. ______ right subclavian vein
12. ______ spleen
13. ______ submandibular nodes
14. ______ thoracic duct
15. ______ thymus

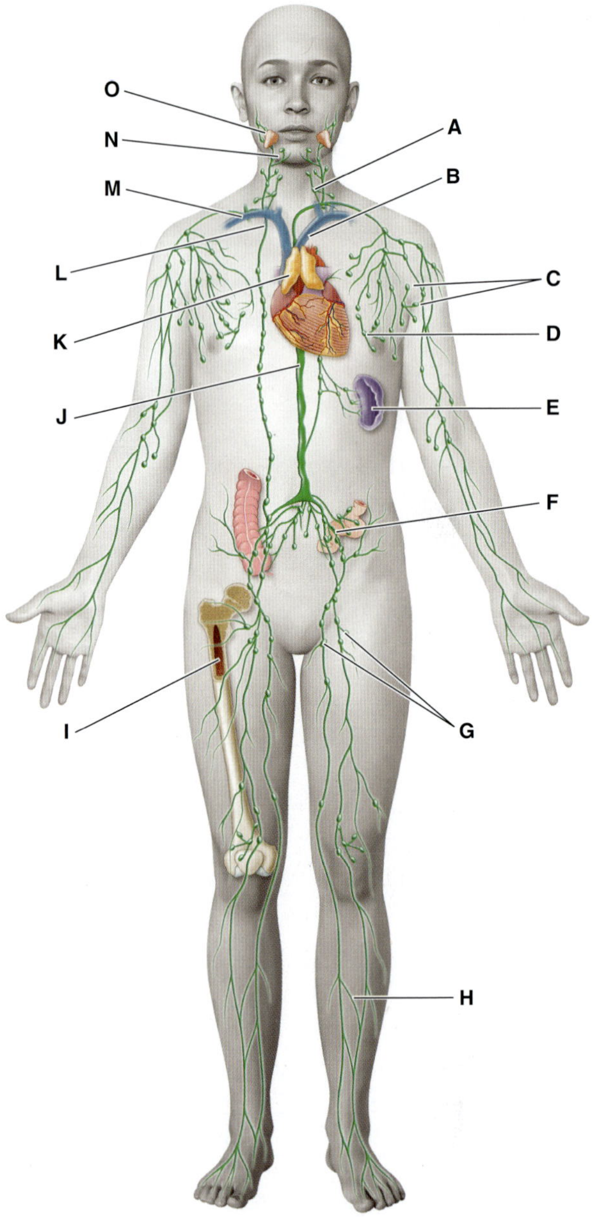

Figure 8-13 Identify the structures of the lymphatic system.

Define the Terms

Identify the word from the following definitions.

1. Substance that can cause disease. ______
2. Accumulation of fluid in tissue spaces. ______
3. State of having a lack of resistance to pathogens. ______
4. Inflammation of lymph glands. ______

5. Collection of blood beneath the skin forming pinpoint hemorrhages. ______________________

6. A decrease in the number of circulating platelets. ______________________

7. A group of bacteria that present as twisted chains. ______________________

8. Granulocyte that stains red or rosy. ______________________

9. Process of stopping or controlling blood. ______________________

10. Chronic hereditary hemolytic anemia where RBCs are shaped like a crescent. ______________________

11. Watery straw-colored fluid of blood that contains fibrin. ______________________

12. Autoimmune disease that blocks or destroys some acetylcholine receptors. ______________________

13. Lymph fluid drains from the left side of the body into the ______________________.

14. Oxygen delivery to the cells of the body is dependent upon this iron-containing protein of RBCs. ______________________

15. The granular white blood cells that are elevated during allergic reactions. ______________________

CHAPTER

9

The Musculoskeletal System

LEARNING OBJECTIVES

Upon completion of the chapter, you will be able to:

1. Identify and define the combining forms, roots, prefixes, and suffixes introduced in the chapter.
2. Spell medical terms related to the musculoskeletal system.
3. Describe the major bones of the skeletal system.
4. Identify the two main divisions of the skeletal system.
5. Describe the three classifications of joints.
6. Identify the five common types of fractures.
7. List the three functions of muscle.
8. Identify the major muscles.
9. Identify and discuss major pathological terms of the musculoskeletal system.
10. Identify and discuss major diagnostic and therapeutic treatments of the musculoskeletal system.
11. Identify the major categories of medications used to treat musculoskeletal pathologies.
12. Define abbreviations of the musculoskeletal system.

We begin this chapter with the story of Jacob, who broke his leg and clavicle in a bicycle accident. The case study introduces some of the medical terms relevant to the musculoskeletal system. After reading this chapter, you will expand your knowledge of medical terms related to the musculoskeletal system. You will understand how the bones, muscles, tendons, and ligaments work together to provide a framework for the body and facilitate movement. You will be able to use the word elements presented to understand unfamiliar terms and to build your medical vocabulary. Throughout the chapter, we will revisit the story of Jacob to understand how an injury can be treated and how a patient can regain function after an injury to the musculoskeletal system.

CASE STUDY

Jacob wakes up in the emergency department. The last thing he remembers is riding his bicycle with his friends Emily and Rob. His head, chest, and shoulder hurt and so does his leg. As he opens his eyes, he sees his mom and dad. He asks them, "What happened?"

His mom starts to cry and says, "Thank God you're awake! You crashed your bicycle. Do you remember anything?"

As Jacob tries to remember, Dr. Fischer, the on-call orthopedic surgeon, walks in and says, "Hello Jacob, it's good to see you awake. When the EMTs brought you in, you were in and out of consciousness. You were smart to wear your helmet; it saved your life."

Jacob's dad, Henry, asks Dr. Fischer, "How bad are his injuries?"

Dr. Fischer explains, "Jacob, you broke your clavicle, which is also called the collarbone. The clavicle sticks up across the side of the upper chest and is the most commonly fractured bone. You also fractured your tibia and fibula, the bones of the lower leg. When the EMTs brought you in, they told me you were at the side of the road and into the woods beyond the guardrail. Emily and Rob called 911 and told the EMTs that you hit the guardrail and tumbled over it, landing on your head and right upper chest. The leg injury was probably from the guardrail and the bike pinning your leg. We gave you 4 mg of morphine, a narcotic pain reliever, which knocked you out. You don't remember talking to me earlier?"

Jacob responds, "No. I remember my head and leg hurting and the EMT looking into my eyes with a penlight."

Ellen, Jacob's mom, asks, "What can you do for him? Does he need surgery?"

Dr. Fischer replies, "We can't do much for the broken clavicle. The fracture is nondisplaced, which means that although it is broken, it didn't shift and will heal in place. It will just take some time in a sling. My bigger concern is his leg."

Ellen and Henry look down at the deep, open wound on Jacob's leg. Dr. Fischer goes on to say, "The tibia and fibula were fractured at the distal end, meaning near his ankle. We x-rayed and saw that the bones are displaced and will need to be aligned with screws and a plate so that they heal properly." Dr. Fischer shows Jacob and his parents the x-ray on the screen. "We can do the procedure today."

Jacob says, "Okay Dr. Fischer, let's do this."

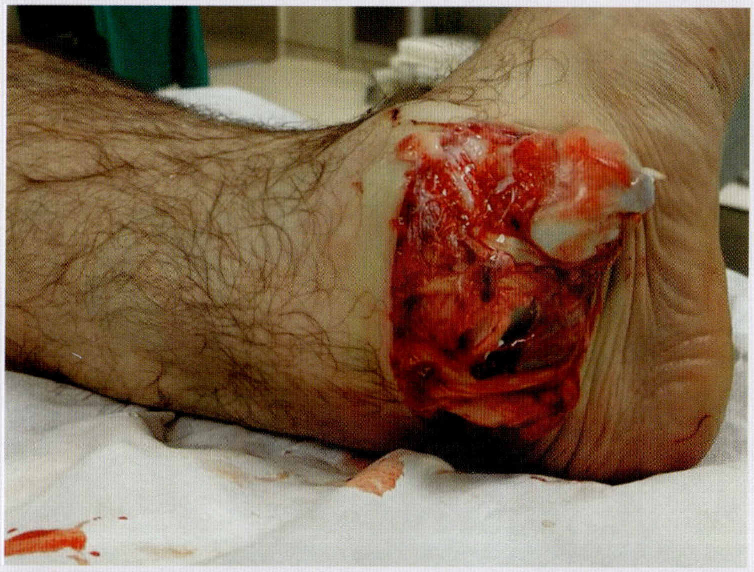

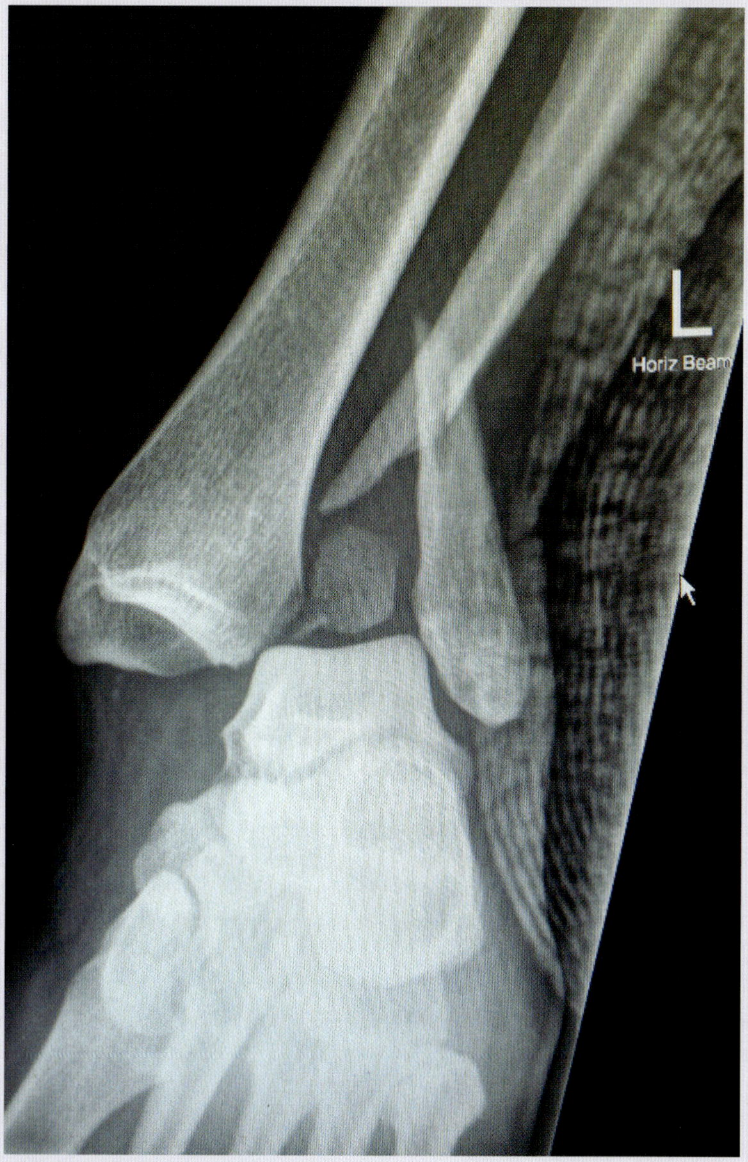
L
Horiz Beam

KEY TERMS

Appendicular skeleton	Endomysium	Matrix	Red marrow
Aponeurosis	Epimysium	Medullary cavity	Sarcomere
Articulation	Epiphyseal plate	Muscles	Sarcolemma
Articular cartilage	Epiphysis	Origin	Sarcoplasm
Axial skeleton	Haversian canals	Osteoblasts	Tarsals
Bursa	Hematopoiesis	Osteoclasts	Tendon
Cancellous bone	Hydroxyapatite	Osteocytes	Trabeculae
Carpals	Insertion	Osteolysis	Trigger points
Diaphysis	Lacunae	Perimysium	Vertebrae
Endosteum	Ligaments	Periosteum	Yellow marrow
			Z line

Structures and Physiology

The musculoskeletal system comprises bones, muscles, tendons, and ligaments.

Bones

Bones have four major functions:

- **Support:** The skeleton is strong and rigid and forms the frame of the body.
- **Protection:** The bones of the cranium protect the brain, the bones of the rib cage protect the heart and lungs, and the vertebrae protect the spinal cord.
- **Movement:** Bones provide a place for attachment of skeletal muscles, enabling coordinated movement to occur. Bones are rigid, which provides a lever for muscles to pull against during contraction.
- **Blood cell formation:** Red bone marrow is a blood-forming tissue inside bone that performs **hematopoiesis**, the production of new blood cells.

Bones have distinctive shapes based on their location and function. There are four main types of bone:

- *Long bones* are longer than they are wide and are designed to absorb stress from body weight. Examples of long bones are the femur, the bone of the upper leg, and the humerus, the bone of the upper arm.
- *Short bones* are equal in length and width. Examples of short bones are the **carpals** (wrist bones) and the **tarsals** (ankle bones). They have a core of spongy bone, also known as **cancellous bone**, and are enclosed in a thin layer of compact bone.
- *Flat bones* are thin and flat and provide broad surfaces for muscular attachment. Examples are the cranium of the head, the ribs, and the sternum, also called the breastbone.
- *Irregular bones* have complex shapes; they include the vertebrae, bones of the inner ear, and facial bones.

Cancellous bone is not as dense as compact bone and has needlelike, spiny, bony spicules called **trabeculae**, giving it a spongy appearance. Thus, cancellous bone is sometimes called spongy bone. The spongy nature of the cancellous bone affords some shock absorption from stresses from multiple angles, maximizing bone strength. The spaces between the trabeculae contain red bone marrow.

Parts of a Long Bone

Long bones comprise the shaft, also known as the diaphysis (Fig. 9-1). The **diaphysis** comprise tightly packed compact bone that offers strength and support. The compact bone contains a system of canals called the **haversian canals**, which contain blood vessels, lymphatic vessels, and nerves. The blood cells transport oxygen and nutrients to bone cells for growth, repair, and maintenance. The haversian canals are surrounded by concentric cylinders of **osteocytes**, also known as bone cells. Inside the diaphysis, there is a large interior cavity called the **medullary cavity**. The medullary cavity is filled with red marrow and yellow marrow. **Red marrow** is the site of hematopoiesis, red blood cell formation. **Yellow marrow** is a fatty tissue for energy storage. The interior surface of the medullary cavity is lined with a membrane called the **endosteum**. The ends of long bones are the **epiphyses**. The epiphyses have a bulb-like end affording space for muscle attachment and made up of cancellous bone. In long bones, growth occurs at a narrow band of cartilage between the diaphysis and the epiphysis, known as the **epiphyseal plate**, or growth plate. Each epiphysis contributes to the structure of the joint, also called an **articulation**. Along the outer surface of the epiphysis, where the joints occur, there is a thin layer of **articular cartilage** that protects the ends of bones.

Except in areas covered by articular cartilage, bone is covered by a thin connective tissue called the **periosteum**. The periosteum is firmly anchored to the surface of the bone by protein fibers, allowing bone to connect to muscle and ligament attachments. The periosteum is highly vascular, meaning it contains many blood vessels and is involved in bone growth and repair.

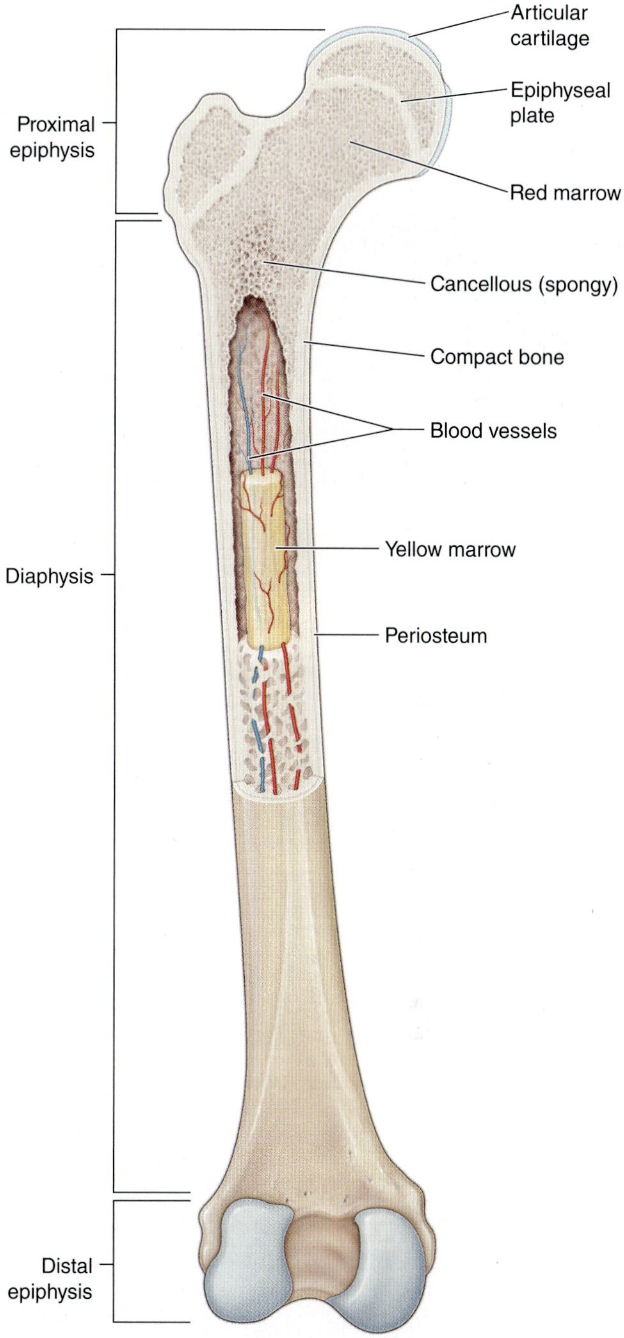

Figure 9-1 Anatomy of a long bone.

PHYSIOLOGY FACT

When a teen has completed skeletal growth, the epiphyseal plate will be completely replaced by bone. X-ray will show that the growth plate has closed.

PHYSIOLOGY FACT

In infancy and childhood, there is a tremendous need for new red blood cells for oxygenation to growing and forming tissues. During this period of growth, almost all the bones contain red bone marrow (Fig. 9-2). As we approach adulthood, the only bones that contain red bone marrow are the ribs, vertebrae, humerus, femur, and pelvis. Red bone marrow is replaced with yellow bone marrow, which stores fat but does not produce blood cells.

ELEMENT REVIEW

-um = noun ending
end/o = with
oste/o = bone
peri- = around

The Chemical Composition of Bone

Bones comprise bone cells called osteocytes as well as a **matrix**, an intercellular arrangement of collagen and mineral salts. The collagen fibers are arranged as a braided rope.

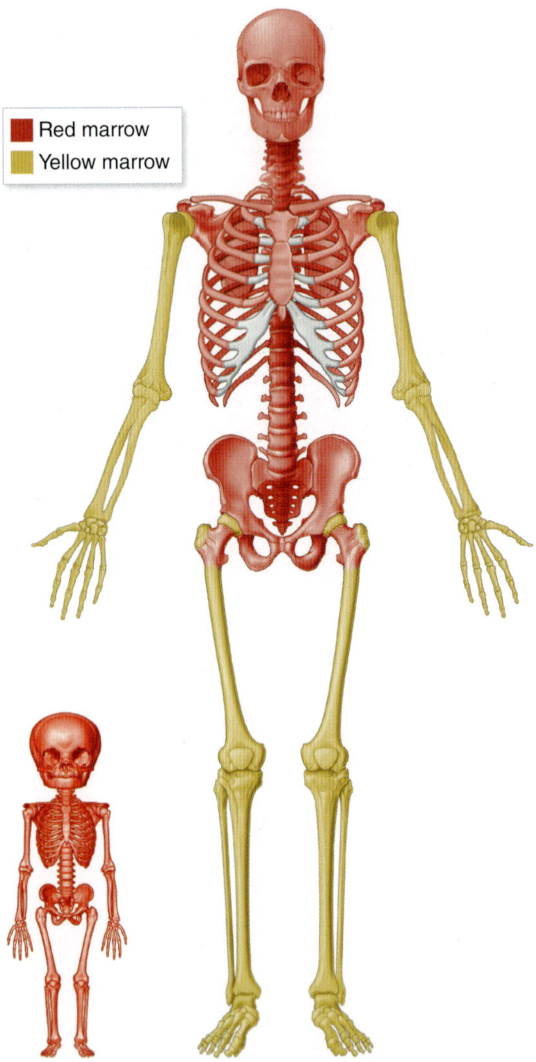

Figure 9-2 Bones containing red bone marrow.

The fibers are slightly flexible and account for almost one-third of the weight of bone. The most abundant of the mineral salts is calcium phosphate, but calcium carbonate and calcium hydroxide are also a part of the bone matrix. Rock-hard crystals of **hydroxyapatite** are formed when calcium phosphate and calcium hydroxide chemically combine. These crystals account for almost two-thirds of the weight of bone and provide strength and durability.

PHYSIOLOGY FACT

Hydroxyapatite crystals are hard but inflexible and are extremely brittle. Alone they would be prone to shatter. The addition of collagen into the bone matrix makes bone slightly flexible and amazingly strong, even stronger than steel.

The bone cells are located in tiny chambers called **lacunae**, which are surrounded by the bone matrix. The primary function of osteocytes is the maintenance of the surrounding matrix. Hormones, such as parathyroid hormone, thyroid hormones, calcitonin, and the sex hormones estrogen and testosterone, direct the osteocytes to release chemicals that can either dissolve bone matrix or form new matrix. Thus, the endocrine system is responsible for growth, maintenance, and repair of bone.

In addition to osteocytes, osteoblast and osteoclast cells play important roles in the maintenance of bone. **Osteoblasts** are young osteocytes found on the surface of bone that migrate to the lacunae as they mature. They secrete collagen and other compounds that form the bone matrix. As they form the matrix, they become trapped in lacunae and become mature osteocytes. **Osteoclasts** are large multinucleated cells formed by red bone marrow and function to break down the bone cells. Osteoclasts secrete acids and enzymes that destroy bone cells in a process known as **osteolysis** to maintain calcium and phosphorus levels in the bloodstream. Surprisingly, the constant creation and destruction of bone cells is a dynamic process with the goal of healthy blood chemistry, not necessarily bone health. This constant cycle of destroying and creating bone cells is called bone remodeling. Osteolysis and the deposition of osteoblasts into the bone matrix are balanced processes that serve to maintain bone size and strength, repair bone in case of injury, and afford growth during infancy and childhood.

ELEMENT REVIEW
oste/o = bone
-lysis = process of destruction
-blast = immature cell
-clast = to break, fracture

The Organization of the Skeleton

The 206 bones of the human body are organized as an interconnected frame called the *skeleton* (Fig. 9-3). The skeleton can be divided into the axial skeleton and the appendicular skeleton. The **axial skeleton** contains the bones of the head, vertebrae, and ribs and lies along the midvertical axis of the body. The **appendicular skeleton** attaches to the axial skeleton and comprises the bones of the upper and lower extremities and their attachments.

The Vertebral Column and Pelvic Girdle

The vertebral column comprises 26 bones called **vertebrae** (Fig. 9-4). The vertebral column supports the body, allows movement, and creates a bony canal that houses and protects the spinal cord. The weight of the body is also supported by the pelvic girdle,

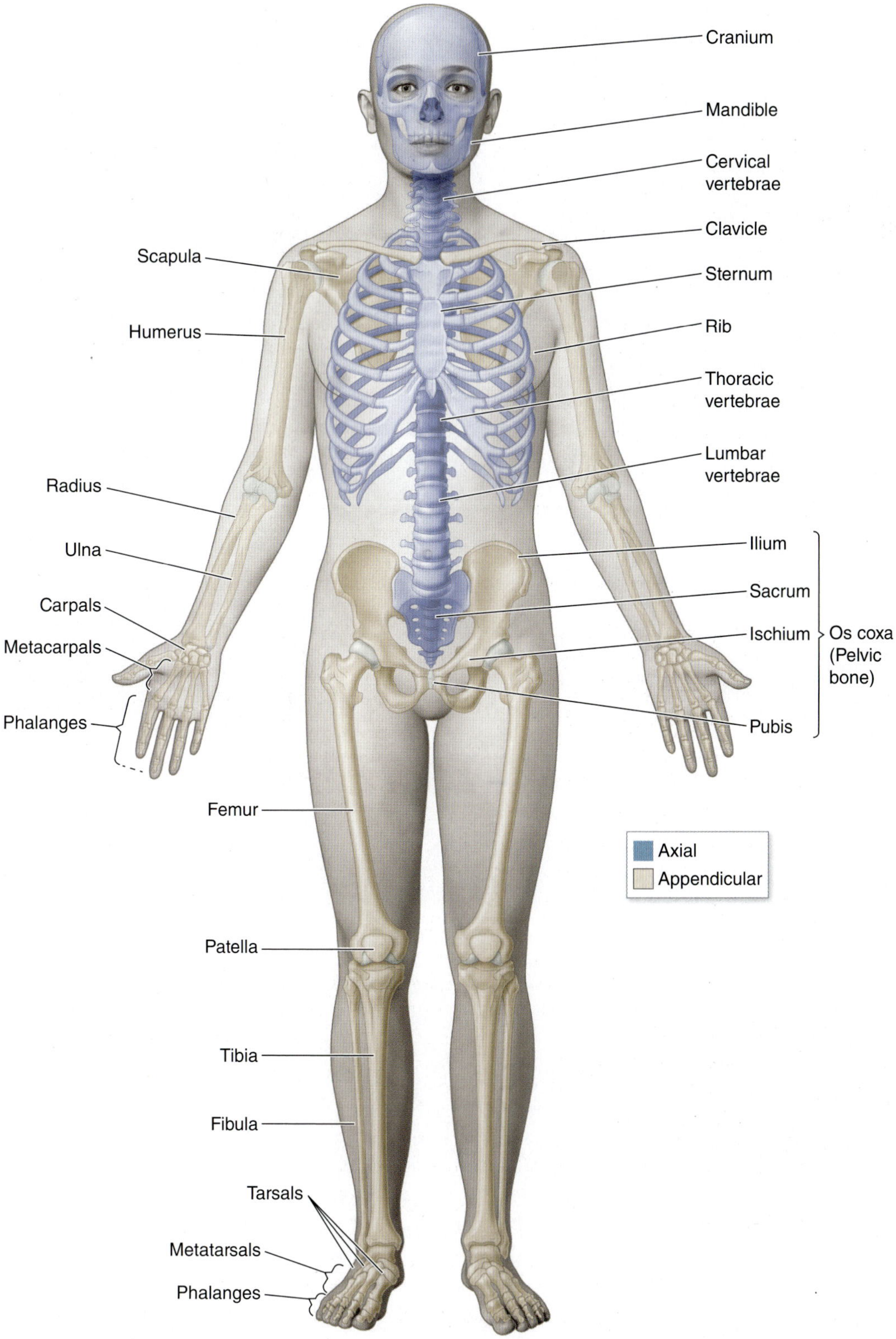

Figure 9-3 The human skeleton.

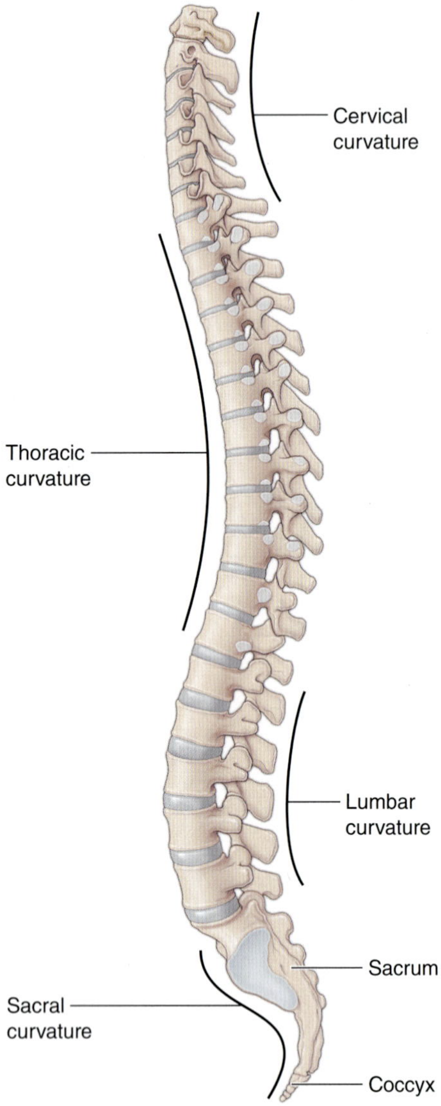

Figure 9-4 The vertebral column.

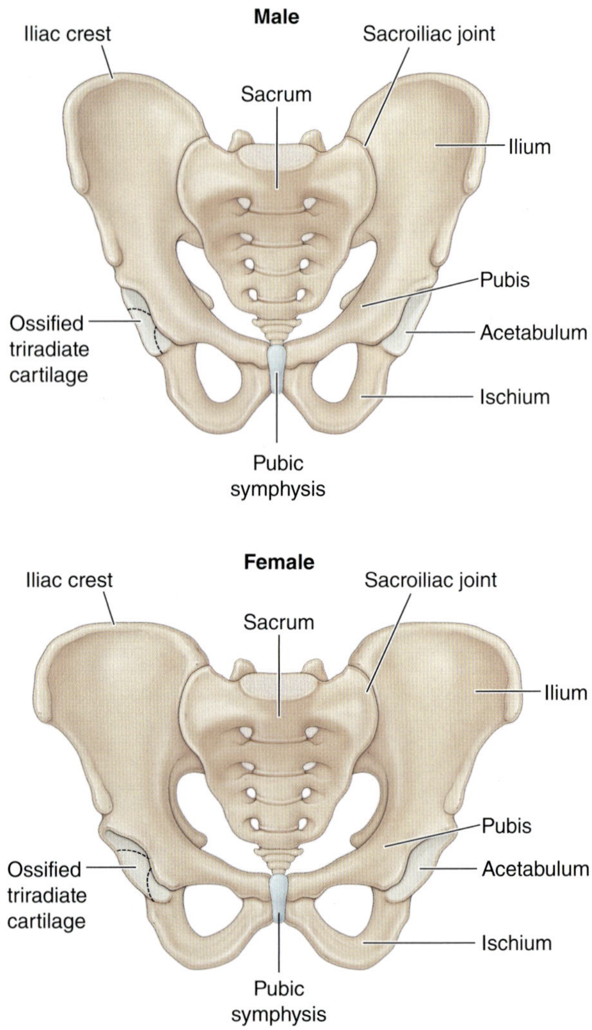

Figure 9-5 The male and female pelvic girdle.

ELEMENT REVIEW
Tri- = three

the basin-shaped structure attached to the sacrum (Fig. 9-5). In childhood, the ilium, ischium, and pubis are separated by the triradiate cartilage. During the teenage years, the triradiate cartilage will harden and the bones will fuse together to form the innominate bone. The three names are still used to describe the respective areas of the pelvic girdle. Although the function of the male and female pelvic girdle is the same, the female pelvic girdle is wider and shallower, affording the passageway for an infant during childbirth.

PHYSIOLOGY FACT

The symphysis pubis comprises cartilage, which will separate in response to relaxin, a hormone secreted at the end of pregnancy to allow delivery of the infant during childbirth. Women sometimes suffer from pubic pain, but the discomfort usually resolves after delivery of the baby.

Surface Features of Bone

The surface of bones includes structural features that correspond to their function. Projections are areas of bone that are enlarged; they stick out and allow an attachment site for ligaments or tendons. Projections can be a variety of shapes. Depressions are the opposite of projections in that they don't stick out but rather are indented. Depressions provide a place for nerves or blood vessels to enter the area. Table 9-1 shows the surface features, descriptions, and examples of processes and depressions.

TABLE 9-1 Surface Features of Processes and Depressions

Surface Feature	Description	Example
Projections		
Head	A rounded proximal end	the head of the femur 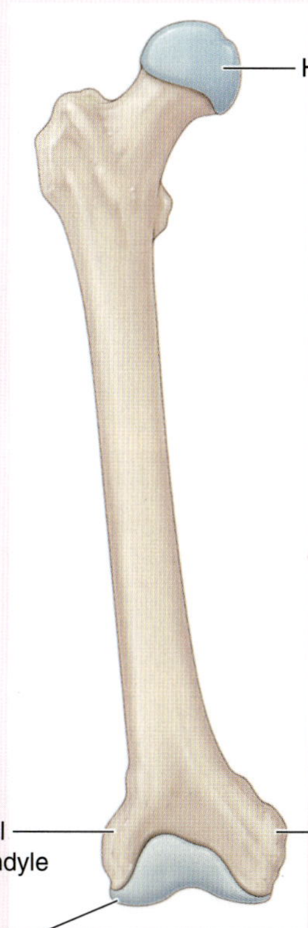
Condyle	A knuckle-like rounded projection	condyle at the distal end of the femur
Epicondyle	A small projection above the condyle that acts as an attachment site	epicondyle of the distal femur

Continued

TABLE 9-1 Surface Features of Processes and Depressions—cont'd

Surface Feature	Description	Example	
Facet	A smooth surface at a joint	Facet at the proximal end of the humerus	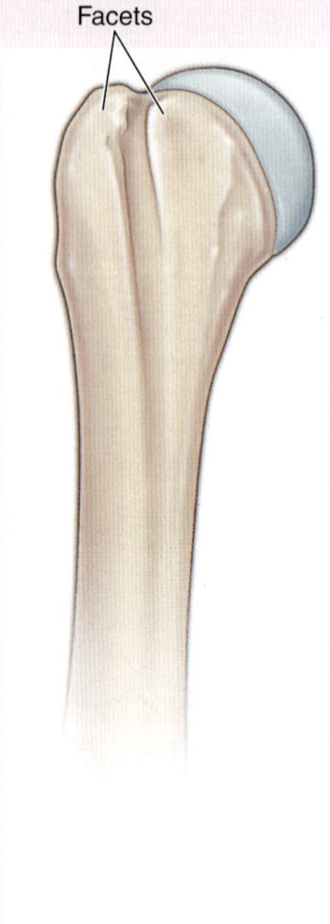
Process	A raised area of bone	Superior articular process	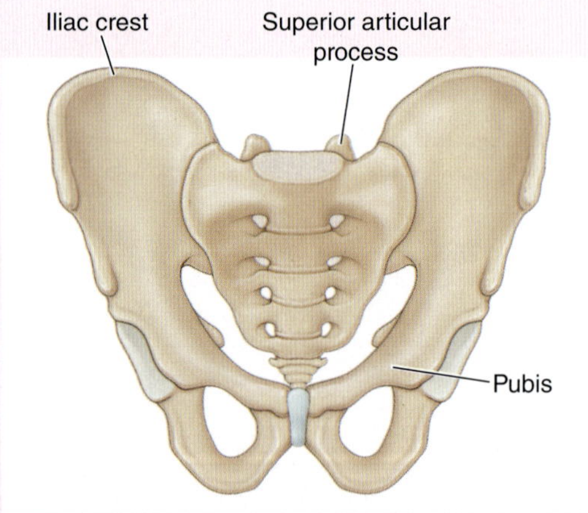
Crest	Superior prominent ridge on a bone	iliac crest	

TABLE 9-1 Surface Features of Processes and Depressions—cont'd

Surface Feature	Description	Example
Depressions		
Foramen	An opening that allows a nerve or blood vessel passage	Mental foramen 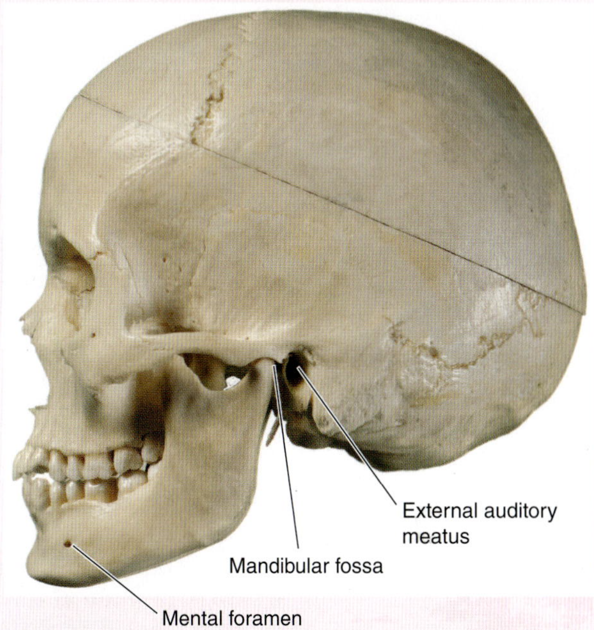
Fossa	A shallow depression	mandibular fossa
Meatus	Opening to an internal channel	external auditory meatus
Sinus	Air-filled pocket within bone	Ethmoid sinus, sphenoid sinus 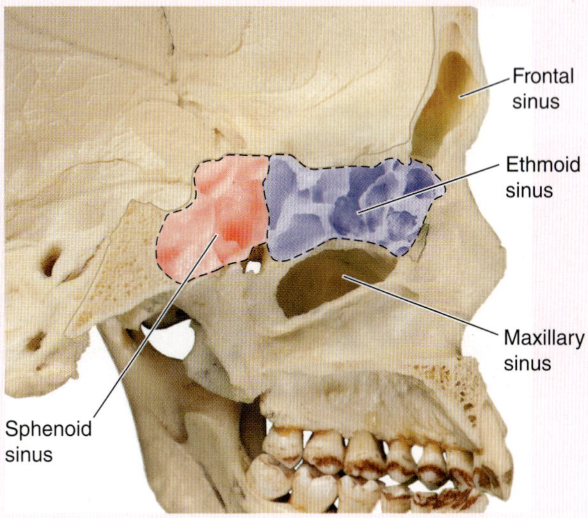

Types of Joints

To allow movement of the body, the bones have areas that join to form articulations, also called joints. Joints are divided into three categories based on the various degrees of movement.

- **Diarthroses** are freely movable joints, such as at the elbow, shoulder, or knee.
- **Amphiarthroses** are slightly movable and are connected by cartilage such as the vertebrae.
- **Synarthroses** are immovable joints such as the sutures in the skull.

Diarthroses are also called synovial joints and contain an extension of the periosteum called the joint capsule. The bones of the joint are bound together by the capsule, and most synovial joints are connected by ligaments and/or sheets of fascia that further stabilize the joint (Fig. 9-6). The inside of the capsule is surrounded by a synovial membrane called a **bursa** and contains synovial fluid. Many joints have more than one bursae to cushion movements of muscles and ligaments at the joint site. Synovial fluid lubricates the joint, allowing for free movement. Cartilage cushions the ends of the bones at the joint.

Muscles, Tendons, and Ligaments

Muscles are the only tissue that can contract, pulling bones across a joint (like a lever) and thus providing movement. Muscle tone also provides posture to the body and promotes a variety of internal functions that require movement. Muscle can be divided into three categories based on their function and organization of the muscle cells (Fig. 9-7).

- Smooth muscles, also called involuntary or visceral muscles, line the visceral organs, the walls of the arteries, the respiratory passages, and the genitourinary ducts. The autonomic nervous system directs the action of smooth muscles and performs their functions without our conscious control.

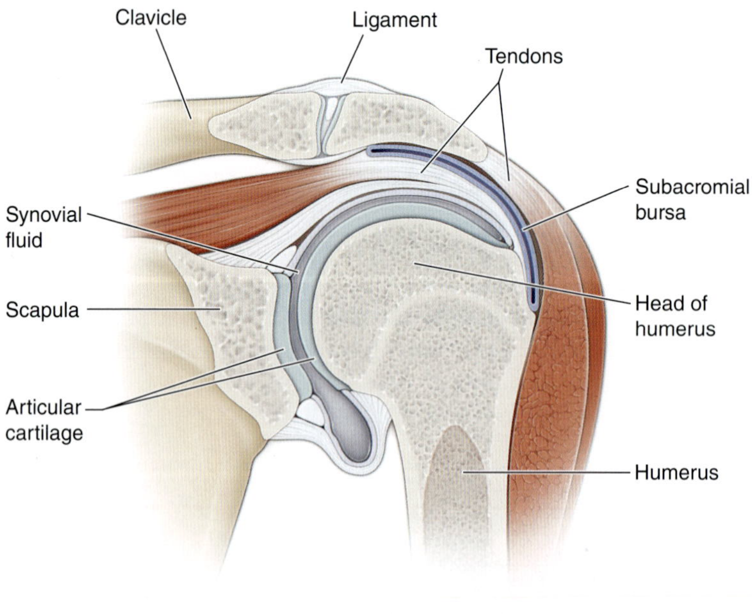

Figure 9-6 The shoulder is an example of a diarthroses (a fully movable joint). The ligaments hold the joint together, the articular cartilage protects the bones at the joint, and the bursae and synovial fluid cushion the joint through its movements.

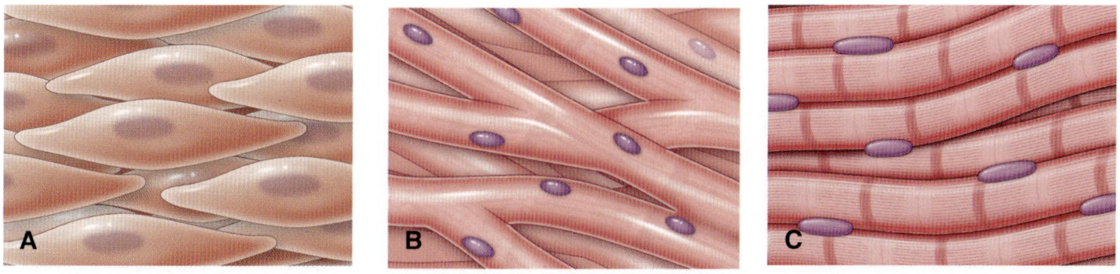

Figure 9-7 The three types of muscles. (A) Smooth muscle: The muscle cells are arranged in spindles and have no striations or nuclei. (B) Cardiac muscle: The cardiac muscle cells are arranged in branches and have striations or nuclei. (C) Skeletal muscle: The muscle cells are grouped into long striated cylinders of multinucleated fibers.

- Cardiac muscle makes up the walls of the heart. Like smooth muscles, cardiac muscle is under the control of the autonomic nervous system and contracts in the rhythmic involuntary pattern known as heartbeats.
- Skeletal muscle, also called voluntary muscle, is controlled by the somatic nervous system. We can deliberately contract these skeletal muscles to provide coordinated movements such as walking or typing. They are the strongest of the three types of muscle, but they fatigue most rapidly. These muscles are also called striated muscles due to their appearance. The voluntary muscles are also found in the tongue, pharynx, and the upper portion of the esophagus. Thus, chewing and swallowing are voluntarily controlled. Once food reaches the lower portion of the esophagus, involuntary (smooth) muscle moves the food through the digestive system.

Muscles attach to bones either by fleshy attachments directly to the periosteum or by fibrous attachments that form three layers: epimysium, perimysium, and endomysium. The **epimysium** is the outermost layer that surrounds the entire muscle. The **perimysium** surrounds groups of muscle fibers, and the **endomysium** is the deepest layer, separating individual muscle fibers. These fibrous attachments are stronger than a fleshy attachment. When the end of a fibrous attachment converges at the end of the muscle, it becomes contiguous and indistinguishable from the periosteum. In some cases, the connective tissue penetrates the surface of the periosteum, contributing to the strength of the attachment. The fibrous end of a muscle that connects to the periosteum often forms a strap called a **tendon**. When the fibrous attachment covers a large area of a bone, the attachment is called an **aponeurosis**. Unlike a tendon, which attaches a muscle to bone, **ligaments** are connective tissue bands that join one bone to another across a joint. Ligaments add stability to joints and limit the range of motion (ROM) of the joint.

ELEMENT REVIEW
mysium = muscle
epi- = around
peri- = around
endo- = within

PHYSIOLOGY FACT

Aponeurosis injury is very rare because the larger attachment area absorbs energy during movement, increasing its stability. Tendons get injured easily because the stress of the movement is concentrated into the "strap" and are present in more injury-prone areas.

Microscopic Structure of Muscle

Skeletal muscle cells are long, cylindrical, usually extend the entire length of the muscle, and have many nuclei. Muscle cells are also called muscle fibers because the thin, long shape resembles a fiber. The fibers are arranged into parallel groups of muscle fibers called bundles. The cell membrane is also called the **sarcolemma**. The body of the cells are called **sarcoplasm** and contain hundreds of mitochondria (also known as the powerhouse of the cell), which furnish 95% of the energy (adenosine triphosphate) necessary for contraction. Within the sarcoplasm, the sarcoplasmic reticulum stores calcium, essential for muscular

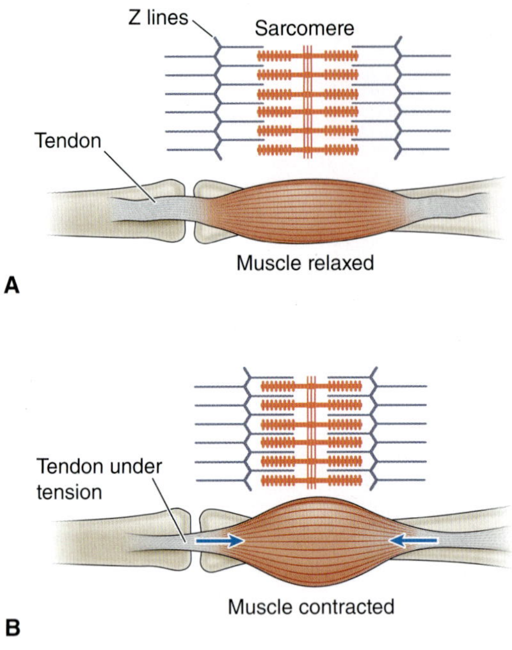

Figure 9-8 The linear arrangement of muscle cells allows sarcomeres to slide along the Z lines contracting or elongating within limits of the Z lines.

contraction. Cylindrical cords of protein, called **myofibrils**, lie parallel to each other throughout the muscle fibers. The linear arrangement of the myofibrils allows the muscle to contract along the length of the muscle. The **sarcomere** is the unit of contraction of the muscle cell's myofibrils between two **Z lines** (Fig. 9-8). The Z line creates the boundary of how far a muscle can contract and elongate. Thus, skeletal muscles contract along one defined direction.

PHYSIOLOGY FACT

Muscle cells of the quadriceps (thigh muscles) can be over 0.5 meters long but are less than 0.1 mm in diameter.

Muscle Movements

Muscles move the body in a variety of movements based on the alignment of the joint and direction of the attached muscles.

Flexion: The act of bending, decreasing the angle between two bones; for example, bending the elbow.

Extension: The act of straightening, increasing the angle between two bones; for example, straightening the elbow.

Circumduction: Movement around an axis. The proximal end of a limb is fixed, and the distal end moves in a circular direction; for example, rotating the arm about the shoulder.

ELEMENT REVIEW
sarc/o = flesh
-lemma = outer shell
-plasm = matter
-mere = part

Abduction: Lateral movement of a limb away from the body, for example, spreading the fingers apart.

Adduction: Lateral movement of a limb toward the body; for example, moving the fingers together.

Pronation: To turn the hand or foot so that the palm or sole is facing downward and inward; for example, turning the hand palm down.

Supination: To turn the hand or foot so that the palm or sole is facing upward and outward, for example, turning the foot to the outside.

Memory Tip

Remember that **supination** contains the word *up*, so the palm or the sole is oriented upward.

Adduction: Add together; for example, bring the fingers together or bring the legs together.

Groups of Muscles

The skeletal muscles of the body allow the coordination of movement. The location and direction of movement of muscles are important to consider when administering intramuscular injections, assessing ROM, or evaluating muscle injuries. The muscles listed in Tables 9-2 to 9-5 and shown in Figures 9-9 to 9-12 are those near the body surface and do not represent all the skeletal muscles; rather, they account for a sample of body movements. The **origin**, where the muscle is attached closest to the midline, and the **insertion**, where the muscle attaches distally from the midline, are included in many of the descriptions.

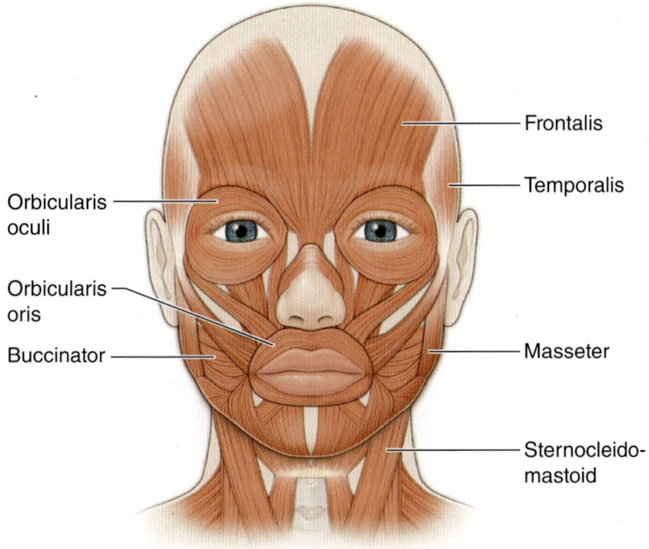

Figure 9-9 Muscles of the head and neck.

TABLE 9-2 Muscles of the Head and Neck

Name	Origin	Insertion	Movement
Buccinator	maxilla, mandible	orbicularis oris	Compresses the cheeks for blowing, whistling, smiling
Frontalis	Galea aponeurotica	skin around the eyebrows and nose	Movement of eyebrows and frowning
Temporalis	temporal bone	mandible	Closes the mouth by raising the mandible
Masseter	zygomatic arch	mandible	Raises the mandible, closes the jaw
Sternocleidomastoid	sternum, clavicle	mastoid bone	Moves the head up and down, side to side and in a circular motion
Orbicularis oculi	maxillary and frontal bones	eyelids	Closes the eyelids
Orbicularis oris	surrounds the mouth	skin at the corner of the mouth	Puckering, closing the mouth, facilitates speech and facial expressions

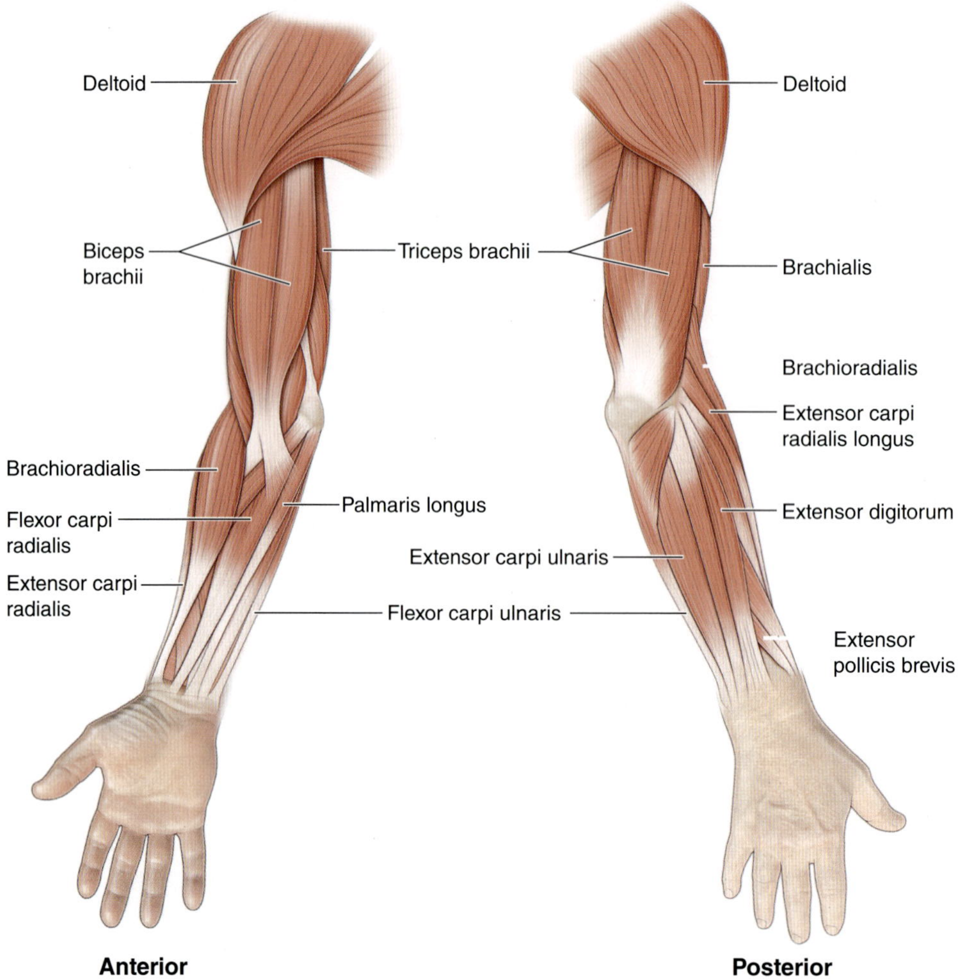

Figure 9-10 Muscles of the upper extremities.

TABLE 9-3 Muscles of the Upper Extremities

Name	Origin	Insertion	Movement
Deltoid	clavicle, scapula	lateral side of the humerus	Abducting (raising) the arm away from the trunk
Biceps brachii	scapula	radius	Bending the elbow brings the lower arm toward the upper arm
Triceps brachii	scapula and humerus	olecranon process of the elbow	Straightens the lower arm away from the upper arm (opposite motion of the biceps brachii)
brachioradialis	lateral supracondylar ridge of the humerus	styloid process of the radius	Flexes the forearm at the elbow
Pronator teres	distal end of the humerus and coronoid process of the ulna	shaft of the radius	Pronates the forearm (turns the medial side downward)
Flexor carpi radialis	distal end of the humerus	second and third metacarpals	Flexes and abducts the hand at the wrist
Extensor carpi radialis	distal end of the humerus	second metacarpal	Extends and abducts the hand at the wrist
Flexor carpi ulnaris	medial epicondyle of the humerus	base of the fifth metacarpal	Flexes and adducts the wrist
Extensor carpi ulnaris	lateral epicondyle of the humerus	bottom of the fifth metacarpal	Extends and adducts the hand and wrist, adds stability to the wrist

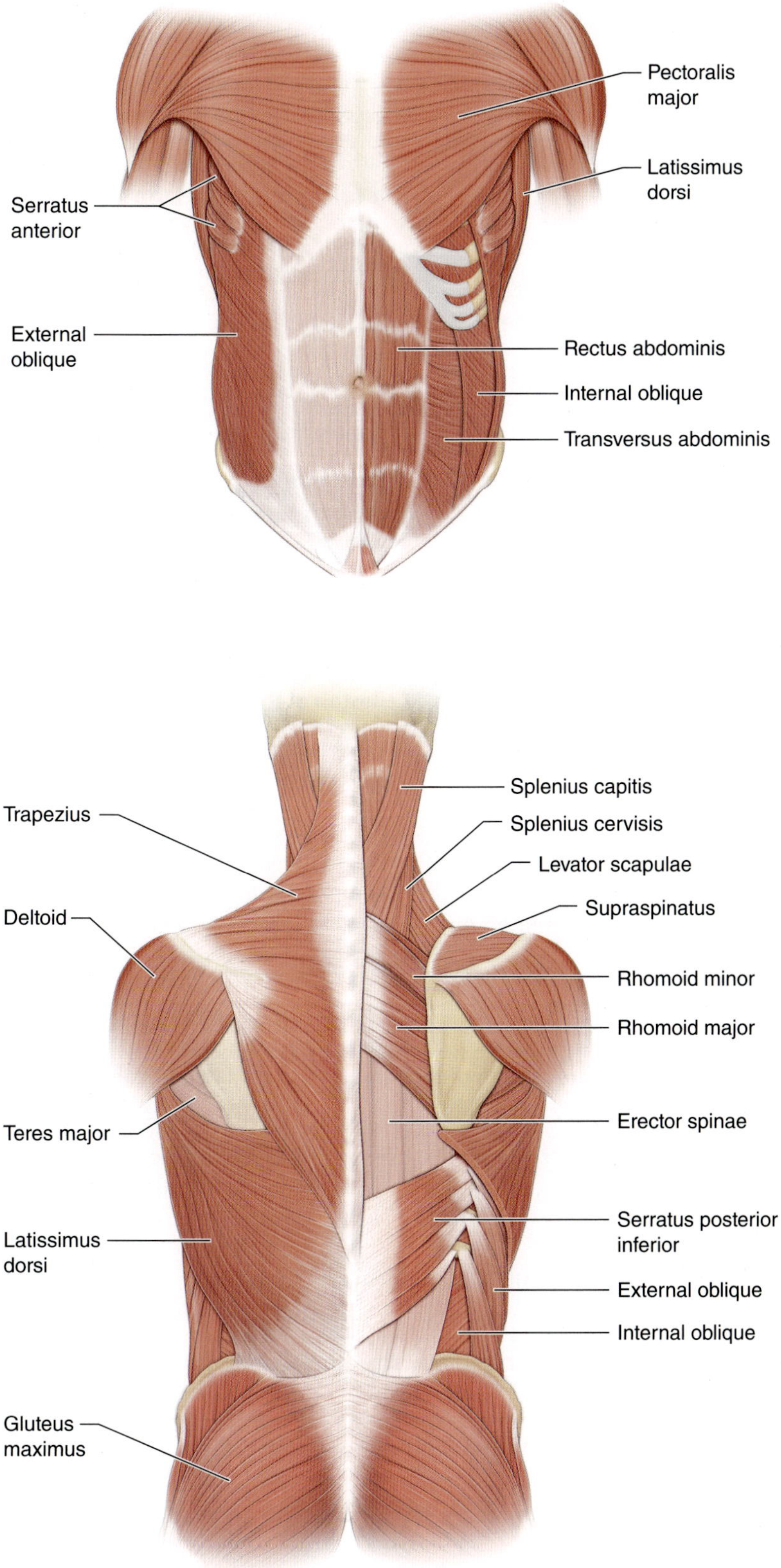

Figure 9-11 Muscles of the trunk.

TABLE 9-4 Muscles of the Trunk (Fig. 9-11)

Name	Origin	Insertion	Movement
Trapezius	occipital bone	acromion and medial scapula	Elevates and rotates the scapula, adducts the scapula, depresses the shoulders, extends the head
Pectoralis major	clavicle, sternum, and costal cartilage	greater tubercles of the humerus	Flexes the arm at the shoulder, adducts and medially rotates the arm
Levator scapulae	cervical vertebrae 1 through 4	scapula	Elevates and adducts the scapula, flexes the head side to side
Supraspinatus	posterior surface of the scapula above the spine	greater tubercle of the humerus	Abducts the arm
Rhomboids	vertebrae c7 through t5	scapula	Adducts the scapula to "square the shoulders," rotates the scapula as in rowing a boat
Latissimus dorsi	lumbodorsal fascia on the lower back, posterior ilium, and sacrum	intertubular sulcus of the humerus (located near the armpit)	Extension, adduction, and internal rotation of the arm
Erector spinae	vertebrae and pelvis	superior vertebrae and ribs	Extends the vertebral column
External oblique	lower eight ribs	iliac crest and linea alba	Aids rectus abdominis in flexing the vertebral column, aids muscles of the trunk in lateral flexion of the vertebrae
Internal oblique and transverse abdominis	aponeurosis of the lower back, iliac crest, costal cartilage of the lower ribs	linea alba and pubic bone	Works with external oblique (same movements)
Rectus abdominis	pubic bone and symphysis pubis	xiphoid process of the sternum, costal cartilage of 5th to 7th ribs	Flexes the vertebral column (as in a sit-up), compresses the abdomen

TABLE 9-5 Muscles of the Lower Extremities

Name	Origin	Insertion	Movement
Iliopsoas	iliac fossa, lumbar vertebrae	lesser trochanter of the femur	Flexes and medially rotates the thigh at the hip
Adductor longus	pubic bone and symphysis pubis	posterior surface of the femur	Adducts, flexes, and laterally rotates the thigh at the hip
Quadriceps Femoris Group			
Rectus femoris	ilium and margin of the acetabulum	patella and tibial tuberosity	Extends the leg at the knee, flexes the thigh at the hip
Vastus lateralis	greater trochanter and posterior surface of the femur	patella and tibial tuberosity	Extends the leg at the knee
Vastus medialis	(deep) medial surface of the femur	patella and tibial tuberosity	Extends the leg at the knee
Vastus intermedius	anterior and lateral surface of the femur	patella and tibial tuberosity	Extends the leg at the knee
Gluteus maximus	ilium, sacrum, and coccyx	posterior surface of the femur and fascia of the thigh	Extends the thigh at the hip
Gluteus medius	ilium	greater trochanter of the femur	Abducts and medially rotates the thigh

TABLE 9-5 Muscles of the Lower Extremities—cont'd

Name	Origin	Insertion	Movement
Hamstring group			
Biceps femoris	ischium and along the linea aspera of the femur	proximal ends of the tibia and fibula	Flexes and rotates the leg at the knee, (laterally) extends the thigh at the knee
Semitendinosus	ischium	medial surface of the tibia	Extends the thigh at the hip, flexes the leg at the knee
Semimembranosus	ischium	proximal end of tibia	Extends the thigh at the hip, flexes the leg at the knee
Tibialis anterior	proximal two-thirds of the tibia	tarsal bone, first metatarsal	Dorsiflexes and inverts the foot at the ankle
Gastrocnemius	distal end of the femur	calcaneus (via the calcaneal tendon)	Plantar flexion, flexes the leg at the knee
Soleus	proximal end of tibia and fibula	calcaneus (via the calcaneal tendon)	Plantar flexion

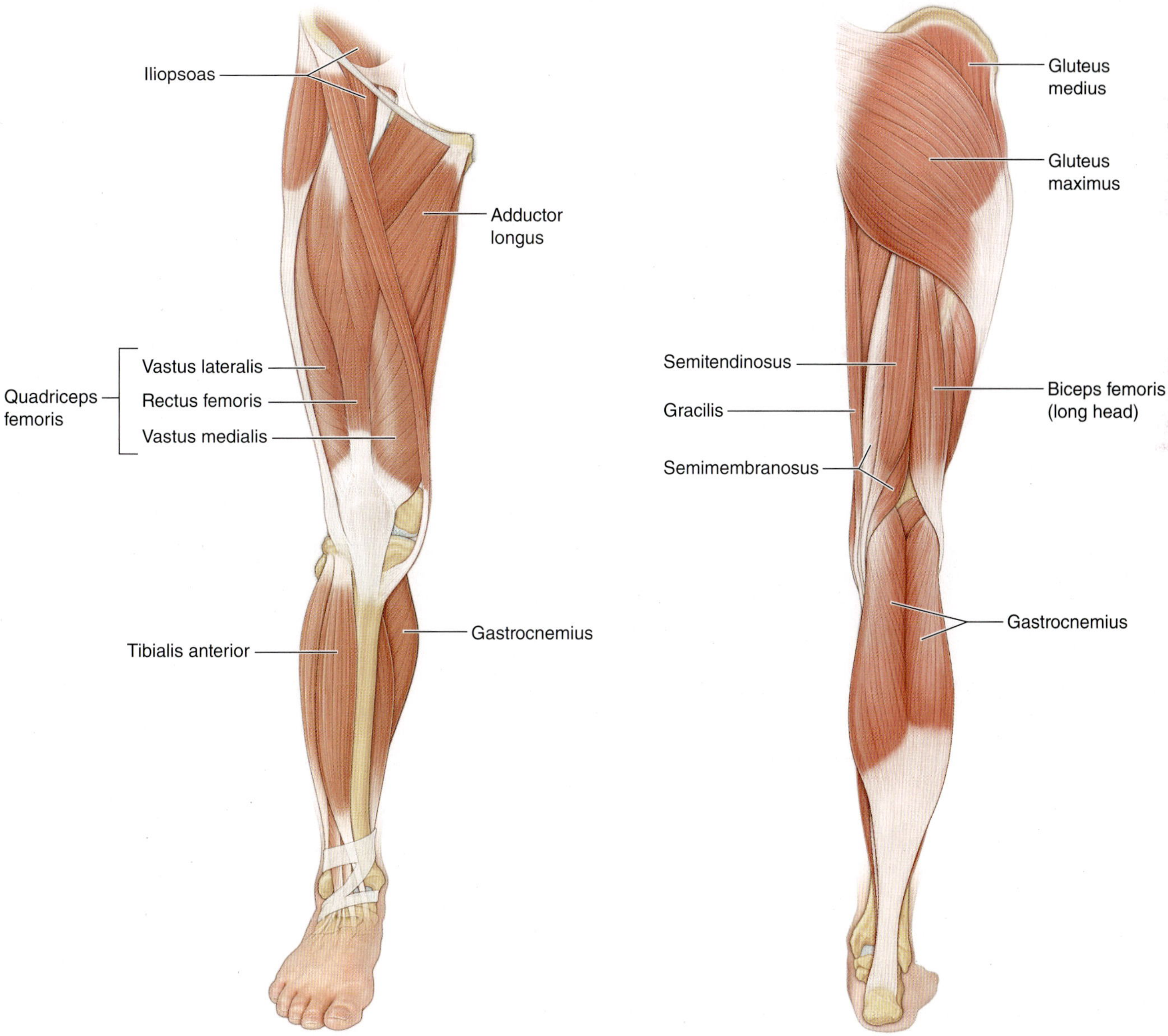

Figure 9-12 Muscles of the lower extremities.

Structures and Physiology Review

Match the Words

Match the word to the description.

aponeurosis	epiphysis	sarcomere
articulation	femur	sarcolemma
articular cartilage	hematopoiesis	sarcoplasm
buccinator	humerus	sternocleidomastoid
bursa	hydroxyapatite	sternum
cancellous bone	masseter	tarsals
carpals	osteoblasts	trabeculae
cranium	orbicularis oculi	vertebrae
diaphysis	periosteum	
epiphyseal plate	red marrow	

1. The covering of bone ____________________
2. The muscle that allows us to whistle and blow ____________________
3. The process of forming new red blood cells ____________________
4. The medical name for the skull ____________________
5. The substance that gives bones their strength ____________________
6. The ends of long bones where growth occurs ____________________
7. Immature bone cells ____________________
8. Large triangular muscle that rotates the head side to side ____________________
9. The bone of the thigh ____________________
10. One of the muscles that closes the mouth ____________________
11. The muscle that closes the eye ____________________
12. The bone of the upper arm ____________________
13. The cell membrane of muscle cells ____________________
14. The breastbone ____________________
15. Synovial membrane that cushions bones at a joint ____________________
16. The irregular bones that protect the spinal cord ____________________
17. The medical term for spongy bone ____________________

18. A broad sheet of connective tissue that attaches muscle to bone ____________________

19. The shaft of a long bone ____________________

20. Needlelike structures that give spongy bone its appearance ____________________

Structures and Physiology Word-Building Practice

1. Nouns and Adjectives

Complete the chart of nouns and adjective forms of words.

Noun	Adjective
vertebra	____________________
____________________	periosteal
tendon	____________________
clavicle	____________________
____________________	sternal
articulation	____________________
muscle	____________________
sacrum	____________________
____________________	iliac
acetabulum	____________________
coccyx	____________________
____________________	femoral

2. Prefixes

Use the listed prefixes to build a word for each definition.

a-	inter-	sub-
dys-	intra-	supra-
hemi-	peri-	
infra-	poly-	

1. Bad growth or development ____________________

2. The outermost covering of bone ____________________

3. Pertaining to within a muscle ______________________
4. Pertaining to above the scapula ______________________
5. Pertaining to below the kneecap ______________________
6. Pertaining to below the sternum ______________________
7. Inflammation of many muscles ______________________
8. Condition of a lack of muscle tone ______________________
9. Paralysis of one side of the body ______________________
10. Pertaining to between two joints ______________________

Singular and Plural Forms

Complete the chart of singular and plural forms.

Singular	**Plural**
vertebra	______________________
epiphysis	______________________
______________________	scapulae
phalanx	______________________
extremity	______________________
______________________	patellae
______________________	aponeuroses
ligament	______________________
______________________	lacunae
bursa	______________________

Word Building With Combining, Prefix, and Suffix Forms

The following word roots, prefixes, and suffixes are commonly used in medical terms for the anatomy and pathology of the musculoskeletal system. Combining vowels for word roots are included. Memorizing these word elements will help you understand new terms that you may encounter as a medical assistant, nurse, physical or occupational therapist, or as another health-care professional.

The lists contain examples of terms that utilize the word elements as well as a pronunciation guide. Be sure to use the pronunciation guide so that you can learn to say the terms correctly.

The Medical Language Lab at medicallanguagelab.com provides audio files to help you practice your pronunciations.

Combining Form	Meaning	Example (Pronunciation)	Definition
acr/o	extremities	acromegaly (ăk-rō-MEG-ă-lē)	enlargement of extremities
ankyl/o	stiff joint	ankylosis (ăng-kĭ-LŌ-sĭs)	abnormal condition of stiff joint
arthr/o	joint	arthrodesis (ar-THRŌD-dĕ-sĭs)	binding, fixation of a joint
articul/o	joint	articular (ăr-TĬK-ū-lăr)	pertaining to a joint
burs/o	bursa	bursitis (bŭr-SĪ-tĭs)	inflammation of a bursa
calcane/o	calcaneous (heel)	calcaneodynia (kal-kā-nē-ō-DIN-ē-ă)	pain in the heel bone
carp/o	wrist	carpal (KĂR-păl)	pertaining to the wrist
cervic/o	neck	cervicodynia (sĕr-vĭ-kō-DĬN-ē-ă)	pain in the neck
chondr/o	cartilage	chondromalacia (kŏn-drō-mă-LĀ-shē-ă)	softening of cartilage
cost/o	ribs	costochondritis (kŏs-tō-kŏn-DRĪ-tĭs)	inflammation of cartilage of ribs
crani/o	cranium	cranial (KRĀ-nē-ăl)	pertaining to the cranium (skull)
fasci/o	fascia	fasciitis (făsh-ē-ĪT-ĭs)	inflammation of fascia
femor/o	femur	femoropatellar (fĕm-ō-rō-pă-TEL-ăr)	pertaining to the femur and patella
fibul/o	fibula	fibular (FĬB-ū-lăr)	pertaining to the fibula
humer/o	humerus	humeral (HŪ-mĕr-ăl)	pertaining to the humerus
ili/o	ilium	iliopelvic (ĭl-ē-ō-PEL-vik)	pertaining to the ilium and pelvis
kinesi/o	movement	kinesiology (kĭ-nē-zē-ŎL-ō-jē)	the study of movement
kyph/o	hump	kyphosis (kī-FŌ-sĭs)	abnormal condition of a hump
lamin/o	lamina	laminectomy (lăm-ĭ-NĔK-tō-mē)	surgical removal of a lamina
lord/o	bent backward	lordosis (lor-DŌ-sĭs)	condition of backward bent (back)

Continued

Combining Form	Meaning	Example (Pronunciation)	Definition
lumb/o	lower back	lumbar (LŬM-băr)	pertaining to the lower back
menisc/o	meniscus	meniscectomy (mĕn-ĭ-SĔK-tō-mē)	surgical excision of a meniscus
metacarp/o	metacarpus	metacarpectomy (met-ă-kăr-PĔK-tō-mē)	surgical excision of the metacarpus
metatars/o	metatarsals	metatarsophalangeal (met-ă-tăr-sō-fă-LAN-jē-ăl)	pertaining to the metatarsals and phalanges
muscul/o	muscle	musculoskeletal (mŭs-kū-lō-SKĔL-ĕ-tăl)	pertaining to the muscles and skeleton
my/o	muscle	myocarditis (mī-ō-kăr-DĪT-ĭs)	inflammation of the heart muscle
myel/o	spinal cord, bone marrow	myelomalacia (mī-ĕl-ō-mă-LĀ-shē-ă)	softening of the spinal cord
orth/o	straight	orthodontist (or-thō-DŎN-tĭst)	specialist who straightens teeth
oste/o	bone	osteocyte (OS-tē-ō-sīt)	a bone cell
patell/o	knee cap, patella	patellectomy (păt-ĕ-LĔK-tō-mē)	surgical removal of the kneecap
ped/i	foot	pedicure (ped-ĭ-KYŪR)	care of the foot
pelv/i	pelvis	pelvic (PĔL-vĭk)	pertaining to the pelvis
phlang/o	phalanges (fingers and toes)	phalangeal (fă-LAN-jē-ăl)	pertaining to the phalanges
pod/o	foot	podiatrist (pō-DĪ-ă-trist)	specialist of the foot
pub/o	pubis	pubalgia (pūb-ĂL-jē-ă)	pain in the groin, pubis
rhabdomy/o	striated muscle	rhabdomyolysis (rab-dō-mī-OL-ĭ-sĭs)	breakdown of skeletal muscle
rad/i	radius	radioulnar (rā-dē-ō-ŬL-năr)	pertaining to the radius and ulna
sacr/o	sacrum	sacroiliac (săk-rō-IL-ē-ak)	pertaining to the sacrum and ilium
sarc/o	flesh	sarcolemma (sar-kŏ-LEM-ă)	cell membrane of a muscle cell
scoli/o	bent, crooked	scoliosis (skō-lē-Ō-sĭs)	lateral curvature of the spine
spondy/o	vertebrae	spondylarthritis (spŏn-dĭl-ar-THRĪT-ĭs)	inflammation of the vertebral joints

Combining Form	Meaning	Example (Pronunciation)	Definition
stern/o	sternum	sternoclavicular (stĕr-nō-klă-VĬK-ū-lăr)	pertaining to the sternum and clavicle
sthen/o	strength	myasthenia (mī-ăs-THĒ-nē-ă)	condition of lack of muscle strength
synovi/o	synovial membrane	synovectomy (sĭn-ō-VĔK-tō-mē)	surgical removal of synovial membrane
tars/o	ankle bones	tarsalgia (tars-ĂL-jē-ă)	pain in the ankle, tarsal bones
ten/o	tendon	tenodynia (tĕn-ō-DĬN-ē-ă)	pain in a tendon
tendin/o	tendon	tendinitis (TĔN-dĭn-Ī-tĭs)	inflammation of a tendon
thorac/o	thorax	thoracocentesis (thō-răk-ō-SEN-tē-sĭs)	puncture and aspiration of the thorax
tibi/o	tibia	tibiofibular (tĭb-ē-ō-FĬB-ū-lăr)	pertaining to the tibia and fibula
uln/a	ulna	ulnar (ŬL-năr)	pertaining to the ulna
vertebr/o	vertebrae	vertebral (VĔR-tĕ-brăl)	pertaining to the vertebrae

ā = say, ă = sofa, ē = meet, ĕ = met, ī = eye, ĭ = in, ō = oh, ŏ = dog, ū = you, ŭ = up, oo = food

Prefix	Meaning	Example (Pronunciation)	Definition
ab-	away from	abducens (ab-DOO-senz)	pertaining to drawing away from the body
ad-	toward, together	adduction (a-DŬK-shŏn)	movement toward the midline
extra-	outside, external	extra-articular (eks-tră ar-TIK-yŭ-lăr)	outside of a joint
inter-	between	interpubic (int-ĕr-PŪ-bĭk)	between the pubic bones
para-	beside, near	paraplegia (păr-ă-PLĒ-jē-ă)	paralysis of the lower body
peri-	around	pericellular (pĕr-ĭ-SĔL-ū-lăr)	pertaining to around a cell
sub-	below, beneath	subchondral (sŭb-KŎN-drăl)	pertaining to under the cartilage
supra-	above	supracostal (soo-pră-KŎS-tăl)	pertaining to above the ribs

ā = say, ă = sofa, ē = meet, ĕ = met, ī = eye, ĭ = in, ō = oh, ŏ = dog, ū = you, ŭ = up, oo = food

Suffix	Meaning	Example (Pronunciation)	Definition
-algia	pain	myalgia (mī-ĂL-jē-ă)	muscle pain
-ar	pertaining to	musculoskeletal (mŭs-kū-lō-SKĔL-ĕ-tăl)	pertaining to muscles and skeleton
-blast	immature cell	myeloblast (MĪ-ĕl-ō-blăst)	immature bone marrow cell
-cele	hernia	myelocele (MĪ-ĕl-ō-sēl)	hernia of the spinal cord
-clasis	to break	osteoclasis (OS-tē-ŏ-klā-sĭs)	surgical fracture of a bone
-desis	surgical fixation	arthrodesis (ar-THROD-ĕ-sĭs)	fusion of two bones
-lysis	destruction	chondrolysis (kŏn-DRŎL-ī-sĭs)	breakdown (destruction) of cartilage
-malacia	softening	osteomalacia (os-tē-ō-mă-LĀ-shē-ă)	softening of bone
-metry	process of measuring	myometry (MĪ-ō-mĕ-trē)	process of measuring muscle strength
-ous	pertaining to	ligamentous (lig-ă-MENT-ŭs)	relating to a ligament
-penia	decreased amount	osteopenia (os-tē-ŏ-PĒ-nē-ă)	bone loss, lack of mineralization

ā = say, ă = sofa, ē = meet, ĕ = met, ī = eye, ĭ = in, ō = oh, ŏ = dog, ū = you, ŭ = up, oo = food

Combining Forms Practice

1. Build the Terms

Using only the word elements listed, create terms to match the definition.

Prefixes	Combining Forms		Suffixes	
ab-	articul/o	maxilla/o	-algia	-itis
ad-	arthr/o	orth/o	-al	-lysis
dys-	bucc/o	oste/o	-ar	-malacia
extra-	carp/o	ped/i	-blast	-oma
peri-	chondr/o	phalang/o	-cele	-ology
sub-	fasci/o	scoli/o	-ectomy	-osis
supra-	kinesi/o			-ous
	kyph/o			-penia
	metacarp/o			

1. condition of being bent ______________________
2. pertaining to the wrist ______________________
3. pertaining to the upper jaw ______________________

4. pertaining to the wrist and fingers ______________________________

5. tumor of the spinal cord ______________________________

6. device to straighten a body part ______________________________

7. study of movement of the body ______________________________

8. condition of a humpback ______________________________

9. destruction of bone ______________________________

10. inflammation of muscle and fascia ______________________________

2. Decipher the Terms

Separate each term into its prefix (if any), combining form, and suffix. Next, translate the word parts and give the common definition of the term. Pulmonary *has been done for you as an example.*

pulmonary

Prefix: *None* *Combining Form:* *Pulmon/o = lungs*

Suffix: *-ary = pertaining to*

Meaning: *referring to the lungs*

1. intramuscular

   Prefix: ______________ *Combining Form:* ______________ *Suffix:* ______________

   Meaning: ______________________________

2. periosteum

   Prefix: ______________ *Combining Form:* ______________ *Suffix:* ______________

   Meaning: ______________________________

3. suprafemoral

   Prefix: ______________ *Combining Form:* ______________ *Suffix:* ______________

   Meaning: ______________________________

4. dyskinesia

   Prefix: ______________ *Combining Form:* ______________ *Suffix:* ______________

   Meaning: ______________________________

5. tibiofemoral

   Prefix: ______________ *Combining Form:* ______________ *Suffix:* ______________

   Meaning: ______________________________

6. subscapular

   Prefix: ______________ *Combining Form:* ______________ *Suffix:* ______________

   Meaning: ____

7. myalgia

   Prefix: ______________ *Combining Form:* ______________ *Suffix:* ______________

   Meaning: ____

8. osteoblast

   Prefix: ______________ *Combining Form:* ______________ *Suffix:* ______________

   Meaning: ____

9. metatarsophalangeal

   Prefix: ______________ *Combining Form:* ______________ *Suffix:* ______________

   Meaning: ____

10. bursitis

   Prefix: ______________ *Combining Form:* ______________ *Suffix:* ______________

   Meaning: ____

CASE STUDY, continued

Dr. Fischer meets Jacob in the operating room. Jacob is placed in the supine position, and Bethany, the CRNA (certified nurse anesthetist), places him under general anesthesia. Jacob's blood pressure, pulse, and respiration is monitored during the 2-hour procedure. Upon conclusion of the surgery, Jacob is sent to the recovery room. Dr. Fischer goes to the waiting room to talk to Ellen and Henry. Jacob's friends Emily and Rob are there too. Dr. Fischer explains that he performed an ORIF, an open reduction and internal fixation, to realign the bones and allow them to heal. He tells them the procedure went well, the wound was debrided (cleaned of debris), and the tibia and fibula were realigned and secured with a plate on the medial side of the lower leg. Five screws were then threaded through the bone on the medial side into the plate and into the bone. The plate will hold the bones in place as they heal and remodel. Emily asks, "Will Jacob need physical therapy? Will he be able to ride again?" Dr. Fischer replies "Yes and yes. He will need PT (physical therapy) to gain strength and stability in the leg. He will be able to ride again, but he will need to stay off the leg for a while. Initially, he will need to use a wheelchair because he will be completely non-weight bearing." Rob tells Ellen and Henry, "I can help Jacob get to PT and drive him to school. My van is equipped for a wheelchair since I take my grandfather to his doctor visits." Emily says, "I can help too. I feel so horrible." Dr. Fischer says, "You two are great friends and did the right thing by calling 911 and not trying to move him. The helmet prevented a head injury but moving someone after a trauma without stabilizing his neck can cause a spinal cord injury."

Musculoskeletal System Diseases and Disorders

Diseases and disorders of the musculoskeletal system can be congenital, due to the aging process, or a traumatic injury or repetitive motion injury. These diseases and disorders can be diagnosed through a variety of imaging techniques and evaluation by a provider. Signs and symptoms are common across a variety of diseases and disorders (Table 9-6).

Pathological Conditions of the Musculoskeletal System

Diseases and disorders of the musculoskeletal system include injuries from trauma, metabolic diseases, autoimmune disorders, cancerous tumors, and progressive degeneration from aging.

Abnormal curvatures of the spine: Can be due to birth defects (congenital), caused by disease such as osteoporosis, or an unknown cause (idiopathic) (Fig. 9-13). Treatment for the underlying cause along with physical therapy, exercises, back bracing, or surgery may correct or minimize the deformity.

Kyphosis: abnormal outward curve of the thoracic spine; commonly called a *humpback*

Lordosis: abnormal inward curvature of the lumbar spine; commonly called a *swayback*

Scoliosis: abnormal lateral curvature of the spine; the curve may be to the right or the left side

Adhesive capsulitis: A condition of the shoulder joint characterized by stiffness, pain, and immobility. Causes include trauma, osteoarthritis, or systemic disease. Treatment is directed at pain reduction and increased ROM of the shoulder joint. Treatments include analgesics, NSAIDs, physical therapy, and exercises to restore normal ROM and strength.

Amyotrophic lateral sclerosis (ALS): A movement disorder or muscle atrophy with degeneration of nerves in the spinal cord and lower region of the brain, which is also known as Lou Gehrig's disease.

Anterior cruciate ligament tear (ACL): A tear of the ligament in the anterior center of the knee (*cruciate* means center). The ACL and posterior cruciate ligament form a cross between the distal end of the femur and proximal end of the tibia/fibula and provide support and limit ROM to the knee joint. The ACL can be torn (partially or completely) by a twisting motion in sports or trauma. Severity of the ACL tear is graded:

- **Grade One**: The ligament has been stretched, but it still does its job of stabilizing the knee joint.
- **Grade Two**: The ligament has been stretched and loosened. It's partially torn. (This grade is rare.)
- **Grade Three**: The ligament is torn and divided into two pieces. This is a very severe injury and will require surgical correction.

An ACL tear is four times more common in women than in men and affects up to 200,000 Americans (mostly athletes) each year. Signs and symptoms include hearing a "pop,"

TABLE 9-6 Common Signs and Symptoms

Symptoms	Signs
Myalgia (muscle pain)	loss of ROM
Arthralgia (joint pain)	edema (swelling)
Myasthenia (muscle weakness)	joint deformities, fractures (traumatic or pathological)
Neuralgia (sharp, stabbing nerve pain that may radiate along the course of a nerve)	changes in gait

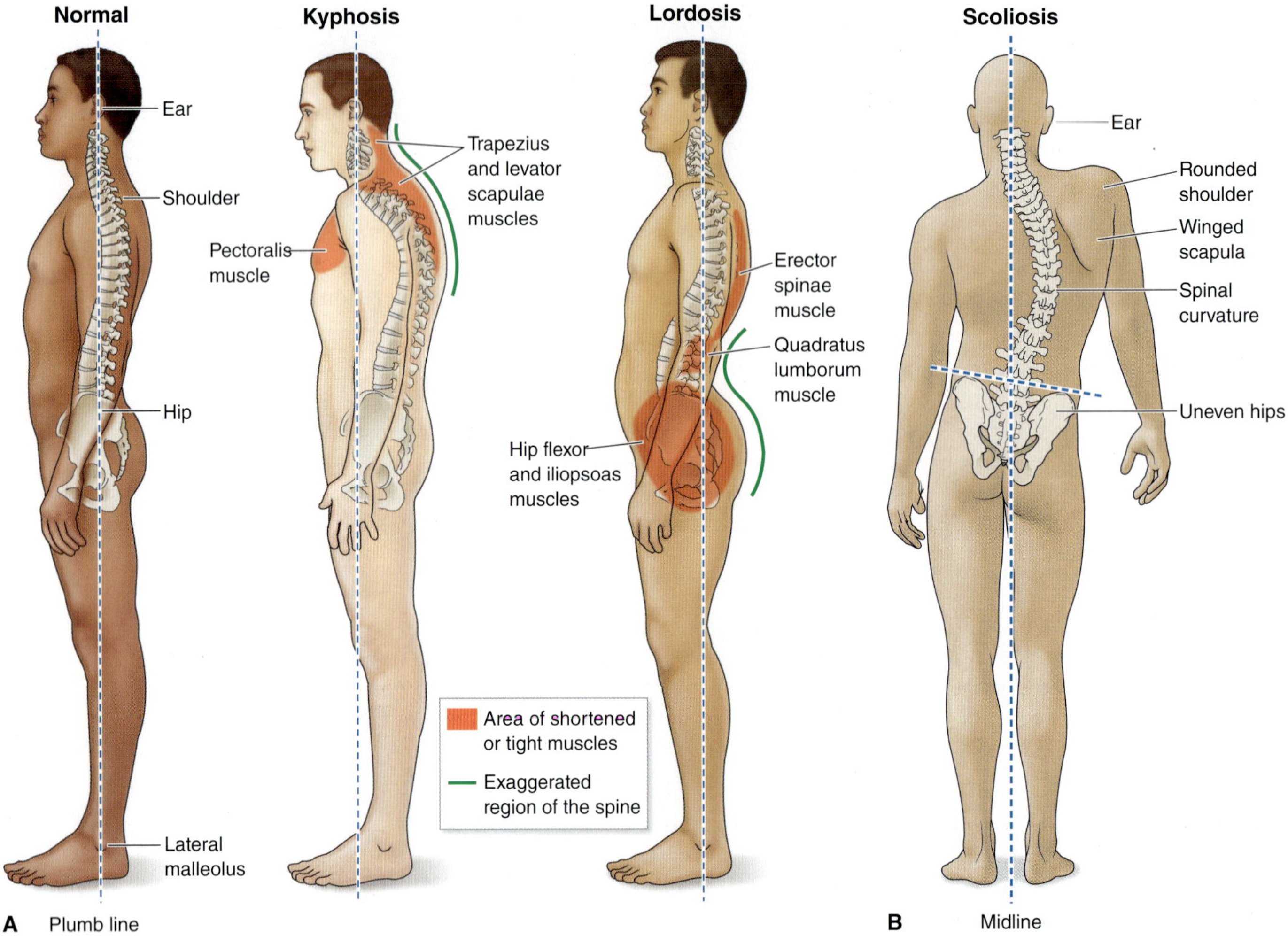

Figure 9-13 (A) Lateral views of normal, kyphosis, lordosis. (B) Posterior view of scoliosis.

immediate pain, swelling, and an inability to bear weight on the leg. Diagnosis is confirmed by an MRI. Treatment includes RICE (rest, ice, compression, and elevation). Surgical reconstruction of the ACL using a portion of the patellar tendon, part of the hamstring muscle, or a cadaver tendon is required for grade three tears. Physical therapy to rebuild strength and ROM about the knee is often painful, and full recovery can be slow, taking up to 6 to 9 months.

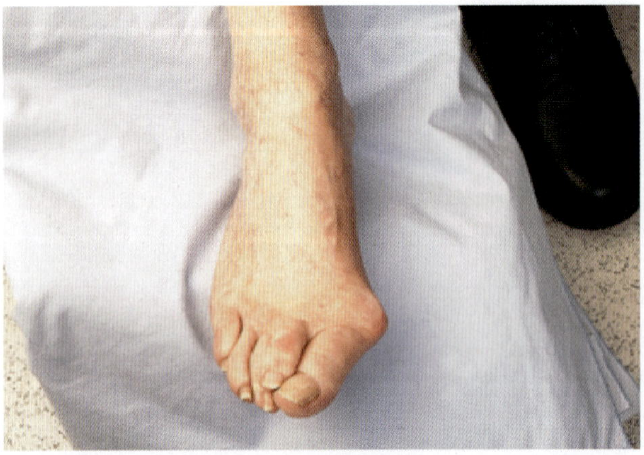

Figure 9-14 Bunion.

Bunion: An abnormal enlargement of the joint at the base of the great toe (Fig. 9-14). The great toe moves laterally toward the second toe. As the condition worsens, the bony prominence enlarges, causing pain and swelling of the joint. Causes include arthritis and wearing tight shoes or high heels, but it can also be congenital. Treatment consists of padding between the toes to alleviate pressure and anti-inflammatory and analgesic medications. A bunionectomy may be performed to remove the bony growth.

Bursitis: The inflammation of a bursa, typically caused by repeated stress to the joint. Commonly seen in shoulders, elbows, and knees.

Carpal tunnel syndrome: Caused when the transverse carpal ligament puts pressure on the median nerve that runs through a narrow passage, the carpal tunnel, at the palm side of the wrist (Fig. 9-15). The disorder is seen in people who use computers, construction workers who use vibrating tools, electricians, and factory workers who repeatedly stress the hands at the wrist. Signs and symptoms include pain, numbness, tingling, weakness, and swelling at the wrist. Treatment is with anti-inflammatory medications or wearing a wrist brace. Taking breaks from repetitive movement may decrease symptoms. Surgical correction where the transverse carpal ligament is cut will allow more room for the nerves and tendons and will relieve pressure, thus relieving symptoms.

Contracture: Fibrosis of connective tissue limiting the normal ROM about a joint.

Crepitation: A clicking or cracking sound heard upon movement of a joint. Commonly heard in the jaw, elbow, and knee joints due to roughness of the articular cartilage.

Degenerative disc: The deterioration of the intervertebral disc, usually due to movement and wear on the disc (Fig. 9-16). Misalignment of the vertebral discs results in friction of the disc and can cause rubbing of the tough outer covering of the disc causing a rupture and/or inflammation. The inflammation crowds and impinges the spinal nerves that extend from the spinal cord between the vertebrae. The primary symptom is pain that is often described as sharp, stabbing, burning, and sometimes radiating down the leg or arm. There may be loss of motor function, and the patient may not be able to perform their normal daily activities or get proper sleep. Conservative treatments consist of chiropractic care or physical therapy, such as traction to open the disc space and relieve nerve impingement. Bed rest, anti-inflammatories, analgesics, back or neck bracing as well as a TENS (transcutaneous electrical nerve stimulation) unit may be effective in reducing pain and inflammation. If conservative care is not effective, laminectomy or spinal fusion are surgical options.

Dislocation: Displacement of a bone from its normal location within a joint. Most common sites of dislocation are the shoulder, finger, hip, or knee. Dislocations accompany sprains, in which the ligaments holding the joint in place are stretched and torn. Signs and symptoms include intense pain, swelling, and altered joint shape. Treatment of dislocation

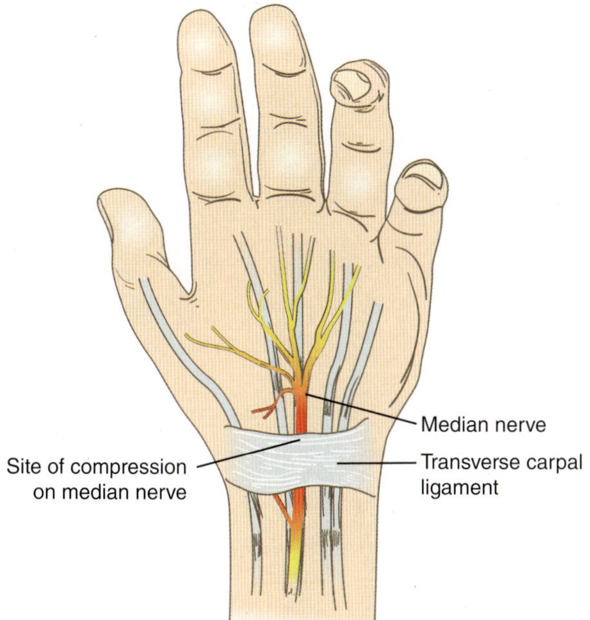

Figure 9-15 Carpal tunnel syndrome.

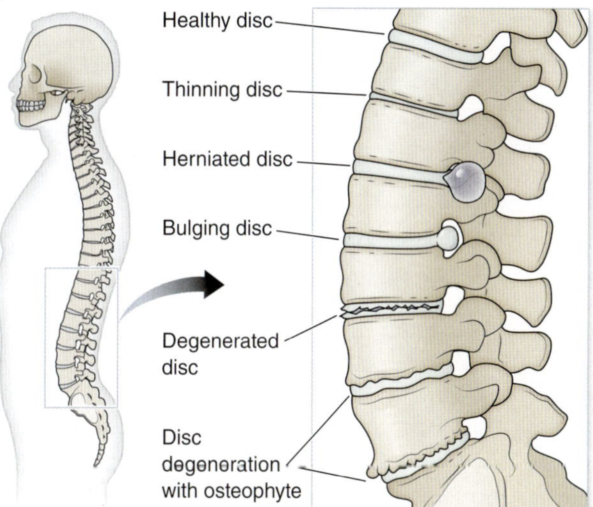

Figure 9-16 Degenerative disc.

consists of a closed manipulation or reduction of the joint in which the provider will move the bones back to the proper position. Ideally, the procedure is done as soon as possible after the injury since extreme swelling of the joint will make the manipulation more difficult with time. Intravenous sedation or general anesthesia is administered for the reduction, and the joint is splinted, casted, or bandaged post procedure to allow healing. Incomplete dislocation is called subluxation, which may be manually manipulated into the normal position without medication.

Dupuytren contracture: Disease affecting the palmar fascia of the hand, causing the ring finger and little finger to contract toward the palm.

Fibromyalgia: A term used to describe a group of symptoms of widespread musculoskeletal pain; chronic fatigue; and sleep, memory, and mood disturbances. Symptoms often begin after a trauma, surgery, psychological stress, or an infection. In other patients, symptoms may gradually increase after no single triggering event. Diagnosis is confirmed by tenderness in 11 out of 18 **trigger points**, which are hypersensitive areas of muscle near a joint (Fig. 9-17). The disorder affects more women than it does men and can be correlated with tension headaches, temporomandibular joint (TMJ) disorders, irritable bowel syndrome, anxiety, and depression. While there is no cure for fibromyalgia, medications to decrease symptoms of pain and swelling, as well as exercise, relaxation, and stress-reduction measures, may help patients manage their symptoms.

Fractures: Can arise from trauma, such as an auto accident or a fall. Some fractures are caused by underlying disease and are called *pathological fractures*. Bone fractures can be classified according to the severity and appearance of the fracture (Fig. 9-18).

Closed fracture: Also called a simple fracture, in a closed fracture the bone is broken, but no open wound is seen.

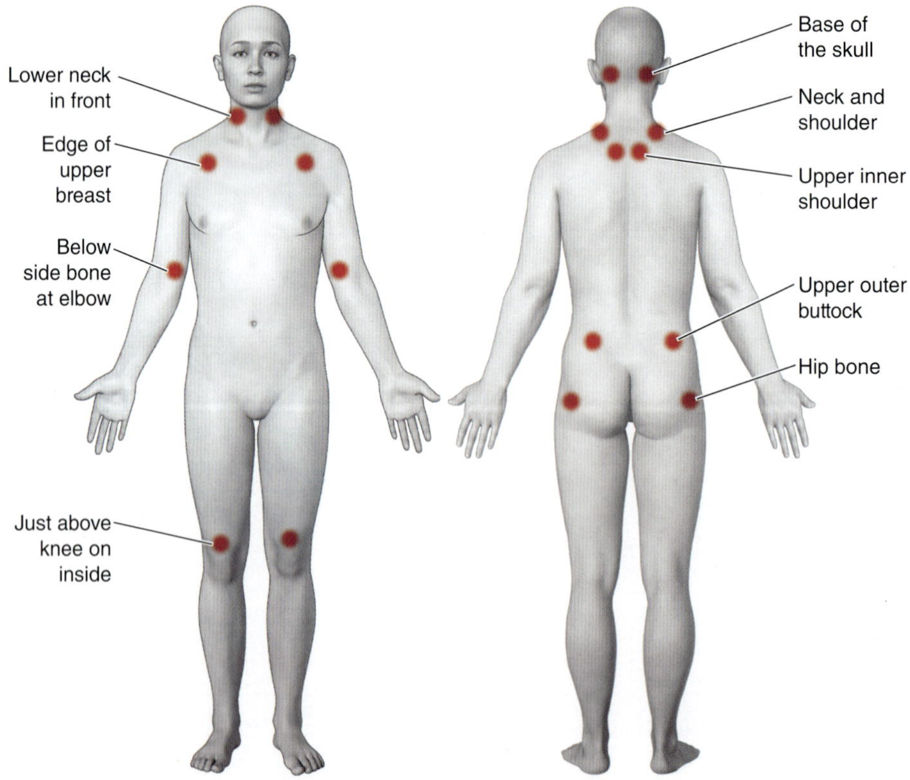

Figure 9-17 Fibromyalgia trigger points.

Open (compound) fracture: The bone is broken and pushes through the skin, forming an open wound. It is a serious condition as blood loss and infection may occur.
Greenstick fracture: An incomplete bone fracture that does not extend through the thickness of the entire bone.

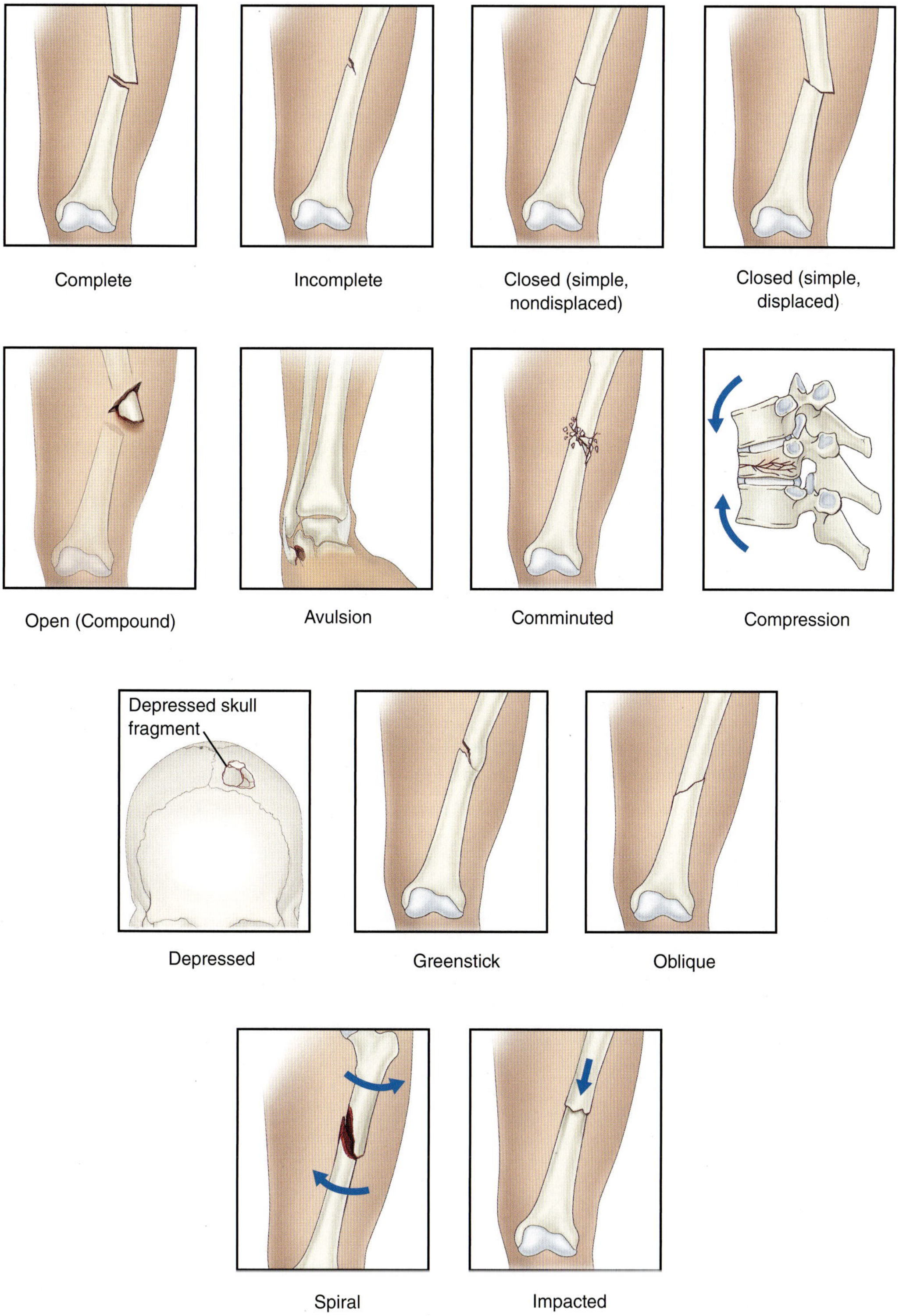

Figure 9-18 Types of fractures.

Comminuted fracture: The force is so great that it splinters or crushes a portion of the bone.
Impacted fracture: Direct force causes the bone to break, forcing the broken end into the break.
Compression fracture: This fracture is caused by bone surfaces being forced against each other, often due to osteoporosis, and it is thus a pathological fracture. Treatment of bone fractures includes casting or surgical correction, depending on the location and type of fracture.

Ganglion cyst: A tumor developing on a tendon or aponeurosis, most commonly on the back of the wrist (Fig. 9-19). The cyst is filled with a jellylike material, causing a smooth lump under the skin. Some ganglion cysts are asymptomatic and require no intervention. Cysts that are painful or that interfere with wrist movement can be surgically removed by ganglionectomy or reduced with a needle aspiration and injection of cortisone to reduce swelling while the area heals.

ELEMENT REVIEW
hyper- = excessive
uric/o = uric acid
-emia = blood condition

Gout: Also called gouty arthritis, gout is a hereditary metabolic disease in which the patient does not metabolize uric acid properly. The uric acid accumulates in the blood (hyperuricemia) and synovial fluid of the joints. The uric acid crystallizes in the joints, causing inflammation, low-grade fever, and intense pain. The most common sites are the first metatarsal joint of the great toe, but uric acid can also be seen in the knee, hands, and the spine. Treatment consists of rest, immobilization of the affected joint, and application of cold packs along with antigout medication (to lower uric acid levels in the blood), NSAIDs, and analgesics. Because the body produces uric acid from the metabolism of purines, a diet low in purines is advised. Avoidance of red meat, alcohol, organ meats (such as liver and heart), some seafoods (such as scallops, tuna, and herring), and sugary drinks. Patients are also advised to increase fluid intake as they are at an increased risk for uric acid kidney stones. Increasing fluid intake will decrease the likelihood of uric acid kidney stones and gout.

Hallux rigidus: A form of degenerative arthritis causing pain and stiffness of the metatarsophalangeal joint of the big toe. Causes of the disorder include overuse of the joint as in squatting or stooping in athletics or working. Treatment includes wearing shoes with ample room for the big toe, analgesics, NSAIDs, foot soaks, and cortisone injections.

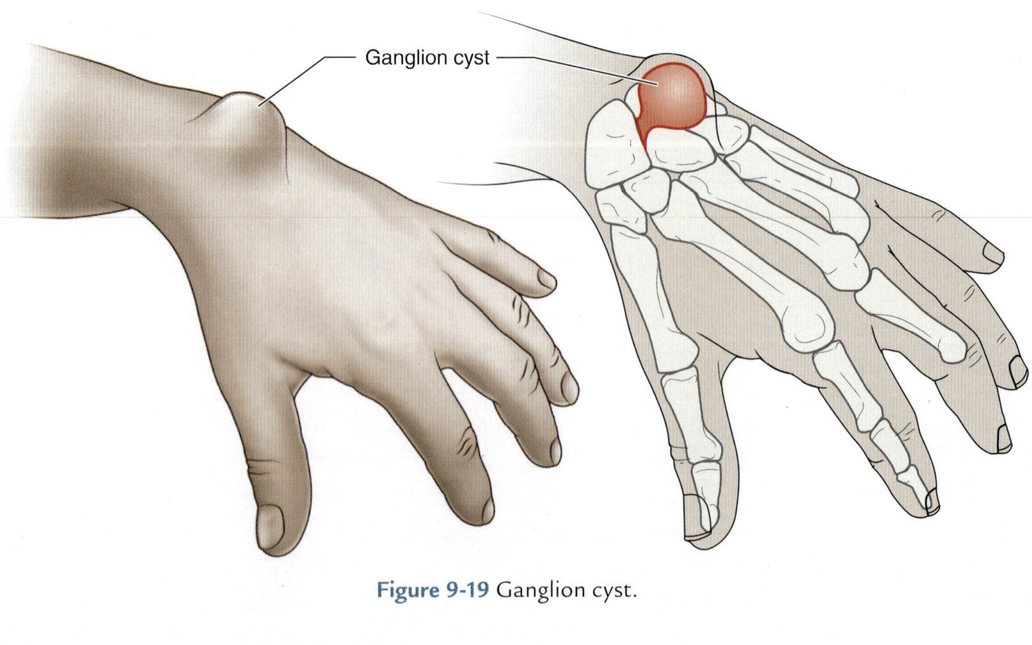

Figure 9-19 Ganglion cyst.

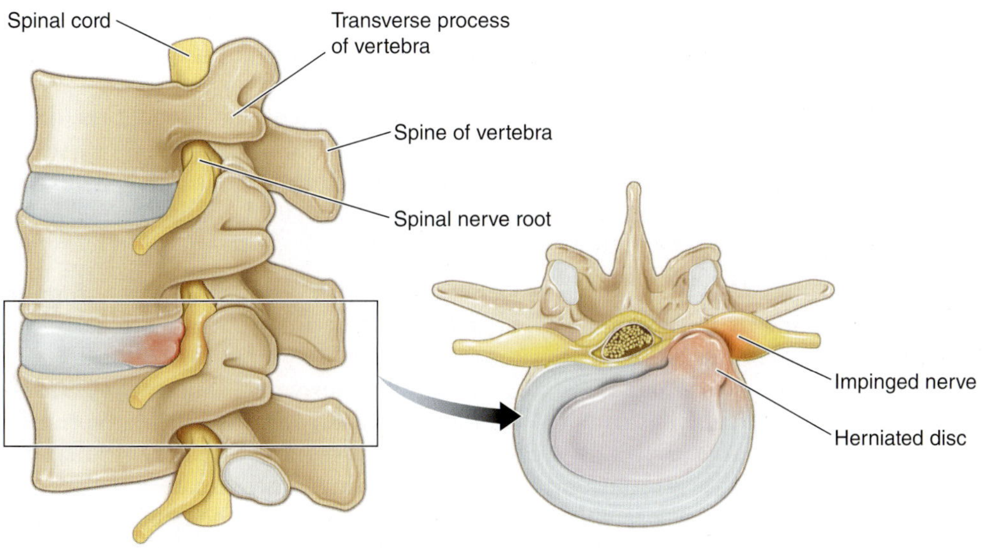

Figure 9-20 Herniated disc.

Herniated disc: A herniated nucleus pulposus is the rupturing of the central portion of the intervertebral disc (Fig. 9-20). Herniation may result from an injury, abrupt movement, or degenerative changes in the vertebra. Obesity and a sedentary lifestyle increase the risk of a herniated disc because extra weight (especially in the abdomen) increases pressure on the discs and lack of exercise creates poor abdominal muscle tone that normally helps relieve pressure on the spine. The disc material leaks into the spinal canal, pressing on the nerves of the spinal cord. Herniation of a lumbar disc can cause burning, stabbing, sharp pain in the back and buttocks and cause radicular pain down the leg called *sciatica*. Herniation of a cervical disc may cause radicular pain down the arm. Treatment consists of bedrest, analgesics, chiropractic manipulation, physical therapy, and muscle relaxants. If conservative care is not successful, surgical removal of the disc may be required.

Juvenile rheumatoid arthritis (JRA): An autoimmune disorder causing pain and joint stiffness, fatigue, and sometimes a fever and a rash. The onset of the disease is varied, but it is normally seen prior to age 16 years. JRA affects approximately 1 in 1,000 children, with girls being affected twice as often as boys. Treatment with anti-inflammatory medications can decrease symptoms of pain and stiffness. Corticosteroids may be used, but caution is advised because they can decrease normal bone growth. Methotrexate can be given to slow disease progression. There is no known cure.

ELEMENT REVIEW
epi- = upon
condyl/o = protuberance of the elbow
-itis = inflammation

ELEMENT REVIEW
peri- = around
oste/o = bone
-itis = inflammation

Lateral epicondylitis: An inflammation of the lateral side of the elbow from repeated use; also known as tennis elbow.

Medial epicondylitis: An inflammation of the medial side of the elbow from repeated use; also known as golfer's elbow.

Medial tibial syndrome: Periostitis of the medial border of the tibia caused by overuse; also known as shin splints. It accounts for 60% of athletic injuries to the lower leg. It can be caused by poor footwear or training on hard surfaces. The pain starts as a dull ache and progresses to sharper pain that limits activity. Treatment consists of rest, analgesics, using proper footwear, and correcting biomechanics.

Meniscal tear: A tear of the crescent-shaped intraarticular cartilage of the knee that cushions the joint (Fig. 9-21). The tear is caused by forceful twisting or rotation of the knee. The movement can cause a "popping" noise and immediate pain. There are two

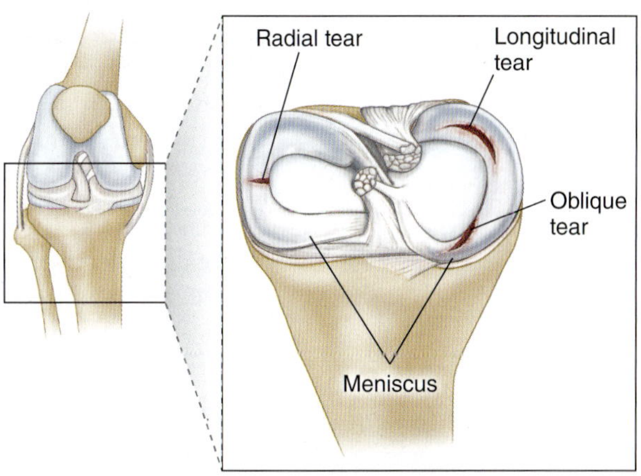

Figure 9-21 Meniscal tears.

menisci in the knee on the lateral and medial side. Diagnosis is confirmed by physical examination and by an MRI. Treatment consists of rest, ice, compression, analgesics, and elevation. Tears may require arthroscopic surgery:

Partial menisectomy: Trimming the edges of the torn meniscus. Done if the damage is less severe.

Total menisectomy: Removing the whole meniscus. Done if it is severely damaged.

Meniscal repair: Suturing (sewing) the torn meniscal edges. Usually done when both the ligament and meniscus need repair.

Muscular dystrophy (MD): A group of genetic disorders characterized by progressive symmetrical wasting of skeletal muscles. Onset usually occurs in infancy to early childhood. Diagnosis is confirmed by physical examination of the infant or child, along with elevation of creatine phosphokinase, abnormal muscle biopsy, and abnormal electromyogram. There are many subtypes of MD; the most common form is Duchenne muscular dystrophy. Symptoms appear by age 3 years, affecting boys more often than girls. As the disease progresses, muscles atrophy and contractures form. Muscle tissue is replaced with fat as the muscle fibers deteriorate. Muscle weakness advances in the pelvis, causing gait abnormalities and eventually loss of the ability to walk. As the muscle weakness continues to progress, the patient loses upper body strength and the ability to breathe as the diaphragm becomes affected. Scoliosis is common in late stages of MD. Treatment consists of controlling symptoms with exercise, surgical correction of scoliosis, braces to support weak limbs, and breathing exercises. Corticosteroids may be used to slow progressive muscle wasting. There is no known cure for MD, and death usually occurs in teen years. Research with stem cell therapy may slow disease progression or even offer a cure in the future.

ELEMENT REVIEW
electr/o = electricity
my/o = muscle
-gram = recording
a- = without
-trophy = growth, development

Myasthenia gravis: An autoimmune neuromuscular disorder characterized by a lack of muscle strength and paralysis. The disorder starts with weakness of muscles of the face and jaw, with difficulty swallowing. The patient may report double vision and have a drooping eyelid. It is caused by destruction of receptors in the synaptic region that respond to acetylcholine, which transmits nerve impulses that tell the muscles to contract. Initially, symptoms improve with application of a cold pack, but as the disorder progresses, muscles become progressively weaker and more muscles are affected. Later stages of the disorder progress to involve the muscles of the limbs. Treatment with corticosteroids and immunosuppressants can be used to suppress the immune response. Cholinesterase inhibitors, such as pyridostigmine (Mestinon) can increase communication between nerves and muscles to improve function.

ELEMENT REVIEW
neur/o = nerves
muscul/o = muscles
-ar = pertaining to
my/o = muscle
-asthenia = weakness, debility

Myosarcoma: Malignant tumor of muscle tissue.

Myositis ossificans progressive: A progressive disease that begins in early life in which muscles gradually convert into bony tissue.

Osteitis deformins: A chronic inflammation of long bones and deformity of flat bones; also called Paget's disease. It affects older people and is of unknown etiology. Signs and symptoms include pain in the tibia, frequent fractures, a waddling gait, and shortened stature. The skull can become enlarged, and hearing may be compromised. Treatment with bisphosphate drugs, over-the-counter analgesics, and NSAIDs is common.

Osteoarthritis: The most common form of arthritis resulting from wear and tear on joints; also called degenerative joint disease. Commonly seen with age, this chronic condition progresses as joints are repeatedly stressed. Signs and symptoms include joint pain and stiffness, especially in the morning upon arising. The joint pain is aggravated by weather, specifically decreases in air pressure from rain or snow. Movements of joints may cause crepitation, a clicking or cracking sound. ROM about the joint may decrease with disease progression. Treatments may include anti-inflammatory and analgesic medications as needed (prn). While osteoarthritis cannot be cured, exercise, stretching, physical therapy, and a healthy diet can slow progression of the disease. If the condition becomes severe, joint replacement surgery can reduce pain and give the patient years of mobility and function.

Osteomalacia: Abnormal softening of bone due to a lack of calcium and phosphorus in the blood. The body will steal calcium and phosphorus from bones to correct the blood chemistry. Bones become soft, flexible, and brittle. Weight-bearing bones, such as the femur, become deformed, causing a bowed leg appearance. When the disease occurs in children, it is called rickets (Fig. 9-22). The deficiency is caused by a lack of vitamin D, which is necessary for the absorption of calcium and phosphorus. Vitamin D deficiency can be attributed to a poor diet, lack of exposure to sunlight, or a metabolic disorder causing malabsorption. Treatment with vitamin D and calcium supplements and a diet that includes calcium, phosphorus, and adequate protein will slow disease progression.

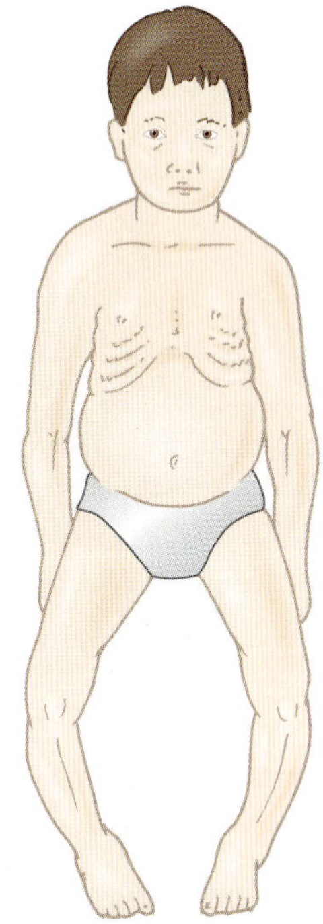

Figure 9-22 Osteomalacia (rickets).

Osteomyelitis: A local or generalized infection of bone and bone marrow caused by a bacterial or, less commonly, a fungal infection or radiation. Disease-causing microorganisms invade bone from the bloodstream (hematogenous spread). Infection can invade bone from an adjacent site, such as an infected tooth, a decubitus ulcer, or a bone fracture. It occurs more commonly in children. The risk of osteomyelitis is increased in patients with peripheral vascular disease, sickle cell disease, urinary tract infections, inadequate nutrition, diabetes mellitus, and prosthetic joints. Signs and symptoms include sudden onset of fever (101°F and above), pain, tenderness, erythema (redness), swelling, anorexia, headache, and fatigue. Treatment consists of high-dose antibiotics, incision and drainage of abscesses, intracavitary instillation of antibiotics, or surgical correction for severe infection.

Osteoporosis: Loss of bone mass, leaving bones susceptible to fracture. The disorder is most common in postmenopausal women due to a decrease in estrogen, which signals bone to store calcium (Fig. 9-23). White and Asian women of small stature are most risk. Lack of exercise or immobilization from other disorders also increases risk. Long-term steroid treatments, Synthroid (prescribed for hypothyroid disease), proton pump inhibitors, alcohol, tobacco, and caffeine also contribute to osteoporosis. Treatment with estrogen replacement drugs, bisphosphonate drugs, calcium and vitamin D supplements, whole-food diets containing calcium, and active weight-bearing exercise will slow the progression of the disease.

ELEMENT REVIEW
hemat/o = blood
gen/o = origination, production
-ous = pertaining to
intra- = within
-cavitary = pertaining to the cavity (of bone)

Plantar fasciitis: Inflammation of the fascia that runs from the heel to the toes. The condition is caused by standing or walking on hard surfaces or by shoes that do not provide cushioning, and it is aggravated by obesity. Rest, analgesics, stretching the Achilles tendon, ice, and wrapping the foot will decrease pain.

Polymyositis: Inflammation of many muscles.

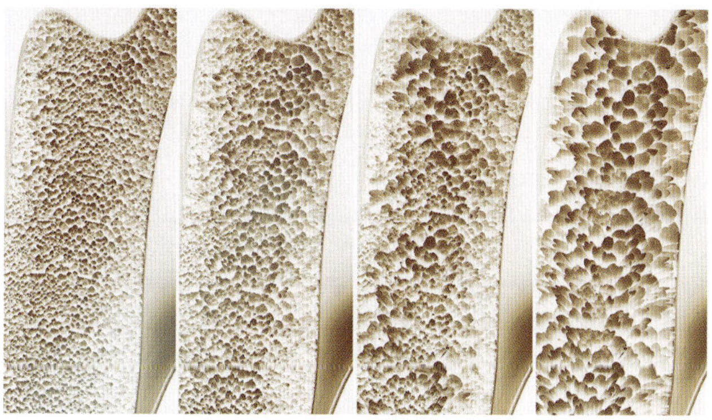

Figure 9-23 Progressive osteoporosis. Healthy bone (left) loses mass, and bones become more porous.

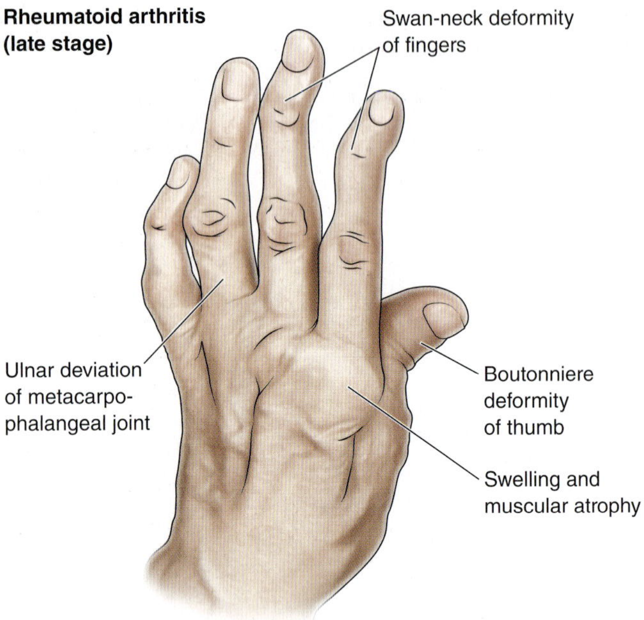

Figure 9-24 Rheumatoid arthritis in the hand.

Rheumatoid arthritis (RA): A chronic, systemic inflammatory disease affecting multiple joints. Common sites are the peripheral joints such as the wrists, elbows, shoulders, ankles, knees, and hips (Fig. 9-24). Onset of RA usually occurs between age 20 to 40 years and affects women more than men. Signs and symptoms include pain, stiffness, loss of ROM, and fatigue. Pain is most prevalent in the morning or after periods of rest. Pain improves with movement. Characteristic changes to the hands and fingers include deviation of the metacarpophalangeal (MCP) joint and hyperextension of the interphalangeal joint and flexion at the distal interphalangeal joint. The pain, stiffness, and deformity of joints progress with age. Treatment consists of aspirin to relieve pain and stiffness, rest, and physical therapy. NSAIDs can be prescribed for patients who cannot tolerate aspirin. Advanced cases of RA may require joint replacement surgery.

Rotator cuff tear: A tearing of one of the group of muscles and tendons that surround the shoulder joint. It can be caused by trauma to the shoulder, such as a dislocation or a broken clavicle. A tear can also occur from repetitive motion, such as throwing a baseball or swinging a golf club. Carpenters, mechanics, and painters can also develop a tear due to repeated shoulder motion associated with their jobs. Signs and symptoms include difficulty and pain while raising the arm, a popping or clicking sound upon shoulder movement, and pain that increases at night or with rest. Diagnosis is confirmed with an x-ray, MRI, or ultrasound. Nonsurgical treatments consist of rest, NSAIDs, wearing an arm sling, physical therapy, or injection of a steroid into the joint capsule. If nonsurgical intervention is ineffective, a tendon repair with removal of accumulated scar tissue may be done arthroscopically.

ELEMENT REVIEW
arthr/o = joint
-scope = instrument to view

Skull fracture: A break in one of the eight bones that form the cranial portion of the skull. It is usually a result of blunt force trauma in an automobile accident, a fall from heights, physical assault, or diving into shallow water. Severity and extent of the injury depends on the location of the fracture and if the brain is injured. Signs and symptoms include, but are not limited to, confusion, loss of consciousness, convulsions, loss of balance and vision, or hearing disturbances. Open or depressed skull fractures will bleed and present with more obvious trauma. The patient must be evaluated for brain damage. Diagnosis is confirmed by neurological examination and CT, MRI, or x-ray. Treatment can include surgical correction to protect the brain. Recovery is based on the extent of damage to the brain. Mild head injuries can result in a full recovery. Of people with moderate to severe head injuries, 25% result in some degree of disability, and 7% to 10% percent remain in a permanent vegetative state or die as a result of their injuries. Thirty-three percent of people with a severe head injury will not survive.

Sprain: An injury to the ligaments surrounding a joint from a twisting motion outside the normal ROM. Common sites are sprained ankles, where the foot inverts (turns inward). A whiplash motion of the head and neck causing overextension of the neck ligaments results in a cervical sprain. Signs and symptoms include pain, swelling, loss of ROM, and muscle weakness. Sprains can be mild, affecting a few fibers of the ligament, or severe, where the ligament may be completely torn from the attachment. Internal bleeding will occur in severe sprains. Treatment consists of elevation and application of ice, joint immobilization, analgesics, and anti-inflammatory medications. X-rays may be ordered to rule out bone fracture.

Strain: An injury to a muscle or attachment of the tendon resulting from an overstretching, overextension; commonly called a "pulled muscle." Causes include vigorous exercise that a person is unaccustomed to or from repetitive motion. Treatment includes rest and application of ice packs for the first 24 to 48 hours after onset. Muscle relaxants and analgesics may be prescribed for severe strains.

Tendinitis: Inflammation of a tendon, most commonly caused by overuse of a joint.

Torticollis: Acute myositis of the cervical muscles; also known as wryneck. Causes include disease of the cervical vertebrae, adenitis, tonsillitis, cerebellar tumor, or rheumatism. Treatment consists of injection of botulinus toxin to the affected muscles or chiropractic manipulation of the cervical spine.

Pathology Word-Building Practice

1. Prefixes

Choose from the list of prefixes to build a word for the definitions below.

a-	hypo-	poly-
epi-	intra-	
hyper-	peri-	

1. Pertaining to within a joint ____________________
2. Lack of growth or development ____________________
3. Pain in many muscles ____________________
4. The covering of bone ____________________
5. Pertaining to a complete lack of muscle tone ____________________
6. Inflammation of protuberance of the elbow ____________________
7. Excessive growth or development ____________________
8. Decreased muscle tone ____________________
9. Pertaining to many joints ____________________
10. Pertaining to within a muscle ____________________

2. Suffixes

Choose from the list of suffixes to build a word for the definitions below.

-blast	-itis	-osis
-clasis	-malacia	-scope
-ectomy	-metry	
-gram	-oma	

1. recording of electrical muscle activity ____________________
2. softening of bone ____________________
3. forward curvature of the spine ____________________

4. inflammation of cartilage ______________________

5. surgical removal of a ganglion cyst ______________________

6. process of measuring the pelvis ______________________

7. tumor of bone and flesh ______________________

8. surgical breaking of a bone ______________________

9. backward curvature of the spine ______________________

10. tumor of the spinal cord ______________________

Musculoskeletal System Diagnostic Procedures

ELEMENT REVIEW
oste/o = bone
myel/o = bone marrow
-itis = inflammation
neutr/o = neutrophils
thromb/o = clotting
cyt/o = cell
-penia = decreased amount

Antinuclear antibody (ANA) test: A blood test that can indicate RA, lupus, multiple sclerosis, or other inflammatory autoimmune disorders.

Arthrography: Process of x-raying a joint after administration of a contrast medium.

Bone marrow aspiration: Removal of a small sample of bone marrow for microscopic analysis. The test is used to diagnose anemia, leukemia, neutropenia, and thrombocytopenia. Sites of bone marrow aspiration include the sternum, iliac crest, or the proximal tibia.

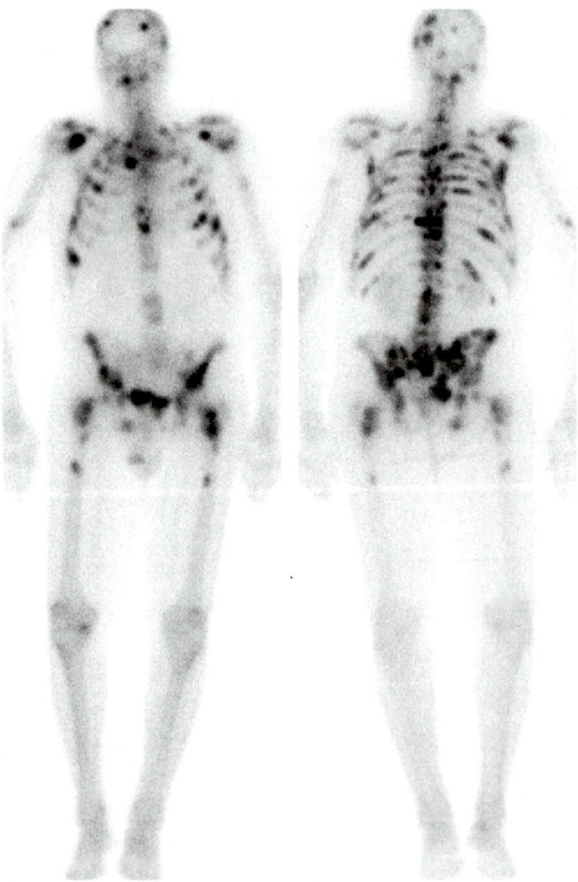

Figure 9-25 Bone scan showing skeletal metastatic lesions in a patient with cancer.

Bone scan: A procedure to detect bone cancer and osteomyelitis (Fig. 9-25). The patient is injected with a radioisotope, which is absorbed into the bone tissue. After approximately 3 hours, the patient is placed into the gamma scanner, which detects areas of radioactive concentration. The image created will show darker hot spots where diseased bone uptakes the radioactive isotope.

C-reactive protein (CRP): A blood test to measure inflammation in the body. The test can help to diagnose RA and lupus, as well as the patient's risk for a heart attack.

Creatine kinase: An enzyme that is found in the skeletal muscles, heart, and brain. Elevated blood levels may indicate muscle injury or disease.

Dual-energy X-ray absorptiometry (DEXA): A noninvasive procedure that uses photons generated by x-ray to evaluate the density of bone. The test is used to diagnose osteoporosis or monitor its progression.

Electromyogram (EMG): A test that measures the strength of contraction of a muscle while it is stimulated with an electric current. A surface electrode or a needle electrode is inserted into the muscle. The muscle is electrically stimulated, and the response is recorded on an oscilloscope, an instrument that displays the electrical action of the muscle on a screen.

Erythrocyte sedimentation rate (ESR): A blood test to measure the rate of erythrocytes (red blood cells) settling to the bottom of an unclotted tube of blood. Elevation in sedimentation rate is associated with inflammatory conditions and thus can help to diagnose disorders such as RA.

Muscle biopsy: A specimen of muscle tissue is removed by a small incision or a biopsy needle for microscopic inspection.

Rheumatoid factor: A blood test to measure antibodies associated with connective tissue diseases such as RA.

CAREER EXPLORATION: PHYSICAL THERAPY ASSISTANT

When I was in high school, I tore my ACL playing basketball. We were in the championship game, after working hard all season. I went to pass the ball to my teammate, pivoting my lower body. I heard a loud snap, and I was suddenly lying on the court. I have never experienced such great pain; my knee was swollen and felt like it was on fire. My coach and my dad helped me off the court, and Dad took me to the emergency department. Dr. Fischer examined my knee and told us it was a grade 3 tear, requiring surgical repair. I had surgery the next morning and wore a leg splint and walked with crutches for 2 weeks; then the hard work began. I had to go to physical therapy three times per week. The therapy was painful, but I regained mobility and strength. My therapist, Rebecca, pushed me to work hard each session. Although it hurt, I enjoyed going to PT and met some great friends, both patients and staff. I hadn't known what I wanted to do after high school, but the PT clinic looked like a great place to work. I met with my guidance counselor at school, and he told me about a local college program where I could become a PTA, a physical therapy assistant. PTAs work under the direction and supervision of a DPT, a doctor of physical therapy. I enrolled in the 2-year program and took some really interesting courses. My anatomy and physiology classes were intense, but my study group worked together, spending long hours in the lab. We studied kinesiology (the study of movement of the body), clinical pathology (the study of disease), and so much more. During the last semester, I did my clinical hours at the same clinic I had gone to for my knee therapy. Rebecca was my preceptor, the DPT who guided me through working with patients. I graduated and took my boards, and now I am a licensed PTA. I got a job working with patients after surgeries and/or orthopedic injuries. I can empathize with them as they work through their pain and regain strength and range of motion. There have been a few basketball players with knee injuries; they appreciate my help in getting them back on the court. One patient hurt his elbow playing golf, a condition called medial epicondylitis. We talked a lot during his therapy sessions and became friends. He is teaching me to play golf, and I remind him of Rebecca's teachings of proper biomechanics as he swings. I love that my career intersects with my love of sports. Someday I may go back to school and pursue a degree as a DPT, but for now I am happy to work as a PTA as I continue to learn.

Musculoskeletal System Therapeutic Procedures

Arthrocentesis: Surgical puncture of a joint with a large needle to withdraw fluid. The procedure not only can be therapeutic to relieve accumulation of fluid, but it also can be diagnostic as the fluid can be analyzed to detect infection.

Arthroplasty: Surgical reconstruction of a joint. The procedure can be performed on joints deformed from disease, such as RA, congenital malformations, or from traumatic injury to a joint.

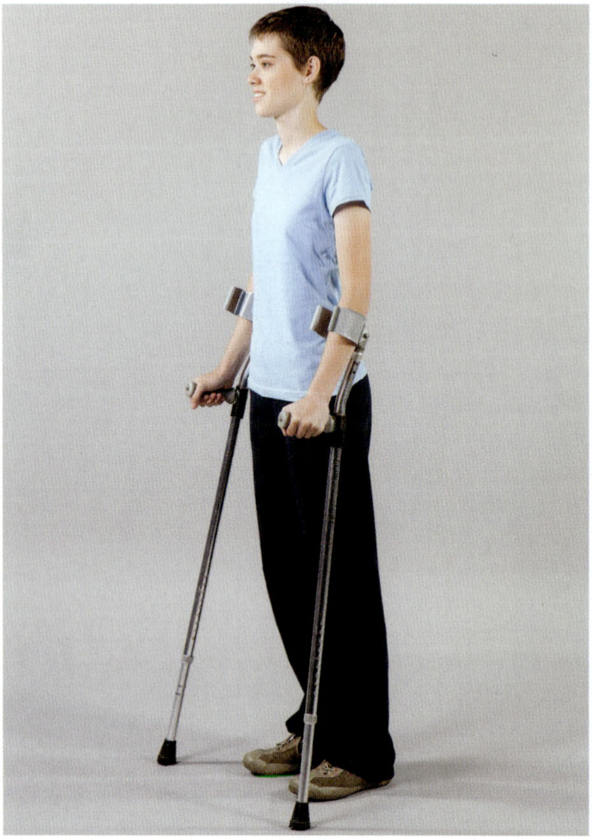

Figure 9-26 Forearm crutches.

Chiropractic care: A system of therapy focused on the structure of the body, particularly the spine. Chiropractors manipulate (a procedure also called an adjustment) the spine to correct body misalignment to relieve pain and restore normal posture. In addition to spinal adjustment, chiropractors advise patients on improving biomechanics and preventing injuries.

Crutches: Devices used by patients to shift weight from the lower extremities to the forearms. The patient must be taught the correct crutch gait to prevent further injury, falls, or arm strain. Four basic types of crutches can be used based on the severity and location of injury and upper body strength of the patient:

Axillary crutches: Wood or aluminum crutches, height can be adjusted to reach the patient's underarm with the elbow flexed to approximately 30 degrees. One or two axillary crutches can be used (when using one crutch, it is used on the uninjured side).

Forearm crutches: Also called an elbow crutch (Fig. 9-26). The cuff of the crutch must be 1 to 1.5 inches below the elbow and allow the patient to flex the elbow 15° to 30°. Patients with lifelong need of crutches may prefer this type of crutch to an axillary crutch as they are smaller and do not create irritation at the underarm.

Gutter crutches: A modification to the forearm crutch that helps the patient maintain balance. The forearms rest on a padding and the adjustable hand grip allows for a broader distribution of weight (along the length of the forearm).

Hands-free crutch: The base of the crutch is designed to sustain the weight of the leg while keeping both hands free.

Gait training: A set of exercises, usually administered by a physical therapist to improve motion of walking, and to prevent exacerbation of injury or reinjury. Gait training may be implemented after a trauma, stroke, or surgery and may include assistive devices such as crutches.

Closed reduction: A procedure performed by an orthopedic surgeon in which a bone fracture is manually manipulated (reduced) into correct alignment without surgery. After the closed reduction is performed, the affected body part is casted or splinted to allow the bone to heal.

Laminectomy: The surgical excision of the posterior arch of a vertebra, usually performed to remove a lesion or a herniated disc. The lesion or herniated disc will cause compression and pain on the spinal cord. The surgery is recommended only after a course of conservative care consisting of physical therapy and anti-inflammatory medications.

Open reduction, internal fixation: A surgical procedure performed by an orthopedic surgeon in which a bone fracture is manipulated into correct alignment (reduced) by an open surgical procedure (Fig. 9-27). Open reduction may include the use of screws or plates to correct bone alignment. External fixation devices may be used to stabilize the bones while they heal.

Physical therapy: A set of exercises administered and monitored by a physical therapist to build strength, decrease pain, increase lost ROM, and reestablish normal gait after an injury or a stroke. Physical therapy is also used to maximize function in infants and children born with neuromuscular disorders.

Total hip replacement: A surgical procedure to remove damaged sections of the hip joint and replace them with metal, ceramic, or a plastic prosthesis. The procedure is also called total hip arthroplasty.

ELEMENT REVIEW
arthr/o = joint
-plasty = surgical correction, repair
prosthe/o = in addition to, replacement
-sis = condition

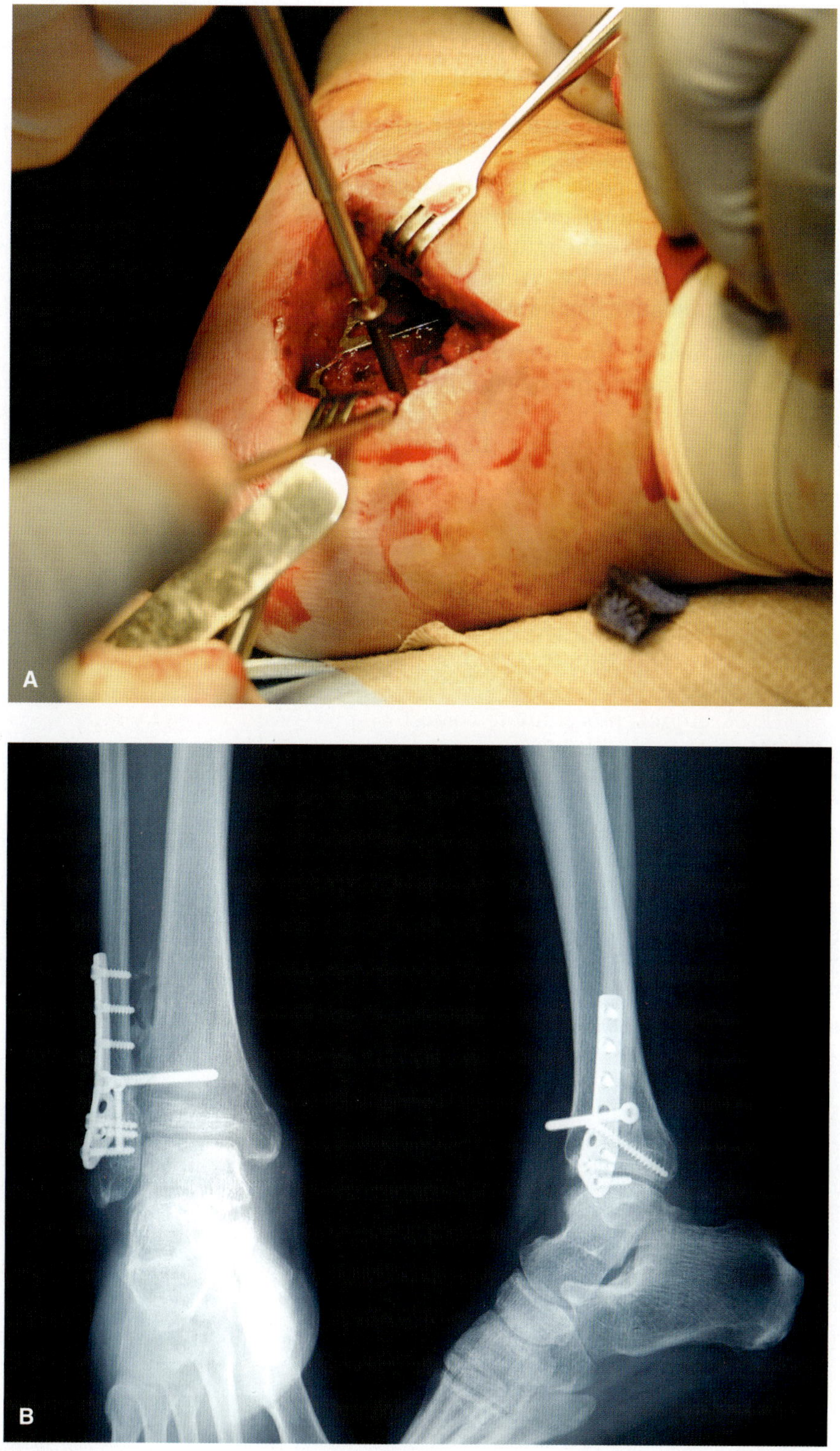

Figure 9-27 (A) Open reduction surgery showing the placement of a screw. (B) X-ray of internal fixation.

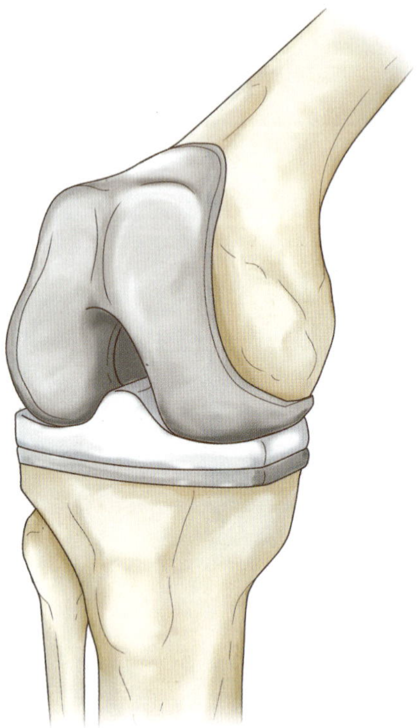

Figure 9-28 Prosthetic knee.

Total knee replacement: A surgical procedure to resurface a knee damaged by arthritis. Metal alloys and high-grade plastic polymer parts are used to cap the ends of the femur and tibia and to resurface the patella (Fig. 9-28).

Transcutaneous electrical nerve stimulation (TENS): The administration of a low-voltage electric current to provide pain relief. The electrodes are placed on or near the nerves where the pain is located or at trigger points. The electrical current stimulates nerve cells that block the transmission of pain signals. The device is also thought to release endorphins, the body's natural pain-killing chemicals. The device can be worn by the patient and the intensity of the electrical stimulation can be adjusted to his/her comfort.

Spinal fusion: The surgical procedure to permanently connect two adjacent vertebrae and maintain stability of the spine. Rods and screws are implanted to prevent movement of the vertebrae and stabilize the joint. Fusion is performed if pressure on the spinal cord is due to degeneration of discs or displacement of a disc from injury and laminectomy will not correct the structural defects.

Procedures and Diagnostics Review

Fill in the blank with the correct term.

1. A surgical procedure to correct/ replace an arthritic joint ________________
2. The density of bone can be measured by ________________
3. A blood test that detects inflammation ________________
4. The type of crutch that is designed to provide the most assistance in balance ________________
5. A device that can be worn for continuous pain control ________________
6. Test that uses a radioactive isotope to detect bone disease or cancer ________________
7. Alignment of a broken bone without surgery ________________
8. A device that measures the force of contraction of a muscle ________________
9. An enzyme found in skeletal muscle ________________
10. Permanent surgical connection of two vertebrae ________________

CASE STUDY, completed

Six weeks later, Jacob has been making great progress at physical therapy. His therapist, Rebecca, created a plan for him to gain strength and balance. Initially, his exercises were active assisted, meaning Rebecca would help him bring his leg through the ranges of motion. As he gained strength and endurance, the exercises were changed to active resistive, where she would oppose his movements to build his strength. Rebecca also has him ride a stationary bicycle and increases the tension as he regains strength. At the end of each PT session, Rebecca applies an ice pack to his leg to decrease swelling and pain. She also inspects the surgical site to look for infection. His leg is looking good, and he is anxious to get rid of the crutches that replaced his wheelchair. His clavicle is healing, but the sling he wears to stabilize the clavicle hurts his neck, and it still hurts a bit when he sneezes. Rebecca recommends that he stop wearing the sling if he feels comfortable without it. He complains that his neck is stiff, so Rebecca recommends he see Dr. Hartell, the chiropractor affiliated with the PT group. Jacob gets his cervical spine, the neck and thoracic spine, and upper back adjusted. An adjustment is a procedure in which sudden force is applied to the spinal joints to improve spinal motion and overall physical function. This helps the upper body pain and stiffness that has occurred from sleeping with the leg injury. Dr. Hartell explains, "Your body is connected, and when you favor the injured leg, you often put more stress on the opposite leg and the upper body. The adjustments will help align your spine and help to balance your posture while you rely on the crutches for support." Jacob feels a bit less pain and more movement each day. He hopes to be back riding his bicycle soon.

CRITICAL THINKING QUESTIONS

1. What is the difference between active-assisted and active-resisted exercises? ______________________
2. What does ROM refer to? ______________________
3. Why is ice applied after PT? ______________________
4. What type of surgeon performs corrective procedures for bone fractures? ______________________
5. What would be some signs of infection at the surgical site? ______________________
6. Jacob complains of muscle pain. What is the medical term? ______________________
7. Why does Jacob's neck hurt? ______________________
8. The clavicle fracture is described as nondisplaced, which means what? ______________________
9. Which two leg bones did Jacob fracture? ______________________
10. Which of the bones is weight bearing? ______________________
11. The leg fracture is at the distal end, which means what? ______________________
12. What does ORIF mean? ______________________
13. What was applied during surgery to stabilize Jacob's leg? ______________________
14. What medication was Jacob given in the emergency department? ______________________
15. Dissect the term *analgesic*. What does it mean? ______________________
16. Why was the analgesic administered? ______________________

Medications for the Musculoskeletal System

Table 9-7 lists medications of the musculoskeletal system that alleviate symptoms of inflammation, pain, muscle spasms, and dystonia (poor muscle tone). Medications can also treat abnormal levels of calcium, deposits of uric acid, phantom limb pain, and autoimmune disorders. Medications are administered topically or orally, depending on their mechanism of action.

Medications Review

Using Table 9-7, complete the chart below. The first one has been done for you as an example.

Medication	Classification (mechanism)	Therapeutic Use
Methotrexate	*DMARDs*	*Rheumatoid arthritis*
1. Flexeril	______________	______________
2. Colchicine	______________	______________
3. Celebrex	______________	______________
4. Prostigmin	______________	______________
5. Fosamax	______________	______________
6. Os-Cal-D	______________	______________
7. Advil	______________	______________

TABLE 9-7 Examples of Medications for the Musculoskeletal System

Classification	Examples	Common Use/Action
Antigout drugs	Allopurinol, Zyloprim, colchicine	gout and kidney stones
Anti-inflammatory drugs (NSAIDS)	aspirin, Bufferin, Motrin, Advil, naproxen, Aleve	swelling, fever
Bisphosphonates	Reclast, Boniva, Fosamax	osteoporosis, with risk of fracture
Calcitonin	calcium carbonate, TUMS, Os-Cal-D	osteoporosis, postmenopause
Cholinesterase inhibitors	neostigmine, Prostigmin	myasthenia gravis
COX-2 inhibitors	Celebrex, celecoxib	arthritis pain and swelling
DMARDs	methotrexate, Imuran	rheumatoid arthritis
Muscle relaxants, antispasmodics	baclofen, Flexeril, Skelexin	muscle pain, stiffness, spasm

DMARD, disease-modifying antirheumatic drug.

Musculoskeletal Abbreviations

The list below provides some common abbreviations pertaining to the musculoskeletal system and their meanings.

ACL	anterior cruciate ligament
ADL	activities of daily living
AKA	above the knee amputation
AP	anteroposterior
BKA	below the knee amputation
BMD	bone mineral density
C1, C2, C3	cervical vertebra
DEXA	dual-energy x-ray absorptiometry
DIP	distal interphalangeal (joint)
DJD	degenerative joint disease
DTR	deep tendon reflexes
EMG	electromyography
ESR	erythrocyte sedimentation rate
Fx	fracture
HNP	herniated nucleus pulposus
IM	intramuscular
JRA	juvenile rheumatoid arthritis
LLE	left lower extremity
L1, L2, L3	lumbar vertebra
L5-S1	disk between L5 (lumbar vertebra and sacrum)
LUE	left upper extremity
MCP	metacarpophalangeal (joint)
MTP	metatarsophalangeal (joint)
OA	osteoarthritis
ORIF	open reduction, internal fixation
ortho	orthopedics
PIP	proximal interphalangeal (joint)
PT	physical therapy
RA	rheumatoid arthritis
RF	rheumatoid factor
RICE	rest, ice, compression, and elevation
RLE	right lower extremity
ROM	range of motion
RUE	right upper extremity
S1	sacrum
SLE	systemic lupus erythematosus
T1, T2, T3	thoracic vertebra
THA	total hip arthroplasty
THR	total hip replacement
TKR	total knee replacement
TMJ	temporomandibular joint

Abbreviations Review

Choose the correct definition for the abbreviation:

1. ORIF
   a. Open reduced internal fracture
   b. Open reduction, internal fixation
   c. Open right internal fracture
   d. Open right internal fixation

2. TMJ
   a. Temporary mobilized joint
   b. Temporary manual joint
   c. Temporomandibular joint
   d. Temporomandibular junction

3. ROM
   a. Range of motion
   b. Range of movements
   c. Radicular osseous movements
   d. Radicular osseous motions

4. BMD
   a. Basal metabolic disease
   b. Bone metabolism disorder
   c. Bone mineral disease
   d. Bone mineral density

5. PIP
   a. Proximal intraphalangeal
   b. Proximal interphalangeal
   c. Proximal interphase
   d. Proximal interpulposus

6. DTR
   a. Dense tendon reflexes
   b. Deficient tendon reflexes
   c. Deep tendon rigidity
   d. Deep tendon reflexes

7. EMG
   a. Electrical movement graph
   b. Electromyography
   c. Electromycography
   d. Electrical muscle graph

8. ADL
   a. Active daily life
   b. Activities of daily living
   c. Absence of directed living
   d. Activities of direct living

9. SLE
   a. Systemic lupus erythematosus
   b. Suspected lupus erythematosus
   c. Systemic lupoid erythematosus
   d. Systemic lupus erythematosis

10. THR
    a. Trabecular hip replacement
    b. Transverse hip replacement
    c. Topical hip replacement
    d. Total hip replacement

11. RA
    a. Rheumatic arthritis
    b. Rheumatoid arthritis
    c. Rheumatoid arthrosis
    d. Rheumatic arthrosis

12. MTP
    a. Metatarsophalangeal
    b. Megatarsophalangeal
    c. Medium tarsophalangeal
    d. Middle tarsophalangeal

13. Fx
    a. Friction
    b. Fixation
    c. Fracture
    d. Fibrous

14. TKR
    a. Transkinetic response
    b. Total knee replacement
    c. Translateral knee replacement
    d. Transkinetic relay

15. DEXA
    a. Dual-energy x-ray absorptiometry
    b. Determined energy x-ray absorptiometry
    c. Density energy x-ray absorptiometry
    d. Degenerative energy x-ray absorptiometry

MEDICAL DOCUMENTATION

Knowledge of terms related to normal anatomy and pathological conditions enables you to understand medical documentation such as history and physical examination, operative reports, discharge summaries, laboratory reports, and x-ray reports. Apply your knowledge by answering the questions that follow the report.

Operative Report

Patient Name: Jacob W.
Date of Operation: April 17, 2023
Preoperative Diagnosis:
Left distal tibia and fibula fracture
Postoperative Diagnosis:
Left distal tibia and fibula fracture
Operation Performed:
Left distal tibia and fibula open reduction internal fixation

Surgeon: Stephen Fischer, MD
Anesthesia: General
Pathology: None
Hemostasis: Left pneumatic thigh tourniquet set at 300 mmHg
Estimated Blood Loss: Less than 15 mL
Materials: 3.5-mm cortical screws ×4, 6.0-mm cancellous screws ×1, 22-gauge surgical steel wire, 1/3 fibular plate with six holes

Identify the Anatomical Structures

Match the structures of the bone from the following list to the letters shown in Figure 9-29.

1. ______ articular cartilage
2. ______ cancellous bone
3. ______ compact bone
4. ______ diaphysis
5. ______ distal epiphysis
6. ______ epiphyseal plate
7. ______ endosteum
8. ______ medullary cavity
9. ______ periosteum
10. ______ proximal epiphysis
11. ______ red marrow
12. ______ yellow bone marrow

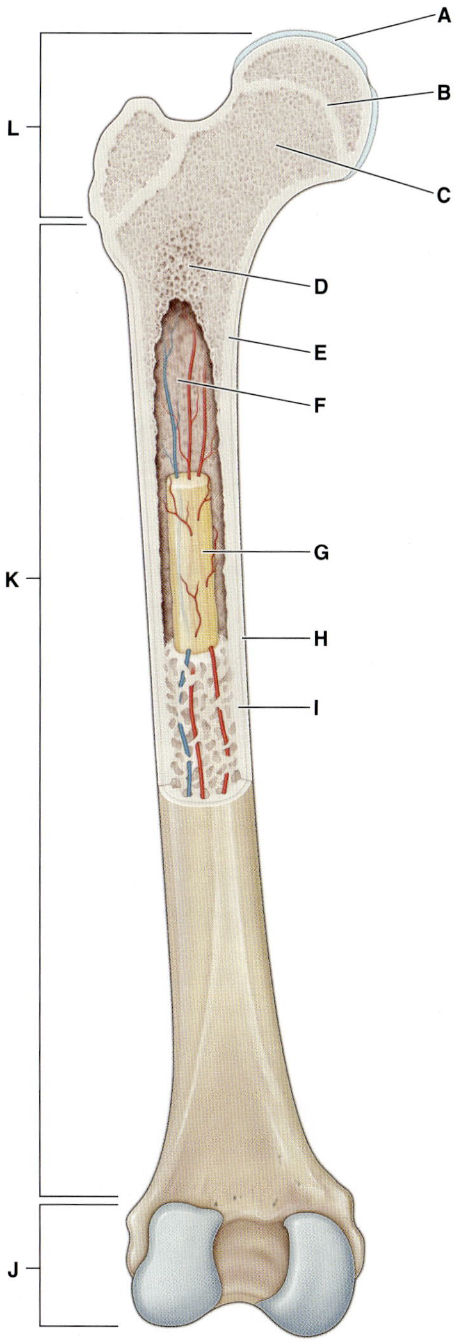

Figure 9-29 Identify the structures of the long bone.

Match the skeletal bones from the following list to the letters shown in Figure 9-30.

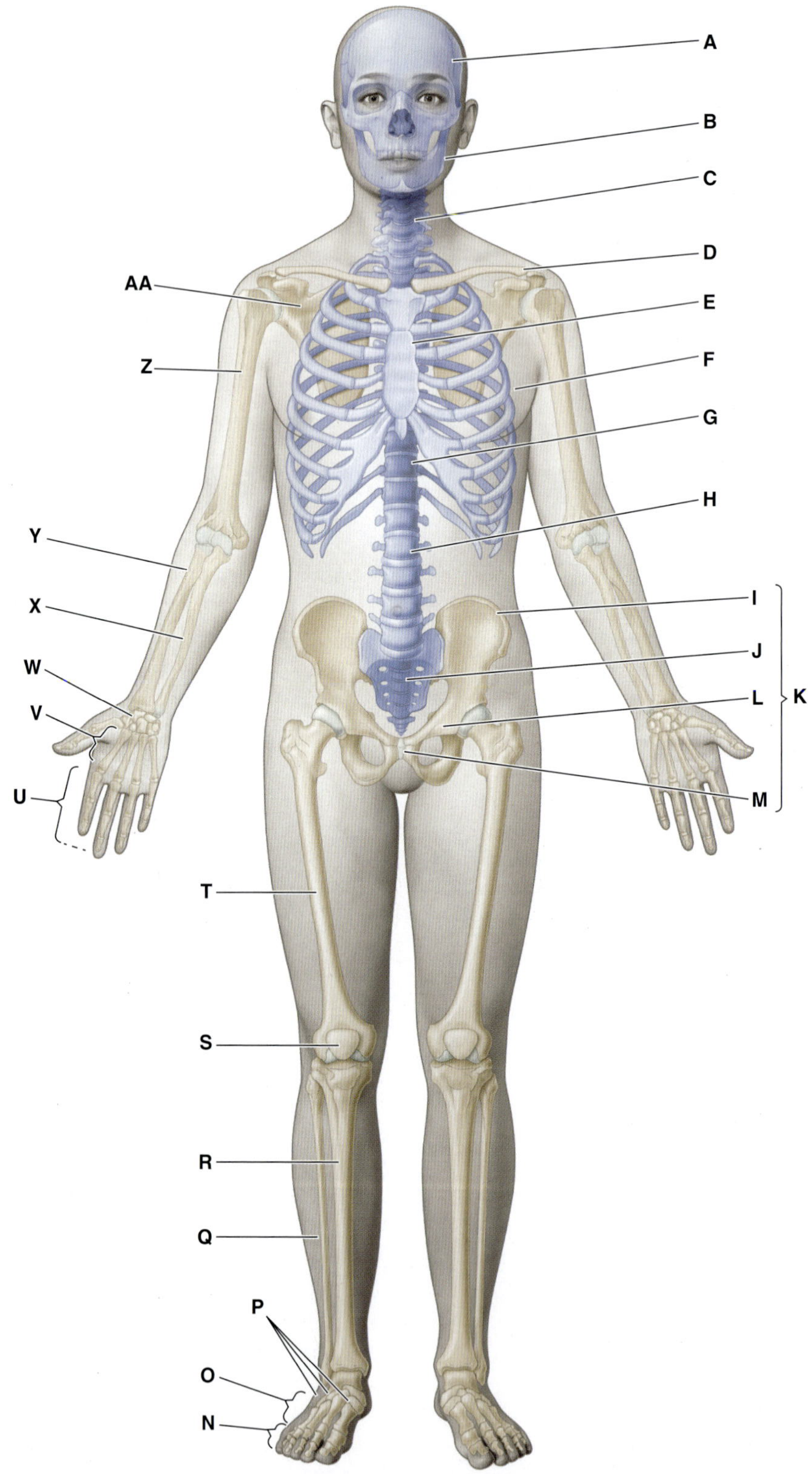

Figure 9-30 Identify the skeletal bones.

1. _______ carpals
2. _______ cervical vertebrae
3. _______ clavicle
4. _______ cranium
5. _______ femur
6. _______ fibula
7. _______ humerus
8. _______ ilium
9. _______ ischium
10. _______ lumbar vertebrae
11. _______ mandible
12. _______ metacarpals
13. _______ metatarsals
14. _______ Os coxa
15. _______ patella
16. _______, _______ phalanges
17. _______ pubis
18. _______ radius
19. _______ rib
20. _______ sacrum
21. _______ scapula
22. _______ sternum
23. _______ tarsals
24. _______ thoracic vertebrae
25. _______ tibia
26. _______ ulna

Match the three types of muscles from the following list to the letters shown in Figure 9-31.

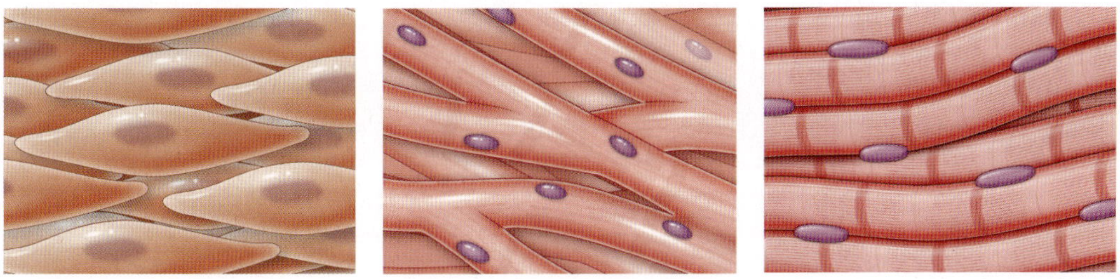

Figure 9-31 Identify the three types of muscles.

1. ______________________________
2. ______________________________
3. ______________________________

Word Building

Separate each term into its prefix (if any), combining form, and suffix. Next, translate the word parts, then give the common definition of the term. Pulmonary *has been done for you as an example.*

pulmonary

Prefix: *None* *Combining Form:* *Pulmon/o = lungs*

Suffix: *-ary = pertaining to*

Meaning: *Referring to the lungs*

1. osteoporosis

Prefix: __________ *Combining Form:* __________ *Suffix:* __________

Meaning: ______________________________

2. rhabdomyosarcoma

Prefix: ______________ *Combining Form:* ______________ *Suffix:* ______________

Meaning: ____

3. chondromalacia

Prefix: ______________ *Combining Form:* ______________ *Suffix:* ______________

Meaning: ____

4. osteolysis

Prefix: ______________ *Combining Form:* ______________ *Suffix:* ______________

Meaning: ____

5. laminectomy

Prefix: ______________ *Combining Form:* ______________ *Suffix:* ______________

Meaning: ____

6. dyskinesia

Prefix: ______________ *Combining Form:* ______________ *Suffix:* ______________

Meaning: ____

7. buccal

Prefix: ______________ *Combining Form:* ______________ *Suffix:* ______________

Meaning: ____

8. metacarpophalangeal

Prefix: ______________ *Combining Form:* ______________ *Suffix:* ______________

Meaning: ____

9. arthrodesis

Prefix: ______________ *Combining Form:* ______________ *Suffix:* ______________

Meaning: ____

10. fibromyalgia

Prefix: ______________ *Combining Form:* ______________ *Suffix:* ______________

Meaning: ____

11. osteogenesis

Prefix: ______________ *Combining Form:* ______________ *Suffix:* ______________

Meaning: ____

12. iliotibial

Prefix: ______________ *Combining Form:* ______________ *Suffix:* ______________

Meaning: ____

13. sternocleidomastoid

Prefix: ______________ *Combining Form:* ______________ *Suffix:* ______________

Meaning: ____

14. calcaneodynia

Prefix: ______________ *Combining Form:* ______________ *Suffix:* ______________

Meaning: ____

15. Endomysium

Prefix: ______________ *Combining Form:* ______________ *Suffix:* ______________

Meaning: ____

16. brachiocephalic

Prefix: ______________ *Combining Form:* ______________ *Suffix:* ______________

Meaning: ____

17. orthopedics

Prefix: ______________ *Combining Form:* ______________ *Suffix:* ______________

Meaning: ____

18. ankylosing spondylitis

Prefix: ______________ *Combining Form:* ______________ *Suffix:* ______________

Meaning: ____

19. hemiparesis

Prefix: ______________ *Combining Form:* ______________ *Suffix:* ______________

Meaning: ____

20. dystonia

Prefix: ______________ *Combining Form:* ______________ *Suffix:* ______________

Meaning: ____

21. hypertrophy

Prefix: ______________ *Combining Form:* ______________ *Suffix:* ______________

Meaning: ____

22. articular

Prefix: ______________ *Combining Form:* ______________ *Suffix:* ______________

Meaning: ____

23. paraplegia

Prefix: ______________ *Combining Form:* ______________ *Suffix:* ______________

Meaning: ____

24. arthroscopy

Prefix: ______________ *Combining Form:* ______________ *Suffix:* ______________

Meaning: ____

25. thoracolumbar

Prefix: ______________ *Combining Form:* ______________ *Suffix:* ______________

Meaning: ____

CHAPTER

10

The Urinary System

LEARNING OBJECTIVES

Upon completion of the chapter, you will be able to:

1. Identify and define the combining forms, roots, prefixes, and suffixes introduced in the chapter.
2. Spell medical terms related to the urinary system.
3. Describe the major organs of the urinary system.
4. Describe the process of urine formation and excretion.
5. Describe the hormonal regulation of water balance and how it affects urine formation.
6. Identify and discuss major pathological terms of the urinary system.
7. Identify and discuss major diagnostic and therapeutic treatments of the urinary system.
8. Identify the major categories of medications used to treat urinary pathologies.
9. Define abbreviations of the urinary system.

We start this chapter with the story of Roger, who has polycystic kidney disease. The case study introduces some of the medical terms relevant to the urinary system. Throughout the chapter, we will revisit the story of Roger to understand his diagnosis and management of his condition to improve his quality of life. This chapter will discuss the normal anatomy and physiology of the urinary system, additional pathologies of the urinary system, and treatments for these conditions. You will be able to use the word elements presented to understand unfamiliar terms and to build your medical vocabulary.

CASE STUDY

Roger is a 43-year-old man who lives in rural Alaska. As an Alaskan native, he follows the traditions of his ancestors by hunting, fishing, and living off the land. Like many people of native origin, he suffers from autosomal dominant polycystic kidney disease (PKD), a genetic disorder that causes many fluid-filled cysts to develop on the kidneys. PKD is one of the most common genetic disorders. PKD affects about 500,000 people in the United States. Roger inherited the gene that causes PKD from his mother. Lately, he has a feeling of fullness and very little appetite. He wakes up in the morning with blood in his urine (hematuria) and excruciating lower back and abdominal pain. He knows that he must get to his provider as he may have a large kidney stone or infected or burst kidney cysts. He takes medication to lower his blood pressure and follows a healthy low-sodium diet. His wife, Annuk, drives him to the hospital where he receives an ultrasound of both kidneys. As suspected, his enlarged kidneys and multiple large cysts are increased compared to the ultrasound he had previously. The emergency department provider admits Roger and calls the renal specialist to evaluate and manage his condition. The renal specialist, Dr. Nassir, orders a magnetic resonance imagining (MRI) of the kidneys. He shows Roger the MRI; the kidneys are extremely large and full of many fluid-filled cysts

Continued

CASE STUDY, continued

that are crowding the peritoneum. He tells Roger, "You aren't very hungry because the kidneys are pushing up into your abdominal cavity." The cysts and back up of fluid have caused the kidneys to struggle to work, perfusing very little urine and causing increasing pressure within the kidneys. Roger's disease has progressed, and now he needs a kidney transplant. Dr. Nassir goes on to suggest that Roger have a bilateral nephrectomy, removal of both diseased kidneys. Annuk asks, "But, Dr. Nassir, without kidneys, how will Roger filter his blood?" Dr. Nassir replies, "He won't filter any blood or produce any urine. We call this being 'anuric,' the complete inability to produce urine. To replace this vital function, Roger will have to have hemodialysis, a procedure that takes his blood out of his body, separates urine out, and returns the cleansed blood to his body. He will have to come to the dialysis clinic every 3 days for the procedure. We will place a port in Roger's arm so that the nurse doesn't have to 'stick' him each time at the dialysis clinic." Dr. Nassir goes on to say, "Roger will continue to have dialysis until a donor kidney is found." Annuk asks, "I don't have kidney disease; can I be Roger's donor?" Dr. Nassir responds "While you don't have kidney disease, you may be a carrier of the genetic defect. We need to check you for genetic kidney disease and your blood type. If you are healthy and a match, you can be Roger's donor." Roger agrees to the nephrectomy and meets with the transplant coordinator to become listed for transplant.

KEY TERMS

Afferent arteriole
Bowman's capsule
Dialysis
Calyx
Distal convoluted tubule
Efferent arteriole
External urethral sphincter
Filtration
Glomerulus
Hilum
Internal urethral sphincter
Kidneys
Loop of Henle
Micturition
Nephron
Renal artery
Renal corpuscle
Renal cortex
Renal fascia
Renal medulla
Renal pyramid
Renal sinuses
Renal tubule
Renal vein
Resorption
Secretion
Ureter
Urethra
Urinary bladder
Urinary meatus
Urine

Structures and Physiology

The urinary system, also called the renal system, works continuously to filter and cleanse the blood by removing metabolic wastes, toxins, excess ions, and water as urine. The renal system filters 150 quarts of blood each day, but only 1 to 2 quarts of urine are formed and excreted. This continuous process is vital to maintaining the purity, pH, and homeostatic balance of the blood and body fluids. The organs of the urinary system are the kidneys, ureters, urethra, and the bladder (Fig. 10-1).

The **kidneys** are two purple-brown bean-shaped organs located on either side of the 12th thoracic vertebra behind the abdominal cavity. They lie outside and behind the peritoneum; thus the positioning is also called retroperitoneal. Each kidney weighs 113 to 170 grams and is approximately 11.4 cm (4½ inches) long and 5 to 7.5 cm wide (2 to 3 inches) and 2.5 cm (1 inch) thick. Each kidney is protected by a thick cushion of adipose tissue. The fatty layer is covered by a fibrous connective tissue, the **renal fascia**, that anchors the kidney to the posterior aspect of the abdominal cavity. Internally, the kidneys are divided into the internal **renal medulla** and the outer **renal cortex**. On the medial side of the kidney, there is an indentation called the hilus or **hilum**, where the renal artery enters. The **renal artery**, like all arteries of the body, supplies the organ with oxygenated blood. As the renal artery approaches the kidney, it branches into five lobar arteries that enter the **renal sinuses**, the spaces between the **renal pyramids** in the renal medulla where the nephrons are arranged (Fig. 10-2). The lobar arteries divide again into interlobar arteries, extending between the renal pyramids. Blood originating from the renal artery flows through this series of arteries to the afferent arteriole of each glomerulus. This supplies blood to each **nephron**, the tiny filtration units of the kidneys.

ELEMENT REVIEW
retro- = behind
peritone/o = peritoneum
-eal = pertaining to

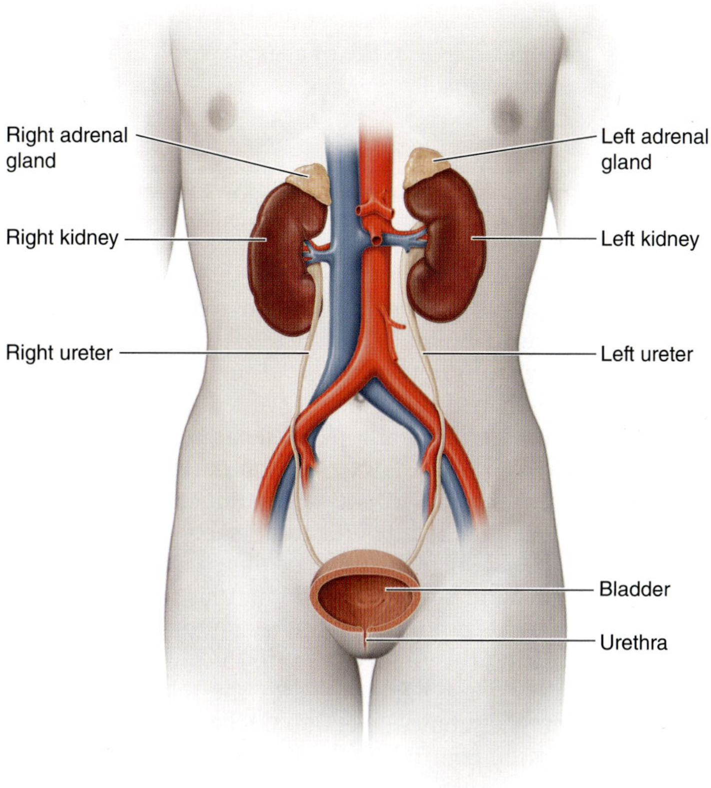

Figure 10-1 The structures of the urinary system.

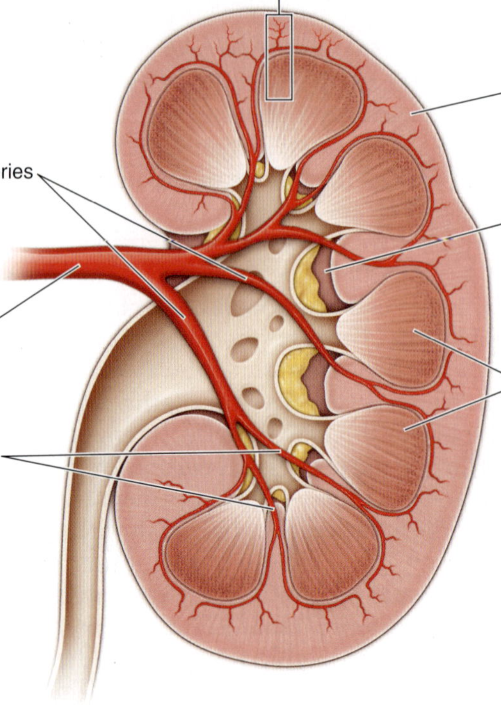

Figure 10-2 The kidney and its renal artery branches.

PHYSIOLOGY FACT

Arterial blood flows from large arteries to the smallest arteriole. The number of arteries increases as they get smaller and smaller:

One renal artery
Five lobar arteries
Hundreds of interlobar arteries
Approximately 1 to 1.3 million afferent arterioles

The nephrons form urine by the process of filtration, reabsorption, and secretion. Each nephron consists of two parts: a bulblike mass called the **renal corpuscle** and a long, twisting tube called the **renal tubule** (Fig. 10-3). The bulb of the renal corpuscle contains the **glomerulus**, a ball-shaped mass of tiny, coiled capillaries. Blood entering the glomerulus from the **afferent arteriole** is filtered to separate fluid and water-soluble waste as **urine** into the renal pelvis. The walls of the glomerulus contain large pores called fenestrations that enable fluid movement out of the lumen of the glomerulus and into the glomerular capsule. Once blood is filtered through the glomerulus, it is drained by a smaller **efferent arteriole**. The smaller diameter of the efferent arteriole causes less fluid to exit, thus creating a higher pressure in the glomerulus. This high blood pressure in the glomerulus is necessary to force fluids and solutes out of the glomerulus and into the glomerular capsule. Fluid exiting the glomerulus into the glomerular capsule flows to the **proximal convoluted tubule**. As the name suggests, the tubule twists and winds, creating a long, large surface area. The tubules extend to the **loop of Henle**, the most distal end of the nephron where resorption continues. The tiny capillaries surrounding the tubules reabsorb much of the fluid to return to the bloodstream. The capillaries are a complex network connected to the **renal vein**, which delivers filtered blood back into circulation.

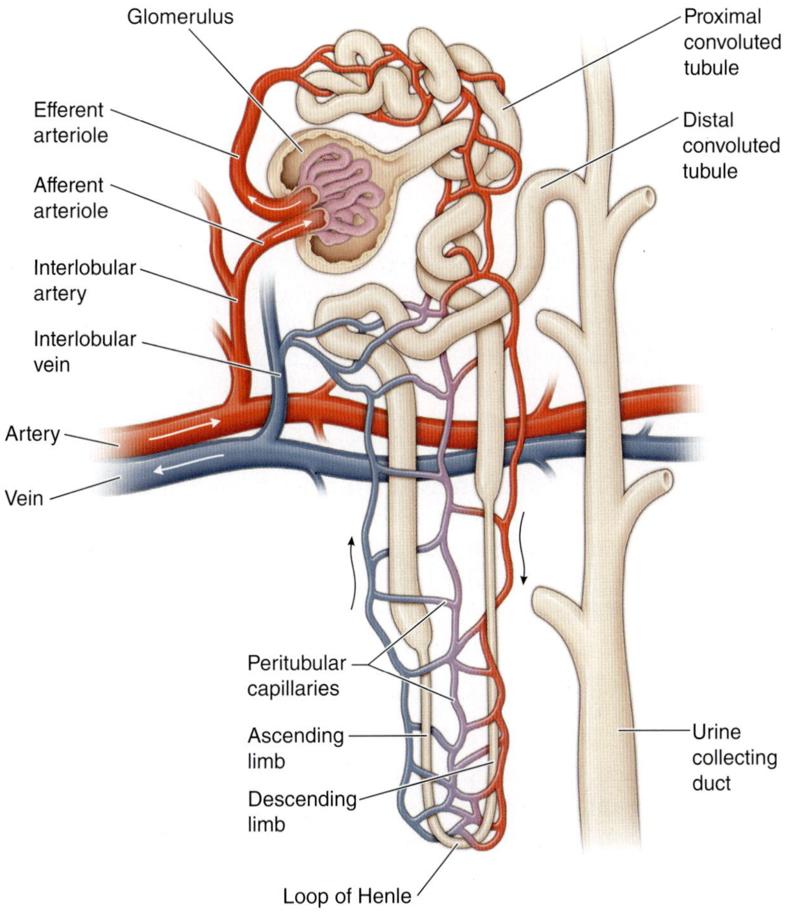

Figure 10-3 The nephron.

The remaining fluid flows from the proximal convoluted tubule to the loop of Henle to the **distal convoluted tubule** to the collecting ducts. The collecting ducts of each nephron join to form a **calyx**. The calyces (plural) hold urine and connect in the hilum to the ureter. The **ureter** of each kidney is a muscular tube from the kidney to the urinary bladder, the collecting organ for urine.

Much of the blood is reabsorbed by the network of arterioles that connect to venules that surround the tubules. The tiny arterioles and venules resorb water, sodium, glucose, amino acids, potassium, and bicarbonate ions. This reabsorption of fluids and ions is directed by adrenal hormones such as ADH (antidiuretic hormone) and aldosterone. The adrenal glands are positioned on top of the kidneys to continuously adjust fluid balance in the body.

PHYSIOLOGY FACT

The kidneys are constantly working (perfusing) to cleanse the blood by separating out waste and excess water to form urine. The ureters continuously push urine into the urinary bladder.

1. **Filtration** = a large quantity of fluid is released out of the glomerulus.
2. **Resorption** = fluid in the tubules is taken back into the bloodstream to the renal vein.
3. **Secretion** = urine flows from the ureters to the bladder to the urethra to the outside of the body.

EPONYM FACT

The glomerular capsule is also called **Bowman's capsule** for Sir William Bowman (1816 to 1892) an English surgeon and anatomist who used a microscope to study various human organs. He is most famous for his work identifying the tiny capsule carrying fluid from the kidney to the urinary system.

The ureters are paired tubular organs that transport urine from the kidneys to the urinary bladder. They originate at the renal pelvis of each kidney, extending inferior to each side of the vertebral column, then curving medially to the urinary bladder. The inner walls of the ureters contain a mucous membrane to protect the organ from the urine that passes through it. The middle layer of the ureters is muscular, and coordinated contractions force the urine downward to the urinary bladder. The outermost layer is a tough fibrous material that protects the organ.

The **urinary bladder** is a hollow muscular organ that functions as a storage area for urine (Fig. 10-4). It is located posterior to the public symphysis and thus is protected by the pelvis. The upper, rounded edge, the fundus, connects to the lower edge, where it unites with the **urethra**, the muscular tube that enables urine to flow out of the body. The urinary bladder walls are elastic, forming wrinkles when it is empty and stretches out when full. The average adult bladder can hold approximately 500 mL of urine. The interior of the bladder contains openings at the lateral edges of the fundus for the two ureters and a single opening at the bladder neck for the urethra. The innermost layer of the bladder contains a mucous membrane that protects the organ from the harmful effects of urine exposure. The bladder walls also consist of longitudinal and circular muscle that enable the intentional release of urine. At the junction of the bladder and the urethra, there is a smooth muscle called the **internal urethral sphincter**. It is an involuntary sphincter that keeps urine in the bladder. The urethra extends downward from the bladder to the floor of the pelvic cavity where the **external urethral sphincter** is located. The external urethral sphincter is composed of voluntary skeletal muscle and enables control of excretion of urine.

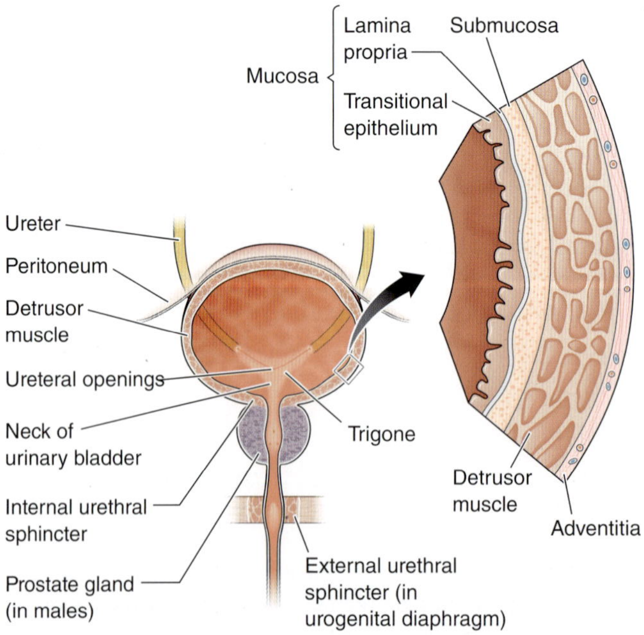

Figure 10-4 The urinary bladder.

PHYSIOLOGY FACT

Positional terms: The kidneys are lateral to the spine. The spine is medial to the kidneys.

The length of the female urethra is approximately 3 to 4 cm (1.5 in.) and is 20 cm (8 in.) in males. The urethra in both females and males opens at the external urethral orifice, also called the **urinary meatus**. **Micturition**, the act of emptying the urinary bladder, is also called urination or voiding the bladder. A person gets the urge to void the bladder as the volume of urine increases and activates stretch receptors in the walls of the bladder. A sensory signal is sent to the spinal cord, and a responding motor signal is sent from the spinal cord to the bladder via a reflex arc. The internal urethral sphincter muscle relaxes and bladder muscles contract to push urine out of the body. If voiding the bladder is not appropriate, skeletal muscles can be consciously controlled to prevent urination until an appropriate time.

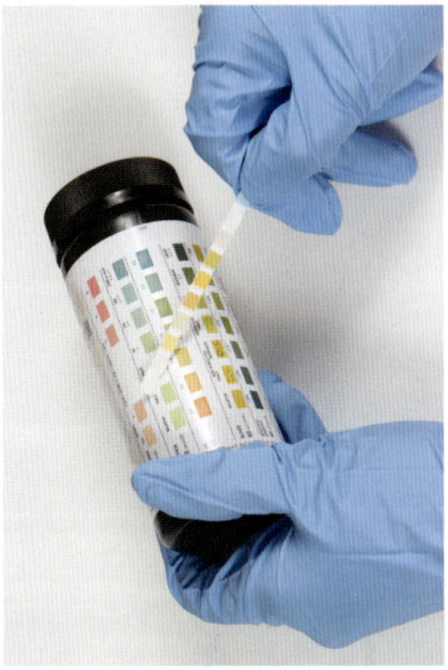

Figure 10-5 The urinalysis test.

Characteristics of Urine

The examination of the composition of urine is an important diagnostic test that can provide information pertinent to the urinary system as well as the health and function of other body systems. A routine urinalysis procedure is a component of both adult and pediatric wellness visits. A random sample of urine is examined for the presence of abnormalities and quantities of normal components of urine. Abnormalities of urine can indicate a variety of pathologies (Table 10-1). Characteristics of urine are observed by visual examination and chemical examination using a reagent strip (Fig. 10-5).

TABLE 10-1 Characteristics of a Urinalysis Test

Parameter	Normal value range	Abnormalities
Color	Pale yellow to deep gold	Dark urine may indicate dehydration. Foods can change urine color; beets turn urine red. Blood in urine (hematuria) can appear red. Excess B-complex vitamins turn urine lemon yellow.
Clarity	Normal urine is clear.	Cloudy (turbid) urine may indicate UTI: pus (pyuria), bacteria (bacteriuria).
Odor	Normal urine has a strong but agreeable odor.	Putrid odor can indicate infection. Fruity odor may indicate diabetes, starvation, or dehydration.
Specific gravity	Normal range = 1.003 to 1.030. It is the amount of solids in solution (pure water = 1.000).	Low specific gravity is found in kidney disease. The urine is very diluted as water is not resorbed in the nephrons. High specific gravity can indicate diabetes mellitus as sugar is present. High specific gravity can indicate dehydration.
pH	Normal range = 4.5 to 8.0	High pH (alkaline) may indicate UTI.
Protein	Normal urine may have trace amounts of protein.	Albumin found in urine (albuminuria) indicates renal disease (the glomerular membrane should filter albumin and other proteins out of urine).
Glucose	Normal urine does not contain glucose.	Glucose in urine can arise from a high-carbohydrate diet, pregnancy, emotional stress. High levels of glucose (glycosuria) indicate diabetes mellitus as renal tubules are unable to resorb sugar from blood with high sugar levels (hyperglycemia).
Ketones	Normal urine does not contain ketone bodies.	Ketones in urine (ketonuria) result from the breakdown of fats for energy and is seen in a ketogenic diet (very low or no carbohydrate), starvation, dehydration, or ingestion of excessive amounts of aspirin.

*Acidic urine inhibits bacterial growth.

Structures and Physiology Practice

Match the Terms

Match the terms to their descriptions.

afferent arteriole	internal urethral sphincter	renal pyramid
Bowman's capsule	kidneys	renal sinuses
calyx	loop of Henle	renal tubule
dialysis	meatus	renal vein
efferent arteriole	micturition	resorption
external urethral sphincter	nephron	specific gravity
filtration	renal artery	ureters
glomerulus	renal cortex	urethra
hilum	renal fascia	urinary bladder
	renal medulla	urinary sphincter
		urine

1. The tube that connects the urinary bladder to the outside of the body ________________
2. The area of the kidney where the renal artery and renal vein enter ________________
3. The amount of solids in solution of urine ________________
4. The process of voiding urine from the body ________________
5. The internal part of the kidneys ________________
6. The external portion of the kidneys ________________
7. The spaces between the nephrons ________________
8. The tubes that carry urine from the kidney to the bladder ________________
9. The microscopic filtration units of the kidneys ________________
10. The fluid released from the cleansing and filtering of blood ________________
11. Another name for glomerular capsule ________________
12. Blood enters the glomerulus from the ________________
13. The small arteriole that raises blood pressure in the glomerulus ________________

14. The process of a large amount of fluid leaving the glomerulus going into the glomerular capsule ______________________

15. The outer portion of the kidney ______________________

16. The holding reservoir for urine ______________________

17. The process of fluid that has been filtrated out of the glomerulus reentering blood supply ______________________

18. Arterioles that deliver blood to be filtered in Bowman's capsule ______________________

19. Fluid flows from the proximal convoluted tubule to the ______________________

20. The structure composed of voluntary skeletal muscle that enables control of excretion of urine ______________________

Structures and Physiology Word-Building Practice

1. Nouns and Adjectives

Complete the chart of nouns and their adjective forms.

1. ______________________ hilar
2. urethra ______________________
3. ______________________ glomerular
4. arteriole ______________________
5. ______________________ lobar

2. Singular and Plural Forms

Complete the chart of singular and plural forms.

1. hilum ______________________
2. nephron ______________________
3. venule ______________________
4. ______________________ arterioles
5. calyx ______________________

Word Building With Combining, Prefix, and Suffix Forms

The following word roots, prefixes, and suffixes are commonly used in medical terms for the anatomy and pathology of the integumentary system. Combining vowels for word roots are included. Memorizing these elements will help you understand new terms that you may encounter as a medical assistant, nurse, or as another health-care professional.

The lists contain examples of terms that use the word elements as well as a pronunciation guide. Be sure to use the pronunciation guide so that you can learn to say the terms correctly.

Medical Language Lab

The Medical Language Lab at medicallanguagelab.com provides audio files to help you practice your pronunciations.

Combining Form	Meaning	Example (Pronunciation)	Definition
azot/o	nitrogenous waste	azotemia (ā-zō-TĒ-mē-ă)	accumulation of nitrogenous waste in the blood
bacteri/o	bacteria	bacterial (bak-TĒR-ē-al)	pertaining to bacteria
cyst/o	bladder, sac	cystitis (sĭs-TĪ-tĭs)	inflammation of the urinary bladder
glomerul/o	glomerulus	glomerular (glō-MER-yŭ-lăr)	pertaining to the glomerulus
keton/o	ketones	ketonuria (kēt-ō-NŪR-rē-ă)	presence of ketones in the urine
lith/o	stone	lithiasis (lĭ THĪ-ă-sĭs)	condition of a stone
nephr/o	kidney	nephritis (nĕ-FRĪ-tĭs)	inflammation of the kidneys
meat/o	meatus	meatotomy (mē-ă-TOT-ō-mē)	incision into the urinary meatus
noct/o	night	nocturia (nŏk-TŪ-rē-ă)	urinating at night
olig/o	scant, diminished amount	oliguria (ōl-ĭg-Ū-rē-ă)	diminished amount of urine excretion
py/o	pus	pyuria (pī-ŪR-ē-ă)	pus in the urine
pyel/o	renal pelvis	pyelonephritis (pī-ĕ-lō-nĕ-FRĪT-ĭs)	inflammation of the renal pelvis and kidney
ren/o	kidney	renal (RĒ-năl)	pertaining to the kidney
ur/o	urine	urology (ū-RŎL-ō-jē)	the study of urine
ureter/o	ureter	ureterocele (ū-RĒ-tĕr-ō-sēl)	herniation of the ureter

Combining Form	Meaning	Example (Pronunciation)	Definition
urethr/o	urethra	urethroscope (ū-RĒ-thrŏ-scōp)	instrument used to view the urethra
urin/o	urine	urinalysis (ū-rĭ-NĂL-ĭ-sĭs)	analysis of urine

ā = say, ă = sofa, ē = meet, ĕ = met, ī = eye, ĭ = in, ō = oh, ŏ = dog, ū = you, ŭ = up, oo = food

Prefix	Meaning	Example (Pronunciation)	Definition
an-	without	anuria (ă-NOOR-ē-ă)	absence of urine formation
anti-	against	antidiuretic (ant-i-dī-yŭ-RET-ik)	medication to decrease urination
dys-	painful, labored	dysuria (dis-ŪR-ē-ă)	difficulty or painful urination
extra-	outside	extracorporeal (eks-tră-kor-POR-ē-ăl)	pertaining to outside the body
poly-	many	polycystic (pŏl-ē-SĬS-tĭk)	pertaining to many cysts
retr/o-	behind	retroperitoneal (re-trō-pĕr-ĭt-ōn-Ē-ăl)	pertaining to behind the peritoneum

ā = say, ă = sofa, ē = meet, ĕ = met, ī = eye, ĭ = in, ō = oh, ŏ = dog, ū = you, ŭ = up, oo = food

Suffix	Meaning	Example (Pronunciation)	Definition
-al	pertaining to	renal (RĒ-năl)	pertaining to the kidneys
-algia	pain	cystalgia (sĭs-TĂL-jē-ă)	urinary bladder pain
-ary	pertaining to	urinary (Ū-rĭ-nār-ē)	pertaining to urine
-lith	stone	nephrolith (nĕf-RŌ-lĭth)	stone in the kidney
-megaly	enlargement	nephromegaly (nĕ-frŏ-MĔG-ăl-ē)	enlargement of the kidney
-meter	instrument to measure	cystometer (sĭs-TŎM-ĕ-tĕr)	device to measure volume of urine in the bladder
-ostomy	create a new opening	cystoproctostomy (sĭs-tŏ-prŏk-TŎS-tō-mē)	surgical formation of a connection between the urinary bladder and rectum
otomy	incision into	nephrotomy (nĕf-RŎT-ō-mē)	surgical incision into the kidney
-oma	tumor	nephroma (nĕ-FRŌ-mă)	tumor of a kidney

Continued

Suffix	Meaning	Example (Pronunciation)	Definition
-osis	condition	nephrosis (nĕ-FRŌ-sĭs)	kidney condition (disease)
-pexy	surgical fixation	cystopexy (SĬS-tō-pĕk-sē)	surgical fixation of the bladder
-tripsy	breakdown, destruction	lithotripsy (LITH-ŏ-trip-sē)	breaking, crushing stones
-uria	condition of urine	dysuria (dis-ŪR-ē-ă)	condition of painful urination

ā = say, ă = sofa, ē = meet, ĕ = met, ī = eye, ĭ = in, ō = oh, ŏ = dog, ū = you, ŭ = up, oo = food

Combining Forms Practice

1. Build the Terms

*Using **only** the word parts in the lists, create medical terms for the indicated meanings.*

Prefixes	Combining Forms		Suffixes	
an-	azot/o	olig/o	-al	-ostomy
anti-	bacteri/o	py/o	-algia	-oma
dys-	cyst/o	pyel/o	-ar	-osis
extra-	glomerul/o	ren/o	-ary	-otomy
hydro-	keton/o	ur/o	-iasis	-pexy
poly-	lith/o	ureter/o	-lith	-rrhea
retro-	meat/o	urethr/o	-megaly	-tripsy
	nephr/o	urin/o	-meter	-uria
	noct/o		-mia	

1. Incision into the urinary meatus ________________
2. Surgical fixation of the bladder ________________
3. Crushing of a stone ________________
4. Stone in the urethra ________________
5. Diminished amount of urine production ________________
6. Discharge, flow of pus ________________
7. Pertaining to the glomerulus ________________
8. Presence of excessive amounts of urea in the bloodstream ________________
9. Instrument to view the interior of the bladder ________________
10. Condition of a kidney stone ________________

2. Decipher the Terms

Separate each term into its prefix (if any), combining form, and suffix. Next, translate the word parts, and then give the common definition of the term.

1. nocturia

   Prefix: ______________________ *Suffix:* ______________________

   Combining Form: ____

   Meaning: ____

2. hydronephrosis

   Prefix: ______________________ *Suffix:* ______________________

   Combining Form: ____

   Meaning: ____

3. azotemia

   Prefix: ______________________ *Suffix:* ______________________

   Combining Form: ____

   Meaning: ____

4. pyelitis

   Prefix: ______________________ *Suffix:* ______________________

   Combining Form: ____

   Meaning: ____

5. urethrostenosis

   Prefix: ______________________ *Suffix:* ______________________

   Combining Form: ____

   Meaning: ____

6. hematuria

   Prefix: ______________________ *Suffix:* ______________________

   Combining Form: ____

   Meaning: ____

7. meatotomy

Prefix: ______________________ *Suffix:* ______________________

Combining Form: ______________________

Meaning: ______________________

8. polydipsia

Prefix: ______________________ *Suffix:* ______________________

Combining Form: ______________________

Meaning: ______________________

9. nephromegaly

Prefix: ______________________ *Suffix:* ______________________

Combining Form: ______________________

Meaning: ______________________

10. urologist

Prefix: ______________________ *Suffix:* ______________________

Combining Form: ______________________

Meaning: ______________________

mll Medical Language Lab

Visit the Medical Language Lab at the website medicallanguagelab.com. Use it to enhance your word-building skills for the word parts covered in this chapter.

CASE STUDY, continued

Dr. Nassir performs Roger's bilateral native nephrectomy, the removal of both of his diseased kidneys. He does well in surgery and is brought to the recovery room. Roger wakes later that day and is transferred to the nephrology unit. Roger's wife, Annuk, has blood testing and a physical examination. Dr. Nassir consults with the couple and says, "I have good news. Annuk, you are healthy, you don't have high blood pressure or diabetes, and you are a blood- and tissue-type match for Roger. You can donate your kidney to Roger. We perform the physical examination and blood work on the donor to make sure that both the donor and recipient can enjoy good health with one healthy kidney." Roger is a little choked up as he says, "Thank you Dr. Nassir, and thank you Annuk; you are saving my life." Annuk replies, "I know you would do the same for me; I love you Roger." Dr. Nassir says, "Now that you do not have kidneys, we will start you on dialysis here in the hospital. We need to make sure that your incision is healing and that your blood pressure doesn't drop too low from blood loss during surgery. We also monitor your bowel function as the trauma to the abdomen can impair function. The nephrectomy is harder on your body than is the transplant." Roger asks, "When will I be ready for the

CASE STUDY, continued

transplant?" Dr. Nassir replies, "We will keep you in the hospital for five days to monitor your response to dialysis and then discharge you to outpatient dialysis. I want you to be on dialysis for 20 cycles, which takes 60 days, with a dialysis every third day. If you are doing well, have good blood counts and blood pressure, we will schedule you and Annuk to be admitted to the hospital for the transplant.

Urinary System Diseases and Disorders

Diseases and disorders of the urinary system can include obstruction (blockages), stone formation, infections, and cancerous or benign tumors. These conditions can occur in the kidneys, ureters, bladder, or the urethra.

Common Signs and Symptoms

Table 10-2 is a list of common complaints, objective signs, and subjective symptoms that patients with urinary system diseases and disorders may describe to their health-care providers and support staff.

Pathological Conditions of the Urinary System

Bladder cancer: The growth of malignant cells of the bladder. The most common form is urothelial carcinoma, cancer of the innermost tissue layer of the bladder. These cells stretch when the bladder is full, shrink when the bladder is empty, and give the signal that urine needs to be voided. Bladder cancer is staged from 1 to 4 as it spreads from the inner lining of the bladder to the muscular layer and finally to adjacent organs of the abdomen. Signs and symptoms of bladder cancer include blood in the urine (hematuria), frequency, urgency, and lower back pain. Factors that increase risk of bladder cancer include smoking and exposure to arsenic and other industrial chemicals used in manufacturing of dyes, rubber,

TABLE 10-2 Examples of Signs and Symptoms

Sign	Symptom
Inability to perfuse urine (anuria)	Urgency
Diminished amount of urine production (oliguria)	Frequency
Urination at night (nocturia)	Kidney pain
Stress incontinence, coughing, laughing	Excessive thirst (polydipsia)
Involuntary release of urine (enuresis)	
Abnormalities of the composition of urine Blood in the urine (hematuria) Protein in the urine (proteinuria) White blood cells in urine Pus (pyuria) Ketones in urine (ketonuria) Bacteria in urine (bacteriuria) Sugar in the urine (glucosuria)	

textiles, and paint. Males suffer from bladder cancer more frequently than females. Less common forms of bladder cancer are squamous cell carcinoma that starts in the bladder lining because of irritation or inflammation; adenocarcinoma, a cancer that starts in the glandular cells; small cell carcinoma that starts in the neuroendocrine cells; and sarcoma, a cancer that starts in the fat or muscle layer of the bladder. Diagnosis is obtained with cystoscopy, in which a transurethral lighted scope is inserted into the bladder in order to view changes to cells of the bladder. During the cystoscopy, the provider may take a biopsy of bladder tissue for microscopic analysis to confirm the diagnosis. CT scan with contrast dye is also used to visualize the structures of the urinary tract. MRI and positron emission tomography scans can also be used to confirm cancer and to determine its spread to adjacent organs. Treatments include transurethral resection of bladder tumor to remove the tumor. For more advanced bladder cancer, a cystectomy, the removal of the bladder, may be necessary. Radial cystectomy in males includes removal of the seminal vesicle and prostate gland. In females it may include removal of the uterus, ovaries, and part of the vagina. After radical cystectomy, the surgeon will create a sphere-shaped reservoir for urine collection from the intestines. Urine may be directed to the urethra so the patient can void urine normally or to an ileal conduit to a urostomy bag for drainage. Chemotherapy, radiation, and immunotherapy may be required after surgery.

Bladder neck obstruction: The inability of the bladder to pass urine into the urethra. It can be caused by prostatic hypertrophy in males, drug therapy, or urethral injury.

Cystitis: Characterized by frequency and urgency of urination. Hematuria and a burning sensation are also observed. It may be caused by a bacterial infection, kidney stone, or a tumor. Diagnosis is confirmed by patient history and urinalysis, which will show bacteria and/or pus. Treatment for cystitis includes oral antibiotics, increased fluid intake, and rest.

Cystocele: Herniation of the urinary bladder that protrudes into the vagina. It occurs primarily in women as a result of weakened muscles from surgical or obstetrical trauma.

End-stage renal disease (renal failure): The progressive development of decreasing kidney function occurring over a period of years. As the kidney function declines, metabolic, fluid, and electrolyte balance fail. Uremia occurs when the waste products of metabolism, such as urea and creatinine, are not filtered out of the blood. The accumulation of these end products of protein metabolism in the blood is called *azotemia*. The most common causes of end-stage renal disease (ESRD) are hypertension and diabetes. Signs and symptoms of ESRD include nausea, vomiting, anorexia, hiccups, and numbness and burning sensations in the legs and feet. Numbness is most pronounced at night. Anemia is caused by a suppression of erythropoietin of the nonfunctioning kidneys. The patient may also suffer from pruritis (itchy skin), polyuria, weight loss, loss of energy, paleness, and mental confusion. Treatment consists of controlling or relieving symptoms to prevent further complications. Antihypertensive medications and a low-protein, low-sodium, and low-potassium diet are advised. Epogen is injected to stimulate red blood cell production. As ESRD progresses, the patient must have dialysis to replace kidney function while awaiting a transplant. Kidney transplantation will allow the patient to lead a more normal life.

Glomerulonephritis: The inflammation of the glomerulus of the kidneys. The acute condition is most commonly seen in children and is characterized by proteinuria, hematuria, and decreased urine output. The urine will have a high specific gravity and will appear dark yellow. Signs and symptoms include headache, hypertension, and edema, seen especially in the face and periorbital (around the eyes) areas. It is caused by beta-hemolytic streptococcal infection, usually from the throat. Poststreptococcal glomerulonephritis typically occurs 2 to 3 weeks after a strep throat infection. Treatment with antibiotics, such as penicillin, protects against recurrence of the infection. Sodium and fluid restriction is advised to control hypertension and fluid overload until clinical signs of nephritis disappear. Ninety percent of children completely recover after antibiotics and bedrest. Thirty percent of adults with acute glomerulonephritis may progress to chronic glomerulonephritis with recurrence.

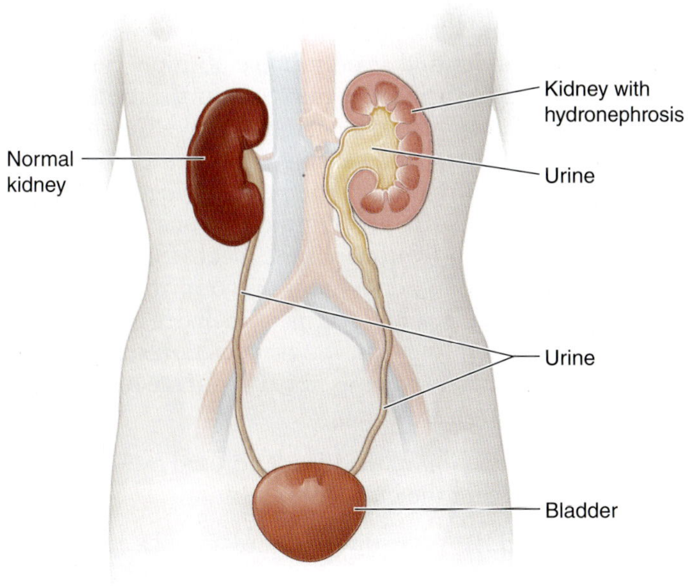

Figure 10-6 Hydronephrosis.

Hydronephrosis: A distention of the calyces of the kidneys caused by an obstruction of the ureter. As urine production in the kidney continues, the urine gets trapped at the point of obstruction. The ureter becomes distended and is called a hydroureter (Fig. 10-6). The obstruction can affect one or both ureters. Signs and symptoms include intense flank pain (unilaterally or bilaterally), nausea, vomiting, and little or no urine output (oliguria or anuria). Surgical treatment to remove the obstruction to the ureter(s) restores urine flow.

Interstitial cystitis: A chronic inflammation of the bladder epithelium and the muscles of the bladder. Ninety percent of patients with interstitial cystitis are women. The cause of the dysfunction is thought to be an abnormal immune reaction of the mucous membrane of the bladder. Signs and symptoms include urinary frequency, increased urgency, pain during intercourse (dyspareunia), and bladder pain and fullness. Diagnosis is obtained by cystoscopy, which will show a reddish mucous membrane and bleeding of the bladder mucosa. Treatment with antiallergic and anti-inflammatory medications offers some relief. Patients are also advised to avoid spicy foods and high-potassium foods. Smoking and drinking alcohol can also irritate the bladder. In severe cases of interstitial cystitis, the spinal cord is stimulated to reduce pain and urgency. Surgical correction can also include bladder dilation (the expansion of the bladder with a liquid or gas), which may reduce symptoms.

Nephrotic syndrome: Caused by damage to the glomerulus, which causes large quantities of protein to be filtered through the glomerular membrane, damaging the nephrons and resulting in severe proteinuria. The excessive loss of proteins, especially albumin, causes low blood albumin levels, which results in generalized edema. Nephrotic syndrome can be caused by glomerulonephritis or diabetes mellitus. Treatment is directed at controlling edema and reducing albuminuria.

Nephrolithiasis: The medical term for kidney stones. Stone formation occurs when there is an excess of crystal-forming substances that cannot be dissolved in urine (Fig. 10-7). High levels of urinary excretion of calcium, oxalate, uric acid, and cysteine can promote stone formation. High urinary pH, low urine volume, and a lack of stone inhibitors also contribute to stone formation. Environmental factors such as decreased fluid intake or living in a hot and dry climate can also contribute to stone formation.

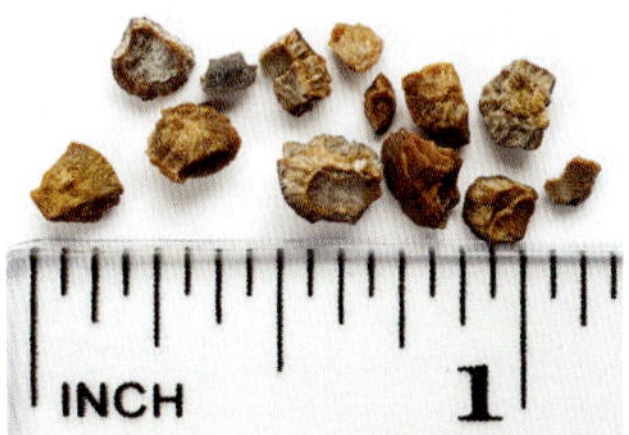

Figure 10-7 Nephrolithiasis.

Signs and symptoms include lower abdominal pain as the stones move from the kidneys to the ureters. As the stone moves down the ureter, it causes increased pressure inside the ureter, followed by spasms and distension of the ureteral walls. The patient experiences severe flank pain and an inability to find a comfortable position. Some patients experience sweating, nausea, and vomiting. As the stone moves from the ureter to the bladder, damage to the ureteral walls and bladder causes hematuria. When the stones reach the bladder, they can obstruct and irritate the bladder, causing pain. If the stones are passed through the urethra and out of the body in the urine, the pain subsides. If the obstruction cannot be resolved, or if the stones are too large or too numerous to pass, complications will ensue. The patient may suffer from hydronephrosis or obstructive pyelonephritis, which can be life-threatening. Diagnosis of kidney stones is confirmed by physical examination and imaging such as x-ray and CT scans. Treatment includes pain control with NSAIDs to reduce inflammation and ureteral spasms, intravenous fluids, and medication to reduce nausea and vomiting. Small stones may be excreted spontaneously; larger stones may be crushed with lithotripsy or be surgically removed.

Neurogenic bladder: Any dysfunction of the bladder caused by a lesion of the central nervous system or the nerves supplying the bladder.

Polycystic kidney disease (PKD): A hereditary disorder of the kidneys that causes fluid-filled cysts to develop and replace normal kidney tissue. As the disease progresses, the kidneys enlarge, causing progressive destruction of the nephrons. Presenting in those in their 30s and 40s, signs and symptoms include loss of appetite, a feeling of abdominal fullness, and flank pain. Some patients report a feeling of heaviness in the kidney region. Pain varies from dull and achy to sharp, stabbing pain. Hematuria is seen in approximately 50% of patients with polycystic kidneys. As the disease progresses, renal function decreases, which leads to kidney failure. Treatment is directed at preventing urinary tract infections (UTIs) and controlling blood pressure as secondary hypertension is common. Eventually the patients' native kidneys must be removed and the patient listed for transplant. Hemodialysis after native nephrectomy is performed until a donor is available and a kidney transplant can be performed.

Pyelonephritis: An acute bacterial infection of the renal pelvis of the kidney. It is one of the more common diseases of the kidney and is caused by an ascending UTI. The infection starts in the bladder and travels up the ureters to the renal pelvis. Acute pyelonephritis often occurs after bacterial contamination from a surgical procedure such as a cystoscopy or catheterization. Signs and symptoms include headache, fever, chills, nausea, flank pain on the affected side, and muscle pain. The urine may appear cloudy with white blood cells and have a foul-smelling odor. Treatment includes antibiotics and rest.

Renal calculi: Term for nephrolithiasis (see above).

Renal cell carcinoma: A malignant tumor of the kidney occurring in adulthood. Most patients are asymptomatic until the latter stages of the disease when painless hematuria is observed. Additional signs and symptoms include flank pain on the affected side, a palpable mass on the kidney, and intermittent fever. Treatment is surgical removal of the tumor with subsequent radiation and/or chemotherapy.

Urinary retention: The feeling of fullness of the bladder with an inability to empty the bladder. It is more common in older men and can be caused by hyperplasia of the prostate. It can also be caused by UTIs, tumors or masses, or stones that obstruct the ureter or urethra. Some medications can cause urinary retention such as NSAIDs, muscle relaxants, medications for urinary incontinence, pseudoephedrine, some antidepressants, medications for Parkinson's disease, some antipsychotics, amphetamines, or opioids. Nerve damage can also cause urinary retention as a complication of multiple sclerosis, diabetes, strokes, and brain or spinal cord injury. Treatment is directed at the cause of urinary retention, such as changing medication or surgical removal of obstructions.

Urinary tract infection (UTI): An infection of any portion of the urinary system, but most often affects the lower urinary tract: the urethra and the bladder. Signs and symptoms include strong urgency to urinate, a burning sensation while urinating, a decreased quantity of urine, cloudy or dark red urine with a strong smell. UTIs typically occur when bacteria enter the urinary tract through the urethra and migrate up toward the bladder. Since the urethra of females is shorter than males, the bacteria reach the bladder in females more often, thus accounting for more female infections. Women may feel pelvic pain, especially around the pelvic bone. *Escherichia coli* (*E. coli*) is a bacteria found in the gastrointestinal tract. Contamination of the urethra from its proximity to the anus can cause bacteria to enter the urinary tract. Infections can also be caused by sexually transmitted infections such as herpes, gonorrhea, chlamydia, and mycoplasma. Treatment with antibiotics and attention to hygiene is advised.

Uremia: The buildup of toxins in the blood caused by kidney failure. It is often a sign of ESRD. Treatments include medication, dialysis, and kidney transplantation. If left untreated, uremia is fatal.

Vesicoureteral reflux: The abnormal backflow of urine from the bladder to the ureters. It may be due to a congenital defect, a UTI, or an obstruction of the bladder outlet. The reflux of urine may cause a bacterial infection in the ureters and kidneys as the hydrostatic pressure increases. Signs and symptoms include flank pain, recurrent UTIs, frequency, urgency, pyuria, and hematuria. Treatment is directed at the underlying cause of the reflux.

Wilms' tumor: A malignant tumor of the kidney occurring most often in childhood. Signs and symptoms include a palpable mass in the abdomen and fever. The child may have abdominal pain, anorexia, nausea, vomiting, and weight loss. Diagnosis is confirmed by imaging, and treatment consists of surgical removal of the tumor followed by radiation and chemotherapy. The cure rate for this form of cancer is high if treated before metastasis to other organs.

Pathology Word-Building Practice

1. Prefixes

Choose from the list of prefixes to build a term for the definitions below.

an-	hydro-	mal-
anti-	hypo-	poly-
dys-	hyper-	retro-
extra-	inter-	semi-

1. An obstruction of the ureter causing fluid backup into the kidneys ____________________
2. The term for many renal cysts ____________________
3. The term that means outside of the body ____________________
4. The hormone that prevents excess water loss ____________________
5. Meaning behind peritoneum ____________________
6. Difficulty urinating ____________________
7. State of complete lack of perfusing urine ____________________

8. Chronic inflammation of the bladder epithelium ______________________

9. Distention of the ureter from fluid backup ______________________

10. Excessive secretion and discharge of urine ______________________

2. Suffixes

Choose from the list of suffixes to build a term for the definitions below.

-al	-megaly	-otomy
-algia	-meter	-pexy
-ary	-oma	-rrhea
-cele	-osis	-tripsy
-itis	-ostomy	-uria

1. Pertaining to the kidney ______________________

2. Enlargement of the kidney ______________________

3. Surgical fixation of a kidney ______________________

4. Pain in the ureter ______________________

5. Hernia of the urinary bladder ______________________

6. Tumor of a kidney ______________________

7. Crushing of a stone ______________________

8. Device for estimating the capacity of the bladder ______________________

9. Formation of an artificial fistula into the renal pelvis ______________________

10. Sugar in the urine ______________________

Urinary System Diagnostic Procedures

Blood urea nitrogen: Blood test performed to determine the amount of urea and nitrogen present in blood. These waste products should be excreted in urine. For this reason, elevated blood levels can indicate kidney malfunction.

Catheterization (urinary): The introduction of a flexible, hollow tube into the urethra up into the urinary bladder for the purpose of removing urine. It can be used diagnostically to collect a sterile specimen of urine or to instill a contrast medium for x-ray examination. It can be used therapeutically to provide relief of urinary retention or to completely empty the bladder before surgery.

Creatinine clearance test: Diagnostic test measuring the filtration rate of creatinine, a waste product of muscle metabolism that should normally be removed by the kidneys.

A 24-hour specimen of urine is collected, and a sample of blood is drawn in the same 24-hour period. If there is an increase in serum creatinine, it is indicative of impaired glomerular filtration.

Cystometrography: Examination of the muscle tone of the bladder. The patient is asked to empty the bladder, and a catheter is inserted through the urethra and into the urinary bladder. The amount of residual urine after voluntary voiding is measured. Saline solution is then instilled into the bladder at a constant rate. The patient is asked to report when they feel the urge to urinate, when the bladder feels completely full, and lastly when it is no longer possible to suppress the urge to void. The cystometer is used to measure the pressure the bladder musculature exerts at intervals of the instillation of 50 mL of fluid.

Cystoscopy: The process of viewing the interior of the urinary bladder with a cystoscope. The cystoscope is a hollow metal or flexible tube introduced through the urinary meatus into the bladder. A light source and magnifying lens enable visualization of the interior of the bladder. The bladder can be inspected for inflammation, tumors, renal calculi, and structural abnormalities. Tissue biopsies can also be obtained during the procedure.

Estimated glomerular filtration rate (eGFR): A fasting blood test that measures the amount of creatinine in the blood. Creatine is a chemical used to provide energy to muscles. As creatine is used by muscles, creatinine is released into the bloodstream. Healthy kidneys filter this toxin out of the blood and into the urine. Elevated creatinine is expressed as a low GFR and is indicative of kidney disease. Chronic kidney disease is diagnosed when eGFR is lower than 60 for 3 months. The five stages of chronic kidney disease can be correlated to the eGFR values:

Stage 1 (eGFR of 90 or higher) is indicative of mild kidney damage, but the kidneys are filtering creatinine out into the urine.

Stage 2 (eGFR of 60 to 89) is indicative of kidney damage, but some kidney function is present. The patient may be asymptomatic.

Stage 3 (eGFR of 30 to 59) is indicative of decreased kidney function, and the patient may be experiencing symptoms such as frequent urination and muscle spasms.

Stage 4 (eGFR of 15 to 29) is indicative of poor kidney function, and moderate to severe kidney damage is present.

Stage 5 (eGFR below 15) is indicative of kidney failure, and dialysis or kidney transplant is necessary.

Extracorporeal lithotripsy: Also called extracorporeal shock-wave lithotripsy. The noninvasive mechanical procedure uses sound waves to break up renal calculi, making them easier to pass through the ureters to the bladder and then to the outside of the body.

Intravenous pyelogram (IVP): A radiographic procedure to visualize the entire urinary tract, including the kidneys, ureters, bladder, and urethra. A contrast dye is administered intravenously, and x-ray films are taken as the medium is cleared from the blood by glomerular filtration in the kidneys. The picture created by the IVP is useful in diagnosing renal calculi, tumors, obstruction, and structural abnormalities such as strictures or nephrosis.

Kidneys, ureters, bladder (KUB): X-ray of the kidneys, ureters, and bladder that shows the outline of these organs. Contrast dye is not used in this procedure; thus, it is noninvasive. KUB is useful in diagnosing malformations of the kidney, soft tissue masses, and renal calculi.

Renal angiography: The x-ray examination of the renal blood vessels after administration of intravenous contrast medium. A catheter is guided up the aorta under fluoroscopy to the level of the renal arteries. A contrast dye is then injected, and a series of x-rays are obtained to visualize the renal blood vessels. The test is useful in detecting narrowing of renal vessels, vascular damage, venous clots (thrombosis), cysts, or tumors.

Renal scan: Procedure in which a radioactive isotope is administered intravenously and the radioactivity into each kidney is measured as the isotope passes through the kidneys. The procedure is used to evaluate renal function, and it provides a picture of the shape of the kidneys. The information is recorded in a graph, and the pattern of the graph is correlated with specific conditions. The isotope is completely excreted within 24 hours.

Retrograde pyelogram: Procedure in which a contrast medium is injected through a small-caliber urinary catheter into the ureters and renal pelvis. X-rays are obtained to show the collecting system of the kidneys. The test is useful in diagnosis of ureteral narrowing or obstruction and is used when IVP cannot be used to visualize the renal collecting structure. It can be used if a patient is allergic to IVP contrast dye as the dye is not absorbed through the mucous membrane by the pyelogram technique.

Ultrasonography: The use of sound waves to visualize internal body structures. The skin is lubricated with a water-soluble gel, and the transducer is placed on the skin. As the sound waves are reflected back to the transducer, they are interpreted by a computer to generate a picture. When examining the kidneys, fluid-filled cysts versus solid masses can be distinguished. Renal calculi and obstructions can be viewed. Additionally, this noninvasive procedure can be used to evaluate a transplanted kidney.

Urinalysis: A general term for the physical and chemical analysis of urine.

Urine culture (and sensitivity) (C&S): The procedure used to cultivate the growth of bacteria present in a urine sample. The procedure is used to identify the specific pathogen that is causing infection. A sample of urine is applied to a culture medium and placed in an incubator for 24 to 72 hours. The plate is then examined for growth on the culture medium. Microscopic analysis of the colony of growth is used to identify the pathogen. Upon identification of the pathogenic organism, sensitivity testing is performed. Various antibiotics are administered to the specimen to determine which medication is most effective in killing the pathogen. The procedure enables providers to treat antibiotic-resistant organisms.

24-hour urine specimen: The collection of all the urine excreted by a patient in a 24-hour period. It is useful in determining the kidney's ability to excrete and/or retain various solutes in urine. Then the concentration of these components will be compared to a blood sample taken at the end of the 24-hour period. The patient is advised to refrigerate and collect urine and store it in a sealed container to prevent contamination.

Catheterized specimen: Urine sample obtained by straight catheter inserted via the urethra and inserted into the bladder. The sample is collected in a sterile specimen container and is used for obtaining a urine culture.

Clean-catch specimen: A sample of urine collected by the patient. The patient is instructed to cleanse the external genitalia with an antiseptic wipe. The patient is then told to void a small quantity of urine into the toilet. The patient then places the sterile collecting container into the urinary stream and collects the sample. The clean-catch specimen is useful in diagnosing UTIs or can be used to obtain a sample for urine culture.

First-voided specimen: A sample of the first morning urine. The patient is instructed to collect the urine and refrigerate it until bringing it to the medical office. The specimen is useful in diagnosing pregnancy and for other tests that require analysis of concentrated urine as first morning urine is the most concentrated sample.

Random specimen: A urine sample that is collected in the physician's office and tested immediately. It is often part of a routine physical examination.

Residual urine specimen: A urine sample obtained by catheterization after the patient has voided. It is useful in diagnosing urinary blockage, enlarged prostate gland, narrowing of the urethra (urethrostenosis), or a neurogenic bladder. Residual urine volume should be less than 100 mL in patients older than 65 and less for younger patients.

ELEMENT REVIEW
urethr/o = urethra
sten/o = narrowing
-osis = condition

24-hour urine specimen: The collection of all the urine excreted by a patient in a 24-hour period. It is useful in determining the kidney's ability to excrete and/or retain various solutes in urine. The concentration of these components will be then compared to a blood sample taken at the end of the 24-hour period. The patient is advised to collect urine, refrigerate it, and store it in a sealed container to prevent contamination.

Voiding cystourethrography: X-ray visualization of the bladder and urethra while the patient is urinating. A radiopaque dye is instilled into the bladder by a catheter. The catheter is then removed, and the patient is asked to void. The x-rays are taken while the patient is urinating. The test is useful in diagnosing lesions of the urethra, strictures, reflux, and obstruction of both the urethra and bladder.

CAREER EXPLORATION: TRANSPLANT COORDINATOR

After graduating from nursing school, I worked in the medical surgical unit. The patients were very sick with a variety of illnesses. One of my patients came in with kidney failure, and the nephrologist came to the floor to consult with the patient. I became interested in kidney physiology and pathology as I cared for the patient. I applied for a nursing position in the transplant unit. The work was very challenging, and I had to learn a lot about pre- and posttransplant care, surgical complications, antirejection medications, and how to educate patients on taking care of themselves after transplant. As I learned more and more about transplants, I worked with the transplant coordinator. Our transplant coordinator left to work at another hospital and approached me to take the job. As an RN with 3 years of experience caring for transplant patients, I was ready for the new challenge of being the coordinator. I studied for and passed the American Board for Transplant Coordinator certification. As the hospital's transplant coordinator, I work closely with recipients, donors, and their families to create a seamless transplant experience. I am in constant contact with the transplant surgeons, and match donors to recipients. Once a donor has cleared the evaluations, I add them to the lists for patients hoping to receive a new kidney. I match the donor and recipient based on several factors, such as blood type, proximity, and how long the patient has been waiting. It is vital to match the donor and the recipient to increase the chances of a successful transplant. I am often "on call" to receive notice of deceased donors resulting from accidents. While it is sad that someone has died, I feel good that I can be a part of saving someone with the gift of a transplanted organ. I have recently started giving talks at our local community center discussing the importance of being an organ donor. One of our kidney transplant recipients and his wife, who was his donor, came and talked to the group. Roger and Annuk's story has prompted many people in our community to become donors.

Urinary System Therapeutic Procedures

Peritoneal dialysis: The process of mechanically filtering blood when the kidneys can no longer adequately perfuse urine. The procedure functions as the native kidney, cleansing the blood of waste products, drawing off excess fluid, and regulating body chemistry. The peritoneal membrane is the thin membrane that lines the peritoneal cavity. It is rich in tiny blood vessels, thus providing continuous blood to be filtered by the dialysate (Fig. 10-8). The procedure requires an access catheter, called a Tenckhoff peritoneal catheter, to be surgically inserted into the lower abdomen. Upon adequate placement, a dialysate solution is administered via the catheter. The infused solution of water and electrolytes will draw excess fluids and toxins out of the peritoneum. The process of infusing and draining fluid is called an *exchange cycle*. There are two types of peritoneal dialysis that can be performed at home by the patient and/or caregiver: continuous ambulatory peritoneal dialysis and continuous cycling peritoneal dialysis.

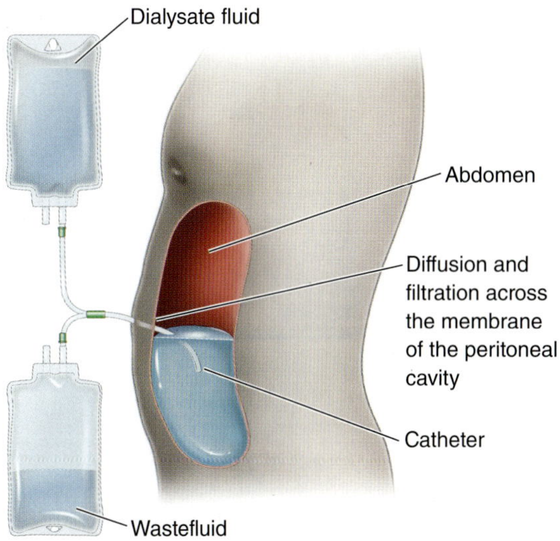

Figure 10-8 Peritoneal dialysis.

Continuous ambulatory peritoneal dialysis (CAPD) can be performed by the patient and does not require a machine. Sterile plastic tubing is used to connect the 2 L bag of sterile, warmed dialysate solution. The dialysate bag is raised above the shoulder height of the patient to enable gravity to aid flow of the solution into the abdomen. During the procedure, the dialysate solution stays in the abdomen for approximately 4 hours. The process is repeated three to five times daily, with the residual fluid from the previous exchange being drained first. The last CAPD of the day can be started at bedtime, and the dialysate is left in the abdomen overnight. Since the CAPD is repeated multiple times each day, it is an intrusive procedure that does not allow the patient to travel and limits activity.

Continuous cycling peritoneal dialysis (CCPD) uses a machine to warm the dialysate solution and cycles it in and out of the peritoneum in several timed cycles as the patient sleeps. The process takes 8 to 10 hours. Upon completion of the cycle, the patient's access tube is clamped, and the infusion tubing is removed. The dialysate solution stays in the patient's abdomen for 12 to 15 hours during the day. Before the patient goes to bed, the access catheter is connected, and the residual abdominal fluid is drained before the fresh dialysate is administered. The advantage of CCPD is that the patient is free of the procedure during the day, making activities more convenient.

The major concern of peritoneal dialysis is inflammation and infection of the peritoneum, called peritonitis. Patients and caregivers are advised to look for and report signs and symptoms of infection such as fever, nausea, redness and tenderness around the access site, weakness, loss of appetite, or a cloudy appearance of the dialysate solution as it drains from the abdomen. Peritonitis can be treated with antibiotics.

Hemodialysis: The process of removing excess fluids and toxins when the kidneys are no longer adequately cleansing the blood. The patient's blood flows out of the body and through the dialysis machine, then it is cleansed and returned to the body. Since hemodialysis will be a repeated procedure that requires blood access, an internal arteriovenous fistula is created in the forearm (Fig. 10-9). The fistula is a connection created to suture the artery and vein together so that blood can cycle continuously. The flow of arterial blood into the venous system at the point of the fistula causes the vein to become distended, providing a large vessel with adequate blood flow for the hemodialysis connection. The arteriovenous

ELEMENT REVIEW
arteri/o = artery
ven/o = vein
-ous = pertaining to

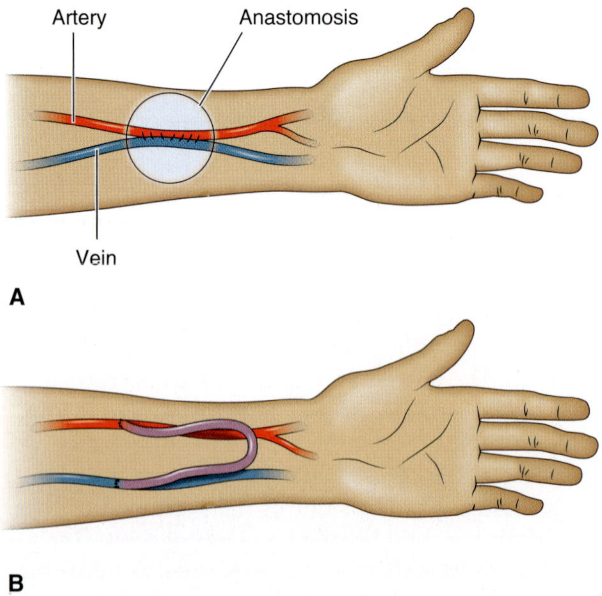

Figure 10-9 Arteriovenous fistula.

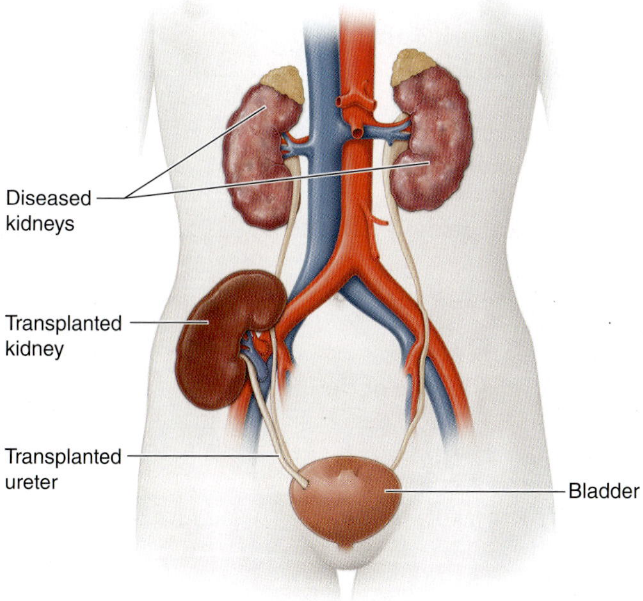

Figure 10-10 Kidney transplant.

fistula must heal for 3 to 6 weeks before it distends and is strong enough for needle insertion. Patients receive hemodialysis three times per week in a hospital or outpatient clinic. Treatment times vary from 3 to 4 hours. With adequate supervision, hemodialysis can be administered at home.

Kidney transplantation: The surgical implantation of a donated kidney to a patient with ESRD. The donor kidney may be obtained from a living donor (usually a blood relative) or a nonliving (cadaver) donor. The recipient's native kidney is not generally removed unless PKD is advanced and the native kidney is massively enlarged. The renal artery of the donor kidney is connected to the recipient's iliac artery, and the iliac vein of the donor kidney is connected to the recipient's iliac vein. As Figure 10-10 indicates, the transplanted kidney is placed in the recipient's iliac fossa and thus protected from injury by the pelvis.

Advances in tissue matching and antirejection medications have improved outcomes for transplant recipients. Survival rates for kidney recipients are 95% for 1 year and 90% for 3 to 5 years. Kidney donors are carefully screened for undiagnosed kidney disease, hypertension, and diabetes as these conditions could compromise their health after kidney donation.

Procedures and Diagnostics Review

1. X-ray examination with contrast of the bladder and urethra while the patient is urinating ____________________

2. A test used to measure urea and toxins in the bloodstream ____________________

3. A 24-hour urine diagnostic test to measure the filtration rate of waste products of muscle metabolism ____________________

4. X-ray examination of renal blood vessels ______________________

5. Use of a catheter to obtain urine after the patient has voided the bladder ______________________

6. A urine sample obtained by the patient after cleansing the external genitalia ______________________

7. The physical and chemical analysis of urine is ______________________

8. Noninvasive procedure using sound waves to break up kidney stones ______________________

9. A test to measure the muscle tone of the urinary bladder ______________________

10. A test that uses intravenous contrast dye to visualize the renal structures ______________________

CASE STUDY, completed

Roger is discharged on postoperative day 5, and he is regaining his strength. Roger and Annuk stay with friends in Anchorage to be near the dialysis clinic, where he goes three times per week for the 2-hour procedure. Annuk has a complete physical examination the day before admission. She is healthy and ready to donate her kidney. Dr. Nassir meets with the couple in their hospital room the night before the transplant surgery. Both patients are told they will be npo past midnight for surgery tomorrow morning. Dr. Nassir says, "Tomorrow is the big day. Do you have any questions?" Roger asks, "How soon will the kidney start working?" Dr. Nassir replies, "I'm glad you asked; transplants are amazing. Annuk's kidney transplanted into your body may start perfusing urine before you are out of the operating room, or a few hours later at most." Roger replies, "That is amazing! Thanks Dr. Nassir. See you early tomorrow." Roger and Annuk both do well in surgery and wake in the recovery room. Dr. Nassir comes in to see them both late in the afternoon to examine them. Roger is already perfusing urine, as the nurse notes from his catheter bag filling. Annuk is feeling well, Roger's pain is much less than after the nephrectomy, and both patients are hungry for dinner.

CRITICAL THINKING QUESTIONS

1. Roger had removal of both kidneys in a procedure called a ______________________.

2. Both Roger and Annuk are npo beginning at midnight before the surgery. What does this mean? ______________________

______________________.

3. The procedure that replaces native kidney function is called ______________________.

4. If a patient cannot make any urine, they are called ______________________.

5. In addition to cysts, Roger suffered from kidney stones, a condition called ______________________.

6. Roger's kidneys stopped working; this condition is called ______________________.

7. While Roger was waiting for his transplant, Dr. Nassir was monitoring him for low blood pressure, which is called

______________________.

CASE STUDY, completed

8. The hospital unit where kidney transplants are performed is called ______________________.

9. What type of specialist is Dr. Nassir? ______________________.

10. Annuk is the ______________ of a kidney. Roger is the ______________ of a kidney.

Medications for the Urinary System

Table 10-3 contains medications used for contraception, to promote abortion, to promote ovulation, to induce labor, or to replace hormones lost during menopause.

TABLE 10-3 Examples of Medications for the Urinary System

Classification	Examples	Common Use/Action
Urinary analgesics	phenazopyridine hydrochloride (AZO)	Urinary pain, urgency, frequency
	methenamine and sodium	
	salicylate (Cystex)	
Antibiotics	nitrofurantoin (Macrobid)	Bacterial UTI
	sulfamethoxazole (Bactrim)	
	ciprofloxacin (Cipro)	
Antispasmodics	oxybutynin (Ditropan, Urotrol)	Incontinence caused by overactive bladder
	solifenacin (VESIcare) (Detrol)	
Loop diuretics	Furosemide (Lasix)	CHF, renal insufficiency
	torsemide (Demadex)	
Osmotic diuretics	mannitol (Osmitrol)	Increased intracranial pressure
		Increased intraocular pressure
Potassium-sparing diuretics	spironolactone (Aldactone)	CHF, PCOS
	triamterene (Dyrenium)	
Thiazide diuretics	chlorothiazide (Diuril)	Hypertension, edema
	hydrochlorothiazide (HydroDIURIL)	

CHF, congestive heart failure; PCOS, polycystic ovary syndrome.

Medications Review

Using the table of medications, complete the chart below. The first one has been done for you.

Medication Name	Classification (mechanism)	Therapeutic Use (What is it used for?)
Diuril	*Thiazide diuretic*	*Hypertension, edema*
Mannitol	______________	______________
Lasix	______________	______________
Bactrim	______________	______________
VESIcare	______________	______________
Aldactone	______________	______________
Ditropan	______________	______________

Urinary System Abbreviations

The list below provides some common abbreviations for terms pertaining to the urinary system.

ADH antidiuretic hormone
AGN acute glomerulonephritis
AKI acute kidney injury
ARF acute renal failure
ATN acute tubular necrosis
BNO bladder neck obstruction
BUN blood urea nitrogen
CAPD continuous ambulatory peritoneal dialysis
Cath catheterization, catheter
CCPD continuous cycling peritoneal dialysis
CRF chronic renal failure
C&S culture and sensitivity
Cysto cystoscopy
EPO erythropoietin
ESRD end-stage renal disease
ESWL extracorporeal shock-wave lithotripsy
GFR glomerular filtration rate
HD hemodialysis
H_2O water
IVP intravenous pyelogram
KUB kidneys, ureters, bladder
pH potential hydrogen (degree of alkalinity or acidity of a fluid)
RP retrograde pyelogram
SG, sp gr specific gravity
TURP transurethral resection of the prostate
UA urinalysis
UC urine culture
UI urinary incontinence
UTI urinary tract infection
VCUG voiding cystourethrogram
VUR vesicourethral reflux

Abbreviations Review

1. UTI
   a. Urine timed input
   b. Urine-tested infection
   c. Urinary tract infection
   d. Urine tract infection

2. KUB
   a. Kidney, ureter, bladder
   b. Kidney, urethra, bladder
   c. Kidney ureter blockage
   d. Kidney urethra blockage

3. UA
   a. Urinary analysis
   b. Urine analysis
   c. Urinalysis
   d. Urinary assessment

4. ESRD
   a. Endosectioned renal disease
   b. End-stage renal disease
   c. End-stage retroperitoneal disease
   d. End-stage retro disease

5. VCUG
   a. Voiding cystourethrogram
   b. Voiding cystoureterogram
   c. Vesicle cystourethrogram
   d. Vesicle cystoureterogram

6. GFR
   a. Glomerular fractional rate
   b. Glomerular fibrotic rate
   c. Glomerulfacial rate
   d. Glomerular filtration rate

7. C&S
   a. Culture and sensitivity
   b. Culture and sedimentation
   c. Culture and systems
   d. Culture and species

8. ADH
   a. Alpha diuretic hormone
   b. Associated diuretic hormone
   c. Antidiuretic hormone
   d. Antediuretic hormone

9. ATN
   a. Antitubular necrosis
   b. Acute tubular necrosis
   c. Antitubular neck
   d. Acute tension necrosis

10. ESWL
    a. extracorporeal shock-wave lithotripsy
    b. enterocorporeal shock-wave lithotripsy
    c. extracorporeal shock-wave lithotomy
    d. enterocorporeal shock-wave lithotomy

MEDICAL DOCUMENTATION

Knowledge of terms related to normal anatomy and pathological conditions enables you to understand medical documentation such as history and physical examinations, operative reports, discharge summaries, laboratory reports, and x-ray reports. Apply your knowledge by answering the questions that follow the report.

Pathology Report

Patient: Roger C
Specimens
  A. Right kidney
  B. Left kidney

Gross Description

- Kidney A is markedly enlarged, with bosselated surface. It weighs 7.8 kg and is composed of numerous subcapsular cysts 2 to 4 cm in diameter. The cysts contain clear to brown fluid.

Continued

MEDICAL DOCUMENTATION—cont'd

- Kidney B is markedly enlarged with bosselated surface. It weighs 7.3 kg and is composed of numerous subcapsular cysts 2 to 4 cm in diameter. The cysts contain clear to brown fluid.

Microscopic (histological) description

- Both kidneys show saccular diverticula of all portions of renal tubule and glomerular capsules that are disconnected and filled with fluid.
- Cysts are lined by flattened epithelium and have papillary projections and polyps.
- Functional nephrons exist between cysts with areas of global sclerosis, tubular atrophy, interstitial fibrosis, and chronic inflammation.
- The right kidney shows renal adenomas at the hilar margin.

Gross diagnoses

Bilateral PKD
Bilateral enlargement and inflammation of the kidneys

Microscopic diagnoses

Global nephrosclerosis
Tubal atrophy
Interstitial fibrosis and inflammation
Renal adenomas, hilar margin of the right kidney

Electronically signed
Kristen Andrews, MD
Pathology

Questions

1. Define the term nephrosclerosis. ______________________
2. Define the word *interstitial*. ______________________
3. Which term in the document means replacement of normal cells with fibers? ______________________
4. What does adenoma mean? ______________________
5. Define the term atrophy. ______________________
6. What does polycystic mean? ______________________
7. Which structures are atrophied? ______________________
8. What do the cysts contain? ______________________

CHAPTER REVIEW

Complete the Sentence

Using medical terms from this chapter, complete the sentences.

1. The ________________________ are the blood filtration units in the kidneys.
2. The term ________________________ means inflammation of the urinary bladder.
3. The term ________________________ means diminished amount of urine production and excretion.
4. The process of filtering the blood by an external machine is called ________________________.
5. Bowman's capsule is also called ________________________.
6. Blood that needs to be filtered by the kidneys enters via the ________________________.
7. Blood that has been filtered exits the kidneys via the ________________________.
8. The kidneys are supported and protected by a fatty layer called the ________________________.
9. Urine exits the kidneys and flows to the bladder in the ________________________.
10. Much of the fluid that is filtered reenters the blood supply by a process called ________________________.
11. Urine exits the body from the ________________________.
12. Examination of the muscle tone of the bladder is called ________________________.
13. A person who cannot perfuse urine is said to be ________________________.
14. The inner section of the kidney is the ________________________.
15. The outer section of the kidney is the ________________________.
16. Much of resorption occurs in the ________________________.
17. The indentation on the medial side of each kidney is called the ________________________.
18. The collecting ducts of each nephron join to form a ________________________.
19. A device used to measure the quantity of urine in the bladder is a ________________________.
20. A device inserted through the urethra and into the bladder to drain urine is a ________________________.

Spelling

Circle the correctly spelled terms in the pairs of terms.

1. anuric	anueric
2. glomerulus	glomerelus
3. vesicouretheral	vesicourethral
4. intrastitial	interstitial
5. nephrosclerosis	nephrasclerosis
6. filtration	filtation
7. cystocele	cystosele
8. extracorporal	extracorporeal
9. lithatripsy	lithotripsy
10. micturition	micturation

Abbreviations

Define the following abbreviations:

1. VUR ____________________
2. AKI ____________________
3. EPO ____________________
4. SG ____________________
5. HD ____________________
6. IVP ____________________
7. UI ____________________
8. RP ____________________
9. C&S ____________________
10. Cysto ____________________

Identify the Anatomical Structures

Match the structures of the urinary system from the following list to the letters shown in Figure 10-11.

1. ______ bladder
2. ______ left adrenal gland
3. ______ left kidney
4. ______ left ureter
5. ______ right adrenal gland
6. ______ right kidney
7. ______ right ureter
8. ______ urethra

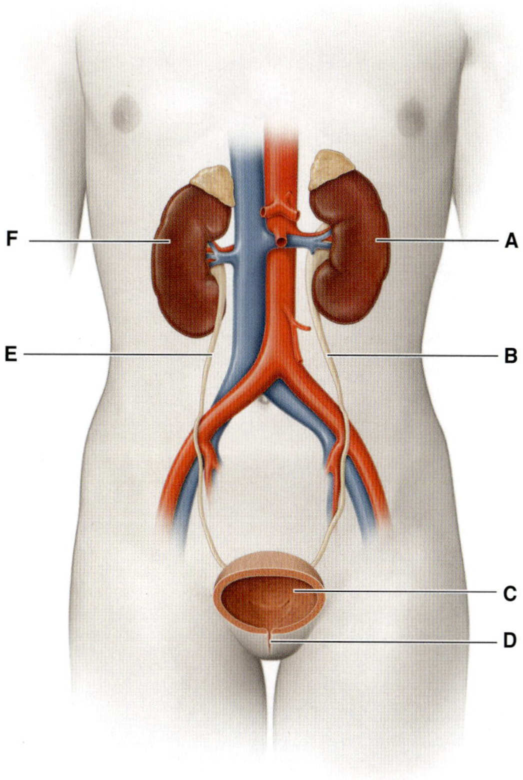

Figure 10-11 Identify the structures of the urinary system.

Match the structures of the kidney from the following list to the letters shown in Figure 10-12.

1. ______ interlobar arteries
2. ______ lobar arteries
3. ______ nephrons
4. ______ renal cortex
5. ______ renal medulla
6. ______ right renal artery
7. ______ right renal vein

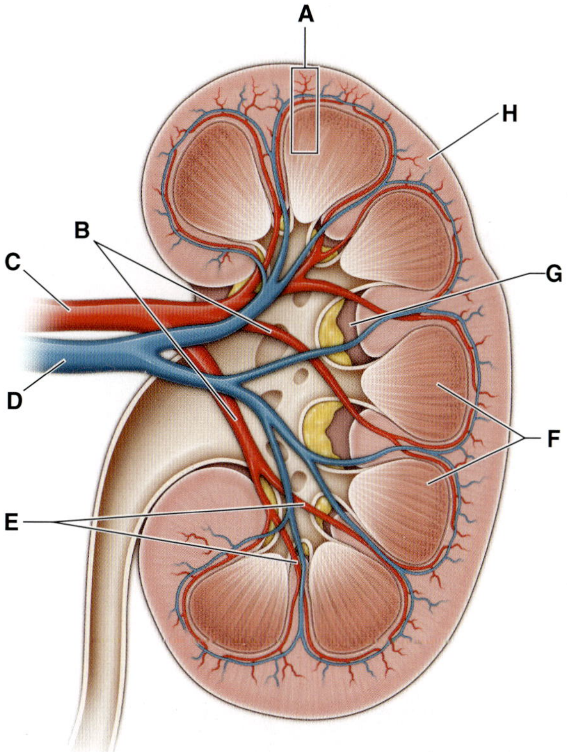

Figure 10-12 Identify the structures of the kidney.

Match the structures of the nephron from the following list to the letters shown in Figure 10-13.

1. _______ afferent arteriole
2. _______ artery
3. _______ ascending limb
4. _______ descending limb
5. _______ distal convoluted tubule
6. _______ efferent arteriole
7. _______ glomerulus
8. _______ interlobular artery
9. _______ interlobular vein
10. _______ loop of Henle
11. _______ peritubular capillaries
12. _______ proximal convoluted tubule
13. _______ urine collecting duct
14. _______ vein

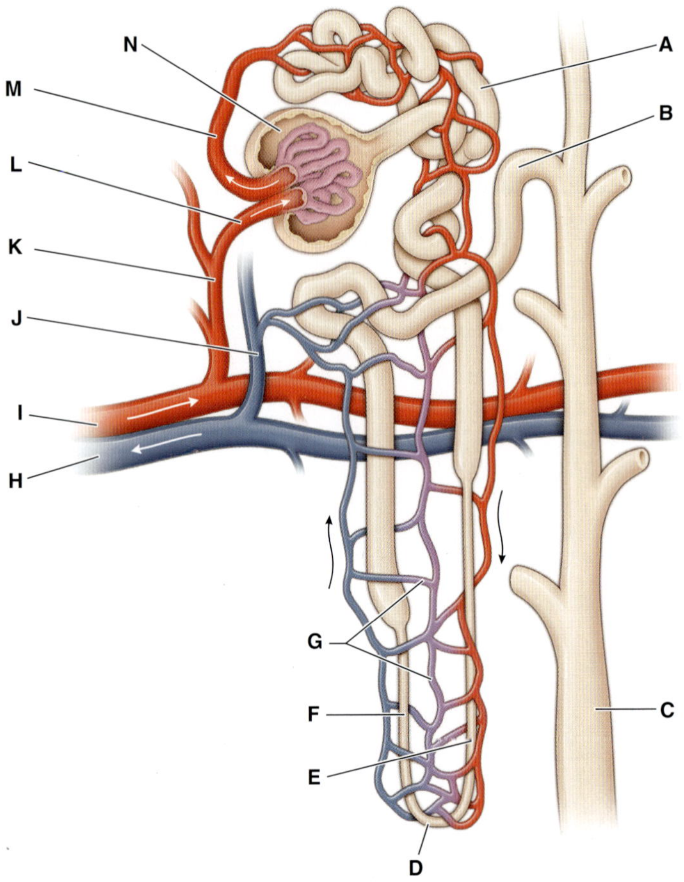

Figure 10-13 Identify the structures of the nephron.

Word Building

Construct a word for the following definitions:

1. blood in the urine _______________
2. disorder of blood in which waste products are not filtered out _______________
3. inflammation of the kidneys _______________
4. process of filtering blood with a machine _______________
5. pertaining to the glomerulus _______________
6. backup of fluid in a ureter _______________
7. crushing of stones _______________
8. inflammation of the urinary bladder _______________

9. process of viewing the urinary tract while the patient is urinating ____________________
10. pertaining to behind the peritoneum ____________________
11. surgical removal of a kidney ____________________
12. inspection of the urinary bladder with a scope ____________________
13. presence of kidney stones ____________________
14. pus in the urine ____________________
15. pertaining to many cysts ____________________
16. presence of sugar in the urine ____________________
17. pain in the bladder ____________________,
18. pertaining to through the urethra ____________________
19. pertaining to outside of the body ____________________
20. surgical fixation of a kidney ____________________

Visit the Medical Language Lab at the website medicallanguagelab.com. Use it to enhance your study and reinforcement of the medical terms and word parts covered in this chapter.

CHAPTER

11

The Endocrine System

LEARNING OBJECTIVES

Upon completion of the chapter, you will be able to:

1. Identify and define the combining forms, roots, prefixes, and suffixes introduced in the chapter.
2. Spell medical terms related to the endocrine system.
3. Describe the major organs of the endocrine system.
4. List the nine endocrine glands and the hormones they release.
5. Describe how the body maintains homeostasis through regulation of hormones.
6. Identify and discuss major pathological terms of the endocrine system.
7. Identify and discuss major diagnostic and therapeutic treatments of the endocrine system.
8. Identify the major categories of medications used to treat endocrine pathologies.
9. Define abbreviations of the endocrine system.

We begin this chapter with a case study of Malik, who is diagnosed with diabetes. The case study introduces some of the medical terms relevant to the endocrine system. Throughout the chapter, we will revisit the story of Malik to understand what happens when someone has an endocrine disorder and how medical interventions can improve the patient's quality of life.

After reading this chapter, you will expand your knowledge of medical terms related to the endocrine system. You will understand how the body maintains homeostasis through several negative feedback loops. You will be able to use the word elements presented in the chapter to understand unfamiliar terms and to build your medical vocabulary.

CASE STUDY

Malik is a 7-year-old boy who recently recovered from a gastrointestinal virus. He had a horribly upset stomach, with vomiting, diarrhea, and a fever. Both the fever and the stomach symptoms resolved a few days ago, but Malik's energy did not return. He was feeling tired and seemed a bit confused. His mother, Shaylah, has also noticed that he is constantly thirsty. He has lost 3 lbs. in the last week. Shaylah and her husband, Roy, are concerned about Malik and take him to his pediatrician. Dr. Carlucci examines Malik and asks Melody, the medical assistant, to draw blood and get a urine sample from Malik. Dr. Carlucci explains that Malik is demonstrating signs and symptoms of diabetes. Roy says, "My mom has diabetes, but it developed when she was in her 50s, and her doctor said it can be controlled if she lost weight. Malik is so skinny; how can he be diabetic too?" Dr. Carlucci explains, "Your mother has the more common form of diabetes known as type 2 diabetes. Type 2 diabetes accounts for 90% of diagnosed cases and occurs most commonly in adults 40 and older. Obesity is the primary risk factor. In type 2 diabetes, the pancreas makes insulin, but the cells of the body are not sensitive to the insulin, a state called 'insulin resistance.' Diet and exercise can reverse the cellular insulin resistance, which is why your mother's doctor recommended exercise and weight loss. Malik has a condition called type 1 diabetes, which has a different mechanism. I suspect that his recent bout with the gastrointestinal virus caused damage to his pancreas. Malik's cells are not resistant to insulin; his pancreas is not producing insulin." Shaylah asks, "Why did the virus attack his pancreas?" Dr. Carlucci says, "I wish I knew; some children develop type 1 diabetes from a genetic predisposition. Does anyone in the family have type 1 diabetes?" Roy replies, "No, my doctor warned me at my last physical to lose some weight, but other than my mother, I can't think of anyone in the family having diabetes." Shaylah adds, "No one in my family has diabetes." Dr. Carlucci replies, "I suspect that the virus triggered an autoimmune response that damaged the beta cells of Malik's pancreas. The beta cells are responsible for insulin production and Malik's are not working. To treat type 1 diabetes, Malik will need to take insulin. This will allow his body to use glucose for energy. I will ask Melody to schedule Malik with our pediatric endocrinologist for an appointment later today. You will learn to administer his insulin and control his diet. Malik's energy should return, and his thirst will decrease. With attention to his diet and monitoring his blood glucose, he should be feeling better soon."

KEY TERMS

Adrenal cortex
Adrenal glands
Adrenal medulla
Aldosterone
Anterior pituitary gland
Antidiuretic hormone
Catecholamines
Circadian rhythm
Corticosterone
Cortisol
Cortisone
Electrolytes
Epinephrine (adrenaline)
Estrogen
Glucagon
Glucocorticoids
Glucose
Glycogen
Gonadocorticoids
Homeostasis
Hormones
Insulin
Metabolism
Mineralocorticoids
Negative feedback loop
Norepinephrine (noradrenalin)
Ovaries
Oxytocin
Pancreas
Parathyroid gland
Pineal gland
Pituitary gland
Positive feedback loop
Posterior pituitary gland
Progesterone
Releasing hormones
Sympathomimetic
Testes
Testosterone
Thymus gland
Thyroid gland
Vasoconstriction

Structures and Physiology

The endocrine system consists of a network of ductless glands that produce and secrete **hormones**. Hormones are chemicals that stimulate specific cells (target cells) to increase or decrease function. While these hormones are secreted directly into the bloodstream, different hormones have different functions and therefore different target cells. The overall goal of the endocrine system is to maintain **homeostasis**, a state of dynamic equilibrium. Dynamic equilibrium means that although our bodies are constantly changing (dynamic), the state of the body exists within a healthy stable range of parameters. The endocrine system maintains blood sugar, blood pressure, and water balance and ensures that the body is not too hot or too cold. Additionally, the endocrine system is responsible for the production and maintenance of sexual characteristics controlled by the sex hormones.

ELEMENT REVIEW
home/o = same
-stasis = stopping, control

The Endocrine Glands

The endocrine glands include the pituitary, pineal, thyroid, parathyroid, thymus, adrenal, pancreas, ovaries, and testes. Figure 11-1 shows the location of the endocrine glands and their hormones. These glands work with the nervous system to regulate a variety of body functions. While signals from the nervous system follow nerve pathways very quickly, the endocrine system communicates more slowly through the release of hormones into the bloodstream. From the bloodstream, the hormone must circulate to its target organ. Thus, hormonal regulation of the body is slower than body changes that occur due to nerve impulses that follow along a nerve.

PHYSIOLOGY FACT

The two major types of hormones are lipid soluble and water soluble. Water-soluble hormones need assistance to pass through the cell membrane whereas lipid-soluble hormones pass easily across the cell membrane.

Pituitary Gland

The **pituitary gland** is approximately the size of a pea, weighs 0.5 g, and is located at the base of the brain. It is attached to the hypothalamus by a narrow stalk called the *infundibulum*. The hypothalamus is part of the nervous system, but it produces hormones that

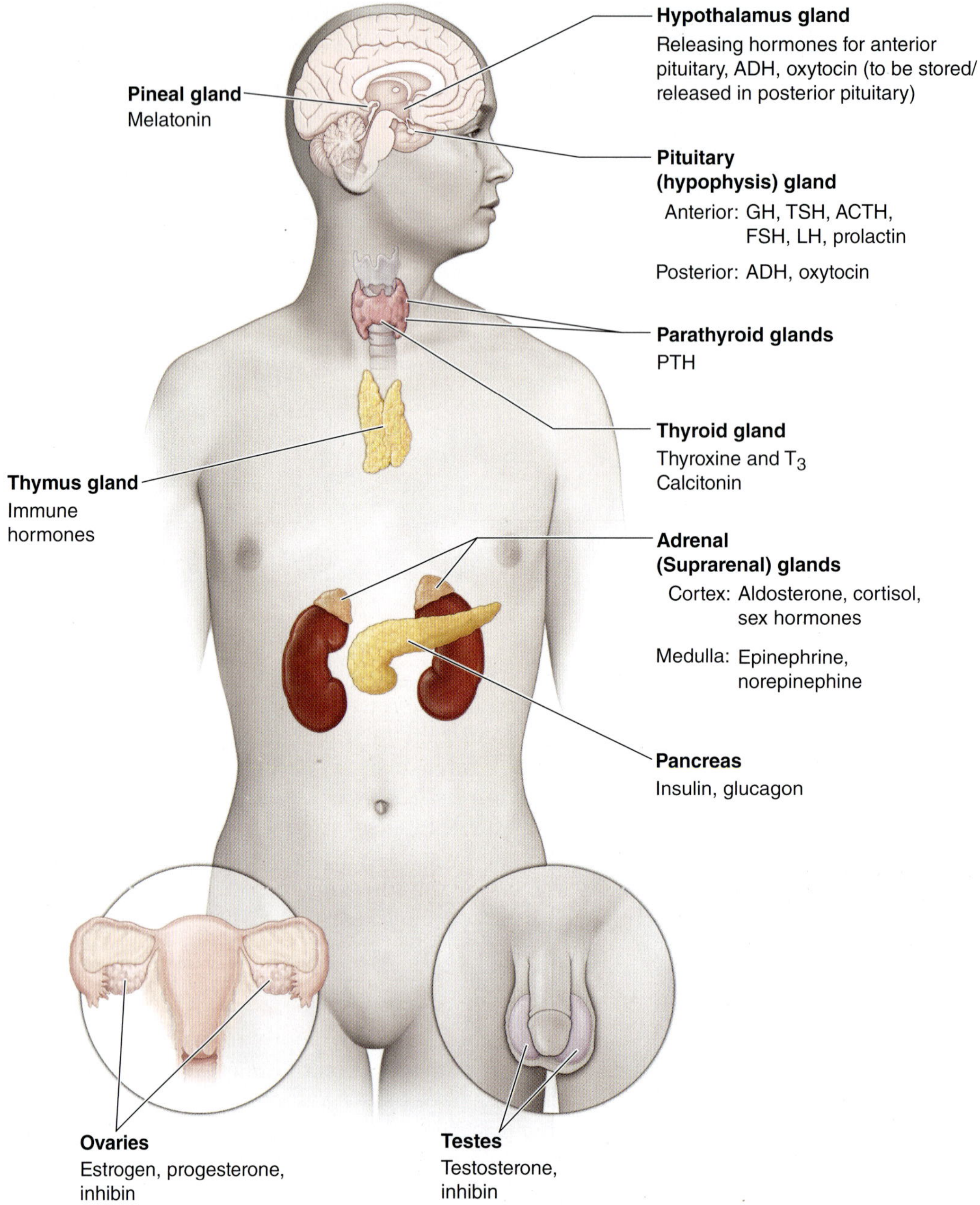

Figure 11-1 The endocrine glands and their hormones.

directly control the anterior pituitary gland's secretion of hormones. Thus, the endocrine and nervous systems are connected in this area of the brain.

The pituitary gland is divided into two lobes, the anterior and the posterior lobes, which produce different hormones (Fig. 11-2). The **anterior pituitary gland** is composed of glandular epithelium enclosed within a capsule of dense connective tissue. Five different types of secretory cells are responsible for secreting six distinct hormones. These six hormones are all **releasing hormones**, meaning these hormones cause target organs to stimulate or inhibit release of their hormones (Table 11-1). The pituitary gland is thus called the master gland as it directs other endocrine glands.

In contrast to the glandular cells of the anterior pituitary gland, the posterior lobe of the pituitary gland is composed of nervous tissue and neurons originating in the hypothalamus. The nerve cells of the hypothalamus extend into the **posterior pituitary gland** and

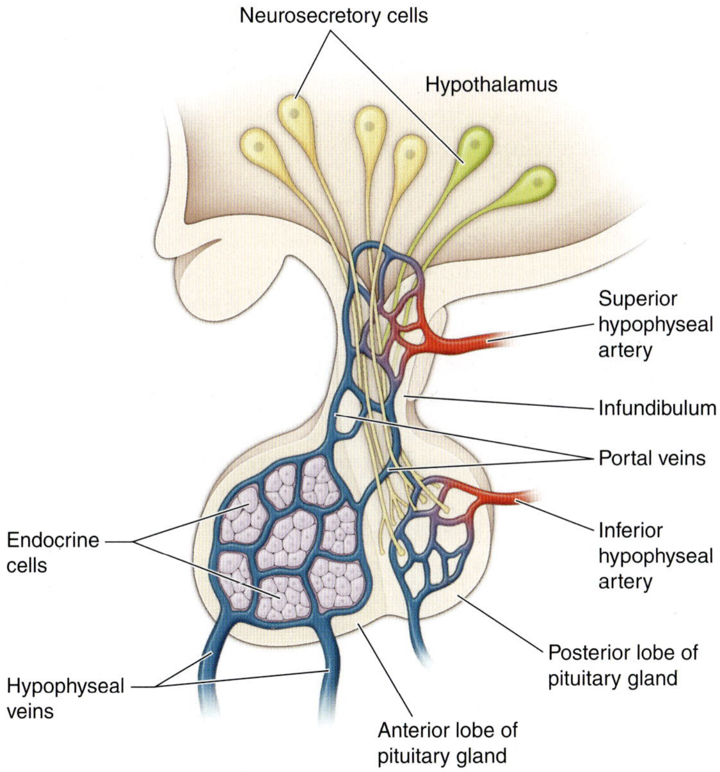

Figure 11-2 Pituitary gland.

TABLE 11-1 Anterior Pituitary Hormones and Target Gland or Tissue

Hormone	Target
Growth hormone (GH)	Bones, muscles
Thyroid-stimulating hormone (TSH)	Thyroid gland
Adrenocorticotropic hormone (ACTH)	Adrenal cortex
Follicle-stimulating hormone and luteinizing hormone (FSH and LH)	Ovaries/testes
Prolactin (PRL)	Breasts

connect to the bloodstream by the inferior hypophyseal artery. These cells secrete oxytocin and antidiuretic hormones. The posterior pituitary gland does not produce any hormones; instead, it stores the two hormones produced by the hypothalamus until it is time to release them into the bloodstream.

Antidiuretic Hormone

Secretion of **antidiuretic hormone (ADH)** is regulated by osmoreceptors in the hypothalamus that detect the amount of osmotic pressure in the bloodstream. When you become dehydrated, the osmotic pressure of your blood rises as the blood becomes less dilute (more solutes, less solution). ADH is stimulated, and the kidneys reduce urine production. The effect is an increase in blood pressure. ADH also triggers sweat glands to reduce sweat production, thus further conserving water. The smooth muscle walls of the arterioles contract, a process called **vasoconstriction**. Thus, ADH is also called *vasopressin*.

Conversely, if you drink an excessive amount of water, the blood becomes more dilute (less solutes in solution) and ADH secretion is inhibited. The kidneys resorb less water,

ELEMENT REVIEW
vas/o = vessel
-pressin = contract, draw together

and more urine is secreted into the ureters. The excess water is eliminated in the urine until normal blood fluid volume is restored. Thus, the maintenance of blood pressure is governed by a **negative feedback loop**, a condition in which the secretion of the hormone provides a reverse response to the stimulus. This is the mechanism that provides homeostasis and is common to most hormonal regulation.

Oxytocin

Oxytocin (OT) is the hormone released to stimulate contractions of the uterus. It also stimulates the cells around the mammary ducts to contract and cause milk to eject. The levels of OT in the bloodstream rise during pregnancy and eventually signal the uterus to begin the birth process. After birth, OT levels decline, but rise again as the mother breastfeeds her baby. Suckling at the breast stimulates neurosecretory cells to secrete OT and stimulate production of prolactin. Additionally, increased OT levels also stimulate uterine contractions after birth, so that the uterus returns to its normal size. The secretion of oxytocin to initiate the birth process is a **positive feedback loop**, a condition in which secretion of the hormone provides a response in the same direction as the stimulus.

OT levels in males are approximately the same as females who are not pregnant. The role in the male body is unknown.

PHYSIOLOGY FACT

Positive feedback systems prompt extreme changes and are unstable and uncommon. Another example of a positive feedback system is blood clotting in response to bleeding. The body releases chemicals to stimulate production of platelets. The presence of platelets activates more platelet production. Thus, the response to the injury (platelet production) prompts more clotting.

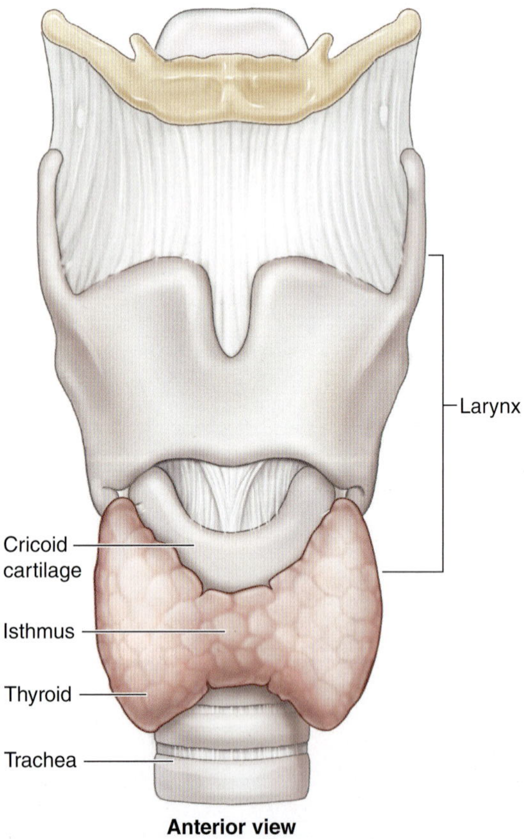

Figure 11-3 Thyroid gland.

Pineal Gland

The **pineal gland** is a small cone-shaped gland that lies above the pituitary gland and is part of the diencephalon, a section of the brain that contains several structures related to both the endocrine and nervous system. It is composed of modified neurons and supportive neuroglial cells. It is innervated by sympathetic neurons. The pineal gland secretes melatonin, a hormone that is thought to induce sleep. Secretion of melatonin fluctuates with day/night cycles, increasing in level as night approaches. This fluctuation ties your circadian rhythm of sleep/wake cycles to your environment. Additionally, melatonin levels vary seasonally as daylight increases or decreases.

Thyroid Gland

The **thyroid gland** is a butterfly-shaped gland located slightly below the larynx anterior to the trachea (Fig. 11-3). The two lateral lobes of the thyroid gland are attached by a narrow structure called the isthmus. The thyroid gland is composed of glandular epithelium within an outer capsule of protective connective tissue. Hollow compartments called thyroid follicles contain follicular cells that produce and secrete the two thyroid hormones:

- **Triiodothyronine** contains three atoms of iodine and is sometimes called T3. It helps to regulate growth and development of the body, and **metabolism**, which is the sum of energy transformations of the body and body temperature.
- **Thyroxine** contains four atoms of iodine and is sometimes called T4. It helps maintain normal body metabolism.

Together, T3 and T4 stimulate the rate of metabolic changes, promote protein synthesis (important for growth and repair), increase the rate of glucose uptake, promote lipid metabolism, and accelerate actions of the nervous system. The effects of the thyroid hormones reach nearly all cells of the body, making thyroid regulation vital for good health. Thyroid hormone levels in the bloodstream are regulated by a negative feedback loop of hormones between the hypothalamus and the anterior pituitary gland. As thyroid hormone levels in the blood decrease, the hypothalamus secretes thyroid-releasing hormone (TRH). This triggers the anterior pituitary gland to secrete TSH, thyroid-stimulating hormone. When TSH reaches the thyroid gland, it stimulates the follicles to release T3 and T4. When T3 and T4 levels in the blood rise, the hypothalamus decreases TRH, and the anterior pituitary gland decreases TSH. Thus, the thyroid hormones are directed by the hypothalamus and anterior pituitary gland.

ELEMENT REVIEW
thyr/o = shield
-oid = resembling

The cells between the thyroid follicles, called parafollicular cells, produce a third hormone, calcitonin (CT), which works with the parathyroid gland to decrease the amount of calcium and phosphate in the blood. Secretion of CT is directed by the hypothalamus and anterior pituitary gland in another negative feedback loop. As calcium levels in the bloodstream rise, the thyroid gland increases its rate of CT secretion. Calcitonin inhibits the action of osteoclasts that dissolve bone matrix. This stimulates bone production by osteoblasts, thus creating new bone matrix. Calcitonin also stimulates the excretion of calcium and phosphate ions by the kidneys. The net effect is more bone production and less calcium and phosphate in circulating blood.

Parathyroid Glands

The **parathyroid glands** are small masses of tissue that are embedded within the posterior thyroid gland. There are usually two to three parathyroid glands on each lobe, and they are composed of secretory cells surrounded by a thin capsule of protective connective tissue. The parathyroid glands secrete parathyroid hormone (PTH), which acts to increase blood calcium levels. PTH increases the action of osteoclasts that, as described earlier, break down old bone and release calcium and phosphate into the bloodstream. PTH enhances the reabsorption of calcium ions in the kidneys, reducing the amount lost in urine. PTH also stimulates formation of vitamin D in the digestive tract, increasing calcium absorption into the bloodstream. Thus, PTH opposes CT, and blood calcium levels are kept within normal levels. Secretion of PTH is regulated by a negative feedback loop of the hypothalamus and anterior pituitary gland in the same manner as CT.

Thymus Gland

The **thymus gland** is a single gland located in the mediastinum, superior to the heart and just below the sternum. During infancy and into childhood, the thymus is prominent, but it decreases in size in early adulthood. It secretes two hormones during early life: thymosin and thymopoietin. Both hormones stimulate the production of T cells, specialized lymphocytes that are important in the immune response. Thus, the thymus gland is part of both the lymphatic and endocrine systems.

Adrenal Glands

The **adrenal glands** are paired, pyramid-shaped, and located on top of the kidneys. They are composed of two parts: the interior adrenal medulla and the outer portion, the adrenal cortex. The divisions have very different functions.

The **adrenal medulla** is composed of modified nervous tissue and works with the nervous system in times of stress. The adrenal medulla secretes two hormones: **epinephrine** and **norepinephrine**. These hormones are very similar in composition and function, and they are an important part of the body's response to stress. These hormones are known as **catecholamines**, biologically active amines that influence the nervous system. Both epinephrine and norepinephrine are **sympathomimetic**, meaning that they cause changes in the body that mimic changes brought on by the sympathetic nervous system. These changes are associated with the fight-or-flight response that occurs when we feel danger.

- Epinephrine, also known as adrenaline, increases the heart rate and the force of the heart contraction. It dilates bronchioles in the lungs, raises blood glucose, and decreases the peristaltic movement of the intestines. These physiological changes help us to prepare for an emergency that requires us to flee or fight.
- Norepinephrine, also known as noradrenaline, produces a vasoconstricting effect on blood vessels, thus raising blood pressure, which also helps us prepare for fight or flight.

In contrast, the adrenal cortex is composed of glandular epithelium, arranged into three layers: the zona glomerulosa, zona fasciculata, and zona reticularis. They secrete corticosteroid hormones that are synthesized from cholesterol and affect our metabolism, fluid balance, and sex hormones.

- **Aldosterone** is a mineralocorticoid secreted by the zona glomerulosa. **Mineralocorticoids** regulate how mineral salts are distributed to our tissues. The concentration of mineral salts, also known as **electrolytes**, must be controlled within defined limits. Aldosterone regulates the concentration of sodium and potassium ions by targeting the kidneys to conserve sodium, which promotes water retention, and to excrete potassium in the urine. Aldosterone also targets sweat glands, salivary glands, and the digestive tract to conserve sodium and remove excess potassium. The retention of sodium allows the body to conserve water, and thus aldosterone has an indirect effect of raising blood pressure by ensuring that blood volume does not get too low. Secretion of aldosterone is activated by a drop in blood pressure, a decrease in sodium blood level, or rising levels of potassium ions in extracellular fluid.
- **Cortisol**, **corticosterone**, and **cortisone** are all glucocorticoids. **Glucocorticoids**, secreted by both the zona fasciculata and zona reticularis, regulate levels of glucose in the bloodstream. The most abundant of the glucocorticoids is cortisone, which is secreted by a negative feedback loop of ACTH (adrenocorticotrophic hormone) from the anterior pituitary gland. The primary function of the glucocorticoids is to promote glucose synthesis in the liver in a process known as gluconeogenesis. As glucose is synthesized in the liver, it is sent into the bloodstream, causing blood glucose levels to rise. Additionally, glucocorticoids inhibit inflammation due to allergic responses. Cortisone creams or oral medications (such as prednisone) are used to decrease rashes and swelling due to allergic reactions. Because glucose is needed in an emergency, the glucocorticoids act as a backup to the stress response of the adrenal medulla.
- **Gonadocorticoids** are sex hormones secreted by the zona fasciculata and zona reticularis. Although these hormones are primarily produced in the ovaries and testes, small amounts from the adrenal cortex are released before puberty to later contribute to the development of secondary sex characteristics in males and females.

ELEMENT REVIEW
gluc/o = sugar
neo- = new
-genesis = production
zona = band, layer
glomerulosa = outer
gasciculata = middle
reticularis = inner

PHYSIOLOGY FACT

The adrenal glands are known as the suprarenal glands because they sit upon the kidneys.
Supra- = above, upon; **-renal** = pertaining to the kidneys

Pancreas

The pancreas is a soft, elongated organ located behind the stomach near its junction with the duodenum (Fig. 11-4). The pancreas can be defined as an exocrine organ because it

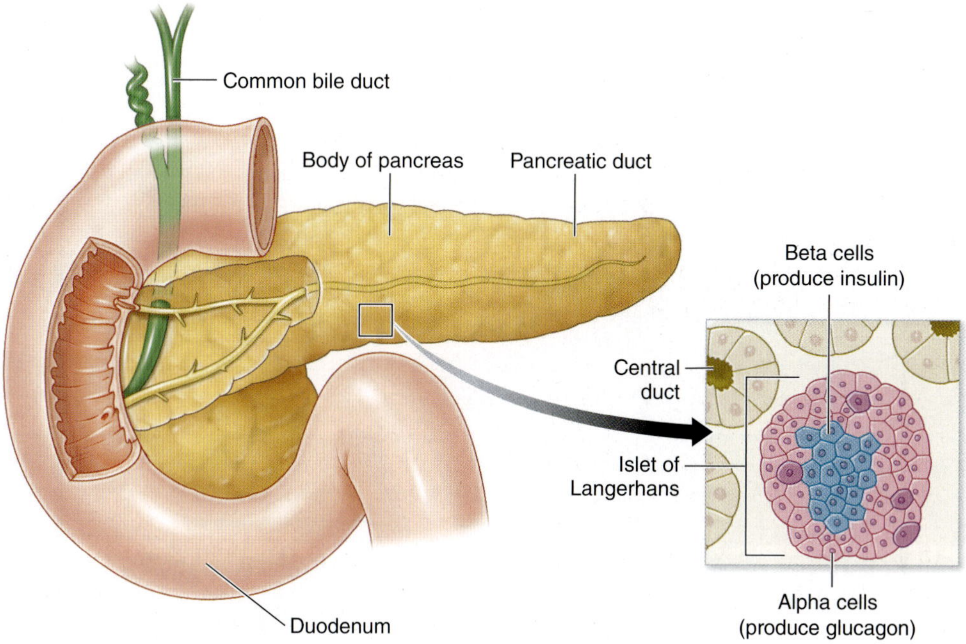

Figure 11-4 Pancreas.

secretes digestive enzymes and bicarbonate ions into the ducts that empty into the duodenum. These secretions aid digestion and neutralize hydrochloric acid from the stomach. Thus, the pancreas is part of the digestive system.

The **pancreas** is also an endocrine organ because it secretes two important hormones that regulate blood glucose. Clusters of cells called pancreatic islets, or islets of Langerhans, contain two distinct types of cells. Approximately 25% of the cells are alpha cells that secrete the hormone **glucagon**. The other 75% of the cells are beta cells that secrete **insulin**. The two hormones work in opposition to stabilize blood glucose levels. **Glucose** is the source of fuel for all metabolic processes of the body.

PHYSIOLOGY FACT

Exocrine glands differ from endocrine glands as they do not secrete hormones into the bloodstream. They secrete a variety of substances externally through ducts. Examples of exocrine glands are sweat and oil glands on the skin, lacrimal glands of the eye that secrete tears, and ceruminous glands of the ear that secrete cerumen (ear wax).

When glucose levels fall below normal, the pancreatic islets detect this change and stimulate the alpha cells to release glucagon. Glucagon stimulates the conversion of glycogen in the liver to glucose. The **glycogen** is stored in the liver as branched chains of glucose that can be cleaved into glucose molecules and released into the bloodstream. This occurs when we are sleeping or during fasting.

Conversely, when a high blood glucose level is detected by the islets of the pancreas, the beta cells are stimulated to release insulin. Insulin has the opposite effect on the liver and stimulates the formation of glycogen to be stored for future use. Insulin binds to receptor sites in skeletal muscle cells, cardiac muscle cells, and adipose cells to uptake glucose from the bloodstream. Thus, the effect of insulin is to reduce blood glucose levels.

The secretion of glucagon and insulin is regulated by two negative feedback loops:

- High blood glucose stimulates beta cells to secrete insulin, and
- Low blood glucose stimulates alpha cells to secrete glucagon.

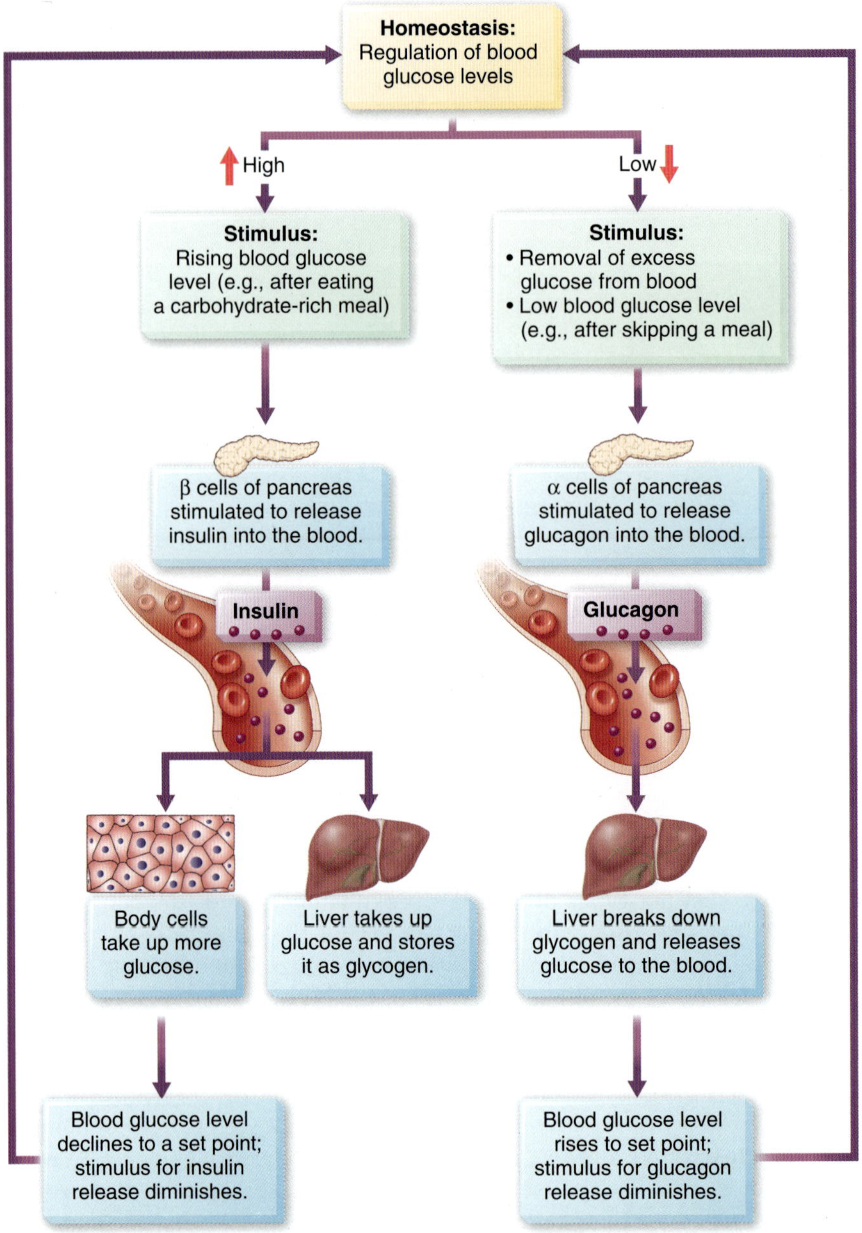

Figure 11-5 The simultaneous actions of insulin and glucagon.

Figure 11-5 shows the simultaneous actions of insulin and glucagon.

> ***Memory Tip***
> Glucagon acts **upon** glycogen to produce glucose.

Ovaries

The gonads are the reproductive organs that produce sex cells and secrete the sex hormones. In the female, the gonads are the paired, almond-shaped **ovaries** located on either side of the uterus. The ovaries are held in place by ligaments near the distal ends of the fallopian tubes. The most notable change during puberty is menarche, the onset of monthly menstruation. At the onset of puberty, follicle-stimulating hormone (FSH) and luteinizing hormone (LH) are secreted by the anterior pituitary gland which stimulates the ovaries to begin secreting estrogen. Estrogen, the primary sex hormone, influences the development of secondary sex characteristics including breast development, widening of the pelvis, deposition of body fat, sexual desires, and pubic and axillary hair.

Estrogen promotes maturation of the ovum and stimulates the uterine lining to prepare for implantation with a fertilized ovum. The ovaries also produce progesterone. As the name implies, **progesterone** is pro gestation, prompting the changes to the uterus that will allow for implantation of a fertilized ovum and development of a placenta. Estrogen and progesterone production are directed by FSH and LH, which are released by the anterior pituitary gland.

Testes

In the male, the gonads are the **testes**. The testes are paired oval organs located within a sac called the scrotum. At the onset of puberty, the testes secrete **testosterone**, the male sex hormone. Testosterone is responsible for the development of sperm and secondary sex characteristics in males, such as deepening of the voice, increased muscle mass, sexual desires, and development of male-pattern body hair. Like the female hormones, testosterone production is stimulated by FSH and LH secreted from the anterior pituitary gland.

Structures and Physiology Review

1. Match the Words

Match the words to their description.

adrenal glands
aldosterone
anterior pituitary gland
antidiuretic hormone (ADH)
calcitonin
circadian rhythm
electrolytes
epinephrine (adrenaline)
follicle-stimulating hormone (FSH)
glucagon
homeostasis
infundibulum
insulin
melatonin
negative feedback loop
norepinephrine (noradrenalin)
oxytocin
parathyroid hormone (PTH)
pineal gland
pituitary gland
positive feedback loop
releasing hormones
sympathomimetic
testosterone
thymosin
thymopoietin
thyroid gland
thyroxine

1. The hormone that regulates sleep-wake cycles ____________________
2. The master gland of the endocrine system ____________________
3. The two hormones that stimulate production of T lymphocytes ____________________
4. The hormone responsible for regulating fluid balance ____________________
5. The hormone that contains four ions of iodine ____________________

6. When a secretion of a hormone provides response in the reverse direction as the stimulus ____________________
7. The hormone that regulates the amount of calcium in the blood ____________________
8. The hormone that is also called vasopressin ____________________
9. The state of dynamic equilibrium is also called ____________________
10. The stalk-like projection that connects the pituitary gland to the hypothalamus ____________________
11. The hormone that stimulates production of estrogen ____________________
12. The hormone that stimulates contractions of the uterus during childbirth ____________________
13. Changes in the body that mimic changes brought on by the sympathetic nervous system ____________________
14. The hormone that is triggered by low blood calcium ____________________
15. The endocrine organ that helps to regulate growth and metabolism ____________________
16. The hormone that is triggered by low blood glucose ____________________
17. The endocrine gland that secretes melatonin ____________________
18. When a secretion of a hormone provides a response in the same direction as the stimulus ____________________
19. The fight-or-flight hormones ____________________
20. The hormone that is triggered by high blood glucose ____________________
21. The sleep/wake cycle is also called the ____________________
22. These glands are also called the suprarenal glands ____________________
23. The hormone responsible for development of secondary male sex characteristics ____________________
24. The hormones that tell target organs to stimulate or inhibit release of their hormones ____________________
25. Releasing hormones all originate from this gland ____________________

Structures and Physiology Word-Building Practice

1. Nouns and Adjectives

Complete the chart of noun and adjective forms.

Noun Form	Adjective Form
1. gland	________________
2. diabetes	________________
3. ________________	hormonal
4. ________________	medullary
5. pancreas	________________

2. Prefixes

Use the prefixes to build a word that corresponds to the definition provided.

a-, an-
endo-
eu-
exo-
hyper-
hypo-
poly-

1. low blood sugar ________________
2. elevated blood calcium ________________
3. excessive thirst ________________
4. absence of urine production ________________
5. pertaining to healthy or normal thyroid ________________
6. the group of glands that secrete hormones into the bloodstream ________________
7. low blood potassium ________________
8. the group of glands that secrete substances outside of the bloodstream ________________
9. condition of an overactive thyroid ________________
10. low parathyroid hormone secretion ________________

Word Building With Combining, Prefix, and Suffix Forms

The following word roots, prefixes, and suffixes are commonly used in medical terms for the anatomy and pathology of the endocrine system. Combining vowels for word roots are included. Memorizing these word elements will help you understand new terms that you may encounter in the field of endocrinology as a medical assistant, medical laboratory technologist, nurse, diabetes educator, or other professional working in endocrinology.

The list contains examples of terms that utilize the combining forms and a pronunciation guide. Be sure to use the pronunciation guide so that you can learn to say the terms correctly.

The Medical Language Lab at medicallanguagelab.com provides audio files to help you practice your pronunciations.

Combining Form	Meaning	Example (Pronunciation)	Example Definition
acr/o	extremities	acromegaly (ac-rō-MEG-ă-lē)	enlargement of the extremities
aden/o	gland	adenopathy (ăd-ĕn-ŎP-ă-thē)	disease of glands
adren/o	adrenal gland	adrenomegaly (ă-drēn-ō-MEG-ă-lē)	enlargement of adrenal glands
adrenal/o	adrenal gland	adrenalectomy (ăd-rē-nă-LEK-tō-mē)	surgical removal of adrenal gland
andr/o	man, male	androgen (AN-drŏ-jĕn)	male hormone
calc/i	calcium	hypercalcemia (hī-pĕr-kăl-SĒ-mē-ă)	elevated blood calcium
cortic/o	cortex	cortical (KOR-tĭ-căl)	pertaining to cortex
crin/o	to secrete, pour	endocrine (EN-dō-krin)	a group of glands that secrete hormones into the bloodstream
dips/o	thirst	polydipsia (pŏl-ē-DĬP-sē-ă)	excessive thirst
gonad/o	sex glands	gonads (GŌ-nads)	ovaries or testes
gluc/o	sugar	glucometer (gloo-KOM-ĕt-ĕr)	device to measure blood sugar
glyc/o	sugar	glycoprotein (glī-kŏ-PRŌ-tēn)	a compound of carbohydrate (sugar) and protein
gynec/o	woman	gynecology (gī-nĕ-KŎL-ō-jē)	the study of women's health care
kal/i	potassium	hyperkalemia (hī-pĕr-kă-LĒ-mē-ă)	elevated blood potassium

Combining Form	Meaning	Example (Pronunciation)	Example Definition
lact/o	milk	lactation (lak-TĀ-shŏn)	production and release of milk
myx/o	relating to mucus	myxedema (mik-sĕ-DĒ-mă)	swelling and mucus production in the skin
natr/i	sodium	hypernatremia (hī-pĕr-nă-TRĒ-mē-ă)	elevated blood sodium
pancreat/o	pancreas	pancreatic (păn-krē-AT-ĭc)	pertaining to the pancreas
somat/o	body	somatic (sō-MAT-ik)	pertaining to the body
thym/o	thymus gland	thymoma (thī-MŌ-mă)	tumor of the thymus gland
thyr/o	thyroid gland	hypothyroidism (hī-pō-THĪ-royd-izm)	condition of low thyroid hormone levels
thyroid/o	thyroid gland	parathyroidectomy (păr-ă-thī-royd-EK-tō-mē)	surgical removal of the parathy-roid gland
toxic/o	poison	toxicology (tŏks-ĭ-KŎL-ō-jē)	the study of poisons

ā = say, ă = sofa, ē = meet, ĕ = met, ī = eye, ĭ = in, ō = oh, ŏ = dog, ū = you, ŭ = up, oo = food

Prefix Form	Meaning	Example (Pronunciation)	Example Definition
anti-	against	antidiuretic (ant-i-dī-yŭ-RET-ik)	lessening the formation of urine
endo-	within	endocrine (EN-dō-krin)	ductless glands that secrete hormones into the blood stream
homo-, homeo-	same	homosexual (hōm-ō-SEK-shoo-ăl)	attraction to the same sex
hyper-	excessive	hyperglycemia (hī-pĕr-glī-SĒ-mē-ă)	high blood sugar
hypo-	under, below	hypothyroidism (hī-pō-THĪ-royd-izm)	condition of low T3, T4
oxy-	sharp, quick	oxytocin (ok-sē-TŌS-ĭn)	hormone that stimulates uterine contractions during birthing
para-	beside	parathyroid gland (păr-ă-THĪ-royd gland)	glands next to the thyroids
poly-	many	polyphagia (pŏl-ē-FĀ-jē-ă)	excessive hunger (eating)

ā = say, ă = sofa, ē = meet, ĕ = met, ī = eye, ĭ = in, ō = oh, ŏ = dog, ū = you, ŭ = up, oo = food

Suffix Form	Meaning	Example (Pronunciation)	Example Definition
-emia	blood condition	hyperglycemia (hī-pĕr-glī-SĒ-mē-ă)	excessive blood sugar
-gen	production	androgen (AN-drŏ-jĕn)	hormone producing male traits
-ism	condition, process	hyperthyroidism (hī-pĕr-THĪ-royd-izm)	condition of excessive thyroid hormone production
-itis	inflammation	pancreatitis (pan-krēa-TĪT-ĭs)	inflammation of the pancreas
-megaly	enlargement	thyromegaly (thī-rō-MEG-ă-lē)	enlargement of the thyroid glands
-oma	tumor	adenoma (ad-ĕn-Ō-mă)	tumor of a gland
-osis	abnormal condition	thyrotoxicosis (thī-rō-tok-sĭ-KŌ-sĭs)	toxicity of thyroid glands
-phagia	eating, swallowing	aphagia (ă-FĀ-jē-ă)	inability to eat or swallow
-stasis	process of stopping, control	hemostasis (hē-mō-STĀ-sĭs)	process of controlling blood flow
-tropin	stimulation of a target organ	gonadotropin (gō-nad-ō-TRO-pĭn)	a hormone that stimulates production of sex hormones
-uria	pertaining to urine	polyuria (pol-ē-YOOR-ē-ă)	excessive secretion and discharge of urine

ā = say, ă = sofa, ē = meet, ĕ = met, ī = eye, ĭ = in, ō = oh, ŏ = dog, ū = you, ŭ = up, oo = food

Combining Forms Practice

1. Build the Terms

Using only the word elements listed, build terms for the definitions in the numbered list.

Prefixes	Combining Forms		Suffixes
anti-	acr/o	gynec/o	-y
dys-	aden/o	hemat/o	-emia
endo-	adrenal/o	kal/i	-gen
homo-, homeo-	calc/i	pancreat/o	-ism
hyper-	cortic/o	somat/o	-itis
hypo-	crin/o	thym/o	-megaly
oxy-	glyc/o	thyr/o	-oma
para-	lact/o	thyroid/o	-phagia
poly-	natr/i	toxic/o	-uria

1. blood in the urine __________
2. inflammation of the pancreas __________
3. condition of low blood calcium __________
4. condition of high blood potassium __________
5. condition of decreased parathyroid hormones __________
6. a substance that stimulates milk production __________
7. surgical removal of thymus gland __________
8. pertaining to toxic activity of the thyroid glands __________
9. surgical removal of the parathyroid glands __________
10. condition of excessive hunger __________

2. Decipher the Terms

Separate each term into its prefix (if any), combining form, and suffix. Next, translate the word parts and then give the common definition of the term.

1. acromegaly

   Prefix: ________ *Combining Form:* ________ *Suffix:* ________

   Meaning: __________

2. exocrine

   Prefix: ________ *Combining Form:* ________ *Suffix:* ________

   Meaning: __________

3. hypernatremia

   Prefix: ________ *Combining Form:* ________ *Suffix:* ________

   Meaning: __________

4. polyadenitis

   Prefix: ________ *Combining Form:* ________ *Suffix:* ________

   Meaning: __________

5. dysphagia

   Prefix: ________ *Combining Form:* ________ *Suffix:* ________

   Meaning: __________

6. polydipsia

Prefix: ______________ *Combining Form:* ______________ *Suffix:* ______________

Meaning: ____

7. thymoma

Prefix: ______________ *Combining Form:* ______________ *Suffix:* ______________

Meaning: ____

8. gonadotropin

Prefix: ______________ *Combining Form:* ______________ *Suffix:* ______________

Meaning: ____

9. hypothyroidism

Prefix: ______________ *Combining Form:* ______________ *Suffix:* ______________

Meaning: ____

10. somatogenic

Prefix: ______________ *Combining Form:* ______________ *Suffix:* ______________

Meaning: ____

Medical Language Lab

Visit the Medical Language Lab at medicallanguagelab.com. Use it to enhance your study and reinforcement of the medical terms and word parts covered in this chapter.

CASE STUDY, continued

Malik and his parents arrive for their appointment with Dr. Lingberg, the pediatric endocrinologist who explains the findings of Malik's blood and urine samples that were taken at Dr. Carlucci's office this morning. She explains, "The urine test showed glucosuria, which means there is glucose in Malik's urine. No sugar should be in a normal urine sample. This means that the bloodstream is 'dumping' the excess sugar into the urine to get rid of it. This is also causing Malik to be polydipsic, or excessively thirsty. His body is trying to get rid of the sugar by secreting large amounts of urine. He urinates frequently, which makes him dehydrated, so he drinks more, and the cycle continues. The blood test shows a glucose level of 150 mg/dL, which means he is hyperglycemic. A normal value for a child Malik's age is 64 to 100 mg/dL. Malik is 46 inches tall and weighs 42 lbs. His BMI, body mass index, is 13.9, which is underweight. I want to start Malik on an insulin pump or injections and a diet that has the proper amounts of protein and fat, along with carbohydrates that will support healthy blood glucose regulation and promote his growth and development." Shaylah asks, "Wow, this is a lot to learn. Who will guide us with Malik's diet and show us how to use the insulin pump?" Dr. Lindberg replies, "Don't worry. Anne, a nurse and one of our diabetes educators, will help you develop a diet comprised of foods Malik enjoys, a schedule of monitoring his insulin, using and wearing the pump or injecting insulin, and even some strategies for school lunches and birthday parties." Roy says, "Thank you Dr. Lindberg, we have a lot to learn, but as a family, we will learn together."

Endocrine System Diseases and Disorders

Endocrine disorders are the result of dysregulation of hormones produced and secreted from the bloodstream to the target organs. Treatment with replacement hormones can often correct these disorders. Some disorders require radiation or surgery to glands or organs in order to promote proper functioning.

Common Signs and Symptoms

Because the endocrine system works to regulate body functions, dysregulation of the endocrine system can present a wide variety of signs and symptoms (Table 11-2).

Pathological Conditions of the Endocrine System

Common disorders of the endocrine system are listed by glands.

Pituitary Gland

Acromegaly: A chronic metabolic disorder characterized by enlargement and elongation of the bones of the face, jaw, and extremities. The condition is caused by a hypersecretion of human growth hormone after puberty is complete. The most common cause is a tumor of the pituitary gland, and treatment with surgical resection of the tumor or radiation can reduce the tumor and stop the excessive growth of the face and extremities.

Diabetes insipidus: A condition caused by a deficiency of antidiuretic hormone secretion by the posterior pituitary gland. The condition causes large amounts of sodium and urine to be excreted. Diabetes insipidus can be caused by brain trauma to the hypothalamus or neurosurgery. It can also be caused by medications that disrupt renal resorption of water, such as lithium or demeclocycline.

The patient will complain of constant thirst and void large amounts of dilute urine. Treatment with vasopressin (antidiuretic hormone) will protect against fluid loss, but the patient must be aware of signs of dehydration.

Dwarfism: Generalized lack of normal growth before puberty due to a lack of growth hormone secretion by the anterior pituitary gland. The abnormal underdevelopment causes the child to be of short stature, with a small body frame. Upon puberty, there is an absence of secondary sex characteristic development. Treatment with supplemental growth hormone before and during puberty can help the child attain a larger size.

Gigantism: Caused by a hypersecretion of human growth hormone by the anterior pituitary gland. The child experiences accelerated growth of long bones, often accompanied by

TABLE 11-2 Common Signs and Symptoms

Common Signs	Common Symptoms
Pyrexia (fever)	Impaired thermoregulation (feeling too hot or cold)
Weight loss or gain	Anorexia (loss of appetite)
Alopecia (hair loss)	Polyphagia (feeling of excessive hunger) Polydipsia (excessive thirst)
Hirsutism (abnormal hair patterns, especially in females)	Insomnia
Dysmenorrhea or amenorrhea (menstrual abnormalities in females)	
Growth abnormalities in children	

pain. Gigantism is most often caused by an adenoma of the anterior pituitary gland. Radiation and/or surgery can reduce the size of the tumor, slow growth, and correct the disorder.

Hypopituitarism: A deficiency of pituitary hormones. The disorder is characterized by metabolic dysregulation, retardation of normal growth, and absence of sexual maturation. Replacement with pituitary hormones can reduce symptoms.

Precocious puberty: Early onset of appearance of secondary sexual characteristics in females or males. Puberty is considered precocious when occurring in girls before age 8 and before age 9 in boys. Symptoms include breast development in girls, and voice changes and growth of the testicles in boys. Both sexes may also present with underarm and pubic hair, acne, and body odor. The disorder is caused by early production and release of gonadotropin-releasing hormone from the anterior pituitary gland. This causes the ovaries and testes to secrete estrogen and testosterone, respectively. Causes of precocious puberty can be a tumor of the anterior pituitary gland, injury to the brain or spinal cord, or congenital abnormalities. Treatment with medications to block puberty can delay onset of puberty to a normal age.

Thyroid Gland

Cancer of thyroid gland: A palpable lump or nodule of the thyroid gland is often the first sign of malignancy. Diagnosis is confirmed by needle aspiration biopsy. Tumors are staged and classified by site of origin, size of the tumor, and metastasis to lymph nodes or other organs. Treatment is partial or complete thyroidectomy. Replacement of thyroid hormones is required for the remainder of the patient's life.

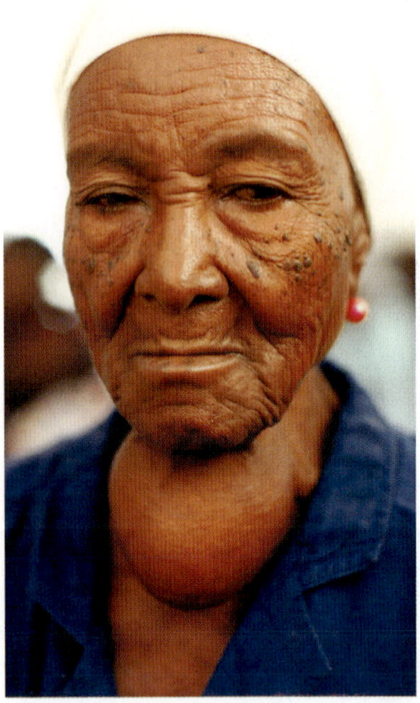

Figure 11-6 Goiter.

Goiter (simple; nontoxic): Enlargement (hyperplasia) of the thyroid gland is visible as the gland protrudes in the anterior neck (Fig. 11-6). The condition is caused by a deficient amount of iodine in the diet, which is required to synthesize T3 and T4. The body responds to low levels of circulating thyroid hormones by the release of thyrotropin by the anterior pituitary gland. As the thyroid gland enlarges, it puts pressure on the trachea and esophagus, causing difficulty breathing and swallowing. Women are more affected than men. Diagnosis is confirmed by physical examination, palpation of the thyroid gland, and decreased T3 and T4 values in blood. Treatment with potassium iodide most often corrects the problem. If thyroid levels do not increase with administration of potassium iodide, a subtotal thyroidectomy may be necessary, and the patient will need to take synthetic thyroid hormones.

Graves' disease (hyperthyroidism): Characterized by hypertrophy of the thyroid gland resulting in an excess secretion of thyroid hormones. Signs and symptoms of Graves' disease include exophthalmia (protrusion of the eyes) and goiter. Patients exhibit rapid heart rate, nervousness, insomnia, excitability, increased appetite, weight loss, nausea, vomiting, excessive thirst, and increased sweating. Mental responses can include hyperactivity and/or delirium. Diagnosis is confirmed by elevation of serum T3 and T4 and increased uptake of radioactive iodine seen on a thyroid scan. Antithyroid immunoglobins may be elevated if the cause is an autoimmune response. Treatments may include antithyroid medication, radioiodine, or surgical removal of part of the thyroid gland (subtotal thyroidectomy). If left untreated, heart disease and thyrotoxicosis (thyroid storm) can occur.

Hypothyroidism: Characterized by a decrease in thyroid hormones causing extremely low metabolism. Signs and symptoms include slowed mental and physical function. Patients exhibit bradycardia, fatigue, apathy, anemia, decreased urination, constipation, musculoskeletal pain, dry and scaly skin, hair loss, and slowed movements. Hypothyroidism causes an increase in serum cholesterol and triglycerides. Severe cases of hypothyroidism lead to myxedema, severe water retention causing puffiness and a thick tongue. This leads to hypoventilation, hypotension, and hypothermia. Diagnosis of hypothyroidism is confirmed by clinical signs and elevated serum TSH level and low T3 and T4 levels. Treatment with replacement thyroid hormones will decrease symptoms. Replacement of thyroid hormones is lifelong, and dosages need to be adjusted to remain in therapeutic range. Hypothyroidism occurs more frequently in females, and age of onset is 30 to 60 years.

Hashimoto thyroiditis (chronic): Chronic inflammation and enlargement of the thyroid gland due to autoimmune destruction of thyroid tissue. The thyroid gland is progressively destroyed and replaced with fibrous tissue. The anterior pituitary gland recognizes the decrease in circulating thyroid hormones and secretes extra thyrotropin. This stimulates the thyroid to continually produce more T3 and T4, increasing the size of the thyroid gland in an attempt to produce more hormones. As the diseased thyroid grows in size, a goiter appears. Diagnosis is confirmed by elevated blood autoantibodies and radioactive iodine uptake testing (RAIU). A needle biopsy of the thyroid gland can also confirm the presence of autoantibodies. Treatment with hormone replacement can control symptoms and prevent further growth of goiter.

Thyrotoxicosis (thyroid storm): An acute, sometimes fatal, overactivity of the thyroid gland resulting in a toxic quantity of thyroid hormones being secreted into the bloodstream. Signs and symptoms include high fever, high pulse rate, dehydration, delirium, and extreme irritability. Thyroid storm is a medical emergency and can be precipitated by surgery, trauma, labor and delivery, myocardial infarction, medication overdose, or undiagnosed hyperthyroidism. Diagnosis is confirmed by clinical presentation and emergency treatment consists of antithyroid medications and beta blockers.

Parathyroid Glands

Hyperparathyroidism: Overactivity of the parathyroid glands resulting in high levels of calcium in the blood and low levels of calcium in the bones. Primary hyperparathyroidism is caused by a tumor or hyperplasia of the gland. Secondary hyperparathyroidism is caused by renal or other endocrine disorders. Signs and symptoms include muscle weakness, atrophy, nausea, vomiting, abdominal pain, cardiac arrhythmia, bone fractures, renal calculi, and lower back pain. Diagnosis is confirmed by elevated PTH on radioimmunoassay and serum elevation of calcium, alkaline phosphatase, and chloride. Blood testing will also show decrease in phosphorus. Demineralization of bone can be viewed on x-ray. Treatment is directed at the cause, resection of tumor, or treatment of renal disease. Surgical removal of parathyroid glands and supplementation with PTH may be required.

Hypoparathyroidism: Decreased production of PTH causes hypocalcemia, a decrease in blood calcium. This causes nerve and muscle weakness with muscle spasms. Tetany, a condition of continuous muscle contraction can also occur. Signs and symptoms include hair loss, brittle nails, arrhythmia, mood swings, and hyperactive reflexes. Serum blood testing shows elevated phosphate and low calcium levels. Treatment with intravenous calcium will decrease tetany. Calcium and vitamin D supplements, exposure to sunlight, and an increase in dietary calcium will increase blood calcium levels and decrease symptoms.

Adrenal Glands

Addison disease: Failure of the adrenal cortex to secrete adequate amounts of mineralocorticoids and glucocorticoids. Causes include autoimmune disorder, tumor, infection, or hemorrhage of the adrenal glands. Signs and symptoms include low blood glucose and sodium, weight loss, dehydration, weakness, digestive complaints, increased skin pigmentation, cold intolerance, anxiety, and depression. Diagnosis is confirmed by ACTH stimulation test. Treatment with replacement of hormones, medications to increase mineralocorticoids and glucocorticoid levels, and diet modification are needed lifelong.

Cushing disease: A condition caused by excess cortisol or ACTH in the bloodstream. Causes of the disorder can be categorized as primary and secondary. Primary Cushing is caused by benign or malignant tumors of the adrenal gland causing increased production of cortisol. Secondary Cushing arises from a disorder of the pituitary gland or hypothalamus where increased ACTH is secreted, triggering adrenal cortex hyperplasia and increased production of cortisol. The disease is more prevalent in females than males and is most commonly diagnosed between ages 20 to 50. Signs and symptoms include abdominal obesity, a round "moon" face, edema, hypertension, cervicodorsal fat deposits (buffalo hump), muscle atrophy, skin infections, fragile skin that is easily bruised, delayed wound healing, decreased sex drive, low serum potassium levels, and emotional changes. Symptoms of diabetes mellitus may also be present as cortisol opposes the action of insulin. Diagnosis is confirmed by a 24-hour urine test for cortisol, a low dose dexamethasone suppression test, and salivary cortisol testing. To differentiate the cause as primary or secondary, a brain MRI to rule out pituitary tumor, blood ACTH levels and corticotropin releasing test are conducted. Treatment is directed at the cause and can include surgical resection of an adrenal tumor and/or radiation. Medications to suppress ACTH secretion can reverse signs and symptoms.

Cushing Syndrome: An exogenous disorder caused by too much glucocorticosteroid intake of prednisolone or Dexamethasone to treat diseases such as asthma, inflammatory bowel disease, arthritis, or malignancies. Signs and symptoms of Cushing syndrome are the same as Cushing disease. Treatment is reduction or elimination of glucocorticosteroid medication if possible. If medication cannot be stopped due to chronic ailments such as diabetes and hypertension, cortisol levels should be closely monitored to identify possible adverse effects.

Pheochromocytoma: A vascular neuroendocrine tumor of the adrenal medulla that results in excess production of epinephrine and norepinephrine leading to hypertension and heart palpitations. Signs and symptoms are episodic or sustained and include headaches, excessive sweating, hyperglycemia, pallor, chest pain, severe anxiety, and muscle weakness. It is often diagnosed between ages 30 to 40 and both men and women are equally affected. It may be a result of an inherited autosomal dominant trait. Diagnosis may be difficult to obtain since signs and symptoms are common to many other disorders such as anxiety disorders, hyperthyroidism, and alcohol withdrawal. Differential diagnosis is obtained by blood and urine testing that shows excess catecholamines (epinephrine and norepinephrine) and/or their metabolites. MRI or radioisotope nuclear scanning is then used to locate the tumor. Treatment is surgical excision of the tumor and follow up care with an endocrinologist to monitor hormone levels. If diagnosed early, cardiovascular damage may not become permanent.

Primary aldosteronism: A condition characterized by excretion of excess amounts of aldosterone; also called Conn disease. The excess aldosterone causes retention of sodium and excretion of potassium in the urine. This causes hypertension due to an increase in blood volume. Signs and symptoms include headache, nocturia, fatigue, ventricular arrythmias, alkalosis, muscle weakness, and tetany. The disorder is caused by adrenal hyperplasia or an adenoma that secretes aldosterone. Surgical removal of one or both adrenal glands is recommended. Medication includes Aldactone, an aldosterone receptor antagonist, to lower blood pressure and raise blood potassium levels. Patients should be educated on dietary management to decrease blood pressure and manage fluid levels. Early diagnosis and treatment will prevent progressive renal and cardiac damage.

Virilism: The development of male secondary sex characteristics in females due to excess secretion of adrenocortical androgens in the adrenal cortex. The most common cause is a tumor of the adrenal gland or adrenal hyperplasia. The disorder commonly presents in females aged 30 to 40 years. Signs and symptoms include excess growth of body hair, male-pattern baldness, clitoral enlargement, amenorrhea, deepening of the voice, and atrophy of breast, uterus, and ovarian tissues. Surgical removal of the tumor will decrease signs and symptoms. The disorder can also be caused by use of anabolic steroids to enhance muscular development.

Pancreas

Diabetes mellitus: The primary disease of the pancreatic islets, it affects more than 25 million Americans of all ages. The disease is caused by a failure of glucose transport in the cells resulting from pancreatic beta cells failing to secrete functional insulin or the inability of cells to recognize insulin and carry glucose into the cytoplasm of cells. The two distinct forms of diabetes are type 1 and type 2 diabetes mellitus:

Type 1 diabetes: Formerly called insulin-dependent diabetes mellitus, usually develops before the age of 40, most frequently during childhood or adolescence. It is characterized by a dramatic decrease in the number of beta cells from the pancreas, resulting in a deficiency of insulin production. The disease is commonly caused by an infection or autoimmune destruction of beta cells. Some research points to genes undergoing a random mutation during development resulting in receptor proteins receiving an incorrect signal causing mutation. The mutation causes production of antibodies in white blood cells that destroy pancreatic beta cells. Signs and symptoms include excessive thirst, hunger, irritability, mental confusion, and weight loss. Diagnosis is confirmed by physical examination and blood testing that shows very low insulin levels and increased blood glucose. Additionally, glucose and ketones are present in the urine (glycosuria and ketonuria). Treatment consists of lifelong regular insulin injections, glucose monitoring, and patient education.

ELEMENT REVIEW
keton/o = ketones
gylcos/o = glucose
-uria = urine
retin/o = retina
-pathy = disease

Type 2 diabetes: Formerly called non-insulin-dependent diabetes mellitus, accounts for 90% of DM diagnoses. Onset of the disease usually develops after age 40, but increasingly obese children are being diagnosed with type 2 DM. Obesity is the primary risk factor in both adults and children. Type 2 diabetes is characterized by the inability of the target cells to take up insulin and use it because of a loss of sensitivity between insulin and the membrane receptors. This decrease in cellular function is called *insulin resistance.* Diagnosis is confirmed by physical examination and blood testing that reveals high glucose levels (hyperglycemia), dehydration, and/or low blood pH (acidosis). Signs and symptoms include BMI of more than 30 (obese), fatigue, and excessive thirst. Treatment with weight loss consisting of diet and increasing exercise can reverse type 2 DM and increase cellular insulin sensitivity. Medications to decrease cellular resistance to insulin can be implemented along with weight loss. If lifestyle changes are not implemented, insulin injections may be required. Uncontrolled type 2 diabetes increases overall risk of death due to the multiple organ systems affected. Complications of type 2 DM include blood vessel damage that may result in kidney damage (or even failure), heart attack, stroke, necrosis of lower limbs (that can lead to amputation of toes, feet, or legs), and loss of vision (due to diabetic retinopathy). The most common acute complication of DM is insulin shock, resulting from a dramatic drop in blood glucose (hypoglycemia). Insulin shock can be caused by decreased food intake or overdose of prescribed insulin. Insulin shock is characterized by cool, damp skin; mental confusion; profuse sweating (diaphoresis); chills, nervousness, and irritability. If left untreated, insulin shock can lead to coma and death. Treatment of insulin shock is a medical emergency requiring immediate administration of glucose. Figure 11-7 illustrates the differences between type 1 and 2 diabetes.

PHYSIOLOGY FACT

Type 1 diabetes cannot be controlled with diet and exercise because the pancreas is unable to produce insulin. Lifelong replacement of insulin (injections) is required. Type 2 diabetes can be controlled or even reversed with diet and exercise as cellular insulin sensitivity increases.

Diabetic retinopathy: A disorder of the blood vessels of the retina of the eye. Capillaries of the retina become congested with blood and form microaneurysms, hemorrhages, leakage, and scarring. Symptoms include a permanent loss of sharpness of vision. The inability of the retina to get blood and oxygen will lead to permanent loss of vision. In the US, diabetic retinopathy is the leading cause of blindness. Control of diabetes mellitus is the only intervention that can slow vision loss.

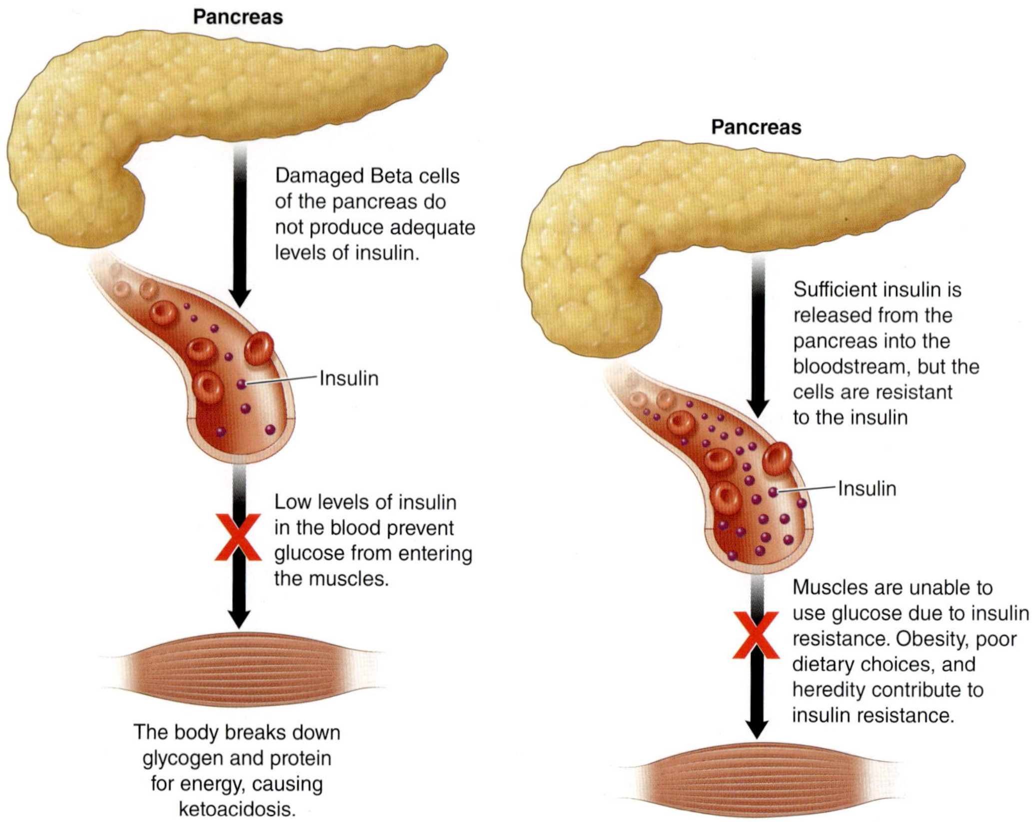

Figure 11-7 The difference between type 1 and 2 diabetes.

ELEMENT REVIEW
hyper- = excessive amount
hypo- = decreased amount
glyc/o = sugar
-emia = blood condition

Gestational diabetes: The development of diabetes in a pregnant woman who was not previously diabetic. Signs and symptoms of diabetes occur in the latter stages of pregnancy as the patient becomes unable to metabolize carbohydrates (glucose intolerance) and develops resulting hyperglycemia. Some women have no symptoms of diabetes and thus all pregnant women are screened for gestational diabetes at 24 to 28 weeks of pregnancy with a glucose tolerance test. Risk factors include previous gestational diabetes, obesity, maternal age of 30+, history of delivering large babies (10+ pounds), a family history of diabetes, previous unexplained stillborn birth, and previous birth with congenital defects. Treatment consists of dietary management and insulin if diet modification does not control blood sugar dysregulation. Diabetes usually resolves after the patient gives birth.

Pancreatic cancer: An acute or chronic inflammation and destruction of the pancreatic cells. Initial signs and symptoms are severe epigastric and abdominal pain, often with radiating pain to the back. The patient reports digestive pain upon eating fatty foods or drinking alcohol and may experience nausea and vomiting. Other signs include rigid abdominal distention, decreased bowel sounds, cold and clammy skin, hypotension, jaundice, and low body temperature. Causes include pancreatitis, alcohol abuse, trauma, metabolic disorders, infection, or a ruptured peptic ulcer. Risk factors include smoking, diabetes, and alcoholism. More women are affected than men, more blacks than whites. Complications may include abscesses, cysts, development of diabetes mellitus, renal failure, heart failure, accumulation of fluid in the abdomen (ascites), and respiratory distress. Treatment by surgical excision of the tumor, radiation, or chemotherapy may prolong life. Medication therapy is directed at decreasing pain and resolving symptoms. Only 4% of patients diagnosed with pancreatic cancer survive 5 years.

Pancreatitis: Inflammation of the pancreas that sometimes can accompany damage to adjacent organs such as the liver, bowel, lungs, and spleen. Inflammation can be chronic or acute.

Acute pancreatitis presents with sudden acute epigastric pain, nausea, and vomiting. Diagnosis is confirmed by physical examination, blood testing showing elevated serum lipase and pancreatic enzymes, and radiographic examination. Complications include necrosis, autodigestion of the pancreas, hemorrhage, gangrene, or development of a pseudocyst. Severe complications can lead to multiple organ failure and 5% of patients will die. Causes include alcohol abuse and gallstones obstructing the pancreatic duct. Acute pancreatitis can also result from use of thiazide diuretics, hypertriglyceridemia, hypercalcemia, abdominal trauma, or viral infection. Treatment consists of hospitalization where nothing is given by mouth until pain, nausea and vomiting resolve and serum lipase and pancreatic enzyme levels normalize. IV fluids and electrolytes are administered to maintain hydration. Antiemetics and pain control medications are administered parenterally. Prognosis varies depending on the amount of damage to the pancreas and adjacent organs.

ELEMENT REVIEW
calc/i = calcium
-emetic = pertaining to vomiting

Chronic pancreatitis is a permanent, progressive destruction of pancreatic cells with fibrosis, atrophy, scar tissue, calcification, and accumulation of fatty deposits. Causes of chronic pancreatitis include alcoholism, neoplasm, malnutrition (often related to alcoholism) and surgery. Signs and symptoms include abdominal pain, steatorrhea (large greasy stools), weight loss, loss of appetite, and development of diabetes. Diagnosis is confirmed by radiography showing pancreatic calcification. Treatment consists of abstaining from alcohol, administration of pancreatic enzymes, antiemetics, and antacids. Insulin is administered if diabetes develops.

ELEMENT REVIEW
steat/o = fat
-rrhea = discharge, flow

Pathology Word-Building Practice

1. Build the Terms

*Using **only** the word parts in the lists, create medical terms for the indicated meanings.*

Prefixes	Combining Forms		Suffixes	
anti-	acro/o	glyc/o	-ia	-osis
dys-	aden/o	gonad/o	-ectomy	-pathy
endo-	adren/o	kal/i	-edema	-phagia
ecto-	adrenal/o	myx/o	-emia	-rrhea
hyper-	andr/o	pancreat/o	-gen	-stasis
hypo-	calc/i	somat/o	-ism	-tropin
homeo-	cortic/o	thyr/o	-itis	-uria
homo-	crin/o	thyroid/o	-megaly	
para-	dips/o	toxic/o	-oma	
poly-	gluc/o			

1. a condition of excessive thirst ____________________________
2. excessive urination ____________________________
3. a condition of excess blood glucose ____________________________
4. a hormone that stimulates production of sex hormones ____________________________
5. the state of dynamic equilibrium ____________________________
6. the glands that sit next to the thyroid glands ____________________________

7. inflammation of the pancreas ______
8. condition of excessive activity in the testes or ovaries ______
9. surgical excision of an adrenal gland ______
10. a tumor of the thyroid gland ______
11. a tumor of the thymus gland ______
12. a condition of excessive production of thyroid hormones ______
13. inflammation of the adrenal glands ______
14. originating in the body ______
15. disease of the adrenal glands ______
16. severe hypothyroidism, puffiness of hands and feet ______

2. Prefixes

Choose from the list of prefixes to build a word for the definitions below.

a, an-	ecto-	hyper-
acro-	endo-	hypo-
anti-	homeo-	para-
dys-	homo-	poly-

1. the hormone that decreases production of urine ______
2. condition of low blood calcium ______
3. condition of increased blood potassium ______
4. excessive excretion of urine ______
5. poor blood sugar regulation ______
6. complete absence of production of urine ______
7. condition of lack of pituitary hormones ______
8. enlargement of the extremities ______
9. medication to reduce vomiting and nausea ______
10. to secrete into the bloodstream ______

3. Suffixes

Choose from the list of suffixes to build a word for the definitions below.

-ectomy	-megaly	-phagia
-emia	-ologist	-rrhea
-gen	-oma	-stasis
-ism	-osis	-tropin
-itis	-pathy	-uria

1. blood in the urine ______________________
2. disease of glands ______________________
3. inability to swallow or eat ______________________
4. condition of excessive growth ______________________
5. stopping or controlling bleeding ______________________
6. inflammation of the pancreas ______________________
7. pus in the urine ______________________
8. passage of large greasy stools ______________________
9. condition of an addiction to alcohol ______________________
10. enlargement of the thyroid glands ______________________
11. surgical removal of the pituitary gland ______________________
12. physician who specializes in treatment of disease and disorders of the endocrine system ______________________

Endocrine System Diagnostic Procedures

Information regarding the function of the endocrine glands can be obtained by blood testing, radioactive scanning procedures, and ultrasound examination of the glands and target organs.

Fasting blood sugar (FBS): A sample of blood taken in the early morning before breakfast. The patient is asked to fast from midnight the night before. Normal fasting blood glucose for an adult is less than 100 mg/dL.

Fingerstick blood glucose (FSBG): Self-monitoring test of blood sugar that can be performed by the patient or caregiver. Home devices (glucometers) are inexpensive, accurate, and easy to use (Fig. 11-8). They are most commonly used by diabetics to determine proper dosing of insulin based on the level of blood sugar.

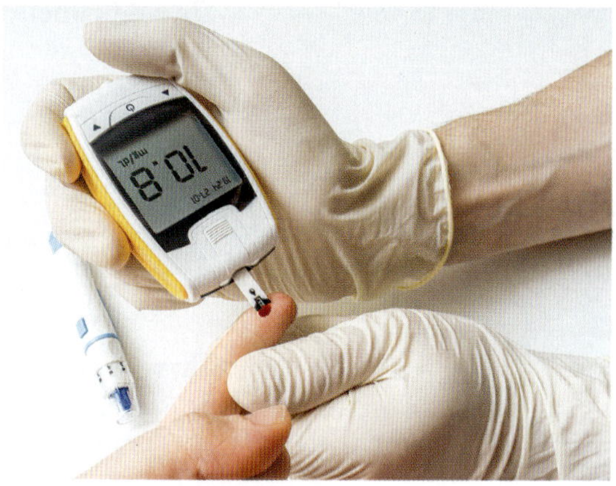

Figure 11-8 Glucometer.

Glucose tolerance test (GTT): This test evaluates the patient's ability to clear a concentrated oral dose of glucose. The patient is asked to fast and then given the glucose solution to drink. Blood glucose levels are measured as follows:

1. Prior to drinking glucose solution
2. 30 minutes after administration
3. 1 hour after administration
4. 2 hours after administration
5. 3 hours after administration

Patients with diabetes mellitus will have serum glucose levels of 200+ mg/dL at the 2-hour mark and later. This shows an inability of glucose to clear the bloodstream. A person without diabetes mellitus will show minimal elevation of blood glucose during the first hour after administration. The body is able to clear the glucose at or before the 1-hour mark. Pregnant patients who may be at risk for gestational diabetes (obesity, previous history of gestational diabetes) are routinely given this test.

Hemoglobin A1c (hbA1c): A blood test that shows the average amount of glucose bound to red blood cells. Glucose chemically binds to the hemoglobin protein at the alpha-1 site to clear the blood of the excess circulating glucose. Because red blood cells have an average life span of 90 days, an elevated level of hemoglobin A1c correlates to elevated glucose for the past 90 days. An increased percentage of red blood cells with bound glucose of greater than 7% is considered a high risk for serious complications of diabetes.

Radioactive iodine uptake test (RAIU): A thyroid function test done by administering a known quantity of radioactive iodine and measuring the uptake of the iodine by the thyroid gland. The gamma ray detector is placed over the thyroid gland, and measurements of uptake are conducted at specified intervals. Patients with hyperthyroidism will uptake increased amounts of iodine. A decrease in uptake can indicate acute thyroiditis and can be treated with oral antibiotics.

Serum glucose test: A measurement of glucose in the bloodstream at the time of sampling. Elevations in random blood glucose measurements can be an indication of diabetes mellitus, but they must be evaluated according to the time of day and time of last meal. Glucose level can be collected in a fingerstick or tube.

Thyroid echogram: An ultrasound examination that distinguishes solid versus cystic thyroid nodules. The picture can show the size, shape, and location of the thyroid gland, nodule(s), and/or goiter.

Thyroid function tests: Blood test that measures levels of T3, T4, and TSH.

Thyroid panel: Blood test similar to thyroid function testing, but also evaluates hormone balance in the thyroid gland and the bloodstream. This test is helpful in differentiating Hashimoto thyroiditis versus Graves' disease (hyperthyroidism).

- TSH level evaluates the overall function of the thyroid gland.
- T4 (total thyroxine) level indicates the quantity produced by the thyroid.
- Free T3 (free triiodothyronine) indicates the amount of T3 present in the cells and tissues, and thus is an indication of hormone balance.
- Free T4 (free thyroxine) indicates the total amount of T4 hormone available to body cells.

Thyroid scan: An image of the thyroid gland that shows the position, size, shape, and physiological function of the gland. Radioactive iodine is administered, and the scan shows uptake in specific regions. The scan is helpful in diagnosing masses, thyroid cancer, nodules, goiter, and cause of hyperthyroidism (Graves' disease versus Hashimoto's thyroiditis).

Thyroid-stimulating hormone (TSH) blood test: A test that measures the concentration of TSH in the bloodstream. The test is useful in differentiating the cause of hypothyroidism. In primary hypothyroidism, a defect in the structure or function of the thyroid gland causes a lack of hormone secretion. Secondary hypothyroidism is caused by insufficient stimulation of the thyroid gland from the anterior pituitary gland. In addition to differentiating primary versus secondary causes of hypothyroidism, serum TSH levels are monitored for patients receiving thyroid replacement hormones. TSH levels are normally decreased in patients with severe illness, and monitoring signs and symptoms along with TSH is vital to maintain healthy T3 and T4 levels.

Endocrine System Therapeutic Procedures

Therapeutic interventions for endocrine disorders include surgical excision of tumors, radiation of glands to decrease overactive glandular activity, and a variety of medications to increase or decrease hormone levels to obtain normal hormone levels.

Adrenalectomy: A surgical procedure to remove one or both adrenal glands. Adrenalectomy is performed if there is an adrenal tumor that secretes excess hormones, is cancerous, or is large (more than 2 inches in diameter). Adrenalectomy is also performed to remove cancer that has spread from other organs such as the kidney or lungs. The surgery can be performed as a minimally invasive procedure by using a robotic laparoscope (anterior approach) or a retroperitoneoscopic adrenalectomy (posterior approach). An open surgical approach may be needed for large tumors. Another surgical procedure uses cryoablation with a computed tomography image to guide the surgeon who inserts a probe that freezes and destroys adrenal tumors. Cryoablation is an option for small tumors that have spread to the adrenal glands from adjacent tumors, especially when surgery carries a high risk. If only one adrenal gland is removed, the other healthy gland will secrete hormones, but if both adrenal glands are removed, then the patient must take replacement hormones for the remainder of life.

ELEMENT REVIEW
retro- = behind
peritone/o = peritoneum
-scopic = pertaining to a scope, to look

Insulin pump: A device that releases insulin as a steady flow throughout the day and night, known as the basal dose (Fig. 11-9). An extra dose is automatically released at mealtime

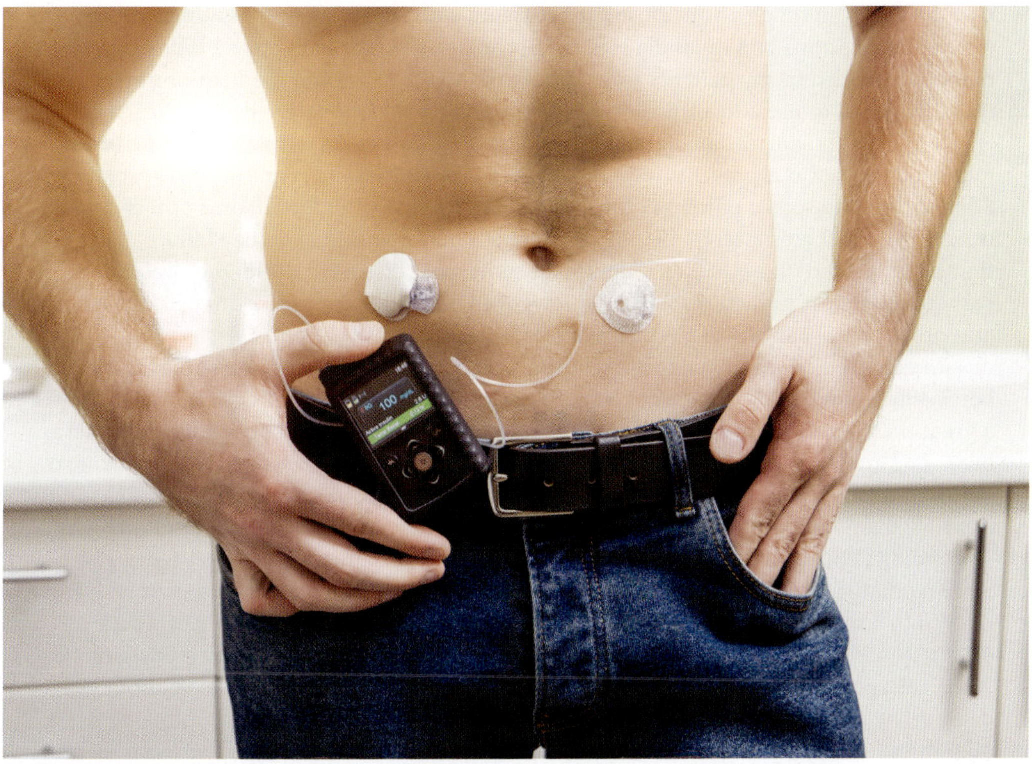

Figure 11-9 Insulin pump.

(called a bolus) to ensure there is adequate insulin to respond to increased blood glucose from meals. The patient, under the direction of a diabetes educator, programs the pump for both the basal and bolus doses. The pump is attached to the patient's body with an infusion set: a thin plastic tube and either a needle or a small cannula placed under the skin. Placement sites are the belly, thigh, or buttock. Insulin pumps use short-acting or rapid-acting insulin, but not long-acting insulin as the device is designed to deliver small amounts of insulin continuously.

Parathyroidectomy: Surgical removal of the parathyroid gland for primary hyperparathyroidism. In 85% to 90% of cases, only one gland is abnormal and needs removal. This approach is called a minimally invasive parathyroidectomy, and patients will not need to take replacement hormones as the normal gland remains functional. A newer transoral vestibular approach (TOVA) removes the diseased parathyroid gland through the oral cavity and thus leaves no surgical scar. If bilateral glands are diseased and require removal, replacement of PTH is necessary for the rest of the patients' life.

Thyroidectomy: Surgical removal of thyroid gland to remove goiters, nodules, tumors, or to correct overactive thyroid glands. Surgical approach through the anterior neck or a TOVA is chosen based on the size of the tumors/gland and surgical risks. After thyroid gland removal, the patient will need to take a synthetic replacement thyroid hormone (Synthroid) for the remainder of life.

Thyroid radiation: Radioactive iodine (RAI) is treatment for hyperthyroidism and some types of thyroid cancer. RAI is administered orally as a capsule, and the patient is encouraged to drink a lot of water to flush the remaining radioactive iodine out of their system. Most patients need one dose of RAI to resolve hyperthyroidism, but testing is recommended to monitor T3, T4, and TSH levels.

CAREER EXPLORATION: DIABETES EDUCATOR

After graduating from nursing school, I worked in a hospital on the kidney transplant unit. I learned so much about caring for patients with renal failure. I administered renal system medications and renal dialysis, and I took care of patients after a kidney transplant. I explained to my patients how important it is to take their medications after transplant and to eat a healthy diet. The surgeons on the floor were great to learn from; we were a great team and helped so many people. My patients were all very sick, and it made me think about prevention of renal disease prior to them requiring a transplant. Some of the transplant patients had type 1 diabetes from childhood, and others developed type 2 diabetes later in life. While there are many causes of kidney failure, I learned that uncontrolled diabetes was a major cause of renal disease. I decided to become a diabetes educator to help my patients prevent the need for dialysis, kidney transplant, and other complications of uncontrolled diabetes.

I investigated continuing education programs for health professionals to become diabetes educators. The Certification Board for Diabetes Care and Education (CBDCE) was a great program. This program is available to clinical psychologists, occupational therapists, optometrists, pharmacists, physicians, and registered nurses like me who want to help educate patients with diabetes. I studied online and took the certification examination. The hospital paid for my certification through their continuing education program.

I give diet education talks to dialysis patients at the outpatient clinic every Saturday. Since working at the Endocrinology Group as a diabetes educator, I have worked with many different patients and have helped patients and families live healthy lives. I especially like working with children like Malik. Malik likes monitoring his blood glucose on his mom's cell phone; he calls it his "blood sugar video game." I help him to think about how he is feeling and the importance of eating protein, carbohydrates, and fats in the right quantities. I design my teaching sessions for each patient; in some ways I feel like a teacher. I hope to continue to work with Malik and other patients and guide them in healthy habits.

Procedures and Diagnostics Review

Identify the Term

Fill in the correct term.

1. An image of the thyroid gland that uses radioactive iodine ____________________
2. A blood test that shows the average amount of glucose bound to red blood cells ____________________
3. A blood test that evaluates the patient's ability to clear glucose ____________________
4. A surgical approach through the mouth that can be used to remove the parathyroid or thyroid glands ____________________
5. Evaluates thyroid hormone balance ____________________
6. A thyroid function test using a known quantity of radioactive iodine and measuring the uptake of the iodine by the thyroid gland ____________________
7. The test that is useful in differentiating primary versus secondary hypothyroidism ____________________
8. Probe that is used to freeze and remove the adrenal glands ____________________
9. Measurement of blood sugar when a patient has not eaten ____________________
10. A device that releases basal and bolus dosages of insulin throughout the day and night ____________________

CASE STUDY, completed

Anne meets with Malik and his parents to discuss options for administering insulin to Malik. The family listens as Anne explains the advantages and disadvantages of an insulin pump versus daily injections of insulin. Anne explains that the insulin pump is a small computer that Malik can wear that delivers insulin every hour. The pump delivers extra insulin at meal and snack times. The insulin will be a short-acting drug because it will be continuously administered. She shows Malik and his family the insulin pump. It is approximately the size of a deck of cards and comes with a clip that Malik can secure to his belt. Anne goes on to explain that the device is connected to a cannula that will be inserted under Malik's skin with adhesive. The insulin pump that Anne recommends also has a continuous glucose monitor, which can adjust insulin dosages automatically. Additionally, Shaylah's cell phone can be connected so that she can monitor Malik's blood sugar readings throughout the day and even at night. Because there is a lot to consider, Anne gives Shaylah and Roy a list of pros and cons of using an insulin pump.

Pros

- Dosages are delivered easily throughout the day.
- Basal rate is automatic and constant.
- Insulin pump infusion sets can be changed every few days.
- Corrections are easily made.
- The basal rate can be suspended, making it easy to adjust dosage during exercise.
- Pumps can be programmed to deliver different doses of insulin automatically at specific times.

Continued

CASE STUDY, completed

Cons

- Changing out infusion sites can be a process.
- Pump problems can occur, such as a kink in the tubing or air bubbles in the insulin cartridge.
- It takes longer to learn the ins and outs of an insulin pump.
- Pump equipment and accessories can be expensive.
- It can be uncomfortable to wear all day.
- Sometimes the pump can be visible.

Anne allows Malik to hold the insulin pump while she goes on to explain the other insulin option of insulin injection with a pen. The insulin pen looks just like a writing pen and delivers insulin by injecting it into the subcutaneous layer of the skin. The insulin injected is long-acting insulin to reduce the number of injections needed per day. A needle is screwed onto the pen, and a dial on the pen is used to measure and deliver the required dosage of insulin. If they choose the insulin pen, Malik will have to rotate the injection sites to avoid pain or skin breakdown. The insulin pen does not monitor glucose levels, so Malik will have to perform fingersticks and use a glucometer to measure his blood glucose. Like the insulin pump, there are some pros and cons to consider with the use of the insulin pen.

Pros

- It is simple to perform injection.
- Injections are inexpensive.
- There's no risk of being away from home and having a pump failure or mechanical issue.
- Nothing is attached to the body, nor is there any tubing involved.
- Injection pens can be used discretely.

Cons

- There will be multiple injections each day.
- The patient cannot change the basal rate once the long-acting insulin has been injected. (The patient must wait 24 hours before making changes to the dose.)
- The background insulin needs to be administered at the same time every day.
- Administering the insulin shot at school will require going to the school nurse each day.

After listening to Anne explain their options, Malik tells his parents he wants the pump because he will have fewer shots and no fingersticks. Roy says to his son, "I agree buddy. Let's get Anne to order your pump and learn more about how to use it. You must promise your mom and me that you will be careful with the pump." Malik responds, "Yes, I want to learn how to eat right and take care of my pump."

Anne says, "Great choice. I can order the pump for you, and we can meet again next week. In the meantime, I will give you an insulin pen and instructions for dosing. Malik, you will need to eat the right amounts of healthy foods. I just sent your mom a link to healthy recipes for diabetic kids and some videos for kids that explain more about diabetes. We can talk about the foods you like each time we meet. Are you ready to learn with me?" Malik replies, "Yes, I want to learn, and I love watching videos."

QUESTIONS

1. Because Malik has type 1 diabetes, what blood abnormality will he have? ______________________
2. If left untreated, what will be his blood insulin level? ______________________
3. Malik presented with what signs of type 1 diabetes? ______________________
4. Malik presented with what symptoms of type 1 diabetes? ______________________
5. To what type of specialist did Malik's pediatrician refer him? ______________________
6. The machine that measures blood glucose levels is called a ______________________

CASE STUDY, completed

7. What type of specialist teaches patients to administer insulin, monitor blood glucose, and choose meals and snacks? ______________________________

8. List three pros of using an insulin pump. ______________________________

____

____

9. List three cons of using an insulin pump. ______________________________

____

____

10. List three pros of using an insulin pen (injection). ______________________________

____

____

11. List three cons of using an insulin pen (injection). ______________________________

____

____

Medications for the Endocrine System

Table 11-3 lists examples of common medications for the endocrine system that help the body maintain homeostasis by regulating hormone levels.

TABLE 11-3 Examples of Medications for the Endocrine System

Classification	Examples	Common Use/Action
Anabolic steroids	Nandrolone decanoate, Oxandrin	Weight gain following severe illness/injury, some forms of anemia
Antithyroid medications	Methimazole, Tapazole, Propylthiouracil 1-131, Iodotope	Hyperthyroidism, Graves' disease
Cortisol inhibitors	Metyrapone, Metopirone	Cushing's disease
Corticosteroids	Hydrocortisone USP, fludrocortisone acetate, Florinef	Severe allergies, asthma, multiple sclerosis, arthritis, Addison's disease
Insulin	Lispro, Humalog, NovoLog, Humulin R, Novolin R, Humulin U, Lantus	Diabetes mellitus

Continued

TABLE 11-3 Examples of Medications for the Endocrine System—cont'd

Classification	Examples	Common Use/Action
Oral antidiabetics	First-generation sulfonylureas: Dymelor, chlorpropamide, tolbutamide	Type 2 diabetes mellitus
	Second-generation sulfonylureas: glipizide, Glucotrol, Diabeta	Type 2 diabetes mellitus
	Biguanides: metformin, Glucophage, Fortamet	Type 2 diabetes mellitus
	Thiazolidinediones: rosiglitazone, Avandia, Actos	Type 2 diabetes mellitus
	Meglitinides: nateglinide, Starlix, Prandin, NovoNorm	Type 2 diabetes mellitus
	GLP-1 agonists: Victoza, Trulicity	Type 2 diabetes mellitus
	DPP-4 inhibitors: anagliptin, Tradjenta, Januvia	Type 2 diabetes mellitus
	SGLT-2 inhibitors: canagliflozin, Invokana, Farxiga, Jardiance	Type 2 diabetes mellitus
Pancreatic enzymes	Pancrelipase, Pancreaze, Creon	Exocrine pancreatic insufficiency
Thyroid hormone replacements	Levothyroxine, Levothroid	Hypothyroidism

Medications Review

Using the table of medications, complete the chart below. The first one has been done for you.

Medication Name	Classification (mechanism)	Therapeutic Use (What is it used for?)
Glucophage	*Oral antidiabetic (biguanide)*	*Type 2 diabetes*
Levothyroxine	______________	______________
Metyrapone	______________	______________
NovoLog	______________	______________
Victoza	______________	______________
Tapazole	______________	______________
Hydrocortisone USP	______________	______________
Creon	______________	______________
Invokana	______________	______________
Humalin U	______________	______________

Endocrine Abbreviations

The list below provides some common cardiovascular abbreviations and their meanings.

ACTH adrenocorticotropic hormone
ADH antidiuretic hormone
BMR basal metabolic rate
Ca calcium
DI diabetes insipidus
DKA diabetic ketoacidosis
DM diabetes mellitus
FBS fasting blood sugar
GH growth hormone
GTT glucose tolerance test
HDL high-density lipoprotein
HbA1c hemoglobin A1c
IDDM insulin-dependent diabetes mellitus (type 1 diabetes)
K potassium
LH luteinizing hormone
LTH lactogenic hormone
MSH melanocyte-stimulating hormone
Na sodium
NIDDM non-insulin-dependent diabetes mellitus (type 2 diabetes)
OT oxytocin
PBI protein-bound iodine
PTH parathyroid hormone
RAI radioactive iodine
RAIU radioactive iodine uptake
T3 triiodothyronine (thyroid hormone)
T4 thyroxine (thyroid hormone)
TFT thyroid function test
TSH thyroid-stimulating hormone
VLDL very low-density lipoprotein

Abbreviations Review

Choose the correct definition for each of the abbreviations.

1. K
   a. sodium
   b. calcium
   c. potassium
   d. iodine

2. PTH
   a. parathyroid hormone
   b. polythyroid hormone
   c. partial thyroid hormone
   d. protein thyroid hormone

3. T3
   a. thyroxine
   b. triiodothyronine
   c. thyroid lipids
   d. thyroid function

4. LH
   a. lipid hormones
   b. low-density hormone
   c. lactogenic hormone
   d. luteinizing hormone

5. LTH
   a. lipid hormones
   b. low-density hormone
   c. lactogenic hormone
   d. luteinizing hormone

6. FBS
   a. fasting blood sugar
   b. first blood sugar
   c. fasting blood status
   d. first blood status

7. RAI
   a. radiation initiation
   b. radioactive iodine
   c. radiation iodine
   d. radicular iodine

8. OT
   a. oxygen test
   b. calcium
   c. oxytocin
   d. oxytocin testing

9. Na
   a. calcium
   b. potassium
   c. iodine
   d. sodium

10. DKA
    a. diabetic analysis
    b. diabetes kinetic assay
    c. diabetic ketoacidosis
    d. diabetic kidney assessment

11. GTT
    a. glucose tolerance test
    b. glucotoxic test
    c. growth tolerance test
    d. growth toxicity test

12. T3
    a. thyroxine
    b. triiodothyronine
    c. thyroid lipids
    d. thyroid function

13. ACTH
    a. adrenal cortisol thyroid hormone
    b. adrenocorticotropic hormone
    c. antidiuretic cortisol thyroid hormone
    d. anticortisol hormone

14. ADH
    a. antidiuretic hormone
    b. adrenal diabetes hormone
    c. antidiabetes hormone
    d. adrenodiuretic hormone

15. GH
    a. glucose hormone
    b. glucose is high
    c. growth hormone
    d. growth of hemoglobin

MEDICAL DOCUMENTATION

Knowledge of terms related to normal anatomy and pathological conditions enables you to understand medical documentation such as the diabetic foot wound consultation that follows. Apply your knowledge by answering the questions that follow this consultation.

Consultation

Patient: Michael K DOB: 08/30/19XX

Reason for Consultation: Nonhealing wound on the plantar aspect of the right foot for 6 weeks duration.

History of Present Illness: The patient is a 79-year-old white male with a past h/o type 2 diabetes, hypertension, chronic renal failure (CRF), and chronic A-fib. The patient reports sustaining a blister on the plantar aspect of his foot approximately 6 weeks ago, which has progressed from a blister to a wound. He was admitted to the hospital 3 weeks ago for pancreatitis and CRF. At that time, podiatry was consulted. X-rays were taken, and an initial debridement was performed. The wound continued to progress, with increasing erythema. It is bleeding, and a pus-filled exudate is present.

The patient denies pyrexia, chills, nausea, or vomiting. He states he does not control his blood sugar and has had readings as high as 300 recently. He states he cannot feel either foot. Accompanied by his daughter, he presents today for evaluation and treatment.

Medications: His current medications include Lantus insulin, Humalog insulin, Lasix, vitamin B, Procrit. He completed a course of Levaquin 2 weeks ago.

Allergies: none

Physical Examination: The patient is an elderly male who is 5' 8" and 190 lbs. Vital signs: temperature: 98.4, pulse: 74, BP 162/82. There is a large ulceration on the plantar aspect

MEDICAL DOCUMENTATION—cont'd

of the right foot measuring 1.4 × 0.8 × 0.4 cm prior to debridement. The ulceration probes 3.6 cm in the 6 o'clock direction. It is covered with necrotic tissue and has an odor of necrosis. There is erythema extending up to the midfoot, but no tenderness is noted in the foot. There is serosanguinous drainage from the wound. There is nonpitting edema in both lower extremities, with superficial eschar in the anterior right tibia.

Imaging studies: Previous x-rays taken 3 weeks ago show no osteomyelitis.

Laboratory Data: WBC 8.4, hemoglobin 11.6, hematocrit 35.3, creatinine 7.6, and BG 342.

Assessment:
1. Cellulitis right foot with diabetic foot infection
2. Ulceration right foot

Plan: I had a discussion with the patient and his daughter and suggested debridement and removal of the infected tissue. The wound was surgically debrided to the level of muscle and fascia. No anesthesia was needed due to his neuropathy. The patient tolerated the procedure well. A Gelfoam was placed over the wound and a below-the-knee bandage applied. He is advised to return in 5 days for a dressing change.

Prescriptions for clindamycin and Levaquin were written. He was advised to control blood sugar more carefully to decrease healing time of the wound.

Signed
Christina Young, DO
Podiatry

Questions

1. Why is Michael unable to feel both feet? ____________
2. What does necrosis mean? ____________
3. What type of medication is clindamycin? ____________
4. What does osteomyelitis mean? ____________
5. What is serosanguinous drainage? ____________
6. Which body systems are affected in the note above? ____________
7. What does neuropathy mean? ____________
8. His blood pressure was measured as 162/82, which is ____________
9. Both lower legs are swollen, a term known as ____________
10. Why is Michael's wound not healing? ____________

Visit the Medical Language Lab at medicallanguagelab.com. Use it to improve your recognition and understanding of terms in medical documentation.

CHAPTER REVIEW

Complete the Sentence

1. The master gland of the endocrine system is the ____________________
2. Hyperplasia of the thyroid gland is referred to as a ____________________
3. A condition caused by deficiency of antidiuretic hormone is called ____________________
4. A condition of excessive cortisol or ACTH in the bloodstream is called ____________________
5. The endocrine organ that secretes insulin and glucagon is the ____________________
6. Development of male secondary sex characteristics in females is known as ____________________
7. The eye disease associated with diabetes is ____________________
8. The name for the laboratory testing of T3, T4, and TSH is ____________________
9. The term for the sum of all physical and chemical processes in the body is ____________________
10. The hormone that stimulates contraction of the uterus for birth is ____________________
11. The study of the endocrine system is ____________________
12. Any disease of glands is referred to as ____________________
13. The gland that secretes thymosin is the ____________________
14. The hormone that regulates fluid and electrolyte balance in the body is ____________________
15. The inner portion of the adrenal gland is called ____________________
16. The outer portion of the adrenal gland is called ____________________
17. The hormone produced by the alpha cells of the pancreas is ____________________
18. The hormone produced by the beta cells of the pancreas is ____________________

19. The hormone that prepares the uterus for pregnancy is ______________________________

20. The blood test that shows the average amount of glucose bound to red blood cells is ______________________________

Spelling

Circle the word that is spelled correctly.

endocrinologist	endicrinologist
diabetes melittus	diabetes mellitus
glycosuria	glucosuria
hyperinsulinemia	hyperinsalinemia
gigantanism	gigantism
virilism	verilism
triiodothyronine	triodiothryonine
polidipsia	polydipsia
anuria	auria
myxedema	mxyedema
glycagenesis	glycogenesis
goiter	gioter
adrenocorticotropic	adrenocorticatropic
melotonin	melatonin
hypothalumus	hypothalamus

Abbreviations

Define the following abbreviations.

1. VLDL ______________________________
2. BMR ______________________________
3. TSH ______________________________
4. HbA1c ______________________________
5. MSH ______________________________
6. RAIU ______________________________

7. TFT ______________________________

8. DM ______________________________

9. DI ______________________________

10. T4 ______________________________

Identify the Anatomical Structures

Match the structures of the endocrine system from the following list to the letters shown in Figure 11-10:

1. _______ adrenal glands
2. _______ hypothalamus
3. _______ ovaries
4. _______ pancreas
5. _______ parathyroid gland
6. _______ pineal gland
7. _______ pituitary gland
8. _______ testes
9. _______ thymus gland
10. _______ thyroid gland

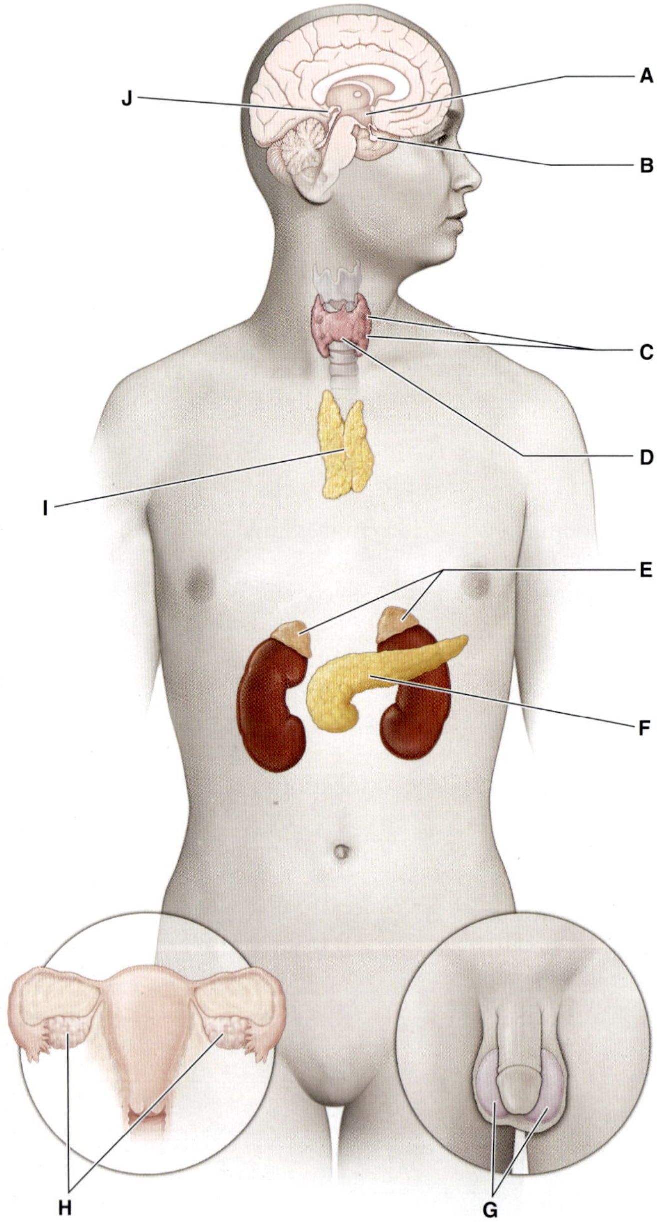

Figure 11-10 Identify the endocrine glands.

Match the structures of the pituitary gland from the following list to the letters shown in Figure 11-11:

1. _______ anterior lobe of pituitary gland
2. _______ endocrine cells
3. _______ hypophyseal veins
4. _______ hypothalamus
5. _______ inferior hypophyseal artery
6. _______ infundibulum
7. _______ neurosecretory cells
8. _______ posterior lobe of pituitary gland
9. _______ superior hypophyseal artery
10. _______ veins

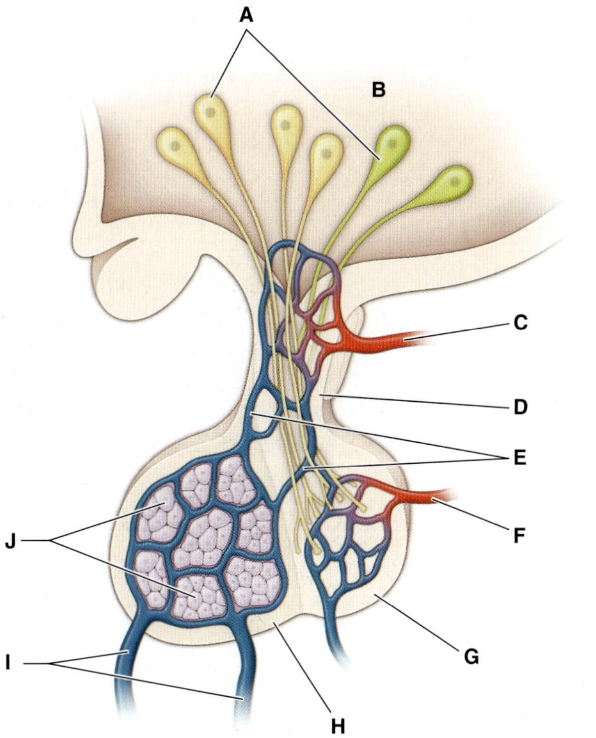

Figure 11-11 Identify the structures of the pituitary gland.

Word Building

Construct a word to fit the definition.

1. surgical removal of a thymus gland ____________________
2. a blood condition of low sugar ____________________
3. urinating at night ____________________
4. located above the kidneys ____________________
5. enlargement of the extremities ____________________
6. condition of elevated blood calcium ____________________
7. the state of dynamic equilibrium ____________________
8. condition of excessive hunger ____________________
9. condition of decreased thyroid hormones ____________________
10. surgical removal of the thyroid gland ____________________

Medical Language Lab

Visit the Medical Language Lab at medicallanguagelab.com. Use it to enhance your study and reinforcement of the medical terms and word parts covered in this chapter.

CHAPTER

12

The Female Reproductive System

LEARNING OBJECTIVES

Upon completion of the chapter, you will be able to:

1. Identify and define the combining forms, roots, prefixes, and suffixes introduced in the chapter.
2. Spell medical terms related to the female reproductive system.
3. Describe the major organs of the female reproductive system.
4. Describe the four phases of the menstrual cycle.
5. Discuss contraceptive methods and prevention of STIs.
6. Describe the process of fertilization and the developmental stages of an embryo to fetus to newborn.
7. Discuss the stages of the birth process.
8. Discuss the changes of a woman's body during menopause.
9. Identify and discuss major pathological terms of the female reproductive system.
10. Identify and discuss major diagnostic and therapeutic treatments of the female reproductive system.
11. Identify the major categories of medications used to treat female reproductive pathologies.
12. Define abbreviations of the female reproductive system.

We begin this chapter with the story of Meredith who is pregnant with her first child. The case study introduces some of the medical terms relevant to the female reproductive system. Throughout the chapter, we will revisit the story of Meredith to understand the stages of pregnancy, nutritional advice given to pregnant women, the preparation for the birth process, and the routine testing during the pregnancy. You will understand the progression of fetal development and how Meredith cares for herself and her developing child. You will see how good prenatal care can promote delivery of a healthy infant. You will understand how a woman's body functions normally for the purpose of reproduction. Additionally, this chapter will discuss the changes in a woman's body as she enters menopause and some pathologies of the female reproductive system and treatments for these conditions. You will be able to use word elements presented to understand unfamiliar terms and to build your medical vocabulary.

CASE STUDY

Meredith and her husband Justin look at the lines on the home pregnancy test and hug each other with excitement. Justin says "We did it! We are going to be parents!" Meredith replies "I'm so happy! I need to call Dr. Johnson's office and make an appointment." At her first obstetrical visit, the medical assistant, Felicity, asks Meredith, "When was your last period?" Meredith replies "I started my last period on September 15th. Today is November 4th, so I think I am 7 weeks pregnant." Felicity says, "I will add that date to your chart." Meredith replies, "I looked up **Naegele's rule**, the mathematical formula to calculate my due date. It is so easy. You add 7 days to the first day of the last menstrual period, add 1 year, and then count back 3 months. This means I should be due on June 22nd." Felicity draws Meredith's blood, takes her vital signs, and asks Meredith to give her a urine sample. She tells Meredith, "The blood and urine tests will confirm that you are pregnant. Dr. Johnson will be in to talk, answer any questions, and give you an examination."

Dr. Johnson comes into the room and says, "Hello Meredith. I see you had a positive home pregnancy test. Have you been taking the prenatal vitamins I prescribed for you at your last visit?" Meredith replies, "Yes, I've been taking prenatal vitamins for 4 months now, and I have not been drinking any alcohol. Justin and I have been talking about starting our family for a while now, and I want to do everything I can to have a healthy baby." Dr. Johnson replies, "That is a great start. I'll have you change into a gown so I can examine your cervix." Meredith replies, "I noticed a white discharge about a month ago; is that normal?" Dr. Johnson says, "Yes, some women see a discharge around the time of ovulation, when you are fertile. This is probably when you became pregnant." Meredith changes into the gown, and Dr. Johnson performs an examination of Meredith's cervix. The doctor says, "I can feel that your cervix, the opening to your uterus, is closed, and I feel no abnormalities." Dr. Johnson completes the exam and tells Meredith, "I want to see you once a month for 5 months, then more often as you get closer to your due date. Continue to take prenatal vitamins, eat whole foods, no alcohol, and get plenty of rest. You may feel extra tired or have an upset stomach. If you have some morning sickness, ginger tea or some saltine crackers may help to settle your stomach. Every woman is different, so listen to your body and enjoy this time in your life." Meredith replies, "Thanks Dr. Johnson. See you next month."

KEY TERMS

Amniotic fluid	Cesarean section	Colostrum	Estrogen
Amniotic sac	Cervix	Contractions	Fallopian tubes
Areola	Chloasma	Corpus luteum	Fertilization
Bartholin's glands	Chorionic villi	Embryo	Fertility
Breast	Clitoris	Endometrium	Fetus

KEY TERMS—cont'd

Fimbriae	Mammary glands	Oocyte	Prolactin
Gynecology	Menarche	Ovaries	Puberty
Gynecologists	Menses	Ovulation	Sexual intercourse
Hymen	Menopause	Ovum	Umbilical cord
Labor	Menstrual cycle	Oxytocin	Uterus
Labia majora	Midwife	Parturition	Vagina
Labia minora	Mons pubis	Perimetrium	Vernix caseosa
Lactation	Myometrium	Placenta	Vulva
Lanugo	Naegele's rule	Pregnancy	Zygote
Linea nigra	Obstetrician	Progesterone	

Structures and Physiology of the Female Reproductive System

The structures of the female reproductive system include internal and external genitalia and the breasts. After the onset of **puberty**, the period of life where a girl becomes able to become pregnant, bodily changes occur, changing the appearance from a girl to a woman. The study of the female reproductive system is called **gynecology**; specialists in this field are **gynecologists**.

ELEMENT REVIEW
gynec/o = female
-logist = specialist
-logy = field of study

External Genitalia

ELEMENT REVIEW
labia = lips
majora = large
minora = small
homo- = same

The external female genitalia are a group of tissues located at the pelvic floor, the region below the abdomen and between the top of the legs. The external genitals are collectively called the **vulva**. It consists of the mons pubis, labia majora, labia minora, clitoris, urethral meatus, the vaginal orifice, Bartholin's glands, and the perineum (Fig. 12-1). The **mons pubis** is the fatty tissue that covers the upper border of the genital region. Upon puberty, a triangular pattern of pubic hair will appear. Extending down from the mons pubis are two narrow folds of skin called the **labia majora**. At the onset of puberty, the labia majora will develop hair that is the mons pubis. The labia majora are the female homolog to the male scrotum. This means that the tissues are derived from the same embryonic tissue during development. Medial to the labia majora are the **labia minora**, the inner fold of moist tissue that is covered in a mucous membrane. The labia minora form the outer margins of a region called the vestibule, the outer chamber that covers and protects the urethra and vaginal opening. At the anterior section of the vestibule is the **clitoris**, the female homolog to the male penis. The clitoris is composed of numerous sensory nerves and erectile tissue, which will engorge with blood upon stimulation, causing the female orgasm. Directly posterior to the clitoris is the urethral meatus, the opening where urine is passed out of the body. Posterior to the urethral meatus is the vaginal orifice, which provides the orifice for sexual intercourse and the passageway for menstrual blood. Two small mucous-secreting glands, **Bartholin's glands**, are located on the lateral walls of the vestibule, and they lubricate the vaginal orifice

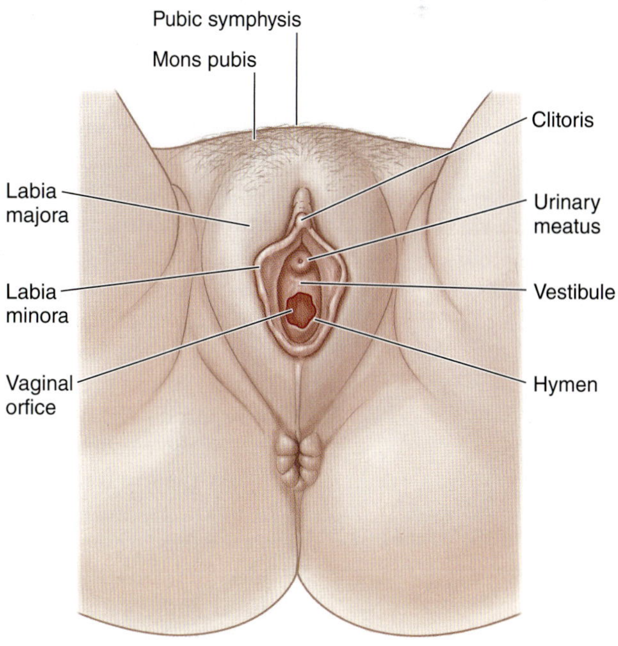

Figure 12-1 The vulva.

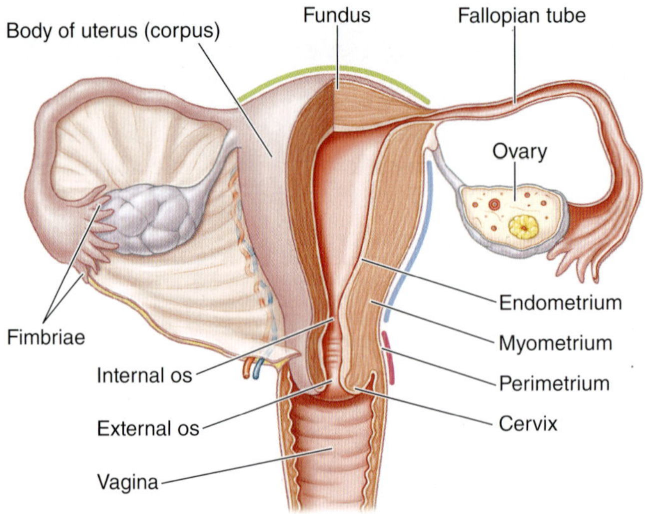

Figure 12-2 The internal female reproductive system.

during sexual intercourse. Posterior to the vaginal orifice is the anus, the last section of the gastrointestinal tract from which feces will leave the body.

Internal Organs of Reproduction

The internal female organs of reproduction consist of the vagina, uterus, fallopian tubes, and the ovaries (Fig. 12-2).

The **vagina** is the muscular tube that connects the uterus with the vulva, the outside of the body. The vagina is approximately 3 inches (7.5 cm) long and rests between the bladder (anteriorly) and the rectum (posteriorly). In young females, the opening may be covered by a thin layer of tissue called the **hymen**. The hymen contains blood vessels, thus it will bleed the first time it is penetrated by either a penis during sexual intercourse or insertion of a tampon. The inner folds of the vagina, called rugae, allow the vagina to expand during childbirth. The vagina is the female organ of copulation, or sexual intercourse, and serves as the passageway for menstrual blood.

At the top of the vagina is the **uterus**, the pear-shaped, hollow muscular organ that will contain an implanted ovum as it develops throughout a pregnancy. If pregnancy does not occur, the uterus will shed its lining as **menses**, the flow of blood out of the uterus into the vagina and out of the body. The uterus consists of three layers: the **perimetrium**, the outermost serous membrane; the **myometrium**, the middle muscular layer; and the **endometrium**, the innermost vascular layer that is designed to give blood and nutrition to a developing fetus. The body of the uterus, the corpus, is the wide central portion near the bladder. The top edge of the bladder is called the fundus, which will rise as a developing pregnancy causes the uterus to grow to accommodate the growing fetus. The lowest portion of the uterus is called the **cervix**, where the vagina and uterus meet. The lower section of the uterus contains two strictures—narrowed sections—called os. The internal os separates the body of the uterus from the cervix, and the external os separates the lower end of the cervical canal to the vagina.

ELEMENT REVIEW
peri- = around
my/o = muscle
endo- = within
metr/i = uterus
-um = noun suffix

At the top lateral edges of the uterus, the **fallopian tubes**, also called the uterine tubes or oviducts, are the passageway for ova to exit the ovaries and enter the uterus. The fallopian tubes are approximately 5 in. (12.5 cm) long and are lined with mucous membrane and cilia, small hairlike projections that will propel the ovum toward the uterus. At the distal ends of the fallopian tubes are **fimbriae**, fingerlike projections that open into the peritoneal cavity. The fimbriae are not connected to the ovaries but rather use a wavelike motion to draw an ovum from the ovary into the tube.

The **ovaries** are two paired almond-shaped organs that are the female gonads, producing ovum, the genetic contribution to a fetus. The ovaries are approximately 1.5 in. (3.5 cm) long and less than 1 in. (2 cm) wide and are supported by ligaments that attach to the pelvic wall and the uterus. The ovary contains numerous saclike ovarian follicles, which each contain a single **oocyte** (**ovum**). Unlike the male sperm cells, which begin developing at puberty, all the female's oocytes are present in her ovaries at birth. By the time a female is born, she may have up to 500,000 oocytes.

Puberty and Menarche

Puberty, the physical changes that prompt sexual maturation of a girl to a woman, can occur from age 9 to 16 and begins with a marked increase in growth. Hormonal changes will prompt the development of secondary sex characteristics such as the development of axillary (underarm) hair, pubic hair, widening of the hips, development of breasts, and the onset of the menstrual cycle. The female's first menstrual cycle is called **menarche** and commonly occurs at age 12 to 15. The menstrual cycle will repeat monthly for approximately 40 years with the maturation and release of the oocytes in a process called **ovulation**. The monthly cycles offer **fertility**, the ability to bear a child.

The Menstrual Cycle

The **menstrual cycle** is influenced by several hormones: follicle-stimulating hormone (FSH), luteinizing hormone (LH), estrogen, estradiol, and progesterone. The coordinated hormonal changes in the anterior pituitary gland and the uterus begin to occur each 28 days after the onset of puberty. The purpose of the monthly cycle is to prepare the uterus for **pregnancy** (Fig. 12-3). In the ovary, the graafian follicle ruptures, ejecting an ovum into the fallopian tube in a process called **ovulation**. A yellowish mass called

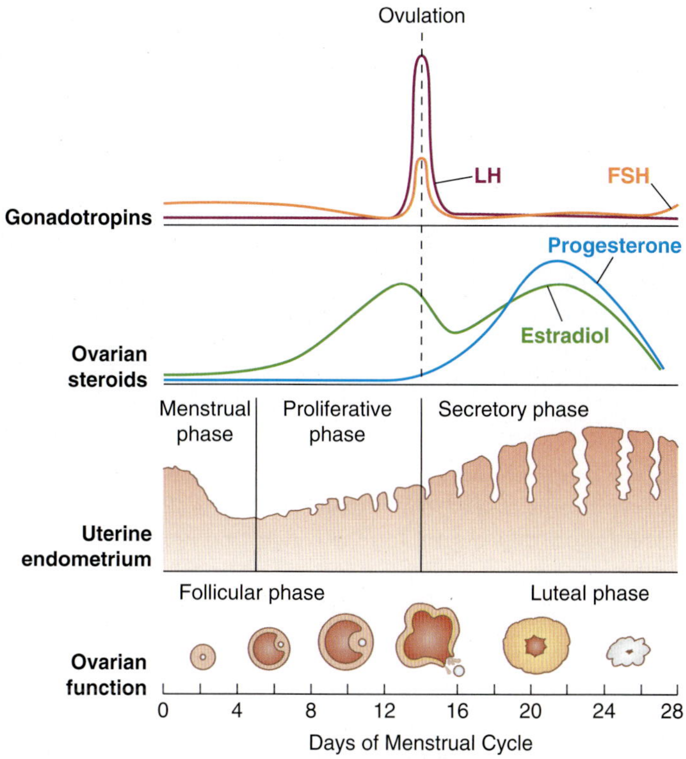

Figure 12-3 The menstrual cycle.

TABLE 12-1 The Menstrual Cycle

Phase	Days 1 Through 28 of Menstrual Cycle	Changes to the Uterus/Ovaries	Hormone Changes
Menstrual phase	Day 1 to day 5	Shedding of lining of the uterus	Drop in estradiol, estrogen, progesterone
Follicular phase	Day 6 to day 12	Several ova begin the maturation process (usually only one will reach full maturity) Uterine lining thickens	Pituitary gland sends FSH and LH to the uterus The ovaries produce estrogen, which tells the pituitary gland to stop FSH
Ovulatory phase	Ovulation occurs on day 13 or 14	Graafian follicle ruptures ejecting an ovum into the fallopian tube	LH increases Progesterone starts to rise
Luteal phase	Day 15 to day 28	Uterine lining thickens	Estrogen and progesterone rise

the **corpus luteum** forms within the ruptured ovarian follicle after ovulation. The corpus luteum contains high levels of progesterone and estrogen and acts as a temporary endocrine gland to secrete large amounts of progesterone. As the name implies, **progesterone** is "pro gestation," or promoting pregnancy. If pregnancy does not occur, the blood-rich environment of the uterus will shed as menses. The menstrual cycle is divided into four phases (see Table 12-1).

Perimenopause to Menopause

The onset of perimenopause occurs by age 45 to 50 and is characterized by a decrease in menses, skipping a cycle, or menstruating for fewer days or having less fluid volume. While pregnancy is less likely to occur beyond age 40, a woman who still menstruates may become pregnant. Perimenopause lasts from 7 to 10 years. The woman may experience menopausal symptoms such as insomnia, vaginal dryness, hot flashes, mood swings, or weight gain. After approximately 40 years from the onset of menarche (age 52 to 55), the menstrual cycles will completely stop in a process called **menopause**. Symptoms will subside as the woman experiences a complete cessation of ovulation and menstruation. Cessation of the menses is caused by changes within the ovary that cause the follicles to be less sensitive to FSH and LH. Consequently, the ovaries will no longer produce estrogen and progesterone, resulting in a decreased size of the uterus and a reduction of the lubricating fluid in the vestibular glands.

PHYSIOLOGY FACT

In some women, the drop in hormone levels during the luteal (premenstrual) phase can cause a group of symptoms called premenstrual syndrome (PMS). Symptoms include irritability, fluid retention, depression, food cravings, and breast tenderness.

Breasts

In children and adult males, the breasts do not function to produce milk. **Mammary glands** of the **breasts** of the mature female function to produce milk in a process called **lactation**. At the onset of puberty in females, under the influence of estrogen and progesterone, the breasts begin to enlarge, accumulating fat beneath the skin layer. The external heavily pigmented central area, the **areola**, surrounds each nipple. Each female mammary gland consists of 15 to 20 lobes. The lobes are arranged in a radiating pattern around the nipple. The lobes are padded with fat, and ligaments attach the breast to the underlying chest muscle (Fig. 12-4). Within each lobe are smaller chambers called lobules, which contain alveolar glands that produce milk. The alveolar glands secrete milk into ducts that open to the outside at the nipple. Production of milk usually follows the birth of the baby as levels of estrogen and progesterone fall and **prolactin** levels increase. As the name implies, prolactin stimulates milk production. During the first few days after giving birth, a substance called **colostrum** is released by the mammary glands. Colostrum contains high levels of antibodies that will protect the nursing baby from infection. Colostrum also contains fat and lactose to nourish the newborn. After a few days, milk production begins. Release of breast milk relies on neural stimulation. The mechanical force of the baby suckling the breast triggers the production of nerve impulses that cause a release of oxytocin from the posterior pituitary gland. **Oxytocin** stimulates the contractile cells around the alveolar glands to contract and push milk through the ducts and out the nipples. The flow of milk, called letdown, may be stimulated by the sound of the baby crying or the breast filling in anticipation of a scheduled feeding. If nursing continues, prolactin and oxytocin will continue to promote the release of milk. When the woman decides to wean the baby, production of prolactin and oxytocin will decrease, and milk production will cease until the next pregnancy.

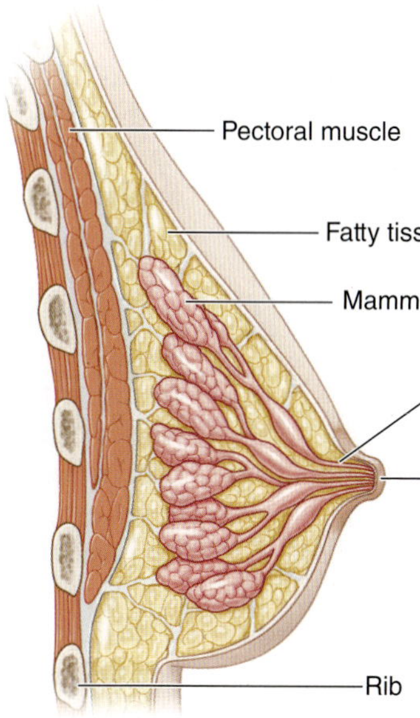

Figure 12-4 The breast.

Pregnancy

The vagina provides the environment for **sexual intercourse**, the insertion of the male's penis and the ejaculation into the vaginal canal. Pregnancy may occur after sexual intercourse. As the pregnancy progresses, hormonal and bodily changes continue until the onset of **parturition**, the process of giving birth. In addition to providing the uterus as the environment for a developing pregnancy, the female will produce breast milk to nurse an offspring. Upon becoming pregnant, women are advised to seek the care of an **obstetrician**, a medical specialist that monitors the health of the mother and developing fetus. OB/GYN is the commonly used abbreviation for a physician who practices as an obstetrician and gynecologist. An obstetrician can deliver the baby and care for the mother in the first 6 weeks following delivery. Many other gynecologists have obstetrics within their practice. Some women may seek a **midwife** for prenatal care and to deliver her child. A midwife is a registered nurse has a specialization in obstetrics and gynecology and often collaborates in the care of patients with an OB/GYN.

Conception

After the male sperm is introduced into the vaginal canal, the sperm cells will migrate through the uterus into the fallopian tube. One sperm cell will penetrate the ovum in a process called **fertilization**. Fertilization occurs in the outer third of the fallopian tube near the ovary. The fertilized ovum is now called a **zygote**. The zygote will travel along the fallopian tube and enter the uterus. It will burrow into the nutrient-rich endometrium in a process called implantation. Upon implantation, the first trimester of pregnancy begins.

First Trimester

The first trimester of pregnancy is the first 13 weeks of pregnancy and is characterized by many changes to the developing embryo as well as to the mother's body. Implantation of the zygote in the uterus relies on enzymes secreted by the endometrium. The enzymes enable the zygote to adhere completely to the nutrient rich lining.

Upon implantation, the zygote is called an **embryo**. The embryonic stage is the first 8 weeks following fertilization. Additionally, around 3 weeks after fertilization, the placenta develops. The **placenta** is the supporting link between the mother and the embryo. It is formed by fingerlike projections from the embryo called **chorionic villi**, which burrow deep into the endometrium to provide nutrients for the developing embryo. In the early stages of placental development, the embryo is connected to the placenta by a primitive stalk. As the embryo continues to grow, the stalk thickens and elongates, forming the **umbilical cord**. The umbilical cord provides the connection of the embryo to the placenta. The umbilical cord contains two umbilical arteries carrying blood from the embryo to the mother and one umbilical vein that carries blood from the mother to the embryo.

From the third to the eighth week of development, the embryo will form the head, the gut, and a tail fold that will eventually regress as the legs form. As the embryo continues to develop, a saclike structure forms called the **amniotic sac**. The sac contains **amniotic fluid**, which will protect the embryo from injury and regulate its temperature. The sac will continue to increase in size as the embryo increases in size. During the fourth to eighth weeks of development the major organs of the body begin to develop in a process called organogenesis. By the end of the seventh week, most organs have formed to the point of beginning their early functions. By week eight the head is well formed, the tail is regressing, and the arms and legs are forming, as are the digits (the fingers and toes).

ELEMENT REVIEW
organ/o = organs
-genesis = development, growth

At the end of the eighth week, the embryo is now called a **fetus** and is approximately 1 in. (2.5 cm) long and weighs 94 g. Approximately one-third of the fetal weight is the head. The neural tube has developed the brain, and spinal cord and bone begins to replace cartilage. The fetal period continues until birth and is characterized by ossification of the bones and development of the chambers of the heart and the organ systems. From the eighth to the thirteenth week, the fetus develops fingernails and teeth buds, and the external ears are formed. The circulatory and urinary systems are functioning, and the reproductive organs are developing. The fetal liver produces bile. By the end of the first trimester, the chances of miscarriage have dropped considerably.

PHYSIOLOGY FACT

Taking 400 mcg of folic acid daily has been found to prevent neural tube defects that can lead to spina bifida and anencephaly. Because the defect will occur in the first 4 weeks of pregnancy, before most women know they are pregnant, supplementation is advised for all women who may become pregnant. In addition to supplements, foods rich in folic acid, such as beans, peas, lentils, orange juice, and fortified cereals, are advised.

During the first trimester, an expectant mother will notice enlargement of her breasts and darkening of the areola, the pigmented area around the nipples. The veins of the breasts will become more pronounced. As the uterus grows to accommodate the growing fetus, it will put pressure on the urinary bladder, causing frequent urination. The mother may experience mood swings and morning sickness from the surge of hormones. The muscular contractions in the intestines are slowed due to the surge of progesterone and may cause constipation. Most expectant mothers feel tired during the first trimester as the hormonal changes and metabolic demands of the developing fetus continue. Increased blood flow to the uterus may cause an elevation in heart rate.

Second Trimester

The second trimester of pregnancy includes weeks 14 through 27. By the 14th week, the fetal kidneys begin to perfuse urine and release it into the amniotic fluid. The skeletal bones harden, and red blood cells form in the spleen. By week 16, the fetus is 4.5 in. long and weighs approximately 4 oz (110 g). Limb movements are coordinated and can be viewed with ultrasound. The sex of the fetus can be seen at approximately week 15 of development. By 18 weeks, the fetus is active in the womb and the mother can feel the movement. The digestive system is working, and the heart is pumping 100 pints of blood each day. By the 19th week, the skin is developing a cheese-like coating called **vernix caseosa** that will protect the fetal skin from abrasion, chaffing, and exposure to amniotic fluid. At 21 weeks, the body is covered by soft hair called **lanugo**, which helps to hold the vernix caseosa on the skin. The sucking reflex is formed, and the fetus may suck the thumb. At approximately 20 weeks, the fetus develops brown adipose tissue in a process called adipogenesis. The deposition of brown fat along the upper back and shoulders will become important for the newborn in order to maintain body heat in a process called *thermogenesis*. At 22 weeks eyebrows and hair are visible; for males, the testes have begun to descend. At week 23, the fetus develops ridges on the palms of the hands and soles of the feet, which will become fingerprints and toe prints. By week 24 the fetus weighs approximately 1.3 lb (630 g) and is 8 in. long. At week 26 the lungs are developing surfactant, a substance needed to allow the alveoli to inflate. By 27 weeks the fetus is gaining body fat, and the nervous system is maturing. The fetus is often sleeping in REM, rapid eye movement, and may smile during sleep.

ELEMENT REVIEW
adip/o = fat
therm/o = heat
-genesis = to produce

During the second trimester, the expectant mother will begin to "show" as the uterus grows to accommodate the developing fetus. Hormonal changes in the first trimester decrease, thus symptoms of morning sickness and fatigue often subside. Many women feel an increase in energy but still require adequate rest. An extra 300 calories per day, along with prenatal vitamins, is advised. Pregnancy symptoms of the second trimester may include lower back pain from the extra weight and pressure on the lumbar spine. Itchy skin and stretch marks appear as the abdomen grows. The mother is producing more melanin and may notice brown patches on the face called **chloasma,** the mask of pregnancy. A dark line, **linea nigra**, may appear from the pubic region to the umbilicus. The darker skin patches often fade after the baby is born.

Third Trimester

The final trimester of pregnancy is week 28 through week 40. By 28 weeks, the fetal central nervous system has matured and can regulate body temperature. The eyelids can open, and eyelashes have formed. By the 30th week, the soft hair, lanugo, is beginning to fall out and is replaced with hair on the head. The fetus may be very active, kicking and rolling as the baby grows. At 33 weeks, the pupils can constrict in response to light. Bones continue to harden, but the skull remains soft to accommodate the narrow birth canal. At approximately 31 weeks gestation, the fetus has completed development and now begins to gain weight quickly. At this stage, a fetus may gain one-half pound of weight per week. By 36 weeks, the fetus has grown so much that he/she is crowded in the uterus; the mother may feel the fetus roll more instead of kick. The fetus will turn its head down, ready to leave the uterus via the vaginal canal. Figure 12-5 shows the entire sequence of fetal development.

During the third trimester, the expectant mother may experience false labor pains, called Braxton Hicks contractions. The growth of the uterus compresses the lungs, making it difficult for the mother to take a deep breath. The breasts will leak colostrum, a fluid that nourishes the baby until the breast milk becomes available. A white vaginal discharge

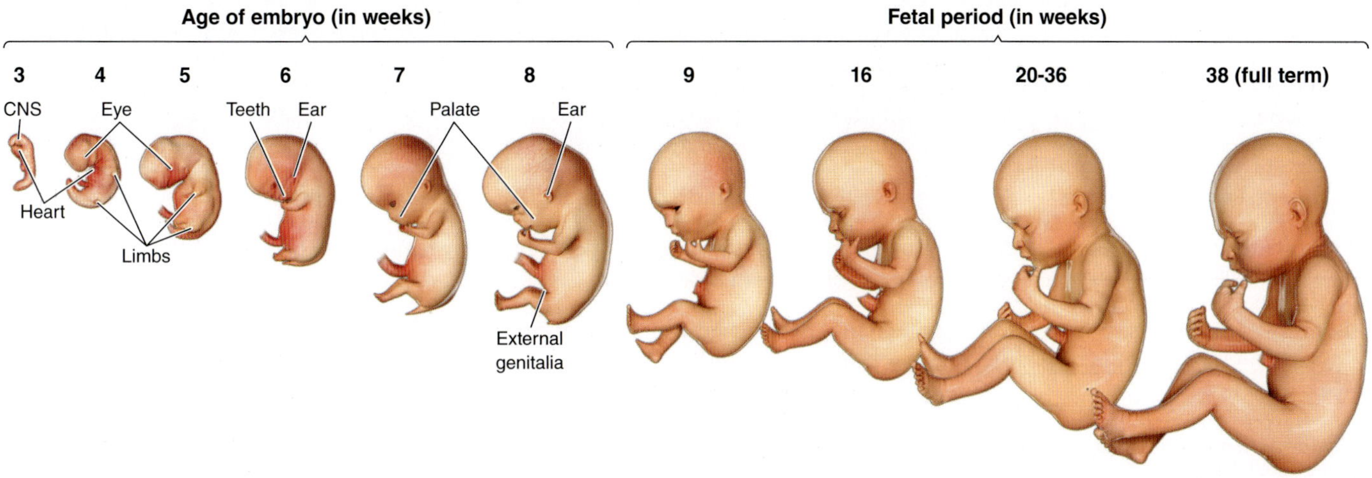

Figure 12-5 Fetal development.

will appear, and the urinary frequency and urgency experienced in the first trimester will return. As the fetus radiates heat, the maternal skin may feel hot. Blood pressure will decrease as the fetus presses on the abdominal veins.

Birth Process

At the end of the third trimester, many women feel an ease of breath as the fetus has moved down and compression of the lungs is decreased. During pregnancy, a thick plug of mucus has developed to protect the cervical opening from bacteria. Nearing the onset of labor, the mucus plug (also called bloody show) may be expelled. It may appear a few days to a few minutes before the onset of labor and is a stringy clear or bloody discharge. Not all women notice this sign. One in 10 women will experience a spontaneous rupture of membranes and a gush of amniotic fluid. During prenatal examinations, the obstetrician will feel for cervical effacement, a thinning of the cervical membrane.

The onset of **labor**, the birth process, is marked by **contractions**. They are the strong tightening of the uterine muscles that feel like menstrual cramping. The contractions will become more intense and more frequent. The obstetrician will palpate the cervix and feel dilation, an increase in the size of the cervical opening that will accommodate the baby leaving the uterus. Ten centimeters in diameter is considered full dilation, and the woman is ready to push the baby out. While labor is unique to each woman, contractions have some common characteristics:

- Contractions are regular.
- The contractions become progressively closer and stronger.
- Contractions are felt in the lower back and radiate to the front or vice versa.
- A change in activity or body position will not slow down or stop the contractions.

During labor, a woman can elect to have medications to decrease pain. Pain medications can be administered intravenously or by an epidural injection. If labor does not progress or the baby is in distress, a patient and her provider may elect to have the baby via **cesarean section**, a surgical procedure in which an incision is made into the uterus and the baby is removed.

Signs and Symptoms of Labor

The onset of labor is different for each woman, but it may include the signs and symptoms listed in Table 12-2.

TABLE 12-2 Signs and Symptoms of Labor

Sign/Symptom	Description
Bloody show	A vaginal discharge of mucus and pink or red blood. It may begin a few days to a few hours prior to the onset of labor.
Braxton Hicks contractions	Mild, irregular uterine contractions that may occur throughout pregnancy. As the pregnancy progresses, the contractions may become more forceful and can be mistaken for labor.
Increased vaginal discharge	As the fetus settles into the birth canal, an increase of clear vaginal secretions may be seen.
Lightening	As the fetus drops into the birth canal, the patient may feel an ease of breathing as the upward pressure on the diaphragm is decreased.
Rupture of amniotic sac	Some women may experience a spontaneous rupture of membranes, and she may say "my water broke." Patients are advised to seek medical care as the amniotic sac serves as a barrier between the fetus and the unsterile outside environment.
Sudden increase in energy	Some women experience an urge to clean, exercise, or prepare for the birth. Caution is advised to reserve some energy for labor.

CASE STUDY, continued

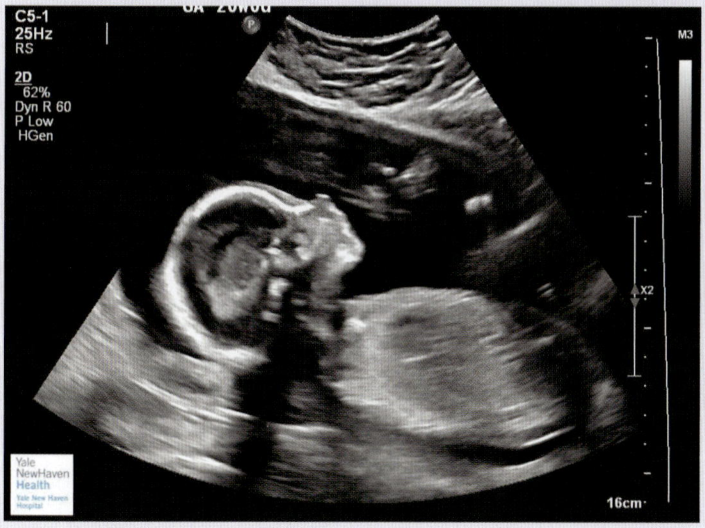

Meredith and Justin are excited for today's appointment. Meredith is 19 weeks pregnant, and the ultrasound may show the sex of the baby. Meredith's morning sickness has subsided, and she is feeling well. After the medical assistant takes Meredith's vital signs, gets a urine sample, and checks her weight, Dr. Johnson comes into the examination room and says, "How are you feeling, Meredith?" Meredith replies, "I am feeling well, tired but able to eat, and no nausea." Justin adds, "Meredith eats pineapple every day. We eat a lot of chicken parmigiana with pasta. I love Italian food, so I am enjoying Meredith's cravings!" Dr. Johnson laughs and says, "Justin, be careful, you wouldn't be the first expectant dad I've seen to gain weight." She then adds, "Let's look at your little one. I will ask Jennifer, our ultrasound technician, to come in. I'll be back to talk after the ultrasound." Jennifer comes into the room and introduces herself to Meredith and Justin. "Is this your first baby?" she asks." Justin replies, "Yes, our first." Jennifer asks, "Do you want to know the sex of the baby?" Meredith says, "Yes, please. We are excited to find out." Jennifer replies, "Okay, I always ask, in case you'd rather be surprised." Jennifer applies Aquasonic gel to Meredith's abdomen. She says, "This gel will help keep contact with your abdomen so I can obtain the pictures. I will take measurements of the baby's skull and body to check development and see if your due date is correct." She applies the wand, and immediately Meredith and Justin can hear the baby's heartbeat. Justin squeezes Meredith's hand with excitement. Jennifer narrates as she views the baby. "The baby measures 17 cm from head to butt (we call that the 'crown-rump length'), and that is perfect. Let's see the skull size. Okay, it's 170 cm in circumference, which is normal. Are you ready to see the sex?" Meredith squeezes Justin's hand, "Oh my, yes!" Jennifer moves the wand. A side view of the baby shows her sucking her thumb. Jennifer says, "Look here at your little girl!" Justin says, "Wow! The picture is so detailed, we can see her!" Jennifer takes the wand off and gives Meredith a towel to wipe the gel off her abdomen. She says, "I will print some ultrasound pictures for you to take home. Congratulations, everything looks normal. Dr. Johnson will be back in to talk and answer any questions."

Dr. Johnson returns and looks at the scan on the screen. She says, "So, we have a little lady in there; she looks healthy and is developing normally. According to the ultrasound, June 22nd is your due date. Now that you are at the halfway point in your pregnancy, I want to see you every 2 weeks for another month, and then every week. I also want to know if you have any bleeding, if you fall, or if you feel dizzy." Meredith asks, "Why would I feel dizzy?" Dr. Johnson replies, "Your blood pressure is normal; your pulse and

Continued

CASE STUDY, continued

respiration are good and show no signs of distress. I see in your chart that your glucose tolerance test was normal, so you do not have gestational diabetes. There was no proteinuria, which means protein in your urine, but dizziness or fainting can be a sign of maternal or fetal distress. No need for you to worry. Keep up your good habits, continue to eat whole foods, drink plenty of water, and get enough rest." Meredith replies "Okay, thanks Dr. Johnson. See you in 2 weeks."

Structures and Physiology Review

1. Match the Terms

Match the terms to their descriptions.

amniotic fluid	external os	lanugo	ovulation
areola	fallopian tubes	linea nigra	oxytocin
Bartholin's glands	fertilization	mammary glands	parturition
cervix	fimbriae	menarche	progesterone
chloasma	fundus	menopause	prolactin
clitoris	OB/GYN gynecologist and obstetrician	menstruation	puberty
colostrum	oxytocin	myometrium	uterus
corpus luteum	hymen	mons pubis	umbilical cord
endometrium	internal os	Naegele's rule	vernix caseosa
estrogen		ovary	vulva
			zygote

1. A dark line on the skin from the pubic region to the umbilicus that may appear during pregnancy __________
2. The protective cheese-like coating on the skin of the fetus __________
3. The glands that secrete a lubricating mucus for sexual intercourse __________
4. The muscular middle layer of the uterus __________
5. The structure that provides a connection of the placenta to the embryo or fetus __________
6. The process of giving birth __________
7. The top edge of the uterus __________
8. The female erectile tissue that is the homolog to the male penis __________
9. The darkly pigmented area around the nipples of the breasts __________

10. The fluid that nourishes a newborn before the breast milk comes in ______________________

11. The fatty tissue that covers the upper border of the genital region ______________________

12. The onset of the first menstrual cycle ______________________

13. The yellowish mass formed by the ruptured ovarian follicle ______________________

14. The mask of pregnancy is also called ______________________

15. The cessation of the menstrual cycles ______________________

16. The external genitals are called the ______________________

17. The formula that uses the date of the last menstrual period to calculate the expected date of birth ______________________

18. The fingerlike projections at the ends of the fallopian tubes ______________________

19. The stricture that separates the body of the uterus from the cervix ______________________

20. The organ that houses a developing fetus ______________________

21. A medical doctor who provides care for both pregnant women and the female reproductive system at times other than pregnancy ______________________

22. Bodily changes from girl to woman that enable her to become pregnant ______________________

23. A fertilized ovum prior to implantation ______________________

24. The hormones that stimulates milk production ______________________

25. The inner lining of the uterus ______________________

Structures and Physiology Word-Building Practice

1. Nouns and Adjectives

Complete the chart of nouns and adjective forms of words.

1. ovary ______________________
2. ______________________ endometrial
3. follicle ______________________

4. ______	embryonic
5. ______	placental
6. menopause	______
7. ______	menstrual
8. cervix	______
9. vagina	______
10. ______	pubic

2. Prefixes

Use the listed prefixes to build a word for each definition.

a-	inter-	primi-
dys-	intra-	sub-
endo-	peri-	supra-
infra-		

1. A painful menstrual period ______
2. The decrease in menstrual cycles before the onset of menopause ______
3. Absence of a menstrual cycle ______
4. Pertaining to above the pubic bone ______
5. Pertaining to within the uterus ______
6. A woman who gives birth for the first time ______
7. Pertaining to below the breast ______
8. The lining of the uterus ______
9. The outside of the uterus ______
10. The period of time after giving birth ______

3. Singular and Plural Forms

Complete the chart of singular and plural forms.

Singular	Plural
1. ovum	______
2. fetus	______

3. ______________________ ovaries

4. ______________________ fimbriae

5. oviduct ______________________

Word Building With Combining, Prefix, and Suffix Forms

The following word roots, prefixes, and suffixes are commonly used in medical terms for the anatomy and pathology of the female reproductive system. Combining vowels for word roots are included. Memorizing these elements will help you understand new terms that you may encounter as a medical assistant, obstetrical nurse, surgical technician, or as another health-care professional working in gynecology, obstetrics, or in a reproductive clinic.

The lists contain examples of terms that use the word element forms and a pronunciation guide. Be sure to use the pronunciation guide so that you can learn to say the terms correctly.

The Medical Language Lab at medicallanguagelab.com provides audio files to help you practice your Pronunciation.

Combining Form	Meaning	Example (Pronunciation)	Definition
cervic/o	cervix	cervical (SĔR-vĭ-kăl)	pertaining to the cervix
colp/o	vagina	colposcopy (kŏl-PŎS-kō-pē)	examination of the vagina with a scope
epis/o	vulva	episiotomy (e-pi-zē-Ă-tə-mē)	incision into the vulva to facilitate birth
gyn/o, gynec/o	woman, female	gynecologist (gīn-ĕ-KOL-ŏ-jĭst)	specialist in women's health
hyster/o	uterus	hysterectomy (his-tĕ-REK-tŏ-mē)	surgical removal of the uterus
lact/o	milk	lactation (lak-TĀ-shŏn)	production and release of milk
mamm/o	breast	mammogram (MĂM-ō-grăm)	x-ray of breast tissue
mast/o	breast	mastectomy (măs-TĔK-tō-mē)	surgical removal of a breast
men/o	menses	menopause (MEN-ŏ-poz)	permanent cessation of menstrual cycle
metr/o, metr/i	uterus	myometrium (mī-ŏ-MĒ-trē-ŭm)	the muscle layer of the uterus
obstetric/o	childbirth, pregnancy	obstetrician (ob-stĕ-TRISH-ăn)	specialist in care of women during pregnancy

Continued

Combining Form	Meaning	Example (Pronunciation)	Definition
oophor/o	ovary	oophoritis (ō-ŏf-ō-RĪ-tĭs)	inflammation of the ovaries
ovari/o	ovary	ovarian (ō-VAR-ē-ăn)	pertaining to the ovaries
salping/o	fallopian tubes, oviducts	salpingitis (săl-pĭn-JĪ-tĭs)	inflammation of the fallopian tubes
uter/o	uterus	uterine (ŪT-ĕ-rīn-, -rĭn)	pertaining to the uterus
vagin/o	vagina	vaginodynia (vaj-ĭ-nō-DIN-ē-ă)	pain in the vagina
vulv/o	vulva	vulvoplasty (vŭl-vŏ-PLAS-tē)	surgical repair of the vulva

ā = say, ă = sofa, ē = meet, ĕ = met, ī = eye, ĭ = in, ō = oh, ŏ = dog, ū = you, ŭ = up, oo = food

Prefix	Meaning	Example (Pronunciation)	Definition
a, an-	without	amenorrhea (ā-men-ŏ-RĒ-ă)	absence of menses
dys-	painful, labored	dysmenorrhea (dis-men-ŏ-RĒ-ă)	painful menstrual cycle
ecto-	outside	ectopic pregnancy (ek-TOP-ik PREG-năn-sē)	pregnancy outside of the uterus
endo-	within	endometrium (en-dŏ-MĒ-trē-ŭm)	the inner lining of the uterus
primi-	first	primigravida (prī-mĭ-GRAV-ĭd-ă)	a woman who is pregnant for the first time
sub-	under, below	subpubic (sŭb-PŪ-bĭk)	beneath the pubic arch

ā = say, ă = sofa, ē = meet, ĕ = met, ī = eye, ĭ = in, ō = oh, ŏ = dog, ū = you, ŭ = up, oo = food

Suffix	Meaning	Example (Pronunciation)	Definition
-al	pertaining to	vaginal (VAJ-in-ăl)	pertaining to the vagina
-arche	beginning	menarche (mĕn-ĂR-kē)	first menstrual period
-gram	record	mammogram (MĂM-ō-grăm)	x-ray of the breast
-graphy	process of recording	mammography (ma-MOG-ră-fē)	process of recording the breast
-gravida	pregnancy	multigravida (mŭl-tĭ-GRĂV-ĭ-dă)	a woman who has been pregnant multiple times

Suffix	Meaning	Example (Pronunciation)	Definition
-logist	specialist	gynecologist (gīn-ĕ-KOL-ŏ-jĭst)	specialist in the diagnosis and treatment of female anatomy
-logy	study of	gynecology (gī-nĕ-KŎL-ō-jē)	study of female anatomy
-para	to bear	primipara (prī-MĬP-ă-ră)	woman who has given birth for the first time
-plasia	formation, development	dysplasia (dis-PLĀ-zh[ē]ă)	formation of abnormal tissue
-rrhagia	excessive flow, discharge	menometrorrhagia (mĕn-ō-mĕt-rō-RĀ-jē-ă)	excessive flow of menses at times other than menstrual period
-rrhexis	rupture	hysterorrhexis (his-tĕ-rō-RĔK-sĭs)	rupture of the uterus
-rrhea	discharge, flow	galactorrhea (gă-lăk-tō-RĒ-ă)	discharge of milk in women not pregnant or breastfeeding

ā = say, ă = sofa, ē = meet, ĕ = met, ī = eye, ĭ = in, ō = oh, ŏ = dog, ū = you, ŭ = up, oo = food

Combining Forms Practice

1. Build the Terms

*Using **only** the word parts in the lists, create medical terms for the indicated meanings.*

Prefixes	Combining Forms		Suffixes	
dys-	cervic/o	men/o	-al	-ology
ecto-	colp/o	metr/o	-ar	-osis
endo-	episi/o	metri/o	-arche	-otomy
nulli-	gyn/o	oophor/o	-cele	-para
primi-	gynec/o	ovari/o	-ectomy	-plasia
	hyster/o	salping/o	-gram	-rrhagia
	lact/o	uter/o	-graphy	-rrhaphy
	mamm/o	vagin/o	-gravida	-rrhexis
	mast/o	vulv/o	-itis	-rrhea
			-ologist	-scopy

1. Discharge of milk from the breast between nursing and after weaning the baby ________________
2. A hernia into the vagina ________________
3. pertaining to the inside of the cervix ________________
4. Inflammation of the fallopian tubes and the ovaries ________________

5. Specialist in the study of female reproductive system ____________________
6. A woman who has never conceived a child ____________________
7. Excessive menstrual bleeding ____________________
8. Excessive bleeding during and between menstrual periods ____________________
9. A condition of the inner lining of the uterus ____________________
10. Incision into a fallopian tube ____________________
11. Inflammation of the breasts ____________________
12. Diagnostic radiography of the uterus and oviducts ____________________
13. Incision into the uterus, also called cesarean section ____________________
14. Suturing of the fallopian tube ____________________
15. Surgical removal of the uterus ____________________

2. Decipher the Terms

Separate each term into its prefix (if any), combining form, and suffix. Next, translate the word parts and then give the common definition of the term. Dysmenorrhea *has been done for you as an example.*

dysmenorrhea

Prefix: *dys = painful* *Suffix:* *-rrhea = discharge, flow*

Combining Form: *men/o = menses*

Meaning: *painful menstrual flow*

1. episiotomy

Prefix: ____________________ *Suffix:* ____________________

Combining Form: ____________________

Meaning: ____________________

2. menarche

Prefix: ____________________ *Suffix:* ____________________

Combining Form: ____________________

Meaning: ____________________

3. multipara

Prefix: ______________________ *Suffix:* ______________________

Combining Form: ______________________

Meaning: ______________________

4. primigravida

Prefix: ______________________ *Suffix:* ______________________

Combining Form: ______________________

Meaning: ______________________

5. salpingectomy

Prefix: ______________________ *Suffix:* ______________________

Combining Form: ______________________

Meaning: ______________________

6. dysplasia

Prefix: ______________________ *Suffix:* ______________________

Combining Form: ______________________

Meaning: ______________________

7. oophorectomy

Prefix: ______________________ *Suffix:* ______________________

Combining Form: ______________________

Meaning: ______________________

8. vulvar

Prefix: ______________________ *Suffix:* ______________________

Combining Form: ______________________

Meaning: ______________________

9. salpingorrhexis

Prefix: ______________________ *Suffix:* ______________________

Combining Form: ______________________

Meaning: ______________________

10. vaginitis

Prefix: ______________________ *Suffix:* ______________________

Combining Form: ______________________

Meaning: ______________________

Visit the Medical Language Lab at the website medicallanguagelab.com. Use it to enhance your word-building skills for the word parts covered in this chapter.

CASE STUDY, completed

Meredith wakes up at 2 a.m. with pain in her abdomen. She thinks, "Could this be labor?" She gets out of bed and goes to the bathroom. She sees some mucus and a bit of blood after she pees. She can't go back to bed; her back aches, and it feels better to walk around. She walks laps in their small apartment and lets Justin sleep. She begins to time the contractions; at 5 am, the contractions are 10 minutes apart. Justin wakes up and sees Meredith hunched over, breathing and blowing like they practiced in Lamaze class. He says to her, "Are you starting labor?" Meredith replies, "Yes, I think so. The pains are getting closer, 10 minutes apart." Justin says "I'll call Dr. Johnson's office and let them know. I'll get your overnight bag." Justin helps Meredith to the car and helps her with her seatbelt. He drives carefully, but Meredith can tell he is nervous. When her next contraction starts, she cries out. He tells her, "Blow, breathe—you can do this. We are almost there."

They pull into the emergency entrance, and Justin gets a wheelchair. He wheels Meredith into the emergency entrance as another contraction starts. ED staff help them to the elevator. The elevator doors open on the labor and delivery floor, and the couple is greeted by a nurse. She introduces herself as Amanda and says, "I'll be your nurse today. Let's get you into your room." Justin helps Meredith out of her clothes and into a gown. Amanda attaches a fetal monitor, and they all can hear the baby's heartbeat. Dr. Johnson arrives and examines Meredith. She says, "Six centimeters dilated; you have some time. How are you feeling?" Meredith replies, "I'm really tired, but I want to deliver naturally if possible." Dr. Johnson says, "Okay, I will give Amanda standing orders for IV pain medication if you need it. You can decide as you progress. I will be on the floor, so I won't be far away." Meredith starts another contraction; Amanda squeezes her hand while Justin rubs Meredith's back.

After 4 more hours, the contractions are close together. Amanda and Dr. Johnson position Meredith, and Dr Johnson feels her cervix. "Good work Meredith, 10 cm. We are ready for delivery. When you feel the next contraction, bear down hard." Meredith feels the next contraction and screams. Justin holds her leg up while Amanda holds the other as Meredith pushes. Dr. Johnson says, "I can see the baby's head crowning. Good work, Meredith. Rest until the next one." The next contraction starts, and Meredith pushes and bears down again. The little girl comes into the world as Dr. Johnson suctions her nose and hands her to Amanda. Amanda wipes the baby and places her on Meredith's chest, skin to skin. Justin hugs his wife and baby daughter. Dr. Johnson delivers the placenta while Amanda assists.

The next day, Meredith, Justin, and baby Sadie are doing well and ready to go home.

CASE STUDY, completed

CRITICAL-THINKING QUESTIONS

1. Meredith was pregnant for the first time, a term known as ______________________.
2. The 6-week period of time after Meredith gives birth to Sadie is the ______________________.
3. The monthly, then weekly visits to Dr. Johnson are what type of care? ______________________.
4. The diagnostic test that allowed Meredith and Justin to know the sex of their baby prior to her birth is called ______________________.
5. Now that Meredith has given birth, her medical record will read G1, P1, which stands for ______________________.
6. Meredith was tested for the presence of protein in her urine, a disorder called ______________________.
7. Meredith had a glucose tolerance test, which is used to diagnose ______________________.
8. Dr. Johnson is a medical doctor that delivers infants, a specialty called ______________________.
9. Dr. Johnson also cares for women with female reproductive disorders; thus she is a ______________________.
10. Meredith had some morning sickness (but not the severe form of vomiting and dehydration) during pregnancy, which is known as ______________________.

Female Reproductive System Diseases and Disorders

Pathological diseases and disorders of the female reproductive system include menstrual disorders, infertility, complications of pregnancy, and cancers.

Common Signs and Symptoms

Table 12-3 is a list of common complaints, objective signs, and subjective symptoms that patients with female reproductive system diseases and disorders may describe to their health-care providers and support staff.

Pathological Conditions of the Female Reproductive System

Amenorrhea: Prior to puberty, amenorrhea is normal, but after the onset of puberty, a woman should have a monthly menstrual cycle if not pregnant or entering menopause. Amenorrhea can be caused by stress or extremely low body mass, due to anorexia or

TABLE 12-3 Common Signs and Symptoms

Signs	Symptoms
Absence of normal menses (amenorrhea)	Painful menses (dysmenorrhea)
Lump in a breast	Inability to hold urine (incontinence)
Excessive menstrual discharge (menorrhagia)	Painful intercourse (dyspareunia)
Discharge of milk in women not pregnant or breastfeeding (galactorrhea)	

competitive athletics. Some women may experience temporary amenorrhea after discontinuing oral birth control pills.

Breast cancer: Malignant carcinoma of the breast tissue most commonly originating in the mammary ducts (ductal carcinoma). If left untreated, the cancer can spread to surrounding tissues, to the axillary lymph nodes in a process called metastasis. Breast cancer is the second most common malignancy in women in the United States and the leading cause of death in women aged 40 to 55. Breast cancer usually presents as a mass in one breast. The less common early signs are nipple retraction or nipple discharge. Women are encouraged to perform a monthly breast self-examination (BSE) to promote early diagnosis. Regular mammography, an x-ray examination, of breast tissue is also advised. Mammography will detect benign and malignant masses, which then are tested and differentiated via a biopsy. Treatments for breast cancer include surgical removal of the breast, radiation, and chemotherapy. Risk factors for breast cancer include family history, smoking, obesity, use of oral birth control pills, and alcohol consumption. White women are more likely to develop breast cancer as compared to Black, Hispanic, and Asian women. Several genes, including BRCA1 and BRCA2 increase a woman's chance of developing breast cancer.

Cervical cancer: A malignant tumor of the cervix; one of the most common malignancies of the female reproductive tract. Signs include bleeding between menstrual periods, bleeding after sexual intercourse and postmenopausal bleeding. Abnormal cells can be seen on a Pap smear, a noninvasive test where cells of the cervix are scraped off and viewed under a microscope. Ninety percent of cervical cancers can be detected by the Pap smear. Following an abnormal Pap smear, a biopsy of cervical tissue is taken to confirm diagnosis of cancer. Factors contributing to the development of cervical cancer include having multiple sexual partners, becoming sexually active before age 18, having STIs, and smoking. Treatment consists of surgical removal of cancerous tissue and a margin of healthy tissue to prevent recurrence. Advanced disease may require a complete hysterectomy with removal of fallopian tubes and the ovaries.

Public Health Tip

The U.S. Food and Drug Administration has approved a vaccine, Gardasil-9, that is effective in preventing human papilloma virus (HPV), a sexually transmitted virus that is implicated in the development of approximately 70% of cervical cancers and 90% of genital warts. The vaccine is administered in three doses over the course of 1 year (0, 6, and 12 months). It is recommended that both boys and girls get the vaccine before becoming sexually active at age 11 to 12, but the vaccine can be started at age 9.

Cervicitis: An acute or chronic inflammation of the cervix. Signs and symptoms may include a thick foul-smelling vaginal discharge, pelvic pain, bleeding after sexual intercourse, itching and burning of the external genitalia. The disorder is commonly caused by *Trichomonas vaginalis*, *Candida albicans*, *Haemophilus vaginalis*, or *Chlamydia trachomatis*.

Diagnosis is confirmed by a Pap smear to identify the offending organism. A cervical biopsy may be ordered to rule out cervical cancer. Once the causative organism is identified, medication is prescribed to fight the infection. A common complication of cervicitis is cervical erosion, in which the tissue becomes raw and ulcerated. Treatment for cervical erosion is cryosurgery to freeze the eroded tissue.

Cystocele: A herniation of the urinary bladder into the vagina. It occurs when the fascia separating the two organs is damaged or weakened from the pressure of pregnancy or surgical trauma.

Dysmenorrhea: An extremely common symptom of pain during menses affecting 200,000 women in the United States each year. Palliative treatments consist of analgesics, NSAIDs, rest, and hot packs applied to the abdomen. Approximately 10% of menstruating women experience temporary disability and lost days of work or school. Dysmenorrhea can be primary, caused by abnormal contractions of the uterus during menses. Primary dysmenorrhea resolves when the menstrual cycle ends. Secondary dysmenorrhea is caused by an underlying disease such as endometriosis, uterine fibroids, pelvic inflammatory disease, or tumors. Treatment for secondary dysmenorrhea is directed at the underlying cause.

Endometrial cancer: A malignancy of the lining of the uterus known as adenocarcinoma of the uterus. It is the most common cancer of the female reproductive tract, occurring most frequently in perimenopausal and menopausal women, with a peak incidence of age 50 to 60 years. The most common sign is abnormal uterine bleeding, bleeding after intercourse, or a watery discharge. Diagnosis is confirmed by an endometrial biopsy by a dilation and curettage (D&C) procedure. The cervical opening is dilated, and the lining of the uterus is scraped off with a spoon-shaped instrument called a curette. Microscopic analysis of the removed tissue will differentiate cancerous versus noncancerous cells. Treatment is a total abdominal hysterectomy with bilateral salpingo-oophorectomy (removal of tubes and ovaries) followed by radiation.

ELEMENT REVIEW
aden/o = gland
carcin/o = cancer
-oma = tumor

Endometriosis: The growth of endometrial tissue outside the lining of the uterus. Endometrial tissue grows on the fallopian tubes, on the small intestines, the bowel, the ovaries, and the surface of the bladder (Fig. 12-6). This common disorder is seen in women 18 to 35 and affects more than 3 million women each year in the United States. Symptoms of endometriosis include lower back and abdominal pain, intermittent diarrhea, and constipation. The pain may begin before menses and continue through the menstrual cycle, offering few days of relief before the next cycle begins. Menses is often heavy and pain during

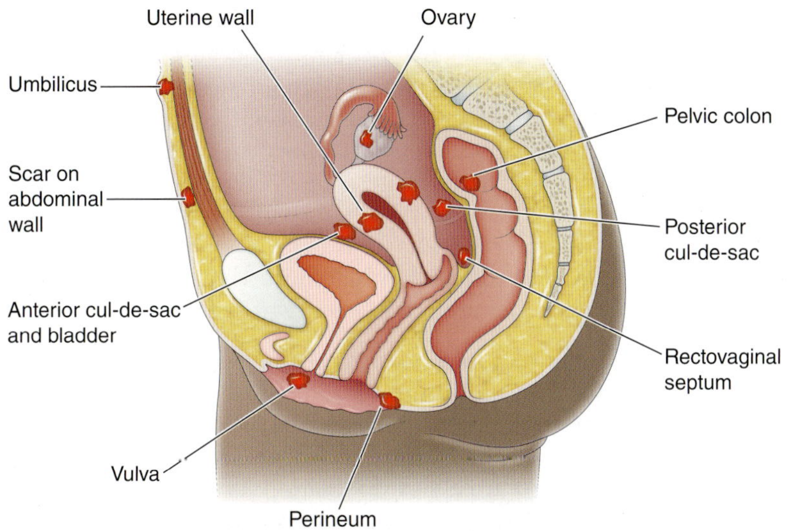

Figure 12-6 Common sites of endometriosis.

intercourse is common. Pain results from a buildup of scar tissue and adhesions in the abdomen. Diagnosis is confirmed by laparoscopy to visualize endometrial tissue on adjacent organs. During the laparoscopy, endometrial tissue can be removed. Additional therapies include NSAIDS to reduce inflammation, analgesics to reduce pain, and oral birth control to suppress growth of endometrial tissue. Endometriosis results in infertility in 30% to 50% of women with the disorder. It can prevent the embryo from implanting in the uterus due to chronic inflammation and hormonal imbalances. Additionally, scarring of the fallopian tube may prevent sperm and ova contact, and thus fertilization is not possible. For severe endometriosis, IVF is recommended if fertility is desired. There is no known cure for endometriosis other than a complete hysterectomy with removal of tubes and ovaries. Most women experience a decrease in symptoms of endometriosis upon menopause as estrogen production decreases.

Fibrocystic breasts: Fibrous breast cysts are benign and change in size during the menstrual period. The breast is most tender just prior to menses, and a lump can be palpated. Upon palpating a lump, many women will seek medical attention. Mammography will show fluid-filled cysts and changes in size during the menstrual cycle. Differential diagnosis of breast cancer versus fibrocystic disease for deep cysts is confirmed by a biopsy. Treatment of fibrocystic breasts is directed at decreasing pain by using a supportive bra, limiting caffeine in the diet, and use of analgesics. Women are advised to perform BSE since cysts versus breast cancer must be assessed. Cysts may continue to occur until menopause but then usually subside.

Fibroid uterine tumors: Noncancerous (benign) tumors of the uterus are common and occur only in premenopausal women. The tumors vary in size, shape, and location in the uterus. They can be embedded in the muscle of the uterus (myometrium), on the inside or outside wall of the uterus, or be attached by a stalk. Patients may be asymptomatic or experience pelvic pain and pressure. Signs include menorrhagia and menometrorrhagia. A detailed patient history and ultrasonography are used to confirm presence of fibroids. Treatments include surgical removal of fibroids, uterine ablation, or hysterectomy. If the patient wants to preserve fertility, surgical removal of large fibroids may be necessary to allow room for a fetus to develop within the uterus.

ELEMENT REVIEW
leio- = smooth
my/o = muscle
men/o = menses
metri/o = uterus
-rrhagia = excessive flow, discharge
-oma = tumor

Leiomyoma: Benign tumor of the smooth muscle of the uterus and presents with the same signs and symptoms as fibroid tumors. Treatment ranges from removing the tumors or hysterectomy depending on severity of symptoms and if the patient wants to preserve fertility.

Ovarian cancer: Malignant tumors of the ovaries most commonly occur in women in their 50s. It is rarely detected early because signs and symptoms do not develop until the disease is advanced. Early symptoms include a bloated feeling in the lower abdomen, mild digestive discomfort, indigestion, loss of appetite, or nausea. Because the signs and symptoms are common to digestive disorders, many women ignore symptoms or change their diet to avoid offending foods. As the tumor increases in size, the feeling of fullness increases and puts pressure on adjacent organs such as the bowel and bladder. Later signs include fluid retention in the abdomen, known as ascites, which increases swelling and discomfort. Diagnosis is confirmed by ultrasound and then biopsy of the tumor. Treatment is surgical removal of the ovary, tubes, and uterus. Metastasis to other organs is evaluated by a biopsy of lymph nodes and a sampling of intraabdominal fluid. Treatment after surgery includes radiation and chemotherapy depending on the severity of the disease.

Ovarian cysts: Fluid-filled sacs that form on or near the ovaries. Cysts can be categorized as a follicular cyst arising from an unruptured graafian follicle or a lutein cyst that arises from residual corpus luteum after ovulation. Signs and symptoms include swelling and firmness of the lower abdomen, pain during sexual intercourse, pelvic and lower back pain. Some ovarian cysts can be assessed by pelvic examination; in some cases a pelvic ultrasound is necessary to confirm the cyst. Most ovarian cysts resolve without medical intervention. Some larger cysts may need to be surgically removed via a laparoscopic cystectomy.

Ovarian torsion: Refers to the complete or partial rotation of the ovary upon its supporting uterosacral ligament. Complete or partial obstruction of blood supply to the ovary causes intense abdominal pain, fever, and nausea without vomiting. A palpable pelvic mass may or may not be present. Ultrasound imaging may show the ovary to be anterior to the uterus rather than its normal lateral positioning. Doppler flow within the torsed ovary is commonly decreased, but blood flow may be present in the case of partial or intermittent occlusion. The most common predisposing factor is the presence of ovarian cysts that may grow and twist the ovary. Eighty five percent of patients with ovarian torsion have ovarian cysts. Surgical treatment involves draining large cysts and fixation of the ovary, oophoropexy, to the uterosacral ligament.

ELEMENT REVIEW
uter/o = uterus
sacr/o = sacrum
-al = pertaining to
oophor/o = ovary
-pexy = surgical fixation

Pelvic inflammatory disease (PID): Infection of the fallopian tubes, also called salpingitis. PID most commonly occurs in women under the age of 30 who are sexually active. The most common causative organisms are *C. trachomatis* and *Neisseria gonorrhoeae,* which are both sexually transmitted. There is a higher incidence of the infection in women who use an intrauterine device for birth control. Signs and symptoms include fever, chills, lethargy, abdominal tenderness, backache, and a foul-smelling vaginal discharge. Laboratory testing will show increased white blood cell count. Diagnosis is confirmed by microscopic analysis of vaginal discharge. Once the causative agent is identified, antibiotic medication is prescribed. Analgesics and bedrest are also advised. Early treatment can preserve fertility, but PID is a major cause of infertility in women.

Polycystic ovarian syndrome (PCOS): Caused by a hormonal imbalance in which androgen (male hormone) levels are too high. It results in a lack of menstrual cycles; women may have only a few menses per year, thus compromising fertility. The ovaries contain multiple small follicular fluid-filled sacs containing immature ova that do not develop and prompt ovulation. The exact cause of PCOS is not known, but some contributing factors include family history of PCOS, insulin resistance, obesity, and chronic inflammation. Signs and symptoms include hirsutism (male pattern hair growth), acne, and a lack of menstrual cycle. Complications can include infertility, type 2 diabetes, sleep apnea, depression, anxiety, and metabolic syndrome. Patients with PCOS who can become pregnant have an increased risk of gestational diabetes, miscarriage, or premature birth. PCOS is also linked to an increased risk of endometrial cancer. Treatment with oral birth control that contains both estrogen and progestin will decrease androgen production. Balancing these hormones will decrease the risk of endometrial cancer. If the patient desires pregnancy, medications to stimulate ovulation are administered.

Urinary stress incontinence: The inability to hold urine when coughing, sneezing, laughing, or lifting. As women age, the bladder sphincter muscle can become weak, especially if she has had multiple pregnancies. The woman is unable to tighten the urethra sufficiently to overcome the pressure on the bladder and a leakage of urine occurs. Treatment may consist of exercises to strengthen perineal muscles. Many women use pads to absorb leaked urine. Medications to reduce urinary frequency and abstaining from caffeine is advised. Surgical correction is not common and reserved for severe incontinence.

Vaginitis: The inflammation of the vagina due to a pH disturbance that allows microorganisms to flourish. The three most common causative organisms are *Candida albicans*, *Trichomonas vaginalis*, and *Gardnerella vaginalis*. Signs and symptoms include an increase in a thin, watery vaginal discharge with a strong fishy odor. Redness and itching of the vulva are common to both bacterial and yeast infections, but it is more pronounced in yeast infections. Diagnosis is confirmed by microscopic analysis of vaginal secretions in a saline wet mount preparation. Treatment with the appropriate antibiotic or antibacterial medication will resolve the infection. There is no need to treat male sexual partners.

Pregnancy-Related Pathologies

During pregnancy, the health of the mother and developing fetus may be at risk from a variety of factors such as hormonal, placental, blood pressure, and glucose abnormalities.

Abortion: The elective or spontaneous end of a pregnancy before fetal viability. The legal definition of viability varies in each U.S. state from 20 to 24 weeks gestation. Signs and symptoms of a spontaneous abortion include abdominal cramping and vaginal bleeding. The most common cause is faulty development of the embryo resulting from chromosomal abnormalities, placental abnormalities, endocrine disturbances, infection, drug abuse, or trauma. Patient care includes assessment of vital signs, vaginal bleeding, fluid balance, and signs of shock and sepsis. If the contents of conception are not completely expelled, surgical completion of the abortion is performed by a D&C. For both elective and spontaneous abortions, health-care professionals monitor the patient for responses such as grief, guilt, anger, sadness, depression, or happiness. The patient is instructed to report any vaginal bleeding or pain and to avoid intercourse until a follow-up examination can be performed.

Abruptio placenta: The premature separation of a normally implanted placenta from the uterine wall after 20 weeks gestation or occurring during the birth process. The condition is life-threatening to both the mother and the fetus due to the risk of hemorrhage. Bleeding on the maternal side of the placenta will cause a hematoma (a clot of blood) to form. Degrees of separation vary from partial to complete and vaginal bleeding can be extensive or completely concealed. Signs and symptoms include uterine tenderness with a rigid abdomen, vaginal bleeding, tachycardia, hypotension, restlessness, cramping, and contractions of the uterus. Abruptio placenta can be caused by cocaine use, trauma to the abdomen from an accident or abuse, or the presence of a short umbilical cord. Treatment is immediate delivery of the fetus by cesarean section and control of bleeding.

ELEMENT REVIEW
tachy- = rapid, fast
-cardia = heart rate
hypo- = under, below
-tension = blood pressure

Eclampsia: A severe complication of hypertension during pregnancy characterized by convulsions and coma. It typically occurs at 20 weeks gestation or later. Risk factors for the condition include advanced maternal age, previous maternal hypertension, renal disease, diabetes mellitus, molar pregnancy, and multiple fetuses. Signs and symptoms include seizure, often without warning, headaches, changes in vision, nausea, edema, abdominal pain, and possibly multiorgan failure. It is a life-threatening condition for both the mother and the fetus. Treatment consists of emergency management of maternal airway, intravenous bolus, and continuous infusion of magnesium sulfate to control blood pressure. Oxygen is administered and continuous fetal monitoring is performed. An indwelling urinary catheter is placed to measure output as oliguria is a sign of renal failure or magnesium toxicity. Once the mother is stabilized, induction of labor or cesarean section is indicated for gestational age 24 weeks+. Regional anesthesia is administered rather than general as the mother is at a high risk of hemorrhage.

ELEMENT REVIEW
olig- = scant, diminished amount
-uria = urination

Ectopic pregnancy: The abnormal implantation of the fertilized ovum outside of the uterine cavity. It is a rare condition affecting 200,000 women in the United States each year. Ninety percent of ectopic pregnancies occur inside the fallopian tube while the other ten percent occur within the ovaries or the abdominal cavity. Causes of the disorder include fallopian tube scarring due to previous infections, inflammation, adhesions due to endometriosis, congenital deformities of the fallopian tubes or pregnancy occurring while an intrauterine device (IUD) is in place. Additionally, ectopic pregnancy risk increases with increased maternal age. Signs and symptoms may be absent or include scant vaginal bleeding, persistent severe abdominal pain, pain in one side of the abdomen, dizziness, or fainting. Blood leaking from the fallopian tube can cause bowel urgency and shoulder tip pain. Diagnosis of an ectopic pregnancy is confirmed by a positive pregnancy test and a transvaginal ultrasound that will show no gestational sac within the uterus. Tubal pregnancies usually spontaneously rupture between 6 to 12 weeks gestation and may be asymptomatic or be marked by dark vaginal spotting and cramping. Treatment with methotrexate can be administered to stop growth of cells, ending the pregnancy. If, however, the fertilized ova continue to grow in the fallopian tube, it will cause a tubal rupture. Heavy bleeding in the abdomen will cause extreme lightheadedness, fainting, and shock. Emergency surgery to remove the products of conception and repair or remove the fallopian tube is necessary to save the life of the mother.

ELEMENT REVIEW
ecto- = outside
-atic = pertaining to

Gestational diabetes: The onset of diabetes during the third trimester of pregnancy in a woman who was previously not diabetic. As the disorder progresses, the woman develops an inability to metabolize carbohydrates known as glucose intolerance and resultant persistent hyperglycemia. Risk factors include obesity, maternal age 30+, polycystic ovarian syndrome (PCOS), a history of birthing large babies (10+ lb), previous unexplained stillborn birth, or having babies with congenital anomalies. Signs and symptoms include excessive thirst, hunger, and frequent urination. Because some women have no symptoms, every pregnant woman is routinely tested for gestational diabetes with a glucose tolerance test at week 24 to 28 of her pregnancy. Treatment consists of dietary changes to promote healthy blood sugar levels including fresh fruits and vegetables, adequate protein, and limiting refined carbohydrates and sweets. Patients are encouraged to get regular exercise for 30 minutes 4 to 6 days per week. Activities such as walking, cycling on a stationary bicycle, and swimming are considered safe. Patients can monitor glucose levels with an at-home finger stick. Antidiabetic medications may be advised if diet and exercise do not control glucose levels. If left untreated, the baby can grow too large making birth difficult and increasing the need for delivery via cesarean section. The baby is at increased risk for breathing disorders, being born with hypoglycemia (low blood sugar), and developing obesity and type 2 diabetes later in life. Untreated gestational diabetes can result in the baby's death either before or shortly after birth. Maternal diabetes usually resolves after the birth of the baby.

Hydatidiform mole: Abnormal condition that starts as a pregnancy, but normal development of the embryo does not occur. The fertilized ovum deteriorates, and the chorionic villi of the placenta forms a small cystic mass that resembles a bunch of grapes. The mass grows quicker than uterine growth of a normal pregnancy. Signs and symptoms include uterine bleeding, extreme nausea, anemia, and an unusually large uterus for the expected date of delivery. There are no fetal heart sounds, and no fetal movement is felt by the mother. Edema and hypertension are common. Diagnosis is confirmed by ultrasound, which shows no fetal skeleton. Treatment options include evacuation of the uterus followed by D&C to ensure that all the tissue is removed. Another option is hysterectomy if future fertility is not desired. The removed tissue is tested for cancerous cells. If cancer is detected, subsequent pregnancy must be avoided. If no cancer is detected, the patient must wait for at least one year to become pregnant again.

Hyperemesis gravidarum: Abnormal condition of pregnancy characterized by severe vomiting that results in maternal weight loss and dehydration. While most women experience some nausea or food sensitivities, especially in the first trimester of pregnancy, hyperemesis gravidarum is much more severe. Risk factors include young maternal age, and first-time pregnancy, hyperthyroidism, elevated estrogen levels, or a multiple pregnancy (twins, triplets). It is characterized by persistent nausea that does not subside, vomiting several times per day, weight loss, low blood sugar, dizziness, and exhaustion. The patient will notice dark urine as she becomes dehydrated. Patients are advised to eat small frequent meals every 2 hours to avoid hunger and thus decrease nausea. Drinking liquids such as lemonade and fruit juices between meals may reduce nausea and vomiting. If dietary strategies do not prevent vomiting and dehydration, intravenous hydration may be required.

Incompetent cervix: A condition where the cervical os (the opening to the cervix) dilates before the fetus reaches term. During the second trimester of pregnancy, the woman will experience uterine contractions. If left untreated, a spontaneous abortion will occur, expelling the developing fetus. Diagnosis is obtained by patient symptoms of cramping, lower back pain, light vaginal bleeding, and confirmed by manual examination that indicates premature dilation of the cervix. A procedure known as cerclage is a suturing of the cervix to prevent opening during pregnancy. If the mother is going to have a vaginal birth, the sutures are removed near the end of pregnancy. If a cesarean delivery is scheduled, the sutures may be left in place.

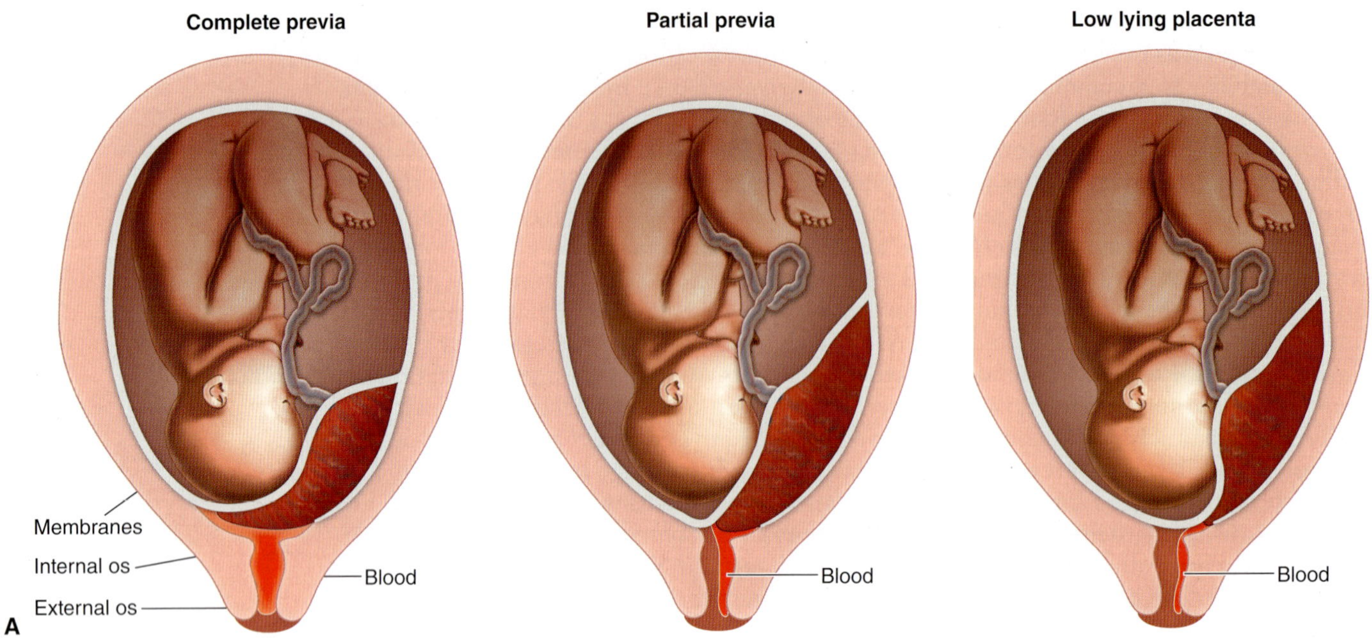

Figure 12-7 Placenta previa. (A) Total (central) placenta previa. (B) Partial placenta previa. (C). Low placenta previa.

ELEMENT REVIEW
multi- = many
primi- = first
-gravida = pregnancy

Placenta previa: Condition of pregnancy where the placenta is implanted in the lower portion of the uterus and precedes the fetus during delivery. The disorder is more common in multigravida than primigravida and occurs in approximately 1 in every 200 pregnancies. The most common sign is bright red vaginal bleeding during the third trimester. If bleeding continues, it becomes more severe and can cause anemia, pallor, a rapid and weak pulse, air hunger, and hypotension. Diagnosis is confirmed by ultrasound. Varying degrees of low placental placement can occur with bleeding and the risk to the fetus being greatest if the cervix is completely blocked (Fig. 12-7). Treatments range from bed rest to immediate delivery by cesarean section depending on the gestational age of the fetus, condition of the mother, and whether fetal distress is observed.

Preeclampsia: An increase in blood pressure, presence of protein in the urine (proteinuria), and edema that affects 3% to 5% of pregnancies. It may progress quickly to eclampsia. Contributing factors include young maternal age (18 or younger), primigravids, smoking, obesity, and diabetes. Signs and symptoms include sudden weight gain, severe headaches, visual disturbances, epigastric pain, facial edema, oliguria, and hyperreflexia. Treatment consists of bedrest, and management of hypertension with intravenous magnesium sulfate. Immediate delivery of the fetus may be required depending on the severity of the disease and the development of the fetus. After a woman is diagnosed with preeclampsia, she is at an increased risk for cardiovascular disease such as heart attack and stroke. She is also at an increased risk for the same complication in future pregnancies.

Rh incompatibility: A Rh-negative woman who becomes pregnant by a Rh-positive man can have a developing fetus with Rh-positive blood. The incompatibility will cause the mother to develop antibodies to the fetal blood. The first Rh-positive baby born from a Rh-negative mother will not be affected by the incompatibility. If, however, a subsequent pregnancy produces a Rh-positive fetus, the maternal antibodies will cross the placental barrier and move into the fetal circulatory system. The antibodies will target and destroy the red blood cells of the developing fetus, prompting fetal death. Treatment for the prevention of Rh incompatibility is an injection of Rh immunoglobulin (RhoGam) given to all Rh-negative patients during the 28th week of pregnancy. If she gives birth to a Rh-positive baby, she will receive another injection of RhoGam within 72 hours of giving birth to stop the continuing formation of antibodies.

Sexually Transmitted Diseases

Sexually transmitted diseases contracted by women can result in infertility, loss of a pregnancy, increased rate of female cancers, and even death. Early diagnosis and treatment of STIs is the best strategy to preserve fertility and health.

Acquired immunodeficiency syndrome (AIDS): HIV (human immunodeficiency virus) is diagnosed by the presence of antibodies to the infection. HIV is a slow-growing virus that typically begins with an acute infection. As the disease progresses, T cells are compromised and their count drops from 1600 (normal) to 800, approximately by one-half. Symptoms of HIV include headache, stiffness in the neck, malaise, fever, night sweats, abdominal cramps, diarrhea, and skin rashes. Patients can stay in this stage of infection for years before T cells decrease to 200 or less, at which point the disease is defined as AIDS. This leaves the patient vulnerable to opportunistic infections and cancers such as Kaposi's sarcoma. The HIV infection is transmitted via blood transfusion, drug use/abuse with contaminated needles, or sexual intercourse with an infected partner. An HIV-positive mother can transmit the virus to her unborn baby during pregnancy. Treatments include a cocktail of several antiviral drugs and management of symptoms as they arise.

Chlamydia: Sexually transmitted bacterial infection that causes inflammation of the urethra (urethritis) and cervix (cervicitis) in females. Symptoms of chlamydia in females include a mucopurulent discharge from the vagina and burning and itching with urination. Preventive measures include barrier protection such as a condom. Treatment with antibiotic therapy and abstinence from sexual contact until treatment is completed is advised.

Genital herpes: Highly contagious viral infection of the male and female genitalia. It is caused by the herpes simplex virus (usually HSV-2). In females, signs include multiple shallow vesicles of the cervix and vulva. The ulcerations resemble cold sores and can be very painful and itchy. Additionally, the patient often experiences fever, headache, swollen glands, painful urination, malaise, and muscle pain. Treatment of genital herpes is symptomatic, with anti-inflammatories and analgesics to reduce pain and swelling until the infection subsides. There is no cure for genital herpes so patients should abstain from sexual contact during active infection. When the ulcerations have healed, sexual activity can resume, but barrier protection should be used during intercourse or sexual contact to prevent infecting a partner.

Genital warts: Small cauliflower-like fleshy growths seen in or near the vagina caused by HPV. Genital warts are transmitted from one person to another through sexual contact and can appear 1 to 6 months after sexual contact. Treatment includes topical medications to destroy the warts or surgical removal by cryosurgery. In some cases, warts may disappear spontaneously. Although use of latex condoms may prevent transmission of genital warts, people are advised to avoid sexual contact with people who have the lesions. Gardasil 9 is a vaccine that protects against some types of human papillomavirus and is recommended by the Centers for Disease Control and Prevention for both girls and boys.

ELEMENT REVIEW
cry/o = cold

Gonorrhea: Sexually transmitted bacterial infection caused by *Neisseria gonorrhoeae* affects the mucous membrane of the genital tract. Females may be asymptomatic or have a green-yellow purulent vaginal discharge and painful urination (dysuria). It is spread through sexual contact with an infected partner and can also be transmitted from mother to infant during the birth process. Diagnosis is confirmed by a culture of the discharge and microscopic examination of a gram-stained specimen of the exudate. Treatment with antibiotics is an effective cure. Patients are simultaneously treated for chlamydial infection as the two often occur concurrently. Newborn infants are routinely treated with erythromycin ophthalmic ointment in their eyes immediately after birth as a prophylactic (preventive) measure against an eye infection with gonorrhea or chlamydia in the vaginal canal.

Syphilis: Highly contagious sexually transmitted infection that presents as lesions on any organ or tissue. The causative organism is the spirochete *Treponema pallidum*. It is spread by sexual contact with an infected partner or passed through the placenta from an infected mother to her unborn infant. If left untreated, it progresses through three stages:

1. Primary syphilis presents as small painless red pustules on the skin or mucous membranes. The highly contagious lesions, known as chancres, appear within 2 weeks of exposure. In females, the chancre usually develops on vagina, lips, in the mouth or anus. Treatment with penicillin effectively treats primary syphilis.
2. Secondary syphilis occurs 2 to 3 months after primary syphilis occurs and is left untreated.
3. Tertiary syphilis is the final and most serious stage of the disease and is most often fatal.

Trichomoniasis: Sexually transmitted infection caused by the protozoa *Trichomonas vaginalis*. Females experience burning and itching with urination and a foul-smelling frothy yellow-green discharge from the vagina. Diagnosis is confirmed by microscopic examination of vaginal secretions of the female (or urethral discharge from the male). If trichomoniasis is present, both sexual partners must be treated to prevent passing the infection back and forth. The treatment of choice is metronidazole (Flagyl), an anti-infective that targets protozoa.

Pathology Word-Building Practice

1. Prefixes

Use the prefixes to build a word that corresponds to the definition provided.

an-	intra-	peri-
dys-	nulli-	pre-
ecto-	post-	primi-
endo-		

1. The term for a pregnancy that starts outside the uterus __________
2. The 6 week period of time after delivery __________
3. A woman who has never been pregnant __________
4. A woman who has given birth several times __________
5. Painful menstrual cycles __________
6. Pertaining to within the cervix __________
7. The term meaning the beginning of changes associated with menopause __________
8. Care offered to women during pregnancy __________
9. Pertaining to within the uterus __________
10. The abnormal absence of a menses __________

2. Suffixes

Use the suffixes to build a word that corresponds to the definition provided.

-al	-gravida	-plasia
-ar	-itis	-rrhagia
-cele	-ologist	-rrhaphy
-centesis	-ology	-rrhea
-ectomy	-osis	-rrhexis
-gram	-otomy	-scopy
-graphy	-para	

1. Surgical removal of the uterus ________________
2. Incision into the vulva to facilitate the birth process ________________
3. Diagnostic x-ray of breast tissue ________________
4. The first time a woman gives birth ________________
5. Surgical removal of the fallopian tubes and ovaries ________________
6. Incision into the uterus to deliver a baby via cesarean section ________________
7. Surgical repair of the vulva after the birth process ________________
8. Puncture and aspiration of the amniotic sac ________________
9. The study of the female reproductive system ________________

Female Reproductive System Diagnostic Procedures

AFP screening: Alpha-fetoprotein (AFP) is a serum screening test that measures the level of AFP in the blood. The AFP score, along with maternal age, allows a provider to estimate the chance that the baby may have birth defects such as spina bifida, trisomy 21 (Down syndrome), or trisomy 18 (severe cognitive impairment and birth defects). The test is conducted between 15 to 21 weeks of gestation and helps to diagnose 80% of cases of spina bifida and 75% to 80% cases of trisomy 21 and 18. Confirmation of diagnosis is obtained by ultrasound or amniocentesis.

Amniocentesis: The surgical puncture and aspiration of amniotic fluid for analysis. A needle is passed into the uterus through the abdominal wall. Amniotic fluid is removed and can be used to diagnose fetal abnormalities, fetal maturity, and maternal-fetal blood incompatibility. An amniocentesis can also be used to determine fetal lung development if an early delivery is medically necessary.

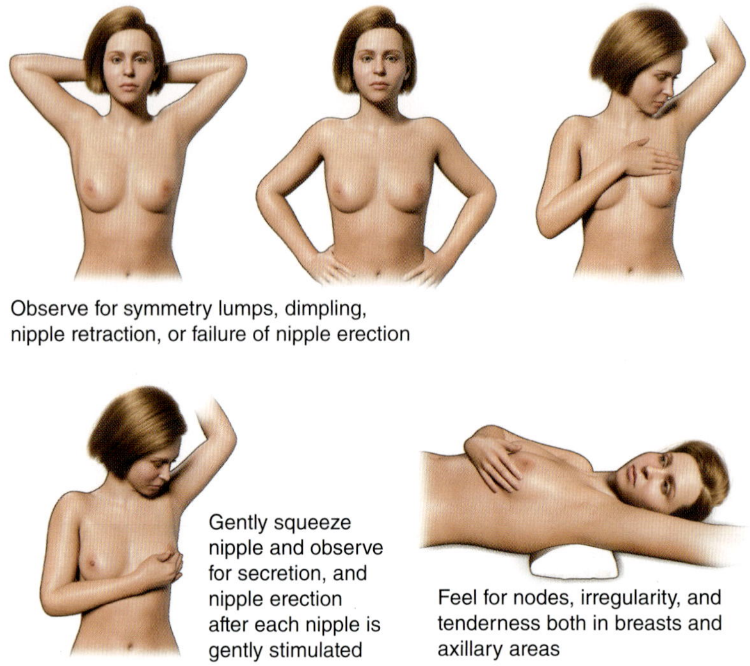

Figure 12-8 Breast self-examination.

Aspiration biopsy: Invasive procedure in which a needle is inserted into an area of the body to assess a small sample of tissue or fluid. It is an outpatient procedure, and a local anesthetic is administered. The procedure can be performed on a breast cyst or lump to diagnose cancer vs benign growth.

Breast self-examination (BSE): Monthly self-examination of breast tissue. Women are advised to perform the evaluation at the end of the menstrual period when breasts are usually soft, making the examination easiest. The examination starts with visual examination, looking for changes in symmetry, puckering of the nipples, discharge, or skin changes (Fig. 12-8). The woman then squeezes each nipple to see if discharge is present. She palpates each breast for the presence of lumps in a clockwise motion around each breast, progressing inward toward the nipple. It is recommended that she then perform the examination again in the shower, using warm water and soap to allow the fingers to glide upon the breasts. After the shower, the examination can again be repeated lying down, flattening the breasts, and using the same clockwise motion. This three-step process will ensure that no segment of the breast is unexamined.

Chorionic villus sampling: A biopsy of a small amount of placental tissue obtained during the 11th to 13th week of gestation. The placental tissue originates from the same fertilized ova as the fetus, thus providing the same genetic material as the developing fetus. A thin needle is inserted either through the cervix or abdominal wall into the uterus to the placenta. The test can detect fetal genetic disorders. The invasive nature of the test has a 1% chance of miscarriage and is therefore not routinely used.

Colposcopy: Visual examination of the vagina with a lighted binocular microscope called a *colposcope*. It is used to directly examine the surface of the vagina and the cervix. After inserting a speculum into the vagina, a 5% acetic acid solution is administered to dehydrate the cells of the cervix. The solution removes mucus and debris that can impede visualization of the cells. The provider inspects the cervix for lesions and cellular changes that may be suspicious for cancer. If changes are noted, a biopsy of tissue is obtained.

Cone biopsy: Surgical removal of a cone-shaped sample of the cervix for diagnosis or treatment. It is recommended when a lesion of the endocervix is noted. The patient will

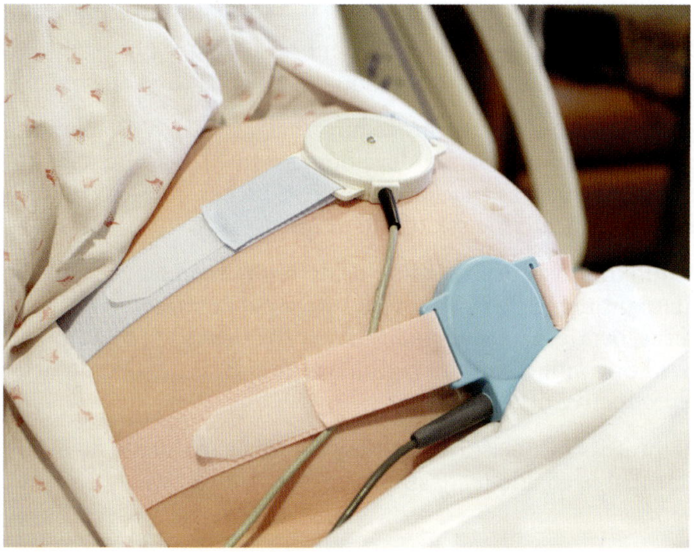

Figure 12-9 Fetal monitoring.

have some spotting but is advised to report any significant bleeding. Biopsied tissue is analyzed to differentiate cancer versus benign lesions.

Endometrial biopsy: Analysis of a sample of endometrial tissue used to diagnose endometrial cancer. The cervix is dilated, and a uterine sound is inserted into the uterus to measure the depth of the uterine cavity. A curet, or aspiration needle, is then inserted into the body of the uterus and a sample of endometrial tissue is retrieved. The patient will experience a pinching sensation and some cramping. Mild analgesics and rest are recommended.

Fetal monitoring (electronic): The use of an electronic device to monitor fetal heart rate and maternal contractions (Fig. 12-9). The procedure can be done with external or internal devices.

Hysterosalpingography: X-ray of the uterus and fallopian tubes. It can be used when a patient has not been able to conceive and a structural anomaly is suspected as the cause of infertility. A contrast medium is injected through a cannula inserted into the cervix, filling the uterus and fallopian tubes. The area is examined by fluoroscopy, looking for structural abnormalities, presence of tumors, or blockage of the fallopian tubes. The patient will experience vaginal draining of the contrast material for a few days after the procedure.

Laparoscopy: The process of viewing the interior of the abdominal cavity with a lighted scope. A small incision is made into the abdomen near the umbilicus. The procedure can be used to diagnose the reason for abdominal pain, and to assess the organs of the female reproductive system to diagnose endometriosis or the cause of infertility. The procedure can be used to perform therapeutic procedures such as tubal ligation, removal of ectopic pregnancies, draining of ovarian cysts, or detorsion of an ovary. The procedure is done under general anesthesia and recovery time varies based on findings.

Mammography: The process of examining the soft tissue of the breasts with an x-ray. The procedure is used to detect benign and cancerous tumors of the breast.

Papanicolaou (Pap) smear: Diagnostic test for cervical cancer. The noninvasive test is performed as part of an annual gynecological examination. The test is performed by obtaining a small sample of secretions of the endocervix and the posterior vaginal area near the cervix. The secretions are placed on two microscope slides labeled cervical and vaginal. Patients are advised not to douche or tub bathe for 24 hours prior to the examination to prevent cells from washing away. The Pap smear is 95% accurate in diagnosing cervical, endocervical, and vaginal cancers.

Liquid-based Pap (LBP): The automated LBP test is similar to the standard Pap smear. The cervical cells are obtained by a brush, and the specimen is placed in a vial of liquid preservative. The specimen is analyzed in the same manner as the Pap smear.

Obstetric ultrasound: Noninvasive procedure that uses high-frequency sound waves to examine the internal structures of the developing fetus. It can be used to diagnose complications of pregnancy such as placenta previa or breech presentation. It is also used to confirm due date and indicate the sex of the fetus.

Pelvic ultrasound: Noninvasive procedure using high-frequency sound waves to create an image of the internal organs. It is used to locate a pelvic mass, an ectopic pregnancy, and to assess the uterus, ovaries, and fallopian tubes. The ultrasound can be obtained through the abdominal wall or conducted transvaginally. The transvaginal approach creates a clearer picture of the reproductive organs.

Pelvimetry: The process of measuring the pelvis either manually or by an x-ray to determine if the birth canal is an adequate size for natural childbirth.

CAREER EXPLORATION: LABOR AND DELIVERY NURSE

In high school, I knew I wanted a career where I could help people. I took classes in early childhood education and psychology, as well as a medical careers course. My teacher took us to the hospital, and I was able to job shadow a labor and delivery nurse. She showed me that being a labor and delivery nurse is a combination of caring for patients' medical and emotional needs. First-time mothers are often scared and need encouragement through the birth process; even women who have given birth previously need care and support. Monitoring the progress of labor involves guiding mothers through the struggle of contractions, administering medications, monitoring vital signs, and assisting in the delivery of the baby. After the birth, the labor and delivery nurse cares for both the newborn and the mother. She will also teach the new mother to breastfeed and care for the newborn. I knew that labor and delivery nursing was the best choice for me. I enrolled in a BSN program and worked hard to pass the NCLEX examination. As a new nurse, I applied to the hospital and was hired on a medical surgical floor. I asked my nurse manager for advice on getting a job in labor and delivery. She suggested that while I work on the med/surg floor, I also study for the inpatient obstetrics examination offered by National Certification Corporation. I also applied to the float pool, working in obstetrics when the floor was short-staffed. I studied and took the online exam, earning the RNC-OB designation—a registered nurse certified in obstetrics. With that certification, I applied to and was hired on the L&D floor for a full-time position. I've been working in labor and delivery now for 5 years. I love my job and helping women bring their little ones into the world. The work is physically challenging; my 8- or 12-hour shifts require me to be on my feet a lot. The hard work and long hours are worth it when I see a new mom with her baby.

Forms of Contraception

Women who can become pregnant have a variety of methods to prevent pregnancy (Table 12-4). It is important to remember that not all contraceptive methods are 100% effective and many forms of birth control do not prevent transmission of STIs, sexually transmitted infections.

TABLE 12-4 Forms of Contraception

Method	How Is It Administered/ Mechanism?	Contraindications	Effectiveness	Side Effects/Comments
Abstinence	Not engaging in sexual intercourse	None	100%	None
Oral contraception	One pill, po (by mouth) once each day, preferably at the same time each day Mechanism: hormones prevent ovulation	History of migraine headaches, breast cancer, estrogen-directed tumors, depression, coronary artery disease	Nearly 100% when taken consistently	**Positive:** Decreased menstrual flow, decreased dysmenorrhea, decrease in iron-deficiency anemia **Negative:** Nausea, headache, weight gain, mild hypertension
Depo-Provera injections	Intramuscular injection administered once every 12 weeks; prevents ovulation	Previous breast cancer, thrombolytic disease, liver disease	99% effective	Weight gain, headaches, osteopenia
Intrauterine device	Implanted into the uterus, the foreign body prevents ovum implanting into the lining of the uterus	History of dysmenorrhea, metrorrhagia, ectopic pregnancy, breast cancer, allergy to the device, fibroid tumors	99% effective	Spotting, uterine cramping, higher risk of tubal pregnancy
Birth control patch	Thin, flexible patch worn on the skin of the buttock, abdomen, or upper arm that administers hormones to prevent pregnancy; changed once per week for 3 weeks, then no patch for 1 week	History of blood clots, breast cancer, estrogen-fed tumors, coronary artery disease	99% effective	**Positive:** Decreased menstrual flow, decreased dysmenorrhea, decreased iron-deficiency anemia **Negative:** Nausea, headache, weight gain, mild hypertension
Contraceptive ring	A flexible ring placed in the vagina that releases low-dose hormones to prevent pregnancy; placed by the patient once per month—left in place for 3 weeks, then 1 week with no ring	Age 35+, heavy smokers, breastfeeding, history of blood clots or coronary artery disease	99% effective	Side effects similar to oral contraceptives If ring slips out of the vagina for 3+ hours, additional form of birth control recommended
Condoms male and female	Male: A thin latex sheath worn on the penis during intercourse Female: Thin latex sheath inserted into the vagina prior to intercourse	Allergy to the condom material the only contradiction	Approximately 82% effective in preventing pregnancy	Male barrier prevents transmission of STIs Both types designed to collect semen and are one-time use
Diaphragm with spermicide	Flexible, circular rubber disc that fits over the cervix; inserted prior to intercourse and primarily used with a spermicidal cream or jelly	None	Approximately 82% effective in preventing pregnancy	Device is fitted by a physician Can be inserted up to 24 hours prior to intercourse Possible cervicitis, increased chance of UTI
Tubal ligation	Surgical procedure in which the fallopian tubes are cut and tied to prevent passage of ova from the tube to the uterus	Not used if future fertility is desired	100% permanent loss of fertility	Scheduled as an outpatient procedure or immediately after giving birth
Micro-insert system	Bilateral occlusion of the fallopian tubes with a soft, flexible micro-insert in each tube	Not used if future fertility is desired	100% permanent loss of fertility	During the first 3 months, alternate form of birth control necessary until body forms the contraceptive tissue barrier

Female Reproductive System Therapeutic Procedures

Cesarean section: Surgical procedure to deliver the baby transabdominally (Fig. 12-10). The uterus is incised to remove the baby, umbilical cord, and the placenta. It can be scheduled near the due date if the mother's pelvis has been measured and will not accommodate the size of the baby. It is also performed if labor is not progressing or if maternal or fetal distress makes quick delivery imperative.

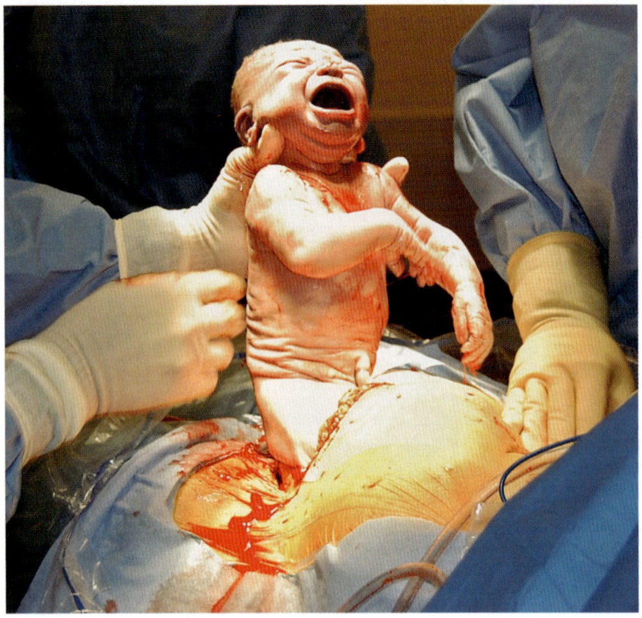

Figure 12-10 Cesarean section.

Cryosurgery: The destruction of tissue by freezing with liquid nitrogen. The procedure can be used to freeze and remove abnormal cells of the cervix detected by a Pap smear. It is also used on other body parts to freeze and remove malignant skin tumors and warts.

Culdocentesis: The surgical puncture through the posterior wall of the vagina into the cul-de-sac, the pouch located between the uterus and the rectum. Because the cul-de-sac is the lowest part of the abdominal cavity, pus and blood may collect there. The culdoscope is inserted and a sample of intraperitoneal fluid is removed. The area is also visually inspected for inflammation, purulent discharge, ectopic pregnancy, ovarian cysts, or ovarian malignancy.

Dilation and curettage: Dilation is the widening of the cervix to allow instruments to be inserted to scrape the lining of the uterus with a curette. During the dilation, the cervix is expanded by inserting a series of probes of increasing diameter. During the curettage, the lining of the uterus is scraped with a spoon-shaped instrument called a curette. The procedure is performed to diagnose uterine disease, to remove an IUD, correct heavy or prolonged uterine bleeding, or to empty retained products of conception after abortion. It can be used to remove infected tissue from pelvic inflammatory disease or to perform an elective abortion. After the procedure, the patient should be monitored for a few hours for excessive uterine bleeding, which is a sign of uterine trauma.

Hysterectomy: The surgical removal of the uterus, which may also include the fallopian tubes and ovaries. Approximately 300,000 American women have the procedure each year, making it the second most common surgical procedure of the female reproductive system. (Cesarean section is the most common.) Indications for hysterectomy include cancer, abnormal bleeding, uterine prolapse, or fibroid tumors. Surgical approaches vary:

Vaginal hysterectomy: Removes the uterus through an incision at the top of the vagina. Dissolvable stitches are placed inside the vagina. This approach is used for a prolapsed uterus or noncancerous conditions. The recovery time is approximately 4 weeks. It is performed in the hospital, but patients often go home on the same day.

Laparoscopic or robotic-assisted laparoscopic hysterectomy: Removes the uterus in small pieces through three to five incisions in the abdomen. The lighted laparoscope is used to visualize the organs. The surgeon may or may not use robotic assistance. Patients often go home the same day as surgery or stay one night. Recovery time is approximately 4 weeks.

Abdominal hysterectomy: Removes the uterus through a 6- to 8-in. incision into the abdomen. The incision is made either vertically from the umbilicus to the pubic bone or laterally across the pubic hairline. This procedure is most used for cancer of the uterus, an enlarged uterus, or a cancer that has spread to other organs. The surgeon uses stitches or staples to close the incision. The patient stays in the hospital for 2 to 3 days, and recovery time is longer than vaginal and laparoscopic approaches.

In addition to removing the uterus, the fallopian tubes and ovaries may be removed based on indications. The cervix may be preserved, removed, or in a radical hysterectomy, the upper portion of the vagina and adjacent lymph node are removed. Radical hysterectomy is commonly performed in cases of cancer.

Loop electrosurgical excision procedure (LEEP): Procedure used to remove abnormal cells from the cervix. A thin wire loop with an electrical current running through it is used to cut away a thin surface layer of cells. A local anesthetic is administered before the loop is inserted into the vagina to the cervix. The LEEP procedure is an office procedure that is the preferred treatment for cervical dysplasia.

ELEMENT REVIEW
dys- = bad
-plasia = formation

Medications for the Female Reproductive System

Table 12-5 contains medications used for contraception, to promote abortion, to promote ovulation, to induce labor, or to replace hormones lost during menopause.

TABLE 12-5 Examples of Medications for the Female Reproductive System

Classification	Examples (Tradename)	Common Use/Action
Abortifacient	Ethinyl estradiol, norgestrel (Cryselle 28, Lo/Orval 28, Ogestrel-28), ethinyl estradiol, norethindrone (Aranelle, Modicon, Ortho-Novum)	Kills fetus within 49 days of menses
Barrier devices (contraception)	Diaphragm, female condom, male condom	Prevent transmission of STIs, birth control
Cervical ripening agents	Dinoprostone (Cervidil, Prepidil)	Inducement of labor
Estrogens	Oral: (Estrace, Premarin) Cream: (Estrace) Patch: (Alora, Estraderm)	Estrogen replacement therapy (ERT)
Implants (contraception)	Etonogestrel (Implanon, Nexplanon)	Prevents ovulation, fertilization, and implantation
IUDs	Levonorgestrel intrauterine system (Mirena), copper IUD	Prevents implantation, kills sperm
Ovulation stimulants	Clomiphene (Clomid, Serophene)	Female infertility
Ovulation prevention	Monophasic: (Cryselle 28, Lo/Orval 28, Ogestrel-28)	Birth control (delivers constant amounts of hormones for the first 21 days of cycle)
	Biphasic: (Apri, Desogen, Mircette, Ortho-Cept)	Birth control (delivers constant dose of estrogen, but two different doses of progestin in the monthly cycle)
	Triphasic: (Aranelle, Junel FE 1/20, Ortho-Novum 7/7/7)	Birth control (delivers varying amount of estrogen and progesterone during cycle)
Oxytocin	Oxytocin (Pitocin, Syntocinon)	Induction of labor
Postcoital contraception	Mifepristone (Mifeprex)	Prevents ovulation, fertilization, and implantation
Progestins	(Errin, Overette, Provera)	Birth control
Spermicides	Nonoxynol-9 (Encare, Conceptrol)	Birth control
Transdermal contraception	Ethinyl estradiol and norelgestromin (Ortho Evra patch)	Prevents ovulation
Vaginal ring	Ethinyl estradiol and etonogestrel (NuvaRing)	Prevents ovulation, fertilization and implantation

Medications Review

Using the table of medications, complete the chart below. The first one has been done for you.

Medication Name	Classification (mechanism)	Therapeutic Use (What is it used for?)
Provera	*Progestin*	*Birth control*
1. NuvaRing	______________	______________
2. Pitocin	______________	______________
3. Clomid	______________	______________
4. Nonoxyl-9	______________	______________
5. Mirena	______________	______________
6. Mifeprex	______________	______________
7. Estrace	______________	______________
8. Ogestrel-28	______________	______________
9. Cervidil	______________	______________
10. Ortho-Novum 7/7/7	______________	______________

Female Reproductive Abbreviations

AB	abortion
BSE	breast self-examination
BSO	bilateral salpingo-oophorectomy
CIS	carcinoma in situ
Cx	cervix
D&C	dilation and curettage
ECC	endocervical curettage
EMB	endometrial biopsy
ERT	estrogen replacement therapy
Gyn	gynecology
HSG	hysterosalpingography
HPV	human papilloma virus
IUD	intrauterine device
LEEP	loop electrosurgical excision procedure
LH	luteinizing hormone
LMP	last menstrual period
LSO	left salpingo-oophorectomy
OB	obstetrics
OB/GYN	obstetrics and gynecology
Pap	Papanicolaou smear
PID	pelvic inflammatory disease
PMS	premenstrual syndrome
RSO	right salpingo-oophorectomy
STI	sexually transmitted infection
TAH	total abdominal hysterectomy
TAH-BSO	total abdominal hysterectomy, bilateral salpingo-oophorectomy
TVH	total vaginal hysterectomy

Abbreviations Review

1. TVH
   a. total vaginal hysterotomy
   b. total vulvar hysterotomy
   c. total vaginal hysterectomy
   d. total vaginal hysterotomy

2. PID
   a. perineum inflammatory disorder
   b. pelvic infectious disease
   c. pelvic inflammatory disease
   d. perineum inflammation disease

3. AB
   a. abortion
   b. able to give birth
   c. abstinence
   d. ablation

4. TAH
   a. transabdominal hysterectomy
   b. total abortion and hysterectomy
   c. targeted abdominal hysterectomy
   d. total abdominal hysterectomy

5. ERT
   a. estrogen replacement therapy
   b. estrogen radiographic tracing
   c. estradiol radiographic tracing
   d. estradiol replacement therapy

6. LMP
   a. liquid menstrual period
   b. last menstrual period
   c. latent menstrual period
   d. lateral menstrual period

7. LEEP
   a. loop electrosurgical procedure
   b. lateral electrosurgical procedure
   c. left-side electrosurgical procedure
   d. liquid electrosurgical procedure

8. EMB
   a. endometered biopsy
   b. endometrial basal cell
   c. endometrial biopsy
   d. endometrial base

9. D&C
   a. dilation and curettage
   b. destruction and curettage
   c. dilation and crushing
   d. destruction and crushing

10. IUD
    a. interuterine damage
    b. intrauterine damage
    c. interuterine device
    d. intrauterine device

11. HSG
    a. hysterosalpingography
    b. hyposalingography
    c. hypersalpingography
    d. hydrosalpingography

12. BSO
    a. biopsy salpingo-ovaries
    b. bilateral salpingo-ovaries
    c. bilateral salpingo-oophorectomy
    d. basal salpingo-oophorectomy

13. Pap
    a. Papain smear
    b. Papin sample
    c. Papanicolaou sample
    d. Papanicolaou smear

14. PMS
    a. perimenstrual symptoms
    b. perimenstrual syndrome
    c. premenstrual syndrome
    d. premenstrual symptoms

15. BSE
    a. breast self-examination
    b. bilateral self-examination
    c. breast symptoms evaluation
    d. breast self-evaluation

MEDICAL DOCUMENTATION

Knowledge of terms related to normal anatomy and pathological conditions enables you to understand medical documentation such as history and physical exams, operative reports, discharge summaries, laboratory reports, and x-ray reports. For the following ultrasound report, Lisa L. presented to the emergency department in acute pain. She was examined, given diagnostic ultrasound and examination, and admitted. Apply your knowledge by answering the questions that follow the report.

Ultrasound Report

Patient: Lisa L.
US non-ob transvaginal with limited Doppler

Impression:

1. The right ovary measures 6.8 × 6 × 4.4 cm. There is arterial flow on pulsed doppler.
2. Partial right fallopian tube torsion with presence of a 1.4 cm right fallopian tube with significant hyperemia and focal tenderness.
3. There is a 5.5 cm simple right ovarian cyst. The right ovary demonstrates normal arterial flow but given the clinical context and above findings of partial torsion, recommend GYN consultation for further evaluation and management.
4. The left ovary measures 2.2 × 3 × 1.4 cm. There is arterial flow on pulsed Doppler.

Plan: Recommend GYN consultation for further evaluation and management.

Wendy Rickert, MD
Radiology

Hospital Course

Lisa L. is a 29 y. o. G0 admitted with waxing and waning RLQ pain of intermittent ovarian torsion. Transvaginal ultrasound done on admission showed partial right fallopian tube torsion and 5.5 cm simple right ovarian cyst with normal arterial flow. The plan is for close monitoring overnight and going to the OR in the AM for diagnostic laparoscopy, possible ovarian/tubal detorsion and ovarian cystectomy and/or salpingectomy.

Subjective

The patient reports worsening RLQ pain to 10/10 this morning with radiation to right lower back. She also felt nauseous which has improved with Zofran.

Objective

Vitals last 24 hours:
Temp: 97.9°F, 99.5°F, 99.5°F
Pulse: 79
Resp: 18
SpO2: 100%
I/Os: No intake or output data in the 24 hours ending 12/08/24 0629

Physical Exam

Gen: well-appearing, lying in bed in pain. Tearful and distressed by her pain.
CV: regular rate and rhythm
Pulm: normal work of breathing
Abdomen: soft, slightly distended, remarkably tender in RLQ, slight rebound tenderness
Neuro: alert and oriented

MEDICAL DOCUMENTATION—cont'd

Assessment and Plan
Partial right fallopian tube torsion with 5.5 cm ovarian cyst.
Laparoscopic detorsion and drainage of ovarian cyst.

Jennifer Wagner, MD
Gynecology

Questions

1. What diagnostic imaging was performed in the emergency department? ____________________
2. A GYN consult was obtained, which means ____________________
3. What type of cyst does Lisa have? ____________________
4. What organ is "torsed?" ____________________
5. What does RLQ stand for? ____________________
6. If the tube needs to be surgically removed, what is the name of the procedure? ____________________
7. If a cyst is surgically removed, what is the name of the procedure? ____________________
8. Break down the word hyperemia, what does it mean? ____________________
9. Break down the word transvaginal, what does it mean? ____________________
10. What type of blood flow was measured by the doppler? ____________________

Visit the Medical Language Lab at medicallanguagelab.com. Use it to improve your recognition and understanding of terms in medical documentation.

CHAPTER REVIEW

Complete the Sentence

Using medical terms from this chapter, complete the sentence.

1. The dark pigmented circular area surrounding the nipple is called the ____________________.
2. Surgical removal of a breast is called ____________________.

3. An x-ray of the uterus and fallopian tubes using a contrast media is called ______________________.

4. The field of medicine that focuses on pregnancy and delivery is ______________________.

5. The muscular tube that connects the uterus with the vulva is called ______________________.

6. The fingerlike projections of the fallopian tubes are called ______________________.

7. The first menstrual period is called ______________________.

8. Maturation and release of an ovum from the ovary is called ______________________.

9. The yellowish mass that forms within a ruptured follicle is the ______________________.

10. The term for acute or chronic inflammation of the cervix is ______________________.

11. A benign smooth-muscle tumor of the uterus is known as a ______________________.

12. The term for abnormally light or infrequent menses is ______________________.

13. The surgical puncture and aspiration of fluid from the amniotic sac is called ______________________.

14. The female erectile tissue that engorges with blood upon orgasm is the ______________________.

15. The process of secreting breast milk is called ______________________.

16. The surgical removal of both fallopian tubes and the ovaries is ______________________.

17. The word that means *through the vagina* is ______________________.

18. The term for the pathologic discharge of milk from women who are not breastfeeding or pregnant is ______________________.

19. The term for inflammation of the breast is ______________________.

20. The period of life when the ability to reproduce begins is ______________________.

21. The term for a woman who has never been pregnant is ______________________.

22. The medical specialist of the female reproductive system is a
_______________________________________.

23. The union of the sperm and an ovum is called
_______________________________________.

24. The upper central portion of the uterus is the
_______________________________________.

25. The two small mucus secreting glands of the vaginal canal are known as the
_______________________________________.

Spelling

Circle the correctly spelled terms in the pairs of terms.

1.	Bartholin's gland	Bantholin's gland
2.	cervix	cerrvix
3.	endomentrial	endometrial
4.	salpingectomy	salpingoectomy
5.	perinuem	perineum
6.	dysmenorrhea	dysmennorrhea
7.	primogravida	primigravida
8.	menstruation	mensturation
9.	hysterasalpingography	hysterosalpingography
10.	gynecalogist	gynecologist

Abbreviations

Define the following abbreviations:

1. TAH-BSO _______________________________________
2. ECC _______________________________________
3. Cx _______________________________________
4. RSO _______________________________________
5. LSO _______________________________________
6. OB/GYN _______________________________________
7. STI _______________________________________
8. HPV _______________________________________

9. CIS ________________

10. HSG ________________

Identify the Anatomical Structures

Match the structures of the vulva from the following list to the letters shown in Figure 12-11.

1. ______ hymen
2. ______ labia majora
3. ______ labia minora
4. ______ mons pubis
5. ______ pubic symphysis
6. ______ urinary meatus
7. ______ vaginal orifice
8. ______ vestibule
9. ______ clitoris

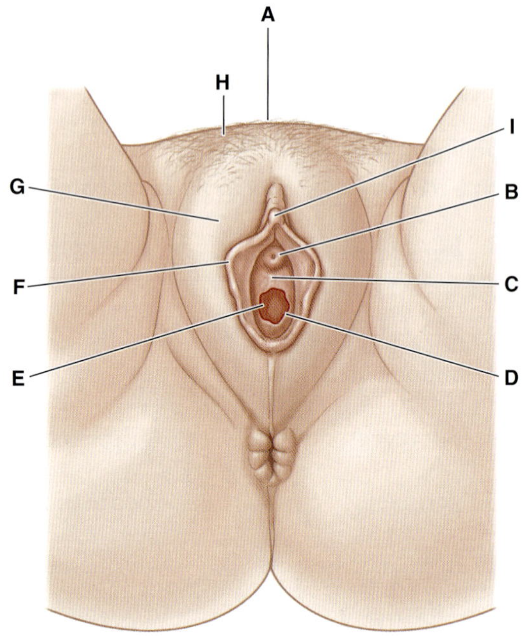

Figure 12-11 Identify the structures of the vulva.

Match the structures of the female reproductive system from the following list to the letters shown in Figure 12-12.

1. ______ body of the uterus (corpus)
2. ______ cervix
3. ______ endometrium
4. ______ external os
5. ______ fallopian tubes
6. ______ fimbriae
7. ______ fundus
8. ______ internal os
9. ______ myometrium
10. ______ ovary
11. ______ perimetrium
12. ______ vagina

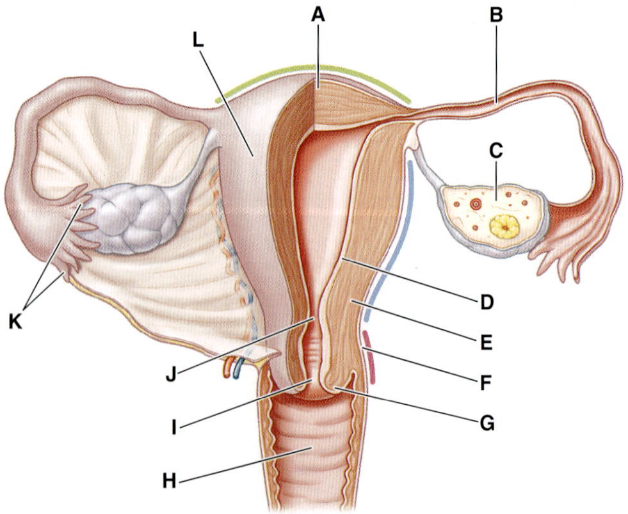

Figure 12-12 Identify the structures of the internal female reproductive system.

Match the structures of the breast from the following list to the letters shown in Figure 12-13.

1. _______ fatty tissue
2. _______ lactiferous duct
3. _______ mammary lobule
4. _______ nipple
5. _______ pectoral muscle
6. _______ rib

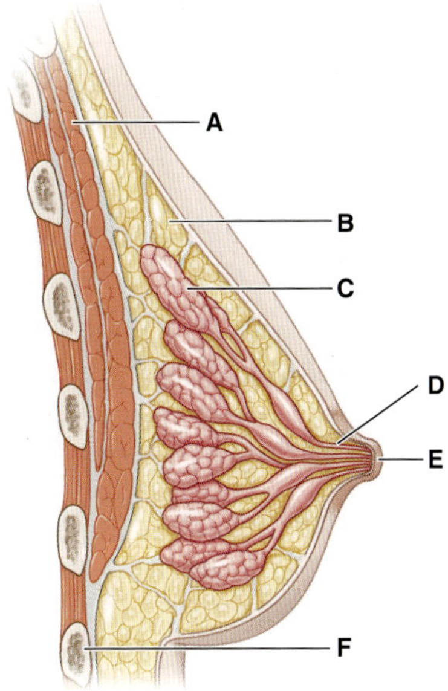

Figure 12-13 Identify the structures of the breast.

Decipher the Terms

Separate each term into its prefix (if any), combining form, and suffix. Next, translate the word parts and then give the common definition of the term.

1. ovarian

   Prefix: ______________________ *Suffix:* ______________________

   Combining Form: ______________________

   Meaning: ______________________

2. polycystic

   Prefix: ______________________ *Suffix:* ______________________

   Combining Form: ______________________

   Meaning: ______________________

3. oophoritis

   Prefix: ______________________ *Suffix:* ______________________

   Combining Form: ______________________

   Meaning: ______________________

4. myometrium

Prefix: ______________________ *Suffix:* ______________________

Combining Form: ____

Meaning: ____

5. mammography

Prefix: ______________________ *Suffix:* ______________________

Combining Form: ____

Meaning: ____

6. episiotomy

Prefix: ______________________ *Suffix:* ______________________

Combining Form: ____

Meaning: ____

7. hysteropexy

Prefix: ______________________ *Suffix:* ______________________

Combining Form: ____

Meaning: ____

8. endometriosis

Prefix: ______________________ *Suffix:* ______________________

Combining Form: ____

Meaning: ____

9. salpingitis

Prefix: ______________________ *Suffix:* ______________________

Combining Form: ____

Meaning: ____

10. pelvimetry

Prefix: ______________________ *Suffix:* ______________________

Combining Form: ____

Meaning: ____

mll Medical Language Lab

Visit the Medical Language Lab at medicallanguagelab.com. Use it to enhance your study and reinforcement of the medical terms and word parts covered in this chapter.

CHAPTER

13

The Male Reproductive System

LEARNING OBJECTIVES

Upon completion of the chapter, you will be able to:

1. Identify and define the combining forms, roots, prefixes, and suffixes introduced in the chapter.
2. Spell medical terms related to the male reproductive system.
3. Describe the major organs of the male reproductive system.
4. Describe the process and location of sperm production.
5. Describe the conditions needed for healthy sperm formation.
6. Identify and discuss major pathological terms of the male reproductive system.
7. Identify and discuss major diagnostic and therapeutic treatments of the male reproductive system.
8. Identify the major categories of medications used to treat male reproductive pathologies.
9. Define abbreviations of the male reproductive system.

KEY TERMS

Bulbourethral gland	Gonads	Rete testis	Spermatogenesis
Ejaculation	Leydig cells	Scrotum	Spermatozoa
Ejaculatory duct	Male orgasm	Semen	Testes
Epididymis	Meiosis	Seminal vesicle	Testosterone
Erection	Penis	Seminiferous tubules	Urethra
Gametes	Prostate gland	Spermatic cord	Vas deferens

We begin this chapter with a case study of Larry, a man who is experiencing urinary symptoms. The case study introduces some of the medical terms relevant to both the male reproductive system and the urinary system. Throughout the chapter, we will revisit the story of Larry to understand his disorder and how medical interventions can improve a patient's quality of life. After reading this chapter, you will expand your knowledge of medical terms related to the male reproductive system. You will understand how a man's body normally functions for the purpose of reproduction. You will be able to use word elements presented to understand unfamiliar terms and to build your medical vocabulary.

CASE STUDY

Larry is a 67-year-old retired brick mason who has always enjoyed good health. He recently has had trouble sleeping. He wakes up several times per night and must go to the bathroom. He feels the need to urinate, but when he goes into the bathroom, he voids only a few drops. He tries to go back to sleep, but the urgent need to void returns several times per night. He is experiencing daytime sleepiness and is becoming very frustrated. He decides to talk with his primary care provider about the problem. Dr. Winslow looks at Larry's blood testing and explains that his prostate-specific antigen (PSA) is elevated. PSA levels for men over age 60 is less than 4 ng/mL; Larry's PSA is 7.9 ng/mL. PSA levels can be elevated from several causes, such as prostate cancer, infection, or recent surgery. Larry's urinalysis shows no white blood cells, so Dr. Winslow does not think the PSA is elevated due to infection. Larry replies, "Wow, could it be cancer?" Dr. Winslow replies, "While it could be cancer, I think it is most likely an enlarged prostate gland, a condition known as BPH, benign prostatic hypertrophy. If your PSA was over 100 ng/mL, I would suspect cancer. I will refer you to Dr. Teegan, the urologist associated with our practice. He will perform some tests and definitively diagnose the problem. In the meantime, I will prescribe Flomax for you. It is a medication that will relax the muscles around the prostate gland and relieve the pressure on the urethra, the tube that urine flows out of. This should allow you to remain asleep, as you will not get that urgent need to pee during the night" Larry replies, "Thanks Dr. Winslow."

Larry goes to see Dr. Teegen, who performs a digital rectal examination by inserting his finger into Larry's rectum to palpate the prostate gland. He explains to Larry, "I can feel that your prostate gland is inflamed. That causes you to urinate frequently at night. Is the Flomax helping?" Larry replies, "Yes, the Flomax helps me stay asleep, but it does make me feel dizzy. I have to get up slowly, or I feel like I will pass out." Dr. Teegan says, "Have you fainted?" Larry says, "No, I just have the feeling that I might faint. It's been okay. The other thing, doc, is that I haven't had sex with my wife since before starting Flomax. At first, I was so tired from not sleeping that I didn't even think of sex. My wife is a great woman. I love her so much, and I don't want this to end our sex life." Dr. Teegan replies, "Let's find out the cause of the enlargement of the prostate and then create a plan to decrease the size. Once the prostate size is decreased, you can stop taking the Flomax and get your energy back. I think your libido, your craving for sex, will return. A lot of guys our age, I'm 61 myself, have an enlarged prostate. Luckily, we have some options to correct the problem." Larry says, "Great. I want to feel like myself again. What are the next steps?" Dr. Teegan replies, "I will perform a prostate biopsy. I won't lie to you; it will be a bit uncomfortable. I will go in through your rectum and cut a small piece of the prostate off to examine it under a microscope. This will tell us if it is BPH or prostate cancer." Larry says, "Will I have to go to the hospital?" Dr. Teegan replies, "Yes, I will do the procedure in the outpatient clinic at the hospital. You won't need to stay overnight, but you will need a ride home. You will want to rest for the remainder of the day." Larry replies, "Okay, doc let's do this."

Structures and Physiology

The male reproductive system functions to produce sperm cells, the genetic contribution that is delivered to the female during intercourse to produce offspring. The organs of the male reproductive system include the testes, vas deferens, prostate gland, bulbourethral gland, seminal vesicles, penis, and urethra.

Both the male and female reproductive organs that produce sex cells (sperm and egg) are called **gonads**. The sex cells, also called **gametes**, upon union in the female body will begin the process of growing into an embryo. The gonads of the male also secrete the primary sex hormone, **testosterone**, which is responsible for the development of sperm and male secondary sex characteristics. Sexual characteristics of a male that present during puberty include increased muscle mass, sexual desires, deepening of the voice, and the development of male-pattern body hair. Production of testosterone is stimulated by the anterior pituitary gland secreting follicle-stimulating hormone (FSH) and luteinizing hormone (LH); this is discussed in Chapter 11, The Endocrine System.

Testes

The gonads of the male are the **testes**, the paired, oval organs that lie suspended within the **scrotum**, a sac-like pouch outside of the abdominopelvic cavity (Fig. 13-1). The location of the scrotum provides a cool temperature necessary to produce sperm cells. Each testis is approximately 1½ inches long and 1 inch wide. It is enclosed by a tough layer of fibrous connective tissue, called lobules, that protects the compartments. Within each of the approximately 250 lobules are one to four **seminiferous tubules**, the sites of sperm production. The tubules are divided by a connective tissue membrane that contains clusters

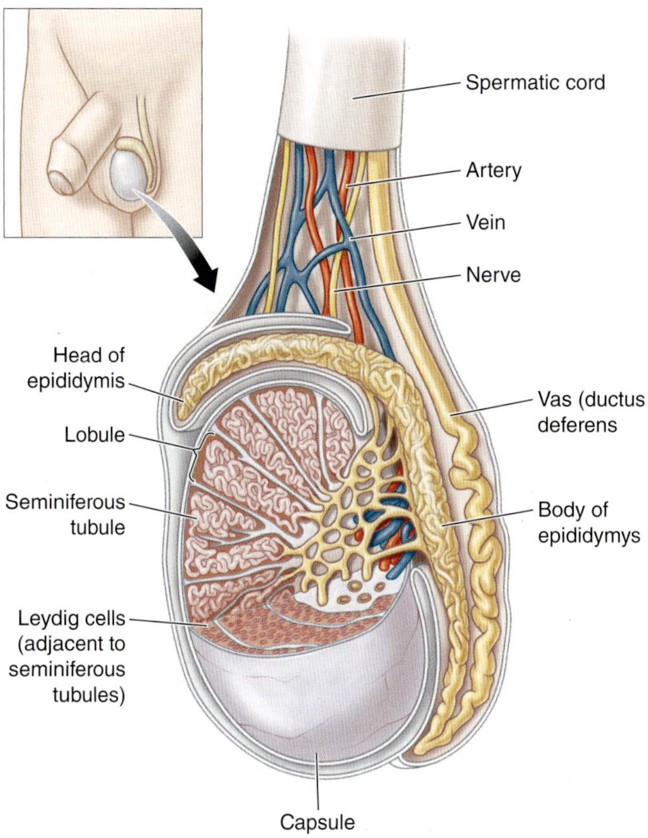

Figure 13-1 The internal structures of the scrotum and testis.

of endocrine cells called **Leydig cells**. The Leydig cells secrete testosterone to promote the production of sperm cells in the adjacent tubules. The walls of the seminiferous tubules are lined with germinal epithelium composed of both supportive cells and germ cells. The supportive cells provide nutrients for the germ cells to produce sperm in a process called **spermatogenesis**. Sperm cells are produced by a process called **meiosis**, which only occurs in the male and female gametes.

ELEMENT REVIEW
spermat/o = sperm
-genesis = production
zo/a = animal, male

Within the germinal epithelium, spermatogonium will divide into primary spermatocytes, secondary spermatocytes, then into spermatids. The resulting cells have only 23 chromosomes. Gamete cells in the female also undergo meiosis and result in cells that have 23 chromosomes. The union of the sperm cell and oocyte results in cells with 46 chromosomes, containing genetic material from both parents; thus, the offspring will have characteristics from both parents but will be a unique human being.

PHYSIOLOGY FACT

Recall from Chapter 3 that all other cells of the body divide and replace themselves by mitosis, creating two daughter cells that are genetically identical to each other and the parent cell. Thus, mitosis results in replacement cells that have 46 chromosomes.

The seminiferous tubules extend posteriorly to the edge of the testes to form the **rete testis**, where the spermatids will continue to develop. The rete testis is met on its posterior margin with a collection of efferent tubules that connect to the **epididymis**. The epididymis is the single, tightly coiled structure at the posterior side of each testis. If stretched out, it would measure approximately 20 feet long. Spermatids arriving in the epididymis lack a flagellum, the tail-like structure that enables them to swim; thus, peristaltic contractions are necessary to move them along through the coils of the epididymis. As the spermatids continue to develop, they form a head, a midpiece, and a flagellum that gives it mobility. Fully formed sperm cells are called **spermatozoa**. The epididymis curves downward and is connected at the base of the testes to the vas deferens. The developmental stages of the sperm cells are shown in Figure 13-2.

PHYSIOLOGY FACT

Spermatogenesis continues from puberty throughout the life of a male. Normal production of sperm cells is millions per day until 70 or even 80 years of age.

Vas Deferens

The **vas deferens**, also called the ductus deferens, carries the spermatozoa from the epididymis to the urethra. It is a single tube with a thick muscular wall that extends from the base of the scrotum upward through the inguinal canal, crossing the lateral wall of the pelvic cavity. It then loops over the posterior side of the urinary bladder. The vas deferens ends at the **ejaculatory duct**, where sperm is carried into the urethra. The vas deferens is part of the **spermatic cord**, which is composed of the vas deferens, the testicular artery and vein, lymph vessels, testicular nerve, cremaster muscle, and connective tissue. The artery carries oxygenated blood to the testes, and the vein carries deoxygenated blood and waste away. The testicular nerve gives tactile and temperature sensation to the testes. The cremaster muscle will elevate the testes in cold temperatures to maintain the narrow temperature limits necessary for developing sperm cells.

Three accessory organs support spermatozoa as they leave the male body. The prostate gland, the seminal vesicle, and the bulbourethral glands all support the transport of viable sperm.

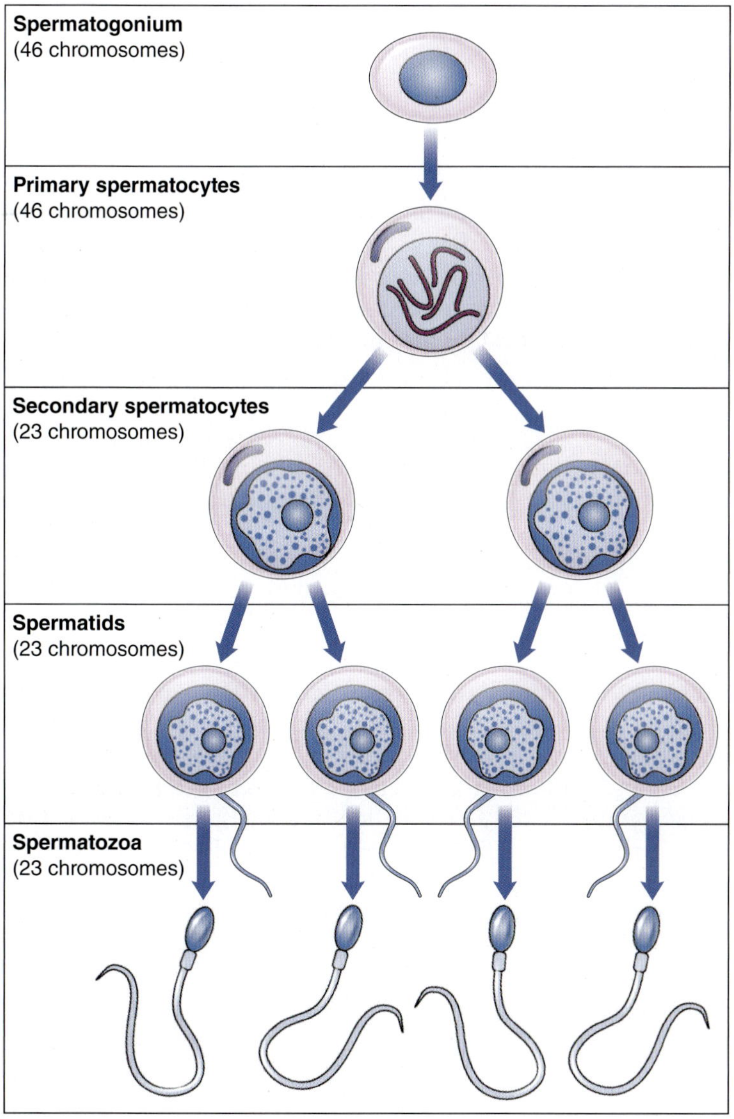

Figure 13-2 At puberty, spermatogonia start dividing and maturing into spermatozoa.

The Prostate Gland

The **prostate gland** is located at the lower margin of the urinary bladder and is approximately 2 cm × 3 cm × 4 cm and weighs 20 g. It is composed of muscular and glandular cells, with ducts that open into the urethra. The prostate secretes a thick alkaline fluid that mixes with spermatozoa. The alkaline fluid aids sperm motility and neutralizes the acidic environment of the female vagina.

The Bulbourethral Glands

The **bulbourethral glands**, also called Cowper's glands, are located inferior to the prostate gland. They are small, round, yellow glands measuring approximately 2.5 cm. The glands secrete a viscous lubricating fluid for sexual intercourse.

The Seminal Vesicles

The **seminal vesicles** are glands located at the base of the urinary bladder. Each gland is composed of numerous sac-like structures that empty secretions into the urethra at the ejaculatory duct. Approximately 60% of fluid volume of ejaculation is from the seminal vesicles and is composed of fructose to nourish and stimulate spermatozoa as they pass through the urethra.

Urethra

The male urethra extends from the distal end of the urinary bladder to the distal end of the penis at the external urethral orifice or urinary meatus. The **urethra** is the passageway for urine in both males and females during urination and for semen in males. Neuronal controls prevent the simultaneous release of urine and semen. The penis is flaccid when voiding urine but erect when ejaculating semen.

Penis

The **penis** is the external cylindrical organ that houses the distal end of the urethra, which carries semen and urine out of the body. During sexual arousal, the penis enlarges and becomes firm in a process called an **erection**. This enables the penis to penetrate the female vagina during sexual intercourse. Three internal columns of sponge-like erectile tissue are covered with a layer of smooth, hairless skin. The skin of the penis contains many sensory receptors that enable sexual stimulation. The erectile tissue contains spaces that fill with blood and enlarge during stimulation and erection. Two of the columns form the dorsal and lateral sides of the penis and are called corpora cavernosa. The third column on the anterior side is called the corpus spongiosum, where the urethra passes through to the urinary meatus. At the distal end of the corpus spongiosum is an enlarged cap called the glans penis. A loose fold of skin, called the prepuce or foreskin, covers the urethral opening. An elective surgical procedure called circumcision is often performed on baby boys shortly after birth. The benefit of circumcision is a decreased chance of infection as the foreskin can be a place for bacteria to collect. Figure 13-3 shows the structures of the male reproductive system.

ELEMENT REVIEW
circum- = around
-cision = to cut

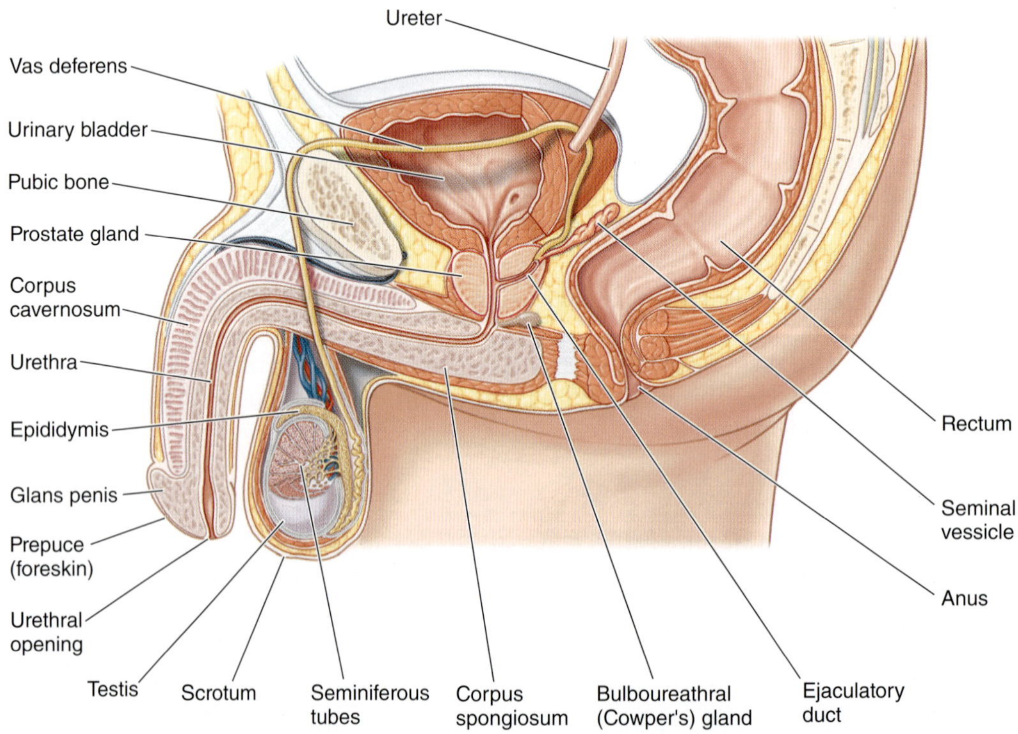

Figure 13-3 The structures of the male reproductive system.

PHYSIOLOGY FACT

- Sperm counts slowly decline after age 35.
- Some research suggests that smoking tobacco can lower sperm counts irrespective of age.
- The generation and release of spermatozoa are controlled by hormonal and neural mechanisms.

Hormonal Mechanisms

Upon puberty, the anterior pituitary gland secretes LH, which promotes the development of Leydig cells in the testes to secrete testosterone. The hormone FSH, also released from the anterior pituitary gland, prepares the germinal cells of the testes to begin spermatogenesis. Thus, the hormonal mechanisms begin spermatogenesis and continue maintenance of testosterone levels in the testes.

Neural Mechanisms

The autonomic nervous system generates impulses upon sexual stimulation. Stimulation can be in the form of touching the body, but it may also be visual stimulation, thinking about sex, or dreams. Originating from the hypothalamus, parasympathetic nerve impulses pass to the walls of the arteries supplying the penis, causing the arteries to dilate. The arterial blood enters the erectile tissue spaces of the corpora cavernosa and compresses the veins that carry blood away from the penis. Thus, the penis swells, becoming erect. Peristalsis of the testicular ducts, the epididymis, and the ejaculatory ducts are stimulated, propelling the semen toward the urethra in contractions called emission. As the urethra fills with semen, sensory and motor impulses are aroused, causing rhythmic contractions, a sensation of pleasure, and finally **ejaculation**, the ejection of semen from the urethra. **Semen** is the thick fluid composed of glandular fluid and spermatozoa. The combination of sensory stimulation, erection, emission, and ejaculation provides a pleasurable experience of physical and mental tension followed by relaxation. This is called the **male orgasm** or climax.

Structures and Physiology Review

Match the Terms

Match the word to the description:

bulbourethral gland	Leydig cells	seminal vesicle
circumcision	male orgasm	seminiferous tubules
ejaculation	meiosis	spermatic cord
ejaculatory duct	penis	spermatozoa
epididymis	prostate gland	testes
erection	rete testis	testosterone
gametes	scrotum	urethra
gonads	semen	vas deferens

1. Cellular division that results in a cell with 23 chromosomes ____________________

2. Provides alkalinity and lubrication to semen ____________________

3. The site of sperm production ______
4. Provides fructose to semen ______
5. The male gonads ______
6. Surgical removal of the foreskin ______
7. Connects seminiferous tubules to the epididymis ______
8. Provides lubrication for sexual intercourse ______
9. Enlargement of the penis upon sexual arousal ______
10. Endocrine cells within the testes that secrete testosterone ______
11. Connection of the testes to the body which contains the vas deferens, the testicular artery, vein, lymph vessels, nerves, and cremaster muscle ______
12. The coiled structure at the posterior side of each testes ______
13. Ejection of seminal fluid from the urethra ______
14. A fully formed sperm cell ______
15. Male organ that becomes erect upon sexual arousal ______
16. Hormone that maintains male sex characteristics ______
17. Passageway for sperm and urine out of the body ______
18. The sac-like pouch that houses the testes ______
19. Carries the spermatozoa from the epididymis to the urethra ______
20. The term that means sperm or egg cells ______

Structures and Physiology Word-Building Practice

1. Nouns and Adjectives

Complete the chart of nouns and their adjective forms.

1. testicle	________________
2. ________________	penile
3. prostate	________________
4. ________________	ejaculatory
5. ________________	scrotal
6. semen	________________
7. meiosis	________________
8. mitosis	________________
9. ________________	urethral
10. ________________	epididymal

2. Prefixes

Choose from the list of prefixes to build a word for the definitions below.

a-, an-	without	hypo-	under, below, decreased amount
crypto-	hidden	macro-	large
epi-	upon	oligo-	decreased number
hyper-	excessive	supra-	above
hydro-	water	trans-	through, across

1. Undescended or "hidden" testicle ________________
2. Absence of one or both testicles ________________
3. Accumulation of fluid in the scrotum or along the spermatic cord ________________
4. Congenital opening of the urethra upon the undersurface of the penis ________________
5. Congenital opening of the urethra on the anterior surface of the penis ________________
6. Decreased number of sperm cells ________________
7. Pertaining to above the pubic bone ________________
8. Pertaining to through the urethra ________________

9. Condition of excessive growth ____________________

10. Absence of sperm in the ejaculate ____________________

3. Singular and Plural Forms

Complete the chart of singular and plural forms.

1. testis ____________________
2. spermatogonium ____________________
3. ____________________ spermatozoa
4. scrotum ____________________
5. ____________________ vas deferens

Word Building With Combining, Prefix, and Suffix Forms

The following word roots, prefixes, and suffixes are commonly used in medical terms for the anatomy and pathology of the male reproductive system. Combining vowels for word roots are included. Memorizing these elements will help you understand new terms that you may encounter as a medical assistant, nurse, surgical or laboratory technician, or as another health-care professional working in urology or in a reproductive clinic.

The list contains examples of terms that use the combining forms as well as a pronunciation guide. Be sure to use the pronunciation guide so that you can learn to say the terms correctly.

The Medical Language Lab at medicallanguagelab.com provides audio files to help you practice your pronunciations.

Combining Form	Meaning	Example (Pronunciation)	Definition
andr/o	man	androgen (AN-drŏ-jĕn)	a hormone that stimulates development of male characteristics
balan/o	penis, male glans	balanitis (bal-ă-NĪT-ĭs)	inflammation of the glans penis
crypt/o	hidden	cryptorchism (krĭpt-OR-kĭd-ĭzm)	failure of testes to descend
epididym/o	epididymi	epididymis (ep-i-DID-ĭ-mĭs)	organ within the testes
noct/o	night	nocturia (nŏk-TŪ-rē-ă)	urinating at night
olig/o	decreased amount	oligospermia (ŏl-ĭ-gō-SPĚR-mē-ă)	decreased sperm count
orchi/o	testicle	orchioplasty (OR-kē-ō-plăs-tē)	surgical repair of the testes

Combining Form	Meaning	Example (Pronunciation)	Definition
orchid/o	testicle	orchidoptosis (or-kĭd-ŏp-TŌ-sĭs)	downward displacement of the testes
pen/i	penis	penile (PĒ-nĭl, -nīl)	pertaining to the penis
pen/o	penis	penoplasty (pē-nō-PLĂS-tē)	surgical repair of penis
phall/o	penis	phallic (făl-ĭk)	pertaining to the penis
prepit/o	prepuce, foreskin	preputial (prē-PŪ-shăl)	pertaining to the prepuce
prostat/o	prostate gland	prostatodynia (pros-tă-tō-DĬN-ē-ă)	pain in the prostate gland
scrot/o	scrotum	scrotal (SKRŌ-tăl)	pertaining to the scrotum
semin/o	semen	seminoma (sĕm-ĭ-NŌ-mă)	cancer of male germ cells
spad/o	split, fissure	hypospadias (hī-pō-SPĀ-dē-ăs)	opening of the male urethra on the underside of the penis
sperm/o	sperm	spermicide (SPĔR-mĭ-sīd)	agent that kills spermatozoa
spermat/o	sperm	spermatogenesis (spĕr-măt-ō-JĔN-ĕ-sĭs)	production of spermatozoa
test/o	testis, testes	testicular (tĕs-TĬK-ū-lăr)	pertaining to the testicles
vas/o	vessel, vas deferens	vasectomy (vă-SEK-tŏ-mē)	removal of a portion of the vas deferens
zo/o	animal, man	spermatozoa (spĕr-măt-ō-ZŌ-ă)	mature male animal gamete

ā = say, ă = sofa, ē = meet, ĕ = met, ī = eye, ĭ = in, ō = oh, ŏ = dog, ū = you, ŭ = up, oo = food

Prefix	Meaning	Example (Pronunciation)	Definition
a, an-	without	anorchism (ă-NOR-kizm)	absence of testes
hyper-	excessive	hypertrophy (hī-PĔR-trŏ-fē)	excessive growth
hypo-	under, below	hypospadias (hī-pō-SPĀ-dē-ăs)	opening of the urethra under surface of the penis
intra-	within	intrapenile (in-tră-PĒ-nĭl, -nīl)	pertaining to within the penis
sub-	under, below	subpubic (sŭb-PŪ-bĭk)	beneath the pubic arch

ā = say, ă = sofa, ē = meet, ĕ = met, ī = eye, ĭ = in, ō = oh, ŏ = dog, ū = you, ŭ = up, oo = food

Suffix	Meaning	Example (Pronunciation)	Definition
-cele	hernia	ureterocele (ū-RĒ-tĕr-ō-sēl)	herniation of the ureter
-ectomy	surgical removal	orchiectomy (or-kĭ-DEK-tŏ-mē)	surgical removal of a testis
-itis	inflammation	epididymitis (ep-ĭ-did-ĭ-MĪT-ĭs)	inflammation of the epididymis
-ology	study of	andrology (an-DROL-ŏ-jē)	the study of the male reproductive system
-osis	condition	phimosis (fī-MŌ-sĭs)	condition of narrowing of the preputial orifice
-pexy	surgical fixation	orchidopexy (OR-kĭd-ō-pĕk-sē)	surgical fixation of a testis
-plasty	surgical repair	balanoplasty (bal-ă-nō-PLĂS-tē)	surgical repair of the penis
-scope	instrument to view	urethroscope (ū-RĒ-thrŏ-skōp)	instrument to view the urethra
-scopy	process of viewing	urethroscopy (ū-rē-THRŎS-kō-pē)	process of viewing the urethra

ā = say, ă = sofa, ē = meet, ĕ = met, ī = eye, ĭ = in, ō = oh, ŏ = dog, ū = you, ŭ = up, oo = food

Combining Forms Practice

1. Build the Terms

*Using **only** the word parts in the lists, create medical terms for the indicated meanings.*

Prefixes	Combining Forms		Suffixes	
an-	andr/o	pen/o	-al	-ile
epi-	balan/o	prostat/o	-cele	-ology
hyper-	crypt/o	scrot/o	-cide	-osis
hypo-	epididym/o	semin/o	-ectomy	-pexy
intra-	hem/o	spermat/o	-genesis	-plasty
	hemat/o	sperm/o	-ia	-scope
	noct/o	testicul/o	-ic	-scopy
	oligi/o	ur/o	-itis	-uria
	orchid/o	vas/o		
	orchi/o			

1. Pertaining to the scrotum ______________________
2. Removal of the prostate gland ______________________
3. Presence of blood in the sperm ______________________

4. Process of production of sperm ______________________
5. Surgical fixation of the testes ______________________
6. Surgical removal of part of the vas deferens ______________________
7. Chemical agent to kill sperm ______________________
8. Condition of a low sperm count ______________________
9. Pertaining to the penis ______________________
10. The study of the male reproductive system ______________________

2. Decipher the Terms

Separate each term into its prefix (if any), combining form, and suffix. Next, translate the word parts and then give the common definition of the term.

balanoplasty

Prefix: None *Combining Form:* balan/o = glans penis

Suffix: -plasty = surgical repair

1. nocturia

Prefix: __________ *Combining Form:* __________ *Suffix:* __________

Meaning: ______________________________

2. balanitis

Prefix: __________ *Combining Form:* __________ *Suffix:* __________

Meaning: ______________________________

3. vasectomy

Prefix: __________ *Combining Form:* __________ *Suffix:* __________

Meaning: ______________________________

4. prostatic

Prefix: __________ *Combining Form:* __________ *Suffix:* __________

Meaning: ______________________________

5. cryptorchidism

Prefix: __________ *Combining Form:* __________ *Suffix:* __________

Meaning: ______________________________

CASE STUDY, continued

Larry has the prostate biopsy and receives a call from Dr. Teegan, who says, "Larry, good news. You don't have cancer, you have BPH." Larry replies, "Doc, that's great news. What can we do for my symptoms?" Dr. Teegan replies "While your prostate is enlarged, it is small enough for me to perform a procedure called a transurethral microwave thermotherapy, TUMT. The healing time is less than a TURP, a transurethral resection of the prostate, where I would cut away some of the prostate tissue. Instead, I will insert an electrode into your urethra into the prostate. Microwave energy will destroy the inner section of the prostate gland, relieving pressure on the urethra. You won't need to be admitted to the hospital, I can do the procedure at the outpatient surgical center, where I did your biopsy." Larry says, "If this will give me good sleep and my sex drive back, I want to do it." Dr. Teegan replies, "Okay, let's get you set up with scheduling and come in for a pre-op visit." Larry replies, "Thanks, doc."

Male Reproductive System Diseases and Disorders

Table 13-1 is a list of common complaints, objective signs, and subjective symptoms that male patients with reproduction system diseases and disorders may describe to their healthcare providers and support staff.

Pathological Conditions of the Male Reproductive System

Diseases and disorders of the male reproductive system include a variety of sexual and urinary complaints or congenital abnormalities of the penis, scrotum, or testes.

Anorchism: Absence of one or both testes. If both testes are absent, the male is impotent, unable to make sperm, and therefore unable to make a woman pregnant.

Anejaculation: The inability to release semen. Commonly caused by a spinal cord injury.

Aspermia: Lack of sperm production.

Balanitis: Inflammation of the glans penis and the mucosal membrane beneath it. It is commonly caused by a bacterial infection. Treatment with the appropriate antibiotic will resolve the infection, but proper hygiene to prevent infection is advised. Balanitis is less common in males who have had a circumcision.

TABLE 13-1 Common Signs and Symptoms

Signs	Symptoms
Inability to maintain an erection	Loss of sex drive (libido)
Elevated PSA	Nocturia (needing to pee at night)
Hypertrophy of the prostate gland	Urinary frequency, urgency
	Incontinence (loss of bladder control)
	Inability to completely empty the bladder

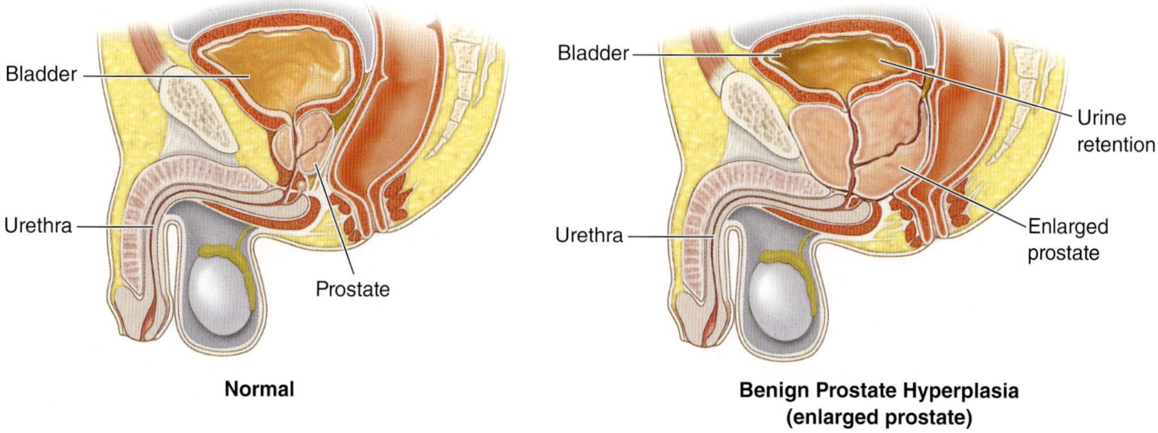

Figure 13-4 A normal and an enlarged prostate gland.

Benign prostatic hypertrophy: The noncancerous growth of the prostate gland (Fig. 13-4). Signs and symptoms include urinary frequency, nocturia (the urge to urinate at night), difficulty starting or stopping urinary stream, weak urinary flow, incomplete emptying of the bladder, and pain or burning during urination. These symptoms are also seen in prostate cancer, so biopsy of the prostate is often used to diagnose BPH vs prostate cancer. Surgical treatments include TURP or TUMT(transurethral microwave thermotherapy). Medication therapy includes tamsulosin (Flomax) to relax the muscles around the prostate and relieve pressure on the urethra.

ELEMENT REVIEW
crypt/o = hidden
orchid/o = testes
-ism = condition
hydro- =water, fluid
-cele = hernia

Carcinoma of the prostate gland: The most common cause of cancer in men and the most common cause of death due to cancer in men 55 and older. The malignant growth within the prostate gland puts pressure on the upper part of the urethra. The increased pressure causes symptoms including urinary frequency, nocturia (the urge to urinate at night), difficulty starting or stopping urinary stream, weak urinary flow, incomplete emptying of the bladder, and pain or burning during urination. Additionally, the patient may have back, leg, or hip pain, and painful ejaculation. Men over the age of 40 are recommended to have a DRE (digital rectal examination) and a PSA test with their yearly physical as early diagnosis of prostate cancer can save lives. Treatments for prostate cancer include prostatectomy, radiation, or hormone therapy. Treatment depends on the patient's age, medical history, and the stage of the cancer.

Cryptorchidism: A condition of an undescended testicle affecting one or both testes (Fig. 13-5). During fetal development, the testes normally move down the inguinal canal into the scrotum. In most babies the testes will descend on their own within the first year of life. If this does not occur, a surgical procedure called orchidopexy is performed. The surgeon makes an incision into the inguinal canal, locating the testicle and bringing it down into the scrotal sac. The surgery is usually performed as an outpatient procedure, and the patient can resume normal activities within a few weeks.

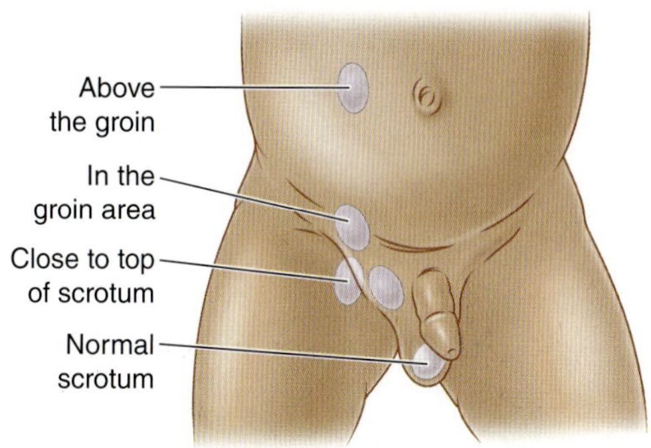

Figure 13-5 Position of the normal testes and the undescended testes.

Epispadias: Congenital condition in which the urethral opening is on the upper (dorsal) side of the penis (Fig. 13-6).

Hydrocele: An accumulation of fluid in the scrotum or along the spermatic cord.

Hypospadias: Congenital condition in which the urethral opening is on the underside of the penis (Fig. 13-7).

Impotence: The inability to achieve or maintain an erection. Also called erectile dysfunction (ED).

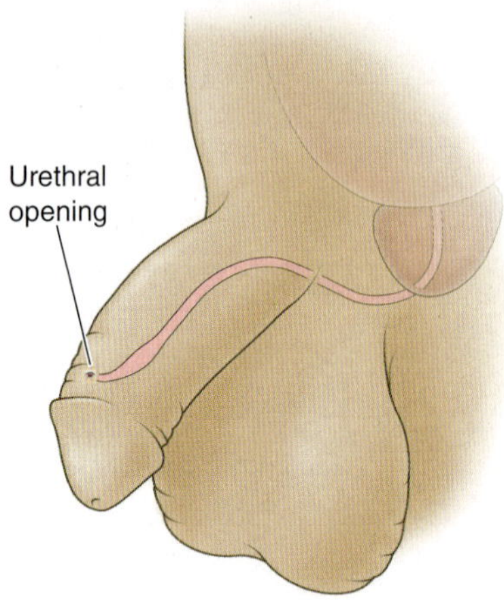

Figure 13-6 Epispadias.

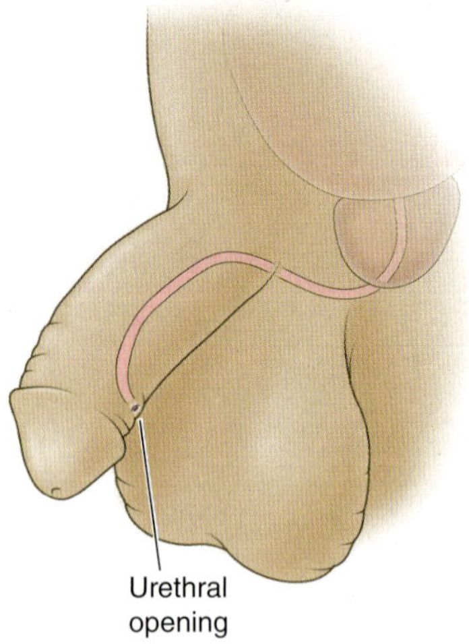

Figure 13-7 Hypospadias.

Inguinal hernia: A protrusion of part of the intestine through the muscular membrane of the inguinal region. The intestine pushes down into the scrotum. Sometimes the patient will notice a bulge on one scrotum. Pain is most often steady and sharp. The patient may be able to temporarily relieve the pain by pressing the hernia back into the abdomen. A support called a truss may be worn to push the intestines up into the abdomen and allow the herniated muscular wall to heal. If the bulge cannot be pressed into the abdomen, the hernia may be strangulated, meaning the intestine is trapped in the scrotum and surgical correction is needed. The surgical procedure is called a herniorrhaphy.

Orchitis: Inflammation of the testes, most commonly from a viral or bacterial infection or trauma. The condition may affect one or both testes. Signs and symptoms include swelling, tenderness, and acute pain. The patient also may experience fever, chills, nausea, and vomiting. Treatment for bacterial orchitis is administration of oral antibiotics. Treatment for viral or traumatic orchitis is palliative, consisting of analgesics and an ice pack to provide symptomatic relief.

Phimosis: A tightness of the foreskin that prevents the foreskin from being pulled back. It can be congenital, being present at birth, or it may develop later in life. It often causes difficulty urinating. Treatment is a circumcision, a surgical procedure to remove the foreskin. Circumcisions are often done on male infants at a very early age, even if phimosis is not present. This prevents the development of phimosis and thus the need for surgery later in life.

Premature ejaculation: The discharge of seminal fluid prior to a complete erection of the penis or immediately after the penis is inserted into the vaginal canal. Causes of premature ejaculation can be psychological (due to anxiety) or a physical cause such as diabetes, prostatitis, or urethritis. A physical examination and a patient interview are required to determine the cause. If the cause is psychological, psychotherapy with or without antianxiety medication may be prescribed. If the cause is physiological, treatment is directed at the underlying cause.

Priapism: A prolonged and unwanted erection of the penis without sexual stimulation. It most commonly affects males 30 years or older, but it can occur in childhood for males with sickle cell disease. Ischemic priapism is the inability of blood to leave the penis due to congestion of the veins that drain blood away. Nonischemic priapism is a disorder of the arteries of the penis where blood continuously enters, and it is most often due to trauma. Treatments are based on cause and may consist of medications such as alpha blockers (tamsulosin [Flomax]), blood thinners, antianxiety medications, or hormones, such as testosterone or gonadotropin-releasing hormone.

Prostatitis: Inflammation of the prostate gland may be acute or chronic and is often due to a bacterial infection. Signs and symptoms include a thick discharge from the urethra, fever, low back pain, fullness or pain in the perineal area, and urinary frequency. Diagnosis is confirmed by urinalysis, urine culture and palpation of the prostate by DRE. Treatment with antibiotics, analgesics, and antipyretics will resolve the condition.

ELEMENT REVIEW
anti- = against
pyret/o = fever
-ic = pertaining to

Sterility: The inability of a man to either produce sperm or to produce viable sperm, therefore being unable to fertilize an ovum. Causes include congenital factors such as cryptorchidism; testicular malformations; or acquired factors such as radiation, testicular cancer, or surgical removal of the testes.

Testicular carcinoma: Cancer of the testes is rare and may initially appear as a painless lump in the testicle. The cancer usually occurs in men under the age of 40. Men are advised to perform a monthly TSE testicular self-examination where the patient feels the testicles for lumps. Diagnosis of testicular cancer is confirmed by a biopsy after a lump has been identified. Treatments include surgical removal of the diseased testicle, followed by radiation and chemotherapy. Although fertility requires only one viable testicle, a man with one testicle being removed may suffer impaired fertility as a side effect of radiation and chemotherapy. If diagnosed early, the chances of a complete recovery are good. If diagnosis is delayed, the cancer can spread throughout the body via the lymphatic vessels and can be fatal.

Testicular torsion: The sudden twisting of the spermatic cord that causes a loss of blood supply to the testicle (Fig. 13-8). Males between ages 12 to 18 years are most affected, and the condition may run in families. Signs and symptoms include swelling of scrotum, abdominal pain, nausea, vomiting, frequent urination, and sudden sharp pain in testicle. The testicle may appear higher on the affected side causing a noticeable asymmetry when observing both testes. Patients are advised to seek immediate medical care for sudden testicular pain as the torsion must be surgically reduced to prevent necrosis and loss of the testicle. Additionally, patients are advised to seek care if sudden sharp testicular pain resolves as this can be a sign of intermittent torsion and then detorsion, which is often followed by another episode of torsion. Surgical correction with orchidopexy will attach both testicles to the inside of the scrotum.

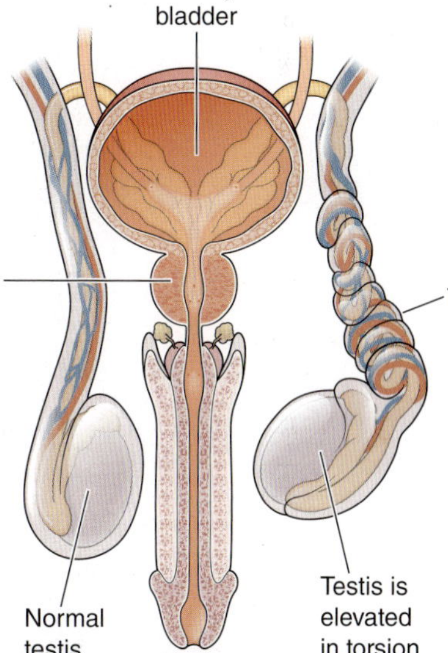

Figure 13-8 Testicular torsion.

Varicocele: Enlarged and twisted veins of the spermatic cord.

Sexually Transmitted Infections

Acquired immunodeficiency syndrome (AIDS): HIV (human immunodeficiency virus) is diagnosed by the presence of antibodies in the blood to the HIV infection. HIV is a slow-growing virus that typically begins with an acute infection. As the disease progresses, T cells are compromised, with their count going from 1600 (normal) to 800, approximately one half the number. Symptoms of HIV include headache, stiffness in the neck, malaise, fever, night sweats, abdominal cramps, diarrhea, and skin rashes. Patients can stay in this stage of infection for years before T cells decrease to 200 or less, which is defined as AIDS. This leaves the patient vulnerable to opportunistic infections and cancers such as Kaposi's sarcoma. The HIV infection is transmitted via blood transfusion, drug use/abuse with contaminated needles, or sexual intercourse with an infected partner. Treatments include a cocktail of several anti-viral drugs and management of symptoms as they arise.

PUBLIC HEALTH FACT

The risk of receiving HIV-infected blood through transfusion has been greatly reduced since screening procedures have been improved.

Chlamydia: The sexually transmitted bacterial infection that causes inflammation of the urethra (urethritis) and epididymis (epididymitis) in males. Symptoms of chlamydia occur 1 to 3 weeks after exposure and include discharge from the penis, with burning and itching. These same symptoms of burning and itching also occur with urination. Preventive measures include barrier protection such as a condom. Treatment with antibiotic therapy and abstinence from sexual contact until treatment is completed is advised.

Genital herpes: A highly contagious viral infection of the male and female genitalia. It is caused by the herpes simplex virus (usually HSV-2). In males, signs include multiple shallow ulcerations of the penis, prepuce, or scrotum. The ulcerations resemble cold sores and can be very painful and itchy. Additionally, the patient often experiences fever, headache, swollen glands, painful urination (dysuria), malaise, and muscle pain. Treatment of genital herpes is symptomatic, with anti-inflammatories and analgesics to reduce pain and swelling until the infection subsides. There is no cure for genital herpes; thus patients should abstain from sexual contact during active infection. When the ulcerations have healed, sexual activity may resume, but barrier protection should be used during intercourse or sexual contact to prevent infecting a partner.

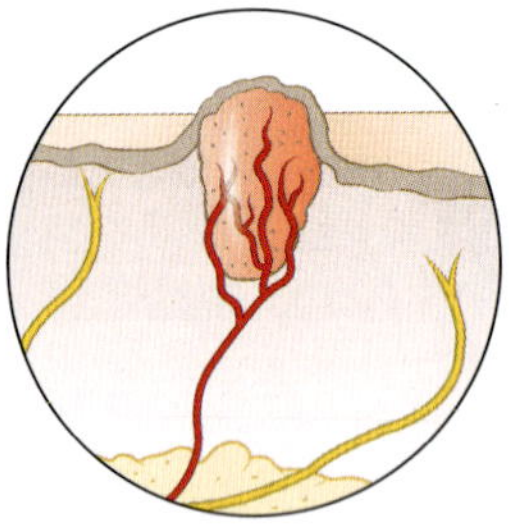

Figure 13-9 Genital warts.

ELEMENT REVIEW
cry/o = cold

Genital warts: Small cauliflower-like fleshy growths seen along the penis, which is caused by the human papilloma virus (HPV) (Fig. 13-9). Genital warts are transmitted from one person to another through sexual contact and can appear 1 to 6 months after sexual contact. Treatment includes topical medications to destroy the warts or surgical removal by cryosurgery. In some cases, warts may disappear spontaneously. Although use of latex condoms may prevent transmission of genital warts, people are advised to avoid sexual contact with people who have the lesions. Gardasil 9 is a vaccine that protects against some types of human papillomavirus, and it is recommended by the Centers for Disease Control and Prevention for both girls and boys.

Gonorrhea: The sexually transmitted bacterial infection caused by *Neisseria gonorrhoeae.* Gonorrhea affects the mucous membrane of the genital tract. In males it presents as a green-yellow drainage of pus from the urethra and painful urination (dysuria). It is spread through sexual contact with an infected partner and can also be transmitted from mother to infant during the birth process. Diagnosis is confirmed by a culture of the discharge and microscopic examination of a gram-stained specimen of the exudate. Treatment with antibiotics is an effective cure. Patients are simultaneously treated for chlamydial infection as the two often occur concurrently.

Syphilis: A highly contagious sexually transmitted infection that presents as lesions on any organ or tissue. The causative organism is the spirochete *T. pallidum*. It is spread by sexual contact with an infected partner or passed through the placenta from an infected mother to her unborn infant. If left untreated, it progresses through three stages:

Primary syphilis presents as small painless red pustules on the skin or mucous membranes. The highly contagious lesions, known as chancres, appear within 2 weeks of exposure. In males, the chancre usually develops on the penis. Treatment with penicillin effectively treats primary syphilis.

Secondary syphilis occurs 2 to 3 months after primary syphilis occurs and is left untreated. During this period of time, the spirochetes have had time to multiply and spread to other parts of the body. The most common sign is a nonitching rash on the palms of the hands and the soles of the feet. Additional signs and symptoms include fever, loss of appetite (anorexia), sore throat, loss of energy, and bone and joint pain. The disease is still very contagious in the secondary stage, but treatment with penicillin is still effective. Following the secondary stage, if the disease is left untreated it may enter a dormant (inactive) phase that may last for up to 20 years before reappearing and entering the third phase.

Tertiary syphilis is the final and most serious stage of the disease and is most often fatal. Tertiary syphilis occurs from not treating the syphilis infection for many years and progressing from primary to secondary to the tertiary stage. Lesions of tertiary syphilis are irreversible and do not respond to treatment with penicillin. The infection can lead to life-threatening disease affecting the brain, spinal cord, and heart.

MEDICAL HISTORY FACT

Notorious gangster and criminal Al Capone suffered from untreated syphilis for many years. As a teenager in New York and later Chicago, he frequently visited sex workers at dance halls, casinos, and social clubs. At the time, sexually transmitted infections were common, and it is estimated that 10% of men had some form of STI and were not aware of their illness. It is not known when Capone contracted syphilis, but his son was born with congenital syphilis in 1918. Later, when he was an inmate at Alcatraz in the early 1930s, he showed signs of dementia caused by tertiary syphilis. He was reported to have delusions and conversations with imaginary people. He continued to decline in both his mental and physical health; he spoke to angels, suffered from slurred speech, and had violent rages. He was transferred to a psychiatric ward at Alcatraz, but he was difficult to manage. In November 1939, he was released from prison and retired to his villa in Miami, Florida. He died in January 1947 from a mix of physical and mental decline.

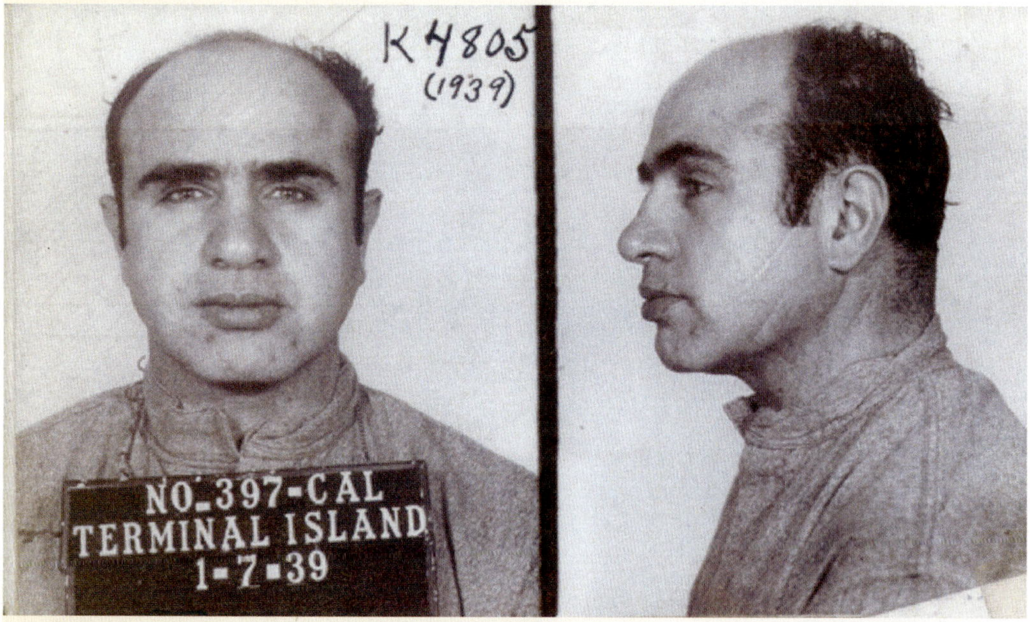

Trichomoniasis: The sexually transmitted infection caused by the protozoa *Trichomonas vaginalis*. Most men are asymptomatic, but some will experience painful urination (dysuria). Diagnosis is confirmed by microscopic examination of vaginal secretions of the female or urethral discharge from the male. If trichomoniasis is present, both sexual partners must be treated to prevent passing the infection back and forth. The treatment of choice is metronidazole (Flagyl), an anti-infective that targets protozoa.

Pathology Word-Building Practice

1. Build the Terms

Using only the word parts in the lists, create medical terms for the indicated meanings.

Prefixes	Combining Forms		Suffixes	
an-	andr/o	orchi/o	-cele	-lysis
dys-	balan/o	prostat/o	-cide	-ology
epi-	crypt/o	scrot/o	-ectomy	-osis
hydro-	cyst/o	spermat/o	-genesis	-pexy
hyper-	epididym/o	sperm/o	-ia	-plasty
hypo-	noct/o	testicul/o	-ic	-scope
intra-	oligi/o	ur/o	-ism	-scopy
	orchid/o	vas/o	-itis	-uria

1. Painful urination ____________________
2. Surgical repair of the penis ____________________
3. Surgical removal of the prostate gland ____________________
4. Destruction of sperm ____________________
5. Condition of a hidden testicle ____________________
6. Surgical removal of the epididymis ____________________
7. The scientific study of men's health ____________________
8. Process of producing sperm ____________________
9. Instrument to view the bladder ____________________
10. Inflammation of the glans penis ____________________

2. Prefixes

Use the prefixes to build a word that corresponds to the definition provided.

a-	epi-	hypo-	oligo-
an-	hydro-	intra-	supra-
dys-	hyper-		

1. A congenital absence of one or both testes __________
2. Condition of a low sperm count __________
3. Congenital opening of the urethra on the upper side of the penis __________
4. Congenital opening of the urethra on the lower side of the penis __________
5. Pertaining to within the penis __________
6. Pertaining to above the pubic bone __________
7. Word to describe increased growth of the prostate gland __________
8. Word meaning without symptoms __________
9. Word meaning within a vein __________
10. Phrase meaning the inability to maintain an erection __________

3. Suffixes

Use the suffixes to build a word that corresponds to the definition provided.

-cele	-ism	-osis	-scope
-cide	-itis	-pexy	-scopy
-ectomy	-lysis	-plasty	-uria
-ic	-ology		

1. Process of examining the bladder __________
2. Surgical fixation of a testicle __________
3. Surgical repair of the scrotum __________
4. Medication to kill sperm __________
5. Surgical removal of part of the vas deferens __________
6. Inability to void urine __________
7. Congenital condition of a narrowing of the preputial orifice __________
8. Pouchlike hernia of the urethra __________
9. Abnormal painful continued erection __________
10. Pertaining to the prostate gland __________

CAREER EXPLORATION: LABORATORY TECHNICIAN

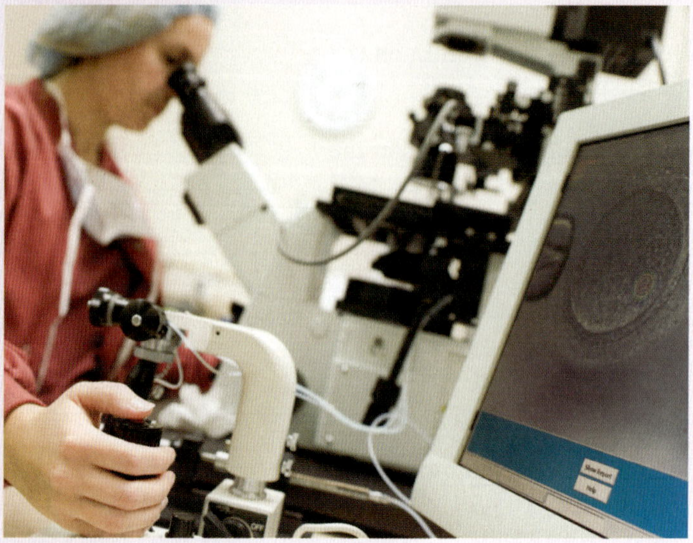

I was a teen when my parents explained how my birth was a bit unusual. My dad had non-Hodgkin lymphoma when my parents first got married. They wanted to have children, but they were young and not ready to start a family. The oncologist explained to my parents that chemotherapy might make my dad sterile. He suggested that my dad freeze his sperm so that if he were sterile after chemo, my mom could be artificially inseminated with my dad's sperm. It seemed to them to be the best way to save my dad from cancer and be able to have children later in life. My dad had several courses of chemotherapy, which saved his life but dramatically decreased his sperm count. When my mom and dad were ready to start a family, they went to the reproductive endocrinology clinic where my mom was inseminated with my dad's previously frozen sperm. Genetically, I am the same as if I were conceived in the normal way. The science of artificial insemination fascinated me. While I hope to someday conceive a child without the use of technology, I am thankful that medical science was able to give me to my parents. I decided to explore working in reproductive endocrinology as a laboratory technician. I went to college and majored in biology and medical laboratory science. The field of medical laboratory science is broad, and some of my friends in school went on to work in a DNA laboratory or work in the pharmaceutical industry. My friend Susan works with the state prosecutor's office collecting DNA at crime scenes. While it is exciting to catch criminals, I wanted to focus on reproductive health. I enjoy helping patients who need IVF (in vitro fertilization) to conceive a child. In the laboratory, we use a process called ICSI (intracytoplasmic sperm injection). It is used when a man has a low sperm count or low sperm motility, or it is used on previously frozen sperm. The woman administers hCG trigger injections at home to promote maturation of the eggs. The physician at our clinic then retrieves the eggs. I use a high-powered microscope to inject the retrieved egg with one sperm in a dish with growth fluids. I must be very careful during the procedure and practice medical aseptic technique. I then transfer the egg and sperm into the incubator overnight. After 24 hours, we look at the growth of the cells. If the cells are dividing normally, the physician transfers the egg and sperm into the mother. Some of the couples who come to the laboratory have been trying to conceive a child for many years. It is so satisfying to be part of a team that helps to make a family, just like mine.

ELEMENT REVIEW
intra- = within
cyt/o = cell
plasm/o = plasma
-ic = pertaining to

Male Reproductive System Diagnostic Procedures

Cystoscopy: The process of viewing the interior of the bladder with an instrument called a cystoscope. Visualization is obtained by a light source at the end of the scope. The procedure is useful in detecting tumors, inflammation, renal calculi, strictures, or other structural abnormalities.

FTA-ABS: A fluorescent treponemal antibody absorption test. It is serological (performed on serum) and checks for the presence of antibodies to *T. pallidum* bacteria, which causes syphilis.

Semen analysis: Performed as part of evaluating the cause of infertility in couples or to confirm that vasectomy has achieved sterility. The specimen should be collected after a period of sexual abstinence of 2 to 5 days and delivered to the physician's office within 2 hours after ejaculation. It should be protected from cold that could destroy the sample. Normal ejaculate should be a viscous, opaque, gray-white fluid with a volume of 3 to 5 mL. A normal sample, upon microscopic analysis, will show 70% normally formed sperm with motility, the ability to move. Specimens with greater than 30% abnormal sperm are considered to be less likely to achieve fertilization. Abnormal sperm can include a head that is too large or too small, a double head, a malformed midpiece, or a twisted or double tail. All of these malformations will render the sperm unable to swim or fertilize an ovum (Fig. 13-10).

A semen analysis can also be performed after a vasectomy to ensure that the vas deferens is cut and male sterility is achieved. Postvasectomy ejaculate should show no sperm, as the vas deferens has been cut and sperm no longer enters the urethra.

VDRL test: A serological test for syphilis. The test is performed on the serum of patients who have a chancre. Microscopic analysis of a heated serum sample is mixed with the VDRL (Venereal Disease Research Laboratory) antigen. If the sample clumps, it is an indication of a reaction and thus syphilis antibodies are reacting with the antigen. In a VDRL

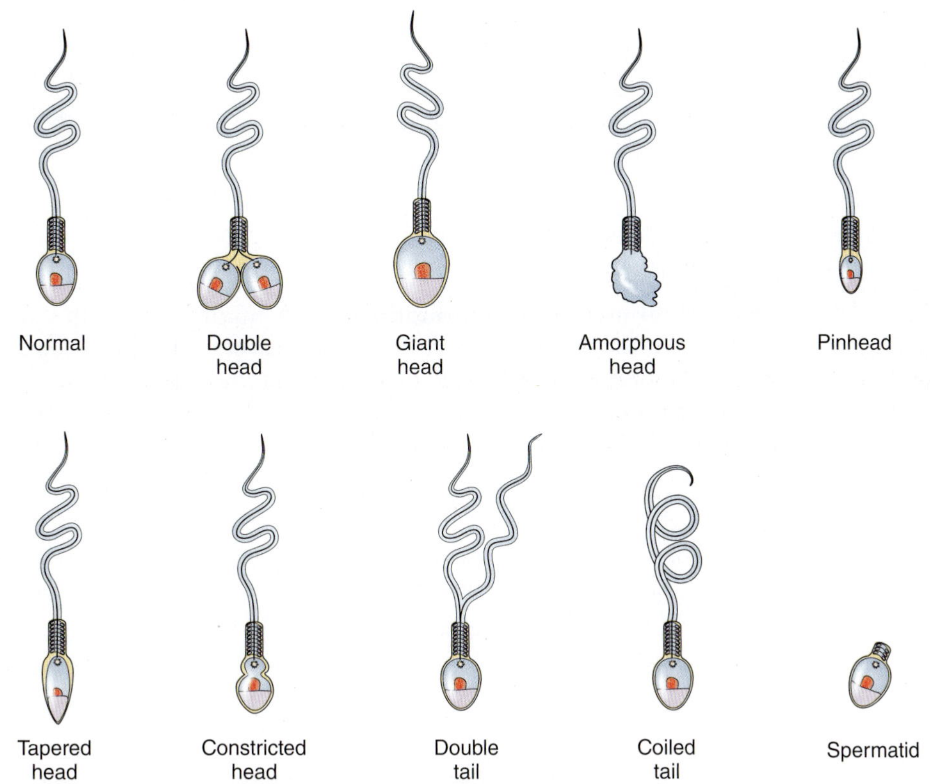

Figure 13-10 Abnormal sperm.

test, both false-positive and false-negative results may occur. If the result is positive, further testing is done to confirm the presence of *T. pallidum* spirochete.

Wet mount, wet prep: The microscopic examination of vaginal or male urethral secretions to test for living organisms. The sample can be mixed with normal saline to look for trichomoniasis or potassium hydroxide to look for yeast or fungi. After the sample is mixed with the solution, a cover slip is placed on the slide, and the sample is immediately observed under the microscope.

Male Reproductive System Therapeutic Procedures

Circumcision: The surgical removal of the foreskin (prepuce) of the penis. The procedure is commonly done on infants to prevent future infection as the uncircumcised penis is more difficult to keep clean and thus is more susceptible to infection. Adult male circumcision is performed if narrowing of the foreskin (phimosis) or inflammation of the glans penis (balanitis) occurs. A patient who is not circumcised and complains of pain with erection or sexual intercourse can benefit from circumcision. The procedure is performed with guided forceps to pull the foreskin over the glans penis, then the foreskin is snipped.

Epididymectomy: Surgical removal of the epididymis may be necessary if there is an injury to the groin, chronic pain after a vasectomy, a pus-filled abscess that does not respond to treatment, or a fluid-filled cyst of the epididymis is present.

Orchidectomy: Surgical removal of a testicle may be performed if the testicle is undescended, painful, or no longer functional. The testicles may be removed if the patient has prostate cancer. This is done not as a cure, but to slow the progression of cancer because the removal of the testes will decrease testosterone levels, which is produced in the testes.

Orchidopexy: The surgical fixation of the testicles. The procedure can be performed if the patient has suffered from testicular torsion. The testes are surgically attached to the inside of the scrotum to prevent the spermatic cord from twisting and depriving the testicle from its blood supply.

ELEMENT REVIEW
therm/o = temperature
resect/o = to cut off
-scope = instrument to view

Radical prostatectomy: The surgical removal of the entire prostate gland through the urethra. It is performed as a treatment for prostate cancer.

Suprapubic prostatectomy: The surgical removal of the prostate gland through an incision made into the abdominal wall above the pubic bone. The prostate gland is removed through the bladder when the gland is too large to remove through the urethra.

Transurethral microwave thermotherapy: A minimally invasive therapy that uses microwave heat energy to remove excess prostate tissue that is blocking the urethra and causing urinary symptoms. The procedure is used for small- to moderate-sized prostates when the patient complains of urinary frequency, urgency, and nocturia.

Transurethral resection of the prostate: TURP, the surgical removal of a portion of the prostate gland by inserting a resectoscope into the urethra and into the bladder. The prostate gland is resected and removed through the urethra, thus decreasing the pressure on the bladder that causes urinary symptoms of urgency and incomplete emptying of the bladder.

Varicocelectomy: Surgical removal of enlarged veins of the scrotum. The procedure is performed to restore normal blood flow to the testes.

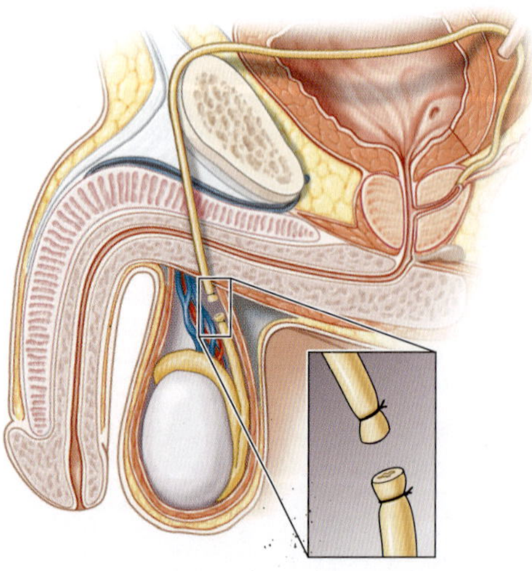

Figure 13-11 Vasectomy.

Vasectomy: The surgical cutting and removal of a portion of the vas deferens to prevent the passage of sperm into the urethra (Fig. 13-11). The procedure is performed via a small incision made into the side of each scrotum to access the vas deferens. A small segment of the vas deferens is removed, and the ends are tied or cauterized separately. Because sperm may remain in the vas deferens for approximately 6 weeks after the procedure, the patient is advised to use contraception until confirmation of no sperm remaining in the semen is achieved. The patient brings a semen sample to the physician's office to be examined for the presence of sperm. The semen analysis is performed twice, at which point, if no sperm are observed, the patient is considered to be sterile. The patient must be counseled prior to the procedure to ensure that he understands that he will no longer be able to make a woman pregnant. While vasectomy reversal is possible, it is not 100% effective and not without surgical risk.

CASE STUDY, completed

Larry wakes up in the outpatient recovery room after the TUMT procedure. He is groggy but tells the nurse that the pain is less than when he had the biopsy. Dr. Teegan comes in and says to Larry, "You should experience minimal pain, and don't worry if you pass a little blood when you urinate. It should resolve itself tomorrow or the next day. The microwave shrank the size of your prostate, but the trauma from the surgery itself causes a bit of swelling. Be patient. I think you will feel increased ease in urinating over the next 3 to 4 days." Larry replies, "My wife, Katie, is here to take me home. When can I get out of here?" Dr. Teegan laughs, "I can see you are anxious to leave. I will tell Katie you are ready to go home. She made an appointment for you to come back to the office next week so that we can talk and I can get a urine sample from you. Going forward, I want to monitor your PSA every 6 months, and please contact me if you have pain or other symptoms." Larry replies, "Thanks doc. See you next week."

CRITICAL-THINKING QUESTIONS

1. Larry had a procedure called a TUMT, which stands for ______________________.
2. Larry complained of having to urinate at night, a medical condition called what? ______________________
3. Larry did not have prostate cancer but what condition did he have? ______________________
4. Larry's prostate gland was pushing on what organ? ______________________
5. Dr. Teegan performed a DRE, which stands for what term? ______________________
6. What abnormality did Larry have on blood testing? ______________________
7. Larry complained of a loss of libido, which means what? ______________________
8. Dr. Teegan performed what diagnostic surgical procedure? ______________________
9. What type of specialist treats prostate symptoms? ______________________
10. Dissect the word thermotherapy into its elements. ______________________

Medications for the Male Reproductive System

Table 13-2 contains medications used to treat diseases and disorders of the male reproductive system, including hormonal imbalances, urinary disorders, sexual disorders.

TABLE 13-2 Medications for the Male Reproductive System

Classification	Examples (Tradename)	Common Use/Action
Androgens	testosterone (AndroGel)	Promote maturation of male sex organs
Estrogen	estradiol (Estrace)	Lower testosterone in men with prostate cancer
BPH medications	doxazosin (Cardura), tamsulosin (Flomax), finasteride (Proscar), dutasteride (Avodart)	Relax smooth muscle of the prostate gland and decrease blockage of the urethra
Erectile dysfunction medications	sildenafil (Viagra), tadalafil (Cialis)	Dilates the arteries of the penis
AIDS medications	emtricitabine and tenofovir alafenamide (Descovy)	Antiretroviral for the AIDS/HIV infection, also used as a prophylaxis for HIV infection

Medications Review

Using the table of medications, complete the chart below. The first one has been done for you.

Medication Name	Classification (mechanism)	Therapeutic Use (What is it used for?)
Viagra	*Vasodilation of the penis*	*Erectile dysfunction (ED)*
Proscar	______________	______________
Estradiol	______________	______________
AndroGel	______________	______________
Descovy	______________	______________

Male Reproductive System Abbreviations

The list below provides some common abbreviations pertaining to the male reproductive system and their meanings.

BPH	benign prostatic hypertrophy
DRE	digital rectal exam
ED	erectile dysfunction
FSH	follicle-stimulating hormone
GnRH	gonadotropin-releasing hormone
GU	genitourinary
HSV-2	herpes simplex virus, strain 2
LH	luteinizing hormone
NSV	no scalpel vasectomy
PSA	prostate-specific antigen
STI	sexually transmitted infection
TSE	testicular self-examination
TUMT	transurethral microwave thermotherapy
TURP	transurethral resection of the prostate
V, Vas	vasectomy
VR	vasectomy reversal

Abbreviations Review

Choose the correct definition for each of the abbreviations listed.

1. VR
   a. venereal rash
   b. vasectomy reversal
   c. vasectomy rash
   d. venereal regimen

2. ED
   a. ejaculatory duct
   b. ejaculation deficiency
   c. erectile duct
   d. erectile dysfunction

3. TURP
   a. transurethral resection of the prostate
   b. transureteral resection of the prostate
   c. transurethral reconstruction of the prostate
   d. transureteral reconstruction of the prostate

4. NSV
   a. nonsteroidal vasectomy
   b. no scalpel vasectomy
   c. nonscarring vasectomy
   d. nonsurgical vasectomy

5. BPH
   a. bilateral prostatic hypertrophy
   b. bilateral prostatic hyperplasia
   c. benign prostatic hypertrophy
   d. benign prostatic hypoplasia

6. GnRH
   a. gonadotropin-releasing hormone
   b. genitourinary-releasing hormone
   c. gonadotropin-receiving hormone
   d. genitourinary-receiving hormone

7. PSA
   a. prostate-specific androgen
   b. prostate-specialized androgen
   c. prostate-specialized antigen
   d. prostate-specific antigen

8. DRE
   a. direct rectal examination
   b. digital rectal examination
   c. digital resection of epididymis
   d. direct resection of epididymis

9. TSE
   a. testicular self-examination
   b. testicular specific examination
   c. testosterone specific examination
   d. testosterone sparing estrogen

10. GU
   a. gonads and ureters
   b. genitoureteral
   c. genitourinary
   d. gonads and urethra

MEDICAL DOCUMENTATION

Knowledge of terms related to normal anatomy and pathologic conditions enables you to understand medical documentation such as History & Physical Exams, operative reports, discharge summaries, laboratory reports, and x-ray reports. Apply your knowledge by answering the questions that follow the report.

Operative Report

DATE: November 12, 2024 DOB: 11/11/2024
PATIENT: Jeremy D.

Operative Note: Circumcision

Preoperative Diagnosis: Congenital phimosis

Continued

MEDICAL DOCUMENTATION—cont'd

Postoperative Diagnosis: Congenital phimosis

Anesthesia: Topical 4% lidocaine cream applied 60 minutes prior to the procedure

Estimated blood loss: Nil

Procedure in Detail: The newborn male infant was taken to the OB procedure room, prepped, and draped in the usual manner. The surgical site was cleansed with chlorhexidine, and the foreskin was grasped at the 2 and 10 o'clock positions. A dorsal crush injury was created, and a dorsal incision was made. The foreskin was bluntly dissected away from the glans penis. It was dissected down to the corona. A 1.1 Gomco bell was placed, and the clamp was applied. The foreskin was sharply dissected away. The clamp was left in place for 5 minutes, then removed. No evidence of hypospadias was observed. The infant tolerated the procedure well. He was taken back to his mother in good condition.

Joesph J, MD, pediatrician

Questions

1. Looking at the word ending of lidocaine, what type of medication is lidocaine? __________
2. Which word in the document means a condition of narrowing of the preputial orifice? __________
3. Which side of the penis is incised? __________
4. Which word in the above document means "cutting around"? __________
5. What does the term congenital mean? __________

CHAPTER REVIEW

Complete the Sentence

Using medical terms from this chapter, complete the sentences.

1. The surgical removal of the prostate gland is called a __________
2. Assessment of a sample of semen is called __________
3. Destruction of tissue by use of freezing is called __________
4. The medical term for inflammation of the testicles is __________
5. An agent to kill sperm cells is a __________

6. The medical term that means through the urethra is ______________________

7. The protrusion of part of an organ or intestine through a membrane is ______________________

8. A medical professional who performs a digital exam is using their ______________________

9. The medical term for an inability to maintain an erection is ______________________

10. Provides nourishment for spermatozoa, prolonging time of viability within the female's body ______________________

11. The inability of a man to fertilize an ovum ______________________

12. The structure that is cut in the vasectomy procedure is the ______________________

13. The medical word that means pertaining to the testicle ______________________

14. The surgical removal of the prepuce is called a ______________________

15. The surgical removal of enlarged veins of the scrotum is called ______________________

Spelling

Circle the correctly spelled terms in the pairs of terms.

1.	balanoplasty	blanoplasty
2.	testicilar	testicular
3.	circumsicion	circumcision
4.	phimosis	fimosis
5.	prostatectomy	prostratectomy
6.	transuretreral	transurethral
7.	spermatogenesis	spermotogenesis
8.	seminiferous	seminaferous
9.	ingunal	inguinal
10.	epididymectomy	epididyimectomy

Abbreviations

1. TUMT ______________________________
2. HSV-2 ______________________________
3. LH ______________________________
4. STI ______________________________
5. V, Vas ______________________________

Identify the Anatomical Structures

Match the structures of the male reproduction system from the following lists to the letters shown in Figure 13-12.

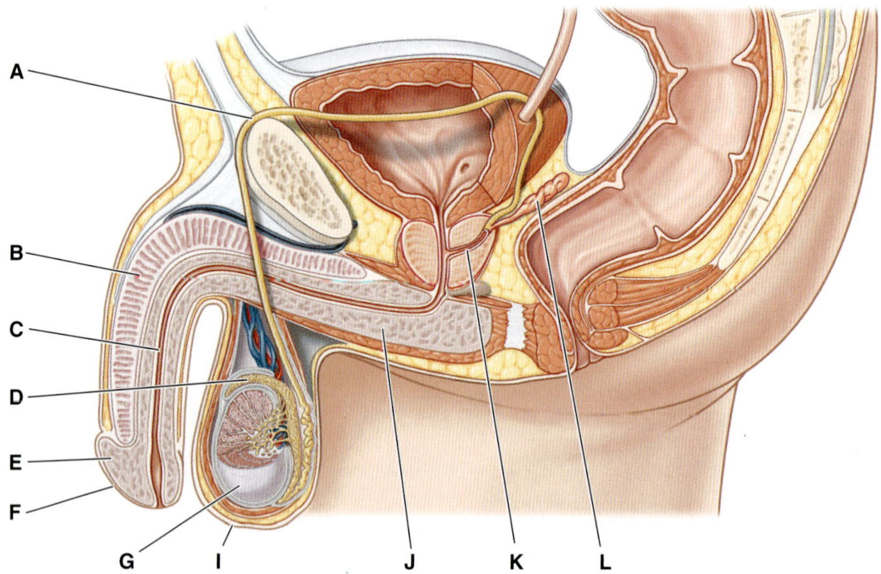

Figure 13-12 Identify the structures of the male reproductive system.

1. ______ bulbourethral (Cowper's) gland
2. ______ corpus cavernosum
3. ______ corpus spongiosum
4. ______ ejaculatory duct
5. ______ epididymis
6. ______ glans penis
7. ______ prepuce (foreskin)
8. ______ prostate gland
9. ______ scrotum
10. ______ seminal vesicle
11. ______ seminiferous tubes
12. ______ testis
13. ______ urethra
14. ______ urethral opening
15. ______ vas deferens

Decipher the Terms

Separate each term into its prefix (if any), combining form, and suffix. Next, translate the word parts and then give the common definition of the term.

1. spermatolysis

   Prefix: ______________ *Combining Form:* ______________ *Suffix:* ______________

   Meaning: ____

2. genitourinary

   Prefix: ______________ *Combining Form:* ______________ *Suffix:* ______________

   Meaning: ____

3. urologist

   Prefix: ______________ *Combining Form:* ______________ *Suffix:* ______________

   Meaning: ____

4. balanitis

   Prefix: ______________ *Combining Form:* ______________ *Suffix:* ______________

   Meaning: ____

5. antipyretic

   Prefix: ______________ *Combining Form:* ______________ *Suffix:* ______________

   Meaning: ____

6. epididymitis

   Prefix: ______________ *Combining Form:* ______________ *Suffix:* ______________

   Meaning: ____

7. orchidopexy

   Prefix: ______________ *Combining Form:* ______________ *Suffix:* ______________

   Meaning: ____

8. ureterocele

   Prefix: ______________ *Combining Form:* ______________ *Suffix:* ______________

   Meaning: ____

9. herniorraphy

   Prefix: ______________ *Combining Form:* ______________ *Suffix:* ______________

   Meaning: ____

10. seminoma

    Prefix: ______________ *Combining Form:* ______________ *Suffix:* ______________

    Meaning: ____

Identify the Correct Term

Identify the correct term for each definition:

1. The inability to void urine ______________
2. Provides nourishment for spermatozoa, prolonging time of viability within the female's body ______________
3. Surgical correction of an inguinal hernia is called a ______________
4. Condition of an unwanted erection of the penis ______________
5. Noncancerous growth of the prostate gland is also called ______________
6. The inability of a man to fertilize an ovum is called ______________
7. The structure that is cut in the vasectomy procedure is the ______________
8. The medical word that means pertaining to the testicle is called ______________
9. The surgical removal of the prepuce is called a ______________
10. The surgical removal of enlarged veins of the scrotum is called ______________
11. The inability of a man to produce viable sperm, therefore being unable to fertilize an ovum, is called ______________
12. Enlargement of the penis during sexual arousal is called ______________

13. The primary sex hormone in males, responsible for the maturation of sperm and male secondary sex characteristics, is called ______________________________

14. The highly contagious sexually transmitted infection that presents as lesions on any organ or tissue, caused by the spirochete *T. pallidum*, is called ______________________________

15. Small cauliflower-like fleshy growths seen along the penis caused by the HPV is called ______________________________

16. The organ that is the reservoir for urine that lies above the prostate gland is the ______________________________

17. Use of a high-powered microscope to inject the retrieved egg with one sperm in a dish with growth fluids is called ______________________________

CHAPTER

14

The Nervous System

LEARNING OBJECTIVES

Upon completion of the chapter, you will be able to:

1. Identify and define the combining forms, roots, prefixes, and suffixes introduced in the chapter.
2. Spell medical terms related to the nervous system.
3. Describe the major organs of the nervous system.
4. Describe the difference between the central and peripheral nervous systems.
5. Describe the difference between afferent and efferent nerves.
6. Describe the differences in the sympathetic and parasympathetic nervous system.
7. Identify and discuss major pathological terms of the nervous system.
8. Identify and discuss major mental health disorders.
9. Identify and discuss major diagnostic and therapeutic treatments of the nervous system.
10. Identify the major categories of medications used to treat nervous and psychological pathologies.
11. Define abbreviations of the nervous system.

We begin this chapter with a case study of Alicia, who is experiencing headaches and loss of sense of smell and who is losing her sense of balance. She seeks diagnosis and treatment with her primary care provider who recognizes that her condition is of a neurological origin and who refers her to a neurologist. The case study introduces some of the medical terms related to the nervous system. Throughout the chapter, we will revisit the story of Alicia to understand her disorder and how medical interventions can improve a patient's quality of life. After reading this chapter, you will expand your knowledge of medical terms related to the nervous system. You will understand how the nervous system functions as the communication center of the body, and you will see how the body receives information, processes information, and initiates responses to move the body in order to interpret sensations, and to maintain the homeostatic environment of the body. You will be able to use word elements presented to understand unfamiliar terms and to build your medical vocabulary.

CASE STUDY

Alicia is a 27-year-old pharmacy technician who has always enjoyed good health. She loves to ride her bicycle; she eats a healthy well-balanced diet, and she is generally an active and happy person. She lives with her younger sister, Christina, who is in college studying nursing. Lately, Alicia has been having headaches, myasthenia (muscle weakness), anosmia (loss of sense of smell), tinnitus (ringing in the ears), and some loss of hearing. When she lost her balance and fell down the stairs, Christina insisted that Alicia go to her primary provider. Alicia meets with Dr. Callahan, who orders magnetic resonance imaging (MRI) of Alicia's brain. When the results of the MRI are available, Dr. Callahan meets with Alicia and Christina to discuss the findings. Alicia and Christina hold hands as Dr. Callahan explains that Alicia's symptoms are caused by a tumor called meningioma. He goes on to explain that meningiomas are the most common form of brain tumors, accounting for 30% of all brain tumors. Dr. Callahan explains that brain tumors occur in 30 out of 100,000 adults each year. Women are diagnosed with meningiomas more often than men, and 85% of meningiomas are noncancerous. Alicia's tumor is located on the underside of her brain and is pressing on her cranial nerves. This pressure is causing her facial pain, anosmia, and her hearing and balance problems. Dr. Callahan refers Alicia to Dr. Singh, a neurosurgeon affiliated with the local hospital, for a consultation and to form a treatment plan. He encourages Alicia and Christina, telling them that since most meningiomas are noncancerous, he is hopeful that with treatment she will recover completely.

KEY TERMS

Afferent nerves	Cerebral cortex	Medulla oblongata	Peripheral nervous system
Arachnoid membrane	Corpus callosum	Meninges	Pia mater
Autonomic nervous system	Dendrite	Neuroglia	Somatic nervous system
Axon	Dura mater	Neurons	Sulci
Basal ganglia	Efferent nerves	Neurotransmitters	Synapse
Brain	Frontal lobe	Occipital lobe	Temporal lobe
Central nervous system	Gyri	Parietal lobe	Thalamus
	Homeostasis	Peduncles	Vermis

Structures and Physiology

The nervous system is the control and communication network of the body that receives, interprets, and transmits information to the entire body. Along with the endocrine system, the nervous system maintains **homeostasis**, the state of dynamic equilibrium. Dynamic equilibrium means that although our bodies are constantly changing (dynamic), the state of the body exists within a healthy and stable range of parameters. The work of the nervous system is to receive information from outside of the body and transmit information to all parts of the body. This allows the nervous system to perform a variety of tasks:

- Regulate all activities of the body,
- Control consciousness,
- Detect environmental stimuli,
- Respond to environmental stimuli,
- Process and store sensory and motor information,
- Transmit sensory and motor impulses between the brain and all parts of the body.

The organs of the nervous system include the nerves, brain, spinal cord, and sensory organs. The nervous system is divided into two parts. The brain and spinal cord are known as the **central nervous system**. The 12 pairs of cranial and the 31 pairs of spinal nerves are called the **peripheral nervous system**.

Nervous Tissue

As discussed in Chapter 3, nervous tissue is one of the four primary types of tissues in the body. Nervous tissue differs from other tissue types because it is designed to respond to changes in the environment surrounding it and to conduct impulses. The two types of cells that compose nervous tissue are neurons and neuroglia.

Although neurons compose only 10% of the cells of the brain and central nervous system (CNS), **neurons** are considered the primary functional cells of the nervous system. Neurons sense changes in the environment, integrate the information, and conduct a motor response. Nerves can be categorized by their function:

- **Afferent nerves** are sensory neurons. They carry impulses from the peripheral parts of the body to the brain or spinal cord; they tell the brain what is felt.
- **Efferent nerves** are motor neurons. They carry impulses from the brain and spinal cord to the peripheral body; they tell the body to move.
- **Interneurons** are association nerves. They form links between neurons and provide a way to relay impulses from one area of the brain or spinal cord to another.

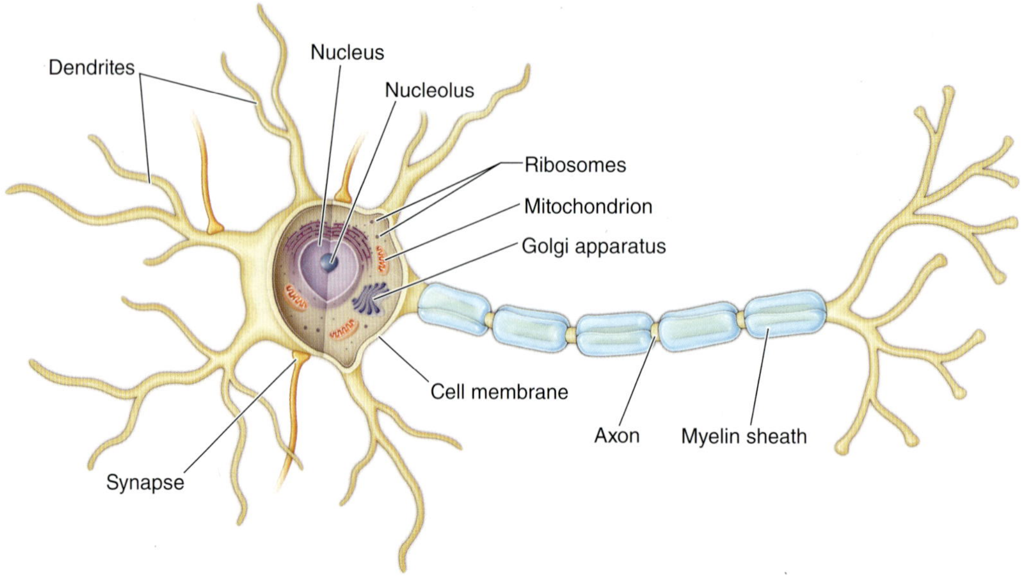

Figure 14-1 A neuron has a cell body, an axon, and dendrites.

Neuron Shape and Structure

The shape and structure of neurons varies, but the general features include a cell body, an axon, and dendrites (Fig. 14-1). The cell body consists of the cell nucleus and nucleolus within the cytoplasm that is surrounded by a cell membrane. Cytoplasmic organelles include mitochondria, ribosomes, lysosomes, and Golgi apparatus. The functions of these organelles are discussed in Chapter 3. Specific to nerve cells, the **axon** is a single slender projection that extends from the cell body. There is only one axon for each neuron. Axons are also called nerve fibers due to their long filament shape. Some axons are covered by an insulation called a **myelin sheath**. The myelin sheath is white; thus, myelinated neurons are called **white matter**. Neurons that do not have myelin on the axons are called **gray matter**, as they appear to be gray in color. Axons conduct impulses away from the cell body and transmit information to the **dendrite** of another neuron. Dendrites are thin, branched structures that resemble the branches of a tree. In most neurons, the dendrites are short in length and highly branched. Dendrites receive impulses and transmit information to the cell body of the neuron. Neurons are not directly connected to each other; rather, they have a space between the axon and dendrite called the **synapse**. Chemical substances called **neurotransmitters** are released into the synapse to activate or inhibit transmission of nerve impulses across the synapse.

> ***Memory Tip***
>
> Axons: *A* for away = sends impulses away from the neuron.
> Dendrites: *D* for deliver = sends impulse toward the neuron.

Neuron Classification

Neurons are classified based on their shape and their specific functions. There are three major structural types of neurons, as shown in Figure 14-2.

- **Multipolar neurons** have many dendrites arising from the cell body. These neurons carry impulses from the CNS to the skeletal muscles.
- **Bipolar neurons** have a single dendrite and a single axon arising from the cell body and pointing in opposite directions. They are found in the special sensory organs such as the eyes, ears, and nose.

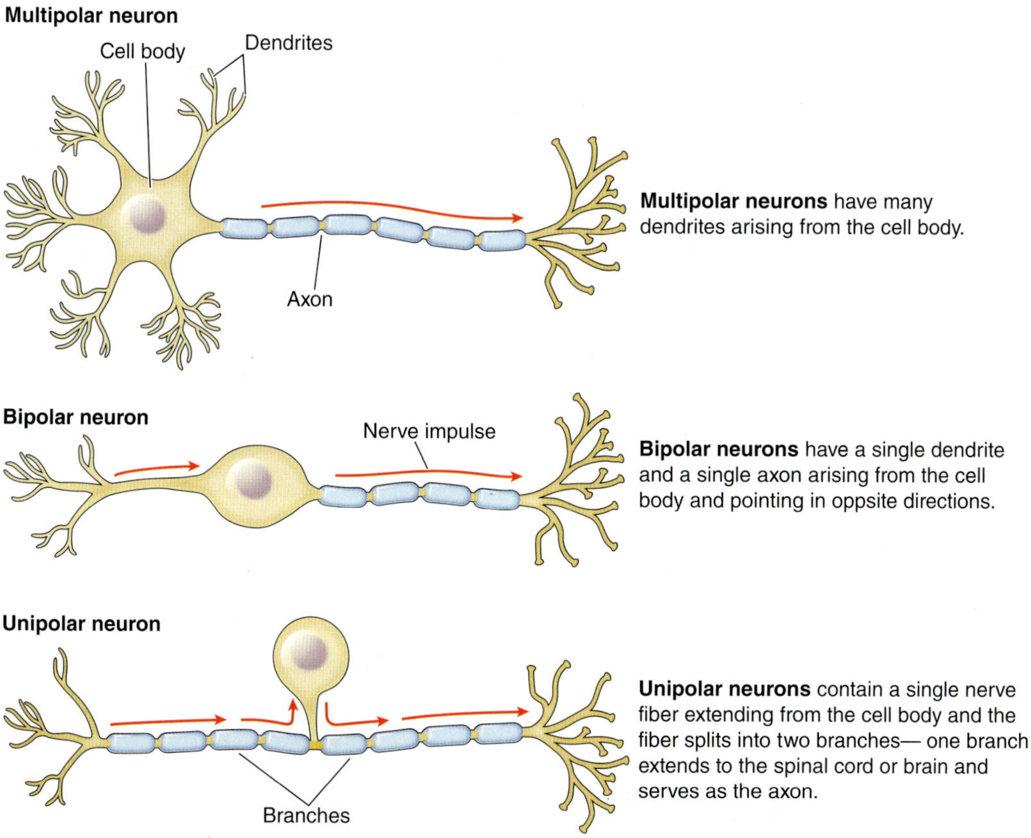

Figure 14-2 The three major structural types of neurons.

- **Unipolar neurons** contain a single nerve fiber extending from the cell body, and the fiber splits into two branches. One branch extends to the spinal cord or brain and serves as the axon, and the other branch extends to the peripheral part of the body and serves as the dendrite. These neurons carry impulses from the skin receptors to the spinal cord.

Neuroglia, sometimes called glial cells, form approximately 90% of the cells of the brain, spinal cord, and some of the peripheral nerves. They anchor and support the function of neurons in a variety of ways. The neuroglia are divided into five types, as shown in Table 14-1.

ELEMENT REVIEW
astr/o = star
oligo- = few, small
dendr/o = branches
-cyte = cell
micro- = small
gli/o = glue
-a = noun ending

TABLE 14-1 The Five Types of Neuroglia

Type of Cell	Location	Function
Astrocyte 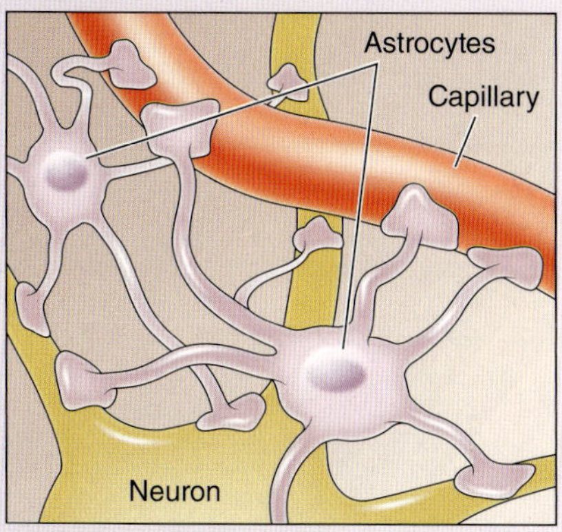	Brain and spinal cord	Anchors neurons to blood capillaries, directs growth of neurons, aids neuron impulse conduction

Continued

TABLE 14-1 The Five Types of Neuroglia—cont'd

Type of Cell	Location	Function
Ependymal cells 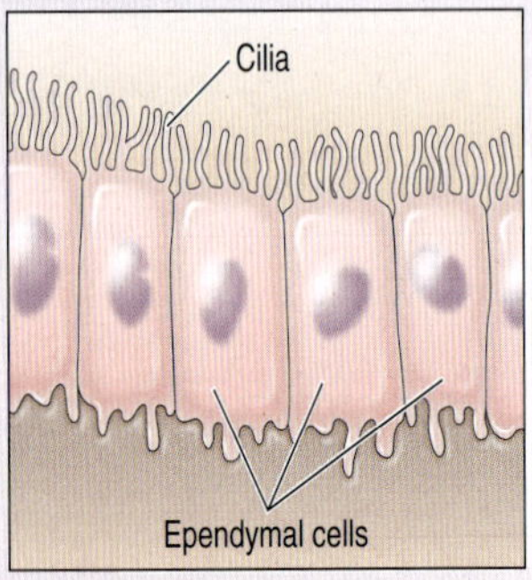	Lines ventricles in the brain	A unicellular layer that contributes to the formation of CSF; establishes part of the blood-brain barrier
Microglia 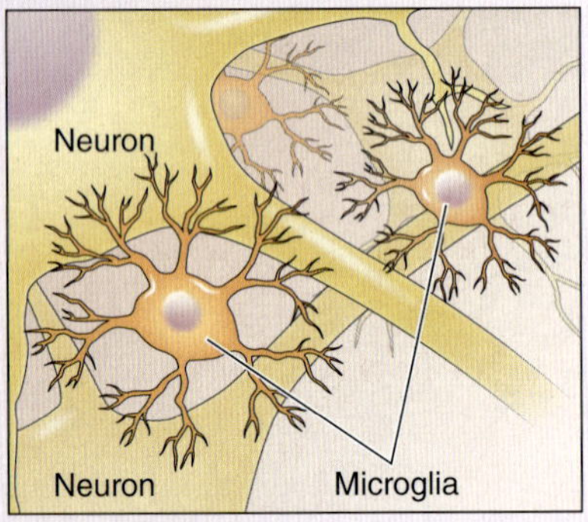	Brain and spinal cord	A phagocyte that removes invading microorganisms and dead cells
Oligodendrocyte 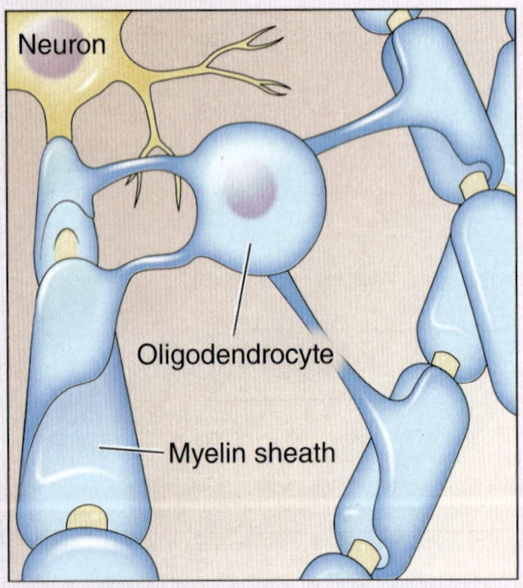	Brain and spinal cord	Small supporting cells that wrap insulation on several adjacent CNS axons, forming a myelin sheath

TABLE 14-2 The Functions of the Cranial Nerves

Cranial Nerve	Name	Type of Nerve	Innervation	Function
I	Olfactory	Sensory	Sensory endings in the nasal epithelium	Sense of smell
II	Optic	Sensory	Sensory cells of the retina	Sense of sight
III	Oculomotor	Motor	Skeletal muscles of the eyeball; smooth muscle within the iris	Movement of the eye; control of the light entering the eye
IV	Trochlear	Motor	Skeletal muscles of the eyeball	Movement of the eye
V	Trigeminal 1. Ophthalmic 2. Maxillary 3. Mandibular	 1. Sensory 2. Sensory 3. Mixed	1. Eyes, tear glands, upper eyelids, skin of the forehead 2. Upper mouth, skin of the face 3. Sensory to the mouth, skin of the jaw. Motor to lower jaw and floor of the mouth	Sensation to innervated areas; movement of the jaw for chewing
VI	Abducens	Motor	Skeletal muscles of the eyeball	Movement of the eye
VII	Facial	Mixed	Sensory to the tongue; motor to facial muscles, tear and salivary glands	Sense of taste; movement of facial muscles, glandular secretions
VIII	Vestibulocochlear	Sensory	Inner ear	Sense of hearing and equilibrium (balance)
IX	Glossopharyngeal	Mixed	Sensory to the tongue and pharynx; motor to pharynx and salivary glands	Sense of taste, sense of touch in pharynx and mouth, movement for swallowing
X	Vagus	Mixed	Sensory to pharynx, larynx, esophagus, organs of thorax and abdomen; motor to larynx, pharynx, heart and visceral organs	Sensations of visceral organs; movement for speech, swallowing, heart function, digestive peristalsis (movement)
XI	Accessory	Motor	Muscles of the upper mouth, pharynx, larynx, neck, and back	Movements of speech, swallowing. Movements of shoulders and head
XII	Hypoglossal	Motor	Muscles of the tongue	Movement of the tongue

mater, the **arachnoid membrane**, and the **pia mater** (Fig. 14-6). The outermost layer, the dura mater, forms a tough protective sheath around the spinal cord. The middle layer, the arachnoid membrane, is made up of collagen fibers and resembles a cobweb. The innermost layer, the pia mater, is directly attached to the outer layer of the spinal cord. Between the arachnoid membrane and the pia mater is the **subarachnoid space**, which is filled with CSF. The CSF circulates around the spinal cord and the brain and provides a shock-absorbing liquid cushion. CSF also transports nutrients and eliminates wastes. The bones of the vertebrae surround the spinal cord adding protection and facilitating movement of the neck and back. The meninges are separated from the vertebrae by a large fat-filled space called the **epidural space**.

ELEMENT REVIEW
arachn/o = spider

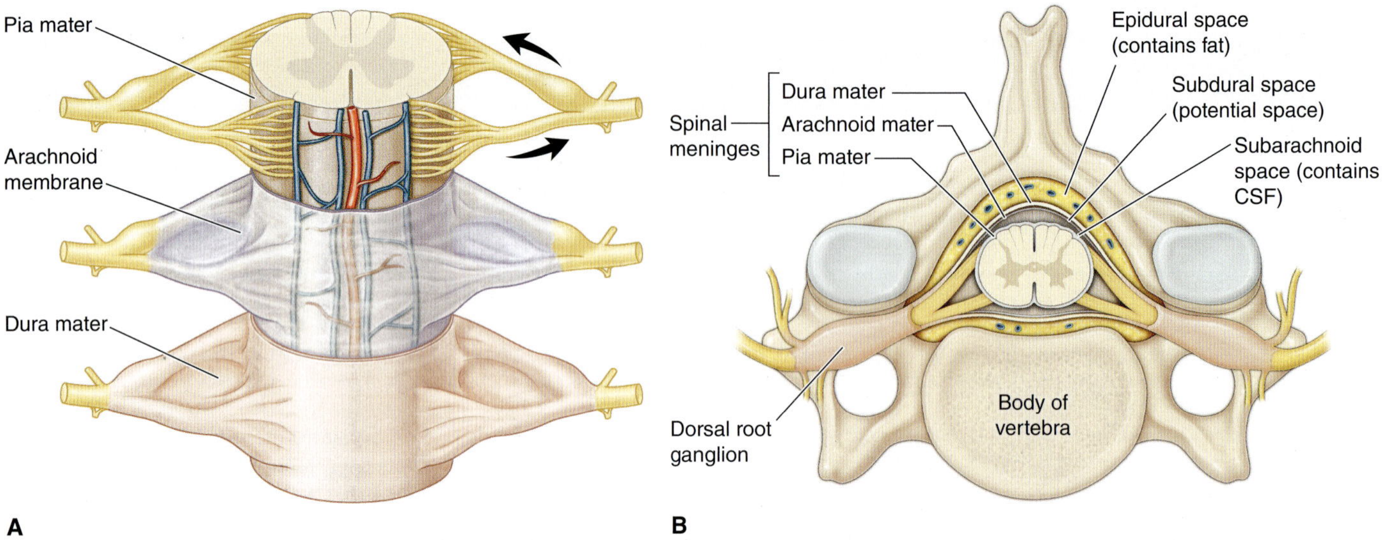

Figure 14-6 (A) Meninges, CSF, and (B) vertebrae protect the spinal cord.

The Spinal Nerves

The spinal cord is arranged into 31 linear segments. Each segment gives rise to paired spinal nerves (Fig. 14-7). The 31 pairs of spinal nerves innervate (supply impulses) to the limbs. The spinal nerves relay information between the spinal cord and the peripheral nervous system. Two distinct tracts compose the nerve pathways. The ascending tracts carry sensory information to the brain, and the descending tracts carry motor information away from the brain. The spinal cord serves as a reflex center for sensory receptors. A reflex is a very rapid response to a danger or emergency, such as touching a hot stove. A reflex does not have to travel all the way to the brain. Within a fraction of a second, the spinal cord will direct the motor nerves to remove your hand from the hot stove.

PHYSIOLOGY FACT

The shape, appearance, or location of structures may appear in their names:

folia = leaves (Greek)
pons = bridge (Latin)
medulla = marrow, inner most (Latin)
cortex = rind, outer layer (Latin)
thalam/o = inner chamber

The peripheral nervous system is further divided into two divisions called the somatic nervous system and autonomic nervous system.

The **somatic nervous system** is the division of the peripheral nervous system that communicates information related to voluntary activities such as walking, typing, or talking. These activities require conscious thought to perform. The somatic division is composed of nerves, ganglia, and sensory receptors that are widely distributed all over the body. There are sensory receptors in the skin, visceral organs, and special sensory organs (eyes, ears). The somatic motor component consists of motor nerves that innervate skeletal muscles and thus enable us to perform coordinated voluntary movements. Both the sensory and the motor pathways of the somatic nervous system are connected via the PNS to the spinal cord and then to the CNS as the brain is ultimately responsible for coordinated movements.

The **autonomic nervous system** is the portion of the PNS that communicates information related to involuntary activities such as digestion, heart rate, and glandular secretions.

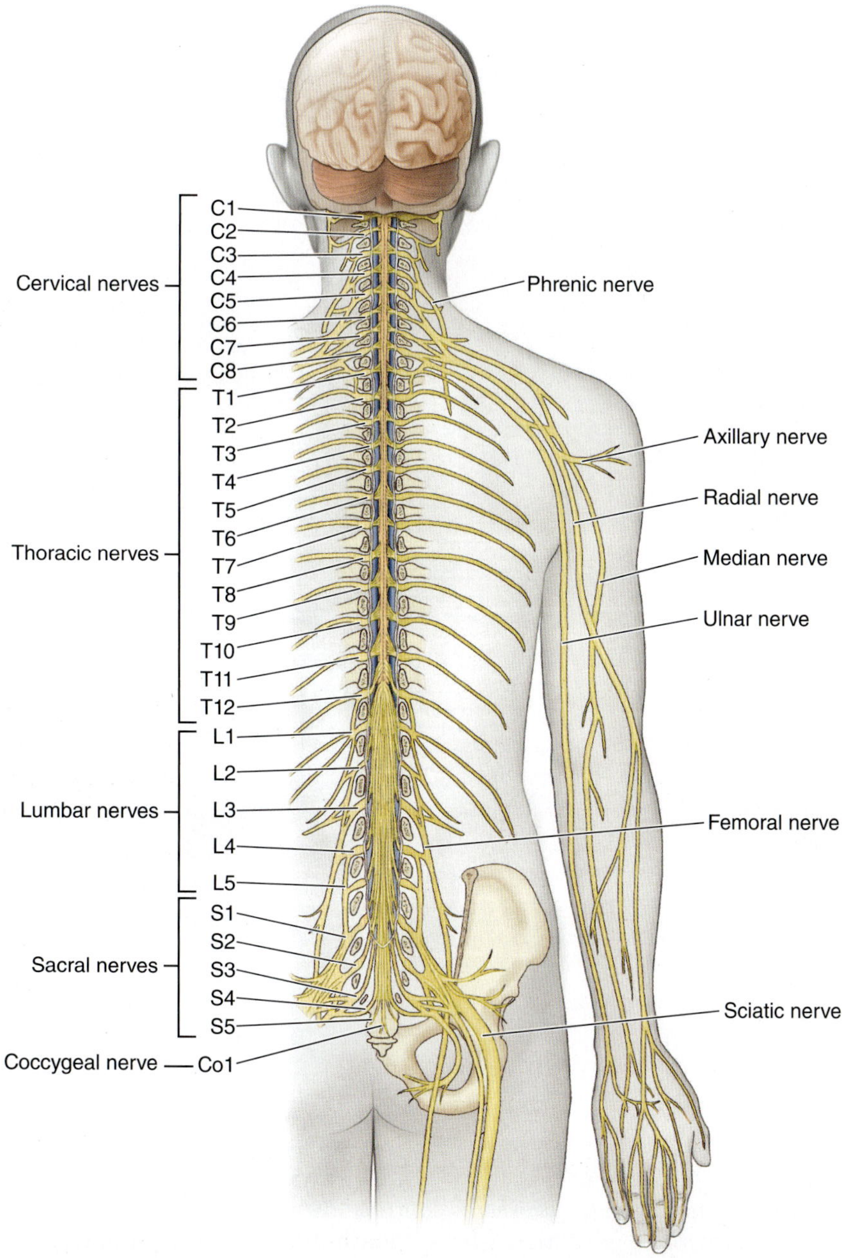

Figure 14-7 The spinal cord and the nerves of the peripheral nervous system.

These functions are performed automatically by reflex actions that are regulated by the hypothalamus and the medulla oblongata. Like the somatic system, the autonomic system contains sensory and motor neurons that carry signals from the skin and visceral organs. The sensory pathways connect to the hypothalamus, brainstem, or spinal cord relaying information. The brain centers perform the integration of the information and relay motor impulses to smooth muscle, cardiac muscle, or glands, as appropriate.

Memory Tip

Somatic = ***s**elf*: We must think about moving: walking, speaking, chewing.

Autonomic = ***auto**matic*: We don't have to think about digestion, breathing, heart rate, or secretion of hormones.

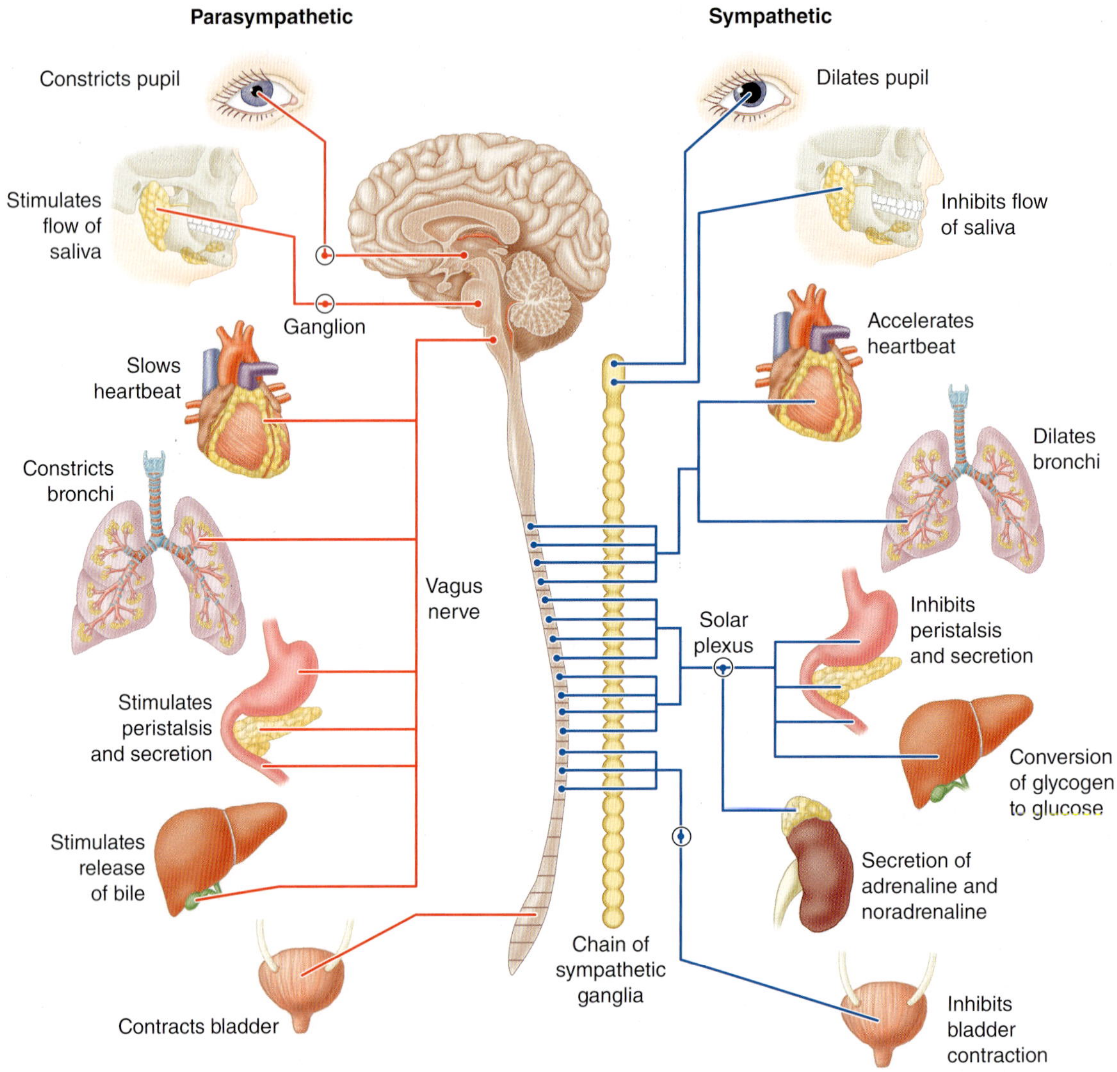

Figure 14-8 The sympathetic and parasympathetic divisions balance the functions regulated by the autonomic nervous system.

Because the autonomic nervous system controls involuntary activities, a control mechanism must balance these activities. The **sympathetic** and **parasympathetic** divisions balance the speeding up and slowing down of the functions regulated by the autonomic nervous system. Stimulation of the sympathetic nervous system prepares us for "fight or flight." Stimulation of the parasympathetic system tells the body to relax and digest food. As such, specific organs of the body are affected (see Fig. 14-8).

Structures and Physiology Review

Match the words to their descriptions.

arachnoid membrane	cerebellum	gyri
autonomic nervous system	corpus callosum	integrative function
	dendrites	meninges
basal ganglia	dura mater	neuroglia
central nervous system	frontal lobe	neurons

neurotransmitters	peripheral nervous system	sulci
occipital lobe	pia mater	synapse
parietal lobe	sensory function	temporal lobe
peduncles	somatic nervous system	thalamus

1. Supportive cells of the nervous system ____________________
2. Lobe of the brain where vision is interpreted ____________________
3. Regulates balance and posture ____________________
4. The involuntary division of the peripheral nervous system ____________________
5. The three-layer membrane that protects the brain and spinal cord ____________________
6. Chemical substances that are released into the synapse to activate or inhibit transmission of nerve impulses ____________________
7. The tough outermost layer of the meninges ____________________
8. The largest portion of the diencephalon that acts as a relay for voluntary motor impulses ____________________
9. Connects the right and left hemispheres of the brain ____________________
10. Shallow grooves of the cerebrum ____________________
11. The layer of the meninges that resembles a spiderweb ____________________
12. The voluntary division of the peripheral nervous system ____________________
13. The primary functional cell of the nervous system ____________________
14. The space between the axon and the dendrite ____________________
15. The innermost layer of the meninges that is directly attached to the outer layer of the spinal cord ____________________
16. Lobe of the brain responsible for language, taste, and smell ____________________
17. Thin branched structures that receive impulses and transmit information to the cell body of the neuron ____________________

18. Connects the cerebellum to the brainstem ____________

19. Masses of gray matter suspended in the white matter of each hemisphere that act as relay stations for motor neurons ____________

20. Lobe of the brain responsible for speech, memory, and emotions ____________

Structures and Physiology Word-Building Practice

1. Nouns and Adjectives

Complete the chart of nouns and adjective forms of words.

Noun	Adjective
1. nerve	____________
2. ____________	axonal
3. ____________	cerebral
4. cerebellum	____________
5. dendrite	____________
6. ____________	astrocytic
7. synapse	____________
8. epilepsy	____________
9. ____________	encephalopathic
10. ____________	narcoleptic

2. Prefixes

Use a listed prefix to build a word for each definition.

a, an-	hemi-	micro-
dura-	hyper-	peri-
dys-	hypo-	quadri-
epi-	intra-	sub-
eu-		

1. Located over or on the dura ____________
2. Pertaining to within the skull ____________
3. Condition of a small brain ____________

4. A condition of decreased or diminished reflexes ______________________

5. Condition of good health; exaggerated feeling of well-being ______________________

6. Either half of the cerebrum or cerebellum ______________________

7. Increased sensitivity to stimuli ______________________

8. Mood disorder, long-lasting bad feelings ______________________

9. Paralysis of all four limbs ______________________

10. Located below the dura ______________________

3. Singular and Plural Forms

Complete the chart of singular and plural forms.

1. nucleus ______________________
2. ______________________ lobes
3. ______________________ sulci
4. ______________________ gyri
5. reflex ______________________
6. ______________________ ganglia
7. stimulus ______________________
8. dendrite ______________________
9. sinus ______________________
10. plexus ______________________

Word Building With Combining, Prefix, and Suffix Forms

The following word roots, prefixes, and suffixes are commonly used in medical terms for the anatomy and pathology of the nervous system. Combining vowels for word roots are included. Memorizing these word elements will help you understand new terms that you may encounter in the field of neurology as a medical assistant, neurological intraoperative monitor, or other professional working in neurology or psychiatry.

The list contains examples of terms that use the combining forms as well as a pronunciation guide. Be sure to use the pronunciation guide so that you can learn to say the terms correctly.

The Medical Language Lab at medicallanguagelab.com provides audio files to help you practice your pronunciations.

Combining Form	Meaning	Example (Pronunciation)	Example Definition
arachn/o	spider, spiderweb	arachnoid membrane (ă-RAK-noyd MEM-brān)	weblike middle layer of the meninges
cephal/o	head	cephalalgia (sĕf-ă-LĂL-jē-ă)	pain of the head, headache
cerebr/o	cerebrum	cerebral (sĕ-RĒ-brĭl)	pertaining to the cerebrum
crani/o	cranium, skull	craniotomy (krā-nē-ŎT-ō-mē)	incision into the skull
dendr/o	branching	dendrite (DEN-drīt)	thin, branched nerve structure resembles branches of a tree
electr/o	electricity	electroneurolysis (ē-LĔK-trō-nū-rōl-ĭ-sĭs)	electrical destruction of a nerve
encephal/o	brain	encephalopathy (en-sef-ă-LOP-ă-thē)	disease of the brain
esthesi/o	sensation	anesthesia (an-ĕs-THĒ-zhă)	medication to reduce sensation
gli/o	glue, gluelike	glioma (glī-Ō-mă)	tumor of a neuroglial cell
kinesi/o	movement	kinesiology (kĭ-nē-sē-OL-ŏ-jē)	the study of movement
mening/o	meninges	meningocele (mĕn-ĬN-gō-sēl)	congenital hernia of the meninges
myel/o	bone marrow, spinal cord	myelomalacia (mī-ĕ-lō-mă-LĀ-shē-ă)	abnormal softening of the spinal cord
narc/o	stupor, numbing	narcotic (năr-KŎT-ĭk)	drug that produces stupor or sleep
neur/o	nerve, nervous system	neurologist (nū-RŎL-ō-jĭst)	specialist in the study of the nervous system
phren/o	mind	schizophrenia (skit-sō-FRĒ-nē-ă)	split from reality, disorganized thoughts, emotions
psych/o	mind	psychology (sī-KOL-ŏ-jē)	the science of mental health
schiz/o	split	schizophrenic (skit-sō-FRĒ-nĭk)	pertaining to split from mind reality
thalam/o	thalamus, chamber	thalamocortical (thăl-ăm-ō-KOR-tĭ-kăl)	pertaining to the thalamus and cerebral cortex
ventricul/o	ventricle (of the brain or heart)	ventriculometry (ven-TRIK-yŭ-lō-met-rē)	measurement of intraventricular cerebral pressure

ā = say, ă = sofa, ē = meet, ĕ = met, ī = eye, ĭ = in, ō = oh, ŏ = dog, ū = you, ŭ = up, oo = food

Prefix Form	Meaning	Example (Pronunciation)	Example Definition
an-	without	anencephaly (an-en-SEF-ă-lē)	congenital absence of the brain
brady-	slow	bradykinesia (brăd-ē-kĭ-NĒ-sē-ă)	abnormally slowed movements
dura-	hard	duraplasty (dū-ră-PLĂS-tē)	plastic repair of the dura mater
epi-	upon	epidural (ep-ĭ-DOOR-ăl)	located over or on the dura
hemi-	half	hemiplegia (hĕm-ē-PLĒ-jē-ă)	paralysis of one side of the body

ā = say, ă = sofa, ē = meet, ĕ = met, ī = eye, ĭ = in, ō = oh, ŏ = dog, ū = you, ŭ = up, oo = food

Suffix Form	Meaning	Example (Pronunciation)	Example Definition
-algia	pain	neuralgia (noo-RAL-jă)	nerve pain
-cele	hernia	encephalocystocele (ĕn-sĕf-ă-lō-SĪS-tō-sēl)	hernia of the brain that contains CSF
-gram	record	electroencephalogram (ĕ-lek-trō-ĕn-SEF-ă-lō-gram)	record of electrical activity of the brain
-graphy	process of recording	electromyography (ē-lĕk-trō-mī-ŎG-ră-fē)	process of recording muscle contractions
-itis	inflammation	meningitis (men-ĭn-JĪT-ĭs)	inflammation of the meninges
-lepsy	seizure	epilepsy (EP-ĭ-lep-sē)	disease of recurrent seizures
-malacia	softening	encephalomalacia (en-sef-ă-lō-mă-LĀ-sh(ē-)ă)	softening of the brain
-oma	tumor	astrocytoma (as-trō-sī-TŌ-mă)	tumor of astrocytes
-osis	condition	psychosis (sī-KŌ-sĭs)	mental disorder, loss of contact with reality
-otomy	incision	craniotomy (krā-nē-ŎT-ō-mē)	incision into the skull
-paresis	partial paralysis	hemiparesis (hĕm-ē-PĂR-ĕ-sĭs)	partial paralysis of ½ of the body
-pathy	disease	neuropathy (noo-ROP-ă-thē)	disease of nerves
-plegia	paralysis	quadriplegia (kwŏd-rĭ-PLĒ-jē-ă)	paralysis of all four limbs
-phoria	feeling, sensation	dysphoria (dis-FŌR-ē-ă)	bad feeling, mood disorder of depression
-phobia	abnormal fear	agoraphobia (ag-ŏr-ă-FŌ-bē-ă)	fear of leaving home, social fear

ā = say, ă = sofa, ē = meet, ĕ = met, ī = eye, ĭ = in, ō = oh, ŏ = dog, ū = you, ŭ = up, oo = food

Combining Forms Practice

1. Build the Terms

Using only the word elements listed, create terms to match the definition in the numbered list.

Prefixes	Combining Forms		Suffixes	
a, an-	arachn/o	esthesi/o	-algia	-oma
epi-	cephal/o	mening/o	-cele	-osis
hemi-	cerebr/o	myel/o	-gram	-otomy
poly-	crani/o	narc/o	-graphy	-ology
sub-	dendr/o	neur/o	-ic	-ologist
	electric/o	phren/o	-itis	-paresis
	encephal/o	psych/o	-lepsy	-plegia
			-malacia	-phobia
			-oid	-phoria

1. The study of the mind ____________________
2. Specialist who treats diseases and disorders of the nervous system ____________________
3. Condition of partial or incomplete paralysis ____________________
4. Recurrent uncontrolled daytime sleepiness ____________________
5. Pain in many nerves ____________________
6. Incision into the skull ____________________
7. Hernia of the meninges and spinal cord ____________________
8. Electrical record of the brain ____________________
9. Inflammation of a nerve ____________________
10. A tumor of the spinal cord ____________________

2. Decipher the Terms

Separate each term into its prefix (if any), combining form, and suffix. Next, translate the word parts, and then give the common definition of the term. Pulmonary has been done for you as an example.

Pulmonary

Prefix: *None* *Combining Form:* *Pulmon/o = lungs*

Suffix: *-ary = pertaining to*

Meaning: *referring to the lungs*

1. electroencephalography

   Prefix: ______________ *Combining Form:* ______________ *Suffix:* ______________

   Meaning: ____

2. psychologist

   Prefix: ______________ *Combining Form:* ______________ *Suffix:* ______________

   Meaning: ____

3. anesthetic

   Prefix: ______________ *Combining Form:* ______________ *Suffix:* ______________

   Meaning: ____

4. arachnophobia

   Prefix: ______________ *Combining Form:* ______________ *Suffix:* ______________

   Meaning: ____

5. polyneuropathy

   Prefix: ______________ *Combining Form:* ______________ *Suffix:* ______________

   Meaning: ____

6. neuralgia

   Prefix: ______________ *Combining Form:* ______________ *Suffix:* ______________

   Meaning: ____

7. myelogram

   Prefix: ______________ *Combining Form:* ______________ *Suffix:* ______________

   Meaning: ____

8. myelopathy

   Prefix: ______________ *Combining Form:* ______________ *Suffix:* ______________

   Meaning: ____

9. subarachnoid

   Prefix: ______________ *Combining Form:* ______________ *Suffix:* ______________

   Meaning: ____

10. anesthesiologist

Prefix: ______________ *Combining Form:* ______________ *Suffix:* ______________

Meaning: ____

CASE STUDY, continued

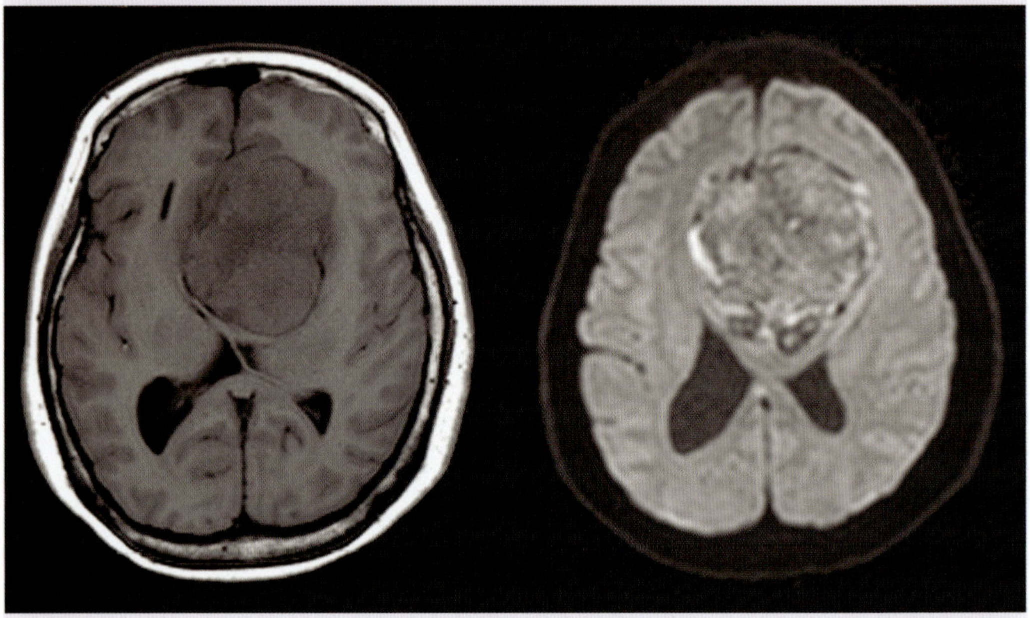

In the car on the way to the neurosurgery appointment, Christina tells Alicia, "When we looked at your MRI scan in the patient mobile app, we could see the location of the tumor. Your cranial nerves come off the base of the brain where your tumor is growing. That explains your headaches, anosmia, hearing loss, and why you have been losing your balance." Alicia replies, "I remember the cranial nerves and their functions from quizzing you last semester. I feel like I am in nursing school too."

Alicia and Christina meet with Dr. Singh who shows them Alicia's MRI. He explains that the tumor location, at the base of the skull, enables him to perform a minimally invasive surgery called an endoscopic endonasal approach (EEA). Dr. Singh explains that he will reach the tumor by going through the nose with a specially designed lighted endoscope. He will insert a tiny blade next to the scope to dissect and remove the tumor. Before the EEA technique was available, surgeons would have to remove part of the skull, called a transcranial approach. The healing time was longer, and the risk of infection was greater. The EEA procedure means that Alicia will not have a surgical incision, which will decrease healing time and decrease the chance of infection. This newer technique will allow Alicia to be in the hospital for a shorter stay and return to her regular activities sooner. After the tumor is removed, it will be sent to pathology to determine if it is malignant or benign. If the tumor is benign, Alicia may not need further treatment, but she will need to return for periodic examinations and MRI scans. If it is malignant, she may require radiation to stop regrowth of the tumor. Dr. Singh says, "Do you have any questions?" Christina asks, "Will my sister need chemotherapy if the tumor is malignant?" Dr. Singh replies, "Chemotherapy is rarely used for malignant meningiomas. Radiation would be the preferred course of treatment, but let's hope that the meningioma is benign. The 10-year survival rate for benign meningiomas is 85%."

Nervous System Diseases and Disorders

Diseases and disorders of the nervous system can be caused by a congenital defect, an injury to the brain or spinal cord, imbalances in brain chemistry, uncontrolled blood pressure or diabetes, and repetitive motion injuries. Treatments vary and include medication to rebalance or replace neurotransmitters, physical therapy, chiropractic care, mental health services, radiation therapy, or surgery. Diagnosis of nervous system disorders is based on clinical, imaging, and laboratory findings.

Common Signs and Symptoms

Because the nervous system works to regulate sensory and motor functions, dysregulation of the nervous system can present a wide variety of signs and symptoms (Table 14-3).

Pathological Conditions of the Nervous System

Alzheimer's disease: A disease characterized by a progressive deterioration of intellectual functions. Onset of symptoms include loss of memory and progress to complete loss of mental, emotional, and physical functions. The three stages of the disease are as follows:

Stage 1 lasts for approximately 1 to 3 years and includes short-term memory loss, inattention, gradual personality changes that include increased irritability, and depression.

Stage 2 lasts for approximately 2 to 10 years when a person loses functions such as writing, getting dressed, and brushing their teeth. Supervision is required to keep the patient safe and to care for their daily needs. The patient will lose communication skills and search for words or use wrong words in attempted conversation. Repetition of conversations is a common feature. At the end of stage 2, the patient will completely lose the ability to speak (aphasia).

Stage 3 lasts for 8 to 10 years and is characterized by a complete loss of communication. The patient is no longer oriented to time, place, and person. Bowel and bladder incontinence is common. The patient often develops limb rigidity and a forward flexion posture. The patient must be cared for by family members or in a long-term care facility. Complications include malnutrition, dehydration, and pneumonia.

Diagnosis of Alzheimer's disease is confirmed by physical, psychological, psychiatric, and neurological examinations with 90% accuracy. Clinical diagnosis is based on observed

TABLE 14-3 Common Signs and Symptoms of Nervous System Disorders

Common Signs	Common Symptoms
Aphasia (inability to speak)	Tinnitus (ringing in the ears)
Ataxia (loss of muscle control, especially voluntary muscles)	Anosmia (loss of sense of smell)
Coma	Dysgeusia (loss or changes in sense of taste)
Loss of consciousness	Depression, elation, improper mood
Paralysis (in two or four limbs)	Feelings of mental confusion
Paresis (partial paralysis, extreme muscle weakness)	Thoughts of suicide or self-harm
Loss of cognitive functions	
Anacusis (measurable hearing loss or deafness)	

findings, but 100% confirmation can only be obtained upon autopsy of brain tissue. While there is no cure, medications to delay symptoms and mental stimulation are advised. Doing crossword puzzles, increasing social interactions, and proper nutrition can delay the onset of symptoms. Treatment protocols include cholinesterase inhibitors such as donepezil or rivastigmine, which prevent the breakdown of acetylcholine in the brain, a neurotransmitter that is thought to be important for memory and thinking. Another medication, Lecanemab, is a monoclonal antibody that blocks the formation of beta-amyloid plaque. Amyloid plaques are brain lesions associated with Alzheimer disease.

Amyotrophic lateral sclerosis (ALS): A progressive weakness and wasting of muscles that usually starts with the hands, progresses to the shoulders and upper arms, and then the legs. The disorder is rare, affecting fewer than 20,000 people in the United States each year. ALS is caused by decreased nerve signaling to the motor neurons arising from the brainstem and spinal cord. As the muscles weaken, the patient complains of fatigue, loss of coordination of movement, spasticity, and eventual paralysis. There is no loss of mental or sensory functions. As the disease progresses, the patient loses the ability to swallow, speak, chew, or clear the airway. Patients experience frustration, depression, malnutrition, pneumonia, and eventually respiratory failure. Most patients die 2 to 5 years after diagnosis; no cure is known for the disease. The disease is also called Lou Gehrig's disease after the New York Yankee baseball player who died from the illness in 1941 at age 37.

Anencephaly: The absence of the brain and spinal cord observed during fetal ultrasound, amniocentesis, or at birth. This congenital disorder is incompatible with life.

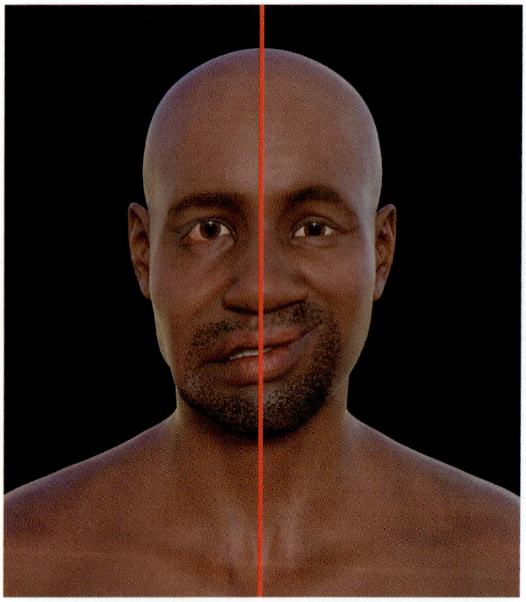

Figure 14-9 Bell's palsy.

Bell's palsy: A temporary or permanent unilateral facial paralysis or weakness of facial muscles that affects 40,000 people in the United States each year (Fig. 14-9). It is seen most often in 15- to 45-year-olds. Causes include trauma to the face, infection, or a tumor pressing on cranial nerve VII (the facial nerve). Infections that can lead to Bell's palsy include herpes simplex, herpes zoster, Epstein-Barr virus, rubella, or mumps. Bell's palsy can also present in the third trimester of pregnancy and often resolves approximately 1 month after delivery. In addition to pregnancy, risk factors include diabetes, obesity, hypertension, and upper respiratory infections. Signs include drooling, asymmetrical facial muscle tone, inability to close the eye on the affected side, and drooping corner of the mouth. Symptoms include loss of appetite and decreased sense of taste. Treatments include gentle facial massage, warm moist compresses, and facial exercises. Analgesics and prednisone are prescribed for pain and swelling. Early treatment usually results in complete recovery.

Brain abscess: A localized accumulation of pus in the brain. It is caused by an infection that is most often from a secondary site, such as a dental abscess, sinusitis, otitis, penetrating head wound, skull fracture, or bacterial endocarditis. It seldom starts in the brain as the primary site. Symptoms present as headache from increased intracranial pressure (ICP), nausea, vomiting, visual disturbances, seizures, neck pain and stiffness, and unequal pupil size. Diagnosis and location of the abscess is confirmed by electroencephalogram (EEG), or computed tomography (CT). Treatment consists of IV antibiotics and mannitol (an osmotic diuretic). Steroids may be prescribed to reduce cerebral edema and ICP. Surgical drainage may be required if the patient does not respond to medication.

Carpal tunnel syndrome: A compression of the median nerve within the carpal tunnel due to inflammation and swelling. It is commonly seen in people who perform repetitive movements of the wrists such as typing, hammering, using screwdrivers or jackhammers. The carpal tunnel is a narrow passage on the anterior surface of the wrist that encloses blood vessels, tendons, and the median nerve. As the tendon becomes inflamed from repetitive movements and compresses the nerve, it causes sharp pain. Often the pain is worse at night, making sleep uncomfortable. Treatment may consist of using a splint to take pressure off the nerve, anti-inflammatory medications, physical therapy, and rest. When conservative care no longer prevents pain and/or the patient cannot perform necessary activities, a surgical procedure called a carpal tunnel release may be performed (Fig. 14-10). The surgery is performed in an outpatient surgical setting and pain relief often occurs within 1 to 2 weeks.

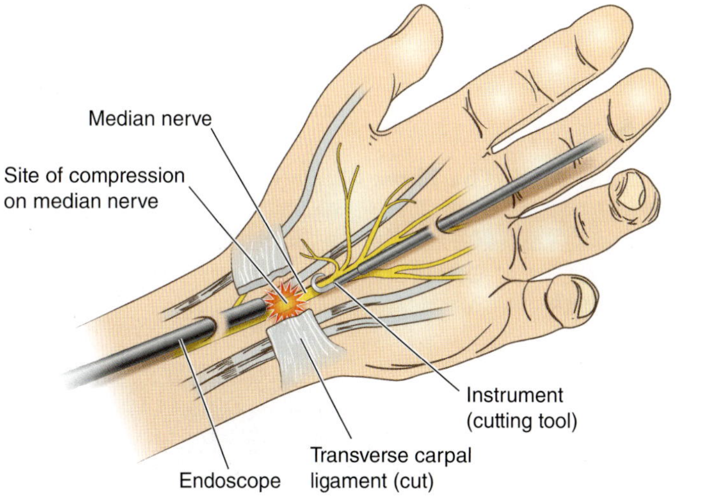

Figure 14-10 Carpal tunnel release.

Cephalalgia (headache): A broad category of pain in the head. The pain may be mild to severe, acute, or chronic and have a variety of causes.

Cluster headache: Occurs typically 2 to 3 hours after falling asleep and is characterized by intense pain in one eye. The patient wakes in response to the severe pain. There are usually no early signs. In addition to the head pain, patients report hyperhidrosis (excessive sweating), runny nose, tearing, facial flushing and edema. Headache usually lasts 30 minutes to several hours, and patients report clusters of recurrent headaches occurring every night for several days to weeks. There is no cure for cluster headaches, and treatment is directed at reducing pain. Treatments can include calcium channel blockers, selective serotonin agonists, or prednisone.

Migraine headache: A recurring, pulsating, vascular headache that affects one side of the head. It usually has a slow onset in which the patient reports an **aura**, a recognized sensation that precedes the head pain. Auras can be visual (i.e., wavy lines), auditory (buzzing or ringing in the ears), olfactory (a distinct smell), or a taste. Patients with chronic migraines learn to take their pain medication upon sensing their aura. Often, patients report needing a dark, silent room to decrease the pain. Migraines can occur at any age; women suffer from migraines more than men, and family history can contribute to their incidence. Women may have an increase in incidence of migraine correlated with their menstrual cycle. In addition to head pain, some patients report nausea and vomiting. Migraines can last from hours to days. Medications can reduce symptoms, but most migraines are recurrent. Dietary avoidance of trigger foods such as chocolate, red wine, sugar substitutes, pork, and corn may decrease the incidence and/or intensity of the headache.

Tension headache: Caused by contraction of skeletal muscles of the face, scalp, upper back, and neck. Pain is brought on by emotional stress, anxiety, or grief. The guarded posture and continued contraction of the musculature results in stiffness and pain. Pain is described as griping, squeezing, vicelike pain. It is most frequent in adolescents to middle-aged adults. Mild analgesics, such as buffered aspirin or acetaminophen, and tranquilizers can decrease pain and tension. Massage, yoga, and relaxation exercises can decrease intensity and frequency of tension headaches.

Cerebral concussion: A violent jarring, shaking, or other nonpenetrating injury to the brain. Concussions usually involve a brief loss of consciousness. Upon regaining consciousness, the patient may not remember what happened (amnesia) and will have a headache. Other symptoms include blurred vision, tinnitus (ringing in the ears), drowsiness, mental confusion, nausea, vomiting, visual disturbances, and dizziness. The patient will be observed for signs of increased ICP or intracranial bleeding. MRI scanning may be required to direct care (such as surgery). In contact sports, such as football or soccer, post-concussion protocols dictate that the player does not return to contact sports for a prescribed period of time. Post-concussion, the patient may complain of difficulty concentrating, but with time, symptoms should subside.

Cerebral palsy (CP): A congenital birth defect that is characterized by damage to cerebrum, cerebellum, or basal ganglia that occurs before birth, during the birth process, or during the child's first 3 to 5 years of life. The disorder is not progressive, but the deficits are permanent. CP affects motor control but not intellectual functions. Children may be very bright, of normal intelligence, or have intellectual disabilities. Other disorders commonly seen are oculomotor impairment, convulsions, hearing or speech deficits. Table 14-4 lists the three major types of CP.

TABLE 14-4 The Three Major Types of Cerebral Palsy

Type	Area of Damage	Resulting Deficits
Spastic 80% of CP	Cortex of the brain 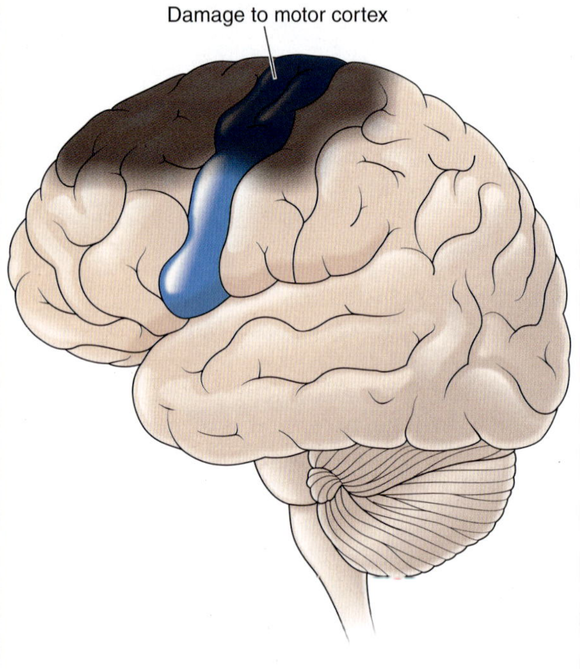 	Tense muscles, tight heel cords that cause the child to walk on the toes. Can affect one to four limbs.
Ataxic	Cortex of the brain	Tremors, loss of equilibrium, difficulty with quick movements, coordination required for walking
Dyskinetic	Basal ganglia 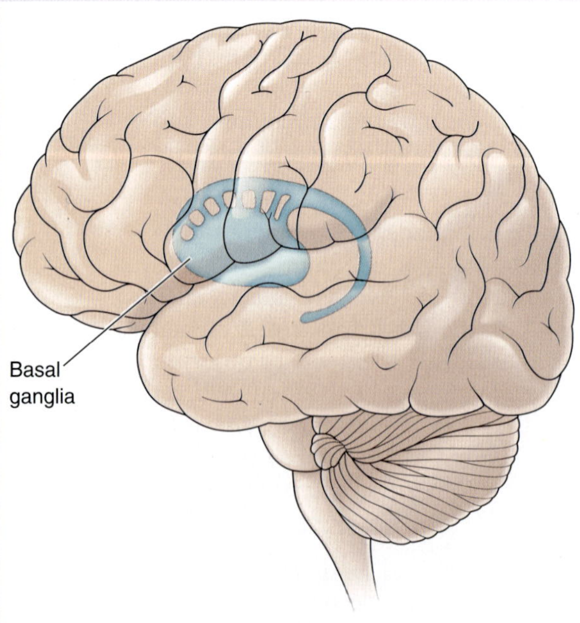 	Abnormal movements such as jerking, twisting. Movements can be brought on by stress.

Cerebrovascular accident (CVA): An occlusion or a rupture of a cerebral blood vessel resulting in decreased blood flow (ischemia) to the affected area of the brain and death of that brain tissue (Fig. 14-11). Also called a stroke. CVA is a broad category and includes cerebral hemorrhage (bleeding), thrombosis (formation of a clot), and embolism (a clot that dislodges).

Cerebral hemorrhage: Occurs when a cerebral blood vessel ruptures and blood spills into the CSF, brain tissue, or the subarachnoid space. It is most commonly caused by hypertension. Other contributing factors are smoking, obesity, liver disease, and drug abuse. Symptoms occur rapidly and include a sudden severe headache, but they may also include other neurological symptoms related to the area of the brain affected. Hemorrhages can occur in various parts of the brain and meninges and include intracerebral, subarachnoid, subdural, or epidural hemorrhages.

Cerebral thrombosis: An accumulation of an atherosclerotic clot in a cerebral blood vessel (artery or vein) that causes death of a specific portion of brain tissue. Causes include hardening of cerebral arteries or veins, hypertension, infections, tumors, surgery to the head or neck, meningitis, thyroid disease, obesity, pregnancy, dehydration, diabetes mellitus, or a violent injury. Signs and symptoms include severe migraine

ELEMENT REVIEW
intra- = within
sub- = under, below
epi- = upon
thromb/o = clot
-lysis = destruction

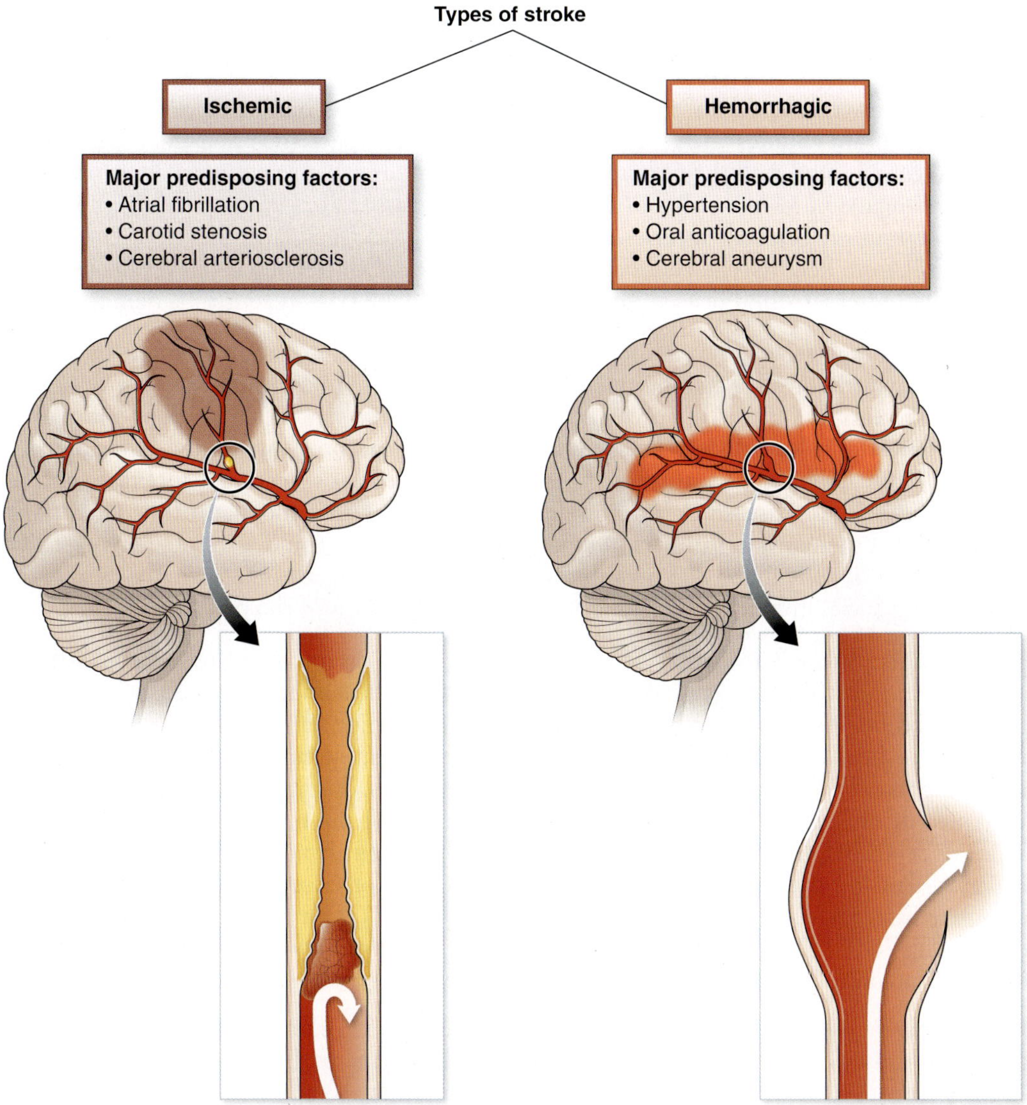

Figure 14-11 Types of cerebrovascular accidents.

headache, nausea, vomiting, eye pain, blurred vision, loss of one-half of visual field, difficulties with speech or language. The signs and symptoms correspond to the functional location of the thrombus in the brain. Diagnosis is confirmed by CT scan or MRI. Treatments vary from administering thrombolytic medications or surgical stenting (opening) of the involved vessel.

Cerebral embolism is a blood clot that occurs elsewhere in the body that travels to the brain and occludes (blocks) blood flow to the brain. Depending on where in the brain the embolism lodges, it can cause paralysis, severe headache, loss of vision, and aphasia (inability to speak).

Complex Regional Pain Syndrome (CRPS): A disorder that causes lasting pain, usually in the arm or leg from a previous injury. The disorder was previously called reflex sympathetic dystrophy. The severity of pain is often greater than the original injury and is of unknown etiology (cause). Injuries that may cause CRPS include burns, fractures, sprains, minor surgery, radiation, and amputations. Pain is described as aching, burning, cold, deep, and throbbing. Other symptoms include muscle weakness, spasms, excessive sweating, and joint stiffness at the affected area. Diagnosis is confirmed by physical examination and medical history. Additionally, a bone scan will show increased wear and/or increased blood flow to the affected area. A sweat test can be used to show increased sweating at the affected area. Treatment includes anti-inflammatory medications, analgesics, antidepressants, NSAIDS, physical therapy, relaxation therapies, and electrodes on the spinal cord to deliver pain relieving electrical stimulation.

Coup and Contrecoup: Two injuries to opposite sides of the brain as a result of a single impact. The brain collides with one side of the skull on impact and then the counterforce causes a second impact on the opposite side of the skull. It can occur during an impact that causes a concussion. Coup and contrecoup injuries are associated with cerebral contusions, where the brain is bruised. Injuries from motorcycle, car, truck, and bicycle accidents, as well as falls from heights, can cause damage to the brain. Contrecoup often results in visual impairment after a frontal head injury as the occipital lobe (vision center) is damaged.

Dementia: Progressive, irreversible deterioration of mental function marked by memory loss, impairment of reasoning, judgment, and abstract thought. Most often occurs in patients 85 years and older. The onset of primary dementia may be slow, taking months or years. Depression, sleep disturbances and paranoia may accompany mental deterioration. Causes may include illnesses, alcoholism, vitamin B12 deficiency, cerebral anoxia, hypothyroidism, Alzheimer's disease, or brain infarcts. Treatment with some medications including donepezil and memantine can improve function. Treatment should also include assistance with activities of daily living and promote as much independence as the patient can tolerate. Maximizing social interaction is thought to delay progression of the disease.

Encephalitis: The inflammation of the brain. It is most often caused by a virus, but can also be due to a parasite, fungi, or bacteria that enters the CNS. The causative organism invades and begins to destroy the brain and spinal cord. Signs and symptoms include seizure, severe headache, fever, neck stiffness, altered mental status, and decreased level of consciousness. The patient may experience facial weakness, dysphagia (difficulty speaking), weakness of one side of the body (opposite to the side of brain inflammation). As nerve cells are destroyed and cerebral edema increases, the patient is at risk for permanent neurological damage and/or a permanent coma. Treatment for encephalitis is directed at the causative infectious agent (antiviral, bacterial, fungal, etc.) with antipyretics (fever reducers), analgesics, anticonvulsants, corticosteroids, and osmotic diuretics to reduce cerebral edema. Outcomes vary based on type of infection and degree of damage to the brain.

Epilepsy is a disease marked by recurrent episodes of irregular electrical activity of the brain that causes involuntary muscle movements called seizures. Epilepsy occurs in 1 to 2% of the population with incidence highest in children under 10 and adults after age 70. The disease may be congenital or acquired from brain disease. Epileptic seizures vary and may affect level of consciousness, skeletal motor function, sensations, or control of autonomic functions of the internal organs. Severe seizures can decrease oxygenation of circulating blood, and cause acidosis and respiratory arrest. Seizures are classified according to the area of the brain involved and the presentation of clinical signs and symptoms. Diagnosis is confirmed by a complete neurological examination, EEG, MRI, and CT scan. Treatment for seizures is anticonvulsant medications (antiepileptics) such as phenytoin or carbamazepine. In the United States, patients who suffer from seizures are unable to obtain a driver's license until they have been seizure-free for one year. The two most common forms of seizures are grand mal and petit mal seizures.

Grand mal seizure: The most common form of epileptic seizure, also called a tonic-clonic seizure. The tonic phase starts with a sudden loss of consciousness, muscle rigidity characterized by extension of the head, legs, and arms, and clenching of the teeth. The eyes roll back, and the pupils will be fixed and dilated. As the patient's diaphragm contracts and air is forced out, a sound like a cry is emitted. Then, breathing suddenly stops. The patient often loses control of both bowel and bladder. This tonic phase may last from 15 seconds to 1 minute. The clonic phase begins with the patient resuming breathing, the muscles of the arms and legs relax. The patient may begin rapid, shallow breathing and have excessive salivation. The patient may be unconscious for 30 to 40 minutes after the clonic phase and upon awakening, is confused, disoriented, and often reports feeling exhausted. The patient will not remember the seizure. Priority of care is to keep the patient safe during the seizure.

Petit mal seizure: A lesser seizure characterized by a decreased attentiveness, lasting only a few seconds. It is often called an absence seizure as the patient appears to "not be in their body." The individual may present with a vacant stare, blank facial expression, and repeated blinking of the eyes. The patient may bob the head up and down or smack their lips. Petit mal seizures mostly affect children aged 4-12 and occur in girls more often than boys. Seizures may be brought on by flashing lights or hyperventilation. Low doses of antiseizure medications such as ethosuximide and valproic acid may be prescribed if seizures are frequent. Up to 75% of children with absence seizures outgrow them and have no permanent disability. Care for the child when experiencing the absence seizure is directed at preventing injury while they are not "present" in their body.

Guillain-Barre syndrome: Autoimmune disorder affecting 1 to 2 people per 100,000 in the United States each year. GB syndrome is acute polyneuritis of the PNS in which the myelin sheaths of axons are destroyed. This prevents the axons from sending nerve impulses and thus a loss of reflex response is noted. Onset of the syndrome often follows an acute viral infection or vaccination. Antibodies react with antigens on the surface of peripheral nerves causing demyelination. The patient will present with symmetric motor and sensory deficits of the lower extremities and the disability will progress to the upper extremities. Pain in the hips, thighs, and back is common as well as bladder and bowel incontinence. This progressive ascending paralysis is potentially fatal if the loss of motor function reaches the diaphragm and causes respiratory failure. Treatment is directed at supporting the patient until motor functions of the PNS return, and minimizing complications. Approximately one-third of patients will require intubation and mechanical ventilation until they can breathe independently. The course of the syndrome can last from a few days to 3 weeks, but full muscle recovery can take months to years.

ELEMENT REVIEW
poly- = many
neur/o = nerves
-itis = inflammation

Hematoma: A swelling from a collection of blood that has left a ruptured artery or vein. Hematomas of the head can occur above or below the dura mater as epidural or subdural (Fig. 14-12).

Epidural hematoma: A collection of blood that pools above the dura mater from a torn meningeal artery or from an injury to the brain such as a cerebral contusion, or from a skull fracture. The hematoma develops quickly, damage from pressure on the brain ensues, and immediate treatment is required to save the patient's life. The first sign is sudden loss of consciousness, followed by a brief period where the patient

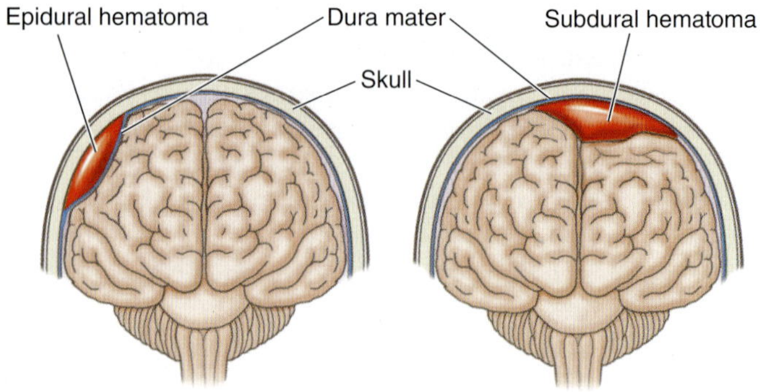

Figure 14-12 Subdural versus epidural hematomas.

appears rational and lucid. The patient may feel well for a period of 1 to 2 hours and then decline rapidly. The patient may lose consciousness. Additional signs and symptoms include seizure, paralysis, sudden intense headache, one fixed pupil, hypertension (increased blood pressure), decreased pulse rate, and even coma. A craniotomy and creation of Burr holes is performed to access the space, repair the damaged blood vessels, and to drain the pooled blood.

Subdural hematoma: A collection of blood located below the dura mater and above the arachnoid layer of the meninges. This injury is usually the result of a closed head injury caused by a hit to the head (contact sports, auto accidents, falls). It can also occur from the use of anticoagulants, or chronic alcoholism. Subdural hematomas are most often from venous bleeding and vary in rate of development. An acute subdural hematoma will develop within a few minutes of the injury and a chronic subdural hematoma will slowly leak blood and evolve over a few weeks. Symptoms include drowsiness, mental confusion, headache, dilation and delayed response of one pupil, possible seizures, paralysis, and signs of increased ICP. Treatment includes diuretics to decrease fluid on the brain and decrease swelling. Surgical evacuation of blood may be done with Burr holes and suction, but an open craniotomy is often required to evacuate coagulating blood.

Memory Tip

Epidural hematoma = arterial blood = vowels E & A
Subdural hematoma = venous blood = consonants S & V

Huntington chorea: A rare inherited neurological disorder of the CNS that affects 5 in 100,000 people in the United States each year. Symptoms usually begin at age 30 to 40 and are characterized by rapid, jerky movements. Emotional, cognitive, and behavioral changes include increased irritability, inability to control emotions, and eventual dementia. Physical symptoms include protrusion of the tongue, dysphasia (difficulty speaking), inability to perform voluntary movements, inability to sit still. As the disability progresses, the patient loses bowel and bladder function, and requires feeding. As movement of the diaphragm decreases, the patient is susceptible to choking, aspiration, poor oxygenation, and malnutrition. Diagnosis is confirmed by genetic testing. People who have the gene but want to start a family often decide to adopt rather than have a child that may suffer from the illness. There is no cure, but supportive care for patients and families can improve quality of life. Most patients die 15 to 20 years after diagnosis, often from aspiration pneumonia or infection.

Hydrocephalus: The accumulation of CSF within the ventricles of the brain as a result of a blockage or destruction of the normal drainage pathways. The disorder is often caused by congenital anomalies such as spina bifida, traumatic lesions, neoplasms, or infectious meningoencephalitis. Often the increased fluid can increase ICP. Diagnosis is obtained by measuring the circumference of the infant's head and observing frontal bossing, where the forehead protrudes. The infant may show signs of increased ICP such as irritability, high-pitched cry, and an inability to sleep for long periods of time. Surgical creation of a shunt from the ventricles of the brain to the peritoneum or the right atrium will direct excess fluid away.

Intracranial tumors: Tumors of the brain can occur in any structure of the brain and can be primary or secondary, arising from another site in the body. Clinical symptoms of intracranial tumors vary according to their location and may include headaches, dizziness, nausea, vomiting, altered mental status, balance and coordination difficulties, paralysis, seizures, and sensory deficits. The tumors can be classified as malignant or benign. Surgical removal of intracranial tumors is desired when possible. Radiation and chemotherapy may be required after a tumor is excised or if removal is not possible.

Primary intracranial tumors: Tumors that begin in the neuroglial cells or the meninges. They are named by the type of cell affected (Table 14-5).

Metastatic intracranial tumors: Occur as a result of metastasis from a primary site of cancer such as the breast or lung. Fifteen percent of all intracranial tumors are secondary, and growth is often rapid. If the patient's health status is stable, and the location of the tumor is accessible, surgical removal of the metastatic tumor offers the best prognosis.

Meningitis, acute bacterial: A medical emergency, fatal in 10% to 40% of cases. Pathogenic bacteria enter the meninges via the bloodstream from an infection from another part of the body. Commonly, upper respiratory infections, skull fractures, or a penetrating wound are the sources of the bacterial infection, making patient history important in the differential diagnosis of meningitis. As the bacteria multiply in the CSF, the brain swells, blood circulation of the CNS becomes congested, clumps of exudate may accumulate around the base of the brain, and ICP increases dramatically. Signs and symptoms of bacterial meningitis include severe headache, neck pain and stiffness, fever, pain with eye movement, nausea, vomiting, diarrhea, drowsiness, confusion, and seizure. Diagnosis is confirmed by lumbar puncture to obtain CSF for culture. Infected CSF will appear cloudy, with increased white cells, increased protein, and decreased glucose. Intravenous antibiotic

TABLE 14-5 Primary Intracranial Tumors

Type of Tumor	Region, Rate of Growth, Prevalence	Survival Rate	Treatment
Glioblastoma	Cerebral hemisphere, rapidly growing	Prognosis is poor. More than 2 years survival is rare.	Radiation and chemotherapy
Astrocytoma	Brain and spinal cord Slow growing Most common form of brain tumor	Average 10 years survival	Surgical excision, may require radiation and chemotherapy
Ependymoma	Fourth ventricle wall to the spinal cord, slow growing 6% of tumors in adults and children	Usually benign 5-year survival rate is 84%.	Surgical excision, may require radiation and chemotherapy
Oligodendroglioma	Frontal lobe, slow growing, 5% of tumors	5-year survival rate is 74%.	Surgical excision, may require radiation and chemotherapy
Medulloblastoma	Cerebellum, most common childhood brain tumor (20%)	Prognosis is poor for children 3 years and younger; 60% survival rate for older children.	Surgical excision, then radiation and chemotherapy
Meningioma	Meninges at the base of the brain; most common tumor in adults	Often benign (90%); prognosis is good with 80% survival 5+ years	Surgical removal

therapy must be administered to avoid permanent damage or even death. The prognosis of bacterial meningitis varies based on the health and age of the patient and how soon antibiotic therapy is started. Severe, long-term complications may include learning disabilities, mental or physical handicaps, cranial nerve malfunction, peripheral circulatory collapse, arthritis, and subdural effusion.

Aseptic or **viral meningitis** is usually clinically mild with a spontaneous recovery. It is commonly caused by an enterovirus transmitted by saliva, sputum, or mucus of an infected person. Lumbar puncture for CSF culture is recommended to rule out bacterial meningitis.

PUBLIC HEALTH FACT

All children in the United States are vaccinated against H. influenzae type B (Hib) and pneumococcus as primary prevention against meningitis.

Multiple sclerosis (MS): An autoimmune disorder that is characterized by inflammation and destruction of the myelin sheath in the brain and spinal cord. As the myelin sheath is destroyed the nerves are hardened (sclerosed) and scarred, interrupting the flow of nerve impulses. MS is most often diagnosed between age 20 to 40 and affects females more than men. Signs and symptoms include progressive weakness in one or more limbs, muscular spasticity, nystagmus (involuntary eye movement), fatigue, tremor, gait instability, irritability, sleep disturbances, depression, and urinary tract infections. Diagnosis is confirmed by MRI, which shows areas of demyelination of the brain and/or spinal cord. While there is no known cure, medications to slow progressive damage to the myelin sheath include corticosteroids to reduce inflammation, and interferon beta blockers to slow disease progression. Patients are advised to avoid exposure to extreme heat or cold and stressful situations and are encouraged to exercise to tolerance. Massage, yoga, and a healthy well-balanced diet may be helpful. The goal of care is to decrease symptoms and maintain as much independence as possible.

Myasthenia gravis: A chronic neuromuscular disorder characterized by skeletal muscle weakness and fatigue of the muscles of the head, neck, and face that progresses to the chest thus affecting breathing. It is a rare progressive autoimmune disease that affects 14 out of 100,000 people. Antibodies block or destroy acetylcholine receptors. Onset in women in usually age 20 to 40 and age 50 to 60 in men. Signs and symptoms include ptosis (drooping) of eyelids, diplopia (double vision), weakness of extraocular muscles, difficulty chewing, and impairment of facial and pharyngeal muscles. Diagnosis is confirmed by patient history, neurological examination, electromyography, and a Tensilon test. Treatment with anticholinesterases and immunosuppressive medications can delay progression of symptoms.

ELEMENT REVIEW
narc/o = sleep
-lepsy = seizure, attack

Narcolepsy: Characterized by recurrent, uncontrollable episodes of daytime sleep. Often cataplexy (temporary muscular paralysis) may occur especially after emotional turmoil. Narcolepsy occurs in families, with 90% of affected people having specific human leukocyte antigen abnormalities. Diagnosis is confirmed by patient history and polysomnography (sleep study) to evaluate sleep disturbances that prevent restful sleep. Treatment includes scheduled naps during the day to prevent attacks and promote safety. Medications to treat narcolepsy include stimulants such as dextroamphetamine sulfate or methylphenidate hydrochloride.

Parkinson disease: A degenerative deterioration of the nerves of the basal ganglia in the brainstem causing motor dysfunction. It is a common disorder affecting 1.5 million Americans with 50,000 new cases being diagnosed each year. Signs and symptoms include gradual onset of fatigue, tremors in one or more extremities, typically the hands when at rest. Patients experience akinesia (inability to begin movements) or bradykinesia (slowed movements). Tremors increase with anxiety and fatigue and purposeful movement becomes progressively more difficult. Patients report an inability to stop movements to sleep. Other symptoms include difficulty arising from a chair or getting out of bed, a shuffling gait, and changes to the voice (loss of volume and lack of variability of tone). Treatment goals are to maintain function for as long as possible and to relieve symptoms. Medications include selegiline and carbidopa/levodopa. Surgical treatments include transplantation of dopamine-secreting cells from other parts of the patient's body or implantation of electrical stimulators to affected areas of the brain. There is no cure for Parkinson's disease; patients must be monitored for safety to prevent injuries from falls and efficacy of medications.

ELEMENT REVIEW
brady- = slow
a- = without
kinesi/o = movement
-ia = noun form

Poliomyelitis: The acute infection and inflammation of the gray matter in the spinal cord caused by the poliovirus. It is an extremely rare disease since the introduction of the polio vaccine in 1955. The World Health Organization reports the incidence of poliomyelitis has been reduced from an estimated 350,000 in 1988 to 6 cases reported in 2021. Signs and symptoms include a severe cold, constipation, a slight elevation in fever, and the onset of paralysis. The degree of paralysis depends on the extent of nerve involvement. Immunization with inactive polio virus vaccine is prophylaxis (prevention) of the disorder. Treatment is supportive; mechanical ventilation for patients whose respiratory muscles are paralyzed. Physical therapy is used to preserve muscular function. Patients are isolated to prevent transmission of poliovirus to others.

Postpolio syndrome: The progressive weakness that occurs 15 to 25 years after initial poliomyelitis infection. Signs and symptoms include uncontrolled, uncoordinated twitching of muscles and muscular weakness and fatigue. There is no cure for postpolio syndrome. Treatment is supportive care with use of mobility aids (walker, wheelchair), regular supervised exercise, planned rest periods and home modification to promote as much independent function as possible.

PUBLIC HEALTH FACT

Jonas Salk, American scientist and virologist invented the polio vaccine in 1955. Prior to the vaccine, infection with poliomyelitis affected many children around the world, causing paralysis and death. President Franklin Roosevelt, who suffered from polio, supported mandating the polio vaccine for all children in the United States. Other countries saw the incidence of polio in the United States decline and began vaccinating their children.

Reye syndrome: An acute encephalopathy with fatty infiltration of the liver, pancreas, heart, kidney, spleen, and lymph nodes. It occurs following viral infection with chicken pox or influenza. It is a rare syndrome with an unknown etiology (cause). Signs and symptoms include nausea, vomiting, altered mental status, seizures, or coma. Children under the age of 18 are most likely to be affected. Mortality rate depends on if the CNS is affected but up to 80% of children die from the syndrome. There is an association with the use of aspirin or salicylates, so parents are advised to administer Tylenol (acetaminophen) rather than aspirin-based analgesics to their children. Treatment consists of intravenous fluids and electrolytes, corticosteroids, and ventilation if needed. Osmotic diuretics are administered to decrease elevated ICP and the head is elevated to 30 degrees.

ELEMENT REVIEW
uni- = one
later/o = side
-al = pertaining to

Shingles (herpes zoster): The acute viral infection caused by a reactivation of the varicella virus (Chicken pox) years after the initial infection. Inflammation of the posterior root ganglia of only a few segments of the spinal cord or cranial peripheral nerves result in a unilateral (one sided) rash (Fig. 14-13). Symptoms include painful vesicles (fluid-filled lesions) that appear along the course of the dermatome of the affected nerve. The patient also reports flu-like symptoms of fatigue, nausea, and diarrhea. The rash is itchy and painful. When the vesicles erupt, the fluid can transmit the virus to others, so patients are advised to wash hands and not share towels or linens with family members. The lesions usually take 3 to 5 days to appear and then dry to a crust. Recovery is in approximately 2 to 3 weeks. The most common area is the trunk, but the face, groin, or limbs may be affected. Ten to twenty percent of the population will

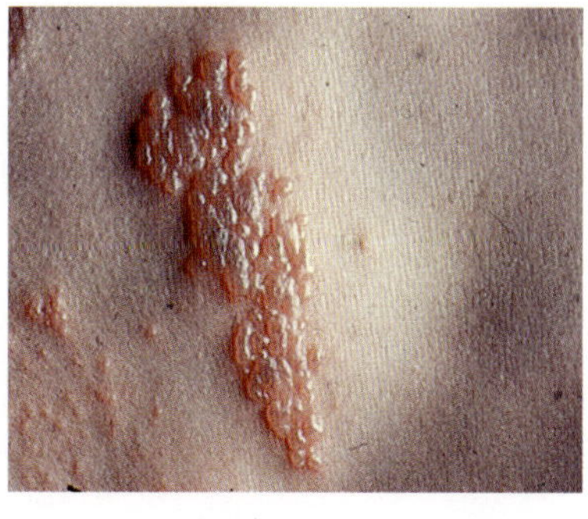

Figure 14-13 Lesions of shingles.

suffer from shingles with the highest incidence occurring in people over age 50. Treatment with antivirals, analgesics, and sometimes corticosteroids is advised. Reactivation of varicella zoster may be prevented with a vaccine. Varicella zoster virus vaccination is approved in the United States for adults 60 and older.

Spina bifida cystica: The congenital defect of the CNS in which the posterior section of one or two vertebrae does not close normally during embryonic development. It is found in 18 out of 100,000 births and like other neural tube defects, it can be prevented with folic acid supplementation (800 mg daily) during pregnancy. A cyst protrudes through the opening between the 5th lumbar and 1st sacral vertebrae. The two forms are meningocele and meningomyelocele. Both defects require surgical closure.

Meningocele: A cyst like sac covered with skin or a thin membrane protruding out of the bony defect in the vertebrae. The defect contains meninges and CSF. Some spinal roots may be displaced, but normal function is intact. Neurological complications may be present, but not as severe as those with meningomyelocele.

Meningomyelocele: A cyst like sac covered with skin or a thin membrane protruding out of the bony defect in the vertebrae. The defect contains meninges, CSF, and spinal cord segment. The patient will have weakness or paralysis of the legs, bowel, and bladder dysfunction. Extreme care must be taken to protect the sac from rupture or injury.

ELEMENT REVIEW
mening/o = meninges
myel/o = spinal cord or bone marrow
-cele = hernia or swelling
lip/o = fat
-oma = tumor

Spina bifida occulta: The congenital defect of the CNS in which the posterior portion of one or more vertebrae do not close properly. The CSF and spinal cord are not displaced posteriorly as in spina bifida cystica. It is most commonly seen on the 5th lumbar and 1st sacral segments, but it may occur on other segments of the spine. Symptoms include a dimple of the skin, a port wine stain, and a tuft of hair growing over the area. A subcutaneous lipoma may be present. No surgical treatment is recommended since neurological symptoms are extremely rare.

Spinal cord injuries: Injuries such as vertebral dislocation or vertebral fractures result in total or partial impairment of spinal cord function below the level of injury. Spinal cord injuries are most commonly the result of trauma from motor vehicle accidents, falls from heights, diving into shallow water, or accidents in contact sports. Trauma to the spinal cord occurring above C3 is often fatal due to a loss of innervation of the diaphragm and intercostal muscles maintaining respiration. In addition to permanent physical disabilities, patients suffer from depression, and psychological counseling and/or medication is advised.

Paraplegia: The paralysis of the legs due to severe injury to the spinal cord in the thoracic or lumbar region. There is a resulting loss of motor and sensory function below the level of injury. The patient will be unable to walk but retains the use of the upper extremities. Loss of control of bowel and bladder function as well as sexual control is present.

Quadriplegia: The paralysis of all four limbs due to a severe injury to the spinal cord at the 4th to 7th cervical vertebrae. Loss of sensory and motor function below the injury causes severe disability. Cardiovascular dysregulation, low body temperature, inability to perspire, impaired gastrointestinal peristalsis, loss of control of bowel and bladder, as well as sexual dysfunction is present.

Tay-Sach disease: The congenital disorder caused by altered lipid metabolism of an enzyme on chromosome 15. The carrier gene is found at a rate of 4% in families of Eastern European Jewish origin. Normal development of the child during the first 6 months of life is followed by profound regression. Signs and symptoms include deafness, enlargement of the head without hydrocephalus, social withdrawal, increased startle response, blindness with cherry red spots on the retinas, convulsions, and paralysis. Death occurs between 2 to 4 years of age. There is no treatment for the disease; thus supportive and symptomatic care are indicated. The disease can be diagnosed in utero by amniocentesis.

Transient ischemic attack (TIA): Brief periods of ischemia (decreased blood flow) in the brain. A TIA can last from minutes to several hours and often occurs prior to a cerebrovascular accident. Neurological symptoms vary depending on the location of ischemia and how many vessels are involved. Signs and symptoms include the patient "feeling funny," numbness, weakness, confusion, and difficulty speaking. Patients should be evaluated by a medical provider as a CVA may be imminent.

Trigeminal neuralgia: A rare condition affecting 150,000 people each year characterized by pain caused by irritation of the 5th cranial nerve. The three branches of the nerve can be affected independently, or all can be involved (Fig. 14-14). Pain in the eye and forehead is caused when the ophthalmic branch is affected. Pain in the lower lip, cheek near the ear, and the lateral portion of the tongue is caused when the mandibular branch is affected. The upper lip, nose, and cheek are painful if the maxillary branch is affected. Pain is exacerbated by heat, chewing, brushing teeth, or touching the affected area. Women are affected more than men, and diagnosis is usually made after age 50. Of patients with MS, 1% to 2% also suffer from trigeminal neuralgia. It can last for years or be lifelong. Treatment includes analgesics for pain control or muscle relaxants to decrease tension in the facial muscles. A botulinum toxin (Botox) injection may also be used to block sensory nerves. Acupuncture and chiropractic adjustments can be used for pain management. Severe cases may require surgery with microvascular decompression to relieve pressure on the nerve.

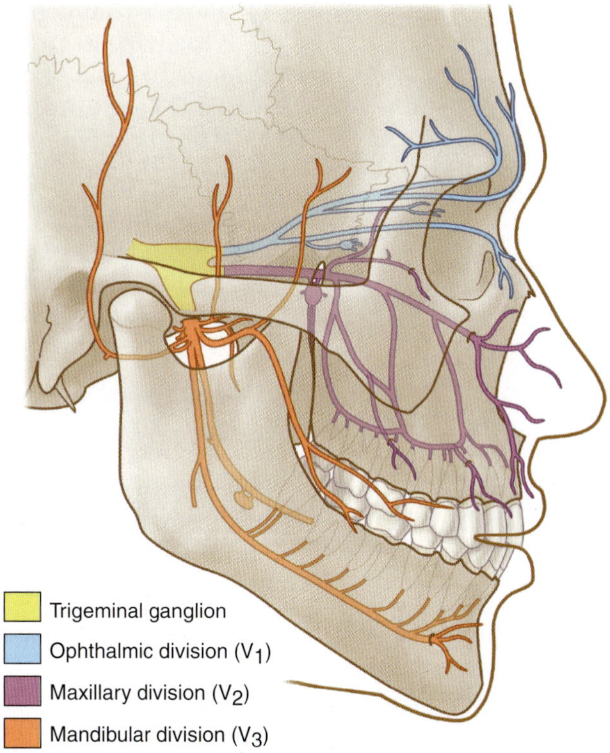

Figure 14-14 The three branches of the trigeminal nerve.

Mental Health Disorders

Mental health disorders can be caused by abnormal brain chemistry, genetics, traumatic events, or injury to the brain. Treatments include medications and counseling and are used to manage and reduce symptoms.

Anxiety: A broad category used to describe uneasy feelings of dread, apprehension, or danger. Sources of anxiety are often nonspecific or unknown to the individual. Recurrent fears impair the patient's ability to live a normal life. Anxiety can manifest as phobias (fears), social anxiety, obsessive compulsive disorder, or generalized anxiety disorder. Treatments for phobias can include controlled exposure to the cause of fear and counseling to change the response to the stimulus. The patient is taught to relax rather than panic upon exposure. Selective serotonin reuptake inhibitors (SSRIs), in addition to cognitive behavioral therapy, can decrease symptoms of anxiety.

ELEMENT REVIEW
-phobia = fear
arachn/o = spiders
ophidi/o = snakes
acr/o = heights
aer/o = air, flying
agora/o = crowds
mys/o = germs

Obsessive compulsive disorder (OCD): Characterized by recurrent thoughts, ideas, feelings, or actions that cause severe psychological distress or interfere with daily living. Common obsessions include cleaning objects, excessive handwashing, compulsive praying, counting, or making things orderly. Diagnosis is confirmed if distress is observed and time-consuming acts take more than 1 hour per day, or if the illness significantly interferes with daily life. It is estimated that 2% to 2.5% of the population suffer from OCD. Treatment with cognitive behavioral therapy and SSRIs are used to decrease symptoms.

Depression: The category of disorders marked by feelings of sadness, loss of energy, loss of interest in activities, changes in weight, insomnia or oversleeping, feelings of worthlessness, and thoughts of suicide or self-harm. Depression can be caused by trauma; psychological, genetic, or environmental causes; as well as biochemical imbalances in the brain. Onset of depression is often age 15 to 30, with women suffering from depression more often than men. Types of depression include:

Seasonal affective disorder (SAD): Serious mood changes that are characterized by feelings of sadness during winter months when sunlight is decreased. Treatment with vitamin D supplementation and light therapy (also called low laser therapy) can decrease symptoms. It usually lifts during spring and summer but may recur each winter.

Postpartum depression: Experienced by new mothers after the birth of her child. Occurring in 10% to 20% of women, the onset is up to 6 months postpartum. Symptoms are that of depression, along with an inability to care for the newborn. Diagnosis is confirmed by administering a postpartum depression screening scale (PDSS). Treatment with tricyclic antidepressants and serotonin uptake inhibitors, along with counseling, are effective therapies.

Bipolar disorder: A serious mental health condition characterized by episodes of severe depression but also an excessively happy mood, known as mania. It is often diagnosed in late teens or early 20s and is lifelong. If left untreated, it can lead to damaged relationships, poor job and/or school performance, and even suicide. Medications, such as lithium, carbamazepine, or anticonvulsant therapies, and talk therapy are used to balance mood.

Posttraumatic stress disorder (PTSD): The intense psychological distress following a traumatic event such as being the victim of a violent crime, natural disaster, or combat. PTSD can also arise from cumulative trauma such as that experienced by first responders (police officers, paramedics, and firefighters) and victims of long-term abuse. Symptoms include flashbacks to the event or events, avoidance of stimuli associated with the trauma, memory disturbance, antisocial behaviors, insomnia, irritability, increased vigilance, and aggression. Treatment with counseling and antidepressant medications are used to manage symptoms.

Schizophrenia: Characterized by a gross distortion of reality, disturbances of language and communication, and withdrawal from social connections. The patient experiences fragmentation of thought, perception, and emotions. Diagnosis usually occurs in people in their 20s and affects 0.4% to 1.2% of the population. Symptoms include delusions, hallucinations, and disorganized speech. Friends and family will observe inappropriate behavior, dysphoric mood, inability to care for the patient, and social withdrawal. Abnormal neurological findings on MRI or brain scan are observed. Medications to control schizophrenia include haloperidol, clozapine, and risperidone. Medications cause significant side effects, making patient compliance difficult. Many patients self-medicate with drugs and alcohol. It is estimated that one-third of homeless people in the United States suffer from schizophrenia.

Pathology Word-Building Practice

1. Build the Terms

*Using **only** the word parts in the lists, create medical terms for the indicated meanings.*

Prefixes	Combining Forms		Suffixes	
a, an-	arachn/o	encephal/o	-al	-osis
dys-	cephal/o	esthesi/o	-algia	–otomy
epi-	cerebr/o	kinesi/o	-cele	-ology
hemi-	crani/o	mening/o	-gram	–ologist
hydro-	dendr/o	meningi/o	-graphy	–paresis
poly-	dur/o	myel/o	-ia	-pathy
sub-	electric/o	narc/o	-ic	–plegia
quadri-		neur/o	-itis	–phobia
		psych/o	-lepsy	–phoria
			-malacia	-us
			-oma	

1. Inflammation of nerves ______________________
2. Condition of excessive water (fluid) on the head (brain) ______________________
3. Condition of difficult movements ______________________
4. Fear of spiders ______________________
5. Paralysis of all four limbs ______________________
6. The study of the mind ______________________
7. Medical term for a headache ______________________
8. Disease of the brain ______________________
9. Softening of the skull ______________________
10. Pertaining to under the dura mater ______________________
11. Process of recording activity of the brain using electricity ______________________
12. Condition of being without sensation ______________________
13. Attacks of daytime sleepiness ______________________
14. Herniation of the meninges and spinal cord ______________________
15. Pertaining to the dendrites ______________________
16. Incision into the skull ______________________
17. Tumor of the meninges ______________________
18. Condition of partial paralysis of one side of the body ______________________
19. Specialist who treats disease/disorders of the nervous system ______________________
20. Related to the skull and brain ______________________

2. Prefixes

Choose from the list of prefixes to build a word for the definitions below.

a, an-	hemi-	poly-
anti-	hyper-	sub-
epi-	hypo-	quadri-
dys-	para-	

1. Pertaining to next to the spinal cord __________
2. Congenital absence of the brain __________
3. Paralysis of one-half of the body __________
4. Condition of poor muscle tone __________
5. Condition of excessive muscular movements __________
6. Medication to decrease epileptic seizures __________
7. Inflammation of many nerves __________
8. Condition of decreased sensations __________
9. Condition of bad feelings, emotions __________
10. Pertaining to upon or above the dura mater __________

3. Suffixes

Choose from the list of suffixes to build a word for the definitions below.

-algia	-itis	-otomy
-cele	-lepsy	-ology
-cyte	-malacia	-paresis
-ectomy	-oma	-plegia
-gram	-osis	-phoria

1. Pain of nerves __________
2. Softening of the spinal cord __________
3. Good feeling __________
4. Star-shaped neuroglial cell __________
5. Herniation of the brain __________
6. The study of the mental health __________
7. Surgical removal of a nerve __________
8. Electrical recording of brain activity __________
9. Recurrent seizure disorder __________
10. Inflammation of the spinal cord __________

Nervous System Diagnostic Procedures

Procedures to diagnose diseases and disorders of the nervous system may include physical assessment, various imaging procedures, analysis of CSF, electrical or sound recording of brain functions, and sleep studies. Correct diagnosis of nervous system pathologies is necessary to direct treatment and afford the patient the best possible outcome.

Babinski reflex: A procedure that involves stroking the sole of the foot, beginning at the midheel and moving upward and lateral to the toes. A positive Babinski occurs when dorsiflexion of the great toe and fanning of the other toes occurs. A positive reflex in newborns up to age 6 months is normal, and the reflex is abnormal if it is positive in adults or children. A positive reflex may indicate a lesion of the corticospinal tract.

Brain scan: A procedure that involves an intravenous injection of a radioisotope to locate abnormal brain tissue. Normally, the blood-brain barrier would prevent uptake of the isotope into the brain. In some pathological conditions, the integrity of the blood-brain barrier is compromised, and thus the isotopes can accumulate. The brain scan can be used to diagnose acute cerebral infarction, cerebral neoplasms, cerebral thrombosis, cerebral hemorrhage, brain abscess, aneurysms, and metastatic cancer to the brain.

Cerebral angiography: A procedure that uses a radiopaque contrast medium injected into an arterial blood vessel, such as the carotid, femoral, or brachial artery. As the contrast medium flows through the brain, x-rays of the cerebrum are used to obtain pictures of arterial, capillary, and venous abnormalities such as occlusions, aneurysms, hematomas, abscesses, and tumors.

Cerebral spinal fluid analysis: Obtained from a **lumbar puncture**, which is the insertion of a hollow needle into the subarachnoid space between the third and fourth lumbar vertebrae. The procedure can be used to obtain a sample of CSF for analysis to diagnose meningitis or encephalitis, to look for the presence of blood, malignant cells, and quantities of protein and glucose. It can be used to draw off excess CSF and decrease ICP.

CT scan (brain): The use of computed tomography to create a three-dimensional view of the brain. A contrast medium is administered intravenously to help identify a variety of pathologies. CT scans can detect intracranial tumors, bleeding, infarctions, ventricular abnormalities, aneurysms, MS, cysts, fractures, and infections (Fig. 14-15). Patients are advised to have no food, or nothing by mouth (npo), for 4 hours prior to the examination as the contrast dye may cause nausea and vomiting.

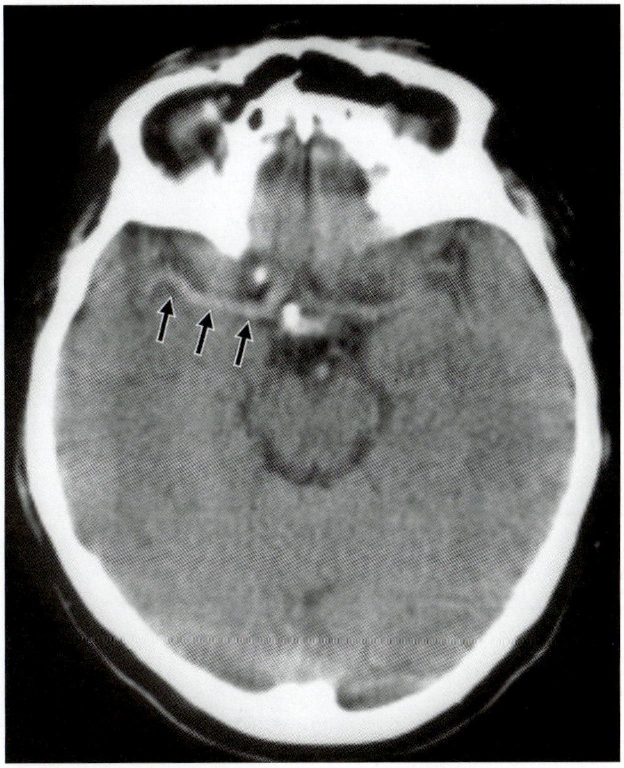

Figure 14-15 CT scan of a stroke.

Echoencephalography: The use of ultrasound to create an image of the brain and analyze its intracranial structures. It is used to diagnose dilation of the ventricles or a shift of the midline structures.

Electroencephalography (EEG): The measurement of electrical activity produced by the brain. Electrodes are applied to the scalp, and recording of the brain activity is translated to a recording device that uses moving paper to create a graph. During the EEG procedure, the patient must remain still. Often the patient is sedated, and the test is performed in a dark, quiet room as the patient falls asleep. A sleep-deprived EEG can be performed after the patient has been awake for 24 hours. The individual should not smoke or consume caffeine for 24 hours prior to the test. Sleep deprivation can increase

EEG abnormalities and help diagnosis of epilepsy, focal damage in the cortex, psychogenic unresponsiveness, and cerebral death.

Magnetic resonance imaging (MRI): Used to diagnose tumors, bleeding, lesions, fractures, and structural abnormalities. The test is not invasive and can be performed on all parts of the body, including the brain. The patient is placed into an electromagnetic tube where radio frequencies are absorbed and the alignment of hydrogen atoms are changed. The absorbed radio frequency is analyzed by a computer generating an image of the structures of the body part. The MRI cannot be used for patients with implanted metal devices as the strong magnetic field will attract the metal, causing injury.

Myelography: The introduction of a contrast medium into the lumbar subarachnoid space to visualize the spinal cord and vertebral canal through x-ray examination. Approximately 10 mL of CSF is removed, and a radiopaque contrast is injected slowly into the subarachnoid space. Care is taken to maintain the pressure of the fluid volume of the CSF. The procedure is conducted on a tilt table to visualize the spinal cord in a variety of positions. The test can help to diagnose adhesions and tumors on the spinal cord or intervertebral disc injuries.

Polysomnography (PSG): Commonly called a sleep study. A PSG is a test used to evaluate the physical factors that affect sleep (Fig. 14-16). Small electrodes are placed on the scalp and the body and attached by flexible wiring to the central monitoring unit. The test is done overnight. A technician monitors the patient while the patient sleeps. Snoring, eye and body movements, respiration, heart rate, and sleep stages are monitored. The test is useful in the diagnosis of sleep apnea, sleepwalking, night terrors, insomnia, narcolepsy, and restless leg syndrome.

Positron emission tomography (PET): A scan that creates radiographic images of various body structures by using an inhaled or injected radioactive marker. The metabolic activity of the brain and other body structures are shown in color and correspond to intensity of metabolic biochemical processes (Fig. 14-17). It is useful in detecting cancer earlier than CT or MRI scans as diseased tissues such as tumors uptake the radiotracer more than healthy

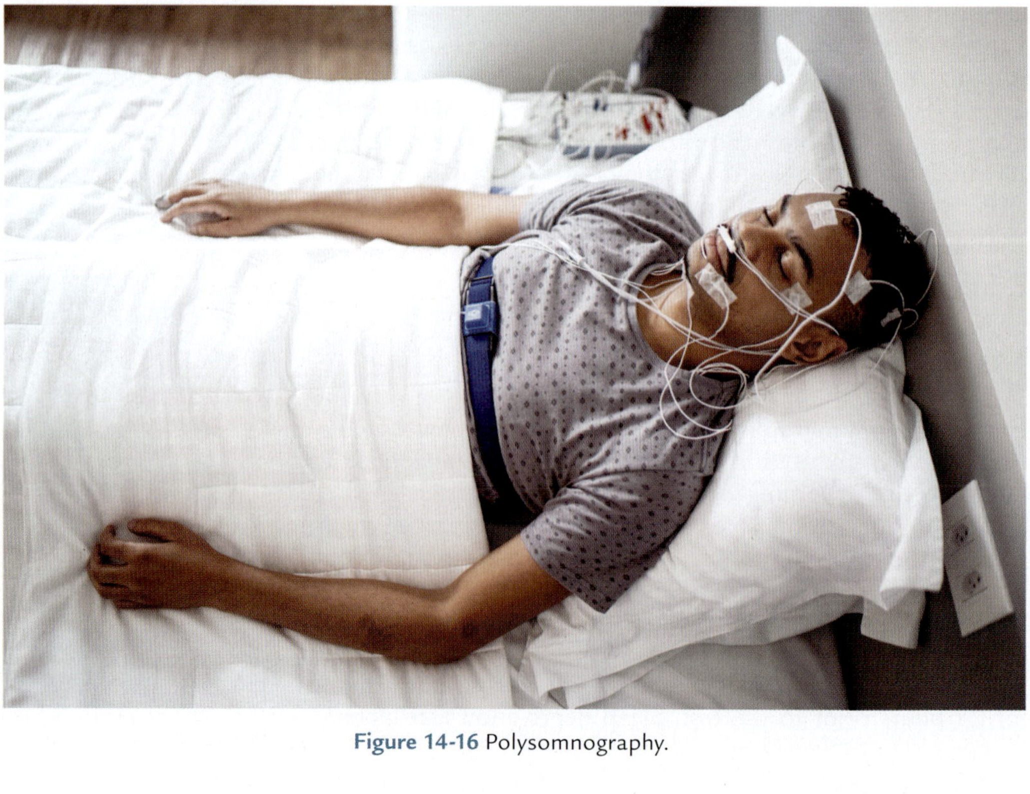

Figure 14-16 Polysomnography.

tissue does. Brain abnormalities caused by cancers, Alzheimer's disease, Parkinson's disease, ADHD, ADD, depression, and substance abuse can be observed. The radioactive markers have a very short half-life, so radiation exposure is minimized.

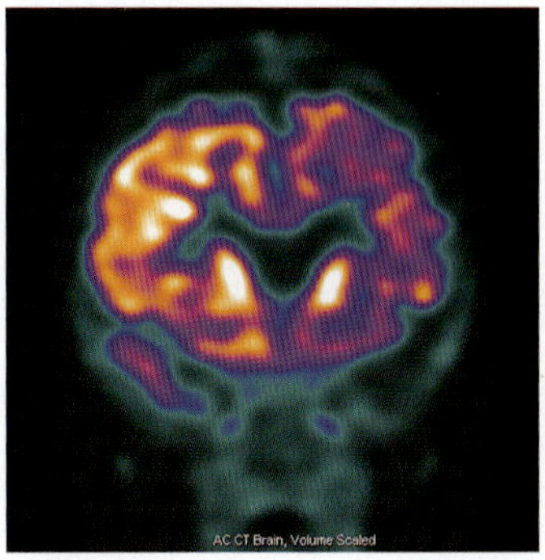

Figure 14-17 PET scan of the brain.

Romberg test: A physical test performed to evaluate cerebellar function. The patient is asked to stand with feet together and hands at their side and attain equilibrium. The patient is asked to close their eyes and maintain equilibrium without swaying or moving. Then the patient is asked to lift their hands to shoulder height without the arms drifting down. If the patient can perform both parts of the evaluation, balance and cerebellar function are considered intact.

Somatosensory evoked potentials (SSEP): Measures the response recorded from the brain, nerve, or spinal cord to electrical stimulation of the peripheral nerve during brain and spinal surgeries.

Tensilon test: Procedure that uses an intravenous administration of the drug Tensilon (edrophonium) to diagnose myasthenia gravis. Confirmation of a diagnosis of myasthenia gravis is obtained if muscular weakness decreases within 60 seconds of administration.

Transcranial electrical motor evoked potentials (TCeMEP): The application of an electrical stimulus to the motor cortex of the brain to record the response from the spinal cord or limb during brain or spinal surgeries.

Nervous System Therapeutic Procedures

Therapeutic procedures for nervous system disorders may include surgeries to relieve pressure on affected nerves, intentional destruction of injured brain cells, craniotomy, or CSF sampling to reduce pressure on the brain and spinal cord, as well as excision of tumors or the use of electrical stimulation to mask the perception of pain. Invasive modalities have risks that must be discussed with the patient to obtain informed consent prior to procedures.

Chordotomy: The disabling of selected pain-conducting tracts of the nervous system that relay sensation from the point of origin to the brain. The procedure is commonly used for patients with cancer or other incurable diseases for permanent pain management.

Cisternal puncture: The insertion of a short, beveled spinal needle into the cisterna magna (the shallow reservoir of CSF between the medulla and the cerebellum). It is used to drain excess CSF or to obtain a sample of CSF for analysis. While post-procedure complications are rare, patients should be observed for cyanosis, dyspnea, or apnea.

Craniotomy: The creation of an opening into the skull. A craniotomy may include creation of a bone flap where one side remains attached and hinged with muscles and other structures to the skull. Alternately, a section of bone may be completely removed from its attachments. A third type of procedure is the creation of a burr hole that allows the brain to be exposed. The purpose of a craniotomy is to access the brain for a surgical procedure or to relieve accumulation of pressure on the brain after an injury. Craniotomy is performed to remove penetrating foreign objects such as bullets. It is used to remove tumors or blood clots or to implant medical devices, such as deep brain stimulators to treat Parkinson's disease, epilepsy, or cerebellar tremor.

Neurectomy: The surgical removal of a small area of a cranial or peripheral nerve to relieve pain. The procedure interrupts the pain signal from the affected body part, preventing the signal from reaching the brain, and thus interferes with the interpretation of pain.

Stereotaxic neurosurgery: The intentional destruction of neurons that control specific functions to create lasting pain relief. Small holes are drilled into the skull, and a probe is used to precisely locate the three-dimensional space. An instrument to destroy the brain tissue is then introduced. Various agents such as heat, cold, and sclerosing (hardening) or corrosive fluids are used to destroy the desired area of the brain. Complications can include postsurgical bleeding or infection.

Sympathectomy: The surgical excision of a portion of the sympathetic division of the autonomic nervous system. It can be used to treat hyperhidrosis (excessive sweating) of the palms or feet. It can be used to treat Raynaud's phenomena or chronic pain. It may include excision of a nerve, plexus, ganglion, or a series of ganglia of the sympathetic trunk based on the intended outcome.

Tractotomy: A surgical division of spinal tracts or portions of nerves of the anterolateral pathway in the brainstem. It is performed to relieve pain without unduly decreasing pressure sensitivity.

Transcutaneous electrical nerve stimulation (TENS): The administration of a low-voltage electric current to provide pain relief. The electrodes are placed on or near the nerves where the pain is located or at trigger points. The electrical current stimulates nerve cells that block the transmission of pain signals. The device is also thought to release endorphins, the body's natural pain-killing chemicals. The device can be worn by the patient, and the intensity of the electrical stimulation can be adjusted to the patient's comfort.

CAREER EXPLORATION: CERTIFIED NEUROPHYSIOLOGIC INTRAOPERATIVE MONITOR

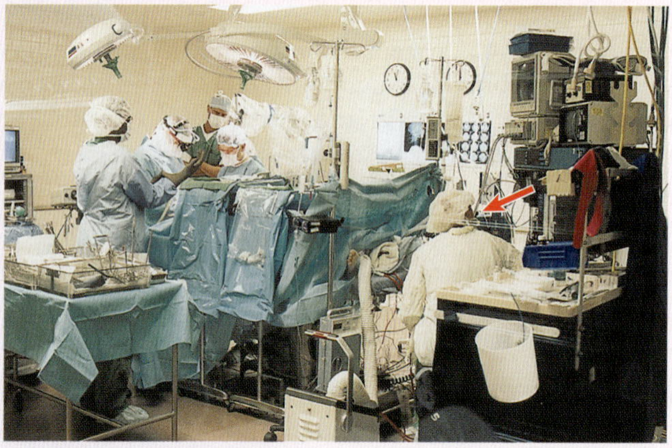

After graduating from high school, I wasn't sure what I wanted to do. But I have always loved science, so I decided to go to college and earned a bachelor's degree in biology. Upon graduation, I thought I would work in a laboratory. During my senior year in college, my cousin Alicia had brain surgery. Alicia was always active and was my fun older cousin; I couldn't believe she had a brain tumor. I visited her when she was home recovering, and she told me about going into surgery. There were so many people in the operating room. Her surgeon is a neurosurgeon, but there were surgical nurses, an anesthesiologist, an otorhinolaryngologist, and an intraoperative neurophysiologist who monitored Alicia's brain during the surgery. Alicia and I looked online to see what intraoperative neurophysiology monitoring (IONM) is and what the technician is responsible for during the surgery. The neurophysiologist, also called a certified neurophysiologic intraoperative monitor (CNIM), performs testing and monitoring of the nervous system during surgery and alerts the surgeon to changes that could result in complications. Continuous monitoring can assist the surgeon in avoiding or reducing complications such as paralysis, hearing loss, or a stroke. The surgical neurophysiologist provides the surgeon information that can direct intraoperative decision-making. I was intrigued by

CAREER EXPLORATION: CERTIFIED NEUROPHYSIOLOGIC INTRAOPERATIVE MONITOR—cont'd

the technology and how it can be used to assist in brain surgery. I investigated hospitals that offer the training and certification program, and I was happy to learn that my bachelors of science degree in biology was the prerequisite for the program. I applied and was accepted to the program. During my training, I learned how to use a variety of modalities in the operating room.

- Somatosensory evoked potentials (SSEP) measures the response recorded from the brain, nerve, or spinal cord to electrical stimulation of the peripheral nerve. We use this in spinal and brain surgeries to monitor the integrity of the sensory nerves.
- We also use a TCeMEP, a transcranial electrical motor evoked potentials device that applies an electrical stimulus to the motor cortex of the brain and records the response from the spinal cord or limb. It works like the SSEP but in the opposite direction, monitoring motor tracts of the spinal cord.
- We also use electroencephalography (EEG) to record brain activity and to avoid injuries caused by ischemia (reduced blood flow) during carotid endarterectomies and aneurysm clipping.

After completing 150 surgical monitoring cases, I became eligible to take the certification examination in neurophysiologic intraoperative monitoring from ABRET. With a lot of studying and prep time, I passed the certification exam, and now I am a CNIM. Every brain or spinal cord surgery must have a CNIM monitoring the patient's nervous system and communicating with the surgeon. After graduation, I got a full-time job at the local hospital and enjoy working with the surgeons and the staff. Technology is constantly changing, so the hospital encourages CNIMs to attend continuing education seminars. The hospital even pays for my continuing education. I love working in the operating room and then seeing the patients recover. Like my cousin Alicia, so many patients can return to a healthy life. I am proud to be part of the team that restores their health.

Procedures and Diagnostics Review

Name the procedure:

1. Disabling of pain-conduction tracts ______________________
2. Electricity applied to the skin used for pain relief ______________________
3. Three-dimensional brain mapping used to guide destruction of specific neurons ______________________
4. Surgical procedure to decrease pain, which can include excision of a nerve, plexus, or ganglia based on the desired effect ______________________
5. Surgical procedure to divide portions of nerves of the anterolateral pathway in the brainstem ______________________
6. Injection of radiopaque contrast medium into an artery to view abnormalities of the brain ______________________

7. This procedure is commonly called a sleep study ____________________

8. A test that quantifies metabolic activity of the brain or other body structures, useful in the early diagnosis of cancerous tumors ____________________

9. A part of a physical examination used to evaluate cerebellar function ____________________

10. Can be used to diagnose meningitis or encephalitis. ____________________

CASE STUDY, completed

Alicia has the surgery and wakes up in the recovery room. She feels well, but her nose is packed with a postsurgical packing. The recovery room nurse tells Alicia she will need to keep the packing in for 2 to 3 days. She is transferred to a step-down unit later that day, and Christina is allowed to visit. Dr. Singh meets with Alicia and Christina and explains that the surgery went well. The tumor was approximately the size of a golf ball and was sectioned and removed through her nose. The sections were sent to pathology and found to be benign. Alicia and Christina are so relieved. Christina asks, "When can I take Alicia home, and what are her restrictions?" Dr Singh explains, "I will discharge Alicia tomorrow so the nurses can monitor her vitals and her pain medication overnight. Alicia, you can return to light-duty work next week, but no heavy lifting for a few weeks. Please don't ride your bicycle or lift weights. Let's give your nose a chance to heal and prevent an injury." Alicia says, "Okay. I guess I can watch movies and relax. I want to stop the pain meds as soon as possible; I hate feeling groggy, and I will feel more comfortable at home." Dr. Singh replies, "I'm glad you are anxious to go home, but let's give it 24 hours to be sure. I want to see you again in the office in 4 weeks to see how you're doing. Additionally, I will want to schedule a follow-up MRI to make sure there is no tumor regrowth." Alicia says "Okay. Thanks Dr. Singh."

CRITICAL-THINKING QUESTIONS

Answer the questions with the correct medical term.

1. What signs did Alicia experience prior to her surgery? ____________________

2. What symptoms did Alicia complain of? ____________________

3. Irritation of Alicia's olfactory nerve caused which symptom? ____________________

4. Dr. Singh performs Alicia's surgery through her nose. The procedure is called EEA, which stands for ____________________.

5. Before the EEA procedure was perfected, surgeons would perform the surgery through the skull. The medical term is ____________________.

6. After surgery, the tumor sections were sent for analysis in what department of the hospital? ____________________

7. Alicia's tumor was assessed and found to be noncancerous. The medical term is ____________________.

CASE STUDY, completed

8. If the tumor was cancerous, the medical term would be ______________________.

9. The tumor affected the covering of the spinal cord at the base of the brain. The medical term for this tumor is ______________________.

10. In the OR, many professionals helped Dr. Singh during the surgery. The physician that is an ear, nose, and throat specialist is called a/an ______________________.

Medications for the Nervous System

Table 14-6 lists common medications for the nervous system that help to control pain, anxiety, depression, mania, insomnia, convulsions, and schizophrenia.

TABLE 14-6 Medications of the Nervous System

Classification	Examples	Common Use/Action
Acetaminophen	Acetaminophen (Tylenol)	Pain, fever
Adrenergics	Norepinephrine, epinephrine	Hypotension, severe wheezing, allergic reactions, anaphylaxis
Adrenergic blockers	Tamsulosin (Flomax), atenolol (Tenormin)	Benign prostatic hypertension, hypertension, cardiac arrythmia, preventing myocardial infarction (MI), migraine headache
Anesthetics (local)	Lidocaine (Xylocaine), prilocaine, benzocaine	Minor surgical procedures, pain, itch relief
Anesthetics (general)	Midazolam, Versed, propofol (Diprivan), ketamine	Sedation for minor to major surgical procedures
Anticholinergics	Atropine (Atro-pen)	Bladder, stomach or intestinal spasms, poisoning
Antiparkinsonian drugs	Ropinole (Requip), selegiline (Eldepryl), carbidopa/levodopa (Sinemet)	Parkinson's disease, acromegaly
Antipsychotics	Clozapine (Clozaril), chlorpromazine (Thorazine)	Schizophrenia, bipolar disorder, severe behavioral disorders in children, nausea, vomiting, severe hiccups
Antiseizure meds	Phenytoin (Dilantin), phenobarbital (Luminal), levetiracetam (Keppra), diazepam (Valium)	Epileptic seizures, nerve pain, anxiety, muscle spasms, alcohol withdrawal
Anxiolytics	Alprazolam (Xanax), diazepam (Valium), lorazepam (Ativan)	Anxiety disorders, panic disorders, alcohol withdrawal, muscle spasms
Barbiturates	Secobarbital (Seconal), pentobarbital (Nembutal)	Insomnia, preoperative sedation, seizures
Cholinergics	Pilocarpine (Salagen), Pilopine, donepezil (Aricept)	Glaucoma, ocular hypertension, dementia associated with Alzheimer's

Continued

TABLE 14-6 Medications of the Nervous System—cont'd

Classification	Examples	Common Use/Action
CNS stimulants	Methylphenidate (Concerta, Ritalin), dextroamphetamine (Adderall)	ADD, ADHD, narcolepsy, obesity
Lithium	Lithium citrate	Bipolar disorder, manic depressive disorder
Monoamine oxidase inhibitors (MAOIs)	Selegiline (Eldepryl)	Parkinson's disease
NSAIDs	Ibuprofen (Advil, Motrin)	Pain, fever, inflammation
Non-narcotic benzodiazepines	Zolpidem (Ambien), eszopiclone (Lunesta)	Insomnia
Opioid analgesics	Morphine, meperidine (Demerol), hydromorphone (Dilaudid), fentanyl (Actiq)	Moderate to severe pain
Salicylates	Aspirin	Pain, fever, inflammation, prevent MI or stroke
Selective serotonin reuptake inhibitors (SSRIs)	Fluoxetine (Prozac), sertraline (Zoloft), paroxetine (Paxil), citalopram (Celexa), escitalopram (Lexapro)	Depression, panic disorders, OCD, bulimia, anxiety disorders, PTSD, PMDD
Selective norepinephrine reuptake inhibitors (SNRIs)	Desvenlafaxine (Pristiq), duloxetine (Cymbalta), venlafaxine (Effexor)	Depression
Tricyclic antidepressants	doxepin hydrochloride (Sinequan), imipramine (Trofranil), nortriptyline (Aventyl HCL)	Depression

Medications Review

Using the table of medications, complete the chart below. The first one has been done for you.

Medication Name	Classification (mechanism)	Therapeutic Use (What is it used for?)
Versed	*General anesthetic*	*Sedation for surgery*
1. Paxil	____________	____________
2. Aspirin	____________	____________
3. Flomax	____________	____________
4. Demerol	____________	____________
5. Ambien	____________	____________
6. Ritalin	____________	____________
7. Cymbalta	____________	____________
8. Trofranil	____________	____________
9. Thorazine	____________	____________
10. Aricept	____________	____________

Nervous System Abbreviations

ADD attention deficit disorder

ADHD attention deficit-hyperactivity disorder

ALS amyotrophic lateral sclerosis

CAT computerized axial tomography

CNS central nervous system

CSF cerebrospinal fluid

CT computed tomography

CRPS complex regional pain syndrome

CVA cerebral vascular accident

ECT electroconvulsive therapy

EEG electroencephalogram

EMG electromyography

ICP intracranial pressure

LOC loss of consciousness

LP lumbar puncture

MRI magnetic resonance imaging

MS multiple sclerosis

NCS nerve conduction study

NREM non-rapid eye movement

OCD obsessive compulsive disorder

PET positron emission tomography

PNS peripheral nervous system

PSG polysomnogram

PTSD posttraumatic stress disorder

REM rapid eye movement

RT reading test

SAD seasonal affective disorder

SNS somatic nervous system

SNRI selective norepinephrine reuptake inhibitor

SSEP Somatosensory evoked potentials

SSRI Selective serotonin reuptake inhibitor

TENS transcutaneous electrical nerve stimulation

TIA transient ischemic attack

TCeMEP Transcranial electrical motor evoked potentials

Abbreviations Review

Choose the correct definition for each of the abbreviations listed.

1. TENS
   a. Transdermal electrical nerve stimulation
   b. Transdural electrical nerve stimulation
   c. Transcutaneous electrical nerve stimulation
   d. Transaxial electrical nerve stimulation

2. PNS
   a. Peripheral nervous system
   b. Parasympathetic nervous system
   c. Perineual symptoms
   d. Peripheral nervous symptoms

3. ALS
   a. Amyloid lateral sclerosis
   b. Amyloid leukocyte scarring
   c. Amyotrophic lateral sclerosis
   d. Amyotrophic leukocyte sclerosis

4. NCS
   a. Nerve conduction study
   b. Neurocognitive study
   c. Neurocognitive scale
   d. Nerve conduction scale

5. ADD
   a. Attention detail disorder
   b. Attention deficit diagnosis
   c. Attention deficit disorder
   d. Attention detail diagnosis

6. MRI
   a. Magnesium radiation imaging
   b. Magnetic radiation imaging
   c. Magnesium resonance imaging
   d. Magnetic resonance imaging

7. LOC
   a. Loss of consciousness
   b. Lack of consciousness
   c. Lack of compassion
   d. Level of compassion

8. CVA
   a. Coronal vascular assessment
   b. Cerebral vascular assessment
   c. Cerebral vascular accident
   d. Coronary vascular accident

9. PET
   a. Positron emission tomography
   b. Positive emission tomography
   c. Positron electromyography
   d. Positive electromyography

10. PSG
   a. Polysomnogram
   b. Parasonmogram
   c. Perisomnogram
   d. Peripheral somnogram

11. CSF
   a. Coronary spinal fluid
   b. Calcium spinal fluid
   c. Cerebrospinal fluid
   d. Cerebrospinal function

12. ICP
   a. Intracranial pressure
   b. Intercranial pressure
   c. Intracerebral pressure
   d. Intercerebral pressure

13. EEG
   a. Electroendocrine graphing
   b. Electroencephalographing
   c. Electroencephalogram
   d. Electroendogram

14. ADHD
   a. Attention deficit-hyperactivity disorder
   b. Attention deficit-hypoactivity disorder
   c. Attention deficit hyperactivity diagnosis
   d. Attention deficit-hypoactivity diagnosis

15. REM
   a. Raised eye movement
   b. Repeated eye movement
   c. Rapid eye movement
   d. Resulting eye movement

MEDICAL DOCUMENTATION

Knowledge of terms related to normal anatomy and pathological conditions enables you to understand medical documentation, such as the consultation that follows, or history and physical examinations, operative reports, discharge summaries, laboratory reports, and x-ray reports. Apply your knowledge by answering the questions that follow the report.

Encephalopathy Consultation

Patient: Hazel M.

History of Present Illness: This is an 83-year-old female with a history of osteoporosis who was recently diagnosed with a seizure disorder. She fell at home, and x-rays revealed lumbar compression fractures and osteopenia. No head injury was noted from the fall. She is acutely confused, and the patient's medical history is obtained from her daughter.

The patient was recently admitted to the hospital for right-sided weakness. She had a generalized seizure on hospital day two and was treated with Dilantin. She remains in the hospital as social services looks for nursing home placement. Over the 24 hours after admission, she has become progressively disoriented to time and place. She is having difficulty sleeping at night. At present she denies pain or headache. She denies weakness but is unwilling to ambulate and refuses physical therapy.

MEDICAL DOCUMENTATION—cont'd

Past medical history:

1. Osteoarthritis
2. Recent questionable transient ischemic attack
3. Seizure disorder recently diagnosed
4. Lumbar compression fracture

Medications: Protonix, Dilantin 100 mg daily, Reglan, Darvocet, Lovenox

Allergies: Penicillin

Social history: The patient is widowed and lives with her daughter and son-in-law. The patient's daughter reports a progressive decline in cognitive functions and activities of daily life. The patient can no longer dress or bathe herself, and her communication has dramatically declined.

Physical Examination: The patient is an elderly female in no acute distress. Temp 97.2°, pulse 80 and regular, respirations 20, and blood pressure 152/74. Head and neck are normocephalic, atraumatic. Oropharynx reveals moist mucosa. Nasopharynx is benign. Neck is supple, with no adenopathy. Chest is clear to auscultation. Heart rate is regular, normal S1 and S2. No murmurs, rubs, or gallops. Abdomen is soft, nontender, and bowel sounds are present. Extremities reveal no cyanosis, clubbing, or edema. Neurological examination reveals patient to be awake but disoriented to place and time. Upon repeated questioning, the patient could not state the year or month. The patient could repeat 3/3 objects but could not recall 3/3 objects. She was unable to perform serial 7s. Cranial nerves are intact. The patient is unable to walk, gait assessment is deferred.

Laboratory Data: WBC is 10.4, hemoglobin 10.2, hematocrit 28.9, platelets 220. Diff WNL, ESR 24, blood glucose 101. Urinalysis reveals 2+ blood, 1+ ketones, 3+ leukocytes, and many bacteria. Urine culture and sensitivity reveals 100,000 streptococci and less than 20,000 mixed flora.

Diagnostic Imaging: Head CT negative for pathology or skull fracture.

Assessment:

1. Encephalopathy consistent with decompensated dementia and urinary tract infection
2. Cognitive decline by history and physical examination
3. Seizure disorder secondary above
4. Gait disorder
5. History of lumbar compression fracture

Recommendations:

1. Physical therapy for gait training with assistive device
2. Antibiotic for UTI
3. Social service placement to residential facility

Electronically signed
Michelle Traynor. MD
Neurology

Questions

1. Hazel does not have any disease of her glands. Which word in the document refers to this? ______________________
2. What does UTI stand for? ______________________

Continued

MEDICAL DOCUMENTATION—cont'd

3. Which word in the document means a disease of the brain? ____________________
4. Hazel does not have any abnormal discoloration to her extremities. What word in the document refers to this? ____________________
5. From what common disorder of "holes in the bones" does Hazel suffer? ____________________
6. Which word in the document means the head is normal? ____________________
7. Hazel had a previous TIA, which stands for what? ____________________
8. Hazel suffers from inflammation of the bone joints, which is known as what? ____________________
9. Leukocytes are found in Hazel's urine; what type of cells are they? ____________________
10. Break down the word hemoglobin into its components ____________________

mll Medical Language Lab

Visit the Medical Language Lab at medicallanguagelab.com. Use it to improve your recognition and understanding of terms in medical documentation.

CHAPTER REVIEW

Identify the Term

Complete the sentence.

1. The basic unit of the nervous system is a ____________________.
2. The space between two nerves over which impulses must cross is ____________________.
3. The fatty insulation that covers some axons is ____________________.
4. Nerves that transmit impulses from the brain to the body are called ____________________.
5. Nerves that transmit impulses from the body to the brain are called ____________________.
6. Voluntary control is governed by which section of the peripheral nervous system? ____________________.
7. Sympathetic and parasympathetic nerves are both part of the ____________________.

8. Axons that are not covered in myelin sheath are ______________________________.

9. The brain and spinal cord are covered by a protective membrane called the ______________________________.

10. The lowest part of the brainstem is the ______________________________.

11. Supporting cells of the nervous system are called ______________________________.

12. Disease of irregular electrical activity of the brain, resulting in seizures, is ______________________________.

13. An inherited neurological disease characterized by rapid, jerky, involuntary movements is ______________________________.

14. Uncontrolled attacks of daytime sleepiness is ______________________________.

15. Degenerative disease of demyelination of nerves of the CNS is ______________________________.

16. Unilateral pain along the 5th cranial nerve is called ______________________________.

17. Surgical procedure to make an opening in the skull is called ______________________________.

18. Visualization of cerebral vascular system using x-ray and radiopaque contrast medium is called ______________________________.

19. Scan that measures metabolic activity of the brain or other structures that is helpful in diagnosing cancer is ______________________________.

20. Progressive deterioration of intellectual function that progresses in stages is ______________________________.

Spelling Review

Circle the word that is spelled correctly.

1. peduncle	pudencle
2. meningeoma	meningioma
3. neuroglia	nueroglia
4. periferal	peripheral
5. encephalopathy	encephalopothy
6. neurovascular	neuravascular

7. subarachnoid   subarchnoid

8. automonic   autonomic

9. corpus callosum   corpus callosem

10. schizophrenia   schizophenia

Abbreviations Review

Define the following abbreviations:

1. RT ____________________
2. CT ____________________
3. ECT ____________________
4. MS ____________________
5. TIA ____________________
6. EMG ____________________
7. CNS ____________________
8. NREM ____________________
9. SNS ____________________
10. LP ____________________

Identify the Anatomical Structures

Match the structures of the nerve cell from the following lists to the letters shown in Figure 14-18.

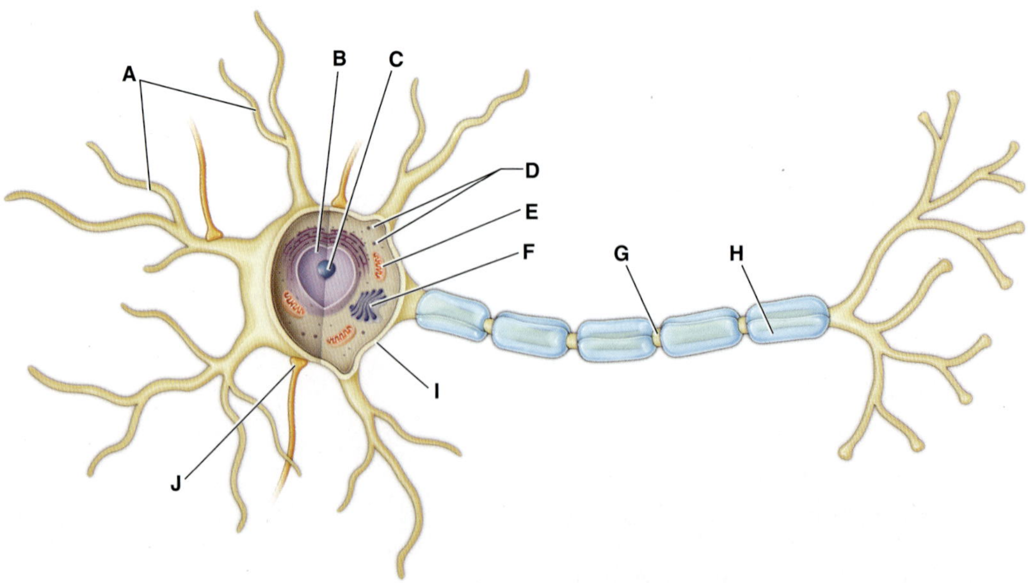

Figure 14-18 Identify the structures of the nerve cell.

1. _______ axon
2. _______ cell membranes
3. _______ dendrites
4. _______ Golgi apparatus
5. _______ microtubule
6. _______ mitochondria
7. _______ mitochondrion
8. _______ myelin sheath
9. _______ node of Ranvier
10. _______ nucleolus
11. _______ nucleus
12. _______ receptors
13. _______ ribosome
14. _______ rough ER
15. _______ smooth ER
16. _______ synapse

Match the structures of the brain from the following lists to the letters shown in Figure 14-19.

1. _______ Cerebellum
2. _______ Cerebrum and cerebral cortex
3. _______ Corpus callosum
4. _______ Diencephalon
5. _______ Hypothalamus
6. _______ Medulla oblongata
7. _______ Midbrain
8. _______ Pineal body
9. _______ Pituitary gland
10. _______ Pons
11. _______ Thalamus

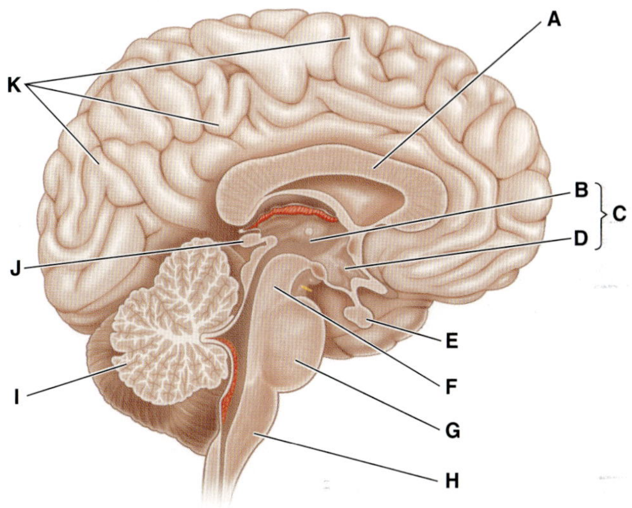

Figure 14-19 Identify the structures of the brain.

Word-Building Exercise

Create a word to fit the definition.

1. Surgical removal of specific nerves of the sympathetic nervous system _______________
2. Process of destruction of the myelin sheath _______________
3. Paralysis of all four limbs _______________
4. Congenital absence of the brain _______________
5. Electrical recording of brain activity _______________
6. Process of recording brain activity with ultrasound _______________
7. Pertaining to the brain and spinal cord _______________
8. Pertaining to above the dura mater _______________
9. Pertaining to the brain and blood vessels _______________

10. Condition of increased fluid in the ventricles of the brain ____________________

11. Condition of a herniation of the meninges and spinal cord ____________________

12. Pain in a nerve ____________________

13. Process of recording the spinal cord ____________________

14. A star-shaped brain tumor ____________________

15. Condition of slowed body movements ____________________

16. Medical term for a headache ____________________

17. Loss of muscle strength and sensation ____________________

18. Condition of poor muscle tone ____________________

19. Pertaining to within the skull ____________________

20. Surgical removal of the bony arch of a vertebra ____________________

CHAPTER

15

The Special Senses

LEARNING OBJECTIVES

Upon completion of the chapter, you will be able to:

1. Identify and define the combining forms, roots, prefixes, and suffixes introduced in the chapter.
2. Spell medical terms related to the eyes and ears.
3. Describe the visual pathway from the eyes to the brain.
4. Describe the hearing pathway from the ears to the brain.
5. Describe the organs of taste and smell and transmission of these sensations to the brain for interpretation.
6. Describe static and dynamic equilibrium and the inner ear structures that control balance.
7. Identify and discuss major pathological terms of the eyes and ears.
8. Identify and discuss major diagnostic and therapeutic treatments of the eyes and ears.
9. Identify the major categories of medications used to treat pathologies of eyes and ears.
10. Define abbreviations of the eyes and ears.

We begin this chapter with the story of Taay, who lost her hearing as a young child. The case study will introduce some of the medical terms relevant to the auditory system. Throughout the chapter, we will revisit the story of Taay to understand her hearing loss and what treatment options are available to her to restore her hearing. You will gain understanding of the organs responsible for hearing and how hearing aids and surgical implants can improve the function of damaged auditory structures. Additionally, this chapter explores the sense of vision and the structures that transmit visual signals from the eyes to the brain for interpretation as sight. Corrective lens, both glasses and contact lenses, will be discussed. This chapter also explores the senses of smell and taste and the organs responsible for these sensations. After reading this chapter, you will understand how vision and hearing are transmitted from the eyes and ears, respectively, to the brain for interpretation. Common pathological conditions affecting vision, hearing, taste, and smell will be explored. You will be able to use word elements presented to understand unfamiliar terms and to build your medical vocabulary.

CASE STUDY

Taay is a 12-year-old sixth grader who has been deaf since the age of 5 years. Born prematurely, Taay had multiple middle ear infections and was prescribed many rounds of antibiotics. Because she had multiple infections, a variety of antibiotics were required to combat the recurrent infections. As a side effect of increasingly stronger antibiotic therapy, Taay's hearing was damaged. She was evaluated by an audiologist and found to be profoundly deaf in her right ear and had lost 80% of her hearing in the left ear. She was fitted with a hearing aid for the left ear but learned sign language and lip reading to be able to communicate with her family and in school. While Taay has learned to communicate and does well in school and sports, she and her parents are interested in a cochlear implant, a device that will enable her to hear. Taay and her parents meet with Dr. Wysenski, an otolaryngologist who specializes in restoring hearing. The medical assistant in Dr. Wysenski's office plays a captioned video presentation that gives Taay and her parents information about the implant and the surgery. The presentation discusses the components of the implant (Fig. 15-1):

1. A microphone designed to pick up sound from the environment.
2. A speech processor, which selects and arranges sound picked up by the microphone.
3. A transmitter and receiver/stimulator that converts the sound into electric impulses.
4. An electrode array, which is a group of electrodes that collect the impulses from the stimulator and send them to the auditory nerve.

The presentation explains that cochlear implants work differently than hearing aids because the components bypass damaged parts of the ear and directly stimulate the auditory nerve. Once implanted, Taay will have to relearn how to hear and to differentiate speech and other sounds in the environment. After viewing the presentation, Dr. Wysenski talked with the family about the surgery with the help of an interpreter who used sign language to make sure Taay understands the steps in the surgery. Taay and her parents agree to the surgery, and Taay is scheduled for the procedure.

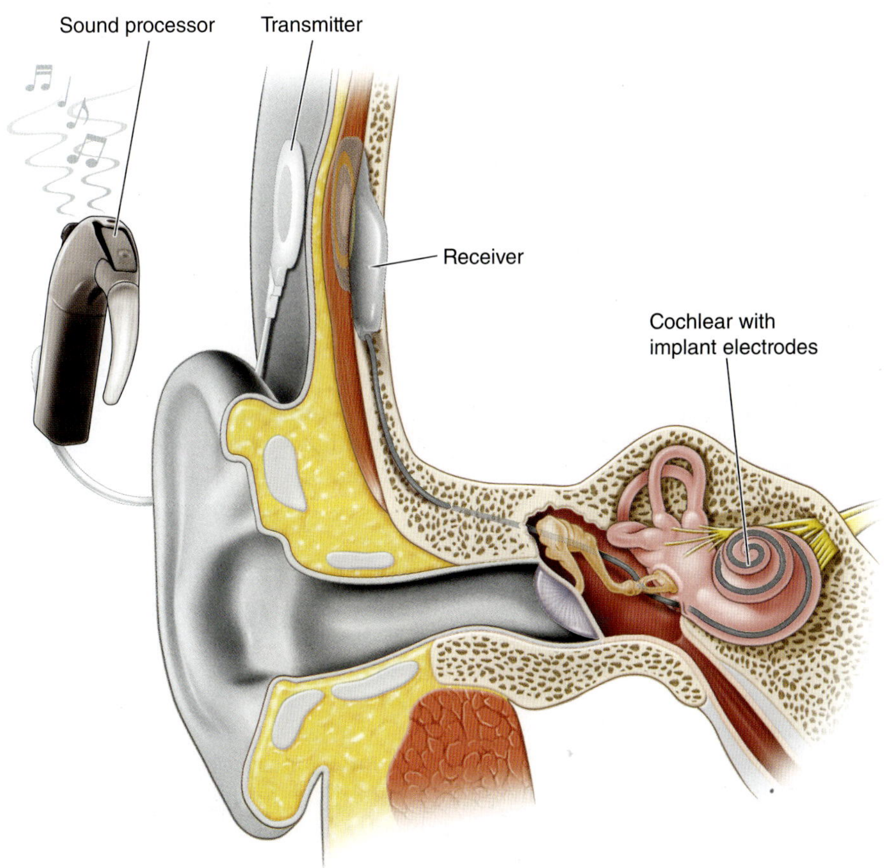

Figure 15-1 The components of a cochlear implant.

KEY TERMS

Accommodation	Endolymph	Macula lutea	Round window
Anterior chamber	Equilibrium	Malleus	Saccule
Aqueous humor	Eustachian tube	Olfaction	Sclera
Auditory nerve	External auditory canal	Optic disc	Semicircular canals
Auricle	Fovea centralis	Organ of Corti	Stapes
Canal of Schlemm	Gustation	Oval window	Suspensory ligaments
Cerumen	Incus	Papillae	Tunics
Choroid	Iris	Perilymph	Tympanic membrane
Ciliary body	Labyrinth	Photoreceptors	Utricle
Cochlea	Lacrimal apparatus	Posterior chamber	Vestibule
Conjunctiva	Lacrimal gland	Pupil	Vision
Cornea	Lens	Retina	Vitreous humor

Structures and Physiology

The special senses are detected by specialized receptors designed to respond to one type of stimuli. These receptors are located in organs of the body such as the eyes, ears, tongue, and nose, but the interpretation of the input occurs in our brains. Thus, the special senses are connected to the nervous system; without such interpretation by the brain, the senses of sight, hearing, equilibrium, taste, and smell would not occur.

The organs responsible for sight are the eyes, the optic nerve, and the visual center of the brain where vision is interpreted.

The organs responsible for hearing and balance are the ears, the auditory nerve, and the brain where sensations of sound and balance are interpreted.

The organs responsible for taste and smell are the tongue and the nose, which contain the gustatory and olfactory nerves that transmit the senses of taste and smell to the brain.

Vision

The sense of sight or **vision** is the most complex sensory system in the body. The **photoreceptors**, the structures that detect light, lie within the eyeball. The eyeball is a complex structure that controls the amount of light to the brain, which will then be interpreted as vision (Fig. 15-2). In addition to the eyeballs, accessory structures protect, move, and lubricate the eyeball. The accessory structures of the eye include the eyelids, lacrimal apparatus, and the external musculature of the eyes.

The eye is a spherical structure measuring approximately 2.5 centimeters (1 inch) in diameter. The wall of the eyeball is comprised of three layers, called **tunics**. The outermost fibrous tunic contains the posterior sclera and the anterior cornea. The **sclera** is a white fibrous connective tissue that can be seen as the "white of the eyes." It provides shape to the eyeball sphere and protects the inner portion of the eye. It is highly vascular, containing many blood vessels, and thus appears red if it is irritated. The posterior surface of the sclera connects to the optic nerve. The **cornea** is the anterior aspect of the tunic where light enters the eye. It is transparent, allowing light to enter, due to the regular arrangement of protein fibers and lack of blood vessels. Lying directly underneath the fibrous tunic is the vascular tunic. As its name suggests, the vascular tunic has an abundance of blood vessels that supply nourishment to all parts of the eye. The vascular tunic contains the choroid, ciliary body, iris, and lens.

ELEMENT REVIEW
vascul/o = blood vessels
-ar = pertaining to

The **choroid** is a thin, dark blue vascular membrane attached to the inner surface of the sclera on the posterior aspect of the eye. Its dark pigment absorbs light rays, minimizing the amount of reflection of light to the retina. This is an important function as too much reflected light would distort the image projected to the retina. Anterior to the choroid, the vascular tunic also contains the **ciliary body**, the thickest part of the tunic. The ciliary

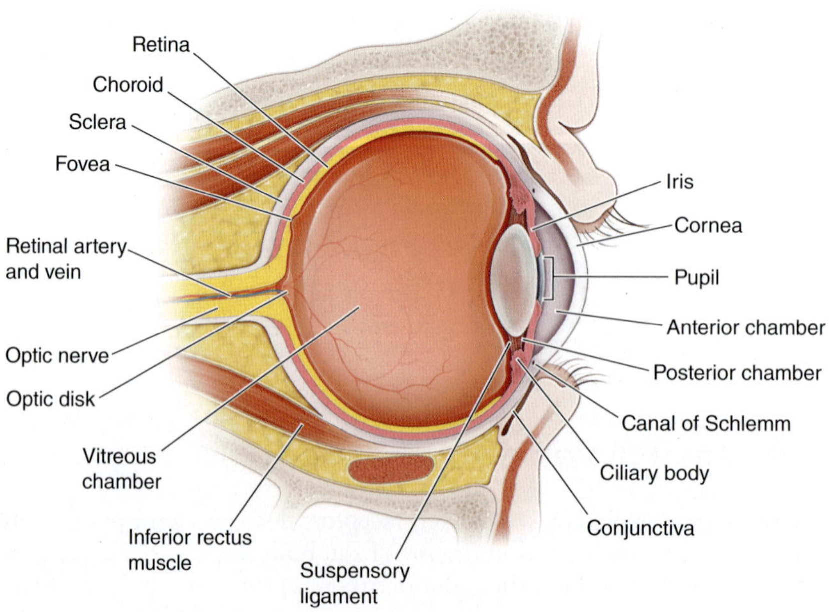

Figure 15-2 The structures of the eye.

body (also called the ciliary muscle) is composed of smooth muscle fibers that connect to the lens by **suspensory ligaments** arranged in a circle around the iris. The function of the ciliary body is to accommodate focal length to see near or far (Fig. 15-3). When the eyes focus on distant objects, the ciliary body relaxes, causing an increased tension on the suspensory ligaments, which causes the lens to flatten. Conversely, to see near objects, the ciliary body contracts, the tension on the suspensory ligaments decreases and the lens becomes more spherical.

The **iris** is the opaque pigmented portion of the eye comprised of smooth muscle that surrounds the pupil. The iris gives the eye its color and gets its name from the Greek word *iris*, meaning goddess of the rainbow. The iris is suspended between the cornea and the lens and controls the amount of light that enters the eye. The muscles of the iris work in opposition; one iris muscle constricts the pupil in bright light, and the other iris muscle dilates the pupil in dim light. The **pupil**, where light enters, is in the center of the iris and appears as the visible black spot in the center of the eye. The **lens** is the transparent structure that sits directly behind the pupil and iris and is composed of interlocking strands of cytoplasm that originate from epithelial cells. The location of the lens creates a separation of the anterior and posterior compartments of the eye. The anterior compartment is divided into two chambers: The **anterior chamber** is located between the cornea and the iris, and the **posterior chamber** is located between the iris and the lens. The two chambers contain a clear, watery fluid called **aqueous humor** that circulates and is continuously recycled by the bloodstream. Fluid pressure is controlled by an expanded vein called the **canal of Schlemm**, which drains excess fluid if pressure increases. The quantity of the fluid and thus the pressure of the fluid within the eyeball is maintained by a homeostatic mechanism. The intraocular pressure exerted by the aqueous humor can be measured in an eye examination. The posterior compartment behind the lens contains a gel-like, thick fluid called **vitreous humor**. The gel is composed of water, collagen fibrils, sugars, electrolytes,

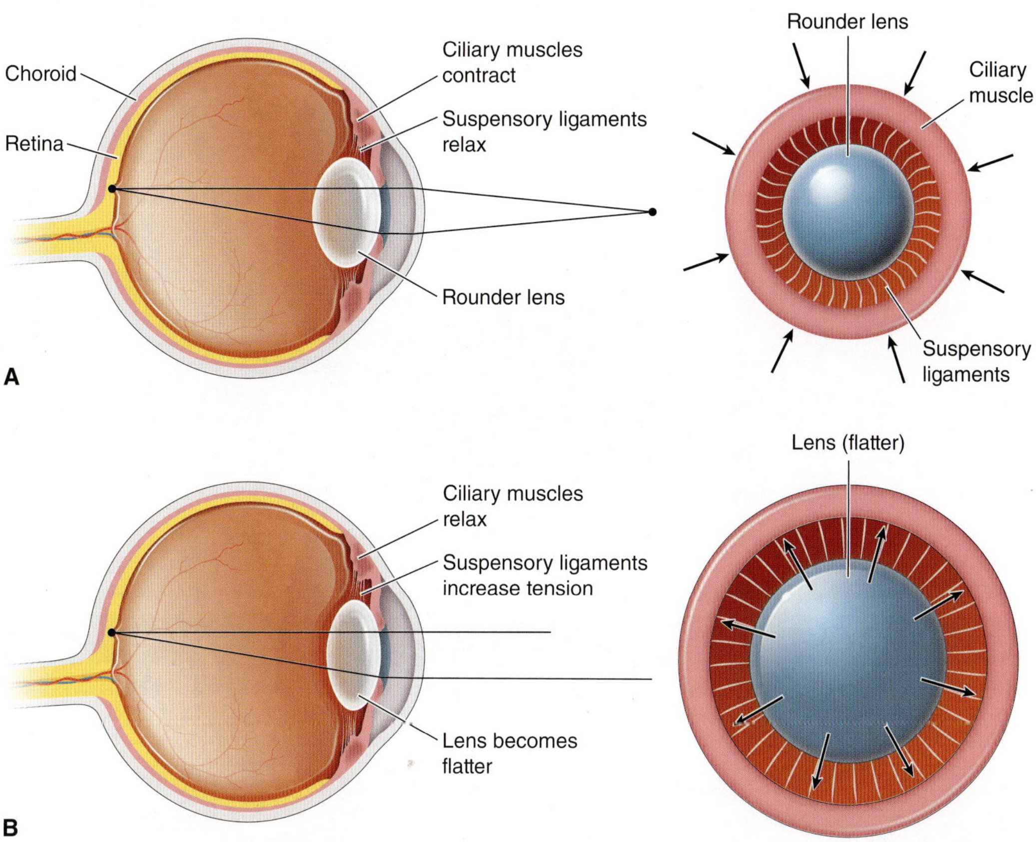

Figure 15-3 The ciliary body accommodates focal length to see near or far. (A) Near vision, (B) distance vision.

ELEMENT REVIEW
phot/o = light
chor/o = membrane
-iod = resembling
intra- = within
ocul/o = eye
-ar = pertaining to

and proteins. It functions to maintain the shape of the eyeball. Unlike aqueous humor, vitreous humor is not continuously recycled by the bloodstream. If vitreous humor is lost through disease or injury, it can be replaced with silicone oil. Vitreous humor fills the entire posterior chamber between the lens and the retina, adhering the retina to the vascular tunic and thus ensuring its blood supply. The **retina** is part of the nervous tunic, a thin fragile layer of neurons forming the inner lining of the posterior wall of the eye. The retina has three distinct layers of nerve cells: rods and cones, bipolar cells, and ganglion cells (Fig. 15-4 and Table 15-1). These nerve cells are photoreceptors that sense light.

Light enters the eye through the pupil and streams into the lens, through the vitreous humor, and on to the retina, where the photoreceptors sense light and send the signal to the **optic nerve**. The optic nerve delivers the signal to the brain, which interprets the signal. At the center of the retina, a structure called the **optic disc** has no photoreceptors and thus produces a "blind spot." Slightly lateral to the optic disc is the **macula lutea**, which means "yellow spot." It has a depression containing cone cells called the **fovea centralis** or central fovea. When light is focused directly on the fovea, a sharp image is created. The sharpness of images is called *visual acuity*.

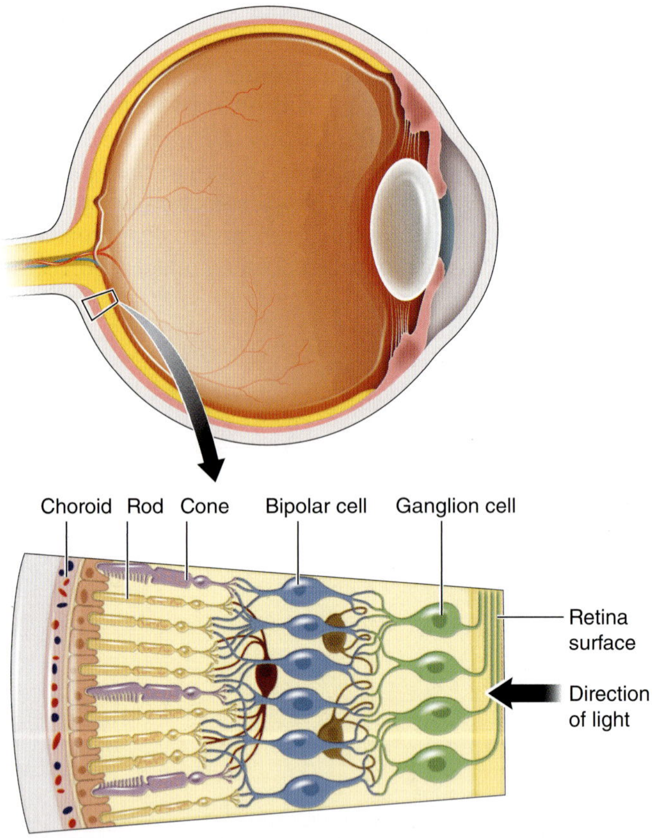

Figure 15-4 The retina has three distinct layers of nerve cells.

TABLE 15-1 The Layers of the Retina

Cell	Function
Rods	Perceive very low levels of light
Cones	Perceive color; require more light
Bipolar cells	Connect rods and cones to the ganglion cells
Ganglion cells	Axons from the ganglion cells converge to form the optic nerve

Refraction and Accommodation

As light rays pass through the eye, the solid and fluid structures of the eye bend the light in a process called **refraction.** The combined refractory effects of the eye to the retina cause the picture on the fovea centralis to be formed. Interestingly, the picture is formed upside down, reduced in size, and reversed from left to right. Our brain learns to coordinate the visual images with the world in early infancy. Thus, our brains orient the image to match the world, and we do not see objects upside down. Simultaneously, the ciliary muscles act upon the lens to bend light for near or far objects to focus on the fovea and create the sharpest image. This action of the ciliary muscle to focus light on the fovea is called **accommodation.**

The accessory structures of the eye protect, lubricate, and move the eye. The **eyelids** are movable, protective folds of skin on the anterior surface of the eye meeting at the medial and lateral corners of each eye. The anterior eyeball and the interior surface of the eyelids are protected and lubricated by a mucous membrane called the **conjunctiva**. Eyelids contain hairs—eyelashes—that sweep debris from the eyes. The **lacrimal apparatus** of each eye comprises the lacrimal gland, lacrimal sac, and nasolacrimal ducts. The **lacrimal glands** secrete tears, a dilute salt solution containing antibacterial enzymes that protect the eyeball from infection and lubricate the eye. As tears flush the anterior surface of the eye, the lacrimal canals channel the fluid to the lacrimal sac. The fluid is then passed into the nasal cavity by way of the nasolacrimal duct. *Crying*, or secreting tears, can be caused by irritants to the eye, for example, as when cutting an onion. Tears can also be in response to emotional upset. Tears contain stress hormones and natural painkillers; thus, emotional crying can make you feel better. The extrinsic muscles of the eye originate from the walls of the eyeball and are inserted at the optic nerve (Fig. 15-5). These six muscles coordinate movement of the eye under the direction of cranial nerves (Table 15-2).

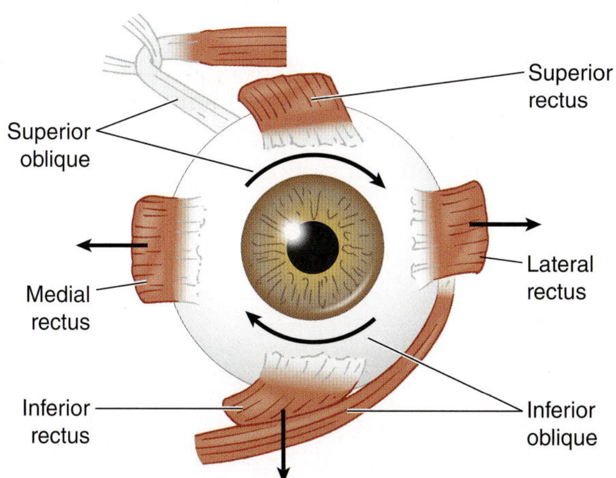

Figure 15-5 The extrinsic muscles of the eye.

TABLE 15-2 The Six Muscles of the Eye

Muscle	Controlling Cranial Nerve	Movement/Action
Lateral rectus	Abducens VI	Moves the eye laterally
Medial rectus	Oculomotor III	Moves the eye medially
Superior rectus	Oculomotor III	Raises and rolls the eye upward
Inferior rectus	Oculomotor III	Lowers and rolls the eye downward
Inferior oblique	Oculomotor III	Raises and turns the eye laterally
Superior oblique	Trochlear IV	Lowers and turns the eye laterally

Hearing and Balance

The sense of hearing and the sense of balance, also called **equilibrium**, are detected by specialized receptors located within the ear. The ear consists of three portions: the external ear, the middle ear, and the inner ear (Fig. 15-6). Each of these sections direct sound waves to the **auditory nerve**, which connects to the brain where sound is interpreted.

The external ear comprises the **auricle**, also called the pinna, the external portion of the ear that extends from the side of the head to the **external auditory canal**. The auricle collects sound waves and transmits the sound to the external auditory canal that extends into the temporal bone. The external auditory canal contains glands that secrete **cerumen**, or ear wax. The waxy substance lubricates and protects the canal. The canal channels the sound to the middle ear.

The middle ear contains an air-filled space within the temporal bone called the tympanic cavity. The tympanic cavity is connected to the throat by the auditory or **eustachian tube**. The tube allows air to flow between the throat and the tympanic cavity, enabling air pressure to equalize on both sides of the tympanic cavity. Without this important ability, changes in atmospheric pressure would cause unequal pressure within the ear. The pressure would result in pain, dizziness, and hearing loss. Because the auditory canal is connected to the throat, infections of the throat may progress and cause middle ear infections, a condition called otitis media (OM). The **tympanic membrane** is a thin, mucus-covered barrier separating the outer and middle ear. It functions to protect the middle and inner ear structures from pathogens. The tympanic membrane is connected to the **malleus**, the first of three auditory ossicles, small bony structures that transmit vibrations to the auditory nerve for interpretation as sound. The three ossicles, the malleus, **incus**, and **stapes** are held in place by tiny muscles and ligaments in the walls of the tympanic cavity. These interconnected ossicles form a connection to the inner ear. When the vibrations (sound waves) cross the ossicles, they are transmitted to the **oval window**, an opening in the wall of the tympanic cavity. The oval window opens to the cochlea of the inner ear. The vibrations from the malleus, incus, and finally the stapes push against the oval window, causing fluid to move in waves within the inner ear. A second opening in the cochlea, called the **round window**, bulges outward in response to pressure from the oval window. This allows fluid to move within the cochlea, activating auditory receptors.

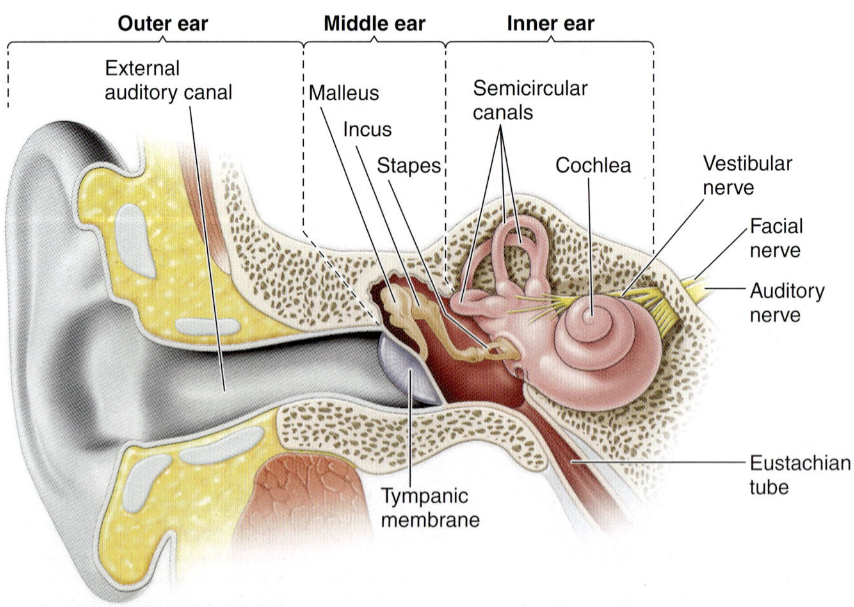

Figure 15-6 The structures of the ear.

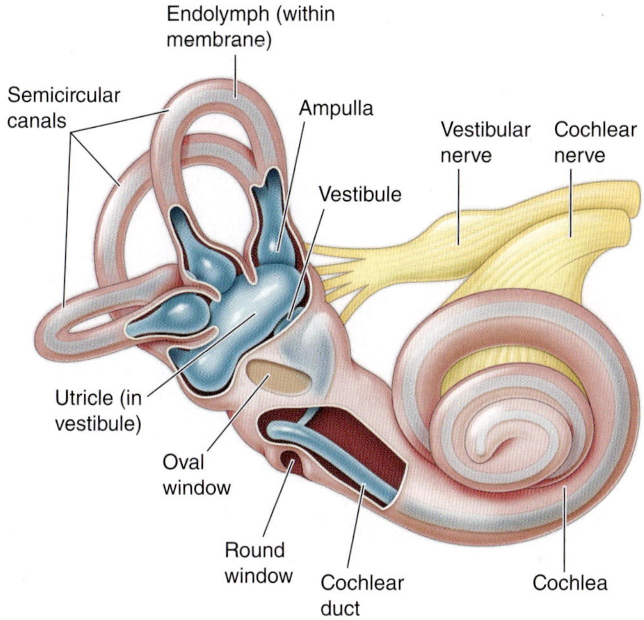

Figure 15-7 The labyrinth of the inner ear.

The inner ear is a winding passageway of canals and is called the **labyrinth**. The **labyrinth** is divided into the outer bony labyrinth and the inner membranous labyrinth (Fig. 15-7). Between the outer wall of the bony labyrinth and the inner wall of the membranous labyrinth, the space is filled with a fluid called the **perilymph**. Within the membranous labyrinth, the space is filled with **endolymph**. This fluid within a fluid system plays an important role in the perception of equilibrium. The canals form three regions: the semicircular canals, the vestibule, and the cochlea. The **semicircular canals** consist of three loops at right angles to each other. The **vestibule** is the chamber where two membranous pouches—the **utricle** and **saccule**—aid in maintaining our balance. Both static (staying still) and dynamic (moving) equilibrium are detected by epithelial and hair cells in the vestibule and the semicircular canals. The vestibule connects the semicircular canals and the **cochlea**. The cochlea is a coiled structure that resembles a snail shell and houses the **organ of Corti**, the true organ of hearing. The spiral structure of the cochlea contains hair cells that are stimulated by sound waves. These sound waves are converted to nerve impulses along the auditory nerve and sent to the cerebral cortex of the brain to be interpreted as sound.

ELEMENT REVIEW
peri- = around
endo- = within
lymph = fluid

PHYSIOLOGY FACT

If you spin on a merry-go-round or spin around while dancing, you may feel dizzy immediately after stopping. The sensation is caused by endolymph movement lagging behind the rate of perilymph movement during the spinning. As soon as you stop, the endolymph continues to move for a while. The nerve cells of the vestibule and semicircular canals continue to send the message to the brain that you are moving. This difference causes you to feel dizzy, but as the endolymph movement slows down, the dizziness subsides. Ballerinas and ice skaters prevent dizziness by specific training. They keep their head and therefore their eyes in a horizontal position during the spin and focus on a fixed spot at the end of spin. This strategy decreases the perception of continuing movement when the spin is completed.

Smell

The sense of smell is known as **olfaction**. Smells are detected by thousands of specialized chemoreceptors in the nose known as olfactory neurons. The neurons are embedded in the mucous membrane of the nasal epithelium of the upper nasal cavity. Forcing air into the nose to "sniff" a scent maximizes sensitivity. As inhaled gas molecules enter the nasal cavity, they become dissolved in the layer of mucus where they reach the olfactory neurons. The smell signal then travels through the nasal epithelium to the cranial cavity. The impulse travels to a paired swelling of olfactory bulbs at the base of the brain. From the olfactory bulbs, the impulse continues along the olfactory nerve to the cerebral cortex, where the interpretation of smell will occur.

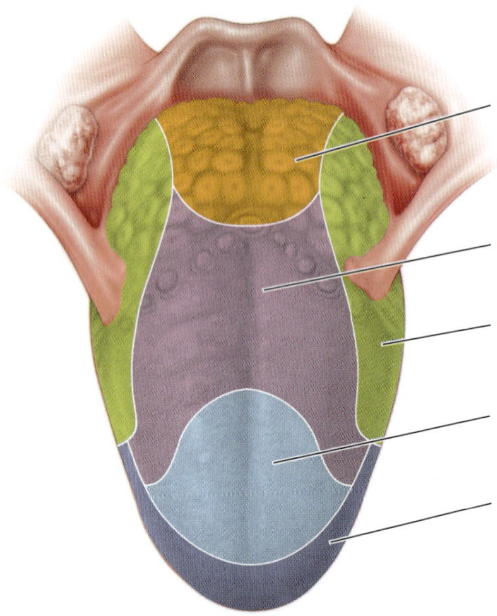

Figure 15-8 The five primary taste sensations.

Taste

The sense of taste is known as **gustation** and is detected by chemoreceptors called taste buds. The taste buds are located in the mouth, with most of them located on the surface of the tongue. The approximately 10,000 raised structures, called **papillae**, on the surface of the tongue house the taste buds. Fewer receptors are found on the roof of the mouth and the walls of the pharynx. Each taste bud contains gustatory cells, surrounded and supported at the base by epithelial cells. The free end of the gustatory cell contains microvilli, tiny hair-like projections connected to the taste pore, the opening on the surface of the tongue. When chemicals in the mouth are dissolved by saliva, they bind to the gustatory cell, creating a nerve impulse in the sensory fibers at the base of the cells. The impulse then travels via cranial nerves VII, IX, and X to the medulla oblongata, the thalamus, and finally the cerebral cortex, where the perception of taste is sensed.

There are five primary types of taste sensation. The location of the taste buds that interpret these tastes are shown in Figure 15-8. *Umami* is the Japanese word for "delicious" and refers to a meaty flavor.

PHYSIOLOGY FACT

Why are taste and smell related? The nose and the mouth are connected. Thus, there are two pathways for the perception of smell; orthonasal olfaction occurs in the nose, and retronasal olfaction occurs in the mouth. In retronasal olfaction, molecules enter the mouth and latch onto olfactory receptors, and they are transmitted to the cerebral cortex in the same way that orthonasal olfaction occurs. As you smell food cooking, you produce saliva, a normal response to anticipating a delicious meal. Conversely, if you have a head cold or sinus infection, your sense of smell is decreased, and food doesn't taste as good. Your sense of taste will be decreased as the flavor of food is no longer enhanced by the smell.

Structures and Physiology Review

1. Match the Words

Match the words to their descriptions.

accommodation	canal of Schlemm	ciliary body	cornea
aqueous humor	cerumen	cochlea	endolymph
auditory nerve	choroid	cones	equilibrium
auricle		conjunctiva	eustachian tube

external auditory canal	macula lutea	photoreceptors	suspensory ligaments
fovea centralis	malleus	pupil	tympanic membrane
gustation	olfaction	retina	utricle
incus	optic disc	rods	vestibule
iris	organ of Corti	saccule	vitreous humor
labyrinth	oval window	sclera	
lacrimal gland	papillae	semicircular canals	
lens	perilymph	stapes	

1. Nerve cells of the eye that detect low light ____________________
2. The external ear is called the ____________________
3. Two membranous pouches that aid in the perception of balance ____________________
4. The "white" of the eye ____________________
5. The structure that separates the outer and middle ear ____________________
6. The sense of taste ____________________
7. The thin dark membrane that lines the internal surface of the sclera of the eye ____________________
8. The colored portion of the eye ____________________
9. The gel-like material of the posterior eye ____________________
10. The sense of smell ____________________
11. The opening at the center of the iris ____________________
12. The process of changing the shape of the lens to create a sharp image ____________________
13. Nerve cells of the eye that detect color ____________________
14. The "blind spot" on the retina ____________________
15. The vein that drains excess fluid in the eye ____________________
16. The three ossicles of the ear ____________________
17. The sense of balance is called ____________________
18. Earwax is also called ____________________
19. The structures of the inner ear are collectively called the ____________________

20. The snail shell–shaped structure of the inner ear ______________________

21. The yellowish spot on the retina ______________________

22. The anterior mucous membrane of the eye ______________________

23. The innermost fluid of the membranous labyrinth ______________________

24. The opening in the wall of the tympanic cavity that receives vibrations from the stapes ______________________

25. The organ of hearing is the ______________________

Structures and Physiology Word-Building Practice

1. Nouns and Adjectives

Complete the chart of nouns and their adjective forms.

	Noun	Adjective
1.	______________________	olfactory
2.	cornea	______________________
3.	______________________	macular
4.	pupil	______________________
5.	cerumen	______________________
6.	______________________	cochlear
7.	______________________	retinal
8.	palpebra	______________________
9.	ophthalmoscope	______________________
10.	nose	______________________

2. Prefixes

Use the listed prefixes to build a word for each definition in the numbered list.

a, an-	entro-	intra-	sub-
dys-	endo-	peri-	supra-
ectro-	infra-	semi-	

1. Deafness ______________________

2. Pertaining to around the eye ______________________

3. Pertaining to within the eye ______________________

4. The outer fluid of the cochlea ______________________

5. The innermost fluid of the cochlea ______________________

6. The canals behind the vestibule ______________________

7. Turning outward of the eyelash margins ______________________

8. Turning inward of the eyelash margins ______________________

9. Discomfort caused by loud noises ______________________

10. Impairment of normal taste sensation ______________________

3. Singular and Plural Forms

Complete the chart of singular and plural forms. Refer to the singular and plural forms table in Chapter 2.

Singular	Plural
1. palpebra	______________________
2. ______________________	sclerae
3. ossicle	______________________
4. ______________________	nares
5. papilla	______________________
6. ______________________	auricla
7. ______________________	microvilli
8. pinna	______________________

Word Building With Combining, Prefix, and Suffix Forms

The following word roots, prefixes, and suffixes are commonly used in medical terms for the anatomy and pathology of the special senses. Combining vowels for word roots are included. Memorizing these elements will help you understand new terms that you may encounter as a medical assistant, optician, audiology technician, or as another health-care professional working in an ophthalmology, audiology, or an eye, ear, nose, and throat specialist's office.

The list contains examples of terms that utilize the combining forms and a pronunciation guide. Be sure to use the pronunciation guide so that you can learn to say the terms correctly.

mll Medical Language Lab

The Medical Language Lab at medicallanguagelab.com provides audio files to help you practice your pronunciations.

Combining Form	Meaning	Example (Pronunciation)	Definition
acous/o	hearing	acoustic (ă-KOOS-tĭk)	pertaining to hearing
ambi/o	both, both sides	ambidextrous (ăm-bē-DEK-strūs)	able to use both hands with equal facility
ambly/o	dull	amblyopia (ăm-blē-Ō-pē-ă)	decrease in corrected vision
aque/o	watery	aqueous humor (Ā-kwē-ŭs HŪ-mŏr)	watery fluid of the posterior chambers of the eye
audi/o	hearing	audiology (aw-dĭ-ŎL-ō-jē)	the study of hearing disorders
audit/o	hearing	auditory (AW-dĭ-tō-rē)	pertaining to the sense of hearing
aur/o	ear	aural (OR-ăl)	pertaining to the ear
auricul/o	ear, earlobe	auriculare (or-IK-yŭ-LĀR-ē)	point at the center of the opening to the external auditory canal
bar/o	pressure	barotitis media (băr-ō-TĪ-tĭs MĒ-dē-ă)	inflammation of the middle ear due to changes in atmospheric pressure
blephar/o	eyelid	blepharoptosis (blĕf-ă-rō-TŌ-sĭs)	drooping of an eyelid
cochle/o	cochlea	cochleitis (KŎK-lē-Ī-tĭs)	inflammation of the cochlea
conjunctiv/o	conjunctiva	conjunctivitis (kŏn-jŭnk-tĭ-VĪ-tĭs)	inflammation of the conjunctiva
cor/o	pupil	anisocoria (ăn-ī-sō-KŌ-rē-ă)	unequal size of the pupils
corne/o	cornea	corneoblepharon (KOR-nē-ō-BLĔF-ă-rŏn)	adhesion of the eyelid to the cornea
dacry/o	tears	dacryostenosis (dăk-rē-ō-stĕ-NŌ-sĭs)	narrowing or obstruction of tear duct
dacryocyst/o	tear sac	dacryocystitis (dăk-rē-ō-sĭs-TĪ-tĭs)	inflammation of tear sac
dipl/o	double	diplopia (dĭp-LŌ-pē-ă)	double vision
glauc/o	gray, silver	glaucoma (glaw-KŌ-mă)	eye disease caused by increased ocular pressure
ir/o	iris	iritis (ī -RĪT-ĭs)	inflammation of the iris
irid/o	iris	iridotomy (ī-RŎT-ō-mē)	surgical puncture through the iris

Combining Form	Meaning	Example (Pronunciation)	Definition
kerat/o	cornea	keratotomy (kĕr-ă-TŎT-ō-mē)	incision of the cornea
labyrinth/o	inner ear	labyrinthotomy (lăb-ĭ-rĭn-THŎT-ō-mē)	surgical incision into the labyrinth
lacrim/o	tears	lacrimation (lăk-rĭ-MĀ-shūn)	secretion of tears
mastoid/o	mastoid process	mastoiditis (măs-toyd-ĪT-ĭs)	inflammation of the mastoid process
myring/o	eardrum	myringoplasty (mĭr-ĬN-gō-plăst-ē)	surgical repair of the eardrum
ocul/o	sight	oculonasal (ŏk-ū-lō-NĀ-zul)	pertaining to the eyes and nose
ophthalm/o	eye	ophthalmologist (ŏf-thăl-MŎL-ō-jĭst)	physician who treats disorders of the eyes
opt/o	eye, vision	optician (ŏp-TĬSH-ăn)	specialist in filling prescriptions for eyeglasses and contact lenses
ot/o	ear	otorrhea (ō-tō-RĒ-ă)	discharge from the ear
palpebr/o	eyelid	palpebral (PAL-pĕ-brăl)	pertaining to the eyelid
phac/o	lens	phacoemulsification (FĂK-ō-ē-mŭl-sĭ-fĭkā-shŭn)	removal of a lens with ultrasound
phot/o	light	photophobia (fō-tō-FŌ-bē-ă)	increased sensitivity to light
presby/o	old age	presbycusis (prĕz-bĭ-KŪ-sĭs)	age-related hearing loss
pupill/o	pupil	pupillary (PŪ-pĭ-lĕr-ē)	pertaining to the pupil
retin/o	retina	retinopexy (rĕt-ĭ-nō-PĔK-sē)	surgical adhesion to correct detached retina
scler/o	sclera	sclerectomy (sklĕ-RĔK-tō-mē)	excision of a portion of the sclera
stape/o	stapes	stapedectomy (stā-pĕ-DĔK-tō-mē)	surgical removal of the staples
tympan/o	eardrum	tympanoplasty (tĭm-păn-ō-PLĂS-tē)	surgical repair of the eardrum
vitre/o	glassy	vitreous humor (VI-trē-ŭs HU-mŏr)	jellylike substance that gives shape to the eyeball

ā = say, ă = sofa, ē = meet, ĕ = met, ī = eye, ĭ = in, ō = oh, ŏ = dog, ū = you, ŭ = up, oo = food

Prefixes	Meaning	Example (Pronunciation)	Definition
aniso-	unequal	anisoaccommodation (AN-Ī-sō-ă-KOM-ă-DĀ-shŏn)	difference in the ability of the eyes to accommodate
eso-	within	esotropia (ĕs-ō-TRŌ-pē-ă)	marked turning inward of the eye
exo-	outward	exotropia (ĕks-ō-TRŌ-pē-ă)	marked turning outward of the eye
extra-	outside, beyond	extraocular (ĕks-tră-ŎK-yū-lăr)	outside of the eye
dys-	bad, abnormal	dyscoria (dĭs-KŌ-rē-ă)	abnormal form or shape of the pupil
hemi-	half	hemianopia (HEM-ē-ă-NŌP-ei-ă)	blindness in one-half of the visual field
intra-	within	intraocular (ĭn-tră-ŎK-yū-lăr)	pertaining to within the eye

ā = say, ă = sofa, ē = meet, ĕ = met, ī = eye, ĭ = in, ō = oh, ŏ = dog, ū = you, ŭ = up, oo = food

Suffix	Meaning	Example (Pronunciation)	Definition
-ectomy	surgical removal	vitrectomy (vĭ-TRĔK-tō-mē)	surgical removal of vitreous humor
-meter	instrument to measure	audiometer (aw-dē-ŎM-ĕ-tĕr)	instrument to measure hearing
-metry	process of measuring	audiometry (ăw-dē-ŎM-ĕ-trē)	process of measuring hearing
-otomy	incision into	keratotomy (kĕr-ă-TŎT-ō-mē)	surgical incision into cornea
-opia	vision	diplopia (dĭp-LŌ-pē-ă)	double vision
-opsia	visual condition	hemianopsia (HEM-ē-ă-NOP-sē-ă)	blindness in one-half of the visual field
-plasty	surgical repair/correction	tympanoplasty (tĭm-păn-ō-PLĂS-tē)	surgical repair/correction of the eardrum
-plegia	paralysis	ophthalmoplegia (ŏf-THĂL-mō-PLĒ-jē-ă)	paralysis of the muscles of the eye
-scope	instrument to view	ophthalmoscope (ŏf-THĂL-mō-skōp)	instrument to view the eye
-scopy	process of viewing	nasal endoscopy (NĀ-zul ĕn-DŎS-kō-pē)	process of viewing the inside of the nose

ā = say, ă = sofa, ē = meet, ĕ = met, ī = eye, ĭ = in, ō = oh, ŏ = dog, ū = you, ŭ = up, oo = food

Combining Forms Practice

1. Build the Terms

*Using **only** the word parts in the lists, create medical terms for the indicated meanings.*

Prefixes	Combining Forms		Suffixes
an-	acous/o	labyrinth/o	-al
dys-	ambi/o	lacrim/o	-ia
ecto-	ambly/o	mastoid/o	-ician
endo-	aque/o	myring/o	-ar
hemi-	audi/o	ocul/o	-ary
hyper-	audit/o	ophthalm/o	-ectomy
intra-	aur/o	opt/o	-itis
peri-	auricul/o	ot/o	-ologist
	blephar/o	palpebr/o	-ology
	cochle/o	phac/o	-opia
	conjunctiv/o	phot/o	-opsia
	cor/o	presby/o	-osis
	corne/o	pupill/o	-otomy
	dacry/o	retin/o	-pathy
	dacryocyst/o	scler/o	-ptosis
	glauc/o	stape/o	-rrhaphy
	ir/o	tympan/o	-rrhea
	irid/o	vitre/o	-rrhexis
	kerat/o		-scopy

1. Another term for nearsightedness ____________________
2. Pertaining to the retina ____________________
3. Specialist who fits eyeglasses and contact lens ____________________
4. Flow of discharge from the eye ____________________
5. Inflammation of the anterior mucous membrane of the eye ____________________
6. Suturing of the eyelid ____________________
7. Age-related loss of vision ____________________
8. Pertaining to tears ____________________
9. Surgical excision of the lacrimal sac ____________________
10. Another term for farsightedness ____________________
11. Loss of vision in one-half of the visual field ____________________

12. Incision into the tympanic membrane ______________________
13. Pertaining to around the ear ______________________
14. Disease of the retina ______________________
15. Pertaining to the pupil ______________________

2. Decipher the Terms

Separate each term into its prefix (if any), combining form, and suffix. Next, translate the word parts and then give the common definition of the term.

1. dacryocystitis

   Prefix: ______________ *Combining Form:* ______________ *Suffix:* ______________

   Meaning: ____

2. otomycosis

   Prefix: ______________ *Combining Form:* ______________ *Suffix:* ______________

   Meaning: ____

3. ophthalmologist

   Prefix: ______________ *Combining Form:* ______________ *Suffix:* ______________

   Meaning: ____

4. blepharoptosis

   Prefix: ______________ *Combining Form:* ______________ *Suffix:* ______________

   Meaning: ____

5. amblyacousia

   Prefix: ______________ *Combining Form:* ______________ *Suffix:* ______________

   Meaning: ____

6. intraocular

   Prefix: ______________ *Combining Form:* ______________ *Suffix:* ______________

   Meaning: ____

7. retinopathy

   Prefix: ______________ *Combining Form:* ______________ *Suffix:* ______________

   Meaning: ____

8. endoscope

Prefix: ______________ *Combining Form:* ______________ *Suffix:* ______________

Meaning: ____

9. otorhinolaryngology

Prefix: ______________ *Combining Form:* ______________ *Suffix:* ______________

Meaning: ____

10. vitrectomy

Prefix: ______________ *Combining Form:* ______________ *Suffix:* ______________

Meaning: ____

Visit the Medical Language Lab at medicallanguagelab.com. Use it to enhance your study and reinforcement of the medical terms and word parts covered in this chapter.

CASE STUDY, continued

After the initial consultation with Dr. Wysenski, Taay's hearing is tested to make sure she is a candidate for cochlear implant. She also has a physical examination, including blood testing, to ensure that she is healthy for surgery. Taay and her parents arrive at the hospital on the morning of the scheduled surgery. Taay is taken to the operating room in the supine position, where she was placed under general anesthesia. Dr. Wysenski begins by making an incision behind her ears and makes a slight indentation in the mastoid bone. He then creates a tiny hole in the cochlea and inserts the electrode into the hole. The receiver is then placed behind the ear under the skin. The device is secured to the skull, and the incision is stitched. Taay does well in surgery, and she is transported to the recovery room in good condition. Dr. Wysenski tells Taay's parents that she did well and will be awake soon. Upon awaking, Taay feels well but does feel a bit nauseous. She drinks some water and eats some applesauce. The recovery room nurse monitors Taay's blood pressure, blood glucose, and urinary output, and she is discharged within a few hours. As Dr. Wysenski had previously explained, the cochlear implant will be turned on in 1 week at her follow-up office visit when her incisions will be evaluated. If no infection is found, the implants will be turned on, but the external device will not yet be added. One month after surgery, the external parts of the device will be added, and the internal component will be activated. While Taay is anxious to begin hearing, she understands that she needs to be patient.

Special Senses Diseases and Disorders

Signs and symptoms of diseases and disorders of the special senses include a variety of deficits in the senses (Table 15-3). While changes in vision or hearing are perceived by the patient and therefore are symptoms, these changes can be measured and thus are also signs.

TABLE 15-3 Common Signs and Symptoms

Signs	Symptoms
Increased intraocular pressure	Itching, burning, of the eyes or ears
Clouding of the lens (cataract)	Changes (usually loss) of vision or hearing
Redness and swelling of the tympanic membrane Redness of the eyes	Loss or change in perception of taste or smell
Fever	Pain: localized at the eye or ear
Exudate from the eye or ear	Ringing in the ears (tinnitus)
Protrusion of the eyeball	

Pathological Conditions of the Special Senses

Eyes

ELEMENT REVIEW
a- = without
chrom/o = color
-opsia = vision

Achromatopsia: Absence of perception of color; color blindness.

Ametropia: The imperfect refractive powers of the eye to focus an image sharply onto the retina (Fig. 15-9). Types of ametropia include hyperopia (farsighted), myopia (nearsighted), and astigmatism (blurred vision).

- **Myopia:** Light rays focus in front of the retina. Objects a short distance away are in focus, and distant objects look blurry; commonly called nearsightedness.
- **Hyperopia:** Light rays focus behind the retina. Objects a short distance away are blurry; commonly called farsightedness.
- **Astigmatism:** Multiple images are refracted on the retina, and close and distant objects look blurry.

Astigmatism: Error of refraction caused by an abnormally shaped cornea or lens. Astigmatism causes blurred vision as images cannot be focused sharply onto the retina. The person may squint to try to focus and suffer from headaches. Diagnosis is confirmed by retinoscopy or automatic refraction test, and treatment with glasses or contact lens often will correct the problem.

Blepharitis: An acute or chronic inflammation of the eyelids. The condition is caused by allergies or bacterial infection. The eyelids appear red, swollen, and the patient complains of itching, burning. There is often a mucous drainage with crusting and a buildup of crusting on the eyelid. Sometimes the condition causes the eyelashes to fall out. Treatment consists of gently cleansing the eyelids and applying warm compresses. Antibiotic eye drops are applied if the cause is a bacterial infection. Topical steroids to reduce inflammation are also prescribed.

Blepharoptosis: The drooping of one or both eyelids, also known as ptosis. The condition is caused by weakened eye muscles and most commonly occurs in older adults (acquired blepharoptosis). The condition may also be congenital, due to trauma, or have a neurological cause. Severe blepharoptosis will completely obstruct vision. Underlying diseases such as myasthenia gravis, muscular dystrophy, diabetes mellitus, or brain tumors may cause the condition. Treatment is directed at the cause of the disease. Other treatment options include surgery to strengthen the muscles of the eyelids. A supportive device called a "crutch" can be attached to eyeglasses to keep the eyelid up.

Blindness: The loss of sight or extreme visual impairment. Total blindness is complete loss of light perception. The term "legally blind" refers to corrected visual acuity in the stronger eye of 20/200 or less or when the visual field is less than 20 degrees. Causes of blindness

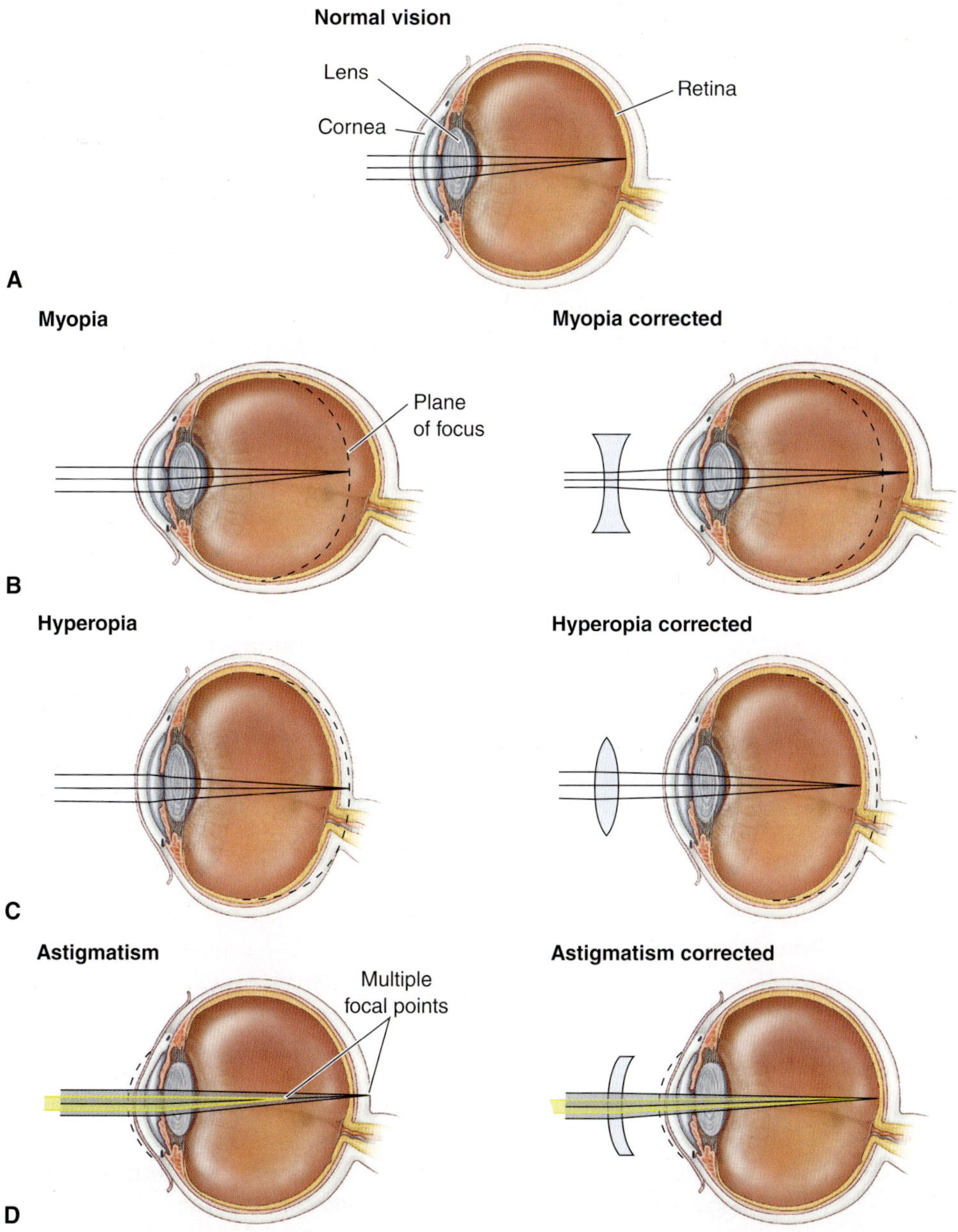

Figure 15-9 Ametropia. (A) Normal eye, (B) myopia, (C) hyperopia, (D) astigmatism.

include trauma, diabetic retinopathy, cataracts, glaucoma, prolonged nutritional deficiencies, or trachoma.

Cataract: The clouding of the lens of the eye that can be observed as it progresses (Fig. 15-10). As the lens loses its transparency, light transmission to the retina is reduced, and sight is progressively lost. Cataracts are classified as senile or secondary. Senile cataracts begin after age 50 when degenerative changes due to wear and tear occur on the crystalline lens. Of people over 65, 95% have some degeneration of the lens. Secondary cataracts can result from trauma, radiation, diabetes mellitus, inflammation, or medications such as corticosteroids. Congenital cataracts, seen in infants, are usually due to a maternal infection and are considered secondary cataracts. Treatment includes surgical removal of the lens by phacoemulsification or extracapsular cataract extraction (ECCE). Surgery is conducted as an outpatient procedure and is indicated when the cataracts impair sight to the extent it impairs daily functions.

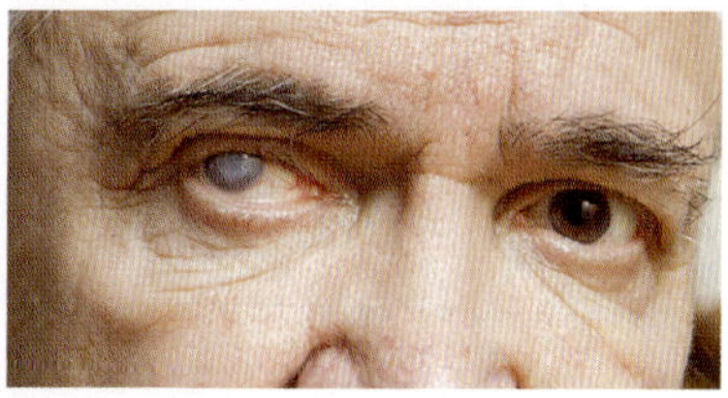

Figure 15-10 Cataract.

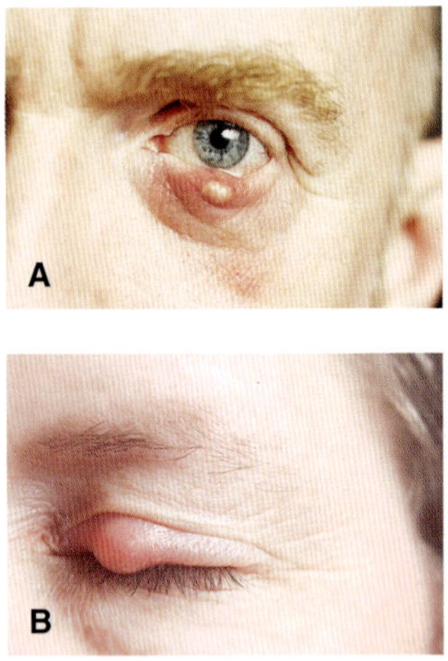

Figure 15-11 (A) Chalazion, (B) stye.

Chalazion: A painless red cyst or nodule that forms on the eyelid (Fig. 15-11). It is caused by an obstruction of a meibomian gland, which provides lubrication to the margin of the eyelid. Diagnosis is obtained by visual examination and patient health history. Chalazions most commonly occur in adults aged 30 to 50 years, vary in size, and usually resolve spontaneously within 6 to 8 weeks. Home treatments include warm compresses, gentle massage, and keeping the face clean. If the chalazion persists, an ophthalmologist may lance the cyst in a minor office procedure.

PHYSIOLOGY FACT

A chalazion is not a stye (hordeolum), but it can form because of a stye. A stye is caused by a bacterial infection and can be painful. Chalazions are not normally painful and occur farther back on the eyelid (farther from the eye).

Conjunctivitis: The inflammation of the anterior mucous membrane that lines the eyelids and covers the front of the eyeball. It is commonly called "pink eye" because the sclera (white) of the eye becomes red or pink due to inflammation. There are three types of conjunctivitis, classified by cause: viral, bacterial, and allergic. Signs and symptoms include redness, tearing, and itching. Viral and bacterial conjunctivitis are also characterized by a yellow discharge that is highly contagious. Upon waking, the discharge may be dry and crusty along the eyelid, making it hard for the patient to open the eye. Warm compresses and gentle cleansing are advised. Patients are also advised not to share bath towels with family members and to wash their hands frequently. The condition may affect one eye or present bilaterally as it is highly contagious. Diagnosis is confirmed by visual examination of the eye, and cause is confirmed by patient history and/or a culture and sensitivity test. Treatment is directed at the cause: antibiotic eyedrops for bacterial infections; ophthalmic drops or ointments for viral infection, and antihistamines for allergic reactions.

Corneal abrasion: An injury to the anterior portion of the eye from a scratch from a hairbrush, fingernail, or other object that contacts the eye. Corneal abrasion can also result from a chemical irritant or dryness of the eye. Signs and symptoms include redness, tearing, sensitivity to light, and sometimes visual impairment. The patient may complain of eye pain in the morning upon opening their eyes. Diagnosis is confirmed by fluorescein staining, which will show an outline of the scratch. Treatment consists of applying an antibiotic ointment or drops to reduce the chance of infection or a contact lens bandage to reduce movement of the cornea against the eyelid. If debris is observed on the eye, it is carefully removed. With prompt treatment, most abrasions heal without complications. If the abrasion is deep, it may require prolonged treatment to prevent infection and scarring, which may affect vision.

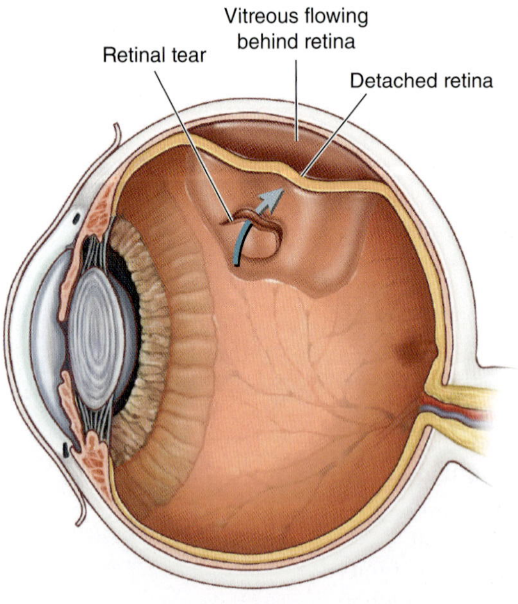

Figure 15-12 Retinal detachment.

Detached retina: An emergency condition in which the retina pulls away from its normal position on the posterior wall of the eyeball (Fig. 15-12). It is a rare condition affecting less than 200,000 Americans each year. It is most common in people over age 50. The longer the retinal detachment goes untreated, the more likely permanent vision loss will occur. Risk factors include previous retinal detachments, eye surgery, family history of retinal detachment, and previous eye injury. Symptoms include the sudden appearance of several floaters drifting through the field of vision, blurred vision, flashes of light, and/or a large shadow over the field of vision. Patients should seek immediate medical care to preserve their sight. Diagnosis is confirmed by patient history and examination of the retina.

Treatment is surgical reattachment of the retina. Several different types of correction are available and are chosen based on the severity and location of the retinal tear:

Pneumatic retinopexy: The injection of a bubble of air to force the retina in place.

Scleral buckling: A piece of silicon is sutured to the sclera to adhere the retina to the back of the eye.

Vitrectomy: The vitreous humor of the eye is drained and replaced with silicone oil to flatten the retina in place. The oil is later removed. The vitrectomy may be performed with scleral buckling.

Retinal photocoagulation: An argon laser is used to create an area of inflammation, which will develop an adhesion, causing the retina to reattach to the posterior choroid.

ELEMENT REVIEW
pneumat/o = air
retin/o = retina
-pexy = surgical fixation
vitre/o = vitreous humor
-ectomy = surgical removal

Diabetic retinopathy: Disease of the retina of the eye that results from long-term, poorly controlled, diabetes mellitus. It is the leading cause of blindness in the United States. The tissue of the retina becomes scarred from abnormal dilation and constriction of blood vessels, hemorrhages, microaneurysms, and blood leaking into the vitreous humor. A permanent loss of sharpness of vision is experienced as the retina cannot get oxygen and nutrients needed for healthy tissue. Diagnosis is confirmed by patient history and examination of the internal eye, which will show hemorrhaging of tiny blood vessels into the vitreous humor. Treatments consist of vitrectomy and replacement with a clear fluid or laser photocoagulation. Controlling blood sugar will slow progression of the disease, but damage to the retina is irreversible.

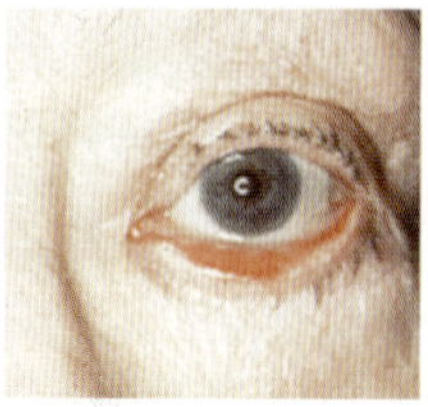

Figure 15-13 Ectropion.

Ectropion: Outward turning of the margin of the eyelash (Fig. 15-13). The condition is a result of weakening of the muscle in the lower lid and can result from aging. The condition causes tears to collect in the eye and not flow to the tear ducts, thus tears run down the face. The condition can be caused by facial nerve paralysis. Diagnosis is confirmed by visual examination. Treatment consists of minor surgical correction.

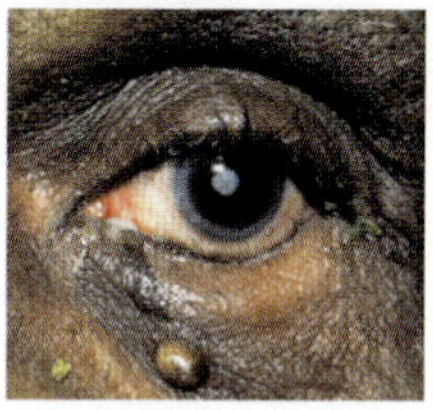

Figure 15-14 Entropion.

Entropion: Inward turning of the margin of the eyelash (Fig. 15-14). This condition is often caused by the aging process. The condition causes an irritation of the eye. The patient feels that there is a foreign body in the eye, causing them to rub the eye. Scratching of the cornea may occur. Diagnosis is confirmed by visual examination. Treatment consists of minor surgical correction.

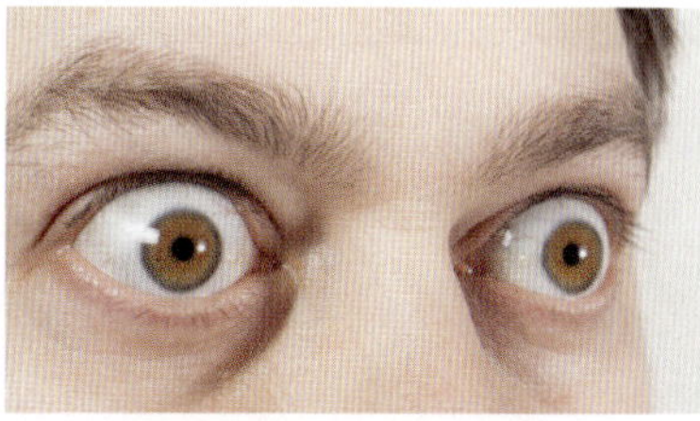

Figure 15-15 Exophthalmia.

Exophthalmia: The abnormal protrusion of the eyeballs (Fig. 15-15). The condition is most commonly associated with hyperthyroidism (Grave's disease) and is also called thyroid eye disease (TED). It may also be caused by a tumor or edema associated with hemorrhage or trauma. Commonly, both eyes are affected, and the onset is gradual. Signs and symptoms include inability to close the eyelids, blurred vision, double vision, restricted eye movement, dryness, and a gritty sensation. Diagnosis is confirmed by ophthalmic examination and testing to determine the underlying cause. Treatment is directed at relief of dryness and irritation and management of the underlying cause. In some cases, surgical decompression of the orbit and systemic corticosteroids are needed to reduce pressure and swelling.

Glaucoma: An increase of intraocular pressure that can cause damage to the optic nerve. The condition can be categorized as primary or secondary, open-angle or closed-angle. It is caused by an inability of aqueous humor to leave the eye. The increased pressure in the eye causes compression of blood supply to the optic neurons, leading to degeneration and atrophy of the optic nerve. If left untreated, it will lead to blindness.

Chronic open-angle glaucoma occurs as a primary disorder from lack of aqueous humor drainage. Gradually, the intraocular pressure increases, damaging the optic nerve and retina. Routine ophthalmic examinations with evaluation of intraocular pressure using a tonometer and retinal and optic nerve examination can detect the onset of open-angle glaucoma. If open-angle glaucoma is detected, medication to open the drainage system or reduce production of aqueous humor can control the disease. If medication does not control intraocular pressure, surgery to aid drainage is advised.

Acute closed-angle glaucoma progresses quickly and is caused by the iris being pushed against the drainage apparatus of the eye. It may be caused by an adhesion of the iris to the cornea (synechia). Signs and symptoms include severe eye pain, blurred vision, photophobia, redness, and seeing "halos" around light. It may cause nausea and vomiting. Acute closed-angle glaucoma is a medical emergency requiring immediate treatment to prevent blindness. Treatment with laser iridotomy will create a channel to allow outflow of aqueous humor. Other surgical interventions include iridectomy, trabeculectomy, and trabeculoplasty.

Hemianopsia: The loss of vision in half of the visual field. It is most commonly caused by a stroke but can result from a brain tumor, bleeding in the brain, seizures, epilepsy, or multiple sclerosis. Diagnosis is confirmed by patient history and an eye examination including a visual field test. MRI, CT scans, and blood testing are used to provide etiology of the sight loss. Treatment is directed at the underlying cause.

Hordeolum (stye): Bacterial infection of an eyelash follicle or sebaceous gland. Signs and symptoms include an acutely tender abscess that usually drains in 3 to 4 days. Treatment includes warm compresses and antibiotic ointment. Patients are advised not to touch the stye and to practice frequent handwashing. If the stye does not resolve, an incision and drainage can be performed in the ophthalmology office.

Hyphema: Bleeding into the anterior chamber of the eye, which can be the result of a blunt force eye injury or postsurgical complication. The condition is a medical emergency because increasing intraocular pressure could lead to blindness. Symptoms include blurred vision, sudden sharp eye pain, and seeing red tint of images. Diagnosis is confirmed by light observation of blood in the lower portion of the anterior chamber when the patient is seated. Treatment consists of bedrest, with elevation of the head of the bed, and administration of sedatives. The blood usually resorbs rapidly. Intraocular pressure is monitored, and diuretics and glaucoma eyedrops may also be administered.

Keratitis: Inflammation of the cornea. Causes include upper respiratory infection, trauma, or a hypersensitivity reaction. Signs and symptoms include irritation, excessive tearing, decreased visual acuity, and sometimes superficial ulcerations of the cornea. Treatment includes eyedrops or ointment and broad-spectrum antibiotics.

Macular degeneration: The progressive deterioration of the retinal cells in the macula due to aging. Age-related macular degeneration (ARMD) begins asymptomatically but progresses to a loss of central vision. The patient may see wavy lines or blurred images in the central field of vision. Diagnosis is obtained by dilated eye examination in which changes to the retina can be observed. Because the disorder affects only the macula, the center of the visual field, the peripheral vision remains intact. There are two forms of macular degeneration: dry and wet (Fig. 15-16).

Dry form causes slow, gradual deterioration of central vision. Patients may report distortion or blind spots in their vision. There is no cure for dry ARMD, but antioxidants and zinc slow the progression of sight loss. There are currently clinical trials using stem cell transplants, which may provide a cure and restore sight.

Wet form is more serious and causes more severe loss of vision. Wet form causes leakage of fluid from blood vessels under the retina. Wet ARMD is treated with intravitreal injections to slow the growth of abnormal blood vessels.

ELEMENT REVIEW
intra- = within
vitre/o = vitreous humor
-al = pertaining to
nyctal/o = night
-opia = pertaining to vision

Nyctalopia (night blindness): Inadequate vision at night or in low light caused by reduced production of rhodopsin, a chemical found in the rods of the retina necessary for vision in low light. Causes include deterioration of the retina, vitamin A deficiency, or congenital defects.

Nystagmus: An involuntary movement of the eyes in a vertical, horizontal, rotary, or mixed pattern. Causes include drug and alcohol abuse, lesions on the brain or inner ear, congenital abnormalities, nerve injury at birth, or retinal malformation. The patient may not be aware

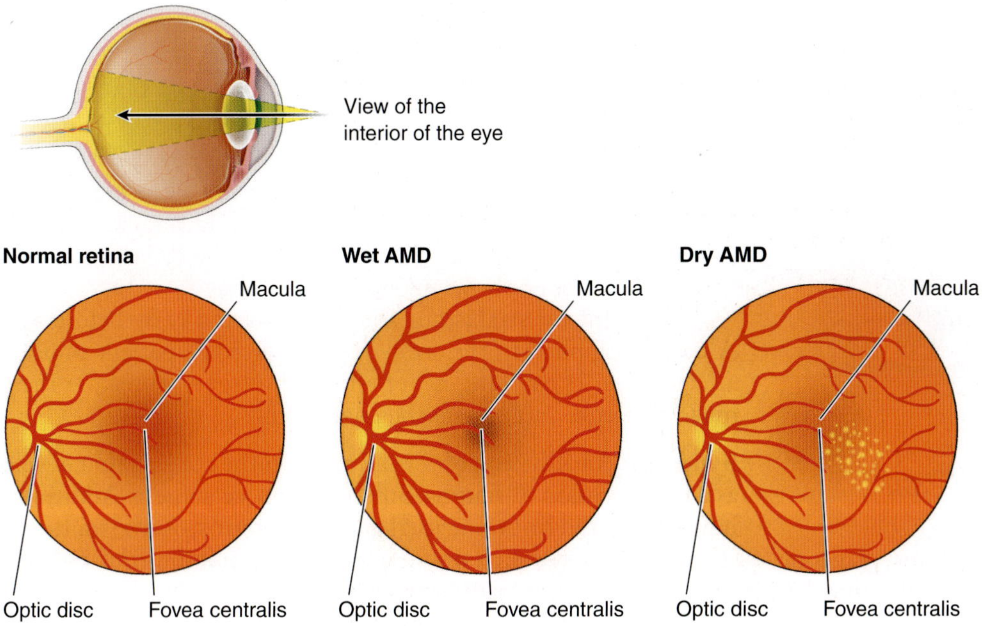

Figure 15-16 Dry and wet age-related macular degeneration.

of the movement. Diagnosis is confirmed by visual examination and observation of the involuntary eye movements. Treatment is directed at the underlying cause. If the cause is congenital, there is no effective treatment.

Ophthalmia neonatorum: Inflammation of the conjunctiva of the newborn. It is caused by the newborn's exposure to viral, bacterial, or chemical agents. In the United States, preventive antibiotic ointment is applied to the eyes of the newborn after birth to prevent *Neisseria* gonorrheal conjunctivitis. Chlamydial conjunctivitis can also be transmitted to the newborn while passing through the birth canal.

Presbyopia: An error of refraction caused by loss of elasticity of the lens due to aging (see Fig. 15-9). The patient notices an inability to focus on near objects and may complain of headaches. Diagnosis is obtained by ophthalmic examination, and treatment with reading glasses or contact lenses is advised.

Pterygium: The growth of irregular fibrovascular tissue on the conjunctiva (Fig. 15-17). It usually appears on the nasal side of the cornea and can disrupt vision if it extends over the pupil. Symptoms include redness, irritation, and itching. Causes include chronic dryness of the eye, allergies, or excessive exposure to ultraviolet light. Treatment with corticosteroids and lubricating ointments usually provides relief. Surgical excision of the tissue can be used if vision is compromised or if the patient seeks cosmetic correction.

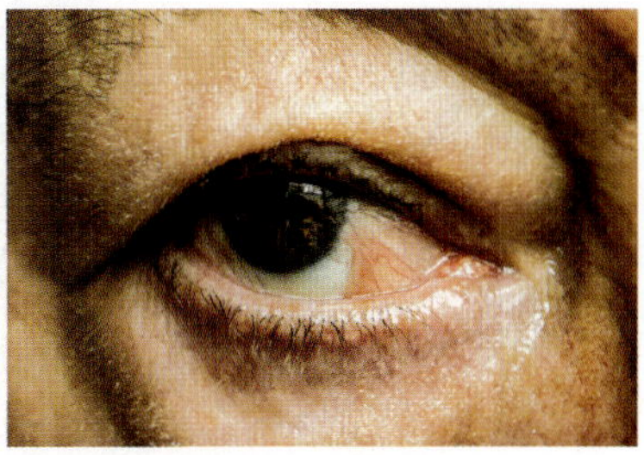

Figure 15-17 Pterygium.

Retinal tear: An opening in the retina that causes vitreous humor to leak under the retina (see Fig. 15-12). Diagnosis is confirmed by ophthalmic examination of the retina. Surgical correction is done with cryosurgery or photocoagulation. Early treatment can prevent recurrence and retinal detachment.

Scleritis: Inflammation of the sclera, the anterior white of the eye. Signs and symptoms include redness, dull pain, and sometimes a loss of vision. Diagnosis is confirmed by visual examination. If left untreated, it can lead to perforation and loss of the eye. Treatments include immunosuppressive medications to decrease inflammation.

Scotoma: An island-like blind spot in the visual field. It can be caused by looking directly into the sun, exposure to chemicals, eye injury, ARMD, or squinting. Additionally, some

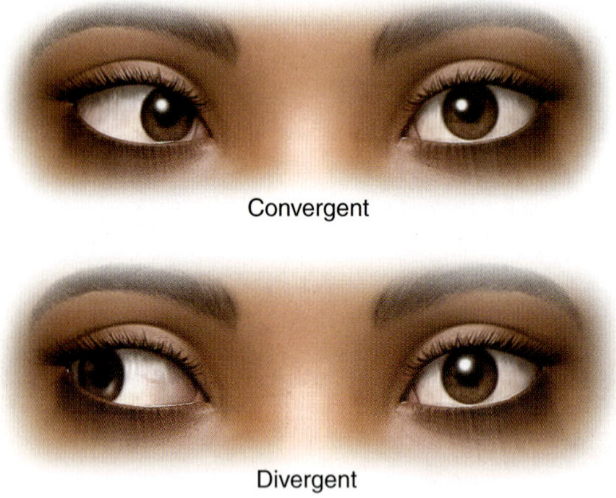

Figure 15-18 Convergent and divergent strabismus.

migraine headaches present with a blind spot. Treatment is directed at the cause of the scotoma.

Strabismus: The failure of the eyes to look in the same direction. It is caused by weakness in the oculomotor muscles that control the position of the eye. Two types of strabismus are convergent and divergent (Fig. 15-18). Convergent strabismus (cross-eye) is also called esotropia, where one eye turns inward. Divergent strabismus (walleye) is also known as exotropia, where one eye turns outward. Strabismus commonly occurs in early childhood.

Treatment for strabismus should be started early before age 5. A patch is applied to the strong eye to force the patient to use the affected eye. If patching is not effective, surgery to restore the eye muscle balance can correct the condition.

Synechia: An adhesion of the iris to the cornea or lens that develops as a complication of trauma, inflammation, or surgery. Additionally, it can be caused by cataracts, glaucoma, keratitis, or uveitis. It causes secondary glaucoma as the adhesion prevents outflow of aqueous humor, thus increasing intraocular pressure. As the pressure rises, rapid loss of vision progresses and can lead to blindness. Treatment of synechia is initiated with dilation of the pupils using a mydriatic. Subsequent treatment is directed at the underlying cause of the adhesion.

Trachoma: A contagious infection caused by *Chlamydia trachomatis*. Signs and symptoms include tearing, photophobia, and inflammation. Treatment with topical sulfonamides and oral erythromycin and tetracycline are effective. If left untreated, it can lead to blindness.

Uveitis: Inflammation of all or part of the iris, ciliary body, and the anterior choroid. It most commonly occurs in one eye, and symptoms include blurred vision, pain, redness, constriction of the pupil, and intense sensitivity to light (photophobia). Causes include autoimmune disorders and infection. Often the cause is unknown. Diagnosis is confirmed by a slit-lamp examination. Treatment includes steroids to reduce inflammation and cycloplegic agents to paralyze the ciliary muscle, allowing it to rest.

ELEMENT REVIEW
cycl/o = cycle, circle
-plegic = pertaining to partial paralysis

Ears

Cholesteatoma: A slow-growing cyst of epithelial cell debris that forms in the middle ear. Cholesteatoma forms as a result of a congenital malformation or results from chronic OM and tympanic membrane perforations. As the scaly epithelial cells migrate to the middle ear, they accumulate and form an infected cyst. Diagnosis is confirmed by patient history, audiometry, otoscopy, and x-ray. Treatment is extraction of the cholesteatoma by cleaning the middle ear canal. Surgical removal of the cholesteatoma is recommended if deterioration of the canal is observed, and repair is required. If left untreated, cholesteatoma can lead to conductive hearing loss, occlusion of the canal, and destruction of ossicles. If the roof of the middle ear cavity deteriorates, an abscess or meningitis may occur.

Deafness (conductive): Conductive deafness is a loss of hearing due to an inability of sound waves to reach the organ of Corti. It is caused by a structural or mechanical abnormality of the oval or round window, tympanic membrane, eustachian tube, ear ossicles, external auditory canal, or the pinna. Causes of the blockage of sound waves include otosclerosis, OM, a ruptured tympanic membrane, or impacted cerumen. Diagnosis is confirmed by audiometry to evaluate the extent of conductive hearing loss. Treatment is directed at the cause of loss of conduction of sound. If the defect cannot be fixed, hearing aids are recommended.

Deafness (sensorineural): Sensorineural hearing loss is caused by the inability of nerve stimuli to reach the brain via the auditory nerve. It is caused by damage or lesions of the auditory nerve, organ of Corti, or the cochlea. The condition can result in mild hearing loss to profound deafness. The condition can be caused by aging (presbycusis) or prolonged exposure to loud noise, loud music, or side effects of medications. It can also be caused by infection, tumors, trauma, vascular disorders, or genetic predisposition. Diagnosis is confirmed by patient history and audiometry to evaluate the extent of hearing loss. Treatment with hearing aids or cochlear implants can restore some hearing. Prevention of sensorineural hearing loss includes wearing ear protection around loud machinery and music. Ototoxic medications should be avoided, if possible.

ELEMENT REVIEW
ot/o = ear, hearing
-toxic = poison
cerumin/o = cerumen
-lytic = pertaining to destruction

Impacted cerumen: The excessive accumulation of cerumen (ear wax) from the ceruminous glands of the external ear canal. Causes include excessive hair or scaly skin in the ear canal or a narrowing of the canal that prevents cerumen from exiting the canal. Signs and symptoms include hearing loss, earache, dizziness, tinnitus (ringing in the ear), and a feeling of a "plugged" ear canal. Treatment consists of irrigation of the ear canal with water, manual removal of the cerumen by a clinician, or use of oil- or water-based ceruminolytic eardrops.

Labyrinthitis: The infection and/or inflammation of the labyrinth or the semicircular canals. Signs and symptoms include dizziness (vertigo), nystagmus (rapid involuntary eye movement), and hearing loss. Causes include viral infection, and rarely, bacterial infection. Diagnosis is confirmed by patient history and physical examination, including a neurological examination. Treatment includes bedrest and medications to lessen symptoms of vertigo. If bacterial infection is the cause, antibiotic therapy is advised.

Mastoiditis: The inflammation of the mastoid process (the bone located posterior and inferior to the ear canal), the mastoid process can be felt behind the ear and is filled with air cavities called the mastoid sinuses. Mastoiditis usually results from expansion of the ear canal due to acute OM. As the middle ear infection progresses, pus can collect in the mastoid sinuses, causing pain and hearing loss. Swelling can be observed over the mastoid process, and the patient may be febrile. It is sometimes associated with cholesteatoma. Diagnosis is confirmed by patient history, x-rays of the mastoid, audiometry, and otoscopy. Blood work and culture and sensitivity of ear exudate can identify a bacterial infection. Treatment with aggressive antibiotic therapy for a 2-week period is often required to prevent bone loss. If antibiotic therapy does not stop the infection, surgical removal of abscessed tissue is required to prevent a brain abscess.

Meniere's disease: The chronic overaccumulation of endolymph causing vertigo (dizziness), hearing loss, feeling of fullness and pressure in the ear, and tinnitus (ringing in the ears). Episodes of vertigo may last for hours or days and be accompanied by nausea, vomiting, loss of balance, and sweating. Most patients have one ear affected, but over time both ears may be affected. Causes of Meniere's disease are unknown but may include stress, excessive salt intake, and menstrual periods. Diagnosis is difficult to discern because the symptoms may be vague and are common to other disorders. Audiometry, x-ray, and patient history can help differential diagnosis of Meniere disease. Treatment includes dietary restriction of sodium, antihistamines, and diuretics and the use of mild sedatives and antiemetics when acute symptoms recur.

Otitis externa: The inflammation of the outer or external ear canal. It is also called "swimmer's ear" because it can be caused by water that remains in the external ear canal, which can create a moist environment that aids the growth of bacteria. Signs and symptoms include otalgia (ear pain), itching, and redness and swelling in the canal. Injury to the ear canal may occur if the patient tries to scratch the canal with a foreign object. Treatment with steroids and antibiotic eardrops are advised.

Otitis media: Inflammation and infection of the middle ear. Acute OM is most seen in infants, toddlers, and preschool age children. Approximately 70% to 80% of children acquire OM by the age of 3 years. It is caused by upper respiratory infection and dysfunction of the auditory tube. In young children, the auditory tubes are small and oriented horizontally, making drainage of fluid difficult. The accumulation of fluid provides an environment for bacteria to grow. The two types of OM are serous and suppurative, and are both treated with antibiotics.

ELEMENT REVIEW
ot/o = ear
-itis = inflammation
medi/o = middle
-a = noun ending
ser/o = blood serum
suppurative = producing pus
-us = noun ending

Serous OM is a collection of clear fluid behind the tympanic membrane. Signs and symptoms include a popping or snapping in the ear, a feeling of fullness and diminished mobility of the tympanic membrane. Diagnosis is confirmed by patient or parent history and examination of the tympanic membrane, which will appear red or pink and is retracted. Sometimes air bubbles can be seen behind the tympanic membrane.

Suppurative OM is a collection of pus behind the tympanic membrane. Signs and symptoms include severe ear pain, fever, vertigo (dizziness), loss of hearing, and tinnitus. The risk of rupture of tympanic membrane is a concern.

Otosclerosis: A condition in which the stapes becomes immobile and does not move the oval window. Thus transmission of sound to the inner ear is impaired. The condition commonly results in conductive hearing loss, but sensorineural hearing loss or mixed hearing loss may occur. Otosclerosis most commonly occurs in females and Caucasians with onset occurring from age 11 to 30. Onset of symptoms include inability to hear soft-spoken tones and tinnitus. Treatment includes use of hearing aids or surgery with stapedectomy and placement of tissue graft.

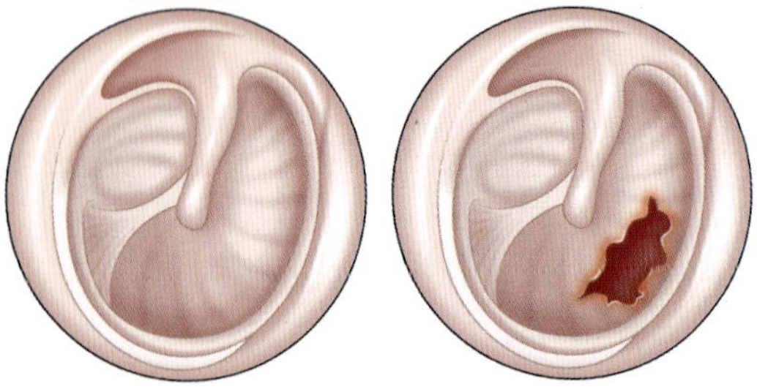

Figure 15-19 Perforation of the tympanic membrane.

Perforation of the tympanic membrane: A rupturing of the tympanic membrane caused by severe middle ear infection, which causes pressure on the tympanic membrane to build (Fig. 15-19). It can also be caused by trauma to the middle ear by a sharp object. Signs and symptoms include partial hearing loss and severe pain that decreases upon rupture as the pressure on the tympanic membrane is decreased. Suppurative drainage may occur. Diagnosis is confirmed by examination with an otoscope, which will show the rupture. Treatment consists of antibiotics to prevent infection because the inner ear is no longer protected by an intact tympanic membrane (TM). A patch may be applied to the eardrum to aid healing and protect the inner ear.

Presbycusis: Age-related hearing loss.

Pathology Word-Building Practice

1. Prefixes

Use the prefixes to build a word that corresponds to the definition provided.

an-	extra-	intra-
eso-	hemi-	presby-
exo-	hyper-	

1. Loss of one-half of the visual field ____________
2. Age-related hearing loss ____________
3. Age-related loss of vision ____________
4. Protrusion of the eyeball ____________
5. Pertaining to outside of the capsule ____________
6. Inward turning of the eyeball ____________
7. Outward turning of the margin of the eyelash ____________

8. Error of refraction caused by an abnormally shaped cornea or lens ____________________
9. Excessive sensitivity to sound ____________________
10. Pertaining to within the retina ____________________

2. Suffixes

Use the suffixes to build a word that corresponds to the definition provided.

-al	-osis	-plasty
-algia	-otomy	-plegia
-itis	-pexy	-rrhea
-meter		

1. Instrument used to measure anterior angle chamber of the eye ____________________
2. Corneal transplant ____________________
3. Inflammation of the middle ear ____________________
4. The process of measuring hearing ____________________
5. Flow discharge from the ear ____________________
6. Paralysis of the eye muscles ____________________
7. Surgical repair of the tympanic membrane ____________________
8. Pain in the ear ____________________
9. Surgical incision into the tympanic membrane ____________________
10. Pertaining to the cornea ____________________

Diagnostic Procedures

Eyes

Errors of refraction and the health of the tissues of the eyes can be evaluated by taking a patient history and using a variety of diagnostic tools. With diagnostic information, a treatment plan for the eye can be created.

Electronystagmography: The group of tests used to evaluate the vestibulo-ocular reflex. Water is instilled into the ear canal and contacts the tympanic membrane. Eye movement is observed and recorded. In healthy patients, the eyes should move in response to the stimuli. Patients with nystagmus will have a loss of reaction. The test should not be conducted on patients with a ruptured eardrum as instillation of water can cause infection.

Electroretinography: The recording of changes in the electrical potential of the retina after stimulation. The procedure is done with a contact lens electrode, which is placed on the cornea under anesthesia. Responses to electrical stimulation are recorded. The procedure is useful in diagnosing retinal disease.

Fluorescein staining: The application of fluorescein-stained sterile filter paper to the lower cul-de-sac of the eye. The paper is moistened with a few drops of sterile saline or sterile anesthetic solution. The eye is viewed under blue light and is useful in diagnosing corneal abrasion.

Gonioscopy: The process of viewing the anterior chamber, the area between the cornea and the iris. It is used to determine the drainage angle of the anterior eye. The procedure is done with a gonioprism, which is a mirrored contact lens and a slit-lamp biomicroscope. After local anesthesia, the gonioprism is placed lightly on the anterior eye and a narrow beam of light is directed at the eye. The ophthalmologist observes the width of the drainage angle, which helps diagnose open- versus closed-angle glaucoma.

Ophthalmoscopy: The examination of the external and internal structures of the eye with the ophthalmoscope. The procedure allows the provider to examine the interior of the eye using a focus dial and lenses of differing magnifications. Abnormalities of the retina can be observed and can indicate glaucoma, diabetic retinopathy, hypertension, brain lesions, and arteriosclerosis.

Pachymetry: A simple, painless process of measuring the thickness of the cornea. The procedure is helpful in diagnosing glaucoma and the patient's eligibility for corrective laser in situ keratomileusis (LASIK) surgery. Thin corneal readings are associated with an increased incidence of glaucoma.

Slit-lamp examination: The examination of the external and internal structures of the eye with a low-power microscope and high-intensity light source focused through a slit beam called a biomicroscope. The examination is used to view the eyelids, sclera, conjunctiva, iris, lens, cornea, and the retina.

ELEMENT REVIEW
ton/o = tension, tone
-metry = process of measuring
-meter = instrument used to measure

Tonometry: The process of measuring intraocular pressure of the eye by calculating resistance of the eyeball to an applied force. Measuring with a noncontact tonometer is conducted by applying a puff of air to the anterior of the eye without touching the eye with the instrument. The tonometer records the resistance of the cornea and thus the intraocular pressure. Alternately, the Goldman applanation tonometer uses a special probe to flatten part of the cornea to measure eye pressure. A drop of anesthetic and fluorescent dye is placed on the cornea. The cornea is then illuminated with a slit-lamp, and the front of the eye is touched by the tonometer.

Ears

The diagnosis of hearing loss, infection, or damage to the ears can be obtained by techniques that include taking a patient history or testing on a variety of equipment.

Audiometry: The process of measuring a patient's ability to hear various frequencies of sound waves. The test is conducted in a soundproof cubicle to eliminate extraneous noises. Patients wear earphones and are instructed to indicate when they hear tones and the duration of the tone. The audiometer delivers single frequencies, beginning with low-frequency tones and progressing to high-frequency tones. The tone is played in each ear, and the volume is slowly lowered. Both the frequency and the volume of the tones perceived in each ear are recorded. The results are recorded on a graph called an audiogram.

Otoscopy: The process of viewing and examining the tympanic membrane and various parts of the outer ear. The lighted otoscope is placed in the external ear canal where the provider can observe color, lesions, tears, or impacted cerumen.

Tuning fork tests: Conducted using a metal tuning fork that is struck, causing it to vibrate. Two tests are used to evaluate conduction hearing loss versus sensorineural hearing loss (Table 15-4).

The Rinne test is conducted by hitting the base of the fork, causing vibration. It is then placed on the patient's mastoid bone and held there until the patient can no longer hear the sound produced. It is then quickly moved to the front of the ear near the ear canal, but not touching the patient. Patients are asked if they can hear the sound. The patient with normal hearing and sensorineural hearing loss will hear the sound longer through the air than through the bone and thus will continue to hear the sound (Table 15-4). If the patient does not hear the sound, conduction hearing loss is present.

The Weber test is conducted by hitting the base of the fork and placing it on the center of the patient's forehead. The patient is asked to report the loudness of sound in each ear. Normally, the loudness of the sound is equal in both ears. Hearing sound more in one ear than the other is indicative of hearing loss. If conductive hearing loss is present, the sound will be heard louder in the affected ear because the patient is unable to hear background noise conducted through the air. If sensorineural hearing loss is present, the sound is heard louder in the unaffected ear.

TABLE 15-4 Comparison of the Rinne and Weber Tests

Test	Normal	Conductive Hearing Loss	Sensorineural Hearing Loss
Rinne 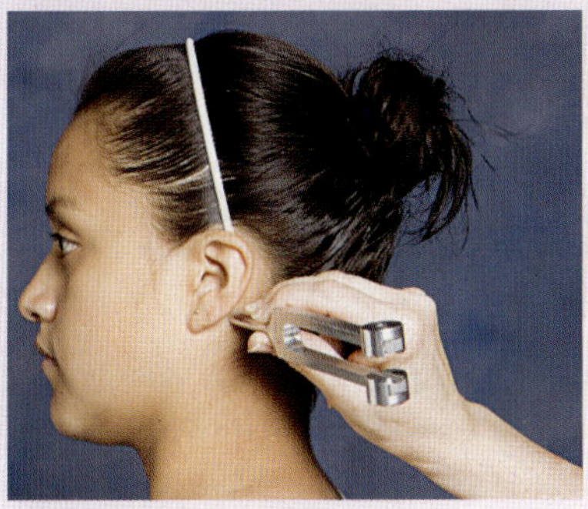	Air louder than bone	Bone louder than air	Air louder than bone
Weber 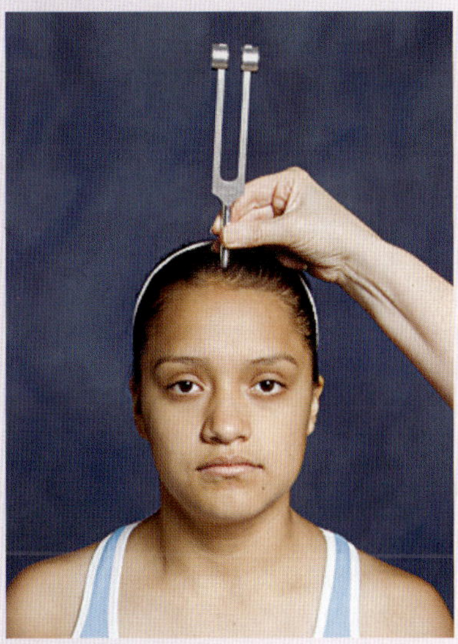	Sound heard in midline	Sound heard louder in bad ear	Sound heard louder in good ear

CAREER EXPLORATION: OPTICIAN

I began wearing glasses in fourth grade. I was having trouble seeing the whiteboard in the classroom, and my teacher noticed that I squinted to see what she was writing. Mrs. Jennings told my mom about my squinting, and mom took me to the optometrist to be evaluated. I remember the machine Dr. Danson had me look through. As she changed the lens, my vision became clear. I was prescribed a pair of glasses for distance vision. After the doctor gave my mom the prescription, we went to the vision store to buy some glasses. I remember the optician, Jeremy, helping me choose frames. Because I was still a child, the frames were small and made of lightweight plastic, so they didn't feel heavy on my face. Jeremy also advised me and my mom to get scratch-resistant lenses, so I wouldn't damage the lens. With my vision corrected, I enjoyed school more, I could read the board easily, and I didn't feel like I had to constantly catch up. I began to love school, especially science and math. I've had many pairs of eyeglasses since then, and Jeremy helped me each time. When I was a senior in high school, Jeremy asked me what career interested me. Because I love science and math, I began to explore becoming an optician. I asked Jeremy about the profession and how to become a licensed optician. He told me about his training to become an optician and how much he enjoys his job. I researched and enrolled in an online program. The training took a year to complete, and I took classes in normal eye anatomy and physiology, pathology of the eyes, and visual acuity. One of the hardest classes was a math class in which students learned the calculations used in optical math, which means how the lens (either glasses or contact lens) corrects a patient's vision. Upon completion of my courses, I took the American Board of Opticianry (ABO) examination, the National Opticianry Competency Examination (NOCE), and the contact lens registry examination (CLRE). With these certifications, I can use the title of licensed optician. Jeremy offered me a job at the vision store, and I love working with my patients. I recently had a 9-year-old patient who came into the store for his first pair of glasses. It made me think of myself at that age and how correcting my vision helped me with my schoolwork and gave me confidence.

Special Senses Therapeutic Procedures

Eyes

Contact lenses: Small round lenses placed directly on the eye's surface. An optometrist prescribes contact lenses to correct errors of refraction, and contact lenses focus light on the retina of the eye, creating a sharp image. Contact lenses may be preferred rather than eyeglasses for contact sports, swimming, and many outdoor activities.

Extracapsular cataract extraction: The surgical removal of the anterior segment of the lens and its capsule, allowing insertion of an intraocular lens implant (IOL) (Fig. 15-20). The procedure requires a larger incision than phacoemulsification of the lens, but it is chosen if cataracts are too advanced for the use of phacoemulsification.

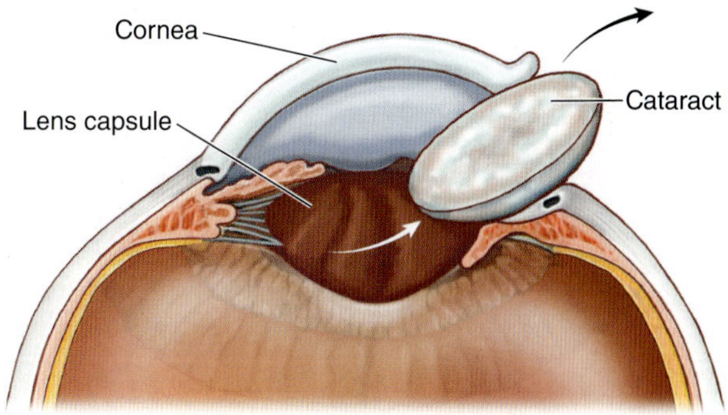

Figure 15-20 Extracapsular cataract extraction.

Eyeglasses: Prescribed by an optometrist and worn to correct vision by focusing light on the retina of the eye, creating a sharp image. Patients can wear either glasses or contact lenses to correct errors of refraction.

IOL implant: The surgical process of inserting an artificial lens after cataract extraction. The procedure restores sight diminished by formation of a cataract.

Iridectomy: The extraction of a small segment of the iris to open the anterior chamber angle and allow flow of aqueous humor into the posterior chamber. It is used as a treatment for closed-angle glaucoma because the procedure lowers intraocular pressure. A similar procedure, a laser iridectomy, is used to create several small openings in the iris.

Keratoplasty: The surgical transplantation of corneal tissue into the eye from a cadaver donor (also called corneal transplant). It is used to replace a cornea that is damaged from dystrophy or scarring due to trauma or infection.

Laser in situ keratomileusis (LASIK): Procedure in which a laser is used to create a flap in the cornea, exposing its inner layers. The flap may be created by either a microkeratome or a femtosecond laser. The surgeon then uses a computer-guided excimer laser, which delivers a series of cool ultraviolet light pulses that vaporize the corneal tissue to correct the refractive error. Once the correction is completed, the flap is reset into its original position. Approximately 90% of patients who have the procedure have postsurgical vision of 20/20 to 20/40.

Phacoemulsification: The use of ultrasound vibrations to split the lens material into tiny particles that can be suctioned out of the eye. After removal of the lens, an IOL implant is placed. Phacoemulsification requires the smallest incision into the cornea; thus, the healing time is shorter than the extracapsular cataract extraction. It is the preferred surgical method.

Photorefractive keratotomy: The surgical procedure in which a few layers of the corneal surface are shaved off by a laser beam. The surgery is performed to flatten the cornea and reduce nearsightedness (myopia).

Retinal photocoagulation: The surgical procedure that uses an argon laser to treat retinopathies such as detached retina or diabetic retinopathy. If detachment is present, the laser is used to create areas of inflammation on the retina and adhere the retina to the choroid. If microaneurysms are present, the laser can be used to seal the leaking vessels and reduce the risk of hemorrhage.

Trabeculectomy: The surgical excision of a portion of the corneoscleral tissue, which allows aqueous humor to flow from the posterior chamber to the anterior chamber, thus decreasing intraocular pressure (Fig. 15-21). The procedure usually includes removal of the trabecular meshwork and the canal of Schlemm.

ELEMENT REVIEW
trabecul/o = trabecular region
-ectomy = surgical excision
corne/o = cornea
scler/o = sclera
-al = pertaining to

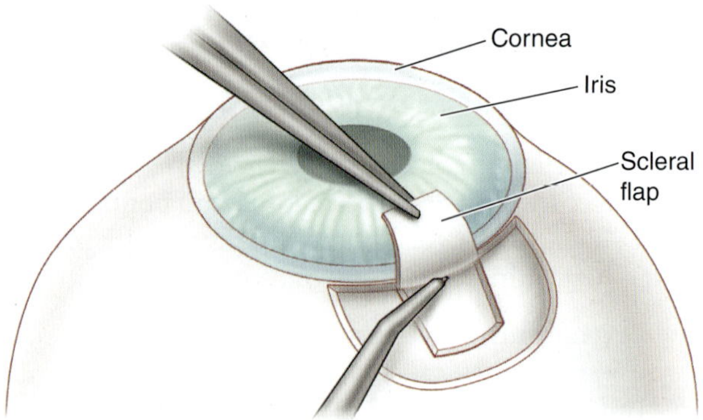

Figure 15-21 Trabeculectomy.

Trabeculoplasty: The surgical creation of a permanent fistula to drain aqueous humor from the anterior chamber. An argon laser is used to blanch the trabecular meshwork, allowing drainage of accumulating fluid out of the eye.

Vitrectomy: The surgical removal of vitreous humor, the gel-like substance that gives the eye its shape. It may be performed to repair a detached retina, remove scar tissue that has formed on the retina or macula, or to evacuate blood from a vitreous hemorrhage that does not spontaneously resorb. Using a microscope, the surgeon suctions out the vitreous gel, repairs damage to the retina (with a laser), and replaces the gel with saline or a gas bubble. Saline or gas restores normal pressure in the eye and preserves the shape of the eyeball. Patients who have a gas bubble placed in the eye cannot fly in an airplane, go into the mountains, or scuba dive for a prescribed postsurgical period because rapid altitude changes can change the size of the gas bubble and cause damage to the retina.

ELEMENT REVIEW
neur/o = nerve
prosthesis = replacement device

Ears

Cochlear implant: The surgically implanted neuroprosthesis that restores hearing to a patient with moderate to severe sensorineural hearing loss (see Fig. 15-1). The device bypasses acoustic hearing by direct electrical stimulation of the auditory nerve. The device has two main components: The outside component is worn behind the ear or can be attached to clothing, and the inside component is the surgically implanted device that contains the coil that receives the sound stimuli. The procedure is performed under general anesthesia and is often performed as an outpatient procedure, with the patient going home the same day. Surgical risks are minimal, but the patient may experience dizziness or, on rare occasions, some tinnitus.

Hearing aids: Small devices, worn in the ear or behind the ear, that amplify sound. Hearing aids contain a microphone that detects sound, an amplifier to increase the volume of the sound, and a receiver that transmits the sound into the ear canal toward the organ of Corti. Hearing aids have different styles to accommodate different types and severities of hearing loss (Fig. 15-22).

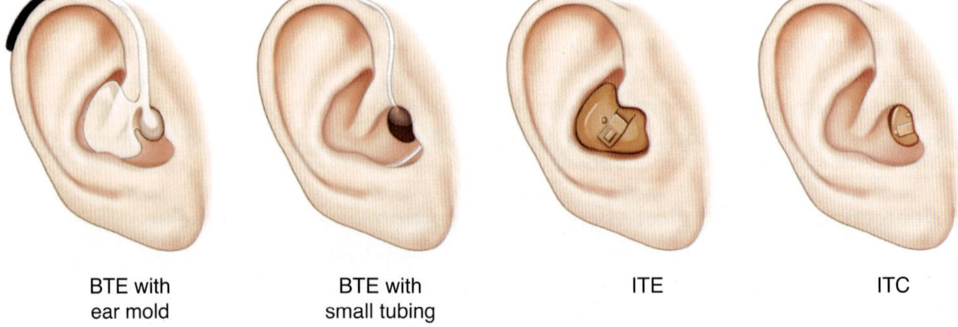

Figure 15-22 Types of hearing aids.

In the ear style hearing aid is worn in the external ear canal and may be full shell or half shell. Advantages of this style include a greater degree of amplification than for other styles and the ability to use the toggle switch in order to use a telephone. It is important to clean the hearing aid because cerumen can collect in it and clog the device.

In the canal style hearing aids are the least conspicuous of the styles because they fit completely into the ear canal; thus, they cannot be seen easily. They are not recommended for patients who do not have good dexterity because the device is very small and must be cleaned and the battery charged.

Behind the ear style hearing aids allow the most amplification and are the most conspicuous device because they are seen outside of the ear. It is the easiest style to care for because it is the largest.

Myringoplasty: The surgical repair of a ruptured tympanic membrane (also called a tympanoplasty). The tympanic membrane is repaired with a tissue graft from the patient or with a gel-like material. The procedure is performed under local or general anesthesia. The surgical site is treated with topical antibiotics and packing material to keep it in place and prevent infection while the graft heals.

ELEMENT REVIEW
myring/o = tympanic membrane
tympan/o = tympanic membrane
ot/o = ear
rhin/o = nose
laryng/o = larynx
-ologist = specialist

Otoplasty: The surgical removal or repositioning of the ear cartilage closer to the head. It is usually performed for cosmetic purposes or correction after trauma.

Stapedectomy: Microsurgery to remove the diseased stapes caused by otosclerosis. The stapes is replaced with a tissue graft and prosthesis to reestablish a pathway for vibrations to deliver sound waves to the oval window. The prothesis is attached to the incus at the superficial end and to the oval window at the deep end. The patient notices a marked improvement in the perception of sound after postsurgical swelling has resolved.

Tympanostomy with tubes: The surgical implantation of a small ventilation tube in the inferior segment of the tympanic membrane (Fig. 15-23). Indications for the procedure include recurrent episodes of OM (more than three episodes in 6 months or more than four episodes in 12 months), poor response to antibiotic therapy for OM, or hearing loss from chronic infections. It is most commonly performed on children aged 1 to 3 years. The

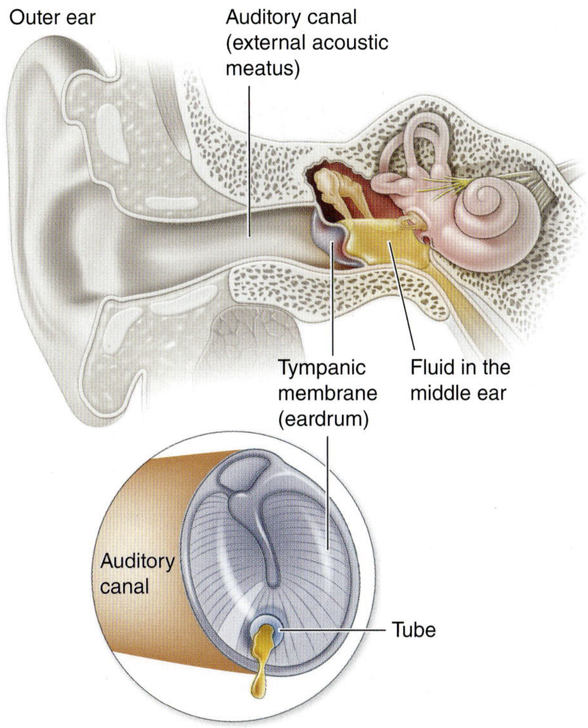

Figure 15-23 Tympanostomy with tubes.

tube provides drainage and decreases the risk of the TM rupturing from pressure and fluid buildup. During the procedure, the otorhinolaryngologist performs a myringotomy, the creation of a small incision into the TM with a scalpel or, in a newer procedure, with a laser (laser-assisted myringotomy [LAM]) and suctions fluid out of the canal. The tubes are then inserted into the incision to allow drainage of fluid. The tubes will spontaneously fall out of the ear within a few months to a year. The patient must avoid getting water in the ear while the tubes are in place as water could carry infectious agents into the inner ear.

Procedures and Diagnostics Review

1. Surgical creation of a fistula to drain aqueous humor from the anterior chamber using an argon laser ____________________
2. Surgical application of a graft to a ruptured tympanic membrane ____________________
3. Abnormal growth of fibrous vascular tissue on the conjunctiva ____________________
4. Surgical procedure that uses an argon laser to treat a detached retina or diabetic retinopathy ____________________
5. Surgical replacement of the stapes with a tissue graft and prosthesis ____________________
6. A painful bacterial infection of an eyelash follicle or sebaceous gland ____________________
7. The instrument used to measure a patient's ability to hear various frequencies of sound waves ____________________
8. Chronic condition of dizziness, vertigo, and nausea caused by excess endolymph ____________________
9. A condition that results in immobility of the stapes ____________________
10. A condition of a plug of wax blocking the ear canal and causing hearing loss ____________________
11. Surgical procedure that uses ultrasound vibrations to split the lens of the eye for removal ____________________
12. Surgical implantation of a neuroprosthesis to restore hearing ____________________
13. Surgical transplantation of a cornea from a cadaver donor ____________________

14. the medical term for night blindness ______________________

15. The process of measuring the thickness of the cornea ______________________

CASE STUDY, completed

Finally, the day for activating the cochlear implant is here! Taay and her parents go to the office for her 1-month postoperative visit. Dr. Wysenski examines both ears and both incisions. He then attaches the external parts of the device and activates the internal device. Taay is startled by the first sounds she hears; everything is so loud! She hears her mom say, "I love you Taay." It is an emotional moment, and both Taay and her mom cry. Her dad gives her a big hug. Dr. Wysenski explains that Taay will need to meet with a speech and language pathologist for therapy that will help with hearing and speech skills. She will also need to come into the office for periodic adjustments to the device. Taay's dad thanks Dr. Wysenski, and they go home with hope for the future.

CRITICAL-THINKING QUESTIONS

1. Dr. Wysenski makes a retromastoid incision, which means ______________________.
2. Taay's procedure is performed bilaterally, which means ______________________.
3. Dr. Wysenski is a surgeon who specializes in the ears, nose, and throat, a specialty called ______________________.
4. Taay is brought to the operating room in the supine position, which means ______________________.
5. The receiver is placed under the skin. How else can you say, "under the skin"? ______________________.
6. Taay suffered from multiple middle ear infections, a condition called ______________________.
7. Some of the antibiotics that were prescribed to Taay were *ototoxic,* which means ______________________.
8. Taay's hearing loss is sensorineural, meaning ______________________.
9. Dissect the word *anesthesia*. ______________________.
10. Dissect the word *audiologist*. ______________________.

Medications for the Special Senses

Table 15-5 lists medications of the special senses, including those that alleviate symptoms of infection and inflammation, reduce intraocular pressure, soften cerumen, provide local anesthesia, or dilate the pupil for an eye examination. Medications are administered in the eye, ear, or orally, depending on their mechanism of action.

TABLE 15-5 Examples of Medications for the Eyes and Eyes

Classification	Examples	Common Use/Action
Antivertigo agents	Meclizine (Anti-Vert, Bonine), diphenhydramine (Benedryl)	Prevention and treatment of motion sickness, vertigo
Cerumenolytics	Carbamide peroxide solution (Auro, Debrox)	Softens earwax
Ophthalmic alpha blockers	Aproclonidine HCL (Lopidine), dipiverfrin (Propine)	Eye irritation
Ophthalmic beta blockers	Betaxolol, levobunolol HCL (Betagan)	Treatment of open-angle glaucoma
Carbonic anhydrase inhibitors	Acetazolamide (Diamox, Sequels, Adopt)	Treatment of glaucoma
Cycloplegic mydriatics	Pilocarpine (Isopto Carpine solution; Scopace)	Dilates the pupil for diagnostic or surgical procedures or to treat inflammation
Immunomodulators	Cyclosporine (Restasis)	To increase tear production
Miotics	Pilocarpine HCL (Isopto Carpine)	Treatment of glaucoma
Ophthalmic antibiotics	Gentamicin Ophthalmic (Garamycin ophthalmic), tobramycin (Tobrex), ciprofloxacin (Ciloxan)	Eye infection
Ophthalmic corticosteroids	Dexamethasone (AK-Dex, Ocu-Dex), prednisone ophthalmic (Pred Forte, Prednisol)	Inflammation and pain caused by injury or surgery
Ophthalmic local anesthetics	Tetracaine (Altacaine, Opticaine), proparacaine (Alcaine, Ophthetic)	Presurgical anesthesia
Ophthalmic anti-inflammatories	Diclofenac 0.1% sol (Cambia, Voltaren)	Inflammation, pain, and chronic dry eye
Osmotic diuretics	Glycerin (Osmoglyn, Ophthalgan solution)	Treatment of glaucoma Decreases intraocular pressure
Ophthalmic prostaglandin agonists	Bimatoprost (Lumigan), Latanoprost (Xalatan solution)	Treatment of open-angle glaucoma and ocular hypertension
Otic antibiotics	Ofloxacin (Floxin), acetic acid (Vosol)	Treatment of ear infection
Otic combination drugs	Ciprofloxacin and dexamethasone (Ciprodex), hydrocortisone and neomycin (Vosol HCL)	Treatment of ear infection with inflammation

Medications Review

Using Table 15-5, complete the chart below. The first one has been done for you.

Medication Name	Classification (mechanism)	Therapeutic Use (What is it used for?)
Vosol	*Otic antibiotic*	*To treat ear infections*
Prednisone ophthalmic (Pred Forte, Prednisol)	______________	______________
Voltaren	______________	______________
Restasis	______________	______________
Pilocarpine HCL	______________	______________
Antivert, Bonine	______________	______________
Glycerin (Osmoglyn, Ophthalgan Solution)	______________	______________
Bimatoprost (Lumigan), Latanoprost (Xalatan solution)	______________	______________
Auro, Debrox	______________	______________
Proparacaine (Alcaine, Ophthetic)	______________	______________

Special Senses Abbreviations

Eye Abbreviations

Acc	accommodation
ARMD	age-related macular degeneration
cc	with correction (glasses)
ECCE	extracapsular cataract extraction
EOM	extraocular movement
ERG	electroretinogram
ICCE	intracapsular cataract extraction
IOL	intraocular lens
IOP	intraocular pressure
LASIK	laser in situ keratomileusis
OD	right cyc (ocular dexter)
OS	left eye (ocular sinister)
OU	both eyes (ocular uterque)
PEARL	pupils equal and reactive to light
PERLA	pupils equal; reactive to light and accommodation
PERRLA	pupils equal, round, reactive to light, and accommodation
PK	penetrating keratoplasty (corneal transplant)
REM	rapid eye movement
sc	without correction
TED	thyroid eye disease
VA	visual acuity
VF	visual field
VTX	vitrectomy

Ear Abbreviations

ABLB alternate binaural loudness balance

ABR auditory brainstem response

AC air conduction

AD right ear (auris dextra)

AS left ear (auris sinistra)

AOM acute otitis media

AU both ears (auris unitas)

BC bone conduction

BOM bilateral otitis media

COM chronic otitis media

db decibel

LAM laser-assisted myringotomy

OE otitis externa

PTS permanent threshold shift

SOM serous otitis media

TM tympanic membrane

TTS temporary threshold shift

Head and Neck Abbreviations

EENT ears, eyes, nose, and throat

ENT ears, nose, and throat

Strept streptococcal infection (of the throat)

Abbreviations Review

Choose the correct definition for the abbreviation:

1. TM
   a. temporomandibular
   b. tympanic membrane
   c. temporal membrane
   d. threshold measurement

2. PK
   a. penetrating keratoplasty
   b. pupils and keratin
   c. penetration of keratin
   d. plastic keratin repair

3. ARMD
   a. age-reduced macular degeneration
   b. age ratio of macular degeneration
   c. age-related macular degeneration
   d. acoustic related macular degeneration

4. BOM
   a. bilateral optic medicine
   b. bilateral otic medicine
   c. bilateral otitis media
   d. biaxial otic medicine

5. LASIK
   a. laser in situ keratomileusis
   b. light in situ keratomileusis
   c. laser in situ keratoplasty
   d. light in situ keratoplasty

6. EOM
   a. extra otic movement
   b. extraocular movement
   c. external otic movement
   d. external ocular movement

7. PERRLA
   a. pupils, eyes, round, react to light and age
   b. pupils, equal, round, react to light and age
   c. pupils, equal, round, react lens to age
   d. pupils, equal, round, react to light and accommodation

8. AD
   a. right eye
   b. right ear
   c. left eye
   d. left ear

9. OS
   a. right eye
   b. right ear
   c. left eye
   d. left ear

10. cc
    a. with correction
    b. without correction
    c. with correlation
    d. without correlation

11. VF
    a. virtual field
    b. visual field
    c. vitreous field
    d. vitrectomy

12. IOP
    a. internal ocular pressure
    b. intraotic pressure
    c. intraocular pressure
    d. intraorbital pressure

13. REM
    a. rapid eye movement
    b. retrograde eye movement
    c. residual eye movement
    d. repeated eye movement

14. db
    a. decibel
    b. double blind
    c. double balance
    d. declaration of blindness

15. ABR
    a. auditory brainstem response
    b. axial brainstem response
    c. aural brainstem response
    d. attention brainstem response

16. VA
    a. Veterans' affairs
    b. visual acuity
    c. vitreous acuity
    d. vitreous alignment

17. ICCE
    a. intracorporeal cataract extraction
    b. intracapsular cataract extraction
    c. intercapsular cataract extraction
    d. intercorporeal cataract extraction

18. ERG
    a. electroretinogram
    b. electroretrogram
    c. elective retinal grading
    d. electroregression grade

19. ABLB
    a. auditory binaural loudness balance
    b. alternate biaural lateral balance
    c. alternate binaural lateral balance
    d. alternate binaural loudness balance

20. TTS
    a. temporary threshold shift
    b. temporal threshold shift
    c. tympanic threshold shift
    d. tonal threshold shift

MEDICAL DOCUMENTATION

Knowledge of terms related to normal anatomy and pathological conditions enables you to understand medical documentation such as the following operative report, or history and physical exams, discharge summaries, laboratory reports, and x-ray reports. Apply your knowledge by answering the questions that follow the report.

Operative Report

Date: February 12, 20XX **Name:** Joseph P.

Preoperative diagnoses:
1. Nuclear sclerotic cataract—right eye
2. Astigmatism—right eye

Postoperative diagnoses:
1. Nuclear sclerotic cataract—right eye
2. Astigmatism—right eye

Continued

MEDICAL DOCUMENTATION—cont'd

Procedures performed:

1. Phacoemulsification with IOL implantation, right eye
2. Limbal relaxing incisions—right eye

Surgeon: David O'Brien, MD
Assistant: Craig Ellison, MD
Anesthesia: Retrobulbar injection with continuous monitoring
Complications: None
Indications for procedure: Poor vision, right eye

Description of procedure: After signing the informed consent, the patient was brought to the operating room and placed in the supine position for phacoemulsification with IOL of the right eye. Blood pressure and cardiac function were monitored for the duration of the procedure. The patient was prepped and draped in the usual sterile fashion for ophthalmic surgery of the right eye. A lid speculum was placed. A 5-mm area was measured traveling in the 95-degree position, and viscoelastic was placed on the cornea. A 550-μm guarded blade was used to make a limbal relaxing incision of 5 mm at the 95-degree axis.

Following this, an eye knife was applied to make a paracentesis wound at the 5 o'clock position. Viscoelastic was then injected into the anterior chamber through the incision. A temporal clear corneal incision was then made using a 2.75-mm keratome blade at the 2 o'clock position. This incision was used to insert a cystitome needle, and a continuous curvilinear capsulorrhexis was made in the anterior lens capsule.

Then the nucleus was hydrodissected and rotated; the phaco needle was placed into the eye. The nucleus was grooved and split into four quadrants. The quadrants were then phacoemulsified and removed from the eye. The I/A handpiece was inserted into the eye, and all remaining cortex was aspirated. The capsular bag was inflated using Healon. An SA60AT lens, measuring 22.5 diopters in strength, was placed into the capsule and rotated into position.

The wounds were checked for leaks and found to have none. A drop of Betadine, 4% pilocarpine, and Lumigan were placed in the eye. The lid speculum was removed, and a sterile patch was applied, along with an eye shield.

The patient was brought to the recovery room in good condition. He was given a follow-up appointment in the office for the following morning.

Electronically signed,
David O'Brien, MD
Ophthalmologist

Questions

1. Joseph's right eye is being operated on. What is the abbreviation for the right eye? ____________________
2. What instrument is used to hold the eyelid up? ____________________
3. What is the word element that means lens? ____________________
4. What does the term capsulorrhexis mean? ____________________
5. Refer to the list of medications in the chapter. Why was Lumigan applied at the conclusion of the procedure? ____________________

MEDICAL DOCUMENTATION—cont'd

6. Joseph was placed in the supine position, which means ______________________
7. Dr. O'Brien is an ophthalmologist, which means ______________________
8. What type of monitoring was conducted throughout the procedure? ______________________
9. Break down the term *hydrodissected*. What does it mean? ______________________
10. An IOL implant was placed, which means ______________________

CHAPTER REVIEW

Complete the Sentence

1. The process of focusing on objects at various distances is called ______________________
2. Hearing loss is caused by the nerve damage to the ______________________
3. The "blind spot" on the retina is called the ______________________
4. The sense of smell is called ______________________
5. Photoreceptors that perceive color are called ______________________
6. The term for the bending of light rays as they pass through the eye is ______________________
7. The malleus, incus, and stapes are collectively called ______________________
8. The lens of the eye is attached to suspensory ligaments of the ______________________
9. The medical physician is called an ENT, which is an abbreviation for ______________________
10. A cyst of epithelial cells that collect in the middle ear is called a ______________________
11. The process of applying a puff of air to the eye to measure intraocular pressure is called ______________________

12. The term for an acute or chronic inflammation and infection of the middle ear is ______________________

13. Progressive loss of vision due to clouding of the lens is known as ______________________

14. The surgical procedure using a laser to remove the lens is a ______________________

15. The medical term for ringing in the ears is ______________________

16. The licensed professional that fills prescriptions for contact lenses and glasses is a ______________________

17. The abbreviation that means both ears is ______________________

18. The category of medications used to soften ear wax is known as ______________________

19. Drooping of an eyelid is called ______________________

20. Involuntary movements of the eye in vertical, horizontal, rotary, or mixed movements are known as ______________________

21. Inflammation of the mastoid process is ______________________

22. The sense of taste is called ______________________

23. The medical term for tear ducts is ______________________

24. The surgeon that corrects pathologies of the eyes is known as ______________________

25. The medical term anterior mucous membrane of the eye is ______________________

Identify the Path of Sound

List the following structures in order of sound vibrations from the ear to the brain:

auditory nerve	1. ______________________
cerebral cortex	2. ______________________
cochlea	3. ______________________
external auditory canal	4. ______________________

incus	5.	____________________
malleus	6.	____________________
organ of Corti	7.	____________________
oval window	8.	____________________
pinna	9.	____________________
stapes	10.	____________________
tympanic membrane	11.	____________________

Spelling Review

Circle the correctly spelled terms in the pairs of terms.

1.	opthalmic	ophthalmic
2.	macular	maculor
3.	pina	pinna
4.	auricular	earicular
5.	lingual	lingaul
6.	glaucoma	glacouma
7.	otittis	otitis
8.	optician	optican
9.	cerumin	cerumen
10.	malleus	maleus

Abbreviations Review

1. Acc ____________________
2. PERLA ____________________
3. AU ____________________
4. OU ____________________
5. VF ____________________
6. ECCE ____________________

7. OE ______________________________

8. BC ______________________________

9. VTX ______________________________

10. HEENT ______________________________

Identify the Anatomical Structures

Match the structures of the eye from the following lists to the letters shown in Figure 15-24.

1. ______ anterior chamber
2. ______ canal of Schlemm
3. ______ choroid
4. ______ ciliary body
5. ______ cornea
6. ______ fovea
7. ______ interior rectus muscle
8. ______ iris
9. ______ lens
10. ______ optic disc
11. ______ optic nerve
12. ______ posterior chamber
13. ______ pupil
14. ______ retina
15. ______ retinal artery and vein
16. ______ sclera
17. ______ suspensory ligament
18. ______ vitreous chamber

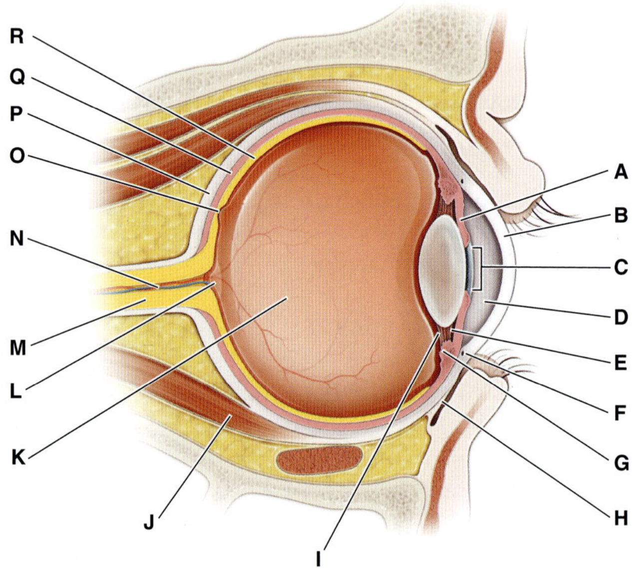

Figure 15-24 Identify the structures of the eye.

Match the structures of the ear from the following lists to the letters shown in Figure 15-25.

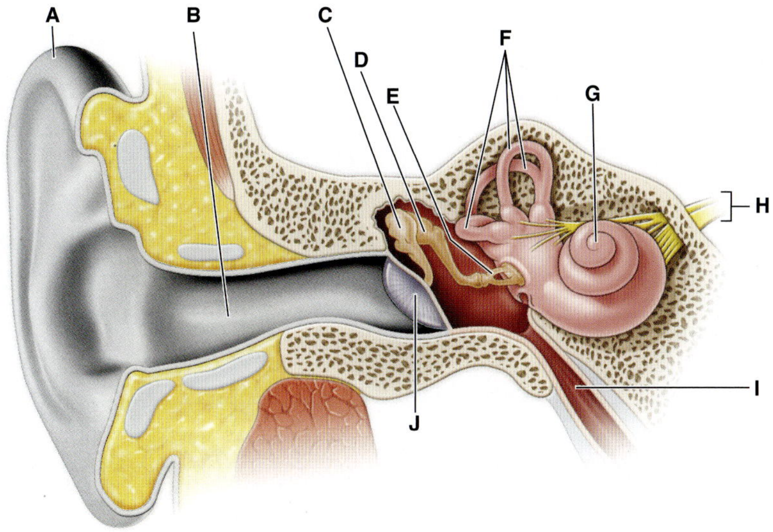

Figure 15-25 Identify the structures of the ear.

1. _______ cochlea
2. _______ eustachian tube
3. _______ external auditory canal
4. _______ incus
5. _______ malleus
6. _______ pinna (auricle)
7. _______ semicircular canals
8. _______ stapes
9. _______ tympanic membrane
10. _______ vestibulocochlear nerve

Decipher the Terms

Separate each term into its prefix (if any), combining form, and suffix. Next, translate the word parts and then give the common definition of the term. Blepharoplasty has been done for you as an example.

blepharoplasty

Prefix: *none* ____________ *Combining Form:* *blephar/o = eyelid* ____________

Suffix: *-plasty = surgical repair* ____________

Meaning: *surgical correction/repair of an eyelid* ____________

1. myringotomy

Prefix: ____________ *Combining Form:* ____________ *Suffix:* ____________

Meaning: ____________

2. exophthalmia

Prefix: ____________ *Combining Form:* ____________ *Suffix:* ____________

Meaning: ____________

3. retinopathy

Prefix: ______________ *Combining Form:* ______________ *Suffix:* ______________

Meaning: ____

4. episcleritis

Prefix: ______________ *Combining Form:* ______________ *Suffix:* ______________

Meaning: ____

5. ophthalmoscope

Prefix: ______________ *Combining Form:* ______________ *Suffix:* ______________

Meaning: ____

6. photophobia

Prefix: ______________ *Combining Form:* ______________ *Suffix:* ______________

Meaning: ____

7. audiometry

Prefix: ______________ *Combining Form:* ______________ *Suffix:* ______________

Meaning: ____

8. amblyopia

Prefix: ______________ *Combining Form:* ______________ *Suffix:* ______________

Meaning: ____

9. monochromatism

Prefix: ______________ *Combining Form:* ______________ *Suffix:* ______________

Meaning: ____

10. iridoplegia

Prefix: ______________ *Combining Form:* ______________ *Suffix:* ______________

Meaning: ____

APPENDIX A

Combining Forms

A

abdomen/o	abdomen
abdomin/o	abdomen
acous/o	hearing
acr/o	extremities
aden/o	gland
adenoid/o	adenoids
adip/o	fat
adren/o	adrenal gland
adrenal/o	adrenal gland
agglutin/o	to clump
albin/o	white
alveol/o	alveolus
ambi/o	both, both sides
ambly/o	dull
amyl/o	starch
andr/o	man
angi/o	vessel
ankyl/o	stiff joint
anter/o	in front
anthrac/o	black, coal
aort/o	aorta
appendic/o	appendix
aque/o	watery
arachn/o	spider
arteri/o	artery
arthr/o	joint
articul/o	joint
atel/o	incomplete
ather/o	thick, fatty
atri/o	atria
audi/o	hearing
audit/o	hearing
aur/o	ear
auricul/o	ear, earlobe
azot/o	nitrogenous waste

B

bacteri/o	bacteria
balan/o	penis, male glans
bar/o	pressure
bas/o	base
bil/i	bile
blephar/o	eyelid
bronch/i	bronchus
bronch/o	bronchus
bronchiol/o	bronchiole
bucc/o	cheek
burs/o	bursa

C

calc/i	calcium
calcane/o	calcaneous (heel)
cardi/o	heart
carp/o	wrist
caud/o	toward the tail
cec/o	cecum
celi/o	abdomen
cephal/o	head, toward the head
cerebr/o	cerebrum
cervic/o	cervix, neck
cheil/o	lips
chir/o	hand
chol/e	bile
cholecyst/o	gallbladder
choledoch/o	common bile duct
chondr/o	cartilage
chromat/o	color
cirrh/o	yellow
coagul/o	clotting
cochle/o	cochlea
col/o	colon
colon/o	colon
colp/o	vagina

coni/o	dust
conjunctiv/o	conjunctiva
cor/o	pupil
corne/o	cornea
coron/o	heart
cortic/o	cortex
cost/o	ribs
crani/o	cranium, skull
crin/o	to secrete, pour
crypt/o	hidden
cutane/o	skin
cyan/o	blue, bluish
cyst/o	bladder, sac
cyt/o	cell

D

dacry/o	tears
dacryocyst/o	tear sac
dendr/o	branching
dent/o	tooth
derm/o	skin
dermat/o	skin
dipl/o	double
dips/o	thirst
dist/o	away from the point of attachment
dors/o	back
duoden/o	duodenum

E

electr/o	electricity
encephal/o	brain
encephala/o	brain
enter/o	intestine
eosin/o	red, rosy
epididym/o	epididymis
epis/o	vulva
erythem/o	red
erythr/o	red
esophag/o	esophagus
esthesi/o	sensation

F

fasci/o	fascia
femor/o	femur
fibul/o	fibula

G

gastr/o	stomach
gingiv/o	gums
glauc/o	gray, silver
gli/o	glue, gluelike
glomerul/o	glomerulus
gloss/o	tongue
gluc/o	sugar
glyc/o	sugar
gonad/o	sex glands
gyn/o	woman, female
gynec/o	woman

H

hem/o	blood
hemat/o	blood
hepat/o	liver
hidr/o	sweat
humer/o	humerus
hyster/o	uterus

I

ili/o	ilium
infer/o	inferior, below
ir/o	iris
irid/o	iris

J

jejun/o	jejunum

K

kal/i	potassium
kary/o	nucleus
kerat/o	horny, hard tissue, cornea
keton/o	ketones
kinesi/o	movement
kyph/o	hump

L

labyrinth/o	inner ear
lacrim/o	tears
lact/o	milk
lamin/o	lamina
lapar/o	abdomen, abdominal wall
laryng/o	larynx (voicebox)
later/o	lateral, away from the midline
leuk/o	white

lingu/o	tongue
lip/o	fat
lith/o	stone
lob/o	lobe
lord/o	bent backward
lumb/o	lower back
lymph/o	lymph
lymphaden/o	lymph gland
lymphangi/o	lymph vessel

M

mamm/o	breast
mast/o	breast
mastoid/o	mastoid process
meat/o	meatus
medi/o	toward the midline, middle
melan/o	black
men/o	menses
mening/o	meninges
menisc/o	meniscus
metacarp/o	metacarpus
metatars/o	metatarsals
metr/o, metr/i	uterus
muscul/o	muscle
my/o	muscle
myc/o	fungus
myel/o	bone marrow, spinal cord
myring/o	eardrum
myx/o	relating to mucus

N

narc/o	stupor, numbing
nas/o	nose
natr/i	sodium
necr/o	dead
nephr/o	kidney
neur/o	nerve, nervous system
noct/o	night
nucle/o	nucleus

O

obstetric/o	childbirth, pregnancy
ocul/o	eye, sight
odont/o	teeth
olig/o	decreased amount, scant
onych/o	nail
oophor/o	ovary
ophthalm/o	eye
opt/o	eye, vision
or/o	mouth
orchi/o	testicle
orchid/o	testicle
organ/o	organ
orth/o	straight
oste/o	bone
ot/o	ear
ovari/o	ovary
ox/o	oxygen

P

palat/o	palate
palpebr/o	eyelid
pancreat/o	pancreas
patell/o	kneecap, patella
pector/o	chest
ped/i	foot; child
pelv/i	pelvis
pen/i	penis
pen/o	penis
peritone/o	peritoneum
phac/o	lens
phag/o	to eat, swallow
phall/o	penis
pharyng/o	pharynx, throat
phalang/o	phalanges (fingers and toes)
phleb/o	vein
phot/o	light
phren/o	diaphragm, mind
pil/o	hair
pleur/o	pleura
pneum/o	air, lung
pneumon/o	air, lung
pod/o	foot
poikil/o	irregular
poster/o	behind, toward the back
prepit/o	prepuce, foreskin
presby/o	old age
proct/o	anus, rectum
prostat/o	prostate gland

proxim/o	toward the point of attachment
psych/o	mind
pub/o	pubis
pulmon/o	lung
pupill/o	pupil
py/o	pus
pyel/o	renal pelvis
pyret/o	fever

R

rad/i	radius
rect/o	rectum
ren/o	kidney
retin/o	retina
rhabdomy/o	striated muscle
rhin/o	nose
rhytid/o	wrinkles

S

sacr/o	sacrum
salping/o	fallopian tubes, oviducts
sarc/o	flesh
schiz/o	split
scler/o	hardening, sclera
scoli/o	bent, crooked
scrot/o	scrotum
seb/o	sebum
semin/o	semen
sial/o	salivary gland
sigmoid/o	sigmoid colon
somat/o	body
spad/o	split, fissure
sperm/o	sperm
spermat/o	sperm
spin/o	spine
spir/o	to breathe
splen/o	spleen
spondy/o	vetebrae
stape/o	stapes
steat/o	fat
stern/o	sternum
steth/o	chest
sthen/o	strength
stomat/o	mouth
synovi/o	synovial membrane

T

tars/o	ankle bones
ten/o	tendon
tendin/o	tendon
test/o	testis, testes
thalam/o	thalamus, chamber
thorac/o	thorax, chest
thromb/o	thrombus (clot)
thym/o	thymus
thyr/o	thyroid
thyroid/o	thyroid
tibi/o	tibia
tonsill/o	tonsil
toxic/o	poison
trache/o	trachea
trich/o	hair
tympan/o	eardrum

U

umbilic/o	navel
ur/o	urine
ureter/o	ureter
urethr/o	urethra
urin/o	urine
uter/o	uterus

V

vagin/o	vagina
valv/o	valve
valvul/o	valve
vas/o	vessel, vas deferens
vascul/o	blood vessel
ven/o	vein
ventr/o	toward the front, belly
ventricul/o	ventricle (of the brain or heart)
vertebr/o	vertebrae
viscer/o	internal organs
vitre/o	glassy
vulv/o	vulva

X

xanth/o	yellow
xer/o	dry

Z

zo/o	animal, man

APPENDIX B

Prefixes

A

a-	without
ab-	away from
ad-	toward, increase, together
alb-	white
ambi-	both, both sides
an-	without, no, not
ana-	not, without
aniso-	unequal
ante-	before, forward, in front
anti-	against

B

bi-	two
bio-	life
brady-	slow

C

circum-	around
con-	together, with
contra-	against

D

dia-	through
dis-	free of, to undo
dura-	hard
dys-	bad, difficult, painful, abnormal, labored

E

ecto-	outside
endo-	within
epi-	above, upon, over
eso-	within
eu-	normal, good
ex-	out, away from, outside
exo-	outside, away from, outward
extra-	outside, beyond

H

hemi-	half
hetero-	different
homeo-	likeness, sameness, same, similar
homo-	same
hydro-	water
hyper-	above, excessive, fast
hypo-	under, below, deficient, decreased, slow, beneath

I

idio-	individual, distinct
im-	not
in-	inside, within, not
infra-	below, inferior, below
inter-	between
intra-	within

J

juxta-	near, beside

M

macro-	large
meso-	middle
meta-	beyond, change
micro-	small
mono-	one
morpho-	shape
multi-	many

N

non-	not
nulli-	none

O

oxy-	sharp, quick

P

para-	near, beside, next to
peri-	around
poly-	many, much
pre-	before, in front of
primi-	first
pro-	before, in front of
pseudo-	false

Q

quadri-	four

R

re-	back, again
retro-	backward, behind

S

semi-	half
sub-	below, beneath, under
super-	above, beyond, superior
supra-	above, beyond, superior, over
sym-	joined, together
syn-	joined, together

T

tachy-	fast, rapid
tetra-	four
trans-	through, across
tri-	three

U

ultra-	beyond, excess
uni-	one

APPENDIX C

Suffixes

A

-a	noun ending
-ac	pertaining to
-al	pertaining to
-algesia	pain
-algesic	pertaining to pain
-algia	pain
-ar	pertaining to
-arche	beginning
-ary	pertaining to
-ase	enzyme
-azole	antifungal

B

-blast	immature, immature cell

C

-capnia	carbon dioxide
-cele	hernia
-centesis	surgical puncture
-cidal	pertaining to causing death
-cide	causing death
-cillin	antibiotic
-clasis	breaking, to break
-cycline	antibiotic
-cyte	cell
-cytosis	condition of cells

D

-desis	binding or surgical fusion, surgical fixation
-dynia	pain

E

-e	noun ending
-eal	pertaining to
-ectasis	expansion, stretching/dilation
-ectomy	surgical removal
-emia	blood condition
-er	person who . . .
-esis	condition

G

-gen	producing, production, forming
-genesis	formation, produce, producing, forming
-genic	pertaining to producing, forming pollution
-glia	glue
-globin	protein
-gram	record or picture
-graph	instrument to record
-graphy	process of recording
-gravida	pregnancy, pregnant

I

-ia	condition, pertaining to
-ial	pertaining to
-iasis	condition
-iatrics	relating to medicine, providers
-iatrist	one who treats, provider
-iatry	medical treatment, profession
-ic	pertaining to
-ical	pertaining to
-ician	specialist in a field of study
-ile	pertaining to
-ion	action, process
-ipramine	antidepressant
-ism	condition, theory, process
-ist	one who treats, provider, practitioner
-itis	inflammation

L

-lepsy	seizure
-lith	stone
-lithiasis	condition of a stone
-logist	specialist in the study of

-logy	study of
-lysis	destruction
-lytic	pertaining to destruction
M	
-malacia	softening
-mania	frenzy, madness
-megaly	enlargement
-meter	instrument to measure
-metry	process of measuring
O	
-oid	resembling
-ole	small
-ology	study of
-olol	antihypertensive
-oma	tumor
-opia	vision
-opsia	visual condition
-opsy	process of viewing
-ory	pertaining to
-osis	abnormal condition
-osmia	smell
-ostomy	create a new opening, new opening
-otomy	incision, incision into
-ous	pertaining to
P	
-para	to bear
-paresis	partial paralysis
-pathic	pertaining to disease
-pathy	disease
-penia	decreased amount
-pepsia	digestion
-pexy	surgical fixation
-phagia	eating, swallowing, to eat, swallow
-phil	love of
-philia	attraction to
-phobia	abnormal fear
-phonia	voice
-phoria	feeling, sensation
-plasia	formation, development
-plasm	formed, plasma
-plasty	surgical repair/correction
-plegia	paralysis, stroke
-plegic	pertaining to paralysis
-pnea	to breath
-poiesis	formation
-practor	specialist
-prazole	proton pump inhibitors
-pril	antihypertensive
-ptosis	downward displacement, drooping
-ptysis	spitting
R	
-rrhage	rupture
-rrhagia	excessive flow, discharge
-rrhaphy	suturing
-rrhea	flow, discharge
-rrhexis	rupture
S	
-sclerosis	condition of hardening
-scope	instrument to view
-stasis	stop, control, process of stopping
-stat	instrument to stop/control
-statin	cholesterol lowering
-stenosis	narrowing
-stomy	creation of a new opening
T	
-terol	bronchodilator
-thorax	chest
-tic	pertaining to
-tion	process of
-tomy	incision into
-tripsy	crushing, breakdown, destruction
-tropin	stimulation of a target organ
U	
-ula	small
-ule	small
-um	singular noun
-uria	pertaining to urine, condition of urine
-us	singular noun
Y	
-y	condition
Z	
-zepam	benzodiazepines
-zosin	antihypertensive

APPENDIX D

Abbreviations and Symbols

A

A&P	anatomy and physiology
ab	abortion
Abd	abdomen
ABGs	arterial blood gases
ablb	alternate binaural loudness balance
ABR	auditory brainstem response
ac	before meals (ante cibum)
AC	air conduction
Acc	accommodation
ACL	anterior cruciate ligament
ACTH	adrenocorticotropic hormone
AD	right ear (auris dextra)
ADD	attention deficit disorder
ADH	antidiuretic hormone
ADHD	attention deficit hyperactivity disorder
ADL	activities of daily living
AED	automated external defibrillator
AF	atrial fibrillation
AFB	acid-fast bacilli
AGN	acute glomerulonephritis
AIDS	acquired immunodeficiency syndrome
AKA	above the knee amputation
AKI	acute kidney injury
ALS	amyotrophic lateral sclerosis
ALT	alanine aminotransferase
AMI	acute myocardial infarction
AOM	acute otitis media
AP	anteroposterior
ARD	acute respiratory disease
ARDS	adult respiratory distress syndrome
ARF	acute renal failure, acute respiratory failure
ARMD	age-related macular degeneration
AS	arteriosclerosis, left ear (auris sinistra)
ASA	acetylsalicylic acid, commonly aspirin
ASD	atrial septal defect
ASHD	arteriosclerotic heart disease
AST	aspartate aminotransferase (formerly called SGOT, serum glutamic-oxaloacetic transaminase)
ATN	acute tubular necrosis
AU	both ears (auris unitas)
AV, A-V	atrioventricular

B

Ba	barium
BBB	bundle branch block
BC	bone conduction
BCC	basal cell carcinoma
BE	barium enema
bid	twice a day
BKA	below the knee amputation
BMD	bone mineral density
BMR	basal metabolic rate
BNO	bladder neck obstruction
BOM	bilateral otitis media
BP	blood pressure
BPH	benign prostatic hypertrophy
bpm	beats per minute
BSE	breast self-examination
BSO	bilateral salpingo-oophorectomy
BUN	blood urea nitrogen
Bx, bx	biopsy

C

C&S	culture and sensitivity
C1, C2, C3	cervical vertebra
Ca	calcium
CABG	coronary bypass graft
CAD	coronary artery disease
CAPD	continuous ambulatory peritoneal dialysis
CAT	computerized axial tomography
Cath	catheterization, catheter
CC	cardiac catheterization, chief complaint

cc	with correction (glasses)
CCPD	continuous cycling peritoneal dialysis
CCU	cardiac care unit
CDC	Centers for Disease Control and Prevention
CF	cystic fibrosis
CHF	congestive heart failure
CIS	carcinoma in situ
CK	creatine kinase
CNS	central nervous system
CO_2	carbon dioxide
CoA	coarctation of the aorta
COM	chronic otitis media
COPD	chronic obstructive pulmonary disease
CP	chest pain
CPAP	continuous positive airway pressure
CPR	cardiopulmonary resuscitation
CRF	chronic renal failure
CRPS	complex regional pain syndrome
CSD	congenital septal defect
CSF	cerebrospinal fluid
CT	computed tomography
CTPA	computed tomography pulmonary angiography
CV	cardiovascular
CVA	cerebral vascular accident
Cx	cervix
CXR	chest x-ray
cysto	cystoscopy

D

D&C	dilation and curettage
db	decibel
decub	decubitus ulcer, pressure sore
derm	dermatology
DEXA	dual-energy x-ray absorptiometry
DI	diabetes insipidus
DIP	distal interphalangeal (joint)
DJD	degenerative joint disease
DKA	diabetic ketoacidosis
DLE	discoid lupus erythematosus
DM	diabetes mellitus
DNA	deoxyribonucleic acid
DPT	diphtheria, pertussis, tetanus
DRE	digital rectal exam
DTR	deep tendon reflexes
DVT	deep vein thrombosis
Dx	diagnosis

E

EAHF	eczema, asthma, and hay fever
ECC	endocervical curettage
ECCE	extracapsular cataract extraction
ECG, EKG	electrocardiogram
ECHO	echocardiography
ECT	electroconvulsive therapy
ED	erectile dysfunction; emergency department
EEG	electroencephalogram
EENT	ears, eyes, nose, and throat
EGD	esophagogastrodudenoscopy
EMB	endometrial biopsy
EMG	electromyography
ENT	ears, nose, and throat
EOM	extraocular movement
EPO	erythropoietin
ERCP	endoscopic retrograde cholangiopancreatotomy
ERG	electroretinogram
ERT	estrogen replacement therapy
ESR	erythrocyte sedimentation rate
ESRD	end-stage renal disease
ESWL	extracorporeal shock-wave lithotripsy

F

FANA	fluorescent antinuclear antibody
FBS	fasting blood sugar
FH	family history
fib	fibrillation
FS	frozen section
FSH	follicle-stimulating hormone
Fx	fracture

G

GB	gallbladder
GBS	gallbladder series
GEBT	gastric emptying breath test
GERD	gastroesophageal reflux disease
GFR	glomerular filtration rate
GH	growth hormone
GI series	gastrointestinal series
GI	gastrointestinal

GnRH	gonadotropin-releasing hormone
GTT	glucose tolerance test
GU	genitourinary
Gyn	gynecology

H

H_2O	water
HAV	hepatitis a virus
HbA1c	hemoglobin a1c
HBV	hepatitis b virus
HCL	hydrochloric acid
HCV	hepatitis c virus
HD	hemodialysis
HDL	high-density lipoprotein
HIV	human immunodeficiency virus
HMD	hyaline membrane disease
HNP	herniated nucleus pulposus
HPV	human papilloma virus
HR	heartrate
HSG	hysterosalpingography
HSV-2	herpes simplex virus, strain 2
Ht	height
HTN	hypertension
Hx	history

I

I&D	incision and drainage
IBS	irritable bowel syndrome
ICCE	intracapsular cataract extraction
ICD	implantable cardioverter-defibrillator
ICP	intracranial pressure
ID	intradermal
IDDM	insulin-dependent diabetes mellitus (type 1 diabetes)
IM	intramuscular
IOL	intraocular lens
IOP	intraocular pressure
IP	ice pack
IPPB	intermittent positive-pressure breathing
IUD	intrauterine device
IV	intravenous
IVC	intravenous cholangiography
IVP	intravenous pyelogram

J

JRA	juvenile rheumatoid arthritis

K

K	potassium
KUB	kidneys, ureters, bladder

L

L1, L2, L3	lumbar vertebra
L5-S1	disk between l5 (lumbar vertebra and sacrum)
LAM	laser-assisted myringotomy
LASIK	laser in situ keratomileusis
LAT	lateral
LEEP	loop electrosurgical procedure
LES	lower esophageal sphincter
LFT	liver function test
LH	luteinizing hormone
LLE	left lower extremity
LLL	left lower lobe (lung)
LLQ	left lower quadrant
LMP	last menstrual period
LOC	loss of consciousness
LP	lumbar puncture
LSO	left salpingo-oophorectomy
LTH	lactogenic hormone
LUE	left upper extremity
LUL	left upper lobe
LUQ	left upper quadrant
LVH	left ventricular hypertrophy

M

MCP	metacarpophalangeal (joint)
MDI	metered dose inhaler
MHP	moist heat pack
MI	myocardial infarction, mitral insufficiency
mm Hg	millimeters of mercury
MM	malignant melanoma
MR	mitral regurgitation
MRI	magnetic resonance imaging
MS	multiple sclerosis, mitral stenosis
MSH	melanocyte-stimulating hormone
MTP	metatarsophalangeal (joint)
MVP	mitral valve prolapse

N

Na	sodium
NCS	nerve conduction study
NG	nasogastric

NIDDM	non-insulin-dependent diabetes mellitus (type 2 diabetes)
NMI	nebulized mist inhaler
npo	nothing by mouth
NREM	non-rapid eye movement
NSV	no-scalpel vasectomy
NVD	nausea, vomiting, diarrhea

O

O_2	oxygen
OA	osteoarthritis
OB	obstetrics
OB/GYN	obstetrics and gynecology
OCD	obsessive-compulsive disorder
OD	right eye (ocular dexter)
OE	otitis externa
ORIF	open reduction, internal fixation
ortho	orthopedics
OS	left eye (ocular sinister)
OSA	obstructive sleep apnea
OT	oxytocin
OTC	over-the-counter
OU	both eyes (ocular uterque)

P

P	pulse
PA	posteroanterior
PAC	premature atrial contraction
Pap	Papanicolaou smear
PBI	protein-bound iodine
pc	after meals (post cibum)
Pco_2	partial pressure of carbon dioxide
PCP	pneumocystis pneumonia, primary care physician
PDA	patent ductus arteriosus
PEARL	pupils equal and reactive to light
PERLA	pupils equal; reactive to light and accommodation
PERRLA	pupils equal; round, reactive to light, and accommodation
PET	positron emission tomography
PFT	pulmonary function test
pH	potential hydrogen (degree of alkalinity or acidity of a fluid)
PID	pelvic inflammatory disease
PIP	proximal interphalangeal (joint)
PK	penetrating keratoplasty (corneal transplant)
PMS	premenstrual syndrome
PNS	peripheral nervous system
Po2	partial pressure of oxygen
pp	postprandial
PPD	purified protein derivative
PPG	postprandial glucose
PSA	prostate-specific antigen
PSG	polysomnogram
PSS	progressive systemic scleroderma
PT	physical therapy
PTC, PTHC	percutaneous transhepatic cholangiogram
PTCA	percutaneous transluminal coronary angioplasty
PTH	parathyroid hormone
PTS	permanent threshold shift
PTSD	posttraumatic stress disorder
PVC	premature ventricular contraction
PVD	peripheral vascular disease

R

R	respiration
RA	rheumatoid arthritis
RAI	radioactive iodine
RAIU	radioactive iodine uptake
REM	rapid eye movement
RF	rheumatoid factor
RICE	rest, ice, compression, and elevation
RLE	right lower extremity
RLL	right lower lobe
RLQ	right lower quadrant
ROM	range of motion
RP	retrograde pyelogram
RR	respiratory rate
RSO	right salpingo-oophorectomy
RT	reading test
RUE	right upper extremity
RUL	right upper lobe
RUQ	right upper quadrant

S

S1	first heart sound
S2	second heart sound
SA, S-A	sinoatrial

SAD	seasonal affective disorder
SBO	small bowel obstruction
SBS	small bowel series
sc	without correction
SCC	squamous cell carcinoma
SG, sp. gr.	specific gravity
SGOT	serum glutamic-oxaloacetic transaminase (now called AST)
SGPT	serum glutamic pyruvic transaminase
SIDS	sudden infant death syndrome
SK	streptokinase
SLE	systemic lupus erythematosus
SNRI	selective norepinephrine reuptake inhibitor
SNS	somatic nervous system
SOB	shortness of breath
SOM	serous otitis media
SpO_2	saturation of peripheral oxygen
SSEP	somatosensory evoked potentials
SSRI	selective serotonin reuptake inhibitor
STI	sexually transmitted infection
Strep	streptococcal infection (of the throat)
Subq, subcu	subcutaneous

T

T and A	tonsillectomy and adenoidectomy
T	temperature
T1, T2, T3	thoracic vertebra
T3	triiodothyronine (thyroid hormone)
T4	thyroxine (thyroid hormone)
TAH	total abdominal hysterectomy
TAH-BSO	total abdominal hysterectomy, bilateral salpingo-oophorectomy
TB	tuberculosis
TCeMEP	transcranial electrical motor-evoked potentials
TED	thyroid eye disease
TENS	transcutaneous electrical nerve stimulation
TFT	thyroid function test
THA	total hip arthroplasty
THR	total hip replacement
TIA	transient ischemic attack
TKR	total knee replacement
TM	tympanic membrane
TMJ	temporomandibular joint
TPN	total parenteral nutrition
TPR	temperature, pulse, respiration
TSE	testicular self-examination
TSH	thyroid-stimulating hormone
TTS	temporary threshold shift
TUMT	transurethral microwave thermotherapy
TURP	transurethral resection of the prostate
TVH	total vaginal hysterectomy

U

UA	urinalysis
UC	urine culture
UGI series	upper gastrointestinal series
UI	urinary incontinence
ung	ointment
URI	upper respiratory infection
UTI	urinary tract infection
UV	ultraviolet

V

V fib	ventricular fibrillation
V, Vas	vasectomy
VA	visual acuity
VCUG	voiding cystourethrogram
VF	visual field
VLDL	very-low-density lipoprotein
VR	vasectomy reversal
VSD	ventricular septal defect
VT	ventricular tachycardia
VTX	vitrectomy
VUR	vesicourethral reflux

W

wt	weight

X

XP, XDP	xeroderma pigmentosum

Symbols

~ or ≈	approximately
Δ	change
↓	down, downward, decreased, diminished
♀	female
♂	male
#	number (#5) or pounds (5# wt.)
×	number of times (×5, 5×) or minutes (×5 min)
1°	primary

2°	secondary, secondary to	ā	before
↔	to and from	c̄	with
→	to, progressing toward, approaching	p̄	after
↑	up, upward, increased	s̄	without

Discontinued Abbreviations

The Joint Commission, an organization focused in part on ensuring safe patient care, has developed a "Do Not Use" list of abbreviations because their use frequently causes errors in transcription or interpretation. In addition, the Institute for Safe Medication Practices (ISMP), which runs the National Medications Errors Reporting Program, publishes their List of Error-Prone Abbreviations, Symbols, and Dose Designations to avoid. The following abbreviations and measurement units are strongly discouraged from use.

Do Not Use	Rationale	Use
AD: right ear	Mistaken for: AS, AU, OD, OS, OU	Use: right ear
AS: left ear	Mistaken for: AD, AU, OD, OS, OU	Use: left ear
AU: both ears	Mistaken for: U (units) when poorly written	Use: both ears
cc: cubic centimeter	Mistaken for: U (units) when poorly written	Use: mL
dc, DC, D/C: discharge or discontinue	Mistaken for: each other	Use: discharge or discontinue
IU: international unit	Mistaken for: IV	Use: international unit
MgSO4: magnesium sulfate	Mistaken for: MSO4	Use: magnesium sulfate
MS, MSO4: morphine	Mistaken for: MgSO4	Use: morphine sulfate
OD: right eye	Mistaken for: AD, AS, AU, OS, OU	Use: right eye
OS: left eye	Mistaken for: AD, AS, AU, OD, OU	Use: left eye
OU: both eyes	Mistaken for: AD, AS, AU, OD, OS	Use: both eyes
qd.: every day	Mistaken for: q.o.d.	Use: daily
qod.: every other day	Mistaken for: q.d. or q.i.d.	Use: every other day
SC, SQ: subcutaneous	Mistaken for: SL (sublingual) or 5 every	Use: subcut. or subcutaneous, SubQ or Sub-Q
ss: sliding scale	Mistaken for: 55	Use: sliding scale
tiw	Mistaken for twice in a week	Use: 3 times weekly
u: unit	Mistaken for: 0, 4, or cc	Use: unit
µg: microgram	Mistaken for: mg	Use: mcg
F or Ø	Mistaken for 4, 6, 8, 9	Use: 0 or zero
/ (slash mark)	Mistake for 1	Use: per when used with doses
<, >: less than, greater than	Mistaken for: each other	Use: less than or greater than
trailing zero (4.0 mg)	Decimal point may be missed, resulting in an overdose of 10 times the prescribed amount	Never write an unnecessary zero after a decimal point.
lack of leading zero (.4 mg)	Decimal point may be missed, resulting in an overdose of 10 times prescribed amount	Always use a zero before a decimal point to indicate its presence (0.4 mg).

Glossary

A

abdominopelvic cavity: The largest cavity of the body, which is divided from the thoracic cavity by the diaphragm.

accessory organs: The liver, the gallbladder, and the pancreas, which add digestive enzymes and chemicals to the digestion process.

accommodation: The adjustment of the lens of the eye by the ciliary muscles to focus images at varying distances on the retina.

acini cells: Portion of the large intestine that begins at the ileocecal junction, curving upward on the right side of the abdomen toward the liver.

acquired immunity: After birth, immunity the body develops to a specific agent.

adenoids: Two masses of lymphatic tissue in the nasopharynx that help filter out bacteria and other foreign substances in the inhaled air; also known as pharyngeal tonsils.

adjective: Word that describes a noun.

adjective suffix: Word element attached to the end of a word that describes the word root to which it is attached.

adrenal cortex: Outer portion of the adrenal glands that secrete corticosteroid hormones.

adrenal glands: Located on top of the kidneys, paired, pyramid-shaped structures called the interior adrenal medulla and the outer adrenal cortex.

adrenal medulla: Interior adrenal gland that secretes epinephrine and norepinephrine.

afferent arteriole: Small arteries that deliver blood to the kidney's glomerulus.

afferent nerves: Sensory neurons that carry impulses from the peripheral parts of the body to the brain or spinal cord.

agglutination: Clumping of cells.

agranulocyte: Type of leukocyte (monocyte or lymphocyte) whose cytoplasm does not contain granules.

albumin: Group of simple proteins in the blood that helps maintain blood pressure to prevent plasma loss from capillaries; acts as a carrier molecule.

aldosterone: Mineralocorticoid secreted by the zona glomerulosa of the adrenal cortex that regulates sodium and potassium concentrations.

alimentary canal: Includes the structures through which food passes: mouth, teeth, esophagus, stomach, small intestines, and large intestines; also known as the intestinal canal.

alveoli: Sacs of air that have extremely thin walls allowing gases to filter to the blood capillaries that surround each alveolus.

amniotic fluid: Watery liquid in which the embryo or fetus is suspended; protects the embryo and fetus from injury and regulates the embryotic or fetal temperature.

amniotic sac: Thin, transparent structure that holds the embryo or fetus suspended in amniotic fluid.

anaphylaxis: Severe and sometimes fatal hypersensitive reaction to previously encountered antigens; also known as anaphylactic shock.

anatomical plane: Imaginary lines on which the body or organ is divided; sagittal, transverse, and coronal.

anatomical position: Standard body view in which the body is erect, with the head facing forward, arms by the sides with the palms forward, and the feet slightly apart with the heels lifted.

anterior chamber: Area of the anterior compartment located between the cornea and the iris.

anterior pituitary gland: Secretes six hormones that cause target organs to stimulate or inhibit release of their hormones; composed of glandular epithelium.

anterior: Directional term meaning toward the front, belly side.

antibodies: Chemical substance programmed to attack a unique foreign antigen.

antidiuretic hormone (ADH): Vasopressin that acts on the kidneys to reduce urine production and triggers sweat glands to reduce sweat production.

antigen: Chemical on the surface of the RBCs that stimulates the production of antibodies and cytotoxic response. Cellular antigens identify the cell surface as self or nonself.

anus: Opening through which feces exit the body.

aorta: Transports blood from the heart to the body; divides into arteries, arterioles, and capillaries.

aortic valve: Heart structure through which blood flows from the left atrium into the aorta.

apex: The tip of the heart's left ventricle. The largest part of the heart.

apical pulse: The site considered the most accurate location for measuring heart rate when listened to for 1 minute.

apocrine glands: One of two types of sudoriferous glands that produce sweat; found in the armpits and groin.

aponeurosis: Fibrous attachment covering a large area of a bone.

appendicular skeleton: The bones of the upper and lower extremities and their attachments; attaches to the axial skeleton.

appendicular: Refers to the limbs and their attachments to either the shoulders or the hips.

aqueous humor: Clear, watery fluid within the anterior compartment of the eye.

arachnoid membrane: The middle layer of the meninges composed of collagen fibers; resembles a cobweb.

areola: Pigmented area around the nipples.

arrector pili: Muscle surrounding each hair follicle that, when contracted, causes the hair to protrude straight up from the skin.

artery: A vessel carrying oxygenated blood away from the heart.

articular cartilage: Protects the ends of bones along the outer surface of the epiphysis.

articulation: The structure of the joint; the movement of joints through their range of motion.

ascending colon: Portion of the colon that begins at the ileocecal junction, curving upward on the right side of the abdomen toward the liver.

aspiration: Pertaining to the respiratory system, inhalation of food or entering the lower respiratory tract.

asymptomatic: A patient who has no indications of the disease or disorder.

atom: The smallest part of an element, consisting of a nucleus and surrounded by electrons.

atrioventricular (AV) node: Specialized cells in the floor of the right atrium that receive electrical impulses from the SA node and transmit those impulse to the ventricles.

auditory nerve: Transmits sound vibrations converted to electrical impulses by the organ of Corti to the brain, where sound is interpreted.

auricle: External portion of the ear that collects and transmits the sound to the external auditory canal. Also known as the pinna.

autonomic nervous system: The peripheral nervous system division that communicates information related to involuntary body functions.

axial skeleton: The bones of the head, vertebrae, and ribs; lies along the midvertical axis of the body.

axial: Refers to the part of the body composed of the head, neck, and trunk.

B

Bartholin's glands: Mucous-secreting glands located on the lateral walls of the female vestibule that lubricate the vagina during sexual intercourse.

basal ganglia: Masses of gray matter cells in the corpus callosum that act as relay stations for motor impulses originating in the cerebral cortex and transmitted to the cerebellum or spinal cord; also known as basal nuclei.

basophil: Granulocytic leukocyte essential to innate immune response of inflammation because they release histamine and other chemicals that dilate blood vessels and make capillaries more permeable.

bicuspid valve: Heart structure through which blood exits the left atrium into the left ventricle; also known as the mitral valve.

bile: Chemical secretion comprised of bile salts, bile pigments and cholesterol that emulsifies fats.

blood: Liquid that circulates through the heart and vessels. Carries oxygen, nourishment, heat, electrolytes, hormones, and antibodies to the tissues and carries away carbon dioxide and waste matter.

blood pressure: Pressure created by pumping blood against artery walls.

body (of the stomach): Portion of the stomach that lies below the fundus and curves to the right.

bolus: The chewed and lubricated ball of food.

Bowman's capsule: Glomerular capsule in the kidney.

brain: Highly organized complex of neuron cell bodies, axons, dendrites, and glia inside the skull that controls the body and processes sensory input.

breast: Mammary gland extending from the upper anterior region of the chest in pubescent and adult females.

bronchi: The two dividing branches of the trachea for the passage of air to the lungs.

bronchial tree: The branching of the bronchi into secondary, tertiary, and bronchiole tubes.

bronchioles: One of the smaller branches of the bronchiole tubes.

bulbourethral gland: Male reproductive organ located inferior to the prostate gland, which secretes a viscous lubricating fluid for sexual intercourse; also called Cowper glands.

bundle of his: Atrioventricular bundle that carries the electrical impulse from the atrioventricular (AV) node and transmits it to both ventricles.

bursa: Synovial membrane surrounding the inside of the joint capsule.

C

calyx: Cavity in the kidney that holds urine; connects in the hilum to the ureter.

canal of Schlemm: Expanded vein within the sclera that drains excess aqueous humor from the eye to maintain fluid homeostasis.

cancellous bone: Bone with a spongy core.

capillaries: The tiniest blood vessels in the body in which the exchange of gases and nutrients occurs.

cardiac cycle: The coordinated contraction and relaxation of the four heart chambers that creates each heartbeat.

carotene: Skin pigment of the stratum corneum and the dermis that gives an orange-yellow hue to the skin.

carpals: The eight short bones of the wrist.

catecholamines: Biologically active amines that influence the nervous system.

cecum: A blind pouch forming the first section of the large intestine beyond the ileocecal sphincter, which receives chyme from the ileum of the small intestine.

cell membrane: Cellular structure that defines the extent of the cell.

cell: The smallest unit of life and the building blocks of all body structures.
cellular respiration: The distribution of oxygen to cells of the body and removal of carbon dioxide from the cells into the bloodstream; also known as internal respiration.
central nervous system: The brain and spinal cord.
cerebral cortex: Surface of the cerebrum made up of convolutions that increase the surface area of the brain for added function.
cerumen: Waxy substance lubricates and protects the ear canal.
cervix: Lowest portion of the uterus where the vagina and uterus meet.
Cesarean section: Surgical procedure where an incision is made into the uterus and the baby is removed.
chloasma: Brown patches on the face that may appear during pregnancy.
chorionic villi: Fingerlike projections from the embryo that form the placenta.
choroid: Dark blue vascular membrane between the sclera and retina that absorbs light rays to minimize the reflection of light to the retina.
chyme: Mixture of partly digested food and digestive secretions in the stomach and small intestine during digestion.
cilia: Hairlike projections lining the interior of the nose, the sinuses, and fallopian tubes.
ciliary body: Smooth muscle fibers arranged in a circle around the iris to accommodate its focal length to see near or far; connects to the lens by suspensory ligaments.
circadian rhythm: Approximately 24-hour sleep/wake cycle.
clitoris: Erectile tissue containing sensory nerves; engorges with blood upon stimulation causing the female orgasm.
coagulation: The process of blood clotting; the clumping of blood cells.
cochlea: Coiled structure lined with hair cells in the inner ear that houses the organ of Corti, the true organ of hearing.
collagen: A strong, fibrous, insoluble protein in connective tissue.
colostrum: Secreted breast fluid that nourishes the baby until the breast milk becomes available.
combined suffix: Suffix made up of two elements, such as combining form and a suffix to create a descriptive suffix.
combining vowel: Vowel that connects a suffix to the word root.
conjunctiva: Mucous membrane that protects and lubricates the anterior eyeball and the interior surface of the eyelids.
connective (tissue): Protects, supports, and connects the other tissues of the body; binds structures together; holds organs in place; separates organs from each other; and provides storage areas.
contractions: Strong tightening of the uterine muscles during labor and delivery.
corium: Region of connective tissue that lies directly beneath the basal layer of the epidermis; also known as the dermis.
cornea: The transparent anterior aspect of the tunic where light enters the eye.
coronal: Imaginary division of the body into anterior (front) and posterior (back) sections, also known as the frontal plane.
corpus callosum: Thick layer of white matter that acts as a bridge between the two hemispheres of the brain, integrating their functions.
corpus luteum: Yellowish mass containing high levels of progesterone and estrogen formed within the ruptured ovarian follicle after ovulation; acts as a temporary endocrine gland to secrete large amounts of progesterone.
corticosterone: Hormone that acts to influence carbohydrate, potassium, and sodium metabolism.
cortisol: Hormone that regulates levels of glucose in the bloodstream.
cortisone: Hormone that regulates the metabolism of fats, carbohydrates, sodium, potassium, and proteins; most abundant of the glucocorticoids.
cranial cavity: Hollow structure defined by the skull, contains the brain.
cuticle: Small flap of stratum corneum that overlies the proximal edge of the nail.
cytoplasm: The mix of inorganic and organic substances of the cell outside the nucleus.

D

deep: Directional term meaning farther from the surface.
defecation: Expulsion of the fecal mass.
dendrite: Thin, branched structure of the neuron that receives impulses and transmits information to the cell body of the neuron.
deoxyribonucleic acid (DNA): Nucleic acid comprising two chains formed in a double helix of deoxyribose and phosphoric acid held together by hydrogen bonds between one of four bases (two purines, adenine and guanine, and two pyrimidines, thymine, and cytosine). The chemical basis of heredity and the carrier of genetic information.
depolarization: The electrical change in cardiac muscle cells in which the inside of the cells become positive in relation to the outside causing individual cardiac muscle cells in the atria to contract in unison.
dermis: Region of connective tissue that lies directly beneath the basal layer of the epidermis; also known as the corium.
descending colon: Portion of colon that turns downward at the splenic flexure on a downward path along the left side of the abdomen.
dialysis: The process of mechanically filtering blood when the kidneys can no longer adequately perfuse urine.
diaphragm: Thin, dome-shaped muscle that lies below the two lungs and separates the lungs from the abdominal cavity.
diaphysis: The shaft of long bone made of tightly packed compact bone that offers strength and support.
diastole: Ventricular relaxation.
diastolic pressure: Lowest pressure exerted against artery walls during ventricular relaxation.

distal convoluted tubule: Structure of the kidney's nephron that receives fluid from the glomerulus.
distal: Farther from the point of attachment (often the shoulder or hip).
dorsal cavity: Hollow structure found in the back of the body that contains the brain and spinal cord
duodenum: The first portion of the small intestines.
dura mater: Outermost layer of meninges that forms a tough protective sheath around the spinal cord.

E

eccrine glands: One of two types of sudoriferous glands found throughout the body that secrete sweat to regulate body temperature.
efferent arteriole: Small arteries that drain fluid from the kidney's glomerulus.
efferent nerves: Motor neurons that carry impulses from the brain and spinal cord to the peripheral body.
ejaculation: The ejection of semen from the urethra.
ejaculatory duct: The structure through which spermatozoa pass from the vas deferens into the urethra.
electrolytes: Ionized mineral salts in blood, tissue fluids, and cells.
embryo: The stage of prenatal development between fertilized ovum and fetus.
endolymph: Fluid within the membranous labyrinth of the ear.
endometrium: The innermost vascular layer of the uterus designed to give blood and nutrition to a developing fetus.
endomysium: Deepest layer of the fibrous muscle attachment, separating individual muscle fibers.
endosteum: Membrane lining the interior surface of the medullary cavity of bones.
enzymes: Pertaining to the digestive system; chemicals that help to break down food into nutrients.
eosinophil: Granulocytic leukocyte that destroys parasites and contributes to allergic reactions by releasing chemicals such as histamine.
epidermis: Water-resistant covering of the body; does not contain blood or nerve supply.
epididymis: Tightly coiled structure at the posterior side of each testis that is the first part of the testis' secretory ducts.
epiglottis: Small tongue-shaped flap of cartilage located at the distal end of the pharynx that covers the glottis.
epimysium: Outermost layer of the fibrous muscle attachment, which surrounds the entire muscle.
epinephrine: Hormone that increases the heart rate and the force of contraction of the heart; dilates bronchioles in the lungs, raises blood glucose, and decreases the peristaltic movement of the intestines as part of the fight or flight response; also known as adrenaline.
epiphyseal plate: Narrow band of cartilage between the diaphysis and the epiphysis; also known as the growth plate.
epiphysis: The bulblike ends of long bones affording space for muscle attachment; contributes to the structure of the joint.
epithelial (tissue): The structure of the outermost layer of skin; the inside lining of the body cavities and hollow organs; the surface of internal organs; and specific membranes, ducts, and glands.
eponym: Name for a disease, organ, function, or procedure adapted from a person's name or, sometimes, a geographical location.
equilibrium: The sense or state of balance.
erection: The engorgement of the penis with blood causing its enlargement and stiffness, generally due to sexual excitement.
erythrocyte: Red blood cell (RBC). Carries oxygen to tissues and picks up carbon dioxide for release via the lungs.
esophagus: Muscular tube that moves food to the stomach.
estrogen: Hormone that stimulates development of female sexual characteristics, maturation of the ovum, and stimulation of the uterine lining to prepare for implantation of the fertilized ovum; secreted by the adrenal cortex, ovaries, and placenta.
etiology: The cause of a disease or disorder.
Eustachian tube: Allows air to flow between the throat and the tympanic cavity, enabling air pressure to equalize on both sides of the tympanic cavity.
exhalation: The forcing of air out of the lungs; also known as expiration.
external auditory canal: The passageway of the ear that extends from the auricle to the tympanic membrane.
external respiration: The exchange of gases from the environment into the body and the body to the environment; also known as ventilation.
external urethral sphincter: Voluntary skeletal muscle that enables control of excretion of urine.

F

fallopian tubes: The passageway for ova to exit the ovaries and enter the uterus.
feces: The solid waste products of digestion.
fertility: The quality of being able to bear a child or produce viable sperm.
fertilization: The process of a sperm cell (spermatozoa) penetrating an ovum, leading to the fusion of the male and female pronuclei.
fetus: Unborn human after the end of the eighth week of gestation until birth.
fibrinogen: Plasma protein essential for the blood-clotting process.
filtration: Removal of particles from a solution by passing the liquid portion through a membrane or other permeable barrier.
fimbriae: Fingerlike projections at the distal ends of the fallopian tubes that open into the peritoneal cavity.
foramen ovale: Small opening in the atrial septum that closes shortly after birth.
fovea centralis: The depression in the macula lutea of the retina containing cone cells that sharpen an image.

frontal (plane): Imaginary division of the body into anterior (front) and posterior (back) sections; also known as the coronal plane.
frontal lobe: One of the four divisions of the cerebrum.
fundus: The upper rounded portion of the stomach.

G

gallbladder: Pear-shaped sac next to the duodenum that stores bile.
gametes: The female ova and male spermatozoa sex cells.
gene: A segment of DNA that contains the instructions for a function; the unit of heredity.
gingivae: Tissue that surround the teeth, anchoring them in place; commonly called the gums.
globulin: Plasma protein created in the liver that has regulatory functions consisting of three types: alpha, beta, and gamma.
glomerulus: Ball-shaped mass of tiny, coiled capillaries within the bulb of the nephron's renal corpuscle.
glottis: The opening of the larynx.
glucagon: Hormone that acts to stimulate the conversion of glycogen in the liver to glucose.
glucocorticoids: Hormones that act to regulate levels of glucose in the bloodstream.
glucose: Simple sugar or monosaccharide that is the product of carbohydrate digestion; the source of fuel for all metabolic processes of the body.
glycogen: The storage form of glucose in the liver and muscles.
glycogenesis: Conversion of glucose into glycogen for storage in the liver.
goblet cells: Unicellular structure that secretes mucus.
gonadocorticoids: Sex hormones primarily produced in the ovaries and testes.
gonads: The female ovaries that form the ova and the male teste that forms the spermatozoa necessary for human reproduction.
granulocyte: Type of leukocyte (neutrophil, eosinophil, or basophil) whose cytoplasm contains granules.
gustation: The sense of taste.
gynecologist: Specialist in the study and treatment of the female reproductive system.
gynecology: The study of the female reproductive system.
gyri: Upward projecting convolutions on the surface of the cerebrum.

H

hair bulb: Distal base of the hair root and hair follicle; the anchoring structure of the hair.
hair follicle: Cavity that contains the hair root.
hair root: Base of a hair cell.
hair shaft: Portion of hair above the skin.
hard palate: Bony hard surface that forms the anterior, upper roof of the mouth.
Haversian canals: The system of canals within compact bone that contains blood vessels, lymphatic vessels, and nerves.
hematopoiesis: The formation and development of blood cells.
hemoglobin: Component of the RBC containing heme (iron) and globin (protein) that carries oxygen from the lungs to the tissues.
hepatic flexure: The bend of the colon under the liver at the junction of the ascending and transverse colon.
hilum: Indentation on the kidney where the renal artery enters the kidney.
homeostasis: The state of dynamic equilibrium in the internal environment of the body.
hormones: Chemicals that stimulate specific cells (target cells) in the body to increase or decrease function.
hydroxyapatite: The hard crystals that provide strength and durability to bone formed from the chemical combination of calcium phosphate and calcium hydroxide.
hymen: Thin layer of tissue partially covering the opening of the vagina.
hypodermis: Area containing connective tissue and adipose (fat) tissue; also known as the subcutaneous layer.

I

ileocecal sphincter: Muscular ring at the ileocecal junction that opens to allow chyme to flow from the ileum to the cecum and closes to prevent the backflow of waste into the ileum.
immune reaction: Defense function of the body in which invading antigens (pathogens) are destroyed.
immunity: State of being protected or resistant to disease; can be natural or acquired.
incisors: Teeth in the front of the mouth used for cutting and tearing food.
incus: The second of three interconnected ossicles that form a connection to the inner ear.
inferior vena cava: The vein that brings deoxygenated blood from the body, excluding the head and neck, to the right atrium.
inferior: Directional term meaning toward the tail, below.
inhalation: The movement of air into the lungs; also known as inspiration.
insertion: The point at which the skeletal muscle attaches distally from the midline.
insulin: Hormone secreted by the beta cells of the pancreas that stimulates cells to take up sugar from the bloodstream, facilitates the storage of excess glucose as glycogen in the liver, and prevents the breakdown of stored fats.
internal respiration: The distribution of oxygen to cells of the body and removal of carbon dioxide from the cells into the bloodstream; also known as cellular respiration.
internal urethral sphincter: Involuntary sphincter at the junction of the bladder and urethra that keeps urine in the bladder.
iris: Opaque, pigmented portion of the eye surrounding the pupil that controls the amount of light entering the eye; suspended between the cornea and the lens.

K

keratin: The waterproofing component of skin that also prevents fluids from evaporating through the skin.
kidneys: Two purple-brown bean-shaped organs that form urine from blood plasma and regulate water, electrolyte, and acid–base content of blood.

L

labia majora: Two narrow folds of skin extending down from the mons pubis.
labia minora: Inner fold of moist tissue medial to the labia majora that is covered in a mucous membrane and that forms the outer margins of a region called the vestibule.
labor: The birth process that begins with contractions and ends with the expulsion of the placenta after birth of the fetus.
labyrinth: The complex passageway of canals in the inner ear.
lacrimal apparatus: Structure within the eye comprising the lacrimal gland, lacrimal sac, and nasolacrimal ducts.
lacrimal gland: Structure within the eye that secretes tears.
lactation: The process of producing breast milk.
lacunae: Tiny chambers with the bone matrix that contain bone cells.
lanugo: Soft hair covering the fetus.
larynx: Airway that begins at the pharynx, through which air passes into the lower respiratory system.
lateral: Directional term meaning further from the midline.
left atrium: The upper chamber of the heart that holds blood prior to its moving to the left ventricle.
left ventricle: The larger and more muscular lower chamber of the heart that holds blood prior to pumping the blood to the body.
lens: transparent structure in the eye that sits directly behind the pupil and iris.
leukocyte: White blood cell (WBC) that protects the body from pathogens or foreign substances, removes debris from injured tissues, and aids in the healing process.
Leydig cells: Endocrine cells adjacent to seminiferous tubules that secrete testosterone to promote the production of sperm cells.
ligaments: Connective tissue bands that join one bone to another across a joint; adds stability to joints and limits the range of motion of the joint.
linea nigra: A dark line on the skin from the pubic region to the umbilicus that may appear during pregnancy.
liver: Largest solid organ in the body; functions as both a digestive and endocrine organ.
loop of Henle: Most distal end of the nephron.
lower esophageal sphincter: Muscular ring controlling the passage of food from the esophagus to the stomach.
lungs: Two spongy organs that lie lateral to the mediastinum and contain the alveoli and capillaries where the work of internal respiration is done.
lunula: The small part of the nail matrix that can be seen through the nail body as a light-colored crescent.
lymph: Clear, colorless fluid that contains proteins, electrolytes, fats, glucose, and lymphocytes; derived from blood and fluids.
lymph node: Specialized group of tissues located at intervals along the path of the lymph vessels that destroys pathogens, filters and removes impurities, and moves the lymph fluid toward venous circulation.
lymphocyte: Agranulocytic leukocyte that is either a T cell or a B cell; 20% to 25% of all white blood cells.

M

macronutrients: An essential nutrient that provides energy as calories; can be categorized as carbohydrates, fats, and proteins.
macrophage: Specialized immune cells located in lymph nodes, liver, spleen, lungs, brain, and spinal cord that kill bacteria.
macula lutea: Area slightly lateral to the optic disc on the retina containing the fovea centralis.
male orgasm: The combination of sensory stimulation, erection, emission, and ejaculation.
malleus: First of three auditory ossicles in the middle ear that transmit vibrations to the auditory nerve for interpretation as sound.
mammary glands: Structures in the female breast that produce milk.
mastication: Process of chewing food.
matrix: The bone's intercellular arrangement of collagen and mineral salts.
medial: Directional term meaning closer to the midline.
mediastinum: An area between the lungs.
medulla oblongata: The most inferior of the brain structures; composed of white matter on the outside and gray matter on the inside; unites with the spinal cord.
medullary cavity: Large interior cavity inside the diaphysis (bone shaft) filled with red and yellow marrow.
meiosis: Cell division process that produces cells with half their number of chromosomes subsequent to the fusion of sperm and ovum nuclei at fertilization.
melanin: Pigment produced by melanin that gives color to skin and hair.
melanocyte: Cell that secretes melanin.
menarche: The female's first menstrual cycle.
meninges: The three protective layers covering the brain and spinal cord.
menopause: Complete cessation of ovulation and menstruation approximately 40 years after the onset of menarche.
menses: The flow of blood out of the uterus into the vagina and out of the body.
menstrual cycle: The periodic changes in the uterus and associated sex organs associated with menstruation and the intermenstrual period averaging 28 days in length.
metabolism: All the chemical processes that occur in the cells and body to sustain life. The energy and material transformations that occur within living cells.

micronutrients: A vitamin or mineral that provides essential components for chemical reactions in the body but does not provide energy.
micturition: The act of emptying the urinary bladder; urination.
midline: The line upon which a midsagittal plane is cut.
midsagittal: The imaginary plane that divides the body into two identical mirror image pieces.
midwife: Registered nurse with a specialization in obstetrics and gynecology.
mineralocorticoids: Hormones that regulate how mineral salts are distributed to the body's tissues.
mitral valve: Heart structure through which blood flows from the left atrium to the left ventricle; also known as the bicuspid valve.
molars: Teeth in the back of the mouth used to grind food for swallowing.
molecule: Two or more atoms bonded together; individual atoms may be of the same element or different elements.
monocyte: Agranulocytic leukocyte and the largest of the white blood cells. Protects the body by engulfing pathogens through phagocytosis.
mons pubis: The fatty tissue that covers the upper border of the female genital region.
muscles: Tissue containing contractile cells.
muscular tissue: Structures in the body that produce movement.
myometrium: The middle muscular layer of the uterus.

N

Naegele's rule: The mathematical formula used to calculate the expected date of birth based on the date of the last menstrual period.
nail plate: Visible portion of the nail that overlies the nail bed.
nail root: Contains active stratum basale known as the nail matrix, which produces new nail cells by mitosis; deep to the cuticle.
natural immunity: The permanent protection present at birth from specific pathogens; also called genetic immunity.
negative feedback loop: Pertaining to hormones, condition in which the secretion of the hormone provides a reverse response to the stimulus.
nephron: Filtration units of the kidney.
nervous tissue: Structures in the body that control and coordinate the activities of the body using electrochemical signals. Composed of neurons and neuroglia.
neuroglia: One of two types of nervous tissue cells that anchor and support the function of neurons; also known as glial cells.
neurons: Nervous systems cell that sense changes in the environment, integrates the information, and conducts a motor response.
neurotransmitters: Chemical substances released into the synapse to activate or inhibit transmission of nerve impulses across the synapse.
neutrophil: Granulocytic leukocyte that has primary role in inflammation and destruction of foreign antigens by phagocytosis; most common type of leukocyte.
norepinephrine: Sympathomimetic hormone that produces a vasoconstricting effect on blood vessels to raise blood pressure; also known as noradrenaline.
nostrils: The opening of the nose; also known as nares.
noun suffix: Word-ending element attached to a combining form to make a term a noun.
noun: Word that names a person, place, or thing.
nucleus (cell): The cellular structure containing the genetic material that controls and directs the cell.
nutrients: Molecules that provide energy or prompt chemical reactions for the metabolic work of the body.

O

obstetrician: Medical specialist that monitors the health of the mother and developing fetus.
occipital lobe: One of the four divisions of the cerebrum.
olfaction: The sense of smell.
oocyte: Stage of an egg cell present in the ovaries.
optic disc: Structure at the center of the retina with no photoreceptors.
oral cavity: The mouth.
organ of Corti: Organ of hearing running along the length of the spiral cochlea.
organ: Anatomically distinct structures that perform specific functions necessary to maintain life.
organelle: Specialized structures inside the cell that perform distinct functions necessary to life.
organism: A living being that can perform all functions of life.
origin: The point where the skeletal muscle attaches closest to the midline.
osteoblasts: Young osteocytes on the surface of bone that migrate to the lacunae as they mature.
osteoclasts: Large multinucleated cells formed by red bone marrow that break down the bone cells.
osteocytes: Bone cells.
osteolysis: Destruction of bone cells.
oval window: Opening in the wall of the tympanic cavity to the cochlea of the inner ear.
ovaries: Female reproductive organs that produce sex cells and secrete sex hormones.
ovulation: The periodic ripening and rupture of the mature graafian follicle and the discharge of the ovum from the ovary.
ovum: Female reproductive cell.
oxytocin: Hormone released to stimulate contractions of the uterus or to contract cells around the alveolar glands to contract and push milk through the ducts.

P

pancreas: Soft, elongated organ located posterior to the stomach that, as an exocrine organ, secretes digestive enzymes and bicarbonate ions and, as an endocrine organ, secretes glucagon and insulin.

pancytopenia: A decrease in all the formed elements, RBCs, WBCs, and platelets.
papillae: Pertaining to the tongue; raised structures on the tongue containing taste buds.
papillary region: Contains fingerlike projections (papillae) that extend toward the epidermis and provide the bumpy surface to the skin.
parathyroid gland: Small masses of tissue embedded within the posterior thyroid gland that secrete parathyroid hormone PTH.
parietal lobe: One of the four divisions of the cerebrum.
parturition: The process of giving birth.
pathogen: Microorganism capable of producing a disease.
peduncles: Myelinated fibers connecting the cerebellum to sensory nerves in muscles, joints, and the inner ear that convey motor impulses, allowing the cerebellum to coordinate voluntary movements.
pelvic cavity: Subdivision of the abdominopelvic cavity containing the organs of reproduction and elimination.
penis: The external cylindrical organ that houses the distal end of the urethra, which carries semen and urine out of the body.
perilymph: Fluid within the space between outer wall of the ear's bony labyrinth and the inner wall of its membranous labyrinth.
perimetrium: The outermost serous membrane of the uterus.
perimysium: Layer of the fibrous muscle attachment that surrounds groups of muscle fibers.
periosteum: Thin connective tissue covering the bone.
peripheral nervous system: The 12 pairs of cranial, 31 pairs of spinal nerves, and the nerves in the arms and legs.
peristalsis: The coordinated contractions of muscles to move food down the esophagus.
phagocytosis: Process by which phagocytes (neutrophils, monocytes, and macrophages) engulf and destroy microorganisms, other foreign antigens, and cell debris.
pharynx: Passageway for food from the mouth to the stomach and air to the larynx; also called the throat.
phlebotomy: Process of withdrawing venous blood from a patient.
photoreceptors: Nerve cells within the eyeball that detect light.
pia mater: Innermost layer of the meninges that directly attaches to the outer layer of the spinal cord.
pineal gland: Small cone-shaped gland superior to the pituitary gland that secretes melatonin.
pituitary gland: Two-lobed structure at the base of the brain that secretes seven hormones.
placenta: The oval structure in the uterus that provides nutrients and oxygen to a developing embryo or fetus.
plasma: Yellow- or straw-colored blood fluid containing electrolytes, proteins, fats, clotting factors, glucose, bilirubin, and dissolved gases.
pleura: Bilayer membrane that covers the lung.
pore: Tiny opening to the surface of the skin.
positive feedback loop: Pertaining to hormones, a condition in which secretion of the hormone provides a response in the same direction as the stimulus.
posterior chamber: Area of the anterior compartment located between the iris and lens.
posterior pituitary gland: Stores oxytocin and antidiuretic hormones; composed of nervous tissue and neurons originating in the hypothalamus.
posterior: Directional term meaning toward the back.
prefix: Word element attached to the beginning of a word to modify it.
pregnancy: The condition of having a developing embryo or fetus in the body lasting, on average, 280 days.
progesterone: Steroid hormone that acts to stimulate contractions of the uterus, facilitate implantation of the zygote (fertilized ovum), stimulates mammary gland development, and to contract and cause milk to eject.
prolactin: Hormone that stimulates the production of breast milk and, with estrogen and progesterone, the development of the breast.
prostate gland: Located at the lower margin of the urinary bladder, male reproductive organ that secretes a thick alkaline fluid that mixes with spermatozoa.
proximal: Directional term meaning toward the point of attachment.
puberty: Life stage during which individuals become capable of reproduction.
pulmonary circulation: The blood flow from the right ventricle to the lungs to exchange carbon dioxide with oxygen and then through the pulmonary veins to the left atrium.
pulmonary valve: Heart structure through which blood exits the right ventricle into the pulmonary artery.
pulse points: Location of large arteries in the body that have a strong pulse and are easily palpated.
pupil: Opening in the center of the iris through which light enters the eye.
Purkinje fibers: Distributes the electrical impulse from the atrioventricular (AV) node through the septum and ventricles.
pylorus: The lower tubular portion of the stomach; ends with the pyloric sphincter that leads to the small intestine.

Q

quadrants: Divisions of the abdominopelvic cavity that enable medical professions to describe the exact location of an area of concern in the cavity.

R

red marrow: Tissue within the bone's medullary cavity that is the site of hematopoiesis, RBC formation.
releasing hormones: Hormones that cause target organs to stimulate or inhibit release of their hormones.
renal artery: Supplies the kidneys with oxygenated blood.
renal corpuscle: Bulblike mass in the kidney's nephron that contains the glomerulus.

renal cortex: The outer area of the kidney.
renal fascia: Fibrous connective tissue covering the adipose tissue surrounding the kidneys; anchors the kidney to the posterior aspect of the abdominal cavity.
renal medulla: The inner area of the kidney.
renal pyramid: The structures in the renal medulla of the kidney where the nephrons are arranged.
renal sinuses: Spaces between the renal pyramids in the renal medulla of the kidneys.
renal tubule: Long, twisting tube forming one part of the nephron.
renal vein: Delivers filtered blood from the kidney back into circulation.
resorption: Removal of fluid by the passage of a substance through a body surface and into fluids and tissue.
respiration: The spontaneous exchange of gases between the air and the body.
respiratory center: Group of neurons in the brainstem that produce rhythmic impulses to initiate the respiratory cycle.
respiratory rate: The number of breaths per minute.
rete testis: Tubules in the mediastinum testis that receives sperm from the seminiferous tubules.
reticular region: Thick elastic area deep in the papillary region with a high concentration of collagen, elastic, and reticular fibers.
retina: Innermost layer of the eye, which contains the receptors for vision, the rods and cones.
right atrium: The upper chamber of the heart that holds blood prior to its moving to the right ventricle.
right atrioventricular valve: Heart structure through which blood exits the right atrium into the right ventricle; also called the tricuspid valve.
right ventricle: Lower chamber of the heart that holds blood prior to pumping the blood to the lungs.
root: The main component of the word.
round window: Opening in the cochlea of the inner ear.
rugae: Folds or depressions of the mucous membrane in the lining of the stomach that allow the stomach to expand in size.

S

saccule: Pouch of the vestibular labyrinth of the inner ear that contains a sensory area with hair cells that respond to movement of the head.
sagittal: The imaginary plane that vertically divides the body into right and left sections.
saliva: Watery fluid from the salivary glands that contains mucus and enzymes.
salivary glands: Secrete saliva.
sarcolemma: Muscle cell membrane.
sarcomere: Unit of contraction of the muscle cell's myofibrils between two z lines.
sarcoplasm: Body of the muscle cells.
sclera: White layer of the eyeball's tunics made of fibrous connective tissue.
scrotum: Sac-like pouch outside the abdominopelvic cavity that contains the testes and epididymis.
sebaceous glands: Exocrine glands that produce sebum, an oily substance that lubricates the hair and skin.
secretion: The making and release of substances by glands or the substance produced by glandular organs.
semen: Thick fluid containing glandular fluid and spermatozoa.
semicircular canals: Region of the inner ear consisting of three loops.
seminal vesicle: Male gland located at the base of the urinary bladder that empties fructose secretions into the urethra to nourish and stimulate spermatozoa.
seminiferous tubules: Site of sperm production within the testes.
septum: A wall of bony tissue that gives structure to the nose; a thick layer of muscle tissue dividing the right and left sides of the heart.
serum: Liquid portion of blood containing no cells or clotting factors.
sexual intercourse: The insertion of the male's penis and ejaculation into the vaginal canal.
sigmoid colon: Portion of colon that connects to the rectum.
sign: An objective deviation from normal health that can be seen or measured by the provider.
sinoatrial (SA) node: Cluster of specialized cells in the right atrium that initiates an electrical impulse to the heart, causing the heart to beat.
soft palate: Posterior and upper portion of the mouth made of skeletal muscle and soft connective tissue.
somatic nervous system: Division of the peripheral nervous system that communicates information related to voluntary activities.
spermatic cord: Male reproductive structure that includes the vas deferens, the testicular artery and vein, lymph vessels, testicular nerve, cremaster muscle, and connective tissue.
spermatogenesis: The formation of mature spermatozoa.
spermatozoa: Mature sperm cells formed within the seminiferous tubules of the testes.
spinal cavity: Defined by the vertebrae of the spinal column; contains the spinal cord.
spirometer: Instrument used to measure the volume of air that the patient can move in and out of the lungs.
spleen: Largest lymph organ that serves as a reservoir for blood. Contains macrophages that remove old RBCs from circulation and forms bile.
splenic flexure: The bend of the colon where the transverse colon bends downward and becomes the descending colon.
stapes: The third of three interconnected ossicles that form a connection to the inner ear.
strata: The five layers of the epidermis.
subcutaneous layer: Area containing connective tissue and adipose (fat) tissue; also known as the hypodermis.
sudoriferous glands: Secrete a watery substance called perspiration; also known as sweat glands.

suffix: Word element attached to the end of a word to indicate if the word is a noun (plural or singular) or an adjective.
sulci: Deep grooves that divide the lobes of the cerebrum.
superficial: Directional term meaning closer to the surface.
superior vena cava: The vein that brings deoxygenated blood from the head and neck to the right atrium.
superior: Directional term meaning toward the head, above.
suspensory ligaments: Connect the ciliary body to the lens.
sympathomimetic: Changes in the body that mimic changes brought on by the sympathetic nervous system.
symptom: A subjective experience that only the patient can detect.
synapse: Space between the neuron's axon and dendrite.
system (organ): A functional group of organs.
systemic circulation: The flow of blood from the left ventricle through the aorta, arteries, and capillaries and its return to the heart through the veins and vena cavae.
systole: Ventricular contraction.
systolic pressure: Measurement of the highest pressure exerted against artery walls during ventricular contraction.

T

tarsals: Ankle bones; type of short bone.
teeth: The hard structures of the lower and upper jaws that are used for tearing, cutting, and chewing.
temporal lobe: One of the four divisions of the cerebrum.
tendon: Fibrous connective tissue that attaches muscle to bones and other parts.
testes: Paired male gonads that produce the male reproductive cells (spermatozoa) and secrete testosterone.
testosterone: Gonadal hormone responsible for the development of sperm and male secondary sex characteristics.
thalamus: Mass of nuclei completely surrounded by the cerebral hemisphere, which filters, processes, and modifies information sensory signals, with the exception of olfaction, and most motor programs.
thoracic cavity: The chest cavity, defined by the rib cage and the diaphragm; contains the heart, lungs, trachea, esophagus, and great blood vessels.
thrombocyte: Cell fragment of a bone marrow cell (megakaryocyte) that initiates the chemical reactions for blood clotting; also known as a platelet.
thymus: Secretes thymosin and thymopoietin during early life; located in the mediastinum, superior to the heart, and just below the sternum.
thyroid: Butterfly-shaped gland located slightly below the larynx anterior to the trachea that secretes triiodothyronine and thyroxine.
tissue: Groups of similar cells that work together to perform a function.
tongue: Solid muscular structure located at the floor of the mouth. The main organ of taste; assists in mastication and swallowing.
tonsils (palantine): Two masses of lymphatic tissue on either side of the soft palate that help filter out bacteria.
tonsils: Three masses of lymphatic tissue at the back of the throat that trap bacteria and other pathogens entering the body through the nose and mouth.
total lung capacity: The maximum quantity of air a person can inhale.
trabeculae: Needlelike, spiny, bony spicules that give cancellous bone its spongy appearance.
trachea: The part of the respiratory tract that carries air through the neck and upper chest.
transverse colon: Portion of the colon that crosses the abdominal cavity horizontally.
transverse: Divides the body into superior (top) and inferior (bottom) sections; also known as a horizontal plane.
tricuspid valve: Heart structure through which blood exits the right atrium into the right ventricle; also called the right atrioventricular valve.
trigger points: Hypersensitive areas of muscle near a joint.
tunics: The three layers of tissue that make up the eyeball wall.
tympanic membrane: Thin, mucus-covered barrier separating the outer and middle ear that protects the middle and inner ear structures from pathogens.

U

umbilical cord: Structure that connects an embryo/fetus to the placenta.
ureter: Muscular tubular organ that transports urine from the kidney to the urinary bladder.
urethra: The passageway for urine in both males and females during urination and for semen in males.
urinary bladder: Hollow muscular organ that functions as a storage area for urine.
urinary meatus: The external urethral orifice.
urine: Fluid- and water-soluble waste filtered and eliminated from the body by the kidneys.
uterus: Pear-shaped, hollow muscular organ that will contain an implanted ovum as it develops throughout a pregnancy.
utricle: One of two pouches in the ear's vestibule labyrinth that aid in maintaining balance.
uvula: Cone-shaped projection that aids in digestion, swallowing, and producing speech.

V

vaccination: Inoculation with any vaccine or toxoid to establish artificial acquired immunity to a specific infectious disease.
vagina: The muscular tube that connects the uterus with the vulva.
vas deferens: Thick muscular tube that carries the spermatozoa from the epididymis to the urethra; also called the ductus deferens. Part of the spermatic cord.
vasoconstriction: Contraction of the arterioles' smooth muscle walls.
vein: Vessel carrying deoxygenated blood toward the heart.
ventilation: The exchange of gases from the environment into the body and the body to the environment; also known as external respiration.

ventral cavity: The space in the torso and abdomen that contains the organs of digestion, respiration, elimination, and reproduction; found in the front of the body; subdivided into the thoracic and abdominopelvic cavities.
venule: The tiny vein originating from a capillary.
vermiform appendix: Worm-shaped structure attached to the colon.
vermis: Central tissue that divides the two hemispheres of the cerebellum.
vernix caseosa: Cheese-like coating covering the skin of a fetus.
vertebrae: The 26 bones that make up the vertebral column.
vestibule: The oval central area of the ear's bony labyrinth.
vision: Sense of sight.
vital signs: Medical measurements used to determine the status of the body's function.
vitreous humor: Gel-like fluid within the posterior chamber of the eyeball that functions to maintain the eyeball's shape; composed of water, collagen fibrils, sugars, electrolytes, and proteins.
vocal cords: Two parallel folds of tissue stretching across the upper larynx generating vibration sound waves that can be converted to speech when air passes between the vocal cords during exhalation.
vulva: The female external genitals consisting of the mons pubis, labia majora, labia minora, clitoris, urethral meatus, the vaginal orifice, Bartholin's glands, and the perineum.

Y

yellow marrow: Fatty tissue for energy storage within the bone's medullary cavity.

Z

z line: The boundary between a muscle cell's myofibrils that determines how far a muscle can contract and elongate.
zygote: Fertilized ovum.

Index

Note: Page numbers with *f* indicate figures; those with *t* indicate tables.

B

C

D

H

I

J

K

L

M

P

T

U

Photo Credits

All art and photographs not listed below are © F.A. Davis, 2025.

Chapter 1

Fig. 1-1 Courtesy of the Library of Congress, Prints and Photographs Division, NYWT&S Collection, LC-USZ62-131540. *World Journal Tribune* photo by Al Ravenna.

Chapter 3

Fig. 3-15 andresr/E+/Getty Images **Fig. 3-16** Getty Images/iStock/wenht

Chapter 4

Fig. 4-6 iStock/Getty Images Plus **Fig. 4-8A** Getty Images/iStockphoto **Fig. 4-8C** Getty Images/iStockphoto **Fig. 4-9** © Thinkstock **Fig. 4-10** Getty Images/iStockphoto **Fig. 4-11** © Thinkstock **Fig. 4-15** © Thinkstock **Fig. 4-17** © Thinkstock **Fig. 4-18** © Thinkstock **Fig. 4-20** GettyImages/iStock/alejandrophotography **Fig. 4-21** Getty Images/iStock/olenagorbenko

Chapter 5

Case Study: Woman on couch, Charday Penn/E+/Getty Images. Laparoscopic Cholecystectomy postsurgery, wanessa-p/iStock/Getty Images Plus **Fig. 5-7** Андрей Клеменков/iStock/Getty Images Plus **Fig. 5-12** kalus/iStock/Getty Images Plus

Chapter 6

Sidebar: Traffic cop, Thidarat Suteeratat/iStock/Getty Images Plus **Fig. 6-6** FG Trade/iStock/Getty Images Plus **Fig. 6-7** Courtesy of the CDC/Donald Kopanoff, Public Health Image Library **Fig. 6-8** smikeymikey1/Shutterstock **Fig. 6-11** grandriver/iStock/Getty Images Plus

Chapter 7

Case Study: Man with chest, iStock **Fig. 7-9** PositiveFocus/iStock/Getty Images Plus **Fig. 7-10** Centers for Disease Control and Prevention. Dr. Edwin P. Ewing, Jr. **Fig. 7-23** Getty Images **Fig. 7-24** Getty Images/iStockphoto

Chapter 8

Case Study: Black woman, Thinkstock/Stockbyte **Fig. 8-9** smartstock/iStock/Getty Images Plus

Chapter 9

Case Study: Bicycle crash, thefurnaceroom/iStock/Getty Images Plus. Open ankle fracture, gubernat/iStock/Getty Images Plus. X-ray of distal fibula fracture, DanBriffa/iStock/Getty Images Plus. **Fig. 9-23** CreVis2/Getty Images/iStock **Fig. 9-27A** simonmack/iStock/Getty Images Plus **Fig. 9-27B** real444/iStock/Getty Images Plus

Chapter 10

Case Study: Ice fisherman, PamelaJoeMcFarlane/E+/Getty Images **Fig. 10-4** daveRN/iStock/Thinkstock **Fig. 10-6** Getty Images/iStock/piotr_malczyk

Chapter 11

Case Study: Young boy, rijayaNita/iStock/Getty Images Plus **Fig. 11-6** James Gray, MissionFoto, Gosport, IN **Fig. 11-8** Getty Images/iStock/vchal **Fig. 11-9** romaset/iStock/Getty Images Plus

Chapter 12

Fig. 12-9 nazdravie/iStock/Getty Images Plus

Chapter 13

Case Study: Black man, ©Photodisc **Sidebar:** Al Capone, Courtesy of the Federal Bureau of Investigation **Career Exploration:** Monkey Business/Getty Images Plus

Chapter 14

Case Study: Two women on couch, Prostock-Studio/iStock/Getty Images Plus. MRI of brain, Tonpor Kasa/iStock/Getty Images Plus **Fig. 14-9** Dr_Microbe/iStock/Getty Images Plus **Fig. 14-16** FG Trade/iStock/Getty Images Plus **Fig. 14-17** Getty Images/iStock/wenht

Chapter 15

Case Study: Young girl with hearing aid, anurakpong/iStock/Getty Images Plus **Career Exploration:** Optician, ©BananaStock **Fig. 15-10** sdigital/Thinkstock **Fig. 15-11A** Getty Images/iStock/RapidEye **Fig. 15-11B** Getty Images/iStock/H. Barth **Fig. 15-15** Zarina Lukash/iStock/Getty Images Plus **Fig. 15-17** flik47 Creative iStock/Getty Images Plus

Stephan Dreyer
Rainer Keppler

W0415835

DAS KOSMOS-BUCH DER AQUARISTIK

FISCHE, PFLANZEN, WASSERTECHNIK

KOSMOS

Umschlaggestaltung von Atelier Reichert, Stuttgart, unter Verwendung von 4 Farbaufnahmen von Burkard Kahl *(Macropodus opercularis* oben links und *Hemigrammus erythrozonus* oben rechts), Bruno Cavignaux *(Aphyosemion gardneri)* und Bernd Greger *(Echinodorus amazonicus).*

Mit 208 Farbaufnahmen, 95 Schwarzweißzeichnungen, 3 Schemata und 5 Tabellen.

Die Deutsche Bibliothek – CIP-Einheitsaufnahme

Das **Kosmos-Buch der Aquaristik**: Fische, Pflanzen, Wassertechnik / Stephan Dreyer; Rainer Keppler. – Stuttgart: Franckh-Kosmos, 1993
ISBN 3-440-06580-4
NE: Dreyer, Stephan; Keppler, Rainer

Informationen senden wir Ihnen gerne zu

Bücher · Kalender · Spiele · Experimentierkästen · CDs · Videos · Seminare

Natur · Garten & Zimmerpflanzen · Heimtiere · Pferde & Reiten · Astronomie · Angeln & Jagd · Eisenbahn & Nutzfahrzeuge · Kinder & Jugend

KOSMOS Postfach 106011
D-70049 Stuttgart
TELEFON +49 (0)711-2191-0
FAX +49 (0)711-2191-422
WEB www.kosmos.de
E-MAIL info@kosmos.de

© 1993, Franckh-Kosmos Verlags-GmbH & Co., Stuttgart
Alle Rechte vorbehalten
ISBN 3-440-06580-4
Lektorat: Angela Wolf
Layout, Herstellung, Satz und Lithografie:
Concept GmbH, Höchberg bei Würzburg
Printed in Italy/Imprimé en Italie
Druck und buchbinderische Verarbeitung:
Tipolitografia G. Canale & C., S. p. A., Borgaro

Alle Angaben in diesem Buch sind sorgfältig geprüft und geben den neuesten Wissensstand bei der Veröffentlichung wieder. Da sich das Wissen aber laufend weiterentwickelt und vergrößert, muß jeder Anwender prüfen, ob die Angaben nicht durch neuere Erkenntnisse überholt sind. Dazu muß er zum Beispiel bei Behandlungsvorschlägen den Tierarzt konsultieren, Beipackzettel zu Medikamenten lesen, Gebrauchsanweisungen und Gesetze beachten.

Fotos: Gerhard Brünner 4m, 66, 67u, 69, 70o, 72u, 73ol, 73or; **Bruno Cavignaux** 1l, 84u, 102r, 109or, 116o, 116ml, 116mr, 121ul, 129ol, 141l, 145ur; **Dr. Stephan Dreyer** 57, 88, 89; **Bernd Greger** 63, 67o, 70u, 71, 72o; **Ludwig Hambsch** 126, 127; **Burkard Kahl** 1r, 4r, 7, 17, 22, 32, 49, 60, 76, 77u, 80, 83, 84o, 95, 96, 97ol, 97u, 98, 99o, 99ul, 100l, 101l, 102l, 103ol, 103u, 104, 105, 108, 109ol, 110u, 112, 113o, 113u, 114o, 115u, 119, 120, 121o, 121ur, 122ol, 122u, 123u, 124o, 124u, 125u, 128, 129u, 130l, 130r, 131ol, 131u, 134ol, 134ur, 135o, 135m, 138, 139u, 140ol, 140or, 142ol, 144, 147, 148u, 149o, 150o, 150u, 151l; **Dr. Rainer Keppler** 3, 13u, 14, 15, 18, 24, 33, 36, 37, 40, 45, 46, 48, 52, 56, 64, 65, 73u, 82, 86, 101r, 106, 107, 139o, 143ur; **Horst Linke** 5m, 5r, 25, 77o, 78, 81, 100ur, 129or, 132r, 133u, 134ul, 137o, 137u, 140ul, 141r, 145ol, 145or, 145ul, 146u, 148o; **Löbbeke-Museum und Aquazoo Düsseldorf/Dr. H. Bosch** 54, 55; **MP-Hetscher Aquarien** 8, 21; **Arend van den Nieuwenhuizen** 4l, 20, 23, 97or, 103or, 109u, 110or, 111, 114u, 115o, 118, 122or, 123o, 131or, 133ol, 134or, 136; **Reinhard-Tierfoto** 5, 13o, 26, 39, 85, 116u, 133ol, 135u, 143l, 146o, 149u; **Dr. G. Schubert/Uni Hohenheim** 93; **Rainer Stawikowski** 140ur, 142or, 142u; **Uni Hohenheim** 92; **Klaus Wilkerling** 28, 31, 34, 99ur, 100or, 110ol, 110m, 125o, 132l, 143or, 151r.

Zeichnungen: Maria Bertsch/Sigrid Haag 61o, 62, 63ol; **aus Engelhardt, Was lebt in Tümpel, Bach und Weiher?** 39, 87; **Marianne Golte-Bechtle** 58, 79; **Reinhild Hofmann** 63r, 66r, 67m, 68ur, 69u, 70; **Kerstin Keppler** 27 Cartoons und 1 Vignette; **Dr. Rainer Keppler** 45, 51; **Peter Löhle** 92, 93o; **Angela Paysan** 61u, 90; **aus Remane/Storch/Welsch, Kurzes Lehrbuch der Zoologie, 5. Aufl.** 75; **Dr. Thomas Romig** 80, 81, 82, 83; **Walter Söllner** 63u, 66l, 66m, 67l, 67r, 68o, 68l, 69or, 69m, 71, 73o, 73u; **Dieter Untergasser** 93u; **Brigitte Zwickel-Noelle** 9r, 9l, 10, 11, 14, 16, 17, 18, 27.

Aquarien-fieber …

Die „Krankheit" steht in keinem medizinischen Lexikon, und kein Arzt kann sie behandeln – schon allein deshalb, weil die „Patienten" überhaupt nicht kuriert werden wollen. Ja, die Betroffenen pflegen ihre ganz spezielle Infektion beinahe schon mit Hingabe: Die Rede ist vom Aquarienfieber.

Oft befällt es einen bereits in der Kindheit, aber auch ältere Semester sind nicht vor der Ansteckung gefeit. Ein Ausbruch ist jederzeit möglich und anscheinend sind männliche Wesen eher infiziert als Mädchen und Frauen. Vielleicht täuscht dies aber auch, und die Wahrheit mag sein, daß (Groß-)Väter, Onkel, Söhne und männliche Enkel etc. mehr von dieser Krankheit reden, weibliche Wesen sie aber versteckt in sich tragen. Doch damit möge sich die Marktforschung herumärgern.

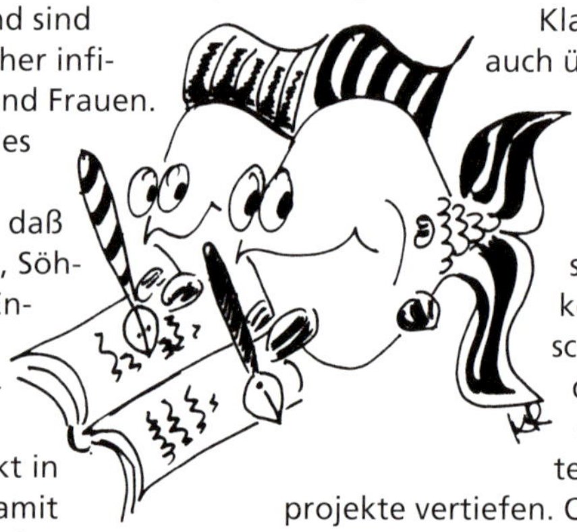

Fest steht, daß einen das Aquarienfieber nicht mehr losläßt, wenn es richtig zugepackt hat. Die Symptome sind sehr unterschiedlich und dringen nicht immer klar nach außen, gemeinsames Merkmal ist aber stets „wäßrig-fischiges" Denken und Handeln. Man frönt der Aquaristik in Theorie und Praxis.

Derzeit gelten mindestens zwei Millionen Mitmenschen allein in Deutschland als befallen. Auch wir gehören dazu, ja, wir müssen eigentlich als besonders hartnäckige Fälle eingeordnet werden. Während nämlich bei den meisten unserer Zeitgenossen das Aquarienfieber nur in der Freizeit so richtig ausbricht, können und dürfen wir sogar beruflich für Erhalt und Ausbreitung dieser Erscheinung sorgen.

Zusammen mit praktisch allen anderen Heim- und Haustieren sind bei uns die Zier- und Nutzfische, dazu natürlich das Wasser mit allem Drum und Dran sowie Futter und Zubehör zu professionellen Aufgaben geworden.

Klar, daß wir uns auch über die berufliche Ausübung der Aquaristik kennengelernt haben. Die ersten Kontakte konnten wir schon bald darauf durch gemeinsam bearbeitete Zierfischfutterprojekte vertiefen. Obwohl Rainer nach dem Studium der Biologie/Zoologie in Karlsruhe zunächst in einem tropischen Speisefischprojekt tätig war (Guramizucht in Thailand) und Stephan sich nach dem Studium der Agrarbiologie/Tierproduktion in Stuttgart (Universität Hohenheim) dem einheimischen Barsch und der Fluß- und Seenfischerei/Fischzucht widmete, waren es aquaristische Themen, die uns beruflich und privat zusammenführten.

Seitdem fiebern wir häufig gemeinsam und wenn dann noch so eine liebe Kollegin wie die Biologin Angela Wolf (Heimtierlektorin bei unserem Verleger) hinzukommt, sind – wie vorliegend zu sehen – nicht nur Fachsimpeleien vorprogrammiert. Rasch wurde es zur gemeinsamen Aufgabe, ein Aquaristikbuch zu fertigen. „Schon wieder eines", fragten wir uns zunächst, aber das „mal etwas andere Sachbuch" in Aufmachung und Darstellungsweise zu machen, reizte uns schnell.

Denn schließlich gehört man als Naturwissenschaftler – gewissermaßen dienstlich – auch immer irgendwie zur „schreibenden Zunft". Zusätzlich wird das ständige Verfolgen von Sach- und Fachliteratur zur Routine. Die gewonnenen Erkenntnisse fließen gemeinsam mit praktischen Erfahrungen aus Hobby, Versuchen und Projekten in entsprechende Auftragsarbeiten ein: Aquaristische Dokumentationen, Vorträge und Seminare zur Aus- und Fortbildung werden so zu gern erledigten Pflichtübungen. Beide waren und sind wir damit immer wieder befaßt, und langweilig ist es nie!

Angela Wolf ermunterte uns, noch darüber hinaus zu gehen, und über ihren Aufgabenbereich hinaus hat sie derartig mitgeholfen, daß sie schon fast Co-Autorin sein müßte. Ohne sie und den Franckh-Kosmos-Verlag, der unsere Wünsche und Ideen stets großzügig unterstützte, wäre dieses Werk nie möglich gewesen.

Angela und allen Mitarbeitern in Stuttgart sei an dieser Stelle recht herzlich gedankt, genau wie unseren doch manchesmal geplagten Ehefrauen, ohne deren Unterstützung (seelisch-moralischer sowie kulinarischer und teils auch aktiv mitwirkender Art) das Buch nicht so geworden wäre, wie es ist.

Daß es dem „Einsteiger" helfen und auch erfahreneren Aquaristikhasen noch manch wertvollen Hinweis geben möge, hoffen wir von ganzem Herzen.

Böhl-Iggelheim und Hockenheim,
im Sommer 1993

Stephan Dreyer
Rainer Keppler

Inhalt

Das Aquarium – Natur zu Hause

Etwa 80 Millionen Zierfische in ca. 2 Millionen Haushalten schwimmen allein in deutschen Aquarien, und mindestens so viele Menschen ließen sich aus freien Stücken vom Aquaristikfieber anstecken. Was haben sie davon?

Haben sie bestimmte (womöglich gemeinsame) Ziele, und was kann und soll Aquaristik bewirken? Welchen Sinn und Zweck kann ein Glaskasten (oder gar mehrere!) haben, den man sich zu Hause oder gar am Arbeitsplatz aufstellt, mit Wasser füllt und mit Pflanzen und Fischen bestückt?

Nun, *die* gemeinsame Antwort auf alle Fragen kann es nicht geben. Es gibt eine ganze Reihe von Gründen, warum Menschen mit Fischen und Wasserpflanzen zusammenleben wollen. Aber allen Aquarianern ist – bewußt oder unbewußt und mehr oder weniger stark ausgeprägt – eines gemeinsam: die Liebe zur belebten Natur sowie die Freude an entsprechenden Beobachtungen.

Ist sie gekoppelt mit einer gewissen Portion „Forschergeist", wird man die mit der aktiven Ausübung der Aquaristik einhergehenden Lehr- und Lerneffekte im Vordergrund sehen. Vor allem aus dem vielfältigen und reizvollen Bereich der Verhaltensforschung läßt sich auch auf begrenztem Raum viel beobachten und analysieren. Gerade Naturkunde- und Biologielehrer machen sich dies bei Schulaquarien zunutze, und manchen Schüler läßt die Thematik nicht mehr los.

Bei keiner Form der Haus- und Heimtierhaltung werden die Wechselbeziehungen zwischen Tier und Umwelt und ihre mannigfaltigen Verflechtungen so deutlich wie in der Aquaristik. Die Ökologie als Lehre dieser Zusammenhänge läßt sich durch die gegebenen Abhängigkeiten (Fisch – Wasser – sonstige Bewohner) trefflich darstellen und vermitteln.

Nur was man in praktischer Erfahrung und direktem Kontakt kennenlernt, wird man auch schätzen können und schützen wollen. Die Aquaristik vermittelt eine Vorstellung davon, was sich draußen in der Natur, mit und ohne Zutun des Menschen, abspielt. Dabei rückt neben den Bewohnern das Wasser selbst mit seiner elementaren Bedeutung für alle Lebensformen in das Zentrum des Interesses.

Fragen und Antworten des Biotop- und Landschaftsschutzes spiegeln sich in Aquarien wider, der Umweltschutzgedanke wird in der Thematik „Wasserqualität, Wasseraufbereitung" greifbar und im Kleinen nachvollzogen. Die Verantwortung für Lebewesen und ihre Umgebung, die Freude, die aus erfolgreicher Hege und Pflege von Wasserbewohnern erwächst, stellen sich als weitere denkbare Aquaristik-Motivationen dar.

Man kann Aquaristik ganz für sich allein, gemeinsam mit Freunden und Bekannten oder als sinnvolle und arbeitsteilige Beschäftigung für die ganze Familie betreiben. Viele Aktive suchen aber auch ganz bewußt den Meinungs- und Erfahrungsaustausch in entsprechend orientierten Interessensgruppen, seien es Arbeitsgemeinschaften an Schulen oder anderen Bildungseinrichtungen oder die zahlreichen Aquarianervereine. Fachsimpeln oder nur zuhören, gemeinsam beobachten oder sich weiterbilden und die geselligen Aspekte dieser Runden genießen – all das kann aus Aquaristik erwachsen, Anlaß für den Einstieg in dieses schöne Hobby sein oder zu seiner Vertiefung führen.

Schließlich seien die Zeitgenossen genannt, die alle zuvor genannten guten Gründe weder brauchen noch wollen: Sie finden es einfach „nur" schön, ein Aquarium zu besitzen und sich daran zu erfreuen: als Zierde einer Wohnung, als Schmuckstück im Zimmer und als Objekt, dessen Betrachtung nach dem hektischen Arbeitstag als entspannend, ja wohltuend empfunden wird.

Zu jeder Form der Ausübung der Aquaristik gehört eine Portion Sachkunde und Fachwissen, um möglichen Fehlern vorzubeugen und Kritikern den Wind aus den Segeln zu nehmen. Bei Durchführung mit Sachverstand gibt es nichts, aber auch gar nichts, das gegen die Aquaristik spricht. Eine sinnvolle Beschäftigung ist sie allemal.

Vorüberlegungen

Wenn wir Lebewesen (Tiere oder Pflanzen) in unsere Obhut nehmen, sollte es selbstverständlich sein, daß wir die Verantwortung für ein ge-

So nicht!

Gesellschaftsaquarium mit Keilfleckbärblingen und Schillerbärblingen.

sundes und artgerechtes Leben dieser Organismen übernehmen. Um im konkreten Fall im Aquarium diese Lebensbedingungen nicht nur kurzfristig, sondern kontinuierlich aufrechterhalten zu können, sind eine Reihe regelmäßiger Pflegearbeiten erforderlich. Sie verursachen ein gewisses Maß an Kosten und nehmen auch einige Zeit in Anspruch.

Da die meisten Mißerfolge in der Aquaristik auf mangelnde oder falsche Pflege zurückzuführen sind, soll hier zunächst einmal der Pflegeaufwand, den ein „durchschnittliches" Aquarium erfordert, besprochen werden. Es liegt dann an Ihnen, sich zu überlegen, ob Sie diese Tätigkeit und den damit verbundenen Kosten- und Zeitaufwand auf sich nehmen wollen. Wenn ja, steht dem Start ins „nasse Hobby" und der damit verbundenen, meist lebenslangen Infektion mit dem Aquaristikvirus nichts mehr im Wege!

Mit der Zeit werden Sie, wie alle Aquarianer, die Erfahrung machen, daß die erforderlichen Pflegemaßnahmen alles andere als lästig sind. Auch die Zeit, die Sie mit „Fische beobachten" verbringen, wird Ihnen nicht als Belastung erscheinen. Im Gegenteil, Sie werden es manchmal bedauern, wenn die Beobachtung interessanter Vorgänge im Aquarium durch berufliche oder sonstige Termine unterbrochen wird.

Der Pflegeaufwand

Hier werden zunächst in allgemeiner Form die erforderlichen Tätigkeiten und der damit verbundene Zeit- und Kostenaufwand beschrieben. Nähere Erläuterungen und Begründungen erfahren Sie dann in den späteren Kapiteln über Wasserpflege und Technik.

Das Füttern Ihrer Pfleglinge ist zweifellos die häufigste Pflegemaßnahme. Eine ein- bis zweimalige Fütterung pro Tag sollte als Anhaltspunkt dienen. Es darf nur soviel gefüttert werden, wie die Fische in wenigen Minuten restlos fressen. Weitere Einzelheiten zur Fütterung finden Sie im entsprechenden Kapitel.

Es ist sinnvoll, während der Fütterung die Fische zu beobachten: Kommt jeder Fisch ans Futter, gibt es Anzeichen von Krankheiten oder Verletzungen, gibt es Unverträglichkeiten zwischen einzelnen Fischen oder liegen sonstige Abweichungen vom normalen Verhalten vor? Gleichzeitig wirft man auch einen Blick aufs Thermometer und prüft, ob alle technischen Geräte ein-

Ein „klassisches" Aquarium.

wandfrei arbeiten. Für diese Tätigkeiten muß mit einem täglichen Zeitaufwand von ca. 10 bis 15 Minuten gerechnet werden.

Die wichtigste, für die Erhaltung eines optimalen Milieus entscheidende Tätigkeit ist die Durchführung eines regelmäßigen Teilwasserwechsels. Um ein stetiges Anhäufen von Schadstoffen im Aquarium zu verhindern, muß regelmäßig alle 14 Tage ein Viertel bis ein Drittel des Wasservolumens abgesaugt und durch frisches Wasser ersetzt werden. Näheres dazu im Kapitel über Wasser. Gleichzeitig werden auch abgestorbene Pflanzenteile und übermäßige Mulmansammlungen entfernt. Falls erforderlich, wird auch ein Teil der Filtermassen im Filter gereinigt. Für diese Tätigkeit muß man bei einem 100-l-Aquarium mit einem Zeitaufwand von ca. 30 Minuten rechnen.

Um sicherzugehen, daß den Aquarieninsassen ihr nasses Element auch zusagt, sollten regelmäßig pH-Wert und Nitrit-Gehalt überprüft werden. Dafür gibt es preiswerte und leicht zu handhabende Testsets im Zoofachhandel. Der Zeitaufwand für eine Messung liegt bei ca. drei bis fünf Minuten.

Bei den Kosten wollen wir uns hier darauf beschränken, nur die Betriebskosten zu behandeln. Anschaffungskosten sind einmalig und hängen letzten Endes davon ab, für welches Aquarium Sie sich entscheiden. Da sich Preise bekanntlich ändern, kann hier nur auf die einzelnen Kostenfaktoren hingewiesen werden. Absolutwerte würden in Kürze nicht mehr der Realität entsprechen.

Prinzipiell entstehen dauernde Kosten an Strom, Wasser, Futter und Pflegemitteln. Die Hauptverursacher von Stromkosten sind Beleuchtung und Heizung. Am Stromverbrauch für Beleuchtung läßt sich nicht sparen, da eine Beleuchtungsdauer von 12 Stunden täglich erforderlich ist. Die Kosten für Heizung richten sich nach der Differenz zwischen Zimmertemperatur und erforderlicher Temperatur des Aquarienwassers. Je kleiner die Differenz, desto geringer die Kosten. Die Stromkosten für Filterung fallen äußerst gering aus, da moderne Aquarienfilter nur sehr wenig Strom verbrauchen (Anschlußwert oft unter 10 W).

Die Wasserkosten für den regelmäßigen Teilwasserwechsel sind praktisch (noch) zu vernachlässigen: Für ein 100-l-Aquarium benötigt man bei 14tägigem Austausch von 30 l Wasser etwa 780 l im Jahr.

Die Kosten für Futter sind von der Zahl und der Größe der gepflegten Fische abhängig. Dazu kommen dann noch Kosten für Pflegemittel, wie z.B. Dünger für Wasserpflanzen, Wasseraufbereiter. Als gelegentliche Kosten kämen noch die erwähnten Testsets hinzu. Bei einer Reichweite von 50–80 Messungen pro Packung (je nach Fabrikat), schlagen sie weniger häufig zu Buche.

Der richtige Standort

Wenn Sie nun die Schilderung des Pflegeaufwandes nicht von Ihrem Entschluß abbringen konnte, sich mit dem Aquaristikvirus infizieren zu lassen, so ist es an der Zeit, den geeigneten Standort für das Aquarium auszusuchen.

Spätestens seit es technisch ausgereifte künstliche Beleuchtungen für Aquarien gibt, hat das Aquarium auf der Fensterbank ausgedient. Der Standort Fensterbank oder auch ein Platz in der Nähe des Fensters, wie er in älterer Aquarienliteratur noch propagiert wird, bringt zu große Lichtprobleme mit sich. Der nur schwer kontrollierbare und nicht kontinuierliche (Sommer/Winter) Lichteinfall fordert Algenprobleme geradezu heraus.

Die dunkelste Ecke eines Zimmers, möglichst ohne Sonneneinstrahlung, ist der ideale Platz für ein Aquarium. Eine gezielt auf die Bedürfnisse der Pflanzen abgestimmte künstliche Beleuchtung sorgt für das richtige Licht in kontinuierlichem Rhythmus. Möglicherweise können Sie dadurch sogar eine ewig dunkle und unbeliebte Ecke im Zimmer aufmöbeln und schlagen so zwei Fliegen mit einer Klappe.

Darüber hinaus sollte der Idealplatz für ein Aquarium aber noch einige weitere Bedingungen erfüllen. Ein elektrischer Anschluß mit mindestens drei Steckdosen sollte sich in der Nähe befinden oder problemlos hergestellt werden können. Die Pflegearbeiten, vor allem aber der nötige regelmäßige Teilwasserwechsel, müssen ohne akro-

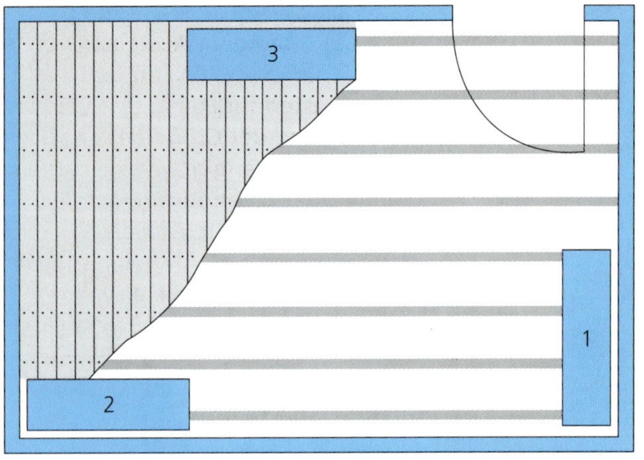

Achten Sie bei der Wahl des Standortes auf den Verlauf der Balken im Fußboden. Quer zur Balkenrichtung ist der ideale Standort (1); in der Ecke (2) ist es immer noch stabiler als parallel zum Balkenverlauf an der Wand (3).

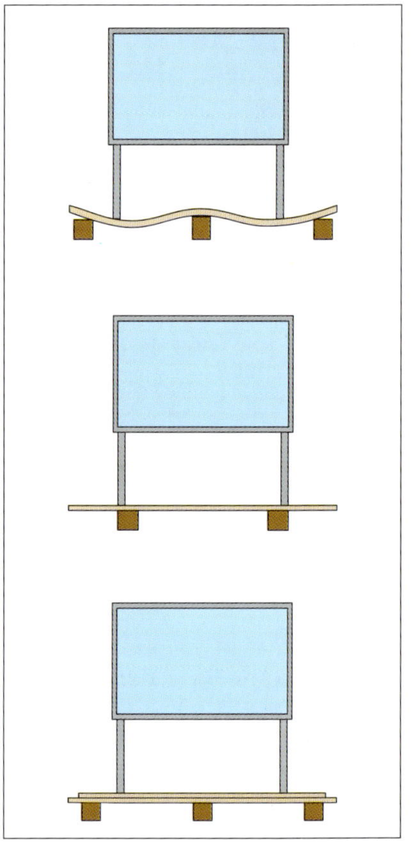

Wenn es nicht möglich ist, das Aquarien-Untergestell über den Balken zu plazieren, hilft eine große Platte als Unterlage, die den Druck über die Balken verteilt.

batische Verrenkungen durchführbar sein.

Die Nähe eines Wasseranschlusses ist nicht unbedingt zwingend erforderlich. Bei kleineren Aquarien wird man den Wassertransport ohnehin per Eimer machen, was einmal in zwei Wochen, auch bei entfernter liegendem Badezimmer, leicht erledigt werden kann.

Bei größeren Aquarien kann die Eimerschlepperei allerdings zur Last werden, zumal zufällig verschwapptes Wasser sicherlich kein Anlaß zu familiären Freudenausbrüchen ist. In einem solchen Fall empfiehlt sich die Anschaffung eines längeren Schlauches (Gartenschlauch). Das eine Ende steckt man ins Aquarium, natürlich nicht ohne Ansaugschutz für die Fische. Das andere Ende klemmt man, nachdem man das Wasser kurz angesaugt hat, unter die Brille des „stillen Örtchens". So kann, ein ausreichender Höhenunterschied vorausgesetzt, jede beliebige Menge Wasser aus dem Aquarium bequem entsorgt werden.

Für den umgekehrten Weg wird der Schlauch mit der Warmwassermischbatterie verbunden (passende Verschraubungen gibt's im Baumarkt) und temperiertes Wasser fließt zurück ins Aquarium. Da man die Eigendynamik von Schläuchen nicht unterschätzen sollte, muß das Schlauchende im Aquarium natürlich entsprechend gesichert werden (Saugnapf, Stein etc.).

Das Gewicht eines gefüllten Aquariums ist nicht zu unterschätzen. Ein 100-l-Aquarium wiegt inklusive Bodengrund, Dekoration und Unterbau ca. 120–150 kg. Bei Aquarien unter 100 l dürfte das Gewicht bei heutigen Deckenkonstruktionen für die Standortwahl unbedeutend sein. Bei größeren Aquarien ist es jedoch ratsam, sich Gedanken über die Tragfähigkeit der Decke zu machen. Sie ist in der Nähe der Wände natürlich höher als in der Mitte des Zimmers. Im Zweifelsfall sollten Sie einen Statiker zu Rate ziehen. Bei Altbauten mit Holzdecke sollte außerdem noch die Laufrichtung der Balken berücksichtigt werden. Steht das Aquarium quer zur Laufrichtung und dazu noch an einer Wand, so ist die Tragfähigkeit am höchsten.

Seinem Gewicht entsprechend, benötigt ein Aquarium natürlich noch einen stabilen Unterbau. Für Aquarien bis ca. 60 l kann dies ein Tisch, Schreibtisch, Regal oder dgl. sein. Für größere Aquarien benötigt man einen eigens für diesen Zweck hergestellten Unterbau. Der Zoofachhandel bietet heute Aquarienunterbauten in zahlreichen Modellen und Ausführungen an. Ein Selbstbau lohnt sich nur bei Sondermaßen, entsprechendes Können natürlich vorausgesetzt.

Es versteht sich natürlich von selbst, daß der Unterbau absolut waagrecht stehen muß. Die eigentliche Fläche, auf die das Aquarium gestellt wird, muß plan und absolut frei von Fremdpartikeln (kleinen Steinchen etc.) sein. Zwischen Stellfläche und Aquarium legt man eine dünne Styroporplatte (Baumarkt) oder eine sog. Polysoftmatte, die es speziell für Aquarien im Zoofachhandel gibt.

Das Aquarium

Größe

Aquaristikeinsteiger stehen allzuoft vor der Gewissensfrage: Zunächst klein beginnen und später evtl. vergrößern oder gleich ein großes Aquarium? Beides hat, offen gesagt, Vor- und Nachteile. Sehen wir uns zunächst einmal die Verhältnisse in der Natur an.

Unsere Pfleglinge schwimmen in ihrer Heimat in riesigen Wassermassen, deren chemische Zusammensetzung sich durch eine ausgeprägte Kontinuität auszeichnet. An diese

Verhältnisse haben sich die Fische mehr oder weniger stark angepaßt (mehr darüber im Kapitel über Fische). Aus diesem Grunde sollte man bestrebt sein, im Aquarium ähnliche kontinuierliche Lebensbedingungen zu bieten. Zumindest sollten sich die Schwankungen in vertretbaren Grenzen bewegen.

Nun ist es nicht zu bestreiten, daß in einem großen Aquarium diese Konstanz der Lebensbedingungen durch versehentliche Pflegefehler nicht ganz so leicht aus dem Gleichgewicht gebracht wird wie in einem kleinen. Andererseits wird man bei einem kleinen Aquarium, sofern man nicht vorzeitig aufgibt, mit den natürlichen Gesetzmäßigkeiten dieses kleinen Lebensraumes eher vertraut als bei einem großen. Pflegefehler werden von einem kleinen Aquarium sofort unerbittlich quittiert.

Hierzu ein Beispiel: Ein unbemerkt gestorbener Fisch wird in einem großen Aquarium keinen Ärger bereiten. Er wird praktisch ohne Auswirkungen auf das Wassermilieu von unzähligen Bakterien und anderen Organismen zersetzt. Im kleinen Aquarium läuft prinzipiell das gleiche ab. Nur kann im hier wesentlich kleineren Wasservolumen die Arbeit der Bakterien zu einem katastrophalen Sauerstoffmangel führen. Die Folgen für die Fische sind wohl jedem klar.

Weiterhin ist auch noch zu bedenken, daß die Anschaffung und auch die Betriebskosten bei einem großen Aquarium natürlich größer sind als bei einem kleinen, zumal der Zoohandel kleinere Aquarien mit durchaus akzeptablen Abmessungen preiswert als Komplettset mit allem erforderlichen Zubehör anbietet. Die Entscheidung liegt letzten Endes bei Ihnen selbst.

Das kleine Aquarium erfordert jedenfalls wesentlich mehr Disziplin und Regelmäßigkeit in der Pflege als ein größeres. Aus diesem Grund könnte man es durchaus als den didaktisch besseren Weg des Einstiegs in die Aquaristik betrachten.

Sollten Sie wider Erwarten nach einiger Zeit feststellen, daß Aquaristik doch nicht das ist, was Sie sich als Hobby vorgestellt haben, dann hält sich zumindestens der finanzielle „Flurschaden" in Grenzen. Wir gehen natürlich davon aus, daß Sie in einem solchen Fall die gepflegten Lebewesen in verantwortungsvolle Hände weitergeben.

Bauart und Form

Am häufigsten findet man heutzutage sogenannte Nur-Glas-Aquarien. Das sind Behälter, die aus exakt zugeschnittenen und diamantgeschliffenen Einzelglasscheiben zusammengeklebt werden. Als Kleber und gleichzeitige Abdichtung dient sogenannter Silikonkautschuk.

Derzeit werden die meisten Becken mit schwarzem Silikon geklebt. Dies soll das „Einwachsen" von Algen in die Grenzflächen zwischen Silikon und Glas verhindern. Andererseits gibt es auch Aquarien, die mit transparentem Silikon geklebt sind, wo auch noch nach 20 Jahren kein nennenswertes Einwachsen von Algen festzustellen ist. Man könnte also die schwarze Klebung eher als Modeerscheinung betrachten.

Die Farbe der Klebung dürfte also letztendlich eine untergeordnete Rolle spielen. Wesentlich wichtiger ist das Vorhandensein von sogenannten Verstärkungsleisten, die auch gleichzeitig als Deckscheibenauflagen dienen. Kaufen Sie nur Becken, die Verstärkungsleisten an den **Längsscheiben** des Aquariums haben!

Bei Becken über ein Meter Länge müssen auch noch, abhängig von der Länge, ein oder mehrere Querstege vorhanden sein, die **auf** die Verstärkungsleisten aufgeklebt sind. Bei großen Aquarien, die nur mit Querstegen versehen sind (ohne Verstärkungsleisten in Längsrichtung), kommt es immer wieder vor, daß die Klebung der Querstege reißt und sich die Längsscheiben dann bedenklich nach außen wölben, wenn nicht sogar platzen.

Geklebte Aquarien haben grundlegende Vorteile gegenüber der früher üblichen „Rahmenbauweise". Durch den Wegfall des aufwendig herzustellenden Metallrahmens, in den anschließend die Scheiben eingekittet wurden, ist es möglich, wesentlich größere Aquarien preiswert zu fertigen. Zudem sind von der herkömmlichen „viereckigen" Form abweichende interessante Formen möglich, die auch als Sonderanfertigungen preislich noch im Rahmen bleiben. Dadurch eröffnet sich eine Fülle neuer Gestaltungsmöglichkeiten im Wohnraum.

Ein kleiner Nachteil dieser Nur-Glas-Aquarien sei jedoch nicht verschwiegen: Vor allem die Kanten sind beim Transport wesentlich leichter zu beschädigen, als die von

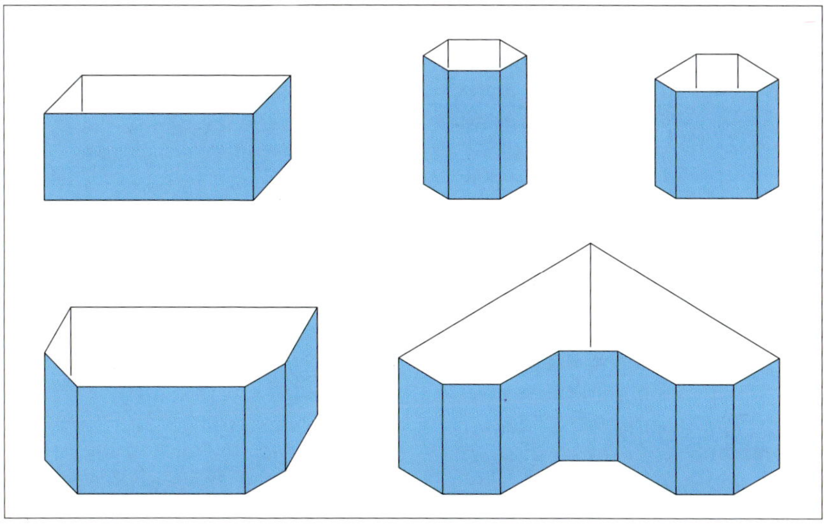

Aquarien gibt es in allen erdenklichen Formen und Größen.

Rahmenaquarien. Mit ein bißchen mehr Vorsicht läßt sich dieses jedoch leicht umgehen.

Bei der Auswahl der geeigneten Beckenform sollte den Ansprüchen der zu pflegenden Fische Vorrang vor innenarchitektonischen „Meisterleistungen" gegeben werden. Langgestreckte Fische, die gern viel schwimmen, sollte man z.B. nicht in kurzen hohen Becken pflegen. Umgekehrt sollten Fische mit hohem Körper nicht in flachen langen Becken gepflegt werden.

Muß das Becken aus irgendeinem Grund (zur Verfügung stehender Platz etc.) eine bestimmte Form haben, so wählen Sie bitte nur solche Fische, denen der angebotene Lebensraum zusagt. Nähere Angaben finden Sie in den Kapiteln über Aquarientypen und Fische sowie in der am Ende des Buches angegebenen Fachliteratur.

Ein weiteres wichtiges Kriterium bei der Auswahl der Beckenform ist die Tiefe des Beckens. Unter Tiefe versteht man die Entfernung zwischen Front- und Rückscheibe. Je tiefer ein Becken ist, desto vielseitiger sind die Gestaltungsmöglichkeiten im Aquarium. Hinzu kommt noch, daß die Entfernung von der Front- zur Rückscheibe, durch das Wasser beobachtet, wesentlich kürzer erscheint als an der Luft.

Ideal wären Aquarien, die tiefer sind als hoch, oder zumindest gleich tief wie hoch. Leider hat die Industrie dies noch nicht erkannt. So sind die allermeisten Aquarien in Standardgrößen höher als tief. Mit etwas Geschick lassen sich jedoch auch solche Aquarien ansprechend gestalten. Für welches Maß Sie sich auch immer entscheiden, achten Sie darauf, nur Fabrikate von renommierten Herstellern mit Garantie auf die Klebung zu kaufen.

Der Vollständigkeit halber seien nun auch noch einige andere Aquarienbauarten genannt. Als die Nur-Glas-Aquarien sich durchzusetzen begannen, fand man eine Zeitlang auch eine Zwischenstufe zwischen Rahmen- und Nur-Glas-Aquarien: Aquarien, die mit Silikon geklebt wurden, auf die jedoch nachträglich ein Rahmen aus Kunststoffprofilen aufgeklebt wurde. Der „Rahmen" dieser Aquarien hat keinerlei tragende Funktion. Er schützt lediglich die Kanten vor Beschädigung. Solche Aquarien sind mittlerweile jedoch wieder „aus der Mode" gekommen. Wer nun um die Kanten seines Nur-Glas-Aquariums fürchtet, kann einen solchen Rahmen aus Kunststoffprofilen (Baumarkt) auch leicht selbst ankleben.

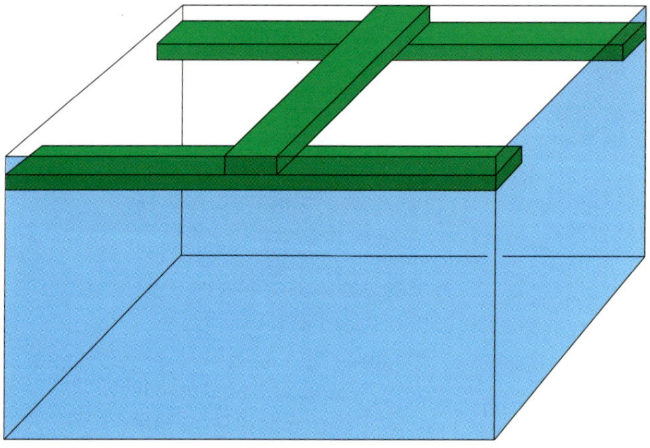

Becken ab 100 cm Länge benötigen einen Mittelsteg zur Stabilisierung, der über den längs verlaufenden Stegen angebracht ist.

Plexiglas ist ebenfalls ein Material, aus dem Aquarien hergestellt werden können. Da es jedoch im Vergleich zu Glas teurer und außerdem sehr kratzempfindlich ist, konnte es sich nicht so recht durchsetzen. Lediglich in einem Stück gegossene, für Quarantäne oder Zucht verwendbare Klein- oder Kleinstbecken aus Plexiglas finden noch Verwendung.

Für extrem große Aquarien kann es aus preislichen Gründen erforderlich sein, auf andere Materialien als Glas zurückzugreifen. Man setzt dann lediglich eine Frontscheibe aus Glas ein. Es wäre z.B. nicht das erste Mal, daß ein Aquarianer sein Traumaquarium betoniert oder mauert und dann das Haus darum herumbaut.

Isolation gegen Wärmeverlust

Bei Aquarien mit tropischen Fischen liegt die Wassertemperatur (zumindest während der kühleren Jahreszeit) um ca. 5–8 °C über der Raumtemperatur. Dies bedingt einen nicht unerheblichen Wärmeverlust nach außen. Nun stehen die wenigsten Aquarien so, daß sie von allen Seiten eingesehen werden können. Es empfiehlt sich also, alle Seiten, die nicht eingesehen werden können, von außen wärmedämmend zu isolieren. Das spart Stromkosten. Als Material eignen sich dazu Styroporplatten oder sogenannte extrudierte Dämmplatten aus Polystyrol (Baumarkt). Extrudierte Dämmplatten sehen eleganter aus und lassen sich mit einem Cuttermesser exakt und fransenfrei zuschneiden. Zur Befestigung verwendet man Silikonkleber oder doppelseitiges Teppichklebeband.

Hintergrund

Der Blick durch ein Aquarium auf die dahinterliegende Tapete paßt in den seltensten Fällen zu der auch noch so gekonnt gestalteten Aquarieninneneinrichtung. Bevor das Aquarium an seinen endgültigen Standort gebracht wird, sollten deshalb alle nicht einzusehenden Scheiben mit einem Hintergrund versehen werden, der natürlich mit der Inneneinrichtung des Aquariums harmonieren sollte.

Die einfachste Art ist ein schlichter Anstrich der betreffenden Scheiben von außen mit handelsüblicher Dispersionsfarbe. Als Farbtöne eignen sich am besten Schwarz oder dunkle erdige Töne. Statt eines direkten Anstrichs der Scheiben können auch die zur Wärmeisolation verwendeten Platten (vorheriger Abschnitt) eingefärbt und dann von außen angeklebt werden.

Aquaristik im Wandel der Zeit

Das Halten und zur Schau stellen von schönen Fischen, die nicht dem Verzehr dienen, hat in Asien, insbesondere China und Japan, eine schon Jahrhunderte alte Tradition. Goldfische und Zierkarpfen standen (und stehen heute noch) dort im Mittelpunkt des züchterischen Interesses. Einfache Tongefäße für den Züchter, verzierte und glasierte Töpfereiwaren für den privaten Halter bis hin zu edelsten, feinen Porzellanbehältern für begüterte Liebhaber kennzeichneten im fernen Osten die aquaristische Praxis.

Noch heute ist dort derartiges in Gebrauch, und alle klassischen Goldfischvarietäten sind auf die Betrachtung von oben ausgesucht und gezielt gezüchtet worden. Die Betrachtung „hinter Glas" im Aquarium kann als westliche Erfindung gelten.

Das waren noch Zeiten, als unsere Vorväter im letzten Jahrhundert die Fischliebhaberei entdeckten. Obwohl wesentliche biologische Bedingungen bekannt waren, so etwa die Temperaturansprüche der tropischen Fische, so waren doch die technischen Möglichkeiten begrenzt, um dies auch erfolgreich in die Praxis umzusetzen.

Historisches „Aquarium" aus dem Artikel „Der See im Glase" von E. A. Rossmässler, der 1856 in der Gartenlaube erschien.

Das „Dampfaquarium"

Die ersten Aquarienheizer waren Petroleum- oder Spiritusfunzeln, die unter das Becken gestellt wurden; später waren dann kleine Gasbrenner schon ein Fortschritt. An den entsprechenden Stellen waren im Metallboden der Becken sogenannte Wärmekuppeln aufgelötet. In ihrer direkten Umgebung wurde mit Bodengrund gespart, um lokale Überhitzungen zu vermeiden.

Damals hat man die Aquarien meist noch selbst gebastelt, und die diesbezüglichen Anleitungen lesen sich für unsere heutigen aquaristischen Begriffe beinahe schon abenteuerlich: Mit Pech- und Teerdichtungsmassen wurde experimentiert, zahlreiche Rezepturänderungen von Fensterkitt sind ausgetauscht und probiert worden. Nach Einbringen der Scheiben in die Rahmung sorgten verschiedene Vergußmassen für zusätzliche Sicherheit.

Die Rahmen überstrich man mit oftmals selbstgerührten „Isolierlacken" auf der Basis von Mennige, einer nicht ganz ungefährlichen Bleiverbindung. Sie wurde durch Beimengungen von Leinölfirnis als Oberflächenschutz „entschärft".

Als Bodengrund dienten schon damals Sand und Kies. Man kommt übrigens heute teilweise auf eine Erkenntnis zurück, die auf erste Beobachtungen in dieser Zeit zurückgeht: Dunkler Bodengrund fördert Ruhe und Farbkraft mancher Fische, die sich bei hellen und reflektierenden Grundmaterialien eher schreckhaft und blaß zeigen. Seinerzeitige Problemlösung: Beimischung von Braunkohlegrieß!

Luft muß sein

War dann das Wasser erst einmal im hoffentlich dichten Aquarium drin, die Pflanzen und Fische eingesetzt, begann auch schon das Bangen um die Flossenträger: Sie schnappten nach Luft, vor allem, wenn man hinsichtlich der Besatzdichte und mangels Filterkenntnis-

Goldfischkugeln sind heutzutage als wenig artgerechte Haltungsmethode glücklicherweise ausgestorben.

sen des Guten zuviel getan hatte. Dringend nötige Luft mußte her, aber wie?

Die ersten Luftspeicher waren Gummischläuche, etwa aus Autoreifen, die ihren Inhalt morgens und abends durch fleißiges Aufpumpen bezogen. In Druckkesseln mit Manometer und Auslaßventil fanden sie ihre vornehmere Variante, aber auch die war nur durch sportliche Betätigung zu füllen. Als Ausströmer dienten bis zum Einsatz von Kieselgurblöcken dicke Filzscheiben.

Keine konstanten Bedingungen

Die ersten Aquarien wurden ohne Beleuchtung betrieben und standen daher auf der Fensterbank. Im Sommer waren Algenprobleme durch zuviel Licht geradezu vorprogrammiert, im Winter war es am Fenster zu kalt, und der Spritverbrauch der primitiven Heizer schoß merklich in die Höhe. Später galt entsprechendes für die ersten Elektroheizungen. Sie wurden als Salzheizer in der Form betrieben, daß in einem U-förmigen Glasrohr Strom durch eine Salzlösung geschickt wurde. Durch Größe der angelegten Kohleelektroden und Konzentration der Lösung war eine gewisse Regulierung der Heizleistung möglich.

Der jahreszeitliche Übergang vom Sommer zum Winter war die kritischste Periode: Unter den Fischen, von denen Makropoden, Kardinalfische und Panzerwelse der Gattung Corydoras zu den Pionieren hiesiger Becken gehörten, grassierte häufig das gefürchtete „Herbststerben". Die Pflanzen ließen mit schwindender Lichtmenge und -intensität in ihrer Sauerstoffproduktion nach, und war die Besatzdichte ohnehin kritisch, kam es rasch zu Ausfällen infolge Verschlechterung der Wasserqualität. Prophylaktisch wurde durch rege Verschenkaktionen im Spätsommer die Fischdichte reduziert, und mancher Zeitgenosse wurde so zum Neu-Aquarianer.

Die Entwicklung geriet kurz auf einen Seitenzweig, der mittlerweile zum Glück fast ausgestorben ist: Man erfand die unselige Goldfischkugel, in der fast keine der zwischenzeitlich verfügbaren, technischen Neuerungen der Aquaristik zur Anwendung kam.

Auf dem Weg zur High-Tech-Aquaristik

Die ersten Filtertöpfe, Glühlampenbeleuchtungen und kleine Luftpumpen kennzeichneten den Weg hin zur modernen Aquaristik. Technologische Verbesserungen fanden und finden statt, begleitet von naturwissenschaftlichen Erkenntnissen aus vielen Fachbereichen.

Trotz idealer Voraussetzungen folgen auch heute noch einige Aquarien-Neulinge dem historischen Prinzip des „Lernens durch Versuch und Irrtum". Damals war nichts anderes möglich, aber heutzutage muß man bei etwas gutem Willen und der Bereitschaft zu einmaligen, sinnvollen Investitionen wirklich nicht viel „Lehrgeld" bezahlen.

Asiatische Zierfischhaltung.

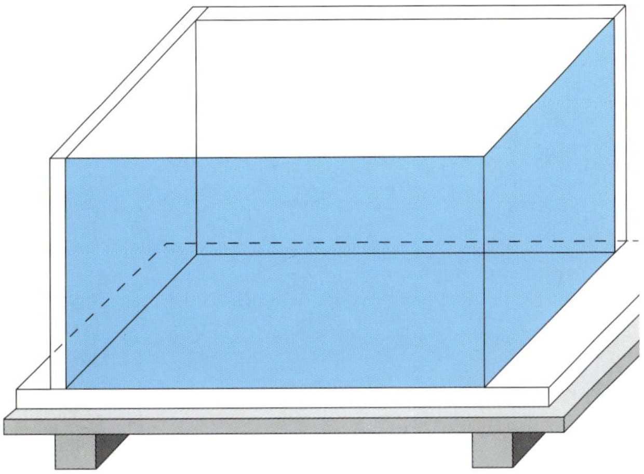

Als Isolation gegen Wärmeverlust werden die dem Betrachter abgewandten Seiten des Aquariums mit einer Styroporplatte verkleidet.

Im Zoofachhandel sind sogenannte Fotorückwände als Meterware in verschiedenen Motiven erhältlich, die dann einfach von außen mit Klebeband befestigt werden. Wer etwas bastlerisches Geschick hat, kann sich aus verschiedensten Naturmaterialien (Steine, Rinde, Schilf etc.) auch eine Rückwand selbst herstellen. Von der Verwendung voluminöser Rückwände innerhalb des Aquariums (z.B. aus bearbeitetem Styropor) raten wir ab, da dadurch, zumindest in kleineren Aquarien, das Wasservolumen zu stark eingeschränkt wird.

Bodengrund

Um den Aquarienpflanzen das erforderliche Pflanzsubstrat und den Fischen den nötigen „Boden unter den Füßen" zu bieten, braucht die künftige Unterwasserwelt einen Bodengrund. Am besten bewährt hat sich kalkfreier, bräunlicher Kies in einer Körnung von 2–3 mm. Meiden Sie reinweißen Kies, wenn er auch noch so schön „clean" aussieht. Fische fühlen sich auf dunklem Bodengrund wesentlich wohler und zeigen schönere Farben.

Achten Sie auch darauf, daß die einzelnen Kieskörnchen rundlich sind. An scharfkantigem Material, wie z.B. Lavabruch oder Basaltsplit, die zwar schön dunkel gefärbt sind, können sich manche Bodenfische empfindliche Verletzungen zuziehen. Weitere Einzelheiten zum Bodengrund erfahren Sie im Kapitel über Wasserpflanzen.

Dekoration

Zur Gestaltung des Lebensraumes Aquarium benötigen Sie natürlich auch noch Wasserpflanzen und bestimmte Dekorationsmaterialien. Damit diese ihrem besonderen Verwendungszweck und nicht zuletzt auch ästhetischen Gesichtspunkten gerecht werden, hier einige grundsätzliche Gedanken vorab.

Da das Aquarium einmal eine kleine, nach biologischen Gesetzmäßigkeiten funktionierende Lebensgemeinschaft werden soll, versteht es sich von selbst, daß Plastikpflanzen absolut tabu sind. Welche wichtigen Funktionen die Pflanzen im Aquarium erfüllen, erfahren Sie im Kapitel über Pflanzen. Auch bei den übrigen Dekorationsmaterialien, die Sie benötigen werden, um z.B. Höhlen, Reviereinteilungen oder Terrassen aufzubauen, bieten sich natürliche Materialien eher an als Plastikkram. Natursteine, Moorkienwurzeln oder Steinholz sind einige Materialien, die sich sehr gut eignen.

Sämtliche Materialien dürfen keine schädlichen Substanzen an das Wasser abgeben. Besonders bei jeglicher Art von Holz ist darauf zu achten, daß nur nicht faulendes, durch jahrzehntelange Lagerung in Mooren mit Huminsäuren imprägniertes Holz Verwendung findet. Bei Materialien aus dem spezialisierten Zoofachgeschäft können Sie sicher sein, daß sie geeignet sind.

Den in der Literatur häufig zu findenden Hinweis, Steine, Wurzeln oder sonstige Materialien vor Verwendung auszukochen, können Sie getrost vergessen. Nicht nur, daß

Geklebtes Aquarium mit zwei Arten von Bodengrund, Polysoftunterlage, verschiedenen Fotorückwänden und rückwärtiger Isolation. Bodengrund links: ideales Material (Kies, Körnung 2–3 mm); Bodengrund rechts: Lavabruch, zwar dunkel, aber scharfkantig. (Polysoftunterlage, Hintergrund und Isolation stehen nur zu Demonstrationszwecken über.)

bei solchen Aktionen meist der Haussegen leidet, auch die Beschaffung passender Töpfe stellt einen normal bestückten Haushalt oft vor unüberwindliche Probleme. Kräftiges Abbürsten unter fließendem Wasser genügt völlig.

Überladen Sie ihr Aquarium nicht mit zu vielen verschiedenen Dekorationsmaterialien. Auch hier gilt der Grundsatz, daß weniger oft mehr ist. Legen Sie also keine Steinsammlung unter Wasser an, sondern verwenden Sie nur Steine einer Art. Mehr über die Aquarieneinrichtung finden Sie im nächsten Kapitel.

Vor dem Aquarium kann man herrlich entspannen.

Nützliche Utensilien

Einige nützliche Dinge, die Ihnen die Arbeit am Aquarium erleichtern, sollten Sie sich gleich von vornherein an einem bestimmten Platz bereithalten. Im wesentlichen sind dies: ein sauberer Eimer, der ausschließlich für die Aquarienpflege benutzt wird und für sonstige Putzaktivitäten im Haushalt absolut tabu ist; dazu ein Absaugschlauch von ca. 2 m Länge mit einem Durchmesser von ca. 15–20 mm. Einen Kescher benötigen Sie, um gegebenenfalls Fische aus dem Aquarium fangen zu können.

Zur Entfernung von Algenbelägen an der Innenseite der Frontscheibe ist ein Scheibenreiniger erforderlich. Außer Eimern (die gibt's im Baumarkt oder Haushaltswarengeschäft) bietet der spezialisierte Zoofachhandel alle genannten Utensilien in verschiedener Qualität und Ausführung an.

Versicherung

Obwohl es, Gott sei Dank, nur sehr selten vorkommt, daß man den Inhalt seines Aquariums auf dem teuren Wohnzimmerteppich findet, sollte man doch für diesen Fall vorgesorgt haben. Stellen Sie sich einmal vor, was ein einziger Eimer Wasser anrichtet, der zufällig aus Versehen im Wohnzimmer umfällt, und rechnen Sie das dann auf den Inhalt Ihres Aquariums hoch! Von dem eigenen Schaden sei hier einmal gar nicht die Rede. In einer Mietwohnung kann das ausgelaufene Wasser eines Aquariums erheblichen Schaden an fremdem Eigentum anrichten.

Am besten, Sie lassen sich von Ihrem Versicherungsfachmann beraten. Eine Haftpflichtversicherung deckt Schäden gegenüber Dritten. Wenn das Aquarium, meist gegen Sonderprämie, in die Hausratversicherung mit eingeschlossen werden kann, sind auch Ihre eigenen Schäden versichert. Mitglieder von Aquarienvereinen, die dem VDA (siehe Adressenverzeichnis) angehören, sind automatisch gegenüber Dritten versichert.

Utensilien zur regelmäßigen Aquarienpflege: Eimer, Fangnetz, Schlauch und Mulmglocke, verschiedene Scheibenreiniger.

Gedankenaustausch

Bevor wir nun in den nächsten Kapiteln tiefer in die aquaristische Materie einsteigen, ein Rat: Ein Aquarium zu pflegen heißt, sich mit einem Komplex sich gegenseitig beeinflussender Lebewesen zu beschäftigen. Und gerade weil es sich um Lebewesen handelt, kann es keine Anleitung wie für eine Maschine geben, der man nur zu folgen braucht, und schon klappt alles.

Dieses Buch will versuchen, Sie in die richtige Richtung zu lenken. Sie werden jedoch früher oder später auf irgendein Problem stoßen, auf das Sie in diesem Buch vielleicht keine Antwort finden. Suchen Sie deshalb den Gedankenaustausch mit Gleichgesinnten.

Ihr erster Ansprechpartner wird Ihr spezialisierter Zoofachhändler sein. Mit der Zeit werden Sie dann sicher auch andere Aquarianer kennenlernen, die vielleicht einem Verein angehören, oder Sie werden selbst Mitglied in einem Aquarienverein. In heißen Diskussionsabenden werden Sie dann feststellen, daß oft viele Wege nach Rom führen und daß manchmal nicht alles so geht, wie man es sich anfangs vorgestellt hat. Aber gerade das ist es, was die Aquaristik so interessant macht.

Für jeden etwas – Aquarientypen

Aquariendekoration und Vorgehensweise

Bevor Sie darangehen, Ihr ganz persönliches Aquarieninterieur zu gestalten, ein Wort vorab: Wollte man den Lebensraum unserer Aquarienfische absolut *naturgetreu* nachbilden, so böte sich in den allermeisten Fällen kein allzu erhebender Anblick. Das muß nicht sein. Die Einrichtung eines Aquariums darf selbstredend durch unser ästhetisches Empfinden geprägt sein.

Wichtig ist lediglich, daß sie trotzdem die Funktion übernimmt, die für ein artgerechtes Leben der Fische erforderlich ist. Das heißt, Fische, die Unterschlupf in Form von Höhlen benötigen, sollten diese auch vorfinden, und Fische, die Pflanzendickichte brauchen, um sich gegebenenfalls zurückziehen zu können, sollten nicht in „Steinwüsten" gepflegt werden, und so weiter.

Im vorangegangenen Kapitel haben Sie bereits erfahren, welche Materialien für eine Dekoration im Aquarium in Frage kommen. Um es noch einmal zu wiederholen: Verwendbar sind grundsätzlich alle natürlichen Materialien, die nicht faulen und keine schädlichen Substanzen an das Wasser abgeben. Taucher, Schiffswracks und sonstige Plastikartikel stören die Fische zwar nicht, aber sie passen nicht so recht zum Bild einer möglichst natürlich wirkenden Unterwasserlandschaft. Über Geschmack läßt sich jedoch bekanntlich nicht streiten.

Die am häufigsten verwendeten Dekorationsmaterialien sind wohl nach wie vor Steine und Moorkienholz. Geeignet sind alle Arten von Steinen, die keine Härtebildner enthalten, also zum Beispiel Granit, Basalt, Schiefer, Lava, Kieselsteine und andere. In Sonderfällen, wie zum Beispiel für ein Aquarium mit Fischen aus den afrikanischen Grabenseen, kann auch Kalkgestein Verwendung finden.

Steine dienen dazu, Höhlen, Reviergrenzen und Terrassen aufzubauen. Terrassen eignen sich sehr gut, um dem Aquarium räumliche Tiefe zu verleihen, wenn sie nicht parallel zum Scheibenverlauf, sondern asymmetrisch nach hinten verlaufend angelegt werden. Um ein Durchrieseln des Bodengrundes durch Lücken in der „Terrassenmauer" zu verhindern, klebt man mit Silikon Glasstreifen hochkant auf die Bodenscheibe, die dann mit Steinen verkleidet werden.

Moorkienwurzeln sind ein hervorragendes Mittel, um im Wasser versunkene Baumteile oder vom Wasser unterspülte Baumwurzeln nachzuahmen. Außerdem bieten sie verschiedenen Harnischwelsen einen wesentlichen Bestandteil ihrer Nahrung, nämlich Cellulose, die diese durch unermüdliches Abraspeln der Wurzeln zu sich nehmen.

Leider haben Moorkienwurzeln eine unangenehme Eigenschaft: sie schwimmen auf, und das unter Umständen noch nach Jahren. Bewährt haben sich folgende Methoden, um die Wurzel unter Wasser zu halten: Die Wurzel so anordnen, daß das obere Ende unter einer Verstärkungsleiste des Beckens zu liegen kommt; das am Boden liegende En-

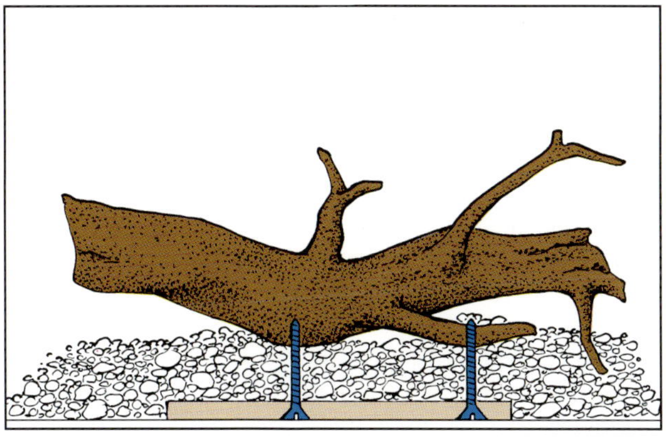

Moorkienwurzeln werden mit nichtrostenden Schrauben auf einer Kunststoffplatte befestigt, die dann mit Bodengrund bedeckt und dadurch gehalten wird.

de mit entsprechend schweren Steinen unten halten. Die Verstärkungsleiste des Beckens soll dabei nur den Auftrieb der Wurzeln abfangen, auf keinen Fall die Wurzel zwischen Boden und Verstärkungsleiste einklemmen – Bruchgefahr!

Mit Edelstahlschrauben kann man eine größere Kunststoffplatte an die Unterseite der Wurzel schrauben. Die Kunststoffplatte wird anschließend im Bodengrund versenkt. Kommen Sie bitte nicht auf die Idee, Wurzeln mit Silikon ankleben zu wollen! Aufgrund der Porosität des Holzes wird nach kurzer Zeit Wasser in die Grenzfläche der Klebung eindringen, die Wurzel macht sich selbständig, und ab geht es nach oben! Wenn die Beleuchtung dabei nicht zu Bruch geht, haben Sie Glück gehabt.

Neuerdings bietet der Zoofachhandel auch tropisches Holz an, das gut für Aquarien geeignet ist und – wesentlicher Vorteil – schwerer ist als Wasser. Es muß allerdings sehr lange vorgewässert werden, da es das Wasser ziemlich stark braun färbt.

Halbierte oder ganze gereinigte Kokosnußschalen mit Öffnung bieten einen idealen Brutplatz für Zwergbuntbarsche. Mit entsprechend zurechtgeschnittenen Bambusstäben kann im Wasser stehendes Schilf oder Gras nachgeahmt werden. Kokosnußschalen und Bambus brauchen, wie Moorkienholz, vor der Verwendung nicht ausgekocht zu werden.

Es gibt sicherlich noch viele weitere wertvolle, natürliche Materialien, deren Aufzählung den Rahmen dieses Buches sprengen würde. Lassen Sie Ihre Phantasie spielen. Vermeiden Sie jedoch die Verwendung zu vieler verschiedener Materialien in einem Becken.

Die Einrichtung des Aquariums erfolgt im wesentlichen nach folgendem Schema:

1. Bodenheizung. Wenn Sie sich zur Verwendung einer Bodenheizung entschlossen haben, muß diese zuerst auf den Glasboden des Aquariums in gleichmäßigen Schlingen verlegt werden. Näheres über Bodenheizungen erfahren Sie im Technik-Kapitel.

2. Einbringen des Bodengrundes. Am besten bewährt hat sich eine 4 bis 6 cm hohe Schicht aus möglichst dunkelfarbigem Quarzkies. Wenn Sie vorgewaschenen Kies aus dem Zoofachgeschäft beziehen, ist es nicht einmal unbedingt erforderlich, ihn auszuwaschen. Eine geringfügige Trübung nach dem Wassereinfüllen verschwindet nach kurzer Zeit wieder. Kies unbekannter Herkunft muß vor der Verwendung im Aquarium unbedingt gewaschen werden.

3. Anbringen von Stabheizer und Filter. Verfahren Sie genau

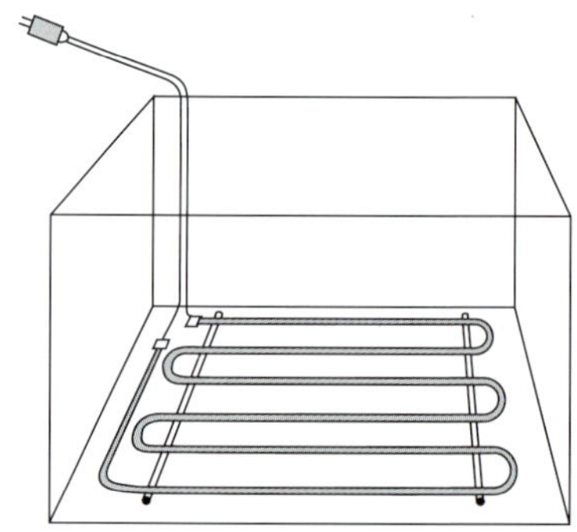

1 Bodenheizung verlegen

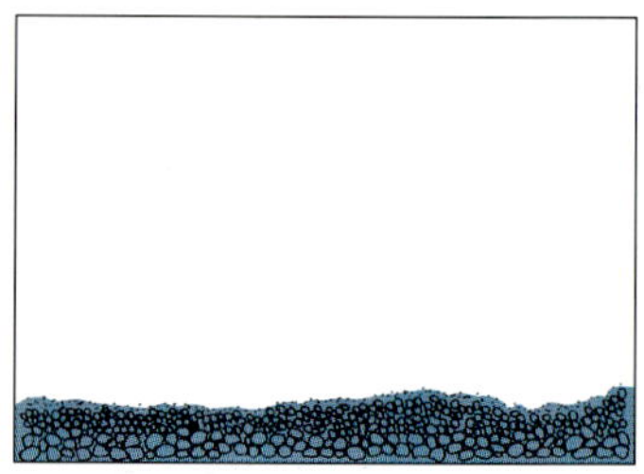

2 Kies einfüllen

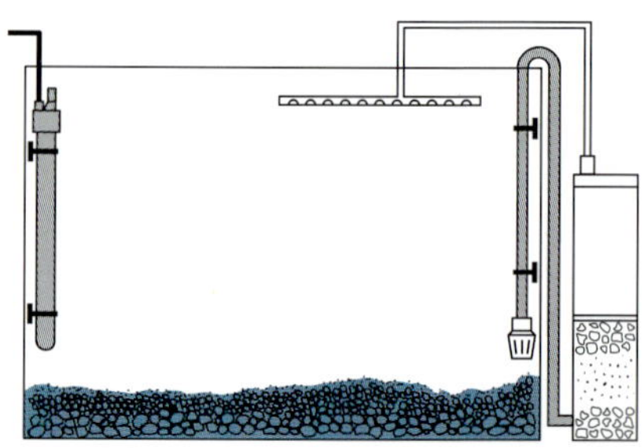

3 Stabheizer und Filter installieren

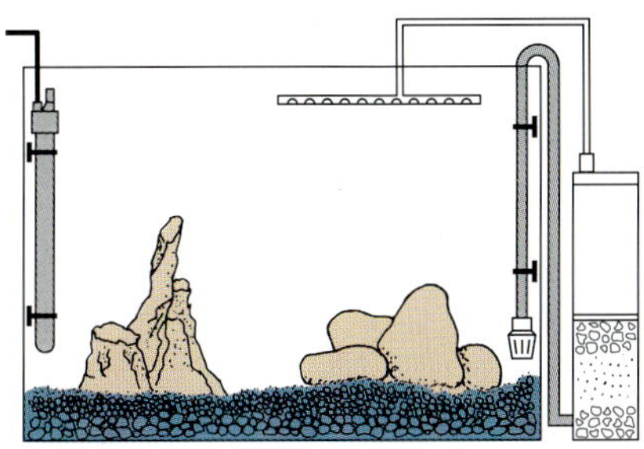

4 Dekoration anordnen

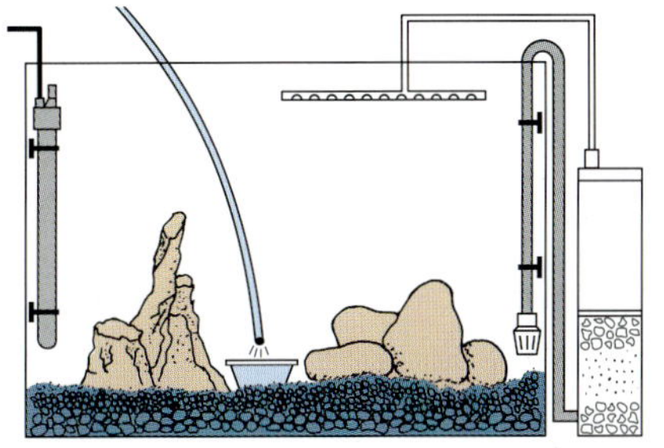

5 Wasser einfüllen

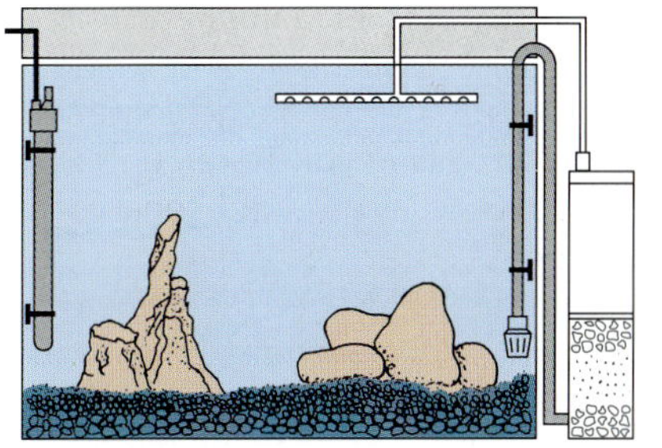

6/7 Beleuchtung anbringen

8 Pflanzen einsetzen

9 Fische einsetzen

Auswahl an Dekorationsmaterialien: Moorkienholz, Korkrinde und verschiedene Steine; das Kunststoffgitter dient als Unterlage für schwere Steinaufbauten (zum Schutz der Scheibe).

nach der Gebrauchsanleitung der einzelnen Geräte. Installieren Sie die Geräte im hinteren Teil des Aquariums so, daß sie später durch Dekorationsgegenstände und Pflanzen möglichst verdeckt werden.

4. Anordnen der Dekorationsgegenstände. Wenn keine besonders stark wühlenden Fische gepflegt werden sollen, können Steine, Wurzeln usw. auf den Bodengrund aufgelegt oder leicht eingegraben werden. Schwere Steinaufbauten für wühlende Fische, z.B. Buntbarsche, müssen *vor* Einbringen des Bodengrundes aufgebaut werden. Um dabei die Bodenscheibe nicht zu beschädigen, ist es ratsam, eine Styroporplatte oder besser ein engmaschiges Kunststoffgitter (Gartenbedarf) unterzulegen.

5. Wasser einfüllen. Um dabei den Bodengrund nicht unnötig aufzuwirbeln, legt man einen flachen Gegenstand (Scheibe, Teller, Stein) auf den Boden und leitet darauf den Wasserstrahl. Das Wasser wird gleich auf 25 °C temperiert (Mischbatterie). Nachdem das Aquarium vollgefüllt ist, werden noch eventuell erforderliche Korrekturen an der Dekoration vorgenommen.

6. Filter und Heizung in Betrieb nehmen, Beleuchtung installieren. Näheres über diese Geräte erfahren Sie im Technik-Kapitel.

7. Animpfen. Nun ist es erforderlich, das Aquarium mit Bakterien „anzuimpfen". Was es mit diesen Bakterien auf sich hat und wozu sie gut sind, erfahren Sie in den folgenden Kapiteln. Die absolut beste Methode der Animpfung ist die: Besorgen Sie sich von einem befreundeten Aquarianer einen Teil eingefahrene Filtermasse und waschen Sie diese in Ihrem Aquarium aus. Die dabei entstehende unschöne Trübung verschwindet rasch wieder, Sie haben praktisch im Handumdrehen einen „eingefahrenen" Filter und können ein bis zwei Tage später bereits Fische einsetzen.

8. Wasserpflanzen einsetzen. Wenn die Technik einwandfrei arbeitet und das Becken angeimpft ist, können die Wasserpflanzen eingesetzt werden. Nähere Einzelheiten dazu im Kapitel über Pflanzen.

9. Einsetzen der Fische einige Tage später. Näheres darüber und über die Fische selbst erfahren Sie in den entsprechenden Kapiteln.

Die richtige Mischung: Gesellschaftsbecken

Sogenannte Gesellschaftsbecken dürften für die meisten Aquarianer der Einstieg in dieses schöne Hobby gewesen sein. Wie der Name schon sagt, werden in einem derartigen

Aquarium verschiedene Bewohner vergesellschaftet.

Generell gilt für die gewollte Vergesellschaftung von Tieren unterschiedlicher Arten – und genau darum geht es hier – eine ganz wichtige Grundregel: Die gemeinsam unterzubringenden Lebewesen müssen sich miteinander vertragen und sie müssen prinzipiell die gleichen Ansprüche an die Umweltbedingungen haben. Nur so ist eine wirklich artgerechte Unterbringung gewährleistet, wie sie zu Recht vom Tierschutz verlangt wird.

Dieser Grundsatz hat natürlich auch in der Aquaristik zu gelten. Eine „wilde Mischung" verschiedenster Fischarten, kombiniert mit diversen Pflanzen und eventuellen weiteren Wasserbewohnern, ausgesucht allein nach Gesichtspunkten des rein persönlichen Geschmacks, geht meistens schief. Zumindest das Wohlbefinden einiger oder gar aller Beckeninsassen wird beeinträchtigt. Wesentliche Lebensfunktionen können schon durch die bloße Anwesenheit ungeeigneter Mitbewohner beträchtlich gestört werden. Streß, Angst und Schmerz kennt man auch von Fischen. Zwingt man ihnen gar völlig unnatürliche Haltungsbedingungen auf, wird das Gesellschaftsbecken leicht zu einem Ort für vorprogrammierte Tierquälerei.

„Schlechte Gesellschaft": Auch bei Fischen kann es Streit geben.

Unsere zuvor genannte Grundregel der gegenseitigen Verträglichkeit unter gleichzeitiger Achtung gleicher Umweltansprüche hilft dies zu vermeiden. Kritikern der Aquaristik wird so das Wasser abgegraben, und man wird langfristig Freude auch an diesem Aquarientyp haben.

Was versteht man nun bei Fischen unter dem Grundsatz des „Sich-miteinander-Vertragens"? Vorab heißt dies, daß Räuber und ihre Beutefische nicht dauerhaft zu vergesellschaften sind. Raubfische, denen ständig maulgerechte Fischchen begegnen, werden diese auch zu schnappen versuchen (und bei häufigem Erfolg vielleicht rasch überernährt), und umgekehrt stehen kleine Beutefischchen selbst bei besten Versteckmöglichkeiten permanent unter Streß, wenn ein Jäger sie stets verfolgt oder belauert.

Verträglichkeit bedeutet auch einmal Verzicht: Langflossige Zuchtformen, die es ja von vielen Fischarten gibt, werden selbst von manchen Friedfischen nur allzugern an den „Schleiern" oder sonstigen Flossenfortsätzen gezupft. Daher gehören derartige Fisch-Spielarten nicht in ein Gesellschaftsbecken.

Die allseitige Zuträglichkeit der Fütterungsmethode und der verabreichten Kost empfiehlt eigentlich die ausschließliche Mischung von Allesfressern oder Gemischtköstlern unter den Fischen. Ansonsten wird ein Gesellschaftsbecken hinsichtlich der Fütterung sehr aufwendig.

Dieser Aspekt leitet zu den Ansprüchen an die Umwelt über, die ja für alle Bewohner dieses Beckentyps unbedingt identisch sein müssen: Setzt man Umwelt zunächst mit Lebens- oder bevorzugtem Aufenthaltsraum einer Fischart gleich, so ist es sinnvoll, wenn man Arten der verschiedenen Schwimmzonen (Wasseroberfläche, freier Schwimmraum und Boden) im Gesellschaftsbecken zusammenbringt. Der vorhandene Raum wird so ideal ausgenutzt. Auch dabei achte man auf Ausgewogenheit: Sowohl innerhalb der Bereiche als auch auf das gesamte Aquarium bezogen, muß die Besatzdichte stimmen! Der Anfänger wird sich mit ein bis zwei Arten pro Beckenzone begnügen müssen.

Die wesentlichen Wasserparameter müssen für alle „Gesellschafter" passen. Glücklicherweise sind bei vielen Fisch- und Pflanzenarten hinsichtlich Temperatur, pH- Wert und Wasserhärte gewisse Bereiche artgerecht und bekömmlich. Innerhalb dieser Grenzen sollte man aber bleiben, und zwar bei allen dreien der genannten Faktoren! Nur wo Sie hierzu anhand des Fisch-Kapitels oder anderer Fachliteratur wirkliche Übereinstimmung feststellen, haben Sie es mit echten Partnern für die Vergesellschaftung zu tun und verhalten sich wie ein wahrer Tierfreund.

Soll man nun bei der Zusammenstellung eines Gesellschaftsbeckens auch noch auf die geographische Herkunft der erwählten Bewohner achten? Oder darf man völlig unabhängig von Erdteil- oder Länderherkunft mischen? Nun, das ist reine Ansichtssache, und die Übergänge zu den nachfolgend behandelten Beckentypen sind fließend. Beim Thema Gesellschaftsbecken scheiden sich nun einmal die Geister und das sollen sie ruhig auch ganz nach Belieben. Wir meinen, erlaubt ist, was gefällt und was hinsichtlich der Ansprüche zusammenpaßt.

Weniger ist (oft) mehr: Aquarien mit Motto

Strenggenommen sind die Aquarien, auf die wir in diesem Abschnitt etwas näher eingehen wollen, auch nichts anderes als Gesellschaftsbekken. Nur, daß eben die Fischgesellschaft in diesen Becken unter einem bestimmten Motto ausgesucht wurde, und auch die Einrichtung der Aquarien entsprechend gestaltet wurde.

War beim „normalen Gesellschaftsbecken" lediglich das Zusammenpassen der Fische, egal woher sie stammten, maßgebend, so beschränkt man sich nun auf eine bestimmte Gruppe oder gar Art, um deren Lebensbedingungen optimal gestalten zu können. In diesem Zusammenhang spricht man von sogenannten Arten-, Biotop- oder Landschaftsaquarien. Als Sonderfall wären dann noch die sogenannten holländischen Aquarien zu nennen.

Mit Aquarien wohnen

Um Aquarien in Wohnräume zu integrieren, gibt es unzählige bauliche und architektonische Möglichkeiten. Ganze Generationen von Raumausstattern und Aquarienmöbelherstellern haben Unmengen von Varianten, Tips und Tricks erdacht, um die Pflege von Fischen und das Wohnen auf praktische und schöne Weise zu kombinieren.

Die Bandbreite reicht von einem unauffälligen, ja fast schon versteckten Unterbringen der Becken bis hin zu ihrer Gestaltung als Blickfang, dekorativer Mittelpunkt des Raumes oder gar Kunstobjekt.

Funktionalität ist das Wichtigste

Ob Fertigprodukte der in dieser Hinsicht sehr phantasievollen Industrie oder Verlaß auf das eigene handwerkliche Geschick – keinesfalls dürfen Optik und angestrebte Wirkung die einwandfreie Funktion beeinträchtigen. Auch „Wohn-Aquarien“ sollen bedienbar sein und bleiben: Zuallererst müssen die aquaristischen Erfordernisse hinsichtlich der Standortwahl, der Technik und der Pflege berücksichtigt werden.

Aquarium als Raumteiler.

Gerade der letzte wichtige Punkt wird leider immer wieder außer acht gelassen: Häufig sind der Filter oder Bereiche der Scheiben so schwer zugänglich, daß selbst für einfache Kontroll- und Pflegearbeiten große Anstrengungen und akrobatische Verrenkungen nötig sind. Doch solcher Leibesübungen wird man rasch überdrüssig und das Aquarium wird dann womöglich vernachlässigt.

Antik oder modern?

Was wird nun für das „Schöner Wohnen mit Aquarium“ angeboten? Die einfachste und naheliegendste Möglichkeit ist, neben „nackten“ Becken, die bewährten Aquarien mit Unterschränken zu versehen, die es in verschiedenen Ausführungen gibt – passend zu jedem Wohnstil oder auch als deutlicher Kontrast. In diesen Schränken können Filter, CO_2-Anlage und weiteres Zubehör griffbereit untergebracht werden.

Becken mit Durchblick

Parallel zur Vervollkommnung dieser Möbelstücke entwickelte sich eine andere, ganz besondere Form des Wohnens mit Aquarium: Das Becken als Raumteiler – wiederum in Stil und Form der sonstigen Einrichtung angepaßt oder im bewußten Kontrast dazu stehend.

Während ein an der Wand stehendes Aquarium von ein bis höchstens drei Seiten einsehbar ist und die Dekoration vor der Rückwand angeordnet wird, besitzt ein Raumteiler-Aquarium praktisch zwei Frontseiten. Dadurch verlagert sich der Raum für „dekoratives Gestalten“ auf einen eng begrenzten Bereich um die Mittelachse des Aquariums. Als Raumteiler sollten deshalb besonders tiefe Aquarien bevorzugt werden.

Das Raumteiler-Aquarium bietet viel freien Schwimmraum für Schwarmfische der oberen und mittleren Wasserzonen. Fischarten, die viele Verstecke und Rückzugs-

Eigenwillige Konstruktion eines freitragenden Aquariums.

möglichkeiten benötigen, werden sich daher in einem Raumteiler-Aquarium weniger wohlfühlen.

Wer unter den vielen angebotenen Beckengrößen und -formen und Aquarienmöbeln nicht das passende findet, kann sich ein Aquarium ganz nach seinen Wünschen selbst bauen oder anfertigen lassen. Übrigens können die meisten Zoofachgeschäfte aus Platzgründen nicht alles ausstellen, was es so gibt. Lassen Sie sich beraten und Prospekte mit weiteren Modellen zeigen!

Thema mit Variationen

Teiche gibt es nicht nur im Garten – auch die Wohnung läßt sich damit verschönern. Hier bietet sich die Möglichkeit, Fische einmal nicht von der Seite, sondern von oben zu betrachten und die Pflanzen aus dem Becken herauswachsen und ihre Blüten treiben zu lassen.

Freistehendes Sechseckaquarium.

Sehr reizvoll können auch „Beckenlandschaften" sein, die Aquarien mit Pflanzbehältern (für Erde, Sumpf oder Hydrokultur) oder Terrarien kombinieren.

Der Weißpunktbrabantbuntbarsch (Tropheus duboisi, *im Bild ein erwachsenes Tier) fühlt sich in einem mit Steinen eingerichteten Artenbecken wohl.*

Artenaquarium

Wohl die meisten Aquarianerneulinge werden mit einem Gesellschaftsbecken beginnen. Früher oder später stellt sich dann (so auch bei den Autoren) die Vorliebe für eine bestimmte Art oder Gattung heraus, über deren Lebensgewohnheiten und Verhalten man etwas mehr wissen oder besser gesagt erleben möchte. Dies ist der Schritt zum Artenbecken, das dann, entsprechend den besonderen Lebensbedingungen dieser Art oder Gattung, hergerichtet wird.

Es gibt jedoch auch Arten und Gattungen, die sich aufgrund ihrer besonderen Anpassungen an bestimmte Lebensräume oder aufgrund bestimmter Verhaltensweisen von vorneherein nur in einem eigens für sie hergerichteten Aquarium pflegen lassen. Zuchterfolge sind dann letztendlich die Bestätigung für die artgerechte Gestaltung des Lebensraumes der betreffenden Fische.

Eine Gruppe von Fischen erfreut sich wie keine andere größter Beliebtheit: die Cichliden oder Buntbarsche. Es gibt ungefähr genauso viele Cichlidenliebhaber wie Liebhaber aller anderen Fischarten zusammen. Cichliden bieten eine ganze Reihe von Besonderheiten, die sie für ein Artenbecken geradezu prädestinieren: Anpassungen an bestimmte Lebensräume, wie z.B. den Malawi- oder Tanganjikasee, ein besonders stark ausgeprägtes Brutpflegeverhalten, das vom Offenbrüten bis hin zur hochspezialisierten Maulbrutpflege reicht, mit mehr oder weniger starker Paarbindung, Vater-Mutter-Familie und vieles mehr. Solche besonderen Verhaltensweisen erfordern natürlich ein entsprechend gestaltetes Aquarium speziell für diese Arten.

Das richtige Aquarium zum richtigen Fisch.

Aber gerade bei Cichliden darf der Begriff des Artaquariums auch nicht zu eng gesehen werden. Viele Cichliden benötigen, um ihr Brutpflegeverhalten voll entfalten zu können, artfremde Beifische, da der angeborene Revierverteidigungstrieb sonst den eigenen Partner treffen kann. So gesehen ist ein solches Aquarium dann auch wieder ein Gesellschaftsbecken. An dieser Stelle noch näher auf die Pflege von Cichliden einzugehen, hieße Eulen nach Athen zu tragen. Der interessierte Leser sei auf die umfangreiche Spezialliteratur hingewiesen.

Biotop- oder Landschaftsaquarien

Im Zuge der immer preiswerteren Fernreisen in tropische Länder haben immer mehr Aquarianer die Gelegenheit, die Lebensräume ihrer Pfleglinge vor Ort genau zu studieren. Was liegt näher, als sich ein solches Biotop in seinen elementaren Teilen zu Hause im Aquarium nachzubilden und die dazugehörigen Fische darin zu pflegen? Schon ist das Biotopaquarium geboren.

Bei der Einrichtung des Biotopaquariums kommt es nicht darauf an, das betreffende Biotop originalgetreu mit Originalmaterialien nachzubilden. In den meisten Fällen sähe ein solches Aquarium wenig einladend aus. Vielmehr müssen die Gestaltungselemente die Funktion erfüllen, an die sich die Fische in ihrem Lebensraum angepaßt haben. So wird zum Beispiel eine Keilfleckbarbe unter dem Blatt einer Amazonasschwertpflanze genauso ablaichen wie unter dem Blatt einer

Cryptocoryne. Wichtig ist lediglich, daß eine Pflanze mit entsprechend breiten Blättern vorhanden ist, die den Ablaichvorgang ermöglicht. Wie die Pflanze heißt und woher sie kommt, ist in diesem Fall gleichgültig.

Auch beim Fischbesatz darf die Biotoptreue nicht übertrieben werden. In einem natürlichen Biotop leben immer verschiedene Vertreter der Nahrungskette zusammen, was dort natürlich seinen Sinn hat. Nun wird keiner auf den Gedanken kommen, Raubfische und deren Beute in ein und demselben Aquarium zu halten, nur weil sie gemeinsam im gleichen Biotop vorkommen.

Wie nun die Gestaltung eines Biotopaquariums konkret aussehen kann, wollen wir an einem Beispiel durchspielen. Weil es die Heimat einer besonders interessanten Fischgruppe, nämlich der Labyrinth- oder Kletterfische ist, haben wir das Biotop „asiatisches Reisfeld mit angrenzenden stehenden oder langsam fließenden Bewässerungsgräben“ ausgesucht. Vielleicht haben auch Sie einmal die Gelegenheit, ein geflutetes Reisfeld und daran angrenzende Bewässerungsgräben mit ihren typischen Bewohnern in Natur zu beobachten.

Der amphibisch wachsende Wasserspinat *(Ipomea sp.)* und zahlreiche Seerosen *(Nymphaea sp.)* bilden ein dichtes Gewirr von Stengeln und Wurzeln unter Wasser. Die großen Schwimmblätter der Seerosen schirmen einen Großteil des einfallenden Lichtes ab. Am Ufer wachsen

Wohnzimmerteiche, Paludarien, Aquaterrarien

In diesem vorbildlich gestalteten Paludarium grünt es über und unter Wasser.

Das an sich schon recht große und vielfältige Gebiet der Süßwasser-Aquaristik läßt sich durch Hinzunahme bestimmter Beckentypen und -ausstattungen noch erheblich variieren. Auch die Wahl der Bewohner spielt dabei eine Rolle.

Wohnzimmerteiche sind eine durchaus ansehnliche „Zwischenlösung“ meist für Kaltwasserfische. Während die klassische Kaltwasseraquaristik (abgesehen vielleicht von der Goldfischhaltung) als fast ausgestorbener Zweig gilt und andererseits die Freilandteiche im Garten „boomen“, entdecken immer mehr Besitzer größerer Wohnzimmer oder Wintergärten die Vorteile der Fischpflege in ebenerdig aufgesetzten oder im Boden eingelassenen Teichbecken, sogenannten **Wohnzimmerteichen.** Anstelle von Kois und Goldfischen oder Orfen (Kaltwasser) könnten darin auch tropische Aquarienfische im Warmwasser leben. Dabei ist die richtige Dimensionierung der technischen Ausstattung wichtig. So eröffnen sich für den Betrachter ganz neue Perspektiven.

Paludarien (Sumpfbehälter) sind etwas für Freunde tropischer Pflanzen, Terrarientiere und Fische. Ein Wasserbereich wird von einem Landteil mit Uferregion überragt oder umgeben, in beiden Bereichen können jeweils typische Bewohner gepflegt werden. Man könnte Paludarien auch als Terrarien mit besonders großem und durch Glas einsehbar gemachtem Wasserbecken bezeichnen, nur daß letzteres von Technik und Pflege her eben wie ein Aquarium betrieben wird.

Aquaterrarien sind dagegen das andere Extrem: Der Landteil ist minimal, meist am Rand angehängt oder als Schwimm-Insel gestaltet. Bei Zwerg-Krallenfröschen und beim Axolotl (einem ständig aquatisch lebenden Molch) z.B. kann auch völlig auf eine trockene Region verzichtet werden. Wasserschildkröten dagegen brauchen einen durch Strahler „besonnten“ Landteil und viel Wasser darum oder darunter zum Schwimmen und Tauchen. Ursprünglich waren Fische hier nur Lebendfutter, Aquaterrarienfans haben aber die Möglichkeiten der Vergesellschaftung von Terrarienbewohnern mit Fischen erkannt und genutzt.

Auch Zimmerspringbrunnen werden ab und zu als Aufenthaltsort für Fische „mißbraucht“. Aufgrund der technischen Ausstattung dürfte das aber nur in den seltensten Fällen sinnvoll und artgemäß sein!

Überschwemmtes Reisfeld in Zentralthailand mit Bewässerungskanal im Vordergrund – ein typischer Lebensraum für viele Labyrinthfische, wie er in diesem Kapitel beschrieben wird.

Schilf und andere Sumpfpflanzen. Etwas weiter treiben die meterlangen schmalen Blätter der Hakenlilie *(Crinum thaianum)* an der Wasseroberfläche. Wurzeln von am Ufer wachsenden Bäumen ragen ins Wasser. Der Boden ist mit einer Schicht abgestorbener Pflanzenteile und in das Wasser gefallener Blätter bedeckt.

An manchen Stellen bilden Schwimmpflanzen wie Muschelblumen *(Pistia sp.)*, Wasserhyazinthen *(Eichhornia sp.)* oder Wasserfarn *(Salvinia sp.)* fast undurchdringliche Polster. Auch zwischen den Reispflanzen finden sich immer wieder Stellen mit Seerosen, Wasserspinat und Schwimmpflanzen. Das meist sehr flache Wasser wird von der tropischen Sonne auf Temperaturen zwischen 28 und 33 °C aufgeheizt.

In diesem Biotop leben, wie bereits erwähnt, verschiedene Arten von Labyrinthfischen, die aufgrund ihrer besonderen Atmungsweise – sie atmen athmosphärische Luft – an das oft relativ sauerstoffarme Wasser gut angepaßt sind. Im gleichen Biotop findet man an weniger dicht bewachsenen Stellen mit leichter Wasserbewegung aber auch verschiedene kleinere Bärblinge wie zum Beispiel den Rotschwanzbärbling *(Rasbora borapetensis)*. An der Wasseroberfläche stehen Trupps von Halbschnabelhechten *(Dermogenys sp.)* und Hechtlingen *(Aplocheilus sp.)*. Die Bodenregion wird von verschiedenen Schmerlen *(Botia sp.)*, kleinen Stachelaalen und unzähligen kleinen glasartigen Garnelen nach Nahrung durchsucht.

Dazwischen lauern aber auch Räuber: An der Wasseroberfläche findet man kleinere Trupps des Nadelhechtes *(Xenentodon sp.)* mit ihren nadelspitzen Zähnen, und am Boden im Pflanzendickicht warten Schlangenkopffische *(Channa sp.)* auf ahnungslos vorbeiziehende Beute.

Ein Aquarium, das diesem Biotop entspricht, könnte folgendermaßen aussehen: Im Hintergrund und an den Seiten repräsentieren hochwachsende Pflanzen wie zum Beispiel Vallisnerien und verschiedene Stengelpflanzen *(Hygrophila, Heteranthera)* den Rand des Reisfeldes mit seinen hoch aufstrebenden Reispflanzen. Dieser Eindruck kann noch durch die Anlage einer Terrasse im Hintergrund betont werden. Einige zurechtgesägte Bambusstäbe stellen Schilf oder andere Sumpfgräser dar, die aus dem Wasser wachsen.

Eine bizarre Moorkienwurzel ersetzt die ins Wasser ragenden Wurzeln der Bäume. Ein oder zwei Tigerlotus (je nach Größe des Aquariums) sorgen mit ihren Schwimmblättern für diffuses Licht. Darüber hinaus können noch einige Schwimmpflanzen wie zum Beispiel der Wasserhornfarn *(Ceratopteris sp.)* eingesetzt werden, zwischen denen die Labyrinthfische dann ihr typisches Schaumnest anlegen werden.

Als niedriger bleibende Bepflanzung im mittleren und vorderen Bereich des Aquariums eignen sich anspruchslose Cryptocorynen wie zum Beispiel *Cryptocoryne wendtii*. Ansammlungen von abgestorbenen Blättern und anderen Pflanzenteilen lassen sich durch getrocknetes Herbstlaub von Buche, Eiche oder Erle sehr gut imitieren. Damit das Laub nicht im Wasser schwimmt,

muß es vorher kurz überbrüht werden.

Ein solches Biotopaquarium kann bereits in kleinen Becken von 60 cm Kantenlänge mit entsprechend klein bleibenden Fischen verwirklicht werden. Als Hauptakteure kämen zum Beispiel ein Pärchen oder besser ein Männchen und zwei Weibchen des Zwergfadenfisches *(Colisa lalia),* des knurrenden Guramis *(Trichopsis vittatus)* oder des Honigguramis *(Colisa chuna)* in Frage. Da die balzenden Männchen bald das ganze Aquarium als ihr Revier betrachten, sollte nur eine Labyrinthfischart gepflegt werden.

Als Beifische eignen sich kleine Barben oder Bärblinge, wie zum Beispiel der Zwergbärbling *(Rasbora maculata)* oder der Rotschwanzbärbling *(Rasbora borapetensis),* von denen man einen Schwarm von 10 bis 15 Stück einsetzt. Die „untere Etage" des Aquariums kann ein Trupp von 5 bis 8 Schachbrettschmerlen *(Botia sidthimunki)* bewohnen. Diese Art war lange Zeit nicht mehr erhältlich und ist in ihrer Heimat vermutlich ausgestorben. Neuerdings wird sie in Thailand nachgezüchtet und kommt dadurch wieder in den Handel.

Die größeren Arten, wie zum Beispiel Mosaikfadenfische *(Trichogaster leeri)* und viele andere erfordern natürlich entsprechend größere Behälter.

Nicht vergessen werden soll natürlich auch der bekannte siamesische Kampffisch. Daß von Kampffischen, aufgrund ihrer Kampfeslust, immer nur ein Männchen mit mehreren Weibchen in einem Aquarium gepflegt werden kann, stimmt nicht ganz. Einander fremde Männchen werden sich natürlich immer erbittert bekämpfen, wenn sie sich begegnen.

Anders jedoch Tiere, die miteinander aufgewachsen sind. Es ist durchaus möglich, mehrere Kampffischmännchen, die sich sozusagen kennen, mit mehreren Weibchen in einem Aquarium, wie es hier vorgestellt wurde, zusammen zu halten und auch zu züchten. Dies trifft für die kurzflossige Wildform noch eher

Fischfang in Nordthailand; viele Aquarienfische sind in ihrer Heimat auch beliebte Speisefische.

zu als für die schleierflossige Form, die leider nur noch ausschließlich im Handel angeboten wird. Da Kampffische den gesamten Wasserraum von der Wasseroberfläche bis fast zum Boden beanspruchen, wird man ihnen, außer ein paar Bodenfischen, keine weiteren Beifische zugesellen.

Es gibt unzählige weitere Möglichkeiten zur Gestaltung von Biotopaquarien, deren Aufzählung den Rahmen dieses Buches überschreiten würde. Der interessierte Leser sei auf das Literaturverzeichnis am Ende dieses Buches verwiesen. Übrigens bieten Aquarienausstellungen hervorragende Gelegenheiten, sich inspirieren zu lassen.

Holländisches Pflanzenaquarium

Hier handelt es sich um Aquarien, bei denen die Pflege von Wasserpflanzen im Vordergrund steht. Diese werden ausschließlich nach besonderen ästhetischen Gesichtspunkten so angeordnet, daß ein harmonisches Gesamtbild entsteht. Da dabei oftmals Pflanzen verschiedenster Pflegeansprüche vergesellschaftet werden, erfordert ein solches Aquarium ein ganz besonderes Fingerspitzengefühl und ein Höchstmaß an pflegerischem Aufwand. Wie bereits der Name besagt, sind solche Aquarien besonders bei unseren holländischen Nachbarn verbreitet.

Holländisches (Pflanzen-)Aquarium.

Ein trockenes Thema: Wasser

Wasser ist *das* Lebenselement unserer Pfleglinge. Durch den innigen Kontakt mit diesem Lebenselement bestehen vielerlei Wechselbeziehungen zwischen dem Wasser und seinen Bewohnern. Die Zusammensetzung des Wassers beeinflußt die Lebensvorgänge von Tieren und Pflanzen einerseits, andererseits werden durch eben diese Lebensvorgänge Stoffe an das Wasser abgegeben, die es verändern. Deshalb sind Wasser und Wasserqualität ein zentrales Thema in der Aquaristik.

Wasser ist nicht gleich Wasser: Nicht immer sieht man so deutliche Unterschiede wie am Zusammenfluß dieser Bäche in Costa Rica.

Wasser ist nicht gleich Wasser

Wasser ist ein ideales Lösungsmittel. Es kann die verschiedensten Stoffe gelöst enthalten, ohne daß man dies äußerlich wahrnehmen könnte. So sieht zum Beispiel ein Liter destilliertes Wasser genauso aus wie ein Liter Meerwasser. Lediglich die Geschmacksprobe (oder eine Messung) verrät den Unterschied. Bereits das Leitungswasser kann aufgrund seiner Herkunft gelöste Stoffe verschiedener Art enthalten.

Darüber hinaus nehmen im Kleinbiotop Aquarium die darin gepflegten Lebewesen auf mannigfache Weise Einfluß auf die Zusammensetzung des Wassers. Verschiedene Stoffe können im Wasser miteinander reagieren oder werden umgebaut. Solche Veränderungen im Wasserchemismus finden leider allzu oft nicht zur positiven Seite hin statt, mit entsprechenden Folgen für die Lebewesen.

Um hier im Bedarfsfall regelnd eingreifen zu können, wollen wir Sie in diesem Kapitel mit einigen wesentlichen Faktoren bekannt machen, die im Wasser ihr „unsichtbares Wesen" treiben. Wir wollen dabei komplizierte chemische Zusammenhänge außer acht lassen und uns – soweit möglich – auf das für die Praxis Wesentliche beschränken. Wer es noch genauer wissen möchte, sei auf das Literaturverzeichnis verwiesen.

Wasserhärte

Sicher haben Sie schon bemerkt, daß man beim Händewaschen in manchen Gebieten viel Seife braucht, um Schaum zu bekommen, während woanders ein bißchen bereits ausreicht. Wo man viel Seife braucht, ist das Wasser hart, wo man wenig braucht, ist es weich.

Verantwortlich für die Härte des Wassers sind bestimmte Mineralsalze, die sogenannten Härtebildner, landläufig auch als Kalk bezeichnet. Wie kommen die nun in das Wasser? Dafür ist es wichtig zu wissen, daß Leitungswasser (in der Regel aus Grundwasser) und das

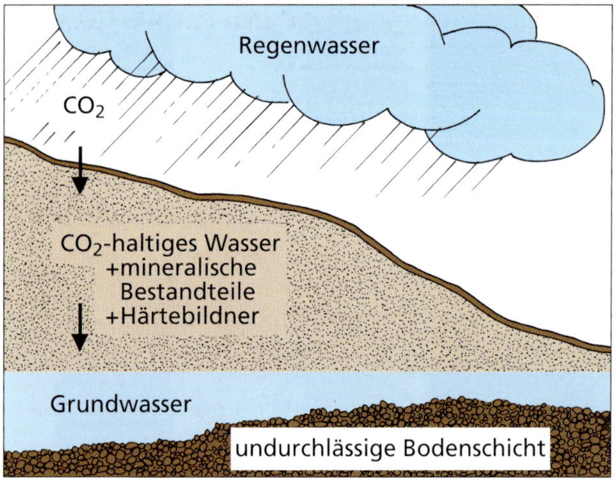

Das kohlendioxidhaltige Regenwasser nimmt auf seinem Weg durch die Humus- und Gesteinsschicht weiteres CO_2 und viele Mineralien auf.

Wasser aus Quellen und Flüssen letztendlich irgendwann einmal Regenwasser war, das durch viele Erdschichten gesickert ist. Über undurchlässigen Bodenschichten sammelt es sich als Grundwasser oder tritt irgendwo als Quelle zutage.

Auf seinem Weg durch die Luft und durch die oberen Humusschichten der Erde nimmt das Wasser CO_2 auf, aus dem im Wasser zum Teil Kohlensäure entsteht. Wenn nun dieses kohlensaure Wasser durch kalkhaltige Schichten sickert, werden durch die Wirkung der Kohlensäure Mineralsalze im Wasser gelöst, es wird hart. Sickert das Regenwasser hingegen durch kalkfreie Schichten aus Urgestein, so wird nichts gelöst und es bleibt weich.

Den Hauptanteil der Wasserinhaltsstoffe bilden Salze der Härtebildner Kalzium und Magnesium.

Man unterscheidet die Begriffe Gesamthärte, Karbonathärte und Nicht-Karbonathärte, die oft aufgrund ihres Hauptbestandteils auch als Sulfathärte bezeichnet wird. Unter Gesamthärte versteht man per Definition den Gehalt eines Wassers an Erdalkali-Ionen, also Kalzium und Magnesium. Seltener vorkommende Ionen, wie zum Beispiel Kalium, Natrium und andere werden dabei außer acht gelassen.

Nun können Ionen nie für sich allein im Wasser vorliegen, da sie nur durch Lösungsvorgänge von Salzen entstehen können. Dabei geht gleichzeitig ein Partner mit in Lösung, mit dem sie sozusagen „verheiratet" sind. Die am häufigsten vorkommenden Partner sind Karbonat- und Hydrogenkarbonationen, die als Bildner der Karbonathärte gelten.

In den meisten Wässern sind etwa 80% der Kalzium- und Magnesiumionen mit Karbonat- und Hydrogenkarbonationen gekoppelt, wodurch man einen Karbonathärteanteil von etwa 80% der Gesamthärte findet. Die restlichen 20% der Kalzium- und Magnesiumionen haben Sulfat-, Chlorid- oder Nitrationen als Partner und repräsentieren die sogenannte Nichtkarbonathärte.

In manchen Gewässern (zum Beispiel in den Tropen) kann es vorkommen, daß außer den Kalzium- und Magnesiumionen auch noch erhebliche Mengen der als Gesamthärte nicht meßbaren Ionen Kalium und Natrium vorhanden sind, die auch noch mit Karbonat- und Hydrogenkarbonationen gekoppelt sind. In diesem Fall ist die Karbonathärte größer als die Gesamthärte. Die in Deutschland übliche Maßeinheit ist Grad deutsche Härte (°d).

Für die Haltung der meisten Aquarienfische und Pflanzen spielt die Härte des Wassers eine untergeordnete Rolle. Es hat sich gezeigt, daß die meisten Weichwasserfische und Pflanzen, die seit Generationen gezüchtet werden, auch in mittelhartem bis hartem Wasser gut zu halten sind. Wesentlich für eine gesunde Haltung von Fischen und Pflanzen ist nicht die ständige Wasserpanscherei, um unerwünscht hohe Härtewerte zu senken (was man dann irgendwann vielleicht aus Bequemlichkeit vergißt), sondern die *Kontinuität* der Bedingungen.

Die Erfahrung hat gelehrt, daß mittelhartes Wasser zwischen 8 und 20 °d Gesamthärte (entsprechend 5–16 °d Karbonathärte) wesentlich „stabiler" (das heißt weniger anfällig gegen Schwankungen der Wasserwerte, vor allem des pH-Werts) ist. Verantwortlich dafür ist die Fähigkeit der Karbonathärte, Säuren zu „puffern". Gibt man zum Beispiel in ein Wasser mit hoher Karbonathärte etwas Salzsäure, so geschieht auf den ersten Blick überhaupt nichts. Die Karbonate haben die Säure gebunden, quasi unschädlich gemacht. Auch der pH-Wert ändert sich nicht. Lediglich die Menge der Karbonate wurde durch die Säure etwas verringert. Die gleiche Menge Säure in karbonatfreies Wasser gegeben, führt sofort zu einem katastrophalen Absinken des pH-Wertes, dem sogenannten Säuresturz, und die Fische sterben. Aus diesem Grund bezeichnet man die Karbonathärte neuerdings als Säurebindungskapazität.

Lediglich zur Zucht sollten annähernd die natürlichen Wasserwerte geboten werden, da die Eier wenig anpassungsfähig sind.

pH-Wert oder Säuregrad

Der pH-Wert ist ein Maß dafür, wie sauer oder alkalisch (basisch, laugig) eine Flüssigkeit ist. Die Werteskala reicht von 0 bis 14. Der Wert 0 entspricht extremer Säure (zum Beispiel Salzsäure) und der Wert 14 extremer Lauge (zum Beispiel Natronlauge). Genau in der Mitte bei 7 liegt der Neutralpunkt, also weder sauer noch alkalisch. Der Säuregrad steigt also, je weiter der Wert *unter* 7 liegt und die Alkalität (Laugigkeit) steigt, je weiter der Wert *über* 7 liegt.

Im alltäglichen Leben werden wir, oft unbewußt, mit dem Phänomen des pH-Wertes konfrontiert.

Huminsäuren färben das Wasser dieses Baches in Zentralborneo braun wie Tee. Hier leben verschiedene Barben und Bärblinge, Schokoladenguramis, Nanderbarsche und Halbschnabelhechte.

↑	0	
	2	
	3	tödlich für alle Fische
zunehmend sauer	4	zunehmend lebensfeindlich für viele Fische
↑	5	
	6	
neutral	7	optimaler Bereich
↓	8	optimal für einige Fische, z. B. aus afrikanischen Seen, optimal für Seewasserfische
zunehmend alkalisch (basisch)	9	
	10	zunehmend lebensfeindlich für viele Fische
	11	tödlich für alle Fische
	12	
	13	
↓	14	

Der ph-Wert des Wassers ist für die Fische von entscheidender Bedeutung.

Extrem sauer geht es zum Beispiel bei der Verdauung in unserem Magen zu. Magensäure hat einen pH-Wert von 1 bis knapp 2. Speisen und Getränke werden von uns als wohlschmeckend empfunden, wenn sie mehr oder weniger sauer sind. Eine Lösung von Natron in Leitungswasser, altbewährtes Mittel gegen Sodbrennen, das durch Magensäure verursacht wird, ist alkalisch und wird als wenig wohlschmeckend empfunden. Leitungswasser liegt in der Regel im neutralen Bereich um 7.

Fische können in einem pH-Bereich zwischen 4,5 und 9 vorkommen. Dabei werden die Extrembereiche (zum Beispiel sehr saure Schwarzwässer des Rio Negro oder alkalische Sodawässer der afrikanischen Seen) jedoch nur von wenigen Spezialisten bevorzugt. Die weitaus meisten Fische, die auch in Aquarien gepflegt werden, leben in pH-Bereichen zwischen 5,5 und 7,5.

In der aquaristischen Praxis hat es sich gezeigt, daß sowohl Arten aus leicht sauren Gewässern mit pH-Werten um 6, als auch Arten aus

neutralen bis leicht alkalischen Gewässern mit einem pH-Wert um 7,5 im neutralen Bereich um pH 7 gut zu pflegen sind. Lediglich zur Zucht sollten die entsprechend bevorzugten pH-Werte eingehalten werden.

Der Grundsatz, möglichst konstante Bedingungen im Aquarium einzuhalten, gilt auch für den pH-Wert. Dies ist einleuchtend, wenn man sich vor Augen hält, daß bei einer Veränderung des pH-Wertes um nur eine Stufe die Säurekonzentration sich nicht etwa um das Doppelte, sondern um das *Zehnfache* ändert. Das heißt, pH 5 ist zehnmal saurer als pH 6 und hundertmal saurer als pH 7. Umgekehrt ist pH 9 zehnmal alkalischer als pH 8 und hundertmal alkalischer als pH 7.

In natürlichen Gewässern wird der pH-Wert hauptsächlich durch das Zusammenspiel zweier Komponenten bestimmt, nämlich Karbonathärte und CO_2, beziehungsweise die daraus entstehende Kohlensäure. Das Mengenverhältnis von Karbonathärte (als alkalischer Komponente) zu Kohlensäure (als saurem Gegenspieler) entscheidet über die Höhe des pH-Wertes. Ist das Mengenverhältnis ausgeglichen, so liegt der pH-Wert bei 7, dem für die Pflege von Fischen und Pflanzen zu bevorzugenden Wert. Als weitere natürliche pH-beeinflussende Substanzen sind noch die in Moor- und Schwarzwässern vorkommenden Humin- oder Fulvosäuren zu nennen.

Im Abschnitt über die Karbonathärte haben Sie bereits erfahren, daß Wässer mit höherer Karbonathärte gegen Säure besser gepuffert sind als weiche. Das gleiche gilt auch für die andere Richtung, nämlich plötzliche pH-Anstiege, die ebenso gefährlich sind: Um den Kalk als Hydrogenkarbonat (doppelt kohlensaurer Kalk) in Lösung und den pH-Wert bei 7 zu halten, ist eine bestimmte Menge gelöstes CO_2 im Wasser erforderlich. Je mehr Kalk im Wasser vorhanden ist, um so mehr CO_2 ist dafür natürlich auch notwendig.

Durch die Assimilation entziehen die Wasserpflanzen am Tage dem Wasser CO_2. Dadurch wird die CO_2-Konzentration unterschritten, die erforderlich ist, um den vorhandenen Kalk in Lösung zu halten. Folge davon: Ein Teil des Hydrogenkarbonats zerfällt in unlösliches Karbonat (einfach kohlensaurer Kalk, der sich als weißlicher Belag auf Pflanzenblättern niederschlägt) und CO_2, wodurch sich ein neues Gleichgewicht einstellt, das den verbliebenen Kalk in Lösung hält.

Wird nicht genügend CO_2 von außen zugeführt, zum Beispiel durch eine CO_2-Düngeanlage, so setzt sich dieser Prozeß fort, bis alles Hydrogenkarbonat aufgebraucht und als unlösliches Karbonat auf den Pflanzenblättern zu finden ist.

Solange noch Hydrogenkarbonat im Wasser vorhanden ist, durch dessen Spaltung sich ein neues Gleichgewicht einstellen kann, wird sich der pH-Wert nur unwesentlich in Richtung 8 verändern. Es gibt jedoch Pflanzen, die nicht aufhören CO_2 aufzunehmen, auch wenn bereits alles Hydrogenkarbonat verbraucht ist. Sie entziehen dann auch noch dem Karbonatniederschlag das darin gebundene CO_2, wodurch der pH-Wert in kürzester Zeit auf Werte bis 10 steigen kann.

Als Folge treten bei den Fischen Verätzungen der Kiemen und Schleimhäute auf, die zum Tode führen können, wenn keine sofortige Abhilfe erfolgt. In weichem Wasser mit wenig Kalk tritt dieses Phänomen natürlich wesentlich leichter und schneller auf als in härterem. Deshalb noch einmal der Hinweis: Härteres Wasser ist pH-stabiler als weiches.

Temperaturabhängigkeit des Sauerstoffgehaltes im Wasser

Temperatur (°C)	Sauerstoffgehalt (mg O_2/l)
10	10,92
11	10,67
12	10,43
13	10,20
14	9,98
15	9,76
16	9,56
17	9,37
18	9,18
19	9,01
20	8,84
21	8,68
22	8,53
23	8,38
24	8,25
25	8,11
26	7,99
27	7,86
28	7,75
29	7,64
30	7,53
31	7,42
32	7,32
33	7,22
34	7,13
35	7,04

Sauerstoff

Sauerstoff ist *das* Lebenselixier für alle tierischen Organismen. Ohne Sauerstoff gäbe es kein tierisches Leben auf der Erde. Sauerstoff ist damit auch für das Aquarium der wichtigste Faktor, von dem das Wohlbefinden unserer Pfleglinge abhängt. Fische benötigen ihn zur Atmung, aber auch Pflanzen benötigen zumindest nachts eine ausreichende Versorgung mit Sauerstoff. Von größter Wichtigkeit ist der Sauerstoff aber für das Millionenheer von Bakterien, die den ganzen anfallenden „Mist" im Aquarium abbauen. Ohne sie wäre eine Aquarienhaltung praktisch undenkbar. Mehr über diese Bakterien und ihre segensreiche Tätigkeit erfahren Sie im nächsten Abschnitt dieses Kapitels.

Gase, so auch der Sauerstoff, haben das Bestreben, zwischen ihren Gehalten (Partialdrücken) in der Luft und einer Flüssigkeit, in unserem Fall Wasser, einen Gleichgewichtszustand herzustellen. Daraus resultiert, je nach Temperatur, ein bestimmter Sauerstoffgehalt im Wasser. Je kälter das Wasser, desto mehr Sauerstoff enthält es im Gleichgewichtszustand. Dies ist auch der maximale Sauerstoffgehalt, der durch Belüftung zu erreichen ist. Bei 25 °C sind es 8,11 mg/l. Die Gehalte für andere Temperaturen zeigt die obenstehende Tabelle.

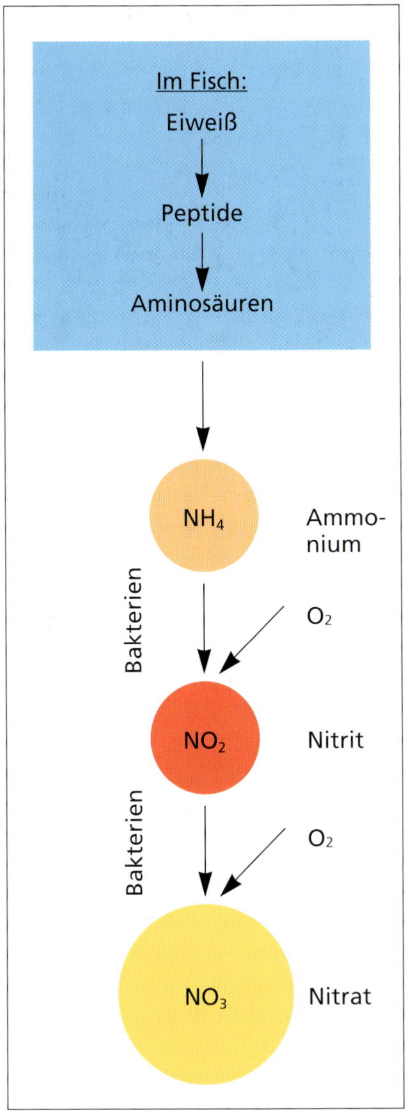

Wenn Sauerstoff vorhanden ist, wird über die Nitrifikation Ammonium zu Nitrat abgebaut.

Im Aquarium sollte man bestrebt sein, den erforderlichen Sauerstoffgehalt auf biologischem Wege, das heißt durch die Assimilationstätigkeit lebender Pflanzen zu erzeugen (Ausnahme: Aquarien mit pflanzenunverträglichen Fischen). Um sich auf der sicheren Seite zu bewegen, ist am Abend (kurz vor Erlöschen der Beleuchtung) ein Sauerstoffgehalt anzustreben, der dem Gleichgewichtszustand bei der gegebenen Temperatur entspricht. Dies ist jedoch nur mit angepaßter Beleuchtungsstärke und optimaler Pflanzenpflege möglich.

Es ist falsch, Sauerstoffwerte der natürlichen Heimat unserer Aquarienfische, die häufig unter Gleichgewichtsniveau liegen, als Vorbild für das Aquarium zu nehmen. Im Gegensatz zum Aquarium sind die Sauerstoffgehalte in der Natur, wenn auch niedrig, so doch von äußerster Gleichmäßigkeit, die durch die Atmung der Tiere nicht beeinflußt wird. Die Tiere haben sich diesem Gehalt angepaßt.

Wollten wir dagegen ein Aquarium mit einem Sauerstoffgehalt von nur 3 oder 4 mg/l „fahren", so würden wir sehr bald ein „blaues Wunder" erleben. Spätestens in der Nacht, wenn Tiere *und* Pflanzen Sauerstoff verbrauchen, wird sich in dem vergleichsweise winzigen Wasservolumen des Aquariums ein katastrophaler Sauerstoffmangel einstellen, mit allen dazugehörigen fatalen Folgen. Von versehentlich zu viel gereichtem Futter oder einem unbemerkt gestorbenen Fisch, die zusätzlich noch Sauerstoff zehren, ganz zu schweigen. Der Lebensraum Aquarium verhält sich anders als ein Naturbiotop und deshalb ist am Abend ein hoher Sauerstoffgehalt in Höhe des Gleichgewichtswertes grundlegende Voraussetzung für das Wohlergehen seiner Insassen!

Auch Fische machen „Mist"

Alle tierischen Organismen benötigen zur Aufrechterhaltung ihrer Lebensvorgänge und zum Wachstum Nahrung, der in einem mehr oder weniger komplizierten Verdauungsvorgang die für den betreffenden Organismus wichtigen Bestandteile entzogen werden. Was nicht gebraucht oder verwertet werden kann, wird ausgeschieden. Die Ausscheidungsprodukte werden über verschiedene Zwischenstufen weiter abgebaut (mineralisiert), von den Pflanzen als Nährstoffe aufgenommen und zum Aufbau von pflanzeneigener Substanz verwendet. Schließlich werden die Pflanzen von Tieren gefressen, und das Ganze beginnt wieder von vorn.

Dieser stark vereinfacht dargestellte Kreislauf spielt sich in einem intakten natürlichen Ökosystem ohne nennenswerte Anhäufung von Zwischenprodukten ab. Das System steht im sogenannten biologischen Gleichgewicht. Im Aquarium besteht eine grundlegend andere Situation. Im Vergleich zu natürlichen Systemen werden hier wesentlich mehr tierische Organismen (Fische) auf engstem Raum mit verhältnismäßig wenigen Pflanzen gehalten.

Die Fische scheiden wesentlich mehr Abfallstoffe aus, als von den Pflanzen im Aquarium verwertet werden können. Es muß im Aquarium also zwangsläufig zu einer Anhäufung von Abfallstoffen aus dem Verdauungsvorgang der Fische kommen. Aus diesem Grund ist es wichtig zu wissen, was mit diesen Stoffwechselprodukten im Aquarium geschieht.

Ammonium, Nitrit, Nitrat

Die größte Bedeutung haben im Aquarium die Stickstoffverbindungen Ammonium, Nitrit und Nitrat, von denen das Nitrit direkt und das Ammonium unter bestimmten Umständen eine Gefahr für die Fische darstellen. Diese Verbindungen entstammen letztendlich der Verdauung von Proteinen (Eiweiß), die im tierischen Organismus bis

zum Ammonium abgebaut werden. Das Ammonium wird als unbrauchbarer Rest ausgeschieden.

Der Abbau der Proteine erfolgt im Prinzip über folgende Stufen: Proteine → Peptide → Aminosäuren → Ammonium → Nitrit → Nitrat. Uns interessieren vor allem die letzten Schritte vom Ammonium bis zum Nitrat, da diese im Aquarienwasser ablaufen und dadurch direkten Einfluß auf die Lebewesen im Aquarium haben können. Auch von Fischen nicht gefressenes Futter wird von verschiedenen Organismen abgebaut, die letztendlich auch wieder Ammonium ausscheiden.

Was geschieht nun mit diesem Ammonium? In der Natur dient es als Hauptpflanzennährstoff und wird dadurch größtenteils „verbraucht". Die Weiterverarbeitung über Nitrit zu Nitrat spielt nur eine geringe Rolle. Im Aquarium kann auch der beste Pflanzenwuchs nicht so viel Ammonium verarbeiten, wie durch die Fische gebildet wird. Deshalb muß es hier durch bestimmte Bakterien unter Verbrauch von Sauerstoff über die Zwischenstufe Nitrit zu Nitrat oxidiert werden. Nitrat kann auch von den Pflanzen als Nährstoff verwendet werden, jedoch wird Ammonium bevorzugt.

Letzten Endes reichert sich also Nitrat im Aquarium an. Das ist auch gut so, denn dieser durch Bakterien bewerkstelligte Umbau von Ammonium zu Nitrat, die sogenannte Nitrifikation, ist praktisch die „Lebensversicherung" für unsere Fische im Aquarium. Warum, ist schnell erklärt.

Das Ammonium selbst ist nicht giftig, kann jedoch pH-Wert-abhängig in das hochgiftige Ammoniak übergehen. Generell gilt: je höher der pH-Wert, desto mehr fischgiftiges Ammoniak liegt vor. Den genauen Zusammenhang zeigt die untenstehende Tabelle.

Ammoniakgehalt in Abhängigkeit vom pH-Wert (geändert nach KRAUSE)

NH_4^+/NH_3 Gesamtgehalt (mg/l)	Anteil des giftigen Ammoniak (mg/l) bei pH-Wert 6,5	7,0	7,5	8,0	8,5	9,0
0,1	< 0,001	0,001	0,002	0,006	0,014	0,035
0,2	< 0,001	0,001	0,004	0,011	0,029	0,069
0,3	0,001	0,002	0,006	0,017	0,043	0,104
0,5	0,001	0,003	0,010	0,029	0,072	0,173
0,8	0,002	0,005	0,015	0,046	0,115	0,277
1,0	0,002	0,006	0,019	0,057	0,144	0,346
1,2	0,002	0,007	0,023	0,069	0,173	0,415
1,5	0,003	0,009	0,029	0,086	0,216	0,519
2,0	0,004	0,012	0,038	0,114	0,288	0,692
4,0	0,008	0,024	0,076	0,229	0,576	1,384
6,0	0,011	0,036	0,114	0,342	0,864	2,076
8,0	0,015	0,048	0,152	0,458	1,152	2,70

Die Tabelle gilt nur bei 24 °C. Je 1 °C höherer/niedrigerer Temperatur sind bis zu 4 % höhere/niedrigere Werte vorhanden.

Bewertung: harmlos kritisch akut gefährlich

Algen im Aquarium

Wer kennt sie nicht, die wohl am meisten gefürchteten Lebewesen im Süßwasseraquarium – die Algen? Sie sind es auch, die leider allzuoft dazu beitragen, daß ein mit Enthusiasmus begonnenes Hobby frühzeitig sein Ende findet.

Am schlimmsten treiben es die blaugrünen bis gelegentlich schmutzig-schwarzen Blau- oder Schmieralgen. Sie überziehen in Windeseile alles, was sich im Aquarium befindet, mit einer schmierigen, glitschigen Schicht, deren penetrant modriger Geruch zuweilen auch noch in einigen Metern Entfernung vom Aquarium wahrzunehmen ist. Befallene Pflanzen können nicht mehr assimilieren und sterben langsam ab.

Die Sauerstoffversorgung der Fische und der wichtigen Bakterien verschlechtert sich. Die Algen scheiden dazu noch schädliche Stoffwechselprodukte aus, und die Katastrophe nimmt ihren Lauf …, wenn nicht durch geeignete Pflegemaßnahmen von vornherein ein übermäßiges Aufkommen von Algen verhindert wird.

Außer Blaualgen gibt es natürlich noch eine ganze Reihe weiterer Algen, die dem Aquarianer mehr oder weniger das Leben schwer machen. Die wichtigsten werden wir noch vorstellen.

Erfolgreiche Gegenmaßnahmen

Was kann nun der Aquarianer tun, um den Algen das Leben schwer zu machen und nicht umgekehrt? Zunächst ist es einmal wichtig zu wissen, daß Algen Pflanzen sind, wenn auch primitive, und im Prinzip die gleichen Nährstoffe brauchen, wie Aquarienpflanzen auch. Allerdings sind Algen geradezu verrückt auf Nitrat und Phosphat, während die sogenannten höheren Pflanzen an geringe Phosphat- und Nitratangebote angepaßt sind. Algen sind als weniger hoch entwickelte Lebensformen auch anspruchsloser und anpassungsfähiger als höhere Pflanzen.

Ganz allgemein kann gesagt werden, daß in einem Aquarium, das dicht mit gut wachsenden Pflanzen besetzt ist, die Algen kaum eine Chance haben, sich stark auszubreiten. Das bedeutet auch, daß die im Kapitel über die Wasserpflanzen beschriebenen Pflegemaßnahmen das beste Algenvorbeugungsmittel sind. Gut wachsende höhere Pflanzen sorgen durch Nährstoffverbrauch dafür, daß für die Algen kaum noch etwas übrig bleibt.

Als oberstes Gebot gilt auch hier: Kontinuität aller Bedingungen. An Veränderungen der Pflegebedingungen müssen sich die höheren Pflanzen erst langsam anpassen. Während dieser Zeit assimilieren sie nicht oder nur wenig. Dies ist dann die Stunde der anpassungsfähigeren Algen, die mit der neuen Situation schneller fertig werden und die von den höheren Pflanzen nicht verbrauchten Nährstoffe für eine starke Vermehrung nutzen.

So sollten zum Beispiel keine Experimente mit der Beleuchtung gemacht werden, wie etwa plötzlicher Wechsel der Lichtfarbe, der Beleuchtungsintensität oder -dauer. Von Leuchtstoffröhren mit rot und blau betontem Spektrum weiß man, daß sie algenfördernd sind. Sie sollten deshalb nicht oder nur in Verbindung mit Tageslichtröhren verwendet werden. Nitrat und Phosphat, die Hauptnährstoffe der Algen, sollten möglichst gering gehalten werden. Dies geschieht am besten durch dichte Bepflanzung von Anfang an und durch regelmäßigen Teilwasserwechsel.

Wehret den Anfängen

In neu eingerichteten Aquarien ist die Gefahr einer Algenplage besonders groß, da die Pflanzen an-

Saugwelse wie dieser **Otocinclus** *sind gute Helfer im Kampf gegen die Algen.*

fänglich nicht in vollem Maße assimilieren, bis das Aquarium „eingefahren“ ist. Während dieser Zeit ist höchste Vorsicht geboten. Jeder sich bildende Algenansatz sollte sofort entfernt werden.

Algenfressende Fische sind eine wertvolle Hilfe im Kampf gegen unerwünschte Algen. Sie sollten gleich von Anfang an bei der „Beckenbesatzung“ mit eingeplant werden. Zu nennen wären verschiedene Saugwelse, wie zum Beispiel *Otocinclus* (auch für kleine Aquarien geeignet), *Ancistrus* (vergreifen sich auch an Wasserpflanzen, wenn nicht genügend Algen vorhanden sind), *Loricaria, Farlowella* und viele andere.

Die siamesische Rüsselbarbe *(Crossocheilus siamensis)* ist vor allem als Jungfisch ein fleißiger Algenfresser. Alle lebendgebärenden Zahnkarpfen zupfen unermüdlich an Algenbelägen. Der Einsatz von Schnecken zur Algenbekämpfung kann leicht zu einer Schneckenplage führen.

Eine chemische Bekämpfung von Algen ist ebenfalls möglich, sollte jedoch nur im Notfall durchgeführt werden. Da Algen, wie bereits erwähnt, auch Pflanzen sind, wirken chemische Algenbekämpfungsmittel natürlich auch gegen Pflanzen. Es ist lediglich eine Frage der Dosis, und wie weit die Empfindlichkeit der Algen und der höheren Pflanzen gegenüber dem entsprechenden Mittel auseinander liegt. Deshalb sind die Dosierungsangaben der Hersteller exakt einzuhalten. Überdosierung ist auf jeden Fall zu vermeiden.

Blatt von **Cryptocoryne pontederiifolia** *mit beginnendem Braunalgenbewuchs und rechts fädige Grünalgen.*

Links: Blatt einer **Cryptocoryne** *mit Blaualgen. Mitte: Blatt eines Zwergspeerblattes* **(Anubias barteri, var. glabra)** *mit Pinselalgen. Rechts: Vallisnerienblatt mit langen Fäden von Bartalgen.*

Algen-Portraits

Die Einteilung der Algen in Grünalgen, Braunalgen, Blaualgen sowie Bart- und Pinselalgen ist wissenschaftlich wenig korrekt, soll jedoch hier beibehalten werden, da jeder Aquarianer sich etwas darunter vorstellen kann.

Grünalgen treten als Belag an den Aquarienscheiben oder als langfädige Gespinste zuweilen an Aquarienpflanzen auf. Sie sind harmlos und zeigen gute Wasserverhältnisse an. Von der Sichtscheibe des Aquariums entfernt man sie mit entsprechenden Reinigungsgeräten (Kapitel Technik). Die fädigen Gespinste lassen sich leicht von Hand oder mit einem rauhen Holzstab beseitigen.

Braunalgen sind eigentlich Kieselalgen und haben mit den echten Braunalgen der Meere nichts zu tun. Kieselalgen sind in der Regel ein Zeichen von Lichtmangel.

Blaualgen treten in der Regel in stark mit organischen Abfallstoffen belastetem Wasser auf. Regelmäßiges gründliches Absaugen der Algenherde mit einem Schlauch und damit verbundener Wasserwechsel lassen diese Algen mit der Zeit verschwinden.

Bart- und Pinselalgen gehören zu den Rotalgen und zählen zu den hartnäckigsten Algen im Aquarium. Sie wurden vermutlich in den sechziger Jahren mit Wasserpflanzen aus den Tropen eingeschleppt. Die Bartalgen bilden lange, blau- bis schwärzlichgrüne Fäden, während die Pinselalgen als schwärzliche, bis etwa 10 mm lange pinselartige Büschel wachsen. Beide Algenarten besiedeln bevorzugt rauhe Substrate, wie die Blattränder zähblättriger Pflanzen oder auch Einrichtungsgegenstände.

Kalkablagerungen auf Pflanzenblättern, hervorgerufen durch CO_2-Mangel, bieten besonders gute Ansiedelungsmöglichkeiten. Dabei ist meist auch der pH-Wert des Wassers erhöht. Die sicherste Bekämpfungsmethode ist die Entfernung befallener Blätter. CO_2-Düngung, verbunden mit einer Absenkung des pH-Wertes, kann eine erneute Ausbreitung meist verhindern.

Durch menschliche Aktivitäten, wie zum Beispiel Wäsche waschen, gelangt Phosphat auch in natürliche Gewässer.

Auch Nitrit ist ein sehr starkes Fischgift. Werte ab 0,5 mg/l sind bedenklich, 2,0 mg/l sind tödlich. Dagegen ist das Endprodukt Nitrat eher fischverträglich. Werte von einigen 100 mg/l können von Fischen noch toleriert werden. In einem gut eingefahrenen Aquarium sollten die Stoffe Ammonium und Nitrit praktisch nicht meßbar sein, lediglich Nitrat darf sich langsam ansammeln. Die Fische wären damit sozusagen „aus dem Schneider". Trotzdem hat der stetig steigende Nitratgehalt einen Haken: Wird nicht durch regelmäßigen Teilwasserwechsel das Nitrat verdünnt, freuen sich ungebetene Gäste über diesen idealen Nährstoff: die Algen. Mehr darüber finden Sie in der Reportage „Algen" auf Seite 32.

Welche Bakterien machen nun diese Nitrifikation und wie kommen sie ins Aquarium? Zwei ganz bestimmte Gruppen von Bakterien haben sich auf die Nitrifikation, also den Abbau von Ammonium zu Nitrat, spezialisiert. Die eine Gruppe baut Ammonium zu Nitrit um und die andere Nitrit zu Nitrat. Die eine Gruppe kann also nicht ohne die andere existieren, da sie von ihr das Substrat (Nitrit) geliefert bekommt.

Um ihre segensreiche Tätigkeit ausführen zu können, stellen diese Bakterien einige Ansprüche an ihre Umwelt: ausreichend Sauerstoff, der zur Oxidation benötigt wird, pH-Wert um den Neutralpunkt bis schwach alkalisch und CO_2 als Nahrung.

Da ein Aquarium kein steriles System darstellt (weshalb das Abkochen von Einrichtungsgegenständen auch Unsinn ist), könnte man nach der Neueinrichtung einfach so lange warten bis sich die Nitrifizierer etabliert haben ..., wenn dem nicht das äußerst langsame Wachstum dieser Bakterien und die (verständliche) Ungeduld des Neuaquarianers entgegenständen.

Der Wasserwechsel ist eine nützliche Pflegemaßnahme – zur Freude der Fische.

Nitrifizierende Bakterien benötigen 10–20 Stunden, um ihre Anzahl einmal zu verdoppeln, was andere Bakterien in wenigen Minuten fertigbringen. Ohne „nachzuhelfen" benötigt daher ein neues Aquarium ca. 2 bis 3 Wochen, bis sich genug Nitrifizierer angesammelt haben. Während dieser Zeit zeigen typische Verläufe der Ammonium-, Nitrit- und Nitratkonzentration den Aufbau der Bakterienkolonie an: Zunächst steigt der Ammoniumspiegel stark an und beginnt nach einiger Zeit zu fallen, während gleichzeitig der Nitritspiegel zu steigen beginnt: Die erste Bakteriengruppe hat sich etabliert und baut Ammonium zu Nitrit um. Es vergeht wieder einige Zeit, bis der Nitritspiegel zu fallen beginnt: Nun nimmt die zweite Bakteriengruppe ihre Arbeit auf und baut Nitrit zu Nitrat um. Wenn der Nitritspiegel sich gegen 0 nähert und ein langsamer Anstieg von Nitrat feststellbar ist, gilt das Aquarium als eingefahren, und es können Fische eingesetzt werden.

Jetzt kann aber ein weiteres Problem auftauchen. Die Anzahl der Bakterien ist vom Substrat abhängig. Wenn das Aquarium praktisch leer, nur mit Pflanzen ohne anfallende Abfallstoffe eingefahren wurde, kann nach Einsetzen der Fische das „Spielchen" erneut losgehen, weil die Bakterienkolonie erst wachsen muß, um sich an das vermehrte Abfallangebot durch die Fische anzupassen.

All das kann Sie kalt lassen, wenn Sie, wie auf Seite 18 bereits angedeutet, Ihr neues Aquarium entsprechend animpfen. Der „Hauptarbeitsplatz" dieser Bakterien ist (außer dem Bodengrund und allem, was sich im Aquarium befindet) der Filter, in dem geeignete Materialien den Bakterien eine geeignete Ansiedlungsfläche bieten. Aus diesem Grunde ist das Auswaschen einer alteingefahrenen Filtermasse (die natürlich nicht ausgetrocknet sein darf) im neueingerichteten Aquarium die absolut beste Animpfungsmethode. Die dabei entstehende „trübe Suppe" klärt sich sehr schnell wieder, und Sie haben vom Augenblick an ein eingefahrenes Aquarium, in das Sie *sofort* Fische einsetzen können.

Aquarienvereine wenden diese Methode seit Jahrzehnten zum Einfahren von Ausstellungsbecken an. Werden Sie mißtrauisch, wenn auf irgendeinem Produkt steht: „Schütten Sie XY ins Wasser, und am nächsten Tag können Sie Fische dazusetzen!" Ganz nebenbei – Nitrifizierer sind „Mimosen" und lassen sich äußerst schlecht konservieren!

Es könnte bisher der Eindruck entstanden sein, daß im Aquarium nur nitrifizierende Bakterien leben. Das stimmt natürlich nicht. Im Aquarium leben eine ganze Reihe verschiedener Bakterien, die am Stoffkreislauf mitbeteiligt sind, nur daß diese Bakterien eben wirklich „von selbst" kommen, ohne unser Zutun.

Gefahr aus der Wasserleitung

Heutzutage werden vor allem in Neubauten, aber auch bei der Altbausanierung, Wasserleitungen aus Kupferrohr verlegt. Von diesen Kupferrohren kann eine ernstzunehmende Gefahr für die Aquarienbewohner ausgehen.

Neuinstallierte Kupferleitungen besitzen noch keine isolierende Kalkschicht im Inneren. Steht nun bei längerer Nichtbenutzung das Wasser in der Leitung, so können sich erhebliche Mengen an Kupfer im Wasser lösen, die bei Aquarienfischen zu Vergiftungserscheinungen und bei Pflanzen zu Wachstumshemmung führen können.

Bei neu installierten oder frisch entkalkten Warmwasserboilern oder Durchlauferhitzern besteht übrigens die gleiche Gefahr. In einem solchen Fall sollte man das Wasser einige Minuten ablaufen lassen, bevor man es für das Aquarium verwendet. Meist hat sich im Leitungssystem nach etwa einem Jahr eine Kalkschicht aufgebaut, die eine weitere Lösung von Kupfer verhindert.

Phosphat

Phosphatverbindungen übernehmen wichtige Funktionen sowohl im tierischen als auch im pflanzlichen Organismus. Energiereiche Phosphate werden als Energielieferant bei der Muskelarbeit oder bei der Pflanze zum Aufbau von Zucker gebraucht. Zum Aufbau von Knochen wird ebenfalls Phosphat benötigt.

Durch die Verdauungsvorgänge der Fische und aus Futterresten gelangt Phosphat ins Aquarienwasser. Die Höhe und die Auswirkung der Phosphatkonzentration im Aquarium werden oft unterschätzt. In der Natur haben sich Pflanzen daran gewöhnt, daß Phosphat Mangelware ist, und besitzen entsprechende Mechanismen, die es ihnen ermöglichen, mit geringsten Phosphatmengen auszukommen.

Was geschieht nun, wenn im Aquarium plötzlich ein Phosphatangebot vorliegt, das den Bedarf der Wasserpflanzen oft um mehr als das Hundertfache übersteigt? Unsere „speziellen Freunde", die Algen, freuen sich und stürzen sich geradezu auf das Phosphat. Wenn dann auch noch entsprechende Mengen an Nitrat vorhanden sind, ist die Algenplage vorprogrammiert. Das Fatale ist, daß Algen Phosphat speichern können, wenn mehr da ist, als sie im Moment brauchen. Dadurch können die Algen auch lange nachdem der Phosphatgehalt gesenkt wurde (Wasserwechsel) noch lustig weiterleben, wodurch das Phosphat als Ursache oft verkannt wird.

Organische Stoffe im Wasser

Alle natürlichen Gewässer enthalten einen hohen Anteil an gelösten hochmolekularen organischen Verbindungen. Diese Stoffe stammen teils aus dem Stoffwechsel der Tiere und teils aus pflanzlichen Abbauprozessen. Im hygienischen Sinn handelt es sich dabei um Verschmutzungsindikatoren,

Ein Schlauch (mit Ansaugschutz) zum nächstgelegenen Abfluß erspart das lästige Eimerschleppen.

die deshalb in unserem Trinkwasser nicht enthalten sein dürfen.

Auf die Fische haben diese Stoffe aber durchaus positive Effekte. Sie bewahren als sogenannte Schutzkolloide zum Beispiel die Schleimhaut vor schädigenden Einflüssen. Huminstoffe, die vor allem in Schwarzwässern enthalten sind, wirken bakterienhemmend und schleimhautverdichtend. Aber auch Wasserpflanzen profitieren von gelösten organischen Substanzen, da viele als natürliche Chelatoren (Nährstoffträger) wirken und so wichtige Nährstoffe pflanzenverfügbar halten.

Es hat sich gezeigt, daß frisches Leitungswasser aggressiv auf Kiemen und Schleimhaut der Fische wirkt. Erst ein Zusatz von organischen Verbindungen macht das Wasser „fischgerecht". Die Zugabe eines der im Zoofachhandel erhältlichen Wasseraufbereitungsmittel behebt dieses Problem.

Wohl bekomm's – Wasseraufbereitung

In diesem Abschnitt wollen wir Ihnen einerseits Tips geben, wie Sie unerwünschte Werte des Leitungswassers verändern können, bevor es ins Aquarium kommt, und andererseits auch aufzeigen, wie Veränderungen der Wasserwerte, die sich während des Betriebs des Aquariums einstellen, durch geeignete Maßnahmen in Grenzen gehalten werden können. Sie erinnern sich doch noch – Kontinuität ist das oberste Gebot!

Bevor Sie jedoch darangehen, die Zusammensetzung des Leitungswassers vor Verwendung zu verändern, sollten Sie sich genau überlegen, ob dies für die Fische, die Sie zu pflegen beabsichtigen, auch wirklich erforderlich ist. Wie gesagt, die meisten Aquarienfische lassen sich im Leitungswasser problemlos pflegen, wenn die Kontinuität der Bedingungen gewahrt bleibt. Und gerade die läßt sich mit Leitungswasser eher einhalten, als mit der dauernden „Wasserpanscherei", die Ihnen vielleicht irgendwann einmal auf die Nerven geht.

Anders bei der Zucht: hier werden möglichst die natürlichen Wasserwerte gefordert, da die Eier der Fische wenig anpassungsfähig sind.

Verändern der Wasserhärte

Aufhärten: Eine Erhöhung der Wasserhärte ist meist nur dann erforderlich, wenn in Weichwasser-Gebieten Fische gepflegt werden sollen, die höhere Härtewerte benötigen, wie zum Beispiel Cichliden aus den afrikanischen Grabenseen oder australische Regenbogenfische.

Filterung über Marmorgrus oder Zugabe von pulverförmigem Kalziumkarbonat erhöht die Gesamt- und Karbonathärte gleichmäßig. Dabei ist die Zufuhr von CO_2 erforderlich, um den Kalk entsprechend in Lösung zu bringen und zu halten. Eine Erhöhung der Resthärte (Gesamthärte ohne Karbonathärte) kann zum Beispiel durch Kalziumsulfat erreicht werden. Bequem zu handhabende Karbonathärte- und Gesamthärtebildner sind auch im Zoofachgeschäft erhältlich.

Enthärten: Das Enthärten von Leitungswasser ist weitaus komplizierter als die Erhöhung der Wasserhärte. Es gibt im Prinzip nur drei Verfahren, die aquaristisch sinnvoll sind. Welches Verfahren man einsetzt, hängt letztlich von den lokalen Gegebenheiten ab. Die Verfahren sollen hier nur im Prinzip vorgestellt werden, da es umfangreiche Fachliteratur gibt, auf die der Interessierte gegebenenfalls zurückgreifen möge.

Zwei Verfahren beruhen auf dem Prinzip des Ionenaustauschs. Es sind dies die **Teilentsalzung** oder Entkarbonisierung und die **Vollentsalzung.** Wie bereits der Name sagt, werden bei diesen Vorgängen bestimmte Ionen gegen andere ausgetauscht, wodurch die Wasserhärte verschwindet. Zentraler Teil solcher Anlagen sind bestimmte Kunstharze mit Austauschereigenschaft, über die das Wasser wie über einen Filter geleitet wird.

Eine Entkarbonisierung ist nur dann sinnvoll, wenn die Karbonathärte im Wasser mindestens 80% der Gesamthärte ausmacht. Da durch die Entkarbonisierung die Ionenverteilung im Wasser verschoben wird und äußerst niedrige Gesamtsalzgehalte, wie sie zur Zucht von Weichwasserfischen gebraucht werden, nicht erreichbar sind, eignet sich diese Methode nur für weniger empfindliche Fische. Bei der Vollentsalzung erhält man praktisch destilliertes Wasser, das man durch Verschneiden auf jeden gewünschten Härtegrad einstellen kann.

Alle Ionenaustauscher haben eine begrenzte Kapazität, die abhängig ist von der Härte des Ausgangswassers und der Menge des verwendeten Harzes. Nach Erschöpfung müssen die Harze mit Salzsäure (Entkarbonisierung) oder mit Salzsäure und Natronlauge (Vollentsalzung) regeneriert werden. Dabei ist mit der bei Chemikalien gebotenen Vorsicht zu arbeiten. Regenerierflüssigkeiten sind Sondermüll und dürfen nicht in den Ausguß geschüttet werden! Es gibt auch Geräte mit Regenerierservice. Das ist zwar etwas teurer als Selbstregenerieren, Sie sparen sich aber die Mühe und das Abfallproblem.

Als dritte Methode wäre noch die **Umkehrosmose** zu nennen. Geräte, die nach diesem Prinzip arbeiten, werden in letzter Zeit immer häufiger im Handel angeboten. Dabei wird durch den im Leitungsnetz herrschenden Druck das Wasser gegen eine Membran gedrückt, die praktisch wie ein mikrofeines Sieb annähernd alles zurückhält, was größer ist als das reine Wassermolekül. Ein geringfügiger Restsalzgehalt bleibt jedoch erhalten.

Der Wirkungsgrad der Umkehrosmoseanlagen hängt von Wasserdruck und Temperatur ab. Er liegt bei Leitungswasserdruck bei etwa 20%. Das heißt, aus 100 Liter Wasser erhält man 20 Liter entsalztes Wasser (Permeat) und 80 Liter Restwasser mit erhöhtem Salzgehalt (Konzentrat), das in den Abguß läuft.

Umkehrosmoseanlagen sollten möglichst permanent in Betrieb sein, um eine möglichst lange Lebensdauer der Membran zu erreichen. Ihre Anschaffung ist also nur sinnvoll, wenn ein kontinuierlicher Wasserbedarf vorhanden ist. Regenerationskosten entfallen, dafür muß von Zeit zu Zeit die Membran gewechselt werden, die teuer ist, und es fallen erhöhte Wasserkosten an.

Vergessen Sie alle anderen Methoden, wie sie zum Beispiel in Spülmaschinen oder bei Haushaltsinstallationen und sonstigen technischen Anwendungen zu finden sind. Enthärtungsanlagen, wie sie z.B. in Spülmaschinen verwendet werden, arbeiten nach dem Prinzip des Neutralaustauschers, kenntlich an der Regeneration mit Salz. Bei dieser Methode werden die Härtebildner letztlich in Salze umgewandelt; das ist reinigungstechnisch sinnvoll, für die Aquaristik jedoch unbrauchbar, da der Gesamtsalzgehalt der gleiche bleibt.

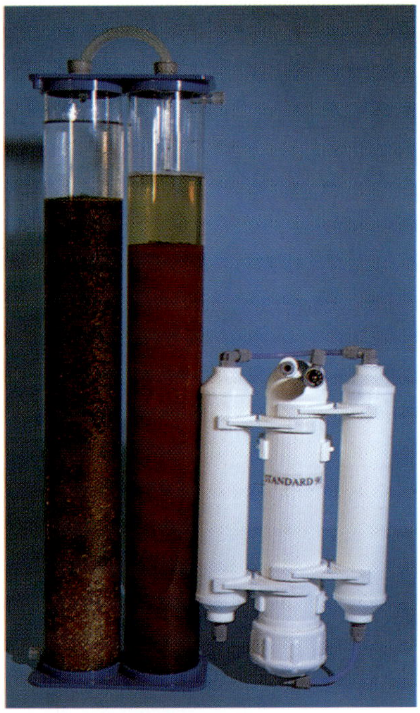

Wasserenthärtung: links Ionenaustauscher (Vollentsalzer) mit Indikatorharz, das durch seine rote Färbung eine anstehende Regeneration anzeigt; rechts Umkehrosmoseanlage.

Verändern des pH-Wertes

Senken: Wie Sie bereits wissen, kommt der pH-Wert in der Natur hauptsächlich durch das Zusammenspiel von Karbonathärte und gelöstem CO_2-Gas zustande. Da im Aquarium meist aufgrund von CO_2-Mangel (es wird durch die Pflanzen verbraucht) der pH-Wert ansteigt, sollte er mit den gleichen natürlichen Mitteln, nämlich Zufuhr von CO_2, gesenkt und auf Werte um den Neutralpunkt eingestellt werden. Gleichzeitig erhalten dabei die Pflanzen lebensnotwendiges CO_2. Bei Wässern mit Karbonathärten über 15 °dKH ist eine Senkung der Karbonathärte auf 10 °dKH sinnvoll, da sonst unnötig viel CO_2 gebraucht würde, um den pH-Wert auf 7 zu senken.

In besonderen Fällen, zum Beispiel zur Zucht, kann der pH-Wert auch durch Torffilterung gesenkt werden. Dies kann jedoch nur im weichen Wasser geschehen, da im härteren Wasser die Säuren des Torfes durch die Karbonathärte abgepuffert werden. Der pH-Wert sollte dabei ständig überprüft werden. Die Wirkung von Torf auf pH-Wert und Karbonathärte ist bei GEISLER ausführlich beschrieben. Es sei noch angemerkt, daß die Filterung über Aktivkohle die Wirkung des Torfes aufhebt.

Erhöhen: Es ist in den seltensten Fällen erforderlich, kann jedoch durch eine Erhöhung der Karbonathärte (siehe dort) erfolgen. Im Zoofachhandel sind auch entsprechende Präparate zur pH-Anhebung erhältlich.

Verändern des CO_2-Gehaltes

Aufgrund des CO_2-Verbrauchs der Wasserpflanzen kommt es in gut bepflanzten Aquarien regelmäßig zu CO_2-Mangel. Die Installation einer CO_2-Düngeanlage schafft hier Abhilfe. Näheres darüber erfahren Sie im nächsten Kapitel. Eine Senkung des CO_2-Gehaltes wird meist nur infolge versehentlich falsch eingestellter Düngegeräte nötig sein und kann durch kräftige Wasserbewegung oder Durchlüftung schnell erreicht werden.

Entfernen von Ammonium und Nitrit

Die Entfernung von Ammonium und Nitrit sollte eigentlich kein Thema sein, da sie, wie bereits geschildert, von Bakterien erledigt wird. Lediglich wenn die Bakterien durch irgend einen Umstand „geärgert" wurden (zum Beispiel durch Behandlung von Fischkrankheiten), das Aquarium katastrophal überbesetzt ist oder zuviel gefüttert wurde, kann der Ammonium- oder Nitritgehalt ansteigen.

In einem solchen Fall kann zunächst ein Teilwasserwechsel vorgenommen werden. Anschließend muß für eine Normalisierung der Verhältnisse gesorgt werden, zum Beispiel durch Herausfiltern von Medikamentenresten über Aktivkohle, weniger füttern und, falls erforderlich, den Fischbesatz verringern.

Entfernen von Nitrat

Die billigste und einfachste Methode das Nitrat loszuwerden, ist der als Pflegemaßnahme bereits bekannte, regelmäßige Teilwasserwechsel. Problematisch wird es allerdings in einigen Gegenden, wo das Leitungswasser bereits Nitrat enthält. Laut Trinkwasserverordnung sind maximal 50 mg/l zulässig. Dies genügt aber schon, um unter Umständen eine Algenplage hervorzurufen.

Es gibt noch einen anderen Weg der Nitratentfernung, den auch die Natur benutzt und der in Kläranlagen mehr und mehr großtechnisch

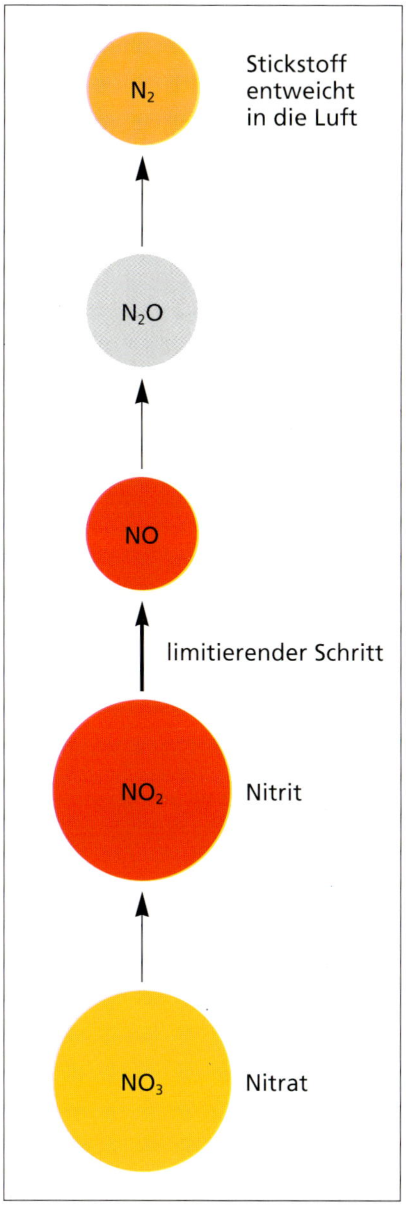

Wenn kein Sauerstoff vorhanden ist, können verschiedene Bakterien den im Nitrat enthaltenen Sauerstoff veratmen und so Nitrat zu Stickstoff abbauen.

angewendet wird: die sogenannte Denitrifikation. Das ist die Fähigkeit verschiedener Bakterien statt des im Wasser gelösten Sauerstoffs den im Nitrat chemisch gebundenen Sauerstoff zur Atmung zu verwenden. Letztendlich entsteht dabei gasförmiger Stickstoff, der in die Atmosphäre entweicht, und schon sind wir das Nitrat los!

Soweit so gut – die Sache hat nur leider einen Haken. Die Bakterien denken unter normalen Aquarienbedingungen im Traum nicht daran, den Sauerstoff aus dem Nitratmolekül zu veratmen, solange noch im Wasser gelöster Sauerstoff wesentlich leichter zu haben ist. Um gleich noch etwas klarzustellen, es handelt sich bei diesen Bakterien nicht um die gleichen, die das Nitrat produzieren und diesen Prozeß etwa nur „rückwärts" ablaufen lassen. Denitrifizierer gibt es in den verschiedensten Bakteriengruppen, die unter bestimmten Umständen eben in der Lage sind, Nitrat zu veratmen. Potentiell denitrifizierende Bakterien sind in jedem Aquarium vorhanden.

Erst wenn praktisch kein freier Sauerstoff im Wasser mehr verfügbar ist und wenn organische Nahrung (zum Beispiel Zucker) vorhanden ist, gehen die Bakterien dazu über, Nitrat zu veratmen. Ähnliche Bedingungen findet man in Mulmansammlungen und im Bodengrund des Aquariums, wenn man nicht in regelmäßigen „Putzanfällen" den Bodengrund umschichtet und jedes bißchen Mulm entfernt. Aquarien mit einer gewissen Portion „Dreck" funktionieren deshalb oft besser als peinlich saubere, die regelrecht „zu Tode geputzt" werden.

In besonders konstruierten Filtern mit extrem geringer Durchflußrate und langem Filterweg können entsprechende Bedingungen künstlich erzeugt werden. Wichtig ist dabei eine regelmäßige Zufuhr von Nahrung für die Bakterien. In Kläranlagen verwendet man Ethanol. Dies ist unter Aquarienbedingungen nicht machbar, da ein „Durchschlagen" des Ethanols ins Aquarium zu einer Massenvermehrung von Bakterien und dadurch zu Sauerstoffmangel führen kann. Für Aquarien geeignete „Bakteriennahrung" muß noch erprobt werden.

Da die Veratmung des Nitrats aber über die Stufe des Nitrits erfolgt, besteht bei hohen Nitratgehalten im Aquarienwasser die Gefahr einer sekundären Nitritanreicherung. Der Schritt Nitrat – Nitrit geschieht nämlich wesentlich schneller als die folgenden Schritte

Ungebetene Gäste

Trotz aller Vorsicht können sich im Aquarium auch manche ungebetenen Gäste einstellen. Als Hauptvertreter wären hier erst einmal verschiedene **Schneckenarten** zu nennen. Meist schleppt man Laich oder Jungtiere mit Wasserpflanzen ein.

Vordergründig haben die zahlreichen kleinen Schneckenarten den Vorteil, daß sie Futterreste und Algen vertilgen. Turmdeckelschnekken lockern auch den Bodengrund auf. Die meisten Aquarianer sind jedoch nicht konsequent genug in der Fütterung der Fische, so daß für die Schnecken der Tisch reichlich gedeckt ist und sie sich zur Plage entwickeln. Manche fressen bei Futtermangel außerdem auch Pflanzen.

Sollte es also einmal soweit gekommen sein, daß der Bodengrund mehr Turmdeckelschnecken als Kies enthält oder Posthornschnecken und andere Kleinschnecken das Aquarium übervölkern, ist Abhilfe nötig. Der Handel bietet Mittel gegen Schnecken an, die allerdings nur im Notfall verwendet werden sollten. Man wird nach einer Behandlung schwerlich alle toten Schnecken im Aquarium finden, die dann empfindlich das Wasser verpesten. Außerdem sind Turmdeckelschnecken weitgehend unempfindlich gegen diese Mittel.

Posthornschnecke mit Gelege.

Es bleibt also nur unermüdliches Absammeln der Schnecken, was sehr lästig ist, oder die Pflege schneckenfressender Fische. Von Kugelfischen raten wir ab. Besser bewährt, weil leichter zu pflegen, haben sich alle Botia-Arten, die mit der Zeit auch Turmdeckelschnecken „erledigen".

Süßwasserpolypen (Hydra) und **Scheibenwürmer** (Planarien) schleppt man sich meistens mit Lebendfutter ein. Sparsame Fütterung läßt diese „Gäste" von selbst wieder verschwinden. Manche anspruchslosen Fische (Makropoden und andere) fressen sie auch. Ganz davon abgesehen, kann Hydra in einem separaten Kleinstaquarium ein interessanter Pflegling sein.

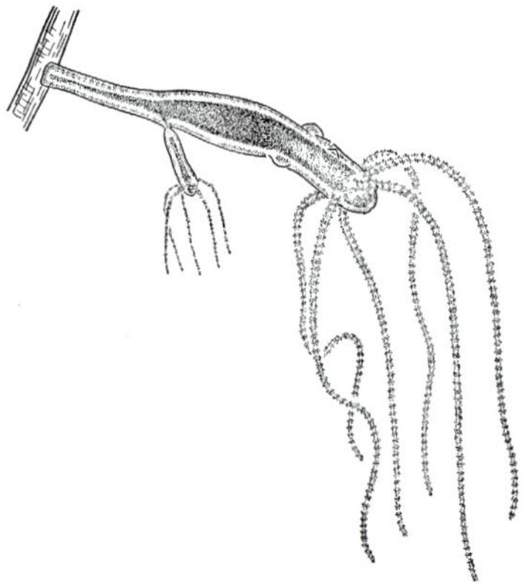

***Süßwasserpolyp* (Hydra)**

von Nitrit über verschiedene Zwischenstufen zu Stickstoff. Ein Denitrifikationsfilter darf deshalb nie direkt am Aquarium angeschlossen werden, sondern muß als „Filter am Filter" betrieben werden.

Nitratentfernung über Austauscherharze ist nicht die Methode der Wahl, da dadurch das Wasser mit anderen Ionen, in der Regel Chlorid, angereichert wird. Dadurch wird die Ionenverteilung im Wasser nachhaltig verändert.

Entfernen von Phosphat

Zu viel Phosphat im Wasser kann praktisch nur durch Wasserwechsel entfernt werden. Durch gezielte, nicht zu gut gemeinte Fütterung und Vermeidung phosphathaltiger Pflegeprodukte läßt sich ein unnötig hoher Anstieg des Phosphatgehaltes vermeiden. Ein üppiger, gesunder Pflanzenwuchs trägt natürlich auch zur Verringerung des Phosphatgehaltes bei.

Leider kommt es immer wieder vor, daß manche Wasserpflanzendünger Phosphate und Nitrate enthalten. Dünger für Zimmerpflanzen hat übrigens im Aquarium absolut nichts verloren! Auch in manchen Wasseraufbereitungsmitteln werden zum Teil noch Polyphosphate als Komplexbildner für Schwermetallionen verwendet. Meiden Sie Pflegepräparate, die Phosphate enthalten! Steigt nach einem Wasserwechsel und Zugabe von Dünger oder Wasseraufbereiter der Phosphatgehalt in kurzer Zeit wieder auf den alten Wert, so enthält zu-

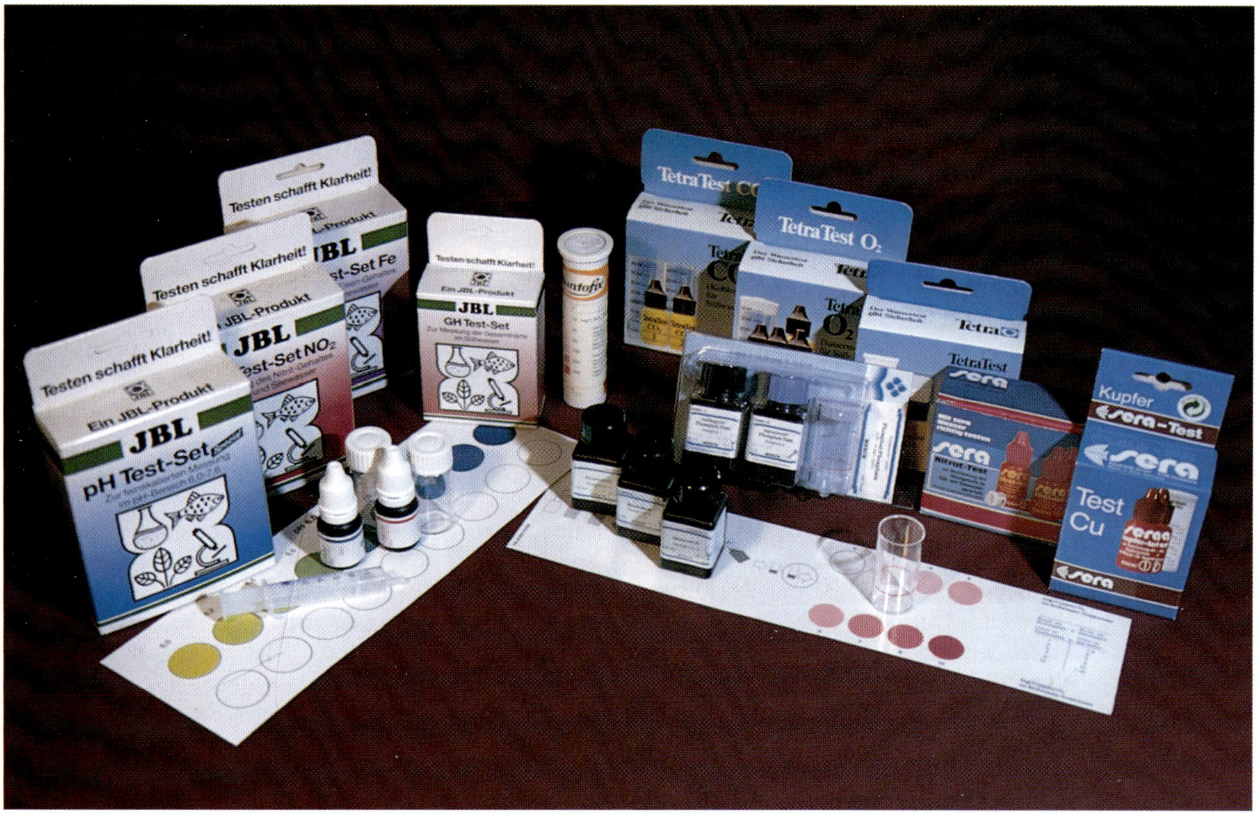

Verschiedene Testsets mit Farbkarten, Reagenzien und Prüfgefäßen.

mindest eines der Produkte Phosphat.

Sie sollten auch einmal den Phosphatgehalt Ihres Leitungswassers prüfen. Oft sind in Hausinstallationen Phosphatdosieranlagen eingebaut, die ein Verkalken der Wasserleitungen verhindern sollen. In einem solchen Fall müßten Sie versuchen, das Wasser für Ihr Aquarium vor dieser Anlage zu entnehmen. Gegebenenfalls den Hausbesitzer um Erlaubnis bitten.

Verändern des Sauerstoffgehaltes

Akute Sauerstoffmangelsituationen können durch Belüftung und starke Wasserbewegung behoben werden. Bei entsprechender Pflege der Wasserpflanzen (Nährstoffe, Beleuchtung) sollten in gut bepflanzten Aquarien eigentlich zumindest tagsüber keine Sauerstoffmangelsituationen vorkommen. Ein eventuell zu starkes Absinken des Sauerstoffgehaltes während der Nacht kann durch leichte Belüftung verhindert werden. (Eine Schaltuhr sorgt dafür, daß die Belüftung nur nachts läuft.) Sauerstoffmangel ist bei Fischen an der beschleunigten Atmung zu erkennen. Im akuten Fall hängen die Fische mit dem Maul an der Wasseroberfläche und führen heftige Atembewegungen aus.

Alles im Griff – Kontrolle des Aquarienwassers

Um gezielte Wasseraufbereitungsmaßnahmen durchführen zu können, oder einfach nur, um zu wissen, ob noch alles in Ordnung ist, müssen die entsprechenden Wasserparameter mit geeigneten Methoden gemessen werden. Der spezialisierte Zoofachhandel bietet eine Reihe von einfach zu handhabenden Schnelltests an, die ausreichend genau und preiswert sind. Für bestimmte Parameter sind auch elektronische Meßgeräte erhältlich, deren Anschaffung sich wegen des vergleichsweise hohen Preises nur bei häufiger Nutzung lohnen wird.

Die Schnelltests beruhen im wesentlichen auf zwei Methoden. Bei der einen Methode (Titration) werden Wasserinhaltsstoffe dadurch gemessen, daß man einer Wasserprobe eine Meßlösung solange zugibt, bis sich ein zugesetzter Indikator verfärbt. Die Anzahl Tropfen der verbrauchten Meßlösung gibt die Konzentration des gesuchten Stoffes an.

Die andere Methode beruht auf dem Prinzip, daß bestimmte Wasserinhaltsstoffe bei Reaktion mit bestimmten Chemikalien eine typische Farbe erzeugen, deren Intensität proportional zur Konzentration der gesuchten Stoffe ist. Durch Vergleich mit geeichten Farbkarten (Colorimetrie) kann die Konzentration ermittelt werden. Gewöhnen Sie sich an, über alle Meßergebnisse Buch zu führen und auch die Tageszeit zu notieren, da sich manche Werte tageszeitlich ändern. So können Sie Veränderungen oder Ten-

denzen schnell erkennen und, falls erforderlich, schnell handeln.

Messen von Härte und Gesamtsalzgehalt

Die Messung der Gesamthärte und der Karbonathärte unterscheiden sich methodisch nicht. Man gibt zu einer Wasserprobe von 5 ml solange ein Reagens zu, bis bei Gesamthärte ein Farbumschlag von rot nach grün und bei Karbonathärte von blau nach gelb erfolgt. Ein Tropfen verbrauchtes Reagens entspricht 1 °d Gesamt- bzw. Karbonathärte. Die Genauigkeit der Methode kann erhöht werden, wenn man das Probenvolumen von 5 auf 10 ml erhöht. Dann entspricht ein Tropfen 0,5 °d. Um die gefundenen Werte mit anderen gebräuchlichen Maßeinheiten, zum Beispiel denen der Wasserchemiker in den Wasserwerken vergleichen zu können, sind die Umrechnungstabellen nützlich.

Zur Messung des Gesamtsalzgehaltes eines Wassers benötigt man ein sogenanntes Leitfähigkeitsmeßgerät oder Konduktometer. Die Messung nutzt die Fähigkeit von Wasser aus, je nach Salzgehalt mehr oder weniger elektrischen Strom zu leiten. Die Maßeinheit ist Mikrosiemens, abgekürzt µS. Geht man davon aus, daß ein Grad deutscher Härte einer Leitfähigkeit von etwa 30 µS entspricht, so kann man durch eine Messung feststellen, ob ein Wasser außer Härtebildnern auch noch andere Salze gelöst enthält. Die Art der Salze kann jedoch nicht festgestellt werden. Von der Härte auf den Gesamtsalzgehalt zu schließen, ist aus diesem Grund nicht möglich! Wer sich genauer für die Leitfähigkeitsmessung interessiert, sei auf das Literaturverzeichnis verwiesen.

Dank ausgereifter Testsets ist das Überwachen der Wasserwerte ganz einfach geworden.

Messen des pH-Wertes

Am weitesten verbreitet sind heute in der Aquaristik pH-Messungen mit Flüssigindikatoren. Einer Wasserprobe (in der Regel 5 ml) werden einige Tropfen Indikator zugesetzt und die entstandene Farbe mit einer Farbskala verglichen. Je nach Anwendungsfall kann man zwischen verschiedenen Meßbereichen und Abstufungen wählen. Tests mit großem Meßbereich (zum Beispiel pH 4–10) messen in der Regel in Abstufungen von 0,5 pH-Einheiten. Zwischenwerte können zur Not geschätzt werden.

Wer es etwas genauer möchte, muß auf Tests mit verringertem Meßbereich (zum Beispiel pH 6–7,6)

Umrechnung der Gesamthärte

	Erdalkaliionen (mmol/l)	Erdalkaliionen (mval/l)	Deutsche Grad (°d)	$CaCO_3$ (ppm)	Englische Grad (°e)	Französische Grad (°f)
1 mmol/l Erdalkaliionen		2,00	5,60	100,0	7,02	10,00
1 mval/l Erdalkaliionen	0,50		2,80	50,0	3,51	5,00
1 Deutsches Grad	0,18	0,357		17,8	1,25	1,78
1 ppm $CaCO_3$	0,01	0,020	0,056		0,0702	0,100
1 Englisches Grad	0,14	0,285	0,798	14,3		1,43
1 Französisches Grad	0,10	0,200	0,560	10,0	0,702	

Umrechnung der Karbonathärte (nach Krause)

	Säurekapazität (mmol/l)	Deutsche Grad (°d)	Französische Grad (°TAC)	Hydrogencarbonat (mg/l)
Säurekapazität 1 mmol/l	–	2,78	4,94	61,0
Deutsche Grad 1 °d	0,36	–	1,78	21,8
Französische Grad 1 °TAC	0,20	0,56	–	12,3
Hydrogencarbonat 1 mg/l	0,016	0,046	0,08	–

zurückgreifen, die dafür aber genauer sind und in Abstufungen von 0,2 oder 0,3 pH-Einheiten messen. Will man die für die Pflege der meisten Fische und Pflanzen günstige pH-Einstellung um 7 überwachen (meist mit der Anwendung einer CO_2-Düngung gekoppelt), so ist die Anschaffung eines Tests mit verringertem Meßbereich und höherer Genauigkeit sinnvoll.

Im spezialisierten Zoofachhandel angebotene Flüssig-pH-Tests haben in der Regel eine Reichweite von 50 bis 80 Messungen pro Packung. Manche Hersteller bieten zusätzlich noch preiswerte Nachfüllungen an, die nur das Reagens enthalten (ohne Probenröhrchen, Farbkarte und so weiter). Hin und wieder werden auch pH-Meßstäbchen angeboten. Sie sind für aquaristische Zwecke zu ungenau und deshalb nur für orientierende Messungen geeignet.

Wer auf häufige und genaue pH-Messungen angewiesen ist (Züchter), wird sicherlich die Anschaffung eines pH-Meters ins Auge fassen. Um keine Fehlmessungen durchzuführen, sollte man sich exakt an die Gebrauchsanleitung halten. Von elementarer Wichtigkeit ist die regelmäßige und gewissenhafte Eichung des Gerätes. Falsch oder längere Zeit nicht geeichte Geräte messen „Hausnummern"!

Die Eichflüssigkeiten sind sorgfältig vor Verunreinigung, insbesondere Verdünnung durch Aquarienwasser, zu bewahren. Nach etwa einem Jahr sollten die Eichflüssigkeiten durch neue ersetzt werden. Die Wassertemperatur hat ebenfalls Einfluß auf die pH-Messung. Bei Geräten mit automatischer Temperaturkompensation braucht man sich dafür nicht zu interessieren. Bei anderen Geräten muß bei jeder Messung am Gerät die Wassertemperatur eingestellt werden.

Der pH-Wert im Aquarium schwankt, je nach Tageszeit, abhängig von der Assimilationstätigkeit der Pflanzen. In Aquarien ohne CO_2-Düngung sollte er gegen Abend nicht höher als 8 bis 8,5 liegen. Gegebenenfalls müssen die

„Wasseraufbereitung"

Beleuchtungsdauer und Intensität entsprechend reguliert werden. Auf schnellwachsende Pflanzen sollte in diesem Fall verzichtet werden, da sie durch ihre starke Assimilation den pH-Wert schnell über 8,5 treiben können.

Bei Verwendung von CO_2-Düngeanlagen ist eine möglichst konstante Einstellung zwischen 6,8 und 7,4 anzustreben. In der ersten Zeit nach der Neueinrichtung eines Aquariums empfiehlt sich eine häufigere Messung des pH-Wertes zu verschiedenen Tageszeiten (Tageszeit immer notieren!). Später, wenn das Aquarium eingefahren ist, genügen eine oder zwei Messungen pro Woche (immer zur gleichen Tageszeit!).

Messen des CO_2-Gehaltes

Sie haben bereits erfahren, daß der pH-Wert im wesentlichen durch das Zusammenspiel der Komponenten Karbonathärte und CO_2 zustandekommt. Aus diesem Grund kann bei bekannter Karbonathärte und bekanntem pH-Wert der CO_2-Gehalt rechnerisch ermittelt werden – unter der Voraussetzung, daß keine weiteren pH-senkenden Stoffe (Huminsäuren) im Wasser vorhanden sind. Um Ihnen die Rechnerei zu ersparen, finden Sie auf Seite 50 eine Tabelle, aus der Sie den CO_2-Gehalt ablesen können.

Es gibt jedoch auch noch die Möglichkeit, den CO_2-Gehalt mit einem Testset direkt zu bestimmen. Einer Wasserprobe wird ein Indikator zugesetzt und anschließend tropfenweise eine Meßlösung zugegeben, bis in der Wasserprobe eine leichte Rosafärbung nicht mehr verschwindet. Meist entspricht ein Tropfen verbrauchter Meßlösung 2 mg CO_2/l.

Sind jedoch außer CO_2 noch andere pH-senkende Substanzen im Wasser vorhanden, so finden Sie sowohl in der Tabelle als auch bei der Messung höhere CO_2-Werte als tatsächlich vorhanden sind. Um eine solche Fehlmessung auszuschließen, gehen Sie folgendermaßen vor: Sie entnehmen zwei gleiche Wasserproben, wovon die erste sofort gemessen wird. Die zweite Probe wird ca. eine Stunde lang belüftet, um alles CO_2 auszutreiben. Bei der nun folgenden Messung der zweiten Probe erfassen Sie den durch andere Substanzen vorgetäuschten CO_2-Gehalt. Das zweite Meßergebnis ziehen Sie vom ersten ab und erhalten so den tatsächlichen CO_2-Gehalt.

Messen des Sauerstoffgehaltes

Die Messung des Sauerstoffgehalts auf chemischem Wege ist ziemlich kompliziert. Auf aquaristische Zwecke zugeschnittene Testsets enthalten deshalb meist 4 Reagenzien. Ihre Anwendung erfordert ein sorgfältiges Vorgehen nach der jeweiligen Gebrauchsanleitung, um verläßliche Ergebnisse zu erhalten. Wesentlich bequemer, aber teuer, ist die Messung mit einem Sauerstoffmeßgerät. Auch diese Geräte erfordern, um einwandfrei zu messen, eine sorgfältige Pflege.

Wie der pH-Wert, so ist auch der Sauerstoffgehalt (zumindest in bepflanzten Aquarien) tageszeitlichen Schwankungen unterworfen – aufgrund der Assimilation der Wasserpflanzen. Bei 25 °C Wassertemperatur sollten abends um 8 mg/l und morgens noch mindestens 4 mg/l meßbar sein. Unter normalen Bedingungen ist eine Messung pro Woche ausreichend.

Messen von Ammonium, Nitrit und Nitrat

Mit diesen drei Messungen hat man den kompletten Abbauweg des „Abfalls" im Überblick. Die Tests bestehen in der Regel aus zwei bis drei Reagenzien (je nach Hersteller) und sind problemlos zu handhaben. In einem gut bepflanzten und eingefahrenen Aquarium sollten Ammonium und Nitrit nicht nachweisbar sein! Bis 0,5 mg/l Ammonium und 0,2 mg/l Nitrit können jedoch noch als normal angesehen werden, wobei eine regelmäßige Kontrolle zeigen muß, ob die Werte stabil sind oder sich erhöhen.

Vor allem nach Behandlungen gegen Fischkrankheiten sind häufigere Messungen empfehlenswert, da die Medikamente oft auch die nitrifizierenden Bakterien in Mitleidenschaft ziehen. Auf die pH-Wert-abhängige Giftigkeit des Ammoniums sei noch einmal verwiesen (Tabelle Seite 31). Nitratgehalte von über 20 mg/l können, wie bereits erwähnt, den Algenwuchs beschleunigen und sollten deshalb vermieden werden, obgleich die Fische auch wesentlich höhere Werte ohne Schaden tolerieren.

Die angebotenen Tests haben Reichweiten von etwa 50 Messungen bei Ammonium und Nitrit und 25 bis 50 bei Nitrat. Unter normalen Bedingungen genügt eine Messung pro Woche. Die Tageszeit spielt dabei keine Rolle. Was den Meßbereich anbelangt, so sollte als untere Grenze bei Ammonium ein Gehalt von 0,2 mg/l noch gut nachweisbar sein. Die Obergrenze des Meßbereichs sollte zwischen 5 und 10 mg/l liegen. Bei Nitrit sollte als untere Grenze 0,05 mg/l noch gut zu erkennen sein, wobei die Obergrenze etwa bei 1–1,5 mg/l liegen kann.

Nitrattests gibt es mit relativ engem Meßbereich von 0,1 bis etwa 10 mg/l und mit weiterem Meßbereich von etwa 10 bis einige 100 mg/l. Tests mit engem Meßbereich sind genauer, erfordern jedoch eine gezielte Verdünnung der Probe mit destilliertem Wasser, wenn man höhere Werte erfassen möchte. Dies entfällt bei den Tests mit höherem Meßbereich, geht jedoch auf Kosten der Genauigkeit im unteren Bereich. Man wird sich also je nach Aufgabenstellung entscheiden müssen.

Messen von Phosphat

Leider sind Phosphattests bei Aquaristikfirmen (noch) dünn gesät. Wenn es Ihnen also nicht gelingen sollte, im spezialisierten Zoofachhandel einen derartigen Test zu erstehen, so wenden Sie sich an den einschlägigen Labor- oder Chemikalienfachhandel. Große Chemiekonzerne bieten schon lange Testsets für das Fischereiwesen an, die auch vorzüglich für die Aquaristik geeignet sind. Da sie jedoch trotz hoher Reichweite (ca. 100 Messungen) relativ teuer sind, wird man nur in Sonderfällen, wie zum Beispiel beim Phosphat, darauf zurückgreifen.

In der Natur gelten Phosphatgehalte von mehr als 0,1 mg/l bereits als hoch und deuten eine beginnende Überdüngung (Eutrophierung) der Gewässer an. Im Aquarium können Werte von 0,5–1 mg/l noch als normal betrachtet werden. Höher sollte der Phosphatgehalt jedoch auf Dauer nicht liegen. In manchen Aquarien konnten wir Gehalte von 10 mg/l und mehr messen!

Messen des Eisengehaltes

Über die Bedeutung des Eisens im Aquarium haben Sie bisher noch nichts erfahren, wir holen dies im Pflanzen-Kapitel nach. Eisentests werden eingesetzt, um die Dosierung eisenhaltiger Düngepräparate zu kontrollieren. Dabei ist es wichtig, daß der Test auch chelatgebundenes Eisen miterfaßt, da alle modernen Wasserpflanzendünger das Eisen in Form von Chelaten enthalten. Dies können Sie überprüfen, wenn Sie eine Wasserprobe mit Eisentestreagens mal für einige Stunden stehen lassen. Nimmt die Farbintensität der Probe während dieser Zeit langsam zu, so ist der Test für aquaristische Zwecke nicht geeignet.

Als Richtwerte für das Aquarium können Gehalte um 0,1 mg/l angesehen werden. Der Test sollte in der Lage sein, noch 0,05 mg/l nachzuweisen. Die Reichweite der aquaristisch gängigen Tests liegt bei etwa 50 Messungen pro Packung.

Der Umgang mit Chemikalien

Wir möchten dieses Kapitel nicht abschließen, ohne noch ein Wort zum Umgang mit den verschiedenen Testsets gesagt zu haben. Sämtliche Testsets bestehen aus Chemikalien, die mehr oder weniger gesundheitsschädlich sein können. Deshalb gehören Tests nicht in Kinderhände und auch nicht in die Nähe von Lebensmitteln.

Vermeiden Sie Hautkontakt sowohl mit den Testflüssigkeiten als auch mit den behandelten Wasserproben; nicht nur, weil verschiedene Testsubstanzen möglicherweise Verätzungen verursachen können, sondern auch, weil durch den Kontakt mit der Haut die Meßergebnisse verfälscht werden können.

Wählen Sie zur Durchführung der Tests einen Platz, der nicht mit Lebensmitteln in Berührung kommt und schütten Sie behandelte, nicht mehr benötigte Wasserproben nicht in den Küchenausguß, sondern in die Toilette oder das Waschbecken im Bad und spülen Sie gut nach.

Die Haltbarkeit der Tests variiert, je nach Art der verwendeten Chemikalien. In der Regel kann eine Mindesthaltbarkeit von zwei Jahren zugrundegelegt werden. Da der Aquarianer jedoch beim Kauf eines Tests nicht weiß, welche Zeit dieser Test bereits in Lagern (Hersteller, Großhändler, Zoofachhandel) zugebracht hat, wäre es wünschenswert, wenn mehr Hersteller dazu übergingen, ein Haltbarkeitsdatum anzugeben.

Für Leute mit Berührungsängsten gegenüber dem „Chemiekram" sei noch erwähnt, daß viele spezialisierte Zoofachhändler entweder als Serviceleistung oder gegen angemessenes Entgelt Wasseranalysen durchführen.

Technik: Der Natur auf die Sprünge helfen

Die Fortschritte in der modernen Aquaristik haben die Aquarienpflege wesentlich einfacher und sicherer gemacht. Denken wir doch daran, wie sich unsere Vorväter noch mit so mancherlei „erfinderischen Konstruktionen" behelfen mußten, die wir uns heute kaum noch vorstellen können.

Trotzdem ist Technik nicht das allein Seligmachende. Ein gewisses Einfühlungsvermögen in die biologischen Vorgänge im Aquarium kann durch keinen noch so großen technischen Aufwand ersetzt werden. Betrachten Sie also die Technik als segensreiches Hilfsmittel, das, mit dem richtigen Augenmaß eingesetzt, der Natur im Aquarium durchaus „auf die Sprünge helfen" kann. Wir wollen versuchen, Ihnen im Laufe dieses Kapitels ein Gefühl für dieses richtige Augenmaß zu vermitteln.

Zuvor jedoch ein Hinweis: Die allermeisten der nachfolgend behandelten technischen Geräte werden mit der üblichen Netzspannung von 220 Volt betrieben. Gerade die Kombination von Wasser und Strom birgt erhebliche Gefahren. Verwenden Sie deshalb nur Geräte, die den geltenden VDE-Richtlinien entsprechen und möglichst noch ein GS-Zeichen haben.

Unterlassen Sie alle Basteleien mit Strom am Aquarium! Wenn sich Eigenbauten nicht umgehen lassen, zum Beispiel bei Beleuchtungen für Aquarien, die von der üblichen Norm abweichen, verwenden Sie nur zugelassene Bauteile und lassen Sie das Ganze von einem Fachmann prüfen, bevor Sie es in Betrieb nehmen. Wer absolut sichergehen möchte, kann die gesamte Elektrik für das Aquarium an einen sogenannten FI-Schalter anschließen, der in Gefahrensituationen (Beleuchtung fällt ins Wasser etc.) abschaltet, bevor es zum Unfall kommen kann. In modernen Neubauten gehören FI-Schalter bereits zur Hausinstallation.

Die unsichtbaren Helfer – Filter

Sie werden sich vielleicht fragen, warum „unsichtbare" Helfer? Filter besitzen nun mal eine gewisse Größe und sind allenfalls nach geschickter Unterbringung oder Verkleidung unsichtbar. Die „unsichtbaren Helfer" sind nicht die Plastikgebilde selbst, die man im Handel erwirbt, sondern sie sitzen im Inneren des Filters, nach einer gewissen Einlaufzeit. Doch darüber später.

Was muß ein Filter leisten?

Ein Filter muß, wie bereits der Name sagt, etwas filtern, nämlich das Aquarienwasser – mit dem Ziel, es sauberzuhalten, was auch immer darunter zu verstehen ist. Darüber hinaus muß er für eine gewisse Strömung im Aquarium sorgen, die gleich mehrere Aufgaben zu erfüllen hat: Gleichmäßige Verteilung der Wärme im Aquarium, Zuführung von nährstoffhaltigem Wasser zu den Aquarienpflanzen, Abtransport von Ausscheidungsprodukten (wuchshemmende Stoffe etc.) und, in wenig bepflanzten Aquarien, Sauerstoffanreicherung des Wassers.

Die Pumpleistung des Filters richtet sich nach den Ansprüchen der zu pflegenden Fische und Pflanzen. Bei strömungsliebenden Arten darf die Stundenleistung dem zwei- bis dreifachen Beckenvolumen entsprechen. Bei weniger strömungsliebenden Arten genügt das halbe bis einfache Beckenvolumen als Stundenleistung. Bedenken Sie bei der Auswahl, daß die Pumpenleistungen immer im Leerlauf angegeben sind und sich nicht selten beim Betrieb mit Filtermasse auf etwa die Hälfte reduzieren.

Mechanische oder biologische Filterung?

Nichts wird in Aquarianerkreisen heftiger und kontroverser diskutiert als die Art und Weise der Filterung. Die einen stehen auf dem Standpunkt, daß ein Filter nicht oft genug gereinigt werden kann und sprechen ihm jede biologische Funktion ab. Der Dreck, der sich im Filter ansammelt, macht ja nur eine Ortsverlagerung durch, befindet sich nach wie vor im System Aquarium und gammelt im Filter vor sich hin, mit allen erdenklich schlechten Folgen für das Aquarium.

Die anderen betrachten eine Filterreinigung so, als müßte eine heilige Kuh in Indien geschlachtet werden, und schwören auf die biologische Reinigungskraft. Die wertvollen nitrifizierenden Bakterien sollen ja so lange wie möglich ungestört ihre segensreiche Tätigkeit der Entgiftung (siehe Seite38) durchführen können, wobei Filterreinigung nur unnötig stört.

Wir haben die beiden Extreme bewußt überspitzt dargestellt. Wie so oft im Leben, ist an beiden Einstellungen „was dran", und der goldene Mittelwert ist mal wieder der richtige. Jeder Filter wird über kurz oder lang biologisch arbeiten, das heißt mit nitrifizierenden Bakterien besiedelt werden, daran

Auswahl an Aquarienfiltern: Geschlossener Topfaußenfilter (hinten links), verschiedene Innenfilter mit Schaumstoffpatronen (hinten Mitte und vorn rechts), offener Außenfilter mit bequem zu reinigenden Patroneneinsätzen (hinten rechts), Rucksackaußenfilter (vorne links), luftbetriebener Innenfilter (vorne Mitte).

gibt es nichts herumzudeuten. Nur sollte man diesen Bakterien ihren „Arbeitsplatz" auch so optimal wie möglich gestalten! Dazu gehört nun einmal, daß man sie einerseits in Ruhe läßt (heilige Kuh), und ihnen andererseits aber auch unnötigen Dreck von der Pelle hält!

Im Klartext heißt das, ein Filter sollte so aufgebaut sein, daß das Wasser zuerst über eine leicht und bequem zu reinigende feine Vorfiltermasse laufen muß, die regelmäßig gereinigt wird, und anschließend über eine etwas gröbere Filtermasse mit möglichst großer innerer Oberfläche, die möglichst selten gereinigt wird und so den Bakterien einen optimalen Arbeitsplatz bietet. Leider läßt sich dieses Prinzip in vielen käuflichen Filtern nicht so einfach verwirklichen.

Unzählige Gespräche mit Kunden in Zoofachgeschäften zeigen immer wieder die gleichen Probleme auf. Leute, die ihren Filter permanent (am liebsten mit Sagrotan) putzen oder jede Woche nagelneues Filtermaterial einsetzen, haben immer Probleme mit zu hohem Nitrit- und Ammoniumgehalt, weil die Nitrifikation nicht richtig in Gang kommen kann. Andererseits hatten die „Nie-Reiniger" immer Probleme mit schnell hoch ansteigendem Nitratgehalt, da der ganze „Dreck" den Bakterien zum Aufarbeiten überlassen wurde.

Filterbauarten

Für welche Filterbauart Sie sich entscheiden, hängt von der Durchführbarkeit des gerade erläuterten Filterprinzips ab, vom zur Verfügung stehenden Platz und nicht zuletzt von Überlegungen, wie man einer versehentlichen Flutung des Wohnzimmers am besten vorbeugt.

Zunächst unterscheidet man Außen- und Innenfilter. **Innenfilter** haben den entscheidenden Vorteil, daß sie sich im Aquarium befinden, also keine wasserführenden Rohre oder Leitungen außerhalb des Aquariums verlegt werden müssen. Nachteil ist das relativ kleine Filtervolumen und der zusätzliche Fremdkörper im Aquarium, der entsprechend verkleidet werden muß. Wenn man ihn für die Reinigung

Das Arbeitsprinzip eines geschlossenen Außenfilters. 1 Vorfiltermasse, 2 Hauptfiltermasse, 3 Pumpenkopf.

entnimmt, wird man naß (sollte für Aquarianer kein Hinderungsgrund sein) und stört eventuell empfindliche Beckeninsassen. Besonders für kleine Aquarien sind genau ins Eck passende, motorbetriebene Innenfilter sehr beliebt. Da hier die Trennung in Vorfiltermasse und Langzeitfiltermasse nicht möglich ist, wird man einen Mittelweg im Reinigungsintervall suchen müssen.

Außenfilter gibt es in geschlossener und offener Bauweise. **Geschlossene Außenfilter** können bequem unter, neben oder hinter dem Aquarium, praktisch unsichtbar, untergebracht werden. Nachteil: Wasserführende Schläuche führen aus dem Aquarium in den Filter und wieder zurück. Die meisten Hersteller haben die Gefahrenquelle erkannt und liefern Filter mit (mehr oder weniger gut bedienbaren) Schlauchverschraubungen. Sehr empfehlenswert für solche Filter ist die Anschaffung von Doppelabsperrhähnen mit dazwischen befindlicher Schnelltrennkupplung, die das An- und Abkuppeln des Filters ohne großen Wasserverlust ermöglicht.

Die meisten dieser Topf-Außenfilter werden von unten nach oben durchströmt, so daß man zur Reinigung der Vorfiltermasse immer erst den gesamten Filterinhalt ausräumen muß. Das ist lästig. Es gibt bereits einigermaßen brauchbare Vorfilter, die man auf das Ansaugrohr aufsteckt. Ihre Reinigung ist auch wieder nicht ganz das „Gelbe vom Ei", da sie sich meist an einer unzugänglichen Stelle im Aquarium befinden. Man will ja das Ansaugrohr mit Vorfilter nicht dauernd vor der Nase haben, wenn man ins Aquarium sieht.

Offene Außenfilter sind oben offene Behälter, die entweder als „Rucksack" für kleinere Aquarien oder als separat stehender Behälter für größere Aquarien so angebracht sein müssen, daß sich die Wasserspiegel im Filter und im Aquarium auf einem Niveau befinden. Ein großvolumiges Überlaufrohr führt das Wasser nach dem Heberprinzip in den Filter, von wo es nach Durchfluß der Filteranlage mit einer Pumpe (Unterwasserpumpe oder Tauchkreiselpumpe) wieder in das Aquarium zurückbefördert werden kann. Gegenüber dem Nachteil des nicht frei wählbaren Aufstellungsortes haben diese Filter den entscheidenden Vorteil des spielend leichten Zugriffs auf die Filtermasse zwecks Reinigung.

Auswahl an Filtermaterialien: Formkohle, verschiedene Plastikfüllkörper, Torfgranulat, verschiedene Schaumstoffzuschnitte, feine und grobe Filterwatte, Lava und Keramikringe.

Filtermassen

Als Vorfiltermasse zum Zurückhalten von groben Verunreinigungen sind Perlonwatte und feinporiger Schaumstoff aus dem spezialisierten Zoofachhandel hervorragend geeignet. Verwenden Sie keinen Schaumstoff aus Verpackungen unbekannter Herkunft, er könnte unerwünschte Stoffe an das Wasser abgeben oder von Bakterien aufgefressen werden.

Als Langzeitfiltermasse zur Besiedelung mit Bakterien bietet sich praktisch jedes offenporige, nicht reagierende Material an. Auf eine gewisse Porenweite bzw. Körnung des Materials ist zu achten. Klassisches und unserer Meinung nach optimales Material ist Schaumstoff mit einer Porenweite von 1–2 mm. Weiterhin geeignet sind Lavabruch, Tongranulat und sogenannte Raschig-Ringe aus Keramik, die gegenüber den anderen Materialien jedoch eine bereits deutlich verringerte Oberfläche besitzen.

Vergessen Sie alles, was sich zur Zeit als Modeerscheinung an Plastikfüllkörpern auf dem Markt herumtreibt. Diese Gebilde haben in der Klärtechnik und bei einigen Spezialaufgaben auch in der Aquaristik durchaus ihre Berechtigung. Als Filtermasse im *untergetauchten* Betrieb sind sie, auch mit noch so tollen Attributen, sehr schlecht geeignet. Die von Bakterien besiedelbare Oberfläche ist im Vergleich zu Schaumstoff bei gleichem Volumen geradezu kläglich.

Selbstverständlich dürfen Filtermassen, gleich welcher Art, nur unter kühlem (25 °C) Wasser ausgespült werden. Ersatz durch neue Filtermasse erfolgt erst, wenn die alte nach häufigem Ausspülen unbrauchbar geworden ist. Niemals die komplette Filtermasse durch neue ersetzen!

Besondere Filtermassen

Torf und Aktivkohle, zwei Filter-

massen mit wichtigen Sonderfunktionen, sollen nicht unerwähnt bleiben. Um eines gleich vorwegzunehmen: Die gleichzeitige Filterung über Torf und Aktivkohle ist Nonsens, geradeso als würden Sie mit Ihrem Auto gleichzeitig vorwärts und rückwärts fahren. Aktivkohle filtert nämlich genau die Bestandteile wieder heraus, die man mit Torf in das Wasser bringen möchte.

Aktivkohle ist eine Sonderfiltermasse, die aufgrund ihrer speziellen Eigenschaften und besonderer Herstellungsweise dazu in der Lage ist, hochmolekulare organische Verbindungen aus dem Wasser adsorptiv zu entfernen. Zu solchen hochmolekularen organischen Verbindungen zählen zum Beispiel Reste von Medikamenten, die nach erfolgter Behandlung aus dem Wasser entfernt werden sollen, aber auch solche erwünschte Stoffe wie zum Beispiel Huminstoffe, Schutzkolloide und Nährstoffträger (natürliche wie künstliche) mitsamt den gebundenen Nährstoffen, die man durch Wasseraufbereitungsmittel und besonders angepaßte Dünger erst mühsam dem Wasser zugesetzt hat.

Aus diesem Grund hat eine *Dauer*filterung über qualitativ hochwertige Aktivkohle im Süßwasseraquarium nichts zu suchen, leistet jedoch als „Feuerwehr" (Medikamentenreste etc.) gute Dienste. Die besten Adsorptionseigenschaften haben sogenannte Formkohlen, das sind Preßlinge verschiedener Größe aus Kohlenstaub. Zerkleinerte Kohle, der man noch die Holzstruktur ansieht, ist vergleichsweise wirkungslos.

Bei der Zucht von Weichwasserfischen ist **Torf** das Mittel der Wahl, um das Zuchtwasser auf natürliche Weise anzusäuern. Gleichzeitig gibt der Torf wertvolle Huminstoffe an das Wasser ab, die durch ihre bakterienhemmende Wirkung die für diese Fische wichtige bakterienarme Umgebung schaffen. Der pH-Wert muß öfters kontrolliert werden, um im weichen Wasser ein zu starkes Absinken zu verhindern. Der Zoohandel bietet verschiedene Torfarten an. Man kann jedoch auch normalen Ballentorf aus Hochmooren verwenden, der jedoch keine Düngezusätze enthalten sollte. Im Zweifelsfall eine Probe im Wasser einweichen und nach einigen Tagen auf Ammonium, Nitrat und Phosphat prüfen.

Egal wie der Filter auch immer aussehen mag, den regelmäßigen Teilwasserwechsel kann er nicht ersetzen.

Es werde Licht – Beleuchtung

Die Beleuchtung ist eines der wichtigsten technischen Hilfsmittel der modernen Aquaristik. Das Aquarium wird damit unabhängig von dem schlecht zu kontrollierenden Tageslicht auf der Fensterbank. Dadurch kann eine den Bedürfnissen der Aquarieninsassen angepaßte Beleuchtung geboten werden, die die Pflege wesentlich erleichtert.

Licht steuert sämtliche Lebensvorgänge bei Fischen, zum Beispiel Nacht- und Tagesaktivitäten verschiedener Arten, den Zeitpunkt des Ablaichens und vieles mehr.

Die wichtigste Funktion ist jedoch die Lieferung von Energie für jenen pflanzlichen Prozeß, den man Assimilation oder Photosynthese nennt, und dessen „Abfallprodukt", der Sauerstoff, tierisches Leben auf unserem Planeten erst ermöglicht.

Genau dieser Funktion, nämlich Energielieferung für die Assimilation der Wasserpflanzen, muß die Beleuchtung durch geeignete Wahl der Leuchtmittel gerecht werden.

Wieviel Licht brauchen Wasserpflanzen?

Hier wäre zunächst einmal die Frage der **Beleuchtungsdauer** zu klären. Nehmen Sie dazu die Verhältnisse in der natürlichen tropischen Heimat unserer Aquarienfische zum Vorbild: Der Lichttag ist dort das ganze Jahr über annähernd gleich. Wechselnde Tageslängen wie in unseren Breiten gibt es nicht. Jahraus, jahrein sind 12 Stunden Tag und 12 Stunden Nacht.

Die Lichtbrechung im Wasser sorgt noch dafür, daß morgens und abends bei niedrigstehender Sonne kaum Licht unter Wasser gelangt. Im Endeffekt findet man unter Wasser eher nur 10 Stunden Tag und 14 Stunden Dunkelheit. Entsprechend sollte das Aquarium höchstens 12 Stunden Licht am Tage erhalten.

Der Einsatz von Zeitschaltuhren sorgt nicht nur für regelmäßiges Ein- und Ausschalten, sondern bei entsprechender Einstellung auch dafür, daß Ihre Fische noch munter sind, wenn Sie es sich abends vor dem Aquarium gemütlich machen. Die Schaltfolge könnte zum Beispiel so aussehen: 11.30/12.00 Uhr an und

Auf die richtige Beleuchtung kommt es an!

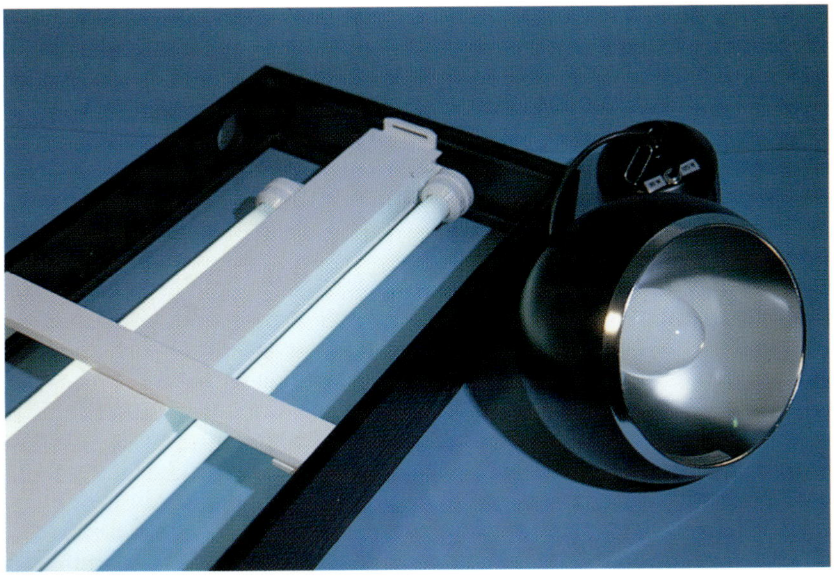

Beleuchtung: links Aquarienabdeckung (Deckel entfernt) mit sicherer Installation zweier Leuchtstoffröhren; rechts eine HQL-Leuchte.

23.00/23.30 Uhr aus. Wenn Sie eine Beleuchtung mit mehreren Lampen installieren, dann empfiehlt es sich, diese so zu schalten, daß nur die Hälfte oder, wenn machbar, nur ein Drittel während 10 bis 12 Stunden angeschaltet ist und die volle Kapazität nur während einer „Kernzeit" von 8 bis 9 Stunden leuchtet.

Was die **Beleuchtungsintensität** angeht, so gilt hier ausnahmsweise der Grundsatz „Viel hilft viel". Gerade die so begehrten rasenbildenden Vordergrundpflanzen sind meist sehr lichthungrig und haben das meiste lichtschluckende Wasser zwischen sich und der Beleuchtung. Die meisten Pflanzen können sich an stärkstes Licht gut anpassen, an zu schwaches jedoch kaum. Dazu kommt noch, daß das Licht oft noch durch Schwimmpflanzen oder an der Wasseroberfläche entlangwachsende Stengelpflanzen abgeschattet wird.

Die Lichtfarbe

Über die Lichtfarbe werden unter Aquarianern nach wie vor heiße, oft nächtelange Diskussionen geführt. Sehr lange galten die rot- und blaubetonten Lampen als das Nonplusultra der Aquarienbeleuchtung und versetzten die Unterwasserwelt in ein unnatürliches, bonbonfarbenes Licht. Die Erkenntnis, daß das Aktivitätsmaximum der Photosynthese im blauen und roten Spektralbereich liegt, führte zu dieser Lichtfarbe.

Mittlerweile weiß man, daß die Pflanzen nicht so sehr auf eine starke Betonung des Rot- und Blauanteils angewiesen sind, vielmehr auf ein ausgeglichenes Spektrum, möglichst mit Tageslichtcharakter, jedoch mit ausreichender Intensität. Außerdem stehen die rot- und blaubetonten Lampen im Ruf, algenfördernd zu sein. Da sich Pflanzen erwiesenermaßen an fast jede Lichtfarbe anpassen können, wenn man ihnen die nötige Ruhe dazu läßt, ist die Auswahl der Lichtfarbe letzten Endes eine Frage des persönlichen Geschmacks und wie „natürlich" das Aquarium aussehen soll.

Die Lampentypen

Wohl am weitesten verbreitet sind heute Leuchtstoffröhren als Aquarienbeleuchtung. Sie haben eine wesentlich bessere Lichtausbeute als die früher verwendeten Glühlampen, „leben" länger und erwärmen sich weniger. Es vergeht kein Jahr, ohne daß nicht irgendeine „sensationelle" neue Röhre mit „nie dagewesenen Eigenschaften" für die Aquaristik auf den Markt kommt.

Mal davon abgesehen, daß die Farbe, wie bereits erwähnt, Geschmackssache ist, seien Sie kritisch! Verschiedene Fabrikate unterscheiden sich ganz erheblich in der Menge Licht, die Sie bei gleichem Stromverbrauch fürs Geld bekommen. Und auf die Intensität kommt es uns ja hauptsächlich an. Sie können sie leicht am Lumenstrom pro Watt errechnen. Der Lumenstrom wird meist auf Merkblättern der Hersteller für die ganze Röhre angegeben. Teilen Sie diesen Wert durch die Leistungsaufnahme. Wenn dann ein Wert um 90 herauskommt, können Sie die Röhre unbesorgt kaufen. Sie werden sehr bald feststellen, daß unter diesen Bedingungen Tageslichtröhren die Nase vorn haben.

Als Faustregel für eine akzeptable Beleuchtungsstärke kann folgendes gelten: Bei 45 bis 50 cm Beckenhöhe rechnet man bei einer Tiefe von 40 cm zwei Röhren von etwa der Länge des Aquariums; pro 10 cm Tiefenzunahme eine Röhre mehr. Geeignete Reflektoren sollten die Lichtabstrahlung nach oben verhindern. Der Fachhandel bietet Reflektorbleche an, die auf die Röh-

re geklipst werden können. Die Leuchtkraft von Leuchtstoffröhren läßt mit der Zeit nach, deshalb sollten sie spätestens nach einem Jahr (auch wenn sie noch brennen!) ausgetauscht werden. Schreiben Sie sich das Datum irgendwo in den Beleuchtungskasten! Mehrere Röhren im Turnus wechseln, damit die Pflanzen keinen Schock bekommen.

Um genügend Licht in das Aquarium zu bekommen, sollten Leuchtstofflampen möglichst nahe an der Wasseroberfläche liegen. Es versteht sich von selbst, daß nur VDE-gerechte, wasserdichte Fassungen verwendet werden dürfen. Lassen Sie, Ihrer Sicherheit zuliebe, die Finger von Eigenkonstruktionen! Es gibt im Zoofachhandel fertige, wasserdichte Einbauleuchten für den selbstgestylten Beleuchtungskasten zu kaufen. Trotz der geringen Wärmeentwicklung der Leuchtstoffröhren kann es bei sommerlichen Außentemperaturen in einem geschlossenen Beleuchtungskasten ganz schön warm werden. Für diesen Fall sollten Lüftungsöffnungen vorgesehen sein.

Die Einführung der **Quecksilberhochdrucklampen** eröffnete neue Perspektiven in der Aquaristik. Mußten Leuchtstofflampen in mehr oder weniger geschlossenen Kästen über dem Aquarium angebracht werden, so ermöglichen die über dem Aquarium angebrachten HQL-Lampen einen ungehinderten Blick auf die Wasseroberfläche. Pflanzen können aus dem Wasser herauswachsen und Blüten bilden. Das Hantieren am Aquarium ist leichter geworden. Durch die stark gebündelte Lichtmenge können auch Becken von mehr als 50 cm Höhe effektiv ausgeleuchtet werden, was mit Leuchtstoffröhren kaum möglich war.

Die Anzahl der Leuchten ist abhängig von der Beckenlänge. Pro 50 cm Länge benötigt man eine Leuchte bei einer Tiefe von 40–50 cm. Die meisten HQL-Leuchten sind umschaltbar von 80 auf 125 Watt, wodurch die Lichtintensität an verschiedene Höhen angepaßt werden kann. Auch die HQL-Leuchtmittel sollte man nach einem Jahr Betriebsdauer austauschen, da sie in der Intensität nachlassen.

Metalldampf-Lampen (HQI) haben sich bisher nur in der Seewasseraquaristik und bei sehr großen Süßwasserbecken etablieren können, wo enorme Lichtintensitäten gebraucht werden.

Auch Pflanzen brauchen Futter – CO_2

Bis vor nicht allzulanger Zeit galt CO_2 als der Fischfeind Nummer eins in den Aquarien und man unternahm alles nur Erdenkliche, um CO_2 aus dem Wasser auszutreiben. Es wurden stark sprudelnde Ausströmersteine installiert, am Filtereinlauf von Motorfiltern wurden Lufteinzugsdüsen angebracht, und mit Strahlrohren und anderen sinnreichen Konstruktionen wurden wasserfallähnliche Einrichtungen geschaffen, deren Geräusch empfindsamere Naturen nach dem nächsten Weg zur Toilette suchen ließ.

Heute weiß man, daß CO_2 als mengenmäßig wichtigster Hauptnährstoff der Pflanzen auch ohne solche Wasserspiele im Aquarium eher Mangelware ist. Deshalb hat sich der Trend umgekehrt und man ist bestrebt, das CO_2, das durch die Atmung der Fische und die Tätigkeit von Bakterien gebildet wird, möglichst wenig aus dem Wasser auszutreiben, ja, man macht sogar erhebliche Anstrengungen, um mehr CO_2 in das Wasser hineinzubekommen, um den Pflanzen ihr nötiges „Futter" zukommen zu lassen.

Um so unverständlicher ist uns deshalb die Werbestrategie mancher Filterhersteller, die immer noch mit möglichst vielen „Wasserspielen" dem Aquarienwasser auch das letzte bißchen CO_2 austreiben und damit den Pflanzen das Leben schwer machen. So können die Pflanzen natürlich auch nicht genügend Sauerstoff liefern und man muß durch Diffusoren und Strahlrohre den Sauerstoffgehalt erhöhen

Dicht bepflanztes Aquarium. Bei der Bepflanzung wurde auf die Kontrastwirkung unterschiedlicher Blattfarben und -formen geachtet.

Bei springfreudigen Fischen braucht man eine Abdeckung, sonst kommt es zu gefährlichen Ausflügen.

– die Katze beißt sich in den Schwanz.

Es ist natürlich auch möglich, erfolgreich Aquarien ohne CO_2-Zufuhr zu fahren, wenn man mit entsprechender Disziplin nur solche Pflanzen wählt, die langsam genug wachsen und so mit dem im Aquarium entstehenden CO_2 auskommen, ohne gegen Abend den pH-Wert in schwindelnde Höhen zu treiben.

Dabei muß man jedoch auf größere Pflanzenvielfalt verzichten. Würde man nämlich schnellwachsende Arten dazusetzen, so würden die in kurzer Zeit das frei verfügbare CO_2 aufbrauchen, den langsam wachsenden bleibt nichts übrig, und da die schnellwachsenden auch das im Karbonat gebundene CO_2 noch angreifen können, steigt der pH-Wert drastisch an und macht das Wassermilieu lebensfeindlich für Fische und Pflanzen.

Dies ist auch der Grund für die häufig geäußerte Meinung, daß sich bestimmte Pflanzen nicht „vertragen". Einfache Erklärung: Die eine macht der anderen das CO_2 streitig. In Aquarien, in denen durch eine CO_2-Zufuhr von außen für ein gleichbleibendes Angebot gesorgt wird, wachsen die „Kontrahenten" meist friedlich nebeneinander. Wir sehen also: Bei ausreichendem CO_2-Angebot lassen sich Pflanzen verschiedener Ansprüche im gleichen Aquarium pflegen. Dadurch erreicht man eine Pflanzenvielfalt, die im Aquarium ohne CO_2-Versorgung von außen nicht möglich ist.

Ist CO_2 für Fische gefährlich?

Um die Antwort gleich vorwegzunehmen: Unter „normalen" Aquarienbedingungen, mit Karbonathärten zwischen 5 bis 15 °d und pH-Werten um den Neutralpunkt, kann CO_2 für Fische grundsätzlich nicht gefährlich werden. Es spielt dabei keine Rolle, ob der CO_2-Gehalt bei 20 oder 60 mg/l liegt – solange die Menge, die nötig ist, um die Karbonathärte in Lösung zu halten, nicht überschritten wird.

Erst wenn darüber hinaus noch mehr CO_2 zugegeben wird, können gefährliche Werte erreicht werden und der pH-Wert stark sinken. Da für ausreichendes Pflanzenwachstum eine gewisse Mindestmenge an CO_2 erforderlich ist, kann bei Karbonathärtewerten unter 4 bis 5 °d zuwenig Karbonat als Gleichgewichtspartner vorhanden sein und der pH-Wert zu stark absinken.

CO_2-Gehalt (mg/l) aus pH-Wert und Härte ermitteln
(geändert nach Krause)

Karbonathärte (°d)	pH-Wert 6,6	6,8	7,0	7,2	7,4	7,6
2	16	10	7	4	3	2
4	32	20	13	8	5	3
6	50	30	20	12	8	5
8	65	40	25	16	10	6
10	80	50	32	20	13	8
12	100	60	40	24	15	10
14	115	70	45	28	18	11
16	130	80	50	32	20	12
18	145	90	58	36	23	14
20	160	100	65	40	25	16

empfohlener Härtebereich
empfohlener pH-Bereich
Bereich mit optimalem CO_2-Gehalt

Umgekehrt würden bei sehr hohen Karbonathärtewerten unwirtschaftlich hohe Mengen an CO_2 gebraucht, um den pH-Wert auf Werte um 7 einzustellen. Das Zusammenspiel zwischen Karbonathärte, pH-Wert und CO_2-Gehalt ist in der Tabelle dargestellt.

Methoden der CO_2-Versorgung

Es gibt verschiedene, mehr oder weniger wirksame Methoden, Aquarienwasser mit CO_2 anzureichern. Von vornherein vergessen sollten Sie Mineralwasser und sogenannte CO_2-Düngetabletten als CO_2-Quelle. Dies entspricht dem berühmten Tropfen auf dem heißen Stein. Durch die Reaktion von Salzsäure mit Marmor in einem Behälter CO_2 herzustellen ist zwar möglich, wegen des Umgangs mit Salzsäure jedoch zu gefährlich. Durch alkoholische Gärung von Hefe in Zuckerlösung ist es möglich, kleine Aquarien für eine Zeitlang einigermaßen mit CO_2 zu versorgen.

Die am weitesten verbreitete und auch effektivste Methode beruht auf der Verwendung von CO_2, das in Druckflaschen in flüssiger Form gespeichert ist. Über eine Druckreduziereinrichtung wird ein geringer, gleichmäßiger Strom ins Aquarium geleitet und dort in Diffusionseinrichtungen verschiedener Art möglichst lange mit Wasser in Kontakt gebracht. Dabei diffundiert das Gas nahezu vollständig in das Aquarienwasser. Durch die Verwendung von Druckflaschen ist es möglich, einen großen Vorrat an CO_2 auf kleinstem Raum bereitzuhalten, wodurch dieses Verfahren das rationellste ist.

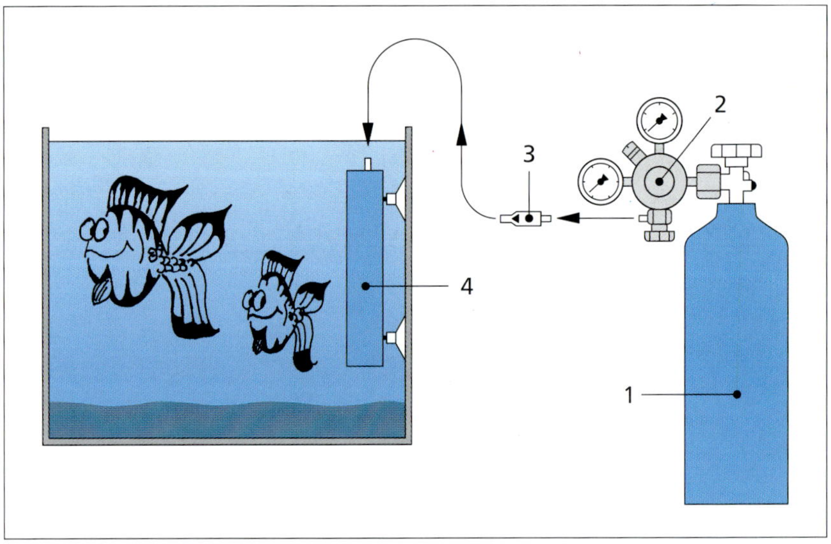

Prinzip einer CO_2-Düngeanlage. 1 CO_2-Druckflasche, 2 Druckminderer mit Arbeits- und Flaschendruck-Manometer, 3 Rücklaufsperre mit Markierung der Durchflußrichtung, 4 Diffusionseinrichtung.

Umgang mit Druckflaschen

Wie alle Druckflaschen, so unterliegen auch CO_2-Druckflaschen in Deutschland einer sehr strengen „Druckbehälterverordnung". Jede Flasche muß mit einem TÜV-Stempel mit Datum versehen sein. Die Flasche darf sich von diesem Datum an gerechnet 10 Jahre im Verkehr befinden und muß dann erneut überprüft werden.

Bei normaler Raumtemperatur beträgt der Innendruck ca. 60 bar. Bei steigender Temperatur nimmt auch der Innendruck schnell zu. Um Unfälle zu vermeiden, sind alle Flaschen mit sogenannten Berstscheiben versehen, die bersten, wenn der Innendruck einen bestimmten Wert übersteigt, um das Gas kontrolliert austreten zu lassen (vergessene Flasche im überhitzten Auto). Defekte Berstscheiben dürfen nur von autorisiertem Fachpersonal gewechselt werden!

Unterlassen Sie in Ihrem eigenen Interesse alle Versuche, leere CO_2-Flaschen selbst zu füllen oder gar andere als die dafür zugelassenen Flaschen mit CO_2 zu befüllen! Obendrein ist es strafbar. Druckflaschen dürfen nur von autorisierten Betrieben (Hersteller oder Kohlensäuredienste) gefüllt werden.

Wie voll oder leer eine Druckflasche ist, kann nur durch Wiegen ermittelt werden. Das Gewicht der leeren Flasche ist als Tara auf jeder Flasche eingestempelt, zusätzlich das zulässige Gasgewicht. Beide Gewichte addiert ergeben das Gewicht der gefüllten Flasche.

Solange sich auch nur ein Tropfen flüssiges CO_2 in der Flasche befindet, herrscht ein Innendruck von 60 bar. Erst wenn kein flüssiges CO_2 mehr vorhanden, die Flasche also praktisch leer ist, beginnt der Druck zu fallen. Um ein Eindringen von Schmutz und Wasser in die Flasche zu verhindern, sollten „leere" Flaschen mit einem Restdruck von ca. 30 bar zum Wiederbefüllen gegeben werden.

Nadelventil oder Druckminderer?

Es gibt zwei Wege, einen einfachen und preiswerten und einen eleganten und kostspieligeren, um aus der unter Druck stehenden Flasche einen langsamen Strom an CO_2 herauszubekommen. Der einfache Weg ist ein sogenanntes Nadelventil, das durch eine feine Nadel, die über eine Gewindespindel bewegt wird, mehr oder weniger CO_2 direkt aus der Flasche ins Aquarium läßt. Die Regulierung solcher Nadelventile erfordert (gleich bei welcher Marke) eine gewisse „liebevolle" Hand, da der volle Flaschendruck von 60 bar direkt geregelt wird, wodurch die kleinste Drehung an der Nadel bereits große Wirkung haben kann. Weiterhin können Schwankungen der Außentemperatur den Gasfluß ebenfalls verändern, da sich der Druck in der Flasche ändert.

All diese Probleme gibt es nicht bei der Verwendung der zwar erheblich teureren, aber eleganteren Druckminderer. Hier gelangt nur ein variabel einstellbarer „Arbeitsdruck" zum Dosierventil, das aufgrund des niederen Druckes wesentlich präziser einzustellen ist. Der eingestellte Arbeitsdruck wird durch ein automatisches Ventil im Inne-

Auswahl an Geräten zur CO_2-Düngung: Links: Druckflaschen verschiedener Größe. Mitte, von oben nach unten: Druckminderer mit Manometern und variabel einstellbarem Arbeitsdruck, Druckminderer ohne Manometer und fest eingestelltem Arbeitsdruck, Magnetventil, Nadelventil und Rücklaufsperren, die ein Rückfließen von Wasser in die Armaturen verhindern. Rechts: Diffusionseinrichtungen für Betrieb ohne Pumpe (ganz außen) und mit Pumpe (übrige).

ren des Druckminderers annähernd konstant gehalten. An zwei Manometern können der Flaschendruck und der Arbeitsdruck abgelesen werden.

Es gibt Druckminderer von verschiedenen Herstellern und in verschiedenen Preislagen. Achten Sie darauf, daß der Druckminderer ein Sicherheitsventil besitzt, das eine Überlastung des Arbeitsdruckmanometers verhindert. Dies tritt häufig auf, wenn eine neugefüllte Flasche schnell aufgedreht wird. Je nach Hersteller kann das System noch durch Nachtabschaltung über ein Magnetventil oder durch pH-Wert-abhängige, vollautomatische Steuerung perfektioniert werden. Solche Steuerungen und Nachtabschaltungen dürfen grundsätzlich nur mit vorgeschaltetem Druckminderer betrieben werden.

Diffusionseinrichtungen

Der Markt bietet Diffusionseinrichtungen verschiedenster Art, die der „Philosophie" der jeweiligen Hersteller entsprechen. Hier gilt: „Es führen viele Wege nach Rom." Es gibt Geräte, die mit Pumpen betrieben werden müssen, solche, die ohne auskommen, solche, die im Aquarium anzubringen sind und solche, die außerhalb angebracht werden. Lassen Sie sich von einem spezialisierten Fachhändler beraten und wählen Sie das für Ihren Bedarf geeignete Gerät.

Für eine optimale Versorgung der Wasserpflanzen sollten Sie bei einer Karbonathärte nicht unter 5 °d und nicht über 15 °d einen pH-Wert zwischen 6,8 und 7,4 einstellen, wobei der niedrigere pH-Wert für die niedrigere Härte und der höhere für die höhere Härte gilt.

Das wohltemperierte Aquarium

Die Aquarienfische haben einen bestimmten Temperaturbereich, in dem sie sich wohlfühlen; die für die Zucht nötigen Temperaturen liegen meistens etwas darüber. Einzelheiten zu den Arten werden bei den Fischbeschreibungen genannt.

Hier geht es nun allgemein darum, welche technischen Möglichkeiten die moderne Aquaristik bietet, um den jeweils benötigten Temperaturrahmen zu schaffen und aufrechtzuerhalten. Da sich die meisten Fische bei einer Temperatur wohlfühlen, die höher als unsere übliche Zimmertemperatur liegt, braucht man eine Aquarienheizung und ein Thermometer, um die Temperatur zu überwachen.

Pflegeplan

Vor allem der Anfänger wird, gerade weil er bemüht ist, alles möglichst gut zu machen, in der Regel zu viel am Aquarium „herumwerkeln". Deshalb haben wir hier noch einmal die erforderlichen Pflegemaßnahmen zusammengestellt. Darüber hinaus sollte das Aquarium Ruhe haben!

Täglich

Ein- bis zweimal so viel füttern, wie in zwei bis drei Minuten aufgefressen wird. Ab und zu einen Fastentag einlegen. Jungfische öfters füttern, natürlich ohne Fastentag.

Fische beobachten: Fressen alle, gibt es Unverträglichkeiten oder Anzeichen von Krankheiten? Tote Fische unverzüglich entfernen.

Kontrollieren: Temperatur, Funktion der Technik.

Wöchentlich, spätestens alle zwei Wochen

Teilwasserwechsel von etwa 1/4 bis 1/3 des Beckenvolumens, verbunden mit Filterreinigung und, falls nötig, Korrektur des Pflanzenwuchses.

„Und was machen Sie mit Ihren Fischen im Urlaub?"

1. Erforderliche Korrekturen an Pflanzen vornehmen.
2. Frontscheibe innen reinigen.
3. Heizung und Filter abschalten.
4. Wasser ablassen, dabei übermäßige Mulmansammlungen im Sichtbereich mit absaugen.
5. Vorfiltermasse des Filters unter fließendem Wasser (kühl!) ausspülen. Falls erforderlich, Pumpengehäuse des Filters reinigen.
6. Falls vorhanden, Deckscheiben reinigen. Kalkablagerungen können mit Essigwasser entfernt werden, danach gut abspülen.
7. Aquarium mit temperiertem Leitungswasser wieder auffüllen.
8. Heizung und Filter wieder einschalten.

Urlaubsvorbereitungen

- Vor Urlaubsbeginn Wasserwechsel in gewohnter Weise.
- Bei Abwesenheit von ein bis zwei Wochen ist keine Fütterung der Fische erforderlich. (Jungfische müssen weiter gefüttert werden.)
- Bei längerer Abwesenheit ist eine sparsame Fütterung mit einem Futterautomaten der Fütterung durch Fremdpersonen vorzuziehen, es sei denn, diese Person ist Aquarianer. Legen Sie für alle Fälle die Telefonnummer eines befreundeten Aquarianers und Ihres Zoofachhändlers bereit.

Wohl dem, der einen Futterautomaten hat.

Zu Besuch im Schauaquarium

Wohlige Wärme, heimeliges Halbdunkel, Stille, vielleicht ein Plätzchen zum Sitzen und ringsum an den Wänden Fenster in eine faszinierende Unterwasserwelt. Korallenfische in leuchtenden, geradezu unwirklichen Farben und bizarren Formen gleiten durchs Wasser, Seeanemonen bewegen anmutig ihre Tentakeln. Die kleinen Polypen, Muscheln und Seesterne geben ihre Schönheit erst bei genauerer Betrachtung preis.

Einige Meter weiter durchstreifen gruselig aussehende Raubfische ihr riesiges, mannshohes Becken, und die spitzen Zähne der Piranhas lassen uns, trotz der trennenden Glasscheibe, eine Gänsehaut den Rücken hinunterlaufen.

Stichlinge, Elritzen und Moderlieschen, die unscheinbaren Bewohner heimischer Gewässer, haben hier ebenso ihren Platz wie „gute alte Bekannte“ aus dem Aquarium – Guppys, Schwertträger, Rote Neon und Keilfleckbarben.

Schauen, staunen, Neues entdecken, Bekanntes beim Namen nennen, von fernen Ländern und Meeren träumen – all das und noch viel mehr kann man in einem Schauaquarium. Auch dann noch, wenn es nicht ganz still und nicht ganz leer ist, weil wir nicht die einzigen Besucher sind, die sich in diese faszinierenden Welten entführen lassen wollen.

Pflege- und Versorgungsgang hinter der Süßwasserabteilung

Der Aufwand lohnt

Nur zoologische Gärten und Parks, Museen und ähnliche Institutionen mit naturwissenschaftlicher Leitung und Betreuung können solche Schauaquarien unterhalten, denn der Aufwand ist groß. Tausende von Fischen, Pflanzen und niederen Tieren mit ganz unterschiedlichen Futter- und Pflegeansprüchen wollen versorgt sein. Die technischen Anlagen müssen überwacht und gepflegt werden.

Der reine Schaucharakter solcher Anlagen, der früher oft mit dem Ausstellen von Skurrilitäten und Sensationen verbunden war, ist in den letzten Jahrzehnten etwas in den Hintergrund getreten. Natürlich möchte man auch heute – zur Freude des Publikums – herzeigen, was man hat. Hinzugekommen sind aber pädagogische Aufgaben: Die Nachbildung natürlicher Lebensräume mit ihren typischen Bewohnern, erläuternde Tafeln, Führungen und Sonderausstellungen gehen über das reine Zeigen von Tieren hinaus.

Neueren Datums sind auch Belange des Arten- und Naturschutzes. Zoos sind oft die einzigen Überlebensstätten von Tierarten, deren Lebensraum in der Natur zerstört worden ist. Tiere, die aufgrund der gesetzlichen Bestimmungen von „Privatleuten“ nicht

gepflegt werden dürfen (z.B. bestimmte Gruppen von Meerwasserfischen), können zumindest in Schauaquarien bewundert werden. Die Zoos tauschen übrigens nachgezüchtete Tiere untereinander aus, so daß immer weniger „Nachschub“ aus der Natur entnommen zu werden braucht.

Seit jeher werden in zoologischen Gärten und Schauaquarien Forschungen angestellt und Erfahrungen gesammelt und ausgetauscht, die nicht nur der weiteren Verbesserung der Pflege und Zucht dienen, sondern von denen auch die Aquaristik profitiert.

Hinter den Kulissen

Sind schon die Schaubecken beeindruckend, so ist es für den Interessierten erst recht ein Blick hinter die Kulissen eines Schauaquariums. Solche Führungen mit sachkundigen Erklärungen werden von manchen Einrichtungen auf Wunsch und nach Anmeldung von Zeit zu Zeit angeboten.

Und was gibt es da nicht alles zu sehen: Dimension und Menge der Leitungen und Ventile, Absperr- und Umleitungshähne an allen Ecken und Enden erinnern an große Wasserversorgungsunternehmen.

Große Filteranlagen halten das Wasser mechanisch und biologisch sauber. Sorgfältig aufbereitetes Frischwasser wird für den Teilwasserwechsel und das Nachfüllen von verdunstetem Wasser bereitgehalten. Alle Wasserwerte werden ständig überwacht, so daß kontinuierliche, optimale Bedingungen für die verschiedenen Pfleglinge gewährleistet sind, die ja ganz unterschiedliche Ansprüche an das Wasser haben – Meerwasser, Brackwasser, Süßwasser mit unterschiedlichen pH- und Härtewerten usw.

Neben den Schaubecken befinden sich hinter den Kulissen weitere Aquarien für die Zucht und Aufzucht von Jungfischen, für Forschungszwecke, die Behandlung kranker Tiere und die Quarantäne von Neuankömmlingen.

Fünf Pumpen versorgen ein Großbecken von 230 000 Liter Inhalt.

Überdimensionale Außenfilter: Rieseltürme.

biologischen System Aquarium existieren jedoch verschiedene Bakterien, die die Chelatoren „knacken" können, und damit sind die Nährstoffe für die Pflanzen erst einmal verloren. Anstelle des oft empfohlenen Verfahrens bei Wasserwechsel nachzudüngen, sollte man lieber häufiger, dafür aber weniger nachdüngen und so für ein gleichmäßiges Nährstoffangebot sorgen. Die optimale Dosierung muß durch Kontrolle mit einem Eisentest „ertastet" werden. Gehalte um 0,1 mg/l sind wünschenswert.

Bodengrund

Der Bodengrund dient nicht nur der Verankerung der Pflanzen, sondern auch als Nährstoffdepot vor allem für solche Pflanzen, die aufgrund ihrer natürlichen Lebensweise als Sumpfpflanzen (*Cryptocoryne, Echinodorus*) an eine Nährstoffzufuhr aus dem Boden gewöhnt sind.

Der Vorteil eisenhaltiger Bodenbeimischungen ist heute unumstritten, entsprechende Produkte werden von verschiedenen Herstellern angeboten. Leider haben sie alle einen Nachteil: Ist man irgendwann einmal gezwungen, Pflanzen zu entfernen oder zu versetzen, geht dies nicht ohne eine unschöne Wassertrübung. Man kann auf solche Beimengungen verzichten, allerdings dauert dann die Anwachsphase wesentlich länger. Als Mittelweg könnte man nur solche Pflanzen, die auf Nährstoffe „von unten" angewiesen sind, mit den zahlreichen im Handel angebotenen Düngekugeln aus Ton oder Laterit versorgen.

Ein wichtiges Kriterium, das der Bodengrund erfüllen muß, ist die Durchlässigkeit, um eine ausreichende Bodenwasserzirkulation zu gewährleisten. Am besten bewährt hat sich dafür feiner Kies mit einer Körnung von 2 bis 3 mm. Die Wasserzirkulation im Boden kann durch Verlegung eines Heizkabels auf der Bodenscheibe optimal gefördert werden. Dadurch werden faulende Stellen im Boden verhindert, den Pflanzen werden neue Nährstoffe zugeführt, und es entsteht kein Temperaturgefälle zwischen Wasser und Bodengrund.

Gestalten mit Pflanzen

Den Fischen wäre die Anordnung und die Auswahl der Pflanzen ja gleichgültig, Hauptsache sie wachsen gut und leisten ihre wertvollen Dienste. Da wir Aquarianer und noch mehr die zu begeisternden (noch) Nichtaquarianer jedoch Wert auf Ästhetik legen, darf und soll das dekorative Potential, das in den zahlreichen verschiedenen Pflanzenarten ruht, auch ruhig ausgenutzt werden.

Eines sollten Sie dabei jedoch lassen: Pflanzen, die eigentlich ans Blumenfenster gehören, zu Wasserpflanzen zu vergewaltigen! Leider werden derartige Gewächse auch immer wieder im Zoofachhandel angeboten. Wie war das doch gleich mit Angebot und Nachfrage? Werden Sie mißtrauisch, wenn eine „Wasserpflanze" verdächtig bunt ist und Sie an Ihr Wohnzimmerfenster erinnert! Solche Pflanzen sind für die Biologie im Aquarium wertlos. Sie sterben nur mehr oder weniger langsam vor sich hin und verpesten das Wasser.

Durch Kombination verschiedener Blattformen und Wuchshöhen können Aquarien spannungsvoll gestaltet werden.

Ein Loch in den Bodengrund drücken, die Wurzeln hineinhalten, vorsichtig das Loch zuschieben und den Bodengrund andrücken. Nicht zu tief pflanzen: Der Wurzelhals muß immer sichtbar bleiben.

Aquarienpflanzen gibt es in verschiedenen Wuchsformen, Farben und Größen. Es gilt, aus diesen Möglichkeiten ein abwechslungsreiches, aber harmonisches Gesamtbild zu gestalten. Dazu einige Tips: Hochwachsende Stengelpflanzen und ausläuferbildende Rosettenpflanzen (zum Beispiel Vallisnerien) verwendet man für den Hintergrund und zum Verdecken von Geräten, wie Heizer, Filteransaugrohr und so weiter.

Mittel- und Vordergrund werden in absteigender Wuchshöhe mit mittelhohen und niedrigen Pflanzen besetzt. Große Einzelpflanzen dienen als Blickfang und sollten nicht genau in die Mitte gepflanzt werden. Stengelpflanzen und ausläuferbildende Pflanzen immer in Gruppen, nie einzeln pflanzen. Schaffen Sie Farb- und Formkontraste: Feinfiedrige Pflanzen neben breitblättrigen, rötliche neben grünen, dunkelgrüne neben hellgrünen und so weiter.

Sparen Sie am Anfang nicht am falschen Ende und bepflanzen Sie Ihr Aquarium von Anfang an dicht, um so schneller werden die Anfangsschwierigkeiten überwunden sein. Wenn Sie sich zum Einsatz einer CO_2-Düngung entschlossen haben, besorgen Sie sich als Erstbesatz möglichst viele schnellwachsende Stengelpflanzen. Damit machen Sie von Anfang an den Algen das Leben schwer. Später können einige schnellwachsende Pflanzen durch langsam wachsende ersetzt werden.

Für ein Aquarium ohne CO_2-Düngung sollten, aus den bereits erwähnten Gründen, nur langsam wachsende Pflanzen verwendet werden. Deshalb muß hier besonders in der Anfangsphase verstärkt auf Algen geachtet werden und es darf nur vorsichtig gedüngt werden.

Einsetzen der Pflanzen

Befreien Sie die Pflanzen nach dem Kauf von allen mitgelieferten Töpfen, Steinwolle, Schaumstoffstreifen und Bleidraht! Steinwolle und Schaumstoffstreifen enthalten oft noch Reste der Nährlösung, in der die Pflanzen in Gärtnereien gezüchtet wurden. Diese Nährlösung enthält Nitrat und Phosphat und darf nicht ins Aquarium gelangen.

Verletzte Blätter und Stengelteile werden sauber abgetrennt. Wurzeln von Rosettenpflanzen auf etwa 3 cm zurückstutzen. Stengelpflanzen werden vorsichtig einzeln in den Kies gedrückt, dabei den Stengel nicht quetschen. Für Rosettenpflanzen bohrt man mit dem Finger ein Loch und setzt die Pflanze tief hinein, deckt mit Kies ab und zieht die Pflanze dann bis zum Wurzelhals wieder heraus.

Verschiedene Aufsitzerpflanzen, wie zum Beispiel der Javafarn *(Microsorium)* oder das Zwergspeerblatt *(Anubias barteri var. nana)* dürfen nicht in den Boden eingepflanzt werden. Man bindet sie mit Nylonfaden auf Moorkienholz oder Steinen fest. Schwimmpflanzen läßt man auf der Wasseroberfläche treiben. Sie benötigen zum Wohlbefinden einen ausreichenden Luftraum über dem Wasser. Am besten gedei-

Beim Neu- und Umpflanzen werden die Wurzeln eingekürzt.

hen sie in Aquarien ohne Abdekkung, mit Hängeleuchten (zum Beispiel HQL).

Wenn Sie alles eingepflanzt haben, benötigen die Pflanzen Ruhe zum Anwachsen. Während der ersten zwei Wochen nur sehr sparsam oder überhaupt nicht düngen, da sich die Pflanzen erst an das neue Milieu anpassen müssen. Viele Pflanzen werden in Gärtnereien außerhalb des Wassers gezüchtet und müssen sich erst durch Bildung von Wasserblättern an die veränderte Situation anpassen. Deshalb wird sich auch der Anblick der Pflanzen mit der Zeit ändern, da die Wasserblätter anders aussehen als die Luftblätter.

Versetzen Sie Ihre Pflanzen (Ausnahme: Stengelpflanzen) so selten wie möglich. Bei jedem Umsetzen bekommen sie einen Umpflanzschock, von dem sie sich erst wieder erholen müssen.

Vermehrung von Pflanzen

Ausläufer: Am einfachsten, weil ohne unser Zutun, geschieht die Vermehrung durch Ausläufer. Wenn

die Pflanzen den Umpflanzschock überwunden haben und einige Zeit kräftig gewachsen sind, bilden sie Ausläufer, an deren Ende sich Jungpflanzen bilden. Dadurch verdichtet sich der Bestand. Wenn er zu dicht geworden ist oder die Pflanzen über den ihnen zugedachten Bereich hinausgewachsen sind, können Jungpflanzen abgetrennt und verpflanzt werden, wenn sie vier bis fünf Blätter haben.

Nach einer gewissen Zeit müssen Altpflanzen aus dem Bestand entfernt und durch junge ersetzt werden, um ein „Vergreisen" des Bestands zu verhindern. Die Ausläuferbildung geht je nach Pflanzenart verschieden schnell vor sich. Cryptocorynen lassen sich eher Zeit, während Vallisnerien in kurzer Zeit dichte Bestände bilden.

Eine besondere Art der Vermehrung zeigt der Hornfarn oder Sumatrafarn *(Ceratopteris)*. Ältere Schwimmblätter bilden am Rand viele kleine Jungpflänzchen, die nach einiger Zeit abgetrennt werden können. Ähnliche Jungpflan-

zen, jedoch wesentlich weniger, bildet der Javafarn *(Microsorium)*.

Pseudoviviparie: Zahlreiche Amazonasschwertpflanzen bilden im Aquarium bereitwillig Blütentriebe. Wenn man diese Blütentriebe daran hindert, die Wasseroberfläche zu erreichen (Beschweren mit einem Stein), bilden sie als „Notlösung" zahlreiche Jungpflanzen aus. Wenn diese kräftig genug sind, kann man sie vorsichtig abtrennen und einpflanzen.

Vermehrung durch Samen: Eine Vermehrung durch Samen kommt im Aquarium relativ selten vor. Einige *Aponogeton*-Arten (Wasserähren) bilden regelmäßig Blütenstände aus, die teils spontan Samen ansetzen oder mit einem weichen Pinsel befruchtet werden können. Für die Aufzucht der Sämlinge finden sich Anweisungen in der einschlägigen Literatur.

Stecklinge: Alle Stengelpflanzen werden mehr oder weniger schnell die Wasseroberfläche erreichen und entweder herauswachsen oder an der Wasseroberfläche entlangwachsen. Man kann auf zweierlei Weise vorgehen: Will man den Bestand vermehren, so trennt man die Stengel etwa in der Mitte durch und setzt die abgeschnittenen Triebspitzen wieder ein. Der verbleibende Stumpf wird zwei oder mehr Neutriebe bringen, die bei Erreichen der Wasseroberfläche ebenfalls abgetrennt und eingepflanzt werden können. Nach einiger Zeit treiben die unteren Stengelteile nicht mehr aus und müssen entfernt werden. Viele Stengelpflanzen bilden auch

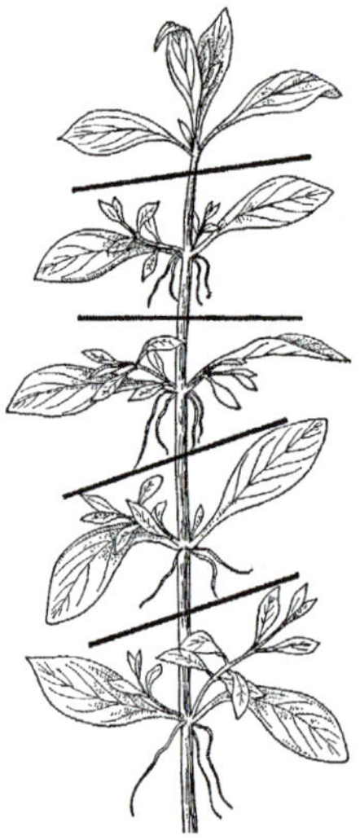

spontan Seitensprosse, die abgetrennt und eingepflanzt werden können.

Will man den Bestand nicht mehr weiter vermehren und immer einen schönen Anblick genießen, so muß man die Stengel regelmäßig herausziehen, unten einkürzen und das obere Teil wieder einpflanzen. Dabei verfährt man so, daß die Höhe der Pflanzen von vorne nach hinten stufenförmig ansteigt. Diese Methode ist allerdings mit relativ viel Arbeit verbunden.

Partner der Fische – ausgewählte Pflanzenarten

In diesem Abschnitt wollen wir Ihnen eine Auswahl gut zu pflegender Pflanzen für das Aquarium vorstellen, die normalerweise das ganze Jahr über zu bekommen sind. Es gibt selbstverständlich wesentlich mehr Arten, die für das Aquarium geeignet sind. Mit der Zeit werden Sie sicher auch Pflanzen finden, die hier nicht erwähnt sind.

Betrachten Sie die folgende Einteilung in Pflanzen für den Hintergrund, mittlere Beckenpartien, Vordergrund und Solitärpflanzen nicht als Evangelium. Ob eine Pflanze für den Hintergrund oder den mittleren Beckenbereich zu verwenden ist, hängt von der beabsichtigten Dekorationswirkung und der Beckengröße ab.

Die nachfolgend aufgeführten Pflanzen sind bei 5 bis 15 °d Karbonathärte, pH-Werten zwischen 6,8 und 7,4 und Temperaturen um 25 °C problemlos zu halten. Pflanzen mit der Angabe „CO_2-Düngung empfehlenswert" können auch ohne CO_2-Düngung wachsen. Dabei muß allerdings damit gerechnet werden, daß manche Pflanzen aufgrund der CO_2-Konkurrenz durch andere das Wachstum einstellen. Die Pflanzen werden meist auch weniger stattlich. Besonderheiten sind bei den jeweiligen Arten angegeben. H = ungefähre Wuchshöhe der Pflanze.

Pflanzen für Hintergrund und Seiten

1 Karolina-Haarnixe
Cabomba caroliniana
Schnellwachsend, hoher Lichtbedarf, CO_2-Düngung erforderlich, bildet bei Erreichen der Wasseroberfläche Seitentriebe, durch feinfiedrige Blätter guter Kontrast zu breitblättrigen Arten, H 45–60 cm.

2 Thailand-Hakenlilie
Crinum thaianum
Sehr groß werdende Pflanze, die jedoch für Aquarien gut geeignet ist, mittlerer bis hoher Lichtbedarf, CO_2-Düngung empfehlenswert, in größeren Becken auch als Solitärpflanze, Blätter treiben an Wasseroberfläche, vertragen zeitweiligen Rückschnitt, Zwiebel braucht tiefen Bodengrund, H bis 200 cm.

3 Seegrasblättriges Trugkölbchen
Heteranthera zosterifolia
Mäßig schnell wachsend, hoher Lichtbedarf, bei Härte unter 10 °d Wachstum ohne CO_2-Düngung möglich, bei sehr starker Beleuchtung gedrungener Wuchs, dadurch auch für Mittelgrund geeignet, H bis 50 cm.

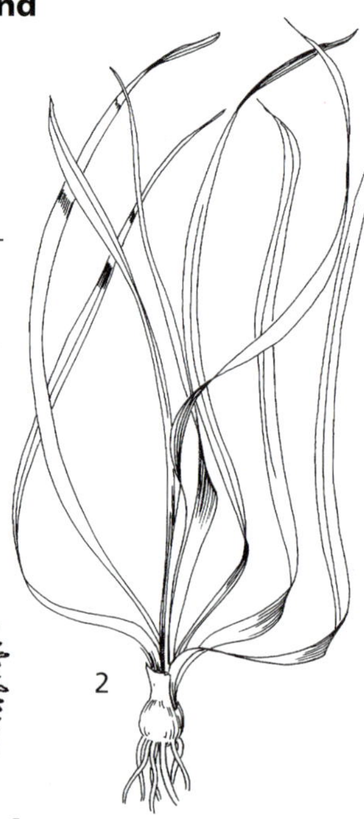

2

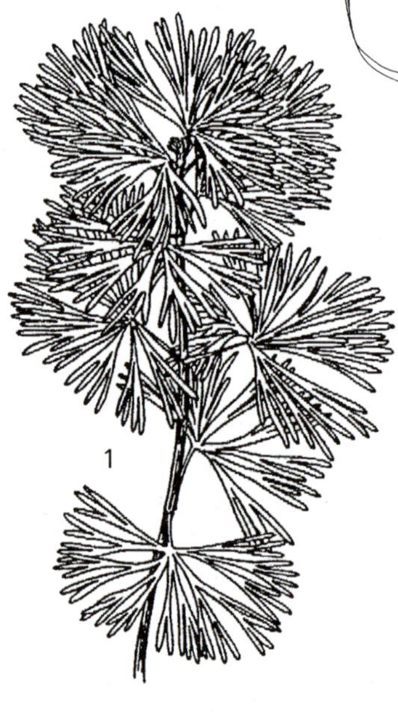

1

3

Ein Besuch beim Wasserpflanzenzüchter

Wir hielten uns wieder einmal zu einem der leider viel zu seltenen Besuche bei unseren thailändischen Freunden in der alten Königsstadt Ayuthaya auf. Eines Tages meinte unser Freund, er müsse einige Riesengurami-Jungfische nach Chachoengsao bringen. Sie würden in Deutschland für wissenschaftliche Untersuchungen benötigt, und der Besitzer einer Wasserpflanzenfarm in Chachoengsao würde den Transport für ihn arrangieren.

Beim Wort Wasserpflanzenfarm wurden wir hellhörig und fragten, ob er denn noch Platz habe, uns mitzunehmen und auch etwas Zeit, so daß wir diese Farm besichtigen könnten. Selbstverständlich konnten wir mitkommen, und zum vereinbarten Termin ging es in einem schlecht gefederten Pick-up, der auch schon bessere Zeiten erlebt hatte, ab nach Chachoengsao.

Unser Freund machte uns zunächst mit dem Besitzer der Farm bekannt und schilderte ihm unser Anliegen. Dieser bedauerte es sehr, uns seine Farm nicht persönlich zeigen zu können, da er geschäftlich zu tun habe, aber wir könnten uns nach Lust und Laune selbst umschauen. Dies taten wir dann auch, während unser Freund seine Fische ablieferte und die nötigen Formalitäten erledigte.

Nachdem man uns durch das Bürogebäude geführt hatte, betraten wir ein riesiges Areal, das, soweit das Auge reichte, mit Schattennetzen auf Holzkonstruktionen überspannt war, um die sengenden Strahlen der tropischen Sonne fernzuhalten. Glashäuser braucht man hier nicht, die Heizung gibt's kostenlos. Wir schlenderten eine ganze Weile mit zwei bis drei herrenlosen Hunden im Schlepp durch das „Schattenreich", bis unserem durch die Tropensonne etwas „ausgedörrtem" Gehirn bewußt wurde, daß wir uns ja in einer Wasserpflanzengärtnerei befinden und bis jetzt noch kein bißchen Wasser gesehen hatten.

Wasserpflanzen auf dem Trockenen

Sämtliche Pflanzen wuchsen in Reih und Glied in säuberlich angelegten Beeten mit hier überall natürlich vorkommendem, zwar recht feuchtem Boden, aber von Wasser konnte keine Rede sein. So langsam arbeiteten unsere grauen Zellen wieder und der biologische Sachverstand setzte sich durch: Die meisten unserer Aquarienpflanzen sind ja Sumpfpflanzen und lassen

Mit Netzen abgeschattete „Trockenbeete".

sich natürlich auch ohne Wasser kultivieren, was wesentlich einfacher und rationeller geht. Außerdem seien sie weniger empfindlich beim Transport, wie uns der Besitzer der Farm später erklärte.

Langsam gewöhnten wir uns an das Bild und nach mehrmaligem Hinsehen erkannten wir auch manch aquaristisch Bekanntes. Die Reihen der mit Netzen beschatteten Beete wurden hin und wieder von idyllisch gelegenen, palmenbeschatteten Teichen unterbrochen. Zwischen herrlich blühenden Seerosen und Lotospflanzen erkannten wir einige Hechtlinge, Bärblinge und Labyrinthfische, aber auch räuberische Schlangenkopffische.

Beim Eintritt in die nächste „Schattengalerie" änderte sich das Bild. Statt der bisher üblichen Beete trafen wir nun auf lange Reihen flacher Betonbecken, teils nur mit einem Gemisch aus Erde und Kies gefüllt. Der überwiegende Teil war jedoch „geflutet", Wasserstand ca. 40 cm, und in dem bereits erwähnten Erde-Kies-Gemisch als Bodengrund standen in Reih und Glied alte Bekannte in verschiedener Größe, angefangen bei winzigen Jungpflanzen bis hin zu verkaufsreifen Exemplaren. Wir fanden verschiedene *Aponogeton*-Arten, *Cryptocorynen, Echinodorus, Hygrophila difformis* und andere.

Hygrophila difformis ***in submerser Kultur.***

In der Mitte jedes dieser Betonbecken stand in schwerem Betonrahmen, mit der Öffnung unter Wasser, ein etwa 60 Liter fassendes Aquarium, dessen Funktion uns anfänglich nicht klar war. Auf unserem weiteren Weg durch die Reihen der Betonbecken begegneten wir einem Angestellten, der aus einer großen Stahlflasche die umgedrehten Aquarien mit CO_2 füllte – jetzt war uns alles klar!

Die „umgedrehten Aquarien" werden mit CO_2 gefüllt.

Nach etwa einer Stunde Rundgang kehrten wir schweißgebadet ins Bürogebäude zurück, wo man uns mit der sprichwörtlichen thailändischen Gastfreundschaft eine Erfrischung kredenzte und sämtliche verfügbaren Ventilatoren auf uns richtete. Es fand sich auch noch die Gelegenheit zu einem kurzen Gespräch mit dem Besitzer. Er zählte uns alle Länder auf, in die er seine Pflanzen exportiert; Deutschland war auch dabei.

Es interessierte uns noch, ob hier alle Pflanzen selbst vermehrt werden oder ob auch Naturentnahmen stattfinden. Bereitwillig erklärte uns der Besitzer, daß vor allem die in Thailand nicht heimischen Pflanzen gezüchtet werden, während verschiedene heimische Arten der Natur entnommen und nur zu Verkaufsgröße herangezogen werden. Unser Freund hatte mittlerweile seine Geschäfte erledigt, so bedankten wir uns und fuhren zurück nach Ayuthaya.

1 Indischer Wasserwedel
Hygrophila difformis
Schnell wachsend, hoher Lichtbedarf, CO_2-Düngung empfehlenswert, sehr dekorativ, bei zu wenig Licht weniger stark geschlitzte Blätter, H 50 cm.

2 Indischer Wasserfreund
Hygrophila polysperma
Schnell wachsend, mittlerer bis hoher Lichtbedarf, CO_2-Düngung empfehlenswert, hellgrüne Blätter, rötliche Blattfärbung nur bei starkem Licht, eine der populärsten Aquarienpflanzen, H 50 cm.

3 Madagaskar Wasserpest
Lagarosiphon madagascariensis
Schnell wachsend, hoher Lichtbedarf, CO_2-Düngung, kann freitreibend oder im Boden verankert kultiviert werden, Beschattung durch andere Gewächse meiden, H variabel.

4 Sumpffreund
Limnophila sessiliflora
Schnell wachsend, hoher Lichtbedarf, CO_2-Düngung empfehlenswert, ähnliche Form wie *Cabomba,* jedoch leichter zu halten, H 60 cm.

Bastardludwigie, Kriechende Ludwigie
Ludwigia repens
Mäßig schnell wachsend, hoher Lichtbedarf, CO_2-Düngung empfehlenswert, rötliche Färbung nur bei genügend Licht, etwas empfindlich gegen Temperaturen über 28 °C, H 50 cm.

5 Rundblättrige Rotala
Rotala rotundifolia
Schnell wachsend, hoher Lichtbedarf, CO_2-Düngung empfehlenswert, rötliche Blattspitzen, H 50 cm.

1

2

3

5

4

6 Mexikanisches Eichenblatt
Shinnersia rivularis
Sehr schnell wachsend, hoher Lichtbedarf, starker CO_2-Verbrauch, Blattform erinnert an Eichenlaub, empfindlich gegen Temperaturen über 25 °C, H 60 cm.

7 Schraubenvallisnerie
Vallisneria asiatica var. biwaensis
Mäßig schnell wachsend, hoher Lichtbedarf, CO_2-Düngung empfehlenswert, in größeren Becken auch für den Mittelgrund geeignet, eng gedrehte Blätter, Ausläuferbildung, H 25–30 cm.

8 Gewöhnliche Sumpfschraube
Vallisneria spiralis
Schnell wachsend, mäßig hoher Lichtbedarf, starker CO_2-Verbrauch, sonst anspruchslos, Ausläuferbildung, H 40–60 cm.

Pflanzen für den mittleren Bereich

Die hier aufgeführten Pflanzen eignen sich in kleineren Aquarien auch für den Hintergrund und können in größeren Becken auch als Solitärpflanze oder in einer Gruppe als Blickfang eingesetzt werden.

Papageienblatt
Alternanthera reineckii
Langsam wachsend, prächtig rot gefärbte Blätter, hoher Lichtbedarf, CO_2-Düngung, nicht durch andere Pflanzen beschatten, Wachstumsstop bei CO_2-Mangel, hoher Dekorationswert in Gruppe mit nach hinten ansteigender Stengellänge, H variabel, um 50 cm.

9 Große Kognakpflanze
Ammania gracilis
Mäßig schnell wachsend, hoher Lichtbedarf, CO_2-Düngung, rötlichbraune Blätter mit guter Kontrastwirkung zu anderen Pflanzen, keine Abschattung durch andere Pflanzen. *Ammania senegalensis:* ähnlich, jedoch kleinere Blätter, H 50 cm

10 Härtels Wasserkelch
Cryptocoryne affinis
Anspruchslos, langsam bis mäßig schnell wachsend, mäßiger Lichtbedarf, Blätter je nach Licht unterschiedlich gefärbt, Ausläufer, H um 20 cm, bei starkem Licht auch größer.

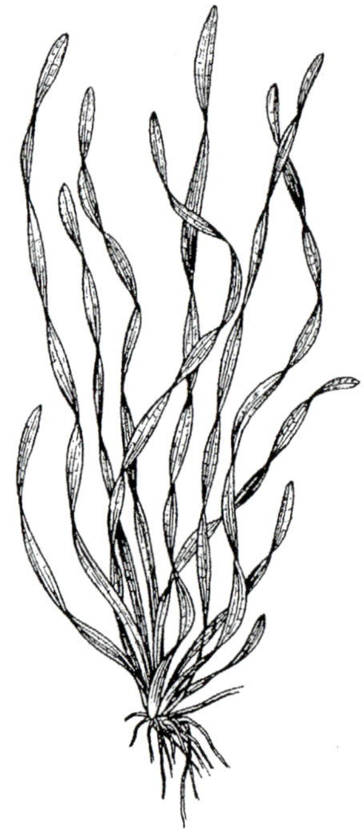

7

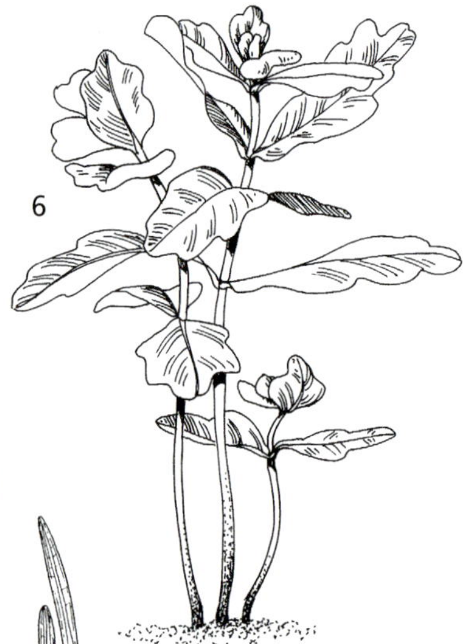

6

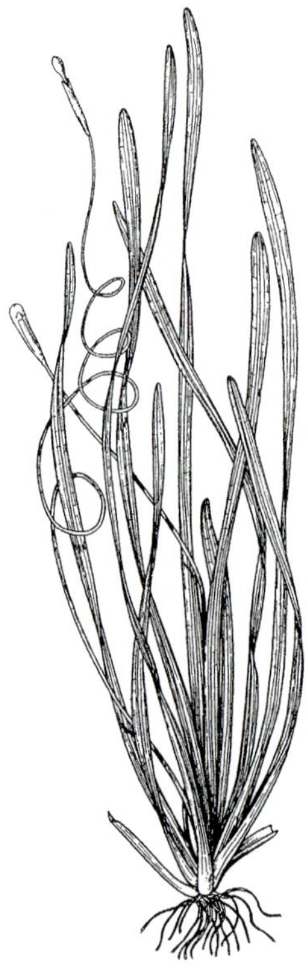

8

9

10

1 Genoppter Wasserkelch
Cryptocoryne crispatula
Langsam wachsend, hoher Lichtbedarf, CO_2-Düngung empfehlenswert, genoppte, schmale, dunkelgrüne Blätter, Ausläufer, H bis 40 cm.

2 Pontederiablättriger Wasserkelch
Cryptocoryne pontederiifolia
Anpassungsfähig, langsam wachsend, mäßiger Lichtbedarf, Blätter leuchtend grün, herzförmig, Ausläufer, H 20–30 cm.

Wendt's Wasserkelch
Cryptocoryne wendtii
Anspruchslos, mäßig schnell wachsend, mäßiger Lichtbedarf, Blätter sehr variabel in Form und Farbe, Ausläufer, in größeren Becken auch als Vordergrundpflanze geeignet, bekannteste und am weitesten verbreitete Cryptocoryne,H 8–15 cm.

3 Kardinalslobelie
Lobelia cardinalis
Steife, langsam wachsende Stengelpflanze, hoher Lichtbedarf, erreicht mit CO_2-Düngung stattliche Größe, sonst zierlicher, Pflanzung in Gruppe mit aufsteigender Höhe, H bis 50 cm.

4 Javafarn
Microsorium pteropus
Langsam bis mäßig schnell wachsend, mäßiger Lichtbedarf, anpassungsfähig, Vermehrung durch Adventivpflanzen an den Blättern, Rhizom darf nicht in den Boden eingegraben werden, auf Steinen oder Wurzelholz befestigen, ältere Blätter können schwärzliche Flecken bekommen, H um 20 cm.

Rotweiderich
Rotala macrandra
Mäßig schnell wachsend, hoher Lichtbedarf, CO_2-Düngung, herrlich rote, rundliche Blätter, gute Kontrastwirkung, ohne CO_2-Düngung schwer zu halten, H 50 cm.

1

3

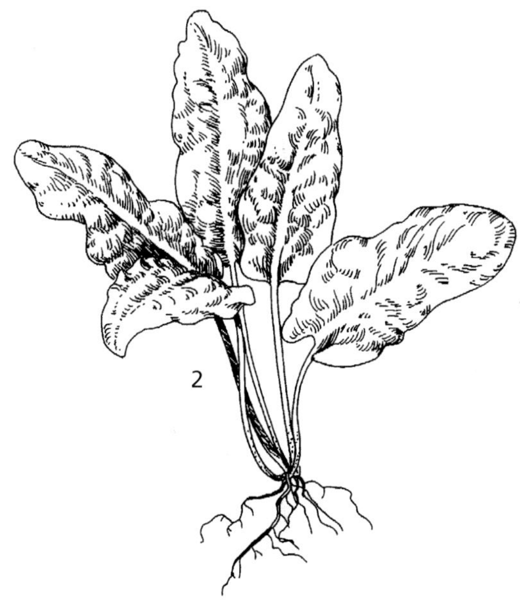
2

5 Breitblättriges Pfeilkraut
Sagittaria graminea var. platyphylla
Mäßig schnell wachsend, hoher Lichtbedarf, CO_2-Düngung empfehlenswert, steife, breitbandförmige Blätter, die auch gegen robustere Fische unempfindlich sind, Ausläufer, H bis 30 cm.

6 Javamoos
Vesicularia dubyana
Mäßig schnell wachsend, mäßiger Lichtbedarf, anspruchslos, hervorragendes Versteck für Jungfische, auf Steinen oder Wurzelholz verankern, H variabel.

Pflanzen für den Vordergrund

7 Zwergspeerblatt
Anubias barteri var. nana
Langsam wachsend, hoher bis mäßiger Lichtbedarf, CO_2-Düngung empfehlenswert, Rhizom darf auf keinen Fall in den Boden eingegraben werden, wächst auch als Aufsitzer auf Steinen oder Wurzelholz, die steifen Blätter werden gern von Pinselalgen besiedelt, H 10–15 cm.

8 Kleiner Wasserkelch
Cryptocoryne x willisii
Langsam wachsend, mäßiger Lichtbedarf, leicht zu pflegende Art, bildet durch Ausläufer dichte Polster, H um 10 cm.

8

4

6

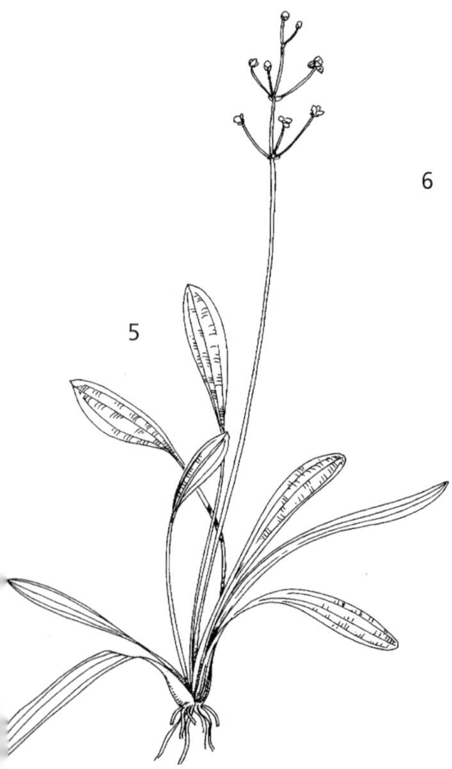

5

7

1 Zwergschwertpflanze
Echinodorus quadricostatus* var. *xinguensis
Mäßig schnell wachsend, hoher Lichtbedarf, keine Abschattung, CO_2-Düngung empfehlenswert, sonst robust, Ausläufer, H 10 cm.

2 Samolusblättrige Schwertpflanze
***Echinodorus parviflorus* „Tropica"**
Langsam wachsend, mäßiger Lichtbedarf, CO_2-Düngung empfehlenswert, neue dekorative Zuchtform mit dichtstehenden, leicht genoppten Blättern, Adventivpflanzen an Blütenstengeln, H bis 10 cm.

Grasartige Schwertpflanze
Echinodorus tenellus
Mäßig schnell wachsend, hoher Lichtbedarf, CO_2-Düngung, anspruchsvoll, keine Abschattung, entwickelt durch Ausläufer niedrigen Rasen, ähnelt *E. quadricostatus,* hat aber schmalere Blätter, H 5 cm.

3 Zwergpfeilkraut
Sagittaria subulata f. pusilla
Mäßig schnell wachsend, mäßiger Lichtbedarf, leicht zu pflegen, Rasenbildung durch Ausläufer, H 5–10 cm.

Solitärpflanzen

Die hier aufgeführten Pflanzen dienen in Einzelexemplaren als Blickfang im Aquarium. Einige können in großen Aquarien auch als Gruppe gepflanzt werden.

4 Salatblättrige Wasserähre
Aponogeton ulvaceus
Sehr schnell wachsend, mäßiger bis hoher Lichtbedarf, CO_2-Düngung empfehlenswert, hellgrüne, dekorative, gewellte Blätter, Knolle nicht ganz eingraben, macht Ruheperiode durch, H 50 cm.

5 Langblättrige Barclaya
Barclaya longifolia
Langsam wachsend, hoher Lichtbedarf, keine Abschattung, CO_2-Düngung, eine der schönsten Aquarienpflanzen überhaupt, olivgrüne bis rötlich getönte, gewellte Blätter, keine „kalten Füße", Höhe bis 30 cm.

1

3

6 Sumatrafarn, Wasserhornfarn
Ceratopteris thalictroides
Schnell wachsend, anspruchslos, CO_2-Düngung empfehlenswert, Schwimmform möglich, kann leicht dominieren, H 40 cm.

2

5

6

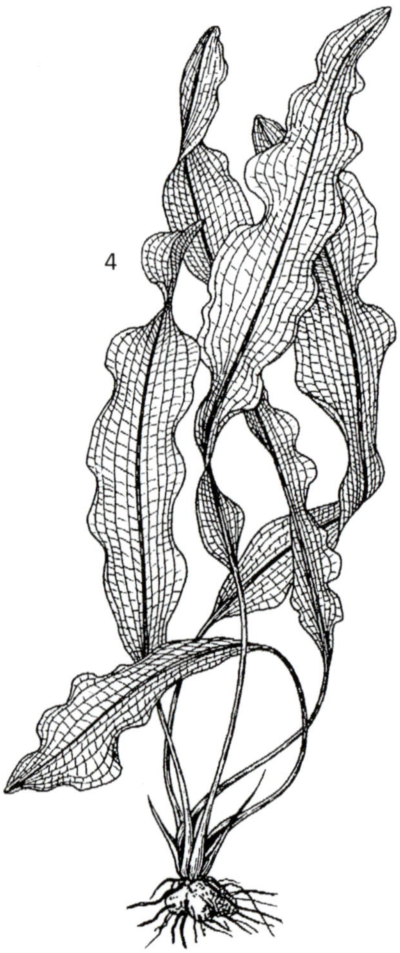

4

Hauptsache pflege-leicht ...

Für den attraktiven Luftbefeuchter mit Fischdekoration gibt es fast keine Accessoires mehr, die es nicht gibt. Sollten Sie keinen grünen Daumen haben und Ihnen das Glück in bezug auf die Unterwassergärtnerei nicht hold sein, dann verzweifeln Sie nicht: Hygienisch, farbenfroh und so lebensnah, wie Plastik nur sein kann, gibt es sie, die Plastikpflanzen! In allen erdenklichen Ausführungen treiben sie unter Wasser bunte Blüten. In „Naturausführung" geht die Natürlichkeit so weit, daß die Plastikstengel bald von Algen besiedelt werden.

So wie der Bodengrund zur Tapete zu passen hat, so läßt auch die Zubehörindustrie in bezug auf die Dekoration keine Wünsche mehr offen. Wer sagt denn, daß Pflanzen nur grün, gelb, rot oder braun auszusehen haben? Pflegeleicht sind sie, bei falscher Beleuchtung nehmen sie kein kümmerliches Aussehen an und verschandeln so die Aussicht auf die Fische. Ausdünnen, umsetzen und düngen braucht man sie jedenfalls nicht.

Und die Vegetarier unter den Fischen können ihnen nicht den Garaus machen: Ein gieriger Goldfisch kann sie ebensowenig verdauen wie die kleine Welsbande, dieses lichtscheue Gesindel, welches mit Vorliebe Blätter durchlöchert ...

Geschmacksache

Doch eines können sie nicht: Sauerstoff produzieren und ein Aquarium zum wirklichen Biotop werden lassen. Doch wozu gibt es Ausströmer?

1 Blass-Wasserkelch
Cryptocoryne cordata blassii
Langsam wachsend, geringer Lichtbedarf, evtl. durch Schwimmpflanzen abschatten, CO_2-Düngung, zwei verschieden hohe Wuchsformen im Handel, braunrote, große Blätter, möglichst wenig stören, H 30–40 cm.

2 Amazonasschwertpflanze
Echinodorus amazonicus
Mäßig schnell wachsend, mäßiger bis hoher Lichtbedarf, CO_2-Düngung empfehlenswert, anpassungsfähig, bekannteste aller Schwertpflanzen, Jungpflanzen an Blütenstiel, H 30–40 cm.

Rotblättrige Amazonasschwertpflanze
Echinodorus osiris
Mäßig schnell wachsend, hoher Lichtbedarf, CO_2-Düngung, sehr dekorative Pflanze, Varianten mit verschieden ausgeprägter Rotfärbung im Handel, keine Abschattung, Jungpflanzen an Blütenstiel, H 30–50 cm.

3 Thailändischer Wasserfreund
Hygrophila stricta
Schnell wachsend, hoher Lichtbedarf, CO_2-Düngung empfehlenswert, Stengelpflanze mit großen, hellgrünen, an Pfirsichlaub erinnernden Blättern, untere Teile verkahlen bei zu wenig Licht oder wenn die Pflanze über den Wasserspiegel wächst, H 50 cm.

4 Roter Tigerlotus
Nymphaea lotus
Mäßig schnell wachsend, hoher Lichtbedarf, keine Abschattung, CO_2-Düngung, herrliche, rote Unterwasserblätter mit dunklen Flecken, Schwimmblätter abtrennen, H 30–50 cm.

Schwimmpflanzen

Schwimmpflanzen tragen durch ihre Saugwurzeln wesentlich zum Abbau von Schadstoffen im Wasser bei. Der CO_2-Bedarf wird, außer bei Riccia, aus der Luft gedeckt. Lichthungrige Unterwasserpflanzen dürfen nicht durch Schwimmpflanzen abgeschattet werden. Bei abgedeckten Aquarien auf genügend Luftraum zwischen Wasser und Abdekkung achten!

1

5 Schwimmender Wasserhornfarn
Ceratopteris pteridioides
Sehr schnell wachsend, Vermehrung durch Adventivpflanzen an den Blatträndern, Jungfische finden gute Verstecke in den Wurzeln, Labyrinthfische bauen gern ihr Nest zwischen den Blättern, Durchmesser bis 40 cm.

6 Südamerikanischer Froschbiß
Limnobium laevigatum
Mäßig schnell wachsend, dunkelgrüne, schwammige Blätter, Vermehrung durch Ausläufer, gedeiht

4

2

3

am besten in offenen Aquarien, Durchmesser 5–8 cm.

7 Flutendes Teichlebermoos
Riccia fluitans
Schnell wachsend, keine echte Schwimmpflanze, da unter dem Wasserspiegel treibend, bildet dichte undurchdringliche Polster, ideal für Jungfische.

5

6

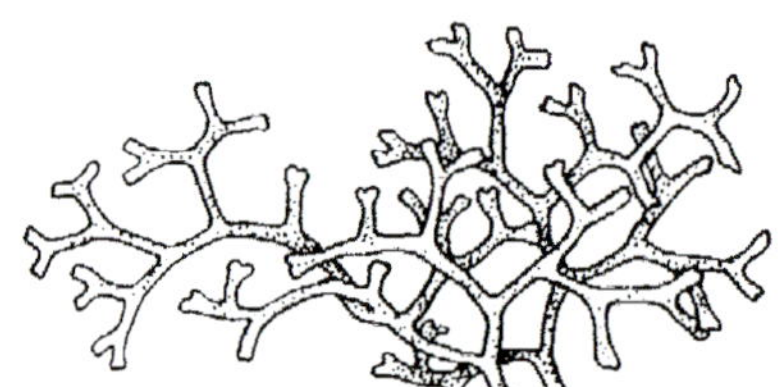

7

Die Hauptdarsteller: Unsere Fische

Der Fisch, ein unbekanntes Wesen?

Sicher nicht! Naturwissenschaftler, Systematiker und nicht zuletzt Aquarianer haben in den letzten Jahren und Jahrzehnten eine Fülle von Informationen über Fische im allgemeinen und die Aquarienfische im besonderen herausgefunden und zusammengetragen.

Zur Systematik

Fische gehören, ebenso wie Lurche (Amphibien), Kriechtiere (Reptilien), Vögel und Säugetiere, zu den Wirbeltieren. (Diesen fünf Tiergruppen ist die Wirbelsäule als zentraler und tragender Bestandteil des Skelettsystems gemeinsam.)

Fische stellen die älteste, artenreichste und von der Individuenzahl häufigste Gruppe unter den Wirbeltieren dar. Ihre Systematik wurde und wird immer wieder diskutiert und abgeändert. Selbst die Gesamtzahl der Fischarten ist unsicher: Die Schätzungen schwanken zwischen 21000 und 25000. Da sicher noch nicht alle Arten entdeckt und beschrieben sind, könnten es sogar 30000 sein.

Die größte und zugleich am besten erforschte Gruppe ist die der echten Knochenfische. Zwischen 5000 und 8000 Arten leben – zeitweise oder immer – im Süßwasser, davon könnten 4000 Arten im Prinzip für eine Pflege im Aquarium geeignet sein. Wirkliche Bedeutung im internationalen Handel haben aber „nur" rund 300 Arten.

Die Körpertemperatur

Fische sind wechselwarm, das heißt, daß sie ihre Körpertemperatur nicht selbst regeln, also keine Körperwärme erzeugen können, sondern so warm bzw. kalt wie ihre Umgebung sind. (Amphibien und Reptilien sind ebenfalls wechselwarm, während Vögel und Säugetiere ihre Körpertemperatur aktiv regulieren.)

Daß Fische wechselwarm sind, bedeutet nun aber nicht, daß sie mit jeder Temperatur zurechtkommen. In Anpassung an ihre jeweiligen natürlichen Lebensräume haben die Fischarten bestimmte Temperaturbereiche, in denen sie sich wohlfühlen und wo ein Überleben möglich ist: Um ein „Temperatur-Optimum" herum liegt ein mehr oder weniger breiter Temperaturbereich, der für die Fische zuträglich ist. Ist es *zu* kalt oder *zu* warm, sterben die Tiere nicht unbedingt sofort, siechen aber dahin, werden krankheitsanfällig und schreiten nicht mehr zur Fortpflanzung.

Die Flossen

Die Flossen sind ein typisches Fischmerkmal. Es handelt sich um Hautflächen, die von Teilen des Skeletts, den sog. Strahlen, gestützt werden und über Muskelstränge bewegt und auf- oder zusammengefaltet werden können.

Man unterscheidet paarige und unpaare Flossen. Meist sind es insgesamt sieben: Je ein Paar Brust- und Bauchflossen sowie die unpaare Rücken-, After- und Schwanzflosse.

Die Rückenflosse kann in mehrere Abschnitte unterteilt sein, die Bauchflossen können völlig zurückgebildet oder zu Haftorganen verwachsen sein (z.B. bei Welsen). Bei den Fadenfischen sind sie zu „Fäden" mit Geschmacks- und Tastsinneszellen umgebildet. Die Männchen der lebendgebärenden Zahnkarpfen haben als Begattungsorgan ein sogenanntes Gonopodium, das aus der umgebildeten Afterflosse hervorgegangen ist.

Oft unterscheiden sich männliche und weibliche Tiere in der Form und Farbe bestimmter Flossen (siehe Artbeschreibungen).

Eine untypische Flosse ist die zwischen Rücken- und Schwanzflosse gelegene Fettflosse vieler Salmler: Sie hat keine stützenden Strahlen und trägt nicht zur Bewegung bei; ihre Funktion ist ungeklärt.

Die Flossen höherer Wirbeltiere, z.B. der Delphine und Wale, weisen die gleiche Funktion wie die Fischflossen auf, sind aber anders gebaut („homolog").

Die Fortbewegung

Fische bewegen sich durch abwechselnden Zug der Seitenmuskeln praktisch „schlängelnd" vorwärts. Rücken-, After- und Schwanzflosse machen diese Wellenbewegung mit oder unterstützen sie aktiv (insbesondere die Schwanzflosse mit ihrer kräftigen Muskulatur). Die Brust- und Bauchflossenpaare steuern, bremsen und halten das Gleichgewicht. Rückwärtsschwimmen ist mit Hilfe der Brustflossen möglich.

Haut und Schuppen

Die Fischhaut ist aus der Oberhaut (Epidermis) und der darunterliegenden Lederhaut aufgebaut. In der Epidermis liegen Drüsen, die den schleimigen „Schutzfilm" absondern, der der Fischhaut einen gewissen Schutz gegen Fremdstoffe, Parasiten, Bakterien und Pilze gibt. Manche Krankheiten, schlechte Wasserqualität und Verletzungen (auch vom unsachgemäßen Han-

tieren) schädigen diese Schleimschicht, so daß Krankheitserreger leichteren Zutritt haben.

Männliche karpfenartige Fische zeigen während der Laichzeit, meist auf Kopf und Rücken, weiße punktförmige Verhornungen der Epidermis. Dieser sog. Laichausschlag kann leicht mit der Weißpünktchenkrankheit *(Ichthyophthirius*, siehe im Krankheitskapitel) verwechselt werden.

Die Schuppen sind verknöcherte Strukturen, die in der Lederhaut gebildet und in Schuppentaschen bis dicht unter die Epidermis vorgeschoben werden. Nicht alle Fische haben Schuppen, so sind z.B. die Welse und einige Schmerlen „nackt". Als Abwandlungen gibt es z.B. sehr kleine, tiefliegende Schuppen, nur teilweise beschuppte Fische (Spiegelkarpfen) und flache Knochenplatten anstelle der Schuppen (Panzerwelse).

Die Seitenlinie

Die Seitenlinie der Fische ist ein Ferntast-Sinnesorgan, das mit Hilfe von Sinneszellen genaue Informationen über Wasserbewegungen aufnehmen kann.

Die Farben

Die Färbung der Fische kommt durch die in der Lederhaut liegenden pigmenthaltigen Farbzellen zustande. Die ganze Farbenpracht entsteht durch nur vier Zelltypen, die unterschiedlich kombiniert sein können: Rot-, Gelb- und Schwarzzellen sowie Glanzzellen mit reflektierenden Kristallen. Blau kommt durch die Mischung von Schwarz- und Glanzzellenpigmenten zustande.

Farbwechsel, Aufhellungen und „Verdunkelungen" entstehen durch Änderung der Lage und der Ausdehnung der Pigmente in den Farbzellen. Bei Albinos fehlen alle Farbpigmente.

Gräten oder Knochen?

Das Knochengerüst der Fische fungiert als Stütze und Muskelansatz. Da das Wasser die Fische trägt, ist ihr Skelett nicht so großen Beanspruchungen ausgesetzt wie das der Landtiere und kann daher relativ zart gebaut sein.

Zentrales Element ist die Wirbelsäule mit ihren Fortsätzen, die sich vom Kopf bis in den Schwanz erstreckt und im vorderen Bereich die Rippen trägt. Alle diese Elemente sind Knochen, nur Feinschmecker bezeichnen die Wirbelsäule als „Mittelgräte". Echte Gräten sind nur die kleinen, frei in der Muskulatur liegenden Stützelemente (verknöcherte Sehnen), die keine Verbindung zu Kopf, Flossen oder Wirbelsäule haben.

Die inneren Organe

Den meisten Platz in der Leibeshöhle nimmt der Verdauungskanal ein. Über Maul und Speiseröhrenschlund gelangt die Nahrung in den Magen, bei einigen Arten direkt in den vordersten Darmteil. Fleischfresser haben einen kurzen, Pflanzenfresser einen stark geschlängelten, langen Darm. Speicheldrüsen haben Fische nicht, wohl aber Leber, Galle und Bauchspeicheldrüse.

Der Bau der Knochenfische am Beispiel eines Barsches.

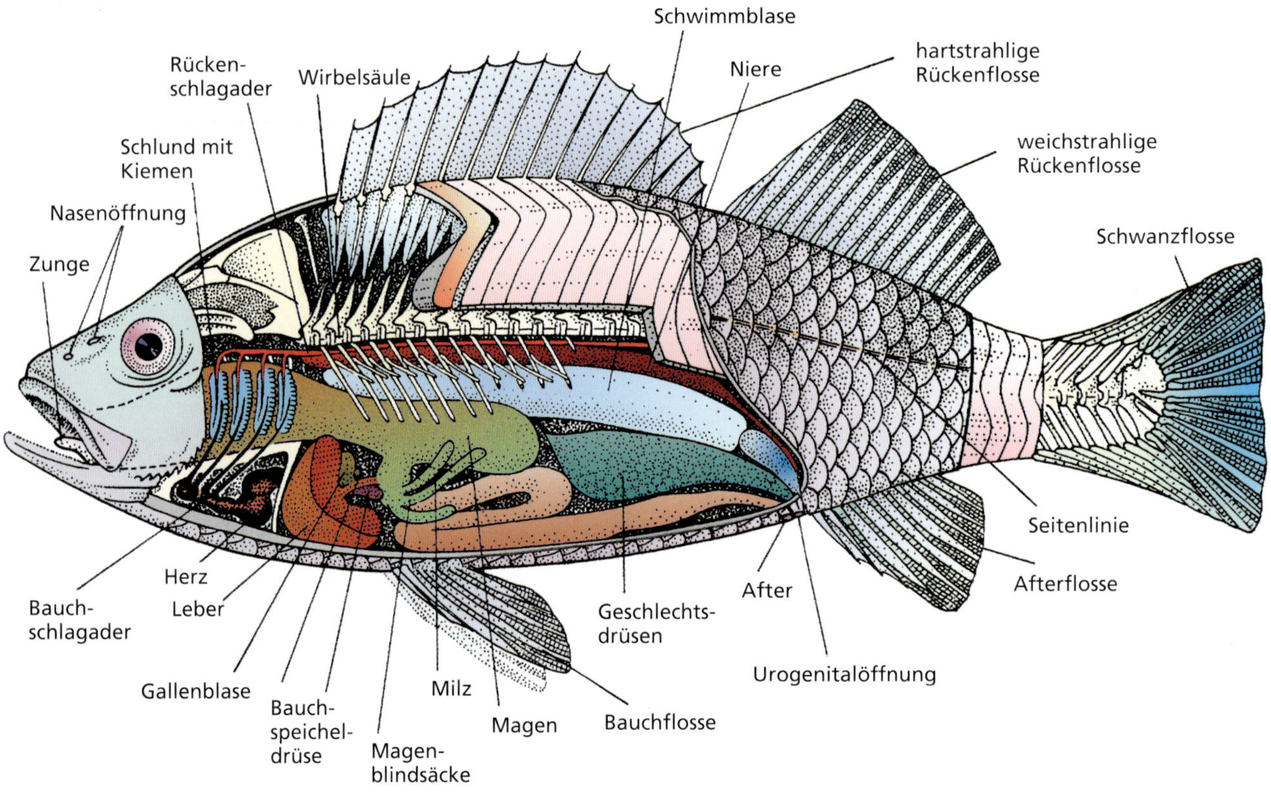

Trinken Fische?

Um diese alte Aquarianer-Frage zu beantworten, muß man zwischen Meerwasser- und Süßwasserfischen unterscheiden: Meerwasserfische ja, Süßwasserfische im Prinzip nicht.
Das Meerwasser ist salziger und enthält mehr gelöste Stoffe als „der Fisch selbst". Da ein Bestreben nach Konzentrationsausgleich besteht (Diffusion, Osmose), verliert der Fisch über seine Körperoberfläche Wasser. Dies gleicht er durch Trinken wieder aus. Das dabei notgedrungen mit aufgenommene Salz wird über die Kiemen und sehr konzentrierten Urin wieder ausgeschieden.
Im Süßwasser ist es umgekehrt: Das „Fischinnere" ist konzentrierter als das umgebende Wasser, es tritt also durch die Körperoberfläche Wasser in den Fisch ein, welches über die Nieren wieder ausgeschieden werden muß. Trinken brauchen Süßwasserfische also nicht; sie nehmen nur eher zufällig kleine Wassermengen auf.

In der Leibeshöhle liegen ferner die Milz, unterhalb der Wirbelsäule die Niere und die inneren Geschlechtsorgane, also Hoden oder Eierstöcke.

Nur bei den Fischen, und auch hier nicht bei allen Arten, findet sich eine **Schwimmblase.** Dieser dünnhäutige Sack enthält ein Gasgemisch aus Sauerstoff, Stickstoff und Kohlendioxid und dient als Schwebeorgan. Bei vielen bodenlebenden Fischen wird die Schwimmblase nach dem Larvenstadium zurückgebildet.

Ihre erste Füllung nach dem Schlupf der Jungfische erhält die Schwimmblase durch aktives Luftschlucken an der Wasseroberfläche; danach findet der Gasaustausch (z.B. zum Druckausgleich in wechselnder Wassertiefe) über den Blutkreislauf statt.

Die Kiemen

Kiemen sind ein typisches Fischmerkmal: Außer bei Amphibienlarven treten sie bei keiner anderen Tiergruppe auf. Einige Fischarten haben noch zusätzliche Atmungsorgane, die bei der Beschreibung der Fischgruppen im folgenden Kapitel vorgestellt werden.

Die Kiemen sind empfindliche, stark durchblutete Hautlamellen (Kiemenblättchen), die ständig von Atemwasser umströmt werden. Seitlich am Kopf gelegen, werden sie durch die Kiemendeckel geschützt. An der Bewegung der Kiemendeckel kann man die Atemfrequenz erkennen.

Das Blut strömt aus dem Körper zum Herzen, wird zu den Kiemen und dort in die feinsten Blutgefäße gepumpt, wodurch eine gewisse Aufenthaltsdauer gegeben ist. Hier gelangt aus dem umgebenden Wasser Sauerstoff ins Blut; gleichzeitig werden Kohlendioxid und „Abfallstoffe" ans Wasser abgegeben. (Die Niere scheidet viel Wasser, aber nur wenig darin gelöste Stoffwechselendprodukte aus.)

Größe und Alter

Alle Fische wachsen Zeit ihres Lebens, nach der Geschlechtsreife allerdings nur noch sehr langsam. Nur ungünstige Lebensbedingungen und der Alterstod beenden dieses potentielle Dauerwachstum. Süßwasserfische erreichen Größen zwischen wenig mehr als einem Zentimeter und über vier Meter (Arapaima).

Die Lebensdauer von Fischen schwankt zwischen einem Jahr und mehreren Jahrzehnten. In der Obhut des Menschen ist meist eine höhere Lebenserwartung als in der freien Natur gegeben.

Nachwuchs im Aquarium

Bei sachgerechter Pflege werden die Fische im Aquarium irgendwann einmal einen körperlichen Reifestatus erreicht haben, wo das Fortpflanzungsverhalten zu den ganz normalen Lebensäußerungen zählt. Andererseits kann die Fortpflanzungstätigkeit auch als Bestätigung dafür gesehen werden, daß man den Fischen zusagende

Die langflossige Form der Prachtbarbe **(Barbus conchonius)** *entstand durch gezielte Zuchtauslese aus der normalflossigen Form.*

Lebensbedingungen geschaffen hat.

Bei vielen Fischen findet die Fortpflanzung spontan im Haltungsbecken statt, andere benötigen dazu bestimmte Auslösereize. Wieder andere Fische werden im Haltungsaquarium zwar geschlechtsreif, laichen unter Umständen auch ab, jedoch sterben die Eier, weil für die *Haltung* der Fische härteres Wasser ausreicht, die Entwicklung der Eier und Jungfische aber weicheres Wasser erfordert. Solche Fische (viele Salmler und Barben) müssen in separat bereitgestellten Zuchtaquarien mit genau vorbereitetem Wasser gezüchtet werden. Uns sollen hier in erster Linie einmal die Fische interessieren, die sich auch im Haltungsbecken fortpflanzen.

Wesentliche Voraussetzung, damit eine Fortpflanzung überhaupt stattfinden kann, ist natürlich das Vorhandensein männlicher und weiblicher Tiere. Nur selten wird man beim Kauf der Tiere im Zoofachhandel bereits erkennen können, was Männlein und Weiblein wird. In der Regel werden Jungtiere verkauft, die sich auch besser in ihre neue Umgebung einleben können.

Beim Guppy gibt es deutliche Geschlechtsunterschiede: Oben das unscheinbarere, größere Weibchen, unten das farbige Männchen mit der zum Gonopodium (Begattungsorgan) umgebildeten Afterflosse.

Wenn Ihnen der Zoohändler also empfiehlt, mehrere Tiere, am besten zehn oder mehr, einer Art zu kaufen, so hat das durchaus seinen Sinn. Bei mehreren Tieren ist die Chance natürlich größer, ein ausgewogenes Verhältnis an Geschlechtern zu erwerben. Außerdem sollten viele beliebte Aquarienfische sowieso nicht „paarweise" gepflegt werden, weil es sich oft um Schwarmtiere handelt, die sich nur unter ihresgleichen wohlfühlen.

Viele Arten sind auch recht wählerisch (zum Beispiel Buntbarsche) was die Wahl des Partners anbelangt. Wenn man mehrere Jungtiere kauft, erhöht sich natürlich die Chance, daß „zwei sich finden".

Tiere nur eines Geschlechts zu halten, aus welchen Gründen auch immer, ist nicht nur unnatürlich, sondern man bringt sich auch um den aufregendsten und interessantesten Teil, den die Aquaristik zu bieten hat, nämlich die Beobachtung der verschiedenen Fortpflanzungsweisen. Viele Fische zeigen auch erst „Farbe", wenn beide Geschlechter vorhanden sind.

Geschlechtsunterschiede

Nun müssen Sie noch wissen, wie man bei Fischen überhaupt Männlein und Weiblein unterscheidet. Das ist nicht immer ganz einfach und kann hier auch nicht bis ins Detail abgehandelt werden. Nähere Einzelheiten sind in der entsprechenden Fachliteratur zu finden. Die folgenden allgemeinen Hinweise können als Anhaltspunkt dienen.

***Flächig rot gefärbte Zuchtform des Zwergfadenfisches* (Colisa lalia, *Männchen*).**

Balzstimmung.

Am sichersten ist die Unterscheidung bei lebendgebärenden Fischen. Die Afterflosse der Männchen ist zu einem typischen Begattungsorgan, dem Gonopodium,

umgestaltet, während die Weibchen eine normale Afterflosse besitzen. Meist werden die Weibchen auch größer als die Männchen. Bei Guppies sind die Männchen außerdem farbenprächtiger und bei Schwertträgern zeigen nur die Männchen den schwertartigen Fortsatz der Schwanzflosse. Schwertträgerweibchen können sich übrigens in Männchen umwandeln, die dann kräftiger sind als Tiere, die von vornherein Männchen waren.

Bei vielen verschiedenen Fischfamilien sind die unpaaren Flossen (Rücken-, After- und Schwanzflosse) der Männchen länger oder spitzer auslaufend als die der Weibchen. Oft sind die Männchen auch farbiger als die Weibchen (viele Labyrinther und Buntbarsche). Bei vielen Zwergbuntbarschen zeigen die Weibchen während der Balz und Brutpflege ein typisches schwarzes Muster auf gelbem Grund, das den Männchen fehlt.

Auslösende Faktoren

Manche Fische vermehren sich spontan, wie bereits erwähnt, ohne daß man etwas dagegen tun könnte. Dazu gehören zum Beispiel fast alle lebendgebärenden Zahnkarpfen, die vor allem dem Anfänger das erste Hochgefühl der eigenen Nachzucht im Aquarium vermitteln.

Andere benötigen bestimmte auslösende Faktoren. Das sind in der Regel Reize aus der Umwelt, die dem Organismus das Signal zur Fortpflanzung geben. Bei vielen tropischen Fischen ist die Regenzeit das auslösende Signal. Durch häufigen Wasserwechsel in kurzen Zeitabständen kann Regenzeit simuliert werden. Wenn dabei die Härte noch etwas abgesenkt und das nachgefüllte Wasser etwas kühler ist, klappt es meistens.

Manche Fische, vor allem Wildfänge, sind noch an die zeitlichen Abläufe ihrer Heimat angepaßt. Sie lassen sich meist nur dann zum Ablaichen stimulieren, wenn in ihrer Heimat auch Regenzeit ist. Bei Panzerwelsen genügt oft bereits eine Temperatursenkung, um die Fortpflanzung anzuregen. Bei Labyrinthfischen sind fallender Wasserstand und Temperaturerhöhung auf bis zu 30 °C der Auslöser.

Vielfach kann auch ein ganz bestimmtes Futter ausschlaggebend sein, daß Fische Laich ansetzen. Schwarze Mückenlarven wirken bei verschiedenen Fischen förderlich. Darüber hinaus gibt es viele Fische, zum Beispiel die Prachtschmerle *(Botia macracantha)*, wo man die auslösenden Faktoren noch nicht genügend kennt oder nicht effektiv genug simulieren kann. Hier ist noch ein weites Betätigungsfeld für forschende Naturen. Es wäre nicht das erste Mal, daß Aquarianer ein solches Geheimnis lüften.

Außer diesen auslösenden Reizen benötigen die meisten Fische auch noch bestimmte Substrate, an die die Eier angeheftet werden. Viele Salmler und Barben brauchen kein direktes Laichsubstrat, bevorzugen aber bestimmte Pflanzen, zwischen denen abgelaicht wird.

Jungfische im Haltungsaquarium

Wer nicht unbedingt Wert auf hohe Jungfischzahlen legt, kann durch geschickte Einrichtung des Haltungsaquariums dafür sorgen, daß immer einige Jungfische hochkommen. Dabei ist es noch nicht einmal erforderlich, spezielles Futter anzubieten. Mit feinfiedrigen Pflanzen dicht bepflanzte Ecken oder dichte Moospolster und ein mit Schwimmpflanzen abgedeckter Teil des

Bevölkerungsexplosion.

Aquariums bieten Jungfischen Schutz vor ihren gefräßigen Mitinsassen und gleichzeitig viele Kleinstlebewesen als ideale Erstnahrung.

Viele anspruchslose Salmler werden in solcher Umgebung regelmäßig für „Verstärkung" im Schwarm sorgen. Auch Regenbogenfische, Hechtlinge und viele andere werden auf diese Weise den Bestand ständig ergänzen oder vergrößern. Lebendgebärende werden Ihnen in einem solchen Aquarium sehr bald mehr Nachwuchs bringen als Ihnen lieb ist. Trächtige Weibchen von Lebendgebärenden in Ablaichkästen zu sperren, um ihre Jungen zu gebären, ist unnatürlich und mit Streß für das Muttertier verbunden.

Zuchtbecken

Wer auf möglichst viele Fischkinder Wert legt, wird um die Einrichtung eines Zuchtbeckens nicht herumkommen. Sei es um den gesamten Fortpflanzungsvorgang von vornherein in diesem Becken ablaufen zu lassen, sei es, um aus dem Haltungsaquarium entnommenen Laich oder Jungfische aufzuziehen.

Weibchen von* Apistogramma cacatuoides *in typischer gelb-schwarzer Brutpflegefärbung mit Jungfischen.

Alle nicht brutpflegenden, eierlegenden Fische (Salmler, Barben und andere) wird man bereits im Zuchtbecken ablaichen lassen, um möglichst zahlreichen Nachwuchs zu erhalten.

Als Zuchtbecken wählt man ein Glasaquarium, das je nach Größe der Fische 10 bis 30 l Fassungsvermögen hat. Das Becken erhält keinen Bodengrund und alle Einrichtungsgegenstände müssen vorher gründlich mit heißem Wasser gesäubert werden. Die Grundeinrichtung besteht aus: Heizung, schwach perlendem Ausströmer und je nach Fischart erforderlichem Laichsubstrat.

Für viele Fische geeignet und praktisch (weil leicht zu reinigen und wiederverwendbar) ist ein Büschel aus zusammengebundenen Wollfäden (Kunstfaser), die man mit einem Sauger am oberen Rand befestigt oder an einem Kork hängend treiben läßt. Boden-, Rück- und Seitenscheiben werden abgedunkelt (dunkle Pappe oder Anstrich).

Da die meisten der in solchen Aquarien zu vermehrenden Fische ihren Laich als willkommene Nahrung ansehen, muß dies möglichst verhindert werden, zum Beispiel durch Auslegen von Glasmurmeln von etwa 20 mm Durchmesser. Die Eier fallen dazwischen und sind weitgehend sicher. Beim Einsetzen der Elterntiere und der Wahl des richtigen Zuchtwassers verfahren Sie nach den Angaben bei unseren Fischbeschreibungen und in der einschlägigen Literatur.

In der Regel werden die Zuchttiere abends eingesetzt, der Laichvorgang findet dann am nächsten Morgen statt. Anschließend müssen die Eltern sofort entfernt werden. Zur Überführung von Laich oder Jungfischen aus dem Haltungsaquarium wird das Zuchtbecken zunächst mit Wasser aus dem Haltungsaquarium gefüllt. Dann wird der Laich mitsamt der Unterlage (Stein, Pflanze etc.) aus dem Haltungsaquarium entnommen und in das Zuchtbekken gebracht.

Panzer- und Harnischwelse laichen oft an der Glasscheibe. Man kann den Laich mit einer Rasierklinge vorsichtig entfernen und in das Zuchtbecken überführen. Bereits schwimmfähige Jungfische saugt man am besten mit einem Schlauch ab und bringt sie dann zusammen mit dem abgesaugten Wasser in das Zuchtbecken.

Ei- und Jungfischentwicklung

Ob nun die Fische direkt im Zuchtbecken abgelaicht haben oder ob Sie Laich aus dem Haltungsaquarium in das Zuchtbecken überführt haben (gleiche Wasserwerte beachten!), in beiden Fällen beginnt nun die erste Phase im Leben der Fische. Innerhalb weniger Stunden bis mehrerer Tage (je nach Art) entwickelt sich im Ei eine kleine Larve. Bei entsprechend großen und transparenten Eiern kann man den Fortschritt der Entwicklung mit der Lupe beobachten.

Nach einer gewissen Zeit sprengen die Larven die Eihüllen. Sie sind zu diesem Zeitpunkt noch nicht in der Lage zu schwimmen oder zu fressen. Je nach Fischart hängen sie mit speziellen Haftorganen an Scheiben und Einrichtungsgegenständen oder liegen auf dem Boden. Einige Tage zehren sie nun von dem im Dottersack „mitgebrachten" Nahrungsvorrat und entwickeln sich weiter, bis sie eines Tages frei im Becken umherschwimmen und nach Nahrung suchen.

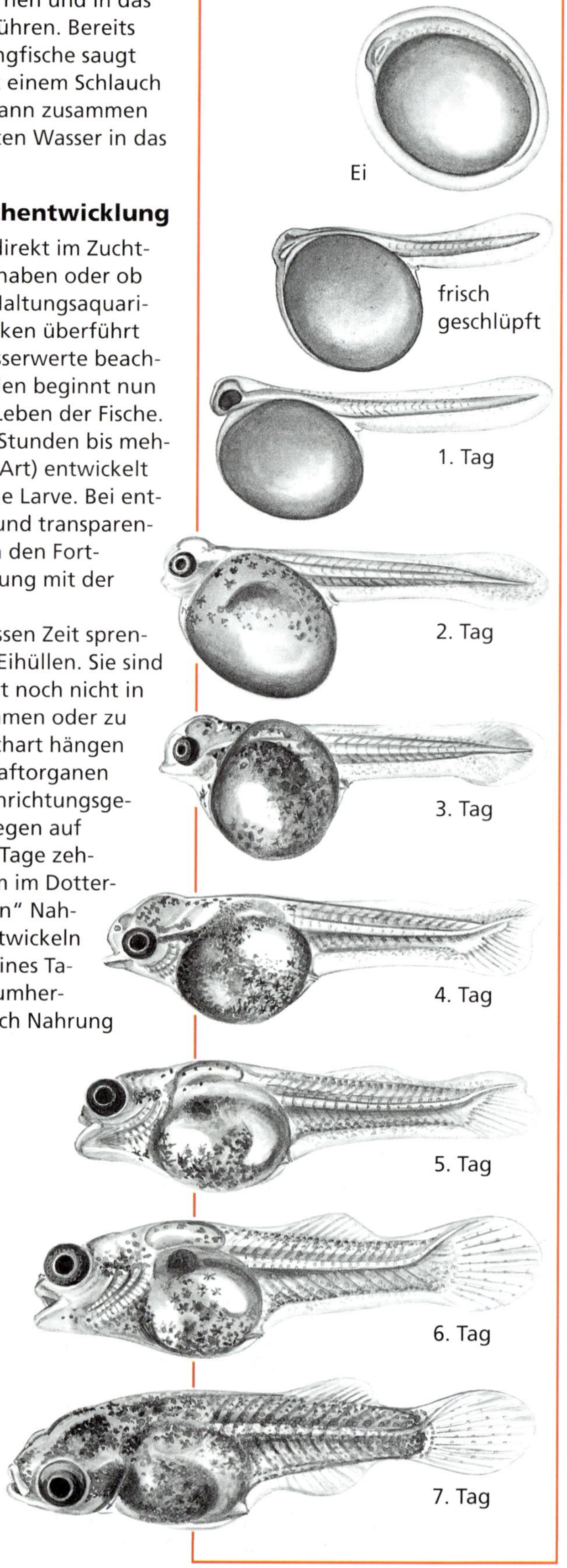

Die Jungfischentwicklung am Beispiel des Riesenguramis. Nach dem Schlüpfen zehren die Larven einige Tage vom Dottervorrat und wachsen heran. Am sechsten Tag beginnen sie umherzuschwimmen und Nahrung zu suchen.

Fortpflanzung und Brutpflege der Fische

Fische haben im Laufe der Evolution die verschiedenartigsten Fortpflanzungsstrategien und damit verbundene Brutpflegeverhalten entwickelt. Die Palette reicht vom einfachen Abgeben der Geschlechtsprodukte ins Wasser bis zu hochspezialisierter Brutpflege oder gar Lebendgebären.

Die allermeisten Fische sind Eierleger. Die Eier werden entweder frei ins Wasser abgegeben oder auf ein Substrat geheftet und anschließend befruchtet. Fische, die keine Brutpflege betreiben, legen pro Laichakt sehr viele kleine Eier, um die hohe Verlustrate während der Entwicklung und dem Heranwachsen der Jungfische auszugleichen.

Je weiter die Brutpflege entwickelt ist, desto weniger und größer werden die Eier. Durch die Brutpflege der Eltern wird die Gefahr des Gefressenwerdens vermindert, so daß geringere Eizahlen genügen, um den Fortbestand der Art zu sichern.

Eine besonders hoch entwickelte Form der Brutpflege findet man bei den lebendgebärenden Fischen, wie zum Beispiel den lebendgebärenden Zahnkarpfen. Hier findet die gesamte Entwicklung von der Besamung bis zum fertigen, selbständig lebensfähigen Jungfisch im Schutz des Mutterleibes statt.
Die Männchen dieser Fische besitzen ein besonderes Begattungsorgan (Gonopodium), das durch

Schmetterlingsbuntbarsch* (Papiliochromis ramirezi), *ein Paar am Gelege.

Das Schmetterlingsbuntbarsch-Weibchen mit Jungfischen.

Umbildung der Afterflosse entstanden ist.

Auch Fische balzen

Am Anfang der Fortpflanzungsaktivitäten steht das Balzverhalten. Bestimmte Verhaltensabläufe, oft gekoppelt mit bestimmten Färbungen und Zeichnungsmustern, dienen dazu, die Abgabe der Geschlechtsprodukte beider Partner zu synchronisieren, das heißt, dafür zu sorgen, daß beide Partner zur gleichen Zeit und am richtigen Ort Eier und Spermien abgeben.

Eng verwandte Arten, die im gleichen Biotop vorkommen, verfügen oft über ein sehr unterschiedliches Balzverhalten, wodurch eine Kreuzung vermieden wird. Je nach Fischgruppe kann das Balzverhalten mehr oder weniger stark ausgeprägt sein. Bei vielen nicht brutpflegenden Arten (Salmler, Barben usw.) ist es wenig auffällig und dauert meist nur wenige Stunden. Arten mit stark ausgeprägter Brutpflege, wie zum Beispiel die Buntbarsche verfügen über ein umfangreiches Repertoire an Balzverhaltensweisen.

Mit dem Balzverhalten geht bei brutpflegenden Arten auch die Besetzung eines Brutterritoriums einher, das heftig gegen Artgenossen verteidigt wird. Wenn dabei nicht selten von einem Paar das ganze Aquarium als eigenes Territorium beansprucht wird, kann es zu erheblichen Komplikationen kommen, da die übrigen Artgenossen nicht ausweichen können und deshalb oft stark verletzt werden.

Der Laichvorgang

Je nachdem, wo die Fische ihre Eier ablegen, unterscheidet man sogenannte Freilaicher und Substratlaicher. **Freilaicher** geben Eier und Spermien einfach ins Wasser ab und kümmern sich nicht weiter darum. Das kann im freien Wasser oder zwischen Pflanzenbeständen geschehen. Die Eier fallen entweder zu Boden oder bleiben an den Pflanzen kleben. Viele Salmler, Barben und Regen-

Nest des Riesenguramis, das aus dem Zuchtteich genommen und geöffnet wurde, um das Gelege zur künstlichen Aufzucht zu entnehmen.

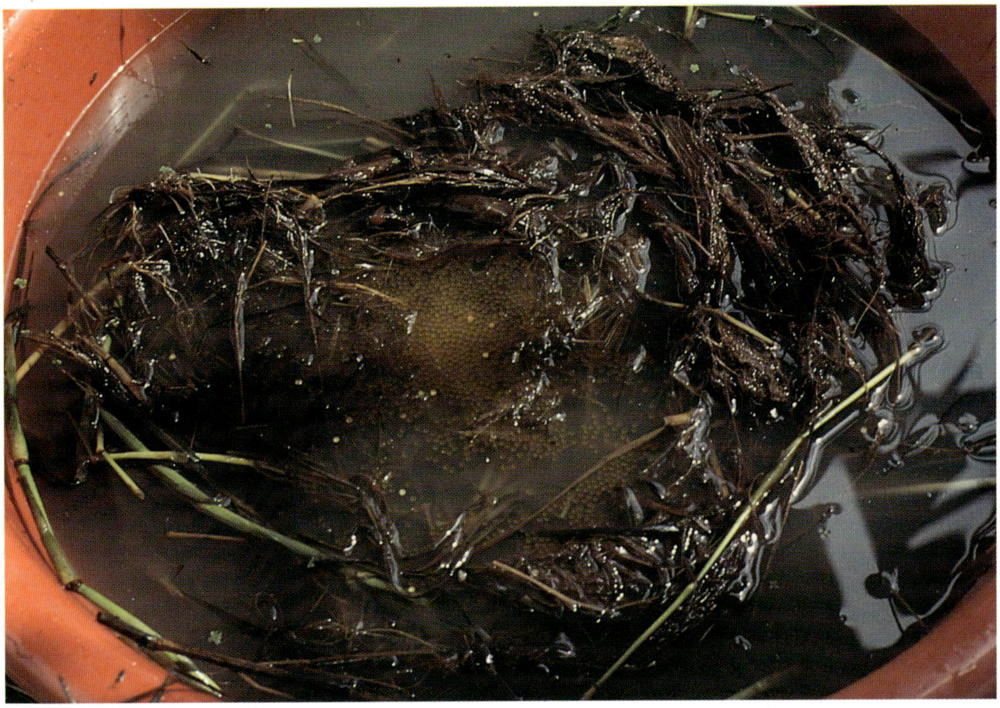

bogenfische laichen auf diese Art und Weise.

Substratlaicher heften ihre Eier auf eine bestimmte Unterlage, ein Substrat. Dazu können Steine, Pflanzenblätter, Holz oder auch Schaumnester dienen. Substratlaicher üben meist eine mehr oder weniger stark ausgeprägte Brutpflege aus. Je nach Art und Dauer unterscheidet man verschiedene Typen der Brutpflege.

Pflege der Eier und Larven

Als sehr interessante Vertreter dieser Gruppe wären die Labyrinthfische zu nennen, die eine besondere Art von Laichsubstrat selbst produzieren: das Schaumnest. Die Männchen nehmen von der Wasseroberfläche Luftblasen ins Maul, umgeben sie mit einem zähen Schleim und spucken sie wieder aus, bis ein dickes Polster von Luftblasen entstanden ist, in das die Weibchen die Eier abgeben.

Nach dem Laichakt wird das Weibchen vom Männchen vertrieben, das dann das Nest mit den Eiern und den später schlüpfenden, noch nicht schwimmfähigen Larven gegen Freßfeinde verteidigt. Während dieser Zeit wird das Nest auch immer wieder durch neue Luftblasen ergänzt.

Der größte Labyrinthfisch, der Riesengurami *(Osphronemus guramí)* zeigt eine besondere Form des Nestbaus. An überhängenden Wurzeln oder an Schilfstengeln wird ein großes Nest aus verschiedenen Pflanzenteilen gebaut, das an ein mit der Öffnung nach unten zeigendes Vogelnest erinnert. Wenn der Laichvorgang abgeschlossen ist, wird die Öffnung vom Männchen verschlossen und das Nest bewacht, bis die Jungfische es verlassen. Der Riesengurami gilt in Asien als beliebter Speisefisch und wird in speziellen Anlagen auch gezüchtet. Die Züchter lassen die Fische auf natürliche Weise ablaichen und entnehmen dann die Nester, um die Jungen künstlich großzuziehen.

Pflege der Jungfische

Zu den Fischen, die auch noch die schwimmfähigen Larven und Jungfische über einen langen Zeitraum betreuen, gehören vor allem die Cichliden (Buntbarsche). Abgelaicht wird auf offenliegenden Steinen, in Höhlen oder an Pflan-

zenblättern. Das Gelege und später auch die geschlüpften Larven und Jungfische werden heftig gegen Eindringlinge verteidigt. Die Eier werden durch „Belutschen" gepflegt und saubergehalten.

Wenn der Zeitpunkt des Schlüpfens gekommen ist, werden die Larven aus den Eihüllen gekaut und in vorbereitete Gruben verfrachtet oder mit speziellen Klebedrüsen an Pflanzenblätter „angeheftet". Während der Entwicklungszeit der frisch geschlüpften Larven bis zum Freischwimmen werden sie öfter umgebettet und von Zeit zu Zeit von den Eltern „belutscht".

Nach dem Freischwimmen zeigen die Eltern besondere Verhaltensweisen und Zeichnungsmuster, über die sie mit den Jungen kommunizieren. Cichlideneltern, die Junge führen, sind besonders aggressiv. Diskusfische sondern ein Hautsekret ab, von dem sich die Jungen während der ersten Lebenstage ernähren.

Maulbrutpflege

Dies ist eine hochspezialisierte Form der Brutpflege, die bei verschiedenen Fischfamilien entwickelt

wurde. Am bekanntesten sind wohl die maulbrütenden Cichliden aus den afrikanischen Seen. Bei der höchstentwickelten Form der Maulbrutpflege werden die Eier sofort nach dem Ablaichen vom Weibchen ins Maul genommen. Die ganze Entwicklung der Eier und der Larven findet im schützenden Maul statt.

Erst die freischwimmenden, sehr weit entwickelten Jungfische werden zur Nahrungssuche aus dem Maul entlassen und flüchten bei Gefahr dorthin zurück, bis sie dafür zu groß sind.

Viele Fischgruppen zeigen Übergangsformen zwischen Offenbrutpflege und Maulbrutpflege. So werden beispielsweise die Eier normal auf dem Substrat gepflegt und erst die geschlüpften Larven werden ins Maul genommen.

Je nachdem, wer sich bei den brutpflegenden Arten um das Gelege und die Jungfische kümmert, unterscheidet man verschiedene Familienformen, wie zum Beispiel Elternfamilie, Mutterfamilie, Vaterfamilie und so weiter. Verständlicherweise kann im vorliegenden Rahmen nicht in letzter Ausführlichkeit auf das gesamte Spektrum von Fortpflanzungs- und Brutpflegeverhalten eingegangen werden. Wer sich näher für dieses aufregende Gebiet der Aquaristik interessiert, sei auf die einschlägige Literatur verwiesen.

Macropodus opercularis: ***Paar am Schaumnest.***

Diese sogenannten Ballon-Mollies sind ein Negativbeispiel für „Zuchtbemühungen". Die Ballonform entstand durch Wirbelsäulenverkrümmung.

Manche Zuchtformen sind nicht mehr fortpflanzungsfähig, wie dieser Schwertträger mit überlangem Gonopodium.

Jetzt muß mit geeignetem Futter mehrmals täglich gefüttert werden. Wenn die Jungfische bereits groß genug sind, um frischgeschlüpfte Artemia-Nauplien bewältigen zu können, so ist die Aufzucht einfach. Dieses Futter kann man sich aus im Zoofachhandel erhältlichen Eiern selbst erbrüten. Das Verfahren ist einfach, und jede Packung enthält eine Gebrauchsanleitung, weshalb wir uns die Erklärung hier sparen wollen.

Die Jungfische vieler Salmler und Barben sind jedoch so winzig klein, daß sie in den ersten Tagen mit Infusorien (Einzeller, meist Pantoffeltierchen) ernährt werden müssen. Pantoffeltierchen muß man selbst züchten (eine Anleitung ist im Werk von Friedrich/Volland zu finden). Wenn die Winzlinge genügend herangewachsen sind, kann mit Artemia-Nauplien weitergefüttert werden. Einige Zeit später können die Tiere dann langsam an andere Futtersorten (Flockenfutter, Mückenlarven usw.) umgewöhnt werden.

Es versteht sich von selbst, daß das Aufzuchtbecken regelmäßig gereinigt werden muß und mit dem Heranwachsen der Jungfische öfter ein Teilwasserwechsel durchzuführen ist. Eine Filterung über einen luftbetriebenen Schaumstoffpatronenfilter ist ebenfalls ratsam. Statt mit Pantoffeltierchen oder Artemia-Nauplien können die Jungfische auch mit verschiedenen Ersatzfuttern, wie zum Beispiel feinst zermahlenem Flockenfutter oder homogenisiertem Flüssigfutter ernährt werden. Der Aufzuchterfolg ist mit den genannten Lebendfuttern in der kritischen Anfangsphase jedoch besser.

Tischlein deck dich ...

Zu einer verantwortungsvollen Aquarienhaltung gehört neben arttypisch gestalteter Umwelt auch eine Ernährung, die den Bedürfnissen der Fische gerecht wird. Da Aquarienfische wohl nur sehr selten die Gelegenheit haben werden, in ihrem Lebensraum das ihrer Gewohnheit entsprechende Futter vorzufinden, sind wir Aquarianer gehalten, es ihnen zu bieten. Welche Futteransprüche die einzelnen Arten stellen, entnehmen Sie bitte den Einzelbeschreibungen im nächsten Kapitel und der einschlägigen Literatur.

Man unterscheidet im wesentlichen drei Ernährungstypen: Karnivore oder Fleischfresser, Omnivore oder Allesfresser und Herbivore oder Pflanzenfresser. Irgendwo zwischen den beiden letztgenannten sind noch die Limnivoren (Aufwuchsfresser) einzuordnen. Selbstverständlich lassen sich nicht alle Fische stur in eine dieser Gruppen pressen. Sehr oft gibt es Übergangsformen.

Das Verdauungssystem der Fische hat sich im Laufe der Entwicklungsgeschichte an die in ihrem speziellen Lebensraum vorkommende Nahrung angepaßt. Das manifestiert sich unter anderem in der Darmlänge, die proportional zur Verdaulichkeit der Nahrung ist.

Rein karnivore Fische, die mehr oder weniger ausschließlich von Fischen und anderen Wassertieren als Beute leben, besitzen einen sehr kurzen Darm mit einem großen Magen, der vor allem der Aufnahme der großen Beutestücke dient. Da diese Nahrung leicht verdaulich ist, ist kein langer Darm erforderlich. Bei Allesfressern wird der Darm bereits länger, weil schon in gewisser Menge schwerer verdauliche, pflanzliche Kost mitgefressen wird. Der Pflanzenfresserdarm schließlich ist extrem lang und auf schwer verdauliche Pflanzenkost eingestellt.

Dies muß bei der Wahl des Futters und bei der Herstellung von industriell gefertigtem Futter berücksichtigt werden, da sonst erhebliche Verdauungsstörungen eintreten

Die heiße Schlacht am kalten Buffet.

können. Auch auf die richtige Art und Zusammenstellung der Rohstoffe für ein Futter kommt es an. Bei industriell gefertigten Markenfuttermitteln können Sie davon ausgehen, daß dem Rechnung getragen wird. Sie müssen lediglich aus dem breiten Angebot das richtige auswählen.

Da trotzdem, vor allem bei selbst gefertigtem Futter, öfter (gut gemeinte) Fehler begangen werden, hier noch einige Hinweise auf mögliche Gefahren: Auf Proteine von Warmblütern, vor allem reines Muskelfleisch, sollte man als ausschließliche Proteinquelle verzichten. Proteine wasserlebender Organismen (insbesondere Fische) sind weitaus besser geeignet. Vor allem einseitige Ernährung mit Rinderherz oder anderem Muskelfleisch kann zu Mangelerscheinungen führen.

Fette können von Fischen nur verwertet werden, wenn sie bei der entsprechenden Haltungstemperatur flüssig bleiben, das heißt sehr viele sogenannte ungesättigte Fettsäuren enthalten. Damit scheidet Fett von Warmblütern von vornherein aus, es wird nahezu unverdaut wieder ausgeschieden, verpestet das Wasser und führt zu Darmentzündungen.

Da Aquarienfische nicht die Bewegungsfreiheit haben wie in der freien Natur und auch eher zu viel als zu wenig gefüttert werden, sollte der Fettgehalt im Futter nicht allzu hoch sein. 3 bis 5% können als Anhaltspunkt dienen.

Kohlenhydrate (typische Vertreter sind Zucker und Stärke) stammen aus dem Pflanzenreich und sollten in Verbindung mit Ballaststoffen (pflanzliche Zellwände etc.) wesentlicher Bestandteil im Futter für Pflanzenfresser sein. Futter mit zuviel Protein und zuwenig Ballaststoffen hält den langen Darm der Pflanzenfresser zu wenig „in Schwung". Manche Fische, die auf pflanzliche Kost angewiesen sind, und die diese nicht in ausreichendem Maße erhalten, werden dies durch entsprechende Selbstbedienung an Aquarienpflanzen zum Ausdruck bringen. Prachtschmerlen können, vor allem als größere Tiere, großblättrige Pflanzen „herrlich perforieren".

Futtertabletten, an die Scheiben geheftet, sind ein willkommener Leckerbissen.

Flockenfutter

Flockenfutter werden heutzutage nach komplizierten Rezepturen hergestellt und sind absolut kein minderwertiges Ersatzfutter, wie es allzuoft hingestellt wird. Ohne die professionell hergestellten Flockenfutter wäre die Aquaristik heute nicht das, was sie ist. Flockenfutter von Markenherstellern enthält alle für die Ernährung der Fische notwendigen Bestandteile. Durch Kombination unzähliger Rohstoffe und gezielte Vitaminisierung ist das Auftreten von Mangelerscheinungen ausgeschlossen.

Flockenfutter gibt es in vielen verschiedenen Formen und Zusammensetzungen, entsprechend den Ernährungsgewohnheiten der

Verschiedene Flockenfutter, Futtertabletten, granuliertes Futter, Staubfutter und gefriergetrocknetes Futter.

Fische. Lassen Sie sich bei Ihrem spezialisierten Zoofachhändler beraten. Zu erwähnen wären unter anderem Flocken verschiedener Größe für große und kleine Fische, unterschiedliche Proteingehalte für mehr „fleischlich" oder mehr „pflanzlich" orientierte Fische. Dann wären noch verschiedene **Futtertabletten** für bodenbewohnende Fische zu erwähnen.

Verschiedene Hersteller bieten Informationsbroschüren an, aus denen Sie mehr über das Futter erfahren, als auf eine kleine Dose gedruckt werden kann. Vor allem für die Analysendaten sollten Sie sich interessieren, die, weil es nicht vorgeschrieben ist, oft nicht auf den Dosen zu finden sind. So können Sie schnell feststellen, ob ein Pflanzenfresserfutter wirklich ein Pflanzenfresserfutter ist, oder nur ein anders eingefärbtes Allesfresserfutter.

Noch ein Wort zu den Futterdosen: Flockenfutter besteht aus Naturprodukten, die verderblich sind. Markenhersteller unternehmen alles Erdenkliche, um durch geeignete Verpackung das Futter vor vorzeitigem Verderb zu schützen. Sie geben auch ein Mindesthaltbarkeitsdatum an, das selbstverständlich nur bei ungeöffneter Dose gilt. Vitamine und freie Fettsäuren sind sehr leicht verderblich. Kaufen Sie deshalb kein Futter, das in Klarsichtbehältnissen (Beutel, Dosen) oder unversiegelt angeboten wird. Futter in einer einmal geöffneten Dose verdirbt schneller. Kaufen Sie also nur solche Gebindegrößen, deren Inhalt Sie in zwei bis drei Monaten verfüttert haben und lagern Sie das Futter möglichst kühl.

„Was es heute wohl gibt?"

Lebendfutter

Trotz aller Vorteile des Flockenfutters – einen Nachteil hat es: Es bewegt sich nicht. Es gibt bestimmte Fische, die partout nicht an Flockenfutter gehen, sei es, weil es sich nicht bewegt, oder weil Geschmack und Form nicht dem gewohnten Futter entsprechen. Viele Importfische kennen gar kein Flockenfutter und müssen erst langsam umgewöhnt werden.

Wer einmal gesehen hat, wie Fische hinter Lebendfutter herjagen, wird diesen Anblick zumindest hin und wieder nicht missen wollen und seinen Fischen diese Abwechslung gönnen. Es gibt verschiedene Wege, an Lebendfutter zu kommen. Man kann es selbst züchten, verschiedene Zuchtansätze sind über den Versand zu beziehen (Adressen in Aquarienzeitschriften), man kann es fangen, oder man kann es (der bequemste Weg) im Zoofachgeschäft kaufen.

Die eigene Zucht von Lebendfutter (vor allem verschiedene Wurmarten und Fliegen) ist sicher nur für Fischzüchter interessant, da sie durchaus zeitaufwendig ist. Selbstfang von Lebendfutter kann eine interessante und gesunde (vor allem mit dem Fahrrad) Freizeitbeschäftigung sein. Aber Vorsicht! Lebendfutter aus Fischgewässern kann Krankheitserreger mit ins Aquarium bringen.

Darüber hinaus werden Sie nur noch selten ein Gewässer finden, wo der Selbstfang von Lebendfutter nicht mit irgendwelchen Eigentums- oder Fischereirechten kollidiert. Wohl dem, der in einem Aquarienverein ist, der eigene Futterteiche hat.

Bleibt also der Gang zum Zoofachhändler als Hauptmöglichkeit, an Lebendfutter zu kommen. Halt, eines hätten wir fast vergessen: Im Sommer können Sie in Regentonnen oder sonstigen Wassergefäßen im Freien schwarze Mückenlarven fangen. Wenn im Aquarium nicht alle gefressen werden, haben Sie jedoch einige Tage später liebe, stechende Zimmergenossen! Die

gängigsten Lebendfuttertiere zeigt der Kasten.

Frostfutter

Unter Frostfutter versteht man tiefgefrorene Lebendfuttertiere oder Teile davon. Außer den im Kasten aufgeführten Mückenlarven und Kleinkrebsen findet man noch eine Reihe weiterer Sorten. Für das Süßwasseraquarium kommen noch ausgewachsene Artemia (Salinenkrebschen), Fischfilet (für Raubfi-

Salinen-krebschen **(Artemia).**

sche) oder Rogen von Fischen (sehr fett!) in Frage!

Frostfutter muß vor Verfütterung komplett aufgetaut werden, um Verdauungsstörungen zu vermeiden. Für die Lagerung gelten die gleichen Regeln wie für tiefgefrorene Lebensmittel. Frostfutter hat, wenn es sachgerecht gelagert und beim Auftauen nicht zu lange gewässert wird, den gleichen Nährstoffgehalt wie Lebendfutter.

Gefriergetrocknetes Futter

Gefriergetrocknetes Futter ist tiefgefrorenes Lebendfutter, dem anschließend unter Vakuum die Feuchtigkeit entzogen wurde. Bei dieser Methode bleibt der volle Nährstoffgehalt erhalten, Krankheitserreger werden abgetötet, und das Futter hat die Haltbarkeit von Flockenfutter. Die meisten Hersteller von Flockenfutter bieten als Sortimentsbereicherung auch gefriergetrocknetes Futter an. Oft wird der Ausdruck FD-Futter verwendet (FD = freeze dried). Mit gefriergetrocknetem Futter lassen sich viele Lebendfutterfresser an Flockenfutter gewöhnen. Außerdem dient es als Abwechslung auf dem Speiseplan.

Lebendfutter

Weiße Mückenlarven

Larven der Büschelmücke *Corethra.* Ausgezeichnetes, unbelastetes Lebendfutter, das nur in sau-

Büschelmückenlarve **(Corethra)**

beren Gewässern vorkommt. Wegen des durchscheinenden Aussehens auch als Glasstäbchen bezeichnet. In feuchtes Zeitungspapier eingeschlagen im Kühlschrank monatelang haltbar. Fertige Mükken stechen nicht.

Rote Mückenlarven

Larven der Zuckmücke *Chironomus.* Rote Mückenlarven werden von allen Fischen sehr gern genommen. Stammen aus belasteten Gewässern, deshalb nur geringe Mengen füttern. Aufbewahrung wie weiße Mückenlarven, jedoch leicht penetranter Ge-

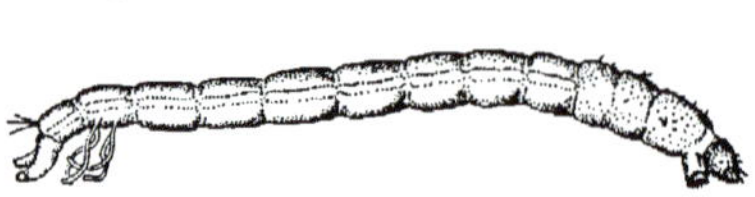

„Rote Mückenlarve" (Zuckmückenlarve, **Chironomus).**

ruch. Fertige Mücken stechen nicht.

Schwarze Mückenlarven

Gibt es wegen der Stechmückengefahr nur gefroren zu kaufen. Lebende müssen Sie auf eigenes Risiko selbst fangen.

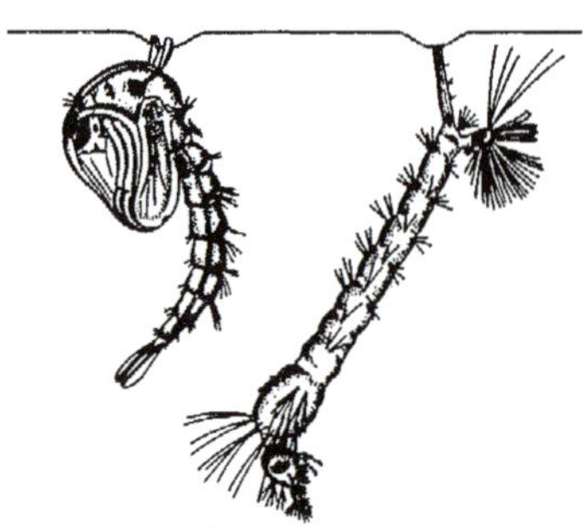

„Schwarze Mückenlarven" sind Larven der Stechmücke **Culex** ***(links eine Puppe).***

Kleinkrebse

Wasserflöhe *(Daphnia)*, Hüpferlinge *(Cyclops)* und Rüsselkrebschen *(Bosmiden)* sind die gängigsten. Sehr kleinen Jungfischen können *Cyclops* gefährlich werden. Klein-

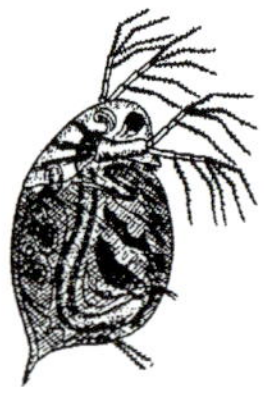

Wasserfloh **(Daphnia)**

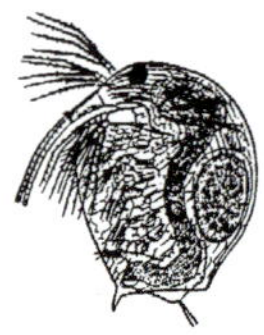

Rüsselkrebschen **(Bosmina)**

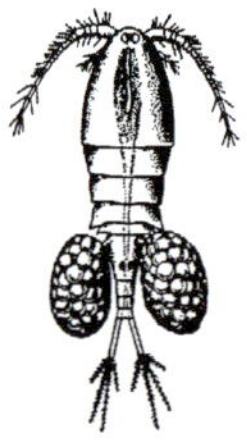

Hüpferling **(Cyclops, *hier ein Weibchen mit Eiersäcken)***

krebse sind ernährungsphysiologisch wertvoll, mit hohem Ballaststoffgehalt; alleinige Verfütterung kann jedoch zu Mangelerscheinungen führen. Aufbewahrung im Eimer mit kühlem Wasser; sehr sauerstoffbedürftig.

Tubifex, Schlammröhrenwürmer

Stammen aus belasteten Gewässern. Durch Wässern unter fließendem Wasser für mehrere Tage kann der Schadstoffgehalt gesenkt werden. Trotzdem nur sparsam

Bachröhrenwurm **(Tubifex)**

füttern, da sehr fett und proteinreich. Nicht gefressene Würmer verkriechen sich schnell im Bodengrund, sterben dort ab und führen zu Fäulnis.

Ein Besuch beim Fischfutter-hersteller

Wir betreten in gespannter Erwartung die „heiligen Hallen“, sprich den Empfangsbereich im Büro- und Verwaltungstrakt einer namhaften Firma der Heimtierbranche. Richtig, wir sind zu Gast in der Produktionsstätte eines auf Zierfischnahrung spezialisierten Futtermittelherstellers.

Natürlich sind schon hier in der Nähe des Eingangs, wie später auch im Labor- und Testbereich, gepflegte Aquarien zu sehen. Ein freundlicher „Weißkittel“ begrüßt uns, um uns nach einigen einführenden Worten und Verhaltensmaßregeln sogleich an den eigentlichen Ort des Geschehens und den Mittelpunkt unseres Interesses zu geleiten.

Vor allem möchten wir die „Dünnschichtflocken“ sehen, die vor Jahrzehnten erfunden und seitdem ständig verbessert wurden. Gerade diese Darreichungsform eines Vollwertfutters hat die Aquaristik ja geradezu revolutioniert und bei vielen Pfleglingen zum züchterischen Durchbruch verholfen. Daher steht zunächst die Besichtigung der Flockenfutterfertigung auf unserem Programm.

Dazu folgen wir dem normalen Produktionsverlauf von den Rohstoffen über die (im Detail natürlich geheime) Rezepturmischung zur eigentlichen technischen Verarbeitung der Komponenten. Im Lager harren die Rohstoffe in Silozellen, auf Paletten gestapelte Säcke, in Hochregalen befindliche Fässer und andere Gebinde wie wir der Dinge, die da kommen werden.

Im Vorbeigehen können wir einen Blick auf einige Beschriftungen werfen: Fisch- und Garnelenerzeugnisse, Getreidemehle, Hefe, Algen und vieles mehr sind zu erkennen. Einige Verpackungseinheiten tragen Abkürzungen und unbekannte Bezeichnungen; allzu neugierige Fragen der Besucher werden lediglich mit einem geheimnisvollen Lächeln beantwortet.

Gänzlich verschlossen bleibt der Raum für die „Zusatzstoffe“. Wir erfahren, daß hier die Vitamine und einzelnen Nähr- und Wirkstoffergänzungen gelagert und abgewogen werden. Gerade verläßt ein Mitarbeiter diesen Raum, aber mehr als einen flüchtigen Eindruck von einer gelblich-hellbraunen, pulverig aussehenden Mischung in einer Kunststofftrommel bekommen wir nicht mit.

Hier kommt die „Riesenflocke“ frisch von der Walze.

Die Futterdosen werden gefüllt und versiegelt.

Tiefer in den Hallen werden die Gerüche noch intensiver als im Warenlager. Der unbedarfte Fremdling würde sagen: Es stinkt! In Sachen Fischfutter versierte Aquarianer sind sich jedoch rasch einig: Es riecht typisch!

Vom Brei zur Flocke

In der Produktionshalle wird gemischt und angerührt, denn Flockenfutter entsteht aus einem fast dünnflüssigen Teig. Den gilt es zunächst mit Wasser optimal anzurühren, ähnlich dem Pfannkuchen- und Waffelteig in unseren Küchen daheim. Unser Führer erzählt von Mischgenauigkeiten und Rührdrehzahlen, doch wir haben kaum Ohren dafür. Es gibt einfach viel zu viel zu sehen.

Wir betrachten in dieser warmen, dampfenden Hexenküche eine komplette Fertigungslinie für eine bestimmte Flockenvariante genauer. Zunächst erkennt man einen großen, zylindrischen Rührbottich, wo gerade Wasser zufließt. Hier entsteht der fragliche Teig und eine Leitung fördert den Teigmix nun auf ein dröhnendes, vor blankem Metall blitzendes Ungetüm von Maschine.

Aha, das also ist ein sogenannter Walzentrockner, eine von innen beheizte, liegend aufgehängte und unermüdlich rotierende Walze. Ein Pendelarm am Ende der Förderleitung verteilt das Material gleichmäßig. Es entsteht ein dünner Film auf der Trocknungswalze. So wird dem Teig Flüssigkeit entzogen und er wird, kontinuierlich von einem scharfen Messerbalken abgeschabt, zu einer breiten, papierähnlichen Futterbahn. Am unteren Ende der Walze verläßt also quasi eine „Riesenflocke am Stück“ diese Produktionsmaschine, um in einem Auffangbehälter zunächst grob zu zerbrechen.

Zur Weiterbehandlung müssen diese großen Flocken nun aber den dampfgeschwängerten Umgebungsbereich der Walzen verlassen, um in dieser hohen Luftfeuchtigkeit nicht wieder zuviel Wasser aufzunehmen. Wir folgen ihnen, das Rauschen und Dröhnen der Technik hinter uns lassend.

Die endgültige Zerkleinerung und Größenklassifizierung sind die nächsten, weit weniger spannenden Schritte. Ein großer Mischer vermengt nun nach den Vorgaben des Produktionsleiters die einzelnen Flockenqualitäten. Aus überdimensionalen Behältern gelangen sie schließlich zur weitgehend automatischen Abfüllung in versiegelte Dosen, wie wir sie aus unserem Zoofachgeschäft kennen.

Andere Futterarten

Zuletzt zeigt man uns noch eine der gerade fleißig vor sich hin stempelnden Tablettenpressen, wo eine andere, besonders bei Bodenfischen beliebte Futtervariante hergestellt wird. Ein völlig trockener Prozeß diesmal, in dem aus mehligpulverigen oder feingrießigen Zutaten durch rein mechanisches Ausformen unter Druck feinste Zierfischhappen entstehen.

Die Besichtigung der Produktionsstraße zur Siebung und Abpackung von (gefrier-)getrockneten, ganzen Futterorganismen wie Wasserflöhen und anderen Kleinkrebsen, Tubifex, diversen Larven und Co. beschließt unseren Besuch. Hier rumpelt und staubt es nicht wenig, und alle Beschäftigten tragen einen Mundschutz.

Tief beeindruckt verlassen wir unsere Gastgeber, nicht ohne uns für das Erlebte zu bedanken. Eins steht fest: Die nächste Portion Futter für unsere Aquarienbewohner betrachten wir mit ganz anderen Augen, ja, vielleicht öffnen wir die Verpackung sogar mit ein bißchen Ehrfurcht.

Auch bei Fischen gibt es Vegetarier.

Flockenfutter füttert man am besten nicht in einem Futterring. Das Futter kann sich so auf der Wasseroberfläche verteilen, und auch scheue und kleinere Fische haben die Möglichkeit, etwas zu erwischen.

Grünfutter

Manche Fische legen Wert auf frisches „Grün", auch wenn sie grünfutterhaltiges Flockenfutter in ausreichender Menge erhalten. Viele Harnischwelse, aber auch Schmerlen nehmen frisches Grünfutter als Abwechslung gern an. Was gefressen wird, hängt oft auch vom Geschmack der Tiere ab, hier gilt es zu experimentieren. Die einen mögen rohe Salatgurkenscheiben, die anderen gekochte Kartoffelstücke, Erbsen, überbrühten Spinat, Salat und was Haus und Garten sonst noch zu bieten haben. Der Auftrieb dieses Grünfutters im Wasser läßt sich durch Festklemmen an einem Stein umgehen.

Frisches Grünfutter (Gurken, Salat etc.) darf bis zu zwei Tage im Wasser verbleiben; wenn dann noch Reste sind, diese entfernen.

Wie oft und wieviel füttern?

Für ausgewachsene oder nahezu ausgewachsene Fische genügen ein bis zwei Fütterungen am Tag. Für halbwüchsige Fische kann eventuell auch eine dritte Fütterung empfehlenswert sein. Kleine Jungfische müssen fünf- bis sechsmal am Tag gefüttert werden, damit sie möglichst schnell wachsen. Was sie in der Jugend versäumt haben, holen sie später nie wieder nach!

Füttern Sie nur soviel, wie die Fische in zwei bis drei Minuten restlos auffressen können. Es sind schon wesentlich mehr Fische zu Tode gefüttert worden, als an Futtermangel gestorben. Nachtaktive Fische, vor allem Bodenbewohner, sollten abends nach Ausschalten der Beleuchtung eine angemessene Extraration Futtertabletten bekommen.

Gesund wie ein Fisch im Wasser?

Leider trifft dieses Sprichwort nicht immer zu. Denn auch im Aquarium können die Fische mitunter alles andere als „gesund wie der Fisch im Wasser" sein. Bevor wir uns jedoch mit möglichen Krankheitserscheinungen bei Aquarienfischen beschäftigen, muß eines von vornher-

Futteraufnahmetypen

Am Körperbau der Fische kann man erkennen, in welcher Wasserregion sie sich bevorzugt aufhalten. Das kann man nicht nur dafür nutzen, ein Aquarium ausgeglichen mit Fischen zu besetzen, son-

dern es läßt auch Rückschlüsse auf die Ernährungsweise zu.

So findet man Fische mit glatter Rückenlinie und nach unten gewölbtem Bauch, die sich an der Wasseroberfläche aufhalten. Das Maul dieser Fische ist schräg nach oben gerichtet (oberständig). Sie suchen ihre Nahrung meist an der Wasseroberfläche. Man kann sie mit Flockenfutter ernähren, lieber fressen sie allerdings gefriergе-

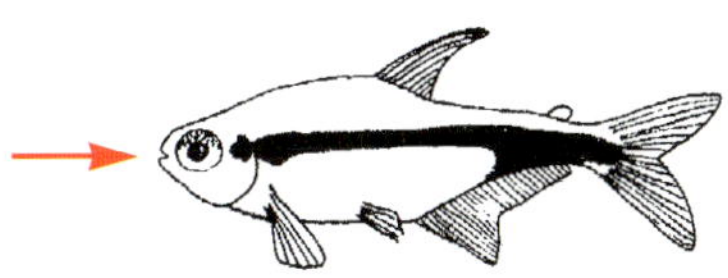

trocknete Insektenlarven und ab und zu auch eine Fliege.

Fische, die sich in den mittleren Wasserschichten aufhalten, haben mehr oder weniger gleichstark gewölbte Rücken- und Bauchlinien. Das Maul steht ziemlich genau waagerecht (endständig). Solche Fische fressen bevorzugt alles, was sich in den mittleren Wasserschichten findet, sei es herabsinkendes Flockenfutter, Lebend- oder Frostfutter.

Am Boden sitzen Fische, die bei ziemlich geradlinigem Bauch eine mehr oder weniger stark gewölbte Rückenpartie haben. Das Maul ist nach unten gerichtet (unterständig) und trägt Barteln, oder es ist zu einem Saugmaul umgebildet. Diese Fische suchen am Boden

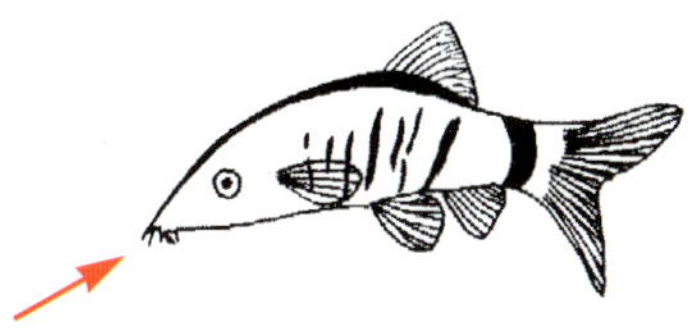

nach Nahrung, die man ihnen in Form von Futtertabletten extra zukommen läßt. Die „Bodenkinder" haben oft auch einen nicht zu unterschätzenden Appetit auf Pflanzliches.

Zwischen diesen drei Typen gibt es natürlich auch Übergangsformen, die mehr nach oben oder nach unten orientiert sind. Reine Oberflächen- und reine Bodenfische verlassen ihr Reich allerdings nur sehr selten.

ein klargestellt werden: Die meisten der in Aquarien auftretenden Krankheiten sind Folgen von nicht zusagenden Haltungsbedingungen.

Das bedeutet aber auch gleichzeitig, daß die beste Krankheitsvorbeugung durch eine den Bedürfnissen der Fische angepaßte Haltung und Fütterung erreicht werden kann. Damit haben Sie als verantwortungsbewußter Aquarianer das beste Mittel in der Hand, Krankheiten erst gar nicht aufkommen zu lassen. Wie heißt doch ein anderes Sprichwort: „Vorbeugen ist besser als heilen."

Eigentlich könnten Sie die Lektüre dieses Kapitels jetzt beenden, denn wenn Sie Ihr Aquarium so pflegen, wie wir bisher versucht haben, Ihnen näherzubringen, sollten Fischkrankheiten eigentlich ein Fremdwort für Sie sein. Trotzdem möchten wir Ihnen für den Fall des Falles hier einige Ratschläge geben und auch einige der häufigsten und vom Aquarianer leicht erkennbaren Krankheiten vorstellen sowie Hinweise zur Heilung geben.

Behandeln Sie Fische nicht auf Verdacht gegen Krankheiten! Jeder Behandlung muß eine einwandfreie Diagnose vorausgehen, der dann eine speziell auf die festgestellte Krankheit abgestimmte Behandlung folgen muß. Bedenken Sie bitte, daß alle Medikamente (auch die bei uns Menschen) nichts anderes als speziell wirksame Gifte sind, die in bestimmter Dosis Erreger abtöten oder lebensunfähig machen, den befallenen Organismus aber (noch) nicht schädigen.

Häufige, grundlose, vorbeugende Behandlung, möglicherweise noch mit reduzierter Dosis, schwächt letztendlich nur den Organismus, den man eigentlich schützen möchte und macht ihn dadurch erst recht anfällig gegen Krankheitserreger. Sie nehmen ja auch nicht laufend vorbeugend Aspirin, nur weil Sie vielleicht nächste Woche Kopfschmerzen bekommen könnten. Ganz davon abgesehen, daß eine Behandlung mit reduzierter Dosis den Erreger oft überhaupt nicht „juckt", weil eine ganz bestimmte wirksame Dosis erforderlich ist, um Erreger zu schädigen. In vielen Fällen werden Erreger durch „Unterdosis" sogar resistent gegen das Medikament, das dann im Ernstfall überhaupt nicht mehr hilft.

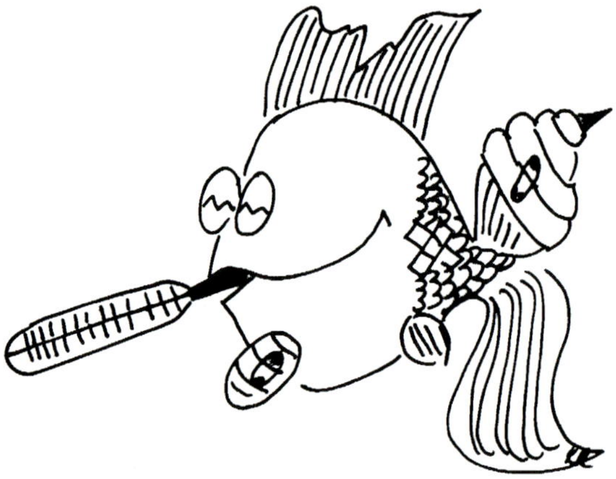

Gesund wie der Fisch im Wasser? Heute leider nicht ...

Die sichere Diagnose einer Krankheit setzt eine eingehende und regelmäßige Beobachtung der Fische voraus. Man muß mit den täglichen Lebensäußerungen seiner Fische soweit vertraut sein, daß einem ungewöhnliche Aussehens- oder Verhaltensänderungen sofort auffallen.

Fischkauf

Bevor Sie Fische einkaufen, sollten Sie bereits eine zu Ihrem Aquarium passende Fischgesellschaft geplant haben. Bedenken Sie bei der Berechnung der Fischanzahl, daß die Jungfische auch später als erwachsene Fische noch genügend Platz im Aquarium haben müssen. Als Anhaltspunkt kann folgendes Schema gelten:
Fische mit 2–3 cm Gesamtlänge: 2 Liter Wasser pro Fisch,
Fische mit 3–5 cm Gesamtlänge: 5–6 Liter Wasser pro Fisch,
Fische mit 5–8 cm Gesamtlänge: 8–10 Liter Wasser pro Fisch,
Fische über 8 cm Gesamtlänge: über 10 Liter Wasser pro Fisch.
Kaufen Sie nur gut genährte und äußerlich gesund aussehende Jungfische mit folgenden Merkmalen:

- gerundete, nicht eingefallene Bäuche
- Flossen ganzrandig, ohne Flekken und weißliche Punkte
- Flossen werden nicht geklemmt
- aktive, dem Temperament entsprechende Schwimmweise,
- kein Scheuern an Gegenständen oder heftiges Atmen
- keine weißlichen Punkte auf dem Körper

Die Färbung braucht bei Jungfischen nicht voll ausgebildet zu sein.
Der Händler wird Ihnen die Fische in speziellen Fischtransportbeuteln verpacken. Bringen Sie diese möglichst schnell nach Hause (im Winter mit entsprechendem Schutz gegen Wärmeverlust). Zu Hause angekommen:

- Beleuchtung ausschalten
- Fische im Beutel auf die Wasseroberfläche legen und 15 Minuten schwimmen lassen
- Anschließend Beutel öffnen und portionsweise Wasser aus dem Aquarium in den Beutel schütten, bis sich der Wasserinhalt im Beutel verdoppelt hat
- Fische vorsichtig über einem Eimer in ein Fangnetz schütten und dann ins Aquarium geben
- Transportwasser wegschütten!
- Einige Stunden später kann die Beleuchtung wieder eingeschaltet werden
- Erst am nächsten Tag füttern!

Beachten Sie dabei auch, daß Fische eine gewisse Bandbreite an normalen Verhaltensweisen und Färbungen aufweisen, wozu auch das Balz- und Brutpflegeverhalten gehört. Vor allem Neuaquarianer sind allzu leicht geneigt, hinter jedem „Flossenzucken" eine Krankheit zu vermuten. In solchen Fällen empfiehlt es sich, Rat bei erfahrenen Aquarianern oder Zoofachhändlern zu suchen.

Erst wenn Sie einige Erfahrung im Beurteilen von Krankheitsbildern und Verhaltensweisen der Fische gewonnen haben, können Sie auch beginnen, sich mit einschlägiger Spezialliteratur über Fischkrankheiten zu beschäftigen.

Vergiftungen

Zunächst wollen wir auf Krankheitserscheinungen aufmerksam machen, die eigentlich gar keine sind, sondern durch äußere Einwirkungen, meist Vergiftungen, entstehen. Charakteristisch für solche Erscheinungen ist, daß plötzlich ausnahmslos alle Fische des Aquariums „befallen" sind, während bei Infektionskrankheiten zunächst einige Fische befallen werden und sich die Krankheit dann allmählich auf den gesamten Bestand ausdehnt.

Typische Anzeichen für Vergiftungen sind ruckartiges Schwimmen, Springen über die Wasseroberfläche, heftige Atmung mit möglicherweise dunkel verfärbten Kiemen oder dunkler Körperfarbe.

Die Gegenmaßnahme ist ein sofortiger, möglichst umfassender Wasserwechsel. Zuvor entnimmt man ca. einen Liter Wasser, das man beiseite stellt und nach Beendigung des Wasserwechsels analysiert, um die mögliche Ursache herauszufinden. Selbstverständlich muß die Ursache dann beseitigt werden.

Häufige Ursache für Vergiftungen sind ein hoher Ammonium- oder Nitritgehalt in zuwenig eingefahrenen oder überbesetzten Aquarien. Auch nach einer Behandlung gegen Krankheiten kann der bakterielle Abbau gestört sein und zu einem Anstieg von Ammonium und Nitrit führen. Nitrit ist direkt giftig, während Ammonium nur bei hohen pH-Werten in das hochgiftige Ammoniak übergeht. Beide Stoffe konkurrieren mit den Sauerstoffbindungsstellen im Blut und rufen praktisch Erstickungserscheinungen hervor.

Ein stark erhöhter oder stark erniedrigter pH-Wert verursacht die Laugen- oder Säurekrankheit. Unvorsichtiges Hantieren mit Insektiziden oder Pflanzenschutzmitteln im Wohnraum kann ebenfalls zu Vergiftungen führen.

Weißpünktchenkrankheit

Diese Krankheit, landläufig „Ichthyo" genannt, wird durch den einzelligen Erreger *Ichthyophthirius multifiliis* verursacht und ist die häufigste Fischkrankheit überhaupt. Leicht erkennbares Merkmal sind kleine, grieskornartige, weißliche Punkte auf Flossen und Körper der befallenen Fische. Die Krankheit ist mit Medikamenten aus dem Zoofachhandel erfolgreich zu behandeln. Haltungsbedingungen überprüfen!

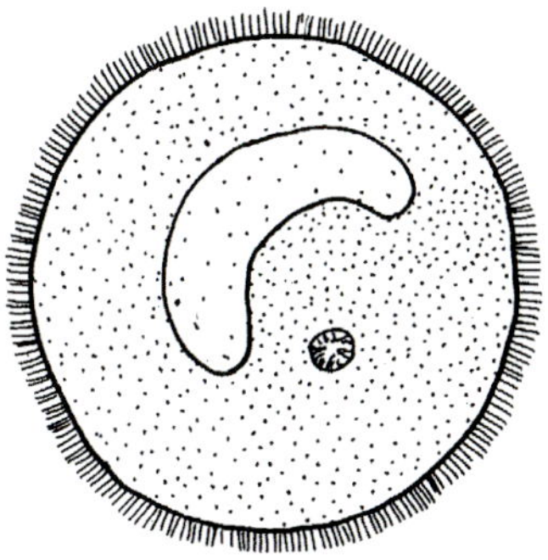

Ichthyophthirius multifiliis.

Pilzbefall

Wattebauschähnliche, weißliche, „haarige" Stellen am Fisch deuten auf einen Befall mit Wasserschimmel *(Saprolegnia)* hin. Befallen werden nur Fische, die bereits durch Verletzungen oder Parasiten vorgeschädigt sind. Der Pilzbefall kann mit Medikamenten aus dem Zoofachhandel leicht behandelt werden. Anschließend muß jedoch die Ursache herausgefunden und beseitigt werden.

Samtkrankheit oder Süßwasseroodinium

Einzellige Erreger der Gattung *Oodinium* sind als kleine, meist gelbliche Pünktchen auf der Haut der Fische zu erkennen. Die Punkte sind wesentlich kleiner als bei *Ichthyophthirius* und rufen ein samtartiges Erscheinungsbild hervor, deshalb der Name Samtkrankheit. Die

Starker Pilzbefall an einem weiblichen Zwergfadenfisch **(Colisa lalia).**

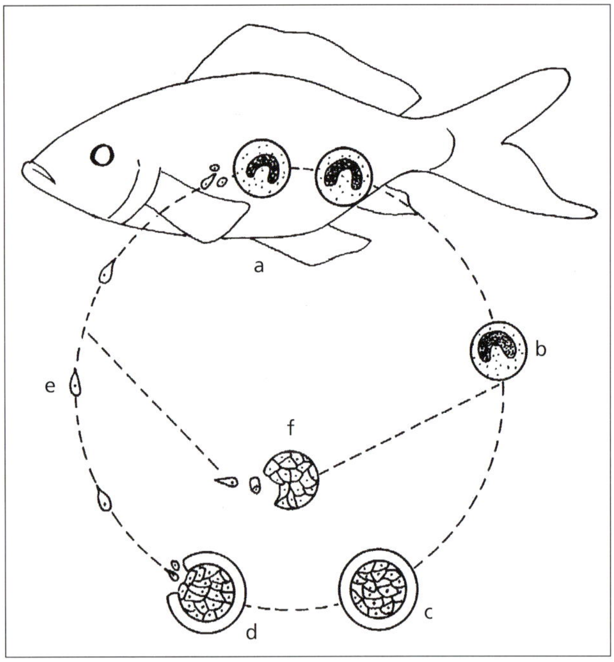

Der Entwicklungszyklus von **Ichthyophthirius multifiliis:**
- *a Fisch mit Parasiten*
- *b abgefallener Parasit*
- *c am Boden abgekapselter Parasit*
- *d schlüpfende Schwärmer*
- *e freie Schwärmer befallen den Fisch*
- *f ein unreif abgestreifter Parasit bildet Schwärmer ohne Abkapselung*

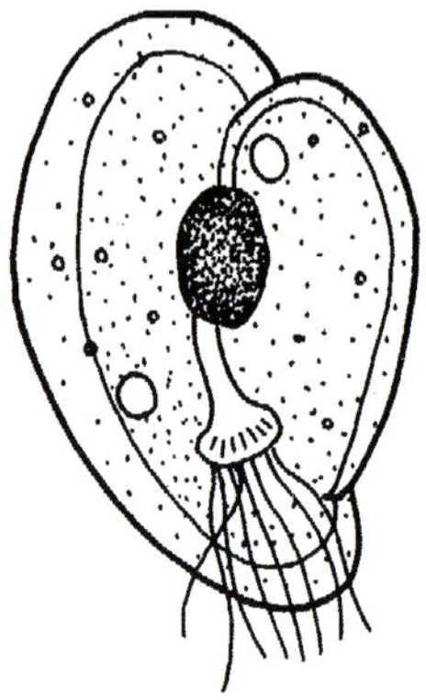

***Großer herzförmiger Hauttrüber* (Chilodonella).**

Krankheit kann mit Medikamenten aus dem Zoofachhandel bekämpft werden. Oft reicht auch eine mehrtägige Abdunkelung des Aquariums, da die Erreger Chlorophyll besitzen.

Hauttrüber

Milchig-bläulichweiße Hautstellen werden durch sogenannte Hauttrüber *(Costia, Chilodonella)* verursacht. Der Zoofachhandel bietet Medikamente an, die üblicherweise auch gegen *Ichthyophthirius* helfen. Die Behandlung kann unter Umständen bis zu zehn Tagen dauern. Temperaturerhöhung ist förderlich.

Damit hätten wir die häufigsten und auch leicht erkennbaren Krankheiten abgehandelt. Alle anderen Krankheiten (es gibt unzählige) kommen im Aquarium relativ selten vor und erfordern meist fachmännische Hilfe zur Diagnose. Viele der selteneren Krankheiten können

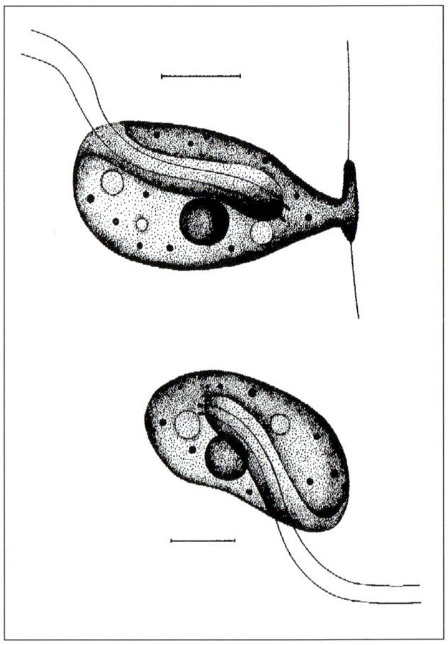

Kleiner bohnenförmiger Hauttrüber* (Costia, *der Maßstab entspricht* 3μm*).

***Starker Befall mit Süßwasseroodinium* (Piscinoodinium pillularis) *an der Rückenflosse von* Aphyosemion gardneri.**

auch mit frei verkäuflichen Medikamenten nicht behandelt werden.

Überlassen Sie den Umgang mit den dafür erforderlichen, verschreibungspflichtigen Medikamenten dem Fachmann. Das ist sicherer, nicht zuletzt auch für Ihre eigene Gesundheit, und erspart Ihnen womöglich auch Ärger mit dem Arzneimittelgesetz. Ein Mittel gegen *Ichthyophthirius* sollten Sie aber auf alle Fälle zu Hause haben. Sie werden sehen, bei artgerechter Pflege Ihrer Fische werden Sie es selten brauchen!

Die Qual der Wahl – die Fischarten

Die hier beschriebenen Fische sind nach ihrer Verwandtschaft in Gruppen zusammengefaßt, und zwar:

- Salmler
- Barben und Bärblinge
- Sonstige Karpfenähnliche
- Schmerlen und Dorngrundeln
- Welse
- Eierlegende Zahnkarpfen
- Lebendgebärende Zahnkarpfen
- Halbschnäbler
- Buntbarsche
- Labyrinthfische
- Ähren- und Regenbogenfische

Innerhalb der Gruppen sind die Arten nach ihren wissenschaftlichen Namen alphabetisch geordnet. Jeder Gruppe ist eine allgemeine Beschreibung vorangestellt, in der gemeinsame Merkmale und allgemeine Pflegehinweise enthalten sind.

In den Artbeschreibungen wird unter dem Stichwort **Herkunft** das ursprüngliche geographische Verbreitungsgebiet der Wildform genannt. In Zeiten des internationalen Handels und der Nachzucht ist damit also nichts über die tatsächliche „Staatsangehörigkeit" eines gerade gekauften Aquarienfisches ausgesagt.

Unter **Lebensraum** werden typische Biotope als bevorzugte Aufenthaltsorte der Wildtiere beschrieben. Doch gibt es unter den tropischen und subtropischen Fischen sehr anpassungsfähige Arten, die sich viele Lebensräume erschlossen haben.

Fische sind in ihrem Äußeren recht variabel, züchterische Veränderungen der Körper- und Flossenformen und der Farben kommen noch hinzu. Die Fotos können daher nicht die ganze „Bandbreite" einer Fischart, wohl aber typische Vertreter zeigen.

Die Größenangaben sind Maximallängen ausgewachsener Tiere.

Fische für jeden Geschmack und passend zur Tapete.

Die im Abschnitt **Haltung** in Klammern gesetzten Angaben beziehen sich auf die Zucht. Dies können keine Patentrezepte für einen garantierten Nachzucht-Erfolg sein – zu mannigfaltig sind die Faktoren, die im Aquarium zusammenwirken. Es sind aber nützliche Hinweise aus dem gesammelten Erfahrungsschatz vieler Aquarianer und Fischzüchter.

Salmler

Innerhalb der Großgruppe der Karpfenartigen im weiteren Sinne gibt es mehrere Familien der Salmler und salmlerähnlichen Fische. Man kennt über 1 000 Arten; die meisten kommen aus Südamerika, der Rest aus Afrika. Viele beliebte Aquarienfischarten gehören in diese Gruppe.

Die überwiegend friedliebenden, meist recht flinken Fische sind wendige Schwimmer, die in der Natur in großen, oft riesigen Schwärmen zusammenleben. Sie bewohnen fließende und stehende Gewässer, schätzen jedoch stets die Nähe von Pflanzen, in deren Dickicht sie sich zurückziehen können.

Die meisten Arten tragen zwischen der Rücken- und Afterflosse eine kleine Fettflosse.

Weiches Wasser bekommt den Salmlern gut; von einigen Arten werden auch höhere Härtewerte vertragen. Zudem sollte das Wasser sauerstoffreich sein.

Stets sind mindestens sechs bis zehn Tiere einer Art gemeinsam zu pflegen, um das Schwarmverhalten aufkommen zu lassen, das den Tieren eine Art Geborgenheit gibt. Die weitaus meisten Arten gründeln und wühlen nicht, so daß das Wasser schön klar bleibt.

1 Prachtkopfsteher
Anostomus anostomus
Herkunft: Nördl. Südamerika: Guayana, Kolumbien, Venezuela; Amazonas.
Lebensraum: Flache Flußufer, Felsspalten schnell fließender Zonen.
Beschreibung: Vor allem bei der Nahrungssuche, aber auch sonst fast

1

Verwendete Abkürzungen

T Wassertemperatur tagsüber
pH pH-Wert bzw. pH-Bereich
Hä Wasserhärte
Er Ernährungstyp und Fütterungshinweise
C Carnivore = Fleischfresser (benötigen überwiegend Lebendfutter)
H Herbivore = Pflanzenfresser (benötigen Pflanzennahrung oder pflanzliches Trockenfutter)
O Omnivore = Allesfresser (benötigen gemischte Kost)
L Limnivore = Aufwuchsfresser (weiden pflanzliche Aufwüchse mit den darin hausenden Kleinlebewesen ab; zusätzliche Futtertabletten sind sinnvoll)
LF Lebendfutter (Tubifex, Mückenlarven, Kleinkrebse; ersatzweise Frostfutter)
TF Trockenfutter (Flocken, Granulate, Pellets, Tabletten; getrocknete oder gefriergetrocknete Futtertiere)

2

senkrecht schwimmend, präsentieren sich diese sehr langgestreckten, lebhaften Schwarmfische in unteren bis mittleren Beckenbereichen. Nur im Schwarm sind die mit 15–18 cm recht großen Fische untereinander verträglich, sonst pflege man ausnahmsweise auch Einzeltiere in Gesellschaft anderer Arten, die aber nicht zu langsam sein dürfen und ebenfalls die Strömung schätzen sollten. In großen Aquarien bietet man neben viel Schwimmraum reichlich Verstecke an, pro Kopfsteher mindestens eines, am besten mit Steinbrocken als Felsspalten modelliert. Dazwischen können sich Wurzeln oder langblättrige Pflanzen befinden. Die in Einzelfällen gelungene Zucht konnte noch nicht standardisiert werden.
Haltung: T: 23–28 °C, **pH:** 5,8–7,5, **Hä:** weich bis mittel, ideal wohl um 8 °dGH; leistungsstarker Filter für Strömung erforderlich, Algenwuchs auf Steinen mit Strahlern fördern. **Er:** L (C, O, H); kleines LF und besonders Frostfutter, TF (auch Tabletten), Algen, Kopfsalat und andere Pflanzenkost.

2 Arnolds Rotaugensalmler, Afrikanischer Großschuppensalmler
Arnoldichthys spilopterus

Herkunft: Westafrika: Südnigeria, Mündungsgebiet des Niger; Lagos.
Lebensraum: Fließgewässer, auch breite Flüsse.
Beschreibung: Die bewegungsliebende Art braucht viel freien Schwimmraum, weshalb sparsame, robuste Randbepflanzung genügt. Ideal sind gut durchströmte, längliche Becken oder große, flache Aquarien mit dunklem Boden. Dann, sowie auch in Gesellschaft mit Welsen und anderen großen afrikanischen Salmlern, ist dieser Schwarmfisch recht ausdauernd. Bevorzugter Aufenthaltsort sind die mittleren und oberen Wasserbereiche. Jungbrut flüchtet bei Störung in den Bodengrund. Bei Zuchtversuchen sollte deshalb weicher Bodengrund verwendet werden. Der äußere Rand der Afterflosse ist beim Weibchen gerade, beim Männchen nach außen gewölbt. Männchen haben auch lebhaftere Farben und einen roten Fleck oder ein rot-gelb-schwarzes Streifenmuster auf der Afterflosse.
Haltung: T: 23–27 °C (bis 28 °C), **pH:** 6–7,5 (6–6,8), **Hä:** bis 20 °dGH (weicher); Torfzusatz, gute Filterung mit Strömungserzeuger. **Er:** C, O; kräftiges LF, Fliegen, kleine Schaben, kleine Regenwürmer oder Stückchen davon, TF (Großflocken).

1

3

1 Marmorierter Beilbauchfisch
Carnegiella strigata
Herkunft: Südamerika: mittlerer und unterer Amazonas.
Lebensraum: Stehende bis leicht fließende Gewässer, die beschattet sind.
Beschreibung: Die bis 4,5 cm langen, hübschen, etwas empfindlichen Schwarmfische mit der auffallenden interessanten Körperform haben keine Fettflosse. Als Fische der oberen Wasserzone halten sie sich bevorzugt zwischen Pflanzen auf und springen gern, daher Becken gut abdecken. Als schnelle Schwimmer „stehen" sie auch oft im Filterstrom. Die empfehlenswerten Schwimmpflanzen sowie feinfiedrige, andere Gewächse müssen vor allem an der Oberfläche des Aquariums genug freien Raum lassen. Nur mit Bodenbewohnern und zarten, anderen Fischen sinnvoll zu vergesellschaften. Die Zucht gelang vereinzelt bei guter Lebendfütterung und in stark abgedunkelten Becken. Nur beim (seltenen) Laichansatz wird das Weibchen runder und manchmal erblickt man durchscheinende Eier, ansonsten sind die Geschlechter nicht zu unterscheiden.
Haltung: T: 24–28 °C (bis 30 °C), **pH:** 6–7,5 (5,5–6,5), **Hä:** bis 10 °dGH, auch bis 20 °dGH (bis 5 °KH); Filterung über Torf oder Zusatz von Torfextrakten. **Er:** C; kleines LF, Kleinstfliegen, TF.

2 Spritzsalmler
Copella arnoldi
Herkunft: Südamerika: Guayana.
Lebensraum: Uferbereich kleiner Bäche.
Beschreibung: Die Männchen dieser interessanten Schwarmfischart erreichen ca. 8 cm, sie sind farbiger, mit ausgeprägterer Flossengestalt als die kleineren Weibchen. Um letztere durch die ständige Paarungsbereitschaft der männlichen Spritzsalmler nicht allzusehr zu stressen, pflege man einen Schwarm mit deutlicher Überzahl der Weibchen (bis zu drei pro Männchen). Laichvorgang und Brutpflege der Art sind biologisch „originell": Im Sprung erfolgen Eiablage und Befruchtung an überhängenden Blättern oder der Deckscheibe außerhalb des Wassers. Allein für das Gelege verantwortlich (Vaterfamilie), bespritzt das Männchen die Eier durch fortlaufende Schläge mit der Schwanzflosse mit Wasser, um sie stets feucht zu halten (Name!). Die gut auch in Gesellschaft zu pflegende Art braucht große, gut abgedeckte helle Becken mit zeitweiliger Sonneneinstrahlung, wo sie sich in den oberen Wasserschichten tummeln kann. Großblättrige Pflanzen, die über die Wasseroberfläche ragen, oder auch eine Schwimmpflanzenecke, kombiniert mit einem abseits davon plazierten Pflanzendickicht, imitieren den Lebensraum ideal. Für die Zucht ist abwechslungsreiches Lebendfutter unabdingbar.
Haltung: T: 22–28 °C (24–29 °C); **pH:** 6,5–7,5 (unter 7), **Hä:** bis 12 °dGH (weicher); Torf, regelmäßige Wasserwechsel. **Er:** O, C: TF, kleines LF, Frucht- und Essigfliegen (Drosophila).

3 Silberbeilbauchfisch
Gasteropelecus sternicla
Herkunft: Südamerika: Amazonas-

2

5

4

Zuflüsse, Brasilien, Guayana, Peru.
Lebensraum: Kleine bis mittelgroße Bäche in der Nähe von Pflanzeninseln und unter überhängenden Uferpflanzen.
Beschreibung: Silberbeilbäuche tragen eine Fettflosse; von oben betrachtet wirken die Männchen schlanker. Zuchten sind noch nicht gelungen. Die 6 bis 7 cm langen Fische sind zunächst meist scheu. Sie brauchen Schwimmraum an der Wasseroberfläche, aber auch Schwimmpflanzen sind beliebt. Becken gut abdecken, da die Schwarmfische gut springen (Raum zwischen Wasser und Abdeckscheibe lassen). Vergesellschaftung möglich, doch haben auch Artbecken (halbhoher Wasserstand) oder Paludarien ihren Reiz. Als Fließgewässer-Bewohner sind Beilbauchfische sehr sauerstoffbedürftig.
Haltung: T: 23–27 °C (Versuche bei 28–30 °C), **pH:** leicht sauer (um 6 probieren), **Hä:** bis 10 °dGH (sehr weich?); Torfzusatz. **Er:** C; kleines LF, TF.

4 Trauermantelsalmler, Schwarzer Tetra
Gymnocorymbus ternetzi

Herkunft: Südamerika: Rio Paraguay, Südbrasilien, Bolivien.
Lebensraum: Schattige, ruhig fließende Gewässerbereiche.
Beschreibung: Revierbildender, aber friedfertiger Schwarmfisch, der bei max. 6 cm Länge durch seine Form auffällt: Die lang heruntergezogene Afterflosse verleiht ihm einen interessanten Umriß. Das kleinere, schlankere Männchen zeigt deutlicheres Weiß in der Schwanzflosse und meist eine spitzere Rückenflosse. Leider geht die schwarze Färbung im Alter zurück. Die ruhigen und anspruchslosen Fische sind überwiegend in der Beckenmitte zu finden. Nicht zu helle Aquarien mit lockerer Bepflanzung und Wurzeln sind günstig. Vergesellschaftung mit Fischen bis 12 cm Körperlänge. Zucht möglich.
Haltung: T: 23–27 °C (bis 28 °C), **pH:** 6–8 (unter 7), **Hä:** weich bis hart (bis 30 °dGH). **Er:** O, TF, LF.

5 Kupfersalmler
Hasemania nana
Herkunft: Südamerika: südliches und südöstliches Brasilien.

Lebensraum: Kleine und kleinste Fließgewässer mit strömungsbedingt hohem Sauerstoffgehalt.
Beschreibung: Die lebhaften, quirligen, um 5 cm langen Schwarmfische tragen keine Fettflosse. Sie halten sich in der mittleren bis oberen Wasserzone auf und sind gut zu vergesellschaften. Die Männchen bilden Territorien. Relativ dunkel in Beleuchtung und Boden, sollte das Aquarium vor allem am Rand bepflanzt sein, damit Freiraum für ausgiebiges Umherschwimmen bleibt. Die Art ist insgesamt farblich recht variabel, die Männchen sind farbiger als die größeren und dickeren Weibchen. Im Schwarm erscheinen männliche Kupfersalmler regelrecht strahlend, mit leuchtendem Flossenweiß.
Haltung: T: 21–26 °C (26–28 °C), **pH:** 6–7,5 (5,8–7), **Hä:** weich bis hart (bis mittelhart); Torf. **Er:** C, O; kleines LF, TF.

1 Rotkopfsalmler
Hemigrammus bleheri
Herkunft: Südamerika: Unterer Amazonas, Rio Negro, Rio Vaupes, Nordbrasilien, Kolumbien.
Lebensraum: Stehende bis leicht fließende, klare Schwarzwässer.
Beschreibung: Dieser schöne, schnelle Schwarmfisch wird bis zu 7 cm lang; bei so großen und etwas dickeren Tieren dürfte es sich um Weibchen handeln. Die Männchen tragen feine Häkchen an der Afterflosse. Die lebhaften, fettflossentragenden Salmler bevorzugen den mittleren Aquarienbereich. In dunkel eingerichteten Becken fühlen sich diese Fische wohl und schreiten eventuell auch zur Zucht. Vergesellschaftung möglich.
Haltung: T: 24–27 °C (bis 28 °C), **pH:** 5–6,5, **Hä:** weich bis mittelhart (bis 10 °dGH, KH unter 4°); öfters Frischwasserzusatz, besonders auf niedrige Nitratwerte achten. **Er:** O, H; TF, kleines LF, pflanzliche Kost.

2 Glühlichtsalmler
Hemigrammus erythrozonus
Herkunft: Nordöstliches Südamerika: Guayana.
Lebensraum: Durch Uferbepflanzung abgeschattete kleinere Gewässer.
Beschreibung: Die friedlichen, schwarm- und revierbildenden, um 4 cm langen Fischlein nutzen die mittlere und untere Wasserzone. Sie tragen eine Fettflosse. Die etwas größeren Weibchen wirken insgesamt rundlicher und füllig. Man sollte die Tiere bei gedämpftem Licht halten und mit ruhigen Schwarmfischen vergesellschaften. Die Bepflanzung soll viel freien Schwimmraum lassen. Zucht möglich.
Haltung: T: 22–26 °C (26–28 °C), **pH:** 6–7,5 (5,5–7), **Hä:** weich bis mittelhart (weich, bis 10 °dGH); Torfzusatz. **Er:** O, H; TF, kleines LF, Kopfsalat.

3 Karfunkelsalmler
Hemigrammus pulcher
Herkunft: Südamerika: Peru und Brasilien, oberer und mittlerer Amazonas.
Lebensraum: Gewässerbereiche mit weichem Wasser.
Beschreibung: In der mittleren Zone dunkel eingerichteter Aquarien entfaltet dieser bis zu 6 cm lange Schwarmfisch am besten seine Farbkraft. Dicht bepflanzte Bereiche müssen sich mit freiem Raum abwechseln, um den ruhigen Fischen gleichermaßen Rückzugs- und Schwimmöglichkeit zu bieten. Die etwas größeren Weibchen machen einen gedrungeneren Eindruck, manchmal zeigen die Männchen weiße Afterflossenbereiche. Revierbildend, aber friedlich; für Gesellschaftsbecken mit weichem Wasser und anderen „zarten" Fischen geeignet.
Haltung: T: 24–28 °C (eher bei 28 °C), **pH:** 5–6,5, **Hä:** bis mittelhart (weich, bis 10 °dGH); möglichst dunkler Boden. **Er:** O, H; TF, kleines LF, pflanzliche Kost.

4 Schmucksalmler
Hyphessobrycon bentosi bentosi
Herkunft: Südamerika: Guayana, unterer Amazonas.
Lebensraum: Klare, besonnte Abschnitte sandiger bis kiesiger Fließgewässer.
Beschreibung: Rot, rötlich oder auch beinahe durchsichtig zeigen

1

2

sich diese prächtigen, 4 bis 5 cm (selten bis 6 cm) langen „Kleinsegler" am besten in Gruppen (mehrere Paare). Anstelle klassischer Schwärme bilden sich im unteren Beckenbereich Balzreviere der sich dabei heftig umkreisenden Männchen. Weibchen sind dicker und ihnen fehlt die fahnenförmig ausgezogene Rückenflosse. Die Schmucksalmler brauchen eine dichte, randständige Bepflanzung, die zum Beckenzentrum hin lockerer und feinfiedriger wird. Leichte Strömung bei dunklem Boden sagt den Schmucksalmlern zu. Zucht und Vergesellschaftung möglich.

Haltung: T: 24–26 °C (26–28 °C), **pH:** 6–7,5 (5,8–7), **Hä:** bis 20 °dGH (möglichst weich); Farbschwankungen je nach Herkunft und Zuchtstamm. **Er:** C, O; kleines LF, TF, pflanzliche Kost.

5 Blutsalmler
Hyphessobrycon callistus

Herkunft: Südamerika: südliches Amazonasbecken, Paraguay, Mato Grosso.

Lebensraum: Schwarzwässer; ruhige, pflanzenreiche Zonen.

Beschreibung: Die schönen, bis 4 cm großen, lebhaften und nicht immer friedlichen Schwarmfische bevorzugen die Beckenmitte und bilden kleine Reviere. Deshalb, und weil sie als Flossenzupfer gelten, werden meist Artbecken mit dichter Bepflanzung und freiem Schwimmraum empfohlen. Ausreichend Lebendfutter vermeidet Raufereien zwischen Artgenossen. Die Weibchen der Blutsalmler sind etwas größer und wirken höher als die Männchen.

Haltung: T: 22–25 °C (25–28 °C), **pH:** 6–7,5 (5,8–6,8), **Hä:** bis 25 °dGH (weich; bis 10 °dGH); zur Zucht Torf, dunkel halten. **Er:** C, O; kleines LF, TF, pflanzliche Kost.

3

4

5

1

2

3

1 Fahnen-Kirschflecksalmler, Perezsalmler
Hyphessobrycon erythrostigma

Herkunft: Südamerika: oberer Amazonas, Peru.
Lebensraum: Ruhige, teils pflanzenreiche Flußabschnitte.
Beschreibung: Ein Schwarmfisch der mittleren bis unteren Wasserzonen, der bei 6 cm Körperlänge (selten mehr) trotz Revierbildung als friedlich gilt. Die Männchen drohen sich durch Spreizen der verlängerten Rücken- und Afterflossen, kämpfen aber nicht miteinander. Die Weibchen sind größer als die Männchen und weniger farbig. Vergesellschaftung empfiehlt sich mit ruhigen Arten; die Zucht ist möglich. Freier Schwimmraum und dichte Pflanzen sollten gleichermaßen vorhanden sein.
Haltung: T: ab 23 °C (bis 25 °C), **pH:** 6–7,2 (5,6–6,8), **Hä:** bis 12 °dGH (weicher); Torfzusatz. **Er:** C, O, H; LF, TF, pflanzliche Zusatznahrung.

2 Roter von Rio (Roter Tetra, Feuersalmler)
Hyphessobrycon flammeus

Herkunft: Südamerika: Ostbrasilien (bei Rio de Janeiro).
Lebensraum: Flache Gewässer.
Beschreibung: Zähe Schwarmfischchen der mittleren bis unteren Wasserbereiche, um 4 cm Länge, friedlich und ohne besondere Ansprüche. Die größeren Weibchen sind matter in der Farbe und zeigen oft schwarze Brustflossenspitzen und eine helle Afterflosse, die der Männchen ist kräftig rot, und die Ränder der Bauch- und Afterflossen sind tiefschwarz gesäumt. Becken mit dichter Bepflanzung der Ecken und Seiten lassen genügend Schwimmöglichkeiten. Die Balz ist gut zu beobachten, und in Artenbecken ist die Zucht einfach. Am besten mit kleinen Fischarten zu vergesellschaften.
Haltung: T: 22–27 °C (bis 28 °C), **pH:** 6–7,5 (5,8–7), **Hä:** verträgt auch hartes Wasser (Zucht in weichem Wasser einfacher und produktiver); Torfzusatz, dunkler Boden und gedämpftes Licht. **Er:** O; TF, kleines LF, pflanzliche Kost.

3 Schwarzer Neon (Schwarzer Flaggensalmler)
Hyphessobrycon herbertaxelrodi

Herkunft: Südamerika: Brasilien, Mato Grosso, Rio Taquary.
Lebensraum: Flachwasserzonen von Bächen und Flüssen.
Beschreibung: Die friedfertigen Schwarmfische sind so lebhaft, daß

4

5

sie fast ständig in den mittleren und oberen Wasserzonen im Aquarium in Bewegung sind. Die bis zu 4,5 cm langen Fische zeigen bei guter Pflege einen starken Farbkontrast auf dem Körper, was einen schönen Gesamteindruck des (möglichst großen) Schwarms ergibt. Dunkler Boden und mattes Licht werden durch satte Färbung honoriert. Die Männchen sind sehr klein und schlank. Die Zucht gelingt vor allem in separaten Zuchtbecken. Vergesellschaftung nur mit wirklich ruhigen Arten, von hektischen Schnellschwimmern werden die Schwarzen Neons geradezu verschreckt.
Haltung: T: 23–26 °C (27–28 °C), **pH:** 5–7 (bis 6,5), **Hä:** weich bis mittelhart (weich); strömungsliebend, Torffilterung. **Er:** C, O; sehr abwechslungsreich mit kleinem LF, TF, Grünzeug.

4 Zitronensalmler (Schönflossensalmler)
Hyphessobrycon pulchripinnis
Herkunft: Südamerika: Mittelbrasilien, Amazonas.
Lebensraum: Kleine Fließgewässer mit krautigen Pflanzen.
Beschreibung: Ein schöner Schwarmfisch, bis 5 cm lang, der dichte Pflanzenbestände am Rand und freien Schwimmraum schätzt. In der Mitte und in Bodennähe stehen die Tiere gern an bestimmten Plätzen, von wo aus sie „Ausflüge" unternehmen. Immer friedlich und lebhaft wirkend, eignen sie sich auch für Gesellschaftsbecken. Der schwarze Saum der Afterflosse ist bei männlichen Tieren kräftiger, die Weibchen erscheinen hochrückiger als ihre Partner. Die Zucht ist möglich.
Haltung: T: 23–25 °C (bis 28 °C), **pH:** 5,5–8 (5,5–6), **Hä:** bis 25 °dGH (möglichst weicher); Torfzusatz und häufige Wasserwechsel in nur kleinen Teilmengen bekommen dem Zitronensalmler gut. **Er:** C, O; kleines LF, TF, pflanzliche Kost.

Salto mortale.

5 Königssalmler
Inpaichthys kerri
Herkunft: Südamerika: Westbrasilien.
Lebensraum: Verschiedene Kleingewässer.
Beschreibung: Bei schlechter Pflege sind diese maximal 4,5 cm langen, friedlichen Schwarmfische unscheinbar und wenig farbenprächtig. In dunkel eingerichteten Aquarien fühlen sich die Königssalmler inmitten des Freiwassers wohl (daher bei gedämpftem Licht nur randständig locker bepflanzen). Die Weibchen sind kleiner und blasser, ihre Schwanzflosse ist schuppenlos und die Seitenlinie nicht durchgehend. Die männlichen Tiere verteidigen auch in Gesellschaft kleiner und friedlicher Fische anderer Arten ihre kleinen Balzreviere, daher gelingt die Zucht am ehesten in separaten, recht dunklen Kleinaquarien.
Haltung: T: 23–27 °C (26–28 °C), **pH:** 6,5–7,5 (6–7), **Hä:** weich bis mit-

telhart (weich, bis 10 °dGH); Torffilterung; zur Zucht feinfiedrige Pflanzen. **Er:** O; alle Arten kleiner Futtersorten gemischt.

1 Schwarzer Phantomsalmler
Megalamphodus megalopterus
Herkunft: Südamerika: Zentralbrasilien.
Lebensraum: In Flüssen und Seen unter Schwimmpflanzen.
Beschreibung: Die Zucht dieser lebhaften, dabei friedlichen und ausdauernden Schwarmfische ist leider schwer. Die schlankeren, mit größeren Flossen (besonders Rückenflosse) versehenen Männchen drohen einander mit gespreizten Flossen und führen Scheingefechte ohne Schäden durch. Nur bei störungsfreier, guter Haltung zeigen sie ihr schönes Schwarz auf kräftig grauem Körper. Dichte Randbepflanzung umgibt den freien Schwimmraum, den die Tiere von ihren Bodenrevieren aus bis in mittlere Wasserzonen durchstreifen. Nicht zu stark beleuchten und nur mit kleinen Arten vergesellschaften! Weibchen eher rötlich.
Haltung: T: 23–26 °C (bis 28 °C), **pH:** 6–7,5 (6–6,5), **Hä:** bis 18 °dGH (bis 10 °dGH); Torfzusatz, Schwimmpflanzen. **Er:** C, O; kleines LF, TF.

2 Roter Phantomsalmler
Megalamphodus sweglesi
Herkunft: Südamerika: Brasilien, Kolumbien.
Lebensraum: Kleingewässer kühlerer Quellgebiete.
Beschreibung: Bei optimaler Pflege der 4 cm langen, ruhigen Schwarmfische sind die Männchen (mit vergrößerter Rückenflosse) intensiv ziegelfarben. Die Weibchen haben zuweilen die Farbkombination rot, schwarz und weiß in der Rückenflosse. Die schwer durchführbare Zucht gelingt am ehesten in abgedunkelten, sauberen Becken. Die Art ist etwas empfindlicher als der schwarze Phantomsalmler, jedoch gleichfalls ausdauernd. Wie bei diesem wird durch Flossenspreizen gedroht, ohne daß ernsthafte Kämpfe entbrennen. Viel Platz zum Schwimmen im unteren und mittleren Aquarienraum ist günstig, eine Vergesellschaftung mit ruhigen und kleinen Arten möglich. Nicht stark beleuchten.
Haltung: T: um 23 °C, **pH:** leicht sauer (5,5–6), **Hä:** bis 10 °dGH (1–2 °dGH); gute Wasserpflege, Torfzusatz. **Er:** C, O; kleines Lebendfutter, TF, häufig in kleinen Portionen verabreicht.

3 Rotaugen-Moenkhausia
Moenkhausia sanctaefilomenae
Herkunft: Zentrales Südamerika: Paraguay, Ostbolivien, Ostperu, Westbrasilien.
Lebensraum: Leicht fließende Gewässer.
Beschreibung: Anspruchsloser, lebhafter und dabei friedlicher Schwarmfisch, der als recht ausdauernd gilt und bis 7 cm lang wird. Bei Bevorzugung der mittleren bis oberen Wasserregionen lieben die Tiere leichte Strömung. In Gesellschaftsbecken nicht mit ruhigen Oberflächenfischen zusammenbringen. Bei teilweise dichter Bepflanzung mit harten Pflanzen soll viel freier Schwimmraum zur Verfügung stehen. Die Zucht ist möglich.
Haltung: T: 22–25 °C (bis 26 °C), **pH:** 5,5–8,5 (unter 7), **Hä:** weich bis hart (weich); Torfzusatz. **Er:** O; TF, kleines LF, kleinste Fliegen.

4 Längsband-Ziersalmler
Nannostomus beckfordi
Herkunft: Südamerika: Guayana, Parana, unterer Rio Negro, mittlerer und unterer Amazonas.
Lebensraum: Ufervegetationsdickicht und zwischen im Wasser

1

2

liegenden Zweigen in fließenden Gewässern.
Beschreibung: Die 4,5 bis 6,5 cm langen, überaus lebhaften Schwarmfische sind dämmerungsaktiv und leider nur kurzlebig. In den mittleren und oberen Wasserregionen bilden die Männchen Kleinreviere, drohen einander und imponieren in Prachtfärbung. In relativ dunkel eingerichteten Gesellschaftsbecken wird auch lebhaftere Gesellschaft akzeptiert. Die Zucht ist möglich. Die unteren Schwanzflossenlappen und die Afterflosse der Männchen sind rot; Weibchen wirken voller. Die Art ist farblich sehr variabel und trägt keine Fettflosse.
Haltung: T: 23–25 °C (bis 30 °C; durch Fortpflanzung wird die Kurzlebigkeit gefördert, was biologisch aber durchaus normal ist), **pH:** 6–7,5 (um 6), **Hä:** bis 10 °dGH, vorsichtig gewöhnbar bis 20 °dGH (extrem weich); klar bleibendes Wasser mit Torfzusatz. **Er:** C, O; kleines LF, Frucht- und Essigfliegen (Drosophila), TF.

5 Kaisertetra (Kaisersalmler)
Nematobrycon palmeri
Herkunft: Südamerika: Westkolumbien.
Lebensraum: Mündungsbereich der Flußsysteme.
Beschreibung: Bis 6 cm lange, friedliche Schwarmfische, die ruhig bis zeitweilig lebhaft sind und aus Revieren im unteren Wasserraum bis in mittlere Wasserzonen streben. Bei der Ausbildung von Balzterritorien drohen die Männchen mit ihren spitzer als bei den Weibchen ausgezogenen Flossen, ohne zu kämpfen.

3

4

5

Ältere „Kaiserinnen" zeigen einen relativ hohen Rücken, die Zucht gelingt mit diesen Tieren gut. Bei dichter Bepflanzung und ausreichend Schwimmraum läßt sich der Kaisertetra auch mit nicht zu lebhaften Fischen vergesellschaften. **Haltung: T:** um 25 °C, **pH:** leicht sauer (5–7), **Hä:** bis 10 °dGH (möglichst weicher); liebt Torf, auf gute Wasseraufbereitung beim Wechseln achten. **Er:** C, O; kleines LF, TF.

2

1

1 Roter Neon
Paracheirodon axelrodi
Herkunft: Südamerika: Venezuela, Nordwestbrasilien, Westkolumbien.
Lebensraum: Schattige Abschnitte von Klarwasserbächen.
Beschreibung: Die durch kräftiges, großflächiges Rot bestechenden, quicklebendigen Schwarmfische werden selten länger als 4 bis 5 cm. Für viele Liebhaber sind rote Neons mit die schönsten Aquarienfische, die ausdauernd mittlere und untere Beckenbereiche besiedeln. Pflanzendickichte mit freiem Schwimmraum dazwischen und eine Vergesellschaftung mit kleinen bis mittelgroßen Fischen sorgen für artgerechte Bedingungen. Nach wie vor werden überwiegend Wildimporte gehandelt. Die Zucht ist nicht leicht, aber bei den genannten Bedingungen durchaus möglich. Weibchen sind etwas voller, Zuchtversuche sollen unter starker Abdunklung erfolgen.
Haltung: T: 23–25 °C (25–27 °C), **pH:** 5–7 (4,5–6), **Hä:** bis 10 °dGH (ganz weich, nur 1–2 °dGH); Torf, gedämpftes Licht. **Er:** C, O; kleines LF, TF.

2 Neonfisch, Neonsalmler
Paracheirodon innesi
Herkunft: Südamerika: Amazonas-Oberlauf, Ostperu.
Lebensraum: Verschiedene Flußsysteme unterschiedlicher Breite.
Beschreibung: Die farbliche Betonung dieser Schwarmfischart, die von den gehandelten Stückzahlen (viele asiatische Nachzuchten!) weltweit als die Nr. 1 gilt, liegt auf dem wunderschön glänzenden, blau-türkisfarbenen Seitenstreifen. Eine schöne optische Wirkung erzielt nur ein großer Schwarm der um 4 cm kleinen Tiere, die nicht mit großen Arten vergesellschaftet werden dürfen. Geschlechtsunterschiede sind nicht einfach zu erkennen, doch achte man bei dicklicheren Tieren auf den seitlichen Leuchtstrich: Ist er etwas blasser und mit Knick, hat man ein Weibchen vor sich. Auch hier sind teils dichte Bepflanzungen und viel freier Raum gefragt, zur Zucht (schwer!) sollten feinfiedrige Wasser-

3

4

gewächse verwendet werden. Dunkler Boden und abgedunkelte Aquarien fördern die Ausdauer der Neons, die bei geeigneten Verhältnissen über 10 Jahre alt werden können.
Haltung: T: 20–24 °C (bis 25 °C), **pH:** 5–7 (5–6), **Hä:** weich bis hart nach sorgfältiger Eingewöhnung (sehr weich, bis 2 °dGH); Torf, regelmäßige Wasserwechsel; Zuchtbecken nur ganz matt beleuchten. **Er:** C, L; kleines LF, TF, besonders Bodentabletten, pflanzliche Kost.

3 Rotmaulsalmler
Petitella georgiae
Herkunft: Südamerika: oberer Amazonas, Kolumbien, Brasilien.
Lebensraum: Kleine Schwarzwasserbäche.
Beschreibung: Die lebhaft-friedlichen Schwarmfische tragen, wie viele Salmler, eine Fettflosse und sind leicht mit Rotkopfsalmlern zu verwechseln (den Rotmaulsalmlern fehlt die schwarze Zeichnung an den Schwanzstielrändern). Die Geschlechter sind schwer zu unterscheiden. Die männlichen Fische zeigen oft kräftigere Kontraste in der Streifenzeichnung der Schwanzflosse. Die Zucht ist bisher wohl noch nicht gelungen. Vergesellschaftung ist auch mit größeren Fischen möglich, solange es sich um friedliche Arten handelt. In Becken mit dichten Pflanzenbeständen wird bei genügend freiem Raum die mittlere bis untere Wasserzone genutzt.
Haltung: T: 23–25 °C, **pH:** 5,5–7, **Hä:** wohl bis 12 °dGH; Torffilter; nur sorgfältig aufbereitetes Wasser zum Wechseln benutzen. **Er:** C, O; kleines LF, TF, pflanzliche Kost.

4 (Blauer) Kongosalmler
Phenacogrammus interruptus
Herkunft: Afrika.
Lebensraum: Flußsystem des Zaire (ehemals Kongo).
Beschreibung: Eine schöne, nur mit ruhigen Fischen zu vergesellschaftende Art, deren „Flossenqualität“ ganz wesentlich von der Wasserbeschaffenheit abhängt. In großen, dunkelbodigen Becken mit lockerer Randbepflanzung können die 8,5 bis 12 cm großen Fische sich ausschwimmen. Abseits einer guten Strömung werden auch Schwimmpflanzen geschätzt, und die durch Sonneneinstrahlung oder erhöhte Beleuchtungsintensität auslösbaren Laichvorbereitungen bieten Zuchtchancen. Rücken-, Schwanz- und Afterflossen der größeren Männchen sind ausgezogen.
Haltung: T: 23–26 °C (24–27 °C), **pH:** 6–7 (6–6,5), **Hä:** bis 10 °dGH (sehr weich); Torfzusatz, das Wasser darf dabei bräunlich werden; dunkler Boden; auf Nitrat und Einhaltung der Härte achten, wobei auch einmal bis 18 °dGH toleriert werden, wenn alles andere stimmt. **Er:** C, O; LF, große und kleine Fliegenarten, TF, Kopfsalat. Bei Mangel an vegetarischer Kost werden Pflanzentriebe verbissen!

Woher sie kommen

Aufgrund der Haltungsbedingungen und Temperaturansprüche weiß jeder, daß die in unseren Aquarien gepflegten Fische aus wärmeren Teilen dieser Erde, also tropischen oder subtropischen Ländern stammen. Aber kommen sie auch wirklich alle von dort, oder genauer gesagt, von den Gebieten, die man in der Literatur als Verbreitungsgebiet angegeben findet? – Um es gleich vorweg zu nehmen: Die wenigsten kommen wirklich von dort, sind also als sogenannte „Wildfänge“ der Natur entnommen.

Die weitaus meisten (etwa 80 %) der Fische, die man heutzutage in Zoofachgeschäften findet, haben ihre Heimat nie gesehen. Sie kamen nicht irgendwo in einem Reisfeld oder einem Seitenarm des Amazonas zur Welt, sondern in den Aquarien und sonstigen Behältnissen von Züchtern.

Vor allem in Südostasien hat die Zucht und der Export von sogenannten Zierfischen eine große Bedeutung erlangt und stellt die Lebensgrundlage vieler Menschen dar. In Singapur hat sich eine regelrechte Zierfischindustrie entwickelt, die durch Forschungsprogramme und Aktivitäten vom Staat gefördert wird. Aber auch in Thailand, Malaysia und anderen Ländern wird fleißig gezüchtet, sei es im Familienbetrieb, wo vom Sohn bis zum Großvater alle mithelfen, oder in großangelegten Zuchtbetrieben.

Gezüchtet werden nicht nur asiatische Fische wie zum Beispiel Fadenfische, sondern auch Salmler, Lebendgebärende, Diskus und viele andere. Von vielen Arten werden die Jungfische in großen Betonbecken oder Freilandteichen großgezogen, wo sie nach Erreichen der Verkaufsgröße regelrecht abgefischt werden. Die Heizung liefert die Tropensonne kostenlos, so daß kostspielige Hallenkonstruktionen entfallen. Allerdings müssen gefiederte „Fischliebhaber“ durch Netze oder andere Maßnahmen ferngehalten weden.

Viele der größeren Zuchtbetriebe exportieren ihre Fische auch selbst oder haben sich mit anderen zu Gemeinschaften zusammengeschlossen. Kleinere Zuchtbetriebe und Fänger, die Fische aus der Natur entnehmen, liefern ihre Fische an Exporteure, wo sie bis zum Versand in Aquarien oder Betonbecken gehältert werden.

Während eines Besuches bei einem Zierfischexporteur in Bangkok trafen wir zum Beispiel auf einen Herrn, der mehrere große Plastiktüten aus seinem Wagen in die Anlage des Exporteurs brachte. Bei näherem Hinsehen erkannten wir unzählige Jungfische der beiden Schmerlenarten *Botia sidthimunki* und *Botia macracanthus.* In einem Gespräch erfuhren wir, daß er diese beiden Arten als einziger in Thailand züchten könne. Wir erfuhren

In Freilandteichen aufgewachsene Fische werden zum Verkauf abgefischt.

von ihm auch noch, daß er Hormone benutzt, um die Tiere zur Fortpflanzung zu bringen. Weitergehende Informationen wollte er uns, verständlicherweise, nicht geben.

Bei der Gelegenheit konnten wir auch gleich sehen, wie eine Sendung von Fischen für einen deutschen Kunden zusammengestellt wurde. Alle Fische wurden, nach Arten getrennt, sorgfältig in unzählige Plastiktüten verpackt. Die Tüten enthielten nur etwa $^1/_3$ Wasser, die restlichen $^2/_3$ waren mit Sauerstoff gefüllt, damit die Fische den langen Transport sicher überstehen. Die einzelnen Tüten wurden sorgfältig in Styroporboxen verpackt, die ein übermäßiges Abkühlen ihres Inhalts verhindern. Schließlich wurden die Boxen von einem Cargofahrzeug der beauftragten Luftfahrtgesellschaft abgeholt und zum Flughafen gebracht.

Da der Transport lebender Tiere per Flugzeug in letzter Zeit stark ins Gerede gekommen ist, fragten wir natürlich den Besitzer der Firma, ob er denn Transportverluste zu beklagen hätte. Er versicherte uns daraufhin, daß die Verlustrate seiner Transporte bei weniger als 3 % liege. Dies ist auch nicht anders zu erwarten, da die Kunden ja Wert darauf legen, lebende Tiere zu erhalten. Ein Exporteur, dessen Sendungen mit hohen Verlustraten am Ziel ankommen, wird schnell Kunden und damit auch seine Existenzgrundlage verlieren.

Die Kunden der Exporteure sind in der Regel Großhändler, die ihrerseits wieder die Zoofacheinzelhändler beliefern, bei denen Sie dann als Aquarianer Ihre weitgereisten Fische erwerben. Es versteht sich von selbst, daß verantwortungsvolle Großhändler bestrebt sein werden, ihre Fische direkt am ersten Zielflughafen (in der Regel Frankfurt) persönlich in Empfang zu nehmen und sie dann schnellstmöglich in eine, den Bedürfnissen der Fische gerechte Hälterungsanlage überführen. Sie werden dann auch erst nach einer gewissen Eingewöhnungszeit, in der sie sich von dem Streß des Transports erholen können, an den Zoofacheinzelhändler weiterverkauft.

Teil der Aufzuchtanlage eines privaten Fischzüchters in Thailand.

Hälterungsanlage eines Fischexporteurs (Thailand).

Daß dies alles, Zucht bzw. Fang, Transport, Eingewöhnung und so weiter, nicht zum Nulltarif geschehen kann, versteht sich von selbst. Aus diesem Grund werden verantwortungsvoll gezüchtete, transportierte und gehaltene Zierfische auch ihren Preis haben. Und den sollte uns das Lebewesen Fisch allemal wert sein. Vergessen wir dabei auch nicht, daß viele Familien in den Herkunftsländern der Fische letztendlich durch unser Hobby ihren Lebensunterhalt verdienen.

Nicht unerwähnt bleiben soll natürlich, daß auch in Deutschland und Europa Zierfische professionell gezüchtet weden. Seit der Öffnung Osteuropas kommen vor allem von dort auch qualitativ hochwertige Nachzuchten zu uns. Dabei fallen die enormen Transportkosten für Flüge aus Übersee natürlich weg. Aufgrund des höheren technischen Aufwandes (Heizung etc.) und der im Vergleich wesentlich höheren Lohnkosten können deutsche und europäische Nachzuchten aber nicht billiger sein als importierte. Da diese Fische aber wesentlich weniger Transportstreß über sich ergehen lassen müssen, wäre ein Trend in diese Richtung sicherlich wünschenswert.

Bleiben zum Schluß noch all diejenigen Fische zu erwähnen, die in den Becken begeisterter Aquarianer und Hobbyzüchter das Licht der Welt erblicken und so den Bestand im Zoofachhandel bereichern.

1 Rotflossen-Glassalmler
Prionobrama filigera
Herkunft: Südamerika: Amazonas und verschiedene Zuflüsse, Argentinien, Südbrasilien.
Lebensraum: Bäche, Nebenflüsse großer Fließgewässer, teils auch in seeartigen Erweiterungen.
Beschreibung: Sehr friedlich und ganz besonders ausdauernd sind diese 6 bis 6,5 cm langen Schwarmfische des mittleren bis unteren Aquarienbereichs. Die Flossen der Männchen sind auffallend fadenförmig verlängert, und hinter dem Weiß der Afterflossenkante verläuft ein paralleler schwarzer Strich. Gut für Gesellschaftsbecken geeignet, genügen den Tieren lockere Pflanzengruppen am Rand des Aquariums. Freie Schwimmregionen sollen durch Schutz bietende, an der Oberfläche treibende Blätter und (besonders zur Zucht) einige Schwimmpflanzen ergänzt werden.
Haltung: T: 24–28 °C (26–30 °C), **pH:** 6–7,8 (bis 7), **Hä:** bis 30 °dGH (weich); halten sich gern in der Strömung eines leistungsstarken Filters auf. **Er:** O; TF, kleines LF.

2 Sternfleckensalmler, Stieglitzsalmler, Wasserstieglitz
Pristella maxillaris
Herkunft: Südamerika: Venezuela, Guayana, Unterer Amazonas.
Lebensraum: Kleingewässer.
Beschreibung: Die um 5 cm kleinen Fische müßte man im Durchlicht betrachten, um eventuell das Geschlecht zu erkennen: Bei männlichen Tieren erscheint der Leibesinhalt besonders im Bereich der Schwimmblase spitz, bei Weibchen präsentiert sich diese Region abgerundet. Die Weibchen sind auch größer und plumper als die Männchen. Lebhaft im Schwarm durch das nur locker am Rand bepflanzte Becken schwimmend, gilt die Art bei nicht zu heller Beleuchtung und dunklem Boden als ausdauernd. Züchtbar und für Gesellschaftsaquarien geeignet.
Haltung: T: 22–27 °C (bis 28 °C), **pH:** 6–8 (um 7), **Hä:** bis 35 °dGH, volle Pracht nur in weichem Wasser. **Er:** O; TF, kleines LF.

1

3 Schrägschwimmer, Schwarzstreifensalmler
Thayeria boehlkei
Herkunft: Südamerika: Amazonasgebiet, Rio Araguaia, Peru.
Lebensraum: Zwischen Pflanzen in ruhigen Gewässerbereichen.
Beschreibung: Um 7 cm lang wird dieser lebhafte Schwarmfisch. Er ist nicht immer ganz so ruhig und friedlich wie oft beschrieben, macht aber im mittleren und oberen Bereich eines Aquariums kaum ernsthafte Schwierigkeiten. Schwimmt (Name!) schräg nach oben geneigt, trägt eine Fettflosse, und weibliche Tiere wirken etwas voller. Die lockere Bepflanzung mit einigen dichten Stellen sollte noch reichlich freien Schwimmraum im Becken übrig lassen.
Haltung: T: 23–27 °C (25–28 °C), **pH:** 6–7,5 /5,5–6,5), **Hä:** 19-20 °dGH (eher weich). **Er:** O, H; TF, kleines LF, auch Frucht- oder Essigfliegen, etwas Pflanzenkost.

Barben und Bärblinge

Diese Fische gehören zu den Karpfenfischen im engeren Sinne, welche die größte Süßwasserfischgruppe bilden. Alle hier beschriebenen Arten sind Angehörige der Familie Cyprinidae (Karpfenfische), die insgesamt über 1400 Vertreter umfaßt. Die in Warmwasser-Aquarien gepflegten Karpfenfische stammen aus Asien und Afrika, aber auch in den mitteleuropäischen Flüssen und Seen gehören die meisten Arten in diese Verwandtschaft. Nordamerika hat ebenfalls seine (Kaltwasser-) Cypriniden, in Südamerika und Australien findet man diese Gruppe dagegen nicht.

Es ist geradezu selbstverständlich, daß eine so große Tiergruppe biologisch sehr verschiedenartige Arten in den unterschiedlichsten Lebensräumen entwickelt hat. Die Einzelbeschreibungen spiegeln dies wider, und meist ging mit der Eroberung unterschiedlicher Biotope auch eine gewisse Anpassungsfähigkeit einher.

Die hier behandelten Barben gelten als recht anspruchslos, Bärblinge dürfen als etwas empfindlicher eingestuft werden. Als gemeinsames Merkmal tragen sie am Körper meist Rundschuppen, während der Kopf unbeschuppt ist.

Barben und Bärblinge sind häufig Schwarmfische, die – wie Salmler – nicht unter 10 Stück pro Becken gehalten werden sollten.

2

4

3

Wegen des bei dieser Gruppe sehr verbreiteten Nahrungserwerbs durch Gründeln, verbunden mit dem Aufwirbeln von Bodenmulm, werden besonders leistungsfähige Filter benötigt.

4 Prachtbarbe

Barbus (Puntius) conchonius

Herkunft: Nord-Vorderindien: Assam, Bengalen.

Lebensraum: Flüsse, Weiher und Tümpel. Bevorzugt etwas kühlere Gewässer als andere Barben.

Beschreibung: In der Aquarienhaltung bereits ab ca. 6 cm fortpflanzungsfähig, kann diese bartellose Barbe doch bis 15 cm lang werden. Als gerne gründelnder Schwarm halten sich die Tiere überwiegend im unteren und mittleren Beckenbereich auf. Sie sind deshalb besondes gut mit nicht so wärmebedürftigen Fischen der oberen Regionen zu vergesellschaften. Großzügige Schwimmflächen über weichem Boden mit Mulm und einzelne Robustpflanzen zusätzlich zum komplett bepflanzten Beckenrand gefallen den Prachtbarben. Zucht leicht (Männchen farbiger, Weibchen etwas dicker).

Haltung: T: 18–22 °C (22–25 °C), **pH:** 6–8 (6–6,5), **Hä:** weich bis hart (8–15 °dGH); häufiger Wasserwechsel in geringen Mengen unter Verwendung eines guten Aufbereitungsmittels. **Er:** O; TF, LF, Kopfsalat und andere pflanzliche Zukost.

1

2

3

4

1 Purpurkopfbarbe
Barbus (Puntius) nigrofasciatus

Herkunft: Sri Lanka: südliche Teile des Landes.
Lebensraum: Gut bewachsene, langsam fließende Waldbäche.
Beschreibung: Ausdauer, Lebhaftigkeit und friedliches Verhalten sind die Merkmale für diese bis 6,5 cm langen Barben ohne Barteln. Als Schwarmfische ziehen sie gern in Beckenmitte umher, um bald darauf intensiv den Boden nach Futter zu durchsuchen. Dieser sollte weich und möglichst mit Mulm bedeckt sein. Das Aquarium wird am Rand gut bepflanzt und ansonsten nur mit einzelnen, robusten Pflanzen bestückt. Schwimmpflanzen sorgen für relativ dunkle Bereiche, dies mögen die Purpurköpfe neben viel Platz zum Schwimmen. Beachtet man die Wasserwerte, gelingt auch die Zucht. Die Männchen zeigen eine schwarze Rückenflosse und sind insgesamt farbiger als die Weibchen.
Haltung: T: 21–25 °C (25–28 °C); mehrwöchige „Winterruhe“ bei ca. 20 °C ist zuträglich und empfehlenswert!, **pH:** 5,5–6,5 (nur bis 6), **Hä:** weich bis mittelhart (bis 12 °dGH); häufiger Wasserwechsel in geringen Mengen unter Verwendung eines guten Aufbereitungsmittels. **Er:** O; TF, LF, pflanzliche Zukost.

2 Eilandbarbe, Perlmuttbarbe
Barbus (Puntius) oligolepis
Herkunft: Südostasien: Indonesien, Sumatra.
Lebensraum: Steh- und Fließgewässer des Hügellandes.
Beschreibung: Die bis zu 5 cm langen Tiere tragen ein Bartelpaar und sind ausdauernde Schwarmfische im unteren und mittleren Beckenbereich. Da die Männchen (Rücken- und Afterflosse mit dunklem Rand) sich ohne ernsthafte Kampfesfolgen drohen, kann man von einer friedlichen Art sprechen. Mit weichem Bodengrund ist das Aquarium richtig ausgestattet und bietet, locker am Rand und im Hintergrund mit robusten Wasserpflanzen versehen, reichen Schwimmraum, den diese Barben brauchen. Die Beleuchtungsintensität scheint diesen Fischen „egal" zu sein und richtet sich daher nach den Pflanzen. Eine Vergesellschaftung, auch mit munteren Fischarten, sowie die Zucht (dann etwas heller gehalten) sind gut möglich.
Haltung: T: 20–24 °C (24–27 °C), **pH:** 6–7,5 (bis 7), **Hä:** weich bis hart (bis 10 °dGH); häufiger Wasserwechsel in geringen Mengen unter Verwendung eines guten Aufbereitungsmittels. **Er:** O; TF, LF, Kopfsalat und Algen.

3 Fünfgürtelbarbe
Barbus (Puntius) pentazona
Herkunft: Südostasien: Singapur, Malayische Halbinsel, Borneo.
Lebensraum: Uferregion ruhiger Tieflandgewässer; Schwarzwasser.
Beschreibung: Daß die 5 cm langen, schön gezeichneten Fische ruhig, ja fast scheu und nicht so schwimmfreudig sind, unterscheidet sie von anderen Barben. Sie sollten über Kies mit weicher Deckschicht (Torf, Laub) und nur in Gesellschaft anderer ruhiger Fische gehalten werden. Relativ dunkle Aquarien, locker bepflanzt und mit Wurzel- und Pflanzenverstecken (besonders am Rand) versehen, sind der richtige Aufenthaltsort für diese anspruchsvolle Art. Im unteren bis mittleren Beckenbereich umwerben die kleineren, stromlinienförmigeren Männchen ihre nicht so ausgeprägt gefärbten Partnerinnen, doch ist die Zucht nicht einfach.
Haltung: T: 22–27 °C (27–30 °C), **pH:** 5,5–7 (bis 6,5), **Hä:** weich bis mittelhart (bis 10 °dGH); nur bei Torffilterung ist das Orange wirklich schön; wöchentlicher Teilwasserwechsel von 1/5 bis 1/4 des Gesamtvolumens ist anzustreben. **Er:** C; anspruchsvoll; vor allem LF, hochwertiges TF probieren; bei Zucht den Elterntieren zusätzlich Enchyträen reichen (ein Tip für viele Barbenarten, doch hier wohl unabdingbar).

4 Brokatbarbe
Barbus (Puntius) semifasciolatus schuberti
Herkunft: Die als Stammform vermutete Messingbarbe *(B. semifasciolatus)* kommt aus Südostchina.
Lebensraum: Brokatbarben kommen in der Natur nicht vor.
Beschreibung: Die Stammform erreicht bis 10 cm Länge, was einzelne Schläge der Zuchtform auch erreichen können. Doch bleiben Brokatbarben mit ihren zwei Bartelpaaren eher um 7 cm groß. Es sind lebhafte, friedliche Schwarmfische, die sich in Beckenmitte und vor allem am Boden recht schwimmfreudig zeigen. Dies muß bei der Gestaltung des Aquariums berücksichtigt werden, so daß sich, außer bei wenigen Einzelexemplaren, die Bepflanzung auf die Randbereiche beschränkt. Dort darf sie teils auch dicht sein und zumindest in Teilbereichen soll der Boden weich sein. Brokatbarben lieben helle, sonnige Becken und sind gute Fresser. Besonders gilt dies für die einfache Zucht, die nicht zu warm erfolgen sollte. Die größeren Weibchen sind an den Seiten dunkel gefleckt.
Haltung: T: 19–23 °C (24 °C), **pH:** 6–7,5 (bis 6,5), **Hä:** weich bis hart (bis 10 °dGH); häufiger Wasserwechsel in geringen Mengen unter Verwendung eines guten Aufbereitungsmittels. **Er:** O; TF, LF, Kopfsalat und andere Pflanzenkost.

5 Sumatrabarbe, Viergürtelbarbe
Barbus (Puntius) tetrazona
Herkunft: Südostasien: Sumatra, Borneo, eventuell auch Thailand.
Lebensraum: Bodenbereiche stehender und langsam fließender Gewässer.
Beschreibung: 5 bis 7 cm lang werden diese sehr lebhaften Barben ohne Barteln. Innerhalb des Schwarmes bildet sich eine sichtbare Rangordnung heraus. Die Fische durchziehen besonders die Beckenmitte und gründeln in weichem, feinsandigem Boden. Nur am Beckenrand braucht es einzelne und robuste Wasserpflanzen. Die Sumatrabarben, von denen viele Farbvarianten

5

gezüchtet wurden, müssen viel schwimmen können. Zur Vergesellschaftung sind sie nur bedingt geeignet: Nur schnelle, kräftige Fische bleiben unbehelligt. Langsame Arten werden ebenso „belästigt" wie alle mit länglichen Flossen, an denen Sumatrabarben leider allzu gerne zupfen. Die Weibchen wirken kräftiger als die Männchen, bei der Naturform spielt die Färbung der Männchen mehr ins rötliche.
Haltung: T: 20–25 °C (26 °C), **pH:** 6–7,5 (5,5–6,5), **Hä:** weich bis hart (bis 10 °dGH); häufiger Wasserwechsel in geringen Mengen unter Verwendung eines guten Aufbereitungsmittels. **Er:** O; TF, LF, Kopfsalat o. a. pflanzliche Beikost.

1 Bitterlingsbarbe
Barbus (Puntius) titteya
Herkunft: Sri Lanka
Lebensraum: Dunkle Bereiche des Bach- und Flußbodens.
Beschreibung: Die 4 bis 5 cm langen Fischlein haben ein Bartelpaar und gelten als lebhaft, dabei ruhig und friedlich. Sehr „schwarmfreudig" sind sie jedoch nicht, so kommt es häufig zu Streitereien unter den Männchen. Bitterlingsbarben bevorzugen weichen, dunklen Boden bei insgesamt relativ dunkler Einrichtung. So sollte man durch überhängende Pflanzen oder Schwimmpflanzen für Abschattung sorgen und neben viel Schwimmplatz auch Verstecke schaffen. Zucht (Weibchen unscheinbarer und dicklicher) und Vergesellschaftung mit ruhigen Fischen sind möglich. Die Eier hängen an einem Faden an Pflanzen.
Haltung: T: 23–26 °C (27 °C), **pH:** 6–7,5 (unter 6,5), **Hä:** weich bis hart (bis 12 °dGH). **Er:** O; TF, LF, pflanzliche Beikost.

2 Schillerbärbling
Brachydanio albolineatus
Herkunft: Südostasien: Hinterindien, Burma, Thailand, Malayische Halbinsel, Sumatra.
Lebensraum: Bäche und Flüsse.
Beschreibung: Die munteren, etwa 6 cm langen Schwarmfische mit zwei Bartelpaaren sind sehr schwimmfreudig. Friedlich durchziehen die hübschen Tiere die mittleren und oberen Aquarienregionen, weshalb man dort für freien Schwimmraum sorgen sollte. Ideal sind längliche Becken mit Kies und Steinen, die am Rand und im Hintergrund bepflanzt sind. Becken gut abdecken (Springer!). Vergesellschaftung ist möglich, die Zucht darf als einfach gelten. Paare zeigen eine gewisse Partnertreue; die kleineren, schlankeren Männchen sind intensiver gefärbt.
Haltung: T: 21–26 °C (26–30 °C), **pH:** 6,5–7,5 (bis 7), **Hä:** weich bis hart (5–12 °dGH); besondere Lebendigkeit und Farbenpracht bei Sonnenlicht-Einfall, ideal von oben. Zuchtansatz in nur 20 cm hohem Frischwasser und kleinblättrigen/gefiederten Pflanzendickichten im Becken. **Er:** C, O; kleines LF, TF, pflanzliche Beikost.

2

1

3

3 Perl-, Tüpfel-, Leopardbärbling
Brachydanio frankei
Herkunft: Südostasien: Vorderindien.
Lebensraum: Rasch fließende Kleingewässer.
Beschreibung: Die auffällig getupften, 5 bis 6 cm langen, sehr lebhaften, aber friedlichen Schwarmfische mit zwei Paar Barteln werden entweder als natürlich auftretende Farbabweichung (Morphe) oder aber als Zuchtform des Zebrabärblings aufgefaßt. Die endgültige Klärung steht noch aus. Gut abgedeckte Aquarien, normal bepflanzt und mit Freiräumen zum Schwimmen (Mitte bis oben) bzw. ein Gesellschaftsbecken sind der richtige Aufenthaltsort für diese das Sonnenlicht liebenden Fische.
Haltung: T: 20–25 °C (24–26 °C), **pH:** 6–8, **Hä:** weich bis hart; Zucht nach Frischwasserzusatz. **Er:** O; alles kleines LF und TF, ab und zu auch Pflanzen.

4 Zebrabärbling
Brachydanio rerio
Herkunft: Indien: vorderindische Ostküste.
Lebensraum: Schnelle, klare Fließgewässer.
Beschreibung: In der Beckenmitte bis hin zur Oberfläche halten sich diese friedlich-munteren Aquarienfische besonders gerne auf. Die schönen und robusten, bis 6 cm langen Tiere tragen zwei Bartelpaare und sind in sehr hellen, gut durchströmten Becken bestens untergebracht. Auch lange, relativ flache Aquarien, gut abgedeckt und normal bepflanzt, lassen reichlich Schwimmraum. Als Gesellschaft für Zebrabärblinge kommen kleine bis mittelgroße Fische in Frage, die ebenfalls lebhaft sind, oder solche, die sich nicht so leicht aus der Ruhe bringen lassen. Die Weibchen sind etwas größer und dicker, ihre Farben blasser. Bei niedrigem Wasserstand nach Frischwassergabe gelingt die Zucht leicht.
Haltung: T: 18–24 °C (24–25 °C), **pH:** 6–8, **Hä:** weich bis hart; die Art liebt Sonnenlicht. **Er:** O; kleines TF und LF, Abwechslung mit pflanzlicher Kost.

5 Malabarbärbling, Malabarkärpfling
Danio aequipinnatus
Herkunft: Asien: Sri Lanka, Westküste Vorderindiens.
Lebensraum: Eher in Fließgewässern, aber auch in stehenden Gewässern.
Beschreibung: Die meist 8 bis 10, aber auch bis 15 cm langen, sehr aktiven Schwarmfische sind stets friedfertig. Als Oberflächenschwarm gehalten, eignen sie sich besonders zur Vergesellschaftung mit Bodenbewohnern oder – gern auch größeren – Fischen, die eher von der Mitte des Aquariums nach unten streben. Sandiger Boden und viel freier Schwimmraum werden benötigt, die Bepflanzung darf nicht zu weich sein, da sonst Fraß droht. Der blaue Mittelstreifen an der Schwanzflosse des dickeren Weibchens biegt nach oben ab, während er beim Männchen weiter gerade verläuft. Die Zucht gelingt in großen Zuchtbecken. Es gibt verschiedene Lokalrassen mit Farbunterschieden.
Haltung: T: 22–24 °C (25–28 °C),

4

5

1

pH: 6,5–8 (bis 7), **Hä:** weich bis hart (5–12 °dGH); Zucht in hohem Frischwasseranteil; sonniger Standort. **Er:** O; LF, auch Drosophila u.a. Fliegen, TF, Pflanzenkost.

1 Hengels Keilfleckbärbling
Rasbora hengeli
Herkunft: Südostasien: Zentral-Sumatra, Thailand.
Lebensraum: Kleinere Gewässer mit Schwarzwasser.
Beschreibung: Nur etwa 3,5 cm lang werden diese schönen Bärblinge, deren Männchen ein leuchtenderes rost-violettes Rot zeigen und die eine größere Keilzeichnung als die Weibchen haben. Zur Aquarienmitte und nach oben orientiert, braucht dieser Schwarmfisch viel Schatten. Dunkle Einrichtung, wenig Licht und eine dichte Randbepflanzung sind angebracht.
Für Zuchtversuche kann eine kleine Cryptocoryne als Ablaichpflanze dienen. Die Zucht ist nicht einfach, eine Vergesellschaftung mit anderen Kleinfischen möglich.
Haltung: T: 23–27 °C (28 °C), **pH:** 6–6,5 (5,3–5,7), **Hä:** weich bis mittelhart, ca. bis 12 °dGH (sehr weich, 2 °dGH); Filterung über Torf.
Er: O; alles kleines TF und LF.

2

2 Keilfleckbärbling
Rasbora heteromorpha
Herkunft: Südostasien: südöstl. Thailand, Westmalaysia, Sumatra, Java, Borneo.
Lebensraum: Uferbereiche klarer, stehender Gewässer mit dichten Pflanzenbeständen über und unter Wasser.
Beschreibung: Die 4,5 cm langen Schwarmfische des oberen bis mittleren Beckenbereichs sind munter und friedlich, wenn auch die Männchen immer wieder einmal einander imponieren. Dunkler Boden und eine Wurzeldekoration sind gemeinsam mit dichten und feinfiedrigen Pflanzengebüschen die richtige Aquarieneinrichtung. Zwischen den Pflanzen muß Schwimmraum bleiben bzw. für die nicht ganz einfache Zucht ein Platz für eine Ablaichpflanze, etwa eine kleine Cryptocoryne. Bei den Männchen ist

der Keilfleck bis zur Bauchkante ausgedehnt und an seinem vorderen Rand gerundet. Die etwas volleren Weibchen haben einen geraden Keilfleck-Vorderrand. Der Zuchtansatz geschieht am besten paarweise, ein junges Weibchen ist mit einem größeren, 2jährigen Männchen zusammenzubringen. Vergesellschaftung mit etwa gleichgroßen Fischen ist zu empfehlen. **Haltung: T:** 22–26 °C (26–28 °C), **pH:** 6–6,5 (5,3–5,7), **Hä:** bis 12 °dGH (2 °dGH); Torffilterung. **Er:** O; kleines TF und LF.

3

3 Zwergbärbling
Rasbora maculata
Herkunft: Südostasien: südwestl. Malaysia, Singapur, Westsumatra.
Lebensraum: Stark pflanzenbewachsene Uferbereiche in stehenden oder sehr langsam fließenden Gewässern, Sümpfe.
Beschreibung: Mit etwa 2,5 cm Körperlänge ein echter Mini-Schwarmfisch, der fast zierlich-zerbrechlich wirkt, aber durchaus als unempfindlich gelten kann, wenn die Wasserwerte beachtet werden. Zwischen dichten, z.T. feinfiedrigen Pflanzen wird die Beckenmitte mit viel freiem Schwimmraum bevorzugt. Dunkler Boden und abgedunkelte Beleuchtung tragen wesentlich zum Wohlbefinden der Zwergbärblinge bei. Nur mit anderen Kleinstfischen ist eine Vergesellschaftung anzuraten. Die Weibchen sind gelber und voller, die Zucht ist möglich.
Haltung: T: 23–25 °C (25–29 °C), **pH:** leicht sauer, um 6,5 (5,8–6,3), **Hä:** bis 10 °dGH (bis 3 °dGH); Torffilterung. **Er:** O; sehr kleines TF und LF.

4

4 Glasbärbling, Dreilinienbärbling
Rasbora trilineata
Herkunft: Südostasien: Sumatra und Borneo, Westmalaysia.
Lebensraum: Trübe Bereiche stehender und leicht fließender Gewässer.
Beschreibung: Trotz der Größe (bis 15 cm) ein relativ ruhiger und friedlicher Schwarmfisch. Strebt von der Beckenmitte aus auch nach oben und braucht reichlich Gelegenheit zum freien Schwimmen. Überhaupt sind große, lange Aquarien ideal für diesen Bärbling, der sich dunklen Boden und eine lockere Randbepflanzung wünscht. Im Hintergrund dürfen auch dichte Pflanzenbestände als Rückzugsmöglichkeit stehen. Nur andere lebhafte Fische, die zum Aquarienbereich „Mitte bis unten“ tendieren, passen zum Glasbärbling. Die Zucht ist möglich.
Haltung: T: 22–25 °C (25–28 °C), **pH:** 6–7 (bis 6,5), **Hä:** weich bis mittelhart (5–8 °dGH); Torffilterung. **Er:** O; TF und LF.

Sonstige Karpfenähnliche

Hier finden sich vier Arten, die ebenfalls Karpfenfische im engeren Sinne, aber keine Barben oder Bärblinge sind. Von daher werden sie getrennt abgehandelt. Auch mit den im Anschluß daran vorgestellten Schmerlen und Dorngrundeln haben sie wenig gemein.

Unter den „sonstigen Karpfenähnlichen“ wird der Kardinalfisch verwandtschaftlich meist in die Nähe unserer einheimischen Weißfische gestellt. („Weißfische“ ist ein fischereibiologisches Kunstwort und

1

umgangssprachlicher Begriff, der „unedle" Klein-Cypriniden zusammenfassend von „edlen" Speisefischen wie Karpfen oder Schleien trennt.)

1 Siamesische Rüsselbarbe, Algenfresser
Crossocheilus siamensis
Herkunft: Südostasien: Thailand, Malayische Halbinsel.
Lebensraum: Mittlere bis große Flüsse in hügeligem Gelände.
Beschreibung: Bisher noch nicht gezüchtet wurden diese nützlichen Cypriniden, die ein Bartelpaar an der Oberlippe tragen und bis 15 cm lang werden. Äußere Geschlechts-

2

4

3

unterschiede sind nicht bekannt. Den Tieren muß man in sehr gepflegten Becken geradezu veralgte Steine und Wurzeln anbieten, damit sie ihrem Bedürfnis, Algen abzuschaben, nachkommen können. Vor allem untereinander sind diese Fische etwas aggressiv und halten sich entweder am Boden oder auf großen Blättern/Wurzeln „aufsitzend" auf. Bei weichem Boden und dichter Bepflanzung sind sie gute und ausdauernde Gesellschaftsfische, lieben jedoch etwas Strömung und gelten als recht sauerstoffbedürftig.
Haltung: T: 23–27 °C, **pH:** 6–7,5, **Hä:** weich bis mittelhart; nach langsamer und vorsichtiger Eingewöhnung im Fachhandel und daheim sind auch Werte bis pH 8 und 20 °dGH möglich. **Er:** H, (C), O; TF, besonders Tabletten, Salat, auch LF.

2 Feuerschwanz, Feuerschwanz-Fransenlipper
Epalzeorhynchus bicolor
Herkunft: Südostasien: Malaysia, Thailand.
Lebensraum: Fließgewässer mit Stein- und Holzablagerungen am Grund.
Beschreibung: Ein imposanter Fisch der unteren Aquarienregionen, der als Einzelgänger gilt und tatsächlich Reviere bildet, die er auch – besonders gegen seinesgleichen – verteidigt. Dabei gehen die 15 bis 20 cm langen Tiere recht ruppig zur Sache, so daß sie nur bei vielen Verstecken aus Wurzeln oder Steinen zu mehreren gehalten werden sollen. Langlebig ist die Art nur, wenn die Verstecke so angeordnet sind, daß Artgenossen sich darin nicht sehen können. In großen, sandigen Becken ist unter diesen Voraussetzungen auch eine Vergesellschaftung mit anderen Arten denkbar. Das Weibchen ist kräftiger und blasser, die Rückenflosse des Männchens läuft spitz aus. Zuchten sind äußerst selten und als Zufall zu bezeichnen, gelaicht wird in kleinen Höhlen.
Haltung: T: 22–26 °C (27–28 °C), **pH:** 6–7,5, **Hä:** bis 15 °dGH (weich); toleriert, vorsichtig eingewöhnt, auch härteres Wasser; Torfzusatz im Filter. **Er:** C, O; LF, TF, Algen, Löwenzahn, Spinat u. a. pflanzliche Beikost.

3 Grüner Fransenlipper
Epalzeorhynchus frenatus
Herkunft: Südostasien: Nordthailand.
Lebensraum: Fließgewässer.
Beschreibung: Die Körperlänge schwankt je nach Herkunft zwischen 8 und 12 cm, manchmal liegt sie auch darüber. Die lebhafte bis aggressive Art ist dämmerungsaktiv und trägt zwei Bartelpaare. Aus Versteckrevieren heraus jagt der grüne Fransenlipper andere Aquarien-Insassen oft herum, jedoch selten in wirklich gefährlicher Form. Er ist insgesamt etwas „umgänglicher" als sein Feuerschwanz-Verwandter und verhält sich mit wachsender Beckengröße immer friedlicher. Verstecke aus Wurzeln oder Steinen und Sichtschutz durch Bepflanzung sind aber immer angebracht. Die seltenen Zuchten sind eher Zufälle. Das männliche Tier zeigt einen schwarzen Saum an der Afterflosse, die Weibchen sind dicker. Vergesellschaftung unter den o.g. Bedingungen möglich.
Haltung: T: 24–29 °C, **pH:** 6–7,5, **Hä:** bis 10 °dGH; Torffilterung. **Er:** O; TF, LF, Algen, Löwenzahn, Kopfsalat.

4 Kardinalfisch
Tanichthys albonubes
Herkunft: Ostasien: Südchina, vor allem bei Kanton.
Lebensraum: Klare Bäche des Berglandes.
Beschreibung: Dieser friedliche und lebhafte Schwarmfisch von 4 bis 5 cm Länge wurde früher auch als Arbeiter-Neon bezeichnet, vermutlich, weil er viel erschwinglicher war als „echte" Neons, die sich nicht jeder leisten konnte. Unterschiedliche Körper- und Flossenfärbungen, auch Schleierformen wurden herausgezüchtet. Die ohnehin farbigeren, kleineren und schlanken Männchen zeigen ein besonders farbintensives Imponiergehabe. Die Tiere schwimmen im Aquarium in der Mitte und oben; feinsandig-dunkler Grund wird bevorzugt. Die anspruchslosen Kardinalfische möchten gern Platz zum Schwimmen haben! Dichte Pflanzen am Rand oder Dickichtgruppen bzw. eine geschlossene Hintergrundbepflanzung ist der richtige Lebensraum im Aquarium. Guter Gesellschaftsfisch und leicht züchtbar.
Haltung: T: 18–22 °C (nie über 24 °C halten, die Tiere werden dabei blaß), **pH:** 6–8, **Hä:** weich bis hart; häufiger Frischwasserzusatz. **Er:** O; TF, kleines LF.

Schmerlen und Dorngrundeln

Die „Cobitidae" sind eine recht kleine Fischfamilie mit nur etwa 100 Arten, alle im Süßwasser der Alten Welt beheimatet und Barteln tragend. Als Tastorgane mit Geschmacksrezeptoren unterstützen sie den Nahrungserwerb. Alle Arten sind kleinschuppige oder „nackte" Bodenbewohner mit unterständigem, zahnlosem Maul, manche mit einem ausklappbaren Dorn unterm Auge und mit der Möglichkeit, Geräusche in Form eines „Knackens" von sich zu geben.

Viele Schmerlen sind Darmatmer, d.h., daß atmosphärischer Sauerstoff nach Abschlucken von Luft (an der Wasseroberfläche geschnappt) in reich durchbluteten Darmabschnitten verwertet werden kann.

Dem „forschenden" Aquarianer tut sich mit der Fortpflanzungsbiologie dieser Fischgruppe ein weites Betätigungsfeld auf – allzuviel liegt da noch im dunkeln. Die meisten Zuchten basieren auf Zufällen.

1

1 Dornaugen
Acanthophthalmus spec.
Herkunft: Verschiedene Arten aus unterschiedlichen Ländern Südostasiens.
Lebensraum: Meist in Bächen, wo die Jungfische als Schwärme in Pflanzenverstecken hausen, um später eher einzelgängerisch zu werden.
Beschreibung: Die Dornaugen, deren Arten nur für Spezialisten auseinanderzuhalten sind, ähneln mit ihrer Schlangenform kleinen Aalen, tragen aber 3 Paar Barteln. Sie haben keine Seitenlinie und halten sich überwiegend am Boden auf. Es gibt allenfalls Zufallszuchten im Aquarium, wobei sich das kräftigere Weibchen durch Laichansatz fast walzenförmig verdickt. Nachtaktiv (abends füttern) und langlebig, mögen Dornaugen keinerlei Störungen (dann springen sie aus dem Becken!). In dunklen Aquarien mit weichem Boden und vielen Pflanzen fühlen sich die Dornaugen wohl. Sie sollten nur mit Fischen der oberen Wasserregionen vergesellschaftet werden.
Haltung: T: 24–30 °C, **pH:** 5,5–6,5, **Hä:** bis 10 °dGH; Torffilterung, **Er:** C, O; sinkendes LF, pflanzliche Kost, TF (Gewöhnung an Tabletten).

2 Prachtschmerle
Botia macracantha
Herkunft: Südostasien: Indo-australischer Archipel, Sumatra, Borneo.
Lebensraum: Seen sowie Überschwemmungsgebiete von Flüssen.
Beschreibung: Prachtschmerlen sind lebhafte Schwarmfische, die in Aquarien selten über 16 cm lang werden, in der Natur aber 30 cm groß anzutreffen sind. Sie tragen vier Paar Barteln und können knackende Laute von sich geben. Die schwimmfreudige und nicht ganz so versteckt wie andere Schmerlen lebende Art ist auch tags unterwegs, die Neigung zu Dämmerungsaktivität ist aber unverkennbar. Die langsam wachsenden Tiere sind empfindlich gegen Chemikalien und anfällig für *Ichthyophtirius.* In ihrer Heimat zählt man sie zu den wohlschmeckenden Speisefischen. Auf

2

3

weichem Aquarienboden biete man Verstecke und Höhlen aus Wurzeln, Steinen oder Bambusröhren. Außer Zufallszuchten weiß man nichts über die Vermehrung in menschlicher Obhut, ältere Weibchen sind in der Aufsicht fülliger, d.h. sie wirken von oben betrachtet dicker. Alte Männchen werden hochrückig und gedrungen, beides sind jedoch sehr unzuverlässige Merkmale. Zum Ablaichen werden in der Natur vermutlich größere Wanderungen bis in die schäumenden, schnellfließenden Quellregionen unternommen. Diesen wohl auslösenden Reiz kann die Aquaristik nur schwerlich bieten.
Haltung: T: 24–30 °C, **pH:** 5–7, **Hä:** nicht über 10 °dGH, eher darunter; nicht in kleinen Becken, Aquarienlängen ab 1,2 m; öfter Frischwasserzusatz. **Er:** O; TF (auch Tabletten), LF mit Würmern, kleinen Schnecken, Algen u.a. Grünzeug.

3 Horas Schmerle
Botia morleti (Botia horae)
Herkunft: Südostasien: Thailand, Hinterindien.
Lebensraum: Bäche und kleine Flüsse.
Beschreibung: Die 7 bis fast 10 cm langen und damit recht klein bleibenden Schmerlen sind lebhaft, aber meist recht friedlich. Die gelegentlichen Aggressionen sind eher ungefährlich, da die Tiere nicht sehr gut schwimmen. Die Nacht- und Dämmerungsaktivität bedingt eine versteckte Lebensweise in der Nähe des Bodens, wo man dem Schwarm mindestens ein Versteck pro Tier anbieten sollte. Weicher Boden, auch feiner Sand, Steine und Wurzeln sind also die richtige Einrichtung. Als Pflanzen sind widerstandsfähige Arten empfehlenswert. Das Licht darf durch Schwimmpflanzen etwas gedämpft werden. Vergesellschaftung vor allem mit größeren Fischen, z.B. Barben oder Panzerwelsen. Geschlechtsunterschiede und Zuchterfolge sind nicht bekannt.
Haltung: T: 26–30 °C, **pH:** 6–7, **Hä:** bis 5 °dGH; öfter Frischwasserzusatz, etwa 20% pro Woche.
Er: C, O; LF, TF, Algen.

1

1 Schachbrettschmerle, Zwergschmerle
Botia sidthimunki
Herkunft: Südostasien: nördliches Thailand, Hinterindien.
Lebensraum: Kleine, schlammhaltige, stehende oder langsam fließende Gewässer.
Beschreibung: Diese reizende Schmerle mit drei Paar Barteln, im tagaktiven Schwarm äußerst schwimmfreudig, lebhaft und friedlich, wird jetzt in Thailand verstärkt nachgezüchtet. Die Schachbrettschmerlen werden 7 bis 9 cm lang. Nur Schwarmhaltung ist artgerecht; dazu gebe man in Bodennähe viele (Höhlen-)Verstecke auf weichem Grund. Teilweise dichte Bepflanzung komplettiert die Beckenausstattung, freier Schwimmraum muß jedoch vorhanden sein. Kleinere, nicht revierbildende Arten oder ruhige größere Fische sind geeignete Partner für gut gepflegte Gesellschaftsbecken. Für Zuchtversuche eignen sich Artenbecken, die Balz kann durch sichtbare Blässe angezeigt werden.
Haltung: T: 25–29 °C, **pH:** 6–7,5, **Hä:** weich bis hart; öfter Frischwasserzusatz. **Er:** C, O; alle kleineren Sorten TF und LF, Algen.

Welse

Aus der sehr vielfältigen Gruppe der weltweit überwiegend in Süßwasser verbreiteten Welsähnlichen (Siluroidei) wollen wir hier nur eine Auswahl der aquaristisch bedeutendsten Vertreter bieten: Von den mindestens 1000 Arten in 15 Familien beschreiben wir 13 Arten aus 4 Familien.

Im Vordergrund stehen die verschiedenen, von den Haltungsbedingungen sehr ähnlichen Panzerwelse, die systematisch zu den Schwielenwelsen (Callichthyidae) gerechnet werden. Harnischwelse (Loricariidae) finden sich 4 Arten und je ein Repräsentant der Antennenwelse (Pimelodidae) und der echten Welse (Siluridae). Zu letzteren gehört auch unser einheimischer Wels (Waller), der mit über zwei Metern Länge (eine südamerikanische Welsart erreicht noch einen Meter mehr!) im Gegensatz zu den nur 2,5 cm „langen" Zwergpanzerwelsen die Variabilität der Welsartigen eindrucksvoll demonstriert.

Manche Welse können Luftsauerstoff verwerten: Wie die Schmerlen schnappen sie an der Oberfläche Luft, aus der dann, meist in der Schwimmblase, Sauerstoff aufgenommen wird.

Schuppen fehlen den Welsen. Wenn der Körper nicht nackt ist, wird er durch einen Panzer aus Knochenplatten geschützt. Die teils auch in anderen Familien zu findenden Barteln sind bei Welsen oft zu längeren Bartfäden ausgezogen, die tastend und schmeckend einen größeren Umgebungsbereich erkunden können.

Wer Welse hält, braucht sich über Futterreste am Boden nicht zu sorgen; sie jedoch ausschließlich als „Müllschlucker" zu halten, ist sicher falsch und nicht wenige Welse werden wohl zu knapp und „so nebenbei" gefüttert. Dämmerungs- und nachtaktive Arten sollen abends eine eigene Futterration erhalten, damit sie bei Kräften bleiben.

Für Zuchtversuche, am besten in Artenbecken, werden bei allen nicht brutpflegenden Arten die Elterntiere nach der Eiablage herausgefangen, oder aber das Gelege wird entnommen und – in Wasser aus dem Ablaichbecken – separat gepflegt.

Bewohner der Unterwelt.

2 Blauer Antennenwels
Ancistrus dolichopterus
Herkunft: Südamerika: Amazonaszuflüsse.
Lebensraum: Bei ins Wasser gefallenen Hölzern in fließendem Gewässer; klare Bäche.
Beschreibung: Mit 13 bis 14 cm Länge fühlen sich diese bizarren Welse in großen, klaren Becken mit guter Filterströmung im unteren Bereich an Holzsubstraten wohl. Die Männchen tragen mehrere der namensgebenden, geweihartigen Gebilde auf dem Kopf. Diese „Antennen" sind bei den Weibchen ganz klein und dünn. Höhlen, Wurzeln und Hölzer bilden dunkle Rückzugsbereiche, wo große Teile des Tages verbracht werden. Die Art ist friedlich und verschont auch kleine Fische, daher gut zu vergesellschaften. Nach dem Laichakt in Höhlen treiben die revierbildenden Männchen Brutpflege.
Haltung: T: 23–27 °C, **pH:** 6–8 (bis 7), **Hä:** weich bis hart (4–10 °dGH); sauerstoffreiches Wasser. **Er:** H; Algen, Pflanzenkost, auch gekochte Möhren und gefrostete Erbsen, TF, LF, braucht Holz zum Abraspeln.

3 Smaragd-Panzerwels, Grüner Panzerwels
Brochis splendens
Herkunft: Südamerika: Amazonas, Peru, Brasilien, Ecuador.
Lebensraum: Langsam fließende Gewässer mit bewachsenen Uferbereichen.
Beschreibung: Wie bei vielen Panzerwelsen wird die kleine Fettflosse durch einen Dorn gestützt; die Gattung *Brochis* hat 10 bis 12 Strahlen in der Rückenflosse, *Corydoras* nur 6 bis 8. Smaragdpanzerwelse haben 3 Paar Barteln, werden 8 cm lang und leben, auch tagsüber munter und gern schwimmend, im Schwarm im unteren Beckenbereich. Der Boden des gut bepflanzten Aquariums wird idealerweise mit feinkörnigem Kies oder grobem Sand (dunkel) bedeckt, Verstecke wie Steine, Wurzeln und große Blätter sollten nicht fehlen. Teilbereiche mit Mulm werden neben freien Grundflächen ebenso geschätzt wie friedliche Mitbewohner. Große Buntbarsche sind keine gute Gesellschaft. Die Zucht ist möglich, wenn auch äußere Geschlechtsunterschiede bis auf die größere Körperfülle reifer Weibchen nicht erkennnbar sind. Ein Teilwasserwechsel mit zunächst etwas kühlerem Wasser löst oft die Laichbereitschaft aus.
Haltung: T: 18–26 °C (23–27 °C), **pH:** 5,8–7,5 (bis 6,5), **Hä:** weich bis hart (bis 4 °dGH); öfters kleine Teilmengen Frischwasser geben. **Er:** O; TF (Tabletten), LF, gelegentlich pflanzliche Zukost.

4 Stromlinien-Panzerwels
Corydoras arcuatus
Herkunft: Südamerika: mittlerer Amazonas.
Lebensraum: Bäche und kleine Flüsse.
Beschreibung: Ein schöner Bodenfisch, der 5 cm lang wird und 2 Bartelpaare trägt. Auf weichem, dunk-

2

3

4

1

3

2

lem Boden und feinem Sand sollte ein Schwarm dieser netten Welse gepflegt werden. Normale Bepflanzung und einige rundliche Kiesel vervollständigen das Aquarium, welches gern auch ein Gesellschaftsbecken sein darf. Die Nachzucht ist schon gelungen.
Haltung: T: 20–24 °C (24–26 °C), **pH:** 6–8 (bis 7), **Hä:** 2–25 °dGH (um 6 °dGH). **Er:** O; LF, TF, auch „pflanzliches".

1 Sichelfleck-Zwergpanzerwels
Corydoras hastatus
Herkunft: Südamerika: Brasilien, Amazonas, Mato Grosso.
Lebensraum: Ufernahes Freiwasser kleiner Bäche und Flüsse.
Beschreibung: Nur 3 bis 3,5 cm erreicht diese kleine und schwimmlustige *Corydoras*-Art, die sich als friedlicher, tagaktiver Schwarmfisch gern auch in mittleren Beckenzonen tummelt. Die dickeren Weibchen sind größer, Männchen werden nur etwa 2,5 cm lang. Die Zucht ist schon gelungen, wobei kühler Wasserwechsel als auslösend gelten darf. In Aquarien mit weichem Bodengrund und Pflanzendickichten ist eine Vergesellschaftung mit Kleinfischen gut möglich.

Haltung: T: 20–26 °C (25–28 °C), **pH:** 6–7,5 (bis 7), **Hä:** weich bis hart (bis 6 °dGH); häufiger Teilwasserwechsel in geringen Mengen. **Er:** O; kleines LF und TF, gelegentlich auch „pflanzliches".

2 Marmorierter (punktierter) Panzerwels
Corydoras paleatus
Herkunft: Südamerika: Südostbrasilien.
Lebensraum: Kleine Fließgewässer.
Beschreibung: Weil sehr unempfindlich, war dieser friedliche und ausdauernde Panzerwels einer der ersten Zierfisch-Pioniere in Europa. Zwei Paar Barteln tragend, bewohnen die Tiere im Schwarm gerne den Aquarienboden. Der sollte mit Sand ausgestattet sein, damit es zu keinen Verletzungen im Maulbereich kommt. Bei Vorhandensein großblättriger Pflanzen können die 7 bis 8 cm großen Fischlein vergesellschaftet werden. Die Zucht hat auch eine albinotische Form hervorgebracht.
Haltung: T: 18–24 °C (24–26 °C), **pH:** 6,5–8 (bis 7), **Hä:** weich bis hart (bis 6 °dGH); häufiger Teilwasserwechsel in geringen Mengen. **Er:** O; kleines TF und LF, Tabletten.

3 Panda-Panzerwels
Corydoras panda
Herkunft: Südamerika: Peru.

Lebensraum: Klare Fließgewässer, über sandigen Stellen.
Beschreibung: Die lustige Zeichnung, die an die Gesichtsmaske der Pandabären erinnert, gab diesem bis maximal 5 cm langen Panzerwels den Namen. Lockere Bepflanzung, in Gruppen angeordnet, und Sandboden gefällt diesen sehr friedlichen, tagaktiven Fischen. Sie lieben etwas Strömung und gut gefiltertes, sauerstoffreiches Wasser. Eine Vergesellschaftung mit nicht zu großen Fischen bietet sich an, auch die Zucht ist schon geglückt. Keine äußeren Geschlechtsunterschiede; auch hier wirkt ein kühler Wasserwechsel laichfördernd. Die Haltung in kleinen Gruppen entspricht der natürlichen Lebensweise.
Haltung: T: 20–25 °C, **pH:** 6,5–7,5, **Hä:** weich bis hart; Wasserwechsel regelmäßig etwa alle 2–3 Wochen. **Er:** L, O; LF und TF (Tabletten).

4 Netz-Panzerwels
Corydoras reticulatus
Herkunft: Südamerika: Peru, Amazonas.
Lebensraum: Kleingewässer.
Beschreibung: Friedlicher und ausdauernder Schwarmfisch mit zwei Paar Barteln, der sich lebhaft über den Boden bewegt, aber auch freischwimmend in mittleren oder gar oberen Aquarienregionen angetroffen wird. Möglichst feiner Sand als Bodenbelag wird mit einigen größeren Steinen kombiniert, die von Netz-Panzerwelsen als Ruhestandorte aufgesucht werden. Bei normaler Bepflanzung ist auch eine Haltung im Gesellschaftsbecken möglich. Die Zucht (Weibchen sind dicker) ist schon gelungen. Die Tiere werden etwa 7 cm lang.
Haltung: T: 20–26 °C (oberer Bereich davon), **pH:** 6–8 (bis 7), **Hä:** 2–25 °dGH (um 6 °dGH); häufiger Teilwasserwechsel in geringen Mengen. **Er:** O; TF, LF, gelegentlich auch vegetarische Kost.

5 Leopard-Panzerwels
Corydoras trilineatus
Herkunft: Südamerika: Peru.
Lebensraum: Weichgründige Flüsse und Seen.

4

5

Beschreibung: In Gruppenhaltung auf teils weichem Boden fühlen sich die 6 cm langen „Leoparden" wohl. Auch tags aktiv, werden Aquarien mit Wurzelverstecken oder entsprechend gestaltete Gesellschaftsbecken mit Bepflanzung überwiegend im unteren Beckenbereich gern bewohnt. Die Zucht mit Laichauslösung durch kühleres Wasser gelingt auch hier. Leopard-Panzerwelse brauchen etwas höhere Wassertemperaturen als viele andere *Corydoras-Arten.*
Haltung: T: 24–26 °C (25–28 °C), **pH:** 6–7,5 (bis 7), **Hä:** weich bis hart (6 °dGH); häufige kleine Teilwasserwechsel. **Er:** O; TF, LF.

1

2

1 Punktierter Harnischwels
Hypostomus punctatus
Herkunft: Südamerika: Süd- und Südostbrasilien.
Lebensraum: Jungtiere in schnell-, Erwachsene in langsamfließenden Flußbereichen.
Beschreibung: Bei 30 cm Körperlänge und mehr trägt dieser stattliche Wels eine Fettflosse, wächst aber nur langsam. Als Einzelgänger des Bodenbereichs ist er scheu und nachtaktiv. Dann wühlt er allerdings stark, weshalb Pflanzen in Schalen gesetzt und durch Steine geschützt werden müssen. Zu der in der Natur in Erdhöhlen stattfindenden Fortpflanzung und zu äußeren Geschlechtsunterschieden ist nichts bekannt. Schwimmpflanzen sorgen für gedämpftes Licht, darunter werden Wurzeln und Steine als Verstecke geboten. Weiches, leicht saures Wasser wird bevorzugt, eine Vergesellschaftung ist möglich.
Haltung: T: 18–26 °C, **pH:** 5–8, **Hä:** weich bis hart; nur für große Becken ab 1,2 m. **Er:** H; Algen, Kopfsalat, aufgeweichte Haferflocken, Spinat, TF, LF.

2 Indischer Glaswels
Kryptopterus bicirrhis
Herkunft: Südostasien: Hinterindien, Malaysia, Thailand, Java, Sumatra, Borneo.
Lebensraum: Im hellen Freiwasser leicht fließender Gewässer.
Beschreibung: Bei diesen 10 cm langen Welsen mit zwei dünnen, langen Bartelfäden hat die Rückenflosse nur eine kleine Strahlstütze, die Afterflosse reicht bis dicht an die Schwanzflosse heran. Die etwas empfindliche Art wirkt wegen der Durchsichtigkeit recht interessant. Als tagaktive Schwarmfische stehen die Glaswelse gern zwischen lichten Pflanzenbeständen, die am Rand des Aquariums auch zu Dickichten werden dürfen. Teilbedeckung mit Schwimmpflanzen, leichte Strömung und Platz zum Schwimmen sind die weiteren Erfordernisse. Mit friedlichen Fischen, auch anderen Welsen und Schwarmfischen, kann vergesellschaftet werden. Allenfalls Zufallszuchten erfolgten im Aquarium, wobei sich Glaswelse als Freilaicher oberhalb von Pflanzen nach der Nachahmung einer „Regenzeit" erwiesen.
Haltung: T: 22–27 °C, **pH:** 6–7,5, **Hä:** weich bis hart; auf besonders gute Wasserqualität achten. **Er:** C, O; LF, TF.

3 Kleiner Saugwels, Gestreifter Otocinclus
Otocinclus affinis
Herkunft: Südamerika: Südostbrasilien.
Lebensraum: Klare, schnellfließende, pflanzenreiche Gewässer.

3

Verkehrte Welt.

4

Beschreibung: Der mit 4 cm recht kleine Wels lebt tagsüber versteckt und trägt keine Fettflosse. Nachts wird er aktiv und „beweidet" verschiedene Substrate. Naturgemäß braucht er klares Wasser mit deutlicher Strömung und bevorzugt veralgte Steine und Wurzeln. Eine dichte Bepflanzung vervollständigt sein Aquarium, in dem er mit bis zu mittelgroßen Fischen (keine räuberischen Arten!) vergesellschaftet werden kann. Die Weibchen sind – wohl durch Laichansatz – zeitweise dicker, ansonsten existieren keine äußeren Geschlechtsmerkmale. Die Zucht (ohne Brutpflege) ist ab und zu schon gelungen.
Haltung: T: 20–26 °C, **pH:** 6–7,5, **Hä:** weich bis hart; sauerstoffbedürftiger als viele andere Welse.
Er: L, H; TF (Tabletten), Algen, LF, pflanzliche Kost.

4 Gebänderter Zwergschilderwels, Zierbinden-Harnischwels
Peckoltia pulcher
Herkunft: Südamerika: Rio Negro und Nebengewässer.
Lebensraum: Flüsse und Bäche.
Beschreibung: Friedlich und gut zu vergesellschaften, ist die widerstandsfähige, 6 bis 8 cm große Art überall dort zu Hause, wo Holz im Wasser liegt. Dem muß im Aquarium Rechnung getragen werden. Ohne Algen im Becken kümmern die Tiere, die ansonsten mit Verstecken aus Wurzeln oder unter Steinen zufrieden sind. Die Zucht gelang noch nicht. Zeitweilig werden, vermutlich von den Männchen, harte, borstige Hautbereiche an Kopf und Schwanz gebildet.
Haltung: T: 24–28 °C, **pH:** 5,5–7,8, **Hä:** weich bis hart; nur bis 10 °dGH.
Er: L, H; TF, Holz zum „Abnagen", Pflanzenkost, LF.

Aquarien-ausstellungen

Vielleicht ist es nicht gerade *das* Jahresereignis für Außenstehende, doch willkommene Abwechslung und Höhepunkt im Vereinsleben ist sie allemal – die Aquarienausstellung. Manchmal liegt auch ein besonderer Anlaß vor, wie zum Beispiel einVereinsjubiläum, doch oft gehört eine Ausstellung und die damit verbundene Plackerei auch zu den regelmäßigen Aktivitäten im Verein.

Geplant muß so eine Ausstellung werden, organisiert und durchdacht. Leicht ist die Sache nicht zu bewältigen! Der finanzielle und technische Rahmen ist weit gesteckt, will man sich nicht nur mit kahlen Aquarien und wenigen Fischarten begnügen.

Schon Wochen vorher, gewöhnlich dann, wenn den kühnen Worten der Vereinsleitung allmählich Taten folgen müssen, hängt bekanntermaßen der Vereinssegen schief. Meist begradigen sich die Schwierigkeiten und es wird bis kurz vor Eröffnung gehämmert, eingerichtet, eingepflanzt, umgesetzt, verkabelt, beleuchtet, geputzt und poliert.

Aquarianer sind auch nur Menschen und manchem liegt die kniffelige Vorplanung nicht, so daß oft planlos drauflosgearbeitet wird.

Zierfischausstellung im Rohbau, noch fehlen die Aquarien.

Irgendwie wird aber dann doch alles rechtzeitig fertig, wenn auch meist in allerletzter Minute.

Endlich ist es dann soweit, und die Menschenmassen strömen herein. Die Inhaber der einzelnen Aquarien mischen sich unters Volk und verdrücken sich unauffällig in die Nähe *ihres* Aquariums, um Worte des Lobes zu erhaschen.

Bald spaltet sich die Menge in Seewasserfans und Süßwasserfans, sofern beide Gattungen von Aquarien vorhanden sind. Die einen stehen begeistert vor dem Aquarium mit lebenden Korallen und Anemonen, andere schwärmen für Pflanzenbecken (mit ein paar Fischen garniert) oder afrikanische Steinepracht mit Buntbarschen.

Endlich ist es soweit, die Besuchermassen strömen.

Fische, deren Namen jeder kennt, sind magischer Anziehungspunkt, obwohl gerade diese sich vielleicht in grünes Pflanzendikkicht zurückziehen und man nur noch die Schwanzflosse sieht. Manche Erwartung, die „blutrünstigen" Piranhas aus nächster Nähe erleben zu können, wird allzuoft nicht erfüllt.

Die Fische gewöhnen sich recht schnell an die veränderten Umstände und reagieren gelassen. Selbst das Patschen von Kinderhänden an die Frontscheiben der Aquarien ist bald kein Grund zur Besorgnis mehr.

Hinter den Kulissen geht die Arbeit für Vereinsmitglieder natürlich weiter. Die Fische wollen gefüttert werden, und die Wasserqualität muß auf optimalem Niveau gehalten werden.

Richtig zur Arbeit ausarten wird es, wenn sich die Ausstellung nicht nur über ein bis zwei Wochen, sondern über mehrere Monate hinzieht. Dann werden die „vollberuflichen Aquarianer" unter den Vereinsmitgliedern, sprich die Rentner, dringend gebraucht. Das Besorgen von Futter aller Art, besonders lebendes, und eine regelmäßige Kontrolle der Aquarien wird ihnen ans Herz gelegt.

Doch auch der „nebenberufliche" Aquarianer wird den nicht fischbegeisterten Teil seiner Familie oder Partnerschaft allzuoft verlassen, um seine flossigen Freunde zu ihrem Recht kommen zu lassen.

Ist endlich der letzte Tag der Ausstellung angebrochen, dann kann man meistens auf eine schöne und interessante Zeit zurückblicken. Doch Moment mal, erst kommt noch das Thema Abbau und der Umzug der Fische ins heimische Aquarium an die Reihe. Erst bei späteren Treffen mit den Aquarianerfreunden kann dann so richtig gefeiert werden. Und bei dieser Gelegenheit werden die Fotos und Videoaufnahmen vom „großen Ereignis" gebührend gewürdigt.

Trotz aller Strapazen, die man während der Ausstellungszeit auf sich genommen hat, werden schon bald Pläne für die nächste Ausstellung geschmiedet ... denn das nächste Mal wird es garantiert noch schöner und noch besser!

1

1 Engel-Antennenwels
Pimelodus pictus
Herkunft: Südamerika: Peru, Amazonas.
Lebensraum: Trübe, flache Gewässer im Amazonas-Einzugsbereich.
Beschreibung: Bei diesen 12 cm, in der Natur aber länger werdenden Tieren sind die Brustflossenstrahlen mit Widerhaken versehen. In Netzkeschern verheddern sich die Engelwelse, sie sollten mit durchsichtigen Gefäßen aus dem Becken gefangen werden. In kleinen Gruppen ziehen sie meist friedlich durch untere und mittlere Aquarienregionen, sehr kleine Fische werden aber verfolgt. Schwimmpflanzen, Wurzel- und Steinhöhlen sind die richtige Beckeneinrichtung, die reichlich Schwimmraum bieten soll, da die Welse viel Bewegung brauchen. Starke Filterung mit leichter Strömung ist vorteilhaft. Zucht und Geschlechtsunterschiede sind unbekannt. Mit genügend großen, nicht mehr als Beute verfolgten Fischen gut zu vergesellschaften.
Haltung: T: 23–27 °C, **pH:** 6–7, **Hä:** weich bevorzugt, obwohl auch an größere Härten gewöhnbar; Torffilterung. **Er:** O; TF (Tabletten), LF.

Eierlegende Zahnkarpfen

Man kennt über 450 Arten dieser auch „Killifische" bezeichneten Familie (Cyprinodontidae) in 5 Untergruppen. Sie kommt auf allen Kontinenten mit Ausnahme Australiens vor, hier werden nur afrikanische und asiatische Vertreter beschrieben. Die Größenvarianz der eierlegenden Zahnkarpfen liegt zwischen 2 und 30 cm Länge. Das Seitenlinienorgan findet sich meist nur am Kopf, das Maul trägt gebogene, spitze Zähnchen.

Je nach Ablageort der Eier unterscheidet man Haftlaicher, die ihre Eier an Pflanzen legen, und Bodenlaicher. Bei Bewohnern zeitweilig austrocknender Gewässer sterben die Alttiere nach dem Laichakt, die Embryonen überdauern innerhalb der Eihülle die Trockenzeit. Man spricht dann von Saisonfischen, wenn die Eier, unabhängig vom Ablageort, eine derartige Ruheperiode („Diapause") brauchen.

2 Gardners, Nigeria- oder stahlblauer Prachtkärpfling
Aphyosemion gardneri
Herkunft: Afrika: Nigeria, Westkamerun.
Lebensraum: Klein- und Kleinstgewässer der Savannen und Urwälder.
Beschreibung: Sehr schön, aber etwas streitbar (vor allem die Männchen untereinander), ist dieser 6 bis 8 cm lange Saisonfisch. Mehrere Unterarten, aber auch herkunftsbedingte Farbabweichungen machen diese Fische sehr variabel im Erscheinungsbild. Die kleineren Weibchen sind schlichter gefärbt. Ein Artenbecken mit dunklem Boden und dichter, auch Schwimmbepflanzung, ist ideal, vielleicht noch eine Gesellschaft mit hier nicht beschriebenen *Aphyosemion*-Arten der Oberfläche, da *A. gardneri* die mittleren bis unteren Aquarienzonen nutzt. Wurzelverstecke werden gern aufgesucht. Zur Zucht dieser Haftlaicher gibt man den Eiern eine vierwöchige Ruhezeit, wobei sie in Torf austrocknen sollten. Licht durch Schwimmpflanzen abdämpfen.
Haltung: T: 21–24 °C (24–26 °C), **pH:** 6–7 (bis 6,5), **Hä:** bis 10 °dGH (5–8 °dGH); Torffilterung; bitte kein Salz zugeben. **Er:** C; LF, Würmer, TF wird selten genommen.

3 Streifenhechtling, Piku
Aplocheilus lineatus
Herkunft: Asien: Vorderindien, Malabar und Madras, Sri Lanka.
Lebensraum: Kleinere, stehende Gewässer.
Beschreibung: Ausdauernder und robuster Oberflächenfisch, der 10 bis 12 cm lang wird und seine Reviere bis in die Beckenmitte ausdehnt. Aggressiv gegen Artgenossen und gleichgeformte Fische, springt der Piku gern, daher auf gute Abdeckung achten! Zur Vergesellschaftung mit größeren Fischen geeignet, die ebenfalls dichte, feinblättrige Pflanzen mit Schwimmplatz dazwischen mögen. Wurzeln und Schwimmpflanzen gehören ebenfalls zur Aquarieneinrichtung. Die kleineren, matter gefärbten Weibchen legen ihre Eier an Pflanzen oder Kunststoffgespinst ab, wenn der Wasserstand auf etwa 20 cm gesenkt wurde. Die Eier bringt man in flachen Gefäßen zur Erbrütung.

Haltung: T: 21–25 °C (25–28 °C), **pH:** 6–7,5 (6–6,8), **Hä:** nicht zu hart (bis 12 °dGH); Sand- oder Kiesboden. **Er:** C: LF, auch Drosophila und größere Fliegen, Regenwürmer, Fische, TF.

4 Gemeiner Hechtling, Panchax
Aplocheilus panchax
Herkunft: Asien: Indien, Burma, Thailand, Malayische Halbinsel und indo-australische Archipel- sowie Sunda-Inseln.
Lebensraum: Reisfelder, Sümpfe; verlandende, bewachsene Stellen.
Beschreibung: Anspruchslose Killis, die mit 7 bis 8 cm Länge je nach Herkunft verschieden gefärbt sein können und die Oberflächenregion bevorzugen. Gute Abdeckung, dichte Bepflanzung und freier Schwimmraum, Schwimmpflanzen und Wurzelverstecke bilden die Aquarienausstattung. Mit größeren Fischen vergesellschaftbar; äußere Geschlechtsunterschiede sind schwer zu erkennen. Die Beflossung der etwas kräftiger wirkenden Weibchen ist kleiner und sie können blasser sein. Die Zucht gilt als nicht allzu schwer und erfolgt wie bei *A. lineatus* beschrieben.
Haltung: T: 20–25 °C (23–29 °C), **pH:** 6–7,5 (6–6,8), **Hä:** weich bis mittel (bis 12 °dGH); Kunststoffgespinst als Laichsubstrat möglich. **Er:** C; LF, Drosophila, andere Fliegen und Kleininsekten, Fische, TF.

2

4

3

1

2

1 Querbandhechtling
Epiplatys dageti
Herkunft: Afrika: Sierra Leone, Liberia, Elfenbeinküste, Ghana.
Lebensraum: Kleine Fließgewässer.
Beschreibung: 6 bis 7 cm lang (die Weibchen etwas kleiner mit schwächer ausgebildeter Beflossung) werden diese zunächst friedlich-lebhaften Hechtlinge. Im Alter zunehmend aggressiv und räuberisch, sollte man sie allenfalls mit gleichgroßen Fischen vergesellschaften (z.B. Schwarmfische des Mittelwassers, Welse oder kleine Buntbarsche). Dichte Bepflanzung der Aquarienseiten, viele Schwimmpflanzen zur dämmrigen Haltung und dunkler Sand sind zur artgerechten Pflege angesagt. Die Zucht dieses Haftlaichers an Pflanzen, die nach der Eiablage zu entnehmen sind, ist möglich. Die Afterflosse der Männchen ist spitz auslaufend.
Haltung: T: 21–24 °C (24–26 °C), **pH:** 6–7 (bis 6,5), **Hä:** bis 10 °dGH; Torfzusatz. **Er:** C, O; LF plus Drosophila, später auch kleine Fische, TF.

2 Reisfische
Oryzias spec.
Herkunft: Ostasien: Indonesien.
Lebensraum: Kleingewässer.
Beschreibung: Es gibt verschiedene Arten, die zwischen 4 und 5,5 cm lang werden. Bei männlichen Tieren sind Rücken- und Afterflosse größer als bei den Weibchen. Als eine der wenigen Gruppen unter den eierlegenden Zahnkarpfen sind *Oryzias*-Arten zeitlebens Schwarmfische. Sie halten sich bevorzugt in der Nähe der Wasseroberfläche auf, wo einige Schwimmpflanzen noch freien Raum lassen sollten. Bei leichter Strömung, feinblättriger Bepflanzung und sonnigem Standort fühlen sich Reisfische wohl. Die Zucht gelingt, doch ist die Aufzucht nicht einfach. Eine Vergesellschaftung empfiehlt sich mit etwa gleichgroßen Fischen der unteren und mittleren Wasserbereiche.
Haltung: T: 23–29 °C (23–25 °C), **pH:** 7–8,5, **Hä:** 10–15 °dGH; das früher empfohlene „Aufsalzen" des Wassers sollte unterbleiben.
Er: C, O; kleines LF, Drosophila, TF.

Lebendgebärende Zahnkarpfen

Vor etwa 30 bis 40 Millionen Jahren entwickelte die Natur ein Fortpflanzungssystem bei Fischen, welches die ständig bedrohten Fischeier zumindest bis zum Schlupf der Außenwelt vorenthält und so einen Schutz vor Laichräubern bietet: Die Weibchen der lebendgebärenden Zahnkarpfen bringen seit dieser Zeit voll entwickelte, sofort freß- und schwimmfähige Jungtiere zur Welt.

Die Wurfgröße schwankt je nach Art, aber auch abhängig von der individuellen Kondition, zwischen 20 und über 100 Jungfischen, die alsbald nach der Geburt ein Pflanzendickicht oder andere Rückzugsräume suchen, wo sie sich bevorzugt aufhalten und bei der geringsten Gefahr sofort Deckung nehmen.

Gegenüber eierlegenden Fischen (tausende bis hunderttausende Eier) erreichen Lebendgebärende mit relativ „wenigen" Jungfischen letztlich den gleichen Fortpflanzungserfolg.

Kennzeichen aller männlichen lebendgebärenden Zahnkarpfen ist die zu einem Begattungsorgan umgewandelte Afterflosse, das Gonopodium. Als deutlich erkennbares äußeres Merkmal ermöglicht es die Unterscheidung der Geschlechter, Spezialisten können dies selbst bei kleinen Arten schon im zarten Alter von drei Wochen erkennen. Eine einmalige Samenübergabe an ein weibliches Tier ermöglicht mehrere Befruchtungen, d.h. einmal besamte Weibchen können Spermienpakete speichern und so mehrere Würfe ohne weitere Anwesenheit von männlichen „Bedrängern" (und genau das sind die meisten Arten fast dauernd) bekommen.

Anpassungsfähig und leicht züchtbar, sind lebendgebärende

An Brackwasser gewöhnte Tiere sind nicht einfach zu vergesellschaften.
Haltung: T: 24–28 °C, **pH:** 7,5–8,5, **Hä:** hart (25–35 °dGH). **Er:** H (O); TF, Algen, eingeweichte Haferflocken und andere pflanzliche Zukost, LF.

3 Schwertträger
Xiphophorus helleri
Herkunft: Mittelamerika: Mexiko, Guatemala.
Lebensraum: Flüsse und Bäche.
Beschreibung: Von diesen 12 bis 15 cm langen lebendgebärenden Zahnkarpfen wurden sehr viele Varianten und Farbschläge mit speziellen Namen herausgezüchtet.
Als sehr lebhafte Schwarmtiere sind manche Männchen streitsüchtig.
Bei dichter Bepflanzung mit freiem Schwimmraum und etwas Strömung gedeihen Schwertträger ausgezeichnet und sind auch gute Vergesellschaftungspartner. Die Aquarienmitte wird bevorzugt. Eine Zucht ist einfach.
Haltung: T: 19–27 °C (bis 28 °C), **pH:** 7–8,3, **Hä:** mittel bis hart (12–30 °dGH); auf Salzzugaben verzichten. **Er:** C, O; LF, TF, Algen, pflanzliche Zukost.

3

3

3

Oben links: Eine rote Zuchtform des Schwertträgers (oben Weibchen, unten Männchen).

Oben: „Tuxedo", eine schwarze Schwertträger-Zuchtform.

Links: Ein Männchen des sog. „grünen" Schwertträgers (Naturform).

1 *Wagtail-Platys.*

1 *Tuxedo-Platys.*

1 *Gelb-rote Platy-Zuchtform.*

2 *Papageienplaty mit Simpson-Rückenflosse.*

1 Platy
Xiphophorus maculatus
Herkunft: Mittelamerika (auf der Atlantikseite).
Lebensraum: Tieflandflüsse und -bäche.
Beschreibung: Die Männchen dieser sehr variablen Art werden nur ca. 3,5 cm, die Weibchen bis 6 cm groß. Friedlich und ausdauernd bevölkern Platies die mittleren Aquarienbezirke und fühlen sich unter Schwimmpflanzen (Jungfisch-Schutz!), zwischen lockeren, teils auch dichten Pflanzenbeständen wohl. Freier Schwimmraum für ausreichend Bewegung muß auch gegeben sein. Gut zur Vergesellschaftung geeignet, die roten Farbvarianten bringen schöne Kontraste zu anderen Fischarten.
Haltung: T: 20–25 °C, **pH:** 7–8,2, **Hä:** mittel bis hart (10–25 °dGH); nicht salzen oder in zu weichem Wasser halten. **Er:** O; TF, LF, Algen, pflanzliche Zusatznahrung.

2 Papageienplaty
Xiphophorus variatus
Herkunft: Mittelamerika: südliches Mexiko.
Lebensraum: Flachwasser; ruhige Bach- und Flußzonen.
Beschreibung: Auch diese Art ist friedlich, ausdauernd und lebhaft und wurde in vielen variablen Farbschlägen gezüchtet. Bei 6 bis 7 cm Länge ist der Papageienplaty recht schwimmfreudig, weshalb man ihm zwischen dichten Pflanzenbeständen auch genügend Freiraum lassen sollte. Die Zucht ist einfach, und die Fische sind sowohl gute Algenvertilger als auch geeignete Vergesellschaftungspartner. Die Aquarienmitte bis hinauf in obere Regionen ist ihr Reich.

2
Marigold-Papageienplatys.

Haltung: T: 20–25 °C, **pH:** 7–8,3, **Hä:** mittel bis hart (15–30 °dGH); bei langsamer Gewöhnung auch unterhalb des oben genannten Temperaturbereichs in ungeheizten Becken zu halten. **Er:** H, O; Algen, TF, LF.

Halbschnäbler

Die Familie der Hemirhamphidae, auch Halbschnabelhechte genannt, ist ebenfalls lebendgebärend, jedoch nicht mit den entsprechenden Zahnkarpfen verwandt.

Halbschnäbler kommen nur in Südostasien vor, wo sie meist dicht unter der Oberfläche kleiner Gewässer angetroffen werden. Ihr Kennzeichen ist der „Halbschnabel", eine Maulform, bei der der Unterkiefer den kurzen Oberkiefer weit überragt. Das Maul ist also extrem oberständig und ermöglicht das Ergreifen von Mückenlarven und Anflugnahrung in ausgezeichneter Weise.

Auch bei dieser Gruppe ist die Afterflosse der Männchen zu einem Begattungsorgan umgebildet, das eine innere Besamung ermöglicht und bei den Halbschnäblern „Andropodium" heißt.

Zur artgerechten Ernährung und erfolgreichen Zucht wird man u.a. auf eine eigene Drosophila-Futterfliegenzucht angewiesen sein, da nur vielseitig ernährte, kleine Futterinsekten ausreichend Nährstoffe für das Heranreifen gesunder, lebenstüchtiger Jungfische bieten.

Sonstige Pfleglinge

Sind Schnecken eher lästige Gäste im Aquarium, so gibt es doch eine Art, die aufgrund ihrer Größe und interessanten Vermehrungsweise ein empfehlenswerter Pflegling ist. Die Rede ist von der **Apfelschnecke** *(Ampullaria spec.)*. Sie erreicht die Größe einer Weinbergschnecke und ist deshalb auch leicht zu finden, wenn der Bestand einmal überhandnehmen sollte.

Apfelschnecken sind gute Restevertilger, die bei Nahrungsmangel auch schon mal an Pflanzen gehen. Als Luftatmer verfügen sie über ein ca. 5 cm langes Atemrohr, das sie zum Luftholen aus dem Wasser strecken. Sie legen ein traubenähnliches Gelege außerhalb des Wassers (Deckscheibe) ab. Nach einer Entwicklungszeit von einigen Wochen fallen die fertigen Jungschnecken ins Wasser und können mit Flockenfutter problemlos großgezogen werden.

Apfelschnecke mit ausgestrecktem Atemrohr.

Glasgarnelen sind ideale Restevertilger für Aquarien mit friedlichen Fischen.

Überzählige Schnecken können an befreundete Aquarianer oder an den Zoohändler abgegeben werden.

In letzter Zeit werden verschiedentlich auch **Süßwassergarnelen** angeboten, die leicht zu pflegen sind und als Restevertilger gute Dienste leisten. Interessant ist die Nahrungsaufnahme der Fächerhandgarnele *(Atyopsis spec.)*: Mit ausgebreiteter Fächerhand filtert sie Nahrungspartikel aus bewegtem Wasser.

Cichliden und lebhafte Fische sollten nicht mit Apfelschnecken und Garnelen zusammen gehalten werden.

1

Selbst hochwertige gefriergetrocknete Mückenlarven sollen nur ein Ersatz sein. Nach Stallknecht liegt das „Geheimnis" in der Verabreichung ungesättigter Fettsäuren über pflanzliche Öle.

1 Halbschnäbler
Dermogenys spec.
Herkunft: Südostasien: Hinterindien, Malayischer Archipel, Thailand, Singapur, Indonesien.
Lebensraum: Flache Fließgewässer in Küstennähe, auch Brackwasser.
Beschreibung: Allgemein recht aggressiv gegenüber Artgenossen, die Männchen der um 7 cm langen Fische kämpfen mit teils bösen Folgen. In großen Becken mit Schwimmpflanzen und bodenständigem, bis zur Oberfläche ragendem Grün hält man Halbschnäbler, eventuell auch bei 20 cm Niedrigwasser über Kies oder Sand. Besonders anfangs sind die Tiere schreckhaft und durch unkontrolliertes Umherschießen besteht erhebliche „Schnabel"-Verletzungsgefahr. Die Aquarienscheiben verhängt man daher in der Eingewöhnungsphase mit Stofftüchern oder läßt sie vor der Anschaffung veralgen. Gegen die gekonnten Sprünge der Halbschnäbler hilft nur eine gute Abdeckung, wenn man sich nicht für die Niedrigwassermethode entschieden hat. Wie eingangs zu dieser Gruppe beschrieben, ist die Zucht nicht leicht. Es wäre wünschenswert, wenn sich wieder mehr Liebhaber um die Vermehrung in menschlicher Obhut kümmern würden und den Lebendfutteraufwand nicht scheuten. Interessante Pfleglinge sind Halbschnäbler allemal und auch eine Vergesellschaftung ist möglich.
Haltung: T: 21–29 °C, **pH:** 7–8, **Hä:** bis 10 °dGH; zumindest zur Eingewöhnung können 2–3 Teelöffel Seesalz auf 10 l Wasser gegeben werden. **Er:** C; LF plus Drosophila u.a. Kleinfliegen sowie andere kleine Insekten, auch TF. Ab und zu Futtertiere mit Vitaminpräparaten in öliger Lösung oder Pflanzenölen mit mehrfach ungesättigten Fettsäuren präparieren.

Buntbarsche

Die Familie der Cichlidae ist mit über 160 Gattungen und mehr als 900 Arten eine der größten und zugleich vielfältigsten Fischfamilien. Bei sehr vielen Gattungen gibt es nur eine Art als Vertreter, die Gattung heißt dann „monotypisch". In Asien findet man nur eine Gattung von Buntbarschen, die Schwerpunkte der Verbreitung liegen in Afrika sowie Mittel- und Südamerika.

Die Körpergestalten sind mit langgestreckten Formen bis hin zu hohen, flachen Körpern recht variabel, die weitaus meisten Cichliden sind jedoch von der landläufig als „typisch" angesehenen Fischform. Die Rückenflosse besteht aus zwei Teilen, der vordere wird von Hart-, der hintere von Weichstrahlern gestützt.

Die unterschiedlichsten Lebensräume werden von dieser entwicklungsbiologisch anpassungsfähigen Fischgruppe besiedelt, auch in extremen Lebensräumen kommen Buntbarsche vor. Einzelheiten hierzu finden sich in der Spezialliteratur.

Körpergrößen zwischen 5 und 80 cm hat die Natur hervorgebracht, auch ganz verschiedene Ernährungsweisen wurden von Cichliden erschlossen und zusammen mit der Vielfalt des Verhaltens sind davon die Aquarianer in aller Welt fasziniert. Die Systematik ist ständig in Überarbeitung.

Zum Verständnis der Einzelbeschreibungen sei hier noch die Vielfalt der Fortpflanzungsmöglichkeiten skizziert. Man unterscheidet zwischen folgenden Brutpflegeformen: **Offenbrüter**, die ihre kleinen, ovalen, an der Längsseite haftenden Eier in großer Zahl an verschiedenen Unterlagen unversteckt ablegen. **Versteckbrüter** dagegen verbergen ihre Eier, entweder in Höhlen **(Höhlenbrüter)** oder im Maul. Dort reifen entweder bereits die Eier oder die gerade geschlüpften bzw. kurz vorm Schlupf stehenden Larven geschützt heran (ovophile bzw. larvophile **Maulbrüter**). Höhlenbrüter haben bei mittlerer

Fisch mit Eigenheim.

Eigröße Gelege mit weniger Eiern als Offenbrüter. Bei Maulbrütern sind noch größere und weniger Eier gegeben als bei den Höhlen-Versteckbrütern. Die Natur reduziert also mit wachsendem Schutz durch die Elterntiere die Nachkommenanzahl.

Weiterhin kennt man bei den Buntbarschen folgende fünf Familienformen:

Bei der **Elternfamilie** teilen sich Männchen und Weibchen die Aufgaben der Brutpflege, beide Elternteile führen die Jungen nach dem Freischwimmen.

In der **Vater-Mutter-Familie** obliegt der Mutter die Pflege, der Vater besorgt die Revierverteidigung, ist also indirekt am Versorgen seiner Nachkommen beteiligt.

Man kann davon bei polygamen Arten, also dort, wo die Männchen stets mehrere Weibchen mit Nachwuchs haben, noch die **Mann-Mutter-Familie** abtrennen: Hier hat das männliche Tier ein Großrevier zu verteidigen, innerhalb dessen alle Brutreviere der Weibchen liegen.

Die **Mutterfamilie** wird nur durch Arten maulbrütender Cichliden gebildet. Dort hat das Männchen weder als Revierverteidiger noch von der Pflege her etwas mit der Nachkommenschaft zu tun.

Schließlich gibt es – vermutlich nur bei einer hier nicht erwähnten Buntbarsch-Art – noch das Extrem der **Vaterfamilie,** wo nach der Eiablage dem Männchen allein die Maulbrutpflege obliegt.

2

3

2 Thomas-Prachtbarsch, Afrikanischer Schmetterlingsbuntbarsch
Anomalochromis thomasi

Herkunft: Afrika: Sierra Leone.
Lebensraum: Klare Bäche und kleine, klare Flüsse.
Beschreibung: Diese sehr friedlichen und ausdauernden Cichliden des mittleren bis unteren Beckenbereichs werden 8 bis 10 cm lang; die Weibchen sind etwas intensiver gefärbt. Das relativ dunkel gehaltene Aquarium sollte neben offenen Kiesflächen dichte Pflanzenbestände und Höhlen aus Steinen und Wurzeln enthalten. Freier Schwimmraum muß aber auch gegeben sein, dann gelingt auch die Zucht dieser Offenbrüter mit Elternfamilie. Mit Oberflächen-Schwarmfischen zu vergesellschaften.
Haltung: T: 23–27 °C (bis 28 °C), **pH:** 6–7,5 (bis 6,5), **Hä:** weich bis mittelhart (weich). **Er:** C, O; LF, TF.

3 Agassiz-Zwergbuntbarsch
Apistogramma agassizii

Herkunft: Südamerika: Paraguay, Parana, Amazonas.
Lebensraum: Kaum durchströmte Flachwasserbereiche, wo der Boden mit Laub und Ästen bedeckt ist.
Beschreibung: Ein schöner, friedlicher, 8 bis 10 cm langer Cichlide, der als etwas empfindlich – vor allem gegen Chemikalien – gilt.
In dicht bepflanzten Aquarien mit Wurzel- und Steinverstecken in der Nähe freien Schwimmraums werden Reviere in Bodennähe gebildet. Der Schwanz des Männchens ist spitzlanzettlich ausgezogen, der der kleineren (ca. 5 cm) Weibchen abgerundet. Man unterscheidet die blau-weiße, die gelbe und die rote Zuchtform. Bei dunklem Boden in abgedunkelten Aquarien schreitet die Art als Höhlenbrüter zur Fortpflanzung. Die nicht ganz einfach aufzuziehenden Jungtiere werden in der Mann-Mutter-Familie betreut. Mit Schwarmfischen des Oberwassers gut zu vergesellschaften.
Haltung: T: 20–25 °C (um 27 °C), **pH:** 5–6,8 (bis 6), **Hä:** bis 10 °dGH (sehr weich); öfters Frischwasserzusatz, Torffilterung. **Er:** C, O; LF, TF.

1

3

2

4

1 Kakadu-Zwergbuntbarsch
Apistogramma cacatuoides
Herkunft: Südamerika: Peru, Amazonasbecken.
Lebensraum: Flache Klar- und Weißwässer in Flußnebenarmen.
Beschreibung: Hübscher Kleincichlide, dessen Männchen 8 bis 9 cm, die Weibchen nur ca. 5 cm Körperlänge erreichen. Letztere haben auch keine verlängerten Rückenflossen-Membranen, welche die männlichen Tiere schmücken. In mehreren Farbvarianten gezüchtet, zeigen die „Kakadu-Männer" z.T. feuerrote, schwarzgeränderte Flecken in Rücken- und Schwanzflosse. In Becken mit gruppenweise dicht gesetzten Pflanzen auf dunklem Feinkies oder Sand, dekoriert mit Holz- oder Steinverstecken, fühlt sich die Art wohl. Bei einem Männchen mit mehreren Weibchen bleibt der Nachwuchs dieser Höhlenbrüter nicht aus. Dazu werden die Eier an der Höhlendecke abgelegt und in der Elternfamilie mit mütterlicher Brutpflege betreut.
Haltung: T: 25–26 °C (bis 29 °C), **pH:** um 7 (gemäß der Fundortwerte neutral bis leicht alkalisch), **Hä:** weich bis mittelhart (bis 10 °dGH); auf sehr gute Wasserqualität achten. **Er:** C; LF.

2 Schwanzstreifenbuntbarsch
Biotodoma cupido
Herkunft: Südamerika: westl. Guayana, mittlerer Amazonas.
Lebensraum: Fließgewässer.
Beschreibung: Buntbarsch von ca. 13 cm Länge, der aggressiv und stark wühlend untere und mittlere Beckenreviere beansprucht. Die äußeren Geschlechtsunterschiede sind unsicher, die farbigeren Männchen zeigen Glanzstreifen unter den Augen. Das Becken (als Artenbecken oder zur Vergesellschaftung mit größeren Welsen oder ruhigen, mittelgroßen Fischen) gestaltet man mit einer Steilufer-Rückwand aus Steinen mit Höhlen und Spalten. Davor sollen sich weicher Sand, einige Kiesel und Steine sowie Wurzeln befinden, seitlich auch robuste Pflanzen. Die Offenbrüter laichen in einer Kuhle und führen die Jungen in einer Elternfamilie.

Haltung: T: 23–25 °C (25–28 °C), **pH:** 6–7,5 (um 7), **Hä:** weich bis hart (um 10 °dGH); bei guter Pflege ausdauernd. **Er:** C; LF, auch Würmer, zusätzlich TF.

3 Feuermaul-Buntbarsch
Cichlasoma (Thorichthys) meeki
Herkunft: Mittel- und Südamerika: Yukatan, Guatemala.
Lebensraum: Flußufer-Flachwassergebiete zwischen Hölzern und Felsbrocken.
Beschreibung: Vorwiegend im unteren Beckenbereich halten sich diese 14 bis 15 cm langen Cichliden, am besten paarweise gehalten, auf. Die oft kleineren Weibchen sind weniger kräftig leuchtend in der Farbe. Die ausdauernden Fische gehören wohl zu den schönsten amerikanischen Buntbarschen, ihre Zucht (Offenbrüter, Elternfamilie) gilt als leicht. Aquarien mit dichter, sauberer Sandschicht, Verstecke aus Steinen und Wurzeln sowie eine harte Randbepflanzung (Wurzeln mit Steinen gegen Wühltätigkeit schützen) sind der ideale Aufenthaltsort. Mit robusten Arten können die revierbildenden Feuermaulbuntbarsche in großen Becken auch vergesellschaftet werden. Wirklich gefährliche Attacken auf andere Aquarieninsassen sind selten, kleinere Artgenossen werden dagegen angegriffen.
Haltung: T: 21–25 °C (bis 27 °C), **pH:** 6,5–8,5 (um 7), **Hä:** weich bis sehr hart (bis 10 °dGH); reichlich freien Schwimmraum lassen. **Er:** C, O; LF, Würmer, TF.

4 Zebrabuntbarsch, Grünflossenbuntbarsch
Cichlasoma nigrofasciatum
Herkunft: Mittelamerika: Panama bis Mexiko.
Lebensraum: Unterschiedliche Biotope.
Beschreibung: Als bissiger, unverträglicher, pflanzenfressender Cichlide von 10 bis 15 cm Länge ist dieser Buntbarsch, paarweise gehalten, ein Fall für das Artenbecken. In großen Aquarien baue man aus schweren Steinen Höhlen und Verstecke, die, unter Schwimmpflanzen und neben einigen Wurzeln gelegen, als Rückzugsgebiete und zum Höhlenbrüten gebraucht werden. Normalerweise in Vater-Mutter-Familie die Jungtiere pflegend, treten zuchtbedingt leider Störungen dieses Verhaltens auf, ebenso Farb- und Größenabweichungen. Die weniger bunten, größeren Männchen haben stärker ausgezogene Flossen und eine steilere Stirn.
Haltung: T: 20–25 °C (bis 27 °C), **pH:** 7–8,5, **Hä:** mittel bis sehr hart; anspruchslose Art. **Er:** O; TF, LF plus Würmer, Fische, Kopfsalat und Haferflocken.

5

6

5 Schachbrett-Schlankcichlide
Julidochromis marlieri
Herkunft: Afrika: Tanganjikasee.
Lebensraum: Felsige Uferzone.
Beschreibung: Mit bis zu 15 cm Länge der größte Schlankcichlide. Die Zeichnung bildet ein schönes Netzmuster auf den oft gegen Artgenossen aggressiven Fischen. Die Art ist in kleinen Aquarien nur paarweise zu halten, während in größeren Aquarien mit genügend Verstecken auch mehrere Tiere zu halten sind. Wie auch für *J. ornatus* gilt die Regel, unverträgliche Paare wegen drohender Verluste zu trennen. Ebenfalls beiden Arten ist die Schwierigkeit der Geschlechterunterscheidung gemeinsam, da man die meist etwas größeren Weibchen nur bei Laichbereitschaft an der Genitalpapille sicher erkennt. Auf durchaus mögliche Kreuzungen beider Arten sollte man verzichten.
Als Höhlenbrüter mit Elternfamilie sind Schachbrett-Schlankcichliden am besten in Aquarien mit Steinaufbauten untergebracht, die zahlreiche Höhlen und Unterstände haben.
Haltung: T: 22–25 °C (24–26 °C), **pH:** 7,5–9, **Hä:** mittelhart (um 12 °dGH); Bepflanzung möglich. **Er:** C, O; LF, TF.

6 Gestreifter oder Gelber Schlankcichlide
Julidochromis ornatus
Herkunft: Afrika: Tanganjikasee.
Lebensraum: Flach abfallende Felsküstenbereiche.
Beschreibung: Revierbildend und gegen Artgenossen oft unverträglich, bevorzugen diese Cichliden untere und mittlere Aquarienbezirke.

1

2

3

4

Paarweise in Felsenbecken gehalten, kann die Art auch vergesellschaftet werden. Freier Schwimmraum zwischen teils dichten Pflanzungen mit harten Arten und Stein- sowie Wurzelhöhlen kennzeichnen die optimale Einrichtung. Die Elternfamilie dieser höhlenbrütenden Fische schützt die sich lange bei der Laich- und Bruthöhle aufhaltenden Jungtiere eher indirekt durch starkes Revierverhalten. **Haltung: T:** 22–25 °C (25–27 °C), **pH:** 7,5–9 (8–9), **Hä:** mittel bis hart (11–20 °dGH); Wurzeln fehlen im natürlichen Biotop; Bepflanzung möglich. **Er:** C, O; LF, Würmer, TF, Kopfsalat.

1 Rotbrustbuntbarsch
Laetacara (Aequidens) dorsigera
Herkunft: Südamerika: Grenzgebiet von Bolivien und Brasilien.
Lebensraum: Schwach durchströmte Buchten und Uferzonen des Amazonasgebietes.
Beschreibung: Nicht nur friedlich, sondern fast schon zurückhaltend und etwas scheu kann man diese kleinen (8 cm, Weibchen nur 6 cm) Cichliden nennen. Die Art ist stark farbwechselnd hin zu intensivem Rot-Schwarz. Der als Männchen-Merkmal genannte dunkle Rückenflossen-Fleck kommt bisweilen bei beiden Geschlechtern vor, die Männchen haben aber längere Bauchflossen. Die Aquarienausstattung mit dunklem, feinkörnigem Kies-Sand-Gemisch muß durch Stein-, Wurzel- und Pflanzenverstecke auch noch Freiraum zum Schwimmen bieten. Mit anderen kleinen Buntbarschen (z.B. *Apistogramma*-Arten), wenigen Salmlern oder Lebendgebärenden kann der Rotbrustbuntbarsch vergesellschaftet werden. Die angegebenen Zucht-Wasserwerte sorgen zusammen mit einer flachen Laichunterlage (etwa einem glatten Stein) für gute Fortpflanzungsbedingungen (Offenbrüter mit Elternfamilie). Der geschlüpfte Nachwuchs wird häufig umgebettet.
Haltung: T: 23–26 °C (26–30 °C), **pH:** um 7 (6,5), **Hä:** bis 20 °dGH (weicher); regelmäßige Wasserwechsel. **Er:** C, O; LF, TF.

2 Türkisgoldbarsch
Melanochromis auratus
Herkunft: Afrika: Malawisee.
Lebensraum: Felsenküste an den Rändern von Bodenablagerungen.
Beschreibung: Die Männchen dieser eindrucksvoll gefärbten Art werden 12, die Weibchen nur etwa 9 cm lang. Männliche Tiere haben einen schwarzen Bauch, bei den Weibchen ist er gelb-weiß. Von diesen sehr lebhaften, aggressiv-unverträglichen Buntbarschen pflegt man ein Männchen und mehrere Weibchen zusammen mit anderen Arten aus dem gleichen Lebensraum in einem Artenbecken. Es wird als Felsenaquarium eingerichtet, Steinhöhlen und steinige Aufbauten hinter einigen robusten Pflanzen sollen viele Verstecke bilden. Diese Maulbrüter mit Mutterfamilie führen die Jungfische ca. eine Woche nach der Freigabe aus dem Maul noch weiter.
Haltung: T: 21–25 °C (25–28 °C), **pH:** 7–8,5 (7,5–8,5), **Hä:** mittel bis hart (10–15 °dGH); kein Gesellschaftsfisch. **Er:** L, O; LF, Würmer, Algen (auch Blaualgen), Salat, TF bei Nachzuchten mit Gewöhnung daran.

5

6

3 Gestreifter oder Glänzender Zwergbuntbarsch
Nannacara anomala
Herkunft: Südamerika: Westguayana.
Lebensraum: Kleine Bäche oder Alt- und Restwasser großer Fluß- und Sumpfgebiete.
Beschreibung: Diese 8 bis 9 cm langen Cichliden, deren Weibchen nur etwa 5 cm Körperlänge erreichen und je nach Gemütszustand einen Farbwechsel zu kontrastreicher Längs- und Querstreifung zeigen, halten sich friedlich in unteren und mittleren Aquarienbezirken auf. Als recht unempfindliche Art kann man sie mit nicht zu großen und aggressiven Fischen vergesellschaften, wenn teilweise dichte Bepflanzung, freier Schwimmraum, einige größere Steine und Verstecke gegeben sind. Oft versteckt laichende Höhlenbrüter; das Weibchen übernimmt die Brutpflege samt Revierverteidigung (Mutterfamilie).
Haltung: T: 22–26 °C (26–29 °C), **pH:** 6–7,5 (bis 6,8), **Hä:** weich bis hart (bis 10 °dGH); wühlt nicht. **Er:** C; LF, geht schwer an TF.

4 Prinzessin von Burundi
Neolamprologus brichardi
Herkunft: Afrika: Tanganjikasee.
Lebensraum: Felsen mit Sedimenten mit 2 bis 3 m Freiwasser darüber.
Beschreibung: Die Gruppe der Gabelschwanzbuntbarsche enthält viele ähnlich aussehende Arten. Die etwa 8 cm langen „Prinzessinnen" und ihre bis 10 cm großen „Prinzen von Burundi" hält man am besten paarweise in versteckreichen Felsaquarien. Die Höhlen und Steinaufbauten sollen eher im Hintergrund plaziert sein, damit vorne genug Schwimmraum bleibt. Die Geschlechter der Fische sind schwer zu unterscheiden, die Rückenflosse der Männchen ist oft spitzer ausgezogen. Die Höhlenbrüter mit Elternfamilie laichen in Spalten zwischen Felsbrocken. Kommen die Eltern erneut in Brutstimmung, lassen sie die heranwachsenden Jungen in Ruhe.
Haltung: T: 25–27 °C (bis 30 °C), **pH:** 7,5–9, **Hä:** mittel bis hart (10–12 °dGH); Aquarium kann auch bepflanzt werden. **Er:** C, O; LF, TF.

5 Schmetterlingsbuntbarsch
Papiliochromis ramirezi
Herkunft: Südamerika: Venezuela, Kolumbien.
Lebensraum: Kleine, klare Bäche mit seeartigen Erweiterungen in „Oasen" der Steppen- und Savannengebiete (Llanos).
Beschreibung: Die Wildtiere dieser bunten Art werden nur 5 bis 6 cm lang, asiatische Nachzuchten auch größer. Von dort kommen auch viele farbenprächtige Zuchtformen, bei denen leider das Brutpflegeverhalten stark gestört oder ganz abhanden gekommen ist. Die Geschlechter sind nicht einfach zu unterscheiden, bei Männchen ist der erste Rückenflossenstrahl länger ausgezogen und die Flossenhäute sind insgesamt größer als bei den etwas kleineren Weibchen. Letztere zeigen bei sexueller Reife einen rosa Bauch. Paarweise hält man die Tiere in dicht bepflanzten, abgeschatteten Aquarien mit Steinhöhlenverstecken, die das Becken in Ruhe- und Schutzzonen mit dazwischenliegendem Schwimmraum gliedern. Empfindlich gegen Chemikalien, verträgt der Schmetterlingsbuntbarsch auch das Umsetzen schlecht und nimmt jeglichen Streß und schlechte Aufteilung des Aquariums übel. Leider ist die Art recht kurzlebig. Offenbrüter mit Elternfamilie.
Haltung: T: 22–26 °C (27–30 °C), **pH:** sauer (6–5,6), **Hä:** bis 10 °dGH (sehr weich, in der Natur unter 1 °dGH und KH); häufig größere Mengen Wasser wechseln; Torffilterung. **Er:** C, O; kleines LF, TF.

6 Purpurprachtbuntbarsch, Königscichlide
Pelvicachromis pulcher
Herkunft: Afrika: südliches Nigeria.
Lebensraum: Geht auch ins Brackwasser, sonst flache Zonen langsam fließender Gewässer.
Beschreibung: Recht verträglich besiedeln die ansprechenden Cichliden mit bis zu 10 cm Größe, paarweise gehalten, eher die Boden- als die Mittelregion des Aquariums. Die kleineren, besonders bei der Balz oft farbigeren Weibchen haben nicht so spitz auslaufende Rücken- und Afterflossen wie männliche Königscichliden. Höhlenbrüter mit

1

2 *Blauer* Pseudotropheus lombardoi.

2 *Rote Farbvariante von* P. lombardoi.

Vater-Mutter-Familie. Die Tiere wühlen gerne in grobem Kies, jedoch ohne die dichte Bepflanzung neben freiem Schwimmraum zu schädigen. Unterstände und Höhlen aus Steinen und Wurzelholz brauchen diese Buntbarsche, die man auch mit Schwarmfischen der oberen Beckenzonen vergesellschaften kann. Oft glänzt die Rückenflosse der Weibchen prächtig.
Haltung: T: 23–25 °C (bis 28 °C), **pH:** 6–7 (bis 6,5), **Hä:** weich bis hart (8–12 °dGH); laicht meist an der Höhlendecke. **Er:** C, O; LF, TF.

1 Streifenpracht(bunt)barsch, Smaragdpracht(bunt)barsch
Pelvicachromis taeniatus
Herkunft: Afrika: südöstliches Nigeria, Kamerun.
Lebensraum: Uferzonen klarer Flüsse, bis ins Brackwasser vordringend.
Beschreibung: Nur etwa 7 cm Länge erreichen die schöneren Weibchen dieser Cichliden, die Männchen mit eckigerer Schwanz- und spitz zulaufender Rücken- und Afterflosse werden 9 cm lang. Obwohl friedlich auch gegen Artgenossen, hält man die Fische am besten paarweise. Sie bilden ihre Reviere im unteren und mittleren Aquarienbereich und werden zur Laichzeit etwas aggressiver. In recht dunkel eingerichteten Becken mit dichter Bepflanzung, Höhlen und anderen Versteck- und Rückzugsmöglichkeiten aus Wurzeln, Holz und Steinen lasse man freien Schwimmplatz über feinem Sand als Bodengrund. Dort wird gern gewühlt, ohne daß dabei die Pflanzen beschädigt werden. Eine Vergesellschaftung ist gut mit Oberflächen-Schwarmfischen möglich. Die Zucht dieser Höhlenbrüter mit Vater-Mutter-Familie ist ebenfalls möglich. Es gibt natürliche und züchterisch bedingte unterschiedliche Farbrassen.
Haltung: T: 22–25 °C (25–28 °C), **pH:** 6,2–6,8, **Hä:** 5–10 °dGH; leichte Strömung bieten. **Er:** C, O; LF, TF.

2 Hellblauer Malawibarsch
Pseudotropheus lombardoi
Herkunft: Afrika: Malawisee
Lebensraum: Geröll-, Felsenregionen.
Beschreibung: Strahlend gelbe Männchen mit Eiflecken auf der Afterflosse und himmelblaue Weibchen mit sechs schwarzen, vertikalen Binden bilden diese 15 cm lange Cichlidenart. Innerartlich (auch die Weibchen) recht aggressiv, besiedeln diese Buntbarsche revierbildend alle Beckenregionen. In großen Aquarien ist eine Vergesellschaftung günstig, wenn genügend Fluchtraum für die Gesellschaftsfische bleibt. Dann wird die Aggression unter den Artgenossen sozusagen umgelenkt. Die Einrichtung besteht aus einer Felsrückwand mit vielen Spaltenverstecken; Steinaufbauten davor bilden weitere Höhlen, die diese Maulbrüter mit Mutterfamilie gern benutzen. Die Art neigt zum Beknabbern von Pflanzen, weshalb allenfalls harte Arten verwendet werden können. Man pflegt stets ein Männchen mit mehreren Weibchen.
Haltung: T: 24–26 °C (25–28 °C),

3

4 *Diskus Royal blue (rechts) und brauner Diskus.*

4 *Diskus Royal blue x Türkis.*

pH: um 8, **Hä:** mittel bis hart (10–20 °dGH); Verzicht auf Pflanzen ist auch artgerecht. **Er:** L, O; TF, LF, Fisch- und Krebsfleisch.

3 Segelflosser, Skalar
Pterophyllum scalare
Herkunft: Südamerika: Amazonas.
Lebensraum: Tiefe, stehende oder ruhig strömende Flußgebiete.
Beschreibung: Die friedlichen Schwarmfische, die während der Laichzeit Reviere bilden, wirken in zahlreichen Farb- und Formspielarten durch ihr außergewöhnliches Erscheinungsbild recht attraktiv. Außerhalb der Brutperiode zeigen sich keine sicheren äußeren Geschlechtsunterschiede. Viele Zuchtformen sind degeneriert und zeigen nicht mehr die arttypische Brutpflege in der Elternfamilie. Eine Vergesellschaftung mit ruhigen, nicht zu kleinen Fischen (Neons werden gefressen!) ist möglich, wenn große Aquarien mit mindestens 50 cm Höhe verwendet werden. Viel Schwimmraum soll von Vallisnerien oder großblättrigen Pflanzen umgeben sein. Holzwurzeln und gedämpfte Beleuchtung ermöglichen auch die Zucht dieser bis 15 cm großen Offenbrüter.
Haltung: T: 23–28 °C (26–29 °C), **pH:** 5,5–7,5 (bis 6,5), **Hä:** weich bis mittelhart (um 5 °dGH); kümmert bei zu kühler Haltung. **Er:** C, O; LF, TF, pflanzliche Beikost wie Salat; neigt zum Überfressen.

4 Diskus, Diskusbuntbarsch
Symphysodon aequifasciatus
Herkunft: Südamerika: Klar- und Weißwasser Amazoniens.
Lebensraum: Ruhige, tiefe Klar- und Weißwässer.
Beschreibung: Ein majestätischer Cichlide, der durch die außergewöhnliche Form besonders in Gruppenhaltung besticht. Er ist ausdauernd, aber aufgrund der Ansprüche kein Anfängerfisch. Bei 15 bis 20 cm Größe werden mindestens 50 cm hohe Becken gebraucht, um bei dichter Randbepflanzung mit großblättrigen Arten, viel Schwimmöglichkeiten, Wurzeldekoration und freistehenden Großpflanzen eine artgerechte Haltung zu ermöglichen. Ein Artenbecken ist die richtige Unterbringung, wo auch eine Zucht dieser Offenbrüter (meist auf senkrechten Flächen) mit Elternfamilie versucht werden kann. Als „Säugefisch" ernährt der Diskus seinen Nachwuchs mit einem hauptsächlich im Rückenbereich gebildeten, schleimigen Hautsekret, welches die Jungtiere abweiden und bis mindestens 10 Tage nach dem Schlupf bekommen sollen.
Haltung: T: 25–29 °C (28–31 °C), **pH:** 5–7,5 (5,5–6,5), **Hä:** bis 10 °dGH (sehr weich, 1–3 °dGH); Torffilterung; oft und regelmäßig Teilwasserwechsel. **Er:** C; abwechslungsreich füttern; LF, Spezial-TF.

1

1 Weißpunkt-Brabantbuntbarsch
Tropheus duboisi
Herkunft: Afrika: Tanganjikasee, Küstenstreifen im Nordwesten sowie zentrale Ostküste.
Lebensraum: Sedimentfreie Felsenzone in 3 bis 15 m Tiefe.
Beschreibung: Diese 12 cm langen Buntbarsche weisen kaum äußere Geschlechtsunterschiede auf, die Männchen sind etwas größer und haben längere Bauchflossen als weibliche Tiere. Letztere zeigen als Erwachsene am Rücken oft weiße Flecken. Im Felsen-Artenaquarium, ohne Pflanzen, aber mit vielen Durchgangshöhlen, sind diese Cichliden bestens untergebracht. Man hält sie paarweise über mittelgrobem Sand, dann schreiten die Maulbrüter mit Mutterfamilie auch zur Fortpflanzung. Interessant ist der altersbedingte Farbwechsel: Nur Jungtiere (siehe Foto oben) haben weiße Punkte auf dunklem Grund, die später verschwinden (Foto Seite 22). Dann wird ein vertikales Körperband als Zeichnung ausgebildet. Nahe verwandt ist *T. moorii,* der Brabantbuntbarsch.
Haltung: T: 24–26 °C (25–28 °C), **pH:** 7,5–9 (8,5–9), **Hä:** mittel bis hart (10–12 °dGH). **Er:** L, O; LF und ballaststoffreiche Kost wie Algen, Salat, Spinat, eingeweichte Vollkorn-Haferflocken ist wichtig; Tubifex nur ab und zu als Leckerbissen.

Labyrinthfische

Als entwicklungsgeschichtlich relativ junge Gruppe entstanden vor etwa 50 Millionen Jahren die Labyrinth- oder Kletterfische. Man rechnet sie zu den weiteren Barschverwandten und die Systematiker kennen vier Familien. Verbreitet sind die Anabantoidei in Afrika und Asien. Hier werden nur asiatische Vertreter vorgestellt.

Biologisch höchst interessant an diesen Fischen ist ein zusätzlich zu den Kiemen vorhandenes Atmungsorgan, das namensgebend für die ganze Gruppe wurde: das Labyrinth. Dabei handelt es sich um eine Ansammlung reich durchbluteter, stark gefalteter Hautschichten und -lamellen, die über den Kiemen im Kopf liegen. Dem Labyrinth wird durch aktive Aufnahme an der Wasseroberfläche Luft zugeführt, und es ermöglicht den Kletterfischen, den atmosphärischen Sauerstoff zu verwerten.

So konnten auch Lebensräume mit kaum im Wasser gelöstem Sauerstoff besiedelt werden, ja, das Labyrinth ermöglicht seinen Trägern sogar einen längeren Aufenthalt außerhalb des nassen Elements, wenn sie nur feucht gehalten werden. Extreme Lebensräume wie Kleinstgewässer, sumpfige Tümpel und überschwemmte Reisfelder, auch in flachsten Bereichen, wurden so durch diese Fischgruppe erobert.

Die Anpassung an diese Art des „Luftschnappens" geht so weit, daß man den Tieren den Zugang zur Wasseroberfläche nicht verwehren darf. Sie würden, allein auf die Kiemenatmung angewiesen, sicher ersticken. Und eine weitere Gefahr birgt diese in der Natur so sinnvolle Methode der Luftverwertung, die der Aquarianer kennen muß: Ist die über dem Wasser stehende Atemluft nicht wohltemperiert, d.h. entspricht ihre Temperatur nicht in etwa der des Wassers, können sich Labyrinthfische schwere Erkältungen zuziehen! Achtet man auf eine gute Abdeckung, dann erwärmt sich die Luft über dem Wasserspiegel schnell und die Gefahr ist gebannt. Damit es nicht stickig wird, sollten einige Luftschlitze in der Beckenabdeckung sein.

Viele Labyrinther treiben intensive Brutpflege, die meisten bauen dazu aus schleimumkleideten Luftblasen ein sogenanntes Schaumnest, das an der Oberfläche schwimmt. Nach Eintrocknen des Schleimes ergibt sich ein recht stabiles Gebilde, das oft durch eingebaute Schwimmpflanzen zusätzliche Festigkeit erhält. Dort hinein werden die Eier verbracht und bis zum Schlupf der Larven umsorgt. Auch die Larven werden noch eine Zeitlang im Schaum verborgen.

Andere Brutpflegetypen oder das Fehlen jeder Aufmerksamkeit für den Nachwuchs sind auch vertreten. Der mit über 70 cm für die private Aquaristik zu große Speisegurami, *Osphronemus gorami,* baut z.B. kein Schaumnest, sondern formt aus Pflanzenteilen ein großes, kuppelartiges Gebilde an der Wasseroberfläche, das einem überdimensionalen umgedrehten Vogelnest gleicht. Darin wachsen aus aufschwimmenden Eiern die Larven heran. (Foto Seite 83)

2 Siamesischer Kampffisch
Betta splendens
Herkunft: Asien: wohl von Mittel- und Westthailand aus weit verbreitet (Schleierformen des kurzflossigen Wildkampffisches).
Lebensraum: Reisfelder, Gräben, Sümpfe.

2 *Kampffischmännchen der Wildform.*

3

2 *Männchen der langflossigen Kampffisch-Zuchtform an seinem Nest.*

4

Beschreibung: Nur *ein* Männchen (erkennbar an prächtiger Farbe und ausgeprägter Beflossung) pro Becken halten! Die Tiere kämpfen sonst nach interessantem Imponiergehabe heftig und oft bis zum Tod miteinander. Nach der Drohphase mit gespreizten Kiemendeckeln und Zeigen der aufgefalteten Flossen folgen Körper- und Flossenschläge bis zum Übergang in die Nahkampfphase. Beißen und Reißen bis zur völligen Erschöpfung und schwere Verletzungen sind die Folge. Die unscheinbaren Weibchen zeigen bei Laichreife eine Genitalpapille. Mehrere, teils dichte Gruppenpflanzungen am Boden und Schwimmpflanzen zur Oberflächenabdeckung kennzeichnen das Kampffischaquarium. Bei Beachtung der o.g. Grundregel ist der Kampffisch ein guter Vergesellschaftungspartner für friedliche, nicht flossenzupfende Arten. Eine Zucht der Schaumnestbauer mit Vaterfamilie ist gut möglich. Einzelhaft der Männchen in Kleinstgefäßen unter einem Liter Inhalt ist Tierquälerei!
Haltung: T: 25–27 °C (30 °C), **pH:** 6–7,5, **Hä:** weich bis hart (bis 25 °dGH); bei Zucht jegliche Wasserbewegung vermeiden, da Schaumnest sehr empfindlich. **Er:** C, O; LF, TF.

3 Dick- oder Wulstlippiger Fadenfisch
Colisa labiosa
Herkunft: Asien: Birma, Bangladesh.
Lebensraum: Klein- und Kleinstgewässer.
Beschreibung: Diese friedlichen, ruhigen Labyrinther werden 9 bis 10 cm lang und sind für Gesellschaftsbecken geeignet. Die Zucht der Schaumnestbauer (Vaterfamilie) erfolgt jedoch besser in einem Artenbecken. In beiden Fällen sind Schwimmpflanzen über dunklem Boden, eine insgesamt dunkle Einrichtung mit schwacher Beleuchtung und einige niedrige Pflanzengruppen die richtige Beckenausstattung. Die Fadenfische bevorzugen obere und mittlere Wasserregionen. Männchen farbiger mit spitz ausgezogener Rückenflosse.
Haltung: T: 23–25 °C (28 °C), **pH:** 6–7,5 (leicht sauer), **Hä:** 4–10 °dGH. **Er:** O; TF, LF.

4 Zwergfadenfisch
Colisa lalia
Herkunft: Asien: Nordostindien, Bangladesh.
Lebensraum: Flüsse, auch im Mündungsbereich und Überschwem-

2

1

mungsgebieten; Kanäle mit Pflanzen.
Beschreibung: Wunderschön und friedlich sind diese kleinen, bis 6 cm langen Kletterfische. Die bunten Männchen haben spitz auslaufende Rücken- und Afterflossen, die Weibchen sind silbrig-grau. Unter Schwimmpflanzen und zwischen dichten, auch feinfiedrigen Pflanzengruppen halten sich die Zwergfadenfische gerne oben und in der Mitte des Aquariums auf. Moorkienholz kann ebenfalls eingebracht werden und eine Vergesellschaftung ist mit Bodenbewohnern oder friedlichen Schwarmfischen möglich. Der brutpflegende Vaterfisch gilt als sorgfältiger Schaumnestbauer, wobei Pflanzenteile integriert werden. Bei guten Wasserbedingungen gelingt auch die Zucht.
Haltung: T: um 25 °C (28–30 °C), **pH:** 6–7,5, **Hä:** weich bis mittel; störungsempfindlich, aber regelmäßiger Wasserwechsel unbedingt nötig. **Er:** O; alles kleine LF und TF.

1 Honigfadenfisch, Honiggurami
Colisa sota (Colisa chuna)
Herkunft: Asien: Nordostindien, Bangladesh.
Lebensraum: Flüsse, in Einzugsgebieten der Deltabereiche.
Beschreibung: Außer den Weibchen zeigen auch unterdrückte männliche Fische eine braun-graue Färbung mit zeitweiligem braunen Längsband, dagegen besticht der Farbkontrast bei leitenden Männchen. Scheu und zurückhaltend, während der Laichzeit aber revierbildend, eignen sich Honiggouramis zur Vergesellschaftung mit kleinen Fischen der Bodenzone und des unteren Aquarienbereichs. Viele feinfiedrige und andere Pflanzengruppen, Schwimmpflanzen oder bis zur Wasseroberfläche wuchernde Pflanzen verwenden. Die Zucht der schaumnestbauenden Art mit Vaterfamilie ist nicht ganz einfach.
Haltung: T: um 25 °C (28–30 °C), **pH:** 6–7,5, **Hä:** nicht zu hart (bis 15 °dGH); relativ abgedunkelt halten.
Er: C, O; kleines LF, TF.

2 Küssender Gurami
Helostoma temminckii
Herkunft: Asien: Sumatra, Borneo, Thailand, Malaysia.
Lebensraum: Sümpfe und Flüsse, auch kleine Seen.
Beschreibung: In seiner Heimat ein beliebter Speisefisch (bis 30 cm lang), wird der Küssende Gurami in Aquarien meist nur 15 bis 20 cm groß. Die Naturform ist grün-silbrig, bekannter ist die rosa-fleischfarbe-

3

4

ne Variante. Große Aquarien (für erwachsene Tiere nicht unter 1 m Länge) mit reichhaltiger Ausstattung durch harte, kräftige Pflanzen sind ein idealer Aufenthaltsort. Schwimmpflanzen und treibende Stengel anderer Wasserpflanzen komplettieren die Einrichtung. Eine Vergesellschaftung mit anderen Labyrinthern ist möglich; Küssende Guramis bewohnen vorwiegend die mittleren Aquarienbereiche. Die nicht einfache Zucht dieser Freilaicher ohne Nestbau und Brutpflege gelingt in großen Becken, wenn die Fische eine Körperlänge von ca. 14 cm haben.
Haltung: T: 21–28 °C, ideal um 25 °C (30 °C), **pH:** 6–7,5, **Hä:** weich bis hart (weich); gute Filterung.
Er: O; LF, TF, Pflanzenkost.

3 Paradiesfisch, Makropode
Makropodus opercularis
Herkunft: Asien: Südchina, Korea, Vietnam, Formosa.
Lebensraum: Wassergräben, Sumpfgebiete, kleine und kleinste Bäche, Reisfelder.
Beschreibung: Die robuste Art, der asiatische Pionier in der europäischen Aquaristik, ist mit maximal 10 bis 12 cm Länge in größeren Becken problemlos zu halten. Das farbigere Männchen hat auch längere Flossen. Gut beleuchtete Aquarien mit stellenweise dichten Pflanzenverstecken und Schwimmpflanzen bekommen dem Paradiesfisch gut, eine Dekoration mit Moorkienholz und darauf angesiedeltem *Microsorium* tut ein weiteres. Man sollte diese Tiere nicht mit kleinen, friedlichen Fischen vergesellschaften; nur Robustarten eignen sich dazu. Der Zuchtansatz erfolgt am besten paarweise, der Vater sorgt für die Eier und Jungen in einem Schaumnest. Manche Makropoden sind leider etwas aggressiv.
Haltung: T: 10–35 °C werden zwar vertragen, doch sind 22–25 °C zu empfehlen (28 °C), **pH:** 6–8, **Hä:** weich bis hart. **Er:** O; TF, LF.

4 Mosaikfadenfisch
Trichogaster leeri
Herkunft: Asien: Malaysia, Sumatra, Borneo.
Lebensraum: Weiche, saure, langsam fließende, oft halbdunkle Flachwässer.
Beschreibung: Diese Labyrinthfische erreichen 12 bis 15 cm Länge, die Geschlechtsunterschiede werden erst ab etwa 8 cm Körpergröße deutlich. Die männlichen Fische zei-

1 *„Cosby", die Marmor-Zuchtform des Blauen Fadenfisches (Männchen).*

1 *Blaue Fadenfische, rechts ein Weibchen.*

gen Orangerot an Kiemen-, Brust- und Bauchpartie und haben eine spitz endende Rückenflosse. Die Art ist sehr friedlich, fast scheu, und fühlt sich nur in großen Aquarien wohl. Dämmrige Haltung unter Schwimmpflanzen, der Boden gut bepflanzt (auch feinfiedrige Arten verwenden), damit Versteckmöglichkeiten zustande kommen, sind Voraussetzungen für die Zucht (Schaumnest, Vaterfamilie). Als Gesellschafter kommen allenfalls ruhige Bodenbewohner in Frage.
Haltung: T: 23–27 °C (30 °C), **pH:** 5,5–7,5 (bis 6,5), **Hä:** 5–30 °dGH (bis 4 °dGH); Torffilterung, ruhig bis zur Braunfärbung des Wassers. **Er:** O; TF, LF.

1 Blauer Fadenfisch
Trichogaster trichopterus sumatranus
Herkunft: Asien: Sumatra.
Lebensraum: Verschiedene Fließgewässer mit schwacher Strömung und ruhigen Zonen.
Beschreibung: Der maximal 12 cm lange blaue Fadenfisch ist eine Unterart von *T. t. trichopterus,* dem punktierten Fadenfisch aus Indonesien und Malaysia, der 15 cm lang wird. Zwischen dichten Planzenbeständen und Schwimmpflanzen halten sich die Tiere gerne in Beckenmitte und oben im Aquarium auf. Männliche Fische haben längere, spitz auslaufende Rückenflossen. Marmorierte und albinotische Zuchtformen sind leider nicht so vital und produktiv wie die Wildform. Die Zucht ist leicht, und außer einer Vergesellschaftung mit zu robusten Fischarten nimmt dieser Labyrinther so schnell nichts übel. Für kräftige und zahlreiche Nachkommenschaft hat sich die exakte Einhaltung der Zucht-Wasserwerte bewährt.
Haltung: T: 22–28 °C werden toleriert, um 27 °C ist besser (30 °C), **pH:** 6–8 (leicht sauer), **Hä:** 5–35 °dGH (sehr weich); Alttiere vertragen das Umsetzen schlecht. **Er:** O; TF, LF, Planzenkost.

Ähren- und Regenbogenfische

Obwohl von Systematikern in zwei verschiedene Familien gestellt, wollen wir hier die Ährenfische (Atherinidae) und die Regenbogenfische (Melanotaeniidae) gemeinsam abhandeln aufgrund der Gemeinsamkeiten in Körperform, Schwarmverhalten und den Grundansprüchen an eine artgerechte Haltung.

Der überwiegende Teil der Ährenfische bewohnt weltweit flache Küstenbereiche der Meere, die Gruppe hat nur wenige Süßwasservertreter. Kennzeichen der Familie ist der Besitz zweier Rückenflossen, die einen weiten Abstand voneinander haben.

Das Verbreitungsgebiet der Regenbogenfische ist mit Australien, Neuguinea und einigen vorgelagerten Inselgruppen sowie einem Seengebiet von Indonesien dagegen recht eingeschränkt. Auch sie tragen zwei Rückenflossen, doch stehen diese dicht hintereinander.

Angehörige beider Fischgruppen haben meist einen länglichen, oval geformten und seitlich zusammengedrückten Körper und sind erst

2

3

als erwachsene Tiere richtig ausgefärbt. Als Schwarmfische fühlen sie sich nur in einer Gruppe von ihresgleichen wohl. Gute Wasserpflege ist gegen vorzeitiges Verblassen unbedingt erforderlich.

Brutbiologisch sind sowohl Regenbogen- als auch Ährenfische sogenannte Dauerlaicher, d.h., daß über die ganze Laichperiode hinweg jeden Tag einige Eier abgelegt werden. Javamoos, Wollfadenbündel oder Kunststoffgespinst geben ein geeignetes Substrat dafür ab. Dieses Material bzw. die vorsichtig von Hand abgesammelten Eier gibt man in ein Aufzuchtbecken, in dem die gleichen Wasserwerte wie im Aquarium gegeben sind. Die langsam wachsenden und sofort freßfähigen Jungfische sind nicht ganz einfach aufzuziehen.

2 Madagaskar-Ährenfisch
Bedotia geayi
Herkunft: Madagaskar.
Lebensraum: Bergbäche mit klarem Wasser.
Beschreibung: Die etwas empfindliche Art wird ca. 15 cm lang, die Zucht gilt jedoch als leicht, wenn auf die Wasserqualität geachtet wird. Die Männchen zeigen rote Säume an Rücken- und Schwanzflosse und sind kräftiger gebaut. Die abgelegten Eier hängen an Fädchen zwischen Pflanzen (feinblättrige Arten am Rand und im Hintergrund anordnen). Lange Becken zum Ausschwimmen und etwas Strömung sind gut, auf klares Wasser, entsprechend dem natürlichen Lebensraum, sollte man achten. Eine Vergesellschaftung ist vor allem mit anderen strömungsliebenden Arten unter den friedlichen Fischen möglich.
Haltung: T: 20–24 °C (22–24 °C), **pH:** 7–8, **Hä:** mittel bis hart (ab 10 °dGH); wöchentlich bis 1/3 Frischwasser. **Er:** C, O; LF, TF, Pflanzenkost.

3 Lachsroter Regenbogenfisch
Glossolepis incisus
Herkunft: Asien: Indonesien.
Lebensraum: In der Nachbarschaft von Pflanzenbeständen im Sentani-See.
Beschreibung: Die kräftig roten, im Alter hochrückigen Männchen (die Farbe ist jedoch auch abhängig von Stimmung und Rangordnung) und die gold-gelb-oliv gefärbten Weibchen dieser bis 15 cm großen Art zeigen – ähnlich wie einige Buntbarsche – einen deutlichen Geschlechtsdichromatismus. Die Ausfärbung der friedlichen, schreck- und lebhaften Schwarmfische beginnt jedoch frühestens ab etwa 5 cm Länge. Bei lockerer Bepflanzung mit viel Platz zum Schwimmen ist die Zucht nicht schwer.
Haltung: T: 22–24 °C (24–26 °C), **pH:** 7–8 (bis 7,5), **Hä:** mittel bis hart (18–25 °dGH); Javamoos als Laichsubstrat. **Er:** C; LF, etwas TF.

2

1 Werners Regenbogenfisch
Iriatherina werneri

Herkunft: Nordaustralien, Süd-Neuguinea.

Lebensraum: Kleine, stehende oder langsam fließende Gewässer mit Pflanzen.

Beschreibung: Deutlich verlängerte Flossenstrahlen sind sichtbares Geschlechtsmerkmal der Männchen. Mit 5 cm Körperlänge bewohnen die friedlichen Schwarmfische die mittleren Aquariumregionen. Feiner Sand als Bodengrund und reichlich freier Schwimmraum kennzeichnen das „Werneri"-Becken, das nur am Rand und im Hintergrund bepflanzt wird. Auch eine Teilabdeckung mit Schwimmpflanzen ist möglich. Die Zucht ist nicht ganz einfach. Man hält diese Fische entweder im Artenbecken oder in Gesellschaft kleiner, zarter Fische bzw. zusammen mit anderen Regenbogenfischen.

Haltung: T: 25–27 °C (bis 28 °C), **pH:** 6–7,5 (um 7), **Hä:** weich bis mittelhart (ab 10 °dGH); wöchentlich $^1/_4$ Teilwasserwechsel. **Er:** C, O; kleines LF, TF.

1

2 Ajamaru-Regenbogenfisch, Bösemans Regenbogenfisch
Melanotaenia boesemani

Herkunft: Indonesien: Ajamaru-Seen (Irian Jaya).

Lebensraum: Flache Seenbereiche mit feinen Pflanzen.

Beschreibung: Die männlichen Tiere dieser 10 bis 14 cm langen Regenbogenfische sind intensiver gefärbt, etwas größer als die Weibchen und hochrückiger. Überwiegend in mittleren bis oberen Bereichen als Schwarm umherziehend, braucht die friedliche Art viel freien Schwimmraum. Deshalb nur eine lockere Randbepflanzung vornehmen, die im Hintergrund dichter sein darf. Der gute Gesellschaftsfisch springt gern und mag sandigen Boden. Obwohl in der Natur in weichem und alkalischem Wasser von pH 9–9,5 vorkommend, haben

sich die unten in Klammern genannten Werte für die an sich leichte Zucht bewährt.
Haltung: T: 24–27 °C (bis 30 °C), **pH:** 7–8,5 (7), **Hä:** mittel bis hart (8–15 °dGH); Dauerlaicher. **Er:** C, O; hauptsächlich LF, TF.

3 Juwelen-Regenbogenfisch
Melanotaenia trifasciata
Herkunft: Nordaustralien.
Lebensraum: Diverse Flußsysteme.
Beschreibung: Von dieser etwa 12 cm langen Art gibt es je nach Herkunft unterschiedlich gefärbte Varianten, die auch von den Ansprüchen an die Wasserparameter etwas verschieden sein können. Fragen Sie beim Kauf danach. Als friedlich-lebhafte Schwarmfische beleben die Tiere die Aquarienmitte. Becken mit dunklem Boden und Bepflanzung am Rand und hinten lassen genug freien Schwimmraum. Die Zucht der Dauerlaicher ist einfach. Es empfehlen sich Artenbecken oder die Vergesellschaftung mit anderen Regenbogenfischen.
Haltung: T: 24–28 °C (25–30 °C), **pH:** 7–8, **Hä:** mittel bis hart; regelmäßig Teilwasserwechsel, was auch die Fortpflanzungsbereitschaft auslöst. **Er:** C, O; LF, TF.

4 Celebes-Sonnenstrahlfisch
Telmatherina ladigesi
Herkunft: Südostasien: Sulawesi (Celebes)
Lebensraum: Bäche in hügeligem Gelände.
Beschreibung: Die 7 bis 8 cm lange Art trägt im männlichen Geschlecht verlängerte Flossenstrahlen und bewohnt friedlich die mittleren Aquarienzonen. Die Schwarmfische lieben die Morgensonne und balzen prächtig in deren Strahlen. Das Becken sollte teils dichte Randbepflanzung und Schwimmpflanzen auf Teilen der Oberfläche aufweisen. In Längsrichtung wird viel freier Schwimmraum gebraucht. Vergesellschaftung ist gut möglich und auch die Zucht gelingt.
Haltung: T: 22–28 °C (unterer Bereich davon), **pH:** 7–8 (7), **Hä:** mittel bis hart (ab 12 °dGH); häufige Frischwassergaben und „klare Verhältnisse" sind unabdingbar. **Er:** C, O; LF, TF.

3

4

Literaturverzeichnis

Aquaristik allgemein

Beck, Peter: Aquarien-ABC. Franckh-Kosmos, Stuttgart 1992.
Friederich, Ursel und Volland, Werner: Futtertierzucht. Ulmer, Stuttgart 1992.
Frey, Hans: Das Aquarium von A bis Z. Neumann, Radebeul 1964.
Frey, Volker: Lexikon der Aquaristik in 3 Bänden. Band 1. Neumann, Radebeul 1992.
Geisler, Rolf: Wasserkunde für die aquaristische Praxis. Kernen, Stuttgart 1964.
Horst, Kaspar: Mein erstes Aquarium. Aquadocumenta, Bielefeld 1992.
Krause, Hanns-Jürgen: Handbuch Aquarienwasser. BeDe, Kollnburg 1990.
– Wasser für unser Aquarium. Franckh-Kosmos, Stuttgart 1991.
Scheurmann, Ines: Aquarium für Süßwasserfische und Pflanzen. Gräfe und Unzer, München 1992.
Schliewen, Ulrich: Wasserwelt Aquarium. Gräfe und Unzer, München 1991.
Seegers, Lothar: Das Aquarium. Ulmer, Stuttgart 1992.
Sterba, Günther, Hrsg.: Enzyklopädie der Aquaristik und speziellen Ichthyologie. Neudamm, Melsungen 1978.
Sterba, Günther: Aquarienkunde. Ulmer, Stuttgart 1989.
Vierke, Jörg: Unser Gesellschaftsaquarium. Franckh-Kosmos, Stuttgart 1989.
Vierke, Jörg: Unser erstes Aquarium. Franckh-Kosmos, Stuttgart 1993.
Wilkerling, Klaus: Die Aquarienfibel. Franckh-Kosmos, Stuttgart 1992.

Fische

Baensch, Hans A. und Riehl, Rüdiger: Aquarienatlas Band 2. Mergus, 5. Aufl., Melle 1992.
Bone, Q. und Marshall, N. B.: Biologie der Fische. Gustav Fischer, Stuttgart, New York 1985.
Herrmann, Hans-Joachim: Die Buntbarsche der alten Welt – Tanganjikasee. Ulmer, Stuttgart 1990.
Hieronimus, Harro: Welse. Ulmer, Stuttgart 1989.
Koslowski, Ingo: Die Buntbarsche der neuen Welt – Zwergcichliden. Edition Kernen, Essen 1985.
Linke, Horst: Labyrinthfische – Farbe im Aquarium. Tetra, Melle 1992.
Muus, B. J. und Dahlström, P.: Süßwasserfische. BLV, München, Wien, Zürich 1981.
Paysan, Klaus: Aquarienfische. Franckh-Kosmos, Stuttgart 1992.
Pinter, Helmut: Handbuch der Aquarienfischzucht. Edition Kernen, Essen.
– Cichliden, Buntbarsche im Aquarium. Ulmer, Stuttgart 1981.
Reichenbach-Klinke, H.-H.: Grundzüge der Fischkunde. Gustav Fischer, Stuttgart 1970.
Riehl, Rüdiger und Baensch, Hans A.: Aquarienatlas Band 1. Mergus, 9. Aufl., Melle 1992.
– Aquarienatlas Band 3. Mergus, Melle 1990.
Sommer, Wolfgang: Nachwuchs im Aquarium. Franckh-Kosmos, Stuttgart 1990.
Staeck, Wolfgang: Cichliden – Verbreitung – Verhalten – Arten, Band I. Engelbert Pfriem, Wuppertal, ohne Jahresangabe.
– Cichliden – Verbreitung – Verhalten – Arten, Band II. Engelbert Pfriem, Wuppertal 1977.
– Cichliden Band III – Entdeckungen und Neuimporte. Engelbert Pfriem, Wuppertal 1983.
Stallknecht, Helmut: Lebendgebärende Zahnkarpfen. Neumann-Neudamm, Radebeul 1989.
– Aquarienfische. Ulmer, Stuttgart 1992.
Stawikowski, Rainer und Werner, Uwe: Die Buntbarsche der neuen Welt – Mittelamerika. Edition Kernen, Essen 1985.
– Die Buntbarsche der neuen Welt – Südamerika. Edition Kernen, Essen 1988.
Stawikowski, Rainer: Fische im Biotopaquarium. Franckh-Kosmos, Stuttgart 1990.
Sterba, Günther: Süßwasserfische der Welt. Ulmer, Stuttgart.
Wickler, Wolfgang: Das Züchten von Aquarienfischen. Franckh-Kosmos, Stuttgart 1968.

Pflanzen

Brünner, Gerhard: Aquarienpflanzen. Franckh-Kosmos, Stuttgart 1983.
– Handbuch der Aquarienpflanzen. Franckh-Kosmos, Stuttgart 1984.
De Wit, Hendrik C. D.: Aquarienpflanzen. Ulmer, Stuttgart 1990.
Greger, Bernd: Aquarienpflanzen. Franckh-Kosmos, Stuttgart 1991.
Horst, Kaspar: Pflanzen im Aquarium. Ulmer, Stuttgart 1986.
Paffrath, Kurt: Bestimmung und Pflege von Aquarienpflanzen. Landbuch, Hannover 1978.

Fischkrankheiten

Bauer, Roland: Erkrankungen der Aquarienfische. Paul Parey, Hamburg 1991.
Reichenbach-Klinke, H.-H.: Krankheiten und Schädigungen der Fische. Gustav Fischer, Stuttgart 1980.
Roberts, R. J. und Schlotfeld, H. J.: Grundlagen der Fischpathologie. Paul Parey, Hamburg 1985.
Schubert, Gottfried und Untergasser, Dieter: Krankheiten der Fische. Franckh-Kosmos, Stuttgart 1991.
Untergasser, Dieter: Krankheiten der Aquarienfische. Franckh-Kosmos, Stuttgart 1989.

Aquarienzeitschriften

Aquarium Heute, Aquadocumenta Verlag, Bielefeld.
das Aquarium, Schmettkamp Verlag, Bornheim.
DATZ, Ulmer Verlag, Stuttgart.
TI international, Tetra-Verlag, Melle.

Nützliche Adressen

Arbeitskreis Fischkrankheiten des VDA
Karl-Wilfried Hamel, Darmstädter Straße 179, 64625 Bensheim-Auerbach, Telefon (0 62 51) 7 36 96.

Deutsche Cichlidengesellschaft (DCG)
Geschäftsführer: Winfried Poesdorf, Parkstraße 21a, 33719 Bielefeld.

Deutsche Gesellschaft für Lebendgebärende Zahnkarpfen (DGLZ)
Geschäftsführer: Dr. Vollrad Etzel, Hamburg-Amerika-Straße 6, 27472 Cuxhaven.

Deutsche Guppy-Föderation e.V.
Vorsitzender: Günter Tischmann, Thyssenstraße 18, 13407 Berlin.

Deutsche Killifisch Gemeinschaft (DKG)
Geschäftsführer: K. Breitfeld, An der Wasge 7, 04416 Markkleeberg.

Informations-Zentrum Heimtiere (IZH)
(beantwortet Fragen zur Aquaristik und zur Heimtierhaltung allgemein)
Postfach 1264, 67456 Böhl-Iggelheim.

Internationale Gemeinschaft für Labyrinthfische (IGL)
Präsident: Michael Kokoscha, Kniestraße 12, 46117 Oberhausen.

Internationale Gesellschaft für Regenbogenfische (IRG)
Geschäftsführer: Andreas Deutrich, Rather Straße 53, 52353 Düren.

Österreichische Guppy-Gesellschaft
Geschäftsstelle: Ingrid Schlögl, Rennbahnweg 27/12/16, A-1222 Wien.

Referent für Fischkrankheiten im VDA
Dieter Untergasser, Schloßstraße 34, 64720 Michelstadt-Steinbach.

Verband Deutscher Vereine für Aquarien- und Terrarienkunde (VDA)
Geschäftsstelle: Hans und Ingrid Stiller, Luxemburger Straße 16, 44789 Bochum.

VDA-Arbeitskreis Barben, Salmler, Schmerlen, Welse (BSSW)
Geschäftsstelle: Uwe Wolf, Lindenwiese 5, 98544 Zella-Mehlis.

VDA-Arbeitskreis Wasserpflanzen
Geschäftsführer: Gerd Eggers, Flachsbleiche 70, 41564 Kaarst.

Register